Professional Sch[ool Counseling:]
A Handbook of Theories, Programs, & Practices

THIRD EDITION

Edited by Bradley T. Erford

CAPS Press
An Independent imprint of

8700 Shoal Creek Boulevard
Austin, Texas 78757-6897
800/897-3202   Fax 800/397-7633
www.proedinc.com

© 2016, 2010, 2004 by PRO-ED, Inc.
8700 Shoal Creek Boulevard
Austin, Texas 78757-6897
800/897-3202   Fax 800/397-7633
www.proedinc.com

All rights reserved. No part of the material protected by this copyright notice may be reproduced or used in any form or by any means, electronic or mechanical, including photocopying, recording, or by any information storage and retrieval system, without prior written permission of the copyright owner.

NOTICE: PRO-ED grants permission to the user of this book to copy the figures and tables for teaching or clinical purposes. Duplication of this material for commercial use is prohibited.

Library of Congress Cataloging-in-Publication Data

Professional School Counseling : a handbook of theories, programs, & practices / edited by Bradley T. Erford.—3rd ed.
    p. cm.
  Includes bibliographical references.
  ISBN 978-1-4164-0689-1 (Print)
  ISBN 978-1-4164-0690-7 (e-book PDF)
    1. Educational counseling—United States—Handbooks, manuals, etc. I. Erford, Bradley T.
LB1027.5.P6593   2016
371.4'220973—dc23
                                          2015000931

This book was developed and produced by CAPS Press, formerly associated with ERIC/CASS, and creator of many titles for the counseling, assessment, and educational fields. In 2004, CAPS Press became an independent imprint of PRO-ED, Inc.

Design: Jan Mullis
Cover: Craig Hattersley and Jan Mullis
This book is designed in ITC Giovanni and Myriad Pro.

Printed in the United States of America
1 2 3 4 5 6 7 8 9 10   24 23 22 21 20 19 18 17 16 15

Table of Contents

Foreword ix

Preface xi

Dedication xiii

About the Editor/Authors xv

Section 1: The Foundations of School Counseling

Chapter 1: Professional School Counseling: Integrating Theory and Practice Into a Data-Driven, Evidence-Based Approach 3
Bradley T. Erford

Chapter 2: The History of School Counseling 9
Mei Tang and Bradley T. Erford

Chapter 3: Current and Future Perspectives on School Counseling 23
Joyce A. DeVoss

Chapter 4: Outcomes Research on School Counseling 35
Qi Shi and Bradley T. Erford

Chapter 5: Codes of Ethics and Ethical and Legal Considerations for Students, Parents, and Professional School Counselors 47
Lynn E. Linde and Carolyn Stone

Chapter 6: Certification, Licensure, and Accreditation in School Counseling 63
Brent M. Snow and C. Marie Jackson

Section 2: Leadership and the Professional School Counselor

Chapter 7: The Professional School Counselor and Leadership 73
Joyce A. DeVoss

Chapter 8: The Professional School Counselor: Cultivating Academic Achievement and College/Career Readiness for All Students 83
Chris Wood

Chapter 9: Organization Development in Schools   95
   Joyce A. DeVoss

Chapter 10: Assessing and Changing School Culture   105
   Mei Tang

Chapter 11: Supervising School Counseling Interns   115
   Gerta Bardhoshi and Bradley T. Erford

Section 3: Comprehensive School Counseling Programs

Chapter 12: The ASCA National Standards and the ASCA National Model   127
   Carol A. Dahir, Trish Hatch, and Lawrence E. Tyson

Chapter 13: Data-Driven School Counseling   145
   Carolyn B. Stone and Carol A. Dahir

Chapter 14: Comprehensive Developmental School Counseling Programs   155
   Bradley T. Erford and Qi Shi

Chapter 15: Needs Assessments: The Key to Successful and Meaningful School Counseling Programs   163
   Bradley T. Erford

Chapter 16: How to Write Learning Objectives   171
   Bradley T. Erford

Chapter 17: Designing Developmental Guidance Lessons   177
   Bradley T. Erford

Chapter 18: Setting Up and Managing a Classroom   187
   Carlen Henington and R. Anthony Doggett

Chapter 19: Program Accountability   209
   Bradley T. Erford

Chapter 20: Career Development Interventions in the Schools   217
   Brian Hutchison, Spencer G. Niles, and Jerry Trusty

Chapter 21: Secondary and Postsecondary Educational Planning   231
   Suzanne M. Dugger and Kalinda R. Jones

Chapter 22: Consulting in the Schools: The Role of the Professional School Counselor   253
   Donna M. Gibson

Chapter 23: Conflict Resolution, Bullying, and Cyberbullying   263
   Nadine E. Garner and Jason B. Baker

Section 4: Techniques and Approaches to Counseling in Schools

Chapter 24: Professional School Counselors and Reality Therapy   279
   Robert E. Wubbolding

Chapter 25: Using Cognitive Behavioral Techniques   291
   Ann Vernon

Chapter 26: Development and Implementation of Behavioral Interventions in Schools: A Function-Based Approach   301
   R. Anthony Doggett and Carl J. Sheperis

Chapter 27: Adlerian Counseling Techniques   313
   Mardi Kay Fallon

Chapter 28: Solution-Focused Brief Counseling   323
   Bradley T. Erford

Chapter 29: Using Family Systems Interventions in Schools   335
   Bradley T. Erford

Chapter 30: Integrating Knowledge of Learning Styles and Multiple Intelligences in Counseling Diverse Students   347
   Bradley T. Erford

Chapter 31: Group Counseling in Schools   357
   Gary E. Goodnough and Vivian V. Lee

Section 5: Assessment in School Counseling

Chapter 32: What Assessment Competencies Are Needed by Professional School Counselors?   369
   Bradley T. Erford

Chapter 33: High-Stakes Testing: What Counselors Need to Know   379
   Patricia Jo McDivitt

Chapter 34: Parents' Questions About Testing in Schools, and Some Answers   387
   Mary Ann Clark and Sandra M. Logan

Chapter 35: What Professional School Counselors Need to Know About Intelligence Tests   397
Bradley T. Erford

Chapter 36: A Practical Approach to Career Assessment in Schools   407
Jerry Trusty, Spencer G. Niles, and ZiYoung Kang

Chapter 37: A Selective Overview of Personality and Its Assessment   419
Ralph L. Piedmont

Chapter 38: Behavior Assessment   431
Carlen Henington

Section 6: Clinical Issues in School Counseling

Chapter 39: Helping Students Who Have Attention-Deficit/Hyperactivity Disorder   449
David J. Carter, Patricia Carter, and Bradley T. Erford

Chapter 40: Helping Students Who Have Alcohol and Other Drug Problems   459
Gerald A. Juhnke and Elias Zambrano

Chapter 41: Helping Students Who Have Eating Disorders   469
Dana Heller Levitt

Chapter 42: Helping Students Who Have Depression   481
Bradley T. Erford

Chapter 43: Helping Students Deal With Obsessive-Compulsive Disorder   493
Bradley T. Erford

Chapter 44: Separation Anxiety Disorder in the Schools   501
Henry L. Harris and Sejal Parikh Foxx

Chapter 45: Test Anxiety   511
Bradley T. Erford

Chapter 46: Helping Students Who Have Posttraumatic Stress Disorder   515
Bradley T. Erford

Chapter 47: Habits, Tics, and Self-Mutilation (Cutting): A Behavioral Approach to Assessment and Treatment   521
Bradley T. Erford

Chapter 48: Reactive Attachment Disorder in Schools: Recommendations for Professional School Counselors   537
Carl J. Sheperis, R. Anthony Doggett, and Robika M. Mylroie

Chapter 49: Students With Learning Disabilities: Counseling Issues and Strategies   545
Adriana G. McEachern

Chapter 50: Helping Students With Severe Behavioral Problems   555
Gregory R. Janson and Jonathan Procter

Chapter 51: Counseling High-Functioning Students With Autism Spectrum Disorder   571
Henry L. Harris

Section 7: Special Issues and Populations in School Counseling

Chapter 52: Helping Students Acquire Time-Management Skills   583
Bradley T. Erford

Chapter 53: Understanding Special Education Policies and Procedures   591
Bradley T. Erford

Chapter 54: Understanding Section 504 Policies and Procedures   599
Amy J. Newmeyer and Mark D. Newmeyer

Chapter 55: School Support for Students Who Have Chronic Illnesses   603
Carol J. Kaffenberger

Chapter 56: Intervention Strategies for Physically or Sexually Abused Students   613
David J. Carter and Patricia Carter

Chapter 57: Counseling Sexual Minority Students in the Schools   623
Mark Pope, Lela Kosteck Bunch, and Michael S. Rankins

Chapter 58: Helping Students From Changing Families   639
Qi Shi and Bradley T. Erford

Chapter 59: Preventing Professional School Counselor Burnout   655
Gerta Bardhoshi and Bradley T. Erford

Chapter 60: The Professional School Counselor in the Rural Setting: Strategies for Meeting Challenges and Maximizing Rewards   663
Deborah L. Drew and Dorothy Breen

Chapter 61: Counseling Multiracial Students 671
   Henry L. Harris, Lyndon P. Abrams, and Edward A. Wierzalis

Chapter 62: Emotional Safety in the Classroom 681
   Gregory R. Janson and Margaret A. King

Chapter 63: Counseling Children of Poverty 689
   Donna S. Sheperis and Belinda J. Lopez

Chapter 64: Parent Involvement in Schools 695
   Henry L. Harris and Edward A. Wierzalis

Chapter 65: Helping Students Manage Stress 705
   Bradley T. Erford

Chapter 66: Helping Students Manage Anger 721
   Carol Z. A. McGinnis and Bradley T. Erford

Chapter 67: Bereavement in Schools: How to Respond 729
   Susan Norris Huss and Melissa Nowicki

Chapter 68: Crisis Intervention With Individuals in the Schools 737
   Gerta Bardhoshi and Bradley T. Erford

Chapter 69: Systemic Crisis Intervention in the Schools 749
   Bradley T. Erford

References 759

Foreword

Almost daily, professional school counselors and counselor educators encounter situations that call for authoritative information on a variety of topics. Typically, they must seek information from multiple sources, often of variable quality and applicability. The task is often time-consuming, and the results can be less than what is needed or expected. This handbook was developed to address this problem by providing a single source that will meet most of the professional school counselor's information needs.

A review of the table of contents will reveal the exceptional breadth and comprehensiveness of this publication. In fact, it is so broad, and the chapters are so authoritatively written, that it would suffice as an excellent source and resource for all of the many topics covered in an accredited school counselor education program. For the practicing counselor, it will provide a highly useful resource for the myriad questions a professional school counselor must respond to in a typical day. Whatever your position, be it professional school counselor, counselor educator, administrator, or interested citizen, this handbook provides an excellent means to update your knowledge about the school counseling profession.

Dr. Bradley Erford is a highly respected leader in counseling, and, as such, he was able to assemble a body of writers of exceptional counseling expertise and writing skill. It is a book that provides a quick (but authoritative) study, and it does so in an interesting and nonpedantic fashion. Unlike some large and impressive-appearing tomes, which are used only once, this book will "hook" the reader, and he or she will want to refer to it again and again. We predict that almost everyone involved or interested in professional school counseling will want to have his or her own copy of this handbook. Why not begin now and reap the benefits of having the all-encompassing resource you've always needed and wanted?

Garry R. Walz and Jeanne C. Bleuer

Preface

The first edition of this Handbook was published in 2004 and the second edition in 2010. Who would have thought so much about school counseling would have changed in just a decade? A dynamic wave of change has swept over school counseling programs all across the country. Since 2003, the American School Counseling Association (ASCA) published three editions of the *National Model for School Counseling Programs* (ASCA, 2003, 2005, 2012), which led to numerous important changes in how school counselors implement their school counseling programs. The model emphasizes four themes (i.e., leadership, advocacy, collaboration, and systemic change) that are infused throughout four elements, which help structure program formation and implementation: foundation, delivery system, management system, and accountability.

This third edition of the Handbook integrates and expands upon the changes brought about by revisions to the *ASCA National Model*. Revisions to each chapter reflect the influence of the model as appropriate. Other chapters give further substance and clarification to implementation of the model, including chapters in the section on Leadership and the Professional School Counselor.

Several other educational initiatives and societal dilemmas have either stemmed from or occurred simultaneously with the model. First, school reform has created a data-driven focus to programmatic changes; that is, data is used to define and demonstrate problems *before* strategies and innovations are implemented to address the problems. In the past, perceptions-based or subjective sources of information were used. Second, more attention is being given to the training of school counselors, particularly during school-based practicum and internship. Third, several clinical problems have received increased prominence in the schools over the past decade. The chapter on Habit Disorders was revised to include self-mutilation, as "cutting" among adolescents has become far too common in our schools. Also, the redefining of the autism spectrum to include children with high-functioning conditions has led to professional school counselors providing more frequent social interventions and academic advocacy to students within this clinical subpopulation. Finally, a number of chapters focusing on a school counselor's work with special populations of students and special topics in schools were updated, including "Counseling Children of Poverty," "Counseling Multiracial Students," and "Emotional Safety in the Classroom."

The section structure of the third edition of the Handbook is as follows:

- Section 1: The Foundations of School Counseling
- Section 2: Leadership and the Professional School Counselor
- Section 3: Comprehensive School Counseling Programs
- Section 4: Techniques and Approaches to Counseling in Schools
- Section 5: Assessment in School Counseling
- Section 6: Clinical Issues in School Counseling
- Section 7: Special Issues and Populations in School Counseling

As society and schools continue to change, a dynamic relationship with school counseling will continue to evolve. To school counseling professionals who use this book to retool and update skills, I hope the excitement of these transitions help you to provide even better services to your students and school community. To students who are entering the field, I hope this book provides you with a strong foundation of the current state of school counseling, but also gives you some perspective as to how the profession evolved to its current state and some insights into where you will take the field in the future. You could not have chosen a more challenging and gratifying career . . . Enjoy!

Bradley T. Erford, PhD, Professor
School Counseling Program, Education Specialties Department
School of Education, Loyola University Maryland
Past President of the American Counseling Association
January 2015

Dedication

This effort is dedicated to The One—the Giver of energy, passion, and understanding—who makes life worth living and endeavors worth pursuing and accomplishing; the Teacher of love and forgiveness.

About the Editor and Authors

About the Editor

Bradley T. Erford, PhD, LCPC, NCC, LPC, LP, LSP, is a professor in the school counseling program of the Education Specialties Department in the School of Education at Loyola University Maryland. He was the 61st President of the American Counseling Association (ACA, 2012–2013). He is the recipient of the ACA Research Award, ACA Extended Research Award, ACA Arthur A. Hitchcock Distinguished Professional Service Award, ACA Professional Development Award, and ACA Carl D. Perkins Government Relations Award. He was also inducted as an ACA Fellow. He has received the Association for Assessment and Research in Counseling (AARC) AARC/MECD Research Award, AARC Exemplary Practices Award, AARC President's Merit Award, the Association for Counselor Education and Supervision's (ACES) Robert O. Stripling Award for Excellence in Standards, Maryland Association for Counseling and Development (MACD) Maryland Counselor of the Year, MACD Counselor Advocacy Award, MACD Professional Development Award, and MACD Counselor Visibility Award. He is the editor of numerous texts including: *Orientation to the Counseling Profession* (Pearson Merrill, 2010, 2014), *Developing Multicultural Counseling Competence: A System's Approach* (Pearson Merrill, 2010, 2014), *Crisis Intervention and Prevention* (Pearson Merrill, 2010, 2014), *Applying Techniques to Common Encounters in School Counseling: A Case-Based Approach* (Pearson Merrill, 2014), *Group Work in the Schools* (Pearson Merrill, 2010), *Group Work: Process and Applications* (Pearson Merrill, 2011), *Transforming the School Counseling Profession* (Pearson Merrill, 2003, 2007, 2011, 2015), *Professional School Counseling: A Handbook of Principles, Programs and Practices* (PRO-ED, 2004, 2010, 2016), *Assessment for Counselors* (Cengage, 2007, 2013), *Research and Evaluation in Counseling* (Cengage, 2008, 2014), and *The Counselor's Guide to Clinical, Personality and Behavioral Assessment* (Cengage, 2006); and co-author of six more books: *Mastering the NCE and CPCE* (Pearson Merrill, 2011, 2015), *40 Techniques Every Counselor Should Know* (Merrill/Prentice-Hall, 2010, 2016), *Free Access Assessment Instruments for Common Mental Health and Addiction Issues* (Routledge, 2013), *Educational Applications of the WISC-IV* (Western Psychological Services, 2006), and *Group Activities: Firing Up for Performance* (Pearson Merrill, 2007). He was the General Editor of *The American Counseling Association Encyclopedia of Counseling* (ACA, 2009). His research specialization falls primarily in development and technical analysis of psycho-educational tests and outcome research and has resulted in the publication of more than 60 refereed journal articles, 100 book chapters, and a dozen published tests. He was a representative to the ACA Governing Council and the ACA 20/20 Visioning Committee. He is a past president and past treasurer of AARC, past chair and parliamentarian of the American Counseling Association–Southern (US) Region; past-chair of ACA's Task Force on High Stakes Testing; past chair of ACA's Standards for Test Users Task Force; past chair of ACA's Interprofessional Committee; past chair of the ACA Public Awareness and Support Committee (co-chair of the National Awards Sub-committee); past-chair of the Convention and past chair of the

Screening Assessment Instruments Committees for AARC; past president of the Maryland Association for Counseling and Development (MACD); past president of Maryland Association for Measurement and Evaluation (MAME); past president of Maryland Association for Counselor Education and Supervision (MACES); and past president of the Maryland Association for Mental Health Counselors (MAMHC). He was also an associate editor of the *Journal of Counseling & Development*. Dr. Erford has been a faculty member at Loyola since 1993 and is a Licensed Clinical Professional Counselor, Licensed Professional Counselor, Nationally Certified Counselor, Licensed Psychologist and Licensed School Psychologist. Prior to arriving at Loyola, Dr. Erford was a school psychologist/counselor in the Chesterfield County (VA) Public Schools. He maintains a private practice specializing in assessment and treatment of children and adolescents. A graduate of The University of Virginia (PhD), Bucknell University (MA), and Grove City College (BS), he teaches courses in Testing and Measurement, Lifespan Development, Research and Evaluation in Counseling, School Counseling, and Stress Management.

About the Authors

Lyndon P. Abrams earned a PhD in counseling from Texas A&M University–Commerce. He is a Nationally Certified Counselor and has professional counseling experience in community settings. Dr. Abrams is currently an associate professor in the Department of Counseling at the University of North Carolina at Charlotte.

Jason B. Baker, PhD, LPC, is an assistant professor in the Department of Psychology at Millersville University. As a licensed professional counselor, Jason has worked therapeutically with children, adolescents, and adults in community, school, and home settings and brings these experiences to his writing and teaching.

Gerta Bardhoshi, PhD, is an assistant professor of counselor education at the University of South Dakota. Her specialty areas include working with children and families in public schools, especially rural areas, as well as comprehensive school counseling program creation and evaluation.

Dorothy Breen, PhD, is a retired professor of counselor education at the University of Maine. She is a psychologist in private practice in rural Maine. She attained her master's degree in counselor education and doctorate in counseling psychology from the University of Wisconsin.

Lela Kosteck Bunch is the executive director of the Missouri School Counselor Association. Prior to taking her current position, she was an assistant professor in the Division of Counseling and Family Therapy at the University of Missouri–St. Louis. She also served for 3 years as the director of guidance and placement for the Missouri Department of Elementary and Secondary Education. She has a PhD in School Psychology with an emphasis in educational and family systems from the University of Missouri–Columbia and a master's degree in School Counseling from Pittsburg State University.

David J. Carter received a PhD from the University of Nebraska at Lincoln. He is the Peter Kiewit Professor and clinical supervisor in counselor education at the University of Nebraska at Omaha. His private practice work is with children and adolescents. He is a past president of the Nebraska Counseling Association and continues to serve on the American Counseling Association's Professional Standards Committee.

Patricia Carter is a Nebraska Licensed Independent Mental Health Practitioner and has accumulated over 20 years of experience in the social services field and as a professional counselor in private practice. She is Board Certified in neurofeedback and founder of the Carter Counseling Center in Omaha, Nebraska.

Mary Ann Clark, PhD, NCC, is a professor emerita in the Counselor Education Program at the University of Florida, Gainesville. She has been a professional school counselor and administrator in stateside and overseas schools prior to her university work. Dr. Clark has served as a consultant and speaker to school and community groups on topics including student assessment, school safety and violence prevention, and small-group counseling. Her areas of special interest include gender differences in educational achievement, student success factors, character education, university/school partnerships, and career development.

Carol A. Dahir is the chair of the School Counseling Department at NYIT. She has extensive experience working with state departments of education, school systems, and school counselor associations and organizations on delivering and evaluating comprehensive school counseling programs. She served as the project director for the ASCA National Standards development and Planning for Life initiative. She also served on the governing boards for the American School Counselor Association and the National Career Development Association. She focuses her research and presentations on college and career readiness, accountability, principal-counselor relationships, cultural competence, and continuous improvement for school counselors.

Joyce A. DeVoss, PhD, is a professor and coordinator of the MEd school counseling program at Northern Arizona University in Tucson. Her research and scholarly interests include school counselor leadership and advocacy and social/emotional learning in K–12. She has also worked as a professional school counselor, agency counselor, psychologist, and organizational consultant. She has written a book, book chapters, and journal articles relevant to school counseling. She is the Chair of the Education and Professional Development Committee for the North American Society for Adlerian Psychology (NASAP) and an active member of the Research Committee for the Arizona School Counselors Association.

R. Anthony Doggett, PhD, is a school psychologist with Fluency Plus, LLC, providing professional consultation services in the areas of school-wide positive behavior interventions and supports, response to intervention, function-based behavioral supports, tiered academic interventions, data-based decision making, and intervention compliance and integrity. He is the former graduate coordinator of the Department of Counseling and Educational Psychology and program coordinator of the School Psychology program at Mississippi State University. Dr. Doggett received his PhD in school psychology from The University of Southern Mississippi. He completed a predoctoral internship and a 1-year postdoctoral fellowship in behavioral pediatrics at the Munroe-Meyer Institute for Genetics and Rehabilitation in Omaha, Nebraska. He has served as the president of the Mississippi Association for Psychology in the Schools and a professional consultant to several school districts or state departments of education.

Deborah L. Drew, EdD, is an associate professor and director of the graduate counseling and human relations program at Husson University in Bangor, Maine. In her private practice, she provides counseling, consultation, and supervision to rural Maine counselors and school systems. Formerly, she was a professional school counselor in rural areas of Maine. She attained her master's degree and doctorate in counselor education from the University of Maine.

Suzanne M. Dugger, EdD, is a professor in the Department of Leadership and Counseling at Eastern Michigan University where she serves as the Coordinator of the School Counseling program. Dr. Dugger also developed EMU's course on postsecondary planning for school counselors and is in the process of finalizing a textbook, *Foundations of Career Counseling: A Case-Based Approach*, which will be published by Pearson. She holds credentials as a school teacher, school counselor and Licensed Professional Counselor in Michigan.

Mardi Kay Fallon has an EdD in counselor education from the University of Cincinnati. She currently works for Central Clinic and is a contract therapist for Hyde Park Counseling Professionals.

Sejal Parikh Foxx is an assistant professor and director of the counseling and school counseling program at the University of North Carolina at Charlotte. As a former school counselor, she developed a passion for multicultural counseling with a special focus in social justice and advocacy. She spends her academic time training school counselors, conducting research, and serving the community. Dr. Parikh Foxx also has experience in building university–school partnerships which keeps her grounded and focused on current issues in education and school counseling. She has presented over 60 conference presentations and invited workshops during the past decade on topics such as multiculturalism, solution-focused counseling, and building comprehensive school programs.

Nadine E. Garner, EdD, LPC, is an associate professor in the school counseling program of the Psychology Department at Millersville University of Pennsylvania. She is the founder and director of the Center for Sustainability and the chair of the Sustainability Committee. Dr. Garner is co-author of the book *A School With Solutions: Implementing a Solution-Focused/Adlerian-Based Comprehensive School Counseling Program* (ASCA, 1998). As a former K–12 professional school counselor at Scotland School for Veterans' Children, Dr. Garner developed a comprehensive conflict resolution/peer mediation program.

Donna M. Gibson is an associate professor of counselor education at Virginia Commonwealth University. She has worked with families and children in public schools, hospitals, private practice, and clinics as a counselor and psychologist.

Gary E. Goodnough is professor and chair of the Counselor Education and School Psychology Department at Plymouth State University. He has worked in public schools as a teacher, professional school counselor, and director of guidance. Gary consults regularly with school districts on comprehensive school counseling programs. He is the author of more than 20 articles and book chapters and is the co-editor of *Leadership, Advocacy and Direct Service Strategies for Professional School Counselors*.

Henry L. Harris is a former secondary school counselor and military veteran. He is a Licensed Professional Counselor and a licensed school counselor in the state of North Carolina. He is also professor and Chair of the Department of Counseling at UNC Charlotte.

Trish Hatch, PhD, is the author of *The Use of Data in School Counseling: Hatching Results for Students, Programs and the Profession* (2014); co-author of the *ASCA National Model: A Framework for School Counseling Programs* (ASCA, 2003, 2005) and co-author of *Evidence-Based Practice in School Counseling: Making a Difference with Data-Driven Practices* (Dimmit, Carey, & Hatch, 2007). Dr. Hatch is the Director of the school counseling program and associate professor at San Diego State University and the Executive Director of the Center for Excellence in School Counseling and Leadership (CESCaL), in the College of Education at SDSU. A former school counselor and administrator, Dr. Hatch has served in multiple leadership roles including Supervisor/Post-Secondary Level Vice President of the American School Counselor Association (ASCA). Multiple state and national awards include ASCA's Administrator of the Year Award and the Mary Gehrke Lifetime Achievement Award. As President and CEO of Hatching Results® LLC, Dr. Hatch provides training and consulting on evidenced-based practice and the use of data to improve outcomes for students, programs, and the profession. (www.hatchingresults.com)

Carlen Henington, PhD, NCSP, is an associate professor in the school psychology program at Mississippi State University, where she is program coordinator and directs the Summer Academic Clinic for children who are referred for academic and behavior concerns. Her research and professional interests include evaluation and implementation of academic and behavioral interventions, and assessment and intervention in early childhood.

Susan Norris Huss, LPC, is an associate professor in the mental health and school counseling program at Bowling Green State University in Ohio. She received her PhD in counselor education from the University of Toledo after being a professional school counselor for 23 years. Dr. Huss has extensive experience in working with bereavement in schools. For 20 years, she led loss support groups for students who experienced a death. She has presented at local, state, and national levels in the area of bereavement and legal and ethical issues and has conducted research related to the efficacy of school-based loss support groups for parentally bereaved students. Dr. Huss is a past president of the Ohio Counseling Association, the Ohio Association of Counselor Education and Supervision and currently serves on the American Counseling Association Ethics Committee.

Brian Hutchison, LPC, NCC, is currently an assistant professor, Coordinator of the School Counseling Program, and International Studies Fellow at the University of Missouri–St. Louis. He received his PhD in counselor education and supervision from Penn State University in 2009. His scholarly work is focused on the study of social class bias in the delivery of school counseling interventions, international school and career counseling, counselor feelings of social class dissonance as it applies to their work, and the delivery of interventions that incorporate the concept of human agency and social justice as it impacts the development of underserved and international populations.

C. Marie Jackson, EdD, is a former counselor education faculty member at the University of West Georgia. She has a master's degree in counseling from Jacksonville State University and a doctoral degree in counselor education from the University of Alabama. She has experience in public schools as a teacher, psychometrist, and a school counselor, K–12. She has been program leader for school counseling training programs in three university settings. In addition to her school counseling credentials and experience, she was a Licensed Professional

Counselor and a Nationally Certified Counselor, and has worked in a psychiatric hospital outpatient setting as a therapist.

Gregory R. Janson is an associate professor of child and family studies at Ohio University, Athens. A Professional Clinical Counselor and Clinical Supervisor, Dr. Janson has worked extensively in community mental health and private practice as a trauma specialist and family counselor with severely disturbed children and adolescents and their families, and as a forensic examiner. A former therapeutic foster parent, his current research interests focus on the impact of emotional maltreatment in classrooms, PTSD, and risk assessment with behavioral intervention teams in higher education. Other research interests focus on issues affecting gay, lesbian, bisexual, and transgendered adolescents and their families

Kalinda R. Jones is an assistant professor of school counseling at Loyola University Maryland. She earned her PhD in Guidance and Psychological Services with a specialization in counseling psychology from Indiana State University. She received her BA in biology education from Olivet Nazarene University and her MA in school counseling at Eastern Michigan University. Drawing on 20 years of experience as an educator and counselor primarily with underserved students and clients, her current research involves the career development of children and adolescents as well as the training of counselors to work cross-culturally.

Gerald A. Juhnke, EdD, LPC, NCC, MAC, LCAS, ACS, is professor at The University of Texas at San Antonio. He is the past president of the International Association for Addictions and Offender Counseling (IAAOC) and the Association for Assessment in Counseling (AAC). Jerry is a former editor of the *Journal of Addictions and Offender Counseling* and a past co-chair of the American Counseling Association's Council of Journal Editors. He has authored or edited eight books and has more than 48 refereed journal articles that have either been published or are currently in press. Jerry's direct clinical counseling and clinical supervision histories includes independent practice, community mental health, corrections, and schools. Jerry's most recent book is *Counseling Addicted Families: An Integrated Assessment and Treatment Model*.

Carol J. Kaffenberger is an associate professor emerita at George Mason University in Fairfax, Virginia. Currently she teaches school counselor preparation courses at Johns Hopkins University and is a consultant for the American School Counselor Association (ASCA) and Virginia school districts, providing training for practicing school counselors in the development of comprehensive school counseling programs and the use of accountability strategies. She is the associate editor for practitioner research for the *Professional School Counseling* journal. Kaffenberger was on the *ASCA National Model* (3rd ed.) Advisory Board and served as a Counselor Educator VP for ASCA. Previously she was an elementary school counselor. She is the co-author of publications developed to help practicing school counselors align their school counseling programs with the *ASCA National Model* and use data. She has also conducted a research study on the school reentry issues of children with cancer and developed a model for school reintegration for students with chronic illnesses. She provides training to practicing school counselors, social workers, and public health nurses. Her writing interests include supporting students with chronic illness, the transformation of school counseling programs, and training school counselors to use data to drive program development and evaluation.

ZiYoung Kang is a doctoral candidate in the counselor education program at the Pennsylvania State University. She earned a master's degree in counseling at Seoul National University (SNU), Korea. Prior to pursuing her doctoral degree, she worked as a counselor and a Campus Mentoring Program coordinator at SNU, and then as a researcher, mentor, and lecturer of Won Coaching Program for Adolescents at the Won Buddhism Bureau of Adolescents, in Seoul, Korea. She is currently a counseling intern at the Penn State Career Services.

Margaret A. King is a professor emerita in early childhood teacher education at Ohio University. Dr. King served as secretary and governing board member of the National Association for the Education of Young Children. She has written and presented on emotional maltreatment by school personnel, boys and guidance, best teaching practices, and teacher development.

Vivian V. Lee is associate professor in the Department of Counselling in the Faculty for Social Wellbeing at the University of Malta. She serves as the Coordinator of Supervision for both the Transcultural Counselling Master's and the Master's in Counselling degrees. Dr. Lee is the past president of the Maryland Association for Counseling and Development and held a leadership position in the Pennsylvania Counseling Association. Lee has authored and co-authored articles and book chapters on conflict resolution and violence, group counseling, and equity-focused systemic and data-driven school counseling programs. Lee recently completed a nine year collaborative library building project in Ghana with colleagues from the United States and Ghana as an outgrowth of a Fulbright-Hays Scholars Group Project. She was a recipient of the O'Hana Award in 2008 by the Counselors for Social Justice. Lee is the former Senior Director, Counselor Advocacy at the National Office for School Counselor Advocacy of The College Board. Lee worked to transform counselor training, practice, and policy at the state and national level. Dr. Lee is an accomplished trainer and presenter at the international and national levels and has held academic posts as a counselor educator at University of Maryland, Old Dominion University, and University of Scranton. She received both master's and doctoral degrees in Counselor Education and Supervision from the University of Virginia.

Dana Heller Levitt is associate professor of counseling at Montclair State University. Dr. Levitt has nearly 20 years of experience in counseling and counselor education. In addition to her previous clinical work and research in the areas of eating disorders and body image, she has contributed to scholarship in areas of ethical practice, counselor development, and religious and spiritual issues in counseling.

Lynn E. Linde is clinical assistant professor and the director of clinical experiences in the school counseling program at Loyola University Maryland. She received her master's degree in school counseling and her doctorate in counseling from George Washington University. She was previously the chief of the Student Services and Alternative Programs Branch at the Maryland State Department of Education, the state specialist for school counseling, a local school system counseling supervisor, a middle and high school counselor, and a special education teacher. Dr. Linde was the 2009–2010 President and the 2012–2013 Treasurer of the American Counseling Association. She is an ACA Fellow and has received a number of awards, including the 2013 ACA President's Award for contributions to the profession, as well as awards from the state of Maryland for her work in student services and youth suicide prevention. She has been a chair and member of the ACA Ethics Committee, Ethics Appeal Panel, and Ethics Revision Task Force for the 2014 ACA *Code of Ethics*. She has made numerous presentations, particularly in the areas of ethics and legal issues for counselors and public policy and legislation, over the course of her career. She has authored or co-authored a number of book chapters and articles on counseling ethics and has taught the Professional Issues and Ethics course in Loyola's school counseling program for over 15 years. Dr. Linde is also a certified True Colors trainer.

Sandra M. Logan is a doctoral fellow in the counselor education and supervision program at the University of Florida. She earned her master's degree and credential in school counseling at Chapman University in California. Prior to pursuing her doctorate, she worked as an elementary and middle school counselor and held the role of district Tobacco Use, Prevention, and Education (TUPE) coordinator. Her specific research interests include school counseling supervision, leadership development, and professional identity development of counselor educators.

Belinda J. Lopez, PhD, LPC-S, NCC, CSC, earned an MS in counseling and a PhD in counselor education from Texas A&M University–Corpus Christi. She is an assistant professor of counselor education at Lamar University. Her experiences include work as a professional school counselor, teaching, supervision of counselor interns for certification and state licensure, and leadership in local, state and national organizations.

Patricia Jo McDivitt began her career as an educator, serving as a classroom teacher and/or counselor for 12 years. In addition to her teaching experience, she is past president of the Association for Assessment in Counseling and Education (AACE). During her year as president, Ms. McDivitt was co-editor of the *Measurement and Evaluation in Counseling and Development* (MECD) special edition, Large-Scale Assessment and High-Stakes Testing. Since 1995, Ms. McDivitt has served as a member of the Joint Committee on Standards for Educational Evaluation (JCSEE) where she was instrumental in the development and launch of *The Student Evaluation Standards*. She most recently served as the Joint Committee's vice chair and is currently serving as the co-chair of the revision task force for the *Classroom Assessment Standards*.

Adriana G. McEachern, PhD, NCC, CRC, LMHC, is a counselor education associate professor and program director in the College of Education at Florida International University. She received her doctorate in counselor education from the University of Florida. She is past president of the Florida Counseling Association and past chair of the American Counseling Association Southern Region. She has published numerous articles in the areas of child abuse, exceptional students and exceptional student education, and multicultural issues.

Carol Z. A. McGinnis, PhD, LCPC, NCC, is a pastoral counselor and assistant professor in the graduate counseling program at Messiah College in Mechanicsburg, PA. Her research and clinical interests relate to anger as a positive emotion and online Xbox video gaming as a factor in young adult and family counseling. She also serves as Clinical Director for the Amazon Warrior Institute (AWI) at Fairview United Methodist Church in Phoenix, MD.

Robika Modak Mylroie, PhD, is an adjunct professor in the counseling and special populations department at Lamar University. Her research interests include childhood obesity and its impact on children personally, socially, and academically.

Amy J. Newmeyer, MD, completed a postdoctoral fellowship at the Kennedy-Krieger Institute at the Johns Hopkins University School of Medicine upon completion of her medical degree from Ohio State University and residency from Akron Children's Hospital. She is double boarded in pediatrics and neuro-development disabilities and is currently on faculty at Children's Hospital of the King's Daughters in Norfolk, VA.

Mark D. Newmeyer, EdD, is an assistant professor in the School of Psychology and Counseling at Regent University where he serves as the coordinator of the PhD program in Counselor Education and Supervision. He has a background in a variety of school settings providing behavioral evaluation, testing, and assessment. His current research efforts include understanding parental stress, training effective group workers, and the protective factors in preventing compassion fatigue among counselors.

Spencer G. Niles is the Dean for the School of Education at The College of William & Mary and previously served as a Distinguished Professor and Department Head for Educational Psychology, Counseling, and Special Education at Pennsylvania State University. Dr. Niles is the recipient of the National Career Development Association's (NCDA) Eminent Career Award, a Fellow of the American Counseling Association (ACA) and NCDA, the recipient of ACA's President's Award, David Brooks Distinguished Mentor Award, Extended Research Award, the Thomas J. Sweeney Visionary Leadership and Advocacy Award, and the University of British Columbia's Noted Scholar Award. He served as President for the National Career Development Association and Editor for *The Career Development Quarterly*. Niles was the Editor of the *Journal of Counseling & Development* and serves on six additional editorial boards for national and international journals. He is also on the advisory board for the International Centre for Career Development and Public Policy. Dr. Niles has authored or co-authored approximately 120 publications and delivered over 125 presentations on career development theory and practice.

Melissa Nowicki is a graduate of Mount Vernon Nazarene University with bachelor's degrees in psychology and sociology. She is currently working on a master's in school counseling at Bowling Green State University.

Ralph L. Piedmont is a professor of pastoral counseling at Loyola University Maryland. His research interests include the five-factor model of personality and its relationship to spiritual phenomena. He has also developed a motivationally based measure of spirituality, the Assessment of Spirituality and Religious Sentiments (ASPIRES) scale, and is interested in documenting its predictive validity in a number of applied contexts.

Mark Pope, EdD, NCC, MCC, ACS, MAC, is professor and chair of the Department of Counseling & Family Therapy in the College of Education at the University of Missouri–Saint Louis, where his specialties include career counseling, addictions counseling, psychological testing, and multicultural counseling, including counseling with sexual minorities. He has written extensively on various aspects of counseling, including the career development of ethnic, racial, and sexual minorities; violence in the schools; teaching career counseling; psychological testing; international issues in counseling; and the history of and public policy issues in professional counseling. He served as the editor of *The Career Development Quarterly*, the premier journal in career counseling, and is the past president of the American Counseling Association; National Career Development Association; Association for Gay, Lesbian, and Bisexual Issues in Counseling, and Society for the Psychological Study of LGBT Issues. He is a Fellow of the American Counseling Association, American Psychological Association, National Career Development Association, Society for the Psychological Study of LGBT Issues, Society for the Psychological Study of Ethnic Minority Issues, and Society of Counseling Psychology.

Jonathan Procter is an assistant professor of psychology at Marist College teaching in both the psychology and mental health programs in the School of Social & Behavioral Sciences. He is a Licensed Professional Counselor, a National Certified Counselor, and an Approved Clinical Supervisor. His research interests include the LGBT community, disability, multiculturalism, and social justice issues. His clinical experience includes both community and in-patient psychiatric populations including children, adolescents, and adults living with formidable behavioral, emotional, and mental disorders. He is active in state and national organizations including the American Counseling Association, Association for Counselor Education and Supervision, and the Association for Contextual Behavioral Science.

Michael S. Rankins, PhD, received his doctoral degree in 2008 from the University of Missouri–St. Louis. A former intern of the Victim Service Council and the Masters & Johnson Institute in St. Louis, Dr. Rankins has also served as a prevention coordinator with St. Louis Effort for AIDS, as a counselor with Hyland Behavioral Health at St. Anthony's Medical Center, as Assistant Director of Student Life at UM–St. Louis, and as founder and Director of the Student Life Resource Centers at UM–St. Louis. Upon completion of his doctoral degree, he joined the faculty at Lindenwood University and is an associate professor in the Division of School and Professional Counseling. He continues to be involved in advocacy and community outreach and also remains dedicated to assisting those affected by HIV/AIDS. He is currently completing a book outlining his experiences with marriage equality efforts in San Francisco.

Carl J. Sheperis is chair of Counseling and Special Populations at Lamar University. He is author of *Counseling Research* and *Foundations of Clinical Mental Health Counseling* for Pearson. He serves as a director for NBCC and as associate editor for the *Journal of Counseling & Development*.

Donna S. Sheperis earned a PhD in counselor education from the University of Mississippi. A core faculty member in the Mental Health Counseling Program of Walden University, Dr. Sheperis is a Licensed Professional Counselor, National Certified Counselor, Certified Clinical Mental Health Counselor, and Approved Clinical Supervisor with over 20 years of experience in counseling settings. She has served as co-chair of the ACA Ethics Committee and is involved with the Association for Assessment and Research in Counseling, the Association for Humanistic Counseling, and the Association for Counselor Education and Supervision. Dr. Sheperis has authored numerous articles in peer-reviewed journals in addition to publishing her own books and chapters in edited texts. Dr. Sheperis presents regularly on topics related to counseling and has received several awards for her teaching, scholarship, and research.

Qi Shi, PhD, is an assistant professor in school counseling in the Education Specialties Department at Loyola University Maryland. Her research interests include using national longitudinal datasets in school counseling research, ESL students' educational attainment, and multicultural competency of school counselors.

Brent Marriott Snow is the Provost and Vice President for Academic Affairs at Texas A&M University–San Antonio. He was the principle investigator of one of the six national transforming school counseling grants funded by the Wallace Reader's Digest Fund administered through The Education Trust while at the University of West Georgia. His previous positions include Associate VPAA and Chair of the Department of Counseling and Educational Psychology at the University of West Georgia, a faculty member and coordinator of the counseling area faculty at Oklahoma State University, and a faculty member at the University of Idaho. He received his PhD from the University of Idaho, his MS degree from Oklahoma State University, his BS degree from Brigham Young University, and his Associate Degree from Boise College (now Boise State University).

Carolyn B. Stone is a professor at the University of North Florida, where she teaches and researches the legal and ethical implications for working with minors in schools. Prior to becoming a counselor educator, Dr. Stone was a supervisor of guidance, an elementary and secondary teacher, and elementary and high school counselor.

Mei Tang, PhD, LPC, is a professor in the counseling program of University of Cincinnati and has been a counselor educator since 1996. She obtained her doctoral degree from the University of Wisconsin–Milwaukee. Her teaching and research areas include multicultural issues in counseling, career development of minorities, assessment and research in counseling, internationalization of counselor training, and school counseling issues. In recent years, Dr. Tang has been applying an ecological counseling approach in her research and collaboration with local school and community agencies as well as cross-cultural settings.

Jerry Trusty is professor of counselor education and coordinator of the Secondary School Counseling Program in the Department of Educational Psychology, Counseling, and Special Education, at The Pennsylvania State University. Dr. Trusty has experience as a middle school and high school counselor. He has published numerous works on adolescents' educational and career development. Dr. Trusty recently completed his second term as Editor of *Career Development Quarterly*.

Lawrence E. Tyson, PhD, is an associate professor in the Department of Human Studies, Counselor Education Program at the University of Alabama at Birmingham. He is the school counseling advisor and was an American School Counselor Association Trainer for National Standards for School Counseling Programs. He is the primary author of *Critical Incidents in School Counseling* (1st & 2nd ed.), *Critical Incidents in Supervision*, and *Critical Incidents in Group Counseling*. Prior to joining the faculty at UAB, he worked as a professional school counselor in central Florida. Dr. Tyson was also a contributing task force member for the development of Alabama's first Comprehensive Counseling and Guidance Model for Alabama Public Schools. Dr. Tyson continues to investigate the effect of Alabama's model on the implementation of school counseling programs in Alabama.

Ann Vernon, PhD, is professor emerita, University of Northern Iowa, where she served as coordinator of the school and mental health counseling programs for many years. Dr. Vernon is the President of the Albert Ellis Board of Trustees and a member of the International Training Standards and Review committee at the Institute. She is the author of numerous books, chapters, and articles, including *Thinking, Feeling, Behaving* and *What Works When With Children and Adolescents*. She is internationally recognized as the leading expert on applications of RE&CBT with children and adolescents and conducts training programs on this topic in South America, Romania, Australia, and the United States.

Edward A. Wierzalis earned a PhD in counseling and supervision from the University of Virginia. He has professional counseling experience in both the school and community settings. He is presently a clinical associate professor and Coordinator of Clinical Field Experiences in the Department of Counseling at the University of North Carolina at Charlotte.

Chris Wood, PhD, is an associate professor in Old Dominion University's Counseling and Human Services department and the graduate program director for the distance learning program. He was most recently an associate professor at Seattle University (SU) and was previously a faculty member at the Ohio State University and the University of Arizona. In addition to being a counselor educator, Dr. Wood has experience as a high school counselor, a counseling/guidance department chair, a counselor/group leader at a residential youth facility for adjudicated youth/troubled teens, and a career counselor at an alternative school serving grades 7–12. He is currently the Head Editor for the *Professional School Counseling* journal, the flagship research journal for the American School Counseling Association (ASCA).

Robert E. Wubbolding, EdD, is the director of the Center for Reality Therapy in Cincinnati, Ohio; former director of training for the William Glasser Institute (1988–2011); and professor emeritus of Xavier University. A former elementary and high school counselor and adult basic education instructor, he is the author of 13 books on reality therapy, including *Reality Therapy for the 21st Century*. He has taught reality therapy in North America, North Africa, Asia, Europe, and the Middle East and has received the Marvin Rammelsberg Award, the Herman Peters Award, the Mary Corre Foster Award, and outstanding alumnus of the University of Cincinnati, College of Education.

Elias Zambrano, MA, is a retired certified school counselor and worked as a professional school counselor for 28 years. During that time, he also served as the Safe and Drug Free Schools and Communities Program Coordinator and then Director of Guidance Services for Northside Independent School District in San Antonio, TX. He currently serves as a clinical assistant professor in the counselor education and supervision program at the University of Texas at San Antonio.

SECTION 1

The Foundations of School Counseling

CHAPTER 1

Professional School Counseling: Integrating Theory and Practice Into a Data-Driven, Evidence-Based Approach

Bradley T. Erford

Preview

The introduction of the American School Counselor Association (ASCA) national model (ASCA, 2012a) and data-driven, evidence-based, and outcome-oriented school counseling practices have dramatically changed how professional school counselors have operated over the past 10 years. The focus of this transformed role is to build on the broad-based theoretical and practical counseling skills that have become the core of a professional school counselor's training and to expand into a more data-driven, systemic orientation to meet the needs of all students. The systemic, data-driven, evidence-based approach highlights comprehensive services, social advocacy, and accountability dimensions to remove barriers to student performance and promote a system of equity and access for all students.

American society in general and school systems in particular continue to change. As a result, the school counseling profession necessarily undergoes a continuous evolution. But the changes during the past 10 years are the most dramatic since those that followed the National Defense Education Act of 1959 in reaction to the Soviet Union's launch of *Sputnik* (Erford, 2015c). This current evolution involves both the traditional roles and functions of professional school counselors, as well as the comprehensive school counseling programs that professional school counselors strive to implement—programs that serve the academic, career, and personal–social needs of every student. The task of meeting the developmental needs of all students is ominous:

- Substance Abuse and Mental Health Services Administration (SAMHSA; 2013) indicated that 3.1 million youths ages 12 to 17 years (12.7%) received counseling or some other form of treatment for emotional or behavior problems in the previous year. Adolescent females were slightly more likely than adolescent males to seek mental health treatment.
- Up to 50% of students with significant emotional impairments drop out of school (U.S. Department of Education, 2009).
- 9.1% of adolescents (2.2 million; 13.7% of females and 4.7% of males) had at least one major depressive episode during the previous year, but less than half sought treatment (SAMHSA, 2013).

- For individuals 10 to 24 years of age, suicide is the third leading cause of death, claiming nearly 30,000 deaths annually (SAMHSA, 2013).
- Between 3% and 5% of children have attention-deficit/hyperactivity disorder (ADHD), or approximately 2 million children in the United States (National Institute of Mental Health, 2012).
- Approximately 8 million children receive special education services annually (U.S. Department of Education, 2009).

Society and governments turn to schools for help in meeting the needs of students. Unfortunately, the ratio of professional school counselors to students is only 1:470 (American Counseling Association [ACA], 2013) and has remained near that level throughout much of the past 2 decades—substantially higher than the 1:250 recommended by ASCA—with no real hope of dramatic improvement in the near future.

Given that the problems continue to mount and service availability remains stagnant, what is the solution? While the answer is in no way simple, the transformed role of the contemporary professional school counselor requires that counselors become agents of social change, school reform, and accountability as well as experts in the traditional theory and practice of individual and small-group counseling (Erford, 2015c; Martin, 2015). This shift from an individual, student-centered focus to a systemic intervention focus stems from the realization that, while essential in some cases, "fixing" students one at a time is akin to sticking one's finger in a dike:

> A look to the left and right will often show other professionals using their fingers to plug a hole. By joining with other professional counselors . . . and speaking with a united voice in advocating for the needs of students, they are seeking solutions not only for the students they are working to help, but for all students—those that colleagues are seeking to serve, and those that will seek help in the future. (Erford, 2015c, p. 19)

The ASCA National Standards and ASCA National Model

Over the years, many have deliberated, evaluated, and argued over the role and professional identity of professional school counselors. Some assert that school counselors are teachers who educate students on how to behave and make better life decisions. Still others maintain that school counselors should focus their attention solely on those students who are at risk and underserved by traditional classroom interventions. Neither of these views accurately reflects the precise knowledge and skills of professional school counselors, and these views confuse important decision makers, including administrators and politicians. Sadly, even some practicing school counselors fail to challenge these misconceptions. Practically speaking, professional school counselors are counselors specifically trained to work in educational settings.

The ASCA national model (2012a) provides a structure for the development of a comprehensive counseling program that permits professional school counselors to draw on their specialized skills to meet the needs of all students. The purpose is to promote academic success and to encourage the implementation of proactive strategies designed to meet the needs of students through the various stages of development. Furthermore, this model incorporates student competencies and measurable performance indicators. Perhaps the most notable distinction is the *encouragement* to transform the role of professional school counselors into effective leaders and advocates of change. Knowledgeable about the challenges and systematic hurdles, professional school counselors may be in the best position to affect changes and limit factors restricting student success.

Transforming the Professional School Counselor's Role: Five Guiding Realizations

Erford (2015c) discussed five realizations that can spawn changes in the ways professional school counselors approach program implementation and service delivery:

1. *Professional school counselors receive extensive training in consultation, collaboration, and team or relationship building.* Professional school counselors can use these skills to reach beyond the counseling office, think systemically, and build partnerships with other educators, mental health resources, community organizations, parents, and others to provide needed services to *all* students, but especially those who have been marginalized or oppressed.

2. *Professional school counselors cannot do it all!* The "lone ranger" approach of a single, autonomous professional school counselor "hanging out a shingle" and providing the equivalent of "private practice services" to a select few students will perpetuate the "finger in the dike" phenomenon. Thinking systemically and building partnerships with valuable internal and external resources will help far more students in the short and long term.

3. *Comprehensive developmental school counseling programs are efficient and effective.* Face it: If a professional school counselor does not implement a comprehensive developmental school counseling program, none will exist in that school! Professional school counselors who spend most of their time engaged in a single activity (e.g., individual counseling, paperwork, classroom guidance) are not implementing a comprehensive program.

4. *All professional school counselors have strengths and weaknesses; thus, each provides services of varying quality to varying clientele.* The key here is to know one's proficiencies and use these strengths to benefit all students while developing strategies and partnerships with other resource providers to cover the other areas of a comprehensive program.

5. *Many students are not getting what they need from our educational and mental health systems.* Professional school counselors need to become skilled social advocates and develop effective referral procedures through partnerships with community organizations. The training of professional school counselors is broad by design so that one can serve in the "triage role," allowing the professional school counselor to prioritize the allocation of services in the most efficient manner. This often means that professional school counselors can best serve the greatest number of students by making referral arrangements for the neediest students or those most able to afford services available in the community, thus freeing the professional school counselor to focus on the students for whom the counselor is the last (and perhaps only) hope for effective treatment.

Ten Current and Emerging Roles and Practices of the Professional School Counselor

The realizations described in the previous section give rise to potential changes in how professional school counselors function. Erford (2015c) proposed 10 roles or functions that should be adopted to varying degrees by professional school counselors. Some of these roles and functions are traditional; some are less so, but are of equal importance: (1) Professional; (2) Developmental classroom guidance specialist; (3) Career-development and educational-planning specialist; (4) School and community agency consultation or collaboration specialist; (5) Provider of individual and group counseling services; (6) Safe schools, violence-prevention, at-risk specialist; (7) Agent of diversity and multicultural sensitivity; (8) Advocate for students with special needs; (9) Advocate for academic and social justice; (10) School reform and accountability expert. While there are those who will argue about which of these 10 roles and functions is most important, each is an essential component of a comprehensive program designed to meet the needs of *all* students. Please note, however, that all subsequent components flow from the first one: "Professional school counselors use effective techniques and practices implemented through legal, ethical, and professional means. Belonging to a profession requires one to adhere to the highest standards of that profession . . . [because] how one behaves, good or bad, reflects on all" (Erford, 2015c, p. 24). All professional school counselors should belong to local, state, and national counseling organizations so that the profession can speak with one voice. Advocacy is sometimes accomplished most effectively with one's money—paying your membership dues could be one of the best advocacy actions of your career and for the future of your profession!

Outcomes-Oriented, Evidence-Based, Data-Driven, Accountable School Counseling Programs

One cannot overemphasize the importance of accountability and data-driven, evidence-based, or outcomes-oriented decision making in the implementation and continuous improvement of any comprehensive developmental school counseling program. A number of comprehensive reviews have been conducted, which have resulted in moderate to strong support for the effectiveness of school counseling services (Sexton, Whiston, Bleuer, & Walz, 1997; Whiston, Feldswich, & James, 2015; Whiston & Sexton, 1998). Other chapters in this book address these summaries more directly. Likewise, data-driven approaches to identifying needs and "closing the gap" between high-achieving and low-achieving students describe how students develop as a result of the school counseling program. In particular, ASCA's national model challenges professional school counselors to determine how counseling programs facilitate student development. The model (ASCA, 2012a) incorporates two different intervals:

Short-term: Data collected at the completion of the program that provide information regarding student progress.
　　　　　Example: Students participating in a counseling group to reduce aggression are able to identify other behavioral responses and coping strategies
Long-term: Data that reflect the effectiveness of a particular intervention or activity.
　　　　　Example: Suspension rates decline for group participants

Over time, the collection of data provides professional school counselors with the information needed to review the effectiveness of school counseling programs and, if necessary, adjust to meet the changing needs of the student population.

The critical issue remains, however, that outcomes research in the school counseling field lags behind that of other counseling specialties, and what the research indicates as effective or not effective is frequently not known by the average practitioner in the field. The uneven application of an evidence-based or outcomes-driven approach by school-based practitioners presents one of the greatest challenges to a profession that strives to meet the academic, career, and personal–social needs of every student. School counseling professionals must strive to (a) conduct more outcomes research to determine which services and strategies are effective and which are not; and (b) disseminate evidence-based information to school-based practitioners, supervisors, and counselor educators so that practitioners' theoretical orientation and practice can be driven by an understanding of what is and is not effective. In many ways, the purpose of this book is to provide a resource that is not just accessible and understandable to the practicing professional school counselor or counselor-in-training, but that is also informed by outcome and evidence-based research, thereby providing a wealth of information for practitioners regarding what is and is not effective in our work with students.

The Future of School Counseling

The school counseling profession has been shaped by numerous events and initiatives, including *Sputnik* and the *National Defense Education Act*, Wrenn's (1962) *The Counselor in a Changing World*, ASCA's *National Standards for School Counseling Programs* (Campbell & Dahir, 1997), The Education Trust's (1999) "Transforming School Counseling Initiative," and *The ASCA National Model: A Framework for School Counseling Programs* (ASCA, 2012a). Throughout the last century, the profession has evolved to meet changing societal and school-system demands. For some time now, doomsayers have predicted the demise of the school counseling profession. Well, the reports of our demise are premature! Perhaps Erford (2015c) said it best:

> The historical roots that have spawned the need for counselors in schools and future issues that remain to be fully resolved at the beginning of the 21st century suggest that the role of the professional counselor is not a rigid and static set of functions. Rather, it is in a constant state of transformation in response to the changing demands on American schools and the factors and influences that affect the growth and development of America's children and youth. Across the one hundred years or so that comprise the history of school counseling in the United States, the questions and issues have changed. However, there is no longer the question of whether professional school counseling will survive or whether it is relevant to the mission of the school. The questions today are how to make its contribution more explicit, how to distribute its effects more evenly across school and student groups, and how to deploy these precious professional resources in the most efficient and effective manner. These are the challenges that the future professional school counselor will face. (p. 25)

The school counseling profession will continue to evolve and thrive so long as professional school counselors strive to meet the academic, career, and personal–social needs of all students.

Summary/Conclusion

The school counseling profession has a rich history of evolving in new and necessary directions to address societal, systemic, and student needs. The current phase of evolution, or transformation, must be driven by data, evidence-based research, and outcome research that identifies effective practices. In addition to the traditional emphasis on theoretical counseling orientations and practices, the contemporary professional school counselor must emphasize accountability, social advocacy, and systemic interventions, all within the umbrella of a comprehensive developmental school counseling program that removes barriers to student success and addresses the academic, career, and personal–social needs of *all* students.

CHAPTER 2

The History of School Counseling

Mei Tang and Bradley T. Erford

Preview

Reviewing the history of a profession generally serves two purposes. One is to understand how the profession came into being and how it reached its current status. The other is to look for a direction for the future. This chapter will focus on the first goal, to explore the roots and developmental stages of school counseling as a profession, providing context for several of the chapters that follow, which address the later purpose. As Erford (2015c) argued, counseling in schools did not arise in a vacuum; it is necessary to review the development of school counseling in the historical context: "The historical moment must be right for the ingredients of change to take root and begin to flourish" (p. 18). This chapter will chronicle school counseling developmental periods through four dimensions: historical context, external forces or significant events that have had momentous impact on the growth and direction of the school counseling profession, theoretical frameworks that have influenced professional school counselors' work, and roles and functions professional school counselors have performed.

Emerging Years (1900–1915)

Historical Context

At the beginning of the 20th century, American society went through vast changes as a result of the Industrial Revolution. The Industrial Revolution resulted in a concentration of the work force, a demand for skilled workers, uncertainty in the labor market, and, consequently, a growth in secondary school enrollment and a challenge to the classical education that was not adequately preparing skilled workers (Dixon, 1987). The other societal and contextual factors for these changes during the early 1900s included urbanization, a large influx of immigrants, the abuses of child labor, city ghettos, and neglect of individual rights and integrity (Herr, 2002; Minkoff & Terres, 1985).

Brewer (1942) identified four important economic and social conditions (i.e., division of labor, technological innovations, vocational education, and modern democracy) that influenced the rise of educational reform and vocational guidance, while Traxler and North (1966) pointed to "philanthropy or humanitarianism, religion, mental hygiene, social change, and the movement to know pupils as individuals" (p. 6). These changes forced schools to address the needs of students and respond to the social, economic, and educational problems.

Bookish learning and impractical instruction were criticized for failing to prepare students adequately to avail themselves of the growing opportunities as they entered into the work force. At the same time, because the labor division was so differentiated and comprehensive, family and friends could no longer provide essential information and assistance for occupational choice (Erford, 2015c). Therefore, it became necessary for schools to provide vocational guidance for these youngsters. *Vocational guidance*, as the root for school counseling, has been well documented in the literature (Erford, 2015c; Gysbers & Henderson, 2012) as a response to the effects of industrial growth in the late 19th and beginning of the 20th century: "Vocational guidance was not only viewed as assisting the development of individuals, but also seen as a means for achieving social goals" (Dixon, 1987, p. 112).

External Forces and Significant Events

The pioneering work of early practitioners created a foundation for vocational guidance and career education that is still useful today. Important figures emerged: George Merrill developed the first systematic vocational guidance program in San Francisco in 1895; Eli W. Weaver authored *Choosing a Career* and organized guidance services for New York City; Frank Goodwin developed a system-wide guidance program for Cincinnati, Ohio; Meyer Bloomfield and Anna Reed established a guidance program with a focus on employability of students and the ethics and practice of business; Jesse B. Davis and Frank Parsons were acknowledged in the literature for their significant ground-breaking work in incorporating vocational guidance programs into school systems (Erford, 2015c; Gysbers & Henderson, 2012).

From 1889 to 1907, Jesse B. Davis was a school administrator and counselor in Detroit and was greatly concerned with students' vocational and social needs. When he became the principal of the high school in Grand Rapids, Michigan, in 1907, Davis introduced the first guidance course as a part of the school's English curriculum—for the first time making guidance an accepted part of the school program (Beale, 1986).

Frank Parsons, known as the "father of guidance," founded the Vocation Bureau of Boston in 1908 and authored *Choosing a Vocation*, a major text in the field, in 1909. Parsons was concerned about the transition from school to the world of work and society's failure to develop resources and services for human growth and development (Erford, 2015c). His work at the bureau aimed to help young students make appropriate choices for a vocation by using a scientific approach (Gysbers & Henderson, 2012). Parsons also designed training programs to help young men become vocational counselors. His work was instrumental in creating the first counselor certification program in Boston and was eventually adopted by Harvard University as the first college-based counselor education program (Miller, 1968). His book "laid out the principles and methods of implementing vocational guidance, collecting and publishing occupational information, conducting a group study of occupations, carrying on individual counseling, and processing individual assessment" (Erford, 2015c, p. 18), which also set the tone for the trait-and-factor approach that later became a major school of career development theories.

In 1913, the National Vocational Guidance Association (NVGA) was founded in Grand Rapids, Michigan. This organization was one of the founding divisions of the American Personnel and Guidance Association (APGA) in 1952 (later renamed the American Association for Counseling Development [AACD], and now called the American Counseling Association

[ACA]). NVGA was also the original publisher for two current important journals: *Career Development Quarterly* and *Journal of Counseling & Development*. The significance of NVGA is its instrumental role in the unification and identification of what has become the counseling profession and, particularly, the school counseling profession.

Theoretical Framework

Parsons (1909) articulated the principles and methods of providing vocational guidance in the most influential theoretical work of that time and for many decades to come. He specified three essential factors in choosing an appropriate vocation: clear self-understanding of one's aptitudes, abilities, interests, resources, limitations, and other qualities; understanding of the requirements and conditions, pros and cons, compensation, opportunities, and prospects of different jobs; and understanding of the relationship between the two groups of factors. The goal of the early guidance movement was to prepare students for the world of work.

Roles and Functions

In the early 1900s, there were no job titles such as *professional school counselor* or even *guidance counselor*. The implementation of guidance was accomplished by appointed teachers who provided guidance and counseling without relief from their regular teaching loads or additional pay (Gysbers & Henderson, 2012). These teachers were given a list of activities relating to vocational guidance but no organized structure in which to work.

Formative Years (1915–1930s)

Historical Context

In the years following the early vocational guidance movement in the 1900s, there was a continual emphasis on vocational guidance within education; however, educational reform and concerns about the dignity and rights of children emerged (Erford, 2015c; Gysbers & Henderson, 2012). The National Education Association supported guidance activities for education but not for vocation or employment, believing that vocational guidance was irrelevant to the needs of college-bound students (Minkoff & Terres, 1985). In the 1920s and 1930s, the school counseling focus was shifted from job-oriented counseling to personal counseling and academic advisement. A number of movements (e.g., mental hygiene, measurement, developmental studies of children, introduction of cumulative records, progressive education) influenced the changing purpose of vocational guidance (Gysbers, 2001). A broader focus including issues of personality and human development beyond vocational guidance started to emerge.

During this period, World War I and the Great Depression were two major events that affected the development of the school counseling profession. World War I affected the development and growth of testing. During the Great Depression, many young people were out of school or work and needed guidance to address livelihood needs.

External Forces and Significant Events

The mental hygiene movement, which reformed mental health services, was influenced by Clifford Beers, a former patient with a mental illness, and his book, *A Mind That Found Itself*. Published in 1908, this book was instrumental in reforming the treatment of patients with mental illness. The mental hygiene movement contributed to the acceptance and understanding of mental illness by society. It also brought rising attention to students' personality and maladjustment issues (Erford, 2015c). As a result, a clinical model of guidance and personal counseling began to dominate practice.

Psychological testing and measurement was another contributing force for counseling development and experienced a tremendous growth during this time. During World War I, the U.S. military began to use group training and testing procedures to screen and classify draftees. This classification provided impetus for further development of aptitude and interest measurement for the subsequent decades. The testing movement served to provide a conceptual strength and methodology to guidance.

Progressive education in the schools, introduced by John Dewey, emphasized the school's roles in guiding students' personal, social, and moral development (Erford, 2015c). Guidance activities were incorporated into the school curriculum to help students develop skills for living. While progressive education was criticized for not attending to the fundamentals of education, the most significant influence of progressive education was supporting the establishment of the guidance counselors.

Several other significant events followed. In 1926, New York became the first state to require certification for guidance workers. In 1938, a Guidance and Personnel branch was created in the U.S. Division of Vocational Education. Finally, in 1939, the first edition of the *Dictionary of Occupational Titles* was published by the U.S. Department of Labor, providing a reference for job descriptions and related job titles (Erford, 2015c).

Theoretical Frameworks

Guidance was less concerned with social and industrial issues than with personal and educational issues during this period, yet there were no major theories or models of school counseling (Erford, 2015c). The rapid development of measurement and subsequent availability of numerous tests saw an increased use of the trait-and-factor approach. Williamson (1939) developed a directive, or counselor-centered approach, which stated that counselors should enlighten students through exposition. In this direct approach, counselors were expected to collect data, synthesize data, and deliver the results with the purpose of motivating students.

Burnham, referred to as the "father of elementary school guidance" (Stone & Bradley, 1994), authored *Great Teachers and Mental Health* (1926), which advocated for the necessity of guidance in elementary schools. He emphasized the critical role of classroom teachers in the mental health of children and the importance of developmental and preventive guidance programs.

Roles and Functions

The work of the pupil personnel, the organizational framework of the time, focused on bringing the pupils of the community to the educational environment and enabled them to maximize their desired development (Myers, 1935). Personnel involved in pupil personnel work included attendance officers, visiting teachers, school nurses, school physicians, and vocational counselors. Erford (2015c) summarized the roles and functions of professional school counselors in the 1920s to 1940s as:

- helping students gain more personalized educational experience (to counteract the insensitive education system);
- helping students sort through educational positions and create a unified course of instruction to discover the student's talents and locate the resources to develop these talents; and
- coordinating the student personnel services to provide integrated support rather than compartmentalized assistance.

Professional Identity and Growth (1940s–1950s)

Historical Context

The onset and end of World War II increased government involvement in the counseling profession. During the war, many psychologists and counselors were needed to help screen and train military and industrial specialists. After the war, many veterans needed services to readjust to civilian life. One particular governmental influence was the George-Barden Act of 1946, which provided funds to develop and support guidance and counseling activities in schools.

The problems in school counseling (such as limited preparation of professional school counselors, lack of advocacy for professional school counselors, no systematic professional organization, and little legislative support for school counseling) began to change (Erford, 2015c). Renewed hope also came from the emergence of person-centered counseling, developed by Carl Rogers, and the first national school counselor organization.

External Forces and Significant Events

Carl Rogers published his monumental books, *Counseling and Psychotherapy: Newer Concepts in Practice* (1942) and *Client-Centered Therapy: Its Current Practice, Implications, and Theory* (1951). Most importantly, Rogerian influences emphasized a growth-oriented counseling relationship as opposed to an informational and problem-solving approach.

In 1948, the *Occupational Outlook Handbook* was first published. In 1949, Robert Mathewson published *Guidance Policy and Practice*, a pioneering work on planning and implementing developmental guidance programs in schools. In 1952, professional school counselors formed their own professional organization, the American School Counselor Association (ASCA). The impetus for the new organization stemmed from school counselors' belief that the National Vocational Guidance Association no longer served the needs of school counseling adequately, given that the professional school counselor's role and responsibilities extended beyond merely vocational guidance (Minkoff & Terres, 1985). ASCA became the fifth division in APGA (now the American Counseling Association [ACA]) in 1953. As professional school counselors became more recognized in schools across the country, ASCA reinforced the unique role professional school counselors performed and provided a forum for communication among professional school counselors (Erford, 2015c).

Theoretical Frameworks

Rogers (1942, 1951) developed one of the most widely used counseling frameworks in history. He encouraged counselors to attend to the person in the process, and his ideas transformed counseling from medical and problem-solving models to a personal-growth model. This theoretical approach fit naturally with the gradually emerging theme since the 1920s—individual counseling that focused on the personal and emotional needs of students.

The pupil personnel work structure continued to dominate guidance and counseling in schools (Gysbers & Henderson, 2012). Counseling services were a subset of services in the educational system to be delivered by professional school counselors. The clinical model of guidance made individual counseling emerge as the central part of guidance. The nature and scope of counseling services expanded, compared to earlier decades, but there was still no unified, systematic, standard framework for what professional school counselors did. As a result, counseling services depended to a large extent on the mandates of local school districts.

Roles and Functions

Professional school counselors started to provide more than just vocational and personal counseling. Their responsibilities included orientation, individual appraisal, information, placement, follow-up, individual and group guidance, and consultation with parents and teachers.

Booming Years (Late 1950s, 1960s, & 1970s)

Historical Context

The late 1950s through the 1960s produced legislation initiatives that served to define school counseling's importance throughout the second half of the 20th century. The 1960s saw the expansion of school counseling across the nation. More training programs for professional school counselors were developed, and professional school counselors were hired. It is interesting that the school counseling movement occurred primarily as a result of the Cold War. After World War II, the United States and Soviet Union became world superpowers, representing two very different ideological frameworks. When the Soviet Union launched *Sputnik* in 1957, the first man-made earth satellite, the United States was alarmed. A serious concern arose as to whether the United States had the scientific and technological capability to compete with the Soviet Union in space programs and eventually win the Cold War. A series of initiatives in the late 1950s and throughout the 1960s increased the competitive ability of the United States (Erford, 2015c). As a result of federal funding and legislative support, school counseling positions expanded to unprecedented levels, as did the quantity and quality of professional school counselor training programs.

External Forces and Significant Events

The passage of the National Defense Education Act (NDEA) in 1958 was one of several legislative initiatives to counteract the perceived threat of the Soviet Union. The NDEA provided funding to enhance school counseling programs in public schools, aiming to identify and encourage talented students to enter science and engineering careers. The funding also benefited new and existing counselor education programs, as the need for training professional school counselors was enormous. Most important for the school counseling profession, the counselor training programs became more systematic and integrated, state certification requirements were established, and many more students were served (Erford, 2015c).

In 1964, the NDEA Title V-A was passed to extend guidance and counseling for all students, including those in elementary schools and various types of postsecondary schools. Despite this addition, elementary school counseling was not yet readily accepted within school systems or by the public. In the mid-1960s, several national studies investigating the functions and roles of elementary school counselors gave visibility, clarity, and direction to elementary school counseling, resulting in more counselors becoming employed in that setting (Erford, 2015c).

In 1966, the U.S. Department of Education established the Educational Resources Information Center (ERIC) to provide for education the same systematic acquisition and dissemination of relevant, quality information that had already been established for the physical sciences. A key feature of the ERIC system was its decentralization, in which individual clearinghouses had the responsibility of ensuring that the ERIC database included the important literature and met the information needs of its designated scope-area constituents. Fourteen clearinghouses were established, with scope areas that included math and science, reading, early childhood education, and others. A proposal by Dr. Garry R. Walz at the University of Michigan led to the establishment of an ERIC Clearinghouse on Counseling and Personnel Services. This assured that all relevant counseling journals and publications—and particularly the school counseling literature—were processed for input into the national database.

At the same time, numerous pieces of legislation were being passed to address social issues such as unemployment, poverty, and civil rights. In response to the Elementary and Secondary Education Act of 1965 and the Vocational Education Amendments of 1968, school counseling services incorporated attention to school dropouts, the economically and academically disadvantaged, and students with disabilities. The myriad legislation enacted in the 1960s also created vocational guidance, career education, and other career-related projects, emphasizing the role of professional school counselors in preparing students for transition from school to work (Erford, 2015c).

In the 1970s, two important pieces of legislation had significant effects on professional school counselors. The first was the Education for All Handicapped Children Act of 1975, which involved professional school counselors in program planning, counseling, consulting, and curriculum monitoring for exceptional children. The other was the Family Educational Rights and Privacy Act of 1974 (known as the Buckley Amendment), which limited access to a student's records.

Other significant events during this period included the emergence of two important and widely read publications. In 1959, *The American High School Today*, authored by James Conant, inspired the idea that all students should have access to counseling and advocated for one full-time professional school counselor for 250 to 300 students (Erford, 2015c). This student-to-counselor ratio is still widely espoused today but is not fully implemented in most states. Also, C. Gilbert Wrenn (1962) wrote *The Counselor in a Changing World*, in which he strongly stressed the importance of building a developmental elementary and secondary school counseling program rather than a crisis-oriented remedial program.

Theoretical Frameworks

Even though there was still no unified and systematic school counseling theory per se, the 1960s saw the rise of several counseling and career development theories. Many counseling theories (e.g., Ellis' rational emotive therapy, Glasser's reality therapy, behavioral counseling introduced by Wolf and Krumboltz, Super's career development theory, Holland's theory of occupational types) familiar to contemporary counselors across practice settings were developed in this period. Other influential approaches to school counseling included Keat's (1974) multimodal counseling approach, which promoted examining and treating the student across several dimensions rather than on the presenting problem alone, and Egan's (1975) concept of stages in the counseling process, which provided professional school counselors a road map for how to counsel.

Roles and Functions

One of the primary goals of increasing the number of professional school counselors was to identify and encourage talented students to pursue science and engineering careers. In addition to the coordination role, which assisted students in achieving educational and vocational goals, professional school counselors continued to provide individual counseling to students, albeit generally in reaction to events or circumstances. In reviewing his professional school counselor job in the 1960s, Baker (2001) stated that

> there was not enough time for proactive guidance programming. [Time was spent] scheduling all students over the summer (without pay) and making schedule adjustments in the fall—all by hand, lunch-room monitoring, student council advising, junior and senior proms, senior-class awards day, and graduation. (p. 76)

Nonetheless, the literature during and following the 1960s emphasized broader programmatic roles and functions for professional school counselors. Preferred services included developing comprehensive guidance programs to incorporate into the school curriculum, individual and group counseling, student assessment, and consultation with parents and teachers. Much of this focus on services stemmed from efforts by the National Association of Guidance Supervisors and Counselor Trainers, which, in 1959, began a 5-year project to construct educational standards for preparing high school counselors.

Challenge, Equity, and Opportunity (Late 1970s–Present)

Historical Context

The years after the boom (between the late 1970s and 1990s) observed several significant events in the United States and the world. In U.S. society, these decades observed the movements of civil rights, women's liberation, school desegregation, a sharp rise in drug abuse, an AIDS epidemic, and the end of the Cold War. Problems of inner-city schools, high dropout rates, diversity of student populations (in terms of racial or ethnic, cultural, and socioeconomic backgrounds), readiness to learn, violence in schools and homes, teenage pregnancy, peer pressure, and limited resources have presented enormous challenges to school counseling professionals and educators in general (Erford, 2015c). The fast-paced social, economic, and technical changes in the 21st century also added another layer of challenges for school counselors as they have to keep updated on using media and communication technology in order to effectively reach youth and accomplish their tasks as school counselors.

In the 1970s, a decade of enrollment decline in schools along with a depressed economy forced local school districts to reduce the numbers of professional school counselors. The fact that professional school counselors are often the victims of budget cuts in school systems has caused the profession to focus on two pertinent issues: role clarification and accountability. The debate about the definition and direction of roles, functions, and responsibilities of professional school counselors has centered on the training, capabilities, and certification of professional school counselors compared to counseling in other settings (Paisley & McMahon, 2001). The focus on accountability has provided evidence of the effectiveness of school counseling services (Erford, 2015c). The last two decades in the 20th century observed the second immigrant influx—different from the first, because a majority of the immigrants were from Asian and Hispanic cultural backgrounds. The diverse school-age population, particularly in urban settings, presented new challenges for professional school counselors.

External Forces and Significant Events

The Career Education Incentive Act of 1978 and the Carl Perkins Vocational Education Act of 1984 steered the development of career education programs in schools. The School to Work Opportunities Act of 1994 "has endeavored to create new models of collaboration between schools, transition mechanisms designed to facilitate the successful movement of students between school and employment, and employers" (Herr, 2002, p. 228).

By 1970, all states had professional school counselor certification. The department of education in each state regulates the requirements of training and experiences for school counseling certification. In 1982, The National Board of Certified Counselors (NBCC) was developed to certify counselors across the states. NBCC provided a consistent credentialing process across the country and offers a National Certified School Counselor (NCSC) credential.

Beginning in the 1980s, the comparison between students in the American education system and those in other developed countries alarmed educational professionals, politicians, and the public. In 1983, the National Commission on Excellence issued the publication *A Nation at Risk* to advocate for more rigorous standards for high school graduation (Herr, 2002). As the 21st century approached, ASCA called for professional school counselors to take action to help students be academically competitive and productive citizens.

Throughout the 1980s and early 1990s, federal funds for school counseling programs were provided primarily through the Carl D. Perkins Vocational Education Act of 1984 and the Carl D. Perkins Vocational and Applied Technology Act of 1990 (Erford, 2015c). The Elementary School Counseling Demonstration Act of 1995 provided federal grants to local school districts to make counseling services available to all students. Counselor preparation programs began to collaborate with K–12 schools to provide assistance to students in school settings. This act provided the impetus for orienting school counseling to include more than just career guidance.

During the 1970s to the present, the ERIC database grew to be the most used education database in the world, eventually containing over 1 million documents. In 1993, Dr. Garry Walz and Dr. Jeanne Bleuer moved the ERIC Clearinghouse on Counseling and Personnel Services (ERIC/CAPS) from the University of Michigan to the University of North Carolina at Greensboro. At that time, the name was changed to the ERIC Clearinghouse on Counseling and Student Services (ERIC/CASS). Although the U.S. Department of Education abolished the decentralized structure of ERIC and closed the 16 ERIC clearinghouses in December of 2003, during its 38 years of existence, ERIC/CAPS (CASS) acquired and processed over 25,000 counseling-related documents, indexed and abstracted over 50 journals, and published over 250 books and 200 ERIC Digests. In addition, the clearinghouse conducted 25 heavily attended national workshops devoted to cutting-edge topics that were relevant to school counseling (e.g., assessment and testing, use of computers and technology in guidance programs, life or career development, and leading and managing comprehensive school counseling programs).

Although the ERIC/CASS Clearinghouse has closed, Drs. Walz and Bleuer have established a new organization, Counseling Outfitters, to continue and, in fact, expand many of the services and products that had been offered by the Clearinghouse. This book is an example of the new line of resources produced by CAPS Press, the publishing division of Counseling Outfitters.

Near the beginning of the third millennium, school reform and accountability movements led a group of forward-thinking, nationally focused school counselors and counselor educators to professionalize and standardize the approach to school counseling. ASCA published the *National Standards for School Counseling Programs* in 1997 (Campbell & Dahir, 1997) and later the *Vision Into Action: Implementing the National Standards for School Counseling Programs* (Dahir, Sheldon, & Valiga, 1998). The standards were aimed at providing guidelines and a framework for professional school counselors to develop and implement comprehensive developmental counseling programs for all students in the personal–social, academic, and career-development areas. It emphasized the importance of assessment of students' needs and evidence-based research to make the school counseling program accountable. At the same time, The Education Trust began a Transforming School Counseling Initiative under the leadership of Patricia Martin. The goal of this initiative was to transform school counselor education to focus on equity, undoing decades of marginalization practices that made only a small proportion of our high school graduates prepared for college. The initiative selected six university school counseling training programs to serve as model programs. Near the end of the first decade of the 21st century, Pat Martin was hired by the College Board and established the National Office of School Counselor Accountability (NOSCA), which was charged with initiating additional practices among professional school counselors to ensure all students graduate from high school college and career ready. The *ASCA National Model* was first published in 2003 and aimed at providing a unifying framework for school counseling programs and streamlining the roles and job duties of school counselors. The third edition of the ASCA model was published in 2012, with focus on a comprehensive developmental guidance program and integration of leadership, advocacy, collaboration, and systemic change (ASCA, 2012a).

Between 2006–2013, ACA and the American Association of State Counseling Boards (AASCB) sponsored a multi-organization task force called 20/20: A Vision for the Future of Counseling. This committee of 31 counseling organizations convened and eventually produced a consensus definition of counseling, statement of principles, licensure title, and scope of practice. All of these efforts were aimed at standardizing the counseling profession and facilitating the portability of counseling licensure across state lines. Unfortunately, the 20/20 committee was unable to agree on a consensus set of educational standards at that time.

Finally, in 2010, the state governor and state school superintendent organizations collaboratively introduced the Common Core State Standards, a comprehensive set of K–12 education standards and goals aimed at standardizing the educational experience of school-aged children across the United States. While the vast majority of states have adopted the standards, this national initiative remains controversial in some states due to the state's pre-eminent and constitutional role in educating students.

Theoretical Frameworks

The concept of comprehensive developmental school counseling programs, rather than a professional school counselor providing an ancillary set of services, has evolved since the 1970s and has become an adopted guideline by ASCA for all professional school counselors to follow. Gysbers and Henderson's (2012) innovative work provided a conceptual and practical guide for the profession to develop and manage a school guidance program.

But a true turning point in the history of school counseling occurred between 1997 and 2003, when ASCA published two important documents: ASCA's *National Standards for School Counseling Programs* in 1997 (Campbell & Dahir, 1997) and *The ASCA National Model: A Framework for School Counseling Programs* in 2003 (ASCA, 2003a, 2005, 2012a). These publications provided a framework for professional school counselors to turn to for defining their job responsibilities. As a result, the school counseling profession now has a unified voice in communicating with other school personnel and the public about what professional school counselors do: develop and manage comprehensive and developmental school counseling programs that help all students with academic, personal–social, and career development areas. A recent multi-state study found that implementation of the ASCA model is effective in decreasing discipline referrals and suspensions, and increasing attendance and student achievement (Carey & Dimmitt, 2012). It is evident that school counselors need to use data; prioritize and wisely use their time on college and career readiness, academic success, and parent involvement; and also find a differentiated delivery mode.

In the past two decades, a particular counseling approach has gained popularity in the school counseling profession: brief, solution-focused counseling (Sklare, 2014). The reason for this approach's appeal to professional school counselors lies in the promise of efficiently resolving concerns in a short time frame. Traditional approaches may be effective, but professional school counselors simply do not have time for long-term therapy. Most recently, with the increasing awareness of contextual influence on counseling practice, an alternative approach called the contextual school counseling approach, was proposed in hopes of bridging school counselors' clinical skills to the school environment (see Baskin & Slaten, 2014).

Roles and Functions

Despite the debate about the roles and functions of professional school counselors, in the past four decades, professional school counselors have performed duties widely perceived as *traditional* (i.e., academic advising, vocational planning, personal–individual counseling, reactive or crisis-oriented counseling, participating in Individualized Education Programs [IEPs], test administration and scoring, and scheduling). At the same time, professional school counselors were torn between providing direct services or working as social change agents to provide a better school environment for students (Whiston, Feldwisch, & James, 2015). It was recommended that professional school counselors need to function as counselor, consultant, facilitator, coordinator, change agent, team player, and leader to successfully develop and implement a comprehensive developmental school counseling program (Erford, 2015c; Paisley & McMahon, 2001). Professional school counselors are also expected to be culturally responsive counselors and to advocate for student needs in the culturally diverse school and community settings. The debate about whether school counselors are mental health service providers first or educators first is ongoing, with each position possessing valuable benefits toward the role and function of professional school counselors. Yet despite the efforts of ASCA, there seems lacking a uniform view of an exact definition of school counseling. Nonetheless, school counselors' roles in helping students achieve their potential and transition well to becoming productive citizens is undeniable, regardless of the position one takes.

To address this problem, the American Counseling Association's (ACA) School Counseling Task Force (2013) created a definition of school counseling:

> Counseling is a professional relationship that empowers diverse individuals, families, and groups to accomplish mental health, wellness, education and career goals. Using counseling theories and techniques, school counselors accomplish these goals by fostering educational and social equity, access, and success. The professional school counselor serves as a leader and an assertive advocate for students, consultant to families and educators, and team member to teachers, administrators and other school personnel to help each student succeed. (p. 2)

Summary/Conclusion

School counseling was rooted in vocational guidance at the beginning of the 20th century as a response to the needs of students in transition from an agricultural to an industrial economy. Over a century, the direction of school counseling was often shaped by social reform, school reform, and the national welfare (see the timeline provided in Table 2.1). The school counseling profession has evolved from "a peripheral, ancillary role in schools to a more central one" (Herr, 2002, p. 230). School counselors need to provide comprehensive, preventive, systematic, culturally appropriate, and accountable programs to serve all the students.

Table 2.1 Timeline of Significant Events in School Counseling History

Timeline	Significant Event and Impact
Emerging Years (1900–1915)	
Late 19th century and early 1900s	Industrialization, urbanization, influx of immigrants, classification of labor, and demand for a skilled work force lead to the need for employment guidance
1908	Frank Parsons founded the Vocational Bureau of the Civic Services in Boston; pioneer work in schools to help students
	Jesse Davis introduced the first guidance course as part of the English curriculum in Detroit, making guidance accepted as part of the school curriculum
	Clifford Beers authored *A Mind That Found Itself*; brought the treatment of mental patients to public attention
1909	Parsons' book *Choosing a Vocation* published 1 year after his death; laid out principles and methods of providing vocational guidance
1913	Founding meeting of National Vocational Guidance Association in Grand Rapids, Michigan; first professional counseling organization—later became a founding division of ACA
Formative Years (1915–1930s)	
1920	Mental hygiene, measurement movement, progressive education
1926	Burnham published *Great Teachers and Mental Health*; first to advocate for elementary school counseling
1926	New York requires certification for guidance workers
1938	A Guidance and Personnel Branch was created in the Vocational Education division in the U.S. Office of Education
1939	First edition of *Dictionary of Occupational Titles* (DOT) was published
Professional Years (1940s–1950s)	
1942	Carl Rogers published *Counseling and Psychotherapy*
1948	*The Occupational Outlook Handbook* was first published
1952	American School Counseling Association (ASCA) was founded
1953	ASCA became the fifth division in the American Personnel and Guidance Association
1958	National Defense Education Act was passed, expanding the training and hiring of school counselors
1959	James Conant published the *American High School Today*, suggesting 1:250 to 1:300 school counselor-to-student ratio
Booming Years (1960s–1970s)	
1962	Wrenn published *The Counselor in a Changing World*; influential guide for the school counseling profession in the years to follow
1964	NDEA Title A—legislation to extend counseling to elementary schools
1966	The U.S. Department of Education established the ERIC Clearinghouse on Counseling and Personnel Services (ERIC/CAPS) at the University of Michigan
1976	Career Education Incentive Act; infusion of career education in schools

(continues)

Table 2.1 (*continued*)

Timeline	Significant Event and Impact
Challenge and Opportunity Years (Late 1970s–Present)	
1988	Gysbers and Henderson published *Developing and Managing Your School Guidance Program*
1993	ERIC/CAPS moved to the University of North Carolina at Greensboro and became ERIC/CASS (Counseling and Student Services)
1994	School to Work Act was passed, reinforcing career guidance and counseling
1995	Elementary School Counseling Demonstration Act provided $20 million to assist schools in making counseling services available
1997	ASCA publishes the *National Standards for School Counseling Programs;* aims at providing benchmark for school counseling programs to promote student competency
Mid-to-Late 1990s	The Education Trust establishes the Transforming School Counseling Initiative and selects six university school counseling training programs to serve as model programs
2002	No Child Left Behind is signed into law
2003	ASCA publishes *The ASCA National Model: A Framework for School Counseling Programs;* it is revised in 2005 and 2012
2006	The 20/20: A Vision for the Future of Counseling committee convenes and eventually produces consensus definition of counseling, statement of principles, licensure title and scope of practice
2007	Pat Martin establishes the National Office of School Counselor Accountability (NOSCA) at the College Board
2010	Common Core State Standards are introduced
2013	ACA's School Counseling Task Force creates a definition of school counseling: Counseling is a professional relationship that empowers diverse individuals, families, and groups to accomplish mental health, wellness, education and career goals. Using counseling theories and techniques, school counselors accomplish these goals by fostering educational and social equity, access, and success. The professional school counselor serves as a leader and an assertive advocate for students, consultant to families and educators, and team member to teachers, administrators and other school personnel to help each student succeed.

CHAPTER 3

Current and Future Perspectives on School Counseling

Joyce A. DeVoss

Preview

Despite significant progress made since the turn of the 21st century in addressing numerous challenges to the profession, school counselors in the United States are faced with additional challenges. Some are completely new and others involve themes from the past. Issues for which professional school counselors have reported progress in the past decade include clarifying role definition; integrating programming; defining delivery systems; deciding on generalist versus specialist roles; attaining reasonable student-to-counselor ratios; accepting leadership, advocacy, and public-relations roles; developing technological competencies; developing data-driven school counseling programs; and obtaining optimal professional development. Through the work of the American School Counselor Association (ASCA) and The Education Trust's Transforming School Counseling Initiative (TSCI), professional school counselors in the United States developed a systematic approach to creating and managing school counseling programs. Key to this accomplishment was the use of data to demonstrate how school counseling programs make a difference for students. While working to maintain the gains in these areas, professional school counselors encounter issues with: closing the gap between schools that fully implement comprehensive school counseling programs and those that do not; integrating the Common Core standards into the counseling curriculum; embracing research on behalf of students and the profession; assessing and addressing the impact of the growth of charter schools across the country; responding to the increase in school crises; and developing leadership in the field. In this chapter, I address current and future challenges for professional school counselors as educational programs become influenced by social changes and socioeconomic pressures and as the profession of school counseling advocates for needed changes

School counseling's origins go back well over 100 years. Its development was influenced by a variety of forces, including the industrial revolution's exploitation of children, population immigration and migration, the educational reform movement at the turn of the 20th century, the evolution of counseling theory, and the national agenda. At the turn of the 21st century, educational reform once again became a primary source of influence on the evolution of the profession. With the influence of the Transforming School Counseling Initiative (Education Trust, 1999) and the American School Counselor Association (ASCA) national model (2012a), professional school counselors joined other educational professionals at the school reform table. They have acted as assertive advocates, both for students and for the school counseling profession.

In February 2002, in Greensboro, North Carolina, a group of approximately 300 counselors, counselor educators, central office personnel, and state-level personnel attending a national conference titled "Leading and Managing Comprehensive School Guidance Programs" documented 10 critical issues in school counseling (ASCA, 2002b). These key challenges and issues for professional school counselors in the 21st century are addressed within this chapter and are organized by the following topics: school counselor role definition, school counselor preparation, school counseling programming, school counseling program delivery system, generalist versus specialist, reasonable student-to-counselor ratios, technological competencies, professional development, and leadership, advocacy, and public relations.

Several authors have identified and discussed more recent current and future challenges for professional school counselors (Erford, 2015c; Lapan, Harrington, Brown, & Manley, 2009). These challenges will be addressed under the previously mentioned 10 topic headings in this chapter and include: closing the gap between schools that fully implement comprehensive school counseling programs and those that do not; embracing research on behalf of students and the school counseling profession; incorporating the Common Core educational standards adopted by most states; and public schools impacted by growth of charter schools.

Professional School Counselor Role Definition

Defining the professional school counselor's role has caused considerable difficulty in daily practice, limiting credibility for the profession. Perceptions of professional school counselor roles have varied widely, even within the same school district. Some professional school counselors reported experiencing a lack of administrative support, confusing expectations, and lack of respect (ASCA, 2002a; Hurst & Eggert, 2006). Sears and Granello (2002) noted that professional school counselors struggled with role definition. Paisley and Borders (1995) stated that professional school counselors experienced a lack of control over day-to-day duties and sometimes had to deal with competing expectations from principals and counseling directors.

Based on results of a Missouri statewide study, which surveyed professional school counselors and administrators about the level of implementation of comprehensive guidance programs during the 2004–2005 school year, Lapan, Gysbers, Cook, Bragg, and Robbins (2006) concluded that implementation is especially a concern in high school, where counselors continue to be inundated with clerical tasks. They noted that non-guidance tasks hurt program implementation. Baker and Gerler (2007) stated that "school counseling, long viewed by some as an ancillary service in the schools, remains unclearly defined both within and outside the profession" (p. v). Baker and Gerler offered the following advice: "The next generation of school counselors will have to be more active than their predecessors if the counselor role challenge is to be resolved" (p. 307). It is important for the role of the professional school counselor to be clear, with some uniformity, yet broad-ranged and not so demanding as to limit effectiveness.

In the early stages of the national Transforming School Counseling Initiative, House and Martin (1998) outlined the new vision of the school counselor role and compared it to the traditional role of the professional school counselor. The new vision professional school counselor is expected to be a proactive leader who is committed to quality education and equity of access to higher education for all students. The professional school counselor is envisioned as an assertive advocate and social activist on behalf of students, parents, schools, and the school counseling profession. The Education Trust (1999) defined school counseling as "a profession that focuses on the relations and interactions between students and their school environment with the expressed purpose of reducing the effect of environmental and institutional barriers that impede student academic success" (p. 1).

The school–community collaboration model (Adelman & Taylor, 2002) also emphasized the school counselor's roles as advocate, collaborator, catalyst, and facilitator of social reform while working to remove barriers to student learning. This approach outlined six objectives for focusing the integration of school and community resources on addressing learning barriers:

- Effectiveness in the classroom
- Support families in transition and increase family support of student learning
- Crisis prevention and intervention services
- Comprehensive social, emotional, and physical health services for families
- Meaningful partnerships with community organizations

Each of the three editions of The ASCA national model furthered the progress of clarifying the roles and responsibilities of professional school counselors. The first edition of the ASCA national model (2003a) listed and described the roles of professional school counselors as designers, coordinators, implementers, managers, and evaluators of their school counseling programs. The second edition of the ASCA national model (2005) included 12 School Counselor Performance Standards that reflect the roles listed above. Within the ASCA model, it was suggested that an evaluation should be developed using the performance standards instead of one designed using teaching standards. The third edition of the ASCA national model (2012a) contains a section on School Counselor Competencies necessary to successfully implement the ASCA model program and a school counselor performance appraisal template which identifies the duties and responsibilities to be rated by the school administrator. Quality graduate training programs provide school counselor trainees with understanding of, and practical experience with, the new vision roles described by the ASCA national model.

A current area of concern relevant to understanding of school counseling role definition is the increasing numbers of charter schools and the limited involvement of school counselors in their development and ongoing operation. Since the first charter school law was passed in 1991 in Minnesota, charter schools have increased to about 6,000 in 42 states and the District of Columbia with more than 2.3 million students attending and nearly a million students on waiting lists (Reichgott Junge, 2014). While charter schools have spurred innovations in education, little information generally exists concerning counseling services in charter schools, according to Urofsky (Rollins, 2006). He compiled the results of a survey of 174 charter schools in 28 states and found that only 44% employed school counselors. Based on the survey results, he concluded that staff at charter schools held misperceptions of what school counselors do. He recommended that the school counseling profession pay closer attention to charter schools as the numbers continue to grow.

Gysbers and Stanley (2014) noted "What was once a position in the schools, with wide-ranging duties, often clerical and administrative in nature, has moved to a comprehensive program approach, allowing school counselors to better meet students' academic, career and social/emotional needs" (p. 22). Gysbers and Stanley credit ASCA for leading the way with this transformation from focus on position to focus on a comprehensive program.

Professional School Counselor Preparation

To effectively carry out the mission of schools and to function optimally as part of school leadership teams, professional school counselor trainees must receive adequate training. Potential professional school counselors have choices from diverse training programs. With some basic knowledge about program accreditation, national trends, and professional standards, potential trainees should be able to locate quality graduate programs that meet the national standards of the Council for the Accreditation of Counseling and Related Educational Programs (CACREP; 2009) as well as incorporate The Education Trust's vision of professional school counselors, the school–community collaboration model (Adelman & Taylor, 2002), and the ASCA national model (2012a) for school counseling programs. Many state departments of education are adopting CACREP standards as minimum standards for certification or licensure (Baker & Gerler, 2007; Sears & Granello, 2002). But even with CACREP standards, there has been little consistency across school counseling training programs. In 1992, although 195 graduate programs in 72 institutions were CACREP accredited (Kandor & Bobby, 1992), the curriculum varied considerably from one graduate school counseling program to another. CACREP (2009) standards for master's level school counseling programs require a minimum of 48 semester hours of graduate study, including the following eight areas: Professional identity; Social and cultural diversity; Human growth and development; Career development; Helping relationships; Group work; Assessment; and Research and program evaluation. In addition, CACREP specifies that professional school counselor trainees must successfully complete a 100-hour practicum and a 600-hour internship in school settings. These are considered minimal standards for counselor preparation.

ASCA (2000) developed a list of professional school counselor competencies that fall into three domains: knowledge competencies, skill competencies, and professional competencies. Some examples of the *knowledge competencies* are human development theories and concepts, career decision-making theories and techniques, and program development models. Some of the *skill competencies* include diagnosing student needs, career and educational counseling and planning, and conducting in-service training for staff. *Professional competencies* include conducting a self-evaluation to determine strengths and areas needing improvement, advocating for appropriate state and national legislation, and adopting a set of professional ethics to guide practice. It is in the best interest of prospective professional school counselors to seek graduate preparation programs that, in addition to being CACREP accredited, have been continuously updated and aligned with national standards and the Transforming School Counseling Initiative. This is one way to help ensure that new school counselors will be well prepared as they enter the workforce.

At the 2014 National Evidence-Based School Counseling Conference, Erford provided a strong rationale for school counselors to embrace research for the benefit of students and the school counseling profession. The trend continues in school counseling programs to train school counselors to conduct action research and to effectively use data for program-related decision making. With the increase in school crises in the past 20 years and the view that school counselors are important in crisis intervention (Jackson-Cherry & Erford, 2014), there has been more emphasis in graduate school counseling programs on training in crisis prevention, preparedness, response, and recovery.

Gysbers and Stanley (2014), in stressing the need to conceptualize school counseling as a program and not a position, emphasized that graduate programs need to insure that school counseling students become familiar with school counseling program language so that they can clearly communicate its concepts. For example, school counseling students need to become very familiar with concepts within the four components and the themes of the ASCA national model in order to design and manage their school counseling program. They also need to learn about teaching and classroom management concepts in order to successfully implement classroom guidance. And, they need to be well versed in concepts of educational leadership in order to function effectively as leaders and advocates on behalf of students. For counselors in the field who need additional education to increase their mastery of important areas in their field, ASCA has created ASCA U where school counselors can receive ASCA Specialist designation in Legal & Ethical, Bullying Prevention, Leadership and Data.

School Counseling Programming

In a 2002 presentation at The Education Trust Summer Academy, in Chicago, ASCA past president, Mark Kuranz, reminded participants of six problems previously identified with school counseling programs (Hart & Jacobi, 1992): lack of basic philosophy, poor integration, insufficient student access, inadequate services for some students, lack of counselor accountability, and failure to use other resources. Although progress has been made in these six areas over the two decades since they were first identified, work continues on these issues today. An example of current school counselors' work on integrating counseling curriculum with academic curriculum involves efforts to incorporate the Common Core State Standards (Hess & Gong, 2014) into the counseling curriculum.

Lapan, Gysbers, Cook, et al. (2006) noted the need to close the gap between schools that fully implement comprehensive school guidance programs and those that do not. When RAMP (Recognized ASCA Model Program) data is reviewed on the ASCA website and considered an indicator of implementation of the ASCA Model, we can note that some states are leading the way in full implementation of the ASCA model with large numbers of RAMP schools, while other states seem not well represented by schools with the RAMP designation.

Basic Beliefs, Vision, and Mission

The ASCA national model (2012a) stresses the need to design a strong foundation for a school counseling program that includes beliefs, a vision, and a mission. These give the program focus and guide program development and implementation. The beliefs relate to student learning, development and achievement, school counselors' roles in promoting student success, the roles of others in the school counseling program, how data will inform program planning, and the incorporation of ethical standards in the program.

The vision statement is influenced by the beliefs and focuses on the preferred future for all students and the school community in terms of outcomes. It should align with the school and the district's vision statements. The mission of a school counseling program should be tied directly to the school and the district's mission as well as the mission of the state department of education. It should focus on all students' academic success and achievement. Examples of desired results that can be written into the mission statement might include improved national and state test results, improved graduation rates, improved attendance, decreased behavioral referrals, decreased dropout rates, increased enrollment in postsecondary education programs, and increased enrollment of poor and minority students in high-level math and advanced placement courses.

Integrated, Longitudinal Developmental Counseling

Integration of school counseling goals, objectives, and activities is a key characteristic of an effective school counseling program. An effectively integrated program needs to be truly longitudinal (Herr, Cramer, & Niles, 2004) and should span from elementary school through secondary school. Sandhu (2001) stressed that, starting with elementary school, counseling programs need to emphasize the interconnections among cognitive, physical, and social development of children. Gysbers (2001; Gysbers & Stanley, 2014) is a leading advocate of fully implemented comprehensive guidance and counseling programs for all U.S. schools. Gysbers and Henderson (2012) described in detail the steps in designing a comprehensive guidance program for a school building or district. The process involves concretely describing the content, organizational framework, time allotted, and resources needed. It is a time-intensive process but is well worth the investment for the program. The ASCA model (2012a) also outlines and describes the components of an ASCA model program.

For maximum effectiveness and relevance to all students, Sandhu (2001) recommended that school counseling programs be proactive and positive in approach. It is reasonable that these programs be comprehensive and well integrated into the mission of the school. The growing numbers of RAMP-designated schools on the ASCA Web site indicate that fully-implemented comprehensive guidance programs are becoming a reality in schools and school districts across the United States. These programs are staffed by professional school counselors concerned with serving all students instead of focusing only on high- and low-achieving students and providing less than adequate services to all others.

Student Accessibility and Services for All Students

The ASCA national standards for school counseling programs (Campbell & Dahir, 1997), now referred to as student competencies (ASCA, 2004), remain the essential elements of an effective school counseling program at any level of K–12 education. They address program content and expected knowledge, attitudes, and skill competencies for all students in schools with comprehensive school counseling programs. Three content areas include academic, career, and personal–social development. Under each of these headings are three standards, which describe the outcomes for students of an effective school counseling program. For example, under the career development domain, Standard B states that "students will employ strategies to achieve future career success and satisfaction" (Campbell & Dahir, 1997, p. 92). The trifold developmental focus, including career development, should start in elementary school and continue through 12th grade (Sandhu, 2001).

Gysbers and Henderson (2012) described in detail how to adapt a school counseling program model to meet the specific needs of a school district or a school building and to balance the use of the professional school counselor's time, according to predetermined priorities. The use of established steering and school–community advisory committees is recommended throughout the decision-making process. This collaborative approach ensures that the school counseling program adopted by the decision makers will adequately address the systemic needs of the district or school.

The ASCA national model for school counseling programs (2012a) creates a common vision for professional school counselors. This model includes four major components: foundation, delivery system, management system, and accountability. The model integrates an emphasis on accountability, advocacy, leadership, and systemic change in keeping with the themes of the school counseling reform movement. It provides professional school counselors with a framework for the development of school counseling programs while allowing flexibility for responsiveness to local community needs. Professional school counselors can achieve Recognized ASCA Model Program (RAMP) status for their school counseling program by meeting the criteria for and having their program reviewed by a designated ASCA review committee. School counselors are responsible for providing a comprehensive school counseling program for all students. This means that counselors in the 21st century must be prepared to provide appropriate school counseling services to students and families of diverse cultural and ethnic backgrounds, learning disabilities, sexual orientations, emotional and physical disabilities, and religious beliefs and practices (Sandhu, 2001). It also means that professional school counselors need to meet the challenge of becoming assertive advocates for all students, especially disadvantaged and minority students, working toward closing any achievement gaps between these students and their peers. Gysbers (2001) contended that professional school counselors can reach all students by using comprehensive school counseling programs with planned guidance activities in the classrooms. He cited research indicating that comprehensive guidance programs do benefit students academically, in career development and in school climate.

Traditionally, stage models of development have been the foundation for school counseling programs. Some question the adequacy of these models for this purpose (Green & Keys, 2001; Sears & Granello, 2002). The models may not sufficiently take into account issues of diversity and other contextual factors important to consider when developing a comprehensive developmental school counseling program.

Green and Keys (2001) recommended using a development in context paradigm in school counseling program designs. This model takes into consideration contextual factors such as culture, values, and living environment that impact student development. Professional school counselors operating from this model facilitate student awareness of self in context, an awareness of the multiple contexts impacting the student's life.

Although the profession emphasizes the role of school counselors in the delivery of comprehensive guidance programs, there are many obstacles (Sandhu, 2001). While the comprehensive guidance approach is preplanned, proactive, and comprehensive in nature, in practice the professional school counselor must constantly strive to achieve and maintain balance in the school counseling program. Despite the best planning efforts, there continues to be many demands on the professional school counselor's time and effort.

Sears and Granello (2002) noted that professional school counselors get pulled in different directions as they attempt to conform to the national reform agenda. For better or worse, professional school counselors respond to more school-based crises and intervene on behalf of both greater numbers of students and students who are more intensely emotionally disturbed or troubled. Baker and Gerler (2007) acknowledged many demands to which counselors in schools are expected to respond. The ASCA national model (2012a) and the student competencies as well as national, state, and local school counseling organizations and departments of education are resources available to help professional school counselors meet the challenges of setting and assertively maintaining priorities for their comprehensive, developmental school counseling programs.

Accountability

Baker and Gerler (2007) explained the difference between the terms *evaluation* and *accountability:* "Evaluation is the act of gathering information about one's services; accountability is the act of reporting the results of the evaluation" (p. 322). They described basic professional school counselor accountability competencies, such as how to do a needs assessment and how to assess consumer satisfaction and cost effectiveness.

Accountability is expected of all educators, including professional school counselors, and data from schools are readily available for professional school counselors to use in evaluating the impact of school counseling programs. Professional school counselors have moved to evidence-based practice (Dimmitt, Carey, & Hatch, 2007) and are expected to access and disaggregate data for developing data-driven school counseling programs. When professional school counselors report the outcomes of their interventions on achievement data, other educators, including administrators, begin to understand the connection between counseling programs and the mission of schools.

In 1970, in the midst of economically hard times, Arbuckle (1970) wrote an article titled "Does the School Really Need Counselors?" which challenged the profession to become more accountable. In response, some individuals developed models of accountability; others reiterated the need for accountability; and some state legislation mandated accountability of school counseling programs and professional school counselors. Yet many professional school counselors resisted instituting evaluation measures. Since that time, the pressure for accountability has mounted to an all-time high.

In the face of current educational reform and the Common Core curriculum that has been approved and implemented by the majority of states, professional school counselors can no longer afford to resist accountability. With the economic stresses and decreased educational funding following the terrorist attacks of September 11, 2001, some school districts again asked Arbuckle's question. Professional school counselors are challenged to advocate for their survival. Advocacy via the use of data that indicate the impact of school counseling programs on achievement can be powerful and gives the profession credibility. Johnson, Lambright, Sparks, Stiff, and Taft (2006), presented a useful guide, including 13 ways to prepare your school or district to implement the ASCA national model.

Other Resources and the Need for Collaboration

Considering the challenge for professional school counselors to meet the needs of all children, success in serving students may best be achieved through a team effort. Because typical school student-to-counselor ratios continue to be far in excess of the ideal ratio of 200:1 and 300:1 recommended by ASCA and Baker and Gerler (2007), professional school counselors cannot adequately meet those needs on their own. An ASCA (2002a) study reported that in 1999–2000, the national average student-to-counselor ratio was 490:1; in 2012 it was 471:1

(ASCA, 2014). These data lend support to professional school counselor efforts to collaborate with others in delivering services to students.

Paisley and McMahon (2001) believed that professional school counselors must foster collaborative relationships with other school personnel, parents, professionals, and other community members to combine efforts and meet student needs. By doing so, professional school counselors enlarge the pool of talent and resources available to the school community. In one example, teachers effectively delivered guidance curriculum in the classroom. Although involvement of others besides professional school counselors in the counseling program can be beneficial to students, ethical and professional practice requirements (ASCA, 2010a) dictate that counseling-related activities performed by noncredentialed personnel be supervised and coordinated by credentialed professional school counselors.

School Counseling Program Delivery System

The ASCA national model (2012a) outlined the delivery system for school counseling programs. Professional school counselors must be competent in the following areas to meet basic practice standards of the profession: implementing developmental guidance curriculum, providing individual planning, offering responsive services to meet immediate needs, and performing systems-support administration and management activities.

Currently, there is considerable consensus in the field of school counseling that the resources of the professional school counselor can best be used with a proactive developmental approach (Erford, 2015c; Gysbers & Henderson, 2012). The professional school counselor is looked upon to coordinate the design, planning, and implementation of the school counseling program with care and flexibility to adequately meet the needs of students, parents, teachers, administrators, and other school community stakeholders.

Generalist Versus Specialist

Professional school counselors must decide on the extent to which they are generalists or specialists (Erford, 2015c). This decision may be made best according to the needs of the school district or individual school and may be influenced based on the degree to which teams are used. If the school building has a counseling department, the professional school counselors may be expected to be part of the departmental team. ASCA U currently offers specialist training and certification in Bullying Prevention, Ethical and Legal, Leadership, and Data. This trend might promote professional school counselor specialization within counseling departments.

Such teams can operate in a variety of ways. In some settings, the most efficient teamwork occurs when members are specialists who continuously hone specific knowledge bases and related skills. In the case of a counseling department team, the counselors might divide the departmental responsibilities based on the specialties of its members. In other settings, professional school counselor team members might work optimally as generalists and provide an array of services to pre-assigned caseloads of students. And in yet other environments, a department may operate most efficiently with a mixture of some specialists and some generalists.

When a school building has only one professional school counselor assigned, that counselor is most likely to function as a generalist. This is frequently the case for elementary school counselors. These professional school counselors can become isolated if they are not proactive in assuring involvement on leadership teams and in other collaborative relationships.

Reasonable Student-to-Counselor Ratios

Reasonable student-to-counselor ratios are essential for professional school counselors to become adequately familiar with students and their needs. Because of the amount of variation in type and intensity of the needs in student populations and in the expectations of professional school counselors, it is difficult and unrealistic to determine a standard student-to-counselor ratio to fit all settings.

In general, however, caseloads of 300 or fewer are seen as optimal (Baker & Gerler, 2007). These ratios are determined primarily by financial conditions and secondarily by the perceived value of the school counseling program. Gysbers and Henderson (2012) offered a formula that calculates approximate student-to-counselor ratios in an optimal school counseling program. The ratio varies, depending on the prearranged counseling program activities for the school and, therefore, the professional school counselor's availability to provide the program activities.

Leadership, Advocacy, Public Relations

Professional school counselors must successfully articulate to policy makers, media, and the public their essential contributions to the mission of their schools. To effectively educate the community about the important role of school counseling, professional school counselors must actively promote the profession and its mission. Baker and Gerler (2007) suggested that social activism is the approach needed to accomplish recognition of the preferred identity for professional school counselors. The Education Trust (2000) outlined "the new vision" role of the professional school counselor as leader, advocate, collaborator, and consultant.

With a clearer definition of school counseling and the roles of professional school counselors, the local and national community can have a better understanding of key contributions made by professional school counselors in achieving educational equity for all children. Erford (2015c) believed that professional school counselors and their supporters needed to join national professional organizations like the American School Counselor Association (ASCA), Association for Counselor Education and Supervision (ACES), and American Counseling Association (ACA), and the regional or state affiliates of these organizations in order to initiate grassroots efforts to achieve dramatic educational change on a national level. He expressed concern that less than half of all professional school counselors are members of any professional organization.

The Education Trust and ASCA have provided a great deal of leadership and advocacy on behalf of the school counseling profession. In 2012, a group known as the Transformed School Counseling & College Access Interest Network (TSCCAIN) was established through ACES. Many leaders in the profession joined the organization and participate in ongoing discussions and initiatives about the future of the profession. Meanwhile, the Center for School

Counseling Outcome Research and Evaluation (CSCORE) continues to lead the promotion of research among school counseling professionals, students, and faculty.

Technological Competence

Professional school counselors are expected to be competent in the use of technology (ASCA, 2012a). The Association for Counselor Education and Supervision (ACES; 2007) established technological competencies for counselors that should be included in counselor education. These competencies are summarized here. Counselors need to be able to do the following:

- Use productivity software to develop Web pages, group presentations, letters, and reports
- Use audiovisual equipment such as video recorders, audio recorders, projection equipment, videoconferencing equipment, and playback units
- Use computerized statistical packages
- Use computerized testing, diagnostic, and career decision-making programs with clients
- Use e-mail
- Help clients search for various types of counseling-related information via the Internet, including information about careers, employment opportunities, educational and training opportunities, financial assistance or scholarships, treatment procedures, and social and personal information
- Subscribe to and participate in counseling-related listservs
- Access and use counseling-related CD-ROM databases
- Know strengths and weaknesses of counseling services provided via the Internet
- Know the legal and ethical codes that relate to counseling services via the Internet
- Use the Internet for finding and using continuing education opportunities in their profession
- Evaluate the quality of Internet information

Tyler and Sabella (2004) provided a detailed description and discussion of each of these competencies. In addition to these competencies, professional school counselors should become familiar with mobile applications such as Twitter and current videoconferencing applications such as Skype and ooVoo. They need to be familiar with Powerpoint and Prezzi for presentations and Facebook, LinkedIn and other social network systems. Current technology skills are necessary tools for supporting effective school counseling services.

Professional Development

Due to the rapidly changing educational environment, professional development is a priority for counselors who can and should use available professional development opportunities to stay current in the profession and to maintain their professional identity. Furthermore, professional school counselors can view professional development as an opportunity to network and exchange innovative ideas in the profession. Hatch and Bowers (2002) strongly urged counselors to become actively involved in professional development and reminded them of state requirements to maintain certification. Some popular topics in professional development currently include how to incorporate the Common Core standards into guidance lessons, upgrading technology skills, teaching approaches to engage students, effective program evaluation, action research skills, and increasing awareness of evidence-based and promising practices in school counseling.

Professional school counselors are encouraged to become members of at least one professional organization. Fewer than half of professional school counselors take advantage of such a membership. The benefits may include subscriptions to the publications of the organization, liability insurance, notices of professional development or networking opportunities as well as discounts on conferences and professional publications. These organizations offer potential leadership roles for professional school counselors along with the opportunity to make a difference at a systemic level. ASCA is the national school counselor professional organization, and nearly every state also has a state school counselor association.

Summary/Conclusion

School counseling in the United States has evolved for more than a century of rapid social, political, and economic change. The profession has been affected by myriad influences, including social reform efforts, immigration, economic changes, national defense issues, and the advancement of psychological and developmental theory. The impact of its meandering evolutionary process left the school counseling profession with numerous challenges at the end of the 20th century, including (a) clarifying role definition; (b) identifying and obtaining optimal preparation; (c) integrating programming; (d) clearly defining program delivery systems; (e) deciding on a generalist versus specialist role; (f) attaining reasonable student-to-counselor ratios; (g) accepting leadership, advocacy, and public relations roles; (h) developing technological competencies; and (i) participating in relevant professional development.

The role of the professional school counselor in the 21st century remains fluid and constantly changing in response to the changing demands of our schools and our local and national communities. However, as the profession continued the transformation process that was begun at the end of the last century, it has become an active participant in the educational reform movement. Aided by the ASCA national model, The Education Trust's Transforming School Counseling Initiative (1999), and the school–community collaboration model (Adelman & Taylor, 2002), professional school counselors have made progress in facing the challenges and issues discussed in this chapter, and are continuing this important work. Through strong professional organizations and a unified approach to school counseling through the ASCA national model, professional school counselors have learned to speak as advocates with one voice toward ensuring that all students have equal access to quality education.

CHAPTER 4

Outcomes Research on School Counseling

Qi Shi and Bradley T. Erford*

Preview

A continuing trend in mental health and education is a push for evidence-based practice and accountability. Professional school counselors have limited outcome research available for practice, which presents both a challenge and an opportunity. We offer a summary of classic and current outcome research in school counseling accumulated over the past four decades, as well as implications and recommendations for practicing professional school counselors.

The school counseling profession has seen a great deal of reform in the last decade. Comprehensive school counseling programs (Gysbers & Henderson, 2012) have helped to organize and professionalize the services that professional school counselors provide, while the American School Counselor Association's (ASCA) national standards have prescribed types of student outcomes school counseling programs should produce (ASCA, 2004; Dahir, 2001). More recently, the Transforming School Counseling Initiative has suggested a stronger focus on academic achievement and increased leadership and advocacy roles (Erford, 2015c). The emergence of the ASCA national model (ASCA, 2012a) builds on these previous efforts and consolidates a comprehensive system of advocacy, collaboration, systemic change, and leadership toward the ASCA national standards. *Accountability*, a familiar word to all school personnel, is a core part of the new ASCA national model. The accountability theme endorses program evaluation, appropriate performance evaluation, and results reports. Within the recommended results reports, effectiveness data for immediate, intermediate, and long-range results serve as tools for advocacy for students and school counseling programs.

In addition to school counseling, research and professional trends in psychotherapy and education have also focused more attention on effectiveness and results. Using rigorous scientific methodology, empirically validated treatments (i.e., interventions shown to be effective) are promoted for psychotherapy and, at times, are the only accepted treatments for managed care. At the same time, the field of education is focused on accountability. While the process or means of determining academic accountability has been debated, the demand for results is inescapable. Many teachers and schools are now measured by student performance on state mandated standardized achievement tests. In fact, in many states, funding and teacher incentives are tied to the outcomes on student tests.

---

*Our gratitude to Patrick Akos, who authored a previous version of this chapter in the first edition of this book.

As teachers and schools are measured by client or student outcomes, so are professional school counselors. More than two decades ago, Fairchild (1993) found that 67% of professional school counselors were involved in some type of accountability effort. They must increasingly describe their contributions to student achievement and validate their time spent with students. This push for counseling science or school accountability requires professional school counselors to measure and determine the effectiveness or outcomes of interventions (Sink, 2009; Stone & Dahir, 2011). Along with the responsibility for accountability comes an ethical duty of making informed decisions about interventions (Sink, 2009; White, 2007). Professional responsibility and the direction of education and counseling reform beg an important yet difficult question: What school counseling services or interventions work to create desired student outcomes? We provide a brief summary of the outcome research, put the findings in perspective, and suggest several implications for professional school counselors.

Major Findings in School Counseling Outcome Research

In general, classic and more recent research has demonstrated that psychotherapy with children and adolescents is effective (Kazdin, 1993). Although school counseling has less empirical evidence to support practice compared to other venues of counseling, several meta-analytic reviews of the outcomes research in school counseling have suggested moderate to positive results (Baker, Swisher, Nadenichek, & Popowicz, 1984; Nearpass, 1990; Prout & DeMartino, 1986; Prout & Prout, 1998; Sprinthall, 1981; Whiston, Tai, Rahardja, & Eder, 2011). Qualitative reviews of school counseling have generally shown positive affects (Borders & Drury, 1992; Carey & Dimmitt, 2012; Whiston & Quinby, 2009; Whiston & Sexton, 1998), specifically for low-achieving students (Wilson, 1986), elementary school students (Gerler, 1985), and middle school students (St. Clair, 1989).

Reviews of school counseling can also be made quantitatively through meta-analyses, a technique that allows empirical studies to be examined across a quantitative index that provides meaning (Erford, 2014). This quantitative index is known as the *effect size* (ES; d). Cohen (1988) specified an effect size of 0 to signify no effect from the treatment, an effect size of .20 to signify a small effect, an effect size of .50 to signify a medium effect, and an effect size of .80 or higher to signify a large effect from the treatment. The calculation of the Pearson r is another way of expressing effect sizes in correlational research (Erford, 2014). In this case, an effect size of $r = .10$ is small, .30 is medium, and .50 is large. Among the many formulas for effect size estimates, d and r are the two principal statistics found in the literature. Effect sizes for empirical studies testing differences between treatment and control conditions are interpreted as the number of standard deviations a given treatment mean score lies above or below the mean score of the control group. Meta-analysis has been employed in counseling and educational research because of its meaningful, generalizable characteristics, allowing summarization of results across a number of studies at once (Ioannidis, Cappelleri, & Lau, 1998; Shadish, 1996; Sharpe, 1997; Sohn, 1997). Research reviews are particularly helpful in evaluating the multitude of duties performed by professional school counselors (Whiston, Feldwisch, & James, 2015). Considering the content areas in the ASCA national model, evidence exists to show that professional school counselors have been effective in promoting academic, career, and personal–social development in students.

Career Development

Career development, it seems, has the greatest amount of outcome or effectiveness evidence. Two meta-analyses provided evidence that career interventions can positively influence students' career development (Oliver & Spokane, 1988; Whiston, Sexton & Lasoff, 1998). Both meta-analyses (Whiston & Sexton, 1998) and narrative reviews (Palmer & Cochran, 1988) have supported the effectiveness of career interventions, especially through individual planning. Individual student planning involves professional school counselors coordinating continuous systemic activities to aid students in deciding on personal goals and evolving plans for the future (ASCA, 2012a). The overall weighted effect size for 10 studies that addressed individual planning was statistically significant (ES = .27). The majority of the studies involved high school students,

Two meta-analyses conducted by Oliver and Spokane (1988) and Whiston et al. (1998) indicated the most effective methods of delivering career counseling services were through individual career counseling or classroom guidance. Programs that employed computer-based career guidance programs or career sources from the Internet lacked the guidance of a professional school counselor and were not as effective (Whiston, Brecheisen, & Stephens, 2003). However, students did gain from the use of these computerized guidance programs when a counselor integrated other activities into the program. Previous literature examined the effectiveness of different computer-based career guidance programs; for example, using the CHOICES program increased the career decision-making commitment of university students (Pinder & Fitzgerald, 1984) and using the DISCOVER program helped middle school students gain career maturity (Luzzo & Pierce, 1996).

Students also benefited from parent consultation about career development. Kush and Cochran (1993) and Palmer and Cochran (1988) found that adolescents' career development was positively affected by teaching parents methods for helping their children in their chosen career path. There is evidence that both parents and students would like more emphasis on career guidance and development activities (Scruggs, Wasielewski, & Ash, 1999).

Gysbers (1988) described various benefits of classroom guidance in outcomes related to developing career goals, college attendance, and career-planning skills. The outcome research also revealed that career services have been useful to a variety of students, including ethnic minorities, the academically gifted, and students with disabilities (Sexton, Whiston, Bleuer, & Walz, 1997).

In addition to the mode of career counseling interventions, students' age was also a factor contributing to career counseling success (Sexton et al., 1997). Oliver and Spokane (1988) concluded that career counseling had the largest effects with pre-teenage students, rather than high school or college students. For middle school and junior high students, the effect size for individual planning activities was 1.01, which indicates the importance and effectiveness of individual planning activities for those students in middle or junior high school (Whiston, Eder, Rahardja, & Tai, 2005). Also, compared with other outcomes, career interventions had the most impact on the development of career decision-making skills (Oliver & Spokane, 1988). In general, professional school counselors can be assured that career development activities are effective (Whiston et al., 2015).

Personal–Social Development

In terms of personal–social development, group counseling was found to be effective in helping elementary students adjust to family difficulties (Whiston & Sexton, 1998). Social skills training also helped many students. Borders and Drury (1992) suggested that attitudes and behaviors toward the students' school improved among students who had undergone counseling services. They also found that small-group counseling helped improve students' attendance, classroom behaviors, self-esteem, self-concept, and attitudes toward themselves and others.

Additional studies showed classroom guidance activities were effective in improving school behavior, attitudes toward school, attendance, and coping skills (Bundy & Boser, 1987; Gerler & Anderson, 1986; Myrick, Merhill, & Swanson, 1986). Students who have access to school counseling programs reported greater feelings of fitting in and safety in their schools (Lapan, Gysbers, & Sun, 1997). These outcomes for personal–social development were found to generalize across widely varying groups of students (e.g., across age, race).

Academic Development

Guidance activities promoted self-esteem and exhibited trends of positive influence on academic achievement (Whiston & Sexton, 1998; Wilson, 1986). Whiston et al. (2011) conducted a meta-analysis examining the school counseling outcome studies and they concluded that school counseling interventions have a small but significant influence on students' GPA and achievement tests.

A causal comparative study was conducted by Sink and Stroh (2003) to determine if the implementation of a comprehensive developmental guidance program produced higher achievement scores in students. The results were inconclusive, although it was clear that elementary students who were enrolled in the same school for three years or longer performed better academically, whether or not the school counseling program was fully implemented.

Another study conducted by Gerler and Herndon (1993) also focused on student academic achievement. After a 10-session guidance curriculum was implemented, students were more aware of how to succeed in school. A replication of this study by Lee (1993) used the same guidance curriculum but split the participants into treatment and control groups. Students who participated in the 10-session guidance curriculum performed significantly higher on posttest math scores than did students who did not participate in the guidance curriculum.

Characteristics of Effective School Counseling

Research suggested that a variety of factors affect school counseling outcomes. Lambert (1986) found that common factors were evident across counseling approaches that were responsible for about 30% of client improvement. Students' characteristics can affect outcomes; for example, outcomes vary depending on level of education (elementary, middle, high; Nearpass, 1990; Prout & DeMartino, 1986; Prout & Prout, 1998; Reese, Prout, Zirkelback, & Anderson, 2010), although it was clear that the least amount of research exists for middle school counseling (St. Clair, 1989; Whiston & Sexton, 1998). Programs that required students to participate in counseling services often were less successful than programs that allowed students to volunteer participation (Wilson, 1986). In addition, while some research suggested that student factors like gender, age, socioeconomic status, parental marital status, academic variables, and referral status (self vs. other) affect outcomes, other research suggested that a variety of demographic and school factors were unrelated to counseling outcomes (Hagborg, 1993).

Students of all ages showed improvements as a result of the implementation of a school counseling program. However, certain age levels were differentially affected. Whiston et al. (2011) found an effect size of .26 for elementary students who were exposed to a school counseling intervention, .42 for middle school students, and .34 for high school students. Prout and DeMartino (1986) suggested that older students benefited more from school counseling interventions than did younger students. Even older high school students, such as 11th and 12th graders, were impacted more by the interventions than were 9th- and 10th-grade high school students. Reese et al. (2010) conducted another meta-analysis which, in contrast, concluded that elementary school students achieved the greatest gains. Elementary students showed improved affective, behavioral, interpersonal, and ethnic identity development as a result of school counseling programs (Cholewa, Smith-Adcock, & Amatea, 2010; Lemberger & Clemens, 2012; Steen, 2009; Webb-Landman, 2012).

The least amount of research regarding effective school counseling has been conducted on middle school students (St. Clair, 1989; Whiston & Sexton, 1998), but the results are consistent with other age groups. In one study, behavior management, daily progress reports, and self-relaxation techniques were found to be beneficial to middle school students who were exposed to a school counseling program (St. Clair, 1989).

Ethnicity was not a significant factor in successful counseling; however, student–counselor ethnic similarity was shown to affect dropout rates (Sexton et al., 1997). Therefore, if outcome is measured by dropout rate, ethnic similarity may be important.

Certain professional characteristics also had an impact on counseling outcome. Qualitative reviews found no relationship between training or experience and outcomes of counseling (Auerbach & Johnson, 1977; Beutler, Crago, & Arizmendi, 1994; Christenson & Jacobson, 1993), while some meta-analytic reviews provided mixed results (Sexton et al., 1997). One meta-analytic study found no relationship between experience and client outcome but did find higher rates of success for counselors who had been professionally trained, regardless of experience (Stein & Lambert, 1995). In a meta-analysis by Whiston et al. (2011), the provider was found to significantly influence effect size, with larger effect size for "other providers" and "teachers."

Therapeutic skills have not always increased with the length of training or experience (Beutler, Machado, & Neufeldt, 1994; Dobson, 1989). Treatment manuals have been integrated into professional practice to enhance standardization of treatment and equalize counselor skill (Erford, 2014). Treatment manuals use a research-based, standardized treatment approach and have been shown to enhance treatment outcome. In contrast, Robinson, Berman, and Neimeyer (1990) determined that the use of treatment manuals was no more effective than counseling without treatment manuals.

Personal characteristics of the counselor, such as self-confidence, self-efficacy, and adjustment level, were significantly related to outcome (Lambert & Bergin, 1983; Maxis, 2013; Sexton & Whiston, 1991). For professional counselors undergoing therapy, there was only a slight relationship with their clients' treatment outcomes (Sexton et al., 1997). However, reasons for professional counselors seeking therapy in these studies may have led to extraneous error; that is, it was not clear whether the counselors in the studies sought counseling for therapeutic and personal insight or because of personal problems.

The therapeutic alliance also may have some effect on counseling outcomes. The American Psychological Association Division 29 Psychotherapy Task Force (Steering Committee, 2002) identified seven therapeutic alliance characteristics that appeared to enhance effectiveness. These included positive regard, genuineness, self-disclosure, repairing alliance breaks, quality of interpretations, management of countertransference by the counselor, and feedback. More recently, six statewide research studies were published, providing valuable evidence of the relationship between positive student educational outcomes and school counseling program organization, counselor time use, and specific school counseling activities (Carey & Dimmitt, 2012). Two meta-analysis studies have been conducted that focused on reviewing the effectiveness of the four components of the ASCA national model separately (Whiston & Quinby, 2009; Whiston et al., 2011).

Classroom Guidance

Classroom guidance is designed to address all students in a developmentally appropriate manner. Guidance curriculum activities form the core of the school counseling program. In a meta-analytic review conducted by Whiston et al. (2011), guidance curriculum ($d = .35$), along with responsive services ($d = .35$), produced the largest effect size among the delivery strategies or intervention approaches.

Some research found that classroom guidance activities can be successfully combined into an academic curriculum with middle and high school students (Hughey, Lapan, & Gysbers, 1993). Collaboration between classroom teachers and professional school counselors to implement a combined language arts and career guidance unit was successful in giving students the opportunity to develop academic proficiency and explore career topics. While some outcome studies have found positive outcomes for classroom guidance, the research is very limited (Whiston et al., 2015).

Group Counseling

Research shows that certain methods of interventions were more frequently researched or had more positive outcomes than other methods of intervention. Although it is not conclusive, it seems that outcome research has examined and supported group counseling as much or more than individual counseling. Wilson (1986) concluded that group counseling was more effective than individual counseling in improving academic achievement for low-achieving students. Group counseling intervention was found to have a positive effect on students' academic achievement and school success behaviors (e.g., cognitive and metacognitive skills, social skills, and self-management skills; Brigman & Campbell, 2003; Webb & Brigman, 2005). One study addressing failing elementary students concluded that 83% of the students placed in small-group counseling experienced improvement in grades (Boutwell & Myrick, 1992). Social skills training and discipline problems were most effectively treated through group counseling (Whiston & Sexton, 1998). Students showed short- and long-term positive effects after participating in parental divorce groups (Omizo & Omizo, 1988; Pedro-Carroll & Alpert-Gillis, 1997; Pedro-Carroll, Sutton, & Wyman, 1999; Ziffer, Crawford, & Penney-Wietor, 2007).

Cognitive-behavioral group counseling has effectively increased high school students' self-esteem and academic self-concept (Bauer, Sapp, & Johnson, 2000; Hyun, Chung, & Lee,

2005; Nelson & Dykeman, 1996; Shechtman, 1993). Racial attitudes of elementary school students also were positively influenced through small-group counseling sessions (Reeder, Douzenis, & Bergin, 1997). Other group counseling studies (a) demonstrated improved self-concept among children of alcoholics, (b) reduced at-risk behaviors among adolescent girls, and (c) reduced aggressive and hostile behavior among elementary students involved in a social skills training group (Riddle, Bergin, & Douzenis, 1997; Whiston & Sexton, 1998; Zinck & Littrell, 2000). Confirmation of the effectiveness of group counseling was largely provided for younger students; the effects on older students need to be studied further (Whiston et al., 2015).

There have been inconsistent findings in terms of the comparison of the effectiveness between individual counseling and group counseling (Whiston & Quinby, 2009). A recent meta-analysis on school counseling interventions (Whiston et al., 2011) found that there were no significant overall differences between individual counseling and small-group counseling even though the effect sizes were varied.

Individual Counseling

In some instances, individual counseling was found to be more effective than group counseling with school-aged students (Nearpass, 1990). Also, counselors who primarily used individual counseling were more effective than counselors who used primarily classroom guidance in achieving positive student outcomes, although methodological problems existed within the study (Wiggins & Wiggins, 1992). However, in a more recent meta-analysis, Whiston et al. (2011) found that individual counseling yielded a slightly smaller effect size ($d = .26$) than guidance curriculum ($d = .35$) and other responsive services ($d = .35$).

For example, an individual dropout prevention program comprised of tutoring and counseling significantly improved school success, confidence, and classroom behavior in at-risk students (Edmonson & White, 1998). Individual counseling does not have to be long term to be effective. Brief individual counseling can be just as effective as long-term counseling. For example, three approaches to brief counseling that address emotional adjustment of high school students were implemented by Littrell, Malia, and Vanderwood (1995). Participants in any of the three conditions reduced worries and were motivated to move closer to their goals. Behavioral approaches in individual counseling were most effective when addressing aggressive behavior (Wilson, Lipsey, & Derzon, 2003), and Lavoritano and Segal (1992) found that misbehavior decreased as individual counseling progressed.

Peer Mediation

Popularity of conflict resolution programs has increased during recent years. During the early 1990s, peer mediation programs increased in schools by about 40% (Sheperd, 1994). Whiston et al. (2005) discovered that peer mediation interventions had an effect size of .39, but Wilson et al. (2003) found that peer mediation programs had little influence on aggressive behavior. Questions about leadership roles and training for these programs have also arisen (Lewis & Lewis, 1996). Gerber and Terry-Day (1999) disputed the amount of empirical evidence to support the popularity of peer mediation programs. More research is necessary before any conclusions can be made about the effectiveness of peer mediation programs.

Consultation or Collaboration

Professional school counselors consult with teachers, parents, and other educators, and by collaborating with these stakeholders, they can implement systemic and programmatic changes in schools and communities to prevent students from dropping out of school. Growing empirical evidence suggests that consultation was effective as a method of resolving problems (Murphy, 2009; Zins, 1993). Elementary school students' behaviors were affected by consultation between teachers and counselors (Gerler, 1985). Borders and Drury (1992) found that consultation was effective for both elementary and middle school students, and, as a result of a counselor's consultation workshop, more students were referred to counseling (Otwell & Mullis, 1997).

Skillful demonstrations by professional school counselors determined the effectiveness of consultation. Gresham and Kendell (1987) concluded that problem identification was the most important factor within the consultation process. If counselors directly trained consultees in problem solving, communication, and intervention techniques, consultation between counselors, parents, and teachers was more successful (Zins, 1993). When counselors modeled the problem-solving process for their consultees, consultation was also more effective. Furthermore, investigation of typical activities led by professional school counselors (e.g., peer mediation, family education, consultation) produced mixed findings, and conclusions were difficult to draw because of the variations in professional school counselor involvement and functioning.

Outcome Research in Perspective

Research on school counseling is based on probabilities, rather than assurances of effectiveness or prescriptive directions (Martin & Hoshmand, 1995), and most of the research is correlational, which does not suggest causality. So, although research is available to support school counseling effectiveness, the research is neither vast nor methodologically strong.

In a comprehensive review of published school counseling literature from 1988 to 1995, Whiston and Sexton (1998) found no consistent type of outcome targeted, no consistent measure or instrument used, and most research focused on responsive services rather than on preventive or developmental activities. With only 22% of the studies incorporating experimental design and the majority focused on remediation, research has not consistently shown the effectiveness of school counseling services nor focused on the preventative or proactive nature of helping (Sexton et al., 1997). Whiston and Sexton's (1998) review suggested no clear trend in the research favoring one method over another (individual, group, classroom). Disturbingly, the review also suggested that the many flaws with the existing research limit confidence in results (e.g., lack of experimental design, convenience samples, nonstandard outcome measures). Even the psychotherapy literature was often based on laboratory research (Sexton, 1999). In fact, most of the research on children and adolescents was conducted in clinical or research settings (Kazdin, 1993). However, in a more recent meta-analysis conducted by Whiston et al. (2011), an overall small to medium average weighted effect size for all school counseling interventions was found ($d = .30$), based on 117 experimental studies that involved 153 interventions.

Additionally, it is a challenge for practicing professional school counselors to keep up with outcome research articles as they appear in journals. Often, results are difficult to decipher, and it is a challenge to find results pertinent to practice (Whiston et al., 2015). Furthermore, choosing interventions from a list often inhibits innovation, dehumanizes students, and puts too much attention on technique (Waehler, Kalodner, Wampold, & Lichtenberg, 2000). This approach of matching treatment or intervention to remedial need dismisses many influences important to professional school counselors, including diversity, career counseling, psychoeducational and developmental concerns, and prevention or proactive programs. Additionally, the counselor must have the knowledge and ability to assess presenting concerns and appropriately apply these treatments (Sexton, 1999).

Implications for Professional School Counselors

Be an Active Consumer of Outcome Research in School Counseling

Although reports of evidence-based interventions for professional school counselors are not conclusive, it is important to be an astute consumer and incorporate research into practice. Research has shown that some practices are more effective than others, and some client problems are helped most by specific counseling models (Sexton, 1999). Professional school counselors must examine a diverse set of published research in a variety of journals and read each study with caution. Therefore, professional school counselors must examine effectiveness research as one step in the decision-making process to determine an appropriate intervention.

Keep Grounded in Core Conditions of Effective Helping

In reality, the great majority of what works will be determined by efforts related to, but distinct from, determining an appropriate intervention. Research has suggested that the specific psychological technique accounts for only 15% of the outcome (Lambert, 1991; Lambert & Barley, 2001). Lambert (1991) suggested that 30% of the outcome in counseling is related to common factors evident in therapy, regardless of type of theory or intervention. These common factors include (a) the supportive value of a collaborative counseling relationship; (b) the value of learning (through affective experiencing, corrective emotional experiences, or skills acquisition); and (c) action (through behavior change, successful experiences, behavioral regulation, and mastery; Sexton, 1999).

Professional school counselors improve the outcome of helping when they work with these common factors. For example, counselors often see challenging students who are referred by teachers or parents. Many counselors scour the research literature for a solution that uses the newest technique, but they often fail first to focus on and establish a collaborative counseling relationship. Research suggests that the type of counseling relationship that is established would dictate the student's value of learning from the counselor and the action taken. Historically, demographic factors, professional identity, and even experience have been thought to influence the effectiveness of the counselor; however, current evidence suggests that, when all things are equal, these three factors are unrelated to the counseling outcome (Sexton, 1999). Instead, counselors' skill level (competence), cognitive complexity (ability to think diversely and complexly about cases), and an ability to relate and relationally match with the clients are important to outcomes.

Although Watsford and Rickwood (2014) did not find any association between young people's expectations and outcome, most studies concluded that clients' expectations for therapeutic gain are related to outcome (Glass, Arnkoff, & Shapiro, 2001). Students view professional school counselors with varying levels of expectation for change. Again, students who are referred by others often have limited desires or expectations for change. Client expectations are shaped by the student's experience, background, and relationship with counselors, and professional school counselors are again challenged to create expectations for change when determining what works (much like how solution-focused counseling builds with the miracle question). Beyond the relationship and client expectations, various factors outside of the counseling dynamics influence outcomes.

In terms of counseling or therapy in general, Lambert (1991) proposed that 40% of outcomes in therapy are attributed to factors outside of the counseling relationship. For professional school counselors, two influential aspects include (a) the systems involved in students' lives and (b) the context or culture of the school and the student. An element that is perhaps unique to the professional school counselor's role (as compared to other types of counselors or therapists) is that professional school counselors often have access to and can influence many of the factors outside of the counseling session. In an ecological framework, this element is where a variety of helping services (e.g., consultation, collaboration, coordination, leadership, advocacy, parent education) may be influential to outcomes in school counseling.

Consider Multiple Systems, Culture, and School Context

Most of the published school counseling outcome studies examine a specific school or district sample, so it is important for professional school counselors to consider how to apply the research to their individual context and students. Schools possess stratified context issues including, but not limited to, structural factors (e.g., urban or rural, public or private, academic grouping, disability services); instructional factors (e.g., teacher expectations, qualifications, behavioral management); and relational factors (e.g., peer rejection, peer influence, school or class social dynamics; Farmer & Farmer, 1999). All of these factors influence the outcomes of a professional school counselor's efforts to help students. For example, the way a professional school counselor helps a student who has a learning disability and exhibits behavioral problems may be differentially effective, depending on whether the student is mainstreamed in the regular classroom or is in a self-contained classroom. In the same way, school climate may dictate the effectiveness of a peer helping program.

The multiple systems in a student's life can reinforce or inhibit professional school counselor practice. Students do not live in a laboratory, nor do they operate only in one type of school. Although scientific research on professional school counselor intervention does not always account for multiple influences inside and outside of the school, professional school counselors can use their understanding of the school context.

Consideration of the developmental forces in children and adolescents is essential to both the school context and the student culture. Students experience a great deal of developmental change that is independent of the professional school counselor intervention. For example, the participants' developmental level will greatly influence a professional school counselor's group intervention to promote healthy body image. Whereas a mixed gender group of elementary school students may focus on generalized self-esteem, a gender-specific middle school group may focus on the messages of popular culture to women and girls. Although both of these groups would be described as a group intervention for personal–social development, the outcomes will be greatly influenced by the developmental stages and needs of the students.

Even when multiple systems and contexts are considered in determining interventions that work, professional school counselors have a responsibility to serve all students in the school. Most of the research about effectiveness or best practices is centered on helping students who demonstrate problems. An effective professional school counselor, when selecting what works, should also consider the effectiveness of proactive activities targeted toward normal or optimal development.

Implement Action Research on Your Own Developmental, Preventive, and Proactive Interventions

Where school counseling research leaves off, professional school counselors can research their own programs. Relevant, simple research designs may not immediately prove useful to the field of school counseling as a whole, but a wealth of information can be maintained by practicing professional school counselors about what works in their own schools. Systematically piecing together smaller studies can show effective school counseling services.

One particularly useful research design includes *action research.* Action research is varied but is used for immediate local needs and applications rather than generalization of results (Ferrance, 2000). For example, a middle school counselor may choose to understand what interventions help English as a second language (ESL) students feel connected and perform well academically in school. Determining a research design (e.g., comparison study), treatment or interventions (e.g., group vs. classroom guidance), data collection (e.g., connectedness measure, grades, test scores), and data analysis (e.g., t test between groups) may allow the professional school counselor to make an informed choice about providing services to ESL students. Collaborative designs with others (i.e., professional school counselor educators, educational or psychology professionals inside and outside of the school) also hold great promise. Many school–university partnerships produce fruitful research and provide both professional school counselors and university faculty a means for professional development.

Summary/Conclusion

Several authors (Allen, 1992; Deck, Cecil, & Cobia, 1990) have suggested that professional school counselors have little interest in the research or science of school counseling, or they see it as beyond their responsibility. Although reforms and national models are useful, professional school counselors cannot establish or maintain an important role in the school without science to validate their presence. At the extreme, several states and districts may have already cut school counseling positions because they are viewed as ancillary services.

"The outcome-based knowledge is currently not, and may never be, refined to the point that it will dictate specific treatments for an individual client" (Sexton, 1996, p. 598). There is no study that dictates how professional school counselors can best help students. Determining what works needs to be contextualized within the student, professional school counselor, school, family, and community framework. Selecting what works is also highly dependent on student needs. Making choices on what works will involve a combination of knowledge and use of current research, a commitment to actively researching what works, and continuing to be an inner-critic to choice of interventions.

CHAPTER 5

Codes of Ethics and Ethical and Legal Considerations for Students, Parents, and Professional School Counselors

Lynn E. Linde and Carolyn Stone

Preview

One of the hardest challenges facing all counselors today, and particularly professional school counselors, is how to determine the best and most appropriate way of working with students who present myriad, complex problems. While federal and state laws apply in some situations, many of the issues with which counselors deal fall into a gray zone: there is no clear guideline for handling the situation. Fortunately, the American Counseling Association (ACA, 2014), the American School Counselor Association (ASCA, 2010a), and the National Board for Certified Counselors (NBCC, 2013) have developed codes of ethics that provide guidelines for ethical behavior. Each section of these codes applies to different situations that counselors face. We also discuss the rights and responsibilities of minors and their parents and the implications of these rights on the professional school counselor's work. Ethical codes, federal statutes, state laws, and court cases that involve student and parental rights are examined. Furthermore, we address complications that professional school counselors encounter as they work to protect students' rights while remaining aware that their obligations extend beyond the minor student to the student's parents.

Whenever supervisors for school counseling programs or professional counselor associations survey members regarding topics for professional development, ethics and legal issues always rank at or near the top of the list. Schools and school systems are no longer immune from the litigious society in which they operate. Parents are fast to complain and hire lawyers when they feel that their rights have been violated or when they question the way in which the school or a staff member has handled a situation. Professional school counselors often feel overwhelmed by the variety of problems that students present each day, and they struggle to find the best legal or ethical way to work with students, continually striving to balance the needs of the students with the needs of the school or family.

The legal and ethical complexities of working with minors in schools require that professional school counselors remain vigilant about the rights and responsibilities of minors and their parents and the implications of these rights on the counselor's work. A school's legal and ethical landscape is complicated because a professional school counselor's obligation extends beyond the minor student to the parents, who have considerable rights. Private and agency counselors who work with minors usually do so because parents seek their help. Students are sent to school for academics, so the dynamics are quite different when they show up at the professional school counselor's door through a teacher's suggestion or self-referral. A professional school counselor's multiplicity of responsibilities to parents, students, administrators, teachers, and others in a setting designed to deliver academic instruction complicates the legal and ethical world of school counseling (Alexander & Alexander, 2012; Imber & Van Geel, 2009; Linde, 2015; Remley & Herlihy, 2013; Stone, 2010).

The very nature and function of school (i.e., to provide a free and appropriate quality education) creates immediate conflict when a student seeks a professional school counselor's help for emotional or social needs. When a student approaches a professional school counselor without his or her parent's knowledge or consent, immediate tension can arise between the student's right to privacy and the parents' right to be the guiding voice in their child's life. Generally, the younger the child, the more rights are vested in the parents. The conflict between a parent's right to be informed about what is happening in the child's personal life and the child's need and right to privacy is a decided challenge for professional school counselors who are charged with protecting the rights of both students and parents (Alexander & Alexander, 2012; Imber & Van Geel, 2009; Linde, 2015; Remley & Herlihy, 2013; Stone, 2009).

We examine some of the ethical codes, federal statutes, laws, and court cases that involve student and parental rights, and this chapter should be augmented by texts that address the legal rights of students and parents and the ethical behavior of professional school counselors. (See Remley and Herlihy [2013] and Alexander and Alexander [2012] for a more thorough review of legal and ethical issues.) Professional school counselors are encouraged to attend legal and ethical workshops and university courses to increase their comfort level and competence in student and parental rights. Consulting with other professionals and seeking guidance is paramount when addressing issues of student and parental rights.

Some, but not all, situations are clearly defined by federal or state law or by local policy. Local boards of education are hesitant to pass policies or procedures for controversial issues, and it is likely if they *did* create such policies, they might significantly limit the ability of professional school counselors to operate without informing parents about everything. Fortunately, the professional associations for counselors have developed codes of ethics and standards that provide a framework for professional conduct. To understand the applicability of the codes of ethics to professional school counselors, it is helpful to understand something about the organizations that create the codes.

Professional Counseling Associations

The American Counseling Association (ACA) is the professional association for all counselors. The mission of the association is to promote public confidence and trust in the counseling profession. Organizationally, ACA is a partnership of associations representing professional counselors who enhance human development. It is composed of 20 divisions that represent specific work settings or interest areas within the field of counseling, and 56 state or affiliate branches that are divided into four regions representing major geographical areas. Through its activities and entities, ACA influences all aspects of professional counseling. These areas include the credentialing of counselors and the accreditation of counselor education programs, developing and promulgating ethical standards, offering professional development, offering professional resources and services, and influencing public policy and legislation.

ACA has 15 active standing committees that address much of the professional business of the association. One of those committees, the Ethics Committee, is responsible for educating members about the association's ethical standards and investigating and adjudicating ethical complaints. Counselors must sign a statement agreeing to abide by the Code of Ethics when they join ACA. Additional information about ethics, ethical issues, and professional behavior is available through a number of services and resources offered by the association. ACA and its entities offer a variety of training and professional development opportunities, some of which are offered at state, regional, and national conferences; others are workshops and learning institutes, which are offered throughout the year.

The journals published by ACA and its divisions provide current research, professional practices, and other information valuable to the practicing counselor. Articles and information about professional behavior is frequently covered in these sources. ACA's monthly newsletter, *Counseling Today*, includes valuable information about general counseling topics as well as covering special topical issues. ACA publishes many books about counseling that cover current trends and topics in the field and which are frequently used as texts in counseling courses. One example is the *ACA Ethical Standards Casebook* (7th ed.), by Herlihy and Corey (2014). This is a valuable resource for all professional counselors and is an excellent supplement to the 2014 *ACA Code of Ethics*. ACA staff is available for consultation on a variety of issues, including legal and ethical questions. In summary, ACA touches all counselors' lives, from the training they receive, the requirements they must achieve to be credentialed, the way in which they conduct themselves across all counseling specialty areas, and the professional development in which they engage. More information about the American Counseling Association is available on their Web site (http://www.counseling.org).

The American School Counselor Association (ASCA) became a division of ACA in 1953. According to ASCA (2010a), its "members are school counselors certified/licensed in school counseling with unique qualifications and skills to address all students' academic, personal/social and career development needs" (p. 1). ASCA focuses its efforts on professional development, publications and other resources, research, and advocacy for school counseling.

The Ethics Chair and the ASCA Board develop the Ethical Standards for School Counselors, give members an opportunity to respond to proposed codes, and then the Delegate Assembly further responds and adopts the code of ethics. ASCA sponsors a national conference and offers a number of professional development activities for professional school counselors. One of the topics covered at some of these events concerns ethics and professional behavior. More information about the American School Counselor Association is available on their Web site (http://www.schoolcounselor.org).

The National Board for Certified Counselors (NBCC) began as a corporate partner of ACA and is now an autonomous organization. While the link between ACA and NBCC remains strong, it was necessary to separate the certifying entity from ACA to eliminate any potential conflicts of interest. Headquartered in Greensboro, North Carolina, NBCC is the only national credentialing organization for professional counselors. All other licenses and certifications for counselors are obtained through state agencies and local organizations. NBCC has established the National Certified Counselor (NCC) credential and several specialty-area certifications. Counselors must pass the National Counselor Exam (NCE) as part of the process to become nationally certified. Many states use the NCE as the exam required for professional counselor licensure or certification; in some states, counselors may be eligible for certification by the state board of education if they are an NCC. The NBCC has also developed a code of ethics that must be followed by counselors who hold this certification. More information about this association and certification is available on their Web site (http://www.nbcc.org).

Purposes of Ethical Standards

Both laws and ethical standards are based on generally accepted societal norms, beliefs, and customs. However, laws are more prescriptive and carry penalties for noncompliance. Laws "dictate the *minimal* standards of behavior that society will tolerate, whereas ethics represent the *ideal* standards expected by the profession" (Remley & Herlihy, 2013, p. 8). Ethical standards are usually developed by professional associations to guide the behavior of a specific group of professionals. Ethical standards are usually divided into two types: mandatory ethics and aspirational ethics. A counselor who adheres to mandatory ethics is following the "musts" of the profession. Counselors who practice aspirational ethics follow the "oughts" of the profession; they must adhere to the highest standards and think about the impact of their actions. Herlihy and Corey (2014) suggested that for a counselor to practice aspirational ethics, the counselor must understand the underlying intent and principles of the ethical standards.

The ACA's (2014) *Code of Ethics* is based on six general moral principles that guide counselors' behavior and decision making. *Autonomy* refers to the clients' ability to choose and make decisions about their behavior and control the direction of their lives. *Monmaleficence* means to do no harm. Counselors always need to ensure that they operate in ways that neither result in harm nor potentially result in harm. *Beneficence* means to always promote that which serves the growth and good of clients and society. *Justice* refers to fairness in counselors' relationships and includes fair treatment and consideration of clients. *Fidelity* refers to honesty in the counselor–client relationship, honoring one's commitment to the client, and establishing an accepting relationship. The last principle is veracity, which was added to the list of ethical principles with the 2014 revision of the code. *Veracity* refers to being truthful in professional relationships.

Within ACA and its divisions, there are multiple codes of ethics. ACA (2014) has the *Code of Ethics* to which members must adhere. Several divisions, specifically the American School Counselor Association, American Rehabilitation Counseling Association (ARCA), American Mental Health Counselors Association (AMHCA), National Career Development Association (NCDA), and International Association for Marriage and Family Counseling (IAMFC) have their own codes. The Association for Specialists in Group Work (ASGW) has developed Best Practice Guidelines to supplement ACA's *Code of Ethics*. These codes of ethics parallel the ACA *Code of Ethics* but speak more directly to practice within the specialty area. For example, ASCA's (2010a) *Ethical Standards for School Counselors* discusses what ethical behavior consists of in a school setting, and the ASGW (2007) Best Practice Guidelines address ethical behavior when conducting groups.

Many counselors belong to multiple organizations, some of which have their own code of ethics. Professional counselors may also hold credentials from organizations or state credentialing boards that either have their own code of ethics or require that a particular code of ethics be followed. It is sometimes confusing and difficult to discern which code takes precedence. While all professional counselors need to make that decision for themselves, there are two general guiding principles represented by the following two questions. First, in what type of setting is the professional counselor practicing, and is there a designated code that applies or that is required for that setting? Second, what is the professional counselor's position in that setting? In reality, all codes of ethics are very similar, are based on the same general principles, and serve the same general functions. But if there continues to be a question, one should adhere to the code that is the most stringent or rigorous for that issue or setting.

All codes of ethics concern behaving in an appropriate and professional manner; always functioning in the best interests of the client or student; and always practicing within the scope of one's education, training, and experience. Counselors who behave ethically should not be concerned about multiple codes of ethics. Codes of ethics serve another important function: they protect and educate the public about the standards of behavior they should expect from counselors.

ACA's 2014 Code of Ethics

The 2014 ACA *Code of Ethics* delineates the responsibilities of professional counselors toward clients, colleagues, workplaces, and themselves by describing the ideal standards for counselors' behavior. All ACA members are required to abide by the 2014 *Code of Ethics*. Any violation of ethical behavior will result in action taken against the member. The ACA cannot take much action against professional counselors who are not members; however, as these are the standards of the profession, all professional counselors are held to them, regardless of their professional association membership status. Failure to be familiar with, use, or comprehend the 2014 *Code of Ethics* is not a legally valid excuse for unethical or inappropriate behavior. In the absence of any law or written policy or procedure, courts will use the 2014 ACA *Code of Ethics* as the standard for all professional counselors. ACA states that the 2014 *Code of Ethics* serves six main purposes:

> 1) The *Code* sets forth the ethical obligations of ACA members and provides guidance to inform the ethical practice of professional counselors; 2) The *Code* identifies ethical considerations relevant to professional counselors and counselors-in-training; 3) The *Code* enables the association to clarify for current and prospective members, and for those served by members, the nature of the ethical responsibilities held in common by its members; 4) The *Code* serves as an ethical guide designed to assist members in constructing a course of action that best serves those utilizing counseling services and establishes expectations of conduct with a primary emphasis on the role of the professional counselor; 5) The *Code* helps support the mission of ACA; and 6) The standards contained in the *Code* serve as the basis for processing inquiries and ethical complaints. (ACA, 2014, p. 3)

The 2014 ACA *Code of Ethics* addresses the responsibilities of professional counselors toward their clients, workplace and colleagues, and themselves. It is divided into nine areas:

- *Section A: The Counseling Relationship* covers all areas related to the nature of the relationship with the clients. It includes the subtopics of client welfare; client rights; clients served by others; personal needs and values; managing and maintaining boundaries and professional relationships; extending boundaries beyond conventional parameters; sexual intimacies with clients or their family members; multiple clients; group work; fees and bartering; termination and referral; and end-of-life issues. In general, counselors must always put the best interests of their clients first and ensure that clients understand the extent and limitations of counseling. The 2014 *Code of Ethics* added language to this section to make it clear that counselors must avoid imposing their personal values and may not refer a client based on any of the counselor's personally held beliefs, values, or behaviors.

- *Section B: Confidentiality and Privacy* covers all areas related to the confidentiality rights of the client or clients and discusses the limits to confidentiality. It includes the subtopics of right to privacy, groups and families, minor or incompetent clients, records, research and training, and consultation. This section clarifies the confidentiality rights of deceased clients and discusses the issues of confidentiality when counseling families. Changes included reinforcing the confidential nature of records kept in any medium and the need for counselors to keep records as appropriate to their practice.
- *Section C: Professional Responsibility* covers counselors' responsibilities toward their clients, themselves, other professionals, and the public. It includes the subtopics of standards of knowledge, professional competence, advertising and soliciting clients, credentials, public responsibility, and responsibility to other professionals. This section also addresses counselor impairment and the transfer of records, using a records custodian, and clients in the event of the death of a counselor and discusses the counselor's responsibility to use a scientific basis for treatment. Counselors must make reasonable efforts to contribute to the good of the public through *pro bono publico* works.
- *Section D: Relationships With Other Professionals* covers work setting issues and includes the subtopics of relationships with employers and employees, consultation, fees for referrals, and subcontractor arrangements and issues related to interdisciplinary teams and the way in which they should function.
- *Section E: Evaluation, Assessment, and Interpretation* covers standards related to the assessment of clients, the counselor's skills, and appropriateness of assessment. It includes the subtopics of general appraisal issues, competence to use and interpret tests, informed consent for appraisal, releasing information, proper diagnosis of mental disorders, test selection, conditions of test administration, diversity in testing, test scoring and interpretation, test security, obsolete tests and outdated test results, test construction, and forensic evaluations.
- *Section F: Supervision, Training, and Teaching* covers issues related to training and supervising counselors and counselor education programs. It covers the subtopics of the supervisory relationship, counselor educators and trainers, counselor education and training programs, and students and supervisees.
- *Section G: Research and Publication* covers issues related to the ethical treatment of participants and ethical research procedures. Subtopics include research responsibilities, informed consent, reporting results, and publication.
- *Section H: Distance Counseling, Technology, and Social Media* covers the increasing use of technology in counseling and the benefits and confidentiality challenges presented by its use. Counselors must strive to become knowledgeable about these resources, the benefits and challenges, and the ethical and legal requirements. This section covers the use of distance counseling and the relevant laws and ethical issues, and the use of social media in counseling. Counselors must keep their personal and professional virtual presences separate and may not view their client's virtual presence without client permission. Counselors

must make clients aware of how they use technology in their counseling practice and its impact on confidentiality.
- *Section I: Resolving Ethical Issues* covers the procedure professional counselors should follow when they suspect another counselor of unethical behavior. Subtopics include knowledge of standards, suspected violations, and cooperation with the ethics committee.

The 2014 ACA *Code of Ethics* reflects some significant changes from the 2005 *Code*. The 2014 *Code of Ethics* clarifies professional values in the preamble; identifies when the counseling relationship begins and when a counselor is able to refer; clarifies boundary issues and extending relationships beyond conventional boundaries; explains that one may not have a professional relationship with someone with whom the counselor is unable to be objective; reinforces the need to keep records in any medium; and addresses the increasing importance of the use of technology in counseling. Additional terms were defined in the glossary, which was expanded. The *Code of Ethics*, resources, and more information can be found on the ACA Ethics Web page (http://www.counseling.org/Resources/CodeofEthics/TP/Home/CT2.aspx).

ASCA Ethical Standards for School Counselors

The American School Counselor Association has developed a parallel set of ethical standards that specifically address professional school counseling. The ASCA (2010a) Code of Ethics and Standards of Practice for professional school counselors is an attempt by the profession to standardize professional practice for the purpose of protecting students, parents, and the professional school counselor. ASCA's ethical standards are a guide to help meet the needs of individual situations, but they are rarely appropriate for rote application, because it is the context of the dilemma that determines appropriate action.

It is only the professional school counselor, in consultation with other professionals, who can determine how to apply an ASCA ethical code to further the best interest of the student. Codes are not intended to be a blueprint that removes the need for judgment and ethical reasoning (Corey, Corey, & Callanan, 2010). A summary of each of the seven sections follows.

- *Section A: Responsibilities to Students* covers the professional school counselor's responsibilities to treat each student as a unique individual; maintain confidentiality as appropriate in the relationship; develop academic, career/college/post-secondary access, and personal/social counseling plans; avoidance of dual relationships that might impair objectivity and increase risk of harm to students, make appropriate referrals; screen prospective group members and maintain awareness of participants' needs, fit, and personal goals in relation to the groups' intention and focus; inform parents/guardians or appropriate authorities of students' intent to endanger themselves or others; maintain and secure student records; use appropriate evaluation, assessment and interpretation techniques, information, and technology; and ensure the welfare of students in peer helper programs. Confidentiality for students is an area that is tough to negotiate while protecting both student and parental rights. Confidentiality is a cornerstone of individual counseling and facilitates a trusting relationship between students and professional school counselors. The ASCA code promotes the philosophy that professional school counselors have a primary obligation and loyalty to students. However, confidentiality is far from absolute for minors in a school setting. Parental rights must also be considered in any value-laden work, such as individual counseling, that a professional school counselor does with a student. Parents are continually vested by our courts with legal rights to be the guiding voice in their children's lives (*Bellotti v. Baird*, 1979; *H. L. v. Matheson*, 1982).

- *Section B: Responsibilities to Parents/Guardians* covers parents'/ guardians' rights and responsibilities regarding the professional school counselor's behavior and confidentiality.
- *Section C: Responsibilities to Colleagues and Professional Associates* covers professional school counselors, the school counseling program director/site supervisor, and the school counselor educators' relationships with other professionals, including sharing information, collaborating, and educating around the role of the school counselor.
- *Section D: Responsibilities to the School, Communities, and Families* covers the professional school counselor's responsibility to support and protect students' best interests and the interests of the school, including advocating for the hiring, training, and development of competent professional school counselors and accepting employment only for which they are qualified. Responsibilities to the community include collaboration with community agencies/organizations for students' best interests while promoting equity for all students and not obtaining personal benefit through the role of a school counselor.
- *Section E: Responsibilities to Self* includes professional competence which covers the professional school counselors' responsibility for maintaining their personal emotional and physical health; professional growth and multicultural, social advocacy, and leadership skills and monitoring their effectiveness; and current membership to professional organizations.
- *Section F: Responsibilities to the Profession* covers ethical behavior and involvement with professional associations, supervision of school counselor candidates pursuing practicum and internship experiences, and collaboration and education about school counselors and school counseling programs with other professionals.
- *Section G: Maintenance of Standards* covers the procedure for dealing with concerns about potential ethical violations and the use of an ethical decision making model, such as the Solutions to Ethical Problems in Schools (STEPS) model.

Codes give professional school counselors guidance in their ethical responsibility to students and parents, but they do not propose or attempt to provide complete answers. Ethics are situational and have to be considered in the context of institutional and community standards, school-board policy, and the circumstances surrounding each ethical dilemma. It is ultimately the responsibility of the professional school counselor to determine the appropriate response for individual students who put their trust in the security of the counseling relationship (Stone, 2010).

Professional school counselors frequently ask what should be done when laws and ethical standards appear to be in conflict. Both laws and ethics are based on the same standards generally accepted by society, but laws are written into statute and therefore carry sanctions for failure to follow them. Usually, the most significant penalty an association can impose on a professional counselor is to revoke membership. Both laws and ethical standards are created to protect the public or society by outlining behavioral expectations for the practitioners. When laws and ethical standards conflict with each other, the professional counselor must attempt to resolve the issue. Because penalties are associated with lawbreaking, professional school counselors will generally choose the legal course of action, provided it does not harm the client. Ethical standards recognize that laws, policies, and procedures must be followed and recommend that professional school counselors advocate changes to any requirements that are not in the best interests of their clients.

Case Study 5.1. When Ethics and Law Collide.

Cedric's mother confides in you, the school counselor, that Cedric was the victim of prolonged sexual abuse at the hands of an older cousin. His mother admonishes you not to tell anyone as they are trying very hard to keep the information confidential. During the course of a child study team meeting for the purpose of evaluating possible special education placement for Cedric, you reveal this information to the multidisciplinary team. Were you legal? Were you ethical?

Substantial interest is the key consideration in this case. In the case of *N.C. v. Bedford Central School District* (2004), social worker Reulbach and school counselor Mackie were at the center of a lawsuit that helped define and refine the limits of counselor's substantial interest.

N.C., the parents of the abused child A.J., had a strong interest in keeping their child's abuse private. His parents feared, because of the nature of the offense, that disclosure to his peers or other members of the community might cause A.J. more trauma. However, Dr. Reulbach and Ms. Mackie, in their respective responsibilities as social worker and school counselor, have a substantial interest in revealing relevant details about events which likely affect the student's emotional well-being. All of the communications cited by the parents occurred during the course of the child study team evaluation, which was conducted at the parents' request. The communications took place only between the educators so they could adequately determine the student's need for exceptional student education. The court found that the social worker and school counselor were engaged in professional communication for the student's benefit outweighing the parents' or student's right to confidentiality (*N.C. v. Bedford Central School District*, 2004).

This is a case of ethics and laws conflicting. The counselor and social worker were legal but it is debatable as to whether they were ethical. Laws and ethics can conflict, and when there is conflict, the law takes priority. The law is the minimum standard of care, and ethics are aspirational. Counselors must always be legal but they do not leave their ethical obligations behind just because they have managed to be legal. Ethically, the school counselor might explain to parents the benefits of disclosure, the fact that the child study team is comprised of caring, educational professionals, and convince the parents to engage the other professionals.

Students' Rights and Responsibilities

The legal and ethical complexities of working with minors in schools require school counselors to remain vigilant about the rights and responsibilities of students and their parents/guardians, as well as the implications of these rights on their work (ASCA, 2010a; Imber & Van Geel, 2009). The numerous responsibilities school counselors have in schools and the complexities of delivering counseling services in a setting designed to deliver academic instruction further complicate the legal and ethical realm of school counseling (Moyer, Sullivan, & Growcock, 2012).

Ethical complications are acutely present in both individual and group counseling. Groups are important tools school counselors use to reach more students, but confidentiality cannot be guaranteed. Counseling, especially group counseling, "can be an effective outlet for promoting [a student's] welfare at both individual and systemic levels" (Hays, Arredondo, Gladding, & Toporek, 2010, p. 179). The astute school counselor will use caution to guard what is said in the group to prevent students from harm due to a breach of confidentiality.

Confidentiality, which is addressed in Standard A.2 of the ASCA Ethical Standards, means that the professional school counselor provides informed consent (i.e., disclosing the terms at or before entering the counseling relationship or at the beginning of counseling sessions to provide the counselee the purposes, goals, techniques, and rules of procedure under which he or she may receive counseling). The school counselor explains the meaning of confidentiality in developmentally appropriate terms and helps the student understand that school counselors will try to keep confidences, except when the school counselor determines that serious and foreseeable harm is present. The use of the terms serious and foreseeable is a shift from the previous idea of "clear and imminent" danger, which after several legal cases was found to be insufficient to cover situations in which the school counselor may know of a danger that is not directly in front of them, but could not be classified as "clear and imminent." Therefore, the term "serious and foreseeable" was adopted to provide a larger blanket of protection for students and counselors.

Legal complications are acutely present because states define the legal status of minors very differently. Typically, 18 years is considered the legal age of majority. For example, 18 years is cited in the Family Educational Rights and Privacy Act (FERPA; 1974) as the age at which the majority of parental rights to records transfer to students. All minors share the legal characteristic that they are unable to make decisions on their own behalf. Minors have few responsibilities, an abundance of restrictions, and a dependency on adults. The legal concept of the age of majority has implications for minor clients' rights to make choices about entering into counseling as well as their rights to privacy and confidentiality. The Supreme Court has upheld parents'/guardians' legal right to make critical decisions about their children (*Bellotti v. Baird,* 1979). Because counseling is considered to be a contractual relationship, minors are not afforded the opportunity to legally agree to counseling on their own (Remley & Herlihy, 2013). There are some exceptions as given in most states' statutes allowing minors younger than 18 years to receive counseling or medical services without parental consent.

The lack of congruency among laws regarding minors adds to the difficulties of working with minors because we are unable to rely on clearly stated principles of legal policy to guide us. Scott (2001) states:

> The legal regulation of children is extremely complex. Much of the complexity can be traced ultimately to a single source—defining the boundary between childhood and adulthood. Thus, the question, "What is a child?" is readily answered by policy makers, but the answer to the question, "When does childhood end?" is different in different policy contexts. This variation makes it very difficult to discern a coherent image of legal childhood. Youths who are in elementary school may be deemed adults for purposes of assigning criminal responsibility and punishment, while seniors in high school cannot vote and most college students are legally prohibited from drinking. (pp. 562–563)

An area of student and parental rights that has far-reaching ramifications for professional school counselors involves the value-laden areas of abortion and sexual activity, which often involve a family's religious beliefs, values about sexual conduct, and parental rights to be the guiding voice in their children's lives. Professional school counselors need to be advocates and sources of strength for students who come to them for help in dealing with areas such as sexual activity and abortion. But principles of law and school board policy must be considered.

For example, states vary on whether or not minors can seek contraceptive help in the absence of parental involvement. The Guttmacher Institute (2013) conducted a study of the state statutes involving minors and contraceptive information. (Find the complete report at http://www.guttmacher.org/statecenter/spibs/spib_MACS.pdf.) In summary:

> Twenty-one states and the District of Columbia explicitly allow all minors to consent to contraceptive services. Twenty-five states explicitly permit minors to consent to contraceptive services in one or more circumstances. Three states allow minors to consent to contraceptive services if a physician determines that the minor would face a health hazard if she is not provided with contraceptive services. Eleven states allow a minor to consent if the minor meets other requirements, including being a high school graduate, reaching a minimum age, demonstrating maturity or receiving a referral from a specified professional, such as a physician or member of the clergy. (p. 1)

Parents' Rights and Responsibilities

The ethical imperative of confidentiality in school settings is complicated because of the school counselor's competing interests and obligations that extend beyond the students to parents/guardians, administrators, and teachers. Working with minor clients always poses special considerations with the client's parents/guardians, but never more so than when the minor client is a student in a setting designed for academic instruction rather than clinical counseling. In some instances, parents/guardians may demand and obtain "maintained" information on their child including case notes. In *Parents v. Williamsport Area School District* (1991), a psychologist could not use his professional confidentiality as a basis for refusing to reveal to parents/guardians what was said in an individual counseling session and recorded in individual case notes. Other court cases have supported the school counselor's ethical and sometimes legal imperative to safeguard the confidentiality of minors; however, the courts tell us to be ready to defend our behavior and to show we are competent to address sensitive subjects with students in isolation from their parents/guardians. Generally speaking, school counselors should feel free to discuss relevant but controversial issues with students, such as drug and alcohol abuse, pregnancy, abortion, and birth control. However, when counseling a student about these sensitive topics, we must carefully consider the student's developmental and chronological levels and the legal status of minors, as well as parents'/guardians' rights to be the guiding voice in their children's lives, especially when it comes to value-laden issues.

The Family Educational Rights and Privacy Act (FERPA) of 1974 (often referred to as the "Buckley Amendment") is the federal law that protects the privacy of all student records in all PreK–12 schools that accept funding from programs administered by the U.S. Department of Education. FERPA defines education records as being all information collected by a school for attendance, achievement, group and individual testing, assessment, behavior, and school activities for all students. Personal notes and some confidential information, such as reports of child abuse and neglect, are not considered part of the educational record. FERPA governs the disclosure of information from education records and gives parents the right to talk to teachers and school administrators about their children, see their children's education records, and decide if their child will participate in a questionnaire, survey, or examination regarding a parent's personal beliefs, sex practices, family life, or religion. If a parent disagrees with something in their child's record, the parent may write a statement which then becomes part of the educational record. Under FERPA, only persons with a "legitimate educational interest" can access a student's record. Some personally identifiable information, referred to as *directory information*, is considered public information and can be released without signed, informed consent by the parent.

The major exception to the confidentiality of student records involves law enforcement issues; the school must comply with a judicial order or legally executed subpoena. Additionally, in the case of an emergency, relevant information can be released without the parent's consent, such as in a medical emergency. In situations in which a referral has been made to Social Services or another agency charged with protecting the child, sufficient information can be released to support the allegation. For example, in the case of a neglect referral, the school could release to the appropriate agency attendance and other information that they used in the development of the referral.

The rights of consent transfer to students upon their 18th birthday or to students under the age of 18 years when they enter a postsecondary program. However, for students still in secondary schools when they turn 18 years old, the law does not limit the rights of the parents to continue to be able to access their child's records. New regulations clarify that information about a student in a postsecondary program can be shared with parents under any circumstances if the student is claimed as a dependent on the parent's tax returns. Non-custodial parents have the same rights under FERPA as custodial parents, unless a court order has limited the rights of one or both parents. Other family members, such as step-parents and grandparents are not recognized as having any rights under FERPA unless they are granted such rights by the courts. More information about FERPA is available on the U.S. Department of Education Family Policy Compliance Office Web site (http://www.ed.gov/policy/gen/guid/fpco/index.html).

A second major law that has implications for records is the Health Insurance Portability and Accountability Act (HIPAA) of 1996. The passage of HIPAA required the U.S. Department of Health and Human Services (HHS) to adopt national standards for the privacy of individually identifiable health information. The law also outlined patients' rights and established criteria for access to health records. The law further required the adoption of national standards for electronic health care transactions. The Privacy Rule, which became effective in 2001, functions for health records much the same way FERPA functions for education records. It gives patients the right to inspect and request corrections to their health records, affords some control over the disclosure of their records, and provides a complaint process. It also requires that health care providers give patients a privacy notice and obtain a signed acknowledgement of this notice.

School systems are required to operate under the guidelines of FERPA, so school records are exempt from HIPAA regulations. However, schools often receive records from outside providers that are covered by HIPAA, so it is helpful to have a basic understanding of this law. School systems are continuing to work with their departments of health and other entities regarding HIPAA's impact on records that schools receive from agencies, organizations, and providers governed by this law. Examples of records governed by HIPAA include outside evaluations, medical and mental health records from agencies or private providers, and other information for students receiving services from non-school system personnel. These records are often sent to the school to be used in the appropriate placement or determination of student services, particularly special education services. Once they are received, they generally become part of the educational record and are governed by FERPA, unless the parent or provider of the record indicates that the information should not be redisclosed.

The mandates of both HIPAA and FERPA are consistent with ethical standards and therefore should not prove to be a barrier to sound professional practice. Informed consent, limits to access to, disclosure and redisclosure of records, review and appeals processes, and the confidentiality of records are all part of ethical standards and should direct the practice of professional school counselors (Linde, 2015).

Minor Consent Laws

All states have a minor consent law that allows certain minors to seek treatment for specific conditions involving substance abuse, mental health, and some reproductive health areas. These laws are based on the federal regulation 42 U.S.C §§ 290dd-3; 42 C.F.R. Part 2, which addresses the confidentiality of patient records for drug and alcohol abuse assessment, referral, diagnosis, and treatment. The law further prohibits the release of these records to anyone without the client's informed consent and includes clients under the age of 18 years, even if they are in school and living with parents or guardians.

As states have incorporated this federal law into their statutes, they have taken different approaches to deciding to whom this law applies and for which conditions or issues. The statutes suggest that the patient must be old enough to understand the problem, the treatment options available, and the possible consequences of each option. Some states may have no age limits and maintain that a minor has the same capacity as an adult to consent to certain services. Other states have designated a specific age at which the minor may consent to mental health treatment, reproductive or substance abuse services, or treatment for sexually transmitted diseases (STDs) and HIV/AIDS. Information about your state's requirements can be found on the Guttmacher Institute Web site (http://www.guttmacher.org).

There is tremendous variability across school districts regarding what is permissible under the law. Medical personnel, including the school nurse, are covered, but it is questionable whether a professional school counselor or school psychologist is covered. It is critical that counselors and other student services personnel become familiar with the minor consent law in the state in which they work and their local school systems policies to ensure compliance (Linde, 2015).

Educators' Rights and Responsibilities Regarding Students and Parents

Educators have a responsibility to provide students with an environment conducive to learning in which sexual harassment is not allowed. The U.S. Supreme Court, in *Davis v. Monroe County Board of Education* (1999), in combination with Title IX of the Education Amendments of 1972, established that public schools may be forced to pay damages for failing to address student-on-student sexual harassment. Sexual harassment can no longer be ignored or given cursory attention by school districts. The Davis case demands advocacy against known sexual harassment. According to the Supreme Court, liability may be imposed when the school district is deliberately indifferent to sexual harassment of which the recipient has actual knowledge (Biskupic, 1999). The harassment must be severe, pervasive, and deprive the victim of access to an equal educational opportunity.

Most states have statutes giving educators the right to conduct searches of students on public school property, school buses, and at school events based on reasonable suspicion of criminal activity. School officials can question students without informing them of their constitutional rights; the constitutional rights of minors are not equated with that of adults in most states. For example, school officials can establish dress codes and grooming requirements as part of the student code of conduct.

Application of Student and Parental Rights Through Case Studies

The following cases are presented to highlight additional legal and ethical principles in an effort to raise awareness, reduce risk, and transfer the principles of these cases to other situations.

Case Study 5.2. Rights For Non-Custodial Parents I.

A student's mother, who is incarcerated, requested copies of her son's education records. Are you legally required to provide her with education records?

Non-custodial parental rights are often misunderstood. FERPA makes it clear that both parents have equal access to education records. Even incarcerated parents, parents who have refused to pay child support, and abusive parents have rights to education records under FERPA unless there is a court order expressly forbidding a parent to have education records.

Case Study 5.3. Rights for Non-Custodial Parents II.

Sharon, a 9-year-old student, occasionally seeks your help with relationship issues with her mother, the custodial parent. Sharon's parents are divorced and generally at war over everything, including how to raise Sharon and her sister. Sharon describes her mother as being very strict. A teacher expressed concern that Sharon's grades have been plummeting and that she seems distracted and withdrawn, a marked contrast to how Sharon usually behaves. After meeting with Sharon, you believe you need to involve her parents. Sharon begs you to call her father instead of her mother. You believe Sharon's mother will be upset that you contacted Sharon's father instead of her. Can you consult Sharon's father without seeking permission or notifying her mother, the custodial parent?

Professional school counselors can find guidance in the court case *Page v. Rotterdam-Mohonasen Central School District* (1981). John Page had visitation rights for his son, Eric, but repeated requests to the school district to provide him with education records went unheeded. Mikado Page, Eric's mother, sent a statement to the school (at what was believed to be the school's request) explaining that she has legal custody of Eric and that she did not want John Page to have Eric's education records, participate in teacher–parent conferences, or in any way engage in the education of Eric. The court found that John Page was not trying to alter custodial rights but simply trying to participate in his son's educational progress. The court found that school districts have a duty to act in the best educational interest of the children committed to their care, which means providing educational information to both parents (Alexander & Alexander, 2012; *Page v. Rotterdam-Mohanasen Central School District*, 1981).

Parents, whether or not they have legal custody, do not have to give up their rights to be involved in their children's education or psychological care. Consulting with your building-level supervisor or your district-level supervisor of guidance can help answer the legal rights of non-custodial parents and also shed light on what is in Sharon's best interest and the best interest of the family.

Case Study 5.4. Runaway Children: Working Through a Case Study.

You have been counseling Whitney for several months. You believe Whitney's parents emotionally abuse her, and you have twice reported this suspicion to the Department of Children and Family Services. Emotional abuse has never been established. You recognize how hard it is to determine emotional abuse, and you believe that Whitney will never find relief from authorities. You believe that at 15 years of age, Whitney's best course of action is to flee the abuse. You have never suggested to Whitney that she leave home, but she has brought it up several times, and you do not encourage or discourage this course of action. You have listened and asked questions about her plans. Whitney finally leaves home, and you learn from her friend that she is safe with friends. Whitney's parents call the school, inquiring if school officials would ask Whitney's friends, teachers, and counselor if they had any information about her whereabouts. When asked, you remain quiet. Have you acted illegally?

In most states, it is unlawful to aid a runaway who is unmarried or a minor. If anyone who is not authorized by the Department of Juvenile Justice or the Department of Children and Family Services knows that a child has left home without parental consent or knows that the child is being provided shelter and does not report this to law enforcement authorities, then that person is guilty of a first-degree misdemeanor in most states (Children and Families in Need Services Act, 2000; Delinquency; Interstate Compact on Juveniles Act, 2000).

Summary/Conclusion

One of the most important sources of information for professional school counselors to use in their practice to ensure appropriate behavior is the code of ethics from a professional association. ACA, ASCA, and NBCC have all developed codes of ethics that cover counselors' responsibilities to themselves, their clients or students, colleagues, other staff in their workplace, and communities in which they work. The ASCA code dictates that professional school counselors have a primary obligation and loyalty to students, but it also states that parents need to be involved, because parents are continually vested by our courts with legal rights to guide their children (*Bellotti v. Baird*, 1979; *H. L. v. Matheson*, 1982). Community standards, a counselor's own personal values, school board policy, the school setting, and state and federal statutes all contribute to the complex nature of working with minors in schools.

The rights and responsibilities of students and their parents have considerable implications for all educators, but in many ways they are even more complicated for professional school counselors because their work involves the personal–social arena. The multiplicity of responsibility to parents, students, administrators, teachers, and others in a setting designed to deliver academic instruction requires a vigilance to not only protect the rights of students but also consider parents and others who have rights to influence students.

Professional school counselors must be constant consumers of legal and ethical information by seeking the counsel of colleagues, administrators, supervisors, school attorneys, and Title IX officers. Such supervision and advice make the legal and ethical world of professional school counselors less daunting. Counselors must become familiar with the specifics of which code they deem most appropriate for them and implement its standards in their practice. When professional school counselors behave ethically, they ensure quality services to their students and limit the possibility of getting into legal difficulty. The final decision regarding one's conduct and course of action always resides with the counselor.

CHAPTER 6

Certification, Licensure, and Accreditation in School Counseling

*Brent M. Snow and C. Marie Jackson**

Preview

In this chapter we present a brief history of credentialing and clarify the confusion and differential requirements related to state certification in school counseling, national certification in counseling, licensure in professional counseling, and national accreditation of graduate programs in school counseling.

School counseling, along with other specialty fields in education, historically has required practitioners to meet certain requirements to work with children in public schools. In addition to teachers, administrators, and other specialists, stakeholders in school counseling have developed standards in every state, requiring a credential to work in the schools as a professional counselor. In addition to a state credential in school counseling, professional school counselors with appropriate training and education are eligible for licensure as professional counselors in most states and also for national certification in counseling. Because of the lack of standardization of terminology and differential requirements between states and credentialing bodies, we will attempt to clarify this confusion. In addition to a brief history of credentialing, we will address state certification in school counseling, licensure in professional counseling, national certification in counseling, and accreditation of graduate programs in counseling.

Why All the Confusion With This Credentialing Stuff?

Until the 1970s, there was very little, if any, confusion about credentials in the field of counseling. That is because until that time there were basically only two credentials that affected counselors: state certification in school counseling (administered by a state department of education or similar body) and licensure as a psychologist (administered by a state licensure board). State certification in school counseling controlled who could be a professional school counselor in a public school, and psychologist licensure controlled who could practice

---

*The authors wish to acknowledge the contributions of Dr. Sally Murphy to this chapter. Dr. Murphy authored the chapter "Professional Training and Regulation in School Counseling," which was published in the first edition of this handbook.

psychology (e.g., counseling, psychotherapy), either independently or in private practice. As a result, if a professional was not interested in working in a school or private practice, credentials were not an issue. State and private agencies and other employers of counselors simply developed their own requirements for hiring counselors. At that time, counselors with doctoral degrees were routinely licensed as psychologists (Snow, 1982). Although school counseling was not particularly affected, Snow (1981) indicated that

> there has been considerable dialogue in recent years alluding to difficulties between psychologists and counselors regarding who should or should not be licensed (as psychologists) and who can do what to whom. The problem seemed to magnify in the early 1970s as state psychology licensing boards became more restrictive in just who they were willing to identify as psychologists. (p. 80)

With licensure as a psychologist (led by the American Psychological Association) becoming more restrictive, *counselors* (led by the American Personnel and Guidance Association, now called the American Counseling Association [ACA]) began to advocate for separate licensing laws that governed private, independent practice. In 1976, Virginia became the first state to enact a separate licensure law that allowed counselors to engage in private practice, and, today, most states license counselors as *professional counselors*. At the same time, other specialties that were represented by professional associations, such as the American Association for Marriage and Family Therapy, began to push for separate licensure as well. Many states now separately license psychologists, professional counselors, marriage and family therapists, and social workers, thus adding to the confusion surrounding licensure relative to private practice in the helping professions.

State Certification in School Counseling

Certification or credentialing is a professional process through which an individual receives recognition for having attained certain professional qualifications and standards. State credentialing for professional school counselors is a statutory process and is a requirement in all states (ACA, 2014). The procedures and requirements for obtaining certification vary from state to state, but they all require a minimum of some graduate education for initial certification in school counseling. Even the training program requirements outlined by state agencies vary across states, with some state education agencies reviewing and approving university programs. A few states continue to require teaching experience prior to certification. Previous teaching experience as a prerequisite is a long-debated issue in the field of school counseling, even though research does not indicate a link between teaching experience and successful counseling practice (Baker, 1994). Counselor educators (i.e., professors who train counselors at colleges and universities) agree that master's degree-level counselors-in-training do not need prior teaching experience to be successful professional school counselors (Smith, 2001).

Some states allow employees to become certified before they complete all requirements, and some states offer provisional certification, allowing counselors-in-training to be placed in professional school counselor positions prior to finishing degree requirements. Provisional certifications often have a limited time frame during which degree requirements must be completed and full certification earned. An overview of state certification requirements in school counseling can be summarized as follows (ACA, 2015a): All states require graduate education in school counseling; 12 states require supplemental graduate education in addition to counseling; 26 states require completion of a school-based practicum or internship; 15 states require previous teaching or counseling experience; 39 states use standardized examinations as part of the certification process; all 50 states require a criminal background check; and 44 states and the District of Columbia require a master's degree in school counseling. The remaining six states require a bachelor's degree in education, with a minimum of 30 hours in graduate-level work in school counseling (American School Counselor Association [ASCA], 2013a).

Once a counselor receives certification, he or she must keep it in effect by acquiring the appropriate continuing education that each state agency requires. Counselors must also apply for renewal, usually every 5 to 8 years. Additional coursework can serve as continuing education for recertification purposes. Credentialing professional school counselors protects the counselor as well as the general public. State certification allows the professional school counselor to practice as a school counselor and, theoretically, prohibits those without appropriate credentials from legitimately being employed in those positions. State school counseling certification is meant to ensure the public (e.g., parents, teachers, students, community members) that counselors who are hired in these positions have had the minimum training required, no character defects, and other necessary qualifications to provide the designated services to students.

National Certification in School Counseling

Unlike state certification, which is mandatory for professional school counselors, national certification is a voluntary professional credential and is not required for the counselor to practice in the schools, in other agencies, or in independent private practice. Rather, it indicates that a professional school counselor meets national standards developed by counselors, for counselors (rather than by legislators or education departments). While it does not or cannot substitute for state credentials, it is an avenue for identifying counselors who meet rigorous national standards.

Presently, the two national organizations that certify professional school counselors are the National Board for Certified Counselors (NBCC) and the National Board for Professional Teaching Standards (NBPTS; see additional information for certification requirements in Table 6.1). Of these two, the oldest, largest, and best known is NBCC, which was created in the early 1980s. This credentialing body certifies *general* counselors who, when certified, are referred to as a National Certified Counselor (NCC). Additionally, the organization also credentials three counseling specialties, referred to as a National Certified School Counselor (NCSC), Certified Clinical Mental Health Counselor (CCMHC), and Master Addictions Counselor (MAC). There are more than 80,000 counselors certified by NBCC, about 2,500 NCSCs, 1,100 CCMHCs, and 700 MACs. Requirements (NBCC, 2014) for becoming a nationally certified or general counselor include a combination of education (at least a master's degree), supervised experience, and passing an examination known as the National Counselor Examination (NCE) for licensure and certification. There are several options that allow for combinations of education and experience, including benefits associated with graduating from a program accredited by the Council for Accreditation of Counseling and Related Educational Programs (CACREP). The specific requirements for obtaining the NCSC credential

Table 6.1 Additional Information

State School Counselor Certification Requirements

www.schoolcounselor.org; 1-800/306-4722; The American School Counselor Association Web site contains State Certification and Continuing Education requirements within the section on Career Roles.

State Professional Counselor Licensure Requirements

www.counseling.org; 1-800/347-6647; The American Counseling Association Web site contains information on licensure and certification.

National Board for Certified Counselors (NBCC) Requirements

www.nbcc.org; 336/547-0607; The National Board for Certification Web site provides information about the various certifications available through NBCC.

National Board for Professional Teaching Standards (NBPTS) Requirements

www.nbpts.owrg; 703/465-2700; The NBPTS Web site provides information about various teacher certifications available and also includes information about the certification of school counselors.

from NBCC include completing a graduate degree in counseling, with 48 semester or 72 quarter hours of coursework covering eight content areas and including six semester hours of field experience (e.g., practicum, internship); 3,000 hours of post–master's degree supervised experience as a professional school counselor; 100 hours of counseling supervision; and passing the National Certified School Counselor Examination. It is possible for applicants to take the school counseling examination only and obtain both the general (NCC) and school counseling certification (NCSC; Schweiger, Henderson, McCaskill, Clawson, & Collins, 2011).

The National Board for Professional Teaching Standards (NBPTS) has developed a strong presence in certifying teachers at the national level. More than 100,000 teachers across the country have met the NBPTS standards since its inception. In 2002, the NBPTS adopted 11 standards of accomplished practice for professional school counselors that serve as the basis for certification. The resulting credential is referred to as the Early Childhood through Young Adulthood/School Counseling (ECYA/School Counseling) certificate. The eligibility requirements include a baccalaureate degree, 3 years of school counseling experience, and state certification or licensure in school counseling. After meeting these requirements, the NBPTS assessment process involves presenting a portfolio with work samples, videotapes, and other evidence demonstrating effectiveness in meeting the 11 standards. The assessment also includes a *test*, which demonstrates the counselor's knowledge in human growth and development, school counseling programs, diverse populations, theories, data and change, and collaboration.

NBPTS (2013) has announced the revision of the certification process in hopes of better meeting its goal of being the norm rather than an exception in certifying professionals. The plans for the revision include incorporating the latest research, allowing the certification process to be completed in one year or over several years, and reducing the cost to no more than $500 per component, with each of the four components to be submitted separately. All components are expected to be available by 2016-2017 (see http:www.nbpts.org/sites/default/files/douets/certification revisions page/certification changes 1pager.pdf).

There were early attempts to unify certification between NBCC and NBPTS and create one national credential and process. While many had hoped that the NBPTS would adopt the requirements already existing in the NBCC and the NCSC credential, this never occurred, leaving these two national certification bodies competing with each other. It remains to be seen which credential, or if both credentials, stand the test of time in influencing national recognition in school counseling.

Licensure in Professional Counseling

All states currently license professional counselors (ACA, 2014). Terminology varies, but the most common titles are *licensed professional counselor (LPC)*, *licensed mental health counselor (LMHC)*, *licensed clinical professional counselor (LCPC)*, or *licensed clinical mental health counselor (LCMHC)*. Licensure laws are passed by state legislatures and, generally, regulate the title and practice of counseling. Essentially, licensure laws govern the independent, private practice of professional counselors. Counselors who work in government agencies and schools are generally exempted from compliance with licensure laws. The ACA has developed model legislation for states to use in developing counseling licensure laws, and many have followed these guidelines. Some states, of course, have not done so, resulting in licensure laws with varying requirements to become licensed and differing definitions of counseling practice. The model law includes the following definitions in the scope of practice of professional counselors (ACA, 1995):

> The practice of professional counseling includes but is not limited to: individual, group, and marriage and family counseling and psychotherapy; assessment; crisis intervention; diagnosis and treatment of persons with mental and emotional disorders; guidance and consulting to facilitate normal growth and development, including educational and career development; utilization of functional assessment and counseling for persons requesting assistance in adjustment to a disability or handicapping condition; consulting; research; and referral. Assessment shall mean selecting, administering, scoring, and interpreting psychological and educational instruments designed to assess an individual's attitudes, abilities, achievements, interests, personal characteristics, disabilities, and mental, emotional, and behavioral disorders and the use of methods and techniques for understanding human behavior in relation to coping with, adapting to, or changing life situations. (p. 3)

All states require a master's degree, supervised experience, and the passing of an examination—most often the NCE, which is developed by the NBCC. All states exempt professional school counselors from the requirement of becoming a licensed professional counselor to practice school counseling. Many professional school counselors, however, qualify and are eligible for state licensure, if they desire it. Professional school counselors who have private, independent practices outside of their employment in the schools must be licensed. About 12 states require passage of a jurisprudence exam testing the applicant's knowledge of rules and regulations (ACA, 2015a). This is an attempt by licensure boards to require that professional counselors understand practice guidelines and restrictions.

Accreditation of Graduate Programs in Counseling

Accreditation is a system for recognizing universities and colleges as well as professional programs affiliated with those higher education institutions for a level of quality performance and integrity based on review and comparison with a set of standards (CACREP, 2014). In the field of counseling, there are two major accrediting bodies: the Council for Accreditation of Counseling and Related Educational Programs (CACREP) and the Council on Rehabilitation Education (CORE). The American Psychological Association also accredits counseling psychology programs at the doctoral level, but only if they are considered a *psychology* program rather than a *counseling* program.

Since 1981, CACREP has been the primary professional counseling accreditation organization (CACREP; 2014). Accreditation of counseling programs continues to grow, as does the associated influence, recognition, and prestige. For example, beginning in 2017, Ohio will require graduation from a CACREP-accredited program to be eligible for licensure as a professional counselor. Many others require graduation from a program with similar standards as those established by CACREP. The authors believe that the trend to require CACREP accreditation will continue to grow and expand. There are other advantages of CACREP as well. For example, NBCC does not require post-degree experience for those graduating from a CACREP program. Program accreditation provides the foundation for graduate-level school counseling programs to achieve and maintain a high level of quality and integrity based on rigorous national standards. In addition to school counseling programs, CACREP also accredits master's degree programs in addictions counseling; career counseling; student affairs and college counseling; marriage, couple and family counseling; and clinical mental health counseling; as well as doctoral programs in counselor education and supervision.

CACREP standards require entry-level (generally at the master's degree level) counselor education programs to have a minimum of 2 full academic years of graduate study to include a minimum of 48 or 60 semester hours of credit, depending on the program. Standards stipulate eight academic common-core areas: professional identity, social and cultural diversity, human growth and development, career development, helping relationships, group work, assessment, research and program evaluation, and specialized studies in school counseling. These additional specialty standards in school counseling include preparation in the foundations of school counseling in areas such as ethical and legal issues, as are addressed in the American Counseling Association and the American School Counselor Association's codes of ethics. Additional areas of preparation are focused on the contextual dimension of school counseling, the knowledge and skill requirements for professional school counselors, and clinical instruction. This *practical* instruction is an important element, and the standards require students to obtain a supervised practicum (a minimum of 100 clock hours) and a 600-hour internship in a school setting, under the site supervision of a qualified professional school counselor.

As of June 2014 (CACREP, 2014), there were 279 institutions of higher education that had CACREP-accredited programs (totaling 634 specialized programs). Of these programs, about 224 were school counseling programs. As there are well over 300 school counselor education programs in the United States, many school counselor education programs do not offer a CACREP-accredited program. Even so, many of these non-accredited programs are aligned with CACREP's core curriculum requirements. However, these programs may significantly differ from the quality curriculum required in a program accredited by CACREP. Cutting-edge school counselor education programs also align themselves with ASCA's national model (ASCA, 2012a), the national standards incorporated within the model, and with the essential elements and focus of the transforming school counseling movement initiated by The Education Trust (2003). These standards and elements are briefly discussed in the next section.

Transforming School Counseling Initiative

Counselor educators, professional school counselors, and other education experts began to examine the role of the professional school counselor in the school reform movement (Bemak, 2000; Burnham & Jackson, 2000; House & Hayes, 2002). The educational reform for professional school counselors not only examined the role of the counselor within the school community but also addresses the training of preservice school counselors based on professional standards and regulations as well as current research and practice. A more comprehensive discussion of this reform is covered in other chapters, but it is important to understand the integral role it has in the training of professional school counselors.

Although CACREP provided the guidelines for core curriculum requirements within a school counselor education program, these core areas only have begun to address the training needs of the professional school counselor for the 21st century. Funded by the DeWitt-Wallace Reader's Digest Fund, The Education Trust, and six universities (University of West Georgia, University of North Florida, California State University–Northridge, Indiana State University, Ohio State University, and the University of Georgia) have played a significant role in the research, dialogue, and training to improve school counseling by focusing particularly on the graduate-level preparation of professional school counselors (Pérusse & Goodnough, 2001). This focus helped to define a new role for professional school counselors and was known as the Transforming School Counseling Initiative (TSCI).

ASCA National Model

ASCA, the primary association for professional school counselors, provides the structure and standards for school counselors and school counseling programs (ASCA, 2013b) and describes the role of the professional school counselor. The structure for school-based counseling programs, which should be part of the counselor education curricula, is found in the third edition of *The ASCA National Model: A Framework for School Counseling Programs* (ASCA, 2012a). The national model presents an organized approach to program foundation, delivery, management, and accountability, which are the four major components for school counseling programs. This model also incorporates four overarching school counselor role description themes of leadership, advocacy, collaboration, and systemic change. These four themes were drawn from The Education Trust, and ASCA worked with those in the Transforming School Counseling Initiative to infuse these themes throughout the second edition model, as they represented the importance of professional school counselors' skills that lead to systemic change and academic achievement. The third edition continues to include these themes from The Education Trust initiative and to intertwine them throughout the model.

ASCA's model incorporates the ASCA national standards, which are categorized as academic development, career development, and personal–social development. The model reflects current education reform initiatives including the No Child Left Behind Act of 2001 and builds upon its philosophy of "one vision and one voice." Thus, ASCA provides all school counselor educators with a professional, organized, and consistent framework for developing, managing, and delivering school counseling programs. By integrating ASCA's national model within a quality school counselor education program, preservice school counselors graduate with the skills and knowledge necessary to work with diverse school communities and student populations.

Summary/Conclusion

With a brief background and understanding of credentialing and accreditation in the field of counseling, professional school counselors in practice as well as aspiring school counselors can better assess the value of the various certifications and licenses. In this chapter, we provided information to help sort out licenses, certifications, and program accreditation in the field of school counseling. All professional school counselors must become state certified in order to practice in the schools. To practice outside of the school in an agency or private practice, most states require an additional license as a professional counselor. Achieving national board certification identifies the professional school counselor as having achieved professional standards and qualifications at the highest level. Graduating from a nationally accredited program in school counseling, such as those approved by CACREP, adds an element of distinction to one's degree and can be a benefit when seeking national certifications. Clearly, professional school counselors can add to their professionalism and credibility through the attainment of professional credentials and this process can be facilitated by graduating from a CACREP-accredited program.

SECTION 2

Leadership and the Professional School Counselor

CHAPTER 7

The Professional School Counselor and Leadership

Joyce A. DeVoss

Preview

Effective professional school counselors accept leadership, advocacy, collaboration, and public relations roles, all of which require specific leadership skills that can be learned. Professional school counselors understand that leadership is a key component of their professional identity, and it is through leadership behavior that school counselors contribute to systemic change for the benefit of all students. Current professional school counselor preparation programs generally incorporate leadership development into their curricula (DeVoss & Andrews, 2006; Murphy, 2004; Young & Miller-Kneale, 2013). Experienced professional school counselors who have found their educational and professional training lacking in leadership have sought specific training through district, state, and national professional development opportunities. A systematic approach to leadership development includes becoming familiar with leadership theories and models, completing leadership assessment, and incorporating feedback, mentoring, and learning into a leadership improvement plan and professional practice. ASCA now offers a structured program of training leading to a School Counseling Leadership Specialist certificate in recognition of the specific skill set required for effective school counseling leadership.

The Call for Professional School Counselor Leadership

A review of the 13 American School Counselor Association (ASCA) school counselor performance standards and the school counselor competencies associated with each of the four components described in the *ASCA National Model* (2012a) clarifies the expectation that professional school counselors act as educational leaders. Professional school counselors are expected to plan, organize, coordinate, and manage the guidance program for their schools. In addition, they are expected to perform educational leadership activities such as establishing and convening a guidance advisory council on a regular basis, collecting and analyzing data to drive the guidance program, and conducting an annual program audit. They are looked upon as student advocates, educational planners and reformers, team members and collaborators, as well as systems change agents. They are members and chairs of school and district committees.

Davis (2005) stated that "the students, their families and the community are the recipients of the benefits of school counselors with strong leadership skills" (p. 220). Without a minimum of basic leadership skills training, professional school counselors lack the essential tools that are needed to adequately perform their jobs. Murray (2010) noted that burnout and attrition is high in the school counseling profession, finding in a review of literature that inadequate job preparation is a crucial variable. Development of school counselor leadership, advocacy, and public relations skills has the potential to benefit the helper and prevent burnout as well as meet the needs of students.

There has been some debate over the question of whether leaders are born or developed. Some who are involved in the debate use a very narrow definition of leadership that includes aspects of dominance and having overt influence over others, and see these as inherited human traits. Others believe that we all have leadership capabilities that need to be developed and strengthened. From this perspective, effective leadership is a result of the use of the best leadership practices in our environment. Good leadership starts from within, through understanding one's own style of leadership. In addition to this understanding, good leaders continue to learn about leadership and to develop their leadership skills (Bennis, 1994).

Educational Leadership Theories Highlighted

Professional school counselors who develop an awareness of some of the contemporary theories and models of leadership that have influenced the field of education position themselves to confidently take their places on school leadership teams. Such a foundation is necessary to share a common understanding and language of leadership with other educational leaders. In addition, knowledge and understanding of theories and models of leadership are useful when a professional school counselor articulates his or her own leadership approach. Some of the currently popular leadership models described in this chapter include the Situational Model of Hersey and Blanchard, the Transformational Model of Bennis and Deming, the Moral Model of Sergiovanni, the Learning Organization Model of Senge, the Servant Leadership Model of Covey, and the Empowerment Models of Bennis and Kouzes and Posner.

Situational Leadership (Hersey and Blanchard)

Hersey and Blanchard (1969) developed a model that was focused on adapting one's approach to situational demands. Such a model requires that the leader determine the readiness level, which involves both ability and the willingness (Hersey, 1984) of people being addressed. Two dimensions of leadership behavior described in this model include *task behavior* and *relationship behavior*. When using a task behavior style, the leader explains the task, how to do it, and when to do it. When using a relationship approach, the leader supports and facilitates the process of task completion.

Transformational Leadership (Deming and Bennis)

Transformational leadership was developed by W. Edwards Deming (1993) and Warren Bennis (1994). It is an approach that views the leader as a change agent who has vision and is inspirational. The leader is responsible for relationship building and involving others in leadership. Deming's Total Quality Management approach emphasized 14 points, which focused on

Table 7.1 The 14 Points of Deming's Total Quality Management

1. Create constancy of purpose for the improvement of product and service.
2. Adopt the new philosophy.
3. Cease dependence on mass inspection.
4. End the practice of awarding business on price tag alone.
5. Constantly improve the system of production and service.
6. Institute training.
7. Institute leadership.
8. Drive out fear.
9. Break down barriers between staff areas.
10. Eliminate slogans, exhortations, and targets for the workforce.
11. Eliminate numerical quotas.
12. Remove barriers to pride of workmanship.
13. Institute a vigorous education and retraining program.
14. Take action to accomplish the transformation.

Note. From *Out of the Crisis* (pp. 23–24), by W. E. Deming, 2000, Cambridge, MA: MIT Press. Copyright 2000 by MIT Press. Reprinted with permission.

process (including teaching and learning), attention to classroom climate, curriculum, and relationship within the school environment (see Table 7.1). Ensuring quality in these areas in the educational setting leads to high-quality outcomes.

Deming believed that his 14 principles must be applied as a whole. However, some educational legislation, such as the No Child Left Behind Act of 2001, makes adoption of this model as a whole by American schools unfeasible. In spite of this, many of Deming's ideas continue to be applied by educational leaders who share a similar philosophy.

Bennis (1994) conceptualized leadership as full expression of oneself. He emphasized ideas, relationships, and adventure—ideas for change; relationships for harmonious and open interactions and empowerment as well as inclusion of all; and adventure for risk, curiosity, and challenge. Leaders are effective when they express themselves well, know their strengths and weaknesses, and manage them well. They know what they want, how to communicate, how to achieve goals, and how to garner support of others. After interviewing 28 leaders, Bennis concluded that leaders are made, and they continue to grow and learn to develop their voice across their life span. They take charge of their lives and their lifestyles. The process of becoming a leader is a transformational process in which there are unlimited opportunities and challenges along the way.

Four basic leadership ingredients of Bennis's (1994) approach include (a) a guiding vision of what the leader wants to do professionally and personally; (b) a passion for life and course of action; (c) integrity including self-knowledge, candor, and maturity; and (d) curiosity and daring. The leader learns to innovate through active and imaginative anticipation, listening to others, participation in shaping events, and self-direction. Leaders learn to lead by listening to one's inner voice and leading. Transformational leadership is a lifelong developmental process of becoming fully oneself, a concept similar to that of self-actualization, as described by Maslow (1968) and Carl Rogers (1980).

Moral Leadership (Sergiovanni)

Sergiovanni (1992), the leading crafter of moral leadership, described this model as one that connects the interactions of the heart, head, and hand. The connection starts with the heart, then the head, and then the hand. The *heart* consists of what one values and believes. The *head* includes one's mental picture of how the world works. The *hand* represents one's decisions, actions, and behaviors. Leadership in this model is a form of behavior and a form of stewardship. Sergiovanni emphasized building a sense of community in schools in which teachers, principals, and counselors are stewards and servant leaders with shared values and a sense of empowerment regarding their duties in the learning community. The focus in the learning community is on sharing a common vision instead of having one leader to follow.

Sergiovanni's (1992, 2001) concept of moral leadership includes emotions, group membership, meaning, morality, intuition, and obligation. Like Bennis, Sergiovanni (1992, 2001) maintained that moral leaders strive to do "the right things" rather than "do things right." He described the virtuous school as one in which the educational leaders believe that every student can learn and the learning community seeks to serve the whole student. Parents, teachers, the community, and school are viewed as partners in the virtuous school.

Learning Organization Leadership (Senge)

Senge (1990) described five disciplines that overcome organizational learning disabilities in his Learning Organization model. Leaders in a learning organization emphasize continuous feedback to foster learning for improvement of the organization as a whole. The first discipline is *personal mastery*, which includes personal growth, learning, and personal vision. The second discipline is *mental models*, which includes one's internal images of how the world works. The third discipline is *a shared vision*, a connection to learning and work that people share in their hearts. The fourth discipline is *team learning*, learning in which a group functions as a whole and synergizes efforts. The fifth discipline is *systems thinking*, an approach to thinking in which the four other disciplines are integrated into the big picture and their interrelationships are considered. Members of learning organizations recognize that, through their connection to their organizations, they affect the world.

Servant Leadership (Covey)

Two significant contributors to the servant leadership model were Thomas J. Sergiovanni (1992), previously mentioned as the creator of the moral leadership model movement, and Stephen Covey (1991), who wrote about principle-centered leadership. Many of Sergiovanni's relevant concepts were addressed in the Moral Leadership section, so this section will focus on Covey's contributions to the servant leadership model.

Covey offered a framework for leadership that focused on relationships, including both personal and professional relationships. The servant leader strives for balance among family, personal, and professional life through effective relationships. Servant leadership is developed from within. It is practiced on four levels: personal, interpersonal, managerial, and organizational.

Servant leaders learn continually. They care about the needs of others. They are service oriented and have a positive outlook and positive energy. They believe in other people. They are willing to take some risks. They believe in synergy, that the whole is more than the sum of parts. Servant leaders exercise for self-renewal and lead balanced lives. They create environments in which others thrive and are empowered to develop as leaders.

Covey (1991) recommended that leaders develop a clear mission statement and described steps for developing a personal and organizational mission statement. Such statements help leaders to gain and maintain awareness of their destinations and to stay focused on the activities designed to get them there. Effective school counseling programs have clear mission statements guiding them. Professional school counselors can apply the idea of a mission statement to their personal as well as professional lives. Some have separate professional and personal mission statements; others have one broad mission that covers all aspects of their lives.

Covey (1991) recommended developing a personal mission statement through a reflective process in which one examines one's roles and the contributions for which one would like to be remembered in each role. He suggested considering the characteristics, values, and principles represented in the contributions. The mission statement should be inspiring and empowering. It should represent the person's higher purpose and alignment with his or her vision and values. Figure 7.1 provides instructions for development of a personal or professional mission statement. A written mission statement represents a personal commitment to oneself to live by one's values and principles to achieve a higher purpose.

Empowerment Leadership (Bennis, Kouzes, and Posner)

Research by Kouzes and Posner (1995) and Bennis (1994) found that effective leaders accept input from others, share power with others, and motivate others toward success. These are empowering behaviors. Bennis made contributions to both transformational leadership and empowerment leadership theories. Some of his concepts were addressed in an earlier section in this chapter, so the focus here will be on the leadership challenge model of Kouzes and Posner (1995). This model recognizes the human need for respect and acknowledgement. It includes five practices and 10 commitments that came out of more than 10 years of study of personal best cases of leadership in accomplishing extraordinary things.

The first of the five practices is *challenging the process*, with the associated two commitments of searching out challenges and taking risks. The second practice is *inspiring a shared vision*, associated with the commitments of envisioning an uplifting future and enlisting others in a common vision. The third practice is *enabling others to act*, with the commitments of fostering collaboration and strengthening people by giving power and support. The fourth practice is *modeling the way*, with the commitments of setting the example and promoting small victories for progress. The fifth practice is *encouraging the heart*, with associated commitments of recognizing individual contributions and celebrating team accomplishments.

Kouzes and Posner's leadership challenge model addresses the potential for leadership development in everyone. A leadership assessment instrument called the *Leadership Practices Inventory* is associated with this model and will be described in the next section. The leadership challenge process includes assessment, review, and analysis of results; development of action plans; and ongoing behavioral changes to improve leadership effectiveness.

Instructions: Follow the steps below to develop a personal or professional mission statement. Write the resulting statement on a large sheet of paper and post prominently.

1. In the first column, list the roles you fill.
2. In the second column, list your contributions for each role.
3. In the third column, list the values, characteristics, and principles reflected in your contributions for each role.
4. Review all columns and summarize in a concise mission statement that you will be able to commit to memory.
5. Post your mission statement in a prominent place where you can review it regularly.

Your roles	Your contributions	Your values, characteristics, and principles
_____	_____	_____
_____	_____	_____
_____	_____	_____
_____	_____	_____
_____	_____	_____
_____	_____	_____
_____	_____	_____

Mission statement: _____

_____

_____

_____

_____

Figure 7.1. Worksheet for development of a mission statement.

Leadership Assessment

Assessment provides the professional school counselor leader with feedback from self and others about his or her leadership characteristics and skills. Feedback is useful in evaluating which areas of leadership capabilities need to be developed and strengthened, thus directing leadership development and improvement. Many leadership assessment instruments are self-assessment devices. It is useful to incorporate with the results of such devices some feedback of others who have observed the professional school counselor in leadership behaviors. This will give a more balanced and objective leadership assessment. Four leadership assessment tools appropriate for professional school counselors will be described in this section. Many other leadership assessment tools are easily accessible to the professional school counselor, and several of these are explained next.

Myers-Briggs Type Indicator

The *Myers-Briggs Type Indicator* (MBTI; Myers, McCaulley, Quenk, & Hammer, 2003) helps professional school counselor leaders to better understand their thinking, behavior, and emotions and identify their strengths and weaknesses as information processors and decision makers. Based on Carl Jung's Jungian analytical psychology theory, the MBTI is a self-report questionnaire of 16 personality types. It assesses psychological type on four dimensions: extraversion–introversion, sensing–intuiting, thinking–feeling, and judging–perceiving.

Each dimension is represented by a letter (i.e., I = Introversion, E = Extraversion, N = Intuition, S = Sensing, T = Thinking, F = Feeling, P = Perceiving, J = Judging), and the professional school counselor who completes the MBTI assessment is assigned four letters based on their preferences on the assessment items. The four letters represent the person's personality type (e.g., INTJ, ESTP, ENFP, INSJ). Each of the types has a corresponding type description. The original purpose of the MBTI was to assist people in career choice. Now it is widely used as a tool for team building and leadership development. It is offered by some university and community college testing centers.

True Colors Self-Assessment System

True Colors was developed by Don Lowry (1990) and has been used by educational personnel, including professional school counselors, to increase self-awareness in themselves and in students. The assessment can be useful in identifying personality characteristics that contribute to leadership practice. This assessment is based on four psychological types and has a foundation in Carl Jung's theory of personality, the work of Katharine Briggs and Isabel Myers in developing the MBTI, and Keirsey's research on temperament and development of the Keirsey Temperament Sorter. The True Colors Assessment assigns a color to each of the four different personality types, reflecting differences in how people of different types think and behave. Each of the personality types and defining characteristics is briefly described in the following list:

Green—analytical, reflective, ingenious, seeks knowledge

Blue—creative, thoughtful, compassionate, inspiring

Gold—organized, traditional, responsible, trustworthy

Orange—playful, fun loving, optimistic, energetic, bold

Two components of the assessment include character cards and a word sort. An additional assessment is available online and consists of multiple-choice responses to 24 questions. The character cards have characters on them demonstrating behaviors associated with each of the four colors. The respondent must choose the color card with the character who behaves most like them. In the word sort, respondents must give weighted scores to groups of words to indicate which words are most like them (4) to which words are least like them (1). The totals from each column correspond to a color. The highest score indicates the person's dominant color, the next highest is the second color in dominance, and so forth. The true colors multiple-choice assessment can be taken online through the True Colors Web site (http://www.mytruecolors.com) after paying a fee. Respondents receive a 20-page report, summarizing the results of this assessment. The results can be used to develop insight into a professional school counselor's personality strengths and how a professional school counselor can best contribute to teamwork and collaboration.

Leadership Practices Inventory

The *Leadership Practices Inventory* (LPI) is based on Kouzes and Posner's (1995, 2001) research on leadership in a variety of settings, including schools, with more than 4,000 cases and 200,000 surveys. The LPI has two versions: one is for self-assessment and the other is for one or more observers to complete. The inventory consists of 30 items that assess the use of the five practices and 10 commitments of the leadership challenge model of leadership development. The items are rated on a 10-point scale, according to the degree to which the leader being assessed uses the skills listed on the questionnaire. This instrument has been found to have high reliability and good validity. The results of the inventory are likely to be a good predictor of leadership behavior, especially when the person who is assessed completes their own assessment and has one or more observers who know the person well also complete the assessment. The LPI can be taken online or purchased as a paper-and-pencil version.

Leaders as Relationship Builders

Dubrin (2004) identified seven relationship-oriented attitudes and behaviors that help to get people working together smoothly. Since their professional role is primarily relationship-oriented, professional school counselors are likely to find a number of their leadership strengths among these attitudes and behaviors. In addition, completing an assessment based on these attitudes and behaviors, professional school counselors may identify some areas for growth and intentional goal setting and action steps. The attitudes and behaviors are listed and described here:

Aligning and mobilizing people—getting people to work together smoothly.

Concert building—building a work group into a well-functioning, ongoing system.

Creating inspiration—triggering powerful emotional experiences in others by building enthusiasm, stimulating thinking, enabling leadership in others, recognizing others' contributions, and developing people's talents. Being visible and accessible reinforces inspiration.

Satisfying higher level needs—learning what is important to others and facilitating opportunities for getting those needs met.

Giving emotional support and encouragement—accomplished by expressing appreciation of others and through the sharing of leadership and decision-making opportunities.

Promoting principles and values—advocating for good causes uplifts and motivates others to care about and act in the interest of the common gouzd.

Being a servant leader—being committed to service and helping others achieve their goals.

An assessment tool for these attitudes and behaviors is provided here. On the Relationship-Oriented Attitudes and Behaviors assessment form provided in Table 7.2, rate yourself on a scale of 1 to 5, where 1 = *very weak* and 5 = *very strong* on these seven attitudes and behaviors described by Dubrin (2004).

When reviewing your scores, consider the leadership relationship dimensions you scored at 4 or 5 as strengths, and those you scored at 1 or 2 as areas that need improvement. Make note of your strengths and areas for improvement on the lines that follow each item. Consider the areas listed for improvement when you review and revise your leadership improvement plan.

Table 7.2 Relationship-Oriented Attitudes and Behaviors

	Very Weak				Very Strong
Aligning and mobilizing people	1	2	3	4	5
Concert building	1	2	3	4	5
Creating inspiration	1	2	3	4	5
Satisfying higher level needs	1	2	3	4	5
Giving emotional support and encouragement	1	2	3	4	5
Promoting principles and values	1	2	3	4	5
Being a servant leader	1	2	3	4	5

Leadership Improvement Plan

Once a professional school counselor becomes familiar with leadership theory and concepts and completes a self-assessment using the instruments previously described or other leadership assessment tools, the professional school counselor can use the results to identify strengths and areas for improvement. From this list, the professional school counselor can choose items to address on a leadership improvement plan, formulate objectives for improvement, and identify specific strategies for improvement. Methods for monitoring progress need to be built into the plan so that the professional school counselor has some way available to obtain ongoing feedback on how well the plan is working and whether adjustments in the strategies need to occur. A sample leadership improvement plan is provided in Figure 7.2. It can be duplicated for more than one behavior or skill for improvement.

The leadership improvement plan should be discussed with a mentor and incorporate the mentor's suggestions. In seeking a mentor, it is helpful to make a list of what is needed from the relationship and what qualities are valued in a mentor. Discuss with a potential mentor what is needed in the relationship and consider together the time commitment involved. The school counselor leader should meet regularly with one or more mentors to update the mentor(s) on progress and to discuss possible adjustments needed in the plan, as necessary.

Journaling is a common approach for reflection on one's progress in leadership skill or behavior improvement. The professional school counselor can document examples of opportunities to practice leadership skills and note how well the opportunity was used. The journal can be used to document feedback from trusted colleagues. The journal provides the professional school counselors with a record of progress to review in meetings with a mentor.

Summary/Conclusion

Bennis (1994) emphasized that leaders learn to lead by leading. Professional school counselors need to develop their own leadership styles and practice acquired leadership skills on a continuous basis. Ongoing mentoring for professional school counselors can be instrumental to growth as a leader when it is related to the specifically identified goals and objectives to which there is commitment indicated on the leadership improvement plan. The professional

> **Professional School Counselor Leadership Improvement Plan**
>
> Behavior or skill to improve
> _____
>
> Objectives
>   1. _____
>   2. _____
>   3. _____
>
> Mentors
> _____
> _____
>
> Strategies to Achieve Objectives
>   1. _____
>   _____
>   2. _____
>   _____
>   3. _____
>   _____
>
> Strategies to Monitor Progress
>   1. _____
>   _____
>   2. _____
>   _____
>   3. _____
>   _____

Figure 7.2. Sample of a leadership improvement plan.

school counselor who is flexible and adaptive can learn to integrate newly acquired leadership knowledge and skills into their unique perspective as an educational leader. This chapter provided both an overview of leadership theories relevant to professional school counseling and resources for leadership training and developing a leadership improvement plan to guide the professional school counselor in realizing his or her full potential as an educational leader.

CHAPTER 8

The Professional School Counselor: Cultivating Academic Achievement and College/Career Readiness for All Students

Chris Wood*

Preview

In this chapter, we describe how professional school counselors can use their skills and knowledge to contribute significantly to the academic mission of the school and help ensure all students become college and career ready. The chapter will examine system-centered and student-centered ways in which professional school counselors can influence student achievement. We will provide examples through the lens of South Middle School (SMS), a fictional middle school (Grades 6–8), with a student body consisting of 25% African American students, 3% Asian American students, 45% European American students, and 27% Hispanic American students. Forty percent of SMS students receive free or reduced-price lunch. At SMS, there are three professional school counselors who loop with their 6th through 8th grade levels. Thus, they work with the same students for 3 years, and over 3 years will work closely with all of the teacher teams in the building. The professional school counselors are in a unique position to understand all of the strengths and weaknesses of both the staff and the students at SMS as well as the South City community. They are well versed in the educational and community resources available for students and their families.

Cultivating Academic Achievement and Career Readiness for All Children

The important contributions school counselors make toward the academic achievement and college or career readiness of students is increasingly being recognized. "School counseling is a necessity to ensure that all our young people get the education they need to succeed in today's economy" (Obama, 2014). In support of the role of school counselors, Secretary of Education Arne Duncan stated

> School counselors are pivotal in helping students manage their academic programs as well as the inevitable life events that may threaten students' ability to succeed in

---

*Special thanks to Peggy LaTurno Hines, Teesue H. Fields, and Lisa Hinkelman for their contributions to previous editions of this chapter. Our eternal gratitude goes to Susan Jones Sears for her contribution to previous editions of this chapter, may she rest in peace.

school. . . . Increasing the number of students who graduate from high school ready for college and careers requires that all students benefit from a holistic support system that ensures consistent access to effective school counselors. (2014, para. 2)

Not everyone consistently views professional school counselors so positively. The Bill & Melinda Gates foundation funded a survey of over 600 young adults ages 22–30 years (Johnson, Rochkind, Ott, DuPont, & Hess, 2011). The majority of these survey respondents were disappointed in the college and career assistance they received from their high school counselor. Equally disturbing, the study claims that students who perceived a lack of "good counseling" (survey respondents chose answers—'another face in the crowd' or 'counselors made an effort to get to know me and treat me as an individual') were less likely to go from high school directly into college. Methodological concerns notwithstanding, there are certainly some points from the report that should resonate with the field of education and professional school counselors. One is surely that professional school counselors can be influential entities within the school system, especially in terms of the academic and career planning of students.

K–12 education in the new millennium has focused upon improving the academic achievement of every student. The U.S. Congress and numerous state legislatures have enacted legislation to hold schools accountable for raising the academic achievement level of all students (Indiana Department of Education, 1999; U.S. Department of Education, 2001). The belief that schools are responsible for teaching all students to reach rigorous academic standards is now the norm by which schools are evaluated (Hines & Fields, 2004).

With the national emphasis on standards-based educational reform, professional school counselors are encouraged to demonstrate how they can contribute to increased student achievement and remove barriers to student learning. Moreover, professional school counselors are urged to help close the achievement gap and advocate for rigorous preparation of all students including low-income and minority youth (The Education Trust, 1997). Reflecting the national interest in educational reform and closing the achievement gap, the American School Counselor Association (ASCA) developed the national standards for school counseling programs (Campbell & Dahir, 1997). The national standards address three domains of development: personal–social, career, and academic. One of the student standards under the academic development domain reads that "students will acquire the attitudes, knowledge, and skills that contribute to effective learning in school and across the life span" (Dahir, Sheldon, & Valiga, 1998, p. 7). More recently ASCA (2012b) articulated school counselor competencies described as the knowledge, skills/abilities, and attitudes requisite for professional school counselors to meet the needs of preK–12 students.

Professional school counselors focus on the academic, career, and personal–social development of all students and are trained to help students who are having difficulty in those areas. However, education reform models omit professional school counselors from the planning process for achieving educational excellence. For example, professional school counselors were not mentioned in the U.S. Department of Education's publication, *School-Based Reform: Lessons from a National Study* (Quellmalz, Shield, & Knapp, 1995). Until recently, when professional school counselors were mentioned in reform models, it was only to include their position on an advisory committee (U.S. Department of Education, 1998). Professional school counselors were seen as peripheral at best, and unnecessary at worst, in the effort to raise student achievement (House & Martin, 1998). But times have changed.

Professional school counselors are the eyes and ears of the school (House, 2002). They know the issues and concerns of students, parents, faculty, administration, and the community. In addition, professional school counselors possess knowledge and skill sets that are unique within the school environment. While both professional school counselors and administrators are trained in leadership and research skills, professional school counselors are the only educators skilled in counseling, group facilitation, collaboration and consultation, and advocacy (Hines & Fields, 2004). Moreover, professional school counselors are being encouraged and trained to develop, manage, and lead comprehensive school counseling programs that help students be college and career ready.

The third edition of *The ASCA National Model: A Framework for School Counseling Programs* (ASCA, 2012a) stresses the importance of the school counseling program's contribution to student achievement. To further school efforts at implementing the model, ASCA developed the Recognized ASCA Model Program (RAMP) to recognize exemplary school counseling programs (ASCA, 2003b). Research consistently supports the efficacy of the model in improving academic achievement at all educational levels (Sink & Stroh, 2003; Sink, Akos, Turnbull, & Mvududu, 2008). Directly related to state standards of achievement, Wilkerson, Perusse, and Hughes (2013) found that students in RAMP program schools had substantially higher achievement in English/language arts and mathematics.

Professional school counselors play a critical role in efforts to raise student achievement through the implementation of system-centered and student-centered activities. *System-centered* activities are designed to influence adult behavior or the educational environment. From a system-centered standpoint, professional school counselors join with building administrators to help facilitate school improvement efforts. A critical system-centered professional school counselor activity is facilitating the creation of interventions designed to remove barriers impeding academic achievement. Additional system-centered activities include using data to spur change, task group facilitation, advocacy, collaboration, and conducting research.

Student-centered interventions are activities created to directly affect students. From a student-centered perspective, professional school counselors work to align their counseling program priorities with the school's academic goals and Common Core State Standards (CCSS) through the design of a continuum of interventions that help students master the school guidance standards and indicators that will help students be successful in school. Student-centered activities include developmental guidance lessons and small-group and individual counseling.

One way for school counselors to conceptualize their role in the academic achievement of students is to pursue the goal of students becoming "college and career ready." ASCA (2012a) states that ". . . college and career readiness is exemplified by students who are prepared for any post-secondary experience without the need for remediation and that all students possess the skills and knowledge needed to qualify for and succeed in their chosen field" (p. 14). Conley (2013) adds to this definition the "habits" students must possess in order to be successful in post-secondary education or training. He describes four areas of readiness: cognitive strategies, content knowledge, transition knowledge and skills, and learning skills/techniques. The University of Chicago Consortium on Chicago School Research (CCSR) identified noncognitive factors in increasing student achievement and helping students attain college/career readiness (Nagaoka et al., 2013). Specifically, five categories of noncognitive factors emerged from their review of hundreds of research studies: (1) academic behaviors, (2) academic perseverance, (3) social skills, (4) learning strategies, and (5) academic mindsets.

Academic behaviors include attending class, completing assignments on time, and engaging in class activities. Academic perseverance can be conceptualized as student tenacity as applied to particular tasks or long-term goals—especially in the face of obstacles or distractions. Social skills are interpersonal abilities as expressed through social interactions including assertiveness, cooperation, personal responsibility/ownership of feelings/behavior, and empathy. Learning strategies (e.g., study skills, mnemonic devices, self-regulation) are those methods used to aid in thinking or learning. And, finally, academic mindset refers to four specific ways of perceiving oneself in the educational context: (a) a sense of belongingness in the academic community, (b) a belief that ability/skills/learning increase with effort, (c) confidence in ability to engage successfully in performance/academic self-efficacy, and (d) a sense that the academic tasks have value. There is supporting research to indicate that noncognitive factors in these areas are related to students' academic performance and other career-related outcomes.

Hines, Lemons, and Crews (2011) published a guide directing professional school counselors working toward college and career readiness for every student. They recommended five steps to enhance the school counselor role in college and career readiness. Step one included revising school counselor job descriptions to focus on educational equity and college or career readiness. Step two involved altering university school counselor preparation programs to center on the school counselor's role in college/career readiness for all students. Step three was raising state licensing/credentialing requirements to include interventions/programming for college/career readiness. Step four provided support for school counselors, including professional development. And step five made professional school counselor evaluations commensurate with academic outcomes/student results. In response to guiding research and the needs of the profession, ASCA is developing the document, *ASCA Mindsets and Behaviors for Student Success: K–12 College and Career Readiness Standards for Every Student*. While still in draft form, these student competencies contain thee domains of academic, career, and social/emotional development. But rather than competencies in strands of each domain, they are organized according to the aforementioned categories of noncogntive factors contributing to academic performance. Professional school counselors can help foster noncognitive factors, assist students acquiring the CCSS, and assist students to become college/career ready through system-centered and student-centered activities inherent in comprehensive school counseling programs.

System-Centered Activities

Professional school counselors understand the process of systemic change and are familiar with education reform models. They know that to raise student achievement the focus must not be solely on helping students gain the knowledge and skills needed to help them achieve. Professional school counselors must also help adults create and implement effective strategies that encourage student achievement. Through the activities of collaboration and teaming, school data analysis, group facilitation, advocacy, and research, professional school counselors can effectively join with building administrators in facilitating the school improvement process.

Collaboration and Teaming

The creation of an effective school improvement plan requires a tremendous amount of collaboration and teaming. It is important for the school to involve faculty, parents, students, and community stakeholders. Professional school counselors know how to form effective task groups and can use their teaming and collaboration skills to bring teachers, parents, and community members together. Professional school counselors are skilled at using a wide variety of resources and are natural liaisons between the school and community. Professional school counselors can be an invaluable resource for involving the broader community in efforts to raise academic achievement. Collaboration will also be necessary during the strategy implementation process. The counselor can help the various constituent groups stay involved in program and strategy implementation and ensure that all groups have an opportunity for continued input. The following is an example:

> SMS is beginning a school improvement process. The principal and professional school counselors work together to create a school improvement team (SIT), consisting of faculty, parents, and community representatives. The principal and professional school counselors collaborate on meeting agendas and take turns facilitating various portions of the meetings. At the same time, they meet with the grade-level instructional teams in the building. They actively collaborate to engage the entire faculty in the school improvement effort.

School Data Analysis

Data-driven decision making is a critical element in successful school improvement efforts (Erford, 2015c). Professional school counselors are skilled in the collection, analysis, and presentation of student achievement and related data. Their skills can help facilitate the school improvement team's examination of data, such as standardized test scores, grades, teacher assessments, and student management data. They also understand the importance of disaggregating data by variables such as gender, ethnicity, and socioeconomic status to discover underlying access and equity issues that influence student achievement. Data analysis is used to drive interventions, programs, and activities that are designed to raise student achievement.

> The SMS counselors may facilitate an in-depth examination of SMS student achievement and related data. The first thing the school improvement team does is look at the standardized test scores, grade reports, and school management data for the current year and for the previous 2 years. This gives the SIT team an overall report on their student outcomes. All the data are disaggregated by gender, ethnicity, and socioeconomic status so the improvement team can look at overall outcomes as well as the outcomes for subgroups of students. The SMS team discovers that, at all grade levels, female students are well below average in math scores. Girls are also underrepresented in pre-algebra and algebra classes. In addition, there is a higher math failure rate for Hispanic girls. The SMS school improvement team shares this information with the entire faculty, who decide to create a goal to improve the math scores of females in general and Hispanic females in particular.

Group Facilitation

Small-task groups perform much of the work in raising student achievement. Although a school administrator often leads the school improvement team, other staff members will lead many of the subgroups and strategy teams. Professional school counselors are logical leaders for these groups due to their task group leadership skills. They understand the stages of group development, the importance of group process, and group-facilitation skills. Professional school counselors expect groups to move through the typical stages of forming, storming, norming, performing, and adjourning (Tuckman, 1965). Professional school counselors help the group move through these stages in a healthy way so that the group task gets accomplished and the group does not get stuck in any stage.

During early meetings, professional school counselors help the members understand themselves in relation to the task and work to establish a sense of trust, thus enabling the group to proceed more smoothly. As experienced group leaders, professional school counselors recognize that a certain amount of disagreement among members is to be expected (Gladding, 2012) and that their job is to normalize this stage and help members use the energy to seek better solutions to the task at hand. As the group works to finalize its report and agree on strategies, it is important that conflicts among various viewpoints be resolved. The steps are essentially the same as in conflict resolution, but the leader's issues revolve around the task rather than personal conflicts. Professional school counselors help members examine various perspectives (e.g., whether or not to require a teacher recommendation for algebra enrollment) and then develop strategies that both sides can accept.

> Jacinda Brown, the seventh-grade SMS professional school counselor is the facilitator of a math curriculum task group. One of the members of the group is Mr. Pi, an experienced math teacher. The group's task is to examine the problem of the low math achievement by female students. The committee is discussing the idea of removing lower level math options for all students as a way of raising the rigor of math. Mr. Pi is adamant that math content not be watered down. He is concerned that any effort to include underprepared students will affect his ability to teach math in a way that will prepare his students for high school math classes. He believes that not all students can learn math and, therefore, lower level math courses are needed. The other group members have heard Mr. Pi repeat this opinion over the years, and they are frustrated with his lack of willingness to try new strategies to reach these students. Ms. Brown carefully facilitates the meeting, making sure that the group hears Mr. Pi. She helps the group begin to brainstorm various strategies, making sure that Mr. Pi's concerns are taken into consideration. Ms. Brown models respect for the opinions of all members and facilitates the resolution of disagreements into the creation of strategies that the group can support.

Advocacy

Many forces influence student achievement. These include school policies, teacher quality, attendance and discipline procedures, parent and community involvement, instruction and assessment methods, expectations, and guidance standards (Haycock, 2002). Professional school counselors advocate for programs and experiences that are needed to lower barriers to learning. They point out inequities and policies that discriminate, and they use their advocacy skills to gain support with parents and community stakeholders (House & Martin, 1998). Professional school counselors are in a prime position to raise probing questions, be a voice for the students most often left behind, and mobilize allies outside the schools.

> At SMS, the eighth-grade counselor, Michael Justice, has noticed that a large number of Latina students have limited English proficiency. He is also aware that math is not considered an important skill for girls to learn in many Hispanic American homes.

Mr. Justice approaches the math curriculum committee with his concerns about the influence of limited English proficiency on the Latina student math achievement levels and actively works to find strategies to address this barrier. He also teams with a Hispanic English teacher. They meet with leaders of the local Hispanic community and provide information about the skills needed by Latinas to be successful in the workforce. They collaborate with the leaders to set up tutoring centers in area churches that will work with Hispanic students.

Action Research

Professional school counselors are trained action researchers. Schools expend many resources on strategies to improve student achievement. It is imperative that the outcomes of these strategies be studied in order to examine their effectiveness. Professional school counselors can help the school plan, collect, and analyze data on school improvement efforts.

As the SMS task groups develop strategies, the professional school counselors collaborate with the groups to develop an evaluation plan. The plan includes the collection of baseline data. The professional school counselors continue to work with the groups through the implementation phase, supporting needed professional development, and working with any resistance.

Student-Centered Activities

Professional school counselors are perhaps more familiar with student-centered activities than with system-centered activities. Student-centered programs and activities are often based on a student needs assessment (Gysbers & Henderson, 2012) and are oriented toward evidence-based practice in student learning and toward helping students to become college or career ready. When professional school counselors are focused on raising student achievement, student-centered activities are designed from a counseling program that is aligned with the academic standards and goals of the school. Student-centered activities affect student knowledge, skills, and behavior. In order to ensure that every student masters CCSS standards and becomes college/career ready, it is important that a continuum of interventions be created. Thus, student-centered activities include aligning the school counseling program with the school's academic goals, creating developmental guidance classroom lessons, conducting small-group counseling sessions, and counseling individual students. Lastly, such student centered activities should be delivered in a fashion that maximizes the proactive and preventative benefits of school counseling program interventions and minimizes time intensive interventions that can keep professional school counselors from helping all students.

As mentioned previously, learning strategies are one of the major categories of non-cognitive factors that increase student achievement. During the last 3 decades, exciting new discoveries about the nature of learning and how students regulate their own learning processes have emerged (Zimmerman & Schunk, 2001). Research on metacognition (i.e., awareness of and knowledge about one's own thinking) and social cognition has resulted in new perspectives about students' individual differences in learning. For example, some researchers attribute individual differences in learning to students' lack of self-regulation. They claim that students need to learn how to manage their limitations during their efforts to learn and thus learn to exert more control over their own learning processes.

One reason many students simply are ineffective learners by the time they have reached middle or high school is that they have not been taught how to learn (Kiewra, 2002). Instruction in learning strategies was not incorporated into the schools' curricula. Educators almost always teach content but don't teach students how to learn, a precursor to acquiring the content students are being asked to master. Students who take control of their own learning are often referred to as *self-regulated learners.* Academic self-regulation refers to self-generated thoughts, feelings, and actions intended to attain specific educational goals, such as analyzing a reading assignment, preparing to take a test, or writing a paper (Zimmerman, Bonner, & Kovach, 1996).

Self-regulated learners engage in a cycle of cognitive activities as they progress through a given task or assignment (Butler & Winne, 1995). First, they analyze task demands. This first step of task analysis is very important because it sets the stage for further learning. Students' subsequent decisions about what learning strategies to use are based on their perception of the task demands (Butler, 2002). Based on their task analysis, self-regulated learners then select, adapt, and may even invent strategic approaches to achieve the objectives related to the task or assignment facing them. In other words, they draw upon prior knowledge and experience to make decisions about what learning strategies to apply to the task at hand. For example, when trying to select learning strategies to apply to their current task, students try to remember approaches that worked for them in past situations with similar requirements or expectations.

When self-regulated learners have chosen and implemented specific learning strategies, they must monitor the outcomes associated with strategy use. Students need to know if the learning strategy or strategies they selected are helping them progress toward completing their tasks or assignments. Smart learners engage in self-evaluation by comparing their progress against criteria for successful completion of the task to generate judgments about how they are progressing. If students see gaps between their desired and actual performance, then they must adjust their learning strategies or activities. In addition, smart learners pay attention to external feedback such as scores and comments on tests and teacher or peer comments on written assignments so they can self-evaluate their performance. They use this feedback to diagnose their difficulties and find possible solutions. Thus, monitoring the outcomes of their learning activities is another very important step because students generate judgments about their progress and then make decisions about what to do next.

To promote or encourage self-regulation in students, professional school counselors, with the help of teachers, can assist students to engage flexibly and adaptively in a cycle of task analysis, strategy selection and use, and self-monitoring (Butler, 2002). Some researchers (Zimmerman et al., 1996) suggested applying cyclic self-regulatory methods to five basic study skills: (1) planning and using study time more effectively, (2) understanding and summarizing text material better, (3) improving methods of note-taking, (4) test anticipation and preparing better for exams, and (5) writing more effectively.

Aligning the School Counseling Program With the School's Academic Goals

The *ASCA National Model* (ASCA, 2012a) emphasizes the importance of aligning the school counseling program with the academic goals of the school. To do this, professional school counselors work with their faculty and advisory council to ensure that the standards with the greatest potential to help students reach the school's academic goals receive the greatest attention. Once the standards are prioritized, the professional school counselor then designs a continuum of interventions designed to make certain that every student masters those standards.

> SMS's sixth-grade team has set a goal to raise math scores on the state standardized test. Ashlyn Glenn is the sixth-grade professional school counselor. She works with the faculty and the school counseling program community council to prioritize the student guidance standards and indicators by answering the question, *Which of our school counseling program standards and indicators do you believe are the most important for our sixth-grade students to master to help them raise their math achievement level?* Ms. Glenn designs the year's guidance curriculum, based upon the established priorities. She then works with the faculty to map how the curriculum will be delivered.

One way that professional school counselors can conceptualize the academic goals of the school is through the Common Core State Standards (CCSS). Ninety percent of the states in the United States have adopted the CCSS as part of efforts to help students be college and career ready by the time they exit the preK–12 educational system. The CCSS is a set of academic standards in the areas of English language arts/literacy and math (see www.corestandards.org).

Achieve (2013) has published a guide to assist professional school counselors in understanding how they may contribute to the academic goals of their school by implementing the CCSS through three action steps: (1) understanding the CCSS and serving as a resource for such understanding, (2) supporting the CCSS at the school level through rigorous course sequencing and delivering classroom guidance lessons in support of CCSS, and (3) implementing and integrating CCSS throughout typical, daily school counseling activities including the development of a "college-going culture."

Classroom Guidance

Once the school's counseling program standards are prioritized based on the school's academic goals, the professional school counselor designs the classroom guidance curriculum, which may be delivered in many ways. Professional school counselors may come into classrooms, faculty may teach the standards through the regular curriculum or by adapting the curriculum to fit the guidance standards, and appropriate community members may deliver the curriculum (ASCA, 2012a).

> Ashlyn Glenn, the sixth-grade SMS professional school counselor, goes into each sixth-grade classroom the first 2 weeks of school and conducts lessons on study skills, time management, and asking for help (ASCA Standard A; Campbell & Dahir, 1997). Each teacher follows up on these lessons by giving each student a planner and helping them map out assignments for the first grading period. The teachers also give tips for studying their particular subject and use many study aids for students during the first grading period. Each teacher also uses strategies to encourage students to ask for help, particularly students who are having difficulty. Thus, all students in sixth grade are getting the same study skills instruction. Because SMS has decided to focus on math achievement, the sixth-grade counselor and the math teacher present some extra lessons on how to study math and how to deal with math anxiety. These supplemental lessons deal with the specific academic goals of the school to improve math skills.

Small-Group Counseling

Professional school counselors conduct small groups, which may be based on a general needs assessment or may be in response to specific problems (Smead, 1995), such as a number of students who continually experience difficulty making friends or developing a sense of belonging. While this is one aspect of a small-group program, professional school counselors offering a continuum of services aligned with the school's academic goals will also use small-group counseling as a follow-up to classroom guidance for those students who experience difficulty in mastering a requisite competency. Using this model, professional school counselors are able to use group counseling to foster social skills, learning strategies, and academic mindsets.

When students begin to learn unfamiliar material, they often cannot break down or analyze the task or assignment into components. Students frequently fail to set specific goals, develop effective learning strategies, or monitor progress. With instruction or training in the self-regulatory cycle, students can learn to analyze tasks, set effective goals, choose appropriate learning strategies, and monitor progress toward task completion. Learning the steps involved in a self-regulatory cycle not only enhances students' learning skills but also increases students' perceptions of control over their learning process.

The small group is an ideal way to work with these types of problems because a level of trust can be established in a small group that is difficult to achieve in the classroom. Professional school counselors can use group counseling leadership skills to establish trust among group members, help the members set individual goals, and provide opportunity for the members to practice new skills (such as asking for help) in the group. Counselors also use basic group work skills in drawing out, connecting, and cutting off to help all members of the group benefit from participation. If personal issues surface in the small group, professional school counselors use evaluation skills to determine the seriousness of such issues and make referrals for individual counseling or other resources as needed.

> After the classroom guidance classes on study skills and the additional lessons on math study skills at SMS are implemented, there is still a group of girls who teachers identify as having difficulty learning math. Ms. Glenn, the sixth-grade counselor, invites the girls to join a group that will focus on applying the self-regulatory cycle to acquiring math skills.

To help professional school counselors conduct small group counseling as an intervention focused on increasing student academic achievement, readers are referred to Sears, Wood, and Hinkelman's chapter in the previous edition of this text (2010). That chapter has an appendix with a small-group counseling plan for either middle or high school. The outline used to describe the small group activity includes (a) the ASCA Standard illustrated; (b) student competencies identified in the activity; (c) background notes to professional school counselors to help them prepare for the group; (d) activities and procedures to be followed in each session; and (e) suggestions for student handouts.

Individual Counseling

Professional school counselors know that some students need individual counseling to work on issues that are negatively influencing their academic achievement or mastery of the school counseling program standards. Assuming that the system barriers have been removed and that adequate support is now available, it is more likely that each student has an idiosyncratic problem. Individual counseling provides an opportunity for more in-depth help with these issues. This type of counseling is usually short term in nature (ASCA, 2012a). Professional school counselors are familiar with community resources and refer students and families appropriately.

> At SMS, even with the systemic changes, classroom guidance lessons, and small-group time, there are still several eighth-grade Hispanic girls who are not achieving well in math. At this point, the eighth-grade counselor, Michael Justice, sees each girl individually to further analyze the issues. Maya is a bright Hispanic student who is still making Cs and Ds in pre-algebra, even though she participates in the new group tutoring and homework sessions and has access to an individual tutor. When Mr. Justice talks with Maya, he discovers that the family has been under a lot of stress because a family member has a chronic illness. Maya has had difficulty concentrating on her schoolwork and, since math is her most difficult subject, the lack of concentration shows up in pre-algebra the most. Mr. Justice works with Maya to devise solutions that will relieve some of her anxiety about the family situation while still giving math some of her energy. They go to the math teacher together and explain the situation. All three agree that if there has been a crisis with the sick family member, Maya can ask to have a test postponed or have an extra day for homework. Just knowing that this is a possibility relieves a lot of Maya's stress, and her grades start to improve almost immediately.

Response to Intervention

One way to conceptualize the implementation of the above student-centered interventions is using the Response to Intervention (RTI) framework (National Center on Response to Intervention, 2014). A comprehensive explanation of RTI is beyond the scope of this chapter, but the above example can be used to illustrate the utility of RTI in discerning the delivery of school counseling program interventions. RTI is a three-tiered approach to intervention delivery where Tier 1 is a school-wide intervention delivered universally to all students (such as classroom guidance lessons described in the examples above). This first tier will generally be effective for the bulk of students; however, some students will require a more time intensive school counseling intervention in order to achieve the desired outcome (for example, see small-group counseling as described above). This second tier will help many of the students who didn't achieve the desired outcome from classroom guidance lessons, but still for a few students even the small-group counseling (see Maya in the example immediately above) will not be effective and an intervention such as individual counseling will be necessary. In short the RTI model can be applied as a way to make sure that student-centered interventions in a school counseling program are delivered in ways that maximize the preventative nature of the guidance curriculum and minimize time intensive responsive services provided on an individual basis in order to maximize the benefits of school counseling for all students in K–12 schools.

Summary/Conclusion

Raising the academic achievement level of all students is the primary goal for K–12 schools. While traditionally left out of school reform legislation and related efforts, professional school counselors are beginning to be recognized as essential resources in raising the academic achievement of all students. Professional school counselors need to be actively engaged in both system-centered and student-centered activities. System-centered activities enact leadership and advocacy (House & Sears, 2002) and ideally position professional school counselors to foster programs, policies, and environments that promote academic growth. Student-centered activities are essential to a school counseling program that is aligned with the academic goals of the school and provide a continuum of strategies designed to help every student reach their learning potential and leave the preK–12 system with college and career readiness. The activities of professional school counselors are beneficial to all students and staff as the education community seeks to help students reach academic, personal/social, and career goals.

CHAPTER 9

Organization Development in Schools

Joyce A. DeVoss

Preview

Organization development in schools is an ongoing effort to create and maintain a model, structure, and environment that produce the highest possible effectiveness in promoting student success. This chapter describes organization development in schools and reviews some models for K–12 school reform along with potential benefits and limitations. Professional school counselors in the 21st century use the ASCA National Model (American School Counselor Association [ASCA], 2012a) for school counseling programs as a guide to their proactive participation in organizational development for school improvement. Professional school counselors align their programs with the mission of schools for the benefit of all students.

School districts across the country continuously try to improve instruction. The extent to which reform efforts affect individual schools or whole districts varies, as do the methods that are used, including new curricula, extensive professional development programs, and comprehensive school reform. The federal government created the Comprehensive School Reform Demonstration Act in 1998 (CSRD), earmarking $145 million for incentives to schools that were using at least one comprehensive improvement plan or developing their own. The CSRD interventions that were used are departures from current practice, requiring all members of school communities to learn new knowledge, skills, and practices. Often, these interventions require organizational changes and incorporate collective learning. The more ambitious and unconventional the interventions, the more learning is necessary; the more comprehensive the approach, the greater the need for organization development.

In the last decade of the 20th century, the school counseling profession began adopting comprehensive school guidance programs that required school organizational changes and promoted collective learning with a focus on fostering the academic and life success of all students. Comprehensive guidance programs are integrated into school curriculum and incorporate a prevention component. The movement toward adopting statewide comprehensive guidance programs positioned professional school counselors to become active participants and leaders in school reform. This movement ultimately led to the creation of the ASCA national model (ASCA, 2003a) by leaders of ASCA. Now, in its third edition (ASCA, 2012a), the ASCA national model has been adopted by many states and school districts.

Comprehensive school reform focuses on reorganizing and revitalizing entire schools rather than implementing isolated reforms. It is a systemic approach to school reform that uses well-researched models for change supported by expert trainers and facilitators. Most comprehensive school reform models include high academic standards, relevant professional development, and community involvement. Schools undergoing reform typically engage in some degree of organization development. Successful organization development in schools is ongoing, organization wide, and supported by school stakeholders, with the overall goal of improving student academic achievement. Professional school counselors support this overall goal.

The professional development component of organization development is critical to comprehensive school reform. Hixson and Tinzmann (1990) identified three challenges for professional development in 21st century schools: (a) meeting the needs of diversity in the student population; (b) adopting appropriate goals for schooling; and (c) implementing organizational structures to promote shared responsibility, collaboration, and a community of continual learning. In light of these challenges, Hixson and Tinzmann identified new priorities for professional development: a focus on systemic change, or change in the *culture* of the school; continuing focus of change at the school level and focus of professional development on developing *learning communities*; learning that is continuous for students, teachers, counselors, and administrators; and responsibility that falls on all educational staff to continue their professional development. These priorities for professional development concepts are consistent with the values of the profession of school counseling.

Models for K–12 School Improvement

In the past, numerous new school reform models have been developed and evaluated. As members or potential members of school improvement leadership teams, professional school counselors should be well versed in the ASCA national model (2012a). Additionally, professional school counselors would be wise to develop a familiarity with some of the current organizational development and school reform models. This section reviews a few of the many models and approaches to organization development available to schools.

Four-Frame Model

A model of leadership and organizational development that has been incorporated into training for professional school counselor leaders is the four-frame approach from Bolman and Deal (2013). In their book, *Reframing Organizations: Artistry, Choice, and Leadership*, Bolman and Deal describe their four-frame model for understanding organizations. Brief descriptions of the four frames are provided here.

- **The Structural Frame** looks at organization structure and explores how to better organize and structure units to be more successful in obtaining results.
- **The Human Resource Frame** views people in organizations, explores how to satisfy their needs and manage people, as well as how to build positive dynamics among people.
- **The Political Frame** views organizational political dynamics and how to understand and deal skillfully with power, conflict, and politics.
- **The Symbolic Frame** views meaning and culture in organizations, and how to shape organizational culture while building spirit through a variety of means.

This framework is included in the ASCA national model (2012a) and also described with examples of a four-framework approach to practice in *School Counselor Leadership* (Young & Miller-Kneale, 2013). Using the four-framework approach perspective, Young and Miller-Kneale (2013) explained that professional school counselors identify their school counseling program focus that is aligned with selected student competencies from the ASCA model. They identify professional development needs and engage in professional development. In addition, professional school counselor leaders communicate their belief in people and connect with stakeholders. Professional school counselors can use negotiation skills, are skilled in the use of metaphors, and model appropriate behaviors to influence followers.

North Central Regional Educational Laboratory

Hassel, Raack, Burkhardt, Chapko, and Blaser (2000) developed a guide for the North Central Regional Educational Laboratory (NCREL) school reform model with the following components:

- Strategizing through goal and standard setting
- Building support from stakeholders
- Facilitating informed choice, with each school developing their own strategy to meet their school's needs
- Forging a new compact with schools, whereby greater authority for reform strategies along with accountability for results are received
- Building capacity for strengthening teaching, learning, and leadership

Each component has related action steps, examples of which for the first component of *strategizing through goal and standard setting* are as follows:

1. Identify the district's key priorities
2. Determine how comprehensive school reform supports the district's mission, vision, and goals
3. Identify the district's assets
4. Determine method and schedule of implementation
5. Identify financial resources for comprehensive school reform efforts
6. Determine evaluation strategies

School counseling programs are currently customized to support district and school missions, visions, goals, and, most important, student performance.

This guide was developed to help districts make comprehensive school reform an integral part of strategies for improving student achievement. When identifying the district's assets, the school reform leadership team should carefully consider the type of leadership needed and the composition of the leadership team, school–media relationship, dedication level of school personnel, level of support of constituents and local businesses, commitment level of teachers and staff, available funding through grants and other sources, potential partnerships, and opportunities for collaboration. Professional school counselors should actively advocate for representation on school leadership teams. They are key relationship and partnership builders for schools.

Vision-Based Leadership and the Learning School

Wallace, Engel, and Mooney (1997) stressed vision-based leadership as critical to school success. They proposed a model of a learning school in which everyone is a learner. Their model demonstrated how theory and research can influence educational vision by incorporating concepts from Senge's (1990) learning organization in the role of leadership in the learning school. For Senge, dialogue is critical among all levels of the organization. Furthermore, he incorporated the disciplinary elements of personal mastery, mental models, shared vision, team learning, and systems thinking in his vision of the learning organization.

Sergiovanni (2001) contributed the moral dimension of leadership in the learning community that complements Senge's (1990) concept of a learning organization. Sergiovanni stated that discussion about attitudes and values inform the role of the leader and also proposed the idea of shared leadership, with emphasis on the content of education. Sergiovanni's moral basis for educational leadership stems from the leader's perceived obligations and duties implied from shared values, ideas, and ideals. The model for the learning school includes integration of elements of a shared vision, authentic teaching and learning, a supportive school organization, and the use of assessment.

Wallace et al. (1997) explained how to achieve shared governance and how leaders can engage others to achieve a shared vision. They discussed how to engage the broader community in the learning community model, borrowing their underlying message from the Bible: "Where there is no vision, people perish" (Proverbs 29:18). Wallace et al. believed that the sharing of a mission should be systemic, and that the values, sentiments, and beliefs of communities connect people in a common cause. Communities give us norms to structure what we do and give us reason why we do what we do. Professional school counselors in the 21st century are key players in the learning community. They promote the development of the whole student. They need to assertively advocate for and accept a place on leadership teams to promote organizational development to reform schools.

New Designs for Learning

New designs for the learning process (Copa, 1999) is a model in which staff, students, community, and a team of school designers work together to discover new ways to design a school's learning experiences and environment. Goals include:

- representing the leading edge of a new breed of schools;
- operating the school as a learning community;
- drawing more attention to learning versus teaching;
- more closely aligning learner expectations with learning process organization and environment;
- promising the idea of a common set of learner outcomes for all;
- relating learner expectations to challenges and opportunities in work, family, community, and personal life;
- providing a positive special school character with more focus, coherence, and spirit to learning; and
- wanting schools that do not cost more to build or operate.

Some of the key learning elements in the new designs for learning model include context, expectations, process, partnerships, staff development, celebration, and accountability. At the inception of the comprehensive school reform process, the formal school leadership carefully chooses a team devoted to the design of the school's learning process and environment. Design group members come from inside and outside the school. The professional school counselor should advocate to become part of the leadership team. Team members are expected to think comprehensively and long term. The model seeks to reawaken learners' potential as well as that of staff and community and fosters a special spirit that gives meaning to all dimensions of learning. This model gives students multiple pathways to learn, thereby leveling the playing field for all learners.

The learning community's attention to learning organization concepts influences organization of time, learners, staff, process, decision-making technology, and settings. Emphasis is given to the learning staff and staff development is focused on current and future needs. Consideration is also given to who can best provide staff training. Design group members act as role models for others, relying on more than one way of doing things, bringing the rest of the learning community along with reform efforts, and thinking comprehensively and long term.

The Coalition of Essential Schools

Theodore R. Sizer founded the Coalition of Essential Schools (CES), a comprehensive school change project, while at Brown University in 1984. CES was influenced by the Model Schools Project movement sponsored by the National Association of Secondary School Principals between 1969 and 1974. CES initially focused on high schools and then expanded to lower grades. CES reform came from the grassroots, including the local community, and maintains that no two good schools are the same.

CES reform principles highlight school climate and a set of organizational principles to govern behavior and beliefs of member schools and the national organization. CES stresses the importance of documenting change, valuing local wisdom, and responding flexibly to local contexts. CES values collaboration and changes to school structures to accommodate CES principles. Advocated school changes include a view of students as workers, smaller class sizes, personalization, professional sharing among teachers, and collaborative conceptions of curriculum, instruction, and assessment. Professional school counselors are trained in relationship building that can lead to collaboration and coordination of services in an effort to bring about the types of changes proposed by the CES model.

Success for All, and Roots and Wings

Success for All (SFA) is a comprehensive school-wide reform model developed by Robert Slavin and colleagues at Johns Hopkins University (Lockwood, 1998) for elementary schools that are focused on reading and students at risk of academic failure. The program stresses that reform efforts must deal with instruction, curriculum, and school organization in order to be successful over time and not regress to the old system. SFA believes that all children must read at grade level by third grade. They use tutors to ensure that students do not fall behind. Furthermore, they administer assessments at 8-week intervals to regularly monitor progress. This model has the advantage of also being available in Spanish.

Roots and Wings (Slavin & Madden, 2000; Slavin, Madden, & Wasik, 1996) is a comprehensive school reform model that incorporates all elements of Success for All. It also includes MathWings, based on the National Council of Teachers of Mathematics standards, and WorldLab, which uses simulations and group-learning projects for social studies and science. Schools implementing Roots and Wings generally do so over a 3-year period, starting with the SFA components in the first year, MathWings in the second year, and WorldLab in the third year.

SFA and Roots and Wings are structured models that provide complete sets of student materials, teacher's manuals, and other support. Furthermore, Roots and Wings uses a Family Support Team in each school, made up of concerned school personnel who are focused on attendance, school-based intervention, parental involvement, and connections with community service providers. Elementary schools are where professional school counselors devote the most time to delivery of school guidance services to students and can offer strong support of this type of school reform effort.

The Paideia Program

The Paideia Program (Lockwood, 1998) was based on the writings and ideas of American educator and philosopher Mortimer Adler, now supported by the National Paideia Center (NPC), founded in 1988 and housed at University of North Carolina at Chapel Hill. It provides training and technical assistance in Paideia methods, researches the results of the methods, and acts as a clearinghouse for schools establishing the Paideia program.

The basic belief of this model is that a democratic society needs to provide excellent education to all students. The program provides a rigorous liberal arts education in K–12 that fosters critical thinking and the necessary skills for full participation in a democratic society. It employs cooperative learning and collaborative seminars and views teachers as facilitators. As with other school reform programs, the Paideia Program could be strengthened with a comprehensive school guidance program, based on the ASCA national model and customized to support the program's goals.

Comer School Development Program

The Comer Process is a school-wide intervention approach developed by Dr. James P. Comer, a professor of child psychiatry at Yale University. This approach maintains that healthy child development is key to academic and life success. Child development is described as occurring along six developmental pathways: physical, cognitive, psychological, language, social, and ethical. These pathways are the framework from which decisions are made to benefit children in Comer School Development Programs. This approach has demonstrated effectiveness in increasing academic achievement, improving behavior and attendance, and improving students' self-concepts. Professional school counselors are trained to take child developmental issues into consideration as they make decisions to choose appropriate interventions for their students. Furthermore, their mission aligns with the school mission to improve student success, as demonstrated by indicators monitored by the Comer Process, as well as other indicators of student success.

The Comer Process emphasizes the need for a team approach and the development of a school culture that is characterized by respectful problem solving, consensus building, and collaboration. These are processes for which professional school counselors are well prepared. They have much to offer to enhance the success of this and other school-wide intervention approaches.

There are many other promising whole-school reform programs, including Schoolwide Projects and eight designs representing diverse approaches within the New American Schools programs. Information on these programs can be found in the ERIC Digest titled *Whole School Reform* (McChesney, 1998) and in other educational publications such as the *Phi Delta Kappan*. A familiarity with current school reform programs can benefit professional school counselors as they contribute to the development of school reform and organizational development efforts and align their school counseling programs with these initiatives.

Limitations of School Reform Efforts

Cohen and Loewenberg Ball (2001) reported that the history of instructional intervention is one of very limited success. They noted that interventions tend to be surface level, do not last long, are affected by rapid staff turnover, and are subject to poorly integrated accumulation of past interventions. They offer three plausible explanations for these observations. First, while no intervention can be totally comprehensive, most have been only partial. Second, many interventions provide principles and directions but leave a lot of specifics to be filled in by teachers and schools. Finally, those who initiate the interventions rarely provide the training needed for school personnel, parents, and students. These observations and explanations offer support for whole-school, systemic approaches to school reform, including comprehensive school counseling programs based on the ASCA national model.

Schwartz (2001) reported that school efforts to close the achievement gap between ethnic and racial minorities and White students have generally been unsuccessful. However, recently developed knowledge-based strategies for school improvement promote optimism. Rose (2001) also contended that policymakers need to listen to the public and improve the public schools that currently exist, to provide all children with education in safe buildings conducive to quality education. However, it may be difficult for policymakers to remain focused on the public school with the charter school and voucher systems on their agenda.

Goertz (2001) observed that while state and federal policies gave strong signals about goals of standards-based reform, they offered limited direction as to its substance. This has led to teacher and district complaints about standards that are too general, leaving the task of developing appropriate curriculum and instruction to teachers. Teachers do not have the time to develop new curriculum to fit under the new standards. Simply setting goals for standards-based reform is not enough to guarantee adequate success in America's schools. Policymakers must consider the benefits of providing more specific standards while allowing enough flexibility in local school improvement efforts.

In past school reform movements, schools were often focused on as the primary unit of change, frequently overlooking the role of the school district. Under these circumstances, states intervene directly in low performing school operations, ignoring district responsibilities for school performance. With the focus on school instead of district accountability, the consequences for individual schools can be more serious than in the past and can include substantial bonuses or school closure and reconstitution. Under the No Child Left Behind Act of 2001, the emphasis shifted back to school-district accountability. In 2009, the emphasis became the state as the National Governors' Association developed Common Core State Standards to outline standards for student expectations in knowledge and application (and for assessments) to determine if students were meeting the standards in all 50 states.

Hatch (2002) identified a paradox in improvement programs. Hatch emphasized that schools are frequently faced with the task of putting more than one improvement program in place at one time. Hatch observed that this can create too much demand on the school's resources, teachers, and administrators. School personnel in this predicament often experience high levels of frustration and anger. Schools often face competing and even conflicting demands from a variety of sources. Hatch recommended that, in order to embrace improvement programs that were likely to be successful, school leaders needed to select appropriate programs based on sufficient knowledge, plan for adequate resources to be devoted to the chosen programs, and figure out how to integrate school improvement interventions into the school. Professional school counselors have a roadmap in the ASCA national model to develop and manage comprehensive school guidance programs that integrate other school reform and organizational development efforts.

The Role of the Professional School Counselor in School Improvement and Organization Development

Historically, professional school counselors were left out of school improvement and organizational development efforts. In the last few decades, however, counselors have begun to participate in comprehensive school reform. They have begun to serve on the school leadership teams. In that leadership role, professional school counselors have assured that comprehensive school guidance programming with the trifold focus on academic, career, and personal–social student needs is integrated into the school improvement plan. Additionally, because of their personal connections and knowledge of the school community, professional school counselors helped foster support for comprehensive school reform from teachers and parents, identified some districts' key resources, and helped craft homegrown comprehensive school reform models (Hassel et al., 2000). Counselors have effectively helped implement action steps and promoted school-wide support for the comprehensive school reform. ASCA's national model (2012a) emphasizes a direct connection between the comprehensive school counseling program and the mission of the school. In addition, the model stresses an organizational framework and accountability system, and positions counselors to integrate school counseling programs with comprehensive school reform.

Johnson (1997) noted that with increasing decentralization of power in school districts, educators have begun to use data not only to assess student performance but also to make changes at a systems level, "to help them make better choices and uncover better ways of serving students and the community" (p. 1). Educators, including professional school counselors, can create databases used to make program changes, to share with other educators, and to adjust teaching styles based on what is learned. These databases hold keys to identifying target areas for school change at a systems level. Johnson suggested making better use of existing data on attendance, grades, referrals, retentions, and standardized test results to make comparisons with other, similar schools.

Schools can begin to make better use of the existing data by first analyzing what the data can reveal as to patterns not previously seen, as well as opportunities for continuous data-driven improvement. The data can be broken down (i.e., disaggregated) by such categories as gender, race, and socioeconomic status. Other data can be collected, such as test results and numbers of books read. Professional school counselors and teachers, individually and collaboratively, are in an excellent position to do small-scale relevant research, called *action research*, to help make informed decisions regarding their work, based on the findings.

By virtue of their unique training and expertise, professional school counselors are excellent resources for providing staff development and facilitation of team process. Such functions are generally important in comprehensive school reform and organization development activities. Professional school counselors' knowledge of systems theory and group dynamics are necessary qualifications for roles as trainers and facilitators.

While professional school counselors have historically been left out of the school reform movement, the profession has recently proactively emphasized the importance of aligning the school counseling program with the mission of the school and school reform efforts. Emphasis has been placed on the role of the professional school counselor as leader, collaborator, change agent, and advocate for quality education for all students. The potential contributions of professional school counselors to school leadership teams, comprehensive school reform, and organizational development are numerous. School leaders can reap benefits for their schools by using professional school counselors as a significant resource when planning for school reform and organization development.

Lapan, Gysbers, Cook, Bragg, and Robbins (2006) believed that it is the critical mission of professional school counselors to fully implement the ASCA national model for all students. Lapan et al. also recommended that professional school counselors communicate with administrators, parents, school board members, and elected officials about their work and the benefits provided to all students. For school districts interested in further development of professional school counselors as resources for leadership teams for school improvement and organizational development, The Education Trust offers specific workshops to professional school counselors and administrators that focus on transforming the work of professional school counselors. The goal is to develop professional school counselors who aggressively support quality education for all students, creating a school climate where access and support for rigorous preparation is expected.

Leadership development workshops within school districts help professional school counselors connect to school reform, become integral members of the school leadership team, and apply skills in teaming and collaboration to increase access and equity for all students. In addition, professional school counselors learn to serve as advocates for success of all students and to design and deliver data-driven counseling programs. To set up training for a school district, contact Peggy Hines (phines@edtrust.org) or Karen Crews (kcrews@edtrust.org) from the National Center for Transforming School Counseling at The Education Trust.

Summary/Conclusion

In this chapter, I defined and described organization development in the context of school reform efforts, provided a brief examination of some models of school improvement, looked at the limitations of reform attempts, and explored the potential for increasing professional school counselors' involvement in school improvement efforts and organization development in schools. The valuable contributions professional school counselors can make to school reform were identified and described.

Successful school improvement takes an investment of resources such as personnel, time, effort, and money, which need to be allocated where they will make the most difference in quality of education and academic results. Professional school counselors are becoming recognized as a viable resource for school leadership teams. A familiarity with current school reform models and the Common Core State Standards that most states have adopted is important for professional school counselors as they participate in school reform and organizational development efforts, and align their school counseling programs with reform initiatives and legislation. ASCA and The Education Trust support professional school counselors as leaders, advocates, and collaborators in school improvement. Professional school counselors contribute a valuable knowledge base and skills to team efforts in comprehensive school reform and organizational development. They are encouraged to continue to work on fully implementing their comprehensive school guidance programs based on the ASCA national model.

CHAPTER 10

Assessing and Changing School Culture

Mei Tang

Preview

School culture is important for professional school counselors because the mission and goals of education cannot be fulfilled if the environment of the school setting does not support high academic achievement and personal growth and development. Professional school counselors, with their special training, are capable of taking a leadership role in making the school culture more accommodating for teacher and staff development, and students' growth and learning. In this chapter, the importance of assessing and changing school culture is discussed and strategies professional school counselors can implement to improve the school climate for quality education are offered.

Definition of School Culture (Structure, Teacher, Student, Process, and Product)

The definition of *school culture* is varied because different people have different understandings of what constitutes *culture*. In the literature, a similar concept, *school climate*, is often used as well. The study of school culture was derived from anthropology and organizational cultural studies, with an intention to improve the school environment by understanding various dimensions of school life. In this sense, school culture is a multifaceted concept that makes a difference in the effectiveness of schooling (Maehr & Midgley, 1996). Each school has distinguishable characteristics and a kind of social-psychological life of its own. These characteristics might be the shared set of organizing principles (Erickson, 1991), beliefs, and values (Cunningham & Cresso, 1993), or accustomed ways of thinking and acting (Sarason, 1995). A school culture is "a system of ordinary, taken-for-granted meanings and symbols with both implicit and explicit content (e.g., norms, values, beliefs, assumptions) that is, deliberately and non-deliberately, learned and shared among members" (Erickson, 1987, p. 1).

From an organizational perspective, school culture includes three levels (Shaw & Reyes, 1992): (a) observable behaviors (i.e., visible but often not decipherable, such as artifacts); (b) shared values (i.e., may or may not be visible, requiring greater awareness; members' sense what ought to be); and (c) organizational assumptions about reality (i.e., invisible and preconscious, such as teachers' orientations and outlooks). The nature of school personnel's shared

---

*Thanks to Barbara L. Carlozzi for her outstanding contributions to the second edition of this chapter.

norms, values, beliefs, and assumptions defines the content of a school's culture (Leithwood, 2002).

School culture is shaped by its members, including teachers, staff, students, parents, and the community. Schools are not separable from social context, and therefore the development of school culture is embedded in the school organization, policies, resources, ethos, school district and state policies, local communities, educational professional environment, occupational systems, and societal cultures (Talbert & McLaughlin, 1999).

Importance of School Culture

The most significant factors in shaping minds are the cultural settings where learning takes place, the activities participants engage in, and discussion among participants (Wells & Claxton, 2008). School culture has been found to affect teacher and staff development and empowerment (Hamilton & Richardson, 1995; Short & Rinehart, 1993), teacher collaboration (Andringa & Fustin, 1991), students' academic and social behavior and performance (McEvoy & Welker, 2000), students' aspiration (Plucker, 1998), and professional school counselors' self-efficacy and outcome expectancy (Sutton & Fall, 1995). Caring school environments profoundly impact a student's understanding of self and others; positive emotions and interactions; and ability to act responsibly, to appreciate a variety of relationships, and to link empathy to moral behavior (Cooper, 2004). School culture is equally important for reform and improvement in schools, because success is not possible if there is no supportive environment or climate to nourish the change.

Maehr and Midgley (1996) argued that the school's cultures directly relate to the purpose of schooling (i.e., motivation and learning). One of the functions of education in the United States is to prepare its citizens to participate in a democratic society. At a minimum, young people should leave school with the knowledge and skills they need to be employable, and they must have the knowledge and motivation to intelligently contribute to a democratic system of government. As noted by Beane (1998), this requires a balance between self-interest and concern for the welfare of others. Of course, many of us expect far more than the minimum from our schools, believing that schools should also cultivate the full potential of each individual; a love of learning; a respect for human dignity, equity, justice, caring, and diversity; and the desire and creativity to create a better world than the one he or she was born into.

Common to differing beliefs about the function of education is the belief that we must prepare students for employment and we must instill in them a desire for the common good. Students' investment in learning, the effort they put forth, whether they feel a sense of belonging, and concern for others in their school community and beyond is related to what schools stress and reward. Schools that emphasize ability and achievement (outcomes) versus task approach and growth (process) are likely to produce students whose aspirations relate more to self-interest and predetermined goals than to concern for others and a desire to improve the world.

According to Marchant, Paulson, and Rothlisberg (2001), school context (teacher responsiveness, school responsiveness, and a supportive social environment) and family context (parental values) have been found to be significantly related to students' motivation, school competence, and academic achievement. Similarly, a school environment promoting academic achievement also promotes higher aspirations of students (Plucker, 1998). The conditions for the positive school environment included having positive relationships with adults, valuing a positive outlook in life, and respecting diversity. Barr and Higgins-D'Alessandro (2009) found that healthy school culture also has a positive impact on students' empathy development. The effects of school climate have been found to lead to students' engagement in learning, which in turn influences their hope and academic achievement overtime (Van Ryzin, 2011). The positive school climate significantly predicted professional commitment of teachers who tend to integrate social-emotional learning in classrooms (Collie, Shapka, & Perry, 2011).

After all, how members in the schools perceive and feel about their interaction with the environment matters. It is the culture that makes the difference in teacher, student, and staff lives in schools. "Greatness does not grow out of a focus on structure and process, but is found in the culture of the organization and the spirit and purposefulness of the lives of people who belong to that organization" (Cunningham & Cresso, 1993, p. 25).

Characteristics of Effective Schools

Research indicates that effective schools are characterized by a culture that focuses on collaboration among all shareholders, open communication, and continuous improvement (Johnson, Snyder, Anderson, & Johnson, 1997). Collaboration between parents, schools, and communities, information sharing, commonly held values, and communication are critical to strong partnerships; and school leadership plays an important role in building school culture and valuing partnerships (Mutch & Collins, 2012). Research also found that healthy school culture encourages teacher involvement in decision making, quality interaction, and teacher empowerment (Rhodes, Camic, Milburn & Lowe, 2009); and that positive teacher-student relationships, school connectedness, academic support, order, and discipline were predictive of school climate satisfaction. Specifically, the characteristics presented in Table 10.1 are considered to define and sustain educational excellence. Schools that foster altruism must facilitate

Table 10.1 Characteristics of Effective Schools.

- Key members work together to develop a collective vision of what school should be like, focusing on a vision, not deficiencies
- Foster individual identities of group members and build a collegial relationship among members
- Trust, support, and mutual understanding of each other within the organization
- Access to quality information for all members
- Open and fluid communication
- Promoting lifelong professional development and personal growth
- Empowerment of individuals to take risks and make a difference
- Collaboration between administrators, teachers, parents, community partners, and students to make a decision
- Face-to-face involvement of appropriate stakeholders
- Shared values, interests, and vision of an ideal school
- Strategic planning by groups within the organization
- Continuous incremental and systematic improvement
- Valuing students' growth and improvement rather than mere achievement
- Every student is important and has equal rights to adequate opportunities
- Accountability and constant feedback on results
- Sustainable changes

students' empathic orientation toward others, since empathy has been strongly related to altruism (Cooper, 2004).

Unfavorable Factors for Effective Schools

DeWit et al. (2000) found that low teacher and classmate support, student conflict, unfair school rules and disciplinary practice, and low student autonomy in decision making were associated with low attachment to learning, behavior problems, attendance, and substance abuse. A similar finding by Plucker (1998) also showed that the lack of support for curiosity, respect for independent thinkers, and care from adults tended to lower students' aspirations for learning. Staub (2005) identified the following factors as detrimental to the development of *altruism*:

- Excessive control, blaming, or scapegoating
- Abuse, neglect, rejection, hostility, or excessive physical punishment
- Barriers to connection with others
- A lack of guidance or permissiveness

And Cooper's (2004) research noted the following impediments to *empathic* environments:

- Unempathic teachers who were aloof, snobby, overbearing, overly authoritarian, or unable or unwilling to relate individually to students
- An overfilled curriculum that left teachers feeling pressure for student achievement
- Overlarge class sizes in which teachers were unable to know and interact individually with students
- Not enough time to tailor instruction to individuals or small groups or for teachers to interact with parents, school personnel, or personnel in community agencies
- Management policies and leaders who failed to demonstrate concern for the needs of individuals and groups
- Highly competitive environments
- Environments that had a high proportion of needy individuals, whether the needs were for social, emotional, physical, or academic support
- School environments with inadequate space, resources, or equipment

Assessing School Culture

"The secret for successful change in a school is to identify an existing school culture and reshape it" (Bulach, 2001, p. 8). Before implementing change, it is necessary to understand what is happening in the school and to have a complete picture of the practice and perceptions of all shareholders. It is important to know what works and what does not work. Otherwise, the change loses its direction.

The other purposes of assessing school culture include providing baseline data for future evaluation, having a need for accountability (Milstein, 1993), identifying positive features and areas for improvement, and providing necessary information for strategic planning. It is important to note that assessment is an integral part of restructuring the school for better results and is not cause for anxiety. Most aspects of school culture measurement in commonly used instruments are stable over time (Kallestad, 2010); therefore, it provides reliable sources of information for program evaluation. Fan, Williams, and Corkin (2011) advocated for multievel, multi-construct assessment of school climate and should include both student and school level of perception.

Methods of Assessing School Culture

The concept of school culture is complex and multifaceted, and no single source or method of assessment can answer all questions. A variety of information as well as multiple ways of collecting the information should be used to obtain a comprehensive understanding of the numerous aspects of school culture. Because *culture* is a product as well as a process, the strategies for assessing school culture should incorporate process into the assessment plan.

Where to look for data. Handbooks, mission statements, announcements, newsletters, school calendars, yearbooks, and annual reports are sources of information for understanding the symbolic aspects of the school environment (Wren, 1999). School rules, ceremonies, rituals, and routines can also provide valuable information about school culture, as can the school policies regarding behaviors and performance (e.g., how students' conduct is rewarded or disciplined in nonacademic and academic domains).

Other sources of data come from the subjective measures of members of the school setting, whose perceptions and observations of the school operation are essential because they construct the *culture*. Members may include, but are not limited to, teachers, administrators, staff, paraprofessionals, students, parents, community partners, custodians, bus drivers, and volunteers. Interactive data are composed of information about interaction among members and practices in various school settings (e.g., interactions among administrators, staff, and teachers in meetings; teacher and student interactions in classrooms; how school personnel interact with parents; how students interact with each other in classrooms, on playgrounds, and on the bus).

How to gather the data. Data-collection methods vary depending on the data needed and the assessment's purpose. The advantages of formal measurement and standardized instruments are the reliability and validity associated with derived scores, but the disadvantages are the costs and amount of time consumed. The following suggestions are easy-to-use and low-cost ways of collecting data:

- Design a chart to collect pertinent information from records and documents about the nature, frequency, intensity, and scope of the event.
- Interview members within the organization regarding their perceptions and insights about the schools or about aspects of school life. The interview should lead to an ecological profile, which would provide valid information about the assets and resources as well as barriers for a change in the school system.
- Develop a questionnaire to solicit participants' input about different aspects of school culture. The content and format of the questionnaire need to be consistent with the purpose of the inquiry as well as the target participants. For instance, a questionnaire about resource allocation might mean different things to teachers and students.
- Go to classrooms, faculty meetings, and student-oriented activities to make an observation as a participant or as an observer. Use field notes and audio or video to document the observation.

- Use informal, cost-effective index card methods (Bulach, 2001) to understand teachers' and students' expectations about the school environment and the leadership styles of administrators. Also use this method to collect information on how a particular change is perceived by the stakeholders in the school. Writing responses to one question on one index card makes it easier and less labor intensive to analyze.
- Collaborate with an outside consultant who is an expert in assessing organizational culture. Outside, objective sources can provide available insights, especially because stakeholders may have limited or biased views of their own contexts.

Table 10.2 provides an informal school culture assessment grid that is helpful in assessing school culture.

Standardized Instruments

The most popular instrument for measuring school climate and environment is the *Charles F. Kettering Ltd. (CFK) School Climate Profile* (Johnson & Johnson, 1995), which has four sections—General Climate Factors, Program Determinants, Process Determinants, and Material Determinants—and a total of 120 questions. The section of General Climate Factors is most frequently used in research and has eight subscales: Respect, Trust, High Morale, Opportunity for Input, Continuous Academic and Social Growth, Cohesiveness, School Renewal, and Caring. Several studies (Dixon & Johnson, 1991; Johnson & Johnson, 1992a, 1995) found the scale to be valid for the intended purpose, but factor analysis revealed the presence of some empirical dimensions or subscales that might not correspond with the original design. *What works* and *what doesn't work* seem to be the two new structures underlying the subscales. Table 10.3 includes other measures used for assessing school climate and environment.

Strategies to Change School Culture

"Culture building requires that school leaders give attention to the informal, subtle and symbolic aspects of school life which shape the beliefs and actions of each employee within the system" (Cunningham & Cresso, 1993, p. 25). It is also important to forge strong partnerships and collaboration between school and community in order to have sustainable positive outcomes (Lorion, 2011; Rhodes, Stevens, & Hemmings, 2011; Ross & Sibbald, 2010). Discussions about school culture are often found in the educational administration literature; principals are not the only ones who can take the leadership role. In fact, professional school counselors can and should take leadership roles to transform the culture of schools (Littrell & Peterson, 2001). Professional school counselors also possess the skills to bridge the school administration rules and the purposes of schooling for students.

Professional school counselors are in the position to help the school community develop a shared mission and goal, and they are in a good position to emphasize the importance of a caring, responsive environment. Many of the constraints to empathic environments are especially relevant to professional school counselors' training. Professional school counselors understand how to demonstrate empathy and how to respond to insensitive communication. They understand the qualities and processes of groups that can be either supportive or

Table 10.2 School Culture Assessment Grid

Area	What Is Now (To what extent has the school attained goals in the *What Should Be* list?)	What Should Be	Strategies to Change (What can be done to change the school culture in this area?)
Vision/Mission		Every student is important and deserves quality education. The school promotes lifelong professional development and personal growth. All members of the school and community are involved in the education process. The reward system is fair and focuses on improvement and growth rather than on mere academic achievement.	
Communication		There are open channels for everyone to voice his or her opinion. There is a system in which all shareholders can exchange information and ideas. All members have equal access to information. The school's mission and policies are clearly communicated to all shareholders via multiple methods.	
Relationships		There is a trust and mutual understanding of each other within the organization. Administrators support teachers' work and vice versa. Teachers and students have a trusting relationship.	
Shared Values		Members within the organization share the values, interests, and vision of an ideal school. Strategic planning is shared by all members. All members believe in the mission of the school.	
Collaboration		Administrators, teachers, parents, community partners, and students collaborate to make all decisions. All shareholders collaborate on strategic planning.	
Structure		The organization is accountable for its mission. Organizational structures are effectively designed and aimed at achieving excellence. Every member within the organization is accountable for his or her responsibility.	
Physical Environment		The school building is clean and safe. The school environment is inviting and friendly for students and parents. The classroom has basic facilities for learning.	

Table 10.3 Other Assessment Instruments for Assessing School Climate and Environment

Litwin and Stringer Climate Questionnaire (Litwin & Stringer, 1968): 50 items assessing eight dimensions (structure, responsibility, reward, risk, support, standards, conflict, and identity).

Halpin's and Croft's *Organizational Climate Description Questionnaire* (Halpin, 1966): 64 items measuring the degree of satisfaction with teacher–principal interaction.

Likert Profile of a School Questionnaire (Likert & Likert, 1972): 100 items measuring goal commitment, decision-making processes, and team cooperation.

High School Characteristics Index (Stern & Richman, 1964): 300 items assessing teachers' perceptions of climate and students' attitudes and feelings about their school's environment, curriculum, staff, student activities, and interests.

Brookover Elementary School Social Climate Questionnaire (Brookover, 1978): 115 items assessing relative contribution of composition and climate variables (pertaining to teacher, students, and principal) to differences in school achievement (Johnson & Johnson, 1992a).

Quality of School Life Scale (Epstein & McPartland, 1976; Johnson & Johnson, 1992b): 27 items measuring students' general reaction to school, levels of students' interests in school work, and nature of student–teacher relationships.

School Administrator Assessment Survey (Braskamp & Maehr, 1985): 19 scales assessing school administrators' perception of the culture of the school district and their perceptions of job opportunities, individual improvement, and personal development, and the culture or climate of the work setting.

---

destructive of community harmony. Professional school counselors are also knowledgeable about discipline and management issues. They understand the strengths and limitations of differing management systems and how the developmental needs of students must be considered when designing a management system. Professional school counselors know about some of the curricular programs that promote empathy. Some of these programs (e.g., literature programs that develop empathy) need not be additional to an already overfilled curriculum. Finally, professional school counselors are trained to facilitate positive, constructive group interaction. These skills are essential for working with parents, students, teachers, administrators, and community members to systematically address factors that contribute to or detract from caring school environments. By interacting with every member in the school system, they are in a unique position to be change agents for school culture (ASCA, 2012a). Their leadership skills can help them develop teams of invested individuals to work on issues such as promoting a quality environment and addressing problems of time, teacher–pupil ratio, and rigid or inflexible curricula.

Other factors also impact school culture: treating each student with dignity and as an individual who can learn and be successful in school; making opportunities for students to identify meaning and relevance in their school experiences and future lives; promoting teacher and student ownership and investment in their own growth; developing open and effective communication skills; solving the problems with a solution rather than focusing on victims; and presenting meaningful and interesting lessons and units of study (Ediger, 1997).

As noted by Erford (2015c), professional school counselors alone cannot assume responsibility for positive school environments and academic achievement. They can, however, function as team facilitators, advocates, and collaborators with families, community members, and school personnel. As team facilitators, professional school counselors can help family–school teams, mental health teams, and action teams by using group process skills to foster productive outcomes and positive relationships. The day-to-day lives of school counselors are full of stories of victimization, stories that provide a window to the inner life of students and place professional school counselors in a unique position to advocate for those who cannot or will not advocate for themselves. Understanding the causes or reasons behind undesirable behavior enhances both problem solving and compassion for those we find difficult to deal with. Finally, as collaborators, school counselors facilitate networking between people and organizations. This role is a natural outgrowth of the multifaceted job of the professional school counselor, which permits interaction with a wide variety of people. Additionally, the communication skills of professional school counselors encourage open and respectful communication between people (see Bryan, 2005, for a more complete explanation of the roles of advocate, facilitator, and collaborator).

Professional school counselors are in a unique position to promote a positive school culture. Their knowledge, skills, and interactions with a wide variety of people have great potential to facilitate changes in school culture (Bryan, 2005). The following activities summarize what professional school counselors can do to promote school culture change:

- Identify the need for change by coordinating assessment and evaluation of school culture.
- Advocate for changes to address the unmet needs of students, teachers, and other members of the school community. In a professional manner, share the personal stories of those whose voice is neglected, misunderstood, or silenced. Every player needs to be healthy and happy to make the system work.
- Collaborate with members of the school community to develop clearly defined and fair school policies and rules for discipline and performance. Encourage management systems that support a cooperative, caring school culture.
- Provide in-service training for members of the school community to promote empathy for one another and help them interact more effectively.
- Coordinate with every member in the school system to find meaning in common experiences and a sense of belonging and community.
- Take the initiative in facilitating proactive teams to develop strategic plans for continuous improvement. Encourage open dialogue and promote respect for the unique contributions of each team member. Facilitate member involvement in school reform and improvement.
- Facilitate networking and member involvement in school reform and improvement.
- Make changes incremental, systematic, and sustainable.

Summary/Conclusion

School culture explicitly or implicitly tells the individuals within the school system what is important, expected, and valued. School culture defines a school, so it is essential for professional school counselors to be cognizant of the various dimensions of school culture and facilitate the necessary changes to provide a healthy, safe, and supportive environment for learning and growth. Professional school counselors should take the leadership role in constructing a school environment with a sense of belonging, in which every member feels safe, valued, cared for, and respected; a context where individuals experience personal and professional development and growth and where every member finds meaning and purpose.

CHAPTER 11

Supervising School Counseling Interns

Gerta Bardhoshi and Bradley T. Erford*

Preview

Providing quality supervision for school counseling interns is both a leadership responsibility and a challenge for professional school counselors in the field. Specific requirements of supervision are presented while offering a supervision format specifically developed within the framework of ASCA's National Model.

Quality Supervision of School Counseling Interns

A critical leadership responsibility of professional school counselors that leads to the training of exemplary professional school counselors is the quality supervision of school counseling interns. As gatekeepers of the profession, on-site school counseling supervisors assume the role of mentor, teacher, evaluator, consultant, facilitator, and administrator (Bernard & Goodyear, 2013) as they work with school counseling students during their field experiences. On-site supervisors provide focused support for school counseling interns who aspire to become high-performing professional school counselors.

A supervision format is presented for professional school counselors who have volunteered to be on-site supervisors for student counselors participating in practicum and internship field experiences. Prerequisites needed to become a site supervisor are outlined and a supervision model described that was developed and structured within the four components of the American School Counselor Association (ASCA) national model (ASCA, 2012a).

Prerequisites for the Supervisory Role

School districts and individual school counselors must know the requirements to become on-site supervisors. These prerequisites are outlined in the Council for Accreditation of Counseling and Related Educational Programs' (CACREP, 2009, Section III) *Standards for School*

---

*Special thanks to Sally Murphy and Carol J. Kaffenberger for their outstanding contributions to the first two editions of this chapter.

Counseling Programs: Clinical Instruction. A site supervisor must possess the following minimum requirements to become an on-site school counselor supervisor:

- Minimum of a master's degree in counseling or a related profession with equivalent qualifications including appropriate certifications and/or licenses.
- Minimum of 2 years pertinent professional experience in the program area in which the student is completing clinical instruction.
- Knowledge of the program's expectations, requirements, and evaluation procedures for students.

In addition, the 2014 American Counseling Association (ACA) *Code of Ethics* advises counselor supervisors to have received training on supervision methods and techniques prior to beginning supervision. Similarly, the ASCA (2012b) Counseling Competencies emphasize knowledge of supervising school counseling interns based on the ASCA national model (Standard IV-B-6c). Familiarity with supervision topics and school counseling best practices, such as those described in this chapter, may better prepare supervisors to effectively deal with the inherent challenges in supervisory relationships.

Definition of Supervision

What is supervision? It is a method of conveying a profession's skills, knowledge, and attitudes to individuals who are or are becoming a part of that profession (Bernard & Goodyear, 2013). Consistent supervision ensures that the student counselor's counseling skills will improve over time. The on-site supervisor should offer constructive and timely feedback, allowing for the mutual sharing of ideas and challenging assumptions. Supervision creates a context in which learning occurs, so on-site supervisors must create a safe environment in which respect, honesty, trustworthiness, and responsiveness are evident. Due to the inherent power differential between the school counseling supervisor and school counseling intern, supervisors need to acknowledge their personal and professional power and establish supervisory relationships that foster the personal and professional functioning of the intern (ACA, 2014; Bernard & Goodyear, 2013). Effective supervision relies on the strength of the professional relationship between the school counselor supervisor and the school counseling intern.

Understanding the meaning of supervision and perceiving the importance of the relationship component in supervision are the beginning of the supervision process. The next step is implementing a model of supervision. This is critical for an organized, intentional, and grounded approach to training school counseling interns.

Supervision Model

Although much has been written about various supervision models (e.g., Bernard & Goodyear, 2013; Erford, 2105b; Studer & Diambra, 2010), the use of the *discrimination model* (Bernard & Goodyear, 2013; Luke & Bernard, 2006) is ideal for professional school counselors to use as on-site supervisors. The discrimination model provides categories of options, or discriminations, supervisors use when training school counseling interns during their clinical field experiences. Because the categories can be selected or combined based on the need or topic of supervision, this type of model is flexible and customizable, allowing the school counseling supervisor latitude in navigating supervision. Supervisor roles include teacher, counselor, and consultant, and the on-site supervisor's focus is on the areas of intervention, conceptualization, personalization, and professional behaviors and standards.

Other variables in supervision. Other variables also influence the supervision used and the supervisor–supervisee relationship. Erford (2015b) stressed the importance of recognizing that process variables (e.g., supervision stages and the student school counseling intern's development) may affect the supervision process. Constant variables (i.e., gender, age, race, ethnicity, and personality characteristics) are also evident in supervision. Cultural beliefs held by the on-site supervisor and the school counseling intern that pertain to diversity issues affect all aspects of supervision and counseling. It is critical that the on-site supervisor and the school counseling intern discuss their diversity perspectives and are aware of the cultural differences between them, as well as the potential differences between the counseling intern and students they are serving (Bernard & Goodyear, 2013). The fundamental question the supervisor must ask is, "Is the school counseling intern a culturally competent counselor?" (Hays & Erford, 2014). In the following section, how to use the ASCA national model (ASCA, 2012a) as the basis for supervision is described and an explanation of the supervision roles and areas of focus are presented, including the key components of the discrimination model (Bernard & Goodyear, 2013).

Introduction to Supervision within ASCA's National Model

It is critical that professional school counselors adhere to ASCA's standards, position statements, and program framework to have uniform quality programs, policies, and procedures. ASCA has developed a third edition of the ASCA national model (ASCA, 2012a) to further assist professional school counselors. Professional school counselors assume the responsibility and challenge of simultaneously managing their school counseling programs per ASCA's national model and authenticating that school counseling interns are trained in the correct method of the implementation of these programs. Relying on their professional organization's direction for effecting change within their school communities, professional school counselors who assume the responsibility of being a supervisor to perspective new counselors are also providing a role model for leadership.

The ASCA national model immediately makes sense to practicing school counselors and provides a framework for organizing what they already do. It is also an ideal basis upon which to structure the supervision of school counseling interns. The four components of the national model—foundation, delivery, management, and accountability—provide opportunities for the site supervisor to structure the internship experience and ensure that school counseling interns are exposed to all aspects of the counseling program.

Foundation. The supervision of school counseling interns starts within the foundation component. On-site supervisors explain the school counseling program focus by sharing their own belief systems with the school counseling interns (e.g., "I believe change occurs when . . .") and highlighting the alignment of the counseling program's mission statement to that of the school's. This critical discussion lays the groundwork for the intern to more fully understand the connection of the school counseling program to the school's overall mission and goals. By talking about their academic qualifications and experiences, supervisors help ensure that interns value the supervision from an experienced on-site supervisor, while also understanding all the skills and experiences that are essential to the implementation of a successful school counseling program. Finally, school counseling supervisors educate interns on the student standards reflected throughout the school counseling program and the importance of incorporating state and district initiatives into their practice.

Delivery system. On-site supervisors use the delivery system component to help the intern focus on both direct and indirect student services. These include the school counseling core curriculum, individual planning, responsive services and referral, consultation, and collaboration. Supervisors ask interns to develop and implement guidance units. Interns should also participate in parent education activities, group counseling, the special education process, crisis response, and/or individual counseling.

Conducting supervision meetings. Embedded within the delivery system component, within the scope of the indirect services school counselors provide for the benefit of students through their interactions, are the underlying elements of clinical supervision. Weekly supervision meetings between the school counseling intern and the on-site supervisor are critical to the overall growth of the intern's field experience (see Figure 11.1 for a checklist of supervision activities). The weekly supervision time (scheduled for at least 1 hour a week, either in a 60-minute or 30-minute blocks) is an essential professional growth experience for the student counselor (ASCA, 2012a). Formal supervision meetings enrich the field experience and pull everything together for the supervisee.

During weekly supervision meetings, the on-site supervisor focuses on the school counseling intern's areas of strength and growth needs. It is critical for the intern to be open to hearing about areas of strength and growth needs for progress to occur. It is more than a question of semantics when the supervisor addresses the intern's *area for growth* instead of calling it an *area of weakness*. It frames the suggestions in a positive light and sets the stage for the intern to more readily hear and implement feedback. An example of highlighting one of the intern's strengths might be, "Your ability to establish a genuine rapport with the students was evident when you worked with . . ." Likewise, the on-site supervisor might need to point out that the school counseling intern needs to talk less and do more listening. By focusing on this as an area for growth (instead of a weakness), the intern is immediately positioned for success. Another important aspect of the weekly supervision meetings is when intern and supervisor both review the intern's log of hours to ensure that a variety of experiences are incorporated into the field experience over the semester. The supervisor and intern also use supervision time to complete short- and long-term planning for the school counseling program.

Supervision meetings can also be used for formal evaluations. The *ACA Code of Ethics* (ACA, 2014) recommends the scheduling of periodic formal evaluation meetings with supervisees. These meetings allow school counseling supervisors the opportunity to provide a summative review of the intern's skills, while also tracking and documenting progress on areas of growth identified during weekly supervision meetings.

On-Site Supervision Checklist

Weekly supervision meetings are required: One 60-minute block or two 30-minute blocks.

School Counseling Intern's Name: _____.

Date: _____.

Time: _____.

Supervision Activities: In Progress (IP) or Completed (C)

Phases of Internship

IP   C
- ☐   ☐   Orientation and shadowing
- ☐   ☐   Cocounseling and coteaching (guidance lessons)
- ☐   ☐   Independence
- ☐   ☐   Closure

Reflective Practice

IP   C
- ☐   ☐   Emphasize intern's areas of *strength* (be specific)
- ☐   ☐   Address intern's areas for *growth* (be specific)
- ☐   ☐   Encourage intern's questions and exchange of ideas
- ☐   ☐   Review counseling (case) interventions and conceptualizations
- ☐   ☐   Review the log of hours to ensure a balance of activities over time
- ☐   ☐   Discuss short-term planning
- ☐   ☐   Discuss long-term planning
- ☐   ☐   Address supervisor's concerns about intern's issues (e.g., promptness, appearance, resistance, ethical issues, professional behavior)

ASCA National Model

Has the intern been exposed to aspects of the school's counseling program that align with the model?

IP   C
- ☐   ☐   Foundation (e.g., counseling program's mission statement)
- ☐   ☐   Delivery
  - School guidance curriculum
    - Classroom instruction, group activities, parent workshops and instruction
  - Individual student planning

Figure 11.1 On-site supervision checklist.   *(continues)*

- Responsive services
    - Individual and small-group counseling, crisis counseling
    - Referrals, peer facilitation, parent education, special education (attends local screen, reviews 504, develops referral lists, reviews school crisis intervention plan)
- System support
    - Professional development, consultation, collaboration, teaming

☐ ☐ Management
   - Use of time, use of data, advisory council, monitoring student progress

☐ ☐ Accountability (e.g., program evaluation)

Observations and Interactions

Has the intern been observed in these situations?

IP C
☐ ☐ Guidance lesson
☐ ☐ Small-group counseling
☐ ☐ Individual counseling
☐ ☐ Parent conference

Has the intern participated in meetings?

IP C
☐ ☐ Faculty
☐ ☐ Guidance
☐ ☐ Team meetings
☐ ☐ Teacher/Administration interaction

University Support (e.g., site visits, e-mails, phone contact, hardcopy correspondence)

IP C
☐ ☐ Communication with the University Supervisor: Initiated by me (M) or University (U)

Figure 11.1 (*continued*)

Supervision roles and focus areas. To determine what role will be prominent at any time during supervision, it is helpful to consider the purpose of the role (see Table 11.1). Supervisors, as teachers, determine what is critical for the school counseling intern to learn during the clinical field experience. They give information, instruction, and guidance to the intern, and it is in this role that supervisors must also evaluate the intern by giving regular verbal and written feedback about the intern's strengths and areas for growth.

When on-site supervisors are engaged in the counselor role, they tap into their own knowledge of counseling to help school counseling interns focus on inter- and intrapersonal interactions. This supervisory role is especially important when helping school counseling interns conduct a self-evaluation. As a *consultant,* the third role used in the discrimination model, the on-site supervisor acknowledges the collegial relationship with the school counseling intern. The intern is encouraged to offer suggestions for treatment of the client and for programmatic changes. The supervisor and the intern have a mutually respectful relationship, in which both benefit.

In addition to the three roles of supervision, supervisors have four focus areas that they address to assess their intern's skills. When focusing on intervention, on-site supervisors help

Table 11.1 Supervision Roles and Areas of Focus: Responsibilities and Examples

Roles	Responsibilities	Examples
Teacher & Evaluator	Provide information about the counseling internship, including an explanation of the supervision and evaluation components. Determine what to include in the field experience. Demonstrate specific techniques. Instruct intern about specific school or district policies and procedures. Use specific, behavioral, observable, and constructive feedback.	Does the intern have the knowledge and information about the role of the school counselor in a school setting? Does the intern understand the rights and responsibilities of an intern to the school community's stakeholders? Does the intern understand the components involved in his or her supervision and evaluation?
Counselor	Addresses the intern's areas of strength and growth regarding specific counseling skills and interventions. Addresses issues concerning the intern's inter- and intrapersonal interactions.	Does the intern have the correct counseling skills and techniques to address student issues? Is the school counseling intern able to conduct a self-evaluation of inter- and intrapersonal interactions?
Consultant	Exchange ideas about interventions, goals, and program plans.	Does the intern have opportunities to exchange ideas and make suggestions about interventions, goals, and program plans?

Focus	Responsibilities	Examples
Intervention	Help intern develop clinical interventions used in counseling. Underscore the importance of using a multicultural counseling approach.	Does the intern have the correct counseling skills and techniques to address student issues? Is the intern culturally competent?
Conceptualization	Help intern understand what is going on in the counseling session. What are the central issues and factors in play?	Does the intern accurately understand the client's issues? Can the intern communicate the appropriate interventions that would best help the client in his or her particular situation?
Personalization	While maintaining a professional approach, address the personal counseling style that school counseling interns implement when working with clients.	Does the intern understand boundary issues and the importance of avoiding counter-transference responses? Does the intern know the importance of limiting or avoiding self-discourse statements?

(continues)

Table 11.1 (continued)

Roles	Responsibilities	Examples
Professional Behaviors and Standards of School Counseling	Address ethical behaviors and standards commensurate with the role of the professional school counselor. Address appropriate professional demeanor and attire.	Does the intern model leadership, advocacy, collaboration, systemic change, and multiculturalism? Does the intern accept feedback, constructive criticism, and suggestions in an open and positive manner? Does the intern consistently wear suitable professional attire? Is the intern prompt?

school counseling interns improve the type of clinical interventions used during a counseling session (e.g., *Does the school counseling intern have the correct counseling skills and techniques to address the client's issues?*).

On-site supervisors focus on conceptualization when they want to determine how well school counseling interns understand what is happening in the counseling session (e.g., *Is the school counseling intern able to articulate the correct areas to be addressed? Can the school counseling intern communicate the appropriate interventions that would best help the client in his or her particular situation?*).

Personalization addresses the personal counseling style that school counseling interns implement when they work with clients while maintaining a professional approach (e.g., *Does the school counseling intern understand boundary issues and the importance of avoiding countertransference responses? Does the school counseling intern know the importance of limiting or avoiding self-discourse statements?*).

Supervisors' focus on their interns' professional behaviors and standards is constant throughout the entire clinical field experience. This concentration highlights the need for school counseling interns to develop ethical behavior and demonstrate appropriate professional demeanor and attire (e.g., *Does the school counseling intern exhibit, on a consistent basis, through verbal and nonverbal behavior, the professional standards commensurate with the role of the professional school counselor? Does the school counseling intern model leadership, advocacy, collaboration, and systemic change? Does the school counseling intern consistently wear suitable professional attire?*). The supervisor addresses these focus areas by alternately using the discrimination model's three roles (Bernard & Goodyear, 2013): teacher, counselor, or consultant. While one role may be primary, all three roles may come into play during a supervision session.

It takes skill, training, practice, and learning to think like a supervisor and to effectively supervise school counseling interns, which is especially important when addressing the school counseling intern's resistance, avoidance, or conflict. It is important that on-site supervisors understand that these behaviors are normal reactions for some beginning student counselors. It is helpful to describe and interpret the resistance, offering specific feedback to the counselor intern in order to clarify or restate the behavior. On-site supervisors are encouraged to frame a school counseling intern's resistant behavior positively (e.g., "*We've been focusing on your need to become more assertive with several of the teachers. I see this as a challenge for you, not a problem."*). Using role-play scenarios helps the supervisor and the intern identify the cause of resistant behaviors. Supervisors can record the supervision sessions so the school counseling intern can review the session. The supervision training stresses the importance of involving the university supervisor in any relevant concerns. On-site supervisors fully understand that supervision is a process and that they are not alone in the supervision of school counseling interns. A collaborative partnership must exist between the university supervisor and the on-site school counseling supervisor.

Ethical and legal issues in clinical supervision are the final, and perhaps the most important, components in the delivery section. The American Counseling Association (ACA, 2014) delineates ethical guidelines for counselor supervisors that include competence to supervise; boundaries of the supervisory relationship; confidentiality, accountability, and liability; and evaluation. ACA also provides direction for legal issues. The on-site supervisor must understand the meaning of *direct liability*—that is, the on-site supervisor is legally and ethically responsible for all of the school counseling intern's actions at the school site. The impact of this issue underscores the need for quality supervision and supervision training.

A good supervisor knows that the more the supervisee is engaged in the process, the more the supervisee will benefit and grow. It is through quality and intentional supervision that school counseling interns learn how to conduct themselves consistent with their professional standards, critically analyze their own efforts, and mature from the constructive feedback of their on-site supervisors.

Management system. Supervision within the third component in the ASCA national model focuses, among other things, on school counselor competency and program assessment, annual agreements with supervisors, planning, an advisory council, and use of data for systemic change. While many on-site supervisors plan their yearly school counseling programs around the school calendar, many are unfamiliar with self-evaluation of themselves and the school counseling program; annual agreements that address how the program will be organized; use of data to measure results; and advisory councils that review and can make recommendations for further improvement of the program. On-site supervisors should discuss these issues with their school counseling interns. The management system component provides an excellent opportunity to ask interns to think about how they communicate with administrators about their program goals, how their programs connect to the mission of the school, and how they collaborate with stakeholders to meet school needs.

Accountability. The fourth and last component of the ASCA (2012a) national model is one with which some on-site supervisors are least familiar. While supervisors understand that schools are in an era of accountability, collecting and disaggregating data traditionally were not part of their counselor role in previous decades. Accountability is described in terms of the three purposes of using data: to monitor student progress, to assess counseling programs, and to demonstrate counselor effectiveness. Each school counseling intern should conduct data collection for the site (e.g., in collaboration with the on-site supervisor, choose an aspect of the site's school counseling program to evaluate). One example would be for the school counseling intern to conduct a needs assessment to determine what new programs or services are needed at the school. Other examples of projects include an evaluation of a career-day program, a needs assessment concerning staff diversity training, and the effectiveness of an 8-week counseling group. Once the purpose of the project is agreed upon, the school counseling intern develops the instruments needed to collect the information, gains approval from administration, gathers the data, analyzes the data (perhaps using R-stat or Excel charts to organize the findings), makes recommendations based on the data, and prepares the documents for a presentation to the on-site supervisor or others at the school. The process of using data to understand school counseling-related educational issues is new to many on-site supervisors, but they are quick to see the power of data.

University Support for On-Site Supervisors

Are you alone in the supervision process? Absolutely not. The ASCA (2010a) Ethical Standards for School Counselors specifies that school counselor supervisors should ensure a site visit by a university supervisor for each supervisee. Even so, the university supervisor should be available to the on-site supervisor throughout the entire field experience. There should be an initial meeting at the site (or via phone) with the school counseling intern, the on-site supervisor, and the university supervisor. At that meeting, the university supervisor should provide a written manual or handbook that includes a description of the program and course requirements, a contract that describes the field experience expectations and responsibilities, an evaluation instrument (see Erford, 2015b), and other pertinent documents needed by the school counseling intern, the on-site supervisor, or the university supervisor. Additional visits and communication via phone and e-mail should continue throughout the field experience. At a minimum, there should be a mid-semester contact to ensure that the school counseling intern is making progress and meeting all program and site requirements. The last contact should be at the end of the field experience. Even though the on-site supervisor will complete a final evaluation of the school counseling intern, the university supervisor should see if there are additional issues to be discussed. The university supervisor should be readily available at all times during the semester to provide support to the on-site supervisor and school counseling intern.

Summary/Conclusion

Providing quality supervision to school counseling interns is critical to their future success as professional school counselors. Most on-site supervisors assume the responsibilities of supervising a counseling student without previous supervision training. The best way to assure that on-site supervisors are prepared, and that school counseling interns are receiving the highest quality of supervision that is consistent with the guidelines provided by professional counseling organizations, is for universities to conduct ongoing supervision training with all site supervisors. As school counseling programs and counselor education programs adopt the ASCA national model (2012a) as the framework for their school counseling programs, it is essential that the ASCA national model be infused into the supervision of school counseling interns.

SECTION 3

Comprehensive School Counseling Programs

CHAPTER 12

The ASCA National Standards and the ASCA National Model

Carol A. Dahir, Trish Hatch, and Lawrence E. Tyson

Preview

In this chapter, we describe the history and impact of the American School Counselor Association (ASCA) Sharing the Vision: The National Standards for School Counseling Programs *(Campbell & Dahir, 1997) and the development of the* ASCA National Model: A Framework for School Counseling Programs *(ASCA, 2003a, 2005, 2012a,) which has become a seminal document for the profession.*

As we progress through the 21st century, new directions are being defined for the profession of school counseling. Historically, professional school counselors have lacked consistent professional identity, been professionally marginalized, and in many states, become expendable personnel with no requirements for their school services or programs (Hatch, 2008). The American School Counselor Association (ASCA) national standards (Campbell & Dahir, 1997) and the ASCA national model (ASCA, 2003a) were written to address these and other professional needs by providing common content, competencies, and one vision, one voice for the profession. In 2012, ASCA released a third edition of the ASCA national model (2012a), and ASCA will soon release a new edition of the ASCA student standards. As we look for the impact and opportunities of these new documents on the school counseling profession's future, it is also crucial that students of the profession understand its past and how we got here.

Exploring our Past

At the turn of the 20th century, professional school counselors did not exist. Instead, teachers used a few minutes of their time to offer vocational guidance to students who were preparing for work in a democratic society (Gysbers & Henderson, 2012). The current school mission is not altogether different than the 1900s. Today, in a world enriched by diversity and technology, professional school counselors' chief mission is still supporting the academic achievement of all students so they are prepared for life beyond school. However, professional school counselors no longer work in isolation; instead, they collaborate with other educational professionals to implement a school counseling program that is integral to the total educational program for student success. This evolution from teachers sparing minutes a day to trained professionals implementing a comprehensive school counseling program did not take place without professional scholars and school counselors having the vision, knowledge, and determination to move forward.

Professional school counselors began as vocational counselors in 1908, and the profession has evolved to incorporate the domains of academic, career, and personal–social development (Campbell & Dahir, 1997). During this evolution, differing philosophical perspectives developed among academic counselors, career counselors, and personal–social or mental health counselors regarding their role and function, purpose, and focus. Lacking clear role definition as a profession, school counseling became a house divided by controversy between those who focused on vocational guidance (which later became educational guidance) and those who attended to the personal–social foundational needs of students in education (Aubrey, 1991).

While procedures were similar, methods were varied. Counseling could be either directive or nondirective—two somewhat opposing methods of delivery. In directive counseling, the focus on intellectual interpretation was counselor directed, while nondirective counseling was client-centered and focused on the release of feelings and the achievement of insight. The counselor delivered the first approach; the student discovered the latter. Most vocational counselors were directive, whereas social workers, mental hygienists, and child-guidance clinicians were nondirective (Warters, 1946). In the 1960s, the directive approach to counseling was encouraged by the National Defense Education Act of 1958. Professional school counselors in U.S. schools identified and herded the best and the brightest students toward math and science majors in college, in an effort to win the Space Race with the Soviet Union. Meanwhile, Carl Rogers (1951) was training counselors in a nondirective, more passive approach.

Counselors who were trained in programs rooted in psychological and clinical paradigms differed greatly from those who were rooted in educational paradigms. Postsecondary training programs contained conflicting and varied theoretical perspectives between and within their programs and, consequently, professional school counselors' training and perspectives about their role and function varied substantially. Not unlike today, professionals within school counseling debated whether counselors are mental health providers within schools or educators who provide mental health support and assist with students' personal–social and emotional well-being.

The counseling and guidance movement was also characterized by a proliferation of competing methodologies that focused more attention on the technique of counselors and the process of counseling and less on the content and objectives of the program. This alteration in counseling methodology led to changes in the substance and priorities that guidance programs were given (Aubrey, 1991). "The focus was on a position (counselor) and a process (counseling), not on a program (guidance)" (Gysbers & Henderson, 2012, p. 1). Consequently, guidance became an ancillary support service and not a program integral to the total educational program of student success. The result was that professional school counselors were (and in some cases still are) more likely to be saddled with administrative tasks and clerical duties.

In the 1970s and 1980s, several attempts were made to unify the profession. Emerging from this movement were several theoretical models of comprehensive programs, many of which were based on the expansion of the career guidance model. Norman Gysbers and Patricia Henderson wrote textbooks and developed and trained districts and states in how to develop and implement comprehensive guidance programs models (Gysbers & Henderson, 2012); C. D. "Curly" Johnson and Sharon Johnson (2001, 2002) focused their counselor training on designing results-based school counseling programs; and Robert Myrick (2010) wrote about planned developmental guidance programs. In addition, the ERIC Clearinghouse on Counseling and Student Services published several books and conducted four national conferences that offered training in the development and implementation of comprehensive school guidance programs. Despite the tremendous impact of these forward thinkers, the legitimization of the school counseling program within schools remained quite tenuous and unevenly developed across the country.

For decades, the school counseling profession attempted to respond to the question, "What do counselors do?" However, that question only confused those within and outside the profession because of the various models in which counselors were trained or committed to. In addition to listing myriad counseling-related duties (e.g., guidance lessons, group counseling, academic planning, individual counseling, consultation, collaboration), professional school counselors were burdened with a variety of quasi-administrative and non-counseling duties. Just as preservice training varied for professional school counselors, so too did administrative expectations for school counselors, based on administrative knowledge, pre-service training, or lack of understanding with regard to school counseling programs (Olson, 1979).

In 1992, Hart and Jacobi wrote *From Gatekeeper to Advocate: Transforming the Role of the School Counselor*, in which they discussed the six problems in school counseling programs, summarized here:

1. *Lack of basic philosophy.* Few professional school counselors are guided by a well-developed philosophy or belief system, one that drives the entire program and the behaviors of the counselors within the program. Rather, they tend to work independently and are often reactive.

2. *Poor integration.* School counseling remains an ancillary rather than a core component of K–12 education. Professional school counselors must connect with other stakeholders in the school system as integral partners in the total educational program.

3. *Insufficient student access.* Student-to-counselor ratios are high, and many students do not have the opportunity to meet with their professional school counselors. High ratios are only part of the problem, however. Another is that some counselors still insist on focusing on individual counseling rather than ensuring that every student receives school counseling services through a school-wide guidance curriculum.

4. *Inadequate guidance for some students.* Economically disadvantaged students and students of color are often denied the opportunity to enroll in rigorous academic coursework at the same level that is often afforded to other students.

5. *Lack of counselor accountability.* There is no common understanding about what constitutes accountability and in what way counselors are to be held accountable for the results of their program.

6. *Failure to use other resources.* Professional school counselors cannot deliver the entire counseling program; rather, they are encouraged to better use school and community resources to create networks, garner referrals, and meet a variety of students' needs.

The Momentum for Change

The school improvement agenda of the 1990s directed the development of national standards across all academic content areas to improve educational practice and pedagogy and identify student outcomes. Concerned about the absence of references to school counseling contributions to the Goals 2000 statute (U.S. Department of Education, 1994), the American School

Counselor Association (ASCA), the national professional association representing professional school counselors, determined it was important for school counselors to have a voice in the educational reform and school improvement agenda, and take a position along with the other associations developing standards across the content areas. The ASCA leaders suggested the development of national standards for school counseling programs would:

- create a framework for a national model for school counseling programs;
- establish school counseling as an integral component of the academic mission of the educational system;
- encourage equitable access to school counseling services for all students, provided by a credentialed professional school counselor;
- identify the knowledge and skills all students should acquire as a result of participation in the school counseling program;
- identify and implement goals for students that were deemed important by the school community;
- clarify the relationship of school counseling to the educational system;
- address the contributions of school counseling to student success in school; and
- ensure that school counseling programs are comprehensive in design and delivered in a systematic fashion for all students (Campbell & Dahir, 1997).

The National Education Goals Panel (1994) described program content standards as specifying what students should know and be able to do. The ASCA Governing Board adopted the definition of the National Goals Panel and determined the development of school counseling content standards would define what students should know and be able to do as a result of participating in a school counseling program (Campbell & Dahir, 1997). As a result of a national survey and extensive field reviews involving thousands of ASCA members, nine national standards, three in each of the areas of academic, career, and personal–social development, became the foundation for the content of school counseling programs.

By 2001, more than 130,000 one-page executive summaries (Dahir, 2001) describing *Sharing the Vision: The National Standards for School Counseling Programs* (Campbell & Dahir, 1997) and listing the national standards were circulating around the country and internationally. Over 35,000 ASCA national standards documents had been sold. The second document, *Vision into Action*, was intended to provide counselors with the direction, guidance, and assistance to implement the standards (Dahir, Sheldon, & Valiga, 1998). According to the *ASCA National Standards for School Counseling Programs Project Impact Report*, presentations were made to 67 professional associations nationwide (Dahir, 2001). By 2001, more than 79 school system implementation workshops had been held and more than 400 school districts throughout the United States established programs based on the national standards Twenty-six states reported incorporating the national standards into their state models and two states (Delaware and New Jersey) completed full state adoptions. At that time, 42 ASCA-certified trainers assisted school systems with the implementation process, and 61 districts reported a standards-based school counseling program was in place. Four states reported cross-walking state counseling standards with their state's academic learning standards; 30 state school counselor associations endorsed the national standards; five states reported legislation incorporating the national standards into legislative code; and 57 counselor education programs incorporated the national standards into their curriculum.

With accountability driving school reform, there was a critical need to inform stakeholders of the relationship of school counseling programs to student learning and achieve-

Table 12.1 National Standards for School Counseling Programs

Domain		Standard
Academic	A	Students will acquire the attitudes, knowledge, and skills contributing to effective learning in school and across the lifespan.
	B	Students will complete school with the academic preparation essential to choose from a wide range of substantial postsecondary options, including college.
	C	Students will understand the relationship of academics to the world of work and to life at home and in the community.
Career	A	Students will acquire the skills to investigate the world of work in relation to knowledge of self and to make informed career decisions.
	B	Students will employ strategies to achieve future career goals with success and satisfaction.
	C	Students will understand the relationship between personal qualities, education, training, and the world of work.
Personal–Social	A	Students will acquire the knowledge, attitudes, and interpersonal skills to help them understand and respect self and others.
	B	Students will make decisions, set goals, and take necessary action to achieve goals.
	C	Students will understand safety and survival skills.

Note. Adapted from *Sharing the Vision: The National Standards for School Counseling Programs*, by C. Campbell and C. Dahir, 1997, Alexandria, VA: American School Counselor Association.

ment (Dahir et al., 1998). These standards offered professional school counselors, administrators, teachers, and counselor educators a common language to promote student success through involvement or participation in school counseling programs. Educational colleagues who were involved in school improvement and the implementation of standards across other disciplines readily understood the concept of standards. Standards-based school counseling programs had characteristics similar to other educational programs, including a scope and sequence, student outcomes or competencies, activities and processes to assist students in achieving these outcomes, professionally credentialed personnel, materials and resources, and accountability methods. The integration of academic, career, and personal–social development assisted students to acquire the attitudes, knowledge, and skills for success in school and success in life (see Figure 12.1).

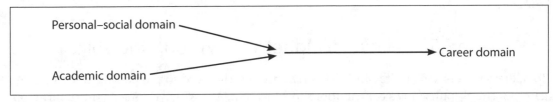

Figure 12.1. Merging of student academic and personal–social domains leading to successful career and life choices.

The student competencies identified specific attitudes, knowledge, and skills students should obtain or be able to demonstrate as a result of participating in a school counseling program. Student competencies supported the goals of the national standards, guided the development of strategies and activities, and were the basis for assessing student growth and development. The 122 ASCA student competencies were arranged in the three domain areas and provide direction to achieving the nine standards.

The standards offered professional school counselors the ability to restructure and improve their school counseling programs based on what students needed to succeed in the three domains (Perusse, Goodnough, & Noel, 2001). It was believed that a school counseling program based on national standards provided all the necessary elements for students to achieve academic, career, and personal–social success in school. This standards-based programmatic approach helped professional school counselors to continuously assess their students' needs, identify the barriers and obstacles that may be hindering student success, and advocate programmatic efforts to eliminate these barriers (Herr, 2001).

According to Schmidt and Ciechalski (2001), the national standards promoted student learning and development while also defining the major components of a comprehensive school counseling program, including the traditional components of counseling (individual and small group), consultation, coordination, case management, guidance curriculum, program evaluation and development, and program delivery. Additionally, professional school counselors were encouraged to shift from a role-and-position focus and the delivery of a menu of student services to the design and implementation of a structured and programmatic approach of school counseling that addresses the needs of all students (Gysbers & Henderson, 2012).

School counseling leaders applied and integrated different paradigms and approaches (e.g., Gysbers & Henderson, 2012; C. D. Johnson & Johnson, 2001, 2002; Myrick, 2010) to the context of school counseling as a program. The developmental school counseling approach (Myrick, 2010) addressed the needs of students consistent with their expected stages of growth and learning. The comprehensive program model (Gysbers & Henderson, 2012) was the first to view school counseling as a system for delivering and organizing the school counseling program. The results-based approach (C. D. Johnson & Johnson, 2002) offered a methodology for demonstrating outcomes and impact. The national standards were designed as "core content" within these established approaches and were not meant as a substitute for a comprehensive, developmental, and results-based program. A comprehensive, developmental, and results-based program provided direction for *what* and *how* services are delivered. The national standards and the student competencies were not only "curriculum," but made up every aspect of professional school counselors' work with students. These approaches independently and collectively complemented each other. However, professional school counselors and counselor educators remained confused and conflicted regarding which approach or system they should use to implement the standards. "Random acts of guidance" were no longer acceptable in 21st century schools (Bilzing, 1996).

The ASCA National Model: One Vision, One Voice

To address the growing professional concerns around the need to provide a unified voice regarding school counseling's contributions to education, ASCA's governing board, at its March 2001 meeting, agreed to develop one national program model. The standards provided content for the foundation of a program; however, board members agreed that the next logical step would be the development of a framework to maximize the full potential of the standards documents. This new document would reflect current education reform movements, including the No Child Left Behind Act of 2001, which mandated all federally funded programs be accountable for and directly connected to student learning and student improvement.

ASCA held a national summit to create an ASCA national model by bringing the leaders in the field together with the goal of creating "One Vision, One Voice!" for all professional school counselors. All attendees agreed: ASCA should move forward to develop the model to address the historical concerns and current challenges, and to assist practicing school counselors in planning for the future of their programs and the profession through one common lens. The *ASCA National Model: A Framework School Counseling Programs* (ASCA, 2003a) connected school counseling to the educational reform movements that emphasized student achievement and success.

Model Development

From the first stages of development, ASCA called upon the expertise of national leaders and practicing school counselors. The first ASCA summit was held June 1 through June 3, 2001, in Tucson, Arizona. The purpose of the summit was to discuss the future of school counseling programs and to develop a framework for a national model. For 2.5 days, summit participants brainstormed, collaborated, and finally achieved consensus on how the model would be structured. Summit participants agreed to develop a model that would consist of three levels of program implementation: foundation, delivery and management, and accountability. There would be four or five components in each of the three levels. The ASCA national standards would be the foundation upon which the building blocks of the program curriculum would be built.

As a basis for a national model, participants incorporated theories, and concepts and generously donated text, training, and resource materials from programs designed by Dr. Norman Gysbers, Dr. C. D. "Curly" Johnson, Dr. Robert Myrick, The Education Trust, and the ASCA national standards. The initial document, written by Trish Hatch and Judy Bowers, included samples of their own work and work created with professional school counselors in the Moreno Valley Unified School District in California, and the Tucson Unified School District in Arizona, respectively. State and school counselor association documents of comprehensive programs were reviewed and used in the development of the document.

In developing the national model, participants agreed on the following assumptions and criteria:

- ASCA's national standards are a framework or foundation for the development of a school counseling program. Many states also have standards that align with the ASCA standards.
- A distinction must be made among the school counseling standards for every student, school counseling standards for the program, and school counseling standards for the professional school counselor.
- A school counseling program provides a framework that allows flexibility for states and school districts to create a program based on the districts' individual needs and accountability.

- Any model must be integral to students' academic achievement, particularly in facilitating improvement in academic achievement, and must help set higher standards for student achievement.
- Any model must be data driven (disaggregated) and results based, and should not focus only on methods and techniques.
- Any model should be developed and implemented district wide, not just at individual schools.
- Any model should provide intentional guidance to specifically address the needs of every student, particularly students of culturally diverse, low socioeconomic status, and other underserved or underperforming populations.
- Any model should empower professional school counselors and teach them how to work with administrators to reassign non-guidance activities such as master scheduling or testing. A school counseling program must include plans for the effective use of a counselor's time within the delivery system.
- Any model should demonstrate evidence of the use of technology to implement the program; to advocate for the program; and to collect, analyze, and interpret data.
- Any model program should be preventive in design and developmental in nature.

Additionally, the summit participants emphasized the design of a school counseling program model must include accountability tools for measuring results. To facilitate the adoption of a school counseling program model by school districts, ASCA would identify and disseminate best practices for designing, developing, coordinating, implementing, evaluating, and enhancing the program. Successful development and implementation of a school counseling program would rely on school–community collaboration. Professional school counselors would play the leadership role in defining and carrying out a school counseling program. Licensed or credentialed professional school counselors must implement a school counseling program. In a school counseling program, professional school counselors would work as change agents within the educational system to advocate for students' needs and students' results. Professional school counselors must use data to advocate for students and the school counseling program, and professional school counselors must strive for continued improvement and use results to continually improve the program for students.

Writing the Model

The co-authors of the model (Hatch & Bowers) researched dozens of state department and state association school counseling documents. Reading, sorting, and sifting through thousands of pages was a daunting task and responsibility. Each document was dissected in light of its possible contribution to the overall, agreed-upon framework. Working with ASCA's graphic artist, several versions of the graphic were reviewed, until the final version was agreed upon.

In November 2001, the first rough draft was reviewed by Summit I members and test-driven by professional school counselors in Tucson, Arizona, and at the Moreno Valley School Counselors Academy in California. Counselors and administrators were trained in the model, reviewed the manuscript, and provided valuable feedback. The authors made revisions and submitted a new draft in May 2002 at Summit II, which was held in Washington, DC. The first public draft was unveiled during ASCA's national school counselor conference, in Miami, in June 2002. Keynote conference speakers included some of the leaders in the school counseling field who attended the initial model development summit meeting, specifically Norman Gysbers, Clarence "Curly" Johnson, and Robert Myrick. Several conference sessions were devoted to providing an overview of the model. An intensive, 3-hour workshop conducted by the draft authors, Judy Bowers and Trish Hatch, drew more than 200 participants. The focus of the workshop was on how professional school counselors could implement the model in their own districts.

ASCA provided an online version of the model and solicited national public comment for the 4-month period following the conference. The document received overwhelmingly positive responses. Professional school counselors and counselor educators nationwide provided praise, helpful and constructive criticism, and made suggestions for improvement. The draft authors analyzed the feedback and provided a revised version to the Summit III participants in November 2002. After a final end of the year rewrite, the authors submitted their gift[1] (a final version) to ASCA for an initial printing to coincide with National School Counselors Week in February 2003.

ASCA National Model (2003)

The ASCA national model is an organizational framework designed to assist professional school counselors to develop or redesign their programs to meet the current educational needs of students. By using the model to align the school counseling program with the school's mission and school improvement plans, professional school counselors partner as leaders in systemic change, ensure equity and access to a rigorous education, and promote academic, career, and personal–social development for *every* student.

The ASCA national standards (revised in the ASCA model to be referred to as ASCA standards for students, or ASCA student standards) and competencies became part of the foundation for ASCA's national model (2003a), which placed the school counseling program in the context of an organized, planned, and intentional program for every student. Implementation required an organizational framework and accountability system to determine how well students met the standards or achieved intended outcomes. The competencies delivered at the building or district level emphasize early intervention, prevention, and responsive services.

The ASCA National Model: A Framework for School Counseling Programs (ASCA, 2003a, 2005, 2012a) was written as a comprehensive approach to program foundation, delivery, management, and accountability. It provides a framework for the program components, the professional school counselor's role in implementation, and the underlying philosophies of leadership, advocacy, and systemic change. The model is the mechanism with which professional school counselors and school counseling teams will design, coordinate, implement, manage, and evaluate their programs for students' success.

Within the national model, professional school counselors switched their emphasis from *service-centered* for some students to *program-centered* for every student. The model not only answered the question, *What do professional school counselors do?*, but it also required a response to the question, *How are students different as a result of the work of professional school*

---

[1]Trish Hatch, PhD, and Judy Bowers, co-authors of the *ASCA National Model: A Framework for School Counseling Programs,* were paid no royalties for their work. They wrote the document as a gift to the profession. ASCA recommended the citing as (ASCA, 2003) to promote "One Vision, One Voice" within the profession.

counselors? School counseling programs based on the national model are designed to ensure every student receives the benefits of the program. Historically, many professional school counselors spent 80% of their time responding to the needs of 20% of their students (i.e., high achieving or high risk). The ASCA national model recommends 80% of the professional school counselor's time be spent in direct service to all students so every student receives the program benefits.

The ASCA national model incorporates school counseling content standards and competencies for every student. These content standards serve as the foundation for the program and focus the direction for an organized, planned, sequential, and flexible school counseling curriculum. The model uses disaggregated data to drive program and activity development, thus enabling professional school counselors to design interventions to meet the needs of all students and to close the gap between specific groups of students and their peers. The model emphasizes an organizational framework and accountability system to determine how well students have met the standards or have achieved intended outcomes. The school counseling program reduces confusion, aligns goals and objectives with the school's mission, and ultimately leads to student achievement, as demonstrated by results data.

The ASCA national model serves as a template for the development of a school counseling program; it is not meant for exact replication. Because attention to local demographic needs and political conditions is necessary for effective school counseling program development, the ASCA national model is meant to integrate with and adapt to the school's current program. There is no one "ideal program" that can or should be used as a "cookie-cutter" approach throughout the nation. Rather, ASCA's goal was to provide professional school counselors with an institutionally consistent document as the framework of a comprehensive school counseling program.

Leadership skills are critical to the successful implementation of new or remodeled programs at the school, district, and state levels. Professional school counselors are change agents, collaborators, and advocates. As professional school counselors become proficient in retrieving and analyzing school data to improve student success, they ensure educational equity for every student. Using strong communication, consultation, and political skills, professional school counselors collaborate with other professionals in the school building to influence systemic change and advocate for every student.

The second edition of the ASCA model was released in 2005. Very few changes were made to the original content; most were made to improve clarity and to correct typographical errors. ASCA inserted a new appendix section written by Dr. Patricia Henderson entitled "The Theory behind the ASCA National Model" to provide readers with additional rationale and background information.

The Third Edition of the ASCA National Model

The third edition of the ASCA national model was revised by ASCA and released in 2012. ASCA members were also invited to provide public comment, after which ASCA released the model during the annual conference in 2012. The third edition of the ASCA national model contained many important changes for school counselors and others supporting the implementation of the ASCA model (e.g., counselors educators and administrators) of which to be aware. These will be described in detail below. The third edition clearly eliminates the word "guidance lesson" and replaces it with "core curriculum." This move aligns with a strong shift by many professionals in the field to eliminate the terminology *guidance counselors, guidance programs,* and *guidance curriculum* in favor of *school counselors, school counseling programs,* and *core curriculum* or *school counseling core curriculum* as common appropriate terminologies.

The 2012 ASCA model provides the strongest language to date regarding the use of data, which is mentioned 124 times in the 161-page document (ASCA, 2012a). The newly revised model incorporates language from the most recent revision of the ethical standards (ASCA, 2010), stressing the responsibility of school counselors to use equity-based data to identify, address, and resolve attainment, achievement, and opportunity gaps. The terms "gap" or "gaps" are mentioned 60 times. Finally, the ASCA model's focus on results (124 mentions) and accountability (48 mentions) is irrefutable. Clearly, ASCA members must understand and answer the question: *How are students different as a result of the school counseling program?*

ASCA Components

The order of the components has been revised from Foundation, Delivery, Management, and Accountability to Foundation, Management, Delivery, and Accountability. Shifts in each component area and detailed explanations of changes are provided below.

Foundation

The Foundation component has been expanded to include three sections: Program Focus, Student Competencies, and Professional Competencies. The Foundation component asks professional school counselors to develop a mission statement that connects school counseling to the school building or district's mission (Hatch & Bowers, 2002). Embedded in every mission statement are the standards and competencies that support student achievement, success in school, and school improvement. School counselors also engage stakeholders in a collaborative school-wide effort that looks at data to identify student needs as the *foundation* for the comprehensive school counseling program (Stone & Dahir, 2004).

The Program Focus keeps the beliefs item of the prior versions, adds a new vision statement, keeps the mission statement, and adds the new item Program Goals. The philosophy is now incorporated into the beliefs and vision. Setting program goals has been added as a new topic in the foundation component of the ASCA national model (2012a). Although prior versions encouraged goal setting through the use of action plans, the third edition increases this focus of goal setting by including a SMART goals example for developing program goals through the use of data.

The Student Competencies section now includes both the ASCA student standards (formerly the ASCA national standards) as well as other student standards, such as state standards and the National Career Development Guidelines. Finally, the new Professional Competencies include the new ASCA school counselor competencies (ASCA, 2012b) and the ASCA *Ethical Standards for School Counselors* (2010a).

Management System

The Management component previously listed the Use-of-Time, Management Agreements, Advisory Council, Use of Data, Action Plans and Calendars as separate topics on the ASCA

Model graphic. These topics are now included in a new graphic under the two sections: Assessments and Tools.

The *Assessments* section contains three items: (a) the new School Counselor Competencies Assessment tool based on the ASCA school counselor competencies which are contained in the Foundation component; (b) the revised School Counseling Program Assessment (formerly called the Program Audit in the Accountability section) was condensed and revised to align with the third edition; and (c) the new Use-of-Time Assessment was created to align with the new language and approach to implementing the Delivery component (direct and indirect services, program management and fair-share responsibilities).

The *Tools* section contains six items: (a) the Annual Agreement (a renamed Management Agreement); (b) the Advisory Council with additional directions to meet at least two times a year; (c) Calendar (annual and weekly) Templates; (d) the new School Data Profile; (e) Action Plans (including a new Closing the Gap Action Plan); and (f) Curriculum Lesson Plan (a new addition).

The new Annual Agreement, revised to address a concern in some states that the term "management" became "complicated" for some states, now includes a space for the mission statement and program goals (ASCA, 2012a). The recommendations for use of time and for when the advisory council meet are included in the template. One important shift in the Annual Agreement is referencing the previous years' results report when developing the annual calendar and action plan. Space is provided for assignments of professional collaborations and responsibilities, budget requirements, office organization (including hours of operation), and clarity for roles of other support service providers. A lesson plan template was added to the third edition. It includes the ASCA student standards used to guide the lesson and provides space for indicating types of data that will be collected.

The third edition of the ASCA national model eliminated the term "achievement-related" and now calls for achievement, attendance, behavior, and school safety data. Behavioral data is defined as "those fields the literature has shown to be correlated to academic achievement" (ASCA, 2012a, p. 50). The term "outcomes" was used instead of "results" to provide a distinction between the results obtained from perception data (pre-post) and results obtained from a change in student behavior or achievement.

The earlier editions of the ASCA national model (ASCA, 2003a, 2005) called for two action plans: guidance curriculum and closing-the-gap. The third edition of the ASCA national model revised the language to core curriculum action plans and added a small group action plan to provide an increased focus on using data to design and evaluate small groups (ASCA, 2012a). The distinction between the Small Group Action Plan and the Closing the Gap Action Plan in the ASCA national model is that the Closing the Gap Action Plan is designed to address equity issues or discrepancies in behavior or academic data between students of different *demographic* groups. In this case, it would be discrepancies between groupings that are attending, behaving, or performing, and those that are not.

Delivery

The new edition has adapted the traditional Gysbers' delivery system in the original ASCA National Model (2003a, 2005), guidance curriculum, individual student planning, responsive services, and system support, into two sections: direct student services and indirect student services. These are further divided into elements and strategies, and recipients and methods.

Methods are divided into interaction "with" students (direct) and those that happen with others "for" students (indirect).

Core curriculum, individual student planning, and responsive services are direct services provided in large group, classroom, small group, and through individual methods directly to and with students. Standards and competency-based curriculum (previously referred to as guidance curriculum) providing students with the knowledge, attitudes and skills appropriate for their developmental level is now referred to as the School Counseling Core Curriculum. Individual Student Planning calls for ongoing systemic activities to ensure students establish goals and plans for the future. Responsive Services are designed to meet the immediate needs of students. Indirect student services provided on behalf of students include activities such as consulting and collaborating with teachers, parents, and community organizations, and providing referrals on behalf of students to appropriate service providers for additional intervention.

In the third edition of the national model (ASCA, 2012a), direct services should compose 80% of the school counselors time, and 20% or less should compose indirect services, such as developing and assessing the foundation, management, and accountability components, and providing fair share responsibilities to support the school system. Previous use-of-time recommendations are considered optional, helpful suggestions, but not promoted as schools are encouraged to make program decisions based on students and site needs. System support, originally in the delivery component of the model has been removed and divided into other components (management and accountability).

Direct Student Services

Individual student planning. This direct service assists the individual student in establishing personal goals and developing future plans. The professional school counselor provides opportunities for students to plan, monitor, and evaluate their progress; learn to take ownership; and assume responsibility for their academic and affective learning and development. Students' activities might include goal setting; career planning; understanding, interpreting, and applying assessment information in a meaningful way to academic planning; postsecondary planning; and course selection. Individual planning should also include parental involvement and provide multiple opportunities to personalize the educational experience. Through the individual planning process, students can set academic, career, or behavioral goals and develop a pathway to realize their dreams. Individual planning documents the achievement of specific competencies that will ultimately support every student's attainment of the national standards. The use of data can present a picture of the struggles and achievements of individual students and groups of students.

Responsive services. Traditional training of professional school counselors, both pre-service and in-service, predominantly focused on interventions for mental health problems. Until recently, many school personnel believed this was the primary orientation for counselors in schools. In a comprehensive school counseling model, responsive services are much broader than individualized interventions for at-risk students. Nearly all students are at risk for academic difficulties at some time during their school careers. The responsive services component consists of activities designed to meet the immediate needs of students. These can consist of individual and group counseling, consultation, referral to community agencies, and crisis intervention and management. The impetus for response and intervention is often dominated by presenting student issues, school building and faculty concerns, parental trepidations, and community matters. Data paint a clear picture of a school and its students, thereby depicting a vivid representation of the successes and failures in school buildings and systems. Responsive services that are data based can address issues such as peer pressure, resolving conflict, family relationships, personal identity issues, substance abuse, motivation, and achievement concerns. Responsive services can be delivered in a direct (e.g., individual counseling, group counseling) or indirect (e.g., consultation, outside referral) manner and facilitate growth and development in academic, career, and personal–social development.

School counseling core curriculum. Professional school counselors provide developmental and sequential information, knowledge, and skills about academic, career, and personal–social development that are frequently delivered through large-group meetings, which offer opportunities to provide guidance to the largest number of students in a school. Usually, professional school counselors first work with students in large groups, when appropriate, because it is the most efficient use of time. Professional school counselors and teachers in classrooms or advisory groups deliver the core school counseling curriculum to students through the use of organized activities. The activities and lessons give attention to particular developmental issues or areas of concern in the school building or district. Professional school counselors regularly partner with teachers and other members of the school community to deliver the school counseling curriculum. This collaborative effort is intended to assure each student achieves specific competencies that will ultimately support attainment of the national standards.

Indirect Services

The coordination of services involves planning and connecting activities and services to the national standards and the goals of the counseling program in the school. For example, hosting an advisory committee helps to inform the direction of the program and provides a sounding board for discussion about what is working, what needs to change, and how the comprehensive school counseling program can better support student success.

Effective professional school counselors possess the attitudes, knowledge, and skills to effectively provide both the direct and indirect components of a comprehensive school counseling program. Direct services, which usually target students, typically include individual counseling, small-group counseling, and classroom guidance. Indirect services include the management of resources, consultation, collaboration and teaming, advocacy, and the coordination of services, and are essential to affect systemic change and support the "new vision" of school counseling (Erford, 2015c). In all instances, student growth and development is monitored by the achievement of competencies, which ultimately result in the attainment of the nine national standards. As a result, professional school counselors can clearly connect their work to the purpose of school and contribute to student success and achievement.

Accountability

The final component, Accountability, has replaced the topic of Results Reports with five topics in three sections. The first section, Data Analysis includes the new School Data Profile analyzing process, perception and outcome (previously referred to as results) data, and the Use-of-Time Analysis Template. The second section, Program Results, includes the Curriculum Results Report analysis and the Small Group Results Report Analysis.

The Evaluation and Improvement section includes the analysis tool for the new School Counselor Competencies Assessment. Originally called the Program Audit, the newly designed School Counseling Program Assessment (now located in the Management component) has an analysis tool located in the Accountability component. This section also includes a new School Counselor Performance Appraisal Template designed to assist in the development, delivery, management, and accountability of the school counseling program and an analysis tool for the School Counseling Program Goals.

ASCA Model Themes

The ASCA (2012a) model themes are presented in more detail in the third edition. Different guest authors address each theme, along with several special topics

Other Changes

System support, now removed from the delivery component and essentially divided or embedded into other components (management and accountability), has often been misunderstood as referring to "non-counseling" assignments in schools, such as hall monitoring, class coverage, or bus duty. In actuality, system support was intended to refer to when school counselors provide ongoing support to their own professional development, their programs, and the school environment, and when they perform activities such as organize, deliver, manage, and evaluate the comprehensive school counseling program. System support also includes fair-share responsibilities provided by the school counselor, opportunities to facilitate discussions about school improvement, examining data that may be affecting the success of students, attending to professional development, and providing in-service activities for the faculty.

Contemporary Challenges and Opportunities Continue

Many recent initiatives have forced educators to rethink and reinvent expectations and outcomes: the school improvement and accountability movement, standards-based education, high-stakes testing, achievement gap issues of equity and access, an increase in legislation supporting student retention, the funding of new programs through block grants, getting all students college and career ready, the use of technology and data to drive decisions and affect change, school safety issues, and the movement from an educational culture of entitlement to one of performance. School counselors, just like every other educator, cannot focus on how hard they work or how well meaning they are; they must continually strive to answer their stakeholders' questions: How are students achieving and succeeding as a result of the school counseling program? How can school counselors use data to become more efficient and effective? How will school counselors partner in reform movements to ensure their program is integral to the total educational program and create outcomes supporting student success?

In a recently released Action Brief, the education organization *Achieve* charged school counselors with recognizing their responsibility to assist in the transformation of schools through the strong implementation of the Common Core State Standards (CCSS; Achieve, 2013). Calling on school counselors to take an "active role" in working with school leaders to support shifts in cultural and instructional environments, the Action Brief offers several recommendations. School counselors need to increase awareness regarding their role in implementing CCSS, understand how schools must change, and understand how the new standards will affect the academic, career, and personal–social domains of school counseling. As uniquely positioned professionals, school counselors are further charged to support and take action on the new CCSS (Hatch, 2014). Action steps for alignment with the ASCA national model (2012a) are recommended in several specific areas, including those for instructional practice:

- Determine the impact of the CCSS on systemic approaches to help students develop appropriate education plans.
- Develop and continually update 6-year individual student educational (learning) plans for every student relating to college- and career-readiness.
- Develop college- and career-readiness lesson plans that align with CCSS college- and career-ready anchor standards, and reinforce subject-specific standards.
- Develop a calendar for when lessons will be conducted and push into classrooms.
- Prepare to present and/or share the action plan for ensuring that all students have a completed and up-to-date Individualized Education Plan (Achieve, 2013).

Recent White House Initiatives are calling for school counselors to support college and career readiness for all students, particularly first generation and low-income students. In the midst of these calls to action, school counselors are called again to shift their program in new directions; to imagine new content, outcomes, and competencies; and develop new ways to coordinate and collaborate with their school staff to seamlessly implement their programs and services. ASCA has recently announced the impending release of the new ASCA student standards.

The future of school counseling is uncertain. After 100 years of marginalization and efforts to operationally legitimize a profession, only time will tell if the ASCA national model and the new ASCA student standards will move the profession closer to accomplishing this vital and daunting task. Research supporting the efficacy of model school counseling programs is vital. A recent National Summit on School Counseling Research was held to begin these conversations. In addition, the National Panel for Evidenced-Based School Counseling Practices is working to design the parameters for research in the field of school counseling by reviewing the research base, determining which practices are evidence based, and identifying areas in which additional research is needed. The goal is to improve the available research within the profession to validate evidenced-based programs and practices. Citing evidenced-based practices is necessary not only for program improvement but also to advocate at the local, state, and national levels for legislation to support and promote school counseling programs.

Summary/Conclusion

Recent school improvement agendas, the No Child Left Behind Act of 2001, and Race to the Top (2010), were intended to close the achievement gap between disadvantaged students and other groups of students. Additionally, the charge of this present decade is for all students to graduate from high school college and career ready. This has presented yet another opportunity for professional school counselors and school counseling programs to vocalize strategies and create meaningful conversations among professional school counselors, school administrators, teachers, parents, and representatives of businesses and communities about expectations for students' academic success and the role of counseling programs in supporting and enhancing student learning (Carey, Dimmit, & Hatch, 2007; Dahir et al., 1998). As powerful allies in school improvement, professional school counselors can document and demonstrate their contribution to student growth and learning, thus supporting the national goals to improve results for every student. The ASCA national standards and the ASCA national model have paved the way for professional school counselors of today to advocate for change and continuous improvement within the profession to help our students succeed in the complex globally connected world of the 21st century.

CHAPTER 13

Data-Driven School Counseling

Carolyn B. Stone and Carol A. Dahir

Preview

In this chapter, we emphasize the powerful influence and impact that using data has on both school counseling practice and programs. In this age of accountability, school counselors must not be left behind. Data-driven school counseling demonstrates the powerful contributions of school counselors to the school success agenda, to successful outcomes for students, and to the goals of school improvement.

The American School Counselor Association (ASCA; 2012a), The Education Trust (1999), Lapan, Gysbers, and Kayson (2006), and countless other leaders in the school counseling field have given the profession accountability: the means and mechanism that enhances school counselor credibility. In the last decade, significant research has demonstrated the positive impact accountability has on student success. Schools with comprehensive school counseling programs have contributed to student success (Carey & Dimmitt, 2012; Erford, 2015c; Lapan, Gysbers, & Kayson, 2006). Accountability has become the cog in the machinery that school counselors use to show how their work advantages students, and it has become more commonplace to find student impact results in the literature.

The *ASCA National Model* (ASCA, 2012a) aligns the school counseling program with the mission of schools, and school counseling has taken a central position in the student's academic success. Data informs and challenges school counselors' thinking and is critical to setting annual priorities for program delivery. Accountability illuminates areas in which systemic change is needed, confirms progress, and reveals shortcomings in student performance (Stone & Dahir, 2011). Closely examining critical data elements in the areas of attendance, socioeconomic impact on class enrollment, graduation and postsecondary planning rates, and standardized testing results not only identify the needs of students but also the school- and system-wide issues that affect success. The resonating question for the school counselor of today is "*How are students different [better off] as a result of what school counselors do*" (ASCA, 2012a, p. 59)? By using data, professional school counselors can present a picture of positive changes in student data and the school counselor practices that have led to higher levels of student success (Dahir & Stone, 2003; Young & Kaffenberger, 2009).

Disaggregating data by variables such as ethnicity, gender, socioeconomic status, or teacher assignment is important in the analysis of student performance. The disaggregation of data makes it possible to determine how policy and practices affect issues of equity. It is now possible to more closely examine which groups of students are successful and which are not.

Using data enables professional school counselors to work closely with building administrators and faculty to close the opportunity, information, intervention, and achievement gaps. Professional school counselors who focus their efforts on moving data in a positive direction demonstrate a strong commitment to sharing the responsibility and accountability for student outcomes. In this chapter, we will address the powerful ways that data can inform a comprehensive school counseling program, organized around seven themes:

1. A Data-Driven Program Initiates a Powerful Comprehensive Program
2. A Data-Driven Program Focuses Our Efforts
3. A Data-Driven Program Affects Student Achievement
4. A Data-Driven Program Supports School, System, and National Improvement Goals
5. A Data-Driven Program Shares Accountability
6. A Data-Driven Program Helps Identify Effective Strategies and Stakeholders
7. A Data-Driven Program Identifies and Rectifies Issues That Stratify Student Opportunities

A Data-Driven Program Initiates a Powerful Comprehensive Program

The comprehensive model is a planned and intentional system to design, develop, implement, and evaluate a school counseling program (Gysbers & Henderson, 2012). Comprehensive school counseling is intended to be similar to other programs in education and includes student outcomes or competencies, activities to achieve the desired results, a system of organization, and specific suggestions as to program delivery.

The ASCA national model (2012a) requires school counselors to use key school-based disaggregated data as the driving force for program and activity development; professional school counselors use the data to design interventions to meet the needs of all students as well as intentionally close the gap between specific groups of students and their peers. The ASCA national model suggests starting with the Foundation component, moving to Management, then Delivery, and then Accountability. For some professional school counselors, developing a comprehensive program can be overwhelming or seem too complicated. We suggest that school counselors can develop a school counseling program by starting with the data. Without data, a comprehensive school counseling program will result in loosely held together components that may be unrelated. Data can be instrumental in evaluating a comprehensive school program, but data can also be the first step in initiating a comprehensive school counseling program. The process of developing a comprehensive program begins with a piece of critical data that needs improvement. To demonstrate this, let us work through an example using discipline referrals as the critical data element.

Beginning With Data: A Discipline Referral Example

Discipline referrals were identified by the school principal on the school improvement plan as an area in need of attention. The professional school counselor, along with other educators, disaggregated the discipline referrals to achieve a better understanding of the problem. The disaggregated data revealed that discipline referrals occurred in every grade level, but they were concentrated in the fourth and fifth grades, especially during lunch, and mostly on Mondays. Rather than separately gathering all the pieces of a comprehensive program to address this issue, the professional school counselor could start with the data element *discipline referrals* and the knowledge gained by looking at the disaggregated data to start to put into place the specific components that are needed, including direct responsive services, individual student planning, and the school counseling core curriculum to move the critical piece of data. The task of beginning to develop a comprehensive program is bite-sized, doable, and generates a good start based on an important school need. Professional school counselors can focus on both the data component (data) and the delivery system without feeling overwhelmed by trying to do everything at once. The focus then becomes what specific interventions in the following areas might be needed for a reduction in discipline referrals.

Foundation. The *foundation* of the program requires the implementation of the belief and mission that every student will benefit from the school counseling program. This component connects the professional school counselor's work to the school's mission by supporting a safer, more respectful school environment and by focusing efforts on reducing the discipline referrals. The foundation also facilitates student development in three broad domains—academic, career, and personal–social development—to promote and enhance the learning process. Using focused strategies to reduce discipline referrals allows work in all three domains.

ASCA national standards and competencies. These elements define the knowledge, attitudes, or skills students should obtain or demonstrate as a result of participating in a school counseling program. Developing in students the skills, attitudes, and knowledge to discontinue or to avoid discipline problems meets the competencies of the ASCA national standards (ASCA, 2004).

Delivery. The *delivery system* defines the implementation process and the ways of delivering the ASCA national model (e.g., school counseling core curriculum, individual student planning, and responsive services). This component encourages school counselors to provide both direct services to students and indirect services for the benefit of students.

School counseling core curriculum. The core curriculum can be developed as the professional school counselor starts to address a focused need. For example, as the professional school counselor works to reduce discipline referrals, he or she may deliver classroom lessons in areas such as helping students respect themselves, understanding diversity, and using bully-proofing strategies. The school counseling core curriculum is designed to assist students in achieving the knowledge and skills that are appropriate for the students' developmental level (ASCA, 2004).

Individual planning with students. The professional school counselor will work in an intentional way to help students understand the interrelationship between school and their future. This is one way the individual planning component assists individual students in establishing personal goals, developing future plans, and making better choices in school that do not include office visits for misbehavior.

Responsive services. With discipline issues as the data-driven focus, the professional school counselor will develop and focus responsive services to meet the immediate needs of students. These needs require individual and group counseling, consultation, referral, conflict resolution, and peer mediation (ASCA, 2012a).

Indirect services. Oftentimes, a whole-school effort is required to create a respectful school climate. School counselors work closely with classroom teachers, administrators, parents, and community organizations to provide services that will help achieve the goal.

Management system. The *management system* presents the organizational processes and tools needed to deliver a comprehensive school counseling program, including mutual planning agreements, use of data, action plans for the core curriculum and closing the gap, and time and task analysis. By disaggregating the data, the professional school counselor is able to understand who the multiple discipline offenders are and become aware of the types of offenses. This helps the professional school counselor to monitor students' progress in order to ensure that each student receives what is needed to achieve success in school. In this example, student discipline data is carefully monitored. However, due to a strong correlation between behavior and achievement, other areas including student achievement data and standards and competency-related data is reviewed. Collection, analysis, and interpretation of student achievement data may be systemic by district or be specific to a school site, grade, class, or individual (Stone & Dahir, 2011).

Accountability system. The *accountability system* helps professional school counselors demonstrate the effectiveness of their work in measurable terms, such as impact over time, performance evaluation, and a program audit. The use of data to affect change within the school system is integral to ensuring that every student receives the benefits of the school counseling program. Professional school counselors must show that each activity implemented as part of the program was developed from a careful analysis of students' needs, achievement, and related data (ASCA, 2012a).

Action plans. By joining with other stakeholders, the professional school counselor can develop an action plan to achieve the desired result (Stone & Dahir, 2011).

Use of data. A comprehensive school counseling program is data driven. The use of data to affect change within the school system is integral to ensuring that every student receives the benefits of the school counseling program. Professional school counselors must show that each activity implemented as part of the program was developed from a careful analysis of students' needs, achievement, and related data (ASCA, 2012a).

A Data-Driven Program Focuses Our Efforts

When professional school counselors focus their efforts on the mission of school improvement, they widen educational opportunities for every student and positively affect student achievement by

- raising student aspirations;
- helping students acquire resiliency and coping skills for school and life success;

- managing and accessing resources for student support;
- collaborating with faculty to share the responsibility for student progress;
- engaging students in educational and career planning that present students with a wide variety of quality postsecondary opportunities; and
- working intentionally toward closing the gap in student performance.

Professional school counselors who embrace a leadership mindset also act on their beliefs and advocate for the removal of institutional and environmental barriers which impede student success. As advocates advancing a social justice agenda, professional school counselors purposely promote equitable access to quality education for all students. Counselor behaviors begin with a commitment to a programmatic approach that is systemic in impact; grounded in social justice; driven by advocacy and equity; aligned with the state, system, and building mission; and collaboratively developed and delivered.

Social advocacy implies questioning the *status quo* and challenging the rules and regulations that decrease opportunities for the underrepresented. Today, we are reminded that "equity means giving students what they need to ensure they have the academic preparation and social capital necessary to remove the racial/ethnic predictability in K–12 and postsecondary educational outcomes" (National Office for School Counselor Advocacy, 2012, p. 1). The American free public school system is a mechanism that should guarantee students from all segments of society an equal chance to develop their talents and achieve success.

Professional school counselors can collect and analyze student data to inform and guide the development of a comprehensive school counseling program based upon school-wide issues. Critical data elements can usually be found on the school's district or building report card. School systems routinely collect and store academic and demographic data in a retrievable form, and professional school counselors have ready access to data in areas that contribute to achievement such as course enrollment patterns and attendance. For example, if a counselor learns that the ninth-grade retention rate is 40%, this is information that can be used to inform and influence this area as an identified need for attention and strategies.

Data help professional school counselors identify the institutional or environmental barriers that may be adversely influencing the data elements and impeding student achievement. Professional school counselors can initially determine which elements to tackle first and which elements can be moved in a positive direction by the school counseling program. A quick look at data alone does not tell the whole story. It is important to disaggregate the critical data elements on which you are focusing in a variety of ways to ensure that the system addresses access and equity issues. When the school-based data is disaggregated by ethnicity, gender, race, socioeconomic status, or teacher assignment, it is possible to identify institutional and environmental barriers impeding student success. Disaggregated data also identifies specific groups of students that professional school counselors can target to ensure that no one is barred from any opportunity (Stone & Turba, 1999).

A Data-Driven Program Affects Student Achievement

The professional school counselor assesses the effectiveness of his/her program in having an impact on students' academic, career and personal/social development through accountability measures especially examining efforts to close achievement, opportunity and attainment gaps (ASCA, 2010a, A.9.g).

The American School Counselor Association's (ASCA) national standards for school counseling programs (ASCA, 2004), the ASCA national model (ASCA, 2003a, 2005, 2012a), and the ASCA *Ethical Standards for School Counselors* (ASCA, 2010a) emphasize the importance of professional school counselors delivering accountable school counseling programs that carefully consider local demographic needs and the political climate of the community.

The ASCA national model (ASCA, 2012a) speaks to the importance of having an accountability system and an organizational framework that documents and demonstrates how students are different as a result of the school counseling program. A commitment to accountability shifts public perception from questions such as *"What do professional school counselors really do?"* to demonstrating that professional school counselors are key players in the academic success story for students and partners in student achievement.

When counselors work with data, they are contributing to each of these critical elements and bringing attention to student progress and results. Professional school counselors can positively affect student achievement by

- working with students to increase their desire to access rigorous academic work;
- motivating students and raising aspirations;
- managing and accessing resources to help students succeed;
- ensuring every student has an educational and career plan;
- encouraging students to achieve good attendance; and
- presenting students with a wide array of postsecondary opportunities.

Professional school counselors who address improving student results will contribute to raising the achievement level for every student. By examining their practice and looking carefully at their way of working, professional school counselors can articulate and communicate how their contributions positively affect student achievement and thus share accountability for school improvement with other members of the faculty. Partnership with education professionals demonstrates a willingness to improve results and to help to close the achievement gap that exists among students of color or students of poverty. Measurable success resulting from a concerted effort on the part of professional school counselors to expand educational opportunities can be documented by an increased number of students completing school with the academic preparation, career awareness, and the personal–social growth that is essential when choosing from a wide range of substantial postsecondary options, including college. Aligning the purpose of the school counseling program with the school improvement plan presents professional school counselors as champions and collaborators who encourage high aspirations and create opportunities for students to realize their dreams.

A comprehensive school counseling program, such as proposed by the ASCA national model (2012a), when aligned with the educational enterprise, is data driven, proactive, and preventive in focus and assists students in acquiring and applying lifelong learning skills. Professional school counselors can advocate for the academic success for every student while delivering the content of the school counseling program in a comprehensive and accountable manner.

A Data-Driven Program Supports School, System, and National Improvement Goals

The No Child Left Behind Act of 2001 (NCLB) was a clear imperative for professional school counselors to accept the responsibility to support academic achievement, share the pressures of school accountability, and demonstrate advocacy for every student to experience success. Traditionally, professional school counselors were not held to the same accountability standards as other educators. They were rarely included in conversations about contributions that affect the critical data elements that are publicly displayed on school report cards. In a climate of school improvement, it has become increasingly important for professional school counselors to play a proactive role in identifying and responding to the issues, policies, and practices that stratify student opportunity and inhibit access to equitable educational opportunities.

Accountability, as defined in NCLB, offers an opportunity for professional school counselors to significantly affect school improvement through targeted interventions that affect important school-based data. Professional school counselors are in a unique position to review data in schools and can identify the gaps that exist in student success. Professional school counselors, using their leadership and advocacy skills, ensure that appropriate resources and programs are in place to offer each student equitable access to a challenging curriculum and all options to access postsecondary opportunities. Professional school counselors can influence the school climate to ensure that high standards are the norm in a safe and respectful environment. Professional school counselors, working together with the school administrators, can focus faculty attention on the importance of creating safe and drug-free communities.

> *Together, we must achieve a new goal, that by 2020, the United States will once again lead the world in college completion. We must raise the expectations for our students, for our schools, and for ourselves—this must be a national priority. We must ensure that every student graduates from high school well prepared for college and a career.*
> —President Barack Obama, March 2010, Blueprint for Reform, p. 1

The U.S. agenda for school improvement continues to progress. The Race to the Top initiative (U.S. Department of Education, 2011) has presented more opportunities for school counselors to support the national agenda to ensure all students are college and career ready!

At the district and building level, stakeholders may no longer be asking *"What do counselors do?"* but rather *"How did the conflict resolution program reduce bullying incidents?"* and *"Did the chronic offenders who are frequently suspended benefit from weekly group counseling?"* Professional school counselors have always supported a student's personal and emotional needs and helped students acquire coping and resiliency skills to stay focused and succeed academically. Looking back at the example scenario presented earlier in this chapter about discipline problems, the greater opportunity for school counselors is to demonstrate how the conflict resolution program contributed to improved school climate, reduced discipline referrals, or improved attendance—all of which contribute to academic success. For example, when a professional school counselor delivers targeted interventions in collaboration with classroom teachers for seven chronic offenders who were frequently suspended, and the suspension rate is reduced, the work of the professional school counselor contributes to the goals of school improvement. When monthly conflict resolution lessons are delivered in collaboration with the seventh-grade teacher teams and a documented reduction in fighting is noted, the data show the contribution to school climate and school improvement.

Professional school counselors are at risk of being viewed as ancillary in the climate of high property tax assessments that support school funding and high stakes testing that is the current barometer of adequate yearly progress. In the past, some school counseling programs have been perceived to be a fiscally irresponsible and ineffective use of resources by some policy makers, school boards, and school system leaders who are held accountable for increasing student achievement (Whiston, 2002). Professional school counselor accountability is a commitment to affecting the key data elements that publicly demonstrate a school's success and the achievement of all of its students.

The Race to the Top agenda (USDOE, 2011) challenges the beliefs and attitudes of every educator to support all students' achievement of high standards. Professional school counselors who purposely promote equitable access to quality education for all students and use data to advance a social justice agenda are key contributors to advancing the national, state, and system goals to improve our schools and close the opportunity gap.

A Data-Driven Program Shares Accountability

Professional school counselors have traditionally offered process data (Gysbers & Henderson, 2012) or a numerical summary of the types of activities they have delivered, how often and to how many, as a means of assessing and evaluating the impact of a school counseling program. Merely presenting the numbers of students seen individually, in groups, or in classrooms is no longer enough; time and task analysis does not show any progress toward affecting student achievement. Sharing accountability for school improvement requires professional school counselors—as it does all educators—to systematically collect, analyze, and use critical data elements to understand, contribute to, and eliminate the achievement gap. When the school counseling program is aligned with the educational enterprise, it is data informed, proactive and preventive in focus; it assists students in acquiring and applying lifelong learning skills and is delivered in a comprehensive and accountable manner (Stone & Dahir, 2011). Professional school counselor accountability involves collaboration with all education professionals to ensure that every student has access to a quality education and opportunity to meet high standards of achievement.

Accountability offers the opportunity for professional school counselors to demonstrate how they can effectively identify and rectify issues that impede student achievement, contribute to each of these critical data elements, and bring attention to student progress and results. Sharing accountability for student success has become a driving force for transforming and reframing the work of school counselors (ASCA, 2012a; Erford, 2015c; Gysbers & Henderson, 2012; Sink, Akos, Turnbull, & Mvududu, 2008; Stone & Dahir, 2011).

A Data-Driven Program Helps Identify Effective Strategies and Stakeholders

Professional school counselors, as managers of resources, join existing groups of stakeholders (such as the school improvement team) or use their leadership skills to bring other stakeholders and resources together to create and implement an action plan. Professional school counselors identify stakeholders to become part of a team to address the movement of the critical data elements. Counselors should include all concerned members of the internal and external school community, secure their commitment, and determine who will bring them together. If possible, an existing school action committee can be used. Accountability for professional school counselors involves teaming and collaborating with other stakeholders and avoiding tackling issues in isolation, which can be accomplished by

- identifying the additional stakeholders from the internal and external school community,

- securing their commitment,
- working with the school leadership team to facilitate this process, and
- involving any existing committees to address the concerns around the critical data elements.

Strategies are developed by the counselor individually and in collaboration with others that will change systems as well as affect individual students and targeted groups of students. *Impacting systems* means: (a) replicating successful programs and interventions; (b) identifying barriers that adversely affect students' opportunities to be successful learners; and (c) developing strategies to:

- change policies, practices, and procedures;
- strengthen curriculum offerings;
- maximize the instructional program;
- enhance the school and classroom culture and climate;
- provide student academic support systems (e.g., safety nets);
- influence course enrollment patterns to widen access to rigorous academics;
- involve parents and other critical stakeholders (internal and external to the school);
- raise aspirations in students, parents, teachers, and the community; and
- change attitudes and beliefs about students and their abilities to learn.

Publicizing the results of an effective school counseling program to stakeholders is a vital step in the accountability model, and it is important to success because stakeholders will have a deeper understanding about the contributions of the school counseling program to student achievement. Professional school counselors will thus be seen as partners in school improvement and will have demonstrated a willingness to be accountable for changing critical data elements.

As an example, at Ribault High School in Jacksonville, Florida, using and monitoring data has focused professional school counselor efforts, and, in collaboration with all stakeholders in the middle feeder school and high school, all have shared responsibility for improving postsecondary admissions. Using and monitoring data clearly demonstrated the intentional focus of the school counseling program on improving the postsecondary admission rate. In 2014, 74% of the graduating class was accepted to enroll in college—a monumental leap from the less than 15% who even applied to college a decade earlier. This collaborative effort made the change happen, and the professional school counselors' commitment as key players in school improvement was well established and acknowledged. As the strategies delivered in K–12 positively moved this data forward, the measurable results showed how the school counseling program can work to increase the postsecondary admission rate through a focused, system-wide effort.

A Data-Driven Program Identifies and Rectifies Issues That Stratify Student Opportunities

Accountability shows that all educators, especially professional school counselors, intentionally and purposely act to close the achievement gap (Topdemir, 2013). If administrators, faculty, and all stakeholders truly believe that all children can learn and achieve, then professional school counselors, by their beliefs and behaviors, demonstrate their willingness to work side by side with colleagues. Professional school counselors form partnerships with principals and key stakeholders to embrace accountability and promote systemic change with the expressed purpose of furthering the academic success of every student (ASCA, 2012a; Hatch, 2014; Hubbard & Hands, 2011). With an accountable, data-driven school counseling program, professional school counselors are seen as powerful partners and collaborators in school improvement and essential to fulfilling the mission of every school. Accepting the challenge of accountability propels professional school counselors to fulfill the responsibility of removing barriers to learning and achievement and raise the level of expectations for all students—especially for whom little was traditionally expected.

Professional school counselors who work within an accountability framework can challenge the pervasive belief that socioeconomic status and color determine a young person's ability to learn. By acting as agents of school and community change, professional school counselors can create a climate in which access and support for quality and rigor is the norm. In doing so, underserved and underrepresented students have a chance at acquiring the education skills necessary to fully participate in the 21st-century economy.

Summary/Conclusion

Closing the gap in student performance is central to affecting systemic change. The use of demographic and performance data makes it possible for counselors to determine how policies and practices are affecting issues of equity. Student achievement data can be collected and analyzed systematically to inform and guide the development and construction of a school counseling program, based upon school-wide issues. Professional school counselors can initiate, develop, and coordinate prevention and intervention systems that are designed to improve the learning success for every student who is experiencing difficulty with challenging academic coursework. Viewing the world of schools through a data-driven perspective helps professional school counselors to act on their belief system and assume a leadership role in identifying and rectifying issues that affect every student's ability to achieve at expected levels.

CHAPTER 14

Comprehensive Developmental School Counseling Programs

Bradley T. Erford and Qi Shi*

Preview

School counseling is an ever-transforming field (Eschenauer & Chen-Hayes, 2005; Leuwerke, Walker, & Shi, 2009; McCurdy, 2003; Paisley, 2001; Paisley & Peace, 1995). Amidst the change in the field, comprehensive developmental school counseling programs have remained central to the work of professional school counselors (Green & Keys, 2001; Gysbers, 2001). In this chapter, we discuss components of comprehensive developmental school counseling programs, including mission, developmental approaches, diversity, student competencies, delivery systems, resources, and program evaluation.

Most professional school counselors are familiar with the phrase "comprehensive developmental school counseling program." Few, however, are able to clearly define it. This is understandable, given the variability and flexibility that exist in effective comprehensive developmental programs. In spite of this variability, effective programs do share some characteristics.

Gysbers and Henderson (2012) suggested that true comprehensive developmental school counseling programs complement the existing academic programs and are well integrated into a curriculum that supports the mission of the school and district. Comprehensive developmental programs also provide a full range of services, including counseling, referral, consultation, information, and assessment, which are implemented through a variety of delivery systems. Inherent in the provision of a full range of counseling services is the understanding that professional school counselors are pivotal to, but not the sole service providers of, a school counseling program Comprehensive developmental school counseling services are most effectively offered through a team approach (Erford, 2015c). Professional school counselors work in consultation and collaboration with guidance advisory committees; school staff (including teachers, resource teachers, principals, school psychologists, social workers, pupil personnel workers, nurses, secretaries, building services workers, and instructional assistants); parents, grandparents, and guardians; and community stakeholders (Gysbers & Henderson, 2012; Erford, 2015c).

---

*Special thanks to Dr. Cheryl Moore-Thomas for her outstanding contributions to the first two editions of this chapter.

School counseling programs are *developmental* in that they provide regular, systematic opportunities for students to achieve competencies that are focused on their growth and development (Gysbers & Henderson, 2012). Effective school counseling programs result from planned, sequential, flexible curricula that complement the academic curriculum and emphasize the life skills and experiences that all students need to become successful in school and adulthood. Further definition of comprehensive developmental school counseling was offered by Borders and Drury (1992), who suggested that comprehensive developmental school counseling programs are proactive, preventative, and aimed at helping all students acquire the knowledge, skills, self-awareness, and attitudes necessary for normal development. In order to determine if comprehensive developmental school counseling programs are in fact meeting these aims, student progress, program results, and other relevant data are collected, analyzed, and effectively used to make warranted program adjustments. Although it is important to understand what comprehensive developmental school counseling programs are doing, it is more important to understand the results of school counseling programs. The "so what" question, answered by results and perception data, is extremely significant for the viability of school counseling programs (American School Counselor Association [ASCA], 2012a); professional school counselors collaborate with others to answer this important question. In summary, comprehensive developmental school counseling programs:

- embody the school mission and philosophy;
- offer students proactive opportunities to learn the skills, knowledge, and attitudes that are necessary for healthy development;
- provide a full range of school counseling services, implemented through varied delivery systems;
- complement other school programs;
- involve advisory committees, school staff, parents, guardians, and community members;
- monitor and support student progress;
- collect and analyze process and results data; and
- evaluate and adjust program elements as warranted.

The ASCA National Model: A Framework for School Counseling Programs (ASCA, 2012a) provides a specific structure for comprehensive developmental school counseling programs. Because it is focused on the national education mission for improved student achievement, this data-driven model ensures access to appropriately rigorous education through the delivery of a systematic knowledge- and skill-based program for students in K–12 (ASCA, 2013b). In this chapter, we discuss the major components of comprehensive developmental school counseling programs and the ASCA national model in more depth.

Program Mission

School counseling programs are an integral component of the education environment (ASCA, 2013b). They are not isolated, stand-alone services or activities. All elements of the school counseling program are meant to support the educational mission of schools in ways that appreciate and facilitate students' development and academic achievement. To ensure that this occurs, professional school counselors work collaboratively with community stakeholders to create clear, concise, student-focused school counseling program mission statements that parallel the local school, district, and national vision of quality education while describing the distinctive purpose, vision, and contributions of school counseling (ASCA, 2013b; Baker & Cato, 2010). Relevant mission statements ground comprehensive developmental school counseling programs and affect and focus program planning, implementation, evaluation, and funding. Extraordinary leadership, advocacy, and courage are therefore required to create a bold and timely vision of school counseling programs that provide appropriate service and opportunities for all students (Dollarhide & Saginak, 2012; Mason, 2010; Shillingford & Lambie, 2010). The following examples of school counseling program mission statements highlight a student focus and appropriate, rigorous education for all.

> The mission of the Lakeside Elementary School Counseling Program is to enable all students to maximize their potential by providing guidance and counseling in the areas of academic, career, and personal–social development that recognizes and respects individual uniqueness and personal worth.

> The mission of the Edgemere Middle School Counseling Program is to help students become successful learners, responsible citizens, and full participants in a diverse and changing world.

> The school counseling program at Hillsdale High School is designed to empower all learners, regardless of individual differences, to lead responsible and fulfilling lives in the present and to make promising and productive linkages to the future.

Developmental Approach

The research and theoretical base for school counseling programs is largely found in the theory and practice of human development. Basically, developmental theory deals with the manner in which individuals change over time. The specific stages, characteristics, and contextual considerations of change are described in a variety of human development theories including, but not limited to, psychosocial development, cognitive development, ethnic identity development, moral development, spiritual development, and self-concept development. Gysbers and Henderson (2012) suggested that a human development approach has specific applicability to school counseling. Their conceptualization of life career development is depicted as "self-development over the lifespan through the integration of roles, settings, and events in a person's life" (p. 49).

Well-planned and well-executed school counseling programs help students gain the knowledge, skills, and attitudes that are necessary for the mastery of normal developmental tasks (Camizzi, Clark, Yacco, & Goodman, 2009). Research suggests that students functioning at high levels of development are better able to handle the tasks of living and learning (Borders & Drury, 1992; Paisley & Peace, 1995). These data appear to strongly support developmental school counseling programs. It is prudent, therefore, that professional school counselors and other school counseling program stakeholders appreciate, understand, and use the principles of human development theory. On a practical level, this process involves the identification and selection of age-appropriate tasks and challenges, which are sequentially organized within a school counseling program at each grade level.

Developmental Approach and Issues of Diversity

Professional school counselors must make certain that the foundational developmental theories of the comprehensive school counseling program are appropriate for *all* students. Professional school counselors ensure that school counseling programs meet the needs of students of all racial, ethnic, and socioeconomic backgrounds and that they serve all students, regardless of achievement level, gender, sexual orientation, family structure, language, or any other aspect of diversity (ASCA, 2009; Aydin, Bryan, & Duys, 2012). This task is challenging due to the rapidly increasing diversity in schools. From 2001 to 2011, the percentage of White student enrollment in prekindergarten through 12th grade in U.S. public schools decreased from 60% to 52% (National Center for Education Statistics, 2013). Population projections indicate that by 2050, the non-Hispanic White population will decline from 64.7% in 2010 to 46.3% in 2050 (Center for Public Education, 2012). The relevance, effectiveness, and ethical standing of comprehensive developmental school counseling programs are therefore dependent upon the critical alignment of culturally relevant developmental approaches and counseling services. The American School Counselor Association (2009) called on professional school counselors to "provide culturally sensitive counseling, consultation, and other services to promote student success; also collaborate with stakeholders to create a school climate that welcomes and appreciates the strengths and gifts of culturally diverse students" (p. 1); however, there are data which suggest all students, especially those of color and those from low socioeconomic statuses, are not receiving adequate services (Dervarics, 2011). Developmental principles cannot be blindly applied. Effective school counseling programs are built on developmental models that are applied and interpreted in the cultural context of students and their communities. To ensure that pertinent diversity aspects are appropriately reflected in the comprehensive developmental school counseling program, professional school counselors and other stakeholders should engage in professional development opportunities related to diversity, consult and collaborate with experts in cultural competence, and use tools like the *Multicultural Competence Checklist* (Holcomb-McCoy & Chen-Hayes, 2015) for self-assessment.

Program Benefits

One of the most valuable benefits of a comprehensive developmental school counseling program is that it provides professional school counselors with a rationale and framework for providing services to students (Erford, 2015c; Camizzi et al., 2009). Furthermore, comprehensive developmental programs move the work of professional school counselors from random, ancillary guidance activities that benefit a few students to focused, mission- and data-driven school counseling services and programs that benefit all students. The systemic, continuous nature of comprehensive developmental school counseling programs decreases the likelihood that needy students will go unserved or underserved while increasing the likelihood that all students will benefit from the developmental and preventative nature of school counseling programs (Studer, Diambra, Breckner, & Heidel, 2011). Clearly, students are the greatest benefactors of comprehensive developmental guidance programs, but the benefits to the entire school community cannot be overlooked. Comprehensive developmental school counseling programs benefit teachers and other educators, parents, and community stakeholders through the implementation of proactive, collaborative programs that provide continuous data regard-

Table 14.1 Terminology

Term	Definition
Competency:	Skill or ability
Domain:	Developmental area
Goal:	Broad statement of desired student achievement that embodies the mission and purpose of the institution or program
Indicator:	Specification or delineation of a student outcome
Objective:	Measurable evidence of students' skills, knowledge, or attitudes
Standard:	Statement of what students should know or be able to do, indicating a level or standard of expected performance

ing student development and performance in a variety of domains, including areas of academic achievement.

Program Competencies

An important initial step in developing a comprehensive developmental school counseling program is identifying student competencies. *Competencies* are the skills or abilities students are expected to acquire as a result of participating in the comprehensive developmental school counseling program. In determining and selecting appropriate competencies for a specific school population, professional school counselors should consult school district goals, needs assessment data, outcome data, professional research literature, and professional organizations' position statements. Table 14.1 provides a brief listing of current curricular terminology and definitions. *The ASCA National Model: A Framework for School Counseling Programs* (ASCA, 2012a) proposes student competencies grouped by the academic, career, and personal–social domains and provides accompanying standards. These resources assist professional school counselors in selecting the complement of competencies that best meets the needs of the students at each developmental level in a particular school community.

Selected student competencies must be further defined by outcomes and indicators, which assist the professional school counselor and other stakeholders in assessing student success. Careful consideration and articulation of "what success will look like" (e.g., evidence of the achievement of the competencies) goes a long way to support school counseling program accountability.

Selection of an appropriate competency, outcome, and indicator is demonstrated in the following example:

> The professional school counselor of a large urban elementary school, in consultation with the school counseling advisory committee, reviewed 2 years of school and district data which seemed to suggest that the local suspension rate increases significantly at the fourth-grade level. Qualitative data revealed that the suspensions were primarily due to student fights and verbal conflicts. These data were troubling, given the school and district's mission of success for all students. The professional school counselor, administrator, and school leadership team decided to address this

Table 14.2 Framework for Addressing Suspension Rates Through a Comprehensive Developmental School Counseling Program

Program Component	Content
School Goal:	Academic success for all students
Domain:	Personal–social
Standard:	Students will make decisions, set goals, and take necessary action to achieve goals (ASCA, 2012a)
Competency:	Self-knowledge application
Indicators:	Students will use a decision-making and problem-solving model
	Students will understand consequences of decisions and choices
	Students will know how to apply conflict resolution skills (ASCA, 2012a)
Objectives:	1. After participating in the school-wide classroom guidance unit on conflict resolution skills, 80% of the school's third-grade students will be able to apply conflict resolutions skills to a given hypothetical situation with 100% accuracy.
	2. Eighty percent of the targeted fourth-grade students, after having participated in small-group counseling on conflict resolution, will be able to identify the three steps of the problem-solving model.

concern through various school programs, including the comprehensive developmental school counseling program. Knowing that a critical step in developing a comprehensive developmental school counseling program is to select competencies that are aligned with institutional goals and data, and undergirded by sound culturally appropriate developmental principles, the professional school counselor used the ASCA national model (ASCA, 2012a) as a blueprint. The counselor incorporated the standards as part of the school counseling plan for the upcoming academic year and highlighted a framework (provided in Table 14.2) for beginning to address the school's troubling suspension rate.

Program Delivery System

Comprehensive developmental school counseling programs are delivered to students through many processes—some of which provide direct service to students; others, indirect. School counseling core curriculum, a *direct* process, consists of classroom lessons, interdisciplinary curricula, and school-wide activities. Individual student planning, another direct service, involves small-group and individual student appraisal and advisement regarding issues such as test results, career awareness, and course selection. Responsive counseling, the most frequently used delivery system, involves a host of counseling services and activities, including individual and group counseling, consultation, crisis counseling, and referral. ASCA suggested that professional school counselors spend 80% of their time in direct service to students through the delivery of a comprehensive developmental school counseling program (ASCA, 2013b).

System-support activities are *indirect* services that maintain and enhance the comprehensive developmental school counseling program. They are defined by the delivery of school counseling services through training and professional development, community outreach, advisory boards and councils, and program and total school management.

The professional school counselor and other stakeholders must select the most appropriate delivery process for each aspect of the comprehensive developmental school counseling program. Student needs determine the most appropriate delivery processes. For example, a group of ninth-grade students in one community may be served best by small-group counseling services that focus on body image and self-esteem, while the developmental needs, regarding the same topic, of a different ninth-grade community may most appropriately be met through an interdisciplinary classroom lesson that is developed and implemented by the professional school counselor and health education teacher. Program delivery systems clearly suggest that professional school counselors are central to the comprehensive developmental school counseling program, but they are not the entire school counseling program. The success of each delivery system is dependent on the support of the entire school community.

Program Resources

Human and financial resources undergird comprehensive developmental school counseling programs. Human resources for counseling programs include the leadership and service of the professional school counselor working in collaboration with students, teachers, administrators, other school staff, advisory committees, parents, and community members (Erford, 2015c; Gysbers & Henderson, 2012). Each has a role and responsibility regarding the development and implementation of effective counseling programs.

Financial resources include district and local dollars and in-kind services provided for school counseling programs. Budget restraints sometimes prohibit school counseling programs from receiving optimal levels of financial support. This demands that all individuals who are responsible for counseling programs engage in creative problem solving to meet the financial needs of programs. This problem solving could lead to advocacy and lobbying for full funding of school counseling and other educational programs; partnerships with community businesses; or the facilitation of school, community, and student-led fundraising activities.

Program Evaluation

Evaluation of comprehensive school counseling programs is an important, multifaceted process (Dimmitt, 2009; Erford, 2015c; Gysbers & Henderson, 2012), and ordinarily framed by at least two questions:

- Does the school have a written, comprehensive program that is fully implemented and aligned with district, state, and national standards?
- Does the program produce the intended outcomes?

Practical guidelines for conducting program evaluations are important and discussed in depth elsewhere (ASCA, 2012a; Dimmitt, 2009; Erford, 2015c; also, see Chapter 19). It is practical and highly desirable to connect program concerns to only one or two well-articulated questions to focus and manage evaluation. It may also work to ensure that the specific program component under evaluation is being fully and appropriately examined.

The school counseling program evaluation process is systematic, ongoing, and cyclical (Dimmitt, 2009; Erford, 2015c). It starts small and builds upon what the data suggest works. Successful methods and delivery processes are determined and replicated so that over time, necessary program refinements work to build a comprehensive developmental school counseling program that fully supports the school's mission and simultaneously meets the needs of all learners.

Effective evaluation always begins with the school's mission. The mission provides the basis from which meaningful, institution-specific assessment questions arise. These assessment questions lead to the determination of what evidence must be collected. Evidence can provide crucial information about program evaluation and program results.

Evidence can be derived from standardized or informal measures, student performances, or student products. Once evidence has been gathered, it must be interpreted. Conclusions can then be drawn regarding the counseling program's value, strengths, weaknesses, and outcomes, and program improvements can be made. As assessment information is used to prompt programmatic changes, goal setting and the posing of new questions begin again. Meaningful, thorough program evaluation provides professional school counselors with opportunities to collaborate with counselor educators, educational accountability experts, consultants, and other program evaluation experts. Collaboration, assessment questioning, data gathering and interpretation, and results reporting can be conducted in clear and practical ways that benefit students and the entire school community.

Important work regarding broad questions of comprehensive developmental school counseling program accountability has been conducted in studies on academic achievement (Carey, Harrington, Martin, & Stevenson, 2012; Sink, Akos, Turnbull, & Mvududu, 2008; Sink & Stroh, 2003; Wilkerson, Pérusse, & Hughes, 2013), student satisfaction (Lapan, Gysbers, & Petroski, 2003), and student preparation for the future (Carey et al., 2012; Lapan, Gysbers & Sun, 1997). Initial results data seem to suggest that comprehensive developmental school counseling programs are making a positive difference in students' lives (Carey & Dimmitt, 2012; Dimmitt & Wilkerson, 2012). This line of inquiry must continue, however, with carefully designed studies of what students know and can do as a result of comprehensive developmental school counseling programs (Brown & Trusty, 2005; Dimmit & Wilkerson, 2012).

Summary/Conclusion

Comprehensive developmental school counseling programs are vital to the work of today's professional school counselors. Rooted in developmental theory, comprehensive programs use well-selected student competencies, delivery systems, resources, and assessment processes to assist students in acquiring the culturally appropriate knowledge, skills, and attitudes needed for healthy development. As professional school counselors, administrators, teachers, parents, and others work together to design and implement comprehensive developmental school counseling programs, continual systematic movement is made toward the healthy development of all students.

CHAPTER 15

Needs Assessments: The Key to Successful and Meaningful School Counseling Programs

*Bradley T. Erford**

Preview

Needs assessments empower professional school counselors through data. By gathering the input of the school's stakeholders, professional school counselors gain the information necessary to create programs that truly reflect the unique needs of their community. In this chapter, the steps necessary to gain support and cooperation from coworkers, administration, community, and the school board are discussed, all aimed at building a strong foundation for conducting a needs assessment.

Community schools, whether rural, urban, or suburban, need to have school counseling programs built on information that is collected and evaluated on a regular basis. By bringing together feedback from students, teachers, parents, school board members, administrators, and community leaders, professional school counselors can develop a program that truly reflects the unique needs of each school community. *Assessment* and *observable outcomes* are key words that are frequently heard in the education field. Increasingly, actions and decisions in our society are guided by findings from collected information, which in turn drive movement and choices. Developing an effective, successful, and meaningful school counseling program is no different. By assessing the specific needs of the community, the professional school counselor gathers significant information that emerges from data, enabling the school counseling program to determine a purposeful path of action. This data, aligned with the American School Counselor Association (ASCA) national model (2012a) for school counseling programs, can create a powerful tool for positive change in the school. A comprehensive and developmental school counseling program is based on research and built with the combined efforts of the professional school counselor and stakeholders of the school and community. Needs assessments empower professional school counselors through data.

Approaches to needs assessment vary, and there are many surveys available for use in schools. The purpose of the survey may be remedial, preventative, or both. Needs assessments may be purchased commercially, borrowed, or adapted from an existing source; a school district may also decide to create a needs assessment for their own use. Surveys are included in

---

*Special thanks to Dr. Jan R. Bartlett for her outstanding contribution to the first two editions of this chapter.

many books that address school counseling program development, and many texts in the school counseling field either include sample needs assessments or address needs assessments in varying detail, including Erford (2015c), Baker and Gerler (2007), Gladding (2013), and J. Schmidt (2010). For a book devoted entirely to the process of developing, administering, and evaluating a needs assessment, Rye and Sparks (1999) is an excellent resource. It provides sample needs assessments for all school levels, an example of results, and a plan developed from the sample data provided.

Needs Assessment Design

Some needs assessment designs promote a comprehensive approach, in which all the elements of goals and topics that might realistically be components of a comprehensive school counseling program are addressed. This approach may be most suitable for school districts that are establishing a baseline and implementing their initial assessment, with no previously collected data. Other designs consider assessing certain topics or concerns explicitly, so they are targeting issues; this would be helpful when a district or school is updating or altering a program based on an existing needs assessment (Erford, 2015c). A number of methods have been used for assessing the needs for a school including: surveys (questionnaires and inventories), analysis of records, personal interviews, visits to classrooms, contracting an outside consultant, counseling statistics, and systematic evaluation of the existing school counseling program. Collecting information using any of these sources is extremely valuable; however, in this chapter the focus is on the most frequently used tool for needs assessments—the survey. Also discussed are factors that are critical to the successful implementation and use of the needs assessment.

Here are some additional ideas that will boost your enthusiasm for this endeavor. Whether you select an existing survey or develop your own, developmental variables and patterns might help you collect valuable information for your survey. For example, a study of needs assessments conducted with students from kindergarten to ninth grade recommended a shift in guidance topics, with an individual and family focus during early elementary years to larger social context issues as students matured (Drefs, 2003). Social context issues might include drug and alcohol use, sexual activity, disease risks and education about HIV/AIDS and hepatitis C, and Internet safety. Topics could also be a call to social and civic responsibility, which might address poverty, social justice topics, energy and sustainability, global warming, and other global or local concerns to engage students in debate, critical thinking, and discussion. The self-reported needs of students in the Drefs (2003) study helped to identify these developmental shifts in the entire school population. Tracking these shifts may prove to be useful for decisions regarding curriculum, resources, community opportunities for mentoring, and the creation of group opportunities.

Another study stressed the need for appropriate school services for homeless children (e.g., children who might be residing in shelters within your district); many of these children had experiences in counseling and reported them positively (Nabors et al., 2004). Examine your survey and consider the viewpoint and perspective of the homeless parent or child to ensure that it is sensitive and relevant. Another key point is that the needs assessment may provide valuable information regarding the varying needs of multicultural and diverse populations within schools and district.

Getting Started: Build a Strong Foundation

When conducting a school-wide needs assessment, a professional school counselor must attend to several considerations. First, gain the support of the entire counseling staff in your building or district. If you succeed in capturing their attention and commitment, the chances for strong involvement and overall success are strengthened. If it is not possible to do a district-wide assessment, then shifting the focus to a specific school may be the best place to start.

Second, after gaining the support of professional school counselors, attempt to gain endorsement and backing of the administration. Not only should the school administration be included in the process, but they must also be made aware of the school counseling program's efforts to improve services.

Once the needs assessment data has been collected and evaluated, plans for program improvement should be developed and implemented. This allows for some sense of permanence and stability for the school counseling program. If, for instance, changes occur within an administration, then less disruption to the school counseling program might occur.

Accountability for the school counseling program is another key reason for involving the administration at the very beginning of the needs assessment process. Data from a needs assessment can be used effectively in establishing priorities for program development (Erford, 2015c). Because of the No Child Left Behind Act of 2001, it is critical that professional school counselors think of their program in terms of accountability. Purposeful programming, based on data collected from the needs assessment, which is tied to the personal–social, career, and academic standards and competencies, indicates and demonstrates the link to a research base. It is essential that the programming be regularly evaluated to demonstrate measurable outcomes and that this information be presented and shared with the staff, administration, school board, and community. Press releases or articles written by professional school counselors or other committee members regarding the goals and objectives for the needs assessment can further expand support, endorsement, and involvement from students, parents, and the community. Also, the membership and involvement of the advisory board or committee working in conjunction with professional school counselors throughout the entire process should be highlighted.

Content of Proposal

The proposal should include at least the following components, accompanied with specific and detailed information:

1. Address the broad aim and purpose for the needs assessment. Discuss general goals for the school counseling program. Topics might include creating the highest quality program; continued improvement for the program; identifying and addressing changes in the student body and community; determining the priorities for services from the stakeholders; and matching services with school and community needs.
2. Address who will be involved in the process. Introduce the advisory board or committee, and discuss the membership of this group. The advisory board is composed of representatives of the stakeholders in the school district: administrators, teachers, staff, students, school board members, parents, and a community representative. This is a good time to discuss the organizational needs of the advisory board. A large school district may need a district-wide steering committee as well.

3. How will the needs assessment be organized? Address in broad terms the responsibilities of the various members, including training, setting goals, conducting needs assessment, planning strategies, and evaluation. Include details for implementing the evaluation data and plans for ongoing revisions.
4. Provide a detailed timeline for the completion of the needs assessment's planning stage. Emphasize that each planning cycle leads to an evaluation of the data, which is the basis for redirection and fine-tuning of the existing program.
5. Estimate how long it will take. Include in the proposal a prediction for when a document will be available for the school board to review and a date for when the plan will be completed.

Include a statement regarding the perceived impact of the resulting plan. Remember to stress the importance and benefits of the planning process; do not only emphasize the outcomes.

Advisory Committee

The advisory committee, sometimes called the "group advisory team" or "advisory board," is composed of representatives of the stakeholders in the school—individuals in the school and community who are committed to the success of the school and students. It is wise to identify a list of potential individuals including students, teachers, administrators, parents, and community leaders (e.g., ministers, business leaders, mental health professionals, law enforcement officers, government officials; Erford, 2015c).

The professional school counselors might organize this group or the school board might appoint it. Alternatively, the group could be selected and organized and then appointed by the school board. Along with the professional school counselors, the committee will be involved in planning, implementing, and evaluating the counseling program. Once the group or committee has been identified, essential communication between the members will be necessary to move the needs assessment forward. This work may be time-consuming, but it will provide a solid foundation for future activities and discussion.

Each community is unique, and the services that are needed from the school counseling program will vary. Because of variables such as the size of the school, socioeconomic status of the community, cultural diversity, concentration of learning problems found in the school, educational backgrounds of parents, community's attitude toward the school and education, and leadership of the school and district (J. Schmidt, 2010), it is essential and advisable that the community be reflected in the advisory committee as closely as possible.

Building a Program Base

By bringing together elements of a school and community to design the comprehensive program, the energies are channeled toward a common goal rather than competing or fragmenting the efforts of the needs assessment (Rye & Sparks, 1999). A comprehensive school counseling program is not the sole domain or responsibility of the professional school counselor. It includes many people to expand the base of support (Erford, 2015c).

Instead of a discussion on the roles and function of professional school counselors, Rye and Sparks (1999) presented fundamental beliefs of a comprehensive school counseling program:

1. Governing values are the foundation of all human endeavors.
2. Education is the top priority for ensuring a positive future for all.
3. Comprehensive counseling programs are essential elements of any quality educational process for students.
4. Quality counseling programs must be developed from explicitly stated value bases and have both administrative and community support.
5. Comprehensive services must be systematically planned, implemented, and evaluated over an extended period of time.
6. Program planning is most effective when it is centered in an informed team of school and community representatives.
7. Effective counseling programs are specifically designed to meet identified needs in the school and community populations.
8. Programs of excellence offer services that build self-understanding and a variety of skills in a pattern of increasing levels of difficulty as students move from grade to grade. (Rye & Sparks, 1999, p. 4)

A decision should be made about whether to look at existing models for school counseling programs or to start fresh. One may consult VanZandt and Hayslip (2001) as a resource that includes information on several models: the Missouri model, the multidimensional model, and the ASCA national model. The professional school counselor should make a basic presentation of the national standards for school counseling programs (Campbell & Dahir, 1997) and the ASCA national model (ASCA, 2012a) to committee members. The national standards provide detailed student competencies for each of the core domains of personal–social, career, and academic success.

Core values. The committee might begin by discussing the core values. Chances for success are further enriched by exploring the values of the school's counseling program. Failure to determine a shared set of values coupled with the lack of a process to resolve value differences can lead to divisiveness within the committee (Rye & Sparks, 1999). The stated and expressed values from the committee should also be reflected within the larger community and within the cultural context surrounding the school; this is essential to attain and retain credibility.

To explore the respective values held by committee members, examine and discuss mission statements for the school, school counseling program, parent–teacher groups, businesses, and any other existing documents. This can help to provide a starting point for processing and clarifying individual values. Are there key words that are prominent in the documents? Is there a common ground? Within the profession there is still some question as to whether there is consensus on core values, but in a school district, the professional school counselors should articulate their own values and link them to those of the community (Rye & Sparks, 1999). Is there a common theme that runs through the community committee members? Work in small groups around general questions, and then chart the key points on large paper to be shared and to organize the discussion. Possible starter questions may include, *What elements do members see as essential in a happy and successful student? What are the core values members want to see delivered through a school counseling program?*

Values to vision. Once the group's values have been clarified, the next step is to connect them to a shared vision for the future. Possible questions for exploring the vision for the program might include, *How are students different because of the school counseling program? When students move on from this school to another level or graduate, what skills do we want them to have? What will be the attributes of this student?* One helpful activity might be to ask committee members to close their eyes for a few minutes and reflect on what an exemplary school counseling program would look like and how it would affect students. Then let the group members spend a few moments writing notes based on their reflections. Encourage the members to share their ideas in small groups, where ideas can be documented and then shared with the larger group. Develop a vision or a mission statement for the school counseling program based on what emerges from the group. It should be a vision that all can agree on and support enthusiastically. In larger communities and communities with diverse students in the school district (e.g., cultural, religious, ethnic, racial, socioeconomic status), the professional school counselor might consider conducting focus groups to gather additional information to ensure all voices are included in the vision.

The Needs Assessment

A needs assessment helps the professional school counselor determine stakeholders' needs and develop or refine program goals and objectives. Considerations for developing a needs assessment include (a) developing a timeline, (b) populations to be assessed, and (c) the instrument used.

Develop a Timeline

Rye and Sparks (1999) stated the time commitment for an in depth and thorough needs assessment process will be 5 to 6 years, with the first year devoted to the following:

1. Preparing and organizing the advisory team into a working group.
2. Reviewing and refining the beliefs, vision, and mission of the counseling program.
3. Conducting a needs assessment among students, parents, and school personnel.
4. Identifying high-priority needs.
5. Writing objectives.
6. Helping the counseling staff develop activities to address identified needs. (Rye & Sparks, 1999, p. 34)

The next 4 years would involve the implementation, monitoring, evaluation, and revision of the plan that was initially developed. In the final year another needs assessment could be conducted and a new plan developed and written, based on emergent needs.

Within the same time frame is another exciting possibility. An approach using a continuous cycle of assessing program needs, which could be tied to the national standards, could allow an assessment of each of the three areas of academic, career, and personal–social to occur on specific years in a 6-year cycle (Erford, 2015c). A possible cycle involves a focus in years 1 and 2 on assessment of academic needs, years 3 and 4 on the needs for career development and educational planning, and years 5 and 6 on personal–social issues. Once a program is clearly established, adjustments might be made in a 3-year improvement cycle. If drastic changes occur within the community, either because of shifts in demographics or some type of national, state, or local crisis of political or natural causes, it may be necessary to respond and adjust in a time frame other than the one planned.

Populations Assessed

All stakeholders in the community will have valuable information and opinions to share regarding the direction for the school counseling program. The groups commonly asked to participate in the needs assessment are students, parents, administrators, and teachers. Critical issues are frequently determined and discovered when surveying these groups (J. Schmidt, 2010). Information from community organizations and local business leaders can be helpful, but it may be difficult to obtain a large enough response sample. Therefore it may be prudent to gather this data through personal interviews and contacts (Erford, 2015c). Additional information may be gleaned from school volunteers, the school nurse, school psychologist, social worker, and professional organizations. Input from these sources can assist in understanding expectations for the services to be provided (J. Schmidt, 2010) and supplement other feedback.

Because the return rate is essential for accurate and meaningful needs assessment results, students should fill out their survey while at school, perhaps at the end of a class period. It is important to share with the students their significant role in the survey. Stress that their opinions and insights are valued and honest responses are important. Teachers and staff generally respond well, especially if the administration is vocally supportive. The challenge is for a high return rate from parents. A "captured audience" can maximize the return rate, so consider gatherings at faculty meetings, class, or parent meetings for distributing and collecting surveys (Erford, 2015c).

Brainstorm ideas with committee members to garner high enthusiasm and participation rates. Free food is always a draw. Consider enlisting the community, students, and faculty in a spaghetti dinner or fish fry. The ticket in could be a completed parent survey; the community could donate food, and students and school personnel could cook and serve. Send the surveys home with students ahead of time and have plenty of extra copies at the door. This gathering would provide a wonderful opportunity for building connections with parents. It would also be a forum for sharing information on a host of issues at the school and enlisting parent support. Student groups could be asked to participate to encourage further parent involvement.

The Instrument

There are many sample surveys available. The survey can address the same content area across levels with minor adjustments. The questions should not use education- and counseling-specific jargon. Some surveys use a Likert-type scale that rates the severity or importance of the issue or concern from 1 to 5 or 1 to 7, using *never* at one end of the spectrum and *always* at the other extreme. Other approaches include answers of *yes, no,* and *sometimes.* Other surveys have boxes to be checked for *rarely, sometimes, frequently, most of the time,* and *almost always.* There are many variations, and the committee may decide either to alter an existing survey to accommodate perceived needs or create their own. The content for the needs assessment should be topical, such as questions related to social skills, changes within families, substance abuse, or college application procedures (Erford, 2015c). The format for the survey may use questions or statements; for example, *How important is it that "jokes" regarding sexual orientation be eliminated from the school community?* or *Students need to be more tolerant of people whose views, appearances, or actions differ from their own.* The committee may also decide to provide a space for collecting qualitative data with an open question (e.g., "Is there anything else you would like to share with the committee?"). This will allow for information to emerge that may have otherwise been missed or overlooked.

The Plan and Evaluation

Once the data have been collected and evaluated, the highest priority needs may be determined and used to establish program goals (Rye & Sparks, 1999). The committee will need to weigh and rank results from the surveyed data and groups. The students' highest priority may be different from that of the parents. The needs assessment may lead the committee to ask further questions in focus groups and individual interviews to clarify the data. Gathering additional information may be critical to goal setting and sorting the priorities. In the first year after the needs assessment, the school counseling program may elect to focus efforts on the top three to five priorities that emerged. These goals should be concentrated on for at least a year before adding additional goals. An exemplary school counseling program evolves over a number of years, not in one year.

Summary/Conclusion

After joining and merging the voices from students, teachers, parents, school-board members, administrators, community leaders, and professional school counselors, the emerging school counseling program will reflect the unique needs of the school community. In turn, by focusing on prevention and developmental goals for students, professional school counselors do more than repair wounds and mend fences; they create healthy school climates and enhance human relationships (J. Schmidt, 2010). Administering a needs assessment is a time-consuming, tedious, and necessary adventure that binds together the school's stakeholders with the professional school counselors in a noble and worthwhile cause: the creation of a meaningful and successful program that makes a real difference in the lives of students, families, and the community.

CHAPTER 16

How to Write Learning Objectives

Bradley T. Erford

Preview

The information in this chapter will help professional school counselors develop measurable learning objectives to guide the activities that comprise developmental guidance programs and individual and group counseling activities. Special emphasis is given to aligning objectives with programmatic standards, competencies, and assessment strategies so that evidence can be generated to document that program standards and student learning outcomes are being met.

If you don't know where you are going, you may have a difficult time getting there. And it probably doesn't matter in which direction you go. Obviously, such an approach is disastrous in the educational setting, because effective instruction is supposed to change behaviors, thoughts, and feelings in a desirable direction. Yet for years, some professional school counselors have entered the classroom to provide developmental guidance activities with wonderfully entertaining materials, interesting activities, or professionally produced videos but no clear understanding or statement of what changes in student thoughts, feelings, and behaviors were to be accomplished. The same was true for individual and small-group work. Professional school counselors have often viewed the provision of these services as ends in themselves rather than as means to an end (Erford, 2015c). Thus, students of divorce participated in a group or individual counseling experience because these were ways to provide services, but little thought was given to what the students were supposed to get out of these services (i.e., the outcomes). Often, these outcomes simply went unstated, but, in many instances, there was no guiding plan to move students in a positive developmental or therapeutic direction. Obviously, this is neither a systematic nor evidence-based approach to providing school counseling services.

This lack of direction was in part due to the lack of an agreed-upon domain of knowledge or of behaviors specific to school counseling programs (Erford, 2015c). Other academic disciplines (e.g., math, social studies, science) have well-defined and agreed-upon domains of knowledge that result, for example, in first-grade teachers across the country teaching basically very similar content and skills. While variations in curriculum no doubt occur—particularly as students get into middle school and high school—all academic disciplines plan for learning to occur in a systematic, sequential, and developmental manner. Until recently, this domain of knowledge and planfulness has been missing in many school counseling programs.

The American School Counselor Association (ASCA) national standards (Campbell & Dahir, 1997) were a positive step toward conceptualizing and establishing a school counseling domain of knowledge. They also provided competencies associated with each standard to further explain what was to be accomplished. In this book, the curriculum development sequence is identified as follows: standards, competencies and outcomes, objectives, activities, and assessment. Whether one uses the ASCA national standards or state or local standards/goals, good curriculum development starts with standards or goals to ensure that the broad domain of knowledge is identified. Competencies (sometimes analogous to the term *outcomes*) capture in broad terms the actions, skills, or abilities students must develop. Objectives help to further define and explain competencies and must be stated in specific, measurable terms to identify what will be accomplished as a result of the student's participation in the planned activities. Lessons or activities are then developed to provide the knowledge or experiences that allow students to accomplish the objectives. Finally, the objectives are assessed to determine the extent to which student learning, skills, and abilities developed during the lessons. If the objective is stated correctly, the professional school counselor will be able to assess whether the objective has actually been met.

The Objective of the Objective

An objective is comprised of words/diagrams/pictures that let learning stakeholders know precisely what the students should achieve (Goodnough, Pérusse, & Erford, 2015). In curriculum development, one first must determine where one wants students to end up (the objective) before creating the means to move them there (lessons and activities) and finally evaluating whether they have arrived (assessment). Thus, objectives are focused on outcomes rather than process, are measurable and specific rather than broad or general, and are student focused rather than teacher focused.

The Purpose of a Learning Objective

Learning objectives serve several purposes (Goodnough et al., 2015). First, objectives help professional school counselors to develop activities and select procedures, resources, and materials. A plumber or carpenter does not select a tool until he or she knows what needs to be accomplished. Likewise, a professional school counselor should not select a favored or entertaining activity or technique and make it "fit" into the curriculum. Second, learning objectives help to obtain consistent results. Objectives serve as road maps leading to a reliable and consistent outcome. Finally, learning objectives make instruction more efficient. When a professional school counselor selects appropriate learning objectives, it is assumed that those objectives serve to structure the available time. If activities do not support a learning objective then the activity becomes nonessential. This is not to say that students will not learn important lessons from nonessential activities, just that what they learn might lie outside of the domain of knowledge that should be mastered.

Types of "Teacher Thinking"

According to Mager (1997), there are five basic types of objectives, and each is linked to a specific purpose that an instructor may have. A *coverage objective* merely involves a description of what will be covered in a lesson (e.g., students will learn to resolve conflict). An *activity objective* designates the actual activities that students will engage in (e.g., students will read pages

54–59). An *involvement objective* specifies what students will "get into" (e.g., students will react to a poem on the virtues of problem solving as opposed to aggression when resolving conflict). *Thinking skills objectives* focus on the thought processes that must be developed in order to achieve mastery objectives (e.g., students will develop the ability to think critically about the causes and solutions to conflict). *Mastery objectives* state in specific, measurable terms what a student will be able to do after a lesson (e.g., after observing four role-plays of students in conflict, 90% of students will be able to list at least three nonviolent ways to resolve a conflict). Most educators tend to think in terms of the first four types of objectives. However, mastery objectives are essential to the curriculum because they relate to outcomes that result in student change and development, thereby subsuming all the other types of objectives.

Qualities of Measurable Learning Objectives

High-quality learning objectives effectively communicate what is to be accomplished in specific terms. As such, some words commonly used in nonspecific learning objectives (e.g., *to know, to understand, to appreciate, to internalize, to believe, to enjoy*) leave one wondering how to demonstrate that the student has accomplished what he or she set out to do. Therefore, words that lead to more specific interpretations and which can be demonstrated through student performance should be used (e.g., *to write, to compare/contrast, to solve, to construct, to identify, to build*).

Teaching the Elusive Intangibles

Historically, many professional school counselors have resisted the accountability movement—some out of frustration of trying to describe the complex developmental change processes that students must undergo to become productive citizens; others take the position that the changes in students are too complex or intangible to measure. After all, how does one measure motivation, self-esteem, and success? This view of school counseling program outcomes as intangible and immeasurable is counterproductive at best, and self-extinctive at worst.

Think about it: How long would a math curriculum (or math teacher) survive if the students did not improve their math skills? Likewise, now that a domain of knowledge and behavior (standards and competencies) has been established for school counseling programs, how long will school counseling programs (or professional school counselors) survive if the students do not improve their academic, career, and personal–social development? The issue is no longer *can* we measure student performance in these three domains but rather *how will* we measure it? The *how* is made possible through writing specific learning objectives. Teachers teaching things that cannot be evaluated are in the inenviable position of demonstrating whether they are teaching anything at all. This is a classic dilemma: If one is teaching something that is intangible, it cannot be evaluated; if it cannot be evaluated, one cannot determine that it has been mastered; and if it cannot be mastered, why would one teach it? What value could it possibly have within a curriculum?

The answer to this dilemma, of course, is to teach what can be mastered and write the learning objective in a way that mastery can be determined. At a basic level, this is the difference between process and outcomes. *Process* has to do with the instructional methodology (e.g., exploring, debating), which is the means and not the end. The *outcome* is the end. The outcome involves the actual learning result that can be demonstrated through assessment of the learning objective. The bottom line is that if one is willing to decide (intuitively) that a student is performing satisfactorily on some intangible process, then with a little more effort, one can understand, describe, and develop criteria to assess the basis for that satisfaction.

The ABCDs of a Well-Written Learning Objective

A well-written learning objective focuses the lesson on specific student outcomes and accomplishments. While experts generally agree on the essential components of a learning objective, they do not always agree on the components that lead to a determination of mastery. Because the emphasis of this chapter is on helping professional school counselors develop mastery objectives, an integrated approach is used (Goodnough et al., 2015; Kellough & Roberts, 2010; Saphier, Haley-Speca, & Gower, 2008). Here is an ABCD model for writing learning objectives: **A**udience, **B**ehavior, **C**onditions, and **D**escription of the expected performance criterion.

Audience

The first essential component of a well-written learning objective involves the audience for whom the objective is intended. Because the primary recipient of an individual or group counseling session or large-group developmental guidance lesson is the student, almost all applicable objectives will be targeted at the student audience. Thus, many learning objectives begin with phrases such as, "Students will . . ." or "Students will be able to . . ." Less frequently used audiences may include teachers, parents, or an entire class or group of students.

Behavior

The second essential component addresses the behavior that the student is expected to engage in to be able to think, solve, or do. "These behaviors are typically descriptive verbs that address the . . . outcome around which the lesson is structured" (Goodnough et al., 2015, p. 221). Here are some examples of objectives using these descriptive verbs: *Students will be able to recognize cooperative group behaviors* or *Students will be able to identify five methods that would help them cope with loss and subsequent grief.* The behavioral component of a learning objective deals with cognitive, affective, or behavioral outcomes.

Conditions

This component describes the conditions under which the behavior is supposed to occur. It is essential to identify *when* or *how* the behavior will be measured. Typical conditions are tests, worksheets, observations, role-plays, or engaging in some structured activity. Here are some examples of the conditions component: *After completing a worksheet listing 10 scenarios of cooperative group behaviors, students will be able to recognize cooperative group behaviors;* or *After reading an article on loss, students will be able to identify five methods that would help them cope with loss and subsequent grief.* Mager (1997) suggested that conditions address three main questions: "What will the learner be expected to use when performing ... not be allowed to use.... What will be the real-world conditions under which the performance will be expected to occur" (p. 87).

Description of the Expected Performance Criterion

The final component of a well-written learning objective, and the one that is most often left out, is a *description of the criterion for expected performance.* Generally, this criterion takes the form of the amount of a task the student must perform successfully (e.g., 90% correct on a test) or the percentage of students that successfully display the behavior under the given conditions (e.g., 80% of students). The criterion sets the level of acceptable performance, the level that students are challenged to surpass. Examples of completed objectives using the ABCD model include, *After completing a worksheet listing 10 scenarios of cooperative group behaviors, 75% of fifth-grade students will be able to recognize one cooperative group behavior in each scenario,* or *After reading an article on loss, 80% of students will be able to identify five methods that would help them cope with loss and subsequent grief.*

The criterion for mastery is an essential part of a learning objective, because, without it, the expectation is for perfection. While it is praiseworthy to strive for perfection, student motivation, preparation, test-taking skills, work habits, instructional strategies, and myriad other potential problems often interfere with performance and lead to some degree of nonmastery.

If one sets the criterion too high, then the objective is not met. If objectives are not met, then no evidence exists that competencies (or outcomes) have been met. If competencies have not been met, this means that the standards (or goals) have gone unmet. In this case, the professional school counselor has no proof that the school counseling program has had any desirable impact—at all! Thus, it is essential to set a reasonable criterion for each objective so that students are challenged and at the same time accurate accountability measurement occurs. The criterion can be qualified to include the number of times a student must perform, the length of time of a performance, an accuracy ratio (percentage of time), the percentage of students who can perform the task, and the quality of the task (generally scored according to some rubric of quality indicators). A criterion provides a standard against which the success of the instruction or intervention can be tested, tells students when they have met or exceeded expectations, and provides a basis for concluding that students can do what an instructor sought to accomplish.

Avoiding the Pitfalls

The preceding sections focused on what professional school counselors should do to write effective learning objectives, but Mager (1997) pointed out a number of important characteristics of ineffective objectives that should be avoided. First, avoid terms that indicate a *false performance*, or no real performance at all. For example, how would one determine whether a thorough understanding of peer mediation ever existed? Second, one should avoid *false givens* (conditions; e.g., "Given adequate practice in time management..."). Third, avoid *gibberish* (e.g., "Demonstrate a comprehensive understanding of..."). Finally, avoid identifying *instructor performance*—what the professional school counselor or teacher is supposed to accomplish (e.g., "The professional school counselor will help students to..."). The emphasis is always on the stakeholder who is to demonstrate mastery. Avoiding the pitfalls will help the professional school counselor construct concise learning objectives that will demonstrate mastery performance and effective school counseling services.

Summary/Conclusion

A well-written learning objective is an essential starting point for demonstrating the effectiveness of a comprehensive developmental school counseling program. The ABCD model (Audience, Behavior, Conditions, and Description of expected performance criterion) has all the components necessary to craft a well-written mastery-level learning objective. Objectives written in this way provide a built-in process for accountability of school counseling programs, particularly when used to structure and guide individual and group counseling sessions and classroom guidance.

CHAPTER 17

Designing Developmental Guidance Lessons

*Bradley T. Erford**

Preview

In this chapter, practical considerations are addressed to help professional school counselors effectively deliver the developmental and preventive components of a comprehensive school counseling program. Specific topics include how to develop grade-level objectives, how to write and adapt lessons using a guidance lesson plan format, and how to determine the scope and sequence of lessons. Sample lessons are provided as well as a discussion about implementing the school counseling curriculum and the role that teachers and professional school counselors should assume.

In the early years of the school counseling profession, guidance was considered an ancillary support service, conceptualized as a position rather than a program (Gysbers & Henderson, 2012). Narrow in scope, the focus was on providing selected services for problem students (Thompson, 2012). However, schools must now be more responsive to the increasing complexity and diversity of our society as well as to changes in personal and social values and social structures. Increasing violence, substance abuse, teenage suicide, sexual experimentation, and a rapidly changing work force, among other factors, have a significant impact on student development (Erford, 2015c). Poverty, child abuse, homelessness, and lack of access to postsecondary education add to the mix (Lee & Goodnough, 2015). Guidance services must be reconceptualized to better address these challenges as well as those brought about by technology and an increasing societal complexity that affects life roles (Erford, 2015c; Gysbers & Henderson, 2012).

A significant aspect of the reconceptualization of guidance services has been the gradual evolution from a "smorgasbord-of-services" approach to a comprehensive program. School counseling programs should be comprehensive and developmental, emphasizing primary prevention and healthy development for all students. In support of the comprehensive program focus, and in an effort to better prepare students to deal with factors that affect their development, the American School Counselor Association (ASCA) assumed a key leadership role in developing national standards for a comprehensive approach to program delivery, management, and accountability. The national model for school counseling programs (ASCA, 2012a) is designed to promote and enhance the learning process by facilitating student development in three domains: academic, career, and personal–social.

---

*Special thanks to Ann Vernon for her outstanding contributions to the first two editions of this chapter.

As professional school counselors transform their programs to reflect the beliefs and practices of a comprehensive developmental program, it becomes increasingly important that they know how to design, develop, and deliver the developmental and preventive component that forms the core curriculum of the comprehensive program. Through the guidance lessons that are integral to this component, students are taught developmentally appropriate personal–social, academic, and career development concepts to increase their knowledge and skills and to help ensure healthy development. As Goodnough, Pérusse, and Erford (2015) noted, professional school counselors have a unique opportunity to help students master these developmental changes through a sequential K–12 core curriculum.

The purpose of this chapter is to describe the process of identifying grade-level competencies and how to develop guidance lessons that address specific competencies. A guidance lesson plan format is described, along with information about scope and sequence of lessons and developmental considerations. In addition, the role of the professional school counselor and teacher in implementing guidance lessons as part of the developmental and preventative component of a comprehensive program will be discussed.

Designing the Developmental Curriculum

Incorporating developmental principles into a comprehensive curriculum is a daunting yet critical task for professional school counselors at all levels. In designing this curriculum, professional school counselors need to assume a leadership role in developing the scope and sequence of the program, in accordance with developmental considerations. The national standards for school counseling programs (Campbell & Dahir, 1997), which are based on extensive research and field reviews, provide professional school counselors with the attitudes, knowledge, and skills that students should acquire in the areas of personal–social, academic, and career development and include examples of three broad standards in each of these domains that can serve as a basis for the curriculum. The ASCA standards also identify competencies, which were developed as a result of extensive research with professional counselors at all levels (Lee & Goodnough, 2015). These are very general, however, and professional school counselors will need to develop more specific grade-level competencies for each of the standards in each domain so that distinct concepts can be presented at each grade level.

In designing these competencies, it is important to consider the developmental tasks students must accomplish in grades K–12 and identify specific competencies accordingly. For example, an appropriate interpersonal relationship competency for kindergartners would be to learn to share and cooperate, whereas an appropriate interpersonal relationship competency for eighth graders would be to learn effective ways to deal with peer pressure, and understanding how to deal with dating relationships would be an appropriate interpersonal relationship competency for 11th graders. It is important to consult child development texts and literature for information about developmental tasks.

In writing the competencies, professional school counselors should be very specific and avoid words like *to understand* or *to appreciate,* because they are harder to measure (see Chapter 16). In this era of accountability, words such as *identify, differentiate,* or *describe* allow practitioners to develop ways to measure what students have learned. It is also easier to design a lesson that addresses the competencies or objectives when they are concrete and specific.

It is necessary to determine the number of competencies per grade level, which is usually based on the number of lessons you intend to deliver throughout the course of a year. Assuming that there will be 30 to 36 lessons (one per week), you would take the three standards (personal–social, academic, career development), decide if you want to give equal emphasis to them (up to 12 competencies per standard) or weigh one more heavily than the others, and then identify specific grade-level competencies accordingly. To illustrate, the ASCA standards (Dahir, Sheldon, & Valiga, 1998, p. 16) for personal–social development include the following:

> Standard A—Students will acquire the attitudes, knowledge, and interpersonal skills to help them understand and respect self and others.
>
> Standard B—Students will make decisions, set goals, and take necessary action to achieve goals.
>
> Standard C—Students will understand safety and survival skills.

There are 21 competencies in Standard A, divided into two categories: acquire self-knowledge and acquire interpersonal skills. There are also 12 competencies in Standard B and 11 in Standard C. Professional school counselors should study these competencies to determine if they want to use them as a basis for developing their own grade-level competencies, if there are others that should be added, or if there are some that would fit better under one standard than another. For example, "learning to cope with peer pressure," which is listed under personal–social development Standard C (*understand safety and survival skills*) could also be included under Standard A (*acquire the attitudes, knowledge and interpersonal skills to help them understand and respect self and others*). Likewise, "demonstrate a respect and appreciation for individual and cultural differences," which is included under Standard B (*students will make decisions, set goals, and take necessary action to achieve goals*) is perhaps better suited for Standard A, since it relates to respecting self and others. As professional school counselors study the competencies, they may also see areas that are not addressed and should be included. This is the process of *personalizing* the curriculum for individual school districts. Also, remember that while the general focus of a comprehensive program is on development, there may also be some situation-specific areas that need to be added to the curriculum to address needs in a particular school district. For example, if students live in a high poverty area, the professional school counselor would want to reword the competency that reads "recognize, accept, and appreciate ethnic and cultural diversity" (Dahir et al., 1998, p. 16) to also include sensitivity to socioeconomic diversity.

After studying the ASCA competencies, you may decide to modify them, not use them at all and write your own, or use them as they are. If you use them verbatim and also incorporate the 43 career development competencies and the 34 academic development competencies, you would have a total of 121 competencies to separate into grade-level categories. This would roughly be the equivalent of 10 competencies for each Grade 1 through 12, or 9 competencies for Grades K–12. Therefore, if you intend to have a year-long curriculum, which would be approximately 30 to 36 weeks, you would either need to have multiple lessons for each competency, add competencies, or address some competencies over multiple grades.

Grade-Level Competencies

To illustrate this process, the following section is part of the personal–social domain, with examples of grade-level competencies. The ASCA Standard A under personal–social development has been rewritten as follows: *Students will acquire the attitudes, knowledge, and skills to help them understand and respect self and others and identify and effectively express feelings.* This standard as reworded includes self-development, emotional development, and social development. Instead of using the ASCA competencies, the following uses specific grade-level competencies or objectives from *The Passport Program: A Journey Through Social, Emotional, Cognitive, and Self-Development* (Vernon, 1998a; 1998b; 1998c). Due to space limitations, Table 17.1 lists only three competencies per grade level, but there are at least six per grade level (with corresponding lessons) in these curriculums. Also due to space restrictions, the self-development competencies will be identified only for Grades 1 through 5, emotional development competencies only for Grades 6 through 8, and social development competencies only for Grades 9 through 12, even though there are competencies for each grade in each of these areas. The intent here is to give the reader an idea of the scope and sequence when developing grade-level competencies. Had there been space to reproduce all the objectives, the reader would be able to see the developmental progression from grade level to grade level as well as recognize that most of the ASCA competencies are represented in the more specific grade-level competencies of *The Passport Program*.

When developing a total comprehensive curriculum, a similar process would include grade-level competencies for decision making (ASCA personal–social Standard B) and safety and survival skills (ASCA personal–social Standard C), as well as competencies for the career and academic development standards.

Developmental Guidance Lessons

After developing the grade-level competencies for personal–social, academic, and career development, the next step is identifying the objectives and activities to achieve the competency. Again, this may seem like a monumental task, but in reality the field is replete with emotional education curricula, career development programs, games, workbooks, and bibliotherapy resources. The problem lies in selecting programs or materials that correspond to the specific competencies and that have been proven effective. One way to address this problem is to write your own lessons. See Vernon's Passport Programs (Vernon 1998a, 1998b, 1998c) for examples of lesson plans.

Lesson Plan Format

The first step in writing a guidance lesson would be to specify the grade level, the standard (personal–social, academic, or career development), the grade-level competency or competencies (usually no more than two per lesson), and the lesson objective(s) (also usually no more than two per lesson). The next step is to create a short (15–20 minutes, depending on the amount of time allotted) stimulus activity that addresses each competency. The stimulus activity might include, for example, bibliotherapy, role-play activities, simulations, games, worksheets, or music and art activities. Professional school counselors can create their own activities or find activities from commercial sources that match their competencies. In selecting activities from commercial sources, it will often be necessary to adapt the activity so that it directly addresses the specific competency. In other words, if the competency is *Students will identify various degrees of anger,* it would not be appropriate to have a general lesson on feelings, because the lesson should specifically relate to anger. Likewise, if the competency is *Students*

Table 17.1 Selected Competencies from *The Passport Program*

Self-Development—Grade 1

   Students will:

      Learn that everyone has strengths and weaknesses.

      Develop an attitude of self-acceptance.

      Identify ways in which they are growing and changing.

Self-Development—Grade 2

   Develop awareness of abilities and attributes.

   Learn to accept oneself with these abilities and attributes.

   Recognize that strengths and limitations are part of one's self-definition and to not put themselves down because of limitations.

Self-Development—Grade 3

   Learn that how one acts does not determine self-worth.

   Learn that nobody is perfect and to accept themselves as less than perfect.

   Identify characteristics of self, including strengths and weaknesses.

Self-Development—Grade 4

   Learn that making mistakes does not make one a bad person.

   Learn that others' approval is not required to be worthwhile.

   Identify individual preferences, characteristics, and abilities.

Self-Development—Grade 5

   Identify specific characteristics that are like or unlike oneself.

   Identify feelings associated with varying rates of development.

   Differentiate between making mistakes and being a total failure.

Emotional Development—Grade 6

   Learn that feelings can change.

   Learn specific ways to feel happier.

   Understand the connection between feelings and behaviors.

Emotional Development—Grade 7

   Identify what experiences trigger anger and how to effectively control and/or express anger.

   Identify ways to increase positive feelings.

   Identify strategies for dealing with intense negative emotions.

Emotional Development—Grade 8

   Learn effective ways to deal with the ups and downs associated with puberty.

   Learn how thinking affects feeling and how to change feelings by changing thoughts.

   Learn how to distinguish between healthy and unhealthy ways to relieve emotional pain.

Social Development—Grade 9

   Develop skills for dealing with interpersonal relationship problems.

   Examine the positive and negative aspects of peer pressure.

   Identify ways to resist peer pressure.

(continues)

Table 17.1 (continued)

Social Development—Grade 10

    Learn how to stop the negative cycle of rumors, gossip, and assumptions that affect relationships.

    Identify feelings and issues involved in the termination of a romantic relationship.

    Identify effective ways to deal with the breakup of a relationship.

Social Development—Grade 11

    Learn to distinguish between healthy and unhealthy dependence in relationships.

    Learn what one can and cannot control in relationships with others.

    Learn to distinguish between healthy and unhealthy ways to deal with relationship issues.

Social Development—Grade 12

    Identify effective strategies for dealing with parent–teen relationships.

    Identify ways to deal with competition in relationships.

    Identify feelings and issues involved in intimate relationships.

Note. Adapted from *The Passport Program: A Journey Through Emotional, Social, Cognitive, and Self-Development* (Grades 1–5); *The Passport Program: A Journey Through Emotional, Social, Cognitive, and Self-Development* (Grades 6–8); and *The Passport Program: A Journey Through Emotional, Social, Cognitive, and Self-Development* (Grades 9–12), by A. Vernon, 1998, Champaign, IL: Research Press. Copyright 1998 by Research Press. Adapted with permission.

will identify five tease tolerance strategies, the lesson should directly address one's tolerance for teasing and not a more general lesson on getting along with others.

After the activity has been written or selected from commercial resources, the next step is to identify two types of discussion questions to help process the lesson. Although the stimulus activity is an important way to introduce the concepts, the discussion is equally important, because it helps students clarify and reinforce what they learned. This part often gets slighted because the activity takes up too much time, so it is critical to allow at least 15 minutes of the allotted lesson time for discussion. The discussion questions developed for this lesson prototype include content questions and personalization questions. Content questions pertain to the content of the activity (e.g., what happened in the story they read, what occurred during the role play, what their responses were on the worksheet they completed). For example, if they had just played a group decision-making game, content questions might be, "How did your group arrive at the decision?" "What was the most challenging part of this decision-making process?" "What was the easiest part of this decision-making process?" Personalization questions help students personalize the information and apply it to their own lives. For instance, if they read a story about a boy who was teased, personalization questions might be, "Have you ever been teased? If so, how did you feel and how did you handle it?" "What does it say about you if you are teased? What can you do next time you are teased?"

The final step in the lesson plan format is the assessment component. This might take the form of a short quiz about the content of the lesson, a homework assignment in which students are asked to apply what they learned and report back in the form of a short report, or having students develop a short skit to convey what they learned from the lesson.

To further illustrate the lesson plan format and the examples of content and personalization questions, a lesson for eighth graders is presented in Figure 17.1. Developmentally, many

Pain Relievers

Competency: To distinguish between healthy and unhealthy ways to relieve emotional pain.

Objective: After completing a tag-board poster, all groups of students will be able to identify at least two healthy and unhealthy ways to deal with a painful emotion.

Materials: A chalkboard and the following for each group of four students: magazines, scissors, glue, a large sheet of tag board, and markers.

Procedure/Activities:

1. Introduce the activity by having students quickly brainstorm examples of painful emotions. As they identify examples, write them on the board. Next, discuss the difference between healthy and unhealthy ways of dealing with painful emotions. For example, anger can be a painful emotion. An unhealthy way to deal with anger would be to get drunk. A healthy way to deal with it would be to talk it out.
2. Divide students into groups of four, and distribute the materials. Instruct them to make two columns on the bottom half of the tag-board poster and to label one side Healthy Ways to Deal With Painful Emotions and the other side Unhealthy Ways to Deal With Painful Emotions. Ask each group to list two or more painful emotions at the top of the poster, then have them look through the magazines for pictures representing at least two healthy and two unhealthy ways to deal with these emotions. If they cannot find appropriate pictures, have them draw pictures or symbols. In either case, students should use words to represent their suggestions.
3. After the posters have been completed, have the small groups share them with the total group.
4. Discuss the content and personalization questions.

Discussion Content Questions:

1. Which are harder to identify: healthy or unhealthy ways to deal with painful emotions?
2. In general, were the small groups in agreement with each other? Were there some ideas that one group labeled unhealthy that you might have considered healthy, or vice versa? (Ask students to share examples and remember that what students identify as healthy and unhealthy may vary depending on culture.)
3. What makes the unhealthy methods unhealthy? Do you really think they help relieve pain in the long term? Why or why not?

Personalization Questions:

1. Are your "pain relievers" generally healthy or unhealthy? How do you feel about that?
2. If you have tried unhealthy methods in the past, how has this affected your life? If you had it to do over, what might you do differently, if anything?
3. Did you learn anything from this lesson that will be helpful to you in dealing with painful emotions? (Invite sharing.)

Assessment: The instructor should collect the tag-board posters to verify that each group of students could list at least two healthy and two unhealthy ways to deal with a painful emotion. If all groups are able to do so, the objective for the session has been met.

Figure 17.1. Example of a lesson plan format for eighth graders. *Note.* Adapted from *The Passport Program: A Journey Through Emotional, Social, Cognitive, and Self-Development (Grades 6–8)* (pp. 203–204), by A. Vernon, 1998, Champaign, IL: Research Press.

adolescents experience discouragement, ambivalence, depression, shame, and confusion that often seem unbearable. Many lack the ability to deal constructively with their feelings and adopt unhealthy ways to relieve their pain. A lesson of this nature helps them learn more effective coping strategies.

Using the lesson plan format shown in Figure 17.1 provides professional school counselors and teachers with a framework that helps organize the lesson and assure greater accountability, because the content and personalization questions relate specifically to the identified competency.

Implementing the School Counseling Curriculum

Although the phrase "for all students" is rooted deep within the philosophy of a comprehensive program and has generally been a characteristic of elementary counseling programs since their conception, this concept necessitates a role change for professional school counselors, particularly at the high school level, where functions have been more traditional. Numerous authors (ASCA, 2012a; Erford, 2015c; Goodnough et al., 2105; Gysbers & Henderson, 2012; Lee & Goodnough, 2015) support this change because it has the potential to impact so many students and assist them with the mastery of developmental tasks.

As professional school counselors transition into the classroom, it is important to remember that classroom developmental guidance needs to be a team effort. Professional school counselors may teach or team-teach the lessons as well as serve as a resource person to the teacher who assumes the leadership role in the delivery process (Gysbers & Henderson, 2012). As specified in the underlying principles of a comprehensive program, this team approach is imperative because the professional school counselor is *not* the counseling program. Although the intent of a comprehensive program that emphasizes prevention is to reduce the focus on crisis and remedial intervention, it is naïve to assume that we can eliminate all problems through prevention. Because professional school counselors, not teachers, are the ones who are trained to do crisis and remedial intervention, school counselors must continue to assume this role. But it is also unreasonable to think that counselors can do this on top of all the prevention. For this reason, training teachers to take an active role in delivering developmental classroom guidance lessons is crucial.

According to Tollerud and Nejedlo (2009), professional school counselors can train teachers in the types of lessons as well as the process. They can model the teaching of personal–social, academic, and career guidance lessons that ultimately enhance development. In addition, professional school counselors can assist teachers in identifying ways to incorporate personal–social, academic, and career development objectives into their specific subject matter.

Tollerud and Nejedlo (2009) outlined several key principles of a counseling curriculum: that they help students cope with normal developmental issues and problems; that they consider the nature of human development, including the general stages and tasks of normal development; and that they not only encompass a remedial and crisis approach but a preventative focus as well. The human development perspective is the foundation for the program and the basis for identifying the competencies that students need to master. Sharing these principles with teachers and administrators will help clarify misconceptions they may have about a guidance curriculum.

Summary/Conclusion

The purpose of this chapter was to give professional school counselors suggestions for promoting healthy development in all students by implementing, in conjunction with teachers, the core component of a comprehensive developmental program: the guidance curriculum. Use of the ASCA standards and broad competencies as a basis for developing specific grade-level competencies was described to help professional school counselors move to the next level: identifying or writing developmentally appropriate guidance activities to achieve the competencies. The lesson plan is a viable format for teachers and professional school counselors to use, and readers are encouraged to use a structure that emphasizes knowledge and skill acquisition and also helps students personalize the information to their own situations for optimal learning.

CHAPTER 18

Setting Up and Managing a Classroom

Carlen Henington and R. Anthony Doggett

Preview

The information in this chapter will provide the professional school counselor with recommendations for school personnel to get the school year off to a good start and to maintain an efficient and effective classroom environment throughout the year. This chapter includes: (a) information about effective physical arrangement of the classroom; (b) procedures to establish and teach classroom rules and procedures; and (c) use of effective behavior management strategies including differential reinforcement, group contingencies, token economies, behavior contracts, overcorrection, time-out, and response-cost procedures. To address recent accountability and response to intervention mandates, we will also offer suggestions for how professional school counselors could make recommendations for tracking children's behavior prior to and during implementation of classroom management strategies (i.e., responsiveness to intervention). To maximize the recommendations presented in this chapter, we advise that professional school counselors assist teachers in developing a comprehensive plan for their classroom at the very beginning of the school year, prior to student attendance. However, the information within this chapter can be implemented with minor modifications at any time during the school year. As such, professional school counselors may want to consult this chapter throughout the academic year as they receive student or classroom referrals.

At the end of the first month of school, Mr. Jones, a new teacher, approached Mrs. Williams, the professional school counselor. He stated that he did not believe he was cut out to be a teacher. Mrs. Williams wondered, "What had gone wrong?" On his first day of school, Mr. Jones had told her that he was looking forward to having his own classroom, meeting the children, and making a difference in their lives. He was finally a teacher! However, he is concerned about the focus on high-stakes testing and the accountability for students' progress as mandated by federal laws. Mr. Jones stated he had recently been informed of several students who had been identified as "at risk," based on grade retention or universal screening measures and knew they were struggling to meet the demands of classroom instruction. As she spoke with Mr. Jones, Mrs. Williams discovered that, like many new teachers, he was having difficulty keeping his students on task. He had spent so much of the day trying to redirect them that he was not able to get through the material he had prepared for the class. He also was concerned about his need to attend and present information at problem-solving meetings for those at-risk students. He asked, "Mrs. Williams, do you have any suggestions?"

This scenario is common in schools across the United States. The professional school counselor may be asked to design a learning environment for students (e.g., a social-skills class for students experiencing peer-relation difficulties), to assist a new teacher in getting the new school year off to a good start, or assist in the school-level meetings for at-risk students (e.g., teacher or student support meetings). Professional school counselors also need to assist in the development of behavior plans and tracking behavior changes in response to required documentation for referrals for assessment. At other times, the professional school counselor might be asked to make a presentation to more seasoned teachers so that they are more likely to have a smooth running classroom during the school year and understand recent changes in school procedures to address behavior and academic concerns for the students in their school.

Recommendations for classroom management start before the first day of class and continue through the school year. This chapter will include suggestions for

- physical classroom structure;
- rules, schedules, and procedures;
- managing transitions;
- enhancing and maintaining student motivation;
- effectively responding to inappropriate behavior; and
- tracking the effectiveness of the procedures through data collection.

Although there are other areas that foster a proficient classroom environment, professional school counselors are frequently asked to address these six areas. A recent trend in classroom management is to consider practices in classroom management in a tier process (Brown-Chidsey & Steege, 2005). This tier process is often referred to as the response to intervention (RTI) model. Although the complete description of the model is beyond the scope of this chapter, the professional school counselor will need a basic understanding of the model. This chapter will therefore begin with a brief overview of the tier model and then will focus on suggestions that the professional school counselor may provide the classroom teacher to address the five previously identified areas. It is important to note that the concepts apply equally to professional school counselors when conducting developmental classroom guidance.

Response to Intervention

The RTI model is founded upon the work of special educators (e.g., Deno's [1970] cascade model of special education service delivery) and a number of mandated regular education initiatives (Brown-Chidsey & Steege, 2005). RTI is believed to address the evidence-based practice requirements for both the No Child Left Behind Act (NCLB) of 2001 and the 2004 reauthorization of the Individuals with Disabilities Education Improvement Act (IDEA; National Association of State Directors of Special Education, 2005). This model is a data-based problem-solving model that, most commonly, uses a three-tiered approach to intervention in regular education classrooms. At each tier, school personnel must rely upon information (i.e., empirically collected data) to make the decision to move to the next tier. A complementary three-tier model is discussed within the School-wide Positive Behavior Interventions and Supports (SW-PBIS) literature and addresses specific behavioral supports required at each tier. The professional school counselor should read Brown-Chidsey and Steege (2005) for complete information and how-to tips and tools for implementation of the complete RTI model, as well as Sailor, Dunlap, Sugai, and Horner (2009) for additional information on a multi-tiered approach to positive behavior support.

Tier 1 is considered to be "good classroom teaching" in the general education curriculum for all students. In this tier, students' needs are anticipated and accommodated by teachers, perhaps with some assistance from the professional school counselor, within a typical classroom environment. The assumption is that students receive adequate education from well-trained teachers in adequately resourced classrooms and includes the use of effective instructional techniques and the good classroom management procedures described in this chapter.

Tier 2 is directed toward students with a need for more intensive and specific instruction in the school environment. This need may be academic or behavioral in nature. For example, a student who is falling behind in his or her class work as a result of noncompletion of homework may be the focus of Tier 2 assistance. The professional school counselor may suggest to the teacher that the student be provided additional instruction in a small group following the presentation of new material and also assist the teacher in the design of a motivation strategy to increase homework completion. Thus, Tier 2 involves supplemental instruction and broad-based intervention provided to the student in the classroom setting. Typically, about 10% to 20% of students in a classroom might receive Tier 2 interventions.

Tier 3 is the provision of more comprehensive and intensive intervention for the individual who does not respond to the Tier 2 interventions and is at risk for significant school failure. Approximately 3% to 5% of students in a classroom may receive Tier 3 interventions. For example, the Tier 2 student is provided small-group instruction and is awarded with stickers for each homework assignment that is turned in. At the end of 9 to 12 weeks, the teacher and professional school counselor determine—based on information collected by the teacher—that the student is not responding adequately to finely tuned interventions. Thus, despite many weeks of appropriate intervention, the student continues to fail. At this point, the student would be referred for Tier 3 intervention. This intervention would be designed by a specially selected group of education personnel (e.g., the school principal, professional school counselor, school psychologist, a curriculum specialist, the classroom teacher). This team is often referred to as a student or teacher assistance team (i.e., SAT or TAT, respectively) or student or teacher support team (i.e., SST or TST, respectively). This team then would complete a series of activities: (a) assess the student's situation (e.g., classroom environment, academic performance, behavioral or discipline referrals, attendance record) and examine detailed records of the past interventions (e.g., progress tracking sheets and integrity records for the interventions); (b) make recommendation for intensive, one-on-one interventions to address the academic and/or behavior concerns identified in the first step; (c) regularly monitor the student's response to the intervention and the integrity with which the intervention is implemented; and (d) make suggested changes to the intervention, if needed. Should the child not respond to this high-intensity, resource-rich intervention, he or she would then be referred for evaluation for eligibility for special education services.

It is important to note that the transition between each of the tiers is reliant upon appropriate documentation of the student's response to the instruction and intervention implemented at each tier. This documentation includes the exact nature of the intervention, the integrity with which it was implemented, and regular monitoring of academic progress (or changes in behavior if appropriate). Thus, each of the following sections might need to be included as documentation as the child moves through the tier process.

Physical Classroom Structure

Organization of a classroom requires planning in a number of areas. The well-prepared professional school counselor will begin preparation tasks long before the first day of school, including gathering information about the students who will be in the classroom. This foreknowledge allows the counselor to anticipate many situations that may cause difficulty later (e.g., behavior or discipline referrals, academic progress, previously implemented special accommodations).

Classroom Arrangement

Researchers have long established that the physical arrangement of a classroom has a direct effect on student behavior (Rathvon, 1999). For example, students with attention-deficit/hyperactivity disorder may respond to preferential seating, in which they are placed near the front of the classroom, away from windows, air conditioners, and other distracting stimuli, and close to the teacher. When careful consideration is made of these situations, a distractible student has been found to be more productive and less disruptive in the classroom. Other reasons to consider room arrangement might include management of noise level and disruptions during activities, facilitation of quality student interactions and deterring inappropriate interactions, effective use of available space, and enhancement of academic productivity. Because large structures such as blackboards and bulletin boards are already in place, furniture placement is usually the primary arrangement consideration in a classroom.

Before considering seating arrangements, however, determine what activities will occur within the classroom (e.g., independent seatwork, small-group, free-time activities). Other space may be required for storage, a quiet time area (e.g., a student retreat), time-out or penalty area, the teacher's desk, computer area, and announcement board. Colvin (2002) provided recommendations and considerations for these and other classroom activities and requirements. Table 18.1 provides information that will assist the professional school counselor and teacher to plan for each of these typical classroom requirements.

Student Seating

Once the classroom functions and requirements have been considered and arrangements have been made for them, it is time to consider student desk arrangement. Strategies for student seating have evolved over the years, with evidence that a wide variety of arrangements are effective.

There are numerous suggestions for seating to facilitate classroom management and student learning. Initially, the teacher should assign seats to the students. However, as the year continues, the teacher may allow the students to participate in seat selection as well as desk arrangements. Some variations to the traditional straight-row layout include semicircular and cluster arrangements or a combination of these. To increase opportunity for development of new friendships, place students next to someone they have not sat next to in the past. The seat-

Table 18.1 Considerations for Classroom Space Arrangement

Task/Function	Considerations	Recommendations
Independent work	Requires minimal distractions	Individual seating, room to spread out, avoid high traffic areas
Small-group work	Requires student attention to teacher and other group members	Consider a circle, semicircle, or similar configuration; be sure teacher is able to monitor the entire room
Free-time area	Usually used when children finish work before other students	Restrict to an area away from the main classroom to minimize distraction; implement specific rules of use for this area
Storage	Requires easy access without disrupting the class	Keep neat and organized; locate in low-traffic area; be sure cabinet does not obstruct view of teacher or students
Quiet area	Often used for students who require a place to retreat when overwhelmed or stressed; is often used at the student's request rather than the teacher's	Place in an isolated area of the classroom to discourage other students from interacting with the child using this area
Time-out area	Used as a consequence for unacceptable behavior	Area requires a desk in a corner or other out-of-the-way place, but where the teacher can closely monitor the child (there may be more than one time-out area)
Teacher's desk	Requires confidentiality and security of contents	Place out of high-traffic area, but in a location where the teacher can supervise and monitor all students at the same time; avoid an obstructed view
Bulletin board	Has multiple purposes including posting rules and announcements such as news events and special projects	Keep up-to-date, attractive, and uncluttered
Computer area	May also serve as a free-time area; chairs and table need to be adequate to allow work space and student collaboration	Place out of high-traffic area but also in a location that can be easily monitored and supervised by the teacher; provide a storage area or shelf for necessary computer hardware (e.g., headphones)

ing arrangement might also depend on the unit being taught in a particular subject. Students become aware of this and anticipate the new arrangement as each unit is finished. The teacher can use student selection as a motivator for doing well on the unit exam (this will be discussed further in the chapter).

Classroom arrangement can be an important tool in facilitating student learning, student cooperation, and enjoyment of the classroom. Be sure to consider the functions and activities that will occur in the class. Avoid placing obstacles to traffic flow in high-traffic areas. Make sure all students can see the instructional area and the teacher can see all areas of the classroom when engaged in a variety of tasks and activities. Be sure to have frequently used supplies and materials well organized and arranged for easy access.

Classroom Rules and Procedures

Determining the classroom schedule and teaching students the rules and procedures at the beginning of the school year are extremely important and necessary. Often, preferred teachers are those who impose structure (i.e., expectations for classroom behavior) and enforce class rules, procedures, and routines. For those students with special needs (e.g., those with developmental delays, mental deficiencies, behavior disorders, learning difficulties), this structure is key in the learning environment. Enforcement of rules and procedures can make the difference between optimal functioning and academic failure and behavior difficulties.

Rules

Much attention in the education literature has been paid to the importance of rules in the management of a classroom. Rules must be taught by teachers and learned by students, and the professional school counselor should remind teachers to include the school rules in their plan and to take time to teach students rules on the first day of class. The most effective classroom managers understand that well-established, effective educational practice must be applied to teaching classroom rules. Any teaching process requires several steps, and it may require the first 2 weeks of the new school year for the students to master all the rules. Colvin (2002) stated that the appropriate behavior of students is dependent upon instruction of the rules and the teacher's expectation for adherence to them.

Rules communicate to students specifically what the teacher expects them to do and not to do in the school environment. A general recommendation is that teachers determine general rules to be implemented, but students should be allowed to participate in the development of the wording for the class rules. This enhances students' sense of 'ownership' in the rules and is likely to increase adherence to the rules. Teachers and students should develop about five proactive classroom rules (e.g., *Use inside voices; Follow teacher directions*). The rules should also be stated in positive terms, observable and measurable, simply stated and age-appropriate, and taught using examples and non-examples of expected behavior (Newcomer, 2008). Furthermore, rules can address both social and academic behaviors. Other examples include, *Keep your eyes on the teacher while he or she is teaching; Raise your hand to speak or request permission; Keep hands, feet, and objects to self; Use appropriate language; Walk in the classroom; Turn assignments in on time;* and *Place your homework in the homework tray*. Rules should be placed in a prominent location in the room and referred to several times throughout the day when praising students and disciplining them. An often-forgotten midyear routine is to reteach the class rules (or even revamp them) following the winter holiday break, and some teachers may find the need to reteach the rules following other breaks during the school year or when behavioral patterns emerge that cause disruption in the classroom environment.

Procedures

A plethora of interruptions and breaks are imposed on the school day. Instruction in the routines and procedures at the beginning of the school year serve three goals: (a) increase time for learning, (b) facilitate access to learning, and (c) foster self-management skills in students. The achievement of these goals is likely to establish and maintain a healthy learning environment, with few behavior problems or other unplanned disruptions to distract the teacher and students.

Teachers allocate a specific amount of time for learning; however, time spent actively learning (engaged time or time on task) is frequently less than allocated time. Additionally, time on task varies considerably from student to student. An important goal is to have all allocated time spent in learning engagement and to have each student engaged for a similar amount of time. An important consideration is that, although students may be on task, they may not be succeeding at the learning task. When students are truly learning and understanding, the time can be termed academic learning time. Researchers have found that of the over 1,000 hours in a school year mandated by most states, only 300 to 400 hours are spent in academic learning time (Weinstein & Mignano, 1997).

Researchers have shown that when students work directly with the teacher they have higher rates of engaged time, whereas students who work on their own are engaged in the task for about half the time (Frick, 1990). Thus, when independent seatwork is assigned, the teacher should carefully monitor the students to increase time on task. Two of the most common losses of time during independent seatwork are a lack of understanding by the student about what to do next and a lack of necessary materials at hand. Therefore, a teacher who is aware of everything that is happening in the classroom (i.e., has 'with-it-ness') is more likely to be able to assist students. Several additional teacher skills include the ability to supervise several activities at once, keep several students involved in activities, and keep the instruction and students (as a group) moving through assigned tasks at an appropriate pace. One method to accomplish these tasks is to have prescribed procedures that students understand and can implement with minimal supervision. This fosters students' self-management of their own learning activities.

Procedures and Rules

The effective classroom manager communicates to students how activities will be accomplished and expectations for behavior in the classroom. It is important to distinguish between classroom procedures and classroom rules. Effective classroom managers develop clear and simple expectations for classroom behavior that are understood by all the students. According to Weinstein and Mignano (1997), a typical day in a classroom might have the following activities:

1. Administrative routines (e.g., attendance taken)
2. Student movement (e.g., changing classes, going to lunch)
3. Housekeeping (e.g., putting away instructional materials)
4. Routines for completing lessons (e.g., collecting assignments)
5. Student–teacher interactions (e.g., asking for help)
6. Student–student interactions (e.g., socializing)

Having clear rules and expectations for these six activities will facilitate effective classroom management. Although some of these activities will have their own rules and procedures, a few general rules will often clarify expectations for appropriate behavior, and procedures for one activity will generalize to other activities. When teaching the procedures to students, be sure to use specific and concrete procedures, model, rehearse, and provide corrective feedback to the students on how well they follow the procedures. Continue to review the procedures for several weeks at the beginning of the school year and again following any major breaks in the school year (winter holidays, fall and spring breaks). It is acceptable to add new procedures as needed, but be sure to follow the same teaching principles. The following are general guidelines for the development and implementation of procedures:

1. Determine procedures for housekeeping activities before the first day of class. Teach the procedures to the students, and reward compliance during the first several weeks of school. Make sure there is a place for everything and that time is allocated to accomplish housekeeping tasks.
2. Decide how students are to enter and leave the classroom. Teach this procedure to students on the first day. Expect compliance every time students enter or leave the class whether they are in a group or by themselves. When students fail to comply, have them come back to enter or leave correctly.
3. Establish a signal to alert the students. There may be more than one signal that students learn (e.g., one each for instructional time, recess, walking in the hall).
4. Be sure all students understand the procedures for participation in class. Will the student raise a hand for assistance or to answer questions? How will students know that a choral response is required? What are the procedures for using the different areas of the room?
5. Teach students the procedure for assignment completion. Where will assignments be posted, where are they to be turned in, and how will the student know how they did on an assignment?

Now that students understand the procedures for engagement in classroom activities, it is time to develop classroom rules. Researchers have found that having students involved in the development of rules increases their motivation to adhere to the rules. Generally, classroom rules address student-to-student interactions (e.g., *Hands and feet to self*) and personal property (e.g., *Ask before borrowing*). Other rules address teacher expectations for student preparation (e.g., *Bring all needed materials to class*). Finally, rules may be intended to facilitate adherence to more general school rules (e.g., dress codes, forbidden items and activities) and school-wide expectations (e.g., be safe, respectful, and responsible). When teaching rules, effective classroom managers provide examples and nonexamples of the rule to facilitate student understanding. Additionally, it is important for students to understand that they will be held accountable for their behavior in following rules and that rules will have consequences.

Consequences for Rule Violations

Generally, it is best to implement a consequence for misbehavior. Alberto and Troutman (2012) outlined the following hierarchy:

1. *Level I*—Differential reinforcement (e.g., reinforcing behavior that is incompatible with problem behavior).
2. *Level II*—Extinction (e.g., withdrawing reinforcement for undesired behavior).
3. *Level III*—Removal of desirable stimuli (e.g., time-out procedures, response-cost procedures, staying in from recess).
4. *Level IV*—Presentation of aversive stimuli (e.g., corporal punishment, spanking). This is the least desirable form of consequence to use for problem behavior and should be avoided if at all possible.

In relation, teachers often develop a hierarchy of consequences for misbehavior that range from least to most intrusive. Options frequently include reminders for the expectation or rule to the whole class or individual violating the rule, brief time-out in class, brief time-out outside of class, different forms of teacher-led detentions (e.g., recess detention, lunch detention, after-school detention), student conference, parent contact or conference, or an Office Discipline Referral (ODR) for continued display of problem behavior. However, use of corrective consequences should be included within a comprehensive behavior management package that leads to the development of a positive classroom atmosphere (Newcomer, 2008). Specific strategies for creating a positive classroom climate, managing transitions, reinforcing appropriate student behavior, and decreasing the display of problem behavior are discussed in the following sections.

Using Rules and Procedures to Prevent Bullying and Create Positive Classroom Climates

Bullying is becoming a concern of parents and educators. In a study of more than 2,200 students, Nickerson, Singleton, Schnurr, and Collen (2014) reported that approximately 30% of students reported being bullied or witnessing bullying. Further, they state "bullying should be viewed from an ecological perspective that considers not only individual variables, but also familial, peer, school, and community factors" (p. 158). In this study, students who experienced or witnessed bullying were more likely to report negative perceptions of school climate. Further, in a study of nearly 2,000 students across 37 schools, Mitchell and Bradshaw (2013) evaluated students' perceptions of classroom climate relative to discipline style and found a positive relationship between positive behavior management techniques and students' ratings of order and discipline, fairness within the classroom, and positive teacher-student relationships.

Thus, it is important that bully prevention procedures and positive classroom management be implemented to avoid situations where children antagonize and/or bully others. Doll, Zucker, and Brehm (2004) maintained that "school classrooms can become resilient communities that provide essential support and guidance so that vulnerable children can learn and be successful" (p. 2). In order to accomplish this, the following essential elements are necessary: (a) academic efficacy, (b) behavioral self-control, (c) academic self-determination, (d) effective teacher-student relationships, (e) effective peer relationships, and (f) effective home-school relationships. Within a resilient classroom, students feel supported, respected, and valued within the environment and across various settings in which they move throughout the day.

The professional school counselor can facilitate positive classroom climates by providing assistance to teachers to contrive positive classroom environments through effective management procedures. For example, setting aside a few minutes each day to have an opportunity for students to talk individually with the teacher allows students to feel that they are listened to and that their concerns are important to the teacher. Establishing norms and rules for how children interact and treat each other is also important. The professional school counselor can also encourage teachers to actively arrange and supervise students' interactions, particularly when discord has occurred. This allows students to develop negotiation skills with the assistance of the teacher who can mediate when disagreements approach high emotionality. Assisting teachers to initiate and maintain effective school-home communication is another important task with which the professional school counselor can assist. This may involve publishing a school newsletter, encouraging parental involvement in school projects, and providing guidance in culturally sensitive policies and procedures. When relationships across the three sets of individuals (peers, teachers, parents) are deliberately cultivated, children are more likely to be academically and socially successful (Doll et al., 2004). Finally, by encouraging teachers to use positive and proactive (or preventative) discipline procedures, the professional school counselor can facilitate students' perceptions of a positive school climate. Additional information on management of behavior is provided below.

Managing Transitions

Anytime a change in activity occurs, it is likely that loss of learning time and behavioral difficulties will also occur. The average classroom makes 8 to 10 transitions per day—the equivalent of a full day each week spent in transitions (Rathvon, 1999). Effective classroom managers limit the number of transitions in a day, and making these transitions smooth will likely result in less lost teaching time. Furthermore, disruptive behavior is more likely to occur during transition times. To reduce the amount of time lost in transitions or when a classroom teacher recognizes that a disruptive behavior pattern has emerged among the students, the professional school counselor should encourage the teacher to use precorrection techniques to address his or her concerns (Newcomer, 2008). In order to effectively use precorrection strategies, the teacher identifies the transition activity and teaches the specific desired replacement behaviors (i.e., rule or routine) for the context. Behavior rehearsals and repeated practice should be used to provide the students with guided opportunities and frequent, overt prompts should be provided to students as they perform the required behaviors (Colvin, 2002). Finally, teaching personnel should be encouraged to actively acknowledge and praise students individually and as a group when they are practicing the transition activity and naturally engaging in the expected behavior throughout the school day. As students become more proficient with the transition, teaching staff should be able to prompt the expected behavior by simply using a precorrection statement (e.g., "Remember to walk on the right side of the hall keeping your hands to yourself and speaking in a low voice tone when going to your next class."). Other effective methods to decrease transition time in the classroom include signs or posters with specific instructions regarding expected behavior during transitions in prominent and relevant locations, step-by-step digital pictures of students following the rule or procedure, questions posted in key places in the classroom (e.g., "Do you have your journal, notebook, calculator, textbook?"), timers to indicate time allowed for different activities, music playing during transitions or specific activities, motivation strategies (i.e., beat-the-clock game), and peer- or self-monitoring strategies linked to contingent reinforcement (i.e., free time) for following procedures correctly.

Methods for Motivating Students and Addressing Behaviors

Difficult to manage behavior is often the result of low student motivation or poor teacher-student relationships. As a first line of intervention, at any of the tiers in the intervention process, the professional school counselor may assist the teacher in developing strategies to

Table 18.2 Tips for Handling Misbehavior in the Classroom Using Classroom Rules

1.	Consistently implement a consequence for a broken rule, and select an appropriate consequence for the infraction.
2.	State the rule and the consequence but nothing else (this prevents arguing and deal making).
3.	Avoid making an example out of the student in front of peers (this avoids making the student or the teacher feel like they need to win) by addressing the behavior privately.
4.	Avoid asking questions to which you already know the answer (e.g., "What are you supposed to be doing right now?").
5.	Control your anger and try to remember that most rule infractions are not personally directed toward you, the teacher.
6.	Remember to use a 4:1 ratio of positive to corrective interactions with students and quickly acknowledge compliance after correcting a student.
7.	Always consider that the preferred outcome is for the student to learn to avoid the infraction in the future as discipline is designed to teach replacement behaviors.
8.	Seek assistance work with other school professionals in a team format to avoid burnout if behavioral problems continue.

increase student motivation and increase the likelihood that a student will engage in appropriate behaviors and actively respond to effective instruction in the classroom. The delivery of high quality instruction is one of the most critical antecedents for the display of appropriate behavior, and the relationship between academic outcomes and performance of appropriate behavior has been established (Newcomer, 2008). One of the most effective methods for decreasing student behavior problems is to increase student engagement in the academic material or lesson by increasing their opportunities to respond (OTR). A comprehensive discussion of instructional practices and instructional management is beyond the scope of this chapter; however, some effective strategies include the use of Direct Instruction (DI), peer tutoring (e.g., Class-wide Peer Tutoring; Peer-Assisted Learning Strategies), computer-assisted instruction (CAI), student response strategies (e.g., choral responding, response cards, clickers, Think-Pair-Share), and incorporation of student interests and choice in academic assignments (Newcomer, 2008). Other critical antecedents include the establishment of a positive learning atmosphere and development of quality relationships with students. Teaching personnel serve as one of the most important role models in assisting students to develop character skills and become self-disciplined in life. The demeanor, values, and personal approach of the teacher creates the atmosphere, or climate, in the classroom. In order to create a positive classroom climate, interactions with students should be conducted in a manner that demonstrates respect, empathy, patience, self-control, fairness, kindness, justice, and caring even in situations in which the student may require correction (Claassen & Claassen, 2008).

In relation, Newcomer (2008) suggested that teachers can engage in behaviors that serve as "climate killers" (e.g., teaching lessons with little or no attention to student emotional states or stress levels, lecturing students about behavior, using sharp or excessive criticism, using humor or sarcasm at the student's expense, talking negatively about students to others, being inconsistent with rule enforcement and reinforcement, providing punitive consequences with no behavioral supports to replace behavior, showing little interest in students' lives, and having no social interaction with students) or 'climate enhancers' (e.g., setting high, yet reasonable and attainable expectations; ensuring academic and behavioral success for students;

consistently modeling respectful and polite behavior; using effective listening skills; genuinely praising students frequently; using concerned, caring, positive language when speaking to others about the student; celebrating student success and achievement; getting to know students and their interests; using humor appropriately; and refraining from over-responding to annoying behaviors or taking student behavior personally). Should these strategies prove to be ineffective and the student engages in undesired behaviors, the goal would be to decrease the likelihood of the undesired or problematic behaviors while still increasing the appropriate behavior. The following sections provide a basic overview of a number of empirically based interventions to address behaviors in the classroom. The first section will assist in development of strategies to increase desired behavior, and the second section will outline strategies to decrease undesired behavior. While research-based, it is important to remember that these procedures should be implemented within the context of a multi-tiered model.

Reinforcement-Based Procedures

One of the most difficult tasks in classroom management is to facilitate and maintain student motivation. However, if students are motivated to do well in the classroom and to follow procedures and rules, the teacher is likely to find that effective classroom management is relatively easy to facilitate. Several methods are available for the teacher to increase students' motivation to follow rules and procedures and engage in academic activities. These include differential reinforcement, the Premack principle, group contingencies, token economies, behavior contracts and charts, time-out, and overcorrection procedures.

Differential reinforcement. One of the most influential management strategies readily available to the teacher throughout the day is the social attention provided to students. Unfortunately, teacher attention can be used to reinforce both appropriate and problem behavior, so the teacher has to be cognizant of the behaviors for which he or she provides attention. Differential reinforcement is a procedure whereby the teacher actively ignores or "extinguishes" the display of problem behavior, and actively provides social attention for the display of appropriate behavior (Alberto & Troutman, 2012). Social attention used in this manner has been labeled *time-in* or *catching them being good* and *strategic attention* (Hembree-Kigin & McNeil, 1995). Generally, teachers are encouraged to use differential reinforcement to teach students to follow rules and display appropriate behaviors in the classroom.

Hembree-Kigin and McNeil (1995) identified four types of social attention teachers used to reinforce rule-following and the performance of appropriate behavior: descriptions, reflections, imitations, and praise. *Descriptions* describe the student's actions that are desirable and conducive to active learning and acknowledge the performance of behavior without directly providing praise statements. For example, the teacher may say, "Timmy, I see that you are looking at the board" while teaching from the front of the room, or "Sally, I see that you have completed five math problems" shortly after handing out a math worksheet.

Reflections demonstrate to the student that the teacher is attentive and listening while, at the same time, increasing communication between the teacher and students. For example, after the student has said "Mrs. Jones, look I made a perfect grade on the spelling test," the teacher may say, "Yes, Sarah, I do see that you made a 100 on your spelling test."

Imitations increase the teacher's involvement with students, improve sharing and turn-taking skills, and increase other students' imitation of appropriate behavior. For example, during an art project a teacher may say, "I'm going to draw a tree in my picture like Josie drew in her picture."

Finally, *praise statements* increase desired behaviors, improve the relationship between the teacher and child, and increase the child's self-esteem. Praise statements can be global and general or very specific. Examples of global praise statements include "great," "good job," or "way to go;" whereas, specific praise statements include "Thank you, Timmy, for sitting quietly," or "Sarah has drawn a beautiful tree." Teachers can also provide praise to students through physical means. For example, teachers can increase desirable behaviors by providing hugs, pats on the head or shoulder, high fives, or other appropriate forms of physical interaction.

Teacher attention should be contingent upon appropriate behavior and provided frequently and enthusiastically. Social attention follows the *if–then* rule: Behaviors that the teacher wants to see repeated should be followed by some positive form of teacher attention. Conversely, most minor problem behaviors should receive no attention or very minimal attention (i.e., mild redirection to task). Appropriate behaviors should receive frequent reinforcement. Teachers should provide attention early and often. In fact, researchers have encouraged teachers to follow a minimum 4:1 ratio of attention for appropriate behavior versus attention for problem behavior (Sprick & Howard, 1995). Finally, teacher attention should be provided genuinely and enthusiastically. Teachers should strive to provide attention with expression in their voice and a varied tone as opposed to using a flat, monotone voice. Most students enjoy receiving attention from teachers; however, use of unconvincing or canned statements or praise can quickly erode the effectiveness of adult attention.

Premack principle. As discussed previously, appropriately scheduled activities and transitions can effectively prevent the display of many problematic behaviors in the classroom. However, the schedule of activities can also be used to motivate the students. For example, teachers can use *grandma's rule*, or the Premack principle (Premack, 1959), to shape the occurrence of appropriate student behavior. The Premack principle involves having the students perform a less preferred activity before being allowed to engage in a more preferred activity. In a sense, this principle is similar to the mealtime rule used by many grandmothers over the generations, who have told children that they must eat their vegetables before being allowed to eat dessert. As such, teachers should schedule more demanding or difficult classes or materials before more socially rewarding activities such as recess, break times, group story times, or individual free time.

This principle also could be incorporated into the scheduled change of seating arrangements in the classroom in the manner previously described in the chapter. For example, the teacher could establish the expectation in the classroom that successful completion of a unit would lead to preferred seating arrangements that are decided collectively by the students. Additionally, with a little scheduling creativity, teachers could intersperse preferred and nonpreferred activities or classes throughout the day both to prevent problem behaviors and reinforce the occurrence of appropriate behaviors.

Group contingency systems. Another classroom management strategy that has proven successful in management of student behavior and improvement in academic performance involves the use of group contingencies. Litow and Pumroy (1975) identified three group contingency systems. The first system, *dependent group-oriented contingency*, uses reinforcement for the entire class contingent on the performance of a selected student or a particular group of students. For example, if Mark and Sally can improve their vocabulary quiz grade by 10% above their scores on the last quiz, then the whole class will get extra free time after lunch.

The second system, *interdependent group-oriented contingency*, provides each member access to reinforcement contingent (or interdependent) upon some group level of performance. For example, if the class average is 80% or higher on the math quiz today, then the students will have extra free time this afternoon.

The third system, *independent group-oriented contingency*, uses reinforcement for each student contingent on their individual performance independent of the group performance or the performance of their peers (e.g., whoever turned their homework in this morning can now go to recess). It is important to note that independent group-oriented contingency is generally the preferred system to use in a classroom to avoid undue pressure on the children's social interaction. It would be easy to imagine the hurt feelings that might arise from denial of a reward to the entire class, based on the actions of just one child.

One example of an interdependent group-oriented contingency system that has been used with great success in classrooms is the *Good Behavior Game*, originally presented by Barrish, Saunders, and Wolf (1969). In the *Good Behavior Game*, the class is divided into two or more teams. Team names are posted on the board beside a list of target behaviors or classroom rules that have been operationally defined (specifically, described with observable and quantifiable behaviors) and discussed with the class. The classroom teacher places a mark under the team name any time a member of the team violates one of the rules. At the end of a predetermined period (academic period, morning, afternoon, end of day), the team or teams scoring below a predetermined criterion wins the game and receives a reward. Although originally developed to increase the performance of prosocial behaviors, replication studies have also found the *Good Behavior Game* to effectively increase the performance of academic behaviors. An attractive aspect of the *Good Behavior Game* is its flexibility; rewards (e.g., extra free time, special jobs, extra recess, special badges, other special privileges) and targeted behavior (e.g., academic performance, compliance with classroom rules and procedures) may be varied. Furthermore, the delivery of rewards may range from several times daily to once per week. For a more thorough review of the *Good Behavior Game*, consult the review by Tingstrom (2002).

Token economy systems. Originally used in residential settings to improve hygiene, social skills, and work skills of individuals with developmental disabilities (Ayllon & Azrin, 1968), the token economy has also proved to be a beneficial addition to group-contingency and other classroom management systems in school settings. A token economy is a reinforcement system in which conditioned reinforcers called tokens are delivered to students contingent upon the display of appropriate behavior. The tokens are then exchanged for backup reinforcers at a later period in the day.

Token economies can be very effective interventions for managing student behavior in the classroom. However, poor planning in the initial stages of development of the program can often lead to failure of the intervention (Moore, Tingstrom, Doggett, & Carlyon, 2001). As such, Miltenberger (2011) effectively discussed several important issues that the professional school counselor should consider when suggesting the implementation of a token economy in a school setting. First, the professional school counselor and classroom teacher should clearly and concretely define the desired behaviors. These behaviors may include academic skills, social skills, vocational skills, self-help skills, or general compliance with classroom rules.

Second, school personnel should identify developmentally appropriate items for use as tokens. Tokens must be tangible objects that can be delivered immediately upon the display of appropriate behavior. Common examples include poker chips, coins, play money, stamps, stickers, stars, check marks on or hole-punches in cards, or puzzle pieces that can be used to complete an entire puzzle.

Third, the professional school counselor and teacher should collaborate to identify effective backup reinforcers. Development of the backup reinforcers should be one of the most important considerations of the system, as the tokens obtain their reinforcement value from the backup reinforcers. In other words, if the students do not view the backup reinforcers as valuable, they will not be motivated to engage in appropriate behavior or to exert effort to earn tokens throughout the day. Identification of such reinforcers does not have to be difficult, as most students are often motivated by activity reinforcers (e.g., free time, computer time, movie time, special jobs) that can easily be incorporated into the regular classroom routine. Other reinforcers could also be incorporated into the system (e.g., snacks, pencils, erasers, movie rentals, restaurant coupons) to provide variety and to avoid satiation by the students.

Fourth, an appropriate schedule of reinforcement must be decided upon. Initially, the classroom teacher should deliver tokens to the students frequently and liberally throughout each period to shape up the display of appropriate behavior. As teachers observe improvement, they can move from a continuous schedule of reinforcement to a more intermittent schedule to maintain improvement in student behavior.

Fifth, the professional school counselor should help the teacher establish the token exchange rate. School personnel should determine how many tokens students might potentially earn in a day and then set the exchange rate based on this criterion. Smaller items (e.g., pencils, erasers) will typically cost less, whereas larger items (e.g., 15 minutes of individual computer time) will require the exchange of more tokens.

Sixth, an appropriate time and place for the exchange of tokens must be decided before the program is implemented. Many teachers have created a school store or treasure chest from which students could purchase backup reinforcers at set periods during the day (e.g., morning or afternoon break).

Seventh, the professional school counselor assists the teacher with decisions of whether the display of undesirable behaviors will compete with the performance of appropriate behaviors in such a manner that a response-cost component is warranted. Response cost is the withdrawal of specific amounts of a reinforcer contingent upon the display of problem behavior. As such, response cost is often viewed as a system of leveling fines for the display of inappropriate behavior, similar to the tickets motorists receive for speeding or parking in a protected parking space. To maximize all parts of the system, the token economy should be implemented for a few weeks before the response-cost component is added to ensure that the tokens are truly functioning as conditioned reinforcers. The undesirable behaviors should then be clearly defined, and appropriate fine levels should be established. As with the delivery of tokens, fines should be delivered contingent upon the display of problem behavior. It is extremely important to remember that, for the entire system to function effectively, the students must earn tokens more frequently than they experience fines.

Overall, school personnel need to examine some practical considerations when implementing a token economy system. For example, the portability and ease of delivery of the actual token should be considered. Additionally, storage of the tokens and the potential of theft must be evaluated. Bartering or trading among students should also be eliminated when

---

Behavior Contract for Homework

I, _____ , agree to complete my homework assignments in _____
with at least _____ % accuracy each night from _____ to _____ .
For meeting the criterion on _____ out of _____ days, I can earn _____
to be delivered on _____ (when) by _____ (person).

_____   _____
            Student Signature   Date

_____   _____
            Teacher Signature   Date

Figure 18.1. Sample behavior contract for homework.

setting up a token economy. Finally, the delivery of tokens should always be paired or associated with teacher praise, as the system will eventually need to be phased out to allow student behavior to be maintained by natural reinforcers, such as teacher praise and attention.

Behavior contracts and charts. Up to this point, this chapter has focused primarily on the motivation of students through reinforcement procedures to the entire group of students in the classroom. However, seasoned professional school counselors and classroom teachers know that some students need individual reinforcement systems to assist in managing behavior. One such system involves the use of behavior contracts or charts. Specifically, a behavior contract is a written document that specifies a particular target behavior for a student and the consequences that will be delivered contingent upon the occurrence or nonoccurrence of the behavior at the end of a predetermined period (Miltenberger, 2011). Generally, these contracts are written in paragraph form, with signature lines at the end of the document. In contrast, behavior charts often specify several behaviors that are evaluated at preset periods during the school day, leading to corrective and reinforcing feedback reliably provided throughout the day and at the end of each day. Generally, these charts are developed as a table with the desired behaviors listed in rows and the evaluation periods grouped in columns next to the behaviors. One example of an empirically based behavior chart is the school–home note developed by Kelley (1990). Examples of each form are presented in Figures 18.1 and 18.2, respectively.

Regardless of which contract system is used, Miltenberger (2011) identified several important steps that must be considered. First, the target behaviors must be clearly defined in proactive terms. In other words, the form should list the behaviors *to be performed* as opposed to specifying behaviors to be eliminated. Second, all parties must agree on a measurement system for monitoring the behaviors. This can be completed through the evaluation of permanent products (e.g., completion of a worksheet) or through direct observation and documentation of the performance of the behavior (e.g., *Stayed in seat throughout the reading period*). Third, the specific times for the performance of the behavior should be clearly stated. Fourth, a reinforcement or punishment contingency must be stated on the form. As with most motivational systems, the use of positive reinforcement is most desirable with behavioral contracting; however, a response-cost component similar to that explained in the token economy

Student Procedures
1. Carry the note to school every day.
2. Have the teacher rate your behavior at the end of each period.
3. Carry the note home each day to be reviewed by your parents.

Classroom Procedures
1. Student behavior is evaluated at the end of each period.
2. Record a "1" if the behavior was displayed.
3. Record a "0" if the behavior was not displayed.
4. Provide social praise for behavior that was displayed.
5. Provide a brief explanation and encouragement for behavior that was not displayed.
6. The last teacher of the day should check to see if minimum points were achieved.
7. Consequences at school should be administered based on number of points earned.
8. The note should be sent home at the end of each day to be reviewed by the parent.

Home Procedures
1. Review the note with your child.
2. Provide praise for behavior that was displayed.
3. Provide the appropriate reward if the criterion was met.
4. Remove the appropriate privileges for lost notes, changed notes, etc.

Name: _____

Date: _____

Behaviors:	Reading	Spelling	Centers	Lunch	Math	Recess
1. Follows directions 1st time given						
2. Keeps hands and feet to self						
3. Uses appropriate language						
Total Points						
Teacher Initials						

Figure 18.2. Sample school–home note.

section could be used with this system as well. Finally, the behavior contract or chart should identify all parties responsible for providing the contingency or reinforcement or punishment; doing so will increase the integrity with which the system is implemented. Readers interested in further learning about contingency contracting and implementing individual management systems should refer to Rhode, Jenson, and Reavis (2010) and Miltenberger (2011).

Punishment-Based Procedures

Other methods used to manage student behavior involve the use of punishment procedures. By strict definition, punishment is a procedure whereby the presentation or removal of a stimulus or event *decreases* the likelihood that a particular behavior will be performed in the future. Two forms of punishment have been identified. Positive punishment refers to *the presentation of an aversive stimulus* following the occurrence of a behavior that leads to a decrease in the likelihood that the behavior will be performed in the future. Negative punishment refers to the *removal of a preferred stimulus* following the occurrence of a behavior that leads to a decrease in the probability that the behavior will occur at a later time.

Positive punishment procedures. Overcorrection is an example of a positive punishment procedure. Originally developed by Foxx and Azrin (1972, 1973) for use with individuals in institutional settings, overcorrection requires a student to engage in a predetermined behavior for an extended period of time contingent upon each occurrence of the problem behavior. Two forms of overcorrection have been identified: positive practice and restitution.

In positive practice, the student is required to engage in the correct form of the appropriate behavior for a specified period of time (e.g., 5–15 minutes) or a specified number of times (e.g., 3 times). For example, a group of students may enter the classroom too loudly. The teacher could have the students go back into the hall and quietly enter the classroom three times. This repetition would provide positive practice of the appropriate behavior. This intervention has application for academic behavior as well. Skinner and colleagues (Skinner, Belfiore, & Pierce, 1992; Skinner, McLaughlin, & Logan, 1997; Skinner, Shapiro, Turco, & Cole, 1992; Skinner, Turco, & Beatty, 1989; Smith, Dittmer, & Skinner, 2002) have used positive practice as an effective component of the cover, copy, and compare academic intervention to increase accuracy rates for students. In this intervention, the student is required to perform an academic task (e.g., take a spelling test). Upon completion of the test, the student compares her words to a list containing the correct spelling of the words. Upon comparison, the student identifies two words that are misspelled. The student is then required to rewrite the misspelled words three times each, which provides for positive practice of the correct spelling of each word. As is illustrated with this example, the goal is to decrease the behavior (i.e., misspelled words) rather than to be punitive toward the student.

Restitution requires students to not only correct the environmental effects of the problem behavior but also to restore the environment to a better condition than before the behavior occurred. For example, two boys were found writing on a wall in a bathroom stall at school. After consultation with the professional school counselor, the teacher decided to have the boys clean not only the wall on which they wrote words but the other walls in the stall as well.

Negative punishment procedure. Negative punishment procedures involve the removal of a stimulus or event in order to reduce the probability of the occurrence of problem behavior. One such procedure has already been discussed in the token economy and behavioral contracting sections and involves the use of response-cost procedures. Another example of a negative punishment procedure involves the use of time-out. Specifically, time-out is a shortened version of the phrase "time-out from positive reinforcement" and has been labeled as a Level III management procedure, and therefore is preferable to the use of aversive procedures (Level IV; Alberto & Troutman, 1995). With the exception of response-cost and overcorrection/restitution procedures, most of this section has focused on reinforcement procedures for motivating students primarily because such procedures must be in place before a punishment procedure such as time-out is used. In other words, the classroom teacher should be discouraged from using time-out until a 'time-in' rich environment has been created through the use of differential attention, Premack principle, group-oriented reinforcement techniques, and behavioral contracting. Furthermore, these more positive procedures are often sufficient to improve a student's behavior to desired levels.

Alberto and Troutman (2012) defined three time-out procedures: seclusionary, nonseclusionary, and exclusionary. In *nonseclusionary time-out*, the teacher denies access to reinforcement; however, the student is not removed from the actual instructional setting (e.g., "Timothy, please place your head on your desk for talking out."). In *exclusionary time-out*, the teacher removes the student from the classroom or activity area (e.g., "Sam, please stand quietly in the hall for pushing Sarah."). In *seclusionary time-out*, the teacher removes the student to a time-out room for a period of time (e.g., in-school detention).

Of the three time-out procedures described, nonseclusionary and exclusionary time-out procedures are easier to implement by teachers and are generally favored over the use of seclusionary time-out. In fact, Erford (1999) presented procedures for a particularly effective version of exclusionary time-out—the contingency-delay model. The professional school counselor should be sure to remind the teacher that time-out is a concept that involves the removal of all forms of reinforcement (e.g., social attention, food, favorite activities) and is not simply a location, such as a chair, corner of the room, or spot on the floor. It is generally suggested that the teacher have a predetermined location for time-out. However, it must be remembered that if the student still receives access to reinforcement in the form of teacher- or peer-provided stares, comments, smiles, or other types of attention, the time-out procedure may become ineffective. Time-out does not have to last long. In fact, releasing the child after a few seconds of quiet behavior can be effective. In most situations, a child should not stay in time-out for longer than 5 minutes after he or she has calmed down and sat quietly in the time-out location. Finally and most important, the professional school counselor should remind the teacher to socially reinforce the child for displaying appropriate behavior as quickly as possible after leaving time-out; doing so will help generate the contrast between receiving reinforcement for appropriate behavior and the loss of reinforcement (i.e., time-out) for problematic behavior. For more assistance with the implementation of time-out in school settings, the professional school counselor is referred to Sterling and Watson (1999).

Restorative Discipline

Unfortunately, discipline and punishment have become synonymous in the educational setting. As mentioned previously, punishment, by strict definition, refers to the delivery of a consequence following an undesired behavior that leads to a decrease in the likelihood that the targeted behavior will be performed in the future. However, many of the punishment techniques that are traditionally viewed as effective by educators (e.g., zero tolerance policies, out-of-school suspension) are actually associated with higher levels of misconduct, higher rates of juvenile incarceration, greater levels of disparity among special education and minority students, and lower rates of academic achievement (American Psychological Association, 2006). Discipline, on the other hand, refers to teaching and instruction that molds, corrects, or perfects the cognitive and academic abilities and moral character of the student (Claassen & Claassen, 2008). All too often, educators are quick to rely on the use of punishment techniques in isolation to try to address student problem behavior because of the frustration and tension associated with the occurrence of the misbehavior. The problem with this approach is that replacement behaviors are often not learned by the offending student and the relationship between the student and the educational personnel is strained, at best, and completely damaged, at worst, due to the use of a reactionary style of management. As such, some educational institutions have started to incorporate restorative discipline techniques in school settings to address student misbehavior (Amstutz & Mullett, 2005; Claassen & Claassen, 2008) in a more proactive manner.

Based on the restorative justice movement (Zehr, 2002), restorative discipline seeks to address three important questions: Was a rule violated? What are the needs and obligations created by the rule violation? And how could things be made as right as possible? (Claassen & Claaseen, 2008). This approach is quite different from the traditional disciplinary approach that asks: Was a rule violated? Who violated the rule? And how should the student be punished? The restorative discipline approach views student-teacher conflicts as normal events that lead to teachable moments and a time of relationship building using inclusive, collaborative processes between the key stakeholders (Claassen & Claassen, 2008). In short, restorative discipline recognizes the purposes of student misbehavior, addresses the needs of those harmed, uses collaborative processes to 'put right' the harm, seeks to heal the relationship, integrates the student back into the educational environment, and improves future behavior and interactions (Amstutz & Mullet, 2005). These outcomes are achieved through the use of several techniques across multiple tiers including student-teacher meetings, problem solving activities, circles, mediation, and family conferencing in addition to using respect agreements, active listening, and I-messages at the classroom level. Interested readers should refer to Amstutz and Mullet (2005), Claassen and Claassen (2008), and Zehr (2002) for specific information on restorative practices and restorative discipline.

Teacher Consultation and Fidelity

Fidelity or treatment integrity refers to the degree to which an intervention or strategy is implemented accurately, consistently, or as planned (Martens & McIntyre, 2009). The aforementioned classroom management strategies have empirical support; however, the intervention techniques can only be proven effective when implemented as intended. Otherwise, it is difficult, if not impossible, to evaluate if the student is responding to intervention. When consulting and evaluating the fidelity with which teachers implement effective classroom management techniques, the school counselor may find it useful to provide feedback using a structured, quantitative approach that directly addresses the use of the behavior management skills discussed in this chapter. Several researchers have offered classroom rating inventories (e.g., Lewis, 2007; Roberts & Doggett, 2011). A sample classroom behavior management rating scale is included in Figure 18.3. This 10-item instrument addresses the physical structure of the classroom, behavioral expectations and routines, student-teacher interactions, pacing of instruction, transitions, active supervision, use of effective instruction delivery and preci-

School: _____	Date of Rating/Observation: _____
Teacher: _____	Time of Observation: _____
Grade: _____	Length of Observation: _____
Subject Area: _____	Rater/Observer: _____

Rate the following behaviors using the scale below for items 1–6, 8, and 10.
0 = rarely happens, 1 = happens some of the time,
2 = happens most of the time, NA = item not applicable

Rating	Item
0 1 2 NA	1. Classroom is organized, seating arrangement and physical structure is conducive to learning (e.g., materials are accessible, students are ready to begin in designated areas, traffic flows smoothly).
0 1 2 NA	2. Teacher states behavioral expectations regarding classwork or routines prior to each lesson / activity or before transition activities (i.e., direct instruction of rules, models with examples, ties instruction to prior knowledge).
0 1 2 NA	3. Teacher actively forges relationships with students prior to (i.e., greets them) and during instruction (e.g., uses names, close proximity, incorporates student interests into lessons when appropriate).
0 1 2 NA	4. Teacher provides appropriate pace of instruction (i.e., effective pacing is maintained throughout lesson, students appear actively engaged) and uses effective instructional techniques (i.e., students have multiple ways to actively respond, teacher regularly checks for understanding, lesson is presented with excitement and enthusiasm, most of allotted time is devoted to instruction).
0 1 2 NA	5. Teacher provides appropriate transition to activities (e.g., quick, quiet, efficient); follows classroom routine as scheduled; provides pre-corrections prior to transitions.
0 1 2 NA	6. Teacher uses active supervision while teaching (e.g., scanning the room to address student needs; moving among students to address needs) and/or during non-classroom transitions (e.g., hallway).
0 1 2 NA Ratio = ____ : ____	7. Teacher uses Effective Instruction Delivery or use of Precision Requests (clear and specific, direct and neutral) versus Vague, Questioning language when directing student behavior. **Note:** 0 = more vague statements than effective instructions; 1 = 1:1 to 3:1 ratio of effective instructions to ineffective instructions; 2 = 4:1 ratio of effective instructions to ineffective instructions
0 1 2 NA	8. Teacher enforces or makes reference to SW-PBIS Expectations (Actively cues or acknowledges the students).

Figure 18.3 Classroom management rating scale. *(continues)*

0 1 2 NA Ratio = ___ : ___	9. Teacher provides Active Acknowledgement for Appropriate Behavior: Praise or Social Recognition to Correction Ratio of 4:1 Positive Interactions: Praise, Noncontingent Attention, Reinforcer/Reward Systems (e.g., behavior bucks) Negative/Corrective Interactions: Reminders, Reprimands, Corrections, Warnings, Consequent Events (e.g., student conference, TO, ASD, ISD) **Note:** 0 = more corrective interactions than positive instructions; 1 = 1:1 to 3:1 ratio of positive to corrective interactions; 2 = 4:1 ratio of positive to corrective interactions
0 1 2 NA	10. Teacher uses effective correction techniques (e.g., delayed responding, effective redirections, extinction for minor problems, limit setting, calm, de-escalating language, restorative practices) or provides other appropriate classroom-based consequence when the student does not respond (e.g., time-out, reflective writing activities, teacher-led ISD, teacher-led ASD, ODR).
___ / ___ = ___	Total Percentage of Fidelity

Figure 18.3 (*continued*)

sion requests, reference to SW-PBIS expectations, student acknowledgement and reinforcement, and use of effective corrective techniques. Raters use a 3-point scale (0 to 2) to rate each item based on a minimum of a 30-minute direct observation. Following the observation, the school counselor should schedule a formal conference with the teacher to provide him or her with direct feedback regarding each of the items, to acknowledge effective use of the management skills, and to provide consultation and guidance regarding the development or enhancement of other skills not observed during the observation. This scale can be used across multiple observations and to document skill development in educational personnel across time.

Summary/Conclusion

With increasing demands placed upon school personnel for the accountability of student progress, it is important for the professional school counselor and teachers to establish a strong working relationship to provide a secure, well-managed learning environment for students. A number of activities and procedures have been discussed within this chapter: use of a tiered model to address teacher concerns, design of a classroom to set up the teacher for success, and use of well-established classroom management and discipline procedures to maintain appropriate behavior in the classroom. According to Alberto and Troutman (2012), those teachers who are most likely to motivate students and to be remembered as special have personal characteristics such as a sense of humor, warmth and caring manifested as sensitivity, and an interest in the personal well-being of the students. One avenue to accomplish this style as a teacher is to have an effectively managed classroom through the use of well-developed rules, effective instructions, well-managed transitions, proper scheduling, differential attention, group-oriented contingencies, behavioral contracting, response cost, time-out procedures, and restorative discipline practices.

CHAPTER 19

Program Accountability

*Bradley T. Erford**

Preview

The information in this chapter gives professional school counselors the basic tools needed to design and conduct effective outcomes assessments and program evaluations to determine and document the quality of comprehensive developmental school counseling programs.

The increasing concern regarding quality education across the nation makes outcome assessment and program evaluation more important than ever. Until recently, however, professional school counselors have provided little evidence that school counseling interventions were achieving intended results; thus, school counseling programs and services lacked substantive accountability. Historically, the response to this criticism was that school counseling services are so complex that evaluating such services and results is difficult, if not impossible (Erford, 2015c). Others noted that school personnel are so busy meeting the needs of students that they shift time that should be spent in evaluation to instruction and programming. Whatever the reason, the lack of accountability threatens the success of students and the future of school counseling programs. Educators are bound by professional and ethical obligations to ensure that educational programs are of high quality and effective in meeting student needs. Without accountability, the determination of program quality will always be suspect.

Generally, program evaluation has at least six purposes: (a) measure the effectiveness of the total program and its activities; (b) collect data that will help determine what program modifications are needed; (c) determine the level of program acceptance and support from stakeholders; (d) obtain information that can be used to inform the public; (e) collect data that add to performance evaluations; and (f) analyze program budget and expenditures. Outcomes assessment and program accountability allow for the documentation and determination of the worth of a school counseling program and are part of a program of continuous quality improvement (Erford, 2015c). Table 19.1 provides definitions of important terms associated with outcomes assessment and program evaluation.

The Assessment Loop

Two key elements of a comprehensive developmental guidance program, as described by Gysbers and Henderson (2012), are program evaluation (process evaluation or audit) and results

---

*Special thanks to Cheryl Moore-Thomas and Lacey L. Wallace for their outstanding contributions to the second edition of this chapter.

Table 19.1 Assessment Terminology

Evaluation is the measurement of worth and indicates that a judgment will be made regarding the effectiveness of a program.

Evidence is qualitative or quantitative data that help make judgments or decisions.

Formative evaluation is evaluative feedback that occurs during the implementation of a program and allows for midcourse corrections to occur.

Summative evaluation is feedback collected at a specified endpoint in an evaluation process.

A *stakeholder* is anyone involved or interested in or potentially benefiting from a program. Students, parents, teachers, professional school counselors, administrators, community leaders, college faculty, and local employers, among others, are potential educational stakeholders.

(outcome) evaluation. *Program evaluation* is the process of systematically determining whether program components have been fully implemented. The process of program evaluation is similar to the concept of content validity. Content validity is a systematic examination of a test's content to answer the question of whether the test measures what it is supposed to measure and in the proper proportion. In the context of school counseling program evaluation, an important guiding question emerges: Is there a preexisting, comprehensive written program that is fully implemented and aligned with district, state, and/or national standards? Simply put, program evaluation involves determining whether written documentation exists and whether implementation of the written program is indeed occurring. Schools and school systems should have well-developed standards/goals, competencies/outcomes, objectives, and curriculum lessons that guide the implementation of a comprehensive developmental guidance program. School-based programs rely on this curricular information to implement consistent and effective developmental services. Unfortunately, this form of program evaluation, while important, only indicates the existence and adherence to a planned program. It does not indicate the results or outcomes of the implemented program. *Outcome evaluation*, on the other hand, answers the question, *Does the program produce the intended outcome?* In order to ensure focused and manageable assessment, it is most practical to connect program concerns to only a few clearly defined questions. Program assessment is cyclical and systematic, a way of answering important questions about a program, and a means to a better education for all students through continuous quality improvement.

Because the assessment process is cyclical and systematic, program evaluation and outcomes assessment processes should start small and build upon successes. Effective methods for individual programs can then be determined and replicated so that, over time, necessary program refinements can be implemented, resulting in a comprehensive developmental school counseling program that meets a school's mission. The assessment loop presented in Figure 19.1 helps to visually conceptualize program evaluation and the ways in which outcome studies can be used to improve educational programs. Assessment is often viewed as a component that concludes a process. However, it should be an integrated part of a continuous process to improve the program. The school's mission drives the program content and therefore drives the assessment process. Then the assessment questions lead to the determination of the kinds of evidence that must be collected. Evidence provides crucial information about program evaluation and results (outcomes).

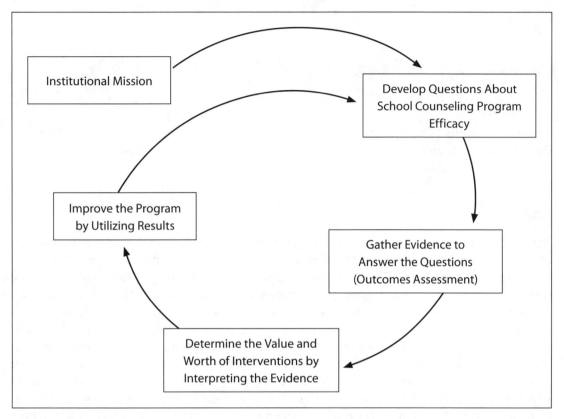

Figure 19.1. Assessment loop.

Evidence can come from numerous and varied sources, including portfolios, external judges or examiners, observations, local tests, purchased tests, student self-assessments, surveys, interviews, focus groups, standardized or informal measures, student performances, or student products. A great deal of evidence is routinely collected in schools. After evidence is collected, interpretation ensues so that conclusions may be reached about the program's value, strengths, weaknesses, and outcomes. As a final step before the process cycles again, interpretations and conclusions are used to adjust to or change program components as needed. Once the changes have been made, new questions can be posed and the cycle begins anew, representing a continuous process of quality improvement.

Results Evaluation

"Questions of worth and effectiveness are derived from a confluence of values, needs, goals, and mission, and these questions lead to the determination of what evidence must be collected" (Erford, 2015c, p. 120). The system chosen for how the evidence is collected warrants further discussion, because how one designs evaluation studies will determine the validity of the findings. At least two primary methods for documenting program effectiveness may be useful to professional school counselors: aggregation and outcome evaluation.

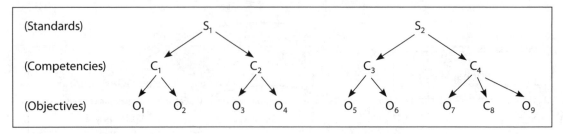

Figure 19.2. Hierarchical structure of a typical curriculum development system.

Aggregation

Aggregation involves a process of combining many small pieces of evidence to document that components of a larger program are indeed effective. A comprehensive developmental school counseling program curriculum is based upon some hierarchical system, usually involving standards (or goals), competencies (or outcomes), and objectives. Figure 19.2 provides a simple hierarchical structure demonstrating this typical system. At the most basic level, demonstrating effectiveness through aggregation depends upon well-written learning objectives.

If a learning objective is written in measurable terms with an appropriate expected performance criterion, it can be determined that the objective has been met. Demonstrating that an objective has been met provides evidence that a competency has been met. Furthermore, when evidence is provided that competencies (or outcomes) have been met, then evidence is also provided that a standard (or goal) has been met. It all starts with measurable learning objectives (see Chapter 16).

Using Figure 19.2, consider an example in which learning objectives O_1–O_6 were met, while learning objectives O_7–O_9 were not. In such a scenario, it is easy to determine that evidence exists that standard 1 (S_1) was met, because objectives 1–4 (O_1–O_4) were met. The first two objectives (O_1 and O_2) were met, providing evidence that the first competency (C_1) was met. The second two objectives (O_3 and O_4) were met, providing evidence that the second competency (C_2) was met. Because both competencies (C_1 and C_2) were met, sufficient evidence exists that the first standard (S_1) was met.

Now consider the scenario for Standard 2, in which the first two objectives (O_5 and O_6) were met, thus providing evidence that the first competency (C_3) was met. The final three objectives (O_7, O_8, and O_9) were not met, thus failing to provide evidence that the final competency (C_4) was met. Because only one of the two competencies (C_3 but not C_4) was met, sufficient evidence does not exist that the second standard (S_2) was met. From this demonstration of the aggregation process, it is easy to conclude that the determination of school counseling program effectiveness begins with learning objectives written in measurable terms, but it also relies heavily on setting a challenging, yet attainable, performance criterion (the "D" component of a learning objective, discussed in Chapter 16).

Conducting Outcome Studies

Outcome studies are generally empirical in nature and involve exercising some control over the conditions under which the evidence is collected (e.g., research design). Campbell and

Table 19.2 Common Research Designs

True Experimental Designs								
A. Posttest-Only Control Group Design					R	T	O	
					R		O	
B. Pretest–Posttest Control Group Design					R	O	T	O
					R	O		O
Quasi-Experimental Designs								
C. Time Series	O	O	O	T	O	O	O	
D. Nonequivalent Control Group Design					O	T	O	
					O		O	
E. Separate-Sample Pretest–Posttest Design					R	O	T	O
					R			
Preexperimental Designs								
F. One-Group Pretest–Posttest Design					O	T	O	
G. One-Shot Case Study						T	O	
H. Static-Group Comparison						T	O	
							O	

Note. R = randomization of participants; O = observation (i.e., data-collection procedure); T = treatment (counseling or learning intervention).

Stanley (1963) wrote the classic work on this topic and provide a helpful summary of research designs that professional school counselors can use to show the effectiveness of interventions. Campbell and Stanley conceptualized research designs as preexperimental, true experimental, and quasi-experimental. Commonly used research designs are presented in Table 19.2.

In general, true experimental designs are characterized by a randomization of participants that controls for all known sources of internal validity. This gives true experimental designs the advantage of allowing causative conclusions to be drawn about the effectiveness of the intervention. For example, if a professional school counselor wanted to know the effectiveness of a group counseling experience for students from changing families, she may choose a pretest–posttest control group design (Design B from Table 19.2), randomly assigning the participants to two or more groups and administering an outcome measure (i.e., a measure of behaviors, thoughts, and feelings that the group counseling intervention was meant to change) to the treatment and control groups before and after treatment. The data can then be analyzed to determine if the participants that received the group counseling intervention changed significantly on the outcome measure (O) as compared to the control group. Of course, if the treatment was effective, the control group should be given the chance to participate in the group counseling intervention.

This example of a group counseling intervention for students from changing families can also be applied to all of the other designs listed in Table 19.2, randomizing, observing, and intervening, as specified. Whenever possible, professional school counselors should collect evidence using a true experimental design; such evidence is conclusive. On the other hand, preexperimental and quasi-experimental designs, while helpful, lead to speculative results that can be questioned and explained through alternative means.

Examples of Program Evaluation

Case Study

A case study was conducted by a professional school counselor to determine if middle school students had improved study skills as a result of the counseling program unit. One group of students was exposed to the 4-week classroom guidance unit, while a comparison group did not participate in the study skills unit. The professional school counselor's goal was for all students involved in the treatment group to improve their study skills and learning. This improvement of learning served as the school counselor's desired competency. To decide if the competency had been met, the professional school counselor must make sure that the objectives under the competency had been met. The school counselor developed objectives to serve as goals for the study skills unit—such as, 80% of students will apply cooperative study skills necessary for academic success by successfully completing a written task with a partner during the group activity, 80% of students will use knowledge of learning styles to achieve a grade of B or better on a social studies test, and 80% of students will become a self-directed and independent learner by completing a homework assignment on their own during the group activity. Students were expected to meet these objectives at the end of the unit to determine whether the academic standard had been met.

After the second session, the professional school counselor collected the activity in which students were required to work with a partner and complete a worksheet by applying necessary study skills. If students scored above 85%, they had met the objective. Once all of the worksheets were corrected, the counselor determined that 80% of students had appropriately applied their study skills; therefore, the objective had been met.

In between sessions, the teacher observed the students take a social studies test. In preparing for the test, the students were to choose and use a specific type of learning style technique introduced in previous sessions. The teacher determined whether students were using their knowledge of a learning style to positively influence their school performance. If 80% of students achieved a grade of B or better, the counselor verified that the objective had been met.

Lastly, students individually completed a homework assignment during the group session by using skills they had learned throughout the group meetings. By observing and correcting the homework assignment, the professional school counselor confirmed that 80% of the students had completed the assignment independently, which met the third objective.

By meeting all three objectives, one may conclude that the students also met the competency of improving learning among students. In order for the competency to have been met, all three of the objectives must be met. If, for some reason, one of the objectives is not met, the professional school counselor may conclude the competency was only partially met.

Program Audit

A program audit was conducted by a professional school counselor at the end of the school year to determine if the comprehensive developmental school counseling program was fully implemented. The program audit provided by the American School Counselor Association (ASCA; 2012a) was used as a comprehensive guide. After examining the program audit, the professional school counselor determined the strengths and weaknesses of the program and created goals for the following school year to address full implementation of curriculum evaluation components that were "in progress" or "completed" but not fully implemented.

Outcome Evaluation

A professional school counselor conducted an outcome evaluation to determine how high school students were different as a result of small-group counseling addressing depression. The professional school counselor set up a nonequivalent control group design, a quasi-experimental design, which did not control for participant randomization during selection. Students were self-referred to participate in the depression group. After 20 were selected, they were split in half and placed into either the control group ($n = 10$) or the treatment group ($n = 10$).

Before treatment began, each participant completed the 30-item *Reynolds Adolescent Depression Scale–Second Edition* (RADS-2; Reynolds, 2001) in order for the professional school counselor to determine each student's pretreatment severity of depression. The average severity of depression for both the treatment and control groups were moderate. After the treatment group had experienced group counseling for 6 weeks and the control group had undergone study skills group training for 6 weeks (the placebo condition), the RADS-2 was re-administered. Students who had participated in the treatment group reported an average of mild levels of depression. In contrast, the control group again reported moderate levels of depression on the posttest. Data were statistically analyzed using R stat, and results indicated significant differences occurred. Thus, the professional school counselor concluded that the group counseling intervention was successful in decreasing levels of depression among high school students (although the quasi-experimental design did not allow for specific causative inference).

Reporting Assessment Results

It is an excellent and essential practice to report assessment findings to administrators, teachers, staff members, parents, students and other appropriate stakeholders. The school counseling program advisory committee and professional school counselor should write the report and be involved in every step of the reporting process. Generally, a comprehensive report is helpful for program analysis and decision making, while a one- or two-page executive summary should be released to system administrators and the general school community. It is important to note that results must be documented, discussed, and reported for accountability to occur.

Summary/Conclusion

Program accountability is one of the most important responsibilities of the professional school counselor. It is essential to understand that assessment is a cyclical process that results in continuous quality improvement. Aggregation and outcome evaluation are strategies for providing documented evidence that the school counseling program is effectively meeting the needs of students and supporting the school's mission.

CHAPTER
20

Career Development Interventions in the Schools

Brian Hutchison, Spencer G. Niles, and Jerry Trusty

Preview

In this chapter, we provide an overview of developmentally appropriate career interventions for students in Grades K–12. The ASCA National Standards for Students (American School Counselor Association, 2004) provided a general starting point for constructing career interventions. Additionally, the U.S. Department of Education Office of Vocational and Adult Education (OVAE) contracted with DTI Associates, Inc., A Haverstick Company, to develop very specific National Career Development Guidelines (NCDG) to help counselors identify developmentally appropriate career development goals and interventions across the life span (America's Career Resource Network [ACRN], 2014). The NCDG guidelines are used as a framework for discussing career interventions across educational levels. A primary theme in this chapter is that career development interventions must help students prepare for the tasks they will encounter as adults. Moreover, career development interventions must help students connect current school activities with their futures. This connection is a key element in increasing school involvement and academic success. Four online activities are recommended throughout the chapter to help readers explore the process of designing and choosing career interventions in schools.

The *ASCA National Standards for Students* (ASCA, 2004) identified career development as an essential element in effective school counseling programs. Specifically, the standards stipulated that, with regard to career development, students will complete the following:

> Standard A . . . acquire the skills to investigate the world of work in relation to knowledge of self and to make informed decisions . . . Standard B . . . employ strategies to achieve future career success and satisfaction . . . [and] . . . Standard C . . . understand the relationship among personal qualities, education and training, and the world of work. (ASCA, 2004, p. 7-8)

These standards make sense because school experiences prepare students for subsequent life experiences, and work is a central life-role for most adults. However, school-based career development interventions have a mixed record of success. In the past, career development programs have not been created systematically, and little attention has been devoted to devising comprehensive career interventions from early childhood through secondary school. Too often, career development programs at one level (e.g., middle school) are not coordinated with programs at another level (e.g., high school). In the 1980s, Gysbers and

Moore (1981) introduced the comprehensive guidance program, a way of organizing guidance activities and services in schools, including competency expectations organized by grade level, that the American School Counselor Association (ASCA) has used to develop the ASCA national model (ASCA, 2012a). This model includes career guidance competencies, activities, and services as part of the comprehensive guidance program (Gysbers, 2005).

Despite recent tools to encourage the practice (Gysbers, Stanley, Kosteck-Bunch, Magnuson, & Starr, 2011; Stone & Dahir, 2011), professional school counselors too often do not evaluate the efficacy of career-related interventions, thereby limiting opportunities for improving services and demonstrating the importance of career interventions to school administrators, parents, teachers, students, and other stakeholders in the educational enterprise. Awareness of the need for intervention efficacy evaluation has been heightened since the initial enactment of the No Child Left Behind Act of 2001 (NCLB) and the more recent Race to the Top (RTT) legislation, which was part of the American Recovery and Reinvestment Act of 2009. For example, NCLB supports four key principles: (a) strong accountability for increased student performance; (b) more freedom at the state and community level; (c) the use of evidence-based education methods; and (d) giving parents more choice in their students' education. As a result of programs funded through NCLB and RTT, a new culture of accountability and evidence-based education has evolved (Stone & Dahir, 2011), giving professional school counselors an opportunity to share the burden of improving schools and student academic performance as well as tying career interventions into the overarching goals of NCLB, RTT, and comprehensive guidance programs.

Many of these challenges confronting professional school counselors emanate from individuals who fail to see the value of career interventions. Those questioning the usefulness of career development interventions assume that career-related activities take students away from time spent focusing on core academic subjects. They assume (incorrectly) that career interventions do not connect to academic subjects when in fact, career-focused interventions are strongly correlated with positive academic outcomes (Carey & Harrington, 2010a, 2010b). Additionally, some career development critics assume that career development programs pressure students to pursue work immediately after high school rather than pursue a college education. Many people who are unfamiliar with how careers develop do not understand why career development interventions are important at the elementary, middle, and high school levels. Those arguing against career interventions for elementary school students often view career decisions as events that occur at particular points during the course of secondary school education (e.g., when students must select a curriculum of study when they leave high school). These perspectives lack an appreciation of the developmental context from which a readiness for career decision-making emerges. Thus, to confront these challenges effectively, many professional school counselors must provide career interventions differently. More specifically, career interventions must be systematic, coordinated, comprehensive, and developmentally appropriate.

Activity 20.1: Exploring School Career Interventions in Your State.

1. Take a few minutes and explore the school counseling pages of the Department of Education Web site in your state. Identify the organizational schema of the site and deter-

mine how you navigate for specific information (e.g., How does one become certified in school counseling?).
2. Navigate the site to determine what content is available specific to the identification, design, implementation, and evaluation of school counseling career interventions.
3. Navigate the site to determine how to identify career interventions that are age appropriate for the school level where you work or wish to work one day (e.g., middle school career interventions).
4. Use your web browser of choice to bookmark pages for future reference or make note of the Web address of these pages in a place where you can easily find them.

Systematic and Coordinated Planning for Career Development Programs in the Schools

Walz and Benjamin (1984) provided important recommendations that professional school counselors can use to address the challenges confronting them as they design career development programs. These recommendations are also useful for creating systematic, coordinated, and developmentally appropriate career development intervention programs. Specifically, Walz and Benjamin recommended the following when implementing career programs in the schools:

- Involve a team of knowledgeable professionals, parents, and representatives from the community in all phases of program planning.
- Use developmentally appropriate interventions.
- Be sure that the program goals and objectives are clearly communicated to all involved in the program.
- Make sure the program is based on student needs.
- Have an evaluation component to determine the degree to which the program goals and objectives have been achieved.
- Make sure that those involved in program delivery are highly competent.

An implicit theme in these recommendations is that program planners need to be sensitive to the political climate in which they operate. For example, in some locations, not clearly connecting career development interventions to student academic achievement will significantly decrease the chances of program success. Also, not adequately communicating successful program outcomes to educational stakeholders (e.g., school board members, parents, administrators, teachers) will result in the program resources being vulnerable to funding cuts. If school personnel view the program as an additional burden to their already heavy workloads, then there is little chance that the program will succeed. Thus, the "marketing" of the program to all stakeholders becomes an important aspect of program development and implementation. Clearly defined behavioral objectives that address the specific needs of students will be useful in marketing the program and providing outcome data that demonstrate program benefits. Lapan (2001) provided six fundamental questions professional school counselors can ask to define their essential work and communicate its importance to constituents:

1. How can counselor roles, duties, functions, and interventions be transformed to be of greater benefit and impact for all students?
2. How can counselor time-on-task be redistributed to maximize benefits for all students?
3. How can a program be tailored to better meet the needs of each school?
4. How can the program become central to the overriding mission of each school?
5. How can better partnerships between school personnel, parents, and business and community leaders be established?
6. How can counselors better advocate for their programs with local, state, and national policymakers?

Another theme implicit in these recommendations for planning career development programs is the importance of taking a team approach to service delivery. One person cannot accomplish all the goals and objectives of an effective career development program. Thus, program personnel need to be clear about their roles and responsibilities. Inevitably, there will be some overlap in the functions performed by program personnel. For example, professional school counselors may, at times, provide classroom instruction and teachers may, at times, perform more career counseling-related functions. Although there is no one prescription for how the roles and responsibilities should be defined, it is logical that professional school counselors take the lead role in developing and implementing career development intervention programs. Professional school counselors are often the only professionals in the school system with specific training in career development. Therefore, professional school counselors possess the knowledge of career development theory and practice that is necessary for formulating appropriate career development program interventions. Moreover, the processes typically used in program delivery relate to counselors' primary areas of expertise. These processes include counseling, assessment, career information services, placement services, consultation procedures, and referrals.

Developing a systematic and coordinated career development program from early childhood through Grade 12 (EC–12) requires understanding the developmental tasks confronting students as they progress through school. Understanding the career development tasks confronting students at all levels of schooling prepares school personnel to work collaboratively in program design and implementation. A comprehensive understanding of the career development process also sets the stage for developing program interventions that are sequential and cohesive. Thus, the following sections of this chapter focus on career development tasks, goals, and interventions for elementary, middle or junior high school, and high school students, respectively.

Constructing Developmentally Appropriate Career Interventions

National Career Development Guidelines

Although the ASCA standards for career development provide general guidelines for career competencies students need to develop, the U.S. Department of Education Office of Vocational and Adult Education contracted with DTI Associates, Inc., A Haverstick Company, to develop very specific National Career Development Guidelines (NCDG; ACRN, 2014). The

NCDG guidelines are used as a framework for discussing career interventions across educational levels to help professional school counselors identify developmentally appropriate career goals and interventions across the life span. The framework is organized into three domains, each with goals that define broad areas of career development competency. Indicators of mastery are highlighted under each goal. These indicators are presented in three learning stages (Knowledge Acquisition, Application, and Reflection) based upon Bloom's Taxonomy (Bloom, 1956). It is important to note that these learning stages are not associated with an individual's age or grade level but instead are a developmental sequence (ACRN, 2014). The specific career development domains and goals are identified as follows:

1. Personal–Social Development Domain
   - Develop understanding of self to build and maintain a positive self-concept.
   - Develop positive interpersonal skills including respect for diversity.
   - Integrate growth and change into your career development.
   - Balance personal, leisure, community, learner, family, and work roles.
2. Educational Achievement and Lifelong Learning Domain
   - Attain educational achievement and performance levels needed to reach your personal and career goals.
   - Participate in ongoing, lifelong learning experiences to enhance your ability to function effectively in a diverse and changing economy.
3. Career Management Domain
   - Create and manage a career plan that meets your career goals.
   - Use a process of decision making as one component of career development.
   - Use accurate, current, and unbiased career information during career planning and management.
   - Master academic, occupational, and general employability skills in order to obtain, create, maintain, or advance your employment.
   - Integrate changing employment trends, societal needs, and economic conditions into your career plans.

Career Development Interventions in the Elementary School

Magnuson and Starr (2000, p. 100) offered the following thoughts to guide professional school counselors as they plan career development interventions at the elementary school level:

1. Become a constant observer of children:
   - Notice how children approach tasks.
   - Notice the activities in which children choose to participate.
   - Observe and encourage the child's initiative-taking.
   - Notice the thematic patterns emerging in each child's activities.
2. Consider the processing of an activity as important as the activity itself:
   - To help children develop a sense of industry rather than inferiority, focus feedback on the specifics of children's efforts.
   - Accompany career awareness and career exploration activities with opportunities for students to express their beliefs about themselves in relation to various occupations. (p. 100)

Personal–social development. Because self-awareness provides the foundation for processing career information, career development interventions in the primary grades can focus on helping students develop more sophisticated self-knowledge. For example, in Grades EC–1, students can increase their self-knowledge by describing themselves through drawings, writing sentences describing the things they like and the things that are important to them, and bringing some of their favorite things to school to show to their classmates. Sharing their self-descriptions with others helps students to clarify their self-concepts. Each of these activities can also emphasize the importance of appreciating the similarities and differences that exist among students in the classroom. Activities that encourage students to focus on clarifying their global self-concepts can be emphasized and easily infused into the curriculum during the first years of school.

Educational achievement and lifelong learning. Activities that help students learn more about themselves can be supplemented with activities that focus on educational and occupational exploration as students progress through the primary and intermediate grades. For example, in the primary grades, students can identify the occupations of their family members (e.g., parents, grandparents, aunts, uncles) as well as the level and type of education each family member has attained. As students share this information, the relationship between education and work can be stressed (e.g., some jobs require a college education, others may require a different type of training, such as trade school or an apprenticeship). Differences in family members' occupations can be discussed as strengths (e.g., it takes people working in a wide variety of occupations to make our society function effectively). To counteract occupational stereotyping, men and women working in gender nontraditional occupations can be invited to school to discuss their work.

Students in Grades K–1 can begin the process of learning about work by focusing on occupations with which they have the most immediate relationship (e.g., occupations of family members, occupations in the school setting, occupations in their neighborhoods and of neighbors). Then, elementary school students can gradually learn about occupations that are more remote (e.g., occupations in the community, occupations in the state, occupations in the nation, occupations throughout the world) as they progress from Grades 2–5. Using a proximity–distance scheme to guide students in the acquisition of occupational information helps students understand the relevance of work in their lives and the ways in which various workers contribute to society. At each level of proximity, the relationship between work and the educational requirements for performing specific occupations can be highlighted. Students can also discuss what is required to perform occupations successfully. Job-content skills (the specific skill requirements for each occupation), functional skills (the skills that are transferable across occupations), and self-management skills (e.g., being reliable, getting along with one's coworkers, being trustworthy, completing assignments on time) can be integrated into these discussions as well.

Activity 20.2: Exploring the Use of the Career Family Tree.

1. Open your Web browser and search using the phrase "career family tree." Refine the search to view images of this career intervention.
2. Select one image of the career family tree and determine how you would describe this career intervention to first, third, and fifth grade students.

3. Reflect upon how the instructions change for each age/developmental level.
4. Working alone or with an elementary-age child, complete the career family tree for 2–3 generations.
5. Upon completion, reflect upon the cross-cultural factors you must consider when using this intervention. For example, are there family dynamics that would require special preparation or cross-cultural considerations?

Career management. Activities to help students learn about the career planning and decision-making process could include the following:

- Having students read biographies and then discuss the important career decisions people made in the biographies they read. Students can be encouraged to consider what constitutes a *good* rather than *bad* career decision as they discuss the biographies they read.
- Students can use a timeline to chart important events that have influenced the life decisions made by the people they read about.
- Encouraging students to read stories about people working in nontraditional occupations can contribute to counteracting the effects of occupational sex stereotyping.
- Discussions of the ways in which culture, gender, and social class may have influenced the career development of the person in the biography.

Parental Involvement

Parents have substantial influence over the career development of their children, and these influences are strong through elementary school, middle school, high school, and into adulthood (Trusty, 1998, 1999). Young (1994) suggested that the influence parents exert on the career development process is most effective when it is planned, intentional, and goal oriented. However, many parents possess minimal knowledge regarding career-development theory and how environmental factors influence the career-development process of children. Thus, it is important that professional school counselors help parents learn ways to contribute positively to the career development of their children. Professional school counselors can begin by providing parents with information about the career development process. Professional school counselors can also explain to parents how the environment impacts options that children are willing to consider (e.g., the influence of occupational stereotyping within the media and gender role stereotyping can be discussed with parents). Finally, professional school counselors can help parents identify specific strategies they can use to facilitate career development in their children. Herr, Cramer, and Niles (2004) identified eight ways parents can help children advance in their careers. These strategies included the following:

- Parents can encourage children to analyze important self-characteristics (e.g., interests, capacities, values).
- When parents are familiar with specific work requirements for jobs, they can communicate these to their children.
- Parents can discuss the importance of work values in work behavior.
- Parents can explain the relationship between work, pay, and the economic condition of the family.
- Parents can connect children with informational resources (e.g., other workers, books, films) for acquiring accurate career information.

- Parents can be careful to avoid stereotyping occupational alternatives and workers.
- Parents can provide children with opportunities for work in the home and community.
- Parents can provide children with opportunities to learn and practice decision-making skills. (p. 349)

Several studies have supported the positive effects of parents' involvement on their children's career development, and parental involvement has been quantified in various ways (e.g., parents' school-based involvement, involvement in school policymaking, help with homework). The type of parental involvement that appears to have the strongest positive effects on children's educational and career development is parents' home-based involvement (Trusty, 1999). Home-based involvement is the degree to which parents communicate positively with their children and support children in their educational and career development. Home-based parental involvement does not appear to be domain specific; that is, through factor analysis using a national sample, Trusty, Watts, and Erdman (1997) found one home-based involvement factor spanning areas of education, vocation, and leisure.

From research on parents and parental involvement (Trusty, 1998, 1999; Trusty et al., 1997; Trusty, Watts, & Crawford, 1996), there are five main reasons that professional school counselors should focus on parents helping their children with their career development:

- There is generally no *generation gap* between parents and children in the area of career development.
- Children and adolescents want parents' help, and parents want to help their children.
- Work with parents promotes positive communication within the family.
- Contact between professional school counselors and parents enhances parents' perceptions of professional school counselors and schools as resources for their children.
- Parents serve as continual resources for their children, whereas professional school counselors' efforts are temporal.

Professional school counselors' helping parents become aware of their own attitudes toward work and occupations, exposing students to work opportunities in the home and community, and providing support to students as they engage in career decision-making tasks are all ways to help students cope effectively with the career development process and lay a solid foundation for coping with the career development tasks of middle or junior high school.

Career Development Interventions in Middle and Junior High School

Thematic consideration of middle and junior high school–level career development goals reveals the importance of students acquiring the necessary knowledge, skills, and understanding to advance in their career development. Based on their literature review of school-based career intervention research, Hughes and Karp (2004) suggested that a greater investment be made in middle school career guidance and academic counseling interventions, because this is potentially the most effective school population for such activities. Sink (2005) offered the following recommendations for middle school counselors wishing to foster academic development and learning when implementing interventions:

- Lessons and activities should be designed to advance student cognition and metacognition.
- Encourage healthy student psychosocial development.

- Partner with teachers to develop and implement lessons and interventions.
- Augment the work of teachers by focusing interventions on enhancing academic skills and student motivation to learn.

Personal–social development. It is also important at this developmental level that career interventions continue to stimulate curiosity in students. Students who are curious about their emerging self-concepts (e.g., their avocational and vocational interests, skills, and values) are more likely to engage in exploratory behavior to acquire the information they need for self-concept clarification. Helping students identify and connect with role models can also facilitate a sense of internal control and future time perspective which can, in turn, lead to *planful* behaviors and the development of effective problem-solving skills (Super, 1990).

Providing career assessment activities (as described in Chapter 36) are essential to helping students expand their self-knowledge in a systematic fashion. Interest and aptitude assessment are particularly useful at this developmental level. In selecting career assessments, it is important that the reading level, language, and normative samples are appropriate for the school population with which the assessments will be used. Interest inventory results can foster more systematic thinking about the activities in which students enjoy participating. Aptitude tests can also help students acquire accurate estimates of their abilities. Interest and aptitude assessments are often administered to students during the middle or junior high school grades. Combining interest inventory with aptitude test results provides a useful foundation for the exploration process.

Educational achievement and lifelong learning. Students will find it useful to explore occupational areas for which they have high interest and high aptitude. When the results of an interest inventory suggest that a student has no area of above-average or high interest, it may be that the student will need exposure to activities across several interest areas to determine if these areas hold any interest for the student. Thus, a key to assessments, especially interest inventories, being useful is that students must have the experiential base to draw upon to respond to assessment items. Students with limited exposure to a variety of activities will be forced to guess at appropriate responses to questions requiring them to identify their likes and dislikes.

When school systems have a systematic career development intervention program in place for all grades, then it is safer to assume that middle and junior high school students have been exposed to activities that have fostered their self- and career exploration. When no such programs exist, then professional school counselors must be especially cognizant of the possibility that many students will need more remedial career development interventions prior to being administered career assessments.

Providing middle school students with exposure to work facilitates the acquisition of knowledge, skills, and awareness related to the career development domains of (a) educational achievement and lifelong learning and (b) career management. Teaching students how families of occupations can be clustered according to factors such as skill requirements, interests, or training helps students organize the world of work and connect their characteristics to occupational options. For example, Holland's (1985) classification system uses six personality types (i.e., Realistic, Investigative, Artistic, Social, Enterprising, and Conventional) to organize the world of work. *Realistic* occupations include skilled trades and technical occupations. *Investigative* occupations include scientific and technical occupations. *Artistic* occupations include creative occupations in the expressive arts. *Social* occupations include the helping professions. *Enterprising* occupations involve managerial and sales occupations. Lastly, *Conventional* occupations include office and clerical occupations. Occupations are classified according to the degree to which the activities of the occupation draw upon the Holland types. The three most dominant types reflected in the occupation are used to classify each occupation.

Clustering systems such as Holland's can be used to guide career exploration by using the types to organize career information resources, career fairs, curricula experiences (e.g., students can be assigned the task of writing an essay about occupations that fall within their dominant Holland type), job-shadowing experiences, participation in extracurricular activities, avocational pursuits, college exploration, and part-time employment experiences. With accurate self-knowledge and systematic educational and career exploration, students develop readiness to engage in career planning.

Activity 20.3: Using the Occupational Outlook Handbook With Middle/Junior High School Students.

1. Visit the Bureau of Labor Statistics Occupational Outlook Handbook (OOH) page at www.bls.gov/ooh/
2. Explore the "Students" resource tab found on the top toolbar of the homepage.
3. If you were working with a middle or junior high school student wishing to explore potential career paths, which of the options would you choose?
4. How would you work with a student using these free resources?
5. Working alone, or with a middle or junior high school student, pick a career that you are unfamiliar with and explore it fully using the OOH Web site.

Career management. Effective career management at the middle school or junior high school level requires students to know how to make decisions, understand the interrelationship of life-roles, know about different occupations and changing male/female roles, and understand the process of career planning. An effective tool for helping middle or junior high school students engage in purposeful planning, exploring, information gathering, decision making, and reality testing related to two prominent life-roles (e.g., student and worker) is an educational and career planning portfolio. Educational and career planning portfolios are typically used to help students chart their academic and career decision making. This charting process can begin in middle or junior high school and continue until the student leaves high school. By making at least annual entries into the portfolio, the student and professional school counselor can track the student's career development progress. They can also make systematic educational and career plans that build upon the student's growing base of self- and occupational knowledge. In essence, the portfolio provides a vehicle for the student and professional school counselor to discuss what the student has done and what the student will do next to advance his or her career development.

To help students focus on the interrelationship of life-roles, and to engage in planning related to their salient life-roles, the educational and career planning portfolio can be expanded to a life-role portfolio by addressing students' readiness for life-roles beyond those of student and worker. Students can be encouraged to plan, explore, and gather information for each of the major roles of life. For example, students who anticipate one day being a parent can plan for this role by considering how parenting interacts with other roles. Students can explore different styles of parenting by interviewing parents about their parenting practices and philosophies. Students can also gather information about the skills required for effective parenting (perhaps by taking a parenting class). Through these activities, students can learn about the factors that are important to consider in making decisions about parenting. Finally, students can reality-test their interest in parenting through participating in childcare activities. Thus, the life-role portfolio serves as a stimulus for meetings between professional school counselors and students that are focused on planning, exploring, information gathering, decision making, and reality testing vis-à-vis the major life-roles. When the portfolio is used over successive years, it also provides developmental documentation of activities and decisions related to major life-roles.

Career Development Interventions in High School

As students transition from middle or junior high school, they focus more directly on the task of identifying occupational preferences and clarifying career or lifestyle choices. According to Super (1955, 1957) the tasks of crystallizing, specifying, and implementing tentative career choices that occur during early (ages 12–15 years), middle (ages 16–18 years), and late (ages 18–24 years) adolescence, will be useful to students as they move forward and will help to normalize the transition process.

The emphasis on knowledge, skills, and understanding that emerged in the middle or junior high school-level domains is continued in the high school domains. The high school domains, however, challenge students to become more focused on making career plans by translating their self- and career information into career goals. At the high school level, students' level of sophistication in the domains of personal–social development, educational achievement and lifelong learning, and career management is such that there is substantial overlap among them. Interventions tend to involve all three domains; this section discusses them collectively.

Savickas (1999) proposed career development interventions that foster the sort of self-knowledge, educational and occupational exploration, and career planning described in the high school competencies. Specifically, these interventions focus on (a) orienting students' comprehension of careers; (b) developing students' competence at planning and exploring; (c) coaching students to develop effective career management techniques; and (d) guiding students in behavioral rehearsals, to become prepared for coping with job problems.

To orient ninth-grade students to the planning tasks they will encounter as they move through high school, Savickas (1999) recommended using a group guidance format to discuss items on career development inventories such as the *Career Maturity Inventory* (Crites, 1978) or the *Adult Career Concerns Inventory* (ACCI; Super, Thompson, & Lindeman, 1988). Using inventory items to orient students to the tasks they need to address in order to manage their career development effectively helps provide a stimulus for planning and exploring behaviors (Savickas, 1990). For example, the ACCI measures developmental task concern for the career stages of Exploration, Establishment, Maintenance, and Disengagement. Reviewing the career stages and tasks within the ACCI teaches high school students about the general process of career development. Using ACCI items, adolescents can identify those career development tasks they are likely to encounter in the near future. Strategies for coping with current and near future career development tasks can be identified. In this way, high school students' understanding of time perspective or *planfulness* can be enhanced (Savickas, Stilling, & Schwartz, 1984).

Results from interest and abilities measures administered at the end of middle school or at the beginning of high school provide direction as to which of the occupational environments offers the best potential for fruitful exploration. The range of career assessment possibilities that can be used systematically with youth is substantial. To measure interests, professional school counselors can use instruments that provide information related to students' Holland types such as the *Self-Directed Search* (Holland, 1985, 1994) and the *Career Assessment Inventory* (Johansson, 1986). Ability measures include the *Differential Aptitude Test* (Bennett, Seashore, & Wesman, 1992), *The Ability Explorer* (Harrington & Harrington, 1996), and assessments of functional skills from school transcripts or educational and career-planning portfolios. Areas of high interest and ability can be matched to occupational clusters and students can identify specific occupations for in-depth exploration.

Although interest and ability assessment results provide important data pertaining to career choice content (i.e., relating students' abilities and interests to occupational options), these data fail to address whether students have developed readiness for career decision making (Super, 1983). Approaches to career assessment must attend to both content and process variables in order to adequately address the needs of youth (Savickas, 1993). Specifically, interests and abilities can be considered as career-choice content data that must be viewed in light of career-choice process data, such as readiness for career decision making, life-role salience, and values, which can be labeled as moderator variables (Super, Osborne, Walsh, Brown, & Niles, 1992). To be ready to effectively choose and adapt to an occupation, it is important for high school students to "see themselves as coping with certain developmental tasks, at a stage in life at which they are expected, and may expect themselves to make certain decisions and acquire certain competencies" (Super, 1983, p. 559). Students who have not successfully accomplished the career-development tasks presented to them at previous educational levels will need remedial interventions (e.g., additional opportunities for self-concept clarification, training in acquiring occupational information) prior to focusing on career decision making.

From this perspective, addressing career choice readiness (Super, 1974) becomes a necessary precursor to the effective use of ability and interest assessment data. According to Super, career choice readiness involves five dimensions: (a) having a *planful* attitude toward coping with career stages and tasks, (b) gathering information about educational and occupational opportunities, (c) exploring the world of work, (d) knowing how to make good career decisions, and (e) being able to make realistic judgments about potential occupations. These dimensions are important because if an adolescent knows little about the world of work, then interest inventories that use occupational titles or activities may produce misleading scores and poor choices may be made (Super, Savickas, & Super, 1996). Likewise, when adolescents do not engage in appropriate career planning, they often encounter career tasks for which they are not prepared (Herr et al., 2004). Thus, assessing high school students' resources for choosing and adapting to an occupation requires conducting appraisals of career-choice content (e.g., abilities, interests, values) and process (e.g., life-role salience, career-choice readiness) variables. When a student is lacking in any of the five dimensions comprising career-choice readiness, then the professional school counselor should focus interventions to help the student progress in that particular domain prior to focusing on career choice content.

It is important to note that traditional assessment approaches focusing only on career-choice content variables assume that all individuals place a high value on work and that all individuals view work as the prime means of values realization. It can be argued that this is a Western middle-class male view of career development and thus is a culturally encapsulated view of life-role salience. Different patterns of life-role salience exist, and they must be considered in helping high school students clarify and articulate their career goals (Niles & Goodnough, 1996). For example, when salience for the work role is high, youth view work as providing meaningful opportunities for self-expression. In such cases, high school students are often motivated to develop the career maturity necessary (e.g., to be *planful*, to explore opportunities, to gather information) for making good career decisions. When work-role salience is low, however, adolescents often lack motivation and career maturity. In the latter instances, professional school counselors need to begin the career development intervention process by arousing the individual's sense of importance for the worker role (Super, 1990). Disputing irrational beliefs, exposing young people to effective role models, and providing mentors are examples of activities that foster career arousal (Krumboltz & Worthington, 1999).

To help students further clarify their life-role self-concepts, professional school counselors can encourage high school students to consider life-role salience questions (e.g., How do I spend my time during the course of a typical week? What changes would I like to make in how I spend my time? How important is each life-role to me? How important is each life-role to my family? What do I like about participating in each life-role? What do I hope to accomplish in each life-role? What does my family expect me to accomplish in each life-role? What life-roles do I think will be important to me in the future? What must I do to become more prepared for the life-roles that will be important to me in the future?). Discussing these questions helps high school students clarify and articulate their life-role self-concepts. Specifically, by discussing these questions during the first years of high school, adolescents can become clearer as to the values they seek to express in each life-role. This information is vital not only for guiding high school students in the selection and pursuit of appropriate educational and occupational options, but also in developing appropriate expectations for values satisfaction within the respective life-roles.

These discussion questions also provide opportunities for exploring the individual's level of acculturation, cultural identity, and worldview. For example, high school students can discuss family expectations and other cultural factors influencing their life-role participation. Finally, discussing these questions helps professional school counselors become aware of potential barriers as well as potential sources of support for students as they move closer to negotiating the school-to-work or school-to-school transition. These discussions also foster the acquisition of the high school-level career development competencies related to understanding the interrelationship of life-roles and understanding the changing nature of male/female roles. This information also helps high school students identify those roles in which they spend most of their time, those that they are emotionally committed to, and those that they expect to be important to them in the future. By clarifying information concerning life-role salience (and the cultural factors influencing role salience), high school students establish the foundation for making accurate self-evaluations and developing career choice readiness.

Clarifying values is an important task in acquiring adequate self-knowledge for effective educational and occupational exploration because values are indications of the qualities people desire and seek, in "the activities in which they engage, in the situations in which they live, and in the objects which they make or acquire" (Super, 1974, p. 4). Because values reflect the individual's goals, they provide a sense of purpose and direction in the career planning process (Super et al., 1996). However, while many agree that values clarification is critical to choosing an occupation, relatively few put forth the effort to examine their values in a systematic way (Harrington & Harrington, 2006). Values card sorts (e.g., *Career Values Card Sort Kit, Non-sexist Vocational Card Sort*) and instruments such as the *Career Orientation Placement and Evaluation Survey* are instruments that are useful in values clarification. Interest inventory results can also be used to identify work-related activities that provide opportunities for values expression.

These interventions represent examples of ways in which high school counselors can help students prepare for a successful school-to-work or school-to-school transition. When professional school counselors at all grade levels work collaboratively to develop systematic career development interventions, there is a greater likelihood that students will be prepared for the career development tasks they will encounter as they move through high school.

Activity 20.4: Selecting and Practicing With a Values Sort Career Intervention.

1. Open your Web browser and search using the phrase "values sort."
2. Review 3–5 of the values sorting approaches that result from your search.
3. If you were to work with a high school age student who is struggling to clarify post-secondary plans, which values sort activity would you select? Why that approach?
4. Working alone, or with a high school age student, complete the values sort exercise that you select.
5. What did you learn about using this type of intervention? What would you do differently in the future?

Summary/Conclusion

More than ever, systematic career development interventions are needed to help young people advance in their career development. The nature of work is changing dramatically, requiring new skills sets (e.g., transition skills, stress management, the ability to engage in lifelong learning, personal flexibility, computer skills) that suggest that change, rather than constancy, will be the norm. Workers in the 21st century will experience multiple career changes that will bring associated levels of stress that must be managed effectively. It is naïve to expect parents, many of whom are struggling to manage their own careers effectively, to provide children and adolescents with the competencies they need to advance in their careers in the 21st century. In light of the challenges that young people face, all stakeholders—especially professional school counselors, parents, and schools—must work together to support students in their career development. Career development interventions must help students prepare for the tasks they will encounter as adults. Moreover, career development interventions must help students connect current school activities with their futures. This connection is key to increasing school involvement and school success.

In many respects, professional school counselors are the human development specialists in the schools. Educating stakeholders about the developmental process students will experience as they move through school helps students, teachers, administrators, and parents develop the awareness to think proactively about the tasks students will encounter. Thus, infusing the curriculum with developmental concepts helps students acquire the awareness that fosters a *planful* approach to coping with career development tasks.

CHAPTER 21

Secondary and Postsecondary Educational Planning

Suzanne M. Dugger and Kalinda R. Jones

Preview

This chapter provides an overview of educational planning in comprehensive school counseling programs. Educational planning is inextricably tied to the career development process and represents an essential component in a school counseling program. The chapter includes step-by-step information that can be used to guide professional school counselors through the educational planning process used for assisting high school students to plan their secondary coursework. It also addresses the planning process for postsecondary education.

The educational planning component is a key component of any successful school counseling program. Whereas the primary mission of professional counselors working in community settings is to promote mental health, the primary mission of professional school counselors is to promote educational achievement. Ultimately, the hope is that educational achievement will serve as the foundation for students' career development and productivity as citizens. Toward this end, professional school counselors systematically assist students and parents with the process of educational planning. The goal is to assist students in preparing for careers and fulfilling lives with intentionality. Rather than finishing school and assuming a job, career, or life by chance (i.e., whatever option happens to be available and accessible at the time), students benefit from engaging in sound educational planning which allows them to exercise choice about their career and life destinations.

Simply put, educational planning can be defined as the process of assisting students and parents in understanding the connection between education and career or life planning, setting goals, making decisions regarding academic course selection and scholastic experiences that will contribute to the achievement of these goals, evaluating progress toward these goals, and modifying educational plans as needed. The purpose of this chapter is to provide an overview of the educational planning process and to offer specific ideas about the integration of educational planning services into an already existing school counseling program. Toward this end, we will address the educational planning process as it pertains both to a high school curriculum and to postsecondary options.

The process of educational planning may be conceptualized as an essential service of a professional school counselor (Hines, Lemons, & Crews, 2011) or as a part of the individual student planning element of a comprehensive guidance and counseling program (Gysbers & Henderson, 2012). The latter conceptualization suggests that professional school counselors work within a programmatic framework. According to the American School Counselor Association (ASCA; 2012a), this framework should include the elements of responsive services (e.g., individual and small-group counseling); individual student planning, which tends to focus on the educational and career planning process; the school counseling core curriculum, in which professional school counselors systematically design and deliver classroom guidance lessons in three broad content areas; and system support (e.g., the managerial aspects of coordinating a program and making fair-share contributions to the school as an organization). Although the individual student planning element is perhaps most closely related to educational planning, the school counseling core curriculum may also be used for this purpose. Specifically, ASCA (2012a) recommends that a K–12 school counselor core curriculum address three content domains: (a) academic development, (b) career development, and (c) personal–social development. Classroom guidance lessons related to educational planning may be included within the academic development domain as well as the career development domain. Additionally, Myrick (2010) delineated several aspects of educational planning. These were to recognize options that are available for planning; illustrate the need to plan ahead; learn a language of educational planning (common terms); learn the sequence of academic courses; identify academic requirements and electives; develop an educational plan for middle or high school; and register for next year's courses.

In approaching the topic of educational planning, we based the information in this chapter on the following assumptions:

- *All students need assistance with educational planning.* Regardless of whether they are college bound, interested in other forms of postsecondary education/training, or looking toward a career that does not require additional education, all students need and deserve assistance with the educational planning process.
- *There is value in all work and no single type of career aspiration is better or worse than another.* It logically follows, then, that the quality of an educational plan is to be judged not by the highest level of education to be achieved by a student but rather by the goodness of fit with the student's aspirations. The critical issue is how well an educational plan prepares a student for whatever career and life he or she has chosen. This second assumption is especially important given that, despite the current 'college for all' movement, "nearly half of the projected job openings requiring postsecondary education will go to people with an associate's degree or occupational certificate" (Symonds, Schwartz, & Ferguson, 2011, p. 2). Although projections are that two thirds of jobs by 2018 will require postsecondary education, this does not mean that all of these jobs will require a bachelor's degree or higher. In fact, the Georgetown Center on Education and the Workforce projects that, of all jobs in the United States in 2018, approximately one third will require a bachelor's degree or higher, approximately one third will require some other form of postsecondary education or training, and approximately one third will require a high school diploma or less (Carnevale, Smith, & Strohl, 2010).
- *Educational planning is necessarily tied to career planning.* Indeed, educational plans should be developed to support a student's career aspirations and interests.

Journeys and Destinations

Before developing an educational plan, professional school counselors must work with students and parents to develop an understanding of the student's long-term goals. If the educational plan is likened to a road map, the student's career aspirations and interests may be likened to the destination. Certainly, it is difficult to develop a detailed road map without a sense of the destination. Because students need more guidance than "go forward," it becomes essential to begin the career exploration and development process early. It is for this reason that ASCA (2012a) recommends career development activities as early as elementary school.

Career development experts and professional school counselors are not alone in their perception of the need for educational and career planning. Students also report a need for more and/or better assistance with their educational and career planning. When surveyed, most students report dissatisfaction with the amount of assistance they receive from their school counselors regarding the educational planning process. Specifically, Johnson, Rochkind, Ott, and DuPont (2010) found that only 30% of students rated their high school guidance counselors as good or excellent with respect to helping them decide which school was right for them, far less than the 67% of students who offered ratings of fair or poor. Although these authors acknowledge that the lack of adequate assistance can be attributed at least in part to "overstretched" counseling programs involving high student-counselor ratios and the assignment of numerous, inappropriate duties, the fact remains that students need and deserve more assistance with educational planning.

As professional school counselors work with students and their parents to look ahead to postsecondary options, it is important to address (a) the amount of formal postsecondary education or training a student is willing to attain; (b) the general career pathway (or specific career) in which the student is interested; and (c) the type of education or training that is best suited to prepare the student for his or her chosen career pathway. When the professional school counselor discusses with students and parents the amount of formal postsecondary education or training a student is willing to complete, it is helpful to review a variety of options rather than to erroneously suggest that a 4-year college degree is the only viable route to a successful career (Carnevale, 2008; Symonds et al., 2011; Unger, 2006). When discussing career options, professional school counselors will do well to use the 16 national career clusters adopted through the State Career Clusters Initiative (SCCI). Prior to this initiative, some states had as few as six career pathways that were used and others had far more. As a result of the SCCI, however, 16 career clusters and 79 associated career pathways (see http://www.careertech.org/sites/default/files/CareerClustersPathways.pdf) are now used nationwide. The 16 career clusters are: (1) Architecture & Construction; (2) Arts, A/V Technology & Communication; (3) Business Management & Administration; (4) Education & Training; (5) Finance; (6) Government & Public Administration; (7) Health Science; (8) Hospitality & Tourism; (9) Human Services; (10) Information Technology; (11) Law, Public Safety, Corrections & Security; (12) Manufacturing; (13) Marketing; (14) Science, Technology, Engineering & Mathematics; (15) Transportation, and (16) Distribution & Logistics.

Because students are generally unable to identify one specific career goal and are better able to identify a grouping of careers in which they are interested and display talent, the use of career clusters is becoming the norm in many school counseling programs. Each cluster includes careers that involve a wide range of postsecondary education and training. Some involve four or more years of college; others involve on-the-job training, and still others require vocational training. In addressing postsecondary options, therefore, professional school counselors will want to work with students and parents to find the length and type of education most likely to assist the student in reaching his or her goals within a given career pathway.

It is essential that the process of discussing postsecondary options begin early—preferably in middle school—in order to develop such an educational plan (Gysbers, 2013).

As Sears (1995) stated, "Students and their parents need to understand . . . that committing to an educational plan, accidentally or on purpose, has long-range consequences" (p. 37). For example, the ability of students who eventually want to go to college to do so will depend greatly upon the selection of courses as early as middle school. Without appropriate coursework and achievement in middle school math and English, a high school freshman will be positioned poorly to begin college preparatory coursework in these subjects. Sears reported on a study conducted by the College Board, which revealed that only half of all high school students who intended to go to college were actually enrolled in courses appropriate for this future plan. These students apparently chose their courses without understanding the implications of their selections on their future educational career. Sears suggested that "many parents are also unaware of the significance of these early decisions" (p. 38).

Further, successful completion of the specific middle school as well as 9th and 10th grade coursework is required for students to enroll in specialized high school courses (i.e., Career & Technical Education [CTE], Advanced Placement [AP], or dual enrollment). CTE programs allow students to complete courses required for certification in technical fields such as auto body repair, cosmetology, and building trades. These programs have been linked to higher rates of high school and adult employment (Stone & Lewis, 2012). In school districts with high school choice, 8th graders can enroll in high schools that house CTE programs. In other high schools, CTE enrollment occurs in 11th and 12th grade for students who have successfully earned credits from 9th and 10th grade courses. However, because many CTE courses comprise elective credits, students who do not earn enough of their core academic requirements in 9th and 10th grade will not be eligible to enroll in CTE classes. Early attention to the importance of educational planning is therefore important to students who may later wish to pursue CTE options.

The same is true for students who may wish to be eligible to earn college credit during high school. This may be achieved by taking AP courses and/or dual enrollment courses. AP courses are taught by high school teachers and cover academic subjects such as biology, English, and calculus. Because AP courses follow rigorous national curricular standards, they are meant to be college-level classes taught within the high school setting. To earn college credits, students may opt to sit for national exams at the completion of AP courses. Students who participate in dual enrollment programs complete college courses, generally on a college campus, while still in high school. Students have the advantage of earning college credit and learning to meet the expectations of college-level courses. In comparison to students who complete traditional high school coursework, students who complete AP or dual enrollment courses have higher high school graduation rates, college-going rates, college GPA, and sustained college enrollment (Allen & Dadgar, 2012; Hargrove, Godin, & Dodd, 2008). Although requirements for enrollment in AP and dual enrollment courses vary across schools, in general, students must maintain a high GPA, complete rigorous 9th and 10th grade coursework, and receive teacher recommendations. These examples illustrate why early educational planning is vital both to students who are planning to enter a technical career and those who will attend college after high school.

Similarly, regardless of whether a student wishes to pursue AP or dual enrollment options during high school, the importance of achieving a sufficient mastery of academic skills in high school cannot be overstated. Although the importance of these issues for college-bound students may seem self-evident, this is not the case. Using the American College Testing Program (ACT) college entrance examination as an example, let's look at the findings regarding college readiness. Between 2006 and 2010, the ACT was taken by approximately

1.57 million students, representing about 47% of the total high school student population in the United States. Although some states (such as Michigan) mandate that all students take the ACT as part of an exit requirement from high school, it is more likely that in other states only those students who plan to attend college will choose to sit for this exam. Reflective of this, 82% of the ACT test takers between 2006 and 2010 expressed an intention of earning at least a bachelor's degree in college (ACT, 2010). If any group of high school students were likely to clearly understand the importance of academic preparation to their postsecondary plans, it would be this group of students. However, although 82% of the test takers planned to go to college for a bachelor's degree, ACT (2010) reported that only "seventy-one percent of all 2010 ACT tested high school graduates took at least a minimum core high school curriculum to prepare them for college" (p. 4). This would seem to suggest that 11% of ACT test takers who aspired to a 4-year college did not understand the importance of taking the appropriate college-bound classes. Even more disappointing is ACTs finding that "only 24% of all 2010 graduates met all four ACT College Readiness Benchmarks, meaning that 76% were not adequately prepared academically for first-year college courses in English Composition, College Algebra, social sciences, and Biology" (p. 19).

These findings point to the importance of both academic preparation and educational planning for all college-bound youth. This includes non-traditional college students who would be the first in their families to attend college; ethnically diverse students; students from low socioeconomic status (SES) backgrounds; and students with special education classifications who may nonetheless have the ability and inclination to pursue college degrees. As compared with Caucasian middle-class students whose parents are college graduates, non-traditional college bound students are less likely to enroll in college and, when enrolled, have lower rates of college persistence and completion (Lombardi, Murray, & Gerdes, 2012; Unverferth, Talbert-Johnson, & Bogard, 2012). Although numerous barriers (related to academic ability, financial resources, and familial/peer support) also contribute to their lack of postsecondary completion, the presence of academic deficits is most frequently a result of not enrolling in rigorous high school courses that prepare students for college (Savitz-Romer, 2012). Educational planning emphasizing the importance of rigorous coursework is essential when working with potential college-bound students who may not yet self-identify as such.

The Early Decision-Making Process

Clearly, early discussion of career interests and aspirations is inextricably tied to the educational planning process. To assist students and their parents in this early career exploration and educational planning process, professional school counselors will want to proactively guide students and parents through a decision-making process. Ideally, this process will include helping students assess their career-related interests, skills, personality styles, and values.

With regard to the assessment of interests, professional school counselors may conduct interviews with students on an individual, small-group, or classroom basis; use formal interest inventories; provide informal interest questionnaires; or facilitate the use of computer software programs that include interest assessment components. Standardized interest inventories most commonly used in the K–12 academic setting include the Self-Directed Search (SDS; Holland, Powell & Fritzsche, 1997) and Self-Directed Search Career Explorer (SDS; Holland & Powell, 1994); the Strong Interest Inventory (Donnay et al., 2005); and the Career Occupational Preferences System (COPS; EdITS, 1995). A number of computer assisted career guidance systems, including Career Cruising (careercruising.com), the Kuder Career Planning System (Kuder Inc., 2012), Naviance (http://www.naviance.com/), and *COIN Educational Inventory* (COIN Educational Products, 2007) also include components that assess students' interests.

The assessment of interests, however, is not sufficient for the career development and educational planning process. Certainly, another important dimension involves skills. Whether these skills are conceptualized as aptitudes, achievement, or ability, it is essential that professional school counselors also assist students in considering the relevance of skills to their future. In assessing skills, professional school counselors tend to rely on student self-report during interviews, on academic performance (as evidenced by GPA), and on standardized test scores. Standardized tests commonly used during the career development and educational planning process include the Differential Aptitude Test (DAT; Psychological Corporation, 1992); the PSAT (College Board, 2014); SAT (College Board, 2014); the PLAN (American College Testing Program, 2013); ACT (American College Testing Program, 2013); and the Armed Services Vocational Aptitude Battery (ASVAB; U.S. Department of Defense, 2005).

Also important to the early decision-making process is the assessment of students' personality styles as they relate to career planning. This is based, in part, on Holland's contention that a match between an individual's personality style and the "personality" of a given occupation or career leads to increased job satisfaction and success (Brown & Brooks, 1990). However, formal personality testing is rarely conducted by professional school counselors. Instead, professional school counselors tend to use career instruments or informal measures to help students identify career-related personality preferences. For example, the SDS (Holland et al., 1997) helps describe student personalities by identifying a student's three-letter preference. Otherwise known as the "Holland Code," these three letters identify the student's personality preference from six possible styles: Realistic, Investigative, Artistic, Social, Enterprising, or Conventional. Some professional school counselors also use tests such as the True Colors program (Imai & Berry, 2001; Kalil & Lowery, 1999) to help students conceptualize aspects of their personality. Still others may use the Kiersey Temperament Sorter (Kiersey, 1998) to help students determine the direction of their preference across four domains: extroversion vs. introversion, sensing vs. intuition, thinking vs. feeling, and judging vs. perceiving.

The final aspect of assessment that generally contributes to the early decision-making process involves the exploration of students' career-related values. In facilitating this exploration, professional school counselors seek to assist students and their parents in identifying and examining values that should contribute to their educational and career decisions. For example, students may value high salaries; prestige associated with a career; flexibility of scheduling; autonomy; the opportunity to make a difference or contribute to society; adventure; or intellectual stimulation. In helping students identify their values and apply them to the career decision-making and educational planning process, professional school counselors may use formal tests such as the Minnesota Importance Questionnaire (Rounds, Henly, Dawis, & Lofquist, 1981), informal checklists, interviews, or value card sorts such as the freely available O*NET Work Importance Locator (U.S. Department of Labor/Employment and Training Administration, 2001).

Through the process of helping students understand how their interests, skills, personality, and values relate to their educational and career decisions, professional school counselors facilitate the early career decision-making process. Specifically, professional school counselors assist students and their parents in applying this knowledge to select an initial career pathway and to estimate the amount and type of postsecondary education that is necessary for the student to reach his or her career and life goals.

The Balancing Act

Helping students make career decisions early enough in their academic career to support the educational planning process for high school course selection requires that professional school counselors successfully negotiate two separate balancing acts. First, because this early decision-making process is ideally completed during the middle school or junior high years, professional school counselors must balance the self-report and autonomy of students (young adolescents) with the influence of others. For example, professional school counselors will want to help students balance their own aspirations, however immature, with the wisdom, caring and, perhaps, dominance of their parents. As another example, it is essential that professional school counselors assist students in ferreting out the influence of their peers when making decisions for themselves. Additionally, professional school counselors will want to proactively assist students in limiting the impact of culturally sanctioned sex-role, race, and media stereotypes when considering various career options (ASCA, 2012a; Bigler, Averhart, & Liben, 2003; Dugger, in press; King, Madsen, Braverman, Paterson & Yancey, 2008).

The second balancing act necessitates an awareness that decisions made by students during middle and even high school may change over time. Whereas a student in middle school may firmly believe that he or she wants to become a physician and seek a medical degree, this same student may alter plans as a result of experiences with college prep coursework. Similarly, another student may initially plan to seek employment immediately following high school graduation but later express an interest in going to college. As students develop their self-awareness, accumulate real-life experience with academic coursework, and improve their understanding of career possibilities, their educational and career goals may change (Schoon, Gutman, & Sabates, 2012). Such changes are commonplace and to be expected. Therefore, professional school counselors must balance the process of helping students make enough of a decision to support educational planning with the importance of also allowing room for students to change their plans.

Matchmaking

Keeping these balancing acts in mind, the professional school counselor's next task is to assist students and their parents in creating an educational plan designed to facilitate students' progress toward their postsecondary educational and career goals. Indeed, it is the process of matching educational plans with student goals that constitutes the majority of a professional school counselor's activities within the educational planning domain.

For the majority of students, graduating from high school constitutes a fundamental goal that serves as a foundation for their future plans. In helping students match their educational plans with this goal, professional school counselors typically engage in a myriad of educational planning activities. First, high school counselors educate students about graduation requirements. This process generally begins in the eighth grade and frequently involves collaboration between the high school and middle school (or junior high) counselors. In helping students understand graduation requirements, it is necessary to teach them about credits (i.e., the curricular requirements necessary for graduation) and the grades needed to achieve credit in any given course. Figure 21.1 provides a sample handout used to explain graduation requirements. Additionally, Sill (1995) suggested that this early orientation should

Graduation Requirements

Credit Rquirements
- 12 Required Credits
- 11 Elective Credits
- 23 Total Credits

Common Learnings
- **3.5 English**
  - 1.0 9th Grade English
  - 1.0 10th Grade English
  - 0.5 Literature
  - 0.5 Composition
  - 0.5 Speech
- **2.5 Mathematics**
- **2.5 Science**
- **2.5 Social Studies**
  - 1.0 U.S. History
  - 0.5 Government
- **0.5 Physical Ed**
- **0.5 Health**
- **0.5 Computers Tech**

Electives
- 11 Elective Credits

Factors for Admission Consideration

1. High school diploma from an accredited high school
2. Grades in academic subjects
3. Grade point average
4. Trend of grades
5. ACT and/or SAT scores
6. Extracurricular activities
7. Community service

Recommended College Preparatory Program

Course	Number of Credits	Comments
English	4	Writing emphasis
Math	4	Algebra 2 and Geometry
Science	3	Biological and Physical Science
Social Studies	3	US History and Government
Foreign Language	2	

Figure 21.1. Sample handout explaining graduation requirements.
Note: From U.S. Government Printing Office.

also address "honors requirements, vocational and college prep information, prerequisite information, and other items of interest" (p. 89).

High School Curricular Planning

Next, the majority of high schools require the preparation of an Educational Development Plan (EDP), also called a 4-year plan, for each student. In addition to ensuring that the EDP includes all graduation requirements, professional school counselors use the EDP process to assist students in selecting curricular options that will best meet their postsecondary educational and career plans. The preparation of an EDP may be accomplished through the individual student planning or the school counseling core curriculum elements of a comprehensive guidance and counseling program (Gysbers & Henderson, 2012).

However, many professional school counselors mistakenly believe that the individual planning activities must be accomplished through the use of individual sessions with students. Such a use of time is inefficient, given the high student–counselor ratios across the country, and the process of assisting with individual student planning can also be achieved through the use of classroom and small-group meetings (Parikh, 2013). Professional school counselors who are interested in quantifying time saved and/or the differential impact of providing individual planning services in classroom or small-group settings are referred to the section on impact analysis in Gysbers and Henderson (2012). Professional school counselors using a small-group format may wish to group students according to postsecondary plans in order to maximize their efficiency. For example, they may meet with students planning for vocational postsecondary training in one group, with students planning for community college in another group, and with students hoping for admission to 4-year colleges in yet another.

Regardless of a student's postsecondary plans, and regardless of the format in which a professional school counselor chooses to discuss EDPs, the EDP form itself is a primary tool. Figure 21.2 offers a sample EDP form. This form offers a simple way to assist students in (a) understanding and tracking their progress toward graduation requirements; (b) understanding general university admission requirements; (c) recording and updating information about educational and career goals; and (d) planning specific coursework for Grades 9 through 12. Within the section General High School Credit Requirements, students are able to check boxes for each half credit earned in a given subject. This allows for a quick visual check on progress toward graduation requirements. Within the section General University Admissions Requirements, professional school counselors should caution students to verify these requirements with the specific colleges they are considering. The section on Career/Educational Goals should serve as a basis for course selection, and it is the professional school counselor's role to assist students in understanding what courses are best suited to the students' goals. Finally, the section reserved for planning specific coursework will need considerable attention. Each grade level has two columns, one for each semester. In assisting students with coursework planning, professional school counselors must be prepared to discuss with students the sequencing of classes, explain the importance of prerequisites, and offer insight regarding the coursework necessary for a variety of postsecondary educational and career plans.

Figures 21.3, 21.4, and 21.5 present sample EDPs that are designed to represent varying postsecondary educational and career plans. Figure 21.3 provides an EDP for Joanie Hansen, a

(text continues on page 244)

Educational Development Plan

Name _____ Student # _____ Professional School Counselor _____ Grade _____
    (last name, first name)

Career/Educational Goals from assessment results.

1. _____
2. _____

Possible Occupations/careers from selected pathway.

1. _____
2. _____
3. _____

Educational/Training Goals

___ High school diploma	___ Tech Prep (2+2, 2+4)
___ Career/Technical Center certificate	___ Four-year bachelor's degree
___ On-the-job training	___ Master's degree
___ Apprenticeship	___ Doctoral degree
___ Trade & technical certification	___ Military
___ Two-year associate's degree	___ Other

General High School Credit Requirements

- 12 Required Units of Credit
- 11 Elective Units of Credit
- **23 Units of Credit Total for Graduation**

- 3.5 **English**
  - 1.0 9th Grade English
  - 1.0 10th Grade English
  - .5 Literature
  - .5 Composition
  - .5 Oral Communication
- 2.5 **Mathematics**
- 2.5 **Science**
- 2.5 **Social Studies**
  - 1.0 Geography
  - 1.0 U.S. History
  - .5 American Government
- .5 **Health**
- .5 **Personal Fitness**

General University Admissions

Required:
- 4.0 English
- 3.0 Mathematics
- 3.0 Science
- 3.0 History/Social Sciences

Recommended:
- 2.0 Foreign Language
- 2.0 Fine & Performing Arts
- 1.0 Computer Literacy

*Athletes Check NCAA Requirements

Grade 9	Grade 10	Grade 11	Grade 12

Alternate _____

Student Signature _____ Professional School Counselor Signature _____ Parent Signature _____

White - File   Yellow - Return with Parent Signature   Pink - Student

Figure 21.2. Educational development plan (EDP).

EDUCATIONAL DEVELOPMENT PLAN

Name __Hansen, Joanie__ Student # __000832__ Professional School Counselor __Phillips__ Grade __9__
(last name, first name)

Career/Educational Goals from assessment results.
1. __4 years of college plus graduate school__
2. __4 years of college plus pharmacology school__

Possible Occupations/careers from selected pathway.
1. __Veterinarian__
2. __Pharmacist__
3. _____

Educational/Training Goals
- ___ High school diploma
- ___ Career/Technical Center certificate
- ___ On-the-job training
- ___ Apprenticeship
- ___ Trade & technical certification
- ___ Two-year associate's degree
- ___ Tech Prep (2+2, 2+4)
- ___ Four-year bachelor's degree
- ___ Master's degree
- _x_ Doctoral degree
- ___ Military
- ___ Other

General High School Credit Requirements
- 12 Required Units of Credit
- 11 Elective Units of Credit
- **23 Units of Credit Total for Graduation**

3.5 English
- 1.0 9th Grade English
- 1.0 10th Grade English
- .5 Literature
- .5 Composition
- .5 Oral Communication

2.5 Mathematics
2.5 Science
2.0 Foreign Language
1.0 Computer Literacy
2.5 Social Studies
- 1.0 Geography
- 1.0 U.S. History
- .5 American Government

.5 Health
.5 Personal Fitness

General University Admissions

Required:
- 4.0 English
- 3.0 Mathematics
- 3.0 Science
- 3.0 History/Social Sciences

Recommended:
- 2.0 Fine & Performing Arts

*Athletes Check NCAA Requirements

Grade 9		Grade 10		Grade 11		Grade 12	
Acc. English 9	Acc. English 9	Acc. English 10	Acc. English 10	Acc. English 11	Acc. English 11	AP English	AP English
World History	World History	AP U.S. History	AP U.S. History	AP Government	AP Government	Indv. Life Sports	Community Service
Molecular Biology	Molecular Biology	Inorganic Chemistry	Inorganic Chemistry	AP Chemistry	AP Chemistry	AP Biology	AP Biology
Acc. Geometry	Acc. Geometry	Acc. Algebra 2	Acc. Algebra 2	Acc. Analysis	Acc. Analysis	AP Calculus	AP Calculus
Physical Education	Information Tech	Health	Zoology	Physics	Physics	AP Physics	AP Physics
Spanish 1	Spanish 1	Spanish 2	Spanish 2	Yearbook	Yearbook	Yearbook	Yearbook
Alternate Chorus	Chorus	Orchestra	Orchestra	Journalism	Info Tech 2	Career Internship	Career Internship

Student Signature _____ Professional School Counselor Signature _____ Parent Signature _____

White - File   Yellow - Return with Parent Signature   Pink - Student

Figure 21.3. EDP for a student pursuing an advanced medical degree.

Educational Development Plan

Name __Brady, Mike__ Student # __000987__ Professional School Counselor __Phillips__ Grade __9__
(last name, first name)

Career/Educational Goals from assessment results.
1. Associate's Degree
2. Trade & Technical Certification

Possible Occupations/careers from selected pathway.
1. Architectural Assistant
2. Computer Aided Designer
3. _____

Educational/Training Goals
- ___ High school diploma
- ___ Career/Technical Center certificate
- ___ On-the-job training
- ___ Apprenticeship
- ___ Trade & technical certification
- _x_ Two-year associate's degree
- ___ Tech Prep (2+2, 2+4)
- ___ Four-year bachelor's degree
- ___ Master's degree
- ___ Doctoral degree
- ___ Military
- ___ Other

General High School Credit Requirements
- 12 Required Units of Credit
- 11 Elective Units of Credit
- **23 Units of Credit Total for Graduation**

3-5 English
- 1.0 9th Grade English
- 1.0 10th Grade English
- .5 Literature
- .5 Composition
- .5 Oral Communication

2.5 Mathematics
2.5 Science
2.0 Foreign Language
1.0 Computer Literacy
2.5 Social Studies
- 1.0 Geography
- 1.0 U.S. History
- .5 American Government

.5 Health
.5 Personal Fitness

General University Admissions

Required:
- 4.0 English
- 3.0 Mathematics
- 3.0 Science
- 3.0 History/Social Sciences

Recommended:
- 2.0 Fine & Performing Arts

*Athletes Check NCAA Requirements

Grade 9		Grade 10		Grade 11		Grade 12	
English 9	English 9	English 10	English 10	Composition	Mythology	Speech	Research Tech
Geography	Geography	U.S. History	U.S. History	Government	Physical Education	Psychology	Health
Physical Science	Physical Science	Biology	Biology	Inorganic Chemistry	Inorganic Chemistry	Physics	Physics
Algebra 1	Algebra 1	Geometry	Geometry	Algebra 2	Algebra 2	Engineering Tech	Engineering Tech
Spanish 1	Spanish 1	Spanish 2	Spanish 2	Architectural Tech	Architectural Tech	Engineering Tech	Engineering Tech
Applied Tech	Manufacturing Tech	Drafting 1	Drafting 1	Architectural Tech	Architectural Tech	Co-Operative Training	Co-Operative Training
Alternate Drawing 1	Drawing 2	Team Sports	Swimming	Photography 1	Photography 2	Information Tech	Dual Enrollment

Student Signature _____ Professional School Counselor Signature _____ Parent Signature _____

White - File   Yellow - Return with Parent Signature   Pink - Student

Figure 21.4. EDP for a student pursuing an associate's degree.

Educational Development Plan

Name: Keaton, Elyse (last name, first name)   Student # 000452   Professional School Counselor: Phillips   Grade: 9

Career/Educational Goals from assessment results.
1. Employment after high school
2. Trade & Technical Certification

Possible Occupations/careers from selected pathway.
1. Child-Care Worker
2. Work in family business
3. ___

Educational/Training Goals
- X High school diploma
- ___ Career/Technical Center certificate
- ___ On-the-job training
- ___ Apprenticeship
- ___ Trade & technical certification
- ___ Two-year associate's degree
- ___ Tech Prep (2+2, 2+4)
- ___ Four-year bachelor's degree
- ___ Master's degree
- ___ Doctoral degree
- ___ Military
- ___ Other

General High School Credit Requirements
- 12 Required Units of Credit
- 11 Elective Units of Credit
- **23 Units of Credit Total for Graduation**

3.5 English
  - 1.0 9th Grade English
  - 1.0 10th Grade English
  - .5 Literature
  - .5 Composition
  - .5 Oral Communication

2.5 Mathematics

2.5 Science

2.5 Social Studies
  - 1.0 Geography
  - 1.0 U.S. History
  - .5 American Government

.5 Health

.5 Personal Fitness

General University Admissions

Required:
- 4.0 English
- 3.0 Mathematics
- 3.0 Science
- 3.0 History/Social Sciences

Recommended:
- 2.0 Foreign Language
- 2.0 Fine & Performing Arts
- 1.0 Computer Literacy

*Athletes Check NCAA Requirements

Grade 9		Grade 10		Grade 11		Grade 12	
English 9	English 9	English 10	English 10	Composition	Short Stories	Speech	Research
Geography	Geography	U.S. History	U.S. History	Government	Physical Education	Psychology	Sociology
Physical Science	Physical Science	Biology	Biology	Hydrology	Information Tech 1	Health	Personal Finance
Algebra 1	Algebra 1	Geometry	Geometry	Cont. Algebra 2	Algebra 2	Marketing	Entrepreneur
Spanish 1	Spanish 1	Spanish 2	Spanish 2	Choir	Choir	Choir	Choir
Choir	Choir	Child Development	Child Development	Child Care Professional	Child Care Professional	Child Care Cooperative	Child Care Cooperative
Alternate Info Tech 1	Info Tech 2	Photography 1	Photography 2	Community Service	Office Assistant	Family Living	Life Management

Student Signature _____   Professional School Counselor Signature _____   Parent Signature _____

White - File   Yellow - Return with Parent Signature   Pink - Student

Figure 21.5. EDP for a student pursuing a career in child care or business.

student intent on pursuing a doctoral degree in veterinary medicine or pharmacology. Figure 21.4 provides an EDP for Mike Brady, a student interested in earning an associate's degree to become an architectural assistant or a computer-aided designer. Figure 21.5 offers an EDP for Elyse Keaton, a student intending to either work in child care or in her family's business immediately following high school graduation. In comparing the three completed example EDPs in Figures 21.3, 21.4, and 21.5, one will note significant differences in course planning. These differences involve both the level of courses planned and the type of courses selected. With regard to the level of courses planned, for example, Joanie's professional school counselor strongly encouraged her to take high-level math classes throughout high school, because she is planning to pursue a doctorate in a medical field. Because Joanie is scheduled to take Accelerated Geometry as a freshman, Joanie will need to have taken prerequisite coursework during middle school. This highlights the importance of early interventions to assist with educational and career planning during middle and even elementary school. In comparison to Joanie's math schedule, both Mike and Elyse have planned to take Algebra I during their freshman year.

The professional school counselor will have worked with these students to assist them in identifying classes related to their postsecondary educational and career plans. Although the majority of classes are selected for the purpose of meeting graduation requirements and of ensuring a well-rounded education for each student, room for electives also generally exists. The choice of electives, therefore, can and should allow students to explore more deeply their tentative postsecondary plans. As an illustration, Mike Brady has expressed interest in both architecture and computer-aided design. In consultation with his professional school counselor, Mike has therefore chosen courses such as manufacturing technology, drafting, and architectural technology as electives. This can be contrasted with Elyse's choice of child development, child care co-op, marketing, and personal finance. Each of these electives is intended to assist Elyse in exploring possible careers in child care and in business.

Turning Vision into Reality

Once the initial EDP has been developed, students are equipped with a road map to a set of possible postsecondary destinations. As students begin taking courses in accordance with their EDP, they will have an opportunity to reaffirm or question their initial postsecondary plans. Again, their reaction may be to the level of difficulty associated with the courses or to the topics addressed in their courses. Additionally, because students are developing and maturing, it is also possible that their interests may change and, as a consequence, it is essential that the educational planning process continue well beyond the completion of the EDP. Professional school counselors will need to periodically meet with students to check on the goodness of fit between the students' EDPs and their developing self-awareness and postsecondary interests and plans. As goals change, of course, it will be appropriate to update the EDP to reflect new postsecondary goals and to identify courses appropriate to the new plans. As the vision changes, a new route must be charted in order to assist the students in turning their vision into reality.

Continued Career Development

In addition to responding to changes in student goals that develop as a result of coursework and maturation, professional school counselors also proactively work with students to facilitate continued career development. They may do so in a variety of ways: through school counseling core curriculum units delivered in classroom settings; through teacher collaborations focused on infusion of career-related information into academic subjects and standards blending (Schellenberg, 2012); through a school-based career development center; through after-school seminars offered to students and their parents; through guest speakers; and through job-shadowing programs. With regard to school counseling core curriculum units, ASCA (2012b) and the National Career Development Association (National Occupational Information Coordinating Committee, 2004) each offered a set of competencies specific to the needs of K–12 students.

School-based career development centers are also common in high schools. Most often, these centers are staffed by a career development paraprofessional or by a professional school counselor. The centers tend to offer a wide variety of career-related resources, including college applications and catalogs, information on scholarships and financial aid, literature about other postsecondary training options, resources about a wide variety of careers, information related to résumé writing and successful interviewing, and employment information.

Educational Planning for Postsecondary Options

To guide students and their families through the process of postsecondary educational planning, a wise professional school counselor will begin early rather than waiting for the "senior stampede" or even the junior interview. Without such systematic planning, professional school counselors will find that, as students near graduation, they and their parents frequently flood into the counseling office, desperate for assistance in finding the right colleges to which to apply, the right training programs to attend, or the right branch of the military in which to serve. Despite even the most careful educational planning process for the EDPs, these students and their parents tend to experience the planning process for postsecondary options as critical to their future. Therefore, specific activities targeting postsecondary educational planning are essential for the high school counselor.

One common method of providing guidance is by offering after-school seminars on topics such as career nights, college nights, and financial aid nights. For each seminar, professional school counselors may serve either as facilitators/coordinators or presenters. Additional topics frequently addressed in after-school or in-school seminars involve military educational and career opportunities, vocational training opportunities, and NCAA eligibility requirements for competing in Division I athletics. Finally, professional school counselors frequently coordinate job-shadowing programs to facilitate student exploration of possible career options. Each of these career development opportunities assists students in testing their initial aspirations and interests against reality.

Another method involves the professional school counselor's library of postsecondary resources. Although such libraries have historically consisted of shelves and shelves of books and college catalogs, technology now allows for Internet-based resources as well. Many school counseling departments now manage a Web site on which students and families can access a wealth of information regarding the postsecondary educational planning process. (For an example of one such Web site, see http://whatcomesnext101.wix.com/psrg/, which was created by Jennifer Horn as a final project for a postsecondary planning course at Eastern Michigan University.) Technological advances have also resulted in significant changes in school-based career centers, as centers now also tend to feature computers equipped with career-related software programs or access to Internet sites relevant to career exploration and planning (Hayden, Poynton, & Sabella, 2008). Examples of widely used programs include Bridges/XAP (bridges.com), Career Cruising (careercruising.com), the Kuder Career Planning System (kuder.com/product/kuder-career-planning-system/), and Naviance (naviance.com).

Most school counseling departments also periodically publish a newsletter, either in hard copy or electronic format, and this is an outstanding way to heighten student and family awareness of issues related to postsecondary planning. It is useful to include sections in the newsletter dedicated to each grade level and to provide postsecondary planning advice for each grade level in each respective section. Electronic listservs to which students and/or parents can subscribe have also become popular ways to disseminate information regarding scholarships, summer opportunities, and other information to specific groups.

Professional school counselors will want to meet with all juniors to discuss their academic record and their preliminary ideas regarding postsecondary options and to provide them with information regarding college entrance examinations and the college search process. Often, they seek the "perfect" option. To assist students, parents, and even fellow professional school counselors in managing this process, Boshoven (2003) cautioned that there is not necessarily a single perfect college or postsecondary training option.

Adapting Mathews' (2003) metaphor likening the college search to a search for a house, Boshoven (2003) suggested that selecting a postsecondary training option is similar to buying a coat. He specifically challenged the notion that there is a perfect college that is somehow perfect for everyone and suggests that colleges, like coats, are not "one size fits all" (p. 8). In working with students and families, he strives to help them find the best fit for them personally rather than applying to the schools everyone else wants to attend. To assist them, Boshoven encourages students and parents to consider the factors related to a goodness of fit. As part of finding the best fit, Boshoven identified the additional factors of feel, fashion/flair, fiscal and other factors as they pertain not only to buying a coat but also to selecting a college or other form of postsecondary education.

In Boshoven's (2003) conceptualization, "fit" may refer to a school's size, geographic location, curricular offerings, extracurricular opportunities, political atmosphere, religious affiliation, or presence of a Greek (fraternity, sorority) system. The "feel" dimension is best captured by student comments such as "the first time I visited, it just felt right!" (p. 8). "Fashion/flair" refers to matching the style of a student to the style of the school. This may relate to average incoming grades and standardized test scores or to career options such as astrophysics, culinary schools, building trades, or pre-med. He cautioned that the fashion/flair of a school needs to suit the specific student, not the student's friends or family members.

The "fiscal" factor, of course, is a pragmatic factor often considered paramount by families as they anticipate the expense of postsecondary educational options. Professional school counselors do not need to become privy to the details of a family's financial situation, but it is essential that a discussion occur between parents and their children as they approach graduation so that the student understands clearly to what degree parents can and will contribute to the costs of postsecondary education. In addition, professional school counselors should educate students and parents about other elements related to financing college. Financial aid workshops are a popular way of doing so, and these workshops should not only include assistance with the completion of the *Free Application for Federal Student Aid* (FAFSA) but should also include a discussion of other issues. Boshoven (2003) offered the following observations:

- Scholarships are available.
- "Private colleges give more money in aid than public universities" (p. 9).
- "Community colleges are less expensive and can offer a number of scholarships" (p. 9).
- Students can work during summers and during the school year to earn money toward the cost of their education.
- Students may look for jobs in which their employers will assist them with the costs of additional education or training.
- Students may consider loans as an option.
- The military, though costing in time, does offer free education.
- Sometimes you get what you pay for. Before gravitating toward the least expensive option, consider factors such as class size and the percentage of courses taught by professors as opposed to teaching assistants.

For students planning to obtain careers that require a college education, professional school counselors become purveyors of college access by providing college knowledge regarding applying for, choosing, and financing college. This knowledge is especially important for students underrepresented in 4-year universities, who are typically first generation college students, ethnically diverse, or from lower socio-economic backgrounds (Conley, 2010). Due to historical exclusion from rigorous K–12 coursework and because their parents are unlikely to possess knowledge of the college access process, such students lack an understanding of the concrete steps required to apply for and enroll in college (Roderick, Nagaoka, & Coca, 2009). School counselors, as advocates for educational equity, should use their ability to identify and meet the college access needs of all students, especially underrepresented students who may otherwise fail to enroll in college. The KnowHow2Go (http://knowhow2go.acenet.edu/) organization offers some particularly useful materials for encouraging students from historically underrepresented populations to consider and achieve college goals.

Developing Your Own Expertise as a Professional School Counselor

In order to be effective in helping students find the "best fit" for postsecondary education, it is essential that professional school counselors develop their own expertise in this area. Fortunately, there are a wide variety of print resources available. Figure 21.6 provides an annotated listing of recommended readings. In addition to relying upon print resources, professional school counselors will want to maintain membership in several professional associations that regularly provide support in the area of educational planning. Figure 21.7 provides a partial listing of such organizations. Additionally, by forming and maintaining working relationships with college personnel, such as financial aid consultants and admissions officers, professional school counselors can obtain updated knowledge concerning postsecondary institutions.

Summary/Conclusion

In this chapter, we provided an overview of the educational planning process and offered specific ideas about the integration of educational planning services into an already existing

(text continues on page 252)

AUCC Publications. (2006). *Directory of Canadian Universities* (40th ed.). Ottawa, Ontario: Author.
   This is a dry but complete listing of programs at Canadian universities.

Antonoff, S. R. (1999). *The College Finder*. New York: Fawcett Books.
   This little gem serves students as the book of college trivia, from kosher kitchens to ping pong and debate championships. It is arranged topically and by school.

Antonoff, S. R., & Friedmann, M. A. (2006). *College Match* (9th ed.). Alexandria, VA: Octameron Associates.
   This is a 150 page, ultra-practical, step-by-step guide for the college bound student and family.

Asher, D. (2000). *Cool Colleges For The Hyper-Intelligent, Self-Directed, Late Blooming, and Just Plain Different*. Toronto: Ten Speed Press.
   This is a nice guide for those "out-of-the-boxers."

Barron's Educational Series. (Ed.). (2006). *Profiles of American Colleges With CD-ROM* (27th ed.). Hauppaugh, NY: Author.
   This is an annual compendium that gives general statistics and overviews of colleges and students.

Coburn, K. L., & Treeger, M. L. (1997). *Letting Go: A Parent's Guide to Understanding the College Years*. New York: HarperCollins.
   This classic book helps parents and students identify and deal with all the emotional issues of separation and change.

College Bound Sports. (2005). *The High School Athlete's Guide to College Sports: How to Market Yourself to the School of Your Dreams*. Lanham, MD: Taylor Trade.
   This is a useful guide for the high school athlete and helps guide them through the complexities of their applications to college.

Dance Magazine. (2005). *Dance Magazine College Guide*. Oakland, CA: Author.
   This is a helpful annual guide of programs and contacts for students interested in a career related to dance.

Everett, C. J., & Topaz, M. (1998). *Guide to Performing Arts Programs*. New York: Princeton Review.
   For our singers, dancers, and thespians, a guide to assist in finding summer programs and college options.

Fiske, E. B. (2006). *The Fiske Guide to Colleges 2006*. Naperville, IL: Sourcebooks.
   This annual guide is written by the former Education Writer for *The New York Times* and is Boshoven's favorite source for looking at great U.S. and Canadian colleges and universities.

Fiske, E. B., & Hammond, B. G. (2001). *Getting Into the Right College* (2nd ed.). Naperville, IL: Sourcebooks.
   A beach read, this tome is written in a practical, sensible manner, allowing students to examine themselves and picking types of colleges that may "match" them best.

Fiske, E. B., & Hammond, B. G. (2005). *Fiske What To Do When For College 2005-2006: A Student and Parent's Guide to Deadlines, Planning and the Last Two Years of High School*. Naperville, IL: Sourcebooks.
   For those students needing definite structure in accomplishing the tasks needed to accomplish the college application process, this little guide can definitely help.

Franek, R., et al. (2003). *The Best Midwestern Colleges: 150 Great Schools to Consider*. New York: Princeton Review.
   A companion to the *Fiske Guide*, these regional books describe the student and academic life of a wider range of selective regional colleges and universities.

Figure 21.6. Annotated listing of recommended readings for professional school counselors. *Note.* The Octameron Series features 16 handy and inexpensive guides covering various college counseling questions. The complete set is available at a discount at http://www.octameron.com.

Greene, R., (2001). *The Teenager's Guide to School Outside the Box*. Minneapolis, MN: Free Spirit.
  Free-spirited students tend to appreciate a book that attempts to engage them in the college process. One student beamed, "You mean there is a college just right for liberal me?"

Hall, C., & Lieber, R. (1996). *Taking Time Off: Inspired Stories of Students Who Enjoyed Successful Breaks From College and How to Plan Your Own*. New York: The Noonday Press.
  Not every student is ready to launch off to college. This book offers good rationale and options for spending productive time between high school and college.

Hammond, B. G. (2005). *Discounts and Deals at the Nation's 360 Best Colleges*. New York: St. Martin's Griffin.
  College is expensive, and families need our help in aiming them at possible scholarships.

Killpatrick, F., & Killpatrick, J. (2002). *The Winning Edge: The Student-Athlete's Guide To College Sports*. Alexandria, VA: Octameron Associates.
  Athletes have double the work in applying to college but also have some definite advantages in admission. The handy guide will help in making sure they've thought of everything.

Kravets, M. B., & Wax, I. F. (2003). *The K & W Guide to Colleges for the Learning Disabled* (7th ed.). New York: Princeton Review.
  An essential resource for assisting students who learn differently with the postsecondary educational planning process. Finding appropriate support at college can be the difference between success and failure.

Leider, A. (2005). *Don't Miss Out: The Ambitious Student's Guide to Financial Aid* (30th ed.). Alexandria, VA: Octameron Associates.
  There's money out there for students willing to work to find it. Here's a helpful start.

Leider, A. (2000). *I Am Somebody: College Knowledge for At-Risk Students* (9th ed.). Alexandria, VA: Octameron Associates.
  A friendly little guide for students wondering if college is appropriate.

Leider, A. (2005). *The A's & B's of Academic Scholarships* (25th ed.). Alexandria, VA: Octameron Associates.
  Merit scholarships are available at many colleges and universities, and this resource provides a helpful and manageable listing of them.

Mathews, J. (2003). *Harvard Schmarvard: Getting Beyond the Ivy League to the College That's Best for You*. New York: Prima.
  The education writer for the *Washington Post* restates Loren Pope's points well.

Mayher, B. (1998). *The College Admissions Mystique*. New York: Noonday Press.
  This expose reveals Brown's strategies for becoming the "hot" Ivy League college prospect and explores the psychology of college admissions marketing.

Pasisk, P. (1998). *Almost Grown: Launching Your Child From High School to College*. New York: Norton.
  This is an outstanding "dealing-with-emotions" book in which the author chronicles her and her son's angst in preparing for the launch to college.

Pintoff, E. (1994). *The Complete Guide to American Film Schools and Cinema and Television Courses*. New York: Penguin Books.
  Although dated, this book provides a good description of the various options for artsy, more hands-on learners.

Pope, L. (2006). *Colleges That Change Lives: 40 Schools You Should Know About Even if You're Not A Straight-A-Student* (3rd ed.). New York: Penguin Books.
  This should be required reading for all students and families. The author examines the fit of colleges and the mission of state universities and private colleges.

(continues)

Pope, L. (2007). *Looking Beyond the Ivy League: Finding the College That's Right for You* (2nd ed.). New York: Penguin Books.
  Pope's research about colleges and the difference they can make if the right fit is there.

Re, J. M. (2005). *Financial Aid Financer: Expert Answers to College Financing Questions* (17th ed.). Alexandria, VA: Octameron Associates.
  Parents get nervous about the costs of college. Here's a handy book to guide them in finding money that may be available to help them.

Ripple, G. G. (2001). *Campus Pursuit: Making the Most of Your Visit and Interview* (9th ed.). Alexandria, VA: Octameron Associates.
  This is a helpful guide to help students learn to "kick the tires" and make the most of a campus visit.

Rogers Publishing, Ltd. (2006). *Maclean's Guide to Canadian Universities.* Toronto, Ontario: Author.
  Although the rankings are suspect, the program descriptions are valuable.

Rubenstone, S., & Dalby, S. (2002). *College Admissions: A Crash Course for Panicked Parents* (3rd ed.). Lawrenceville, NJ: Thomson Peterson's.
  This sensible guide is a terrific reference for families wondering what to do and when to do it.

Rugg, F. E. (2006). *Rugg's recommendations on the colleges* (23rd ed.). Fallbrook, CA: Ruggs Recommendations.
  This trade publication can help counselors get college lists started for students with particular academic interests.

Seghers, L. (Ed.). (2005). *Peterson's Professional Degree Programs in the Visual & Performing Arts 2006.* Lawrenceville, NJ: Thomson Peterson's.
  A specific guide for artists and performers.

Steinberg, J. (2002). *The Gatekeepers: Inside the Admissions Process of a Premier College.* New York: Penguin Books.
  Not for the faint of heart, this scary book highlights the subjective world of the admissions office of Wesleyan University.

Suskind, R. (1999). *A Hope in the Unseen: An American Odyssey From the Inner City to the Ivy League.* New York: Broadway Books.
  This sensitive book follows a first generation African American student in an Ivy League college.

Thacker, L. (2004). *College Unranked: Affirming Educational Values in College Admissions.* Portland, OR: The Education Conservancy.
  This book normalizes student confusion about the college admissions process. In it, seasoned admissions folks put it all into perspective.

The College Board. (2004). *The College Board Index of Majors & Graduate Degrees 2004: All-New Twenty-Sixth Edition.* New York: Author.
  What college offers what major? The complete list by subject relates to the college search engine on their Web site.

Wildavsky, B. (2004). *Ultimate Guide to Becoming a Teacher.* Naperville, IL: Sourcebooks.
  This is a helpful listing of teacher-preparation programs in colleges and universities.

Yale Daily News. (2006). *The Insider's Guide to the Colleges* (32nd ed.). New York: St. Martin's Griffin.
  Students like the gritty social-life reviews, but counselors find the reviews inconsistent and slanted.

Figure 21.6 (*continued*)

American Counseling Association
5999 Stevenson Ave. Alexandria, VA 22304
800/347-6647
http://www.counseling.org

The American Counseling Association (ACA) is a not-for-profit, professional and educational organization that is dedicated to the growth and enhancement of the counseling profession. Founded in 1952, ACA is the world's largest association, exclusively representing professional counselors in various practice settings. By providing leadership training, publications, continuing education opportunities, and advocacy services to nearly 45,000 members, ACA helps counseling professionals develop their skills and expand their knowledge base. ACA has been instrumental in setting professional and ethical standards for the counseling profession. The association has made considerable strides in accreditation, licensure, and national certification. It also represents the interests of the profession before Congress and federal agencies, and strives to promote recognition of professional counselors to the public and the media. One of the two general organizations serving professional school counselors, the national organization sponsors local and state branches that are instrumental in networking and professional development opportunities.

American School Counselor Association
1101 King St., Suite 625
Alexandria, VA 22314
703/683-ASCA or 800/306-4722
http://www.schoolcounselor.org

The American School Counselor Association (ASCA) supports professional school counselors' efforts to help students focus on academic, personal–social, and career development so they achieve success in school and are prepared to lead fulfilling lives as responsible members of society. ASCA provides professional development, publications and other resources, research and advocacy to more than 18,000 professional school counselors around the globe. The other professional association specializing in serving school counselors, ASCA sponsors local and state branches that are instrumental in networking and professional development opportunities.

National Association for College Admission Counseling
1631 Prince Street
Alexandria, VA 22314-2828
703/836-2222
http://www.nacacnet.org

The National Association for College Admission Counseling (NACAC) is an organization of more than 10,000 professionals from around the world, dedicated to serving students as they make choices about pursuing postsecondary education. NACAC is committed to maintaining high standards that foster ethical and social responsibility among those involved in the transition process, as outlined in the NACAC Statement of Principles of Good Practice (SPGP). NACAC's award-winning publications and other media resources, professional development programs and practical research efforts have all been designed to give counseling and admission professionals the tools they need to improve the counseling services they provide to students. NACAC sponsors many college and performing arts fairs nationwide and beyond. The Web site is a valuable resource for counselors, and the E-List helps counselors connect with questions and resources.

Figure 21.7. National organizational resources for professional school counselors.

school counseling program. We emphasized the inextricable link between career development and educational planning and encouraged professional school counselors to incorporate educational planning into their career exploration, development, and planning activities. Toward this end, we recommend helping students explore their interests, skills, values, and personality styles; facilitating student exploration and selection of career pathways; assisting students with development of an Educational Development Plan (EDP) that is consistent with their preferred career pathway(s); and providing substantial guidance related to postsecondary educational planning. Finally, we emphasized the importance of involving parents and families in the overall process of career development and educational planning.

CHAPTER 22

Consulting in the Schools: The Role of the Professional School Counselor

Donna M. Gibson

Preview

Consultation with parents and teachers is one of the most important services provided by the professional school counselor because it bridges the communication gap among adults that can directly affect the life of a student. This chapter focuses on the consultation process and offers guidelines to professional school counselors conducting parent and teacher consultation conferences.

According to the American School Counselor Association (ASCA; 2012a), the professional school counselor as a consultant engages in both student and systems advocacy in acting on behalf of students. Due to the inherent role as an internal consultant, school counselors become an expert resource for various constituents in the school setting (Erford, 2015c; Young & Basham, 2014). It is the consulting role of the professional school counselor that is more observable by administrators, parents, and teachers. Thus, it is imperative for professional school counselors to understand the purpose of consulting and how to make these experiences meaningful, especially for parents and teachers.

The Purpose of Consulting

There are several purposes and settings for consulting (Brown, Pryzwansky, & Schulte, 2010; Dinkmeyer, Carlson, & Dinkmeyer, 2005; Gladding, 2013; Kampwirth, 2011). In general, most consultations are conducted to solve a problem (Dougherty, 2013). This is similar to some of the goals of counseling. Both counselors and consultants use communication skills such as listening, attending, questioning, clarifying, confronting, and summarizing. However, consultation is different from counseling in two important ways. First, the counseling process involves two parties, the counselor and client. In contrast, consultation involves more than two people; generally, the professional school counselor (consultant), teacher or parent (consultee), and student (client). Second, counseling involves dealing with personal problems. In consultation, the process involves work-related or caretaking-related concerns. The teacher (consultee), for example, would be consulting with the professional school counselor (consultant) about the student's (client) behavior in class. The teacher would be consulting with the professional school counselor about alternative behavior management strategies for dealing with the student in the classroom. Therefore, the focus is not on the personal problems of the child as much as the work-related/caretaking concerns of the teacher. Hence, professional school counselors need to monitor their consultation behaviors to prevent consulting from becoming counseling.

Although the general purpose of consultation may be to solve a problem, professional school counselors need to look at consultation as a systematic process that can be used in a variety of situations. Professional school counselors usually consult with administrators, parents, and teachers. Holding conferences with parents and teachers, however, can provoke the anxiety for all parties involved. To reduce or eliminate this anxiety, the professional school counselor needs to establish the goal for the consultation.

To establish a consultation goal, the professional school counselor needs to assess the expectations and purpose of the consultation with the individual he or she is meeting (Erford, 2015c; Hall & Lin, 1994). Goals will vary based on the theoretical orientation of the professional school counselor to the stage of the consultation process. For example, if the problem is not clear to the individuals in the consultation, then the goal may be to identify and clarify the problem. Follow-up meetings may focus on the goal of evaluating the progress that has been made in working or caring for the student by the consultee.

When establishing consultation goals, the parent or teacher (consultee) needs to be aware of his or her role in this process. In this process, the consultee is a collaborator with the consultant (professional school counselor), working in a partnership with shared responsibilities (Dougherty, 2013). If the professional school counselor is offering information in advisement to help the consultee, the consultee is not obligated to follow that advice. However, the consultee is ultimately responsible for the client. In this case, the parent or teacher is responsible for the welfare of the student.

As the professional school counselor and consultee are working on goals in consultation, they are working on building a relationship with each other (Hall & Lin, 1994). At this point, it is also important to consider the role of culture in this relationship (Holcomb-McCoy & Bryan, 2010). If necessary, collaborating and arranging for interpreters to be present in consultation meetings will help meet the needs of linguistically diverse families. Professional school counselors should also be able to identify any prejudicial attitudes that affect the consultation process and act to modify them (Holcomb-McCoy, 2004). Additionally, issues related to cultural influence on how to handle emotional issues should be considered. This relationship evolves as consultant and consultee progress through the stages of consultation.

Hall and Lin (1994) outlined four stages of consultation: entry, diagnosis, process, and disengagement. During the *entry* stage, the primary task of the professional school counselor is to assess the situation. The advantage of the professional school counselor is that he or she is physically located at the school and is available to teachers and parents. In this assessment process, the professional school counselor needs to determine if he or she is prepared to handle the situation. If necessary, appropriate referrals can be made at this time.

If the situation is appropriate for the professional school counselor, then he or she can outline expectations to the teacher or parent. This could include meeting to identify concerns and goals for the client. While many students (clients) are not mature enough to understand and contribute to consultation meetings, it may be appropriate to invite mature students to attend early meetings to provide their perception of the problem. Consultants must use listening skills, such as empathy, genuineness, and respect, to enlist the consultee's help, lessen anxiety, and avoid resistance to the process (Hall & Lin, 1994).

The purpose of the *diagnosis* stage is to define the problem and any relevant factors related to the situation. First, the consultant must gather information about the situation, which could include information about the client's behavior, feelings, aptitude, achievement, or social skills. Second, the consultant and consultee must mutually agree on a definition of the problem. This definition needs to be created in concrete terms so that interventions and evaluations to address the problem can be formulated. Third, goals need to be written in specific terms from the definition. Fourth, interventions need to be designed from the goal statements.

The third stage of the consultation, *process*, involves implementation of the consultation plan. Dougherty (2013) outlined four questions the consultant must ask the consultee to complete this stage: (a) What are we going to do? (b) How are we going to do it? (c) When and where are we going to do it? and (d) How well did we do it? To address the first question, the consultant and consultee can review the interventions planned during the diagnosis stage. Part of planning interventions is to address who will carry them out, when they will occur, and how they will occur. Since consultees have the most responsibility for students, consultees direct most interventions. When professional school counselors meet with parents about their children, parents are responsible for carrying out interventions at home. If necessary, the professional school counselor and parent may have to consult with the child's teacher in order to carry out interventions at school. Of course, these interventions should be evaluated for effectiveness as they are carried out and adjusted to meet the consultation goals. The consultation form provided in Table 22.1 can be copied and used for the planning and implementation of consultation in the schools.

The *disengagement* stage is the ending stage of the consultation process. This stage includes an overall evaluation of the effectiveness of the consultation. This can be a formal or informal process whereby the professional school counselor interviews the consultee about the process or requests that the consultee complete a questionnaire or rating form. It is also during this stage that the consultant and consultee decrease or cease the consulting relationship. In the school, it is not necessary to terminate a relationship, but consultation about a student for a specific problem should decrease.

This systematic consultation process can vary in the amount of time allotted for one problem. It is necessary to understand the process, however, and use the designed activities to help the consultee. In the following sections, the role of the professional school counselor in parent and teacher consultations is explained, and specific recommendations are made to promote effective conferences.

Consulting With Parents

Professional school counselors have several opportunities to consult with parents. Within the realm of a comprehensive developmental counseling program, counseling activities and programs often induce some form of parental consultation. It may be introduced by either the parent or the professional school counselor. Although attitudes and communication issues by both parents and schools may hinder effective communication, there should not be an assumption that parents do not want to help their children (Erford, 2015c). In contrast, the majority of parents want the school's guidance in how to help their children learn and develop. If an initial phone call to a parent to begin the consultation process does not

Table 22.1. Consultation Planning and Intervention Form

Consultant's name: _____

Consultee's name: _____

Client's name: _____

Reason for Consultation: _____
_____
_____

Identification of Issue/Problem: _____
_____
_____

Definition of Problem: _____
_____
_____

Goals and Interventions for Implementation: _____
_____
_____

Implementation Evaluation

Goals	Who Will Implement Goal?	When Will Intervention Begin?	When Will Intervention Be Assessed?	How Will Intervention Be Assessed? Specific Measures.	Outcomes Measured

Evaluation of Consultation Process: _____
_____
_____
_____
_____

©2016 by PRO-ED, Inc.

succeed, emails, letters, text messages, and more phone calls may be more effective in reaching them.

In initial meetings with parents, the professional school counselor should minimize the use of technical jargon and attempt to understand any social language or jargon used by parents (Knotek, 2003). Doing this will help to eliminate confusion and build the partnership between the consultant and consultees during the consultation process (Putnam, Handler, Rey, & McCarty, 2005). Although the majority of professional school counselors do not conduct family counseling within the schools, it is important to understand the functioning of families and family dynamics within the context of cultural influences (Holcomb-McCoy & Bryan, 2010). Understanding that affecting one family member's behavior will usually have an effect on another family member's behavior will enable the counselor to convey the importance of intervention and will allow the interventions to have a better chance of being supported by the family (Mullis & Edwards, 2001). Understanding the cultural influence on the family will help the consultant assess how to empower the family to enable a successful intervention for the student. Professional school counselors can gain the support of faculty and staff when they offer an explanation of the effects of family dynamics on student behavior.

Professional school counselors can serve as primary resources for parents who are trying to sort through various issues, such as divorce, grief, disability, and illness (Mullis & Otwell, 1998). Parents look to schools for information about these issues, and professional school counselors can provide information and resources. In addition, parents look to schools for both cognitive and emotional support. Consider the following case example:

> Ms. Taylor, the professional school counselor, had an appointment to meet with Jacob's mother. Jacob is a 10-year-old fifth-grade student who identifies as Hispanic American. Jacob's grades had dropped significantly over the last 9-week grading period, and he was reported by his teacher to be withdrawn in class. When Ms. Turner, Jacob's mother, arrived, she appeared upset about the appointment. After Ms. Taylor reviewed the purpose for the meeting, she asked Ms. Turner how things were at home. With some hesitation, Ms. Turner reported that Jacob's father had moved out of the house. She reported being so preoccupied with her own thoughts and feelings about this change that she assumed Jacob was doing well. After some discussion about economic issues in the home due to the father leaving and the meaning of "no man has head of the house," Ms. Taylor and Ms. Turner agreed that Jacob may be exhibiting some of these behaviors because of his parent's separation. Ms. Taylor provided some information about the effects of separation and divorce and agreed to see Jacob in counseling. She encouraged Ms. Turner to consult with her husband and possibly seek family counseling.

In this scenario, it took minimal discussion to discover the family dynamics that may have been affecting Jacob's behavior. For the mother, this could have been the first opportunity to discuss his separation with her husband and how it has affected her own life. The professional school counselor provided both cognitive and emotional support in this one brief session. However, follow-up consultation will allow the professional school counselor to determine if the simple interventions discussed in the first session have met the desired goal of improved grades and better class participation for Jacob.

Although professional school counselors can be resources for parents, many parents bring anxiety and anger to consultation. This anxiety and anger needs to be evaluated by the professional school counselor to determine the appropriate response to parents. In many cases, anxiety appears as anger or aggression. The majority of parents are worried about their children, and this worry can prevent them from hearing or understanding the purpose of the consultation. Anger can be a natural response for parents who see their children as an extension of themselves and are asking, "What are they saying is wrong with my child (me)?" The following case example illustrates this point:

> Tamara, a 10-year-old girl, was reported by her teacher for bullying a younger girl in the hall at school. After discussing this with her, the professional school counselor decided to contact her parents, as per the school policy on bullying. When Tamara's mother arrived, she immediately voiced her annoyance at the school for calling her in because she believes her child needs to take up for herself. Allowing the mother to vocalize her objections, the professional school counselor was able to assess that the mother may have issues of feeling like she needs to defend herself. Instead of revealing her insight, the professional school counselor reflected the mother's objections and spent some time establishing rapport with her. After discussion of the details of the bullying incidences, the mother admitted that she had misinterpreted Tamara's disclosure of these incidences. She reported that she had inadvertently supported Tamara's behavior at home. The professional school counselor and Tamara's mother discussed ways that the mother could discuss bullying behaviors with Tamara at home.

When parents appear to take the student's problem on as their own, they may need to vent their frustration and anger initially in the consultation session. Professional school counselors can help diffuse these feelings by engaging in active listening and not becoming defensive. Often, the professional school counselor can spend an initial consultation session normalizing behavior or helping parents perceive their children's behaviors, emotions, and attitudes as normal (Mullis & Edwards, 2001).

Parents may see their children in a negative way, so professional school counselors may have to reframe their statements to put a positive light on the problem or situation. Reframing can act as another resource for parents, because they may not have been able to see the positiveness of the situation prior to the consultation. It is the encouragement from these reframes that provides parents with the incentive to carry out interventions that will help their children at home and school.

Consulting With Teachers

Similar to consulting with parents, the professional school counselor's schedule offers several opportunities for teachers to consult with the counselor and vice versa. In fact, professional school counselors strongly rely on teachers for referrals of students in order to prevent issues from worsening (Gansle & Noell, 2008). Therefore, one of the first steps in consulting with teachers occurs prior to the actual consultation. The most important step is establishing strong rapport and mutual understanding between counselor and teacher.

In attempts to establish this relationship, professional school counselors need to make their services known to the faculty of the school. In a study of future school administrators, 100 participants ranked consulting with teachers as the fifth most important duty of professional school counselors (Fitch, Newby, Ballestero, & Marshall, 2001). Enlisting the support of the school administrator in publicizing the duties of the professional school counselor may help endorse these activities for the teachers. Additionally, the professional school counselor can introduce himself or herself at faculty meetings, create and distribute an electronic brochure about the role of the professional school counselor, and visit each teacher individually to discuss the professional school counselor's role and any concerns of the teacher (Davis & Garrett, 1998).

Professional school counselors are at an advantage because they are based in schools. The majority of consultations are usually about students' problem academic or social behaviors in the school, and their teachers usually have a wealth of knowledge about the students and these behaviors (Gansle & Noell, 2008). Although the professional school counselor may be initiating the consultation process, the teacher actually began it when initiating a referral about the student. It is useful to remember that teachers may feel similar to parents when consulting with the professional school counselor. The following case example illustrates this:

> Ms. Allen, the professional school counselor, stopped by Ms. Henry's class during her planning period at an appointed time to discuss Michael's behavior. As they discussed Ms. Henry's observations, Ms. Henry became upset and started to cry. Ms. Allen attempted to understand Ms. Henry's observations and began to reflect her feelings. She reflected that Ms. Henry seemed to be frustrated with Michael's behavior and was afraid that she could not help him learn anything. After Ms. Henry calmed down, Ms. Allen suggested that she, as the professional school counselor, observe Michael. After this observation, they would meet again to plan some interventions for him in Ms. Henry's classroom.

In this example, it became clear that Ms. Henry was placing a lot of responsibility for Michael's behavior on herself. This is not uncommon for teachers, especially in current educational systems where accountability is stressed. Many teachers feel that their self-worth is based on teaching students to learn. When those students are not learning, it can affect the self-worth of those teachers. Hence, we saw and heard Ms. Henry's self-worth being affected by her frustration with Michael's behavior.

However, research also indicated that teachers perceive family and student-centered issues to contribute more to the students' problems than the teachers' contributions (Athanasiou, Geil, Hazel, & Copeland, 2002). Considering this, it may be necessary to help teachers gain different perspectives on students' problems. Professional school counselors can offer to provide services to teachers in order to help them gain a different perspective on the situation, such as observation. Classroom observation is a way of gathering data and providing additional information to the parties involved in consultation. In general, teachers do not take issue with the professional school counselor making observations because it indicates the counselor's level of commitment to helping the child and the teacher.

In consulting with teachers, professional school counselors need to be mindful of the teacher's schedule when planning meetings and not assume that the teacher has access to resources and/or knowledge necessary to implementing interventions developed in consultation (Gansle & Noell, 2008). Additionally, professional school counselors should remember that consultation is a partnership that is based on trust and respect. Therefore, teachers should be made to feel trusted and respected as they are asked for their own expertise in creating, implementing, and evaluating interventions that will help students. Assessing what resources

Table 22.2 Consultation Suggestions

Determine the purpose of the consultation meeting and what needs to be discussed and done during the consultation.

Be mindful of parents' or teachers' schedules when planning the consultation meeting. Be flexible in scheduling conferences before or after school hours to meet these needs.

When notifying parents or teachers of a needed meeting, explain the purpose and reason for the meeting. This can decrease the anxiety of all individuals involved in the conference.

Hold conferences in a comfortable atmosphere, with adult-sized chairs and a table, if needed. In meeting with teachers, their classroom may be the most convenient and comfortable.

Greet parents and teachers in a friendly manner. For parents, professional school counselors should introduce themselves immediately and shake the hands of all the individuals attending the meeting. Thank parents and teachers for making the time to meet.

Re-explain the purpose and reason for the meeting. Go straight to the point, and do not use technical or educational jargon when explaining information. Be honest about the school's concerns.

Encourage parents and teachers to provide their perspective of the student's behavior. Use active listening skills, especially when emotions run high. Make sure to have tissues on hand.

Provide positive examples when describing the student's behavior. You want to provide another perspective to the student. However, you are emphasizing the behavior that needs to be addressed, which is often not positive.

Establish a supportive relationship with parents or teachers in conferences. Do not become defensive, and continue active listening in order to collect more information about the student.

Create and maintain equal working relationships by encouraging parents or teachers to co-create intervention ideas that can be used at home or school. Set up the plan for implementing and evaluating the interventions.

Provide resources for parents and teachers, such as handouts and books about the specific behavior being exhibited, including a bibliography of references.

Thank parents and teachers again at the end of the meeting for investing time into the student's needs.

Follow up with parents and teachers to review the child's progress, and make needed adjustments to the interventions being implemented.

Document all of your contacts with parents and teachers to review when following up or in future consultations about the student.

---

are available to them and what is needed will help the school counselor and teacher plan for the implementation of the intervention.

The Nuts and Bolts of Parent and Teacher Consultation

In helping students achieve success in and out of school, professional school counselors have the distinction of bridging the communication gap between family and school. Communication between the professional school counselor and faculty is also effective in planning appropriate services for the needs of students in the school. Table 22.2 provides a list of suggestions for professional school counselors to review as they plan consultations with parents and teachers. Since many consultations take place in a conference format, logistical recommendations are listed.

Summary/Conclusion

Consulting with parents and teachers is an important part of the role of the professional school counselor. As consultant, one can be the catalyst for change in the lives of the families and faculty of students. The change created through consultation can help students become more academically and interpersonally successful.

CHAPTER 23

Conflict Resolution, Bullying, and Cyberbullying

Nadine E. Garner and Jason B. Baker

Preview

In this chapter, we present an overview of conflict-resolution programs in the schools, research on their effectiveness, and both immediate and long-range strategies for designing a conflict-resolution program. Using a multiple intelligences approach, techniques that professional school counselors can readily integrate into their work with individuals, groups, and guidance experiences are provided. Further, we include cyberbullying and bullying, relevant implications from research, the professional school counselor's role, and prevention/intervention strategies.

There is a real need for comprehensive conflict-resolution programs in the schools. The summary of the position statement on safe schools through conflict resolution by the American School Counselor Association (ASCA) declared, "comprehensive school counseling programs include anti-bullying/harassment and violence-prevention programs along with comprehensive conflict-resolution programs to foster a positive school climate. A safe school environment is essential for effective learning" (ASCA, 2011a, para. 1). The ability to effectively and peacefully handle conflict is not necessarily intuitive; rather, it is a learned skill. Johnson and Johnson (1991) echoed these sentiments when, after more than 30 years of research, they stated that "most students simply do not know how to manage their conflicts constructively" (p. 3). They found that students struggled with issues of verbal harassment, verbal arguments, rumors, gossip, and dating or relationship issues.

Conflict-Resolution Programs

Conflict-resolution programs have various names, including Conflict Resolution Education (CRE), Peace Education, Peacemaking, Violence Prevention, or Violence Reduction. Conflict-resolution models have common goals because they seek to create opportunities for students and other members of the school community to (a) recognize that conflict is a natural part of life and that it can be resolved peacefully, (b) develop awareness of their own unique responses to conflict and to understand the diversity with which others respond, (c) learn and practice the principles of conflict resolution and the skills of peaceful problem-solving processes, (d) empower themselves to be individually and cooperatively responsible for resolving conflicts peacefully, and (e) integrate this responsibility in their daily lives.

An authentic conflict-resolution program contains two key elements: (a) the *principles* of conflict resolution (separate the people from the problem; focus on interests, not positions; invent options for mutual gain; use objective criteria as the basis of decision making) and (b) a *problem-solving process* (negotiation, mediation, or consensus decision making; Crawford & Bodine, 1997). These two components are common factors in the following four approaches to conflict resolution that are currently used in the schools:

1. *Process curriculum*—A specific time (e.g., separate course, distinct curriculum, daily lesson plan) is dedicated to teaching conflict resolution.
2. *Mediation program*—Adults or students who are trained in conflict-resolution principles and the problem-solving process of mediation act as neutral third-party facilitators to help disputants reach a resolution.
3. *Peaceable classroom*—Conflict resolution is integrated into the core curriculum and classroom management. Peaceable classrooms form the foundation for the peaceable school.
4. *Peaceable school*—All members of the school community (teachers, staff, students, administrators, parents) receive training in conflict resolution (Crawford & Bodine, 1997).

The Professional School Counselor's Role

School-based conflict-resolution programs have been implemented in the majority of schools, and professional school counselors often take a leading role in implementation. The specialized expertise of professional school counselors places them in a distinct position to facilitate change in the school culture (Hovland, Peterson, & Smaby, 1996).

ASCA (2011a) recommended the professional school counselor assume the leading role in the following components of school-wide comprehensive anti-bullying and conflict-resolution programs: data-driven decision making, coordination, instruction, and program evaluation. Furthermore, ASCA recommended that professional school counselors include the following elements in such programs:

- Prevention/intervention services
- Building positive staff and student relationships
- Education in recognition of early warning signs of violence
- Intervention strategies
- Crisis response and follow-up
- Community involvement
- Evaluation of program effectiveness

Indications From the Research

Research indicates it may take 1 to 2 years for teachers to feel comfortable integrating the concepts of conflict resolution into classroom activities (Johnson & Johnson, 1991), and it may take 3 to 5 years for it to take hold in the larger school environment. As such, it is not uncommon for programs to be disbanded or deemed failures before even given a chance.

Lindsay (1998) suggested that the elements of high-quality conflict-resolution programs include recognition that school programs alone are no panacea, given the influence of families and communities on students. Programs in the schools should be part of a larger strategy that includes addressing conflict resolution in families and in the community. Sandy (2001) reported that conflict-resolution programs can positively affect the school and classroom climate most strongly when there is an involvement of the total school community.

Immediate and Long-Range Strategies for Implementing a Conflict-Resolution Program

Due to the multidimensional nature of conflict-resolution programs, the prospect of implementing a comprehensive conflict-resolution program can appear to be an overwhelming task for professional school counselors. A more manageable approach to developing a comprehensive conflict-resolution program is to plan for its development by using both long-range and immediate strategies.

Long-Range Strategies

"It takes a village." Research indicates that the most successful conflict-resolution programs are in whole-school communities that actively participate in the process of training, practice, and evaluation and that link with mediation agencies to develop training programs for the entire school community.

Conflict-resolution committee. Instead of handling such a large task alone, professional school counselors may organize a conflict-resolution committee to plan and implement the long-range conflict-resolution program goals for the school. Membership on this committee builds a foundation of supporters and should include professional school counselors, teachers, students, administrators, parents, and community members. The conflict-resolution program should be seen as a shared opportunity. By involving members from all segments of the school community, the professional school counselor is not viewed as the sole proponent of the conflict-resolution program.

Exploration of available curricula. There are numerous programs available that are designed specifically for elementary, middle, or high school levels. Many programs offer comprehensive curricula complete with lesson plans, training materials, reproducible handouts, videos, instructor's guides, and evaluation tools. Some programs are tailored to specific areas of conflict resolution such as bullying and relational aggression.

Immediate Strategies

Small changes lead to larger changes. Using Milton Erickson's analogy of a hole in a dam, in which even a small hole may lead to changing the structure of the whole dam (Haley, 1973), look for opportunities to integrate concepts that focus on conflict resolution into your existing work with students. When consulting with teachers, ask them what small steps they would be willing to take now to infuse conflict-resolution concepts into their existing curriculum. In so doing, when it is time to implement a comprehensive curriculum, there will already be a core group of people who are taking proactive steps.

A multiple intelligences approach to conflict resolution. Garner (1996) introduced a training program for counselors to use with students titled *A Multiple Intelligences Approach to Conflict Resolution*. Using Howard Gardner's (2011) theory of multiple intelligences to draw out students' differing learning styles, the program encourages students to develop an increased awareness of how they use the various intelligences to think about and deal with conflict and conflict resolution. The program teaches students about the multiple intelligences, presents activities that need one or more of the intelligences to be activated in order to complete them, and asks students to reflect on which intelligences and activities are strengths for them. Armstrong (1993), one of the pioneering authors to apply the use of multiple intelligences to educational settings, supported the use of the intelligences as an effective way to teach the most students through a variety of learning pathways. The following section describes the intelligences used in each of the four activities presented in the chapter. (See Table 30.1 in Chapter 30 for a brief description of how each of the intelligences relates to different types of learners.) Although Gardner has recently proposed two additional intelligences (naturalist and existential), only the original seven intelligences are addressed in this chapter.

Application to real life. Students are better able to synthesize and retain concepts when they make personal or real-life connections to the material. The four activities presented in this chapter provide opportunities for students to make these important connections.

Sample Techniques for Immediate Integration

The following four activities are techniques that professional school counselors can readily integrate into their work with individuals, groups, and guidance experiences and can be adapted to suit elementary, middle, and high school settings.

Activity 23.1: Applying Glasser's Psychological Needs

Intelligences Addressed: Logical–Mathematical, Verbal–Linguistic, Intrapersonal, Interpersonal

Teach students about Glasser's (2011) explanation of psychological needs and their relationship to conflict. Copy and use "The Four Psychological Needs," located in Figure 23.1, as an overhead or handout. According to Glasser, we are driven by the needs for *belonging/love* (belonging, sharing, and cooperating with others); *power* (achieving, accomplishing, being recognized and respected); *freedom* (making choices in our lives); and *fun* (laughing and playing). In order to be psychologically healthy, we need to find responsible ways to have these needs met. Conflicts arise, among other reasons, when one does not fulfill one or more of these needs. Figure 23.2, titled "Applying the Four Psychological Needs: Belonging, Power, Freedom, Fun," provides students the opportunity to respond to scenarios as part of a classroom guidance lesson, based on real-life experiences of students. Students can discuss why they chose their answers and how they can relate the concepts of psychological needs and conflict to their own lives. It also asks them to identify which of the multiple intelligences are used to complete the activities.

According to William Glasser, these four psychological needs must be fulfilled in order to be psychologically healthy:

1. Belonging/Love
   - Belonging
   - Sharing
   - Cooperating with others

2. Power
   - Achieving
   - Accomplishing
   - Being recognized and respected
   - Being responsible for something/someone
   - Being dependable

3. Freedom
   - Making choices in our lives

4. Fun
   - Laughing
   - Playing
   - Finding Humor

In order to be psychologically healthy, we need to find responsible ways to have these needs met. Conflicts may arise when we do not fulfill one or more of these needs.

Figure 23.1. The four psychological needs.

Read each scene. Then write down the psychological need that fits. You may find that there is more than one correct answer.

1. Julio does not feel wanted at home. His parents are divorced and have new families now. He does not feel part of either family. He joins a gang where he feels needed and wanted. What psychological need is he filling? _____

2. Kim likes to be in charge of things. She likes responsibility and needs to have a say in what goes on at school. She runs for class president. What psychological need is she filling? _____

3. Takeda has to baby-sit for her three younger siblings while her mom works. She likes being part of a family and enjoys taking care of the kids, but she gets upset when she can't go to the mall with her friends because of her responsibilities to her family. What psychological need is she not having fulfilled? _____ What psychological need is she filling? _____

Briefly describe a conflict that you are experiencing (or have experienced) in your own life:

What psychological need(s) might not be filled in this situation?

Describe a positive situation or relationship that you currently have (or have had):

What psychological need(s) was filled in this situation?

Which of the multiple intelligences did you use in order to complete the activities on this page?

Which of these intelligences do you feel are strengths for you?

Figure 23.2. Applying the four psychological needs: belonging, power, freedom, fun.

Activity 23.2: Needs Circle

Intelligences Addressed: Visual–Spatial, Intrapersonal, Interpersonal, Verbal–Linguistic

Figure 23.3, titled "My Needs Circle," can be reproduced as an overhead or handout for immediate use. Begin the activity by having students draw a vertical and horizontal line inside the circle to divide it into four quadrants. Label each quadrant on the outside of the circle with one of Glasser's psychological needs. In each quadrant, students list how they get this particular need filled in their lives and answer the reflective questions below the circle. Students then share with a partner or small group the elements of their needs circle. This activity can be used in individual, group, or classroom guidance experiences to help students identify how they are fulfilling their psychological needs. The needs circle is a helpful illustration for a professional school counselor to see what areas of a student's life are strengths for the student and which areas are a cause for concern and may be potential areas of conflict. This is an especially useful activity for a student who has moved or experienced a recent life change. The student can complete two circles: one before the change and one that represents the present time. This activity may also act as a springboard for discussion with a student who is reticent to disclose personal information verbally or who is better able to organize information and communicate with visual–spatial aids. (I would like to acknowledge Ella Kwisnek, a graduate counselor-in-training at Duquesne University in the late 1990s, for presenting the basic diagram of the Needs Circle).

Activity 23.3: Draw a Picture of Conflict

Intelligences Addressed: Visual–Spatial, Intrapersonal, Interpersonal

Students draw a picture of what conflict looks like to them. They share the pictures and try to understand others' meaning of conflict. Ask students to discuss which of the multiple intelligences they activated in order to accomplish the activity. Younger students are often better able to synthesize their understanding of conflict by creating pictures first and then explaining them.

Activity 23.4: Folding Paper Cranes for Peace

Intelligences Addressed: Bodily–Kinesthetic, Verbal–Linguistic, Logical–Mathematical, Visual–Spatial, Interpersonal, Intrapersonal

For more information on this origami activity, visit www.sadako.com. This activity borrows from the true story of Sadako Sasaki, a girl who developed leukemia in 1955 from the effects of radiation caused by the bombing of Hiroshima. There is an ancient Japanese legend that says that by folding 1,000 paper cranes, your wish will come true. Sadako began folding a thousand cranes while hospitalized, wishing for world peace and personal health, but she died before the project was completed. To this day, people all over the world are still folding cranes and sending them to Hiroshima's Peace Park.

My Needs Circle

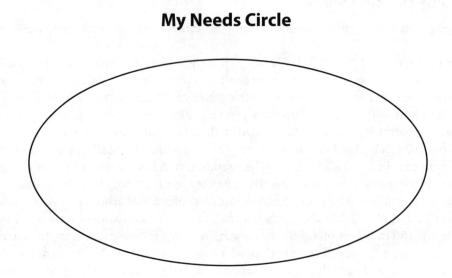

What are some positive ways that you meet your four psychological needs?

What are some possible areas of conflict in your Needs Circle? What changes would you like to make in the way that you meet your needs?

What interesting patterns do you notice about your Needs Circle? (Which areas of the circle are more full/less full? Did you list some things in more than one part of the circle?)

Which of the multiple intelligences did you need to use to complete the Needs Circle activity?

Figure 23.3. My needs circle.

©2016 by PRO-ED, Inc. #14017

Schools often use this activity to unite the school community with a common theme around peace (Levenson, 2006). One memorable example is from Millersville University, in which the Department of Housing and Residential Programs coordinated a project to enlist the campus in making 3,022 paper cranes, each representing a life lost in the World Trade Center tragedy of September 11, 2001. The cranes were fashioned into large mobiles and displayed in the Multipurpose Room on September 11, 2002, during a Remembrance Ceremony. Since then, the mobiles have been permanently installed on campus. This activity is easily integrated into the curriculum as students learn about history and multicultural issues and need to use math and cooperation skills.

Bullying: The Professional School Counselor's Role and Research Implications

As professionals trained in both mental health and education, school counselors play a unique role in creating safe, supportive, and non-threatening learning environments that promote the broader mission of the school (ASCA, 2012a). Further, the work of the school counselor, vertically articulated across the developmental spectrum, allows for a unique angle of intervention in addressing developmental concerns, transitions, and context-based issues. Research has consistently indicated that students' perceptions of the school environment and climate play an important role in the development and maintenance of bullying behaviors; specifically, bullying is more of a problem in those schools where students do not feel supported, accepted, respected, and treated fairly (Bradshaw, Sawyer, & O'Brennan, 2009). Thus, one goal of the school counselor in addressing bullying is to strengthen the pillars of climate support through the application and maintenance of a comprehensive school counseling program, which includes a school-wide anti-bullying program that is regularly evaluated.

A second goal of the school counselor in addressing the problem of bullying is identifying and intervening with target groups. Research has indicated that individuals who suffer from a rejected social status are more likely to be victims of bullying, and non-behavioral characteristics which increase the risk of being bullied include: obesity, off-time pubertal maturation, physical disability, and LGBT status (Juvonen & Graham, 2014). Further, students who display certain emotional or behavioral problems (e.g., depression, lack of friends, marginal social status) are more likely to be victims of bullying, particularly when perceived to be of lower social status by peers (Hodges & Perry, 1999). Finally, while having a supportive friend may not disrupt the bullying, the emotional support provided by a single close friend seems to play an especially important role in mediating the long-term emotional sting and related deleterious potential outcomes (Yeung Thompson, & Leadbeater, 2013). These implications from the research lead to an opportunity for school counselors to identify, organize, and intervene with target groups through various modes of the delivery system (e.g., small groups, individual counseling, classroom guidance lessons).

While these two specific goals for the school counselor (addressing the school climate and intervening with target groups) emerge in the literature, it is also important to consider the role of evidence-based practices and site-specific evaluation strategies as the extant literature is, at times, equivocal. For example, while school-wide anti-bullying programs have become popular as the result of Olweus's (1993) foundational work, more recent attempts to synthesize the literature base on the effectiveness of school-wide programs discovered that 7 of 10 published studies reported decreased bullying (Vreeman & Carroll, 2007). The same study showed even less consistent support for curricular interventions, where 4 of the 10 included studies resulted in decreased bullying. These findings, while only the result of one meta-analytic review, mirror other reviews (e.g., Smith, Schneider, Smith, & Ananiadou, 2004; Merrell, Gueldner, Ross, & Isava, 2008) and provide context for the discerning school counselor to consider when selecting evidence-based practices that can be evaluated locally.

Prevention/Intervention Strategies

There are a number of ways that school counselors can work to prevent bullying and intervene when cases of bullying arise:

1. School counselors can develop, implement, and evaluate school-wide anti-bullying programs and work to create evaluation strategies that reflect the local goals, objectives, and contexts. A number of well-researched and emerging programs exist in the literature (e.g., OBPP [Olweus, 1993]; KiVa [Karna et al., 2011]; Steps to Respect [Frey, Hirschstein, Edstrom, & Snell, 2009]).
2. School counselors can become more strategic in choosing, implementing, and evaluating programs. Research suggests that many school counselors are not actively involved in choosing anti-bullying programs, and even fewer seem intentional about supporting evidence-based programs (Lund, Blake, Ewing, & Banks, 2012).
3. School counselors can be deliberate about goals, objectives, and evaluation strategies, as some programs that have "face validity" are contraindicated in the literature (e.g., group therapy for bullies).
4. School counselors can work to create safe and supportive learning environments for all students by conducting ecological surveys of learning spaces and using the results to create targeted inventions/goals.
5. School counselors can work to identify students who may have developed a hostile attributional bias and use various modalities of the delivery system (e.g., classroom lessons, small group sessions, individual counseling) to attend to those "at-risk" for becoming bullies.
6. School counselors can work to ease transitions, as bullying often peaks at times when social hierarchies are being constructed and defined (Juvonen & Graham, 2014).
7. School counselors can work to be sensitive to "in-groups" and "out-groups," particularly those identified in the literature as being especially susceptible to bullying.

Cyberbullying and the Professional School Counselor

With the introduction and maturation of the Internet, mobile devices, and other electronic means of communicating and sharing information, communication patterns have changed in ways that require the sensitive attention of the professional school counselor. Recent surveys have noted about 6% of children ages 12–18 years reported being cyberbullied during the 2008–2009 school year (National Center for Education Statistics [NCES], 2011b). While this percentage is significantly less than the 28% of the children ages 12–18 years who reported being bullied in general, students who reported being cyberbullied also populated the categories of "engaging in a fight on school grounds" and "skipping school" at higher percentages than students not identified as being cyberbullied (NCES, 2011). The emotional response undergirding these objective observations include anger, sadness, worrying, loneliness, and frustration (Slonje, Smith, & Frisen, 2013).

These systemic changes in communication patterns and resultant student effects often place the school district, in general, and the school counselor, in particular, in a challenging position as various stakeholder groups redefine lines of influence in this virtual space. These technological advancements have come amidst controversy, concern for ethical practice, and an underscoring of best practices.

As noted in the bullying section, school counselors play a unique role in creating safe, supportive, non-threatening learning environments that promote the broader mission of the school (ASCA, 2012a). In blurring the lines of defined "learning spaces" and funneling streams of targeted information that often originate outside of the school setting, modern communication modalities have extended and, in some cases, strained the reach of school counselors focused on meeting this important mission. The chief controversy and related concern for ethical practice in this extended reach relates to the role of the school district in addressing disruptive or offensive patterns of electronic communication that originate and are maintained outside of the school environment. On this point, recent court decisions have provided unclear messages about the degree to which actions in these individual cases reach the point of "substantial disruption" to the mission of the school (Stone, 2010). Thus, school officials are left balancing the free speech rights of individuals with the broader mission of providing safe learning environments for students and faculty.

Indications From Research

Cyberbullying as a phenomenon has recently gained much attention in the research literature and mainstream media. While specificity and consistency in constructs and definitions still remain elusive in the research literature (Kowalski, Giumetti, Schroeder, & Lattanner, 2014), some commonalities in activities and actions fitting under the broad term of "cyberbullying" are available. For example, Willard (2007) created a taxonomy that includes flaming, harassment, outing and trickery, exclusion, impersonation, cyber-stalking, and sexting.

Cyberbullying shares many similarities to traditional forms of bullying. In particular each involves three specific elements: (1) an act of aggression, (2) a power differential, and (3) a repeated or systemic attack (Olweus, 1993). However, the nature of the environment, medium, and process create qualitative differences between cyberbullying and physical bullying. Smith (2012) identified seven specific qualitative differences, including that cyberbullying: (1) is relatively dependent on the technological expertise of the perpetrator; (2) is primarily indirect, thus anonymity is possible; (3) distances the perpetrator from the victim in that short-term reactions/emotional expressions are often not seen; (4) complicates the role of the bystander as the nature/medium of the message (e.g., private messaging, public internet sites, targeted online groups, etc.) allows for selected/differential exposure; (5) lacks the physical display of abusive power over others in front of witnesses; (6) allows for an increased breadth of potential audience members; and (7) increases the difficulty in escaping messages or finding "safe haven."

Prevention/Intervention Strategies

There are a number of ways that professional school counselors can work to prevent cyberbullying and intervene when cases of cyberbullying arise.

1. School counselors can work to insure that current school-wide anti-bullying programs also work to incorporate language and situational demonstrations of cyberbullying. This would work to address the obscurity of the event and provide opportunities for situation-specific discussions of recent and pertinent instances.
2. School counselors can work to use and promote computer-based classroom activities and support for victims from high status peers. Examples of programs effectively using these interventions exist in the literature (e.g., Salmivalli & Poyhonen, 2012).
3. School counselors can work to provide curricular materials and program interventions which specifically address the link between emotional experiences and computer-mediated communication.
4. School counselors can work to provide curricular materials and program interventions which support and promote personal ownership of and empowerment in communication. School counselors can provide creative interventions to specifically address the veil of anonymity in computer-mediated communication.
5. School counselors can work to provide and promote peer mentoring programs both in traditional settings and cyber-settings. An example of a program in this area is Cyber-Mentors (Banerjee, Robinson, & Smalley, 2010). This would work to address issues related to escape and "safe haven."
6. School counselors can continue to work to promote healthy values (e.g., compassion, empathy, sensitivity) and pro-social behaviors through curricular materials and program interventions. This specifically addresses the susceptibility of and support for individual students.
7. School counselors can continue to work to disseminate cyberbullying information to various stakeholder groups. This addresses the elusive nature of the process and helps parents, teachers, and students recognize the importance of awareness and sensitivity.

Summary/Conclusion

Conflict-resolution programs encourage the development of useful skills for resolving conflict peacefully that can be applied across the life span. When implemented comprehensively, such programs promote a positive school climate. There are a variety of approaches from which to choose. The most effective program is a comprehensive one that strives to train and support all members of the school community. A conflict-resolution program is not an instant solution—it is a long-term commitment requiring patience, training, support at all levels of the school community, and ongoing evaluation to tailor the program to the needs of the school.

Bullying is in no way a new phenomenon, though recent legislative attention (anti-bullying laws have been enacted in 49 of 50 states), mainstream media attention, and research attention has brought the issue into sharper focus on the broad horizon of school-wide and developmental concerns. School counselors are in a unique position to address these concerns and will seemingly find continued support from various stakeholder groups as anti-bullying programs are developed, implemented, and evaluated. By strategically sharing evaluation data in ways that demonstrate the influence, responsiveness, and effectiveness of anti-bullying programs, school counselors might better position themselves to meet the needs of a new generation of concerned students, parents, and legislators.

While the phenomenon of cyberbullying, in many ways, represents "old wine in a new bottle" (Li, 2007), research has continued to parse the unique elements of this dynamic, computer-mediated experience. As research allows school counselors to see the experiences of various stakeholder groups (e.g., students, victims, bystanders, bullies, parents) with greater clarity, interventions can grow more focused, more responsive, and more adaptable to the unique needs of student populations. In addition, as technology continues to advance, school counselors will continue to be aware of emerging methods and mediums for perpetuating this antisocial and aggressive behavior. Further, new technologies might well help school counselors create novel interventions, explore new avenues, and reinvest in the two human sides of the computer-mediated interactions.

SECTION 4

Techniques and Approaches to Counseling in Schools

CHAPTER 24

Professional School Counselors and Reality Therapy

Robert E. Wubbolding

Preview

The WDEP (Wants, Direction or Doing, Evaluation, Plans) system of reality therapy provides a practical, useable system for professional school counselors in their many roles. When implementing this system, counselors help students, clients, staff, and parents to conduct inner self-evaluations of their behaviors. Reality therapy also focuses on the overall atmosphere of the classroom and school building through the use of class meetings that have a clearly defined and readily adaptable format.

Most, but not all, human problems are rooted in dysfunctional, disturbed, or out-of-balance relationships. Effective participant interdependence, on the other hand, facilitates and supports the success of most human endeavors. William Glasser (2005) described healthy human relationships as the cornerstone of mental health: "You are mentally healthy if you enjoy being with most of the people you know, especially with the important people in your life" (p. 2). The school setting is one of the most important venues in which human relationships provide a foundational and crucial position. When a school faculty "get along well" with each other, the school is a joyful place, and students learn at a higher level (McClung & Hoglund, 2013). If students believe their teachers care about them, respect their opinions, listen to them, and try to make learning fun, they are more inclined to want to learn and, in turn, get along with each other. Therefore, school achievement and healthy relationships are interconnected (Glasser, 2011). Wubbolding (2005) added, "a job successfully performed results in the satisfaction of power (achievement) and sometimes belonging" (p. 43).

The results of using reality therapy, called *lead management* in schools, are not perfect, but a total immersion can result in major improvements for individual students and for the entire organization. Chaddock School, a residential school for court-referred students in Quincy, Illinois, reduced behavioral incidents to an insignificant level in just over three years (Wubbolding, 2000). Hinton, Warnke, and Wubbolding (2011) found major differences in outcome when they compared students who learned the basics of choice theory and reality therapy with a group lacking exposure to this theory and method. The principal of the freshman academy noted, "This approach made a difference in achievement and discipline" (p. 94).

Clearly, the professional school counselor's mission in the context of reality therapy is the enhancement of relationships. This does not imply a blind, cultic uniformity of viewpoints, but rather a healthy give and take, based on respect for diverse ways of doing things. A key question professional school counselors ask of students and staff is, "Are our current actions bringing us closer together, or are they distancing us from each other?" One of the appealing aspects of reality therapy is its practicality and usefulness with individuals and groups of students, faculty, and parents as well as its organizational applications.

The acronym WDEP summarizes the professional school counselor's use of reality therapy and helps the user remember the concepts. It serves as a pedagogical tool, providing all staff members with a common language as well as a structure for intervening in their classrooms and in all their human interactions. The professional school counselor wears many hats and has a variety of overlapping roles: counselor, consultant, parent educator, in-service trainer, personal-growth facilitator, advocate, community leader. The WDEP system of reality therapy applies to each of these roles in that it is based on universal principles that are applicable to virtually every human interaction (Wubbolding, 2011, 2015).

The WDEP System

Grounded in choice theory, the WDEP system assists human beings to satisfy five generic human motivators or needs: (a) survival or self-preservation, (b) love or belonging, (c) power or achievement, (d) freedom or independence, and (e) fun or enjoyment. When people interact with their environment, they build an internal collection of specific wants or pictures that are related to the motivators or needs (Glasser, 2011). Addressing the WDEP system (W–*wants*), a professional school counselor usually begins by helping students define and clarify their wants, goals, hopes, and dreams related to belonging, power, freedom, and fun. For example, students define what they want from school, parents, teachers, and friends. In consulting with teachers, professional school counselors assist them to define what they want from students and parents as well as to disclose their own expectations (wants) to their students in direct, firm, but non-punitive ways. When children are obstinate, uncooperative, and resistant, teachers and parents are astounded to see such behaviors diminish or vanish when they ask, "What do you want right now?" or "How hard do you want to work at changing your situation?" Of course, interventions based on this question do not produce a magical, immediate, or total reversal of behavior. Rather, such interventions need to be habitual.

Professional school counselors encourage teachers to teach the five motivators and ask students what they want from themselves, by defining their levels of commitment regarding how hard they want to work at satisfying their needs and get what they want. If professional school counselors and teachers visibly display the levels of commitment for all to see, they can reinforce their teaching at strategic moments (Wubbolding, 2000, 2011). For an exercise in applying the needs to yourself and to several cases, see Table 24.1 and Activities 24.1 and 24.2.

Activity 24.1: **Apply the Four Psychological Needs**

Read each scene. Then write down the psychological need that fits. You may find that there is more than one correct answer.

1. Julio does not feel wanted at home. His parents are divorced and have new families now. He does not feel part of either family. He joins a gang where he feels needed and wanted. What psychological need is he filling?

Table 24.1. The Four Psychological Needs

According to choice theory as described by William Glasser, in addition to survival or self-preservation needs, we need to have these four other psychological needs fulfilled in order to be psychologically healthy:

1.	Belonging/Love	Connectedness with other people; Interacting with others; Cooperating with others
2.	Power	Having a sense of inner control; Achieving; Accomplishing; Being recognized and respected; Being responsible for something/someone
3.	Freedom	Making choices in our lives; Being independent
4.	Fun	Having a sense of enjoyment; Gaining satisfaction from learning

In order to be psychologically healthy, we need to find responsible ways to have these needs met. Conflicts may arise when we do not fulfill one or more of these needs.

2. Kim likes to be in charge of things. She likes responsibility and needs to have a say in what goes on at school. She runs for class president. What psychological need is she filling?
3. Takeda has to baby-sit for her three younger siblings while her mom works. She likes being part of a family and enjoys taking care of the kids, but she gets upset when she can't go to the mall with her friends, because of her responsibilities to her family. What psychological need is she *not* having fulfilled? What psychological need *is* she filling?

Briefly describe a conflict that you are experiencing (or have experienced) in your own life: What psychological need(s) might *not* be filled in this situation?
Describe a positive situation or relationship that you currently have (or have had): What psychological need(s) were filled in this situation?

Activity 24.2: My Needs

What are some positive ways that you meet your four psychological needs?
What are some possible areas of conflict in your needs?
What changes would you like to make in the way that you meet your needs?
What interesting patterns do you notice about your needs?
Which areas are more fulfilled or less fulfilled?

Commitment Level I: "I Don't Want To Do Anything."

This is, in fact, no commitment at all, but resistant students, parents, and even teachers often manifest little or no commitment to improve. Professional school counselors using the WDEP system see these behaviors not as mere obstacles but as opportunities to raise their skills to a higher level. Oftentimes, the most negative adults become enthusiastic supporters and users of reality therapy in education.

Commitment Level II: "I'll Try." "I Might." "I Could."

This middle level of commitment is more likely to succeed but still retains an escape hatch to failure. "Trying" to study, be patient, or develop better interpersonal relationships is not identical with successful follow through. Professional school counselors need to encourage everyone to raise his or her level of commitment. "I know you'll try, but will you do it?" School personnel realize that athletic team members describing their commitment as "We will try to win" appears less confident than the team who yells "We're number one" or "We *will* win."

Commitment Level III: "I Will."

Here, the person expresses a genuine desire to move forward, solve a problem, and take effective action. A school faculty might agree to implement the quality school philosophy (Glasser, 1998) and to use the WDEP system to focus on classroom management, absenteeism, raising test scores, or a variety of other objectives. The levels of commitment provide a language for counselors' own use as well as a system for assisting teachers to elicit a higher level of student motivation. As Wubbolding and Brickell (2005) stated, "The levels of commitment . . . operationalize the proven fact that strong and explicit statements bring about change in behavior" (p. 41). Consequently, the WDEP system is more than a vague "What do you want?" approach. It can get as intricate and extensive as is necessary for initiating and accomplishing the many tasks involved in school improvement. "What are you doing?" (D) represents a simplified question related to the exploration of four aspects of behavior:

Physiology—"Does anything hurt?"

Feelings—"How do you feel?"

Thinking—"What are you telling yourself about your current situation?"

Actions (the most changeable part of this suitcase of behavior)—"Tell me what's going on now." "What did she say?" "What happened?"

Emphasizing actions in counseling and consultation draws attention to the most easily changed component of the behavioral system. When a person chooses to change his or her actions, the other components are brought along. When a person acts enthusiastic, tagging along behind is a change in feelings. Genuine feelings of enthusiasm are likely to be a consequence of the initial change in actions. Teachers, parents, and others learn that effective change in students' attitudes follow upon a change in students' actions.

Professional school counselors who work with children or adults do not ignore feelings; rather, they listen empathically to the emotional level. They acknowledge feelings, help clients accept their feelings, and discuss them as openly as is reasonable. Yet, as quickly as possible, they encourage clients to discuss the components of human behavior over which they have most control, actions, and secondarily, thinking. They emphasize that behavior is a choice, especially *actions*, the most clearly chosen aspect of behavior. Though no one explicitly chooses anger, shame, rage, guilt, loneliness, or depression, many individuals choose an action that brings pain along with it, as a car brings along a trunk filled with baggage. Thus, a student cursing a teacher in anger and rage chooses the action. An inseparable part of the total behavior is the feeling of rage and accompanying self-talk or inner discourse.

Reality therapy lends itself to a discussion of students' thinking as well as to actions and feelings. Wubbolding (2000, 2011) identified several negative or less effective self-talk statements concomitant with less effective actions:

A. "I am powerless and have no choices" accompanies depression.
B. "No one can tell me what to do" accompanies antisocial actions.
C. "Even though what I'm currently doing is not effective, still I will choose it again and again" accompanies repeated self-destructive actions.

Professional school counselors using the WDEP system of reality therapy teach this recent addition to students, faculty, parents, and the public. The final and most important self-talk statement is operationalized in many ways: "If I'm frustrating myself by doing something which is ineffective or harmful in order to improve, I will do more of what has not helped me."

Professional school counselors teach more effective cognitive statements to their various groups of consumers. These include:

A. "I have choices and I choose my behaviors."
B. "I am happy when I live within reasonable boundaries."
C. "If my current behavior is not working for me, I'll choose a different action."

Implementing the "D" (*doing*) of the WDEP system means that each component of the behavior is discussed with emphasis on the action element. It is as though the action is the handle of the suitcase of human behavior. When someone chooses to grab the handle and lift, the entire suitcase (thinking, feeling, and physiology) follows.

Self-Evaluation (E) is the cornerstone of the WDEP delivery system and constitutes the major prerequisite for change. No one changes a behavior or makes a better choice until he or she judges that the current course of action is not helpful. In describing the process of how to take charge of our lives Glasser (2011) says, "Ask yourself this question: Is what I am choosing to do now helping me . . . or is my behavior hurting my chances of getting what I so desperately need and want" (p. 221). Students not studying, wasting time by hanging out, or yielding to harmful impulses do not change a direction until they formulate a want, look searchingly at their choices, and make a firm judgment about the usefulness of their behavior. Working in groups or individually, professional school counselors help students, faculty, or parents describe what they want and connect their actions to their wants by assisting them to courageously evaluate whether their actions are helping or hurting.

Wubbolding (2015) has enumerated 22 kinds of self-evaluation. The following are among the most important questions, statements, and interventions:

- Tell me how your current behavior is bringing you closer or further away from the people around you.
- Is what you are doing getting you what you want?
- Describe how what you are doing is helping or hurting the people around you.
- Is what you are doing against the law, the rules—written or unwritten?
- Is what you want realistic or attainable?
- Describe how what you want really and truly is good for you in the long run, not merely in the short run.

- Is your current level of commitment high enough to get you what you want and to help others get what they want?
- Help me understand how your plan for improvement will be effective for you.

In any role, the professional school counselor facilitates a discussion of current wants and behaviors, an inner self-evaluation of them, and a plan of action (P). Effective plans need not be grandiose. In formulating treatment plans, Fulkerson (2013) described action plans as a way to achieve treatment objectives. Useful plans are SAMIC plans:

Simple—not complicated

Attainable—realistically doable

Measurable—answers the question, "When will you do it?"

Immediate—performed sooner rather than later

Controlled by the planner—not dependent on someone else's plans

While asking the question "What's your plan?" seems clear and direct, there is an underlying metacommunication present. The person asked this simple question and other questions in the WDEP system gains a sense of hope and a belief in personal responsibility through an implicit awakening: "Change is possible and I can make it happen. I cannot blame others for my plight."

Case Example 1: Jamal

Jamal, age 11, says he "hates school." It is evident to all that he has no friends in school, is a discipline problem for teachers, and has poor grades. The professional school counselor helps Jamal define his wants regarding (a) having more friends and getting along with his teachers (belonging), (b) getting better grades and learning school subject matter (power), and (c) making school more enjoyable (fun). Jamal describes his current behavioral choices as the counselor helps him evaluate them with such questions as, "If you tell off the teacher, will you get what you want from her?" and "If you fight with the other students, will you gain any friends?" If Jamal is amenable to the idea, the professional school counselor helps him make a realistic, doable plan perhaps to act appropriately for 1 hour a day or to attempt to befriend one student. The counselor might tell him, "A journey of a thousand miles is begun with a single step." Consequently, this realistic plan is a beginning. If his teachers are learning the WDEP system, they too realize that Jamal will not make an immediate turn-around. The philosophy underlying this effort is based on the principle that when Jamal fulfills his needs within the school setting, his failure choices will diminish, and he will be on the road of continuous improvement.

Case Example 2: Teacher Group

Seven English teachers in a large high school seek better behavior management skills for their classes. The professional school counselor leads a discussion about the ABC toxic behaviors—behaviors that damage relationships and chill warm friendships. These include (a) arguing, attacking, accusing; (b) bossing, blaming, belittling; and (c) criticizing, coercing, condemning.

Using the WDEP system, the professional school counselor helps the teachers define what they want from the students, what they can settle for, and what they're doing to get what they want. In a nonjudgmental atmosphere, they evaluate whether and to what degree they are succeeding in achieving their goals. The professional school counselor facilitates making plans and provides many resources, such as the *Phi Delta Kappan* article "Choices for Children: Why and How to Let Students Decide," by Alfie Kohn (1993). This article provides a review of studies showing that when students are accorded choices in classrooms, their overall performance improves.

Case Example 3: Middle School Teachers

Eight middle school teachers seeking ways to prevent problems and increase students' curiosity for learning meet with the professional school counselor to brainstorm solutions and explore the possibility of coordinated action. They have heard about class meetings as a central component of Glasser's quality school (Glasser, 2001). They ask the professional school counselor to discuss the mechanics and the benefits of implementing this strategy. The professional school counselor, serving as in-service trainer, teaches about class meetings from the outline provided in the following section.

Class Meetings

Class meetings provide a structure for discussion of timely and relevant topics and are designed to help students satisfy one or more of the five human needs or motivators. Carleen Glasser (2004) developed resource materials on class meetings for teachers that professional school counselors can also use as they consult with teachers. The teacher helps students gain a sense of belonging, a feeling of inner control (as one student stated, "The teacher respects my opinion"), fun (the reward of learning), and freedom or independence. In general, as Erwin (2006) stated, "holding regular class meetings can develop and maintain a strong sense of community" (p. 13). It should be noted that while the class meeting leader is most often a teacher, a professional school counselor might also volunteer to conduct class meetings. Thus, the following discussion provides the professional school counselor with knowledge that will help him or her in either a direct intervention role or in the role of consultant.

Topics

Students begin use of class meetings by discussing more intellectual topics, especially if this structure is new to them. Only when they become comfortable with this format should the teacher use the meetings for more emotional topics or problem solving. Consequently, meetings are *not* therapy sessions in which there is confrontation, personal self-disclosure, catharsis, or direct disputation of others' judgments. Selected topics may include value of homework, need for rules, friendship, respect for property (especially computers), quality of work, and effort. Topics related to curriculum may be why one should study math, definitions of old age, the value of knowing history, and various topics related to science.

Process

The teacher plays an unambiguous role as a leader, asking students to express their opinions or to simply "pass" if they do not want to speak aloud. Teachers need to realize that during the class meeting the emphasis is on opinions; therefore, there is no need to correct factual inaccuracies. More direct pedagogy is reserved for the major part of the students' school time outside class meetings. The 3-step process, Define, Personalize, and Challenge, provides a clear, nonthreatening format.

Define. Many teachers find a discussion of *effort* useful. This topic could be repeated occasionally when appropriate (e.g., at the start of the school year, after holidays, during the midwinter letdown). Questions focus on "What is effort?" "How do you know you are making a good effort to do quality work?" "What is quality?" In a science class, a teacher might ask students to define *fire*. In one school, there had been a fire across from the school, making the meeting even more relevant. "What are helpful fires (e.g., the sun) and harmful fires (e.g., a house fire)?"

Teacher creativity and ingenuity usually produce many extensions of this component. In another meeting, students defined what old age means to them. Some responded that anyone who is 18 years of age or older is old. Others had grandparents or even great grandparents and saw old age as 70, 80, or older.

Personalize. An effective meeting on *effort* involves questions such as, "What motivates you to put forth extra or high-quality effort?" "If someone were to see you exerting low-, middle-, or high-quality effort, what would they see?" A skilled teacher or professional school counselor demonstrating a class meeting asks such questions as, "Have you ever seen a fire?" "What treasures would you take with you if you had to escape from a fire?" "Do you know what to do if we had to leave this building because of fire?" Questions centering on the meeting about old age could include, "Do you know anyone who is old?" "What do people who are old do for fun?" "How are they the same or different from anyone else?"

Challenge. In this step, teachers push students to reflect on their knowledge, to reevaluate it, and to further develop it. Three types of questions constitute the *challenge* phase of the meeting. Keep in mind the focus is on opinions and questions to which there need not be correct answers.

- *Why?* Students are challenged to examine the basis of their beliefs. Some "Why?" questions are unanswerable, are beyond the current intellectual level of students, or require additional thought. "Why do people exert high or low levels of effort?" "Why does fire exist?" "What would we do without fire?" "Why do people grow old?" "If you could drink a potion and live to be 200 years old, would you drink it? Why or why not?" "Would you drink if there were only enough for the members of this class? Why or why not?"
- *What if?* Another challenge question revolves around imaginative thinking: "What if people always make the lowest or highest effort possible?" "How would your life be different if everyone made a high-level effort to be your friend, to play the athletic game to the best of their ability, to provide the best service possible?" "What if you could start or stop a fire just by thinking about it?" "What would life be like if the sun became much hotter or cooler?" "What if there were two suns instead of one sun?" "What if no one would grow old?" "What if all diseases were curable?"
- *What's the difference?* In "What's the difference between . . . ?" questions, students learn to make distinctions in their thinking as a result of class meetings. "What's the difference

between low-level effort and high-level effort?" "What's the difference between high-quality and low-quality relationships, toys, bicycles, schoolwork, and so on?" "What's the difference between a helpful fire and a harmful fire?" "Could a helpful fire ever become a harmful one?" In one class, students talked about the dangers of sunburn and how to take precautionary steps to avoid it. "What's the difference between maturity and old age?" "Does wisdom always come with age?" "Can a young person be wise and an older person not so wise?" "How could people in this class become wiser?"

Goals

As a result of stimulating intellectual discussions in which students express a wide range of viewpoints, experiences, and opinions, they learn respect for each other, gain a genuine appreciation of diversity, experience an increase in self-confidence, and develop deeper humanistic values. When students feel a sense of interdependence and connection, they grow in knowledge and their behavior improves. Additionally, they develop an appreciation for ideas and for intellectual discussions. This is especially valuable in an age when many kids' discussions and interactions often consist of demeaning and sarcastic humor.

Types of Meetings

Professional school counselors understand the value, purpose, and process of class meetings. They provide demonstrations for teachers and coach teachers to conduct three types of meetings: open-ended, educational/diagnostic, and problem solving.

Open-ended meetings. The previously described meetings on the topics of old age and effort/quality are open ended, opinion centered, "no-correct answers" meetings. Teachers should conduct these meetings until the students and teachers feel comfortable with such discussions and they come to realize that, regardless of their opinions, they will not be criticized or put down.

Educational/diagnostic meetings. Some teachers using educational/diagnostic meetings begin each new study unit with a series of questions related to the topic. In these meetings, teachers conduct an informal verbal assessment of students' prior knowledge of the topic. The meeting centering on *fire* could be such a meeting, though it could also be an open-ended meeting. A history teacher could begin the school year with a meeting built around such questions as *What is history? Do you have your own personal history? Of what value is history? Why do we study history? What if you didn't know anything that happened prior to today?* Science, language, and computer teachers could begin their courses with similar questions. Revisiting these general topics throughout the school year is also useful.

Problem-solving meetings. Teachers wishing to solve problems often initiate class meetings focused on antisocial behavior and irresponsible behavior such as class disruption, respect for adults, drug use, homework, or others. These are the most difficult to conduct because of emotional overtones and the tendency for participants to blame individuals.

One teacher, a union leader in a junior high school who taught difficult classes with hard-to-reach students, told me in October, "I hate to come to this class," when referring to a class of seventh graders. In April, he related that he looked forward to this same class of seventh-graders. Describing interventions causing this change, he related that he started with open-ended meetings during which students learned to respect various viewpoints. Then they discussed a school policy regarded as unfair (i.e., punishing all students sitting at a table in the cafeteria when only one student acted out). The class agreed to approach the student council, which presented the class consensus to the assistant principal, who agreed to change this ineffective and unfair rule. The teacher related that the students came to believe their judgment was worthy of respect. Their effective choices fulfilled their need for power or achievement in a positive way. They were then less inclined to choose self-defeating actions.

Guidelines and Cautions

The following guidelines are useful for professional school counselors who are either modeling class meetings or teaching other school staff members the art of conducting them.

- Make every attempt to sit in a circle. Ideal and desirable, this rearrangement of chairs might be time-consuming, inconvenient, and even impossible. Students should know that "we're having a meeting"—even if adherence to a circled discussion is impractical. Nor should teachers rigidly wed themselves to the large circle structure when variations prove to be useful adjuncts. Some teachers train students to lead the meetings, split the group into two smaller groups, or combine the class meeting with cooperative learning activities (Wubbolding & Brickell, 2001). Buzzwords for teachers to consider are *flexibility, creativity, reevaluation, outcome focused,* and *consultation* with other professional school counselors and teachers. Meetings can be brief; they need not be lengthy. It is better for students to need more time than to be bored.
- Problem-solving meetings should focus on *conditions,* not the behavior of specific students. Emphasizing the negative behavior of specific students can result in criticism, embarrassment, and even humiliation for scapegoated children. Effective meetings emphasize positive outcomes and specific ways to improve the school atmosphere.
- A helpful first meeting for professional school counselors who are demonstrating class meetings or coaching teachers is a "meeting on rules" or a "meeting on meetings." Useful questions include, *What is a rule? What are rules you find helpful? What is your favorite rule? What's the difference between a rule, a law, and a suggestion? What if we had no rules? How would this class function without rules? How would society function? What rules do we need for our class meetings?* Meetings focusing on the nature of a meeting could emphasize questions such as, *What is a meeting? Do your parents go to meetings? Why do people have meetings? What if no one ever went to a meeting? What do meetings accomplish? What makes for a good meeting?*
- Do not allow meetings to degenerate into gripe sessions. School rules, antisocial behavior, homework, the role of authority, and other topics can easily deteriorate if students and teachers are inexperienced in the art of group meetings. The structured process of *define, personalize, and challenge* combined with the WDEP system provide a viable alternative to such disasters.
- Class meetings enable students to develop appropriate language for expressing their opinions, to appreciate a diversity of worldviews and experiences, to enjoy intellectual conversations, to gain a feeling of respect from other students and teachers, and to en-

gage in behaviors that enhance interpersonal relationships. These characteristics of class meetings are at the core of mental health. As Wubbolding (2006) stated, "Mental health has many implications: helping friends and family, acceptance of people who are different without demeaning criticism, and willingness to contribute to society" (p. 6).

With its emphasis on building relationships (belonging) as well as helping students to be concerned for people and issues outside themselves, reality therapy is an effective method for operationalizing recent research findings related to neurobiology. Siegel (2012) described the human mind as a process that "regulates energy and information flow" (p. 43–46). Reality therapy provides a method for helping students deepen their self-awareness and to become attuned to others and feel more connected with them as well as being receptive to the information they receive and the energy they direct outwardly.

Summary/Conclusion

Professional school counselors interface with virtually every person associated with the school—students, faculty, administrators, parents, and community. The WDEP system provides a practical, research-based structure for counseling and consultation as well as content for in-service training. It also enriches the *"define, personalize, and challenge"* format for problem-solving class meetings. Asking students, "What do you want?" helps them to focus their attention on themselves and their own personal responsibility rather than on what they perceive to be the ineffective behavior of others. Asking students, "What are you doing?" narrows the discussion by focusing on the most easily controllable component of human behavior—actions. The pre-eminent question, "Is what you're doing bringing you closer to or distancing you from other people?" illustrates self-evaluation as the necessary prelude to any change. Planning means taking responsibility for the future. Professional school counselors adopting the WDEP system of reality therapy have a comprehensive and programmatic basis for school improvement that is congruent with current brain research.

CHAPTER 25

Using Cognitive Behavioral Techniques

Ann Vernon

Preview

The purpose of this chapter is to provide an overview of cognitive behavioral principles, with specific emphasis on practical applications of rational emotive and cognitive behavior therapy (RE&CBT) that professional school counselors can use in working with students in individual and small-group counseling, as well as in classroom guidance. The focus is on both intervention and prevention approaches. Further applications with parents and teachers are also highlighted.

Rational emotive behavior therapy (REBT) was founded by Dr. Albert Ellis, who is considered the grandfather of cognitive behavior therapy. REBT was the first of the cognitive behavior therapies to be developed and has been in existence since 1955 (DiGiuseppe, Doyle, Dryden, & Backx, 2014). After Ellis originated REBT, Beck developed his approach, known as *cognitive therapy* (CT), and Meichenbaum followed with another alternative, *cognitive behavior modification* (CBM), which focused on changing clients' self-verbalizations (Corey, 2013). Also under the cognitive "umbrella" are more recent cognitive therapies such as mindfulness and acceptance and commitment therapy (ACT; McMahon & Woo, 2012; O'Kelly, 2010).

A fundamental assumption of cognitive behavioral therapies is that emotions and behavior are influenced by cognitions, whether adaptive or dysfunctional, and that thoughts, emotions, and behaviors are all interrelated (DiGiuseppe et al., 2014; Mennuti, Freeman, & Christner, 2012). Because emotional and behavioral problems are influenced by how events are perceived, they can be addressed most effectively through cognitive restructuring—that is, showing people how their irrational beliefs or distorted cognitions upset them and how they can modify this inaccurate thinking using a variety of methods. Cognitive therapies emphasize the present, are time limited, and are solution focused (DiGiuseppe et al., 2014; Kalodner, 2011; Mennuti et al., 2012).

Although REBT and CBT share this common philosophical basis concerning the effect of beliefs on feelings and behaviors, REBT is considered more comprehensive and integrative than most other cognitive therapies because unlike the other CBT therapies, REBT has very strong emotional and behavioral components in addition to the cognitive components. As such, it is considered more multimodal in nature (Ellis & Poppa, 2001), as well as holistic (Vernon, 2011).

Cognitive therapies are increasing in popularity and are used extensively throughout the world—not only with adults, but also with children and adolescents (Bernard, Ellis, & Terjesen, 2006; Vernon, 2009a, 2011). Bernard et al. (2006) outlined several distinctive aspects of child and adolescent REBT that have helped define the field of CBT, including teaching young clients an emotional vocabulary and emotional schema, using the ABC framework, explicitly teaching the concept of emotional responsibility, and helping them develop self-acceptance, other-acceptance, and frustration tolerance.

REBT has a long-standing history of application with children, most notably through The Living School that Ellis established in 1971 to help young people learn rational principles. Since that time, it has been applied to children of all ages for a variety of problems, including school phobia, depression, anger, underachievement, acting out, anxiety, perfectionism, and procrastination, as well as typical developmental issues (Bernard et al., 2006; Vernon, 2009a).

An integral part of REBT is its strong emphasis on prevention and emotional education. Several programs have been designed to help children and adolescents apply rational thinking skills to promote emotional and behavioral well-being (Bernard, 2001; Knaus, 1974; Vernon, 1998a, 1998b, 1998c, 2006a, 2006b). These programs can be used in classroom and small-group counseling settings to teach rational principles (Vernon, 2007).

The purpose of this chapter is to describe practical applications of RE&CBT that professional school counselors can use in individual and small-group counseling. Classroom guidance applications that emphasize prevention will also be addressed, as well as how to employ these principles with parents and teachers.

Cognitive Theory: A Brief Overview

"What we feel is what we think" is a simplistic way of describing the philosophic basis of the cognitive behavior therapies. Maladaptive thoughts affect how people perceive activating events and result in distressing emotions. Beck (1989), Burns (2008), Ellis (2001a), and Meichenbaum (1977) all identified overgeneralizing, awfulizing, and musturbating as key dysfunctional beliefs as well as mind reading, focusing on the negative, dichotomous thinking, personalizing, magnification, arbitrary inference, and perfectionizing (Beck, Rush, Shaw, & Emery, 1987; Ellis, 2001b). According to these experts, dysfunctional beliefs have to be challenged or restructured in order for individuals to experience less intense negative emotions, behave in more self-enhancing ways, and think more functionally and rationally.

Cognitive restructuring can be accomplished in a variety of ways, depending on the professional counselor and the specific orientation. Ellis, for example, favored a very active-directive and oftentimes confrontational method of disputing (DiGiuseppe et al., 2014; Ellis, 2001b; Vernon, 2011). However, Ellis acknowledged that the degree to which the professional counselor is active-directive is a choice (Dryden, David, & Ellis, 2010), and practitioners working with children and adolescents would be well advised to be flexible and less directive in addition to employing a wide range of disputing strategies (Bernard et al., 2006; Vernon, 2009a). Beck used more of a reflective questioning process that helped the clients discover their own misconceptions, while Meichenbaum's self-instructional therapy helped young clients gain awareness of their own self-talk (Corey, 2013). This overview of the basic premises of CBT is simplistic and the major focus of this chapter is on practical applications with children and adolescents. Readers are therefore encouraged to engage in further study and training in the theory and practice of RE&CBT.

Effectiveness With School-Age Populations

Use of RE&CBT approaches with children and adolescents increased rapidly during the 1990s through the present (Bernard et al., 2006) and have received considerable attention and support for a variety of presenting problems experienced by youth (Ollendick & King, 2004). They are very effective with children and adolescents for the following reasons (Vernon, 2009a).

- The concepts are easily understood and can be adapted to children of most ages, cultures, and intelligence levels.
- RE&CBT emphasize short-term problem-solving forms of counseling, which makes it particularly applicable in school settings, where time for counseling is often limited.
- Briefer forms of counseling are especially important for young clients whose sense of time is immediate (i.e., young clients need something to help them now).
- The teachable concepts readily lend themselves to skill acquisition.
- RE&CBT approaches teach behavioral and emotional self-control by helping children understand the connection between thoughts, feelings, and behaviors.
- This approach helps children deal realistically with what they can change in their lives and cope more effectively with what they cannot change.
- The cognitive principles empower children to deal not only with present concerns but also give them tools to use for solving future problems.
- This approach is particularly effective with children in the concrete operational stage of development, because children in this developmental stage have a natural tendency to think dichotomously and lack the ability to reason abstractly. Teaching students to challenge their cognitive distortions helps minimize cognitive deficiencies.

In addition, educators are more accepting of RE&CBT because the structure parallels other educational services (Mennuti et al., 2012; Vernon, 2007). It can be readily adapted to provide interventions on a "continuum from prevention to early identification to direct individual service" (Mennuti et al., 2012, p. 7), which is particularly advantageous in school settings.

Cognitive therapies promote skill acquisition by helping children acquire practical coping skills. More important, they teach children how to *think* better. As a result, youngsters do not just *feel better*, they also *get better*, because they correct the faulty thinking that creates and perpetuates problems. For this reason, as well as for those previously mentioned, professional school counselors will see that using cognitive behavioral approaches with children and adolescents is an efficient and effective approach for problem remediation and prevention.

Individual Counseling Applications

Children and adolescents have to deal with typical developmental problems, and many have to deal with more serious situational problems stemming from dysfunctional family environments, death, illness, abuse, or other major issues. Because their sense of time is more immediate and their array of coping skills may be limited, it is critical to employ developmentally appropriate strategies that address the specific problem. Establishing a good therapeutic alliance is the first step of the process.

Establishing the Therapeutic Alliance

Practitioners working with children and adolescents place strong importance on relationship building, creating an atmosphere in which young clients feel free to share their problems and trust the practitioner to help them work through difficulties (Young, 2006). Stewart, Christner, and Freeman (2007) concluded that the most important tool practitioners can rely on is the working relationship with the young client. Vernon (2004, 2009a) developed numerous rapport-building strategies to facilitate this process, the goal being to put children and adolescents at ease. The ultimate goal is to develop a good working relationship so that students are more willing to work on their problems, learn the key RE&CBT concepts, and do homework assignments to facilitate problem resolution. The next phase of the process is problem assessment.

Problem Assessment

Problem assessment consists of assessing cognitive distortions and irrational beliefs as well as negative feelings and problematic behaviors. Since children (and many adolescents as well) may not be verbally adept and will struggle to label their feelings or articulate their thoughts, professional school counselors have to be creative and use a variety of methods in the assessment process. Inviting younger clients to draw, role-play, or use puppets to describe the problem may be necessary. Likewise, using techniques such as feeling flash cards, unfinished sentences, or feeling games may be good assessment strategies.

After getting a sense of the problem and how the child feels and behaves, it is important to determine the frequency, intensity, and duration of the problem: How long has it been going on, how often does it occur, and how intense is it? It may be helpful to ask clients to fill out a feeling–behaving chart, in which they rate the frequency of the problematic feeling or behavior every hour of the day for a week. This visual record is an excellent way for the student and the young client to better understand the problem. Another effective strategy is to use an *emotional pie* (Merrell, 2008), in which the client draws a circle and divides it into pie-shaped spaces of differing sizes, representing how they felt that week. For example, a small sliver of the pie might be labeled with an *A* for "anger," a larger portion might be identified with a *W* for "worry," and an even larger segment might be a *D* for "depression." This visual not only is an effective assessment technique but it also can be used as a springboard for initiating discussion about how to decrease the negative feelings during the intervention stage.

After establishing what the problem is, how the student feels and behaves, and how intense the problematic emotions and behaviors are, it is time to assess the beliefs. Keep in mind that not all beliefs are dysfunctional or irrational. For example, it is perfectly normal for a 10-year-old student to feel worried about her sister who just had an operation. One would detect the presence of irrational beliefs by asking her what she is thinking about her sister's situation. If she says that all she can think about is that her sister will die and that when that happens she wants to die too because she could not stand to live without her, the professional school counselor would know that this student was *catastrophizing*, since she is predicting that her sister will die from a not-so-serious operation and that if this happens, *she* cannot go on living. On the other hand, if the student is thinking that her sister could possibly die and that if this occurs she would be very sad because she loves her, there is little that is irrational or dysfunctional about her thinking. The same holds true for an adolescent who was not accepted into the university he had his heart set on attending. He naturally would feel disappointed, but if he were devastated, he would be telling himself that this was the worst thing that could ever happen to him, that it proves he is worthless, and that it will do no good to apply to another university because he would never be accepted at any of them. These cognitive distortions contribute to his extreme emotional reaction.

In assessing irrational and cognitive distortions, the professional school counselor needs to detect musts (e.g., I *must* always do well; others *must* treat me as I deserve to be treated), *catastrophizing, awfulizing* (e.g., This is so awful, nothing could be worse), frustration intolerance (e.g., Things should come easily to me; I shouldn't have to work too hard at anything), dichotomous thinking (e.g., It's either this way or that way), overgeneralizing (e.g., She will always be mean), personalizing (e.g., It's all my fault she ignored me), and self-downing (e.g., I'm no good if I got a bad grade on an exam).

Individual Interventions for Children

As previously noted, cognitive interventions can address a wide array of childhood problems ranging from typical developmental problems, such as fighting with friends, to more serious situational problems, such as coping with the death of a parent. Following is an intervention that helps children understand the cognitive theory concepts.

Don't blow it out of proportion (Vernon, 2007). To promote understanding of the concept of dichotomous thinking, put a long strip of masking tape on the floor. Use a typical example, such as "I know I will fail the math test." On an index card write "fail the test," and put this card at one end of the masking tape strip. Then, involve students in helping to identify at least 4 or 5 other points along the strip. For example, "getting a super good grade on the test" could be at the other end, "missing only a few questions," could be somewhere in between, and so forth. Process this by pointing out that there are more than two ways of looking at most situations. Have them give you examples as they apply this process to personal situations. In addition to employing interventions that help children understand the general cognitive concepts, interventions such as the following can be developed for a variety of typical childhood problems.

Adios anxiety (Vernon, 2002). This is a concrete way to help a young student deal with anxiety. The professional school counselor will need a plastic tablecloth with a large hopscotch board drawn on it. When a student describes things he or she is anxious about (e.g., taking a test, moving to a new school, riding in an airplane, doing something for the first time), indicate that you will be the student's secretary and write down all the thoughts he or she has about one of these anxious events. Next, invite the student to stand on the first square of the hopscotch board and read off something he or she was anxious about. If the student can think of a positive statement that will help to decrease the level of anxiety, he or she can hop to the next square. Read the next item, and ask the student to think of something that would make the student less anxious in that context. If he or she can, have the student hop to the next square. You may have to offer suggestions if the student does not understand the task or concept. For example, if a student were anxious about taking a test, the student could tell herself that if she studies hard she has a better chance of doing well, that because she has never done poorly on a test before, chances are that she will do alright this time, and that even if she does not do well on this one test, it doesn't mean she will not do better next time.

Rational coping statements. Rational coping statements are self-talk statements students can say to themselves to counter a fear. For example, if a student was afraid he would drown in a lake while swimming, a rational coping statement might be, "If I don't go past the rope, I should be safe; I can always yell for help." The purpose of rational coping statements is to help students identify less anxious self-talk and more effective coping strategies.

Individual Interventions for Adolescents

To help adolescents learn the basic principles of cognitive behavior therapy, the following intervention has proven effective.

Thoughts and feelings (Vernon, 2006a). To help adolescents learn that emotional problems are caused by their thoughts, invite them to write responses to stimulus questions. The following are examples.

- The principal announces there will be no junior–senior prom this year. How do you feel, and what are your thoughts about this?
- The person you are going with starts dating someone else. How do you feel, and what are your thoughts about this?
- Your mother announces you will be moving to a different town, and next week is the last time you will attend your present school. How do you feel, and what are your thoughts about this?

After they have written their responses, give them a blank copy of the situations and have them ask a friend to complete it (without seeing how your student responded). After your student has both sets of responses, have the student compare them to see if they are similar, and if not, describe what the differences are. Help the student understand that the reason there might be differences is that people think differently, and how they think affects how they feel. For example, if your student felt angry about the prom being canceled, she would have been thinking things such as, "This isn't fair; this will ruin my whole year." In contrast, if she had felt mildly irritated, the thoughts would be something like, "It's not that big of a deal; I can find something else to do." Continue to help the student see how thoughts cause feelings.

Cognitive therapies embrace a variety of methods and strategies to help young clients deal with their concerns. The following intervention illustrates how to help adolescents deal with procrastination.

Put it off (Vernon, 2002). This intervention helps adolescents learn that procrastinating is self-defeating and how to overcome it. To implement this intervention, the practitioner will need a pile of newspapers, pen, and paper. After first discussing with the student his or her problems with procrastination, including irrational thinking that might contribute to procrastination as well as negative consequences, the professional counselor asks the student to make a list of things he or she procrastinates about, discussing each in some detail to understand more about the student's thinking that contributes to this behavior. Then invite the student to lie down on the floor, face up. The professional counselor explains that he or she will read the list the student developed, one item at a time, and for each item, a large stack of newspapers will be placed on the student's chest to symbolize how things "pile up" when one procrastinates.

After everything on the list has been read, the professional counselor then tells the student that he or she can get out from under this pile symbolizing procrastination by identifying more effective things he or she could think and do to overcome it. One by one the professional counselor again reads each of the items from the student's list, but this time, the student needs to identify rational thoughts and constructive behaviors that would help him or her overcome the tendency to procrastinate. As the student identifies more effective thoughts and behaviors, the counselor gradually takes away the pile of newspapers. Discussion can focus on what the student learned and what might be helpful to him or her in dealing with this problem.

There are numerous other cognitive behavioral techniques that can be used to help young people learn to change their maladaptive thinking and, consequently, cope more effectively with problems they encounter. Role-playing, rational emotive imagery, rational role reversal, assertiveness training, bibliotherapy, self-help materials, and homework assignments can all be employed and readily adapted, depending on the developmental level of the child (Bernard, 2001; Vernon, 2002, 2009a).

Small-Group Counseling

Cognitive behavioral techniques are also very effective in group counseling situations. There are two formats that are generally employed: a problem-centered group in which all group members have a similar problem, or an open-ended group in which students take turns presenting problems they would like help with, but the problems are not necessarily similar (DiGiuseppe, 2007; Vernon, 2007). The open-ended group is much less structured in that students come to each session prepared to share a current problem and the group leader and other students help the targeted student apply RE&CBT concepts to help him or her deal more effectively with the issue.

Problem-solving groups, in which all members would have problems relative to the topic, can focus on typical developmental problems, such as getting along with friends or dealing with the emotional ups and downs of adolescence. They might also emphasize skill development, such as anger management or academic underachievement. They could also address specific situational stressors, such as divorce or living in an alcoholic family. Regardless of the focus, this type of group would have more structure than the open-ended group in that various activities would be introduced to help participants learn more about the topic and develop effective coping skills. The emphasis would be on introducing cognitive behavioral principles such as the connection between what they think and how they feel; the connection between how they think and feel to how they behave; and, ultimately, helping them apply these principles to the specific issue so that they have less intense negative emotions and more adaptive behavior. An advantage of the group approach is that participants can help each other develop the cognitive behavioral skills and apply them to their individual situation.

To illustrate, the leader of a divorce group for children would elicit feelings from participants about how their family situation is affecting them. In turn, the leader would probe for children's beliefs about this situation that could pertain to overgeneralizing, awfulizing, demanding, catastrophizing, and low frustration tolerance, such as, "This is the worst thing that could ever happen; it is unfair"; "Nothing will ever be the same again"; "They will never get over it"; "It is too painful to deal with"; and so forth. Using a variety of techniques such as bibliotherapy, journaling, rational role reversal, and feeling games, the leader would help students see that divorce can be a very upsetting circumstance, but, for example, wouldn't it be worse if one of their parents died? And even though it is painful, is it possible that in time they will adjust and feel somewhat better at least? The ultimate goal would be to help children deal with this unfortunate circumstance by recognizing that they can reduce the intensity of their negative emotions by changing their thinking about this event. Through the group format, children help each other challenge their irrational beliefs and identify effective coping strategies.

In an open-ended group, individuals bring present-day problems to the table, and the leader integrates cognitive behavioral principles into the discussion to help them think more clearly about the situation, experience more moderate as opposed to intensely negative emotions, and develop an array of coping strategies. For example, an adolescent might introduce the problem of feeling anxious about calling someone for a date. With the assistance of other group members, the leader would help this student identify his or her disturbing thoughts, such as "What if I get rejected?" "What if I stumble over my words?" "What if they laugh at me or hang up?" They would then help the client learn to dispute them. Different techniques such as role playing, writing rational limericks or stories, or identifying rational coping statements could be used with group members.

Classroom Applications

Of the cognitive therapies, REBT in particular has been psychoeducational in nature from its inception. From 1971 to 1975, The Institute for Advanced Study in Rational Psychotherapy (now called the Albert Ellis Institute) ran an elementary school in the building. The focus was on teaching rational thinking as a preventive mental health program in addition to the regular subjects (Vernon, 2007). The staff developed activities to help teach children effective thinking, feeling, and behaving strategies, and from these activities, Knaus (1974) developed a curriculum that would educate children in the ABCs of REBT. Since that time, other curricula (Vernon, 1998a, 1998b, 2006a, 2006b) have been developed that teach children to develop critical thinking skills, differentiate between facts and assumptions, distinguish between thoughts and feelings, link thoughts and feelings, identify what leads to emotional upset, distinguish between rational and irrational beliefs, and learn to challenge irrational beliefs. Vernon (1998a, 1998b, 1998c) also developed curricula to help children apply rational thinking concepts to typical developmental problems, and Bernard (2001) developed a comprehensive program that applies rational thinking concepts to improving school achievement.

The purpose of introducing these concepts in the classroom is to teach children principles they can apply to problems of daily living as well as to give them tools to use in solving future problems. A wide variety of cognitive behavioral methods are employed in delivering these lessons, including rational role reversal; self-help materials; worksheets; rational emotive imagery; thinking, feeling and behaving games; music and art activities; experiential activities; and didactic approaches. The primary focus is on prevention.

Applications With Parents and Teachers

Parents and teachers can also benefit from cognitive behavioral therapy in several ways. First, they can learn to apply the principles to their own issues, irrespective of their parenting or teaching. Second, they can recognize how cognitive distortions affect their parenting and teaching and learn to function more effectively by challenging these distorted thoughts. Finally, they can serve as rational role models for their children and the students they teach. Christner, Stewart, and Lennon (2012) discussed how RE&CBT techniques can be incorporated into the consultative process, whereby the consultant and parent can "collaboratively explore how the parent's thoughts, behaviors, feelings, and physiological reactions influence the problematic situations" (p. 352). In addition to parent (or teacher) consultation, parent education is also a viable way to introduce RE&CBT principles. Parents and teachers unwittingly fall victim to a number of dysfunctional beliefs, including uncertainty, self-condemnation, demands, and low frustration tolerance (Vernon, 2009a).

- *Uncertainty* (anxiety). It is not uncommon for parents and teachers to be uncertain about what to do in certain situations involving children. Adults often think they should know exactly what to do and what the outcome will be.
- *Self-condemnation*. When children have problems at home or in the classroom, adults often blame themselves. For example, if Juan did poorly on his basic skills tests, his teacher might put herself down, thinking that this reflects on her poor teaching. Parents of children who turn to drugs condemn themselves for their poor parenting. In reality, parents and teachers cannot be totally responsible for a child's behavior or performance.
- *Demanding*. Parents and teachers often demand that children must behave a certain way, and if they don't, it is awful. These adults are often very authoritarian and have little tolerance for children who don't always put forth their very best effort. Needless to say, this has a negative effect on their relationships with children.
- *Low frustration tolerance*. Low frustration tolerance is related to the idea that children, as well as adults, should not have to experience any frustration or discomfort. These adults consequently try to make life easy for children, which means rescuing them and failing to follow through with reasonable consequences for misbehavior.

Professional school counselors can assist parents and teachers by helping them identify these cognitive distortions as well as others such as overgeneralizing or awfulizing, tunnel vision (e.g., only seeing the negative), and the like. Concepts can be presented through parent group meetings and teacher in-services.

Summary/Conclusion

A brief overview of cognitive behavioral therapy was presented, which has successfully been employed with children and adolescents in school settings. Perhaps the most compelling reason for using a cognitive behavioral approach is that it can be used both for remediation and prevention in that it teaches children to identify and challenge the thoughts that create and perpetuate problems. Long-lasting change is more likely than with many other theoretical approaches.

CHAPTER 26

Development and Implementation of Behavioral Interventions in Schools: A Function-Based Approach

*R. Anthony Doggett and Carl J. Sheperis**

Preview

School personnel are increasingly faced with the responsibility of teaching students important social and behavioral skills in addition to providing instruction in traditional academic material. In fact, government agencies have mandated that proactive interventions be developed and implemented for students with disabilities who display problematic behavior. Such suggestions have also been strongly recommended for individuals without documented disabilities who have long histories of displaying problem behavior. We review the motivating factors for engaging in problem behavior; methods for identifying the purpose of problem behavior; and intervention development, implementation, and monitoring guidelines for teaching proactive, replacement behaviors.

Professional school counselors often interact with teachers, administrators, parents, and other applied personnel in designing interventions for students who display problem behaviors in the school setting. Traditionally, professional school counselors have been encouraged to generate interventions based on the topography of the behavior (i.e., how the behavior looks) rather than the function of the behavior (i.e., the purpose that the behavior serves for the individual). Because the interventions developed to teach important behavioral skills need to be as idiosyncratic as the students displaying the problem behaviors, we will take a functional approach to intervention development. Readers interested in more traditional approaches to the implementation of behavioral techniques (e.g., group contingencies, token economies, Premack principle, overcorrection, response cost, time-out) should refer to Chapter 18, "Setting Up and Managing a Classroom." Specifically, we will discuss the motivating factors associated with problem behaviors, best practices in functional behavioral assessment, and proper methods for intervention development, implementation, and monitoring. Such knowledge will enable the professional school counselor to serve as a vital resource to schools and families and assist in improving the behavioral and academic skills of the children they serve.

---

*We wish to thank Daniel J. Krenzler for his contributions to this chapter during the second edition.

School professionals are faced with the increasing responsibility for providing safe school environments in addition to providing academic instruction. As a result, schools have developed zero-tolerance policies, implemented target hardening procedures (e.g., controlled access entrances, metal detectors, body searches), and used segregation procedures (e.g., suspension, expulsion, alternative placements, self-contained classrooms) as methods for trying to control the display of disruptive behavior on school grounds (Teske, 2011). Unfortunately, such restrictive or get-tough responses have proven ineffective (i.e., led to increased levels of student misbehavior, higher rates of suspensions and juvenile incarceration, greater levels of racial disparity for special education and minority students) and the continued display of problematic behavior has served to threaten the process of schooling for all children (Chen & Vazsonyi, 2013). As such, representatives of government agencies (e.g., Department of Education, National Institutes of Health) have advocated for more emphasis on the development of proactive procedures that are designed to provide social and academic skill acquisition (Dupper, 2010). In addition, these representatives have opposed methods solely designed to reduce or eliminate the display of disruptive behavior without an alternative or replacement skill development component. In an effort to promote best practice among professional school counselors related to behavioral problems in children, we discuss potential reasons for the display of problem behavior, assessment strategies for discovering the purpose of problem behavior, and intervention strategies for both reducing the display of disruptive behavior and promoting the occurrence of more adaptive behaviors.

Reasons for the Display of Problem Behavior

Understanding the assessment of disruptive behavior and the implementation of proactive interventions requires a discussion about potential functions of problem behavior. *Function* refers to the purpose that the behavior serves for the student (Dunlap & Fox, 2011). A student can choose to engage in any given behavior in a classroom setting (Quinn et al., 2001). However, the particular behaviors that the student chooses to engage in are greatly affected by learning history or the previous interactions that one has had with significant others or events in their environment (Martens, Witt, Daly, & Vollmer, 1999). For example, one student may immediately begin working on a new math assignment once it has been passed out by the teacher because completing similar academic assignments in the past has led to social praise from teachers. However, another student may look out the window, flip through pages of a book, or walk around the classroom before beginning the math assignment. Eventually, the teacher redirects this student to his or her seat and provides assistance in completing the worksheet. As such, this student conceivably avoids working on the worksheet until social attention is provided in the forms of redirection and assistance. Both students obtained and were reinforced by social attention from the teacher. In addition, both students were faced with the same set of choices when given the worksheet. However, their responses to the worksheet were greatly influenced by their prior history with similar academic demands. Potential functions of behavior have previously been divided into five general categories:

- Positive social reinforcement (e.g., social attention from teachers or peers)
- Material or activity reinforcement (e.g., access to preferred items or activities)

- Negative reinforcement (e.g., escape or avoidance of aversive instructional tasks or activities)
- Negative social reinforcement (e.g., escape or avoidance of nonpreferred individuals)
- Automatic or sensory reinforcement (e.g., internal stimulation; Carr, 1994)

Of these potential functions, obtaining social attention from teachers or peers and avoiding or escaping instructional demands appear to be the most common motivators for engaging in disruptive behavior in classroom settings (Lancioni, Singh, O'Reilly, Sigafoos, & Didden, 2012). A particular problem behavior or several behaviors may serve the same function or each could serve a different function (Doggett, Edwards, Moore, Tingstrom, & Wilczynski, 2001). The task of the professional school counselor is not only to obtain detailed information about the problem behavior but, more important, to obtain information about the motivation for performing the problem behavior.

Reasons for Failed Behavioral Interventions

Teachers and other school personnel often report that they spend a significant amount of time and effort trying to reduce the occurrence of problem behavior that is exhibited by students in their classrooms. Traditionally, treatment efforts aimed at reducing the problem behavior have focused more on the topography of the problem behavior rather than on the function or purpose of the behavior (Hoff, Ervin, & Friman, 2005). In other words, textbook interventions have been universally applied to individuals who have demonstrated similar behaviors or been diagnosed with the same or similar disorders. However, reported research results have indicated that many universally applied school-based interventions have proven ineffective (Newcomer & Lewis, 2004). Although several reasons for ineffective intervention results could be identified for a student, treatment selection without reference to the behavioral function of the problem behavior has been identified as a significant limitation. According to Vollmer and Northup (1996), at least four problems may arise when behavioral interventions are selected without reference to behavioral function. First, the problem behavior may inadvertently be strengthened through positive reinforcement. An example includes the use of reprimands delivered by a classroom teacher in an effort to reduce disruptive behavior. In fact, research has demonstrated that the increased use of reprimands by teachers often leads to a direct escalation in problem behavior by students whose behavior is maintained by obtaining teacher attention (Doggett et al., 2001; Kehle, Bray, Theodore, Jenson, & Clark, 2000; Musser, Bray, Kehle, & Jenson, 2001).

Second, the behavior may inadvertently be strengthened through negative reinforcement (e.g., avoidance or escape). A commonly used classroom management strategy that may strengthen problem behavior through negative reinforcement is the use of time-out. Studies have shown that time-out, or the removal of demands or attention, may negatively reinforce problem behaviors by allowing students to escape tasks or other individuals viewed as aversive or nonpreferred (Everett et al., 2007). Third, the intervention may be functionally irrelevant to the problem behavior. For example, an intervention aimed at reducing teacher attention for problem behavior would be functionally irrelevant for a student whose behavior is primarily maintained by escape from academic demands. Finally, an intervention may not provide alternative sources of reinforcement for more proactive replacement behaviors. For example, in-school suspension, out-of-school suspension, and detention are commonly used punitive procedures designed to reduce problem behavior. However, such procedures do not teach alternative behaviors, nor do they provide reinforcement for the display of proactive behaviors.

Because approaches based solely on topography or diagnosis have proven ineffective in leading to positive outcomes, recent literature has been proliferated with assessment strategies that focus on identifying the function of problem behavior (Newcomer & Lewis, 2004). One such procedure is functional behavioral assessment (FBA). FBA has been defined as a collection of methods for gathering information about target behaviors, events in the environment that precede the target behaviors (antecedents), and events in the environments that follow the target behaviors (consequences). This information is then used to determine the reason for the performance of problem behavior (Gresham, Watson, & Skinner, 2001). Federal law requires FBA for students who are verified with disabilities and who display problem behaviors at school (Individuals with Disabilities Education Improvement Act of 2004) that have manifested into a pattern of behavior which violates the code of conduct or are of a specific nature (e.g., possession of weapons or drugs, aggression that leads to serious bodily injury). Furthermore, FBA is strongly recommended for individuals without disabilities who have a history of displaying disruptive behavior that impedes learning in the school environment (McIntosh, Brown, & Borgmeier, 2008). In recent years, multi-tier intervention models have been recommended for addressing the problem behavior of identified students (Brown-Chidsey, & Steege, 2010; Sailor, Doolittle, Bradley, & Danielson, 2009). These models are frequently referred to as the response to intervention (RTI) model as well as the complementary school-wide positive behavior interventions and supports (SW-PBIS) models. Both models use a three-tier model of academic and behavioral support to address identified student needs and require the employment of research-based or evidence-based interventions with adequate levels of compliance and integrity in addition to ongoing student progress monitoring. At Tier 1, approximately 80% of students respond to empirically based instructional methods and behavior management techniques employed by highly qualified teaching staff. At Tier 2, approximately 10–15% of the students require supplemental or secondary level supports (e.g., mentoring, social skills instruction, academic remediation). At Tier 3, about 5–10% of the school population requires intensive, individualized, tertiary interventions and potential mental health supports. Students with behavioral concerns at Tier 3 require function-based behavioral interventions and supports based on a FBA. In summary, the primary goal of FBA is to identify the specific environmental events associated with the performance of problem behavior to enhance the probability of treatment effectiveness and to prevent a series of ineffective interventions based on best guesses and unconfirmed hypotheses (McComas, Hoch, & Mace, 2000).

Best Practices in Functional Behavioral Assessment

Best practice in FBA occurs in a 4-phase process: (a) description; (b) interpretation; (c) verification; and (d) intervention development, implementation, and monitoring (Ervin et al., 2001; Sterling-Turner, Robinson, & Wilczynski, 2001).

Phase I: Description

The descriptive phase involves both indirect and direct procedures and is used to generate hypotheses about the environmental events that may be triggering or maintaining problem behavior. Indirect methods are used to obtain information from archival data or important others (e.g., teachers, administrators, parents) about the display of problem behavior and the potential functions of problem behavior. Traditionally, indirect methods have included record reviews, rating scales, and interviews. When evaluating student records, professional school counselors should review grade reports, group and individual standardized test results, curriculum-based assessment results, discipline records, attendance records, medical history, Individualized Education Programs (IEPs), and previous interventions. Appropriate use of rating scales requires individuals familiar with the student to rate the perceived impact of specific environmental events (i.e., antecedents and consequences) on the performance of problem behavior. Some of the more commonly used rating scales include the *Motivation Assessment Scale* (Durand & Crimmins, 1988), the *Problem Behavior Questionnaire* (Lewis, Scott, & Sugai, 1994), and the *Functional Analysis Screening Tool* (Goh, Iwata, & DeLeon, 1996). Other indirect methods for gathering information about the functional relationship between problem behaviors and environmental events are teacher and student interviews. Examples of structured or semi-structured interviews include the Functional Assessment Interview (O'Neill et al., 1997), the Preliminary Functional Assessment Survey (Dunlap et al., 1993), the Functional Assessment Information Record for Teachers (Edwards, 2002; Doggett, Mueller, & Moore, 2002), and the Student Assisted Functional Assessment Interview (Kern, Dunlap, Clarke, & Childs, 1994).

The second aspect of the descriptive phase in FBA involves the use of direct methods. Direct descriptive assessment involves the collection of data on the performance of target behaviors and environmental events via direct observation. The most common type of direct observation technique used to obtain data about behaviors and functional relationships is an A-B-C assessment or contingency analysis (Cooper, Heron, & Heward, 2007). A-B-C observations require that the observer record data on the occurrence of antecedent events (e.g., potential triggers, setting events), target behaviors, and consequent events (e.g., potential reinforcers). Direct descriptive data can be collected through narrative recording, event recording, or time-sampling procedures. Review of these procedures is beyond the scope of this chapter, and professional school counselors are encouraged to consult Alberto and Troutman (2012) or Miltenberger (2004) for additional information about these observation methods.

Phase II: Interpretation

Data obtained from the indirect and direct methods are used during the second phase, or interpretive phase, to develop hypotheses about functional relationships between the problem behaviors and the events that precede or follow the behaviors. In fact, McComas et al. (2000) recommended that summary statements be developed for each hypothesis. To illustrate, consider the student who had difficulty attending to the math assignment. One potential summary statement could be, "When the student is given a math worksheet (antecedent event), he or she will look out the window, flip through pages of a book, and walk around the room (observable behaviors) in order to obtain social attention from the teacher (i.e., assistance with the task as a consequent event)." However, another summary statement could be, "When the student is given a math worksheet (antecedent event), he or she will look out the window, flip through pages of a book, and walk around the room (observable behavior) in order to briefly escape from the academic task demand (termination of the task as a consequent event)." It is important to remember that information collected during the descriptive assessment phase is only correlational in nature. In other words, the school-based professional can only make informed suggestions about potential relationships between environmental events and problem behaviors. However, definitive statements about the specific events that occasion or maintain the occurrence of problem behavior cannot be made at this stage. To make statements about causal relationships, progression to the third phase must occur.

Phase III: Verification

Verification of hypotheses developed during the interpretation phase occurs via experimental or functional analysis or through implementation of a function-based intervention. A functional or experimental analysis is a brief experiment designed to confirm or disconfirm prior suggestions made about potential functional relationships between environmental events and problem behaviors. In other words, predictable changes are purposely made in the student's environment to see how those changes affect the performance of problem behavior. As in the case described earlier, the teacher may be instructed to attend to the student every time he or she engages in problem behavior (usually through reprimands or redirections) during a 10-minute functional or experimental analysis condition to evaluate the effect of teacher attention on problem behavior. In another condition, the teacher may be instructed to only attend to appropriate behavior (usually through praise statements) during a 10-minute condition to see if teacher praise, in fact, does increase the display of appropriate behavior. In relation, a student may be given grade level material in one condition and instructional level material in another condition to evaluate potential differences in off-task behavior across each condition.

Most functional analysis research has been based on the work of Iwata et al. (1994) or Carr and Durand (1985) and has been expanded for proper use in classroom settings (Radford, Aldrich, & Ervin, 2000). Functional or experimental analysis conditions can be conducted in analogue settings (i.e., contrived settings designed to approximate the typical classroom setting) or in naturalistic settings (i.e., the child's actual classroom during regular academic instruction). Furthermore, functional or experimental analysis conditions have included manipulation of both antecedent conditions (e.g., level of task demand, amount of attention, presence or absence of peers) and consequent conditions (e.g., social attention for disruptive behavior, removal of task contingent upon the display of problem behavior). For a complete review of school-based experimental analysis conditions, professional school counselors are referred to Carter (2009).

A primary advantage of experimental analysis is that it is the only method for demonstrating a causal relationship between target behaviors and antecedent and consequent events. Major disadvantages include the effort, time, and professional expertise required to implement such procedures (Miltenberger, 2004). In fact, researchers have suggested that many school-based professionals proceed to intervention after completing record reviews, rating scales, interviews, and direct observations if a clear relationship can be hypothesized from the descriptive methods (Doggett et al., 2001). Furthermore, researchers have demonstrated that function-based interventions can be used to validate the hypotheses generated from descriptive methods often making functional or experimental analyses unnecessary (Doggett et al., 2002).

Phase IV: Treatment Development, Implementation, and Monitoring

The last phase of FBA involves treatment development, implementation, and monitoring. Treatment should not consist of a single technique that is designed to simply eliminate the problem behavior. Instead, the behavioral intervention should be composed of a set of antecedent- and consequent-based strategies designed to reduce the problem behavior and, more importantly, increase the performance of alternative replacement behaviors (McComas et al., 2000). Such interventions have been referred to as *positive behavioral supports* and are mandated by federal law for students with disabilities and strongly encouraged for nondisabled students with histories of problem behavior (Brown-Chidsey & Steege, 2010; Drasgow & Yell, 2001; Sailor, Doolittle, et al., 2009). McComas et al. (2000) posited that interventions should match the values, resources, and skills of those persons who would be required to implement the procedures. They also emphasized that positive behavior supports should make the display of problem behaviors irrelevant, inefficient, and ineffective if the student is highly motivated to engage in the alternative behaviors that serve the same function or purpose as the problem behaviors.

Treatment development: Linking assessment to intervention. As was mentioned previously, positive behavior supports or proactive interventions will be composed of intervention elements designed to increase the display of appropriate behavior. These elements will include both antecedent- and consequent-based strategies. More attention has been given to antecedent strategies that could serve to prevent the problem behavior from occurring (Kern & Clemens, 2007). Typically, variables that often trigger the display of inappropriate behavior are broadly defined as the curriculum. Once the curricular variables that occasion the occurrence of problem behavior have been identified through FBA methods, changes can be made to increase the probability that appropriate behavior will be displayed. While not exhaustive, modifications to the curriculum have included changing task difficulty, modifying task size or duration, changing the instructional media, incorporating the student's personal interests in the task, allowing the individual to choose the order of the tasks, changing the pacing of the instruction, and interspersing different tasks (e.g., short vs. long, varied vs. repetitive, long vs. short) over the academic period.

In contrast to antecedent strategies, consequent-based interventions have typically focused on contingencies of reinforcement (i.e., positive and negative reinforcement) in order to increase the display of appropriate behavior. Reinforcement, by definition, increases the probability that a certain behavior will be performed in the future (Skinner, 1953). Positive reinforcement refers to the presentation of a stimulus or event that increases the likelihood that a target behavior will be performed at a later time. Negative reinforcement refers to the removal of a stimulus or event that increases the likelihood that a target behavior will be performed in the future. Thus, both positive and negative reinforcement increase the probability that some target behavior will be displayed over time. Furthermore, it is important to note that negative reinforcement is not punishment (which decreases the probability that a behavior will be displayed in the future).

The most common classroom applications of positive reinforcement include differential reinforcement of alternative behavior (DRA) or differential reinforcement of other behavior (DRO; Mildon, Moore, & Dixon, 2004). DRA involves reinforcing the alternative behavior and ignoring or extinguishing the inappropriate behavior. Using the same example of the student engaging in the math assignment, a teacher using DRA would increase her social praise for working on the math assignment and systematically ignore the off-task behaviors. Conversely, DRO is used to provide reinforcement for a set interval of time that the problem behavior has not been displayed. In this case, the teacher using DRO would calculate the time between distributing the math assignment and initial off-task behavior. If the student gets out of his desk within approximately 5 minutes after being given the assignment, then the teacher would set the interval at 5 minutes. Positive social attention (e.g., verbal and physical praise) would be provided to the student after the 5-minute interval only if he or she worked on the assignment for the entire interval.

Thus far, the discussion of differential reinforcement has focused on providing attention contingent upon the display of appropriate behavior. However, differential reinforcement can be used to reduce the occurrence of escape-maintained behavior and increase the occurrence of working on a task or interacting with a nonpreferred individual. When negative reinforcement is applied, the terms *differential negative reinforcement of alternative behavior* (DNRA) and *differential negative reinforcement of other behavior* (DNRO) are used (Miltenberger, 2004). DNRA or DNRO could be used so that the problem behavior no longer produces escape from or avoidance of task demands or nonpreferred individuals. In other words, the contingencies could be arranged such that longer periods of on-task behavior, work completion, or social interactions lead to escape from the demand. For example, the student who avoided the math assignment could be taught to request a break after working on the worksheet for an appropriate period of time.

Another form of differential reinforcement that is gaining attention in the literature is noncontingent reinforcement (NCR), which refers to the delivery of reinforcers on a fixed schedule, independent of the display of problem behavior. For attention-maintained behavior, the teacher could provide social attention at set periods throughout the day, regardless of the display of problem behavior. For escape-maintained behavior, the teacher could provide scheduled breaks throughout the day that are noncontingent on the display of problem behavior. Mildon et al. (2004) suggested that NCR could serve as a viable intervention alternative for two reasons. First, NCR reduces the student's motivation to engage in the problem behavior because he or she is obtaining the desired reinforcer (e.g., attention or escape) on a predictable schedule. Second, NCR disrupts the contingency between the problem behavior and the maintaining consequence, because the reinforcer is delivered independent of the display of problem behavior. One caution is that NCR procedures have not been researched as thoroughly as other differential reinforcement procedures, and the effectiveness of such a procedure is not as well established.

Finally, the implementation of traditional behavioral techniques can be very useful in managing student behavior as long as the interventions are related to the function of the problem behavior. For example, group-oriented contingencies can be very effective procedures for reducing peer attention for problem behavior and increasing peer attention for appropriate behavior, especially if the students earn free time together for following classroom rules. Furthermore, behavioral charts and school–home notes can often serve to provide social attention or other desired activities to students for engaging in appropriate behavior. Additionally, response-cost and time-out procedures can be useful additions to differential reinforcement for managing problem behavior maintained by social attention. Finally, other punishment-based procedures, such as overcorrection, can be a useful addition to curricular changes in the environment for reducing escape-maintained behaviors. For more guidance on implementing these traditional behavioral techniques, see Chapter 50, "Helping Students with Severe Behavioral Problems."

Once the antecedent and consequent-based strategies have been appropriately identified for implementation based on the function of the behavior, the school counselor will work collaboratively with the student's IEP committee for a special education student or student assistance team for a Tier 3 student to develop a formal behavior intervention plan (BIP) or behavior support plan (BSP). While the formatting of BIPs and BSPs will vary, they all should include the following essential components: (a) summary statements from the FBA, (b) operational definitions of each desired replacement behavior, (c) specific proactive (i.e., antecedent) strategies used to potentially prevent the occurrence of behavior, (d) specific teaching strategies used to teach social skills and identified replacement behaviors, (e) specific consequent strategies used to reinforce the display of appropriate behavior as well as corrective strategies used to address the continued display of problem behavior, (f) identification of when, who, and where all intervention techniques will be employed, and (g) plans for the evaluation of intervention compliance and integrity as well as student progress monitoring methods to evaluate student response to intervention. For special education students, information from the FBA and BIP should be included on the present levels of performance section of the IEP and used in selecting appropriate accommodations and modifications as well as in making decisions regarding the provision of counseling or psychological services as a related service. Finally, appropriate social, emotional, or behavioral goals should be developed and included on the IEP that are directly linked to each desired replacement behavior included on the BIP.

Treatment implementation and monitoring: Increasing treatment integrity and evaluating student progress. After the target behaviors and alternative behaviors have been clearly defined, the functions of the problem behavior have been verified, and the treatment protocol has been developed, the professional school counselor will have to work closely with other school personnel to ensure that the intervention procedures are implemented properly (Sterling-Turner et al., 2001). The amount of time devoted to ensuring that the intervention is implemented properly will vary with each student and teacher. However, proper training is crucial for proper intervention implementation (Sterling-Turner, Watson, & Moore, 2000). When interventions are not implemented properly, the true impact of the intervention remains unknown. In other words, it will be difficult to determine if the FBA results were incorrect and led to inappropriate intervention design or if improper treatment implementation led to the failed efforts and nonresponse to intervention. If the results of FBA were incorrect, then the professional school personnel need to review the FBA data in order to generate and test other hypotheses. If the treatment was implemented with poor integrity, then the professional school counselor needs to determine if the teacher lacked the skills to implement the intervention or the motivation to implement the procedures.

BIP development date: _____ BIP implementation date: _____
Student Name: _____ Student #: _____ DOB: _____
Eligibility: _____ School: _____ Grade: _____
IEP Teacher: _____ Student Removal Dates: _____
Method of Evaluation of Intervention Integrity: ❏ Direct Observation ❏ Self-Report
BIP Integrity Checklist completed by: _____ Date: _____

Behavior Intervention Plan Development

Item #	Item Description	Rating
1	Student has a Functional Behavioral Assessment which identifies all problem behaviors (including operational definitions) and has summary statements regarding all potential functions of behavior.	1 0 NA
2	Student has an active Behavior Intervention Plan (BIP) with clearly defined replacement behaviors and preventative, teaching, reinforcement/reward, and corrective strategies that have been clearly explained to school personnel by appropriate behavioral support personnel.	1 0 NA
3	Relevant school personnel (certified teaching personnel, certified behavioral support personnel, noncertified personnel) have a copy of the current BIP and can clearly articulate the strategies in the plan.	1 0 NA
4	School administrators have a copy of the current BIP and can clearly articulate the strategies in the plan.	1 0 NA

Behavior Intervention Plan Implementation

Item #	Item Description	Rating
5	All school personnel implement designated behavioral preventative strategies consistently.	1 0 NA
6	All school personnel implement designated academic preventative strategies consistently.	1 0 NA
7	All school personnel implement designated behavioral teaching strategies consistently.	1 0 NA
8	All school personnel implement designated reinforcement/reward strategies consistently.	1 0 NA
9	All school personnel implement designated corrective strategies (including alternatives to removal) consistently.	1 0 NA
10	All school personnel rate the student's behavior at the designated times on the Daily Behavior Rating Form.	1 0 NA
11	All school personnel provide feedback to the student regarding his or her behavior at the designated times on the Daily Behavior Rating Form.	1 0 NA

Behavior Intervention Plan Evaluation

Item #	Item Description	Rating
12	Points from the Daily Behavior Report Form are tallied daily and entered into the database weekly.	1 0 NA
13	Student behavior is graphed weekly and visually evaluated for changes in performance.	1 0 NA
14	School personnel reconvened IEP to review/revise BIP as designated by the Code of Conduct and/or to recommend a FBA (if appropriate).	1 0 NA
15	School personnel reconvened IEP to review/revise BIP if graphed performance indicates that student is not responding to designated intervention strategies within the plan.	1 0 NA

At least _____% intervention compliance and integrity is required to document appropriate implementation of the BIP. Total Percentage of Intervention Compliance and Integrity = _____ / _____ = _____%

_____, Teacher or Other School Personnel _____, Administrator

Figure 26.1 Behavior Intervention Plan (BIP) Integrity Checklist.

In order to ensure proper treatment implementation, direct behavioral consultation (DBC) has been suggested (Sterling-Turner et al., 2001). First, the teacher should be provided with a rationale for implementing the treatment that is linked directly to the results of the FBA. Second, the intervention should be modeled for the teacher, and the teacher should be allowed to practice implementation of the intervention while receiving reinforcing and corrective feedback. Once the teacher becomes more proficient in implementing the intervention, then assistance can be faded. However, it would still be important to have the teacher monitor his or her own integrity in implementing the intervention over time. Both the school counselor and teaching personnel may find a structured, quantitative approach to the evaluation of intervention implementation useful. As such, an example intervention integrity form developed by Fluency Plus, LLC has been provided for review in Figure 26.1.

School personnel will need to collect behavioral data regularly (i.e., daily) in order to evaluate student response to intervention. One of the most effective methods for gathering information regarding the display of replacement behaviors by identified students is through the use of behavior tracking forms, typically referred to as daily behavior report cards and school-home notes (Kelley & Jurbergs, 2009). These forms are used to track the display of appropriate behavior throughout the day as teaching personnel rate the display of behavior using a rubric and then provide specific feedback to the student regarding his or her behavior at each identified period on the form. This method of data collection is efficient for teachers and desirable because the information can be quantified and placed on a graph for visual inspection by school personnel on a weekly basis. In addition, the information can be shared with other school personnel on the IEP committee or student assistance team when reviewing student behavioral progress and with parents or guardians to inform them of student skill development at planned intervals during the school year.

Summary/Conclusion

Functional behavioral assessment seeks to answer the questions, *What is triggering the problem behavior?* and *What is maintaining the problem behavior?* Once these questions are answered, function-based interventions can be developed to increase the display of appropriate, replacement behaviors and decrease the display of problem behaviors by making them ineffective, inefficient, and irrelevant. Interventions or positive behavior supports are not composed of one technique but include antecedent- and consequent-based strategies as well as instructional methods for increasing the display of appropriate behavior. Finally, intervention implementation and monitoring are also crucial components for ensuring treatment success and evaluating student response to intervention. Table 26.1 (see next page) reviews the steps in conducting FBAs and implementing function-based interventions.

Table 26.1 Steps in Conducting a Functional Behavioral Analysis (FBA)

Phase I: Description

Step I:	Conduct record reviews, interviews, and complete rating scales.
Step II:	Identify and clearly define problem behaviors.
Step III:	Conduct A-B-C observations or other direct observations.

Phase II: Interpretation

Step I:	Review all data obtained from the FBA.
Step II:	Develop hypothesis statements about antecedent events that could be setting off or triggering each problem behavior.
Step III:	Develop hypothesis statements about consequent events that could be maintaining each problem behavior.

Phase III: Verification

Step I:	Conduct experimental or functional analysis conditions, if necessary.

Step II:	Develop function-based interventions, if satisfied with results from the preceding phases.
	    Identify and clearly define replacement behaviors and related behavioral goals.
	    Identify antecedent strategies.
	    Identify teaching strategies.
	    Identify consequent strategies.
	    Identify progress monitoring and intervention integrity strategies.
	    Provide consultation and training to teacher.

Phase IV: Treatment Development, Implementation, and Monitoring

Step I:	Develop BIP or BSP in collaboration with the IEP committee or student assistance team.
Step II:	If you did not implement BIP strategies following consultation with the IEP committee or student assistance team in the verification phase, then implement comprehensive intervention package here, following the above-mentioned steps.
Step III:	Monitor the intervention for proper implementation through direct observations and treatment integrity checklists. Monitor student response to intervention by tracking student behavior daily and graphing behavioral outcomes weekly.

CHAPTER 27

Adlerian Counseling Techniques

Mardi Kay Fallon

Preview

Adlerian theory has been used for decades to help school counselors and educators understand the behavior and motivation of the student. By exploring how a student understands and experiences the world, the professional school counselor can develop effective interventions that teach the child how to adapt to and cope with life's difficulties in a cooperative and socially responsible manner. In the Adlerian perspective, misbehavior is seen as a learning issue, and all students are seen as desiring to belong and interact in a healthy and beneficial manner with others. Adlerian interventions seek to help the student understand his misbehavior and learn how to develop greater self-control. Professional school counselors can use a variety of interesting and creative techniques to help the student to achieve this level of self-awareness. The Adlerian approach works well with today's multicultural student population and can be adapted to work with special needs populations.

Proponents of Adlerian counseling have developed several principles regarding students and student behavior that are of practical use to the professional school counselor. These principles are also applicable to students with special needs and from diverse backgrounds, making Adlerian theory a viable option for today's school populations.

A basic tenet of Adlerian theory is that all behavior is purposeful. A student is a social being, someone who observes the environment, forms opinions about how things work, and acts upon those (often faulty) assumptions. Therefore, every behavior, no matter how unusual or dysfunctional, has a goal and a purpose. If one can understand the goal and purpose of a student's behavior, then one is able to understand the motives of that student. Understanding a student's motives helps the professional school counselor to understand how best to help the child change problem behavior (Pryor & Tollerud, 1999).

Because children are social beings, they have a need to belong and live cooperatively with others. Indeed, Adlerians consider the ability of a child to engage positively with others (e.g., sharing, showing concern for others, developing empathy) as a measure of that child's mental health. However, because of the natural conditions of childhood, all students experience a sense of inferiority and of being weak and vulnerable. Thus, they strive to achieve superiority, which is seen as working to obtain a sense of mastery and self-control (Carlson & Sperry, 2001).

Children live within a subjective world and tend to distort what they see and experience in order to fit that subjective worldview. They develop a form of private logic, which helps them to make sense of themselves and their world (Sapp, 1997). Students begin by observing their families and developing a set of beliefs and expectations based upon those experiences. This sets up a paradigm through which the student seeks to find meaning as well as ways to belong and achieve a sense of mastery and self-control.

Essentially, in a school setting, students choose their behaviors as a means to obtain goals. However, a student may make decisions that are based on faulty assumptions, leading to misbehavior that is problematic. Misbehavior, then, is viewed more as a learning difficulty than as a character flaw. Indeed, misbehavior is believed to arise from discouragement, from a student having the belief that he is not able to find a way to meet his needs and goals in a cooperative and beneficial manner (Dreikurs & Stolz, 1991).

Understanding Misbehavior

There are essentially four main goals of misbehavior, each of which has specific qualities and attributes that can alert the professional school counselor to the particular intervention that may be most beneficial to the student in question. The four goals of misbehavior are attention, power, revenge, and inadequacy.

The goal of *attention* is very common with students in a school setting. Here, students feel that they are only of value if they can get others to notice or serve them (Sweeney, 2009). When a student is seeking attention, an adult's tendency is to feel annoyed. This is, in fact, one way to assess what a student's motives may be, to determine from the beleaguered adult just what feelings the student's behavior has elicited. The student seeking attention will initially tend to stop misbehaving when first corrected and then begin repeating the attention-seeking behavior soon after (Dinkmeyer, Dinkmeyer, & Sperry, 1987). Corrective action for attention-seeking would be to withhold attention until the student behaves appropriately (Pryor & Tollerud, 1999). Here, bad behavior (that is not dangerous) is ignored, and good behavior is rewarded by giving the student attention. Eventually, the student should learn that the best way to obtain positive attention is to act appropriately and cooperatively.

The goal of *power* is the most likely misbehavior to result in a student being referred to the professional school counselor for intervention. With a power motive, the student feels that she only counts if she can force others to do what she wants (Sweeney, 2009). Students acting on a desire for power elicit in the adult a sense of being challenged and wanting to engage in a power struggle with that student. The adult will want to show the student that she cannot get away with that kind of behavior. If the motive is indeed power, the student's behavior will tend to worsen as corrective action is taken (Dinkmeyer et al., 1987).

The way to correct power misbehavior is to avoid engaging in a power struggle. The professional school counselor will need to set clear limits (e.g., not hurting self, others, or acting destructively). No limits should be set upon the student's speech, however, since the goal of counseling is to help the child express his thoughts and feelings. When limits are set, the professional school counselor must be careful not to convey a sense of being punitive or judgmental. If a student continues to misbehave, the professional school counselor can give the child choices regarding which appropriate behavior he can engage in. Otherwise, the professional school counselor could decide to use logical or natural consequences (Kottman & Johnson, 1993).

Logical consequences are statements of an expected outcome for a student's misbehavior that is fair and consistent. These consequences must be related to what a student actually has done and be geared to help the child understand her misbehavior and to see the benefits of behaving properly. The student needs to feel that she is respected and approved of despite the misbehavior. Punishment and rewards are to be avoided, as the student needs to learn to behave properly for the intrinsic value of cooperating with others. This will teach the student to learn responsibility and cooperate with others without seeking to be rewarded for good behavior (Pryor & Tollerud, 1999). Examples of logical consequences include the following:

- A student who throws a tantrum over a candy bar will not get that candy bar.
- If a student does not turn in his homework on time, he can expect to get a lesser grade for the work.
- A student who does not cooperate with other students will have to leave the game until she can agree to play cooperatively.

Natural consequences are events that can be expected to happen if the adult does not intervene. Most adults will tend to want to protect the student from natural consequences, but allowing a student to experience a natural consequence allows that student to learn how to grow and prepares him for the realities of life. If adults try to protect a student from these natural consequences, the student might get the message that he is inferior and unable to cope on his own (Dreikurs & Stolz, 1991). Examples of natural consequences are:

- A student who goes out without a rain coat is allowed to experience getting wet.
- A student who forgets lunch money misses lunch.
- A student who does not put a bike away either has the bike stolen or it gets rusty and broken down being outside.

The final two goals of misbehavior are revenge and inadequacy. Both of these goals may indicate significant problems or issues, and the professional school counselor may wish to refer such a student to community counseling where more time and attention can be spent on any underlying problems (Kottman & Johnson, 1993).

With the goal of *revenge*, the student believes that she must hurt others, because the student does not feel likable (Sweeney, 2009). The goal of revenge is common among students who are the victims of physical or sexual abuse (Kottman & Johnson, 1993). When a student is acting out of a goal for revenge, the adult will feel hurt and outraged. Initially, any attempt to correct her will result in violent behavior (Dinkmeyer, Dinkmeyer, & Sperry, 1987). Corrective action would involve setting fair and clear rules and imposing natural consequences. The adult needs to take care not to give the student a sense of being disliked. This student will tend to respond better to encouragement, persuasion, and a sense that she is liked by others (Pryor & Tollerud, 1999).

Finally, the student who misbehaves due to a goal of *inadequacy* has learned to feel that he does not matter to others due to being stupid or hopeless. This student feels too discouraged to try, believing that he would fail, and then everyone would know just how inadequate he really is (Sweeney, 2009). Often, this type of student has experienced some history of abuse (Kottman & Johnson, 1993). Adults working with this kind of student often feel like giving up on the child. Any attempt to correct this student's behavior is likely to be met with futile, insincere attempts to change or try things (Dinkmeyer et al., 1987). A way to correct the misbehavior of inadequacy is to use a lot of encouragement and to help the student to see that he is valued (Pryor & Tollerud, 1999).

Encouragement is a specific technique geared to help a student understand that she is likable and helps a student change her motivation to misbehave. Adlerians believe that a student will learn better in an accepting, democratic environment, where the setting optimizes that particular student's ability to grow and develop. In such a nurturing setting, students tend to automatically change misbehavior into something more acceptable and constructive (Pryor & Tollerud, 1999). Encouragement does not refer to simple praise or reward but rather to statements that convey to the student a sense of respect and recognition that she is a competent, acceptable person. Encouragement can be used to build rapport with a student by showing the student that the professional school counselor has faith in the student's ability to do things. An Adlerian-style counselor will allow a student to do things on her own that the student is capable of doing. If the professional school counselor believes the student cannot do a task, the counselor can suggest that the student agree to do it together with the counselor. This is an opportunity to show the student how to problem solve. As the student works on a task, the professional school counselor can acknowledge the effort and improvements made, and encourage the student to continue to try (Kottman & Johnson, 1993).

Through encouragement, a student who misbehaves learns to put forth effort to change and is motivated to remain on task. Providing praise before the student has learned these steps may not help the student to learn these necessary skills (Ehly & Dustin, 1989). Allowing a student to do things on his own and encouraging the student to accept the problems inherent in doing difficult things helps him to grow and develop in a healthy manner. Since students often have trouble separating what they do from who they are, they tend to judge their value by how competent they are. If a student is allowed to develop competence and to learn to deal with life consequences, the student develops a positive sense of self. Students cannot be effectively shielded from life consequences; they need to be taught how to cope with them rather than be kept from them (Dreikurs & Stolz, 1991).

Goals of Counseling

The goals of Adlerian counseling involve helping the student to develop a healthier way of being involved with others, greater self-awareness, and challenging and changing faulty goals and assumptions about life. Counseling involves a form of reeducation in which the student learns new ways to act, to feel self-esteem, and to decrease a sense of being inadequate or inferior. As the student learns to identify her own mistakes in thinking and behaving, she will be able to self-correct and start behaving more appropriately (Carlson & Sperry, 2001).

These goals involve developing an empathic relationship in which the student feels understood and accepted by the professional school counselor. This provides an environment in which the student can be led to explore and understand his beliefs, feelings, motives, and goals regarding life. This exploration helps the student to develop insight into his own mistaken attitudes regarding goals, as well as how he has been acting in a self-defeating manner. Finally, the student learns to identify and consider new, viable ways to change problem behaviors and commit to actually changing misbehavior (Dinkmeyer et al., 1987).

Therapeutic Techniques

Adlerian therapy uses a multitude of techniques to aid the student in self-exploration of behavior. Some of these techniques are appropriate to counseling in general, and others are more appropriate for individual or group settings. Some brief explanations of general techniques follow.

Tracking

As a student moves about the room, the professional school counselor tells the student what she is doing, such as, "You are picking up the truck and taking it over there." This can be used to develop a relationship with the student and to convey to the student that what she does is of importance. This technique works well in play therapy (Kottman & Johnson, 1993).

Restatement

Restate the content of what the student says. If the student says, "The doll wants to hug you," the professional school counselor can respond with, "The doll wants to hug me." Restatement would be most appropriate in play therapy and is a way to convey interest, develop rapport, and help the student to develop self-awareness (Kottman & Johnson, 1993).

Reflection

Reflect the emotion of the student to help him become more aware and understand his own feelings. The professional school counselor should seek to reflect both the surface level of the emotion as well as underlying feelings. An example might be a student throwing down a broken toy, kicking it, and saying, "That always happens to me!" The professional school counselor might say, "Sometimes you feel angry because things don't work, and you feel like that often happens to you" (Kottman & Johnson, 1993).

Early Recollections

This technique requires the student to recall several early life events (which usually come from the time the student was 4 to 6 years old). These recollections help the professional school counselor to identify what the student has come to believe about the world, oneself, and others. These recollections can reflect themes as well as specific emotions that are important to understanding the student. The professional school counselor can identify if the student conveys a sense of being safe, cared for, and able to control things (Kottman & Johnson, 1993).

Therapeutic Metaphors

Students will often use metaphor and symbolism in play, and the professional school counselor can use the student's metaphor to facilitate self-understanding. This can be used in play therapy, in which a student will spontaneously use a metaphor such as, "Here's the daddy doll. He comes home and turns into a monster and eats up the whole family" (Kottman & Johnson,

1993). Obviously, this example provides the professional school counselor with a great deal of information about how the student feels and perceives the world.

Mutual Storytelling

The student's metaphors can also be used to help a student understand his beliefs and views of life. The professional school counselor can have a child tell a story with a beginning, middle, and end. The student's story may contain some mistaken beliefs or perceptions, and the professional school counselor can take the opportunity to retell the story in a more positive and adaptive light to help the student develop a new perspective (Erford, 2015a).

Therapeutic Games

Older students often do not wish to attend counseling or are unwilling to either discuss their emotions or to change their behaviors. Games that are bought in the stores and special games designed for counseling, can be used to engage the reluctant student. Playing games can afford the professional school counselor an opportunity to observe the student's behavior and to identify some of the student's attitudes about herself and others. Game-playing in groups, particularly, can provide information regarding social skills, ability to wait, taking turns, coping with disappointment, and so forth. The professional school counselor can use these opportunities to help the student explore his thoughts, feelings, and behaviors, develop a sense of competence, and build his self-esteem. Sometimes a student may talk while playing the game and provide more information than he would in a formal face-to-face session (Erford, 2010).

Role-Play and Simulation

Using creative dramatics can work to motivate older students in a group setting. Group members can use role-play to explore different behaviors and to observe how these behaviors affect others. Role-play and simulation can also help group members develop empathy for others, develop social skills, explore their inner world with others, develop listening and attending skills, cooperate with others, learn decision-making skills, and develop the ability to observe and evaluate both self and others (Erford, 2015a).

"Could It Be" Questions

"Could it be" questions involve the professional school counselor being aware of the feelings a student's misbehavior is eliciting and help the student to identify his misbehavior. So, if a professional school counselor is feeling annoyed by a student's obvious attempts to get the counselor to watch him, the counselor could say, "Could it be you are keeping me busy with you because you want me to pay attention to you?" This would help the student to become more aware of the goals of his misbehavior.

Paradoxical Intention

As an experiment, the professional school counselor can have the student do the opposite of what she would expect, to emphasize the symptoms or misbehavior. This could help the student develop a greater awareness of the consequences of her misbehavior if she does not *resist* doing it but instead *deliberately* does it. For example, if a counselor tells a student, as an experiment, to deliberately not do her homework for one night, this might help the student become aware of the fact that she chooses her own behavior, that not doing homework is less attractive when it is permitted, and often help the student see how silly or ridiculous that misbehavior may be (Erford, 2015a). This technique must be used carefully, for a limited time, with the appropriate student (and with the approval and support of the student's teacher) to work effectively.

Spitting in the Client's Soup

This technique refers to an old boarding-school activity where a student would spit in another child's soup in order to get that child to give up the soup. Here, the professional school counselor identifies the purpose of, and payoff for, a certain misbehavior and spoils the fun for the student by decreasing the pleasure he may derive from misbehaving. For example, the professional school counselor may reflect to an older student that his drinking problem may be a way for the student to keep connected to the father he claims to hate, because the father is an alcoholic and that is something they can share (Erford, 2015a).

Acting "As If"

The professional school counselor can have the student, as an exercise or assignment, act the way she would like to act. The student may initially resist, saying that it's just pretending and not real. However, the professional school counselor could relate it to trying on a new outfit or suit of clothes. The student could try it on and see if it works. If the student does try and feels better, she may decide to behave differently. This can be done for a certain period of time, and then the student can return to the counselor to discuss the results (Erford, 2015a). An example would be that a shy student could act as if she was friendly and say "hi" to everyone she meets.

Catching Oneself

As the student becomes more aware or his misbehavior and is more motivated to change, the professional school counselor can suggest that the student catch himself doing something that he wants to do differently. At first, the student will tend to catch himself too late to make the change. As the student practices, however, he learns to anticipate and avoid certain situations and to change his behavior. This can be done with a sense of humor and works well if the student can laugh at himself (Dinkmeyer et al., 1987).

Creating Movement

Sometimes a student needs to be motivated to change. This tactic must be used carefully and in light of a sense of trust and the relationship the professional school counselor has developed with the student. To create movement, the counselor can use surprise to jar a student out of inaction. For example, if a student decided she wanted to give up trying, the professional school counselor may agree with her (Dinkmeyer et al., 1987). If used properly, not saying the expected thing could result in a moment of deeper self-awareness.

Avoiding Power Struggles

Often, a child will try to fit the professional school counselor into a role based upon that student's expectations and beliefs about the world. Thus, a student may try to provoke the counselor into validating that he is unlovable. The professional school counselor must avoid falling into this trap or risk confirming to the child that he is, indeed, unlovable. The counselor must keep aware of the feelings the child is attempting to elicit and avoid giving in to feelings of being hurt or discouraged. In particular, the professional school counselor needs to avoid any power struggles with the child (Dinkmeyer et al., 1987).

Task Setting and Commitment

The professional school counselor helps a student to identify what she can do about a problem and commit to doing it for a specific time. If the student is successful, she may feel encouraged and continue to change. If not, new behaviors could be explored, and the student could try again in a different way (Dinkmeyer et al., 1987).

Push-Button Technique

Students need to understand that they are responsible for both the good and bad feelings they experience. Humans create their own moods. In this technique, the student could be directed to mentally re-experience something that gave him a very good feeling. Then, the student could visualize an experience that made him feel very bad. As the child does this, the professional school counselor could help the student to learn to connect how one's thoughts about an experience lead to one's feelings about that experience (Carlson & Sperry, 2001).

Group-Specific Techniques

In groups, the group member gets to interact with peers in such a way as to be able to work on specific ideas and issues. To do this in a safe environment, group members must develop acceptance for each other (have respect and empathy). Acceptance would be modeled by the group leader who could also help specific group members develop their own ability to accept others.

- *Altruism* is the natural tendency in humans to seek to help each other. Group counseling provides an opportunity for group members to extend help to each other. This can be modeled by the group leader, who can also encourage altruism and provide the group opportunities to use and develop this skill.
- *Spectator therapy* refers to the observation that some group members may interact little with the group, but may still be listening and developing a greater understanding of self. Just listening to others in a group situation can help a group member see himself in others and develop self-awareness.
- *Universalization* involves helping group members to understand that their problems are not unique, that they are not as alone as they thought. To understand that they share problems with others can help group members feel less alienated and lonely and thus

able to look at various solutions. This sharing can be used to encourage exploration and discussion.
- *Feedback* helps group members understand how others experience them. This can help develop insight and greater self-awareness. It also helps the group member challenge her faulty beliefs and perceptions. Honest, authentic feedback can also convey to a group member that she is important to others and that others care and are concerned about the student.
- *Ventilation* provides group members the opportunity to express normally inhibited emotions. It also provides an outlet for internal pressures, promotes the expression and exploration of feelings, and helps the group member develop greater insight.
- *Reality testing* helps a group member test a faulty perception or belief within the group setting. For example, if a boy has developed a belief that girls are enemies and that he could never come to understand them, he could test this theory in the group by learning to talk to girls in the group. As he develops an ability to accept that his first assumptions were wrong, the boy may learn to look at other misperceptions or faulty assumptions and develop an ability to be self-aware (Dinkmeyer et al., 1987).

Consultation

Adlerian principles also apply to consultation with teachers and parents. Parents need to understand their child's behavior and can benefit from learning about the four goals of misbehavior and ways to intervene with difficult behaviors. Weekly face-to-face consultations are optimal, but they are not usually practical. Therefore, the professional school counselor may have to seek some other way to consult with the parents, such as by phone. Contact with parents is an important way for the counselor to gather more information regarding the student and to suggest to the parents ways to deal with the student's misbehavior (Kottman & Johnson, 1993). Teachers, also, often can benefit from learning about the goals of misbehavior and identify new, creative ways to intervene with problem behaviors.

Adlerians avoid assigning blame for a student's problems (as so often happens when parents blame schools, schools blame parents, and the student escapes responsibility for her behavior). Sometimes, a meeting with all parties (student, parents, and teachers) is advisable in order to improve communication and cooperation to deal more effectively with the student's misbehavior. Adlerian counselors also avoid using labels or overestimating evaluations and test scores. Each student is seen as an individual and not compared with others (Dinkmeyer et al., 1987).

Special Topics

Adlerian theory seeks to understand the individual within a social context; it is therefore conducive to ethnic and multicultural issues. A student with a diverse background may develop a sense of inferiority and become pessimistic about being able to meet life goals. Adlerians focus on understanding a student's subjective view of the world, respecting the individual student, believing that each student can learn and grow, and developing a student's ability to be cooperative and socially responsible. All of these tenets work well with multicultural and special needs issues. Many cultures value community and social cooperation, but the professional school counselor must operate from a sound understanding of the student's background as well as a sensitivity and respect for that student's culture in order to be responsible and effective in helping that student (Sapp, 1997). Children with special needs may also suffer from feelings of inferiority or faulty beliefs about how the world works and can also benefit from the Adlerian focus on self-worth of the individual student.

Summary/Conclusion

The professional school counselor will find that Adlerian theory and therapeutic techniques are applicable to the work they do. This chapter has provided a brief review of some of the basic tenets of Adlerian theory and how they apply to counseling children within a school setting. The professional school counselor can use the ideas presented in this chapter to identify the goal of a student's misbehavior and to develop an intervention that is specific and appropriate to the needs of that individual student. This chapter also includes some guidelines for consultation, with a special emphasis to avoid placing blame and keeping the child responsible for his or her own behavior. Interested readers can consult references from this chapter for further readings.

CHAPTER 28

Solution-Focused Brief Counseling

Bradley T. Erford*

Preview

Solution-focused brief counseling is presented as an efficient and effective model that professional school counselors can use to meet the needs of students. A general overview, the structure of the model, and its basic steps and techniques are presented.

Solution-focused brief counseling (SFBC) is a counseling approach based on a newly evolving resource-oriented constructivist theory. It is an outgrowth of a wellness system to counseling rather than an approach based on mental health disorders or dysfunctional behaviors. This method builds upon existing "positives"—the strengths of the individual, the present resources, and the solutions already occurring for these individuals. It is solution focused rather than problem oriented and brief in terms of the number of sessions required, from the initial meeting to termination. This counseling model has been deemed appropriate for schools for several reasons:

- SFBC is conceptually simple and easy to learn.
- SFBC is perceived as more effective and more practical since the focus is on *what works* rather than *why* something is a problem.
- SFBC's emphasis on strengths, successes, resources, and hope is a useful element for schools.
- The model spotlights small changes and reasonable co-constructed goals.
- SFBC encourages the acceptance and accommodation of diverse opinions and beliefs, which is appropriate for today's professional school counselors who operate in complex arenas with diverse student bodies.
- According to Murphy (2008), drawing upon past successes, existing positive attitudes, and effective working behaviors is more practical and less time-consuming than attempting to teach new behaviors, so SFBC is especially useful for the school counseling setting.
- A brief approach is crucial for the professional school counselor who has little time to give to individual counseling and must make a difference quickly out of necessity or refer a student to an outside resource who will have more time available for individual counseling.

---

*Special thanks to John R. Charlesworth and C. Marie Jackson for their outstanding contributions to the first two editions of this chapter.

Development of the SFBC Model

Historically, the development of the SFBC model has been attributed to many counseling and psychology practitioners including Berg and Miller (1992), deShazer (1985), O'Hanlon and Weiner-Davis (2003), and Walter and Peller (1992). Books specifically written for the professional school counselor are also available. Murphy (2008) has written for middle and high school counselors, while Sklare (2014) has provided an easy, step-by-step, readable short text explaining a solution-focused approach for professional school counselors.

According to Sklare (2014), it was deShazer who first developed the SFBC approach. Sklare pointed out that the SFBC model encompasses techniques learned in other counseling approaches, thereby making it easier to master than the more traditional approaches. Techniques used in SFBC that are common to many other counseling theories are listening, responding with empathy, asking open-ended questions, supporting, reinforcing, identifying goals, and applying scaling methods.

Central Philosophy and Basic Assumptions

Understanding the basic rules and the assumptions on which SFBC is based is crucial for professional school counselors to "own the model" and accept it as effective.

Central Guiding Philosophy

De Shazer (1985) and Berg and Miller (1992) proposed three basic SFBC rules as the central guiding philosophy for the model. These rules are: (a) If it ain't broke, don't fix it; (b) Once you know what works, do more of it; and (c) If it doesn't work, don't do it again. Do something different.

Assumptions

The number of assumptions purportedly underlying SFBC varies by author. Walter and Peller (1992) presented 12 assumptions of SFBC, and Murphy (2008) presented six assumptions. Sklare (2014) presented five assumptions, but added four guiding concepts. After reviewing all of the foregoing, the most obvious commonalties among them are as follows:

1. Counseling should focus on solutions rather than problems for beneficial change to occur.
2. An effective counseling strategy is to find and transform "exceptions" (i.e., those times when the problem is not present) into solutions.
3. Small changes lead to bigger changes.
4. Counselees have all the necessary resources to resolve concerns.
5. The counselor should focus on developing meaningful counselor–student co-constructed goals with an emphasis on what the counselee wants rather than on the counselor's ideas or opinions.

Guiding Concepts

Sklare's (2014) addition of guiding concepts is useful to the school counselor beginning to use SFBC; one might refer to them as rules for the professional school counselor to follow. The first one reminds the counselor to avoid exploration of the problem. A second reminder, to be efficient with interventions, suggests that the professional school counselor should accomplish as much as possible with the fewest number of interventions. Another concept is that insight does not provide solutions. Sklare reminded the counselor that it is more important to take action than to discuss how counselees became the way they are. The final guiding concept presented by Sklare is to focus on the present and the future. Having students think about what will be different in the future when the solutions are in place builds a belief that things will be better. Acknowledging the times in the present when solutions already exist increases the student's self-efficacy.

An SFBC Model

There are several approaches to brief counseling found in the literature. These various models generally contain similar elements, although there may be slight differences in the terminology and sequencing of steps. The general organization of Sklare's (2014) approach has been selected to acquaint the reader with implementing SFBC.

Initiating the First Session

Since SFBC counselors assume that rapport with the student exists from the moment they meet, little time is spent attempting to develop it, unless it does not appear to be present. In those instances, additional time is spent developing rapport before proceeding. Once good rapport has been established, counselors provide their students with an overview of how the sessions will proceed. Sklare (2014) included the following information:

- The student will be asked a lot of questions, some a little strange and others challenging.
- The counselor will be taking notes during the session.
- Near the end of the session, the counselor will move to another part of the room to write the student a message.
- The counselor will return and read the message to the student, then provide the student with a copy of the message while keeping one for the records.
- The counselor will ensure the student's understanding of the purpose of the message and its contents and provide the student an opportunity to ask questions and make comments.

Identifying Student Goals

One of the most significant predictors of success in any counseling approach is the ability to help the student formulate clear goals. According to Sklare (2014), well-established goals add to the efficiency and effectiveness of SFBC. The goals established in this approach must, of necessity, be stated in small steps of obtainable, observable, measurable, behaviorally specific actions that the students are to "begin doing." Because of SFBC's focus on goals, when students present with problems, rather than pursuing the how and why of the problems, counselors help reframe the problems as goals.

The emphasis in SFBC is on helping students develop positive goals rather than negative "stop doing" goals. Counselors initiate goal-oriented thinking by asking questions such as, *"What is your goal in coming for counseling?"* or *"What would need to happen for you to consider your counseling sessions with me a success?"* Questions such as these frequently lead to student goal statements that Sklare (2014) has classified as (a) positive, (b) negative, (c) harmful, or (d) "I don't know" goals.

Positive goals. These goals are stated as what the student wants to achieve in an observable, behaviorally specific, measurable, and attainable manner. When a student presents with a vague, general positive goal such as *I want to behave better in class*, the counselor must use appropriate questions to define the goal in more specific, concrete terms. Questions such as *What would you be doing that would indicate you are behaving better?* or *What would your teacher say you are doing when you are behaving better in class?* help produce concrete, explicit descriptions of what the student will be doing when making progress toward goals. The student will create clear images of the desired solutions. By continuing to emphasize what the student will be doing when he or she is moving toward goals, the counselor is implicitly suggesting to the student that success is possible. For additional detail for the goal picture, follow-up questions can be asked related to what the achieved goals will look like to the student or significant others.

Negative goals. Sklare (2014) defined negative goals as those stated as the absence of something. They typically refer to the student wanting self or others to stop doing something. Examples of these two types of negative goals are, *I want to stop making bad grades* and *I want my teacher to quit making me stay in during recess*. Such goals are very difficult to accomplish and, in most instances, are unattainable. To reframe negative goals into positive ones, the student must replace the "stop doing" behaviors (negative goals) with the presence of desired behaviors. Questions that assist students in reframing what they do not want into what they do want include, *If you stopped getting bad grades, what would you be doing?* and *What would you rather be doing instead of staying in at recess?* When the student has responded with a positive goal statement, professional school counselors will frequently need to use additional *What else would you be doing?* questions to elicit more specific details of the positive goal.

When a student presents with a negative goal that expresses the desire for others to change or stop doing something, the student is placing the responsibility for achieving the goal on someone other than himself or herself. Frequently the student is either requiring the other person to initiate change or expecting the counselor to "fix things." When presented with a negative (others) goal, such as the one previously stated (*I want my teacher to quit making me stay in during recess*), the professional school counselor must assist the student to reframe the goals into positive ones in which the student assumes responsibility for change. Questions that can help professional school counselors understand the student's motivation for wanting others to change include, *If they did change, what would that do for you?* and *How can I help you with this?* Such questions may lead a student, like the one with the negative goal, to respond that he would like to be able to go to recess to play with friends. With that as the student's positive goal, the professional school counselor could begin to obtain specific details of what the student would be doing to achieve that goal.

Harmful goals. Sometimes, students respond with harmful goal statements involving behavior that would be illegal, harmful, or not in their best interest. Such behaviors as becoming a prostitute, stealing, quitting school, taking drugs, selling drugs, hurting others, damaging property, and the like would not be supported by ethical professional school counselors. When helping students to modify destructive goals into productive positive goals, counselors need to uncover how these destructive goals are symptoms of students' unmet needs. Once the need is identified, professional school counselors help students establish healthy, attainable, positive goals to better meet their needs. As an example, if a student presents with a goal of wanting to sell some drugs, the professional school counselor could attempt to identify the student's unmet need by using a question such as, *What will selling drugs do for you?* If the student responds with the explanation, "I want to get money so I can go to the prom," the counselor could then use this information to help the student identify more appropriate behaviors to attain the positive goal. When students present with impossible goals, such as wanting their separated parents to reunite, professional school counselors address these goals in a similar fashion as when working with negative goals.

"I don't know" goals. Quite frequently, students come to counseling not because they made the choice but because parents, administrators, teachers, or others have referred them. Sklare (2014) insisted that for change to occur, the student must be the customer. When the student is referred by another, the real customers are the ones who made the referral. Other-referred students are often difficult and resistant, acting as if they are merely visitors to the counselor's office. When these students are asked for their goal in coming to counseling, they commonly respond with the phrase, "I don't know." Other-referred students will typically identify the reason for their referral when the professional school counselor uses hypothetical "if" questions, such as *"If you did know* (or, *If you could guess*), *why do you think you've been referred?"* In some instances, obtaining from the student an underlying reason for being sent for counseling may require the use of repeated "if" questions. Using the "if" questions allows the student to "not know" and, in essence, to appear to guess the answer.

Some students have little, if any, motivation for counseling even when they have been able to identify why others have referred them for help. To convert such students from being reluctant to being more cooperative generally requires that the professional school counselor sell them on the benefits they will receive from counseling. For example, a student may have little motivation to get along better with a teacher, even though the consequence of undesirable behaviors is repeated stays in in-school suspension. A question to the student such as, *If we could help you get along better with your teacher so that you wouldn't have to spend so much time in in-school suspension, would that be something you would like to work on?* can be effective in increasing motivation for counseling. The success of this intervention depends upon the counselor's ability to recognize what students want and to help them to understand how counseling can help them get what they want.

Sklare (2014) described another approach for dealing with a reluctant student who believes the reason for being referred was due to an inaccurate assessment by the person making the referral. He identified this approach as the *they're wrong, you're right technique.* When a student strongly stresses that the referring person has made a mistake and that no problem for which the student needs help exists, the professional school counselor should respond, *"So, you're convinced that you don't need help with getting along with your classmates. If we could find a way to prove that your teacher was wrong about you needing help in getting along with other children and that you were right about not having a problem all along, would that be something you would like to work on?"* When a student indicates that he or she would like to correct the teacher's wrong impression, the professional school counselor can then help the student establish positive goals. By having the student elaborate on the question, *What would the teacher need to see you doing that would convince her that she was wrong and you were right?*, positive goals are likely to evolve.

Even though the focus of the early phases of goal identification is to clearly outline measurable goals, it is not always accomplished at this phase. Other techniques such as the "miracle question" are used to build a picture of how the solution or solutions might look and thereby aid the development of concrete behavioral goals.

Using the Miracle Question

During the student goal identification process, the emphasis is on helping the student identify positive goals and the "doing" behaviors needed to accomplish the desired solutions. Frequently, hypothetical questions are needed to help students fully develop specific, observable, concrete, behavioral goals and to gain a clear vision of what life will be like when they have attained these positive goals. According to Sklare (2014), because of its success, the miracle question is one of the more frequently used hypothetical questions. Following is an example of a miracle question:

Suppose you go to sleep tonight and while you are sleeping a miracle happens without you knowing about it. When you awaken the problem that brought you here has been solved. What's the first thing you would notice that would tell you the problem has been solved? What would be different?

Sklare (2014) suggested using an alternative hypothetical question with younger children who may not understand the concept of miracles. One example is as follows: *Suppose I had a magic wand and waved it over your head and your problem was solved. What would be different? What would you see yourself doing differently?* Another alternative hypothetical question is, *Imagine that it is 6 months from now and you have solved the problem that brought you for counseling. What would you notice that was different, and what would tell you that you no longer needed help with that problem?*

Whichever hypothetical question the professional school counselor uses, the student's responses need persistent clarification, using the student's own words or language to ultimately form detailed, specific, well-developed goals. Often students respond to one of the hypothetical miracle questions with a vague response, such as "I'd wake up and I'd be nicer to my brother." A question using the student's own words, such as *"And when you are being nicer to your brother, what would you see yourself doing?"* is likely to lead to a more specific goal. Further questioning about how others might react to these changes helps students to see how making little changes may produce favorable changes in others. For example, asking the question *"If you started being nicer to your brother by helping him with his chores, how do you think he would respond?"* might help the student to recognize the benefit of a simple change in his own behavior and also might help increase the student's motivation for change.

Sometimes students answer miracle-type questions by stating impossible goals, or goals that have little chance of being attained. They may want their parent's chronic illness to be cured, to have their lost pet returned, or to have a favorite relative move to their city. Frequently, students realize the professional school counselor cannot produce these results, but if a miracle could happen, that is what they would want. By responding to the student's impossible wishes with questions such as *"How would things be different for you if your miracle happened?"* professional school counselors can discover the student's real desires and help identify realistic goals.

Identifying Instances and Exceptions

After using the miracle question and constructing a clear vision of a successful resolution of a problem, the professional school counselor's next task is to help the student identify instances when he or she has been successful or partially successful at solving the problem. SFBC counselors believe that, regardless of the presenting problem, there are always times when the problem is either absent or less severe. These times are referred to as *exceptions*. Because students are often unaware of these occurrences, the professional school counselor must help them recall these exceptions and identify what they were doing that led to them.

Students' language often provides cues as to when these instances or exceptions have occurred. For example, when students use words or phrases such as *generally, sometimes, almost always,* and *most of the time,* it suggests there are times when the solution is already occurring to some degree. For example, if a student remarks that he almost always has trouble getting along with Mrs. Jones, it suggests that there are times when he does get along with her. The professional school counselor can help the student become more aware of these unrecognized successes through responses such as *"Tell me about the times you were getting along better with Mrs. Jones"* or by using questions that imply some degree of success.

Mindmapping

After professional school counselors have helped students to identify their unrecognized successes, the next step is to help students identify what they were doing that contributed to those successes. Students' responses to professional school counselors' questions about what they did to accomplish a goal provide the counselor with specific behaviors the student has used successfully. By continuing this process, professional school counselors help students develop mindmaps, which are like roadmaps, to guide students' approaches to solving their problems. Mindmapping is one of several techniques useful to the SFBC counselor.

Cheerleading

Another technique characteristic of SFBC is *cheerleading* as a way to acknowledge students' success and encourage more of it. Professional school counselors sincerely praise or cheerlead any success students demonstrate, no matter how small. The cheerleading helps educate students about what they did to make things better. It also provides encouragement and support for continued success and increases a sense of personal control and self-esteem. Professional school counselors are cheerleading when they praise students, using genuine enthusiasm shown in their voice inflections, facial expressions, and bodily movements. For example, a student might report an instance in which she went to bed without her mother having to make her. The professional school counselor could cheerlead by responding with comments such as, *"You mean you went to bed without your mother even having to tell you?"* or *"How did you manage to do that?"*

Scaling

Professional school counselors use scaling questions with students for a number of reasons, including establishing a baseline to determine students' progress toward their goals. Students are asked to imagine or are shown a scale from zero (lowest) to 10 (highest) and asked to rate their perceived level of goal attainment at that time. Students generally provide a rating greater than zero, which indicates that things could have been worse. Questioning the student about what they did to progress from zero to their current position helps students realize unrecognized personal resources and builds their confidence that they can make progress toward their goals.

Even when students report their current position on the scale as a 0 or a 1, professional school counselors can provide complimentary feedback that highlights students' strengths and bolsters their hope. For example, if a student initially responds that his position on the scale is a zero, the professional school counselor could comment, *"Considering what you have been facing, how have you managed to avoid being at a minus 10?"* Such a response highlights the student's ability to cope with a difficult situation. For a student providing a low initial rating of 1 or 2, the professional school counselor might respond with *"That's great! What did you do to move from a zero to a 2?"*

Once an initial baseline is determined, professional school counselors can encourage a student's further progress by asking, *"What would you need to do to move up one number?"* Through follow-up questions, professional school counselors can help students clarify what behavior or behaviors are needed to make various degrees (i.e., 10%, or a 3 to a 4) of improvement toward their goals. The scale ratings also provide the student and counselor with feedback about progress and reinforce both the student and counselor for their continued efforts for improvement.

Identifying and Overcoming Obstacles to Student Success

To prevent students from becoming discouraged as they pursue their goals, professional school counselors help them identify possible obstacles they might experience. Once obstacles are identified, possible courses of action to avoid or overcome them are explored. Questions such as, *What have you used successfully in the past to keep from getting off track?* are useful in initiating solution-focused discussions.

Concluding the Initial Session

The initial SFBC session is concluded by informing the student that the professional school counselor is going to move to another part of the room for a few minutes in order to reflect on and review the session notes before writing the student a brief message. The message is an extremely important step in SFBC and is comprised of three parts: compliments, bridging statements, and task assignments.

Compliments. Effective messages include a minimum of three compliments that recognize and reinforce the student's strengths, resources, and accomplishments that were identified during the initial session. Using the student's own words that were used during the session makes the message powerful and meaningful. These compliments frequently address a student's desired behaviors, efforts, commitments, attitudes, thoughts, decisions, and attributes. The following is an example of the compliments part of a message: *Your decision to seek counseling demonstrates your maturity and genuine desire to learn how to express your anger in appropriate ways. I'm really impressed with your effort and ability to identify ways you have effectively expressed your anger appropriately in the past. Your insights, intelligence, and flexible thinking all reflect your desire and commitment for positive change.*

Bridging statements. The second part of the message is composed of bridging statements, which connect the compliments to the task part. Bridging statements provide students with a rationale for engaging in tasks that relate to the accomplishment of their goals. The following is a bridging statement that connects what the student wants (goals and solutions) to homework tasks: *Because of your strong desire to express your anger more appropriately, I would encourage you to engage in identified, assigned tasks.*

Tasks. The final part of the message contains task statements. Sklare (2014) recommended that the student's assigned homework tasks be intentionally vague, thereby, indicating confidence and trust in the student's ability to make responsible decisions about what tasks need to be completed to attain the goals. If concerns exist about a student's ability to benefit from vague tasks, the professional school counselor assigns tasks that make reference to the student's successful behaviors that were previously mentioned in the compliments portion of the message. Referring back to the compliments portion of the message written for the student with the anger management problem, the appropriate task portion of this message might include the following: *Because of your strong desire to express your anger more appropriately, I would encourage you to use more of the strategies that you identified that have worked for you in the past, and notice and continue to do what has been working for you.*

Before the initial SFBC session ends, the professional school counselor asks the student if there is any additional information he would like the counselor to know. Professional school counselors conclude the session by having the student assess the need for any additional sessions to accomplish the identified goals.

Subsequent SFBC Sessions

Sklare (2014) used EARS, an acronym for a sequence of steps attributed to Berg, to guide the second and succeeding sessions: **E**licit, **A**mplify, **R**einforce, and **S**tart. Professional school counselors begin these sessions by *eliciting* or asking "What's better or different since the last session?" When students respond by identifying what is better, the professional school counselor *amplifies* these improvements by asking questions that help students recognize how changes in their behavior have favorably affected the behaviors of others. The letter *R* in EARS reminds the professional school counselor to *reinforce* or cheerlead the student for the changes in their behaviors that "made things better." The last step in the EARS sequence is *starting* over again by attempting to elicit, amplify, and reinforce additional student changes that have enabled the student to make progress toward their counseling goals. Following the EARS sequence, *scaling* is once again used to assess progress toward a goal that was achieved since the last session. Students should not be reminded of their previous session scaling responses in order to obtain the most objective assessment of current position.

The additional session's assessment is once again used to determine the need for other meetings. The professional school counselor should begin to spread the sessions and plan for ending sessions completely. The message format continues to be the method for concluding sessions and, if follow-up sessions are necessary, the professional school counselor will continue to use the SFBC approach as outlined in this chapter. Figure 28.1 provides a helpful SFBC template that professional school counselors can use in sessions to keep the counseling process on track.

Summary/Conclusion

This chapter provided an overview of solution-focused brief counseling concepts for the professional school counselor. A quick look at the steps in SFBC has been presented to encourage professional school counselors to try this approach with students. It is efficient, effective, and versatile. SFBC acknowledges the power of focusing on the solution rather than the problem.

Student's Initials _____ Age _____ Gender _____

Session # _____ Date of Session _____ Counselor _____

The Central Philosophy of the SFBC Approach

> 1. If it's not broken, don't fix it.
> 2. If it works, do more of it.
> 3. If it doesn't work, stop doing it. Do something different.

First Session Format: Explain the process including use of questions, note taking, and messages, and provide student opportunity for asking questions.

I. **Obtain presenting goal(s):** (If more than one goal, have student identify the highest priority goal and mark it #1)

   a. "What is/are your goal(s) in coming here?"; "What's the reason you've come to see me?"

   a. *Validate* student's problem/goal and compliment them for wanting to make things better.

   Restate Presenting Goal as a Positive Goal (if needed).

   If Negative (Self): "What would you be doing instead," "if you weren't . . . then what would you . . . ," "be doing differently," "in place of," "rather than," "start doing."

   If Negative (Others): *Change to goals that give the student responsibility.* "If they did change, what would that do for you?" "How can I help you with this?" "How is this a problem for you?" "What difference does this make for you?" "What's the reason for that?"

   If Harmful: *Determine student's reason for wanting harmful goal, reframe as identify healthy goals which meet their needs.* "What's the reason you don't want to . . . ?" "What's the reason you want to . . . ?"

   If Involuntary Student: *Help recognize what they will gain by changing.* "If you were to make this change, what effect would it have on you?" "Would it be in your best interest to want these changes?" "Is what they want for you something that you want as well—especially if it will help solve the problem of . . . ?"

   Detail Goal Solution Steps/Cheerlead/Determine Others Responses

   Use questions to help student describe detailed solutions for goals. "What would you be thinking/doing that show you were working toward or accomplishing . . . ?"; "First thing you would notice you were doing differently/that others would notice?" "If you did that/if that happened how do you think your teacher/etc. would respond to you?"

II. **Ask Solution Question:** "Suppose that during the night, while you were sleeping, *you* solved the problem. What is the first thing you would notice that was different once your awoke?" "What would you be doing differently?"

Figure 28.1. Solution-focused brief counseling template. *(continues)*

III. **Instances–Exceptions/How Brought About/Cheerlead:** (When are some of these things happening already or have happened even just a little bit then how brought about "How did you DO that?" followed by Cheerleading student's successes.)

IV. **Student's Scaling:** (Identify student's current position on a 10-point scale: 0 = *problem worst*; 10 = *problem solved*.) **Cheerlead behaviors that lead to current position.**

(***problem worst***) 0 1 2 3 4 5 6 7 8 9 10 (***problem solved***)

Student's ideas for improving one number on the 10-point scale (What are you going to DO to get from a ___ to a ___?)

Flagging the Minefield (Student's identification of and methods for overcoming obstacles to progress)

V. **Student's Questions About Session/Process, and Counselor's Responses**

VI. **Message:** (Compliments/Bridging Statement/Task) (Provide copy of actual message)

Risk Assessment:

Checked for ABUSE?   Yes/No   If signs or claims of ABUSE report IMMEDIATELY to appropriate authority.

Checked for suicidal/homicidal risk?   Yes/No   Depression Inventory Score _____

If risk, action taken: _____

Additional Assessments:

Troubling Emotion: _____

Behaviors: Needing to be Increased/Taught and/or Decreased: _____

Faulty/Inaccurate or Flawed Cognitions: _____

How would you rate the overall benefit of this counseling session for the student on a scale of 1 to 10? _____

Counselor Notes/Comments: _____

Figure 28.1. (*continued*)

CHAPTER 29

Using Family Systems Interventions in Schools

Bradley T. Erford*

Preview

In this chapter, family systems concepts and strategies that are useful to the professional school counselor are described. Strategies are illustrated by a dozen actual school cases. A four-step initial family systems interview model is presented that is specifically designed to allow for an integrated use of strategies drawn from diverse family systems models.

When families come to me for help, I assume they have problems not because there is something inherently wrong with them but because they've gotten stuck—stuck with a structure whose time has passed and stuck with a story that doesn't work. To discover what's bogging them down, I look for patterns that connect. (Minuchin & Nichols, 1998, p. 43)

Professional school counselors understand that students bring the problems of life outside the school into the school, where problems can negatively influence the educational process. Professional school counselors can employ brief family interventions with students and their families to address educational issues that are linked to the home. Conceptualizing a school problem by its connections to the family system and using family systems techniques to address the problem offers a practical set of strategies for helping students.

Four Categories of Family Adjustment

Family systems interventions are helpful when the student's behavior is a response to stresses and changes with which the family is attempting to cope. When this is the case, it does not necessarily mean there is anything wrong with the family. Rather, it means that the family finds itself in a tough patch on its journey through life.

Pittman's (1987) classic book on treating families in crisis and transition described four categories for thinking about the ways families get stuck in tough patches. First, a family can get stuck trying to cope with a normal task of family development. For example, maybe the family was doing well before the first child had to go to school, but the transition to school for the child is proving a difficult challenge for the family. Second, a family can become stuck

---

*The first edition version of this chapter was written by Dr. Estes J. Lockhart. May he rest in peace.

trying to use a structure with rules that are outdated for the challenges they face. For example, when children enter adolescence, the family faces the task of having to reorganize their rules. Third, a family may be hit with one or more "bolts from the blue"—unexpected stresses, traumas, or discontinuities. For example, a family member may be lost through death, divorce may occur, or the family may be overwhelmed through job loss or illness, causing the family to have trouble coping. A family may find itself in trouble through the stress of having to be a caretaker for another family member with a disability or illness. Finally, whenever stress affects a family system and requires a change to the system's usual repertoire, a crisis can result. Such a crisis can cause nonspecific changes in the family, such as the loosening of boundaries, changing of rules, relaxation of expectations and prohibitions, loss of goals and values, revival of unresolved conflicts, and heightened tension between family members. A student may carry the stress and tension from any of these nonspecific changes resulting from a family crisis into the classroom, where a crisis for the student may result.

Example 1: An Eating Disorder and Decreased Academic Performance

A young girl in elementary school began exhibiting eating problems and decreased academic performance. Her classroom problem was directly related to living alternating weeks in the homes of the two blended families of her divorced, and subsequently remarried, biological parents. The systems intervention was to bring in both biological parents with their new mates, who were now stepparents for the girl, and help the two sets of parents to align their discipline systems. The student was experiencing high anxiety by switching each week from a set of very loose family rules to a set of very rigid family rules. Also, the student was attempting to relate to new stepparents and new stepsiblings. To intervene, the student was informed of the new procedures by both sets of parents in front of the professional school counselor. The professional school counselor then followed up with the girl and checked in by telephone with the two families.

Example 2: A Divorce and Anticipation of Decreased School Performance

The family may inform the professional school counselor of a crisis that is either anticipated or ongoing in the home, and the counselor can then work proactively and collaboratively with the family to prevent the crisis from seriously affecting the student at school. For example, consider a case in which a parent contacted the school counselor seeking help and worried that her child in middle school might be experiencing academic or social problems at school because the student's mother had divorced the student's father. The professional school counselor met with the student using a family systems perspective to address the issue. Together, the father and mother assured the student that the student didn't cause the problem and couldn't cure the problem, but he could cope with it. Coping is a standard message that is helpful for students to hear from divorcing parents. Both the father and mother reassured their son they would be there to support him. The professional school counselor also obtained agreement from both parents that they would not use the student in any way as a pawn, message carrier, or person upon whom to vent on issues related to the failed marriage and divorce. The father arranged his schedule to meet regularly with the son. The purpose of this intervention was to make the changing complexity of the family crisis into a more specific, manageable reality, thus allowing the student to focus on schoolwork.

Example 3: Loss of a Father Through the Catastrophic Illness of AIDS

Sometimes the professional school counselor can help the student by simply conceptualizing that a student's dysfunction at school does not reside solely with the student and by providing resources, including referral information, to the family. For example, consider the case of a bright, very talented student who began to shut down and even become verbally aggressive when given negative feedback in school. The student had lost his father first to marital separation and then to death from AIDS. Prior to the parents' separation, the student felt they blamed him for much of their anger. During the final days of helping his mother take care of his father, the student experienced renewed fights between the three of them, along with negative interactions with his dying, bedridden father (e.g., statements of his failure as a son). The student viewed his situation as one in which he was constantly on edge, feeling rejected by a parent whom he mourned and also felt he had failed at the worst possible moment. The student was helped by having his mother seek his assistance in the grieving process and by her helping him to see that much of the rejection and failure he felt resulted from the failed marriage and his father's depression and pain as he approached death. Feeling blame in the home led to the student acting out at school. There was caretaker stress, bolt-from-the-blue stress, and the structural stress of a family that produced conflict by *triangulation*—in this case, forming an *alliance* between two members to blame a third. It was helpful to have the mother clarify that the son did not cause the divorce. Further, it was helpful for mother and son to understand that classic psychiatric syndromes such as dementia, anxiety, and depressive and psychotic disorders are commonly associated with HIV-related disorders. This made some of the father's behaviors understandable and helped explain the mother's and son's stressful relationships with the father near the end of his life. In this complex case, it was important for the counselor to refer the mother to a family counselor in the community. The professional school counselor then became a case manager, serving as a liaison between school staff, mental health counselor, student, and family. It is important to note that the professional school counselor's initial family session led to the referral to an outside counselor. At home, in counseling, and at school the same message was reinforced: "Don't play the blame game with self or others."

Example 4: The Power of Context in Racial Victimization at School

The unique *context* in connection with *family beliefs,* in this case forces operating within the school, can lead to problems in school. For example, consider the case of a young African American male high school student who was being racially victimized by a group of White students in a school that had only a few minority students. The African American student refused to report verbal assaults against him by the White students and instead let verbal insults continue until they reached the level of physical confrontation. When the student's family was contacted, it was learned that the parents had told the son that racial victimization was simply a fact of life in the United States. They instructed him that in their family the way to handle racial victimization is to pay no attention to it and walk away. The student had been trying to follow his family beliefs. Unfortunately, the White students continued to name-call. The African American student, unable to take it any longer, stood his ground and prepared to fight. Luckily, the principal intervened. A single-session intervention with the African American student's family helped them to see that their response of putting up with racial victimization would not work in the context of their son's school. Unlike the context in their youth, their son had little to no support from peers and was assaulted by students who did not respect the boundaries of others. The intervention was to *challenge family assumptions* in an appropriate and respectful way. The family changed their belief as related to the new school context. The son was encouraged to contact administrators and professional school counselors, who then intervened.

The Family Systems Process

The family is a *self-organizing system* that adapts to the stresses the family faces by sometimes having to reorganize its rules significantly. An example would be the death of a grandmother who had parented the children while both parents worked long hours. It is a system in which various members are connected more or less closely in *subgroups*, for example the parental subgroup or the sibling subgroup. It is a system that draws *boundaries* to control the degree to which those outside any subgroup will communicate or interact with those inside the subgroup. For example, parents might tell their children not to go to a certain place or not to talk with certain people. It is a system in which family members set emotional boundaries to protect individual autonomy, which if too open or too closed, can lead to problems. Where boundaries are too open or loose, relationships can be dysfunctionally cohesive (*enmeshed*). For example, parents of a child with a serious mental health disorder or disability, in an effort to protect the child, may become enmeshed, fearing to set more open boundaries that allow for the child to be independent. The family is a system in which the leadership *hierarchy*, whether weak or strong, rigid or flexible, structured or chaotic, affects all members. Since *family rules* are not always explicit and may be very complex, professional school counselors can not assume anything about the family.

Also, the family is a system that the student cannot ever really leave completely in the sense that we can leave a job. We may attempt to disengage, separate or *cut off* from the family in some way, but we will never completely escape all of its influences. In fact, one of the major challenges that adolescent students in America face is learning how to begin to leave the family appropriately. The families of adolescents may have difficulty helping their children to leave, and this can lead to struggles for power, with ramifications in the schoolhouse. Also, *cultural issues* must be taken into account. For example, a family from South America or Turkey may be sad that their child would even want to think about leaving the family prior to marriage.

The family organizes itself to adapt to environmental challenges and, subsequently, transcends the separate characteristics of individual family members. In one family this might mean individuals would engage in *complementary relationships*, strengthening each other and the family as a whole by providing that which each of the individual members attempting to adjust alone would have trouble providing for themselves. In another family, the attempt to adapt might lead to them getting stuck in a power struggle or some other dilemma.

> Example 5: Preparing to Leave Home Influencing Student Achievement
> Consider the case of a student whose family complained that their daughter wanted to be on her own and was no longer committed to the educational goals she once shared with her family, nor did she want to follow family rules. In this case, there was another issue combined with the normal developmental task of preparing to leave home. The girl served as a

parental child, spending much time after school taking care of her younger siblings. This girl felt undervalued by her parents because she felt they continued to treat her as a child, making rules for her as though she was just another one of their children when she was on the verge of adulthood and parenting the other children. She wanted the freedom of an adult both at home and at school since she took on a parental role at home. Not getting what she expected led to a loss of commitment to the expectations of her parents and a desire to find a way out of the home so that she could be her own person. The student showed lack of motivation in school and began having conflicts with authority figures. The family reorganized positively in several ways. The family changed communication styles with the girl to more resemble those with their adult friends. The family *renegotiated family rules*. The parents remained in charge of the family *hierarchy,* leadership, and decision making but adjusted the rules to recognize their daughter's developmental needs. They also took her out of the role of a parental child so that she was able to enjoy a normal life as an adolescent without the stress of intense parenting responsibilities.

Example 6: Student Violence Ignited by an Extended Family Member

Increasingly, those who take the family systems view address other contexts in the student's life besides the nuclear family. These may include, but are not limited to, in-laws; peer networks; and welfare, health, cultural, racial, ethnic, political, social, legal, sports, and school systems. Consider the following rare and unusual example of the power of an in-law to affect the student's behavior at school. The student would violently attack other students at the drop of a hat. The student had been referred to the county neurological clinic where the examining physician determined that he appeared to have a seizure disorder that would need to be evaluated in a residential center. While waiting for a bed in the residential program, the student was enrolled in an alternative school for troubled youth for part of the day and his regular school part of the day. The widowed mother of the student, who allowed an uncle to live with them, was never able to attend meetings at the school. One day, a school social worker dropped by the mother's home, explaining that she just happened to be in the neighborhood. During the visit, she learned that the uncle was a psychopath whom the mother had taken in as a deathbed request from her husband. This student went to school everyday wondering if his mother would be alive when he returned home and wondering what stress the evening would hold for both of them. Once the mother was helped to report the psychopathic uncle's behavior to the police, he was removed from the home, and the student ceased the violent attacks on other students. The student returned to his regular school full-time without ever needing to attend a residential program. While this example is a rare case, it is not rare for the professional school counselor to intervene with students who act out who live in stressful homes where alcohol, substance abuse, physical abuse, and severe mental health issues of family members produce high anxiety and affect student school performance.

Example 7: Parental Substance Abuse Affecting School Performance

An elementary student was refusing to do classwork and reacting in a hostile way when anyone attempted to make him work. This young elementary student lived with his mother and father in public housing where the parents were doing illegal hard drugs and the young boy was being intimidated daily. He was not able to do well at school because he sat wondering if he would return home to find his parents arrested and removed from the home and his favorite possessions removed from the house. Poverty and illegal drug activity are but two powerful influences in *the larger system*—outside home and school—that the school counselor had to deal with in order to help the student address educational issues. In this case, the counselor first *joined* with the family so that the family respected the professional school counselor as a trusted family member. Joining was a major family systems intervention in that it represented the first time this family, in serious violation of the law, had trusted anyone in the school system. Communication with the family and the school administration had resulted in angry conflicts. The professional school counselor helped the family to agree to *shelve their issues* temporarily with the school administration in order to do what was needed for their child. Next the professional school counselor suggested local resources the family could trust in helping them address their substance abuse issues, realizing that any progress in this area would likely take much time. Collaboration between family and counselor led to the student moving in with a nearby relative for a short time.

Example 8: Student Refusal to Attend School

There can be many possible forces driving a student's dysfunctional behavior. For example, a student may refuse to attend school because he wants to avoid the stress of schoolwork. On the other hand, the student might be experiencing anxiety about separation from a major attachment figure, or worrying about harm befalling a major attachment figure while the student is at school. The student might even fear attack from a gang, or simply find that the long day or interactions with classmates produce anxiety. There are many and varied reasons that might influence a student's refusal to attend school, and they might work in combination. The father of the student may have recently been diagnosed with cancer or there may be an impending parental divorce or loss of income. Any of these family systems dynamics might cause a reorganization of the family that results in anxiety for the student and can be inseparable from other forces working against the student attending school.

For example, consider a case in which a high school student's deceased grandfather had previously lived in the student's home prior to his death. The student's father had a heart attack a few months prior to the student complaining of intense fear upon trying to enter the high school. This was a student who wanted to be in school. He was a high school senior with a high grade point average, a girlfriend at school, and a position on the varsity basketball team. He complained of desperately wanting to be at school, but being terrified by a feeling that all the energy in his body was leaving him as he tried to walk from his car into the school. He said that this had been coming on slowly in other settings like restaurants, and he had been coping by ceasing to visit settings that made him anxious. Now the problem had generalized to his school. The professional school counselor carried out individual desensitization and relaxation training with the student, combined with strengthening the family hierarchy and setting boundaries with his mother, who was enmeshed emotionally with the student. In this case, school refusal was driven by separation anxiety. The student feared that if he left home and became locked into a full day of school, something might happen to someone he loved away from school that would be catastrophic (i.e., his father might suffer another heart attack or his mother with whom he was enmeshed might become ill). He could say that he knew these were irrational fears, but that didn't stop him from having them. His fears led to panic, resulting in a catastrophic feeling of a loss of all the energy in his body. It was important that he be given permission to leave class at any time and check in with parents and that he be allowed to go to the counselor's office as needed to listen to a relaxation tape.

Family Members in Attendance During a Family Systems Intervention

Although it is often helpful to bring in other family members when carrying out a family systems intervention, it is not always necessary. One reason that it can be helpful to bring in other family members is that people have difficulty reporting accurately on their own social situations. Another reason is to engage significant others directly in the support of the student. However, family systems interventions often do not require the attendance of family members. Also, taking a family systems perspective does not mean that the professional school counselor stops thinking about the individual student as an individual, with an individual's own heart, mind, temperament, will, and dreams. One can work individually while using a systems perspective.

For example, if the professional counselor wishes to encourage the student to respond more appropriately in an individual session, the counselor may use the family system intervention of asking the student how his deceased grandmother would advise the student if she were here. In this family systems intervention without any family members present, the influence of a deceased family member can hold great power. This type of family intervention could be referred to as an *invocation of significant others*, and is powerful with students who might otherwise resist or detour around challenging issues. Obviously, the counselor could ask, "If your mother and father or sister or brother were here, would they agree with you?" These are the kinds of questions that allow for the family systems perspective to influence the intervention without any family member present.

Three Models of Family Systems Interventions

There are a wide variety of family systems intervention models. However, today there are few purists, meaning those who rigidly stick to one family system model (Nichols, 2012). The following three models can be useful for the professional school counselor. However, the brief descriptions that follow give only a general sense of each model.

Strategic Family System Interventions

Strategic family therapy describes family problems as being maintained by some combination of unsuccessful problem solving, weak leadership or hierarchy, inability to adjust to transitions in the family life cycle, interactive communication patterns that support dysfunctional interactions, or triangulation relationships that result in coalitions of family members against each other. Problems are resolved by altering the above factors through techniques strategically applied, which often take the form of a directive to be practiced outside of the counseling session. For example, the father and mother might be advised when feeling stress while parenting to avoid any anger at the moment. Instead, the two could meet for 14 minutes in the evening away from the child and each spend 7 minutes explaining his or her thoughts and feelings to the other while the other writes them down and gives no nonverbal or verbal responses. When someone is writing down what is said, it lends support to the feeling of being heard.

When developing strategic family systems, Haley was heavily influenced by a medical doctor and brilliantly creative psychotherapist named Milton Erickson with whom Haley collaborated and about whom Haley wrote (Haley, 1973). Milton Erickson, a hypnotherapist, had an uncanny ability to use language creatively to enlist a client's support in the process of change. One of Erickson's most powerful skills was to use metaphors and stories to engage the client and make indirect suggestions, often below the level of consciousness during an intervention. Haley suggested becoming a "metaphor enthusiast." Using metaphors, or recalling an interesting story analogous to the student's own situation, encourages increased engagement of the student in the intervention. The following application of the strategic model demonstrates the application of major strategic techniques in a school setting, including the use of therapeutic metaphor.

Example 9: Adolescent Who Fights With Peers

This case involves the family of an adolescent son who had begun to engage in serious fights with peers. A conversation with the family led to the conclusion that since the student had not had this anger problem prior to adolescence, it was possible that something could be happening with the family's adaptation to adolescence. This helped to *normalize* the situation by helping the family move from thinking of the adolescent as being abnormal and their family as dysfunctional to thinking of the family as needing to make a perfectly normal adjustment to a common life-cycle event, adolescence. The family set more appropriate limits and response costs and the parents were encouraged to continue to reach out to the son by telling him they were there to help him. The family needed to learn how to avoid getting into *triangular relationships* in which one parent would side with the son against the other when discipline issues at school were reported to the family. They needed support to believe that they still had influence on this young man.

Example 10: Strategic Use of Metaphor to Support Parents

The parents in the previous example stated that they were worried about making decisions for their son. They said he was always accusing them of disrespecting him by setting all the rules rather than letting him take care of himself. But they said they felt caught in a bind because while they wanted to give him more freedom, they feared the outcome if they did, and they lost power through inaction. The metaphor of a ship at sea in a threatening storm was used to drive home the importance of the parents taking charge in the family. They were told to imagine they were out at sea on an ocean liner and a big storm threatens. They were asked which of the following statements from the captain would make them feel more secure: "Relax, stay inside. We have been through many of these storms before, and we know what to do," or "Look, I'd like to get your opinion on what would be the best course of action." And just imagine one's anxiety if the captain actually offered one control of the ship in such a situation. The family said they came back to this metaphor over and over again when feeling under duress from their son.

Also, this family had a *repetitive sequence of behavior* which they continued to try even though it failed them. The mother and father, unable to decide what to do about the son's anger at home and school, would sometimes begin to argue with each other over how to respond to their son's behavior. The mother would call for the father's help in disciplining the son. As the father, a rather quiet and analytical man, attempted to reason with his son, the mother would tell the father that he was not being tough enough in supporting her. Soon the parents would be fighting with each other as the son with the anger problem looked on and criticized them. The parents were challenged to communicate in a way that would break this repetitive cycle and be a better model for their son. A metaphor of a real experiment was used in which two rats in a cage receiving electric shock first tried to avoid the shocks by running around, and then, when the shocks continued, turned on each other. The parents said that was exactly how they felt. It was suggested that, when feeling at their wit's end, unlike the rats they could take a break and, when feeling a bit less stressed, return to problem-solving in a better state of mind.

Structural Family Systems Intervention

The professional school counselor using structural family systems interventions looks for maladaptive boundaries, maladaptive hierarchy, or maladaptive reactions to changing developmental or social conditions as factors that can maintain problems. Problems are resolved by creating clear, flexible boundaries and more adaptive and flexible hierarchy responses to changing developmental or social conditions. The sequence of change in the structural model is to (a) join and accommodate to the family and (b) help the family change its structure.

Example 11: A Gender Issue in a Stepfamily and at School

A young man from a blended family was disrespectful to female classmates. The professional school counselor helped the family to focus on the need for the student to learn more appropriate *boundaries*. For example, boundaries between the mother and student were nonexistent, leaving them emotionally fused or *enmeshed*. The student and mother would talk to each other as friends or equals, and the student would speak to her not as a respected woman, but as a buddy. This made it difficult for the mother to separate herself as the parent. Meanwhile, the boundaries between student and stepfather were closed, resulting in disengagement with little communication. In this situation, the professional school counselor invited the parents in and set an initial goal of *joining* with them. Once joined with the family, the professional school counselor was able to *reframe* the mother's enmeshment in a positive light. This parent behavior of being overly protective of her child, was reframed as, *You just seem to love your child too much*. The mother accepted this. The professional school counselor *highlighted strengths and weaknesses*, such as the need for a discussion and reinforcement of appropriate boundaries for their son with regard to interactions with females. After joining sufficiently to be able to give negative feedback without loss of family respect, the counselor suggested that the stepfather and son spend more time together having fun and discussing, among other things, how to act appropriately with females. This helped by *shifting the family members' relative positions* to interrupt the pattern in which the stepfather and son interacted only for discipline reasons.

Constructivist Family Systems Interventions

In a constructivist approach, the intervention is conceived as a collaboration in which the professional school counselor and student together construct a more desirable reality. Two examples of constructivist theory are solution-focused interventions and narrative-focused interventions. The professional school counselor's role in the constructivist approach is to acknowledge, praise and in other ways highlight and punctuate strengths of the family and collaborate with the family to arrive at resources and solutions for facing the family's challenging situation. The constructivist tends to ask questions more about what has gone right rather than what has gone wrong. They tend to collaborate rather than direct or coach. Virginia Satir (1988) anticipated the constructivist way of viewing the problem when she would refer to a problem as an accident in the interest of the self. The attempt by Satir was to normalize a situation by making it an accident that happened for the best of reasons, the needs of the self.

Constructivist interventions make much use of *looking for exceptions,* in which the student and/or family act competently. The family is then encouraged to do more of their competent-type behavior. Both solution-focused and narrative-focused constructivist approaches make use of the *miracle question* in which the family imagines awaking one morning and finding everything is as it should be (see Chapter 28). This allows the family to begin building a vision more consistent with their ideal of how they would like to live. Solution-focused interventions are one of the most popular of our day because they are cognitive in emphasis, easy to teach, and promise quick solutions (Nichols, 2012).

In constructivist approaches, the attempt is to help the family construct a sense of hope for the future out of the current situation based on successes in other situations. Both solution-focused and narrative-focused interventions give much attention to the language used to communicate about the situation that is presented. This involves the way in which a family conceives their situation and the language they use will either empower them to find the resources they need to succeed or disempower them. Haley (1973) anticipated this concern of the constructivists when he said, "The way one labels a human dilemma can crystallize a problem and make it chronic" (p. 3).

Example 12: A Middle School Student With ADHD

A middle school student was not staying on task in class. The family said that the main problem was ADHD. The student indicated in the session that either she was being unfairly picked on by the teacher or the work was boring and she got fidgety. The parents said that she had told them the main problems were the teacher doesn't like the student, the student can't get any help from the teacher, and the work is either too easy or too difficult. The professional school counselor, using a narrative intervention, asked the whole family for a meeting to discuss the way they would like their story to proceed. In the narrative approach, the counselor *stayed one down,* on an equal footing or below the power level of the family. The counselor's goal was simply to carry on a conversation to help the family determine how they would like to rewrite their family story so that it fit with their view of how they would like to be as a family.

The family preferred a story in which the student would heroically begin to complete homework, stay on task in school doing what she was directed to do, and actively seek help from the teacher when needed. The professional school counselor, using the narrative approach, helped the family to *externalize* the off-task behavior as a monster that would require the family working together to defeat. This *externalization of the problem* is a powerful technique for placing the problem outside the family and removing debilitating blame.

The professional school counselor used *language that suggested a successful ending* by saying to the student and family, "Well, when you are no longer having conflicts with the teacher and you are performing regularly, what kinds of relationships will you then have with your family or teacher?" The parents were also asked how they would feel when all of them had succeeded in defeating the monster. They talked of happiness, relief, joy, and a desire to do more interesting and fun things together. The professional school counselor *celebrated small changes* and approximations toward the desired behavior so that successes could begin to be experienced by the student and family. The counselor also worked with the psychiatrist to give feedback on the effects of the medication.

To clarify differing opinions, family members used a scaling intervention. Scaling is a technique regularly used in solution-focused interventions to encourage clearer more concrete understandings of how each situation is viewed by family members. Scaling can also be used as a baseline against which to measure change as student, teacher, and family report improvement or lack of progress. The student was also helped to *deconstruct a myth* the student had been using to cope with feelings of incompetence. The myth was that it is better to act out than to fail, look foolish, and take another blow to her self-esteem. This myth made its appearance in statements by the student, such as "What's the use anyway?" The teacher also indicated the student's lack of self-esteem by saying, "When she gets a little help at the start of a new lesson, she does well, but when she doesn't, she will just give up after hardly trying." The professional school counselor suggested that learning patience and delaying gratification is a sign of increasing maturity. The parents agreed. The goal of the constructivist approach is that the family will have renewed hope.

Initial Family Systems Interview for Professional School Counselors

The *initial family interview* is important because it is the first step in meeting the family and attempting to intervene. Following is a four-step initial interview model for professional school counselors using strategic, structural, and constructivist techniques and interventions.

Four-Step Initial Family Intervention Model

Step one: Welcoming, joining, and reassuring. Begin the interview by making sure everyone feels as comfortable as possible, connect with all individuals in a way that helps to establish rapport, and communicate reassurance that the professional school counselor cares about the pain in the family and is here to help all of them. A good reassuring statement to the family by the counselor is, "I am sorry this is happening to you, and I am going to work hard to help you." *Stay one down* and *listen empathetically.*

Step two: Interacting, normalizing, and collaborating. Encourage family interaction and discussion around what has been attempted in the family effort to get unstuck and how the family is succeeding in difficult situations. Often it can help to view the situation as a normal part of the family life cycle, individual development, or a bolt from the blue no one could predict which precipitated a crisis. *Highlight family strengths and encourage more of what works.* Discourage continuing what has failed. Treat the family with respect and parents as experts on their child.

Step three: Searching for patterns that connect and planning a new vision. Listen to the family for their story of the situation. Whether through directives, coaching, or collaboration, help them to *frame, reframe, dream* or in some way *construct a more useful family story* along with concrete goals to make their vision a reality. Metaphors can help make a vision clear. For example, where blame has been a problem, the metaphor "Sounds like you are hoping future sights along the way won't be colored by earlier accidents" could be used. Or one might say, "It is hard to drive a car forward when looking through the rearview mirror."

Step four: Agreeing on a plan of positive action. This step involves the family planning the necessary action for getting back on the road to a hopeful future. It can be helpful to provide a way to monitor the intervention, perhaps through brief phone calls.

Summary/Conclusion

"Families don't walk in and hand you the underlying structural patterns that are keeping them stuck. What they bring is the noise—their own confusion and pain" (Minuchin & Nichols, 1998, p. 46). The task of the professional school counselor is to join with the family and look for the patterns that connect. Family members often reveal these patterns in stories that are memories connected to the situation at hand. These stories provide a map of the implicit rules of the family as they attempt to cope with their child's difficulties at school. Many times, the family presents the story of their child's school problem as a crisis in their family. Often this crisis of the family involves worrying how to respond to a current demand for changes to their rules and roles. In responding to the family crisis, the professional school counselor must integrate family systems techniques and interventions wisely in a way that empowers the family to help the student cope in school. This is a difficult task. It requires an appreciation of the complexity of family systems. It requires skill to encourage families to alter repetitive patterns of interaction that keep them stuck. Helping families requires the professional school counselor to respect the family's dreams and beliefs while helping them access their own resources to achieve positive change.

CHAPTER 30

Integrating Knowledge of Learning Styles and Multiple Intelligences in Counseling Diverse Students

*Bradley T. Erford**

Preview

Implementing the concepts of learning styles and multiple intelligences theory into counseling practice provides professional school counselors with additional tools for working with diverse students by encouraging students to view themselves broadly and develop their abilities in wide-ranging areas. Resultant techniques can provide a practical means to enrich the counseling process and empower individual students by approaching them in readily understandable ways as well as encourage less competitive, more productive, team-oriented approaches to life and work.

Using Multiple Intelligences Perspectives in Counseling Diverse Youth

Much of the effectiveness in counseling and teaching comes from the ability to see human beings from different perspectives and to interact in ways that are appropriate to each person's individuality. Much of the harm that results from stereotyping and prejudice springs from viewing people from narrow perspectives and losing sight of that individuality. Theories of multiple intelligences have become more widely used in educational classrooms and offer school personnel important considerations for effective practice. The central theme of these theories is that intelligence is more than a single, unitary factor, such as the intelligence quotient (IQ). Several researchers (Cattell, 1987; Guilford, 1982; Thurstone, 1938) have attempted to identify different kinds of intelligences. However, the most specific theoretical frameworks have come from the work of Howard Gardner and Robert Sternberg.

Gardner's Developmental Framework

Gardner (2011) suggested that the definition of intelligence using traditional quantitative measures, such as the IQ test, was far too narrow in scope. Gardner defined intelligence as

---

*Special thanks to David J. Lundberg and Brenda S. Hall for their outstanding contributions to the first edition of this chapter.

Table 30.1 Gardner's Multiple Intelligences

Linguistic/Verbal intelligence focuses on the production and use of words and language used in listening, speaking, reading, and writing. Example occupations: writers, poets, journalists, politicians, orators.

Logical/Mathematical intelligence pertains to higher order thinking, inductive and deductive reasoning, manipulation of numbers, the capacity to recognize patterns, and the ability to connect logical mathematical operations. Example occupations: mathematicians, engineers, microbiologists.

Visual/Spatial intelligence uses skills involving spatial configurations, such as visualizing an object and creating mental images such as pictures, paintings, diagrams, or maps. Example occupations: artists, navigators, designers, topologists.

Bodily/Kinesthetic intelligence addresses skills using the entire body or parts of the body through physical movement. It involves knowledge of the body, how it moves, and how it can be used to express emotion, solve motor problems, or construct products or displays. Example occupations: dancers, athletes, actors, builders.

Musical/Rhythmical intelligence relates to music such as tonal patterns, rhythm, and beat. It involves recognizing, manipulating, and repeating musical sounds and rhythms. Example occupations: musicians, singers, musical performers.

Interpersonal intelligence addresses skills in interactions with others and involves the ability to get along with others, communication, and sensitivity to the concerns of other people. Example occupations: counselors, teachers, salespeople.

Intrapersonal intelligence centers around knowledge of oneself and involves awareness of one's internal aspects. It includes access to one's own feelings and emotions as well as an understanding of metacognition (how one thinks about thinking). Individuals who share themselves through literature, art, and speech display this intelligence.

Naturalist intelligence addresses the ability to recognize and classify living things and features of the natural world (e.g., animals, minerals, plants). Example occupations: farmers, biologists, chefs.

problem-solving abilities valued in one or more cultural or community contexts. This definition expanded intelligence to include cultural and motivational factors. Gardner rejected the notion that there is only one form of intelligence, arguing that all individuals possess several intelligences with specific types of intelligence stronger in different persons. He maintained the importance of hereditary factors but insisted that societal values, cultural resources, and individual opportunities are paramount in understanding and recognizing intelligences. Gardner's perspective is multifaceted and pluralistic. Within his developmental framework are eight independent abilities, summarized in Table 30.1. Gardner believed individuals are born with the capacity to develop all eight intelligences, although cultural, social, and personal contexts determine how each intelligence is manifested. Thus, because each student's experience in the world is different, each will display a unique range of intellectual strengths and weaknesses. As such, students should not be categorized as being high or low in an intelligence area, but rather appreciated for the full range of their various intellectual abilities, each of which can be strengthened and expanded.

Sternberg's Triarchic Framework

Robert Sternberg's early work on intelligence supported the view that traditional intelligence testing was too narrow. He sought to understand the information processing components re-

Table 30.2 Sternberg's Triarchic Model

Analytical Intelligence is similar to traditionally valued analytic ability and involves problem solving, monitoring solutions, and evaluating results. It refers to how individuals process information and relate to the external world.

Creative Intelligence uses insight and original thought. It reflects how individuals use what they already know and develop new and different ways to complete tasks. Creative intelligence involves using imagination, innovation, and creativity to see the world in different ways.

Practical Intelligence can be referred to as "street smarts"—the ability to take what is learned and apply it to everyday living. This involves the ability to assess a situation and decide how to respond.

lated to the standard intelligence trait (Spearman's g). Sternberg (2007) outlined a theory of intelligence emphasizing three distinct, yet interrelated patterns that can be measured and developed. These facets are summarized in Table 30.2. Like Gardner, Sternberg emphasized the cultural, social, and personal influences on intelligence. Sternberg's theory of intelligence incorporated universal aspects of cognition as well as sources of group and individual differences.

Gardner and Sternberg: Common Ground

Gardner and Sternberg arrived at their conclusions about intelligence in very different ways. Sternberg worked from a more traditional scientific base and emphasized the empirical foundation for his theory of intelligence. Gardner emphasized the use of data. Gardner and Sternberg shared the idea that this broader view of intelligences can be translated into educational practice. Sternberg (1998) has formulated specific principles of teaching for developing successful intelligences and reforming education. Many educators have discussed the applications of Gardner's work to instructional practices in schools and the implementation of multiple intelligences principles has occurred in schools across the country. Commonalities from the work of Sternberg (2007) and Gardner (2011) include the following:

1. All individuals have different minds with varying strengths and weaknesses.
2. People use aspects or types of intelligences based on a multitude of factors (e.g., cultural, social, personal) and experiences.
3. Intelligences can be developed and strengthened.
4. Intelligences can be assessed (although a widely accepted single instrument has not been developed).
5. It is important for educators and counselors to recognize and pay attention to different intellectual abilities.
6. Educators should develop educational strategies and use multiple approaches that encourage the use and development of various aspects of intelligences.

Recommended Counseling Actions and Strategies Using Multiple Intelligences

Table 30.3 provides suggestions for using multiple intelligences to enhance the counseling process in three major areas: self-knowledge, possible courses of action, and self-esteem.

Table 30.3 Counseling Applications of Multiple Intelligence Theories

Self-Knowledge

Find out about the student's culture, including values, resources, and opportunities.

Pay attention to the specific needs and talents of each child.

Help students examine their own assumptions about their potential, achievement, environment, thoughts, feelings, behaviors, needs, and concerns.

Create an environment that exposes individuals to the various intelligences through a variety of activities and a multitude of resources.

Provide opportunities for students to express themselves through diverse interventions and strategies such as talking, writing, drawing, puppets, role play, music, poetry, and small-group interaction.

Promote the awareness of individual strengths and weaknesses and the development of hidden talents.

Involve students in both individual and group interaction so that interpersonal and intrapersonal talents are discovered.

Possible Courses of Action

Encourage students to use self-knowledge and provide opportunities for them to practice new knowledge of self.

Help students reframe a problem using multiple intelligences to achieve a positive outcome. Once students realize that there is more than one way to resolve an issue or complete a task, they can use their self-knowledge, various talents, and resources to successfully address the concern.

Show students how to synthesize self-knowledge, possible courses of action, and evaluate which talents are most appropriate in specific situations. Synthesizing this information opens eyes to new and different possibilities and allows for new perspectives.

Self-Esteem

Plan activities that allow students to express and apply various types of intelligences that lead students to understand the relationship between their intelligences and their work in school.

Through interaction in small groups and other intrapersonal activities, individuals build social skills, learn to control their behavior, and enhance their self-esteem with peers. As students gain self-awareness they can appreciate and feel good about themselves as unique individuals. Students, especially low achievers, can build on successes and set goals that allow them to accomplish something meaningful in school.

Using Learning Styles in Counseling

Understanding the concept of learning styles opens another avenue for interacting with diverse clients in a way that values each as a unique individual and allows a fresh and different way to expand counseling approaches to the helping process. The concept of learning styles, like that of multiple intelligences, offers a specific framework to interact with diverse students in ways that are harmonious and natural for those clients. These approaches promise not only increased effectiveness for professional school counselors but also refreshing and stimulating methods to invigorate the counseling process.

Learning Styles: How They Differ From Multiple Intelligences

Learning styles theory is concerned with differences in the process of learning, emphasizing the ways individuals think and feel as they absorb, process, and internalize information.

An individual learning style is a unique collection of skills and preferences that affect how a person perceives, gathers, and processes information. Learning styles models seek to identify affinities for specific instructional environments, strategies, and resources. While learning styles and multiple intelligences are well documented, hold widespread interest in the educational community, and provide important implications for student development, they are very different concepts. Multiple intelligences theory is an effort to understand how culture and experiences shape human potential. Multiple intelligences focus on the content and products of education but do not address the individualized process of learning. Gardner (2011) explained that

> in MI theory, I begin with a human organism that responds (or fails to respond) to different kinds of contents in the world such as language, number, and other human beings. . . . Those who speak of learning styles are searching for approaches that ought to characterize all contents: a person who is deliberate with respect to music as well as to mathematics, a person who sees the "big picture" whether he is doing physics or painting. (pp. 44–45)

While both constructs promote a multifaceted approach to learning, their differences can be summarized as follows:

- Multiple intelligences theory focuses on the unique talents and strengths of students. Learning styles theories focus on individual preferences in the learning process.
- Multiple intelligences theory is an outgrowth of cognitive theory, related to intelligence testing; learning styles theories have roots in personality theory.
- Multiple intelligences theory addresses what is taught (content); learning styles theories emphasize how it is taught (process).
- Empirical studies relating multiple intelligences and student achievement are limited, while the impact of learning styles on student achievement is well documented statistically.
- Specific instruments for measures of multiple intelligences are being developed and tested. Learning styles assessments yielding valid and reliable scores already exist.

Models of Learning Styles

Learning style is broadly defined as the individual differences in the way learners approach the task of learning. More specifically, a learning style is the way each person begins to concentrate on, process, internalize, and retain difficult and new information (Dunn, Denig, & Lovelace, 2001). One's learning style preferences affect how a person learns, solves problems, and relates to others. Styles of learning tend to change and develop as people grow. Learning style models recognize the role of cognitive and affective processes, and they bring attention to issues related to motivation and student achievement.

Understanding learning styles can be useful to students and professionals in several ways. Knowing their preferences helps students to plan for learning and to develop personal study strategies. Professionals can use individual learning preferences to design and implement effective instructional environments, strategies, and resources. Research supports the idea that when students are taught new and different information through instructional approaches that respond to their learning style preference, they score higher on achievement tests (Dunn et al., 2001).

One of the most widely recognized and researched learning styles models for elementary and secondary school students is the Dunn and Dunn (1992, 1993) framework. It focuses on 21 unique elements that can be classified into five distinct categories:

- *Classroom environment* elements include light (bright/soft), sound (sounds/silence), room temperature (cool/warm), and seating (formal/casual).
- *Emotionality* elements include levels of motivation, persistence, responsibility, conformity, and preferences for structure. Some students are persistent in terms of high levels of motivation or focus, and they provide their own structure. Others need direction for task initiation, focus, and structure.
- *Sociological* elements include learning alone, with peers, with collegial or authoritative adults, and the need for variety versus routine.
- *Physiological* elements include perceptual elements (auditory, visual, tactile, kinesthetic), time-of-day energy highs and lows, preference for snacks or fluids while learning, and the need for mobility versus passivity.
- *Psychological* elements include several methods of processing information. Individuals with strongly analytic preferences approach facts in a step-by-step sequence by first examining specific facts and then gradually integrating them into a whole concept. Global learners first address the overall concept before mastering the specific facts.

Learning Styles Assessment

School professionals can assess a few characteristics of learning style preferences through observation, but there are specific instruments designed to examine the multidimensional characteristics of learning. Each learning styles model has its own assessment tool. Dunn, Dunn, and Price (1989) developed the *Learning Style Inventory* (LSI) to correspond with the 21 elements in their model. This questionnaire is the predominant learning preference assessment for school-age children. It was developed using content and factor analysis, and consists of 104 self-reported questions. The LSI uses a 3-point scale for Grades 3 through 4 and a 5-point scale for Grades 5 through 12. Completion time is 30 to 40 minutes. Research supported the LSI as an instrument yielding reliable and valid scores (Dunn & DeBello, 1999). Adaptations of the LSI are *Our Wonderful Learning Styles* (OWLS) for Grades 2 through 5 and *Learning Style: The Clue To You* (LS:CY) for Grades 6 through 8. These tools identify elements associated with processing information from a broad perspective prior to examining the specific facts (global learning). Both assessments use various methods such as imagery, humor, fantasy, and imagination (Dunn, 1999).

Learning Styles and School Counseling

Current school counseling practices require that professional school counselors actively engage in the ongoing development of students. By understanding, assessing, and using learning styles, counselors are better equipped to design and facilitate developmental strategies and interventions that meet the needs of diverse students. Inclusion of learning styles into counseling practice requires an understanding of learning styles models. Conceptualization of specific learning characteristics and preferences provides a framework for addressing individual student differences. With this knowledge, professional school counselors can assess individual learning styles and choose appropriate strategies and interventions.

In consultation with teachers and administrators, professional school counselors can use learning styles to develop optimal instructional practices for individual students and assist parents and caregivers in the understanding and accommodation of the child's educational and personal needs. Research in the area of counseling interventions and learning style preferences was limited, but Griggs (1991) provided a system for matching specific counseling interventions with individual students' learning style preferences. Learning styles models provide professional school counselors with the opportunity to try a multitude of techniques.

Recommended Counseling Actions and Strategies Using Learning Style Models

Griggs (1985, 1991) suggested that the learning style elements of structure, perceptual strength, motivation, the sociological preferences, and the psychological factors are particularly relevant to counseling. The corresponding categories for these characteristics as outlined in the Dunn and Dunn model are emotionality, sociological, physiological, and psychological. The following are examples of possible counseling interventions to accommodate different modes within these areas.

Emotionality

With students who exhibit a need for more structure and motivation, professional school counselors may find that behavioral approaches are more suitable. The counselor and student may meet to set specific goals, using structured resources and techniques such as behavioral contracts. This type of learner tends to expect the professional school counselor to initiate tasks and provide concrete solutions to issues. For students who are not likely to seek additional assistance, it is beneficial for the counselor to actively follow up on pending issues. Counselors should provide structured exercises as well as expectations for listening and talking for those students engaged in group work. Students preferring less structure may benefit from person-centered approaches, which allow feelings and desires to be expressed freely. Opportunities can be provided by the counselor for the student to initiate new behaviors and solutions.

Sociological

Students who prefer learning alone may reject group methods and not respond well to group counseling. Others may respond well in a group setting but have more difficulty with individual modalities. For the group-oriented student, peer groups can be effectively used to promote participation and growth. Group counseling techniques for peer-oriented preferences may include dramatization of past experiences and present situations. Through role-playing and mime, students can safely express emotions, portray various aspects of their personhood, and practice how to handle confrontations. For the student with a preference for learning on an individual basis, bibliotherapy is an effective strategy. The professional school counselor may choose several types of reading materials through which the counseling theme will be centered, basing the choices on the age, specific concerns, and needs of the individual students. It is important that the counselor be able to discern whether the student is one who prefers the rhythm and routine of regular, predetermined group and individual sessions, or one who is more comfortable "dropping-in" to see the counselor without a scheduled appointment.

Physiological

The auditory, visual, tactile, and kinesthetic senses have a great impact on learning. Auditorily-perceptive students filter information using their listening skills, preferring to accept data by hearing it. Auditory learners find it easier to repeat words, recall conversations, and recite lines from reading materials. Traditional "talking through" counseling approaches often work best with these individuals. Visual learners most often think by using images and pictures. They translate what is heard into images in their minds. Counseling strategies centered on observation, written materials, and imagery fit the visual preference. It is important for counselors to serve as role models and provide opportunities for observing the behaviors of others, such as peers and family members. Use of videotapes, films, books, and other written texts help individuals in the imagery of desired behaviors and solutions to problems. Once visualized, the behavior is often easily carried out.

Tactile and kinesthetic perceptual styles overlap. Having a tactile learning style means that the person learns best by touching. The kinesthetic style requires that the learner becomes physically involved in the experience for best results. These types of students often prefer to learn through movements that involve gross motor skills. Active learners thrive with "hands on" counseling approaches. The use of puppetry, drawing, painting, dance, and other creative art interventions provide alternative ways for emotional release and communication. Movement and manipulation of objects throughout the counseling session may assist kinesthetic learners to share their feelings and thoughts.

Psychological

Analytic processors think in a step-by-step sequential pattern. They examine the facts, absorb them, and formulate a conceptual framework. Global learners must understand the concept or idea first; then they attend to specifics. When working with analytic thinkers it is important to be concrete and focus on details. Professional school counselors should be direct and ask pointed questions. Strongly analytic individuals prefer a more formal interaction. Students who process globally need to gain an understanding of a situation before giving attention to its particular components. Professional school counselors can help these individuals by allowing them to talk in general terms about their concerns before identifying specific aspects they wish to address. The use of illustrations and the sharing of anecdotes are methods counselors can use to help clients determine the focus of their counseling experience. Global thinkers feel comfortable in a more casual environment; nondirective strategies work best.

Summary/Conclusion

Continual assessment of multiple intelligences in counseling enhances the interaction between student and counselor, creating an environment that allows comfort, expression of the whole person, and maximum growth. Through the counseling process, individuals can become aware of the types of intelligences, identify their stronger talents, and develop strategies to effectively use those skills. Equally important is the opportunity for students to build on prominent intelligences and try new ways of expression, thus using one intelligence area to strengthen another. Professional school counselors who continually evaluate client development within the multiple intelligences framework can promote a fuller spectrum of personal, social, and intellectual capabilities in students. Beyond the school setting, this can lead to less competitive, more productive, team-oriented approaches to life and work. Combining learning styles and multiple intelligences can provide holistic models that reflect diversity and individual uniqueness. Attention to these models provides professional school counselors with multidimensional strategies to fulfill their mission of fostering learning and growth in all students. Multiple intelligences represent individual talents reflected by cultural, social and personal influences. Learning styles define how students acquire, store, and present information. Integration of these theories allows professional school counselors to understand both the broader context of each student's unique personal environment as well as the individualized processes of learning.

CHAPTER 31

Group Counseling in Schools

Gary E. Goodnough and Vivian V. Lee

Preview

In this chapter, we discuss the different kinds of group counseling experiences offered in schools and examine strategies professional school counselors use to form groups and collaborate with other leaders in the school. We also provide a rationale for why professional school counselors need to offer a full menu of groups and information that will help implement group counseling as a central component of a systemic school counseling program.

To understand the role of group counseling in schools, professional school counselors must first understand systemic data-driven school counseling programs. The purpose of these programs is to promote academic success by supporting and enhancing the academic, career, and personal–social development needs of all students. These needs are identified through the examination of data, based on a systemic assessment of all constituencies within the school community (Lee & Goodnough, 2015). Goals are formulated and competencies are developed from the identified needs. These competencies identify what students should learn as a result of participating in a systemic data-driven school counseling program. Competencies are delivered to students via levels of programmatic intervention. Group counseling is one level of intervention or service delivery within the structure of school counseling programs.

Within a systemic data-driven school counseling program, group counseling is a means of delivering direct, targeted, and more intensive services to K–12 students. In this way, group counseling, like other aspects of the school counseling program, is data driven and linked to the mission of schools. The professional literature suggests that group counseling is helpful to students (Erford, 2014; Whiston, Feldwisch, & James, 2015). Increasingly, such group counseling interventions have solid empirical research to back claims of promoting social, career, and academic development (e.g., Muris, Meesters, Vincken, & Eijkelenboom, 2005; Paone, Packman, Maddux, & Rothman, 2008; Webb, Brigman, & Campbell, 2005; Webb & Myrick, 2003). First, group counseling is an efficient intervention when compared to individual counseling, as the counselor can see multiple students simultaneously. Second, from a developmental and pedagogical perspective, students often learn best from each other. Group counseling provides an excellent forum to promote such student-to-student learning. Related to this, the power of the peer group can be garnered for positive growth and development under the skillful leadership of the professional school counselor. Finally, groups are a microcosm of society and as such provide real-life settings in which students can work out issues and problems (Corey, 2013; Gladding, 2012). Group counseling is a major function endorsed by the American

School Counselor Association (ASCA), and research suggests that 90% of professional school counselors spend some time providing group counseling to students (ASCA, 2012a).

Group counseling is one of the professional school counselor's most highly specialized skills. As such, it is important for counselors to have a thorough grounding in group counseling theory and practice. In addition, professional school counselors need to know how to take a leadership role and successfully implement group counseling into school counseling programs. Therefore, we will examine the different kinds of groups offered in schools, types of group interventions, strategies to use in forming groups, and how to collaborate with other school leaders to offer a full menu of group topics that have the potential to benefit all in the school system.

Group Counseling: Developmental, Targeted Needs, and School Climate Groups

What is group counseling in schools? Group counseling initiatives within a larger systemic data-driven school counseling program address developmental milestones, provide remediation, and promote a healthy climate within the school. By "developmental milestones" we mean that professional school counselors can reasonably expect that most or all students would benefit from participating in groups designed to promote academic, career, and personal–social development (see Stein, Henfield, & Booker, 2014). For example, developmental groups that address academic development include study skills, test-taking strategies, and transition to middle or high school. Career development groups include goal setting and decision making, transitions to postsecondary options, career exploration, and college planning. Personal–social groups include peer relationships, friendship, self-esteem, forming safe-healthy romantic relationships, personal empowerment, and accepting a newborn sibling.

Group counseling is targeted in nature when it addresses topics or issues that affect only subgroups of students and which may impair the learning and development of specific groups of students. Targeted groups help subgroups of students develop coping skills to assist them in coming to terms with difficult personal and social issues. These groups seek to empower students to regain control over their lives and engage (or reengage) in the learning process. Groups that address targeted issues may include divorce and family separation, sexual identity, substance use (self, family member, or friend), grief and loss, coping with HIV/AIDS in the family, anger management, conflict resolution, and learning to live in a blended family. Some groups are offered around issues that affect a large group of students. For instance, in regions where the military has bases, parents and family members frequently must leave home to serve in the military. Such deployments cause upheaval and uncertainty in a large number of homes and impede the learning process of many students.

Targeted group counseling also dovetails with contemporary school intervention models. Response to Intervention (RTI) is a system of interventions used in schools that organizes interventions according to need (Ehren, 2013). Level I interventions are available to all students. For instance, all students receive reading instruction in the regular classroom. Those who have difficulty are given more intensive (Level II) interventions. Thus, those who have difficulty reading get pulled out of class for more targeted instruction in a smaller group. The parallel to school counseling is that Level I interventions, such as classroom guidance in bullying prevention, are available to everyone. Those who have difficulty learning and applying the learning might need a more targeted intervention, such as group counseling.

Finally, some targeted group topics may include issues that affect all students. These issues might be natural disasters such as a hurricanes, tornadoes, or wildfires, or traumatic events such as mass shootings, school violence, or student deaths. Targeted group counseling can help students debrief the trauma they experience in the immediate aftermath of these and other tragedies. The issues that arise from these events, when unresolved, impair personal growth and impede the learning process. By responding to the targeted needs of students through group counseling, professional school counselors deliver an important and highly specialized service.

A third category of groups that professional school counselors offer addresses the culture and climate of the school. Some of these groups include issues related to diversity awareness, bias and prejudice reduction, conflict resolution, and respect of self and others (see Tauriac, Kim, Lambe Sarinana, Tawa, & Kahn, 2013). These groups may also address the cultural and institutional barriers to learning of certain groups of students (e.g., students of color; students who are gay, lesbian, bisexual or transgendered; students from lower socioeconomic status groups). Professional school counselors provide the needed support to these and other student groups (e.g., Edwards, Adams, Waldo, Hadfield, & Biegel, 2014; Shin et al., 2010) to help remove individual and systemic barriers and provide for equitable learning conditions and access to the best that school and society offer. (See Table 31.1 for an overview of different types of groups presented in the professional literature.)

To form groups in all three categories, professional school counselors need to assess students' needs broadly through a systemic assessment (Lee & Goodnough, 2015). The institutional culture and overall climate of the school can limit the access to and equity of group counseling to all student groups. Professional school counselors need to reach out to underserved populations in ways that are relevant and consistent with their needs. In this way, counselors can encourage students to consider group counseling as a safe and viable means of assistance in making decisions and solving problems.

Previous experiences with societal and institutionalized barriers and biases can diminish trust and cause students to doubt that the school and its representatives have their best interests at heart. In forming relationships with students, it is essential for professional school counselors to validate concerns, earn trust, and advocate for needs. This builds the professional school counselor's credibility and assists in creating a sense of inclusion for all students.

Psychoeducation and Counseling: Group Interventions

Groups in schools led by professional school counselors exist on a continuum from being primarily didactic and psychoeducational in nature to being primarily therapeutic counseling experiences. Most groups have some elements of each, and some vary from session to session. Many developmental groups are primarily psychoeducational and focus on providing topic-specific information to small groups of students. The presentation of the information is carefully designed to directly apply to students' lives, to enhance age-appropriate development and academic success. For example, transitioning students can be taught about the environment they are transitioning into—whether it is middle school, high school, or a 2- or 4-year college.

Table 31.1 Group Counseling: Information From the Literature and Recent Publications

Author(s)	Topic
Edwards, Adams, Waldo, Hadfield, & Biegel (2014)	Mindfulness based stress reduction, self-compassion, and symptom reduction for Latino students
Steen, Henfield, & Booker (2014)	Model for academic and personal social group counseling
Vassilopoulos, Brouzos, Damer, Mellou, & Mitropoulou (2013)	Social anxiety
Tauriac et al. (2013)	Reducing intergroup conflict in high school setting
Ware, Ohrt, & Swank (2012)	Social skills
Hall, Rushing, & Khurshid (2011)	Negative peer pressure
Shin et al. (2010)	Critical consciousness raising for middle school youth of color
Hines & Fields (2004)	Task management skills, asking for help, and developing academic persistence for ninth grade students
Lee (2004)	Conflict management
LaFountain, Garner, & Eliason (1996)	Heterogeneously grouped solution-focused group counseling
Erford, Moore-Thomas, & Mazzuca (2004)	Understanding learning styles
Riddle, Bergin, & Douzenis (1997)	Lowering the anxiety levels and improving the self-concepts of elementary school children of alcoholics
Arman & McNair (2000)	Elementary school-age children of alcoholics
Akos (2000)	A psychoeducational group that helps develop empathy in children
Akos & Martin (2003)	Transition to middle school
Kizner & Kizner (1999)	Adopted children
Bradley (2001)	African American males
Bailey & Bradford-Bailey (2004)	African American males
Smith & Chen-Hayes (2004)	Gay, lesbian, bisexual, transgendered, and questioning youth
Zinck & Littrell (2000)	Adolescent at-risk girls
Goodnough & Ripley (1997)	High school seniors transitioning to postsecondary schools and the military
Coker (2004)	Substance abuse prevention
Brooks (2004)	Stress management
Stone (2004)	Perpetrators of sexual harassment
Jackson & Grant (2004)	The influence of culture, gender, race, and ability on the career development of high school students

Psychoeducation also has a place in targeted groups. Students coping with the loss of a loved one need to be taught about the stages of grieving, because such knowledge is helpful to the healing process. In groups dealing with the school climate, information is frequently taught to students (e.g., in a group on conflict resolution, students need to be taught about the characteristics of conflict and the different types of conflict; Lee, 2004). Thus, the provision of psychoeducation to students in all types of counseling groups is common in schools and fits in well with the culture of K–12 education, as students learn new information (e.g., Vassilopoulos et al., 2013).

As we stated, psychoeducation can be presented in all three group categories. Typically, the provision of psychoeducation leads students to apply information to themselves. They often need assistance to do this. Such processing leads into the second aspect of group work in schools: counseling. It is in the processing that the professional school counselor's unique skill set is used. When students process information, they often reveal confidential information about themselves, thus opening themselves up to psychological risk. Professional school counselors are trained to manage this risk in culturally sensitive ways, thereby helping to promote growth and development through risk taking and sharing.

As students share and process together, the professional school counselor uses counseling skills to promote mutual trust and to help members develop a sense of inclusion within the group. Effective group counselors help to create an environment in which members become known to each other in meaningful ways. In a targeted group for children dealing with family situations in which alcohol or other drugs are being abused, a professional school counselor will not only use psychoeducation (i.e., the professional school counselor might teach about the roles taken in alcoholic families and the addictive nature of substances) but will also help promote healing by helping all students share their particular situations. By working with all members in this way, the professional school counselor helps students know they are not alone. In sum, professional school counselors provide psychoeducation to students and help them process that information in personally meaningful ways. Further, they harness the power of the group to provide an avenue for growth, remediation, and the improvement of the school climate.

Two Ways to Form Groups: Homogeneous and Heterogeneous

The aforementioned groups are homogeneous groups, in which all students are dealing with similar issues. For several reasons, it is appropriate that membership in some groups be restricted. First, students who share a common concern are able to identify with each other and help one another in ways that others might not. While group counseling is not about giving others advice, group members do provide their own unique perspectives; within these perspectives may be information and coping strategies that members find helpful. Related to providing support is the concept of *universality*; the knowledge that others share certain experiences and feelings reduces the sense of isolation that many students feel so they know that they are not alone. This process of universality is one of the key group process factors that promote growth and healing (Yalom & Leszcz, 2005). Finally, when groups are homogeneously formed, topic-specific psychoeducation can be provided in a manner that is beneficial to all.

While the benefits of homogeneously formed groups are evident, there are several reasons why groups might have a heterogeneous composition. In these groups, similarity of presenting concern is not necessary because students learn a method (e.g., solution-focused, problem solving, cognitive behavioral) whereby a variety of problems can be addressed. They also learn that the chosen method can be transferred to other situations with which they might be faced. These types of groups help to decompartmentalize learning and help empower students as they gain confidence to draw on their new skills to solve problems in a variety of challenging situations.

Another way heterogeneous groups are used is by having one or more group members serve as models for targeted students. For instance, an elementary school social-skills group might be less effective if all members have poor social skills. One of the reasons that group counseling works is that students learn from each other. If all students in a group are deficient in social skills, they cannot learn appropriate or positive skills from each other. Because of this, elementary school counselors frequently have behavioral models in social skills groups. These model students are children who have good social skills; the target students can learn from them. As a result, this group is made up of a heterogeneous group of students, not all of whom need remediation in social skills.

Group Counseling Skills

To effectively lead groups in schools, professional school counselors need to have skills in the following four dimensions of group counseling: (a) be knowledgeable about the interrelationship between developmental theory and counseling theory (e.g., how might we best apply solution-focused interventions to fourth-grade students), (b) have knowledge about the topic or content of the group, (c) understand group dynamics, and (d) understand the contextual factors that influence what their students' behavior means. First, professional school counselors must understand students from multiple developmental perspectives (e.g., cognitive, psychosocial, and racial or ethnic identity). From these related perspectives, professional school counselors select group counseling strategies and interventions that are appropriate to the developmental sophistication of students. For example, elementary school counselors may choose to use Adlerian strategies, because many Adlerian concepts are applicable to the developmental needs of young children.

Professional school counselors need to understand theoretical applications well enough to feel confident that selected strategies and techniques are within accepted methods of practice and are robust enough to achieve the objectives of the group. Second, competence in the content or topic to be addressed is essential. While it is not necessary for professional school counselors to be experts in every area of group they offer, they do need specific knowledge (e.g., they need to know how the topic tends to manifest in the population with which they are working). For example, to lead a group on bereavement, professional school counselors need not be experts on issues of loss and grieving, but they do need to be quite knowledgeable about it and, in particular, how processing grief and loss is mediated by factors such as the child's cognitive development and cultural and religious beliefs. This relates to the third group counseling skill: understanding the multiple contexts of children's lives.

The multiple contextual factors that impact the lives of students shape the ways in which students process the content and dynamic interactions in groups. For example, factors such as socioeconomic status, race or ethnicity, gender, religious or spiritual beliefs and practices, sexual orientation, institutional barriers to learning, and family composition all become screens through which students filter the content of the group and the process dynamics that exist within the group. These interdependent and interrelated factors challenge professional school counselors to continually engage in professional development to competently and ethically meet the group counseling needs of students.

Finally, professional school counselors need to keep all of this in mind as they hypothesize about group members' behaviors and facilitate the growth of the group. In doing so, professional school counselors are able to encourage group members to participate fully in the group and respect students' varied and diverse styles of meaningful participation. By attending to these dimensions of group counseling, professional school counselors build cohesion and keep the group focused on the task or topic at hand.

The Context of Public School

Much has been written about the barriers that prevent effective group work in schools. Some of the obstructive forces described are scheduling problems, teacher and administrator attitudes, school policies and practices that limit student access, and the overall culture of schools (Williams, McMahon, McLeod, & Rice, 2013). To overcome these barriers, professional school counselors need to honor and understand the context in which they work. They need to understand that administrators and teachers are held accountable for students' academic performance—often as measured by standardized test scores. Additionally, the work of the professional school counselor when conducting groups is not traditionally seen as enhancing the academic achievement of students or presenting skills such as higher order thinking skills or learning styles that can be effectively used across academic disciplines by students. Additionally, teacher and administrator preservice training does not focus heavily on the role and function of systemic data-driven school counseling programs, methods of service delivery, and the appropriate duties of the professional school counselor (Fitch, Newby, Ballestero, & Marshall, 2001; Pérusse & Goodnough, 2002). As a result, many administrators' perceptions of school counseling reflect their own experiences with school counseling, many of which are older, traditional notions of school counseling. When administrators assume leadership positions in schools, they often perpetuate these past practices.

There are three main ways professional school counselors can attend to the legitimate concerns of administrators and help them envision and facilitate the counselor's implementation of group counseling in a contemporary and appropriate manner. The first concerns professional preparation. Prior to initiating a series of group offerings, professional school counselors need to commit themselves and their time to preparing and scheduling group counseling. This requires counselors to include group counseling in the strategic plan of the school counseling program. Additionally, as one of the programmatic levels of intervention (Lee & Goodnough, 2015), group counseling is an established part of the school counseling program calendar and therefore requires professional school counselors to allot significant time for group counseling. When a programmatic calendar is shared with stakeholders, it sends a message that group counseling is a priority. Additionally, professional school counselors plan for their groups in the same way teachers plan for an academic unit. For example, math teachers do not create their plans in secret, and neither should professional school counselors.

Professional school counselors make their group goals, objectives, and supporting materials available to the public as part of their school counseling program. In accordance with the ASCA (2010a) ethical standards, counselors honor parental–guardian knowledge of their children and seek to team and collaborate with parents to assist in student development. As part of the collaborative effort, professional school counselors seek out parent–guardian permission for their child's participation in group counseling. By preparing well for group counseling, they bring professionalism and rigor to this important method of service delivery.

The second way professional school counselors facilitate the implementation of group counseling is by collaborating and teaming with administrators to address, reinterpret, or revise salient school policies. School counseling interventions perceived by administrators to be outside the academic mission, such as group counseling, are often denied class time to meet so that students' focus remains on academic tasks. As a result of policies such as this, group counseling is oftentimes only offered during lunch, study hall, or before and after school. A school policy that posits *unconditionally* that instructional time cannot be compromised derails effective group counseling initiatives, unless counselors can demonstrate how group counseling can enhance academic achievement. For example, through leadership and advocacy, professional school counselors need to help teachers and administrators see that exceptions to such an important policy are already granted through other school-sponsored activities (e.g., in high schools, athletes in a variety of sports typically miss their last class of the day to travel to away games). This is permitted because participation in interscholastic sports is deemed beneficial for student growth and development—so much so that it supersedes academic time for certain students. It is an accepted belief that athletics offers students benefits that enhance academic achievement by fostering positive peer interactions, learning new skills that foster self-control, and developing a sense of empowerment by accomplishing challenging endeavors.

The task for professional school counselors is to influence and inform policy revisions or reinterpretations that allow all students to have the opportunity to gain similar benefits through group counseling, if they so desire. To do this, professional school counselors have to remind teachers and administrators that group counseling is part of the larger systemic data-driven school counseling program and shares the school's mission for academic success. More specifically, helping students effectively cope with grief and loss so that they can refocus on academic pursuits is as important for some students' personal–social and academic development as wrestling or volleyball is for others.

Thus, when school policy is reviewed, reinterpreted, or revised, professional school counselors collaborate with administrators and teachers to help shift the questions from "When can groups be run?" and "Do they take away from academic time?" to "How can we implement group counseling as a means of improving the quality of students' 'time on task' in math?" Additionally, once policies are reinterpreted or revised, they need to be adhered to by all teachers. This means that teachers' ability to deny students the right to attend groups must be prohibited, and they must not be permitted to count students as absent if they are attending a group meeting. Moreover, students should be given the same amount of time to do makeup work as they would for any other school-sponsored activity (Ripley & Goodnough, 2001).

Finally, professional school counselors and students must honor the privilege that comes with policy revision or reinterpretation. Care must be taken so that neither students nor professional school counselors abuse the system. When applied to attending group counseling during class time, this means that group members must arrive to the group session on time, the same as they would for class. It also means that students who abuse or ignore the rules of the school or the group forfeit their participation in group counseling.

Attending carefully to rules such as these and publicizing them broadly creates consistent behavioral expectations for students and reduces the ambiguity of the consequences of failure to follow school policy. Professional school counselors need to navigate dual role issues involved here. In all ways, they must enforce school policies while also being the group leader and embodying the characteristics and skills necessary for effective group leadership. When group counseling is implemented as described in this section, this powerful intervention becomes a valued part of the systemic data-driven school counseling program.

Summary/Conclusion

Professional school counselors at all levels who do not lead groups are not adequately performing their jobs. This is because group counseling in schools is a central means of delivering a systemic data-driven school counseling program. Providing effective group counseling experiences to students requires leadership, specialized knowledge and skills, and the ability to advocate effectively for the inclusion of a program of group counseling within schools.

SECTION 5

Assessment in School Counseling

CHAPTER 32

What Assessment Competencies Are Needed by Professional School Counselors?

*Bradley T. Erford**

Preview

The assessment competencies used and needed by today's professional school counselors were identified through research conducted by a joint committee of the American School Counselor Association (ASCA) and the Association for Assessment and Research in Counseling (AARC).

Assessment and evaluation skills are important facets of counseling covered in school counselor training programs and in counselor certification requirements. The role of assessment in the work of professional school counselors can be found in models of school counseling work and in studies of school counselors. Work behaviors related to assessment are fundamental to the general practice of counseling.

ASCA/AARC Joint Committee

What are the assessment competencies needed by today's professional school counselors? This was the question put to a joint committee of the American School Counselor Association (ASCA) and the Association for Assessment in Counseling (AAC; now known as the Association for Assessment and Research in Counseling [AARC]). These two professional organizations appointed a joint committee to develop a statement, in collaboration with practicing school counselors, about the assessment competencies needed to work as a professional school counselor.

The committee began discovering what others have said about the role of the professional school counselor and the assessment competencies needed in this role. Organizations and groups concerned with the preparation and certification of professional school counselors have given considerable attention to the assessment competencies needed by counselors. The following paragraphs summarize what the committee found and also include more recent information about professional school counselors and assessment.

---

*Special thanks to Ruth B. Ekstrom and Patricia B. Elmore for their outstanding contributions to the first two editions of this chapter.

The committee began by looking at the Standards of the Council for Accreditation of Counseling and Related Educational Programs (CACREP; 2009). These Standards lists *assessment* as one of the eight common core areas in which all counseling students are expected to have curricular experiences and demonstrated knowledge. According to these Standards, counseling students should have an understanding of individual and group approaches to assessment and evaluation, including: historical perspectives about assessment; basic concepts of standardized and nonstandardized testing and other assessment techniques; statistical concepts; reliability; validity; how age, gender, sexual orientation, ethnicity, language, disability, culture, spirituality, and other factors are related to the assessment and evaluation; strategies for selecting, administering, and interpreting assessment and evaluation instruments; and ethical and legal considerations in assessment.

In addition, CACREP expects that all professional school counselors know about program evaluation and research—two areas that are closely related to assessment. The CACREP Standards include a section about what professional school counselors are expected to know regarding the development, implementation, and evaluation of school counseling programs; counseling and guidance; and consultation. The development and evaluation of counseling programs often require that professional school counselors use data from standardized testing and needs assessments so as to improve student outcomes. The complete CACREP statement about the skills expected of all counselors, and specifically professional school counselors, can be found at the CACREP Web site (http://www.cacrep.org).

The ASCA/AAC joint committee also reviewed each state's requirements for the certification of professional school counselors. The state requirements are available on ASCA's Web site (http://www.schoolcounselor.org) in the section on Careers/Roles under the section for School Counselors and Members. Most public school systems require that counselors take advanced degree courses in testing/assessment and in program evaluation and research. The National Board for Professional Teaching Standards (NBPTS) has also developed standards for the certification of professional school counselors (NBPTS, 2014). The section on student assessment reads, "Accomplished school counselors understand the principles and purposes of assessment, and the collection and use of data. They regularly monitor student progress and communicate the purpose, design, and results of assessments to various audiences." (The complete section on school counselor standards can be viewed at http://www.nbpts.org/sites/default/files/documents/certificates/nbpts-certificate-ecya-sc-standards.pdf.) As you read the CACREP Standards, the certification requirements for your state, and the NBPTS Standards, think about your own counseling skills. Are there areas in which you might benefit from additional training?

Current Assessment Activities

Assessment is one of five major activities of professional school counselors according to Burnham and Jackson (2000), who found that 90% of the professional school counselors in their sample interpreted tests individually for students, parents, and teachers and that 81% conducted in-service training with school faculty about assessment instruments and procedures. A survey of professional school counselors in California (Blacher, Murray-Ward, & Uellendahl, 2005) found that they used a variety of standardized and nonstandardized assessment techniques including observing students individually or in groups and conducting structured student interviews four or more times a week; teacher- or counselor-completed student behavior rating scales about twice a week; and standardized achievement tests, student-completed ratings, and career inventories about once a week. The professional school counselors felt their training for carrying out observations and structured interviews had been good. They rated their training in using standardized tests and in the use of teacher- or student-completed rating scales as adequate. The counselors spent a good deal of time using assessment information. They interpreted assessments to students and parents about three times a week; they also used assessment information to identify students' academic achievement levels, career aptitudes and interests, and levels of social skills, each, about twice a week.

A national survey of high school guidance counseling in 2001–2002 (Parsad, Alexander, Farris, & Hudson, 2003) found that academic testing took between 10% and 19% of the time for 30% of the professional school counselors and more than 20% of the time for 19% of the counselors. Testing and interpretation of tests for career planning purposes was available in 93% of the high schools; this service was used by 56% of the students in grades 11 and 12. Helping students with their academic achievement was the most emphasized goal of high school counseling programs. On the survey, public high school counselors were asked if their state or school district provided in-service training or professional development training on how to interpret test scores and assess student achievement. Overall, 52% of the counselors said they had received such training in the preceding 12 months.

ASCA National Model

In 1997, ASCA developed the *National Standards for School Counseling Programs* (Campbell & Dahir, 1997). The Standards addressed students' academic development, career development, and personal–social development, specifying competencies in each area that are defined by knowledge, attitudes, or skills that the student should acquire and be able to demonstrate. These ASCA standards are the foundation of the ASCA national model's core curriculum (ASCA, 2012a; also see Chapter 12). Accountability requires that professional school counselors collect and use data to evaluate the counseling program and to link it to student achievement. The ASCA standards and the national model make it clear that assessment and evaluation are important parts of the role of the professional school counselor, citing activities such as collecting data from a student needs assessment or disseminating information to help students interpret standardized tests. Professional school counselors are often asked to serve in these roles because they have a better understanding of assessment information than do teachers or secondary school principals, especially when assessment involves test selection, validity, communication of test results, and ethical practices.

Questionnaire Results

After having reviewed the research about professional school counselors and assessment, the ASCA/AAC joint committee developed a list of 39 assessment-related activities that professional school counselors are often expected to do. This list was based primarily on the CACREP standards and state certification requirements. All of the 39 activities appear in one or more state descriptions of professional school counselor work, although they may not always be *typical* of the work of professional school counselors. These assessment-related activities became the basis of a questionnaire that was administered to a random sample of counselor educators and professional school counselors selected from the ASCA membership list. Both the counselor educators and the professional school counselors were asked to indicate how important it is for professional school counselors to be able to carry out each activity (using the scale 3 = *essential*, 2 = *desirable*, and 1 = *not necessary*). Responses were received from 179 professional school counselors and from 63 counselor educators (Ekstrom, Elmore, Schafer, Trotter, & Webster, 2004).

Ten skills and abilities to carry out certain activities were rated as *essential* by 65% or more of both the counselor educators and professional school counselors. These essential skills and abilities are as follows:

- Referring students to other professionals, when appropriate, for additional assessment/appraisal
- Communicating and interpreting test/assessment information to students and helping them use it for educational and career planning
- Making decisions about the type(s) of assessments to use in counseling groups or for individual students
- Interpreting scores from tests/assessments and using the information in counseling
- Reading about and being aware of ethical issues in assessment
- Communicating and interpreting test/assessment information to parents
- Communicating and interpreting test/assessment information to teachers, school administrators, and other professionals
- Making decisions about the type(s) of assessments to use in planning and evaluating counseling programs
- Reading about and being aware of current issues involving multicultural assessment, the assessment of students with disabilities and other special needs, and the assessment of language minorities
- Synthesizing and integrating test and nontest data to make decisions about individuals

In addition, the counselor educators rated eight other skills and abilities as *essential*, including several related to counseling program planning and evaluation:

- Selecting, administering, and interpreting instruments for use in career counseling
- Reading or referring to test use standards such as *Responsibilities of Users of Standardized Tests* (AACE, 2004) or the *Code of Fair Testing Practices in Education* (Joint Committee on Testing Practices, 2004)
- Selecting assessment instruments to use with counseling groups and individual students
- Interpreting data from needs assessments and other counseling program planning assessments
- Selecting assessment instruments to use in planning and evaluating counseling programs
- Adapting or designing surveys or other instruments to use in needs assessment for counseling program planning and/or in counseling program evaluation
- Designing and implementing plans to collect data for use in counseling program planning and evaluation

Many of the skills rated as essential by both professional school counselors and counselor educators are similar in content to parts of the ASCA (2010a) ethical standards (see http://www.schoolcounselor.org/asca/media/asca/Resource%20Center/Legal%20and%20Ethical%20Issues/Sample%20Documents/EthicalStandards2010.pdf).

Survey results show that the counselor educators reported it was essential for professional school counselors to have the skills needed to develop and evaluate school counseling programs. They also reported it was essential for professional school counselors to be familiar with test standards such as the *Code of Fair Testing Practices in Education* (Joint Committee on Testing Practices, 2004), *Responsibilities of Users of Standardized Tests* (3rd ed.; AACE, 2004), and other key testing documents.

The results of this survey were used by the ASCA/AAC Joint Committee to develop a statement of Competencies in Assessment and Evaluation for School Counselors approved by both ASCA and AAC and which can be found in Figure 32.1 (see next page).

This statement is intended to help professional school counselors review and evaluate their own skills in the areas of assessment and evaluation to be able to determine their own professional development and continuing education needs in these areas. After you have read the competencies, ask yourself how your assessment skills measure up to these standards. Then decide what steps to take to improve your own assessment skills.

Improving Assessment Skills

Here are some suggestions to improve assessment competencies. First, check with ASCA and ACA at both the state and national levels to see what in-service training programs are available. Check also with area universities to see if courses in assessment skills for professional school counselors are offered. Finally, explore the AARC Web site (http://aarc-counseling.org/) and look for links to helpful topics.

Summary/Conclusion

Assessment competencies needed by professional school counselors were identified. Professional school counselors are encouraged to engage in self-evaluation to determine if they have these competencies and to use the identified resources to improve their assessment skills.

Competencies in Assessment and Evaluation for School Counselors

Approved by the American School Counselor Association on September 21, 1998, and by the Association for Assessment in Counseling on September 10, 1998[1]

The purpose of these competencies is to provide a description of the knowledge and skills that school counselors need in the areas of assessment and evaluation. Because effectiveness in assessment and evaluation is critical to effective counseling, these competencies are important for school counselor education and practice. Although consistent with existing Council for Accreditation of Counseling and Related Educational Programs (CACREP) and National Association of State Directors of Teacher Education and Certification (NASDTEC) standards for preparing counselors, they focus on competencies of individual counselors rather than content of counselor education programs.

The competencies can be used by counselor and assessment educators as a guide in the development and evaluation of school counselor preparation programs, workshops, inservice, and other continuing education opportunities. They may also be used by school counselors to evaluate their own professional development and continuing education needs.

School counselors should meet each of the nine numbered competencies and have the specific skills listed under each competency.

Competency 1. School counselors are skilled in choosing assessment strategies.

  a. They can describe the nature and use of different types of formal and informal assessments, including questionnaires, checklists, interviews, inventories, tests, observations, surveys, and performance assessments, and work with individuals skilled in clinical assessment.

  b. They can specify the types of information most readily obtained from different assessment approaches.

  c. They are familiar with resources for critically evaluating each type of assessment and can use them in choosing appropriate assessment strategies.

  d. They are able to advise and assist others (e.g., a school district) in choosing appropriate assessment strategies.

Competency 2. School counselors can identify, access, and evaluate the most commonly used assessment instruments.

  a. They know which assessment instruments are most commonly used in school settings to assess intelligence, aptitude, achievement, personality, work values, and interests, including computer-assisted versions and other alternate formats.

---

[1] A joint committee of the American School Counselor Association (ASCA) and the Association for Assessment in Counseling (AAC) was appointed by the respective presidents in 1993 with the charge to draft a statement about school counselor preparation in assessment and evaluation. Committee members were Ruth Ekstrom (AAC), Patricia Elmore (AAC, Chair, 1997-1999), Daren Hutchinson (ASCA), Marjorie Mastie (AAC), Kathy O'Rourke (ASCA), William Schafer (AAC, Chair, 1993-1997), Thomas Trotter (ASCA), and Barbara Webster (ASCA).

Figure 32.1. Statement of Competencies in Assessment and Evaluation for School Counselors. Reprinted with permission from the Association for Assessment and Research in Counseling.

b. They know the dimensions along which assessment instruments should be evaluated, including purpose, validity, utility, norms, reliability and measurement error, score reporting method, and consequences of use.
c. They can obtain and evaluate information about the quality of those assessment instruments.

Competency 3. School counselors are skilled in the techniques of administration and methods of scoring assessment instruments.
  a. They can implement appropriate administration procedures, including administration using computers.
  b. They can standardize administration of assessments when interpretation is in relation to external norms.
  c. They can modify administration of assessments to accommodate individual differences consistent with publisher recommendations and current statements of professional practice.
  d. They can provide consultation, information, and training to others who assist with administration and scoring.
  e. They know when it is necessary to obtain informed consent from parents or guardians before administering an assessment.

Competency 4. School counselors are skilled in interpreting and reporting assessment results.
  a. They can explain scores that are commonly reported, such as percentile ranks, standard scores, and grade equivalents. They can interpret a confidence interval for an individual score based on a standard error of measurement.
  b. They can evaluate the appropriateness of a norm group when interpreting the scores of an individual or a group.
  c. They are skilled in communicating assessment information to others, including teachers, administrators, students, parents, and the community. They are aware of the rights students and parents have to know assessment results and decisions made as a consequence of any assessment.
  d. They can evaluate their own strengths and limitations in the use of assessment instruments and in assessing students with disabilities or linguistic or cultural differences. They know how to identify professionals with appropriate training and experience for consultation.
  e. They know the legal and ethical principles about confidentiality and disclosure of assessment information and recognize the need to abide by district policy on retention and use of assessment information.

Competency 5. School counselors are skilled in using assessment results in decision-making.
  a. They recognize the limitations of using a single score in making an educational decision and know how to obtain multiple sources of information to improve such decisions.
  b. They can evaluate their own expertise for making decisions based on assessment results. They also can evaluate the limitations of conclusions provided by others, including the reliability and validity of computer-assisted assessment interpretations.

(continues)

c. They can evaluate whether the available evidence is adequate to support the intended use of an assessment result for decision-making, particularly when that use has not been recommended by the developer of the assessment instrument.
d. They can evaluate the rationale underlying the use of qualifying scores for placement in educational programs or courses of study.
e. They can evaluate the consequences of assessment-related decisions and avoid actions that would have unintended negative consequences.

Competency 6. School counselors are skilled in producing, interpreting, and presenting statistical information about assessment results.

a. They can describe data (e.g., test scores, grades, demographic information) by forming frequency distributions, preparing tables, drawing graphs, and calculating descriptive indices of central tendency, variability, and relationship.
b. They can compare a score from an assessment instrument with an existing distribution, describe the placement of a score within a normal distribution, and draw appropriate inferences.
c. They can interpret statistics used to describe characteristics of assessment instruments, including difficulty and discrimination indices, reliability and validity coefficients, and standard errors of measurement.
d. They can identify and interpret inferential statistics when comparing groups, making predictions, and drawing conclusions needed for educational planning and decisions.
e. They can use computers for data management, statistical analysis, and production of tables and graphs for reporting and interpreting results.

Competency 7. School counselors are skilled in conducting and interpreting evaluations of school counseling programs and counseling-related interventions.

a. They understand and appreciate the role that evaluation plays in the program development process throughout the life of a program.
b. They can describe the purposes of an evaluation and the types of decisions to be based on evaluation information.
c. They can evaluate the degree to which information can justify conclusions and decisions about a program.
d. They can evaluate the extent to which student outcome measures match program goals.
e. They can identify and evaluate possibilities for unintended outcomes and possible impacts of one program on other programs.
f. They can recognize potential conflicts of interest and other factors that may bias the results of evaluations.

Competency 8. School counselors are skilled in adapting and using questionnaires, surveys, and other assessments to meet local needs.

a. They can write specifications and questions for local assessments.
b. They can assemble an assessment into a usable format and provide directions for its use.

Figure 32.1 (*continued*)

c. They can design and implement scoring processes and procedures for information feedback.

Competency 9. School counselors know how to engage in professionally responsible assessment and evaluation practices.
   a. They understand how to act in accordance with ACA's *Code of Ethics and Standards of Practice* and ASCA's *Ethical Standards for School Counselors*.
   b. They can use professional codes and standards, including the *Code of Fair Testing Practices in Education, Code of Professional Responsibilities in Educational Measurement, Responsibilities of Users of Standardized Tests,* and *Standards for Educational and Psychological Testing*, to evaluate counseling practices using assessments.
   c. They understand test fairness and can avoid the selection of biased assessment instruments and biased uses of assessment instruments. They can evaluate the potential for unfairness when tests are used incorrectly and for possible bias in the interpretation of assessment results.
   d. They understand the legal and ethical principles and practices regarding test security, copying copyrighted materials, and unsupervised use of assessment instruments that are not intended for self-administration.
   e. They can obtain and maintain available credentialing that demonstrates their skills in assessment and evaluation.
   f. They know how to identify and participate in educational and training opportunities to maintain competence and acquire new skills in assessment and evaluation.

Definitions of Terms

Competencies describe skills or understandings that a school counselor should possess to perform assessment and evaluation activities effectively.

Assessment is the gathering of information for decision making about individuals, groups, programs, or processes. Assessment targets include abilities, achievements, personality variables, aptitudes, attitudes, preferences, interests, values, demographics, and other characteristics. Assessment procedures include but are not limited to standardized and unstandardized tests, questionnaires, inventories, checklists, observations, portfolios, performance assessments, rating scales, surveys, interviews, and other clinical measures.

Evaluation is the collection and interpretation of information to make judgments about individuals, programs, or processes that lead to decisions and future actions.

CHAPTER 33

High-Stakes Testing: What Counselors Need to Know

Patricia Jo McDivitt

Preview

The scores on many of the tests currently administered in classrooms are tied to accountability systems whose results might have an impact upon the life chances of students. This chapter serves to inform professional school counselors of what they need to know about high-stakes testing, including understanding the purpose and the link to the standards-based educational reform movement.

A heavy focus is placed on the use of high-stakes testing to determine what students should know and be able to do. The scores on these tests are now tied to accountability systems on which the results might affect teaching and learning. The changing purpose and use of tests over the past few years serve to underscore how important it is for professional school counselors and all assessment professionals to understand the role that high-stakes testing plays in the classroom, including its link to curriculum content standards, teaching, and learning.

As a result of high-stakes testing, professional school counselors and other assessment professionals are challenged not only to be actively engaged in understanding the use of high-stakes tests and the interpretation of the results but also to learn more about what these tests actually measure and whether students have had the opportunity to learn what the test questions are asking. I will summarize what professional school counselors need to know about high-stakes testing, including understanding the purpose and the link to the standards-based educational reform movement, a movement which today focuses heavily upon a set of college- and career-ready standards for all students.

Defining the Purpose of Accountability

It is important for professional school counselors and assessment professionals to understand the definition of high-stakes testing and its purpose in current educational settings. "High-stakes assessments have always had the goal of helping to improve the educational process be it through accountability, helping to focus instruction, providing diagnostic information, or evaluating educational programs" (Reckase, 2011, p. 1). In the past, students' test results were often used to determine their academic strengths and weaknesses so that teachers could plan instruction. Other test results might help students understand their aptitudes and interests in order to explore possible career options or future educational plans. However, in the current educational setting, a great deal of the testing involves the use of tests that are directly tied to school accountability systems, where the results are used to make major decisions about an individual—decisions that might have a direct impact on the individual's future life opportunities.

A test is defined as "high stakes" if it carries with it serious consequences for students or others in the educational community, including teachers and administrators. For example, the results of high-stakes tests are sometimes used, along with other requirements, to determine whether a student is promoted to the next grade or graduates from high school. In addition, a classroom set of students' scores on a high-stakes test may be used along with other information to determine teacher effectiveness. On the other hand, students' average scores on this same test may also be used to judge an entire school's academic performance. For example, a school's high scores on a given high-stakes test might receive praise and financial awards from the community at large; low scores on the same test might bring heavy sanctions. High-stakes testing applications, such as those previously outlined, often put pressure on students, parents, teachers, and others in the educational community. For example, professional school counselors are now becoming more aware of the added pressure and impact that high-stakes tests are having on opportunities for students. In fact, while many students are becoming desensitized to the entire testing process, once they become aware of what is really at stake, the pressure to pass the test can be overwhelming.

Parents and guardians are also experiencing new pressures because states' high-stakes assessments will allow parents, as well as educators and other stakeholders, to see how children are progressing in school and whether they are on track for postsecondary success. The results of school-wide, high-stakes tests may then provide parents and guardians with the opportunity to make important decisions concerning the best educational opportunities for their children. For example, parents and guardians of students in low-performing schools might have to decide whether to enroll their children in a different school or a charter school, or they might be given the opportunity to use federal or state funds to provide their children with additional special training. These decisions may well have a direct impact on a student's future opportunities. Teachers also face significant added pressure because they are more challenged to help all students achieve the level of performance expected by administrators, parents and guardians, and the community at large. Today there is a tremendous push to expand national and state testing to all students—including testing students with disabilities or who are English language learners. According to Marion (2013), all educators must understand that it is a social justice issue to ensure that all students have opportunities to learn the knowledge and skills that will provide them with viable options after they leave school. "On the other hand, some are concerned that, given the limited resources of public schools, focusing on having all students reach an important performance threshold will necessarily limit the attention teachers provide to students who are high performing" (Marion, 2013, p. 3).

High-Stakes Testing: Raising Academic Achievement for All Students

High-stakes testing is also a key component of the educational reform movement, a movement that began several decades ago and culminated in 2001 when President George W. Bush signed into law the No Child Left Behind Act of 2001 (NCLB). NCLB significantly strengthened the federal government's role in both elementary and secondary education and included a plan for educational reform that focused on accountability and the use of high-stakes test results to help raise the academic achievement for all students. NCLB outlined the requirements that all states were to implement reading and mathematics tests in grades 3 through 8 and once again during grades 10 through 12. Science tests were also to be administered to all students at least once in the elementary, middle, and high school years. In addition, NCLB required that high-stakes tests be aligned with state content curriculum standards and designed to provide results concerning each student's progression toward mastery of the defined state-specific standards. As a result, over the past few years, NCLB has required all public schools to be held accountable for meeting very strict high-stakes accountability requirements, and all educators, including professional school counselors, continue to be challenged to support how the requirements are met.

Curriculum Content Standards: What Students Should Know and Be Able To Do

The use of high-stakes tests in the educational setting has its roots within the larger movement of the educational standards-based reform. The reform movement that emerged in the 1990s called for high standards for all students, centering on challenging subject matter and students' acquisition of a rigorous set of content standards designed to prepare them for the next century. Basically, the reform movement was based upon the following premise:

> All students must learn at high levels, regardless of such factors as race, ethnicity, socioeconomic status, native language or gender. Too often, disparities in achievement among urban, rural, and suburban schools, or between schools in rich and poor neighborhoods, or even between schools from seemingly similar communities are accepted as inevitable. Expectations from some students are often lower than for others, frequently leading to a narrowly defined curriculum for those students. Defining what students need to know and be able to do is intended to facilitate holding all students accountable for the same high learning, no matter what their background or particular school. (Woodward, 1999, p. 19)

In 1993, a Technical Planning Group for the National Education Goals Panel published *Promises to Keep: Creating High Standards for American Students.* The publication served to outline the establishment of curriculum content standards or what students should know and be expected to do. In most educational settings, the term *standard,* much like the term *objective,* entails a process of coming to an agreement about what should be taught. Traditionally, the content curriculum standards or learning targets would parallel educational goals, teaching objectives, and outcomes. However, the term *standard* in the current educational setting, where the focus is now upon college and career readiness, has an implication of even higher levels of expectations. For example, college and career readiness for all students has become the fundamental underpinning of the Common Core State Standards educational reform movement. While the goal of the educational reform movement in the 1990s has been to encourage each state's development of new and rigorous academic expectations that all students within a given state should meet, the goal of the college and career readiness standards educational reform movement (i.e., Common Core State Standards) is to ensure that there is a common set of standards that are not only rigorous but also designed to prepare all students equally across the country for college and career readiness (Hess & Gong, 2014).

In response to the national standards-based reform movement that took place in the early 1990s, states did adopt their own state-specific curriculum content standards. Many states also developed their own high-stakes tests, designed specifically to measure students' mastery of the state-specific content curriculum standards. These high-stakes tests are called *criterion-referenced tests* or *standards-based assessments*. Traditional norm-referenced tests are used to compare performance and to determine students' relative strengths and weaknesses, based on the generalized set of objectives that are common across the country for a given content area. Standards-based assessments are used to determine what students can do and what they should know, not how they performed compared to other students who took the same test at a given grade level. However, while these state-specific standards-based assessments were developed to provide information regarding how well students were doing relative to a predetermined performance level on the specified set of educational goals, skills, or outcomes included in the specific state curriculum, critics argued that there was no standardized definition across the country of what it meant for a student to progress toward mastery of the set of each state's standards. In other words, a concern arose over the lack of consistency among state definitions of what it meant for a student to be proficient (Hess & Gong, 2014). In order to deal with these issues, and also to continue to raise expectations for all students, in 2010, the National Governors Association and the Council of Chief State School Officers (2014) created the Common Core State Standards. The Common Core State Standards serve to define the knowledge and skills all students across the country need for college and career readiness, while also providing a common definition of students' readiness for the states that adopt these college- and career-ready standards.

To understand high-stakes testing and its impact on teaching and learning, professional school counselors and all assessment professionals need to become familiar with the content curriculum standards upon which the high-stakes test questions are based. This is true regardless of whether the standards are existing state-specific standards, newly developed state-specific college and career-readiness standards, or the Common Core State Standards. The analysis of the content curriculum standards will provide the professional school counselor with the opportunity to gain a full understanding of the fundamental principles underlying what is to be taught. When examining content curriculum standards, professional school counselors might want to follow the guidelines outlined in the report on the review of education standards from the Goals 3 and 4 of the Technical Planning Group to the National Education Goals Panel (1993). These guidelines provided in 1993 are still relevant today and can be used to examine existing or newly developed state-specific standards, as well as the Common Core State Standards. A summary of the guidelines follows. Are the content standards:

- challenging, or do they simply hold students accountable to minimum acceptance levels of competency?
- useful for helping students to attain career or educational goals, including becoming productive citizens and lifelong learners?
- accurate, and do they reflect sound instructional practices?
- clear and usable so that students, teachers, and parents can easily understand what the standards mean and what they require?

- assessable for all students and specific so that the attainment of the standards can be measured?
- adaptable and able to be implemented in a number of ways depending upon the needs of the students?
- developmentally appropriate?

Performance Standards: Understanding Levels of Performance

The National Education Goals Panel's (1993) publication, *Promises to Keep: Creating High Standards for American Students,* also served to outline the establishment of performance standards, also known as academic proficiency levels. It is very important that professional counselors understand the difference between a content curriculum standard and a performance standard. *Content standards* refer to what students should know and be expected to do. On the other hand, a *performance standard* is a statement that refers to the level of performance that is expected of students to demonstrate in relation to the content curriculum standard (Hambleton, 2013).

In terms of high-stakes testing, performance standards are also translated into scoring guidelines or performance-level descriptors. Performance-level descriptors are typically written to provide clear guidelines for what should constitute the different levels of performance (e.g., Advanced, Proficient, and Below Proficient) on the high-stakes test. They form the foundation for determining what and how much students are expected to know and be able to do in a given content domain for a particular subject area.

Performance standards can be defined in a number of ways. For example, in a physical education class, a performance-level descriptor or standard might be defined by whether a student can perform a set of physical activities to perfection (e.g., running in place for several minutes, walking on a balance beam without falling, jumping rope for a specified number of minutes). If the student is able to perform all of these physical activities to perfection, he or she would be deemed as having mastery of the standard. In this example, even if every student does not successfully complete each activity, the standard is obvious and easy to understand.

Developing good performance level descriptors involves a careful analysis of the curriculum content standards in order to summarize dimensions of performance. McMillan (2013) outlined six steps to follow when summarizing the dimensions of performance that are used to assign student work to a given level: (1) Identify dimensions of excellence; (2) Categorize and prioritize dimensions; (3) Clearly define each dimension: (4) Identify examples; (5) Describe performance continuums; and (6) Try out and refine the continuums.

It is important to know that both curriculum content standards and performance standards have been articulated at a national level in documents published by national organizations, including the National Council of Teachers of Mathematics, the National Council of Teachers of English, the National Council of Teachers of Social Studies, the American Association for the Advancement of Science, and the National Science Teachers Association. Curriculum content standards and performance standards have also been articulated in documents published by the Common Core State Standards Initiative, the Partnership for Assessment of Readiness for College and Careers (PARCC, 2013), and the Smarter Balanced Assessment

Consortium (Smarter Balanced, 2014). Both PARCC and Smarter Balanced each consist of a group of states working together to develop a set of assessments that measure college and career readiness for all students, including defining performance standards or what it means for students to build toward mastery of those standards.

In addition to understanding the performance standards or what is to be expected, professional school counselors also need to have some knowledge of how the standards for performance, or the "cut scores," for those who pass or fail are established. Establishing cut scores is directly tied to the purpose of the test. According to the American Educational Research Association (AERA; 2002, p. 5) policy statement:

> There is often confusion among minimum competency levels (traditionally required for grade-to-grade promotion), grade level (traditionally defined as a range of scores around the national average on standardized tests), and "world-class" standards (set at the top of the distribution, anywhere from the 70th to the 99th percentile). Once the purpose is clearly established, sound and appropriate procedures must be followed in setting passing scores or proficiency levels.

With high-stakes testing, performance standards are typically set by a group of educators or panelists during a standard-setting process. The performance-level descriptors that serve to describe the knowledge and skills expected at the different performance levels are used by the panelists during this activity to guide where the cut scores should be placed from an academic content standard perspective. The panelists are first asked to carefully review each description of performance and consider the following questions:

> How does each performance level descriptor (i.e., Advanced, Proficient, and Below Proficient) generally address the academic content standards or what students should know and be able to do?
>
> What are the general skills implied by each descriptor?
>
> What are the major differences involving what students should know and be expected to do for each level of performance?

Professional school counselors need to verify that the process by which the cut scores are determined is clearly documented and defensible. Such activities are necessary to ensure that proficiency expectations are realistic and score-based inferences accurately represent the competencies measured by the test (Domaleski & Hall, 2013). The purpose and meaning of the scores or performance standards needs to be clearly stated, and validity evidence must be gathered and reported, consistent with the test's stated purpose.

Recommended Actions and Strategies: Technical Quality and What Counselors Need to Know

High-stakes tests need to be fair, and all students should be given the opportunity to learn the material covered in the test. As a result, educational assessment policy must produce measures of performance that are fair and accurate for all students, in order to convey clear, helpful information to educators, parents and guardians, and the students themselves (Linquanti, 2011). A fair test is also one that provides all students with an equal opportunity to demonstrate achievement. For example, in high-stakes testing, fairness refers to students having the right to an opportunity to learn the material that will be on the test. As stated in the *Code of Fair Testing Practices in Education* (American Psychological Association, 2014), fairness implies that every test taker has the opportunity to prepare for the test and is informed about the general nature and content of the test, as appropriate to the purpose of the test.

In addition to the need for high-stakes tests to be fair, they must also yield valid scores. It is important for professional school counselors to know that whether a high-stakes test does in fact measure what it is intended to measure depends upon its clearly defined purpose and the domains of content that serve as the foundation for guiding the entire test development process. McMillan (2013) provided the following questions to help professional school counselors and other assessment professionals determine whether or not a test is valid: (a) What is the extent to which the test matches what is taught and what is assessed?; (b) How closely does the test correspond to what has been covered in class and in assignments?; and (c) Have students had the opportunity to learn what has been assessed?

In the development of any high-stakes test, professional school counselors need to understand that the development process must begin with a clear vision of what it means to succeed within a given context. Knowing what is to be asked of students and what students will be taught is important, because different achievement targets require the application of different assessment methods. The nature of learning is also qualitatively and quantitatively different for certain disciplines. For example, teaching and learning in the subject area of mathematics is often tied to a specified instructional sequence. Therefore, what students should know and be able to do is usually tied directly to the level and quality of the instruction in the classroom. However, when developing a high-stakes test to assess third-grade English/language arts standards, the learning targets might be more generalized and not tied to a specified instructional sequence. Therefore, once a standard by which students are measured is established, then analysis of student results can take place. In other words, did the students meet the standard; and, if so, are they significantly above the standard or simply at or below the standard? Students exceeding the standard should be provided additional learning opportunities so that their potential can be maximized. Those students at the standard or below the standard should be challenged so that they can continue to build toward future mastery of the standard (Hess & Robbins, 2012).

In addition to being fair and valid, high-stakes tests must follow all relevant professional standards as outlined in *The Standards for Educational and Psychological Testing* (AERA, APA, & National Council on Measurement in Education [NCME], 1999). The Standards covers major aspects of assessment including validity, reliability, standard setting, item development, bias, and fairness review. The AERA (2002) has also issued guidelines on high-stakes testing. The following is a summary of these guidelines, with a special focus on those most applicable to the work of the professional school counselor.

1. *Protection against high-stakes decisions based on a single test.* Decisions that affect individual student's life chances or educational opportunities should not be made on the basis of a single test score or test scores alone.
2. *Adequate resources and opportunity to learn.* When curriculum content standards are introduced as a component of educational reform and to improve teaching and learning in the educational setting, students must have adequate resources and the opportunity to learn.

3. *Alignment between the test and the curriculum.* If a high-stakes test is going to be used to measure students' mastery of curriculum content standards, the test questions must validly measure the content standard as required by the test blueprint.
4. *Validity of passing scores and achievement levels.* When high-stakes tests use specific scores to determine whether or not a student passes, the purpose and meaning of the passing scores must be clearly stated. The validity of the scores must also be established.
5. *Opportunities for meaningful remediation for examinees who fail high-stakes tests.* Students who do not pass a high-stakes test should be given opportunities for remediation. Remediation should focus upon the knowledge and skills the high-stakes test is intended to measure, not just the performance itself.
6. *Sufficient reliability for each intended use.* Scores must be reliable. "Reliability is concerned with the consistency, stability, and dependability of the results. In other words, a reliable result is one that shows similar performance at different times or under different conditions" (McMillan, 2013, p. 60).
7. *Ongoing evaluation of intended and unintended effects of high-stakes testing.* Ongoing evaluation is necessary. Professional school counselors need to be aware of both the positive and negative effects of high-stakes tests.

Additional information that serves to describe how a given guideline might apply to the professional school counselor as a test user and assessment leader in the educational and counseling setting is also provided. Finally, the American Counseling Association (2004) presented a *Position Statement on High Stakes Testing* similar in many regards to the area guidelines and still relevant today.

Summary/Conclusion

The standards-based educational reform movement, the No Child Left Behind Act of 2001 with its major focus on high-stakes testing and accountability, and today's educational reform movement that focuses upon college and career readiness for all students have had and will continue to have a major impact on professional school counselors and assessment professionals. In summary, professional school counselors need to make sure that the high-stakes test that is used to measure either existing state content standards or newly developed college- and career-readiness standards, such as the Common Core State Standards, is fair, and students have the opportunity to learn the material covered by the test questions; yields valid scores and measures what it is intended to measure; includes the purpose and meaning of the scores or performance standards that are clearly stated; and follows all relevant professional standards as outlined in the Standards (AERA, APA, & NCME, 1999).

CHAPTER 34

Parents' Questions About Testing in Schools, and Some Answers

Mary Ann Clark and Sandra M. Logan

Preview

Testing in schools is both extensive and complex and, consequently, parents have many questions about testing and their child's part in it. We present some of the questions most frequently asked by parents about testing and some effective responses to those questions that can be used by professional school counselors.

Testing, or assessment, plays a vital role in education and is used for a variety of purposes. For example, assessment results may be used to monitor student performance, assess student potential, improve teaching and learning activities, evaluate programs and schools, and serve as the basis upon which to make school policy decisions. Test results also are often a major criterion upon which public perception about the quality of schools is based. Thus, testing is a fundamental activity in every school and a vital component for setting educational standards and monitoring progress toward them.

Why Do We Have Testing in the Schools?

Tests yield individual and group student data that can be helpful in educational decision making and planning. Of course, each student is unique and varies in characteristics and range of abilities, talents, and achievements. For example, some students are good at reading while others excel in math, and some achieve at their current grade level while others function above or below their current grade level. Because of the individuality and associated range of possibilities, school teachers, professional school counselors, administrators, and parents need as much information as possible about students in order to provide the best teaching and learning environments and activities for each student and classroom group. Testing is an effective and efficient way to obtain useful information about students. Some more specific reasons for testing include the following.

To Increase Learning for Each Student

Education is most effective when it is tailored to the greatest extent possible to the specific needs and abilities of each student. Test data can help to pinpoint each student's strengths and areas in need of improvement and to identify the best ways for each student to be taught and to learn.

To Compare Students With Others and With Themselves

Educators and others responsible for making decisions that affect a child's education need comparative information—that is, it is important to know how each student is performing in specific learning and skill areas relative to other students in his or her grade as well as how the student is performing over time. Such educational decisions include which principles and competencies are to be taught, which activities and materials are to be used, which curriculum is to be followed, and how students should be organized in a classroom or school. Assessment data can provide decision makers with such comparative information. Of course, the information also is helpful as feedback for students, parents, and teachers.

To Facilitate Appropriate Educational Placement

Test scores are one type of information (among others, such as grades and teacher and parent observations and information) that helps to place each student in the most appropriate educational situation. For example, although standardized test data may not be used as the sole criterion to enroll a student in a specific educational placement, they may be used for initial screening for further, more comprehensive evaluations, as well as subsequently to determine the effectiveness of the placement.

To Improve Instruction

Test results are perhaps the most common way to determine if learning objectives are being met, including learning objectives developed at the local, state, or national levels. Examination of total test and individual item results can help educators adjust teaching methods to achieve the highest possible learning benefits for each student. Also, grade- and school-wide test results may be used to assist in planning school improvements and curriculum modifications.

To Inform Parents

Parents have both a right and a desire to know how their child is performing in school, particularly in regard to the child's level of mastery of specific learning and performance objectives in relation to the student's grade level or to the student's peers, either locally, statewide, or nationally. Standardized test results are an objective way to provide such information to parents.

To Inform Community Members

Test data help all members of a school community be informed about the performance of students in the community's schools in both absolute (i.e., how much knowledge and how many skills are actually being learned) and relative (i.e., compared to similar students at the state or national level) contexts. With this information, areas of both strength and concern at classroom, school, and district levels can be readily identified.

What Kinds of Tests Are Given, at What Grade Levels, and When?

A wide variety of tests are administered in schools and for an equally wide variety of reasons. In general, tests may be administered in schools to assess a student's general cognitive ability (i.e., intelligence), academic and other aptitudes, achievement in various academic areas, career and leisure interests, and personal characteristics. All but one of these types of tests usually are administered only by student-services specialists, such as professional school counselors or school psychologists, in response to the unique needs and circumstances of individual students (e.g., for identification of learning problems or placement in specialized instructional circumstances, assistance with career planning, or application for postsecondary education). Most of these assessments are administered individually by the school specialists mentioned above. The following chart identifies a few of the common assessments used in the school setting.

Intelligence	The *Wechsler Intelligence Scale for Children* (WISC) is a norm-referenced test used to assess the general thinking and reasoning skills of children aged 6 years to 16 years. It has five main areas: Verbal Comprehension, Visual Spatial, Fluid Reasoning, Working Memory, and Processing Speed.
	The *Kaufman-Brief Intelligence Test* (K-BIT) is a norm-referenced test of general intelligence and aptitude. It can be used for a variety of screening purposes, as well as assessing cognitive functioning.
Achievement	The *Wechsler Individual Achievement Test* (WIAT) is an academic achievement test for individuals ages 4 years through adulthood. The skills are organized into four categories: • Reading: Word Reading, Reading Comprehension, Pseudoword Decoding • Mathematics: Numerical Operations, Mathematics Reasoning • Written Language: Spelling, Written Expression • Oral Language: Listening Comprehension, Oral Expression
	Woodcock-Johnson Tests of Achievement are comprehensive tests of academic achievement and scholastic aptitude, measuring skills in reading, mathematics, and writing, as well as important oral language abilities and academic knowledge.
	Kaufman Test of Educational Achievement (KTEA) is a test of academic achievement in areas of reading, math, written language, and oral language, for ages 5 years through adult.
Personal Characteristics (Developmental & Behavioral)	*Ages & Stages Questionnaire: A Parent Completed, Child Monitoring System* (ASQ) is a developmental screening questionnaire, designed to screen and monitor infants and young children who may be "at risk" for developmental delays during the first 5 years of life. This assessment may also be used for progress monitoring.
	Behavior Assessment System for Children (BASC) is an ecological, multi-method/multi-dimensional evaluation system intended to assess behavior and self-perceptions of individuals ages 2 to 25 years. This assessment helps in the determination and classification of emotional and behavioral disorders.
	Screening Assessment for Gifted Elementary and Middle School Students (SAGES) is a norm-referenced measure used to identify students, ages 5 to 14 years, who are gifted in targeted academic areas and reasoning.
	Conners-3 is an integrated behavior rating system targeting attention-deficit/hyperactivity disorder (ADHD) and its most common co-morbid disorders in children and adolescents, ages 6 to 18 years.

The notable exception is achievement testing, which is by far the most common type of testing done in schools. Achievement tests typically are either nationally standardized tests, which are purchased by the local school system or statewide from commercial testing companies, or mandated tests, which are created and distributed by the state educational agency and administered in all public schools in the state. Most achievement tests are administered in a group format in the schools.

The achievement tests selected by districts or states usually have been chosen because they closely reflect the learning objectives of the school system at the various grade levels in which the tests are administered and are used to measure learning in areas such as reading comprehension, mathematics, science, and language arts skills. Many states now combine the two types of tests (i.e., national and state) under the umbrella of the statewide achievement testing program, and scores compare students to national norms.

All states have their own state-specific testing programs, but there are many commonalities among statewide testing programs. For example, most states administer their own (i.e., developed by the state's education agency) tests to measure the mastery of student competencies deemed by the state education agency to be necessary at particular grade levels. In the vast majority of states, mastery at minimum criterion levels also is required for high school graduation. Frequently, students are given multiple opportunities to pass the tests or are given alternative test choices. With the No Child Left Behind Act (2001) and the Common Core State Standards Initiative (2009), attempts are being made to provide a more unified set of expectations for all students, regardless of their geographic location or particular school environment. The Common Core Standards were drafted by experts and teachers across the country and focus on critical-thinking, problem-solving, and analytical skills that students will need to be successful. They provide a means to measure student progress throughout the school year and establish consistent guidelines for what every student should be able to do in math and language arts from kindergarten to grade 12. At this writing, 44 states, the District of Columbia, four U.S. territories, and the Department of Defense Education Activities (DoDEA) have adopted and are moving forward with implementing the Common Core Standards (2009).

What Are All the Different Types of Test Scores?

In general, there are two major types of achievement tests. The most common type is known as *norm-referenced* tests, which yield scores that compare a child's performance to that of a much larger group of other children at the same grade or ability level who took the same test at approximately the same time in the school year. This larger group is called the *norm group*. A student's test scores are often reported in percentile ranks, which tell where the student's score is in relation to the larger standardization group. Percentile ranks range from a low of 1 to a high of 99, with 50 representing the middle (and average) score. For example, if a student has a percentile rank of 75, it means that 75% of the norm group students achieved a score lower than the student's score, and 25% of the norm group students achieved a score higher than the student's score. Of course, the greater the similarity between the student and the norm group members, the more valid the comparison.

Students do not pass or fail a norm-referenced test. Scores from norm-referenced tests are intended to give educators and parents an objective picture of how a particular student at a specific grade level is progressing in a specific subject or in school in general. Typically, norm-referenced scores can show whether a student is doing better in some academic areas rather than others or if the student is improving his or her relative standing in specific subject matter or skill areas over time.

Sometimes percentiles are reported for several norm groups, allowing a student's score(s) to be compared simultaneously to, for example, national, state, or local-area norm groups. Although a student's actual (or *raw*) score is the same on a particular test, the percentile corresponding to that score may vary, depending on the norm group to which it is compared.

The results of a norm-referenced test are sometimes reported as stanines instead of as percentile ranks. *Stanine* is an abbreviation for "standard nine," because the range of percentiles is divided into nine groups of percentile ranks. Thus, a stanine is actually a grouping of percentiles. Stanines vary from a low of 1 to a high of 9. The *approximate* percentile-rank bands represented by stanines 1 through 9 are 4, 8, 12, 16, 20, 16, 12, 8, and 4, respectively. For example, a student performing in the first stanine may have a percentile rank of 1, 2, 3, or 4. A student in the ninth stanine may have a percentile rank of 97, 98, 99 or higher. A student whose score is reported as the fifth stanine has achieved a score that is between the 40th and 60th percentile. Stanines provide much less specific information than percentiles because each student's score lies within a band of percentiles.

Another frequently reported type of score is the *grade equivalent,* which shows the grade level of students for whom a score is considered average or typical. For example, a grade equivalent of 4.5 means that the student's score is the same as what the average score of students in the fifth month of the fourth grade would have been if those students had taken the same test. Grade-equivalent scores should not be compared across test takers, because the same grade-equivalent score may not always stand for the same amount of learning for the students compared. In general, grade-equivalent scores are quite frequently misrepresented or misinterpreted and therefore should be used only with persons who have full understanding of what they mean.

The other major type of achievement tests is known as *criterion-referenced tests*. The "criteria" to which the title refers are statements of *very* specific skills or competencies for particular curricular areas, such as mathematics, science, or language arts. Although the scores from criterion-referenced tests may be reported in different ways, all of them basically reflect the numbers of skills or competencies the student has mastered in a particular educational area (i.e., subject). These scores are most often reported as percentage of correct answers achieved on a particular criterion-referenced test. In addition, the number of specific criteria met for each curricular area also usually is reported. Each score thus represents an individual level of achievement rather than a comparison to a norm group.

Many statewide testing programs use criterion-referenced tests and have a specific score that must be equaled or exceeded (often called a "cut" score) for the student to pass the test. A student's score for these tests also may be reported as percentile ranks to show how the student scored compared to a statewide norm group.

Both norm-referenced and criterion-referenced tests provide information about each individual student's level of performance and that of the student's peer group. Although one type is not necessarily better than the other, it is important to know which type of test is used to be able to interpret the resulting scores correctly.

How Are Achievement Tests Different From College Admissions Tests?

Achievement tests are used for a variety of educational purposes in schools and are administered at various grade levels. In contrast, college admissions tests are intended to predict success in college and therefore often have the very specific purpose to assist in determining who is to be admitted to a college or university and who is not. College admission tests are administered to high school students, usually juniors or seniors, seeking admission to an institution of higher education. The students' test results are usually submitted with their college or university applications.

The *Scholastic Assessment Test* (SAT) *Reasoning Test*, administered by a commercial testing company called the College Board (2014), is a 3 hour 45 minute test that yields three main scores. The Critical Reading section assesses ability to use vocabulary and to comprehend written text effectively. The Math section assesses understandings of and ability to apply principles of mathematics. The Writing section assesses the ability to develop and communicate ideas effectively and will become optional beginning in 2016. Scores on each section, Critical Reading and Math, of the SAT are reported using a scale of 200 to 800, with an intended mean of 500, while the Writing Test is scored 0–12. A percentile rank also is given on the student's score report, with the norm group being college applicants. Printed information and videos about the SAT can be found on the College Board Web site (http://sat.collegeboard.org/about-tests/sat). The College Board also administers the SAT *Subject Tests*, a set of achievement tests in subject areas such as history, mathematics, foreign languages, and science. Students usually have a choice of which SAT *Subject Tests* they take, although the tests taken may be specified or required by the college or university to which admission or advanced placement is sought.

The *American College Test* (ACT) is produced and administered by the American College Testing Program, another commercial testing company. The ACT's *Tests of Educational Development* are curriculum-based achievement tests covering four subject areas: mathematics, reading, English, and science, which are completed in 2 hours and 55 minutes (or 3 hours 25 minutes if the optional Writing Test is included.) Each of the four subject tests yields a score on a scale between 1 and 36, while the Writing test is on a scale of 0–12. A composite score, which is the average of the four sections, also is reported. Unlike the SAT's scoring, which deducts ¼ of a point for each incorrect multiple choice answer, the ACT has no penalty for wrong answers. One point for each correct answer is awarded. The national ACT (2013) composite score for high school graduates was 20.9. More information about the ACT can be found at the American College Test Web site (http://www.act.org).

More than ever, colleges and universities are giving applicants the choice of taking either the SAT or the ACT. However, some 800 colleges do not require either for admission and are identified as 'test optional' universities. For a current list of these institutions, go to www.fairtest.org/university/optional. Others may simply require these tests only for placement purposes once the student has been admitted and enrolled. SAT or ACT scores also often are used for academic advising and scholarship or loan applications prior to or soon after admission to a college or university.

The *Preliminary Scholastic Aptitude Test* (PSAT)/*National Merit Scholarship Qualifying Test* (NMSQT) is administered each October to high school sophomores and/or juniors. It is designed to give students practice for the SAT Test. However, the scores earned during the junior year also are frequently used as criteria for students to qualify for scholarship and recognition programs.

What Other Types of Assessment Are Used in the Schools?

One type of assessment becoming more widely used in schools is writing samples, and in fact, many statewide testing programs now require students to write narrative answers to questions. Another approach to assessment used more frequently is a portfolio of student work. With a focus on the outcomes of educational experiences, students use portfolios to display samples of their work in various subject-matter areas and are evaluated in regard to the final products of their efforts. Many educators believe it is important to look at the whole student, and work samples provide for such an approach to evaluation of student performance. Unfortunately, portfolio assessment is notoriously unreliable (i.e., yields inconsistent evaluations), and therefore the results of portfolio assessment techniques should be considered cautiously.

Are Testing Accommodations Made for Children Who Have a Disability?

In accord with the Americans with Disabilities Act of 1990 and Section 504 of the Rehabilitation Act of 1973 (as well as other applicable laws), any student who has a documented physical, emotional, or cognitive (e.g., learning) disability *may* be given special accommodations during testing. To receive accommodations or modifications, evidence of the disability must be presented to the school system or other agency administering the test *before* a test is administered. It is important to note the difference of these two adaptations. According to the National Center for Learning Disabilities (2014), while accommodations change how a student accesses information and demonstrates learning, modifications change what a student is expected to learn. Typically, a student who has a disability that would qualify for a testing accommodation or modification also will have either an Individualized Education Program (IEP) or be on a Section 504 plan at the school. Therefore, the planning team that worked with the parents, teachers, and child to develop the IEP or 504 plan will have given consideration to accommodations for the student's involvement in any testing situation. The college testing programs described previously mostly provide accommodations for students with documented disabilities, as a modification would alter the expectations of what is learned by the student. Such documentation of disability and needed test accommodations must be updated at a minimum of every 3 years for the college testing programs. The trend in testing is moving toward more inclusiveness meaning that most students will be required to take tests and appropriate accommodations will be provided when documentation is given. English Language Learners (ELL) and limited English Proficiency (ELP) students are included in the testing program.

The testing accommodations provided to a student are determined on an individual basis and depend on the nature of the individual student's disability. Typical accommodations for students with disabilities include extending testing time, administering the test in an isolated (i.e., distraction-free) environment, using a large print version of the test, having a reader present the items to the student orally, use of a calculator, or allowing responding on a computer instead of paper-and-pencil form of the test. Testing companies or agencies are aware of when a student is given a testing accommodation in order to score the test properly. However, test accommodation information may or may not be disclosed to test score recipients.

What Can Parents Do to Help Their Child Do Well on Tests?

One of the best things parents can do to help their student do well on tests is to become informed about the testing being conducted in their child's school. Parents should talk with professional school counselors, teachers, and administrators to learn which tests will be administered to their child, when, and most importantly, for what purposes. Parents who are knowledgeable about the testing done in schools are the best possible test preparation and performance resources for their child.

Another important thing parents can do is to help their child adopt an appropriate attitude about participation in the testing process. Children do best on tests when they have a clear sense of why it is important to perform well. Parents can help their child achieve this perspective by talking with students about the testing process, its purposes, and how the results will and will not be used. In the ideal situation, the child will have a *little* anxiety about participating in the test(s) (because a *little* anxiety enhances motivation to do well) but not be so anxious as to inhibit performance on the test(s). School counselors can hold parent information meetings about the testing program to facilitate understanding of these test basics and to help them communicate this information to their children.

Children will do best on national or statewide tests when they are well prepared in regard to the material or skills being assessed. Therefore, parents can help children perform well on these tests by helping them to regularly keep up with their schoolwork. There is a strong, positive relationship between how well children do in school and how they perform on tests. In general, good students are good test takers.

Parents also can help children do well on tests by helping them review what is to be covered on the tests. For example, parents can help their children review what they have learned in their classes at school, organize class notes and study aids, and develop a schedule for preparation. In other words, parents can help children develop good study habits, which are similar in many ways to good test-preparation habits. Many schools currently send home a booklet prior to test taking for parents to review with their child that contains sample test instructions and questions. Going over such materials can help familiarize a child with the format and sample content of tests they will be taking. It also can help parents become more familiar with what to expect with regard to the testing program.

Human performance of any kind has the greatest chance for success when the human body is well prepared to function. Test taking is no exception. Therefore, parents can help children do better on tests by ensuring that they are well rested and well fed prior to the testing period. Sufficient sleep and appropriate nourishment are essential for maximized mental performance, and parents can have a direct influence on these conditions for their child as the testing time approaches. Parents also can advise their child about good test-taking practices. For example, they can advise their child to arrive at an appropriate time before the test, have the appropriate test-taking materials ready, and listen to or read the test directions carefully. They can help their child with a time-management plan for taking the test, such as helping the child determine the average time for response to each item while allowing some time at the end for review of responses. Parents also can advise their child to find a sitting position of good posture and to shift sitting positions as necessary during the testing. They can discuss with their child whether guessing at answer choices is appropriate for the test, based on information that can be obtained from the test administrator before the testing. And finally, parents can talk to their child about reading each item and response choice carefully before selecting an answer.

What Are Some Other Good Sources of Help About Tests and Test Preparation for Parents?

The Internet provides a wealth of information that can be current and useful. A good tactic is to do a keyword search using any of the major Internet search engines and using phrases such as *educational testing, test taking, test preparation, study skills,* or *learning skills.* Also, investigate Web sites of the testing companies that produce and provide the tests to be taken. In addition, most states have a Web site for their department/division of education that usually contains information about state testing programs. Finally, local school systems and individual schools have their own Web sites that describe information and test dates concerning local testing programs. One note of caution about the use of the Internet for information: there are no quality controls on what is placed on the Internet, so exercise care in interpreting what is found.

Summary/Conclusion

Tests yield individual and group student data that can be helpful in educational decision making and planning for students, teachers, administrators, and parents. To make assessment data as valid and useful as possible, it is essential that all stakeholders understand the basic reasons for testing, basic information on the nature of the tests, meaning of scores, and how the results will be used. These principles are necessary to help students put forth their best efforts as well as to make the best use of test results.

CHAPTER 35

What Professional School Counselors Need to Know About Intelligence Tests

*Bradley T. Erford**

Preview

Professional school counselors need to understand the basic concepts of intelligence testing. General information, types and characteristics, ethical guidelines, multicultural aspects, and the responsibilities of professional school counselors with regard to intelligence tests are presented.

Cognitive and general ability instruments, or intelligence tests (IQ tests), form the basis for most psychoeducational reports. Psychological reports for individual students present data and recommendations related to special education services and Section 504 accommodations for which students may be eligible (Villalba & Sheperis, 2004). Although most educators have received some type of basic instruction regarding assessment, instrument development, and working with individuals with special needs, professional school counselors who have a master's degree have advanced coursework in assessment and are able to demonstrate their awareness and understanding of intelligence tests (i.e., IQ tests, cognitive ability measures) and how they affect school students.

School psychologists receive specific training and are typically responsible for administering and interpreting most intelligence tests in school settings (DeThorne & Schaefer, 2004; Villalba & Sheperis, 2004). However, most school psychologists are assigned to several schools within a district and may only visit one particular school once or twice per week. Professional school counselors also receive training in assessment and are often the most knowledgeable on-site staff members when it comes to intelligence tests. Professional school counselors' advanced training in assessment may lead some to become coordinators or cocoordinators of special education identification programs in their schools (Monteiro-Leitner, Asner-Self, Milde, Leitner, & Skelton, 2006). In addition, some professional school counselors who serve on school-based student assistance teams also are given the responsibility for administering brief intelligence tests for screening purposes. Consequently, professional school counselors become the person many colleagues and parents turn to when a concern arises about intelligence tests, psychological reports, or special education services.

---

*Special thanks to Jose Arley Villalba and Peggy S. Byrer for their outstanding contributions to the first two editions of this chapter.

Since most professional school counselors already have had one or more college-level courses in assessment, this chapter will focus on basic characteristics of the more widely used intelligence instruments, how to understand test results, and how to use test results to develop an appropriate educational plan for students. In addition, an outline for presenting intelligence test information to parents and colleagues is provided. Ethical and multicultural considerations also are discussed.

Basic Characteristics of Intelligence Tests

Before the subject of common characteristics can be addressed, the types of intelligence tests must be explained. Basically, there are two types of intelligence tests: (a) brief tests, which are frequently used for screening purposes; and (b) comprehensive tests, which are commonly used for diagnosis, educational placement, and which form the cornerstone of most psychological evaluations and psychoeducational reports. Many professional school counselors, who have completed a master's degree and have taken a course in assessment, may administer a brief test, such as the *Slosson Intelligence Test–Revised* (SIT-R; Nicholson & Hibpshman, 1998) or *Kaufman-Brief Intelligence Test* (K-BIT-2; Kaufman & Kaufman, 2004b). Comprehensive tests such as the *Wechsler Intelligence Scale for Children–Fifth Edition* (WISC-V; Wechsler, 2014), *Wechsler Adult Intelligence Scale–Fourth Edition* (WAIS-IV; Wechsler, 2008), *Kaufman Assessment Battery for Children–Second Edition* (K-ABC-II; Kaufman & Kaufman, 2004a), *Stanford-Binet 5* (SB-5; Roid, 2003), and *Woodcock-Johnson Tests of Cognitive Ability–Third Edition* (WJ-III COG; Woodcock, McGrew, & Mather, 2001) are generally considered "level C tests" (Erford, 2013) and are administered and interpreted by certified or licensed school psychologists or other licensed professionals, including licensed professional counselors (LPCs), depending upon licensure laws and regulations in various states. These comprehensive intelligence assessments are mentioned here because they are the most frequently used intelligence tests for assessing children and adolescents (Erford, 2013).

Whether an IQ test falls under the category of brief or comprehensive, the instrument is used to assess the cognitive ability of individuals (Cohen, Swerdlik, & Sturman, 2012). Perhaps a better way of interpreting the previous statement is that intelligence tests are used to gauge someone's *current ability*, the combined effect of potential and past experiences. Most of the instruments used to assess intelligence are indirectly or directly based on theories of intelligence. However, regardless of the particular theory an instrument is based on, most tests of cognitive ability share a few common characteristics.

Intelligence tests, whether they are administered to an individual or a group, rely on normative data and statistical analysis to determine their usefulness and appropriateness for measuring intelligence. From this data, test administrators are able to determine if test scores are valid and reliable and therefore applicable for administration to children, adolescents, and adults. For example, SIT-R normative data were collected from a sample of 1,800 individuals in preschool through adulthood (Nicholson & Hibpshman, 1998). The WISC-V was normed using 2,200 children ages 6–16 years before it was published and made available for use by professionals (Wechsler, 2014). The SIT-R primarily measures verbal ability through a combination of items that assess vocabulary, word similarities and differences, memory for sentences, memory for digits, comprehension, quantitative reasoning, and general information. The K-BIT-2 (Kaufman & Kaufman, 2004b) uses a nonverbal scale (comprised of the Matrices subtest) and verbal scale (comprised of the Verbal Knowledge and Riddles subtests) to determine an individual's full scale intelligence score. Used in conjunction with information from teachers, academic performance, observations, and achievement test scores, results from a brief intelligence test can be used by professional school counselors and other educators to determine appropriate educational options for students.

Most comprehensive intelligence tests provide a global, overall IQ score, in addition to scores for specific dimensions or categorical components of intelligence through the use of subtests. The subtests combine to provide the overall IQ score and factors (e.g., areas of specific cognitive ability, such as verbal reasoning, short-term memory, processing speed, organizational skills). For example, the K-ABC-II derives an IQ score from how a person performs on two factors: sequential processing facets and simultaneous processing facets (Kaufman & Kaufman, 2004a). For the WISC-V, the overall IQ score is based on how a person performs on the verbal comprehension, visual spatial, fluid reasoning, working memory, and processing speed indexes (Wechsler, 2014). In another example, the SB-5 derives an overall IQ score from up to five different areas, if all five areas are assessed (Roid, 2003): fluid reasoning, knowledge, quantitative reasoning, visual–spatial processing, and working memory.

Regardless of the comprehensive intelligence test used to determine a student's ability, professional school counselors should recognize that IQ scores are not derived from only one area or type of intelligence, but rather efforts are made to test a child's full range of abilities (e.g., verbal reasoning, short-term memory, auditory processing, mathematical ability). Even more important, professional school counselors need to understand how these test results can be used in establishing a child's educational plan.

Understanding Intelligence Test Results

Professional school counselors are responsible for familiarizing themselves with the more frequently used intelligence tests, even though they may not ever administer them (Erford, 2013). The more comfortable a professional school counselor becomes with the different components of intelligence tests, background information on how tests were developed, what population the tests are intended for, and the significance of the results, the more effective they will become at understanding intelligence tests as well as helping others (e.g., students, parents, teachers) understand the results on a particular test. Familiarity with intelligence tests starts with the understanding of how IQ scores are calculated and what the scores mean.

The calculation of IQ scores depends on two factors: (a) the chronological age of the person taking the test, and (b) the raw score received on the instrument administered. These two parts are used to determine the person's IQ score, or standard score (Erford, 2013). A person's chronological age is how old one is in years and months. A person's raw score is simply how many questions (or points) were correctly answered. Using these two pieces of information, the test administrator compares a test taker's raw score to other people in the same age range, as established by the test's developer and reported in the test manual. Age ranges and corresponding standard scores are determined by test developers based on how the normative sample performed on each part (subtest, subscale, index, factor, or total scale) of the intelligence test. This information, usually presented as a series of norm tables, is provided in the administrator's manual as part of the instrument kit. Once standard scores have been established, it is possible for professionals familiar with the test and general assessment procedures

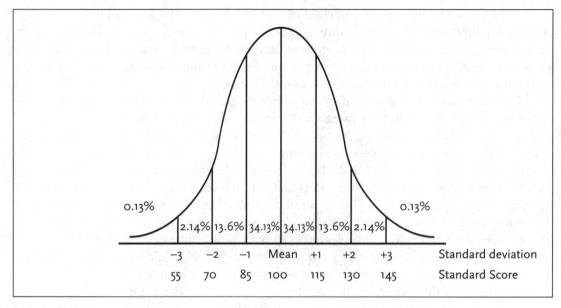

Figure 35.1. Normal distribution of a bell-shaped curve ($M = 100$, $SD = 15$).

to interpret the scores. In essence, it becomes fundamental that professional school counselors understand what these standard scores mean before they can interpret them or help others (e.g., colleagues, parents) understand the significance of the scores.

To understand the significance of a student's standard score (IQ score), a professional school counselor must comprehend three things: the mean of the standardized test score in use, the standard deviation of the standardized test score in use, and the bell-shaped normal curve (see Figure 35.1). For an IQ score to signify something, it must be compared to the mean score on that test. The mean standard score for the WISC-V, WAIS-IV, K-ABC-II, SB-5, SIT-R, WJ-III COG, and K-BIT-2 is 100. In addition, one must also know the standard deviation of the standardized scores used on these tests. With the case of the aforementioned instruments, the standard deviation is 15 points, with the exception of the SIT-R, which has a standard deviation of 16 points. Without getting too mired in statistical jargon, these two components, the mean and standard deviation of a particular intelligence test standardized score, allow the test administrator to determine if a test taker's score is above or below the average score and by how much.

An individual's results on a comprehensive intelligence test are used as one of the principle determinants for special education program qualification (Erford, 2013). Eligibility for special education services also is dependent on teacher observations, academic achievement/performance, adaptive behavior, and social and emotional functioning. The location that a student's IQ score falls on the normal distribution curve can help determine if a child is of average, above-average, or below-average ability. For the purpose of special education, it may also help determine if the test taker is functioning in the gifted range (typically an IQ score of 130 and above), intellectually disabled range (typically an IQ score of about 70 or lower), or if there is a significant difference between cognitive ability (e.g., IQ score) and achievement—as represented by a standardized achievement test score—thereby suggesting the presence of a specific learning disability.

Results on IQ tests and other psychoeducational tests also can assist professional school counselors and other educators in determining the most effective way to teach a particular student, even if he or she does not qualify for specific special education services. The information gained from tests provides a wide array of information for how a student learns best, student strengths and weaknesses, and perhaps for how proficient students are at grasping, retaining, and retrieving new information. Intelligence test scores also can assist in determining what types of classroom accommodations and curriculum modifications may be warranted for the student to be successful in the school setting. All of these data may be used by the professional school counselor to advocate for students and their families.

Helping Others Understand Intelligence Tests

The mere fact that intelligence tests are based on statistical principles and use professional jargon is enough to confuse most teachers and parents. Professional school counselors must be attuned to the confusion, frustration, fear, or indifference that is related to a student's intelligence test results. Also, professional school counselors may need to help teachers, parents, and students make sense of test scores and how the information will be used to alter a student's educational options.

Although it typically is not the responsibility of a professional school counselor to interpret the results of a comprehensive intelligence test to parents and colleagues, one should be aware of and ready to discuss what the results of the assessment mean for a specific student. Most parents want to know if their children are fine, how intelligence test results may affect their children's future, or perhaps even if they are possibly genetically or environmentally responsible for their children's IQ scores.

Professional school counselors should make themselves available to answer teachers' questions about intelligence tests. Professional school counselors must be supportive and nonthreatening when responding to questions about intelligence. Not only can professional school counselors be instrumental in explaining what the scores mean and test administration issues, professional school counselors can also help teachers understand how to best use the test results to augment their teaching strategy toward a particular student. Examples of how professional school counselors can communicate with parents and teachers to help them better understand intelligence tests include the following:

- Explaining the idea of *intellectual ability* (standard IQ scores) as *potential*, perhaps by comparing it to how many ounces of liquid a container can potentially hold (capacity), or how fast a car is capable of driving (velocity).
- Oftentimes, parents or teachers may be confused by the phrase, "Your child's IQ is in the 75th percentile" and left wondering, "Is that good or bad?" When explaining percentile ranks, it is helpful to have stakeholders imagine a line of 100 students the same age or grade as the child, with the first student in the line being the lowest performer and the 100th student being the highest performer. The child's percentile rank indicates the child's position in that line. For example, if a student is performing at the 75th percentile this means his or her performance exceeded 75% of other children of his or her age or

grade. Likewise, it is also sometimes helpful to look at the *unmentioned number* by subtracting the percentile from 100 and stating that new number along with the percentile rank. In the case of an IQ standard score in the 75th percentile, saying "In other words, your child's score is in the top 25%, when compared to other children his age" may be easier to comprehend.

- Using common, interpretative labels to categorize IQ standard scores—such as *average* for IQ scores between 90–109, *high average* for scores between 110–119, *very superior* for scores above 130, or *below average* for scores of 80–89—is helpful when discussing a student's IQ.
- Although individual achievement tests are not discussed in this chapter, it may be necessary for parents and teachers to understand more clearly how achievement tests and ability tests are related. If a child has an IQ standard score of 109 and a reading achievement standard score of 79, then the professional school counselor may help the parent and teacher understand the discrepancy by saying, "The closer your child's reading score is to his potential, the IQ score, the more certain we can be that he is working to his potential. The 30-point difference between these two scores tells us we need to help your child read closer to his potential."
- Finally, parents and teachers should understand that IQ scores are neither *good* nor *bad*. In other words, it is not fair to attach a letter grade of "A" to a score above a 130 of a grade of "F" to a score below 70. Professional school counselors can help parents and teachers attain more realistic expectations by using what the percentage of the population actually scores in certain ranges (i.e., only 2% of the population is in the *very superior* intellectual range; half of all children [50%] score in the *average* range of intelligence) instead of referring to a particular score as *really good* or *not so great*.

Professional school counselors who administer brief intelligence tests as screening tools also must effectively explain the results of screening tests to parents. In addition, students taking the test may also want to know what the scores mean. Figures 35.2 and 35.3 include examples of English and Spanish versions, respectively, of forms professional school counselors can share with parents and students to help them understand intelligence test results. Professional school counselors may also want to share this form with the school psychologist to get additional feedback or suggestions for sharing results with parents and students.

Professional School Counselors and Ethical Issues Regarding Intelligence Tests

Professional school counselors are responsible for proper use and interpretation of assessment instruments (Erford, 2013); furthermore, it is up to the professional school counselor to gauge his or her own limits (ACA, 2014). For these reasons, professional school counselors must determine for themselves what tests they are competent to use, comfortable using, and have the ethical right to use. In addition, professional school counselors must be knowledgeable of when they cannot administer or interpret a particular instrument.

Most professional school counselors have the knowledge and training necessary to administer B-level brief intelligence tests (Erford, 2013), such as the K-BIT-2 and SIT-R. A Level B test can be administered and interpreted by individuals with a master's degree in education or psychology who have also had graduate-level coursework in psychological appraisal. However, Level C tests (comprehensive intelligence tests such as the WISC-V or SB-5)

> **Making Sense of Brief Intelligence Test Results**
>
> Recently (*student's name*) took the (*name of brief intelligence tests*), which was administered by (*school counselor's name*) after parent/guardian permission was granted. This form includes the results of the test, what the score means, and how these results will be used. Test results are used as a screening tool to see if additional testing from (*insert title of educator, such as school psychologist*) is needed, in order to develop the best educational program for (*student's name*).
>
> A person's score on an intelligence test is typically called an "IQ score." An IQ score is used to measure a person's cognitive ability, or rather, their potential and capacity to learn new ideas. Typically, tests that measure a person's intelligence use puzzles, memory tasks, math problems, logic and reasoning games, and pictures to come up with an IQ score. Because these tests measure potential, and not exactly how good someone is at school work, there are no such things as "perfect" scores or "100%." The *average* score on this test is 100, and most children (about 68%) score between 85 and 115. Scores between 116 and 130 are considered *above average* and scores between 84 and 70 are considered *below average*.
>
> (*Student's name*) received a total score of (*score*) on the (*name of brief intelligence test*).
>
> Due to (*student's name*) results on this intelligence test, the school counselor (*school counselor's name*) would like to recommend _____
>
> _____
>
> _____
>
> _____
>
> As you are sure to have questions about this recommendation, please contact me at (*school counseling office phone number*). You can also contact me if you have additional questions or would like further information about the test. Thank you for carefully reading over this form. I look forward to answering your questions and being as helpful as possible.
>
> (*Name of School Counselor, Name of School, Phone number*)

Figure 35.2. Making sense of brief intelligence test results.

require specific coursework related to particular instruments, as well as advanced knowledge in psychometrics, and should only be administered and interpreted by appropriately trained professionals, such as licensed counselors or psychologists and certified school psychologists. Usually, professional school counselors should know their limits when it comes to Level C tests and let colleagues and parents know about these ethical limits. Letting others know the ethical guidelines of the professional school counselor with regard to cognitive ability instruments should assist in clarifying to others what professional school counselors are and are not responsible for.

Intelligence Tests and Multicultural Populations

Developers of current editions of the more commonly used intelligence tests have accounted for increased numbers of minority children in the schools. Test developers of the Wechsler,

> **Haciendo Sentido de los Resultados de un Examen de Inteligencia Breve**
>
> Recientemente (*student's name*) tomo un examen llamado (*name of brief intelligence test*), cual fue administrado por (*name of school counselor*) después de recibir permiso de el padre/la madre/ el guardián. Esta forma incluye los resultados de este examen, lo que significan los resultados, y como usaremos los resultados. Los resultados de este examen se usan de una manera preeliminaría para determinar si es necesario administrar exámenes y pruebas más compresivas. (*Insert title of educator, such as school psychologist*) es en individuo que administrara estas pruebas adicionales, si son necesarias.
>
> Los resultados de un examen de inteligencia típicamente se llaman "IQ score." Un "IQ score" es usado para medir la habilidad cognitiva de una persona, o de otra manera, el potencial y la capacidad para aprender nuevas ideas. Típicamente, exámenes que miden la inteligencia de una persona están compuestos de varias partes como rompecabezas, ejercicios de memoria, matemática, juegos de lógica, y fotos, para determinar un "IQ score." Como estos exámenes miden potencial en vez de determinar el nivel de progreso académico de su hijo/hija, no hay semejante cosa como un valor de 100% o una evaluación perfecta. Es mas, el valor "average" en esta examen que su hijo/hija tomo es 100, y la mayoría de los niños (68%) obtienen valores entre 85 puntos y 115 puntos. Valores entre 116 y 130 puntos se consideran "sobre average" y valores entre 84 y 70 se consideran "bajo average."
>
> (*Student's name*) recibió un valor total de (*score*) como su "IQ score" en el examen (*name of brief intelligence test*).
>
> Debido a los resultados de (*student's name*) en este examen de inteligencia, en consejero escolar (*school counselor's name*) quisiera recomendar: _____
> _____
> _____
> _____
>
> Como es seguro que usted tendrá preguntas sobre esta recomendación, por favor llámeme a este teléfono (*school counseling office phone number*). Usted también me puede contactar si tiene otro tipo de pregunta o quisiera información adicional sobre este examen. Muchas gracias por prestarle atención a esta forma. Anticipo la oportunidad para contestar sus preguntas y para ayudarlo lo mejor posible.
>
> (*Name of School Counselor, Name of Schoo, Phone Number*)

Figure 35.3. Making sense of brief intelligence test results (Spanish version).

Stanford-Binet, and Kaufman tests have made strides to include significant numbers of African American, Hispanic American, and Asian American children in the normative samples for these tests (Erford, 2013). However, that does not signify that these intelligence tests are completely applicable for use with racial minority populations.

Although most current editions of intelligence tests contain statistical information specific to most major ethnic groups, Cohen et al. (2012) believed these tests still show bias against some ethnic groups, such as African American and Hispanic American children and, more specifically, children from families with lower socioeconomic status. These are some of the reasons intelligence tests are multidimensional (contain various subtests) and contribute to the rationale and legal precedent that placement in special education programs cannot be based on IQ scores alone.

Even though most of the items on intelligence tests have been designed to be culture-fair (i.e., without showing a positive or negative slant to a particular culture), none are culture-free (Erford, 2013). Tests that are culture-free (i.e., not impacted by the culture of the person completing the test) are very difficult to find. After all, psychological tests measure behavior, and culture influences behavior. For this reason, professional school counselors must try to find those brief tests that are as culture-fair as possible. In addition, when possible, professional school counselors must make sure that a child's ethnicity or race does not negatively affect his or her scores on a comprehensive intelligence test. Again, it is the responsibility of professional school counselors to familiarize themselves with the more popular IQ tests, even if they are not responsible for administering them, in order to best advocate for children—particularly for children from diverse backgrounds and their families.

Summary/Conclusion

Professional school counselors are responsible for many aspects of a child's educational development. Being knowledgeable of intelligence tests is part of this responsibility. Professional school counselors must be familiar with IQ tests and how they affect children and families. They also must be aware of the expectations their colleagues may have with regard to cognitive testing. A key step toward meeting this responsibility is to understand how best to present intelligence and other test information to children, parents, and teachers. Professional school counselors have the skills to advocate for fair testing practices and ensure that all educators use intelligence test results to help and benefit all students. Together with the appropriate school personnel, professional school counselors can ensure that intelligence test data are used to help students, parents, and teachers in providing the very best educational plan.

CHAPTER 36

A Practical Approach to Career Assessment in Schools

Jerry Trusty, Spencer G. Niles, and ZiYoung Kang

Preview

In this chapter, we present a practical framework for career assessment in schools and take a comprehensive, developmental perspective on career assessment. We discuss various areas of career assessment and present priority areas for assessment at various developmental levels. Formal and informal career assessments are included, and the use of career development portfolios is described. We particularly focus on using existing student data and employing assessment methods that are inexpensive and practical in terms of professional school counselors' budgetary and time constraints.

According to the American School Counselor Association (ASCA; 2011a), the average ratio of professional school counselors to students in U.S. schools in 2010–2011 was 1 to 471. Traditional, individual-based career assessment for every student is not practical for most counselors. Professional school counselors' time and budgets are likely limited, and assessment materials can be expensive. Thus, we offer effective methods of career assessment that are inexpensive in terms of time and money, and we offer a practical and flexible framework for assessment.

Assessment can be defined as the use of any formal or informal technique or instrument to collect data about a student (Niles & Harris-Bowlsbey, 2013). There are five basic reasons for using assessment to help students advance in their career development:

- Counselors can learn more about the needs of students.
- Counselors can learn more about the characteristics of students (e.g., interests, abilities, skills, values).
- Counselors can address environmental pressures that affect career development.
- Counselors can measure students' progress in their career development.
- Students can learn more about themselves and increase their understanding of the career-development process.

Career assessment is something that professional school counselors definitely need to do. The national model (School Counselor Competencies; ASCA, 2012b) and the *ASCA National Standards for Students* (ASCA, 2004) speak directly to career assessment. If school counselors are to have comprehensive school counseling programs, as described in the ASCA

(2012a) national model, systematic career assessment is necessary. Career assessment data are a major component in *data-driven* school counseling program development. When general needs assessments are administered to students in schools, students generally indicate a high degree of need in career development areas. In fact, in our experiences, career-related needs are consistently the highest priority indicated by students overall. Career assessment data, therefore, are *accountability data*.

Career assessments can be formal or informal. Formal assessments have psychometric evidence such as reliability and validity data and normative data appropriate for the group with which the measure will be used. Because formal assessments often have a standard way for interpreting scores, the results can be reviewed, at least initially, with a large group of students. Examples of formal career assessments include the *Strong Interest Inventory* (Consulting Psychologists Press, 2014), the *Differential Aptitude Test Battery* (Pearson, 2014b), and the *Career Maturity Inventory* (Crites & Savickas, 1996).

Although data from informal assessments are more subjective, they can be informative—but in ways different from formal assessments. The results of informal assessments should not be used for comparisons of students, and informal assessments often have no standard way for interpreting the results. The results of informal assessments are often reviewed in a collaborative way between the counselor and an individual student or a group of students (e.g., in small groups, in classroom guidance) and, thus, informal assessments are flexible. Examples of informal assessments include checklists, games, career fantasies, interviews, projects and products, and card sorts (Niles & Harris-Bowlsbey, 2013). Both informal and formal career assessments provide important and useful information to the counselor and student, and informal and formal assessments often complement one another.

Our career assessment framework stresses the use of career development portfolios for students. These portfolios—including collections of formal and informal assessment results, products resulting from guidance activities, samples of academic performance, and so forth—would follow students through elementary, middle, and high schools. At first thought, this might seem burdensome for professional school counselors. But these data are easy to collect; they are valuable data for students, parents, teachers, and counselors; they provide information across transitions from school to school; and these data can help professional school counselors develop and evaluate their programs across students' early childhood through 12th-grade (EC–12) development.

Although career development and career assessment become more focused as students progress to middle and high school, an EC–12 approach to career development and assessment is needed (Starr, 1996). That is, professional school counselors need to take a longitudinal view on career development and career assessment. Experiences and assessments of elementary school students should articulate well with their middle and high school experiences and assessments. In reality, all career assessments are formative evaluations, and none of the assessment data we use should be conceptualized as static outcomes, including assessments in the 12th grade.

Career development and career assessment should also be comprehensive. Although professional school counselors use the categories of students' (a) academic development, (b) career development, and (c) personal–social development, all areas are conceptualized as career development, because all are naturally related. To illustrate, Stone and Bradley (1994) noted that practically everything that elementary counselors do for students is for students' career development. For example, when elementary counselors deliver classroom guidance targeting study strategies or group counseling focused on social competency, they provide students with activities that promote skills needed for their career development. Other authors and practitioners (e.g., Erford, 2015c; Gysbers & Henderson, 2012) take a similar holistic and comprehensive view on career development across the life span. Additionally, research (e.g., Trusty, 2004; Trusty & Niles, 2003, 2004) has demonstrated the importance of students' middle and high school achievement and experiences on later completion of the bachelor's degree.

In this chapter, a practical, flexible, developmental, and comprehensive approach to career assessment for elementary, middle, and high school students is presented. Readers may be tempted to only devote attention to sections that pertain to the students they serve directly, but we assume and encourage an EC–12 perspective. (Actually, the perspective is more of an EC–16 and life-span perspective.) In the last section of this chapter, we present a qualitative, flexible method for career assessment at the middle school and high school levels.

Career Assessment Areas

The Career Assessment Priority Matrix is presented in Table 36.1. This matrix does not include all possible areas of career assessment. However, it is fairly comprehensive, covering skills and abilities, self-perceptions, perceptions of the world of work, self-awareness, decision making, goal setting, and environments and perceptions of environments. In the columns on the right, the priority of the assessment area at the particular grade level is indicated (*low, moderate, high*). If the assessment area is not appropriate at the particular grade level, NA (not a priority) is indicated.

Academic Achievement

Of the areas in the matrix in Table 36.1, the first, *academic achievement*, is very important from the elementary level onward. Researchers have found that early academic achievement has long-lasting effects on students' career development. For example, school grades, even in the early elementary school years, are strongly related to whether students complete high school (Barrington & Hendricks, 1989); and achievement test scores in middle school strongly predict what postsecondary majors students choose (Trusty, Robinson, Plata, & Ng, 2000) and how much postsecondary education they pursue (Trusty, 2002). Achievement in middle school is clearly the result of what students learned in elementary school. The courses that students complete in high school—particularly intensive science and math courses—heavily influence students' success or lack of success in college (Trusty, 2004; Trusty & Niles, 2003, 2004).

Professional school counselors generally have access to achievement data at the elementary, middle, and high school levels. Criterion-referenced, basic skills mastery tests supply limited information because of their nature. Information from these instruments will be less useful for students who are achieving at moderate or high levels. Group-administered formal ability assessments are used in many schools to determine which students should be tested further for gifted or enrichment programs (e.g., *Otis-Lennon School Ability Test* [Pearson Education, 2014c]; *Cognitive Abilities Test* [Riverside, 2014a]), and these supply some information. However, the best sources of achievement information are generally: (a) scores on some national, standardized, norm-referenced comprehensive achievement instrument (e.g., *Iowa*

Table 36.1 Career Assessment Priority Matrix

Assessment areas	Priority/appropriateness at grade levels		
	Elementary	Middle school	High school
Academic achievement	high	high	high
Career exploration behavior	high	moderate	moderate
Perceptions of careers	high	high	moderate
Self-perceptions	moderate	high	high
Interpersonal skills	high	high	high
Environments (e.g., families)	high	moderate	moderate
Perceptions of environments (e.g., barriers, opportunities)	low	high	high
Self-awareness:			
strengths and obstacles	low	high	high
interests	NA	high	high
values	NA	moderate	high
Career awareness	NA	moderate	high
Decision making	NA	moderate	high
Goal setting	NA	moderate	high
Ability self-estimates	NA	moderate	high

Note. NA = not a priority.

Test of Basic Skills [Riverside, 2014b]; *Stanford Achievement Test* [Pearson Education, 2014d]); (b) school grades and other in-school performance criteria; and (c) the intensity of students' curricula. Score reports on standardized achievement instruments generally identify degrees of competence and obstacles in several specific academic areas. School grades are often inconsistent across schools and across teachers, but they may hold valuable information for identifying students' strengths and obstacles. Local performance criteria and students' performance products might become part of the career development portfolio that follows students through schools. Students' curricular experiences should always be a component of the career development portfolio. When professional school counselors, teachers, parents, and students have access to comprehensive data regarding students' achievement, all people involved in students' education are better prepared to make decisions (e.g., special programs, appropriate courses).

In high school, the most important gauge of achievement is the academic rigor of courses completed by students. In large national studies, researchers (Adelman, 1999; Trusty 2004; Trusty & Niles, 2003, 2004) reported that U.S. college students who completed more academically intensive coursework in high school were much more likely to graduate from college. The positive effects of rigorous high-school coursework on degree completion were evident for all major U.S. racial–ethnic groups. With regard to particular courses, completing advanced high school math courses had a particularly strong influence on college success. Students' grades in these rigorous courses mattered little. Academic achievement is also related to most other aspects of career development and career assessment. For example, environments, and especially parents, have a strong influence on achievement.

Career Exploration Behavior

The elementary school years should be a time of open exploration of careers. Career-related fantasy should be encouraged. As Herr, Cramer, and Niles (2004) maintained, the elementary school years are not a time in which children are encouraged to narrow their career options but a time when they are encouraged to broaden their perspectives. Across the elementary grades, the range of careers familiar to students should grow exponentially. Assessment of exploratory behavior might be reflected in students' knowledge of various careers and career areas, their fantasy or enthusiasm reflected in products they create, or in the career-related stories they tell or understand. At the middle- and high-school levels, career exploration may be needed for some students, but as students develop they generally become more focused on particular careers or career areas. Professional school counselors, however, should be cautious, because adolescents are often overly restrictive in their perceived range of desirable or possible careers.

Perceptions of Careers

Students' exploratory behavior and perceptions of careers are closely related. Students often form perceptions of careers early. For example, students often form ideas about occupational prestige and gender roles when they are in elementary school. At the elementary level, students should begin learning various educational opportunities and, in a general way, begin connecting educational tasks to careers. Students should also begin connecting occupations and educational and training requirements. In middle and high school, and even into college, students are susceptible to overgeneralized or otherwise faulty perceptions of careers. At the more advanced educational levels, perceptions of careers are generally conceptualized as *career awareness*, an area discussed later in this chapter.

One critical area is students' perceptions based on gender roles. Students very early on develop ideas about the association between genders and careers (Helwig, 1998). Additionally, gender seems to be a primal basis for eliminating and choosing careers (Gottfredson, 1981), and students may limit their ranges of desired occupations very early in their lives. Therefore, assessments and activities that are focused on gender stereotyping of careers are appropriate at the elementary level and onward. And efforts should focus on both girls and boys. Over the last several years, girls and women have become less gender-stereotypical in their career aspirations and postsecondary educational choices, whereas boys and men have remained relatively gender-traditional in their aspirations and choices (Helwig, 1998; Trusty et al., 2000). The issue of traditional versus nontraditional gender roles is often political and controversial, and likely cultural. However, a system that functions best for individuals and society as a whole is one that uses all its talent and potential effectively. It seems that if this perspective is taken by professional school counselors, their work with students on gender roles would be less controversial for parents, teachers, school administrators, and communities. Professional school counselors should always consider the caveat that in traditional cultures, gender roles may be highly delineated.

Students' perceptions of careers and occupations can be readily assessed simply by having them indicate if they perceive particular careers or occupations positively, negatively, or neutrally. Also, having students relate the positive, negative, and neutral-specific aspects of careers would provide more data on their perceptions. Students' ability to connect occupations, tasks, and education/training requirements is also easily assessed in a classroom guidance format.

Self-Perceptions

A fairly high level of cognitive development is required for young people to reflect on themselves, reflect on the world of work, and match self and work. This requires abstract, second-order thinking, which is associated with the *formal operations* level of cognitive development, a level that is generally reached in adolescence (Muuss, 1996). However, children do develop self-perceptions and self-awareness, albeit at a more concrete level, through the elementary years (Herr et al., 2004). In the elementary grades, students begin to make concrete connections between their performance and their self-perceptions, and these early self-perceptions are the foundation for later, more complex and specific self-perceptions, career-related values, and ability self-estimates, which in turn are the bases for choices.

In recent years, professional counselors and researchers have come to focus on students' self-competence and self-confidence in their academic skills and other career-related areas of performance. Social self-perceptions are also important to young people's learning and functioning. There are various instruments that measure either general self-perceptions (e.g., self-concept, self-esteem) or specific self-perceptions (e.g., self-efficacy for specific tasks, domain-specific self-esteem or self-competence). Self-perceptions could also be assessed in a less formal manner. For example, a professional school counselor might ask an eighth-grader, "On a scale of 1 to 10, with 10 being the best, how good are you at making things with your hands?" Special types of self-perceptions (e.g., career self-awareness, interests, values, ability self-estimates) become more important in middle and high school, and are discussed later in this chapter.

Interpersonal Skills

Children learn and refine cooperation and teamwork skills in elementary school, and according to the ASCA standards, competencies, and indicators (ASCA, 2004; Campbell & Dahir, 1997), these are career-development skills. In fact, it is usually advantageous for professional school counselors to categorize interpersonal skills as career development skills. In the first author's experience as a professional school counselor in a middle school, a teacher once stated, "These kids don't need interpersonal skills, they need academic skills." Obviously, the teacher was not making the connections between interpersonal skills and education and work, and perhaps the teacher would have been more cooperative himself if he had. The message of this interchange was that interpersonal skills and social skills activities could accurately be labeled as *career skills activities*.

Cooperative skills and teamwork skills can be assessed best through observations by teachers and counselors. A brief rating of students' strengths and obstacles would provide important data in students' career development portfolios. Often, teamwork and interpersonal skills receive more attention in elementary and middle schools. The authors' contention is that interpersonal skills for high school students are often ignored, and that interpersonal skills are necessary for advanced levels of career development. For example, interpersonal skills are actually the major part of job interviewing or college interviewing, and interpersonal skills are often a major contributor to occupational advancement.

Environments

Students' environments have powerful influences on their career development. Students in communities of lower socioeconomic status are likely limited in career-related resources. For example, youth clubs and organizations may not be available in particular communities; rural or otherwise isolated areas may be limited in career options; parents may not have access to professionals or extended family with knowledge of particular careers; mentors may not be available for children; or schools may not have budgets sufficient for extracurricular activities. School counselors themselves become an important source of social capital for students in lower socioeconomic status environments (see Bryan, Moore-Thomas, Day-Vines, & Holcomb-McCoy, 2011).

The most influential environmental force is students' parents. The educational goal transmission process in families is very strong (Trusty & Pirtle, 1998). That is, the educational goals that parents hold for their children correspond highly to the goals that children hold for themselves. Parents want to help their children, and children rely on parents for career development help. In addition to parents' expectations for their children, parents' involvement in their children's education also carries strong influence. Parents' school-based involvement (e.g., involvement in parent–teacher organizations) carries some positive influence, but the major influence is from parents' home-based involvement. Home-based involvement includes: (a) parents' regular communication with children regarding school and career, and (b) parents' support of their children's educational and career development. The influences of parental involvement carry into adulthood (Trusty, 1998, 2004).

First-generation college students, or students whose parents did not attend college, present some unique challenges. These students are likely to enter college with limited access to information about the college experience (Thayer, 2000), and they are likely to have low levels of social integration in college (Nunez & Cuccaro-Alamin, 1998). First-generation college students are likely to have conflicting obligations, such as significant work and family responsibilities that might interfere with career development. First-generation college freshmen are two times more likely than their non first-generation counterparts to leave college before their second year, even when factors such as delayed enrollment and working full time are considered (Choy, 2001). Thus, these students and families will need to develop high levels of resilience if students are to be successful.

Data on environments can be assessed relatively easily. Teachers and professional school counselors, after working with students for a few months, will have a good idea of the resources, supports, situations, characteristics, and difficulties in students' environments. Some environmental characteristics are obvious, whereas others are not. For example, if a student is not receiving adequate physical care, problems are easily recognized. However, the emotional climate in families is not often readily recognized. Data on students' environments would identify opportunities and barriers to learning and to career development, and should provide professional school counselors with important contextual information.

Perceptions of Environments

At the middle school level and beyond, young people begin to have some comparative gauge of the positive and negative influences from their environments. In fact, middle school students' perceptions of parents' home-based involvement are more reliable than parents' reports of their involvement. Parents tend to positively bias reports of their own involvement (Trusty, 1996). Perceptions of environments have often been conceptualized as barriers and opportunities. Barriers are frequently described as *real barriers* and *perceived barriers*. If barriers to career development are perceived by a student as real, then barriers are real for that student; and barriers function to block the student's development, although other people may not perceive the barrier to be an actual barrier. Students' perceived barriers and opportunities can easily be assessed. Needs assessments administered to high school students often reveal perceived barriers. Also, the classroom guidance session is an appropriate format for assessing barriers and opportunities, although students may want to keep private their perceptions of some environmental barriers. Counselors should be aware that lack of information (e.g., financial aid information for postsecondary education or training) causes students to perceive barriers.

Self-Awareness: Strengths and Obstacles, Interests, Values

In middle school, students are forced to make decisions about the high school program they will pursue. These decisions are coming progressively earlier in middle schools. High schools are requiring more and more credits for graduation; more students are taking high school credit courses in middle school; and decisions are pushed deeper into the middle school years. For example, in many school systems, students and parents must decide during the sixth grade if students will take pre-algebra in the seventh grade, so they can take high-school Algebra I in the eighth grade, so they can take Calculus in the 12th grade. In the context of increased credits for graduation and an increasingly prescriptive high school curriculum required by colleges and universities, there is little flexibility once students have begun a particular high school program track. Add to this mixture the cognitive developmental level of middle school students (concrete operations) and the psychosocial developmental crisis of students (identity vs. role confusion—if prior development was optimal), and it is clear that students are not ready for these decisions. However, this is the current reality in most schools.

Students' awareness of their own strengths and obstacles, interests and preferences, and values is necessary for effective decision making and goal setting. The correspondence of skills and abilities, interests, and values is salient for decision making and goals. It is important to remember that students and assessments of students are not static. For example, a student may lack skill and interest in mechanics because the student has not had learning experiences associated with mechanics. The interest inventory score and mechanical aptitude score are low because of lack of learning opportunity. Therefore, scores should be a starting point for new learning experiences, and not a static judgment of the young person's characteristics.

Aptitudes, interests, and values can be measured fairly quickly with a battery like the *COPS System* (i.e., COPS-Interests, CAPS-Abilities, and COPES-Values; EdITS, 2014), *CDM System* (Pearson Education, 2014a), or with other instruments. Some companies (e.g., Kuder, 2014) offer well-researched assessments of interests, skills, and values in an online format, and online assessments are often less expensive than printed ones. Computer Assisted Career Guidance Systems (e.g., SIGI 3 [Valpar, 2014]; CHOICES [Bridges Transitions, 2014]) also include assessments of interests and values and may incorporate aptitude scores from other instruments. Some commercial instruments and computer programs have versions specific to elementary and middle school students (e.g., Kuder Galaxy and Navigator). With regard to interest inventories, the *Self-Directed Search* (2014) and the *Vocational Preference Inventory* (Psychological Assessment Resources, 2014) are relatively inexpensive.

However, the school or counseling program may not have budgets to cover commercial instruments or computer programs. There are alternatives. For example, *card sorts* are inexpensive and can be used in a group format for prioritizing career-related interests and values. The *Guide for Occupational Exploration* (GOE; JIST, 2014) is fairly inexpensive. Work-values exercises, along with other activities, are included in the book, and these may be copied and used in a classroom guidance format with middle school or high school students. There are additional resources that are free on the Internet, through U.S. government Web sites, state sites, and university sites (e.g., O*net, http://www.onetonline.org/). Professional school counselors are encouraged to search the Internet for usable resources. Some instruments available through the Internet may not have the psychometric strength of some published, commercially available instruments, but several noncommercial instruments would likely be very useful for professional school counselors and their students (e.g., http://www.freeteachingaids.com). The *Educators Guide to Free Guidance Materials* (Saterstrom & Steph, 2014), among several other guides to free resources, may be accessed.

Career Awareness

If students have access to the Internet, there are many resources that can be used for occupational, educational, and leisure information. For example, the *Occupational Outlook Handbook* (U.S. Bureau of Labor Statistics, 2014) is accessible through the Internet, along with many other government materials. Various national associations and societies representing numerous fields also have useful Web sites. Commercial materials (e.g., occupational card files, books) are available from vendors. However, printed materials on occupations often become quickly outdated and are a substantial investment.

Professional school counselors' assessments of students' career awareness might be connected to classroom guidance activities aimed at career awareness, or degrees of awareness might be evidenced through products students produce. Assessments might be as simple as recording students' frequencies of accessing materials. Assessment may also include assignments connected to regular classes. For example, students in mathematics classes could be required to research surveyors' use of global positioning system (GPS) technology.

Decision Making

It is fortunate that most decisions required of middle school students are not highly specific (an exception might be decisions on what foreign language to take). However, several general educational decisions do come in middle school, and more specific decisions (e.g., part-time work, postsecondary education or work) are rapidly approaching. What is important for students in middle school and high school is that they learn decision-making models and apply models to the decision-making process (see Hirschi & Lage, 2007). Students then have a template for decision making throughout their career development. It is difficult for professional school counselors to assess the wisdom of students' decisions. However, counselors can and should assess if students have learned and applied decision-making models. These data might simply be represented by a check on a checklist (e.g., student applied the decision-making model to the decision process). Similar to other data, these data are included in students' career development portfolios. Professional school counselors should be aware that students vary widely in their decision-making styles, and therefore, a variety of decision-making strategies should be presented to students.

Goal Setting

Decision making and goal setting are closely related. When students make decisions, they are often deciding on goals. Setting goals comes easily for some students, but is difficult for others. Some students experience high levels of ambiguity and discomfort when engaging in goal-setting tasks. For some, there is a real fear to decide. Assessing if students have goals is relatively easy. An assessment of the clarity, consistency, and detail in long-term, intermediate, and short-term goals is straightforward. Assessing how realistic and appropriate those goals are is more difficult and requires professional school counselors to make judgments regarding the consistency among students' goals, potential, previous behavior, personality, and so forth.

Ability Self-Estimates

Ability self-estimates are a special type of self-perception. They relate strongly to students' learning experiences, achievement, and choices. In fact, ability self-estimates are generally a better predictor of career choices than scores on aptitude instruments (Prediger, 1999). This is good news for professional school counselors, because ability self-estimates are easy to assess quickly. Also, ability self-estimates can target work-relevant abilities that are not generally assessed in aptitude or achievement tests. The typical format for ability self-estimates is having students rate, on a scale of 5 or 10 degrees, their abilities in 10 or 15 areas. For example, professional school counselors could easily construct assessments for students to estimate their abilities in the following areas:

Mathematics	Writing	Reading
Organization	Teamwork	Selling things
Cooking	Carpentry	Growing things
Mechanics	Caring for others	Electronics

Generally, each listed area is accompanied by a two- or three-sentence description of the tasks associated with the area. This list is by no means exhaustive, and students could supply ability self-estimates not included in a list but deemed important to them. Professional school counselors could easily tailor assessments to students in their schools. Ability self-estimates will be most accurate for students at more advanced levels (e.g., later high school grades and beyond) and should be relied upon more at these higher levels. The American College Testing Program (ACT) has an *Inventory of Work-Relevant Abilities* (ACT, 2008), which is available commercially, and several Internet-based assessment sites include ability self-assessment instruments.

Another format for ability self-estimates is to have students do comparisons of their abilities. For example, students are asked their level of agreement with statements such as, "Math is one of my best subjects." Using a national sample of high school students, Trusty and Ng (2000) found that 10th-graders' comparative perceptions of math and English as best subjects were highly predictive of types of college majors chosen after high school. These intra-individual, comparative self-perceptions seem to guide young people's choices, and they are included in the qualitative career assessment structure presented below.

Qualitative, Group-Format Career Assessment

The *Life Career Assessment* (LCA; McDaniels & Gysbers, 1992) is a qualitative form of career assessment based on Adlerian theory. It is generally used in an individual counseling setting. Because of high student-to-counselor ratios in schools, we adapted the LCA to a classroom guidance format. We have found adaptations of the LCA to be very effective, providing rich data on adolescents' career development. It is effective for middle school students, but more useful for high school students. The data provide professional school counselors with a deeper understanding of students and provide students with a deeper self-understanding. The LCA is a sequence of items for assessing students' experiences and perceptions. In individual counseling, these questions are intermixed with counselors' reflections and empathy responses. In a classroom guidance format, these questions are presented to students on paper, and students write their responses. Students' responses then go into their career development portfolios. When professional school counselors meet with students for individual counseling or individual planning, professional school counselors use the data to facilitate students in self-awareness and career awareness, career planning, decision making, goal setting, and so forth. An outline for the Group-Format LCA is presented in Table 36.2 (see next page).

Table 36.2 Outline For Group-Format Life Career Assessment

I. Educational Experiences
   A. General appraisal of your educational experiences
      1. dislikes
      2. likes
   B. Particular subjects/classes
      1. dislikes
      2. likes
      3. your best subject(s)
   C. Teacher characteristics
      1. dislikes
      2. likes
      3. your favorite teacher
   D. Learning setting preferences
      1. independent versus collaborative learning
      2. experiential versus didactic learning
      3. study style
      4. memorable learning experiences within and outside school

II. Work Experiences
   A. Last job
      1. dislikes
      2. likes
   B. Job supervisor/supervision style
      1. likes
      2. dislikes
   C. Repeat for previous jobs

III. Leisure
   A. Describe weekend, weekday, evening activities
   B. Fun and relaxation
   C. Friends and social life

IV. Strengths and Obstacles
   A. Three main obstacles
   B. Three main personal (intrinsic) strengths
   C. People who are resources for you

CHAPTER 37

A Selective Overview of Personality and Its Assessment

Ralph L. Piedmont

Preview

This chapter presents an overview of what personality is and summarizes this concept from the perspective of the psychoanalytic and trait schools. Strengths and weaknesses of the two schools are outlined and relevant measurement issues are discussed. The practical value of personality theory for counselors is highlighted.

Perhaps one of the most important concepts we have for understanding people is that of *personality*. However, as a term with widespread colloquial use, it has lost some of its professional precision. The purpose of this chapter is to provide some clarity as to how this term is used in the social sciences, including a basic definition of what personality is as well as providing a synopsis of two major schools of thought in the area. Also, I will discuss some of the measurement issues that coincide with these different theoretical schools. I hope that this chapter will give readers a general sense of the term's value as well as a framework for thinking critically about people: who they are, how they got here, and where they seem to be going.

Personality: A Definition

The term *personality* is certainly applied often. Pets are frequently said to have personality. Some people seem to lack this important characteristic, while others just seem to "ooze" personality. Personality is often thought of as the ultimate definition of who each of us is as a person, but many believe that it is always changing. Such varied connotations underscore just how diffuse our understanding of the term really is. We all know personality when we see it, but it may be hard to put our fingers on what exactly we mean by "it." As such, a basic definition is in order.

Personality can be defined as the intrinsic, adaptive organization of the individual that is stable over time and consistent across situations (Piedmont, 1998). There are four important points to this definition. First, personality represents some structured system by which individuals organize themselves and orient to the world around them. This system is clearly located *within* the person and is not imposed by the environment.

Second, personality is an adaptive structure, which means that it enables us to manage effectively the many competing, often conflicting, demands we encounter from both within ourselves and from the environment. As such, we should not think about personality as being *good* or *bad*. It is what it is—a systematic way of optimizing our ability to survive and thrive in the world in which we live. Rather, the question we need to ask occurs when people wish to change their environments: Will their personalities work as well in the new context as in the original?

Third, personality is stable over time. This means that there is something about who we are and what we are that remains consistent throughout our lives. There is more to say about personality change, but for now we can say that despite all the "change" we may have experienced over our lifetimes, there is some thread that seems to tie together all our developmental experiences around consistent themes. There is something about who we were as children or adolescents that lingers with us today. Finally, personality is consistent from one situation to another. Although specific behaviors may change from one context to another, our view of the world and the personal goals we are pursuing remain essentially unchanged.

This definition should not be interpreted as saying that the environment does not have anything to do with how our personality develops. Culture, context, and situation all have an influence on our development and how we may express our personality. But there does lie within us some kind of psychological "stuff" that provides our basic needs, shapes how we perceive and interpret our external world, and selects the goals we ultimately pursue in our lives. Nor should this definition be construed as arguing that personality is a static quality. To the contrary, personality is a dynamic structure. It is always responding to the demands that develop from both within us and from the world around us. Adaptation is an active process in which we continually contour ourselves to the changing features of our environment. Further, there is a developmental aspect to personality. Just as humans are not born physically mature, so, too, personality is something that begins in a simple form and becomes progressively more sophisticated as it ages. These changes follow an orderly and lawful path, so that when one looks back over life, there can be seen patterns in behavior that lend a sense of continuity to one's life.

With this basic definition in mind, it should be evident that personality is a scientific construct that helps to organize the many diverse, and sometimes conflicting, behaviors and feelings of people into a more organized system that both promotes understanding and increases predictiveness. We now turn to a brief overview of two major schools of thought concerning how personality is defined and understood. These major schools are the psychoanalytic and trait perspectives. Of course, there are many other theoretical orientations, but these two were selected for three reasons: (a) these two approaches represent popular perspectives on personality and assessment; (b) they are perhaps maximally different from each other; and (c) they are particularly relevant to counseling professionals, who are most likely to encounter both of these perspectives in their own work. For those interested in learning more about personality theories from other perspectives, as well as to learn more details about the theories presented here, the reader is referred to more specific texts on the topic (e.g., Cloninger, 2000; Monte, 1998).

The Psychoanalytic Perspective

The first person to provide a comprehensive, scientific description of personality was Sigmund Freud (1916, 1923, 1924). Freud is perhaps the best known of all the personality theorists. Although originally formulated over a century ago, Freud's ideas continue to affect how we think about people today. Freud's theory was revolutionary for his time and made three great contributions to our understanding of people. First was his notion of the *unconscious*. The unconscious represents a region of our psychological world that is outside of our immediate sense of awareness and control. Despite its absence from our daily sense of experiencing, the unconscious has a direct and powerful impact on our behavior. For Freud, all of our motivations for life come from the unconscious regions of our mind. Freud likened the human personality to an iceberg. Just as most of the ice in the berg is located under water, most of the important aspects of who we are reside in the unconscious. Thus, for Freud, it is not what our conscious minds say that is important, rather it is what emerges from the dark recesses of our unconscious that is valuable.

The second great insight that Freud provided was the notion of *childhood sexuality*. For centuries, children were seen as just miniature adults, but without the same passions and motivations that characterize adult life. There was very little recognition that children had their own psychological needs. Freud pointed out that children are very sensual creatures. Having a limited cognitive capacity, children rely more on their feelings and emotions to guide them through their interactions with the world. The most important instinct is the one defined by the pleasure–pain continuum. Children always seek to find gratification for their pleasure needs (e.g., to be fed, held, relieved, comforted) and to reduce the tensions associated with unfulfilled desires. Whether or not these needs to avoid pain and to obtain pleasure are gratified has important implications for how the child's personality will develop.

The third contribution that Freud made was the idea of *psychic determinism*. This is the belief that there is a reason for every action a person performs. Just as in nature there is a reason for everything, so, too, in our inner minds there is a logic and consistency to what we do. That logic, especially of the unconscious mind, may not always appear as rational, but there are essential patterns and meanings to things in the inner world that, once known, can unlock our understanding of the person. These three ideas were revolutionary for their time and helped to significantly stretch our understandings of how the mind works. These concepts also define how Freud looked at people, as organic machines following an innate set of commands in an effort to find security and comfort. To understand psychoanalysis, there are two basic ideas to grasp: the structure of the mind and the processes by which it operates.

The Structure and Process of Psychoanalysis

Psychoanalytic model of the mind. Every personality theory posits an underlying structure to personality. For psychoanalysis, there is a tripartite structure that describes our inner world. The first structure is called the *id*. This is the basic element of personality and is the source of all our psychic energies and motivations (which Freud referred to as *instincts*). The id contains the basic impulses that drive our behavior. There is no logic or sense of order to the id. It runs on what Freud termed *primary process energy*. This is our basic, instinctual need to attain pleasure and to avoid pain.

The second structure is the *ego*. The ego represents our more conscious processes; it embodies the logic and order of conscious thought and operates on what is termed *secondary process energy*. The function of the ego is to gratify the needs of our psychic system in ways that are appropriate and respectful of environmental realities. Two qualities of a healthy ego are its abilities to tolerate tension (e.g., go without meeting or satisfying our needs) and synthesize diverse needs into a more unified set of goal strivings.

The third structure is termed the *superego*. The superego contains our moral values or conscience. The superego, like the id, is very demanding and requires an individual to provide immediate gratification of its needs. In the case of the superego, it demands that the person live up to very high levels of virtuous behavior.

The process of personality. What is of central interest to psychoanalysts is the dynamic way each of these three structures relates to one another. Each part of the mind has its own needs and drives. Both the id and the superego are very demanding and require instant gratification. The ego has the arduous task of working hard to gratify those needs, along with its own, in the context of specific environmental demands. There is no doubt that this system generates much conflict and tension. However, it is in the process of successfully resolving these tensions/conflicts that one's personality develops and creatively engages the external world. For example, the id always wants to have immediate sensual satisfaction; in this case, let us say that it wants to eat. You are shopping at the supermarket and the id is demanding food NOW. The ego must provide it because not satisfying an instinctual need only makes it grow stronger. To satisfy the id, the ego could just reach out and take that bag of potato chips sitting on the supermarket shelf and start eating. However, the superego realizes that stealing is morally wrong—someone has to pay for those potato chips first. The superego chastises severely, creating more demands on the ego. The environment poses its own challenges: The security guard will arrest you if you do not pay for the chips. So, the id has to wait (which it does not like to do), and the longer it has to wait, the more demanding it becomes. The ego has to devise clever and effective strategies for managing all these conflicting desires. This is where *defense mechanisms* come in.

Defense mechanisms are ego-based methods individuals use to help gratify the basic instinctual desires of the id. Defense mechanisms allow the ego to gratify needs, either directly (through consuming some object that provides satisfaction) or indirectly (through the use of imagery, ideas, or other substitutes to "fool" the id or superego into thinking the need has been gratified). For example, say we are back walking through the supermarket and the hunger demands begin. You know this is not the time or place for eating. What does the ego do? Well, it reaches into the pocket and pulls out a piece of gum to chew on. It is not food that fills the belly, but it could help the id believe that it is eating something, thus partially gratifying the instinct. This takes some pressure off the ego. Also, it is not morally wrong to chew gum, so the superego remains contented, and more tension is reduced (keep in mind that reducing tension is very pleasurable). If there is no gum, perhaps putting a pencil in the mouth, or maybe drinking a glass of water will work. All of these behaviors are substitute actions that help defend the ego against the ranting id's need for food. Then, once we have bought the chips and are outside in the car, we reach in and take a big handful of those salty, tasty taters; ultimate satisfaction is attained! In each instance, the ego has worked to reduce the conflicting needs of the psychic world in ways that are appropriate and effective.

In understanding a person, a psychoanalyst wishes to know how the individual copes with the stresses and conflicts associated with instinct gratification. What types of defense mechanisms are used? There are all different kinds, ranging from very simple or childish—*repression*, where you just unconsciously deny the existence of something—to more sophisticated techniques, like *sublimation*. With sublimation, a basic primitive impulse is transformed into a more mature, sophisticated impulse that is socially accepted and valued. For example, a sadistic need to cut and destroy animals gets turned into a desire to become a surgeon. The former, something scorned and infantile, gets changed into a noble urge to want to help others in pain. For Freud, there is not much difference between the little boy who likes to pull the wings off of flies and the surgeon who operates on people in order to manipulate various body parts. Sublimation helps us to live effectively in social groupings by transforming baser instincts into urges that promote a greater social interest. Other defense mechanisms include displacement, projection, reaction formation, isolation, and rationalization.

Measuring the Psychoanalytic Personality

How does one go about measuring these levels of conflict and types of defense mechanisms? How does one gain access to a person's unconscious? To accomplish this, psychoanalysts use *projective testing*. A projective test is based on the principle of psychic determinism; that everything we do bears our characteristic stamp. If we put a person in an unstructured situation and ask that she make sense of this chaos, anything that the person creates will be an expression of her own internal, unconscious view of the world.

Perhaps the most well-known projective test is the *Rorschach Inkblot Test* (Rorschach, 1921/1998). Here, individuals are presented with essentially meaningless inkblots. The designs are basically random, but respondents are asked to create a meaningful picture. The only way for them to make sense of this nonsense stimulus is to project some of their own inner organization onto it; respondents provide their own frame of reference for the interpretation. Therefore, when we look at the response, it tells us something about how the respondents structure their psychological worlds. People are not aware that they are projecting something of themselves onto the inkblot, but to the skilled interpreter, the Rorshach is like an X-ray of the personality, revealing the details of the unconscious domain. However, to interpret those responses requires an extensive amount of training and experience. The language of the mind, from the psychoanalytic perspective, is quite sophisticated and complex. It is a world of symbols and disguised meanings that do not always conform to the rules of logic adhered to in our conscious reality.

There are a number of different projective tests, and what characterizes most of them is their unstructured, fluid format. Most of these tests allow individuals to make as many or as few responses as they wish. Also, there is no right or wrong answers, and respondents are free to give any response they choose. The goal of this class of measures is to make plain the many hidden wishes residing in the unconscious. Another popular projective test is the *Thematic Apperception Test* (TAT; Murray & Bellak, 1973). Individuals are shown a picture and asked to relate what led up to the situation pictured, what is happening now, and what the outcome will be. Again, responses are evaluated for emotional conflicts and how they are handled by the person. *The House-Tree-Person Test* (HTP; Buck, 1964) is another commonly used projective technique. Here, a person (usually a child) is asked to draw a picture of a person, a house, and a tree. The drawing is evaluated for the size of the respective elements, their location on the page, and the details that are present or absent (e.g., the person has no hands, the house has no door). These details are sometimes referred to as emotional indicators. Whether or not they are present says much about the emotional world of the artist (e.g., figures that do not have hands may indicate the presence of depression). Again, it requires much training and experience to interpret this test. Nonetheless, any situation that is unstructured and allows a person to create something can be considered a projective test. Interpreting what is created is believed to reveal important aspects of a person's unconscious world.

Strengths and Weaknesses of Psychoanalytic Personality Theory

Psychoanalysis is valuable because it is a quite comprehensive theory that explains virtually everything about people. It offers insights that link together in meaningful ways behaviors and actions that on the surface may appear contradictory and counterproductive. The theory can highlight the clever and creative ways individuals find to cope with the worlds they live in. However, the theory is quite complex and requires much study to master.

That the psychoanalytic orientation is mostly clinically oriented is both a strength and a weakness. Its focus on conflict and primitive instincts provides rich material for weaving an understanding of a person's adaptive struggles with reality. This provides a clear point of departure for developing and implementing interventions. However, these interpretations usually stress personal weaknesses and inadequacies of the individual. Truly mature and healthy functioning is experienced by only a lucky few. Thus, the theory is lacking in its ability to document true strengths.

It also makes some assumptions about men and women that may be considered objectionable today. In fact, some see the theory as being a product of late Victorian Age thinking, but the entire theory developed out of the observations of one man, usually in response to experiences with only a single patient. Although important and insightful, it is not clear whether all of these insights are valid and generalizable to today. Few aspects of psychoanalysis are amenable to true scientific testing, and, therefore, there are few data available to speak about the ultimate utility of the theory. Yet, despite very little supporting empirical data, psychoanalysis is still one of the dominant scientific theories in the field today.

The Trait Approach

The trait approach to personality takes a very different perspective to understanding the individual. Unlike psychoanalytic constructs, traits are empirically developed variables. Using sophisticated statistical analyses, trait researchers identify behaviors, attitudes, and beliefs that appear to covary with one another. In other words, seemingly diverse behaviors are identified that are observed to occur together frequently. A trait is then developed to explain or define why these various behaviors and attitudes cluster together. For example, we may notice that people who are very talkative also tend to be outgoing and sociable and like going to parties and being the center of attention. They also seem to be very perky and energetic, and they can also be very welcoming and approachable. To understand why these different behaviors go together, we may develop the trait of *extraversion*. Extraversion is a psychological construct that refers to an innate tendency of people to orient themselves to the actions and activities of the outer world of people and events. Behaviors such as time spent talking on the telephone, enjoying the presence of other people, and feeling upbeat and positive can all be linked together because they all reflect this underlying characteristic of extraversion.

McCrae and Costa (2010) have defined traits as "dimensions of individual differences in tendencies to show consistent patterns of thoughts, feelings, and actions" (p. 23). There are two points of interest in this definition. First, traits are dimensions, empirically constructed labels that help us organize human behavior along meaningful lines. Second, traits are referred to as individual differences, qualities that describe people and upon which people vary in terms of how much they possess. Thus, when people talk about extraversion, it is recognized that not everyone has the same desire to talk on the phone and spend time in the company of others. Some people may, in fact, avoid doing those types of activities. These individuals would be considered *low* on extraversion (i.e., they are introverted). Traits are frequently bipolar in nature—that is, the two ends of the dimension represent opposite qualities (e.g., organized vs. sloppy).

One major characteristic of trait psychology is its emphasis on measuring people on specific traits and then determining how much of the trait the person has by comparing his or her score to the scores of some group (known as a *normative sample*). Individuals are considered *high* on the trait if they score higher than many of the people in the normative sample, and *low* if they do not. Most people usually fall in the middle of this distribution and are said to be *ambiverts* (this term refers to someone who can exhibit both aspects of the trait, depending upon the context). For example, an ambivert on the extraversion trait would be someone who, at times, may like going out and meeting others, but can also, at times, have a desire for privacy and solitude.

But traits are more than just descriptive labels for organizing clusters of behaviors. They provide information about people that enables us to accurately predict outcomes in other aspects of the psychosocial world. In short, traits have been shown to carry impressive *surplus meaning*. Given the scientific basis of traits, much research has been done examining their predictive utility. We know that one's tendency to talk on the phone and desire to be with other people (i.e., one's level of extraversion) is linked to levels of happiness a person will experience in mid to later adulthood; it will predict levels of job success in certain types of jobs as well as predict specific types of occupational aspirations. Other traits (e.g., neuroticism and conscientiousness) have been shown to be powerful predictors of competitive performance outcomes in the academic, athletic, and occupational areas.

Traits have been linked to one's genetic makeup. It appears that about one half of the variance observed in traits is inherited genetically from our parents. Traits also have been shown to generalize cross culturally, so the same patterns in behaviors, attitudes, and actions we see in Western culture are also found to occur in other cultural contexts, such as in Asia and Africa. Thus, traits seem to be human universals for understanding human behavior. Perhaps the most intriguing aspect of research on traits has been the discovery that one's trait profile does *not* change in adulthood. After 30 years of age, all things being equal (e.g., no psychotherapy or religious conversions), personality seems to be pretty much set; our trait dispositions will remain stable over our adult lives. The value of this finding is that it tells us that once we know someone's trait standing, we can make accurate predictions about behavior well into the future. Until age 30 years, our personality is still in flux and capable of modification. But after 30 years of age, we have created for ourselves an adaptive orientation to the world that will lead us in very specific directions to pursue personal goals that are the most satisfying to our needs (e.g., the achievement-oriented person will seek out competitive situations; the extravert will seek out the company of others).

There are thousands of personality trait variables available today in hundreds of different inventories and scales. Such a cornucopia of constructs can easily lead to confusion when deciding which traits to use. Fortunately, recent research has discovered that the majority of these traits cluster themselves around five broader dimensions know as the *Big Five personality domains*:

Neuroticism—The tendency to experience negative affect

Extraversion—Reflects the quantity and intensity of one's interpersonal interactions

Openness to experience—The proactive seeking and appreciation of new experiences

Agreeableness—The quality of one's interpersonal interactions along a continuum from compassion to antagonism

Conscientiousness—The persistence, organization, and motivation exhibited in goal-directed behaviors (McCrae & Costa, 2010)

Research has shown that these five dimensions do provide a useful language for talking about trait variables and that these factors do predict a wide range of important psychosocial outcomes, including mental and physical health and occupational, academic, and intrapersonal criteria. See Piedmont (1998) for an overview.

Measuring Traits

Trait-based measures are perhaps the most common type of tests used today. They are frequently referred to as *objective tests*. Unlike the projective tests discussed previously, objective instruments provide the test taker with very specific questions and a provided response format (e.g., from *strongly agree* to *strongly disagree*). There is no room for individualized responses on these types of tests. Scores are presented numerically, usually in the form of a T score. A T score is a standardized score that has a mean of 50 and a standard deviation of 10. Scores between 45 and 55 are considered normative (these are people who are in the middle of the distribution and are considered ambiverts). Scores above 55 are considered *high* (the individual scores higher than most in the normative sample), while scores below 45 are *low*. Only scores in the high or low ranges are seen as interpretable and defining of the person.

Perhaps one of the most widely used objective-type measures is the *Minnesota Multiphasic Personality Inventory–Second Edition* (MMPI-2; Butcher et al., 1989). This scale is widely used to assess *pathological functioning*, although scores on the instrument also can be used to assess normal levels of functioning. When looking at a trait scale, it is important to determine what level of functioning is being assessed, normal or clinical. Normal traits refer to characteristics that define everyday traits in people not suffering from a mental disorder. Clinical traits represent aspects of psychological functioning that characterize more dysfunctional patterns of behaving. Although the two types of traits are related to one another (pathological traits are usually just more extreme versions of nonclinical traits), they do capture very different dynamics of the person. One should generally not use a clinical index to make hypotheses about nonclinical qualities. The MMPI-2 is most adept at capturing these more dysfunctional elements of personality. There are 10 clinical scales that capture broad aspects of psychopathology (e.g., depression, psychosis) as well as hundreds of smaller scales aimed at more specific traits (e.g., masculinity, somatic complaints). The instrument is used routinely by psychologists and psychiatrists in making psychological diagnoses. It also provides insights into one's psychological capacities and soundness.

The *NEO Personality Inventory-3* (NEO PI-3; Costa & McCrae, 2010) is the only commercially available instrument designed to capture the Big Five personality domains. This instrument contains 240 items that measure each of the broad personality domains as well as more specific traits that underlie each of these five broad domains. Each domain has six sub-facet scales. For example, the Conscientiousness domain is broken down into the facet scales of Competence, Order, Dutifulness, Achievement Striving, Self-Discipline, and Deliberation. These subscales can provide specific information on traits that may be directly relevant to specific counseling outcomes (e.g., academic success, interpersonal skills, self-esteem). Costa and McCrae (2010) have outlined the value of the NEO PI-3 for counselors in diverse contexts.

Strengths and Weaknesses of the Trait Approach

The relative omnipresence of self-report trait measures is testimony to the popularity and utility of this approach to understanding personality. The value of trait measures is that they are empirically derived constructs, so they do represent something that does exist in nature. Further, trait measures provide an efficient method for collecting systematic information about people. Easy to administer and score, these scales can provide a wide range of information that has significant implications for predicting future behavior. Scores from trait scales are readily interpreted by comparison to normative samples, and information obtained from one respondent can be readily compared to another respondent, thus facilitating comparative assessments.

However, trait theory does not have the same interpretive depth as psychoanalysis. The psychoanalytic perspective provides detailed insights into the inner world of the individual. Issues surrounding emotional conflicts and maturity are central to psychoanalytic interpretations. Trait theory is still in its infancy and needs to generate more insights into how traits are acquired, both from genetic and environmental sources. Many questions still remain to be answered, including how traits develop over time and identifying the factors that influence how and when they become expressed.

Because traits reflect self-reported regularities in people's perceptions of their own behaviors, attitudes, and actions, there is no consideration of the unconscious. From the psychoanalytic perspective, self-report measures only tell you about superficial aspects of functioning. The more important, latent aspects of personality are not touched upon. If the unconscious is important to your understanding of a client, then trait measures may have limited utility. However, trait measures do have empirically documented predictive validity. Even if traits only capture more superficial aspects of personality, research shows that these dimensions can explain significant amounts of the variance in a wide range of outcomes. Projective tests, on the other hand, are hard to quantify and do not show as high levels of predictiveness as traits. Trait advocates still need to see some empirical support for the notion of an unconscious as well as some empirical justification for the interpretations that are generated by projective tests.

Another value of traits is their focus on mostly nonclinical characteristics. Traits provide useful summary descriptions of normal functioning. Although traits do have implications for clinical issues (e.g., differential diagnosis, treatment selection, and response to treatment), they also help us to understand a student's strengths. Projective testing frequently results in interpretations that are problem-focused, highlighting the weaknesses and vulnerabilities of the student. Even "normal" individuals can appear pathological on a projective report. Trait measures allow for a more circumspect examination of both the liabilities and assets of a student. However, unlike the psychoanalytic approach, trait theory does not have built into it a methodology for making clinical interventions. Although traits can describe what a student is like and the types of treatments that may be helpful, there are no current techniques for changing actual trait levels.

Implications for the Professional School Counselor

The value of personality theory and measurement for professional school counselors cannot be understated. A personality theory provides a framework for systematically integrating the multidimensional nature of an individual into a form that promotes a sophisticated understanding of the developmental/adaptive journey of the student and provides a platform for intervening purposefully and effectively in the student's life. There are three benefits to using personality theories. First, professional school counselors can develop an appreciation for both the emotional weaknesses of a student as well as the psychological resources the student has available to draw upon. All too often, difficult students are seen only in terms of what they lack or what limitations they have. Personality theories cast an eye toward the possibilities for growth and development and thus promote a more holistic, integrative understanding of the individual.

Second, personality theory provides an explanation for behavior that speaks to the fundamental motivations of the student. Understanding what needs a student is trying to have gratified in the school environment can enable the professional school counselor to anticipate the kinds of problems a student may encounter. Personality theory can outline the typical ways which a student will cope with stress or react to pressured situations. It can also outline the types of instructional climates that may be most conducive for optimizing a student's learning.

Finally, personality theories can enable a professional school counselor to identify strategies for engaging students in meaningful dialogues and for selecting appropriate intervention strategies that will be more readily accepted by the student. By understanding how personality develops and influences behavior, professional school counselors can develop a realistic appreciation for which aspects of personality are changeable and which are not. Using personality theories as a way to understand how and why students struggle to adapt to their worlds, professional school counselors can provide the "intrapsychic lubricant" needed to smooth out problems and to enable healthy adjustment and personal growth.

Summary/Conclusion

This necessarily brief overview of these two major schools of thought only scratches the surface of what each approach has to offer in terms of understanding our inner adaptive worlds. There is much more to know about each of them. These two theoretical models are only a limited sampling of the larger number of such theories that exist in the field of personality. The Humanistic, Psychosocial, Cognitive, Behavioral, and Biological approaches, to name a few, provide rich insights into who we are that do not overlap with those contained in the psychoanalytic and trait perspectives reviewed here. There is much to be learned from studying personality theories. Although no one theory may have all the answers, learning about personality teaches the right questions to ask.

Professional school counselors should be strongly encouraged to learn a variety of personality theories and models of the mind. Learning and applying personality theories can greatly enhance the quality of counseling services. A personality theory provides a framework for systematically integrating the multidimensional nature of an individual into a form that promotes a sophisticated understanding of the developmental/adaptive journey of the student, and provides a platform for intervening purposefully and effectively in the student's life. Further, many personality theories also have associated measurement models and scales that help one collect and collate relevant information about an individual. There are six advantages to using personality measures in counseling practice:

1. Measures of personality help promote an understanding of the student in terms of both strengths and weaknesses. Personality assessment can provide a holistic evaluation of the student in terms that are clinically relevant.
2. Such an understanding can breed increased empathy and rapport with the student. A better understanding of the student's conflicts, struggles, and aspirations helps to present a more nuanced portrait of the issues that surround the student's seeking treatment. Such information highlights multiple ways of engaging a student.
3. The results of personality assessment can be used to provide the student with feedback and insight into his or her life patterns. Using a particular measurement model can provide both the student and the professional school counselor with a common language for describing and discussing the conflicts, problems, and issues that the student is experiencing. This language can be used by the professional school counselor for making interventions and providing insights.
4. Data from personality assessments can also aid in differential diagnosis. Test scores provide an independent source of information about a student's behaviors and attitudes that is relevant for nosological classification. The information contained in such scores can help clarify underlying issues that may not be evident upon initial examination.
5. Test information can be used to anticipate the course of treatment for a student. Knowing the personality styles of the student can help the professional school counselor anticipate potential problems and conflicts that may emerge in the therapeutic relationship (e.g., a person low in Agreeableness may frequently challenge the professional school counselor because such a person tends to hold a skeptical and suspicious outlook toward others). Professional school counselors can then either move to head off such potential disruptions or at least prepare for their emergence.
6. The results of personality assessment can also be used to match students to treatments from which they are most likely to benefit. For example, individuals high on Extraversion, who are sociable and talkative, will find interventions that require interpersonal interactions more helpful than do introverts, who may prefer and benefit from individual-based approaches.

Perhaps the most important benefit of personality assessment is what it affords our field as a whole. Using personality assessments enables us as professional school counselors to obtain objective, scientifically based information on students that can allow us to empirically document the value of our services. Regardless of what type of professional context one is in, the pressure is always on for counselors to do more and more in shorter and shorter periods of time. Through it all, both the providers and the consumers of our services are continuously exhorting us to demonstrate the impact of our interventions. How effective are our counseling services? In what ways do we impact our students? How much do we impact them? These are important, empirical questions that need to be answered. Personality measurements are one way of addressing these concerns. Working from a conceptual model that is consistent with the professional philosophy of the professional school counselor, personality measures provide systematic, verifiable data that can document the extent of our impact and the practical value of our services.

CHAPTER 38

Behavior Assessment

Carlen Henington

Preview

School personnel in education have increasingly focused on behavior assessment because of behavioral problems in the educational environment and accountability in educational outcomes as mandated by education policies at the state and national level (Reschly, 2008). Although personality characteristics have, in the past, been an important consideration of problematic behavior for many professional school counselors, current emphasis has been placed on a problem-solving approach (Deno, 2013) within which behavior and associated characteristics are directly and accurately assessed (Ollendick & Hersen, 1984; Shapiro & Kratochwill, 2000) so that responsiveness to intervention can be more readily obtained (Brown-Chidsey & Steege, 2010). To increase the accuracy of behavior assessment, procedures must be systematic, objective, and multidimensional.

Models of Behavior Assessment

Behavior assessment is used to determine the nature of behavior difficulties of a child and to provide information in the development and effectiveness of an intervention plan to address the behaviors. The selection of an assessment model and the assessment techniques are key to an accurate and informative behavior assessment. As such, it is important to consider the nature (e.g., ongoing vs. a one-time assessment) and the goal (e.g., screening, diagnosis, prognosis, treatment design, intervention evaluation) of the assessment. Although there is no perfect assessment system or method, the information (or data) provided by the assessment must be reliable, valid, and useful in a problem-solving approach to assessment. It is important to note that, at times, individuals disagree on the nature of a difficulty, the severity of the difficulty, and even if the difficulty actually exists. Therefore, it is important to carefully document the facts of the situation through identifying the difficulty and its existence, the desired behavior, and any contributing factors to the situation. The goal of administering each assessment component is to compare and contrast the obtained information in a methodical examination of unfolding hypotheses, much like the informed decision making that one uses when completing a difficult jigsaw puzzle. The question might be, "Where does each piece of information fit, and what does it tell us about our next move?"

In part, assessment of behavior is difficult because there are broad ranges of behavior that may be considered for assessment and a variety of classification systems used to describe problematic behavior in the problem-solving approach. Furthermore, there is often no clear distinction between normal and abnormal behavior and whether the behavior is or is not maladaptive to the situation; neither is there always a clear agreement between respondents and interviewees. One person may label a behavior as *difficult* and another may indicate it as *acceptable*. To address this disagreement that may be a part of a discussion during the problem-solving process, Deno (2013, p. 12) identified three initial steps within the assessment process: (a) provide a "factual description of the child's *current level* and *rate of development*," (b) specify "the *desired level* and *rate of development* by parents and teacher," and (c) discuss "the *importance of the difference* between the child's current rate of development and the rate desired." In this manner, it can be determined what specifically is the difficulty in the child's behavior, what is the desired outcome for intervention(s), and what would be acceptable progress toward that outcome as the intervention is provided. The discussion between parents and educational professionals can also reveal conjoint behavior difficulties (i.e., those that occur in the home and school setting). An additional benefit of using this three-step process is that it is responsive to the need to be sensitive to cultural differences in an increasingly diverse society. Discussions between parents and educational personnel can explore differences in expectations, and the facts of the situation can make that discussion more productive, likely leading to more effective communication between those involved.

There are two broad models that can be used to evaluate a student's behavior. The first, the medical model, assumes sharp distinctions between normal and abnormal behavior with the cause of the difficult behavior lying within the child. This model is best characterized through the *Diagnostic and Statistical Manual of Mental Disorders* (5th ed.; *DSM-V*; American Psychiatric Association, 2013) and tied to the *International Classification of Diseases* (World Health Organization, 2007). Alternatively, the multivariate model uses statistical or psychometric properties to compare behavior of an individual to the general population with emphasis on quantitative differences between normal and abnormal behavior. Most experts in assessment of behavior use a combination of these two models to design the assessment process, or system, with the goal of interpreting the assessment results from a specific theoretical perspective.

Although there are a number of theoretical perspectives from which to choose, behavior theory is particularly useful for assessing behavior in children and for use within the problem-solving approach. The information obtained through behavioral techniques can be used in a variety of ways, a broad range of useful information can be gathered, and the techniques allow ongoing evaluation such that change over time can be monitored. Furthermore, multiple informants can be used to provide a broad picture of the behavior in question, the results lead directly to intervention, and the same assessment techniques can be used to evaluate intervention effectiveness (e.g., responsiveness to intervention). This responsiveness has recently become a focus of educators and interventionists through new legislation and an increase in accountability expected by parents and other professionals.

One addition to behavior assessment is the concept of functional behavior assessment. Mandated by the 1997 reauthorization of the Individuals with Disabilities Education Act (IDEA), this assessment process is intended to examine behavior problems through a functional understanding of the behavior, whether it is related to academic or behavioral difficulties. The functional approach involves the generation of a hypothesized function for the problem: academic (e.g., performance vs. skill deficit) or behavioral (e.g., escape, avoidance, attention, automatic) for the engagement of a behavior. This hypothesis is then tested through a series of assessment activities to examine each of the potential functions (Merrell, Ervin, &

Gimpel-Peacock, 2012). From this information about the potential function of the behavior, a behavior intervention plan (BIP) can be developed that is believed to more directly address the underlying problem. For example, a child who is disruptive in the classroom may engage in the disruptive behavior for a number of reasons: (a) he or she cannot do the work (a skill deficit) and needs extra assistance from the teacher (in this case, the function may be to avoid or escape the class work) or (b) he or she may be able to do the work but does not (performance deficit) and instead engages in behavior to gain attention from his or her peers or the teacher or to avoid/escape the work. Using a functional approach to the evaluation of the behavior problem can assist the counselor in making recommendations to more directly address the issue that lies beneath the problem behavior and to develop an intervention that is likely to be more efficacious.

Methods of Assessment

Each method of behavior assessment provides different and important information and, therefore, each of the methods described within this chapter offers information that will be useful in determining the behavior and is likely to be valuable in the design of an intervention to address the behavior. Generally, a preferred method is to directly assess the behavior as it occurs. An example of direct assessment would involve a classroom observation of the child with behavior difficulties, whereas an indirect assessment would involve asking the teacher to describe the child's problematic behavior. It is also preferable to assess the behavior in the natural environment. There are times, however, that this direct assessment in the natural environment is not possible (e.g., too difficult or too dangerous).

This chapter will briefly present four common direct and indirect behavior assessment methods: direct observation, self-monitoring, self-report, and informant report. These methods will be presented in sequence starting with the most direct and ending with the most indirect. When several variations of a particular method are presented, those that can be considered more direct will be presented first, followed by the indirect methods. For each method, a brief description will be provided, followed by an example typical to the school environment. Each example will build on information presented such that a comprehensive assessment may be illustrated at the end of the chapter. Although some instructions for the methods will be provided, it is beyond the scope of this chapter to provide detailed instructions. Therefore, interested professional school counselors are directed to the annotated bibliography located in Table 38.1, which provides additional resources to assist in learning more about each method.

Direct Observation

Direct observation involves assessment of behavior at the time it occurs and is the most direct of the behavior assessment methods or procedures. There are two forms of direct observation: observation in the setting where it naturally occurs, and observation conducted in a contrived or analogue setting. Direct observation in a natural setting is typically a preferred component in all methods or procedures of assessment. In this method, the behavior is observed by a trained individual (e.g., a professional school counselor, teacher, teacher's aide), who observes the child in a natural environment (e.g., classroom, playground, lunchroom).

Table 38.1 Annotated Bibliography for Direct and Indirect Behavior Assessment Methods

Assessment: In Special and Inclusive Education (12th ed.; Salvia, Ysseldyke, & Bolt, 2013, Publisher: Cengage)

    Provides a comprehensive examination of a variety of assessment techniques and procedures, including traditional standardized, norm-referenced measures, and nontraditional measures.

Assessment of Children: Behavioral, Social, and Clinical Foundation (5th ed.; Sattler, 2006, Publisher: Author)

    This is the latest version of this classic in assessment of children. Provides useful descriptions of instruments, extensive lists of resources, and a wide array of tables and appendices to assist in the selection of assessment instruments and methods, understanding of key concepts of assessment and evaluation across a large number of disorders and disabilities, and translation of the assessment into a clear report.

Assessment for Intervention: A Problem-Solving Approach (2nd ed.; Brown-Chidsey, Andren, & Harrison, 2013; Publisher: Guilford Press)

    An informative guide to conducting problem-solving-based assessments in school and clinical settings through examination of environmental factors that may contribute to a child's difficulties. Includes descriptions of application, tools, and methods with case example to assist in understanding the process.

Building Positive Behavior Support Systems in Schools (Crone & Horner, 2003; Publisher: Guilford Press)

    This book provides guidance on conducting functional assessment at a system level. Case examples and a variety of illustrated forms are provided.

Clinical Interview for Children and Adolescents: Assessment to Intervention (McConaughy; 2013; Publisher: Guilford Press)

    Provides a detailed set of guidelines for interviewing children of various ages, including sample questions and examples of rapport building.

Conducting School-Based Assessments of Child and Adolescent Behavior (Shapiro & Kratochwill, 2000; Publisher: Guilford Press)

    This edited book compiles useful, detailed information for the professional school counselor in the four areas briefly described in this chapter.

Conducting School-Based Functional Assessments (2nd ed.; Steege & Watson, 2009; Publisher: Guilford Press)

    This book provides useful, detailed information for the professional school counselor in conducting a functional behavioral assessment, complete with reproducible forms.

School-Based Behavioral Assessment: Informing Intervention and Instruction (Chafouleas, Riley-Tillman, & Sugai, 2007; Publisher: Guilford Press)

    This book is an excellent resource that provides a guide for conducting assessments that lead to intervention development. Provides detailed instructions on observational assessment.

This procedure is time intensive but allows the greatest flexibility in collection of valuable data related to problematic behaviors. Direct observation is particularly useful for determining the precise behavior with information regarding its pattern, level, and likelihood of occurrence (i.e., the specifics of the situation) and allows for assessment of contextual variables (McCurdy, Coutts, Sheridan, & Campbell, 2013). Observation is also useful to determine levels of the behavior prior to, during (i.e., the eliciting and maintaining events for the behavior; Skinner, Rhymer, & McDaniel, 2000), and following intervention to determine treatment effectiveness (Brown-Chidsey et al., 2013). Aspects of the context for behavior can also be noted. These include the structure and discipline within the environment, the support for eliciting and maintaining appropriate behavior, and the presence of positive affective environment (McCurdy et al., 2013).

Case Example

Although there are a number of observation procedures that are commonly used in the schools, the following example uses a momentary time-sampling procedure to directly observe disruptive behavior in the classroom. The disruptive behavior is described as *calling out without permission during teacher lecture*. The professional school counselor, asked to conduct a behavior assessment, would observe the child on several occasions in the classroom at a time that the teacher has identified as a time the disruption is most likely to occur. At 1-minute intervals, the professional school counselor observes the child and determines whether the behavior is occurring at that precise time. The counselor probably would use a clipboard with an observation sheet in this situation; however, another simple method of tallying the behavior is to move a paperclip from one pocket to another if the behavior has occurred at the precise moment of the observation. At the end of the time allotted for the observation (e.g., 20 minutes), the number of tally marks, or paperclips in the "observed" pocket, is counted and noted. The same procedure is followed on at least one more day. This procedure provides a direct, empirical method for assessing the number of times disruptive behavior occurs. To determine the effectiveness of an intervention, the number of tally marks during initial assessment can be compared to the number count collected after intervention is implemented. This could then be used to determine the effectiveness of the intervention as to whether the disruptive behavior has decreased to an acceptable rate or is likely to with continued use of the intervention. Additional information gathered within the process might include the frequency and/or number of supportive interactions between the teacher and the child (e.g., praise statements), presence of a routine within the environment including statements of expected behavior and consistency in enforcement of these routines, and opportunities for early correction of problematic behavior (e.g., positive prompts for the desired behavior).

Alternative Observation Methods

Another assessment procedure is to observe the problem behavior using narrative recording. This is a less direct assessment method, potentially offering rich information, but requires further assessment of the behavior. This method requires the professional school counselor to use a clipboard to write down as much information about the disruptive behavior (such as calling out in the classroom) as possible using the previously presented case example. This information includes what happens before, during, and after the child yells. This information is also known as the *antecedent, behavior,* and *consequence(s)*. For example, if the child disrupts the class only when frustrated, the professional school counselor might suggest that the teacher monitor the student's understanding of the material prior to assigning individual seatwork. In directly observing the behavior, the professional school counselor may notice that when the student yells there are a number of behaviors that also occur. In another example, the professional school counselor may notice that, frequently, when the student yells across the room, the teacher has left the room and the teacher's aide is in charge. This is another example of an antecedent to the behavior. In a third example, when the student yells out in the classroom, he looks around at the other students to see if they are watching. This information provides a hint that the student is yelling to obtain peer attention, and an appropriate intervention may be to encourage other students to ignore this student when he yells in the classroom. It is important for the professional school counselor to note what happens after the student yells. For example, if the teacher sends the student out of the room and to the principal's office, it may be that the student is allowed to avoid school work when he or she yells out and, therefore, yelling serves the function of escape from the classroom and the required class work. Thus, from this information, the professional school counselor can determine what might need to change in the environment to assist the student in changing the disruptive behavior.

Not all behaviors can be easily assessed using observation methods. For example, internal conditions such as fear cannot be observed. However, there are physical indicators of fear, and these can be directly observed (e.g., changes in breathing or heart-rate). Another behavior that cannot be readily observed is an individual's thought process or behaviors that occur outside the typical school environment (e.g., nighttime sleep patterns of a student who falls asleep in the classroom). A possible alternative, less direct than observation in the natural environment, is assessment of the behavior in a contrived situation that is engineered to simulate the natural setting; however, any departure from direct observation of behavior in the natural environment requires inference about the behavior. In this situation, additional data about the behavior must be collected from multiple sources to reduce the likelihood of error and to support the inferences. For example, using the example of the student who yells out in the classroom to illustrate, it may not be possible to observe the student in the classroom, or, when the observer is in the classroom, the behavior may not occur. Then, a contrived situation may be constructed. For example, based on the information provided by the teacher, the professional school counselor suspects that the student is able to avoid or escape schoolwork when he or she is disruptive (i.e., the function of the behavior is to avoid class work). To test this hypothesis, the professional school counselor may be required to provide the student with an academic task to be completed. Because the situation does not directly reflect actual occurrences in the classroom, the professional school counselor may have to collect additional data. An example of such data might be to determine the amount, difficulty, and type of academic work that the student is likely to attempt to avoid.

Self-Monitoring

Self-monitoring is a procedure that uses the individual to observe, record, and report behavior. Researchers have shown that a variety of populations can effectively use self-monitoring to assess behavior (e.g., individuals with developmental delays, learning disabilities, emotional–behavioral disorders; Henington & Skinner, 1998). Self-monitoring was effective in assessing academic and nonacademic behavior. Nearly any behavior that occurs in a school setting can be assessed using self-monitoring (Cole, Marder, & McCann, 2000). Unlike direct observation, self-monitoring requires very little of the professional school counselor's resources. This procedure can be used either as a behavior assessment tool or as an intervention.

One key asset is that self-monitoring can be used when direct observation is not possible (e.g., an adult is not present; the behavior is nonobservable, such as anger).

When using self-monitoring to assess behavior, it is important to provide the student with instruction about the procedures. The first step in the instruction is to describe self-monitoring to the student and suggest when it might be useful. This allows the student to understand that he or she is going to be working on the problem *situation*. Next, be sure that the student understands what the behavior is that will be monitored. It is important to be specific in the description of the behavior and, perhaps, to provide examples and nonexamples to assist the student in discerning the exact behavior to be monitored. Then, explain that when it is time to monitor the behavior, the student, using an internal dialogue, will ask himself if the behavior was occurring; if so, he is to record the behavior. Generally, it is helpful to problem-solve with the student how the behavior will be recorded (e.g., an observation form, or the 'paperclip' method previously described). Once the student understands the self-monitoring procedure, it will be necessary to practice. Initially, the professional school counselor may find it helpful to model self-monitoring using the already provided example and nonexample behaviors. Then, have the student practice the procedure in as natural a setting as possible, with the professional school counselor providing feedback. This step is important because it increases the likelihood of accurate monitoring. However, if the student understands and accuracy is still a concern (e.g., due to the student's noncompliance or truthfulness), then the professional school counselor may want to add a systematic check that another individual conducts. For example, every so often, when the time to monitor occurs, the professional school counselor also records his or her observation, and a comparison is made between the two observers. To increase the student's motivation to accurately self-monitor, the professional school counselor may wish to provide the student with a reward for matching the observation of the professional school counselor.

When a student uses self-monitoring, it may be helpful to implement a reminder (a cue or prompt) to alert the student when to observe the behavior. This can be done with a verbal or nonverbal signal from another individual or through self-prompting (the student checks his or her own behavior). The observation can be done using a schedule (e.g., momentary time sampling described in direct observation or a less formal system, such as when he or she finishes a page of problems).

Case Example

In the following example, a 6-year-old boy often forgets to turn off the water in the boys' bathroom after he washes his hands. The female professional school counselor cannot accompany him into the bathroom to observe his behavior. Therefore, self-monitoring is an appropriate assessment technique. The professional school counselor discusses the problem with the student early in the morning or after school when others are not present. She describes self-monitoring. Then, the counselor models self-monitoring by enacting a scenario were she uses the bathroom to wash her hands. The boy stands outside the bathroom. When the professional school counselor leaves the bathroom, she asks herself if she has remembered to turn off the water. If she has, she says "Good" and makes a note of it by marking on a card taped to her desk. Then, the student enacts the same scenario, following all the steps. If he forgets, the professional school counselor reminds him. If he does it correctly, the professional school counselor praises him and rewards him with a star on top of his tally mark.

Alternatives to Self-Monitoring

A common variation of self-monitoring is peer monitoring (Henington & Skinner, 1998). In peer monitoring, a peer observes and records the data, whereas in self-monitoring, the student implements the procedures himself or herself. It is important to remember that the more complex or difficult the behavior being assessed, the more training time will be needed. In some cases, the behavior may not be appropriate for self-monitoring.

Self-Report Measures of Behavior

There are two broad methods of obtaining information from the individual with the problematic behavior: individual interviews and self-report rating scales. It is generally believed that the individual may be a better reporter of their nonobservable and nondisruptive (internalized) behaviors such as fears, anxiety, and depression. Conversely, it is also generally believed that individuals with observable and more disruptive (externalized) behaviors such as oppositional, attentional, overactivity, and conduct problems are less reliable in their reports of their behavior. Although at times self-report data may be questionable in its validity, when other methods of behavior assessment are also used, self-report can add information that will be helpful in the assessment process and in development of potential interventions.

Individual Interview

This method assesses the individual's perceptions of the behavior in question. Interviews can be viewed on a continuum, with structured interviews at one end and unstructured interviews at the other end. Structured interviews provide preset questions asked by the professional school counselor. The interview generally starts with collection of broad information about the individual and progresses to information about the problematic behavior. The information about the individual assists in building an understanding of events, characteristics, and other relevant issues that may assist in assessing the behavior. Information obtained about the behavior may include (a) a description of the setting and/or circumstances surrounding the behavior, including the response of the individual and others to the behavior; (b) the onset, duration, frequency, and severity of the behavior; and (c) the history of the behavior and presence of the behavior in other family members (Lane, Gresham, & O'Shaughnessy, 2002). Structured interviews can be completed by the professional school counselor during a meeting with the informant; they also can be completed independently with the individual using a written form or computer program.

In unstructured interviews, the professional school counselor might begin with broad questions and then follow the response with additional questions to provide detailed information. The same general information obtained in the structured interview can be collected, but the professional school counselor allows the individual to provide the information with less direction and in a more flexible manner. Most professional school counselors use a combination of the structured and unstructured interview. In this case, the interview might be considered semi-structured. The professional school counselor follows a general outline for obtaining information but pauses to ask follow-up questions as needed.

Self-Report Measures

Self-report measures, also called self-report ratings, provide information regarding an individual's perceptions of his or her behavior. Self-report measures, similar to interviews, provide qualitative information; but quantitative data is often also available. There are as many types of self-report measures as there are types of behavior disorders and concerns. Some measures assess only one aspect of behavior (e.g., depression, anxiety, self-esteem). These measures are considered narrow-band measures. Conversely, some self-report measures assess a broad spectrum of behaviors (i.e., broad-band) and are often referred to as omnibus measures. These broad measures are generally used as screening tools and are often followed by the more specific measures to closely assess for specific difficulties.

Self-report measures can be based on two models to evaluate the behavior: (a) a theoretical model (use of a specific theory about behavior) or (b) a psychometric model (use of a statistical analysis). When the measure is based on theory, often the questions or statements on which the individual self rates are taken directly from the diagnostic criteria for the disorder or problem. For example, a question related to depression would state *I am often sad*, a criterion characteristic from the *DSM*. The individual would rate how valid this response is for him or her. For young children, a forced choice is often used (e.g., true or false). For older individuals, the choices are more expansive and placed on a continuum. In both cases, a number value is assigned to the response (i.e., *very true* = 3, *somewhat true* = 2, *not usually true* = 1, *rarely true* = 0). The number of items within the measure often depends on the criteria and the desired amount of specificity, information, and reliability of the measure. Each item will have a number value that is dependent upon the individual's response, and the total of the number values is then calculated (i.e., simple sum of scores). The subsequent total is usually compared to a set of reference scores that indicate whether the reported behavior perceptions are noteworthy.

The psychometric procedure often uses the same rating format and varies very little in appearance from the theoretically based measures. The questions are often constructed from a theoretical perspective; however, the set of reference scores is empirically derived. In general terms, during instrument development, the measure is administered to a large number of individuals considered to exhibit a broad range of possible behaviors and responses, typical and atypical (e.g., a norm sample). The data from all of these individuals could then be statistically examined in two ways. Without going into great detail, the purpose of these analyses will be described. The first analysis, a factor analysis, determines what questions are related to each other in some statistically systematic way. Using this information, the questions are usually refined and those that are related are considered to assess a specific behavior or characteristic as determined by an examination of the items themselves. The second analysis determines a *typical score* and (what might be considered) an *atypical score*. Using the numbers assigned to specifically grouped items, a derived score, usually a *T* score (a mean of 50 and a standard deviation of 10) is expressed as a cut score (similar to the theoretically derived scales) to indicate noteworthy response patterns. A percentile score is also often provided within a table to indicate where the individual would be placed in the norm sample if he or she had been in the original norm sample. For example, a percentile score of 60 would place the individual's score as exceeding 60 out of 100 individuals' scores in the norm sample.

Because self-report measures usually compare an individual to a preselected group or norm sample, the norm sample should be as similar to the individual as possible. For example, a child from a rural Southern state should not be compared to children from a large urban setting. Likewise, it would be inappropriate for a young child to be compared to adolescents.

Case Example

The following example illustrates a combination of an individual interview, an omnibus self-report assessment measure, and follow-up narrow-band measures. The professional school counselor has received a referral for a preadolescent girl for whom her teacher has concerns about a recent change in the student's demeanor, falling grades, and sudden social isolation.

Once proper consent and assent has been obtained, the professional school counselor meets with the student and conducts a semi-structured interview. In the interview, the professional school counselor obtains information that leads him or her to believe that the student may be experiencing moderate to significant emotional distress. After collecting information about the child's perception of his or her behavior, the professional school counselor then asks the child to complete a broad-based screening measure used by the school district to evaluate children. The professional school counselor scores the broad measure and confirms that there are a number of concerns uncovered by the screener related to depression and anxiety. It is important to note that screening instruments often do not distinguish the fine differences between anxiety and depression. The professional school counselor then follows the screening measure with two separate measures for children—one that specifically assesses depression and another that assesses anxiety. The professional school counselor then scores the narrow-band measures. If the scores are consistent with those of children the same age in the norm sample who have been diagnosed with either disorder, the professional school counselor can be reasonably assured that the child is experiencing distress similar to that of children with either depression and/or anxiety (whichever is indicated by the scores). The professional school counselor can then determine an appropriate intervention to assist the student with reasonable certainty that the intervention will target the correct behavior. As a follow-up to the intervention, the professional school counselor can then reevaluate using the same instruments, a self-monitoring technique, or an observation of specific behavior to determine if the intervention has been effective.

Other-Report Measures of Behavior

The other-report method of assessing behavior, especially children's behavior, is the most frequently used assessment method. One of the reasons for this popularity is that, by their nature, report measures are a relatively brief method of obtaining information across a broad range of behaviors from multiple informants. This method is flexible enough to be applied to nearly any type of behavior without losing the integrity of the assessment process.

Other-report measures, also known as an informant report, are similar to self-report measures. Interviews are conducted with an individual familiar with the child to determine his or her perceptions of the behavior. The informant can also complete rating forms. Those individuals most likely to provide appropriate information include parents, caretakers, and teachers. Generally, informant-report measures are conducted with adults only; however, peers can also be asked to evaluate behavior. When peers are used, special care must be taken to protect the relationship of the child and his or her peers. When such risk occurs, use of the other measures described in this chapter may provide suitable and sufficient information to avoid risk to peer relationships. Thus, only in rare circumstances is the information provided by peers of sufficient importance that risk to the child is outweighed by the need for the additional information. Similar to self-report measures, there are two broad types of informant-report measures: informant-report interviews and informant-report rating scales. It is important to consider the language of the informant, and, in recent years, many measures are available in other languages, with the most typical language being Spanish.

Informant-Report Interviews

According to Sattler (2006), the goal of assessment is to "obtain relevant, reliable, and valid information about the interviewees and their problems" (p. 3). The focus of the interview is determined by the nature of the behavior. Great diversity exists within interview techniques and, frequently, the form and structure of the interview is based on the theoretical training of the professional school counselor. Similar to student interviews, informant interviews can be structured, semi-structured, or unstructured. When the professional school counselor is unsure of the problem behavior or questions the proposed referral question, he or she is likely to use a structured interview to gather a broad range of information. This increases the possibility of determining alternative hypotheses about the behavior and allows a more flexible approach to problem solving in behavior assessment. A professional school counselor who uses an unstructured interview method is more likely to focus on obtaining information directly related to a specific behavior or problem.

Generally, key informants of a student's behavior are those who are most likely to be in a position to observe the behavior, primarily parents and teachers. Information obtained in a parent interview should include the following: family and developmental history of the child and a history of the behavior (e.g., symptom description, onset, duration, intensity or severity, past interventions). Teacher interviews are more likely to be behavior-specific, narrow in scope, and focus on obtaining detailed information about the behavior. Information obtained in a behavior-specific interview should include an exact definition of the behavior, a history of the problem behavior (e.g., setting(s), surrounding events—antecedents and consequences), past interventions and their effectiveness, the goal of the assessment/intervention, potential incentives to use during intervention, and other available resources.

When conducting an interview with the parents, it is desirable to have both parents present to obtain the perspectives of the mother and father. Some professional school counselors may also want the student present for a part of the interview to allow direct observation of the parent–child interaction. Another variation is to have the entire family present. This allows observation of family interaction. Another alternative is to conduct a conjoint interview with the parents and the teacher. Sheridan, Kratochwill, and Bergan (1996) described a procedure for conjoint meetings. In any case, when the student is present, care should be taken to protect the professional school counselor's relationship with the student, and, when appropriate, the student should be excused so that the student does not perceive the adults to be talking about him or her with no regard to vulnerable feelings.

Informant-Report Rating Scales

Although informant-report rating scales are considered to be the least direct form of behavior assessment, they are one of the most used assessment methods because they have strong psychometric properties and are relatively objective. Merrell (2000) described these strengths, stating that rating forms have been shown to have the same rater consistency across time, items, and situations (i.e., reliability). He also stated that rating scales provide consistent information across respondents (i.e., validity). Additionally, they can be used for comparison across individuals and behaviors (i.e., norm-referenced) and can be applied in meaningful ways (i.e., used to develop treatment and interventions). Other researchers have also discussed the strengths of the rating scale method (Shaffer, Fisher, & Lucas, 1999). Relatively little training is required to administer and score rating measures. Additionally, informant-rating measures can provide information about behaviors that are difficult to assess more directly (e.g., low-occurrence behaviors, behaviors that the child may not accurately report). Rating scales often provide information about behavior that has been observed across long periods of time. This allows the professional school counselor to determine the presence of the behavior at other times in the child's development.

Potential problems with rating scales are predominately related to the vulnerability to rater bias. These biases include the halo effect (e.g., a tendency to view a child in a more positive way than would typically occur) and leniency or severity effect (e.g., a tendency to be too easy or too difficult in evaluation of the behavior). It is important that the professional school counselor remembers that ratings are perceptions and, therefore, as stated previously, must be compared for consistency with other data collected about the behavior and the child. Table 38.2 provides annotated bibliographies of commonly used behavior assessments.

Case Example

In this example, a third-grade teacher has approached the school's professional school counselor about classroom management. The professional school counselor uses a brief behavior-specific interview, obtaining the teacher's perceptions of the behavior of her students. He discovers that the teacher has concerns about only one student in her class and that she has spoken with the parents about the student's behavior. The teacher reports that the parents have similar concerns.

The teacher is concerned about a student's variable grades and motivation, disruptive behavior, and lack of friends. This behavior assessment potentially will require a formal assessment and intervention with the student. The professional school counselor then contacts the parents to obtain permission for a formal assessment. He sends some broad-based parent-report measures to the parents and asks them to complete and bring them in when they come for an interview. The professional school counselor then asks the teacher to complete similar broad-based report measures. During the parent interview, the professional school counselor asks that the teacher be present for part of the interview (a conjoint interview) so that more comprehensive information can be collected about the behavior. The parents and the teacher agree and the professional school counselor uses the rating scale responses of the parents and teacher to conduct a behavior-specific interview.

The professional school counselor has now built a team of problem solvers to address the behavior. The team determines that a comprehensive assessment should be conducted.

(text continues on page 446)

Table 38.2 Annotated Bibliography for Commonly Used Behavior Assessments

Self-Report Inventories

Beck Youth Inventories **(2nd ed.; BYI-II; Beck, Beck, & Jolly, 2005; Publisher: Pearson)**

Self-report measure assesses youth aged 7–18 years with five inventories (Depression Inventory, Anxiety Inventory, Anger Inventory, Behavior Inventory, Self-Concept Inventory) each with 20 questions. Individual reports how true each item is for them in the past 2 weeks. Strengths are each inventory can be used individually or together, allows assessment of individuals with special needs and low reading ability, allows progress monitoring for intervention effectiveness.

Behavior Assessment System for Children, Second Edition–Self-Report of Personality **(BASC-2-SRP; Reynolds & Kamphaus, 2004; Publisher: American Guidance Service)**

Available in English and Spanish, assesses student's perceptions and feelings about school, parents, peers, and one's own behavior problems. Two forms: Child—ages 8–11 years (SRP-C); adolescent—ages 12–18 years (SRP-A); and young adults—ages 18–25 years (COL). The SRP-C and SRP-A have identical composite scores (School Problems, Internalizing Problems, Inattention/Hyperactivity, Personal Adjustment, and the Emotional Symptoms Index—ESI, a composite score that consists of positive [adaptive] and negative [clinical] scores). The COL, excluding School Problems, has the same composite scores with slightly different subscales (e.g., Alcohol Abuse, School Adjustment). Includes 14 to 16 subscales (dependent upon the age level) with two new subscales added (Attention Problems and Hyperactivity) beyond those offered by the first edition. For the SRP-A and COL, four content subscales have also been added (Anger Control, Ego Strength, Mania, and Test Anxiety) to broaden content. Yields *T* scores for the 139 to 185 items using norms for the general population, males, females, and a clinical population. Strengths are the ability to assess response sets or validity indices (e.g., "fake good," "fake bad") and use as a multi-informant instrument when combined with other BASC-2 measures.

Children's Depression Inventory 2 **(CDI 2; Kovacs, 2010; Publisher: PsychCorp)**

A multi-rater measure consisting of a 28-item scale appropriate for individuals ages 7–17 years. Contains two scales (Emotional Problems and Functional Problems). Strengths are low reading level (second grade) and ease of administration and scoring either as a screener or diagnostic tool; a short form is available with 10 items for screening purposes. Uses cut scores rather than derived scores.

Reynolds Adolescent Depression Scale **(2nd ed.; RADS-2; Reynolds, 2002; Publisher: Psychological Assessment Resources)**

A 30-item instrument appropriate for ages 11–20 years. Uses a 4- or 5-point rating scale to assess depressive symptomology. Strength is ease of administration and scoring.

Reynolds Child Depression Scale **(2nd ed.; RCDS-2; Reynolds, 2010; Publisher: Psychological Assessment Resources)**

A 30-item instrument appropriate for ages 7–13 years. Uses a 4- or 5-point rating scale to assess depressive symptomology. Strength is ease of administration and scoring.

Revised Children's Manifest Anxiety Scale **(2nd ed.; RCMAS-2; Reynolds & Richmond, 2008; Publisher: Western Psychological Services)**

Assesses state and trait symptoms of anxiety. Appropriate for ages 6–19 years using 49 items to yield *T* scores on three subscales (Physiological Anxiety, Worry, Social Anxiety). Strengths include broad number of anxiety symptoms assessed, and ease of administration and scoring.

(continues)

Table 38.2 (*continued*)

Informant Inventories

Achenbach System of Empirically Based Assessment (ASEBA; Achenbach & Rescorla, 2000; 2001; Publisher: Western Psychological Services)

This revised system includes a variety of new tools for use in assessment including School-Age and Preschool forms. The Child Behavior Checklist/1½–5/LDS and the Caregiver-Teacher Report Form 1½–5 (C-TRF; Achenbach & Rescorla, 2000) are for very young children. The Child Behavior Checklist for Ages 6 to 18 (CBCL/6–18) and Teacher Report Form (TRF; Achenbach & Rescorla, 2001) are for school-age children. All versions provide cross-informant scores on syndromes (e.g., internalizing, externalizing problems), scales consistent with diagnostic categories of the *Diagnostic and Statistical Manual* (DSM-IV-TR), as well as competencies. Strengths include a large research base to support validity of the instrument, wide familiarity to a number of professions in the mental health fields, and translation into numerous languages with input from professionals from 16 cultures to validate diagnostic categories. Useful tools (ASEBA Quick References Guides) are available to assist the practitioner in using the ASEBA forms.

Behavior Assessment System for Children, Second Edition–Parent Rating Scale (BASC-2-PRS) and *Behavior Assessment System for Children, Second Edition—Teacher Rating Scale* (BASC-2-TRS; Reynolds & Kamphaus, 2004; Publisher: American Guidance Service)

Published concurrently with the BASC-2-SRF, these two versions of the BASC-2 are intended to assess a child's clinical and adaptive behavior in the home and community (Parent Rating Scale) and school environment (Teacher Rating Scale). Both measures have three forms: preschool (ages 2–5 years), child (ages 6–11 years), and adolescent (ages 12–21 years). Requires approximately 10–20 minutes to complete. These measures have been expanded beyond the original BASC with extension of ages at both ends of the spectrum; added subscales for Adaptability (to the adolescent level), Activities of Daily Living (to BASC-2-PRS), and Functional Communication (to all levels); and the Content Scale (to all levels; i.e., Anger Control, Bullying, Developmental Social Disorders, Emotional Self-Control, Executive Functioning, Negative Emotionality, Resiliency). Yields T scores using norms for the general population, males, females, and a clinical population. Strengths are the variety of scales for differential diagnosis, validity indices, strong psychometric properties, and use as a multi-informant instrument.

BASC-2 Behavior and Emotional Screening System (BASC-2 BESS; Kamphaus & Reynolds, 2007; Publisher: Pearson)

Multi-informant (students in second grade and beyond, and parent and teacher versions), brief universal screener. Assesses emotional and behavior strengths and weakness of children preschool age to grade 12. Strengths are brief administration, single T score, and Spanish version available.

Devereux Scales of Mental Disorder (DSMD; Naglieri, LeBuffe, & Pfeiffer, 1994; Publisher: Pearson)

New version of the *Devereux Scales* (School Form) with two forms: 111-item scale for ages 5–12 years and 110-item scale for ages 13–18 years. Either parents or teachers can complete this new version that provides T scores on six clinical scales, Attention (ages 5–12 years, only) and Delinquency (ages 13–18 years, only). Strengths include ratings that can be compared across informants and good discrimination between emotionally disturbed and nondisturbed children.

Functional Assessment Informant Record for Teachers (FAIR-T; Doggett, Mueller, & Moore, 2002; Edwards, 2002; Publisher: Author)

Uses teacher provided information to assist in developing hypotheses about the function of students' behavior in the school environment including additional information about the problem behavior, antecedent events (task information, preceding activity), maintaining functions (persons present/absent), consequences of behavior and other actions, and past interventions. Strengths include ease of administration, direct link to behavior that either will supplement direct observation or allow hypotheses generation when observation is not an option.

Specialty or Narrow-band Informant Rating Scales

Attention Deficit Disorders Evaluation Scale–School and Home Versions (ADDES-3; McCarney & Arthaud, 2004; Publisher: Hawthorne Educational Services)

This rating scale has two versions: Home (46 items) and School (60 items); and yields two subscale scores: Inattentive, Hyperactive-Impulsive. Although lacking in construct validity for the subscales, internal consistency tends to be high. Strengths include support materials for interventions and a large nationwide normative base.

Social Skills Improvement System Rating System (SSIS; Gresham & Elliot, 2008; Publisher: Pearson)

This instrument includes self-, parent-, and teacher-rating forms to assess children's social skills, competing problem behaviors, and academic competence. Useful for screening purposes for social difficulties and intervention planning, but behavioral and emotional problem scales may be less useful and valid than other instruments. Strengths are multi-informant measure, provides intervention recommendations for 10 social skills, an available Spanish version, and an available class-wide version.

Sutter-Eyberg Student Behavior Inventory–Revised (SESBI-R; Sutter & Eyberg, 1984; Publisher: Author)

Designed to be the companion to the *Eyberg Child Behavior Inventory* (Eyberg & Robinson, 1982), the SESBI focuses specifically on 36 behavior problems using a 7-point rating scale and yes–no problem identification system. Strength of this measure is that its use facilitates identification of problematic behavior for direct intervention. Spanish version will soon be available.

Formal Behavior Observation Systems

Behavior Assessment System for Children, Second Edition—Student Observation System (BASC-2-BOS; Reynolds & Kamphaus, 2004; Publisher: Pearson)

Also available in an electronic version (BASC Portable Observation Program–BASC POP) in which observations are entered into a computer or PDA, allowing storage of five observation sessions from which to generate reports. Brief observation system that allows for examination of 13 specific categories of behaviors (4 categories of positive–adaptive behaviors and 9 categories of problematic behaviors). Uses a momentary time sampling procedure, narrative procedure, and a checklist of behaviors. Strengths include ease of use, time efficiency, and direct observation of children and adolescents.

Behavior Observation of Students in Schools (BOSS; Shapiro, 1996; Publisher: Guilford Press)

Assesses key components of a student's academic behavior including three types of off-task behavior (i.e., verbal, motor, passive), as well as active and passive on-task behavior. Uses a time-sampling procedure. Teacher's direct behavior toward the target students is also tracked. A comparison peer is also observed. Strengths include distinction between active and passive behavior and focus on academic behavior.

Direct Observation Form (DOF; Achenbach, 1986)

Intended to be integrated with information obtained with other ASEBA products, this observation system examines 96 problems, many of which have overlap with items on the ASEBA rating forms completed by parents, teachers, caregivers, and youth.

State-Event Classroom Observation System (SECOS; Saudargas, 1992; Publisher: Author)

Observational coding procedure with a long history that uses a brief observation and a time sampling procedure. Provides for assessment of instructional situations, categories of student behavior (states and events), and teacher behavior. Strengths include the ability to assess a wide range of classroom occurrences, including peer and teacher behavior.

The professional school counselor makes arrangements to observe the student in the classroom and to interview the student. When the team completes their conjoint meeting, they leave with a belief that the behavior will be properly assessed and will lead to an effective intervention that will improve the student's behavior. The professional school counselor then selects from a variety of assessment tools described within this chapter to collect information and inform him of potential interventions to address the teacher's and parents' concerns.

Summary/Conclusion

A comprehensive behavior assessment is likely to include most if not all four components of behavior assessment: direct observation, self-monitoring, self-report measures, and informant-report measures. The more comprehensive the behavior assessment, the more likely important information will be collected and used to correctly identify the problem; and based on this information, the more likely an appropriate intervention will be developed to address the problem behavior. That is the ultimate goal of a behavior assessment—to address the behavior and alleviate distress that may either be a symptom or a cause of the behavior.

SECTION 6

Clinical Issues in School Counseling

CHAPTER 39

Helping Students Who Have Attention-Deficit/Hyperactivity Disorder

David J. Carter, Patricia Carter, and Bradley T. Erford

Preview

This chapter provides information for increasing awareness, knowledge, and skill levels for addressing the specific needs of students with attention-deficit/hyperactivity disorder (ADHD) using a team approach. In most cases, students affected by this complex disorder are disadvantaged in school, home, and social settings. We provide facts and strategies to dispel myths, support for addressing the needs of students with ADHD, and user-friendly strategies for parents, teachers, and the professional school counselor.

Attention-deficit/hyperactivity disorder (ADHD) is a complex medical condition affecting about 3 million school-age children (about 3%–5% of the school-age population) and is so multifaceted that one student with ADHD may have very different symptoms than another student. This complexity can make navigating the academic arena very frustrating—so much so that 35% of students with ADHD fail to finish high school (Lawlis, 2005).

History of ADHD

Over the years, the terms used to describe ADHD have changed (Barkley, 2006). During the first half of the 20th century, children who had ADHD were described as brain injured or brain damaged. During the 1950s and 1960s, the terms *minimal brain dysfunction* (MBD), *hyperactive child syndrome*, and *hyperkinetic reaction of childhood* were introduced into the literature. In 1980, the third edition of the American Psychiatric Association's (APA) *Diagnostic and Statistical Manual of Mental Disorders* (*DSM-III*) introduced the term *attention deficit disorder* (ADD). *ADD with hyperactivity* was used to describe students with characteristic distractibility, impulsivity, and overactivity. ADD *without hyperactivity* described the distractible and impulsive children who lacked significant hyperactivity. In 1987, APA's *DSM-III-R* introduced the term *attention deficit hyperactivity disorder* (ADHD) and listed 14 criteria. This conceptualization did not distinguish subtypes based on activity levels and reflected the thinking of the time that distractibility in and of itself was not characteristic of a mental disorder. In 1994 with the release of the *DSM-IV*, the current term *attention-deficit/hyperactivity disorder* (ADHD) was introduced.

In the *DSM-5* (APA, 2013), ADHD is currently composed of three subtypes. Students with *predominantly inattentive presentation* have little or no problem sitting still but may have difficulty with organizational skills or staying focused on a task or activity. Other students with *predominately hyperactive-impulsive presentation* may be able to pay attention to a task but have significant difficulty controlling their impulses and motor activity. The most commonly diagnosed form of ADHD is the *combined presentation*; these students have significant symptoms of both the inattentive and hyperactive-impulsive subtypes.

Not all professionals distinguish between types of ADHD in the same way; therefore, addressing the student's specific individual symptoms is most effective. This requires a team approach, in which all significant observers and participants in a student's treatment provide information on how to best support the student. Professional school counselors, school psychologists, teachers, school administrators, and parents are all key members of the team who observe and report on the student's progress. Professional school counselors have the responsibility of selecting and monitoring the student's treatment, making referrals, and linking parents to community resources. Parents should be encouraged to learn about and advocate for their child's rights within the educational system, including rights to an appropriate education in the least restrictive environment and any needed accommodations or special services (Erford, 2015c). When parents know their role on the team, they are empowered to seek the best support for the student.

Common Myths Surrounding ADHD

A number of myths continue to permeate society. Following are nine commonly regarded myths about ADHD.

   1. *ADHD is an "imitation disorder" and is not a real or recognized condition.* ADHD has been recognized as a debilitating disorder and disability by all major professional medical, psychiatric, psychological, legal, and educational associations (Lougy, DeRuvo, & Rosenthal, 2009; Tartakovsky, 2011).
   2. *Stimulant medications cure ADHD.* Research has shown that children and adolescents diagnosed with ADHD benefit from therapeutic treatment with stimulant medications, which have been used safely and studied for more than 50 years. However, medication only reduces symptoms during treatment. "Skills, not pills" create lasting changes in the lives of students with ADHD.
   3. *Individualized Education Programs (IEPs) will always be provided for students with ADHD.* In most school districts, unless a diagnosis of ADHD has been provided by a physician or by a mental health professional after a psychological assessment, an IEP will not be initiated. In these cases, the professional school counselor can recommend intervention strategies to the teacher or advocate for appropriate referral and treatment. Students with ADHD are often given accommodations through Section 504 of the Rehabilitation Act of 1973 or, when eligible, special education services through the Individuals with Disabilities Education Improvement Act of 2004, usually with a handicapping condition of "other health impaired" or learning disability, if such a disability exists.
   4. *A diagnosis of ADHD allows students to make excuses rather than take responsibility for their actions.* Counselors, educators, and physicians routinely teach students and parents that ADHD is a challenge, not an excuse. Medication may address an underlying chemical imbalance, but coping skills give students a fair chance of facing the challenges of growing up to become productive adults.

5. *ADHD is the parent's fault and due to bad parenting and lack of discipline. All that students with ADHD need is old-fashioned discipline.* Faraone and Biederman (1998) demonstrated that while ADHD may be an inherited condition, not all children in a family will develop it. While each child has different experiences within the family framework, primary parental disciplinary styles do not change from child to child. Quite often, however, the parent of a child with ADHD will shift toward an authoritative parenting style in an effort to control the child's behaviors. Simply providing more discipline without any other interventions generally worsens rather than improves the behavior of students with ADHD (Lougy et al., 2009). This only serves to exasperate a child who is already experiencing frustration. Traditionally, parenting styles have been categorized as Permissive, Authoritative, and Authoritarian, with the Authoritative parent being the ideal. Lawlis (2005) suggested a more comprehensive classification: the *Teacher*, who focuses on teaching a specific culturally accepted philosophy and values; the *Supporter*, who provides only support, believing the child's fate is out of anyone's control; the *Molder*, who attempts to form the child to their specific expectations and hopes; the *Guide*, who is passive, allowing the child to have self-expression without control or interference; the *Monarch*, who places their own needs before the student's and views every behavior as a reflection on themselves; and the *Dependent*, who sees the child as a commodity for serving their needs. Lawlis believed the *Teacher* to be ideal.

6. *Teachers and professional school counselors around the country routinely advocate for medication for students who are even a little inattentive or overactive.* When teachers and professional school counselors see students who are struggling to pay attention, concentrate, or are fidgety and disruptive, it is their responsibility to bring this behavior to parents' attention so that parents can make an informed decision and take appropriate action. The majority of professional school counselors and teachers do not simply promote medication; they provide information so that parents can seek out appropriate diagnostic and treatment services. Professional school counselors do not ordinarily diagnose students with ADHD; however, they are the professionals who have the most direct contact with the student, teachers, and the parents. This places them in a position to observe behaviors, collect information, raise the possibility of ADHD, and bring information to the attention of parents. The parents should then have psychological and medical evaluations conducted, either privately or in cooperation with school personnel.

7. *Children will eventually outgrow ADHD.* ADHD may not disappear as a student grows older. Seventy percent of students with ADHD continue to manifest the full clinical syndrome in adolescence. Anywhere from 15% to 50% will continue to manifest the full clinical syndrome in adulthood (Lougy et al., 2009). Generally, hyperactive symptoms are likely to decline in adulthood while symptoms of distractibility and disorganization remain.

8. *Sugar, food dyes, and additives will increase ADHD activity.* Sugar causes a burst of energy (in anyone, not just students with ADHD). Restricting sugar intake will not reduce ADHD symptoms. Food dyes and additives should be eliminated from everyone's diet, but this is becoming more difficult because of current food processing methods. Studies have shown that some students (perhaps 20%) have allergic reactions to these substances. However, food dyes and additives do not cause hyperactive symptoms in the vast majority of students with ADHD (Lougy et al., 2009).

9. *It is not possible to accurately diagnose ADHD in children.* Although scientists have not yet developed a single medical test for diagnosing ADHD, diagnostic criteria have been developed, researched, and refined over several decades. The current generally accepted diagnostic criteria for ADHD are listed in the *DSM-5* (APA, 2013). Using these criteria and multiple methods to collect comprehensive information from several informants, ADHD can be reliably and accurately diagnosed.

Diagnosis

When diagnosing ADHD, professional school counselors can help uncover evidence of clinically significant impairment in a child's social or academic functioning as well as document that the symptoms were evident prior to 7 years of age and were present in more than one setting. A common ADHD assessment used is the *Conners' Ratings Scales–Third Edition* (Conners, 2008). Intelligence tests, such as the Kaufman (Kaufman & Kaufman, 2004b) and Wechsler Intelligence Test Series (Wechsler, 2008, 2014), along with achievement tests, such as the *Woodcock–Johnson III* (Woodcock, Mather, & McGrew, 2001), can be administered to assess for possible cognitive discrepancies and learning disabilities. In order to differentiate between ADHD and other behavioral disorders, omnibus or multidimensional assessments such as the *Child Behavior Checklist* (Achenbach & Rescorla, 2001) should be administered. Symptoms of ADHD must persist for at least 6 months and to a degree that is maladaptive and inconsistent with the student's developmental level.

It is widely believed that many students are misdiagnosed with ADHD because they have medical or psychological conditions that mask or mimic the symptoms of ADHD (Erford, 2013). Comprehensive medical and psychological evaluations are essential in differentiating between conditions that mimic ADHD and comorbid conditions that coexist along with ADHD. This increases confidence in the student's ADHD diagnosis.

Following are medical and psychological conditions that often cause students to behave in a distractible or overactive manner (Erford, 2013): oppositional defiant disorder, conduct disorder, generalized anxiety disorder, dysthymic disorder, bipolar disorder, posttraumatic stress disorder, major depressive disorder, manic episode, schizoid personality disorder (and schizophrenia, schizotypal, and schizo-affective disorders), physical or sexual abuse, grand mal seizures, petite mal seizures, substance use or abuse, asthma (actually the use of the inhaler causes overactivity in some), lead poisoning, hyperactive thyroid, anemia, allergies, autism spectrum disorder, auditory processing disorder, visual processing disorder, and motor coordination disorder. When diagnosing ADHD, each of these conditions should be considered and ruled out during clinical interviewing.

How Educators and Parents Can Help Students With ADHD

Teachers, parents, administrators, and professional school counselors can enact numerous strategies to help students with ADHD experience academic and behavioral success at school and home. These strategies are typically aimed at reducing inappropriate symptoms of distractibility/disorganization and impulsiveness/hyperactivity. Table 39.1 presents strategies that may be used to help students with ADHD. Parents play a key role in the academic and personal success of their children. Professional school counselors can reassure parents that ADHD is not their fault and that it can be treated effectively through parent training, family education, regular monitoring, behavior management, and medication, neurofeedback or natural treatments, when appropriate. Parents can complement the team process and provide continuity between the school and home.

(text continues on page 456)

Table 39.1 Strategies for Helping Students With ADHD

General Suggestions to Help Parents
- Break down target skills into steps that can be taught and practiced.
- Provide student-centered rationales for desired behaviors.
- Be consistent in expectations and tolerances.
- Establish a nonverbal cue (touch or signal) to let the student know when he or she is inattentive or behaving improperly and to prompt attention to desired behaviors.
- Acknowledge appropriate behavior immediately, being specific and genuine in your praise.
- Initially establish lower accuracy expectations that increase over time with the students' success.
- Give positive attention through the use of verbal praise and tangible rewards for behaviors you want to see more often and for approximations of desired behaviors until new behaviors are formed.
- Allow access to rewards at multiple points during the day for achieving or reaching target goals.
- Catch problem behavior as soon as it begins. Give corrective feedback privately. Be brief, specific, and matter of fact.
- Use response-cost behavioral monitoring (e.g., remove a leaf or apple from a constructed tree for each infraction. Once the leaves or apples are gone, a privilege is lost).
- Recommend parent support group association meetings.
- Recommend parenting classes to aid parents in the skills needed for addressing inappropriate behaviors or acquisition of desire behaviors.

Distractibility and Difficulty Focusing
- Maintain a consistent and predictable schedule.
- Realize that the student will be more inattentive just before lunch and late in the afternoon. Plan instruction accordingly.
- Provide short breaks with plenty of performance feedback and encouragement between tasks.
- Encourage parents to set up a recognized routine for home activities, including study time.
- Encourage parents to set up home study spaces with minimum distractions, and parent monitoring and availability.
- Allow preferential seating to lower distractions
  - near the primary area of instruction.
  - with distracting visual stimuli placed behind the student.
  - in a study carrel for independent work or test taking.
  - away from doors, windows, and other distractions.
  - surrounded by focused role-models who will neither distract the student nor allow the student to distract them.
- Keep materials in cabinets when not in use to decrease visual distractions.
- Use earphones (white noise, soft instrumental music) to keep down auditory distractions.
- Teach self-monitoring. Use tape-recorded time prompts, digital watches, special watches made for students with ADHD, such as those available at www.watchminder.com (Sonna, 2005). When the tone beeps or vibrates have the students self-monitor and self-reward to determine if he or she is on task.
- Provide a timeframe for specific steps or instructions (e.g., "10 seconds to get your name on the paper").
- Match academic assignments to the student's level of ability and attention span.
- Cut back on repetitive homework assignments beyond the point of mastery.
- Visually divide worksheets into blocks and columns to prevent the student from becoming visually overwhelmed.

(continues)

Table 39.1 (*continued*)

- Provide more spacing on paper to improve visual organization.
- Limit the number of problems on a page to provide a sense of accomplishment.
- Use a timer to break assignments into smaller, more focused units. For elementary students, timed units should generally not exceed 10 or 15 minutes; for middle and high school students, 15 to 30 minutes.
- Give only one task or instruction at a time.
- Have the student rephrase the directions in his or her own words to be sure he or she understands.
- Alternate between low- and high-interest activities to sustain attention.
- Provide visual–tactile and multisensory approaches to instruction, such as story boards for recording sequence of events in language arts (Hartman & Bowman, 1996).
- Use classification strategies to aid in recall of information, such as the use of word families for spelling and reading (Hartman & Bowman, 1996).
- Make learning fun by creating life-like play in which desired skills are incorporated (e.g., setting up a post office to provide an opportunity to write, send, mail, and receive letters; Hartman & Bowman, 1996).
- Teach students to repeat the question or problem before attempting to answer it (Lougy et al., 2009).
- Increase novelty and stimulation through the use of color, shape, and texture enhancements (Honos-Webb, 2010). For example, use brightly colored instructional materials with a clear and specific instructional purpose to engage the student's attention.
- Hold a review session at the end of the day for homework assignments, key points, and so on prior to tests.
- Give extra time to complete standardized tests, subject tests, projects, and assignments to ensure that grades reflect mastery of content rather than time constraints.
- Due to visual distractions limiting focusing ability, the student may need to be tested orally rather than through traditional written techniques.
- Give multiple-choice tests as opposed to fill-in-the-blank or essay tests to benefit these contextual learners.
- Allow middle and high school students the use of tape recorders to provide a reference to materials at a later time (Lougy et al., 2009).
- Provide older students with copies of notes or allow other students to share their notes (Alexander-Roberts, 1995).
- Incorporate different learning styles into note-taking; for example, have students draw a pictorial representation of the concept (Alexander-Roberts, 1995).
- Teach and model the SQ3R method for reading and comprehending instructional material from texts (Alexander-Roberts, 1995).

Poor Organization
- Create tools to help students improve organizational skills.
- Have student write descriptions of daily and long-term goals.
- Color-code assignment folders and notebooks using a different color for each subject.
- Create checklists for daily chores and tasks.
- Provide a separate homework folder. Label one side *Homework to Be Completed* and the other side *Completed Homework Ready to Turn In*.
- Have student regularly compose To Do lists.
- Have student use an assignment notebook to dictate daily and long-term assignments. Check the notebook at the end of each class period to ensure student has documented homework

assignments and notes completely and thoroughly. This will aid students and the parents who may be monitoring and assisting them with assignments at home.
- Maintain and post a consistent and predictable routine and schedule to promote the student's mental organization.
- Set time limits for chores/tasks to help the student develop a sense of time management.
- Have a well-organized student help transition the student with ADHD from step to step.
- Set up appropriate home and school study schedules with set times and a recognized routine.
- Break down long-term assignments and projects into logical organized steps:
  - List the tasks needing completion.
  - List all needed resources and materials.
  - List tasks in order.
  - Break down difficult tasks into smaller tasks (Sonna, 2005).

Task Incompletion
- Match academic assignments to the student's level of ability and attention span.
- Stress comprehension and application rather than memorization (Sonna, 2005).
- Allow ample opportunity for students to pursue their own areas of interests when possible (Sonna, 2005).
- Allow students to learn at their own pace; comparable to Montessori learning (Sonna, 2005).
- Incorporate the student's preferred learning style into lesson plans and assignments (Sonna, 2005).
- Give only one task at a time.
- Give adequate "getting started" instructions.
- Give an example of what the student is to do.
- Make sure multistep directions are written down, whether on the paper, chalkboard, or an index card.
- Make sure the student is on the right track when starting an assignment.
- Check progress frequently.
  - Have the student do 2 or 3 examples under supervision of a teacher, parent, or student helper to be sure he or she understands the process before completing items independently.
  - Maintain close proximity to the child to provide assistance, feedback, and redirection as needed.
  - Compliment the student when proceeding correctly and redirect his or her performance when off track.
  - Have the student check with you after completing the first item, at the half-way point, and upon conclusion.
- Allow the student to seek assistance from designated peer tutors if needed.
- Involve peers in the learning process. Designate study buddies for tests and long-term projects.
- Insist that the student follow through and finish each task correctly before moving onto a more desired activity. This is called the Premack principle—high frequency behaviors must follow low frequency behaviors. For example, have the student finish language homework BEFORE engaging in a play activity.
- Use the word processor to compose written work. This will help counterbalance the frustration that stems from slow writing speed and rewriting handwritten compositions for editing and final drafts.
- Have the student divide long-term assignments into sections, setting a due date for each section and complying with each due date.
- Have the student rework all errors on tests and assignments to reinforce mastery and stress careful initial work habits.
- Require a daily assignment notebook that allows daily or at least weekly communication between the parent and teachers. This notebook should be signed by teachers and parents.

(continues)

Table 39.1 (*continued*)

- Cut back on repetitive homework assignments beyond the point of mastery.
- Set time limits for work completion.
- Have the student complete a shortened version of a class project.
- Avoid heavy doses of desk work.
- For young students, tape record the homework and schoolwork instructions for moderate to complex assignments so the student can go back to listen to them later in class or at home.

Restlessness and Excessive Movement
- Alternate between low and high movement activities.
- Incorporate movement into activities as much as possible.
  - Give the student specific times when it is appropriate to get up out of his or her seat.
  - Provide opportunities for purposeful movement.
  - Provide a free-movement area in the back of the room where children can stretch or complete jumping jacks when restless (Sonna, 2005).
- Role-play action scenes that emphasize patient, deliberate activities.
- Provide many opportunities for kinesthetic activity during instruction.
- Change activities and posture frequently.
- Alternate between desk, floor, standing, group, and movement activities.
- Give the student sanctioned times out of his or her seat to let off energy.
- Provide short breaks involving physical movement between tasks.
- Allow students to move around while keeping them in the general proximity of their work, by requiring students to have only one body part touching their desk or chair (Sonna, 2005).
- Give ample warning prior to transitions, and guide students throughout (Sonna, 2005).

Impulsiveness
- Establish consistent routines, rules, and procedures.
- Facilitate rule internalization by
  - creating posters with rules for various work periods.
  - asking the student to occasionally restate rules.
  - teaching the student to use self-instruction during work.
  - having the student recite rules to another student before beginning an assignment.
  - using tape-recorded cues or reminders.
  - defining clear and reasonable limits.
- Increase supervision at transition times (e.g., lunch, recess, specials).
- Have the student redo a messy or incorrect assignment to understand that carefulness and accuracy are more important work habits than quickness.
- Teach and reinforce problem-solving strategies.

Medication and Neurofeedback

Medication is effective for treating impulsivity, inattention, and hyperactivity. But medication alone is not the long-term solution (Lawlis, 2005). The use of behavioral and specific academic strategies in conjunction with medication will aid in preparing the student with ADHD for continued academic success. Neurofeedback has also been found effective for the treatment of ADHD. Studies reported improved cognitive performance and decreased behavioral problems in children with ADHD after neurofeedback for up to two years and beyond (Drechsler et al., 2007; Gani, Birbaumer, & Strehl, 2008; Gevensleben et al., 2010; Heinrich, Gevensleben, Freisleder, Moll, & Rothenberger, 2004). Neurofeedback is based on operant conditioning, with the aim of developing skills of self-regulation in regard to brainwave activity. During neurofeedback, simultaneous, contingent feedback responds to neurophysiological signals in order to teach the student to learn self-regulation of brainwave processes. Typical results include improved behavioral, cognitive, and emotional self-regulation. As with medication, the use of behavioral and specific academic strategies enhances the effects of neurofeedback.

Sleep Patterns

Children with ADHD often have difficulty sleeping at night. Children who are not getting enough sleep are not able to manage their ADHD symptoms to the best of their ability. In addition, their ADHD symptoms are frequently exacerbated by their lack of sleep. Sleep difficulties may be partially due to the ADHD or a side effect of medication. Regardless, bedtime behavior can be difficult to manage. A few tips for parents follow:

- Establish daytime routines with regular activities and mealtimes.
- Establish a regular bedtime routine in regard to schedule and bedtime tasks.
- Avoid giving caffeinated drinks in the afternoon and evening (if at all).
- Pay special attention to all the variables associated with a relaxing sleep environment, such as noise, room temperature, bedding, toys, aroma, and lighting. Some children benefit from soothing music as they fall asleep, others need complete quiet. The scent of lavender or use of blue light has also been found useful in inducing sleep.
- Keep the bedroom a sleep-specific area—no television, radio, games, and other distractions. A good night's sleep for a child and adolescent is 9 or 10 hours, with the same bedtime and wake time, 7 days a week.
- Keep track of sleep patterns with a progress chart and reinforce your child each morning.
- Talk to your healthcare provider about your child's sleep concerns. There may be supplements or medications that can help.

Case Vignette

The following vignette is typical of the type of behavior students with ADHD will exhibit in the classroom. It is important to recognize that although these behaviors are typical of a student with ADHD, not all students who exhibit these behaviors have ADHD.

> Mark has more energy than most boys his age, but, then again, he's always been overly active. Starting at age 3 years, he was a human tornado, dashing around and disrupting everything in his path. At home, he went from one activity to the next, leaving a trail of toys behind him. At meals, he upset dishes and chattered nonstop. He was reckless and impulsive, even running into the street with oncoming cars no matter how many times his mother explained the danger or scolded him.
>
> On the playground, he seemed no wilder than the other kids. But his tendency to overreact, like hitting playmates simply for bumping into him, had already gotten him into

trouble several times. His parents didn't know what to do. Mark's caring grandparents reassured them that "Boys will be boys, he'll grow out of it"—but he didn't. In third grade, Mark's teacher threw up her hands and said, *"Enough!"* In one morning, Mark had jumped out of his seat to sharpen his pencil six times, each time accidentally knocking into other children's desks and toppling books and papers. He was finally sent to the principal's office when he began kicking a desk he had overturned. In sheer frustration, his teacher called a meeting with his parents and the professional school counselor. But even after they developed a plan for managing Mark's behavior in class, Mark showed little improvement. Finally, after an extensive assessment, they found that Mark had ADHD–combined presentation. He was given medication to control the hyperactivity during school hours. With the professional school counselor's help, Mark's parents learned to reward desirable behaviors and send Mark to time-out when he refused to follow parental directions (Erford, 1999). Soon, Mark was able to sit still and focus on learning. Today, at age 14 years, Mark is doing much better in school. He channels his energy into sports and is a star player on the football team. Although Mark still gets into scuffles now and then, the professional school counselor is helping him learn to control his tantrums and frustration, and he is able to make and keep friends.

Summary/Conclusion

ADHD is a chronic behavior disorder of uncertain etiology that always begins in childhood. ADHD is most commonly diagnosed in boys, and the disorder often continues into adulthood. The central aspects include inattention/disorganization and hyperactivity/impulsiveness, and the student can exhibit one or both of these difficulties. Three typically used interventions for ADHD include specifically designed school services such as a structured classroom for children with behavior disorders, behavior management techniques, and medications. Classroom and home techniques include securing attention before directions, checking for comprehension, reducing environmental distractions, shortening assignments, and assigning work that is interesting. A collaborative team approach provides educators, family members, and the student with ADHD with a mechanism for new possibilities. Working together will enable each member to grow through the team process toward a common purpose—to enhance the life of the student affected by ADHD.

CHAPTER 40

Helping Students Who Have Alcohol and Other Drug Problems

Gerald A. Juhnke and Elias Zambrano

Preview

Alcohol and other drug (AOD) abuse continues to be a major problem for high school and middle school students and is even becoming problematic at the elementary-school level. The more routinely correlated negative effects of such abuse by students are well documented within existing literature (e.g., poor academic performance, student retention). However, more severe and sensational negative effects often reported via the news media are also related to AOD abuse among this population (e.g., bullying, suicide, aggravated assault). The cognitive-behavioral and adjunctive interventions described herein provide professional school counselors practical and effective treatment options that can be readily implemented with students who abuse AODs.

Helping Students With AOD Problems

Existing literature clearly supports many professional school counselors' perceptions and beliefs that high school and middle school students are: (a) abusing alcohol and other drugs (AODs) more frequently than ever before, (b) beginning AOD abuse at earlier ages, and (c) ignoring the inherent dangers associated with AOD abuse. An example of research reflecting such student AOD abuse and attitudinal deterioration is the National Institute on Drug Abuse (NIDA) annual survey, *Monitoring the Future* (NIDA, 2014). This research surveyed nationally representative samples of 8th-, 10th-, and 12th-grade classes and included almost 42,000 students from 389 public and private secondary schools. Survey results among 12th-grade participants indicate: (a) 39% had used alcohol 30 days prior to survey participation, (b) the percentage of seniors who had used illicit drugs within 30 days prior to survey participation increased from 23% in 2004 to 26% in 2013, and (c) 60% of seniors did not view marijuana as harmful, almost doubling this perception in the last 20 years.

The Substance Abuse and Mental Health Services Administration (SAMHSA; 2013) provided data specific to tobacco, alcohol, marijuana, and other illicit drug use among 12- to 17-year-olds. Whereas cigarette use decreased 50% over the past 10 years, past month use of cigarettes was still reported at 7%. Current alcohol use among this population was 12.6% among males and 13.2% among females. Overall marijuana use among this age group was 7.2%, while the current use of illicit drugs (inhalants, hallucinogens, cocaine, etc.) was 9.5%.

Interestingly, illicit drug use spiked among 16-year-olds to 17%, and 48% of the sample reported obtaining marijuana was easy and 16% indicated ease in obtaining cocaine.

Alcohol is not the only substance abused by students. Inhalant use is fast becoming one of the first substances abused by preadolescent and younger students (Hogan, 2000). Inhalant use is also prominent among adolescent students. Concomitantly, hallucinogens are also used with increased frequency among adolescent students. However, among adolescent students, marijuana still accounts for 75% of all illicit drug abuse. This data clearly demonstrates the need for professional school counselors to be able to effectively intervene with AOD-abusing students.

Cognitive-Behavioral Counseling Interventions

Cognitive-behavioral counseling interventions have significant utility for professional school counselors due to their emphasis upon brief, time-limited interventions directed toward immediate student concerns. Three primary cognitive-behavioral counseling goals exist for professional school counselors helping AOD-abusing students (Nystul, 2006). First, professional school counselors help students understand how the students' thoughts, feelings, and behaviors engender AOD abuse. In other words, professional school counselors help students better understand what students say to themselves (e.g., "If I do drugs, others will think I'm cool and like me"); how they feel (e.g., anxiety, depression, anger); or what they do (e.g., argue, fight, withdraw) immediately before they AOD abuse. Second, professional school counselors promote understanding of how the students' AOD abuse is connected to negative consequences (e.g., failing grades, arguments with peers) and positive consequences (e.g., interactions with peers, feelings of confidence). Finally, professional school counselors help students explore new, healthier ways of thinking and acting, which reduce the probability of continued AOD abuse.

Understanding the AOD Abuse Sequence

Professional school counselors need to understand the AOD abuse sequence in order to help students. This sequence includes recognizing triggers, establishing trigger baselines, nonuse lists, positive consequences, and negative consequences

Recognizing triggers. Professional school counselors who treat students abusing AODs first need to help them recognize triggers (e.g., thoughts, feelings, behaviors, situations) that occur immediately prior to the students' AOD abuse (see Table 40.1). Commonly, students abusing AODs will be able to describe the internal dialogue they have with themselves or the physical or psychological signals that foretell their upcoming AOD abuse. For example, a student might indicate her internal dialogue just before abusing:

> "I'm stressed. There is no way I can get through the rest of this calculus class without taking a hit to calm myself down."

Additionally, she may describe physical feelings such as an inability to relax or concentrate, and physical behaviors such as involuntary muscle contractions or psychomotor agitation (e.g., tapping her fingers, bouncing her leg). Psychological signals might include remem-

Table 40.1 Alcohol and Other Drug Triggers and Nonuse Sequence-Outcome List

Thought triggers	Feeling triggers	Behavior triggers	Situation triggers	Positive outcome	Negative outcome
Nonuse thoughts	Nonuse feelings	Nonuse behaviors	Nonuse situations	Positive outcome	Negative outcome

bering how calming it was when she smoked marijuana the previous day or describing the depressed symptomology experienced most days when she is AOD abstinent. Furthermore, she might be able to identify specific situations or circumstances that increase the probability of her AOD abuse (e.g., the class prior to each Friday's calculus quiz, the nights before her calculus tests, the days in which she receives her calculus quiz scores).

Once students recognize triggers, they make trigger lists. Students rank order the triggers on the lists, indicating which triggers are the most powerful and which are most frequently encountered. Thus, students first rank the strength of the individual triggers from zero (*When I experience this, I will not use at all*) to 10 (*When I experience this, I am inevitably going to use*) and rank the trigger frequency from zero (*I never experienced this trigger*) to 10 (*This trigger occurs constantly throughout my awake hours*). Students give priority to the most powerful triggers and those occurring most often. In other words, triggers that students identify as indicating both inevitable AOD use and that constantly occur are the triggers that warrant the most attention at the onset of the counseling process.

Establishing trigger baselines. Concomitantly, the self-described severity and frequency of triggers presented by students serve as baselines that can be used to measure progress. In other words, these baselines allow both students and counselors to track treatment efficacy. Should students report a decrease in severity and frequency of triggers, progress is occurring and the interventions used should be continued. However, should the severity and frequency of triggers increase, treatment and interventions warrant revision.

Nonuse lists. In addition to the trigger list, professional school counselors may wish to help students construct a "nonuse list," which emphasizes identifying thoughts, feelings, behaviors, and situations occurring when students don't abuse AODs. The purpose of this list is to help students identify different ways of positively experiencing life without the need to abuse AODs.

Many professional school counselors with whom we have spoken have noted that many of their students who frequently abuse AODs will be AOD abstinent when they: (a) are interacting with respected and admired peers who don't use, (b) are participating in activities they are invested in and find interesting (e.g., athletics, engine repair class, choir), and (c) don't experience overwhelming anxiety related to future performance (e.g., upcoming examinations, athletic events in which the student is participating). Thus, a nonuse list provides students with ideas on how they might better cope with experiences that commonly lead to AOD abuse by describing how they think, feel, and behave when they are not driven by the urge to use.

Positive consequences. Unfortunately, helping professionals often ignore or inappropriately minimize positive consequences resulting from student AOD abuse. This is a significant treatment error that dilutes counseling efficacy and disinvests student participation.

Students frequently experience multiple positive consequences as a result of their AOD abuse. These positive consequences can vary greatly depending upon the individual. Perceived peer support provided by other AOD-abusing students, escape from pressing concerns, and pure enjoyment of being under the influence are key reasons students abuse AODs. Honest discussion regarding the potential loss of these perceived positive consequences is necessary before students can begin the abstinence process. Therefore, statements such as, "Tell me about the positive things you experience when you use" or "Help me understand what it is like drinking with your peers" are helpful.

The intent of these questions is not to have students romantically portray AOD abuse. Instead, professional school counselors are learning *why* AOD abuse and AOD experiences are important to the individual. Once the *why* is answered, counselors can begin working to appropriately address the void that will inevitably be created should students eliminate their AOD-abusing behaviors.

For example, if a 13-year-old male indicates that drinking with other teens provides him friendships, the professional school counselor and the student may need to identify other ways that the student can secure friendships without AOD abuse. Given the importance students place upon their acceptance by peers and their desire to fit in, securing alternative friendships can be daunting. However, failing to address this student's need for new friends who are non AOD-abusing, at best, destines the counseling process to limited success.

Negative consequences. When reviewing negative consequences resulting from student AOD abuse, it is helpful to first ask about the presenting circumstances that brought students to counseling and then link these to other academic, family, peer, psychological, or legal problems resulting from or potentially linked to their AOD abuse:

COUNSELOR: Shondra, I know that Vice Principal Myers referred you to my office. As I understand the situation, you had consumed alcohol and then had gotten sick at last Saturday night's homecoming game. Help me understand what that was like for you.

SHONDRA: It was awful. I was trying to be cool and instead I got drunk. When I got to the game, everything started spinning, and I threw up in the stands. I was so embarrassed. Now my parents know I was drinking and I'm grounded, and the people I was trying to impress laugh at me.

COUNSELOR: That sounds rough.

SHONDRA: Yeah . . . it is.

COUNSELOR: What have you learned from all of this?

SHONDRA: Well, I've learned that I don't want to drink anymore before games.

COUNSELOR:	Tell me about other times you had some bad things happen when you drank alcohol or used drugs.
SHONDRA:	I can't think of any.
COUNSELOR:	Sometimes people tell me that they perform badly on tests or get bad grades because they were under the influence of alcohol when they took their tests or because they missed a lot of school due to their drinking. Has anything like that ever happened to you?
SHONDRA:	Naw, nothing like that.
COUNSELOR:	At other times students tell me that when they drink they get into arguments with their parents or family members.
SHONDRA:	Well, a couple weeks ago, when my friends and I had been out drinking, I ran my mom's car into a ditch. I had to call my dad to get the car out. He was really upset. He said I'd have to pay the $480 to get the car fixed.
COUNSELOR:	So, your drinking got you into trouble with your dad and caused you to pay the expenses for repairing your mom's car?
SHONDRA:	Yeah, I guess I'm learning that drinking costs me a lot.

Within this vignette, the professional school counselor first attempts to help Shondra begin understanding the link between her drinking behaviors and other potential negative consequences. The professional school counselor describes the primary reason Shondra came for counseling, the vice principal's referral. Shondra reports two specific problems resulting from this incident (e.g., embarrassment, parental punishment [grounding]). The counselor then investigates potential negative consequences of alcohol consumption related to Shondra's school experience. This is denied. Therefore, the professional school counselor continues asking about other potential negative consequences of alcohol consumption occurring within Shondra's relationship with her parents. Toward the end of this session, the professional school counselor would likely summarize the problems reported by the student as linked to her alcohol use and ask the student to clarify how continued alcohol consumption is helpful.

COUNSELOR:	Shondra, help me understand. You say that you were terminated from Wal-Mart because you've been too drunk to work your scheduled shift. You've said that you've gotten in trouble with the police for drinking and driving and had to pay over $400 to get your mom's car repaired. And, you've told me that you get real anxious when you buy beer, because your mom and dad would kick you out of the house if they knew you were continuing to drink. How is it helpful to you to continue drinking alcohol?
SHONDRA:	I guess it's not.
COUNSELOR:	Based upon your trigger list, you've basically said you consume alcohol when you get bored. So, what will you do differently when you get bored in the future?
SHONDRA:	Well, I guess I'm not going to drink.

COUNSELOR: Okay, what will you do instead when you find yourself becoming bored or thinking that you may become bored.

SHONDRA: I don't know.

COUNSELOR: Well, on your nonuse list, you said when you are with Stacey, you don't use alcohol, because she is fun and she doesn't like beer. I'm wondering if you would be willing to call Stacey if you begin to feel bored.

SHONDRA: Yeah, I could do that.

COUNSELOR: What else could you do?

SHONDRA: I guess I could do some of the other things I said in my nonuse list, like take my dog for a walk or practice my clarinet.

At the conclusion of this vignette, the professional school counselor gently confronts Shondra by asking how continued drinking is helpful. Instead of dropping the discussion when Shondra reports her alcohol consumption is not helpful, the counselor uses the client's trigger list to help Shondra recognize one of the primary reasons she reportedly consumes alcohol (e.g., to escape boredom). Therefore, the counselor is therapeutically using both the student's trigger list and nonuse lists to help provide appropriate interventions.

Sometimes students are either unaware of potential negative consequences of their AOD abuse or purposely deny any negative consequences. Under these circumstances, professional school counselors may wish to use circular questioning. The intent is to learn how students believe they are perceived, valued, and respected by significant others. Thus, professional school counselors might ask a question such as, "Shondra, who is the most important person in your life." Once students identify their most important significant others, counselors can ask, "Based upon what you've told me, your mother is very important to you. Tell me, what would she say were the negative consequences of your drinking and drug behaviors?"

Assorted Adjunctive Interventions

Using cognitive-behavioral interventions to help students more thoroughly understand their AOD abuse sequence (i.e., triggers, nontriggers, positive consequences, and negative consequences) is helpful. Three other adjunctive interventions warrant discussion when counseling AOD-abusing students.

Psychoeducational interventions. Professional school counselors can plan and implement psychoeducational interventions using a cognitive-behavioral approach. Using cognitive-behavioral strategies, the counselor can assist students in understanding that their thinking influences how they feel, which in turn affects what they do, with substance abuse being one possible outcome of this chain of events. Such structured and concrete strategies can assist the professional school counselor in helping young people learn about themselves regarding AOD issues. This is especially helpful when professional school counselors are responding to pre- and early adolescent referrals, when the young client may benefit from developmentally appropriate interventions that are presented in visual and concrete terms. Such activities can be used in individual and group counseling with some modification. Following are two examples of such cognitive behavioral activities.

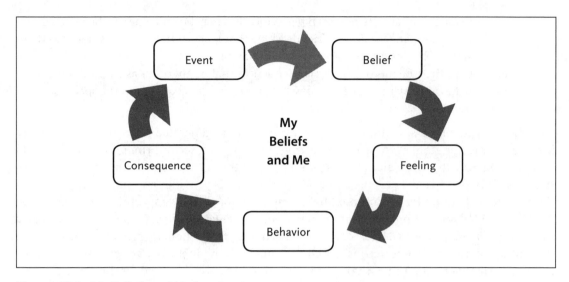

Figure 40.1. My Beliefs and Me handout.

Feeling cards. Construct feeling cards by placing words that label a breadth of emotions (e.g., joy, excitement, fear, sadness, anger) on index cards. As in a card game, have the student take a card from the stack without being able to see the word on the card. Ask the student to turn the card over to see the feeling word and then have the student write a situation on the card that might engender the emotion expressed on the card. Then ask the student to identify an action (or reaction) that might take place in response to the situation identified on the card. After an action has been identified, ask the student to identify a thought or belief about the event that might have engendered the emotional reaction (feeling) to the event. Once an opportunity has been provided to articulate a belief about the situation, ask the student to consider an alternative thought or belief about the situation. Following the identification of an alternative thought or belief, ask the student to consider how the feeling and action might have been different. Allow a second round if time allows.

My-beliefs-and-me wheel. This activity borrows from an illustration to demonstrate the role of cognition on self-perpetuating cycles (Freeman, Pretzer, Fleming, & Simon, 2004) that can be created in response to given situations:

1. Ask the student to identify a recent situation that might trigger the use of AOD. Using the handout titled My Beliefs and Me (see Figure 40.1), ask the student to write words that describe the situation in the space labeled "Event."
2. Ask the student to consider the event and describe beliefs or thoughts about the situation (e.g., how it may affect personal worth or relationships, or how it may illicit negative consequences). After discussion, assist the student in identifying the dominant (irrational) belief at play, and describe it on the handout in the space labeled "Belief." (A list of irrational beliefs that can assist you in guiding this discussion can be found in Freeman et al., 2004.)
3. After discussion, ask the student to identify and describe feelings that might be experienced in response to the identified belief. Ask the student to write a word describing their selected feeling (e.g., sadness, anger, excitement) in the space labeled "Feeling."

4. Ask the student to identify potential behaviors that may be outcomes of the selected emotion (e.g., separate self from friends, skip school, use AOD). Ask the student to write the selected behavior in the space labeled "Behavior."
5. Finally, ask the student to consider consequences that might occur as a result of the selected behavior. Ask the student to describe a selected consequence in the space marked "Consequence."

Repeat this process, using a newly identified event (generated from the Consequence box) as the precipitating event. After repeating the process a second time, assist the student in analyzing how this cycle stemming from irrational thoughts or beliefs can continue, with the possibility that negative events will also continue. This provides an opportunity to introduce the concept of faulty or irrational beliefs in developmentally appropriate terms. Vernon (1989) provided such a presentation in her book *Thinking, Feeling, Behaving: An Emotional Curriculum for Adolescents, Grades 7–12*. After discussing faulty beliefs, provide demonstrated examples. Ask the student to reconsider choices made in the first two cycles. Using a new *My Beliefs and Me Wheel* handout with the same situation initially identified for the "Event" space, coach the student to consider other beliefs or thoughts that may be chosen regarding this event. A student-identified belief that demonstrates rational thinking is selected, discussed, and placed in the "Belief" section of the new handout. As before, the student then identifies emotions that the selected rational thought might stimulate, and selects one to place in the "Feeling" box. The student then identifies behaviors that may occur resulting from that feeling, and the selection of one behavior (more positive than before) is selected and placed in the "Behavior" box. Once again, ask the student to consider consequences to this behavior, and then write the selected consequence as a new entry in the "Event" box. Move through another cycle using the student's newly identified (and more positive) consequence as the precipitating event. To further empower the student with the concept of personal control, use additional practice cycles. Each cycle reinforces the student's power over an event through the interpretation (or belief) of that event.

Contingency contracting. Many professional school counselors use contingency contracting when counseling AOD-abusing students. Contingency contracts are clearly worded contracts that describe acceptable and unacceptable student behaviors. Professional school counselors and their students jointly develop an outline indicating that AOD abuse will not be tolerated. Sanctions are stated (e.g., expulsion from school, specialized placement) as well as rewards for contract compliance (e.g., the student can attend shop class at no cost for materials, the student can participate in athletics).

Sobriety contracts are one form of contingency contract. For example, a professional school counselor may have a student who is prescribed both Ritalin for attention-deficit/hyperactivity disorder and Topomax for AOD abuse. The professional school counselor and the student can identify a time at the beginning of each school day when they can meet for approximately 10 minutes or longer if necessary. During the scheduled meetings, the student verbally commits to remaining alcohol free and achieving academically so that he may graduate from school. Thus, the student may say something like, "Ms. Penn, I'm going to stay drug free today and promise to do my very best at learning so I will graduate and attend college." The professional school counselor then voices any specific concerns she might have about upcoming events that day which may trigger an alcohol use relapse. Here, Ms. Penn might say, "Charlie, I know you want to stay alcohol free and are committed to graduating, but I also know that midterm exams begin today. I am concerned you might feel overwhelmed or anxious and begin using alcohol to cope." The student then responds with how he anticipates handling the noted concern, "Oh, Ms. Penn, if I feel anxious or overwhelmed because of the midterms, I promise to speak with you first. I know I can handle it." Once the student indicates how he will respond the counselor is not allowed to ask further questions that day. The student then takes his medications in front of the professional school counselor (if appropriate) and places an "X" on the Sobriety Contract Calendar for that specific day. At the conclusion of each week, the professional school counselor and the student identify the progress made and discuss any changes warranted for the following week. The intent of this experience, then, is to ritualize this daily experience and encourage students to direct their own recovery.

12-step support groups. Another intervention that warrants discussion is the use of support groups. Incorporating a 12-step recovery program into a student's treatment for AOD abuse may enhance his or her chances of maintaining sobriety (Elliott, Orr, Watson, & Jackson, 2005). Twelve-step groups such as Alcoholics Anonymous, Narcotics Anonymous, Al-Anon, and Alateen are all based on the premise that by sharing and challenging one another, sobriety among group members can be both achieved and maintained. Affiliation in a 12-step program along with other youth may meet several needs for the student, such as modeling, mutual support, shared experiences, sense of belonging, skill acquisition, and strategies to help maintain sobriety (Bristow-Braitman, 1995; Robinson, 1996). Moreover, a central tenet of 12-step programs is living "one day at a time." This seems particularly relevant to a youth who tends to live in the moment. Rational recovery is founded upon rational emotive behavior therapy and encourages members to combat irrational thoughts related to their personal recovery.

Referrals. A final intervention that may be necessary when adolescent AOD abuse escalates and concerns arise about dependency is a referral for either outpatient or inpatient treatment. There are times when professional school counselors may be called upon to refer a student for further treatment. Referrals may require serious consideration when parents or school personnel raise concerns, or when the student self-refers. If a referral is necessary, it is important that professional school counselors have access to resources for both outpatient and inpatient treatment programs. Additionally, it is important for the professional school counselor to be cognizant of how payments for services are to be made if required by those resources. For example, do the resources have established straight fees, or are sliding fee scales use? Also, are there resources within the community that offer *pro bono* services? The United Way (2005) provides such information through a community resource book that can direct the professional school counselor to treatment providers in their cities and counties. In addition, Substance Abuse and Mental Health Services Administration (2005) published a list of more than 11,000 treatment programs across the country to assist the professional school counselor in locating an appropriate treatment program for the AOD student.

Summary/Conclusion

We described literature indicating the prominence of AOD abuse among middle and high school students. Practical cognitive-behavioral interventions were described. Specifically, readers learned about the AOD abuse sequence and gained intervention ideas on how to help students (a) recognize AOD triggers, (b) recognize nonuse triggers, (c) discuss perceived positive AOD abuse consequences and cope with the potential loss of these positive consequences, and (d) link AOD abuse to negative consequences. Concomitantly, three adjunctive intervention techniques were described. These included contingency contracting, 12-step programming, and more intensive treatment. Although counseling AOD-abusing students is challenging, these interventions clearly provide a fundamental approach that can be helpful.

CHAPTER 41

Helping Students Who Have Eating Disorders

Dana Heller Levitt

Preview

Eating disorders and their less clinical forms of disordered eating and body image preoccupation continue to be on the rise. Professional school counselors are likely to see students presenting with such issues from elementary through high school. This chapter provides a brief overview of the symptoms and behaviors of eating disorders followed by a discussion of counseling and prevention strategies. Attention to developmental differences is provided, including manifestations and interventions. A final section provides resources for counselors as well as students, teachers, and parents.

Clinical eating disorders (e.g., anorexia nervosa, bulimia nervosa, binge eating disorders) can be found in about 5% of the general population. A greater number of people are included when the definition is expanded to include those with subclinical manifestations, such as disordered eating and disturbances in body image. Disorders that do not meet standard diagnostic criteria can affect 4% to 16% of the general population, with such cases being two to five times more common among adolescent girls (Mussell, Binford, & Fulkerson, 2000). Neumark-Sztainer, Wall, Larson, Eisenberg, and Loth (2011) determined that 50% of young girls (mean age of 12.8 years) had dieted within the previous 12 months, often using unhealthy measures such as diet pills or purging. Clinical eating disorders may be visualized as on one end of a continuum, healthy eating attitudes and body image on the other end, and differing values on each lying in between. Students who are dissatisfied with their bodies, dieting, or even at the healthiest point all have the potential to develop more serious problems.

The most common forms of clinical eating disorders are anorexia nervosa, bulimia nervosa, and binge eating disorder. Anorexia is marked by three attributes: (a) a sustained reduction in caloric consumption, (b) an extreme fear of gaining weight or ongoing behaviors that prevent weight gain, and (c) misperceptions about one's actual weight (American Psychiatric Association [APA], 2013). In addition, the severity of the condition is determined by the student's body mass index (BMI) percentile. Students with anorexia may intentionally fast and avoid food and may or may not engage in compensatory activities, such as excessive exercise or self-induced vomiting after periods of feeling that they have eaten too much.

Such acts of purging are a defining point of bulimia nervosa, a cycle of binge eating and purging. A *binge* is defined as eating an excessive amount of food in a discrete period of time, such as 2,000 calories in a 2-hour period, while experiencing a loss of control and an inability to take control of what is being consumed. This should be differentiated from normative binges, such as snacking with friends or eating a lot of food at a social event. Purging, such as self-induced vomiting, use of laxatives or diuretics, or excessive exercise, is used as a means of compensating for the binge or may simply be a way to alleviate feelings of guilt, stress, anxiety, or another feeling that is released through this activity following a binge. Binge eating disorder is similarly characterized by binge episodes but does not include the purging cycle (APA, 2013).

Almost every student is susceptible to disordered eating, with some children as young as fifth grade reporting binge-purge behavior (Combs, Pearson Zapolski, & Smith, 2013). Disordered eating (i.e., dieting or in some other way modifying food intake to lose weight) affects children and students of all ages (Equit et al., 2013). Other factors must also be considered, including the evaluation of body size and negative attitudes toward the body (Pesa, Syre, & Jones, 2000). Body image dissatisfaction has been reported as the strongest predictor of eating disorders (Phelps, Sapia, Nathanson, & Nelson, 2000). For example, young non-overweight females with a high body image distortion are likely to use unsafe weight loss measures (Liechty, 2010). Eating disorders or their subclinical manifestations may have little or nothing to do with eating or body image. Sometimes, they are responses to traumatic events or feelings of losing control, and manipulation of eating may be one means of establishing a sense of identity or personal power. There is a direct link between self-esteem and body perceptions (van den Berg, Mond, Eisenberg, Ackard, & Neumark-Sztainer, 2010), and, as a result, little argument that eating disorders need attention in schools.

Identification of At-Risk Students

Eating disorders and related issues still predominantly affect females, with gender differences emerging at around 8 to 10 years of age (Ricciardelli & McCabe, 2001). Many counselors perceive that eating disorders are limited to young European American females and overlook the effects of the issue on young African American females (Talleyrand, 2010). Male body image ideals and values have more recently spurred development of such concerns among boys and young men. One team of researchers discovered that 63% of their young male sample experienced dissatisfaction with their bodies (Jung & Forbes, 2012). The primary concern for boys is about being underdeveloped or not muscular enough, while girls are drawn toward thinness. Poor coping strategies are related to eating-disorder risk in adolescent males and females alike (Garcia-Grau, Fuste, Miro, Saldana, & Bados, 2004). Eating pathology and appearance preoccupation are associated with depression and dysfunctional thinking, both of which affect students' overall self-esteem and well-being (Franko & Omori, 1999). There are numerous warning signs of eating disorders on any point along the continuum beyond dieting such as weight concerns, drives for thinness, feeling inadequate, and negative self-evaluation. Table 41.1 provides a brief overview of warning signs along the different dimensions of physical, behavioral, and psychological symptoms. If a student presents with any of these warning signs (particularly the physical and behavioral symptoms), it is important for the professional school counselor to ensure that the student consults a health care professional. In addition, important developmental issues arise at the elementary, middle, and high school levels.

Table 41.1 Physical, Behavioral, and Psychological Warning Signs of Eating Disorders

Physical	Behavioral	Psychological
weight loss	frequent trips to the bathroom	low self-esteem
hair loss	avoiding snack foods	external locus of control
edema (swelling)	frequent weighing	perfectionism
skin abnormalities	substance abuse	helplessness
discolored teeth	social avoidance	depression
scarring on the backs of hands	isolation	anxiety
self-injury signs	abnormal eating habits	anger

Elementary School

Although they are at an age when their focus should be on making friends and growth, boys and girls in elementary school worry about appearance and fitting in:

- Children as young as age 5 years express concerns about body image and becoming fat (Maine, 2000; Shapiro, Newcomb, & Loeb, 1997).
- The thin-ideal may be internalized as young as age 7 years, and children at this age are beginning to show signs of body-dissatisfaction (Evans, Tovee, Boothroyd, & Drewett, 2013).
- By age 6 years, children use adult cultural criteria to judge physical attractiveness (Gabel & Kearney, 1998).
- Children tease, shame, and avoid friendships with peers who are fat or who are not conventionally attractive.
- Children imitate actions and attitudes of parents and adults; what messages are they sending about dieting and appearance?

Middle School

Dissatisfaction with body shape and size worsens as children age and enter middle school:

- Body image dissatisfaction increased from 40% in third graders to 79% in sixth graders (Ricciardelli & McCabe, 2001).
- Self-esteem is directly linked to body satisfaction.
- The top wish for 11- to 17-year-old girls is to lose weight (Maine, 2000).

High School

High school students have the increased burden of beginning to make adult decisions as well as the stress of trying to fit in both socially and physically.

- Discontent about their bodies and feeling fat has become normative, particularly for girls (Maine, 2000).

- Underweight females are more likely to have a more positive body image than underweight boys (Vilhjalmsson, Kristjansdottir, & Ward, 2012).
- Sixty-seven percent of females and 82% of males in high school believe appearance influences romantic appeal; 72% and 68%, respectively, attribute happiness to appearance (O'Dea & Abraham, 1999).
- Forty-six percent of students in Grades 9–12 are trying to lose weight with more than 12% going more than 24-hours without food within a 30-day period either to lose weight or stop from gaining weight (Centers for Disease Control and Prevention, 2011).
- High school students have lower physical self-esteem and more unhealthy weight control behaviors than middle school students (Cohane & Pope, 2001; Israel & Ivanova, 2002; McCabe & Ricciardelli, 2001).

Counseling and Prevention Strategies

The most widely used approaches to address eating disorders in the schools are individual and group counseling, involvement of family members, and classroom guidance programs. Professional school counselors can also implement school-based changes to create a more safe and accepting environment around the issues of eating disorders, weightism, and physical and overall self-esteem.

Prevention efforts that are generally centered on body satisfaction and education may be conceived at primary (e.g., curb dieting behaviors, concerns about weight/shape), secondary (e.g., reduce the duration of eating disorders), and tertiary (e.g., address and reduce impairment of established disorders) levels (Gabel & Kearney, 1998).

Activities should address all of the systems at play in the development of eating disturbances: family, sociocultural, self-deficits, body image concerns, self-esteem, and peer and parental involvement (O'Dea, 2000, 2004). Attempts should address the negative consequences of unhealthy weight control as well as encourage healthy eating and exercise (Mussell et al., 2000). Programs aimed at promoting body and self-acceptance and decreasing unhealthy weight loss have demonstrated success (Weiss & Wertheim, 2005).

Professional school counselors and other personnel must first examine their own beliefs and feelings about weight, shape, appearance, and self-esteem. Regardless of the form of intervention or age group to which it applies, professional school counselors' work should foremost focus on promoting body satisfaction. Counselors may then help students enhance self-esteem and personal efficacy by recognizing positive aspects of their physical appearance (O'Dea, 2004; Phelps et al., 2000; Weiss & Wertheim, 2005).

Some approaches, particularly peer-led approaches, can have negative effects. Programs that provide information about eating disorders led by "recovered peers" increase students' knowledge of eating disorders but also sometimes lead to an increase in symptoms (O'Dea, 2000). Students introduced to beliefs, attitudes, and behaviors preceding eating disorders may hear suggestions of the desirability to lose weight and the means for doing so. For younger children, frequent coverage of eating disorders in this manner can normalize the problem and thereby create longer term difficulties.

A positive approach providing information on body image can be more beneficial. Addressing what makes students satisfied and dissatisfied with their bodies and introducing activities that desensitize them to the events eliciting body image dissatisfaction and eating disorders are useful tools (Gore, Vander Wal, & Thelen, 2009). Helpful activities may include guided imagery and relaxation, envisioning oneself as brave and strong, and encouraging pleasurable body-related activities (e.g., bike riding, getting a haircut, wearing favorite clothes).

Individual Counseling

The professional school counselor must be mindful of one's limits and be prepared to refer students who have severe impairments to counselors in the community who may offer more constant and intensive care. In addition to community-based mental health counselors, professional school counselors should become familiar with other helping professionals who can assist with eating disorders, such as nutritionists, dieticians, physicians, exercise physiologists, and psychiatrists.

Counseling the student with an eating disorder can be tricky. Education about nutrition, exercise, self-acceptance, and the physical dangers associated with eating disorders is essential. At the same time, the student's emotional distress and academic performance need to be addressed as well as development of identity and appropriate coping mechanisms (Levine & Smolak, 2009). Many students with eating disorders may be defensive and resistant to help because they believe that their behavior has been effective in getting what they want (e.g., attention from peers, parental affection, a socially acceptable body size). Other times, students will refer themselves because their eating problems have gotten out of control. In these cases, the student's willingness to seek help to deal with the eating disorder and other problems in the student's life should be acknowledged and praised.

Garner, Garfinkel, and Irvine (1986), pioneers in eating disorder treatment, suggested that there are two tracks to consider: behavioral context and emotional context. The behavioral context involves issues of weight, starvation, erratic eating, bingeing, vomiting, strenuous exercise, or whatever the student's physical manifestation of the eating disorder may be. Cognitive-behavioral approaches might include restructuring thoughts, assistance with meal planning, and challenging distorted attitudes about weight and shape. The emotional context involves underlying developmental issues, personality, and family and peer themes. A psychodynamic approach might include a developmental understanding of eating disorders as a type of fear, family separation issues, parental inattention to the student's needs, and a lack of self-regulation. Garner et al. suggested that eating disorders can be dealt with initially from either track, as each communicates to the student a desire to help and a commitment to ensuring that both physical and emotional health is restored. Cognitive-behavioral and psychodynamic approaches are the most widely used with individuals with eating disorders; the affective level should be a particular focus among pre-adult populations.

Counseling should match student development levels. The use of journals can be particularly helpful in tracking feelings and behaviors. For younger students with less cognitive capacity, simply keeping a "food-mood" diary may be enough. Professional school counselors working with older students in middle and high school may be successful in eliciting more complex processing by examining what was happening during periods of wanting to binge, purge, abstain from eating, and so forth. Engaging students in the process of analyzing, identifying, and transforming their environments is empowering at any developmental level (Levine & Smolak, 2009).

Group Counseling

Social influence and norms are critical for many school-age youth and are a significant correlate to unhealthy weight management (Eisenberg, Neumark-Sztainer, & Perry, 2005). Groups that focus on body image and the factors that lead to eating disorders are more likely to occur within the school setting. These groups provide students with opportunities to engage in activities and practice new behaviors with peers at a time when they are vulnerable to peer influences (Levine & Smolak, 2009). Students in body image awareness groups build support systems and facilitate connections with one another. It is important for counselors leading groups to ensure that they are being positive role models by addressing their own issues on the subject.

Structured group counseling gives students a focused means of talking about ways to promote positive body image. Several approaches incorporate education, insight, and action. Groups can focus on realistic goal setting, healthy body image, assertiveness, and perfectionism over 8 to 10 sessions (Rhyne-Winkler & Hubbard, 1994). Games, role-plays, and activities that encourage putting into perspective sociocultural and media messages about the importance of appearance empower students to feel good about themselves while contributing to the self-esteem of their peers. Activities may include identifying characteristics of admired people or collecting advertisements that teach students that fat is bad. Group sessions may include information on dieting and exercising, developing a food log, healthy exercise, eating behaviors, emotions associated with eating, self-esteem and autonomy, body image and goal setting, and develop coping skills. In all likelihood, this information will be most effective with students in elementary and middle school.

Students learn about advocacy and the forces that influence their feelings about their bodies while learning how to cope with everyday interactions with others and teasing about their bodies. These protective factors and the immediate feedback from peers in groups enable students to be more proactive in preventing their own and peers' eating-disorder risks. There are dangers in counseling groups of this nature, however, as they can at times be explosive, heavily emotionally laden, or it may be difficult to get students to share openly about their private feelings. The professional school counselor should therefore exercise caution and patience and have appropriate supports in place for students in these groups.

Involving Family Members

Interventions for students with eating disorders are often ineffective without the support of parents and family members. Parents and other family members have a significant effect on students' self-image and self-esteem. Family members may contribute to unhealthy attitudes and behaviors about the body by modeling dieting and disordered eating as well as comments about students' and others' appearances and criticism of their students' changing bodies (Kluck, 2010; Rodgers, Paxton, & Chabrol, 2009). Family dynamics have also been implicated in the development of eating disorders. Girls who report high levels of eating problems live in families marked by lower levels of cohesion, organization, and expressiveness. Families of students with eating disorders are more conflictual, lacking in secure attachments and warmth (Byely, Archibald, Graber, & Brooks-Gunn, 2000). Parents should always be involved in treatment. Consult the American Counseling Association and the American School Counselor Association's codes of ethics and local school policies for guidance on informed consent.

Table 41.2 How to Help Families Cope With Eating Disorders

Educate families about eating disorders.
Send written correspondence home with students.
Facilitate family discussions about weight and health.
Alert families to how they might unintentionally send harmful messages.
Set limits, and openly discuss issues.
Ascertain eating habits, and foster family relationships by suggesting that they spend mealtimes together.
Facilitate an examination of family members' own feelings and prejudices about weight.
Make appropriate referrals to community medical and mental health professionals.
Emphasize that spending time with children can foster cohesive, warm relationships that protect students from eating disorders.
Discourage dieting.
Plan programs through parent–teacher association meetings.
Educate families about normal puberty and developmental changes.

Because of the nature of eating disorders, family therapy is often highly recommended to explore the student's expression of anger, conflict, depression, anxiety, and any feelings that may be influenced by the home and family environment. This is further cause for professional school counselors to know community resources and make referrals for needed services. Professional school counselors must also work collaboratively with the students, mental health counselors, and medical doctors when applicable. Also, it is important that professional school counselors recognize their limits and make referrals as necessary. Table 41.2 includes activities that professional school counselors can engage in to help families cope with eating issues. Within the school setting, professional school counselors can take on a number of roles to prevent, identify, and provide services for students with eating disorders.

Classroom Guidance Programs

The topic of eating disorders can be covered within several elective courses as well as health and physical education curricula. Professional school counselors can encourage teachers to combine issues of nutrition, exercise, and self-acceptance into appropriate classes such that children learn about healthy, positive, and active lifestyles (Gabel & Kearney, 1998). Students can also be educated about the negative effects of starvation, erratic eating, and bingeing, including depression, anxiety, irritability, feelings of inadequacy, fatigue, preoccupation with food, poor concentration, and social withdrawal (Garner et al., 1986). Other content to address with students in classrooms includes body esteem and self-esteem, locus of control, approval-seeking behavior, body image and nutrition, excessive exercise, and perfectionism (Rhyne-Winkler & Hubbard, 1994).

Weiss and Wertheim (2005) proposed a four-session, large-group prevention program that may be likened to classroom guidance. The Making Choices program promotes self-acceptance through discussion of self-esteem, healthy dieting, and exercise. The unique aspect of this program that is most relevant to professional school counselors is its facilitation of full-class and small-group discussions. This may be a helpful means of encouraging dialogue in the classroom setting.

Classroom guidance programs addressing these topics create an environment in which students examine knowledge and attitudes about food and eating, develop positive and realistic attitudes toward their bodies, and gain accurate information (Rhyne-Winkler & Hubbard, 1994). Given the influence of peers, training students to provide peer-led programs might be a useful means of disseminating such information effectively. Students will be more likely to listen to each other on most issues. A select group of students to teach others about eating disorders and positive body image can be empowering for both leaders and recipients. Such opportunities serve as protective factors, much in the same way as peer mentoring programs on other issues, such as substance abuse, violence, and transition to new schools. In one such program, the Ophelia Project (www.opheliaproject.org), high school girls mentor middle school students to prevent and process relational aggression. Program coordinators found that increasing self-esteem in another realm creates more positive body image among participants. Students involved with the program also had significant influences on the school environment as a whole.

School-Based Changes

Professional school counselors should become knowledgeable about eating disorders and provide information and consultation to school personnel, parents, and students (Carney & Scott, 2012). Discussions about biases and views can take place with teachers, coaches, and administrators who address weight reduction (Gabel & Kearney, 1998). Teachers may also be trained to infuse eating disorders into curricula and to listen actively, provide feedback nonjudgmentally, and teach without lecturing so that they are more likely to identify students at risk and refer them for help. Given the developmental concerns of students at each level, professional school counselors must help to create a safe and nonjudgmental environment for students to feel healthy and grow (Akos & Levitt, 2002).

A safe school environment can begin with the professional school counselor, who is a resource to students, teachers, parents, and administrators and helps to ensure timely and appropriate interventions for at-risk students (Bardick et al., 2004; Giles & Hass, 2008). Table 41.3 addresses continuing initiatives that will prompt systemic changes and reduce prevalence of eating disorders (Rhyne-Winkler & Hubbard, 1994).

Developmental Considerations

In order to best help students who are developing tendencies toward eating disorders, professional school counselors must consider developmental issues. Following is a review of differential considerations at the elementary, middle, and high school levels.

Elementary School

Researchers determined that children as young as fifth grade have engaged in binge and purge behaviors (Combs, Person, & Smith, 2011), suggesting early education is warranted. Teaching students early about eating disorders, body-esteem, and self-esteem maximizes positive

Table 41.3 Initiatives to Enhance Systemic Change

- Provide training to become aware of the signs and symptoms of eating disorders.
- Promote activities that foster healthy and realistic attitudes about weight, shape, growth, and nutrition.
- Monitor how health and physical activity requirements are communicated to students and families.
- Create an atmosphere in which students confront negative body talk.
- Advocate for nutritional food and snack offerings.
- Encourage the purchase of library and classroom materials with positive images about self-esteem and body image.
- Encourage use of the term *fat* as neutral and nonderogatory.
- Create a wellness program that will accomplish the following:
  - Focus on prevention and early intervention.
  - Involve teachers and administrators.
  - Promote healthy attitudes and habits toward eating.
  - Encourage self-control.
  - Focus on improving self-esteem and autonomy.
  - Make appropriate materials available in easily accessible areas.
  - Foster discussions among the whole school community.
  - Continually focus on the overall well-being of students.

influences and decreases the likelihood of issues later in childhood and adolescence (Ohring, Graber, & Brooks-Gunn, 2002). Because young children respond well to action-oriented approaches, experiential components such as poetry, humor, and games in prevention curricula and interventions have proven successful (Mussell et al., 2000).

Young children have likely not experienced unsuccessful or chronic dieting and may not understand the concept of bingeing (Ricciardelli & McCabe, 2001). For those who show early signs of disordered eating, gradual exposure to feared foods with relaxation training, role-playing to address social and familial problems, and development of alternative ways of thinking about problems are helpful elements (Gore et al., 2009).

Middle School

Perhaps the most important event at this level is the normalization of physical changes that take place in puberty (Ohring et al., 2002). Bodily changes, especially for students who mature earlier than others, are unfamiliar and create differences. Peer support is vital in middle school, particularly for students with eating disorders. Peer-led programs—whether they are groups, prevention workshops, or merely facilitated small-group discussions—allow students to promote sensitivity and positive body talk while learning that they may seek one another for support (Mussell et al., 2000). Because peers are so influential during middle school, encouraging students to talk sensitively and providing training for peer mentoring and facilitation to teach others about these issues can be an empowering and positive use of peer influence.

O'Dea (2004) described a 9-week program based solely on self-esteem that was effective in improving body image and offsetting dieting, weight loss, and eating-disordered behavior among female middle school participants. Based on the principle of student-centered learning, students worked in groups and incorporated teamwork, games, play, and drama in this content-free curriculum. The program was intended to foster a positive sense of self, positive and safe student environment, vicarious learning, feedback exchange, and a positive and supportive environment. The success of this program in modifying body image without directly addressing the topic demonstrates the benefits of self-esteem–based programming.

High School

It is important to target high school students with low self-esteem and other early signs of eating disorders, and small groups are particularly useful in facilitating intimate discussions among high school peers about these issues (Mussell et al., 2000). Peers help to debunk myths about appearance and offer alternative ways of handling difficult problems.

It is also useful to incorporate activities and introduce resources that have an activist twist, enabling students to work productively toward a solution to eating disorders, the pressures to be thin, and the negative attributions placed on overweight people by society. An interactive Web site developed by the National Eating Disorders Association, *Proud2Bme*, teaches teens about media awareness, activism, and advocacy while increasing self-esteem and preventing eating disorders (see www.nationaleatingdisorders.org or www.proud2bme.org). Proud2Bme posts discussions on social pressures from media and peers, along with information on eating disorders, body image, and perfectionism.

Using group discussions with young adults who have recovered from eating disorders might also be included in school programs (Phelps et al., 2000) but should be done cautiously and under supervision because students are particularly vulnerable when they hear others' experiences with eating disorders. This is especially true as students have access to other attitudes about eating disorders. For example, pro-anorexic and pro-bulimic Web sites are extremely dangerous places where people with active eating disorders attempt to convince others that these are positive and adaptive ways of coping and promote the ultra-thin, sickly, emaciated appearance of anorexia. Students have greater access to these sites with increased unsupervised time on the Internet, and the popularity of the chat sessions within them is high. Professional school counselors should be aware that such propaganda exists and that students are readily able to find, access, and be subject to the dangerous content therein.

Most counseling interventions for eating disorders are designed for work with adults. Adolescents who have the ability to think abstractly are likely to respond well to such approaches. The professional school counselor should be mindful of the developmental level and pressures that the student faces. Challenging students to think about the connection between their thoughts, problems, fears, or pressures and their eating disordered behaviors must be accompanied by the generation of alternatives that can be directly applied.

Resources for Students, Parents, and Other Personnel

Professional school counselors have a tremendous effect on students and the school community by being intentional about helping students with eating disorders and related image concerns. Interventions at individual, group, familial, classroom, and school-wide levels can be challenging and require appropriate resources. "How to Help a Friend" (Table 41.4) is a useful

Table 41.4 How to Help a Friend With Body Image and Eating Difficulties

DO...

Create a safe environment to talk.

Encourage the person to seek help from a professional counselor, physician, or friend.

Expect anger or rejection at first; this may be an embarrassing or frightening first encounter.

Be patient—this is a long process and difficult issue.

Express your concern and desire to help.

Plan your approach carefully.

Speak with compassion and concern.

Model positive actions.

Provide specific information and resources.

Be willing to spend time listening and talking about related personal problems.

Take a look at your own attitudes toward weight, shape, and dieting.

Attempt to discuss feelings.

Explain your concerns with specific observations.

Offer support.

DON'T...

Nag, argue, plead, or bribe.

Criticize yourself or anyone else for being over- or underweight.

Blame yourself or anyone else for the person's difficulties.

Give simplistic suggestions about nutrition or self-control.

Comment positively or negatively about others' sizes and shapes.

Comment on the person's appearance.

Use scare tactics.

Become involved in a power struggle.

Spy or interfere.

Monitor eating.

Use food as a socializing agent.

Discuss weight, amount of calories or fat being consumed, or particular eating and exercise habits.

Expect 100% recovery immediately.

---

tool to share with students who are concerned about friends and peers that will help them identify their own strategies for intervention. The following resources may also be shared with students, parents, and school personnel. Professional school counselors should consult these and other resources in their efforts to combat eating disorders.

- AboutFace: Combating Negative and Distorted Images of Women (www.about-face.org)
- Body Image. 1-800-994-9662 (http://www.womenshealth.gov/body-image)
- Choate, L. H. (2013). *Eating disorders and obesity: A counselor's guide to treatment and prevention.* Alexandria, VA: American Counseling Association.
- Maine, M. (2000). *Body wars: Making peace with women's bodies.* Carlsbad, CA: Gurze Books.

- National Eating Disorders Association. 212-575-6200 (www.nationaleatingdisorders.org)
- National Eating Disorders Association. (2005). *Eating disorders survival guide.* Available online (www.nationaleatingdisorders.org)
- The Ophelia Project. (www.opheliaproject.org)
- Pipher, M. (1994). *Reviving Ophelia: Saving the selves of adolescent girls.* New York, NY: Ballantine Books.

Summary/Conclusion

Eating disorders and their subclinical manifestations do not appear to be diminishing in our society. Professional school counselors are on the front line to intervene in and prevent the development of eating disorders among students. At all developmental levels, students need attention and education about eating disorders, which can be addressed through classroom guidance, individual counseling, and group counseling. Parents can be educated about eating disorders, how to detect them in their students, and how home can either be a safe haven or contribute to these disorders.

As agents of change, professional school counselors are likewise encouraged to educate teachers and other administrative personnel about eating disorders—for example, how to detect and approach students about whom they have concerns and ways to make the school a safe environment, accepting of all body shapes. It is incumbent upon professional school counselors to attend to the reality of eating disorders in their schools, whether they are overt or more subtle manifestations among their students. Through prevention, education, and intervention, professional school counselors play an integral role for students, their families, the school, and the greater community to appropriately and effectively address this dangerous phenomenon.

CHAPTER 42

Helping Students Who Have Depression

Bradley T. Erford*

Preview

Depression in youth has been the focus of increased concern during the past 3 decades. Whereas it used to be considered a disorder of adulthood, current researchers and mental health professionals are aware that many children and adolescents also deal with depression, a serious, complex, and treatable disorder (Merrell, 2008). Young adolescents, in particular, are susceptible to depression because of the intense biological, social, and psychological changes that occur from late childhood to early adulthood. Professional school counselors are in a unique position to initiate activities and services designed to help prevent, identify, and coordinate the treatment of depression in youth. Information about depression is presented, including types of depression, signs and symptoms, factors influencing its onset, and associated risks. Suggested interventions based on outcome studies and research are described, including a list of resources to help professional school counselors to design preventive and remedial activities.

I'm normal, sort of. I take honors and advance placement courses. I was in the marching band, and I played varsity soccer for two years, but I have a distinct quality that separates me from the masses—I am sad most of the time. I don't sulk around or constantly plot ways to end my life; instead, I withdraw from regular activities a lot and spend a good deal of time thinking about my life and my purpose here. Somewhere down the line, amidst all the action and continuous responsibility, I lost track of myself. I felt trapped in all my relationships and virtually had no time to myself. I discontinued communication with my best friends, and my goal every week was to survive to the weekend, where I could relax and put everything on hold. I viewed myself as capable but also as always fallible. By November of my junior year, I was a wreck. Still, I refused to acknowledge my feelings as depression. I didn't think it could happen to me.

—17-year-old high school student who was treated for depression

Depression Defined

According to the National Institute of Mental Health (NIMH; 2013a, 2014), depression is a condition that can affect thoughts, feelings, behaviors, and overall health. It can affect sleeping and appetite, the way one feels about oneself, and the manner in which one thinks about

---

*Special thanks to Debbie W. Newsome for her outstanding contributions to the first edition of this chapter and Julia A. Southern for her contributions to the second edition of this chapter.

things. In addition to affecting a student's current quality of life, depressive symptoms and disorders that begin during childhood or adolescence predict recurring or ongoing depression in adulthood. Unless treated, early onset of the disorder can predict more severe and negative symptoms later in life.

Depression is an internalizing disorder, as are anxiety disorders, social withdrawal, and somatic problems (Merrell, 2008). Internalizing disorders are characterized by overcontrol, which implies that individuals may overregulate or inappropriately control their emotions. In the case of internalizing disorders, the problems are maintained *within* the individual, in contrast to externalizing disorders, such as oppositional defiant disorder and attention-deficit/hyperactivity disorder (ADHD), which are characterized by acting out. The defining characteristic of the internalizing problem of depression is mood disturbance. Depressed youth experience difficulty regulating negative emotions.

Whereas much of the research on depression refers to clinical depressive disorders, other manifestations of depression, while not severe enough to merit a clinical diagnosis, can cause distress in young people and call for the attention of professional school counselors. For depression to be considered a clinical disorder, a collection of symptoms must be evidenced that meet specific diagnostic criteria according to standardized classification systems, such as the *Diagnostic and Statistical Manual of Mental Disorders* (5th ed.; *DSM-5*; American Psychiatric Association [APA], 2013). Diagnosis is based on the intensity and duration of a set of symptoms that are serious enough to interfere with one's level of functioning. Examples of depressive disorders include major depressive disorder and chronic depressive (dysthymic) disorder. Adjustment disorder with depressed mood (or mixed anxiety and depressed mood) also is marked by depressive symptoms, as are bipolar disorders, cyclothymic disorder, and mood disorder due to medical condition or substance use. In this chapter, specific recommendations for helping students with bipolar, cyclothymic, or substance abuse–related disorders will *not* be addressed; instead, the focus is on helping students who struggle with depressive symptoms, major depressive disorder, chronic depressive (dysthymic) disorder, or adjustment disorder with depressed mood. It is likely that professional school counselors will encounter students dealing with depressed mood and depressive disorders. Therefore, it is important to be knowledgeable of the diagnostic criteria for depression and other mood disorders so that appropriate interventions and/or referrals can be made (Erford, 2015c).

Signs and Symptoms of Depression

Identifying depression in young people may be challenging because symptoms are often masked. Although the diagnostic criteria and key defining features of major depressive disorder are the same for youth as for adults, it may be difficult for them to identify or describe their feelings (NIMH, 2013). Instead, depressed students may appear irritable, act out, or withdraw from family and friends. Also, anxiety symptoms and somatic complaints are more common in depressed children and adolescents than in adults. A list of common signs and symptoms of depression in young people is presented in Table 42.1 (NIMH, 2013, 2014).

The diagnostic criteria for major depressive disorder and chronic depressive (dysthymic) disorder are outlined in the *DSM-5* (APA, 2013) as are the criteria for bipolar disorder, cyclothymic disorder, and adjustment disorder with depressed mood. The primary features of each

Table 42.1 Signs and Symptoms of Depression in Children and Adolescents

Feeling sad, empty, or hopeless
Increased emotional sensitivity
Lack of interest or ability to engage in pleasurable activities
Decreased energy level
Physical complaints (headaches, stomachaches, tiredness)
Frequent absences from school (or poor performance)
Outbursts (shouting, complaining, crying)
Boredom
Substance abuse
Fear of death
Suicidal ideation
Sleep/appetite disturbances
Reduced ability to think clearly and make decisions
Increased irritability, anger, or restlessness
Failure to make expected weight gains
Reckless behavior
Difficulty with relationships

disorder are summarized in Table 42.2; however, students may exhibit signs of depression without meeting the full diagnostic criteria for these disorders. These students, as well as students who are clinically depressed, are likely to benefit from early intervention by professional school counselors.

Depression in children and adolescents often is accompanied by other problems, some of which are clinically diagnosable. Examples of disorders that frequently co-occur with depression in youth are anxiety disorders, conduct disorder, eating disorders, personality disorders, and substance use disorders. Particularly high rates of comorbidity exist between depression and anxiety disorders (APA, 2013). In studies of individuals ranging in age from 12 to 21 years, individuals with depression had rates of comorbidity with anxiety ranging from 33% to 75%. Also, depression may accompany medical conditions such as diabetes or other illnesses. Given the high rate of co-occurrence, professional school counselors will want to be sensitive to the possibility that the depressed student may also be struggling with one or more other conditions and plan interventions accordingly.

Prevalence

It is difficult to estimate rates of depression in children and adolescents with certainty (Merrell, 2008). A conservative estimate of 5% to 8% of adolescents struggle with either clinical depression or depressive syndrome (NIMH, 2013, 2014). According to a NIMH (2013) report, approximately 2.5% of children and between 3% and 5% of adolescents experience clinical depression each year. Ten percent to 40% of youth report depressed or unhappy mood, with

Table 42.2 DSM-5 Disorders that Have Depressed Mood as a Symptom

Type of Disorder	Characteristics
Major Depressive Disorder (MDD)	Uncommon in young children but increases in prevalence after puberty, the life-time risk is 10% to 25% in women and 5% to 12% in men. MDD involves at least one major depressive episode (extreme sadness and lack of interest in normal activities for 2 or more weeks at a time) without the occurrence of a manic episode or another disorder that better accounts for the depression.
Chronic Depressive (Dysthymic) Disorder	Common in children and adolescents (lifetime prevalence of 6%), but not diagnosed if a major depressive disorder is evidenced. Depressed mood most days for at least 2 years (1 year in children and adolescents). Symptoms may include poor appetite or overeating, poor sleeping or oversleeping, fatigue, poor concentration, and feelings of hopelessness.
Bipolar Disorder	Rare in young children but can appear in children and adolescents. Involves unusual shifts in mood, energy, and functioning. May begin with manic, depressive, or mixed manic and depressive symptoms. When the onset is before or soon after puberty, it may be characterized by a continuous, rapid-cycling, irritable, mixed symptom state and may co-occur with attention-deficit/hyperactivity disorder or conduct disorder.
Cyclothymic Disorder	Onset typically is early adulthood, but the disorder can occur at younger ages. Characterized by chronic, fluctuating mood disturbance with many periods of hypomanic symptoms and many periods of depressive symptoms. During the initial 1-year period (for children and adolescents), any symptom-free periods do not last longer than 2 months.
Adjustment Disorder with Depressed Mood	An adjustment disorder is a psychological response to an identified stressor that results in the development of emotional or psychological symptoms that are distressing to the individual. The symptoms must develop within 3 months after the stressor occurs and should resolve within 6 months after the stressor or its consequences have ended, unless the stressor is chronic. The predominant characteristics of adjustment disorder with depressed mood are tearfulness, feelings of hopelessness, and depressed mood.

the rates increasing throughout adolescence. The onset of depressive disorders appears to be occurring earlier in life than in previous decades. Early diagnosis and treatment can help offset difficulties that are associated with untreated depression when children reach adulthood.

Prior to age 13 years, the rates of depression for boys and girls are similar. However, gender differences emerge between the ages of 13 and 14 years, with girls twice as likely to report substantive symptoms of depression as boys (Merrell, 2008). One hypothesis for this difference is that girls tend to experience more challenges and stressors in early adolescence than boys, causing girls' depressive symptoms to increase more significantly during this time and throughout adulthood. Some theorists have suggested that these elevated levels of depression are rooted in girls' adherence to the female gender role, beginning during puberty and the concurrent transition from elementary to secondary school. Additionally, physical changes during puberty often cause girls to develop body image concerns and dissatisfaction with their appearance. Deviance from the perceived "thin ideal" often sparks feelings of depressed mood and can in some cases result in the development of other harmful disorders. Regardless of the reasons for the differences, the increased rate of depression in girls may make it more likely that professional school counselors will work with girls struggling with depressive symptoms.

Factors Associated With Depression

Several models of depression have been proposed, many of which have reciprocal components. Recognizing that interaction among causal factors is likely and that research on the etiology of depression is ongoing, current research on biological and psychosocial factors associated with depression in youth is presented next.

Biological factors. Much of the research about biological influences on depression has been conducted with adults rather than youth. Consequently, it is important to keep in mind when reading this section that generalizations about biological influences on depression may not be completely applicable to young people. Specific biological factors associated with the development of depression include abnormalities in the functioning of neurotransmitters and/or the endocrine system. In many cases, individuals may have a genetic predisposition to such abnormalities (Merrell, 2008).

Certain brain chemicals, including serotonin and norepinephrine, affect mood and have been linked with mood disorders (Merrell, 2008). When there are abnormalities in the level or function of these neurotransmitters, mood disorders can develop. Antidepressant medications such as fluoxetine (Prozac), fluvoxamine (Luvox), sertraline (Zoloft), and paroxetine (Paxil) block the reuptake of serotonin, thereby increasing its availability to brain cells. Other medications, such as venlafaxine (Effexor) and nefazodone (Serzone) affect the transmission of both serotonin and norepinephrine and can bring about relief from depressive symptoms.

Also associated with depression is abnormal functioning of the endocrine system, which releases hormones into the bloodstream. Various abnormalities in the functioning of the pituitary gland, thyroid gland, adrenal gland, and glands that release sex hormones have been linked with mood disturbances in youth and adults (Merrell, 2008; NIMH, 2013, 2014). In particular, hormonal changes during puberty may be associated with depressive symptoms.

Genetics play an important role in a person's vulnerability to depression and other mental disorders. It is theorized that multiple gene variants, rather than a single gene, act in conjunction with environmental factors and developmental events, thus making a person more likely to experience depressive symptoms (NIMH, 2013, 2014).

Cognitive and behavioral factors. Cognitive theory describes a strong link between an individual's cognitions, emotions, and behaviors. According to cognitive theory, people's interpretations of events, rather than the events themselves, trigger emotional upsets and mood disturbances. Such interpretations affect one's view of self, the world, and the future. Inaccurate interpretations or faulty information processing can lead to depressive symptoms in youth and adults (Kendall, 2011). Examples of faulty information processing include negative attributions and cognitive distortions.

Children with negative attribution styles may believe that they are helpless to influence events in their lives. They may also believe that they are responsible for any failures and problems that are experienced but not for successful, positive events (Merrell, 2008). For example, a student may believe that she is responsible for her parents' divorce and thus continually blame herself for the breakup of their marriage; or when something positive happens, like winning an award for achievement, the student attributes the event to luck.

Cognitive dysfunctions refer to negative, inaccurate biases that can result in unhealthy misperceptions of events. Studies have found that clinically depressed youth view themselves as less capable than their classmates, even though their IQ and academic performance does not differ significantly. Their negative perceptions often improve with the remittance of their depressive symptoms, indicating that these self-assessments may be dependent on the adolescent's state of mind during a given time (McGrath & Repetti, 2002). Cognitive theorists have identified several types of cognitive dysfunctions, including exaggerating the negative, minimizing the positive, overgeneralizing, catastrophizing, and personalizing. Cognitive distortions also are evidenced when young people engage in all-or-nothing thinking or selective abstraction, such as when taking a detail out of context and using it to negate an entire experience. Such distortions can result in negative automatic thoughts, which then affect emotions and mood states. Teaching students ways to correct faulty information processing is one way to effectively help young people who are depressed (Kendall, 2011).

Behaviors associated with negative cognitions and feelings can both contribute to and maintain depressive symptoms in children and adolescents. In particular, withdrawing from peers and family members can exacerbate feelings of depression and loneliness through the resulting lack of social reinforcement (Merrell, 2008). Related to social withdrawal is the tendency of depressed individuals to quit engaging in activities that formerly were pleasurable, such as athletics or hobbies, thereby creating a cycle that makes it difficult to alleviate depressive symptoms. To break the cycle, professional school counselors can help children identify activities they consider pleasurable and make commitments to participate in those activities between sessions.

Challenges and stressors. Youth who experience numerous stressors may be more likely to experience depression than those who do not. It is likely that the number and timing of changes and challenges in early adolescence affect mental health. Challenges can be categorized as normative life events (expected changes, such as school entry and puberty), nonnormative events (e.g., divorce, abuse, moving away), and daily hassles (e.g., conflict with friends, excessive schoolwork). The manner in which stress is experienced varies greatly from student to student. Recognizing the potential detrimental effects of stress, professional school counselors can conduct classroom guidance lessons and group sessions to teach students ways to manage stress effectively (see Chapter 65, "Helping Students Manage Stress," for specific examples).

Family and peer influences. A number of family-related factors are associated with depression, including extensive conflict, poor communication patterns, low family cohesion, and the emotional unavailability of parents (Merrell, 2008). Having a parent with a mood disorder increases a young person's risk of experiencing depression, due in part to heredity and in part to the family interactions that occur if the parent's condition is not being treated successfully. In community settings, family counseling is often recommended when a member of the family is depressed; however, this option may not be available in the school setting. If not, professional school counselors can be instrumental in helping families become aware of opportunities for family counseling in the community.

Poor relationships with peers, not having a close friend, and being considered unpopular or different also can lead to depressive symptoms in students. Certain populations, includ-

Table 42.3 Risk Factors for Depression

Family history of mood disorders
Gender (adolescent girls twice as likely as boys to develop depression)
Stress
Loss of parent or loved one
Breakup of a romantic relationship
ADHD, conduct disorder, or learning disorder
Cigarette smoking
Chronic illness (e.g., diabetes)
Abuse or neglect
Other trauma, including natural disasters

ing gay, lesbian, and bisexual youth, may experience a greater degree of peer rejection and isolation, thus increasing their vulnerability to depression (NIMH, 2014). A critical role of the professional school counselor is to serve as an advocate for all students. Tolerance and acceptance can be demonstrated and taught in multiple ways, including parent and teacher training programs, classroom guidance lessons, and small-group sessions. See Table 42.3 for a list of risk factors for depression (NIMH, 2013, 2014).

Consequences of Depression

A wide range of intrapersonal and interpersonal problems can arise when depression goes undiagnosed and untreated in young people. A diminished sense of self-worth, a lack of confidence, and a general tendency to view oneself negatively often go hand in hand with depression (Merrell, 2008). For some students, the depression and ensuing fatigue can result in difficulties in concentration, motivation, and academic performance. Impaired relationships with peers and family members can both lead to and become a consequence of depression. The onset of depression is often correlated with interpersonal struggles, such as interpersonal deficits, role transitions, interpersonal role disputes, or grief (Mellin & Beamish, 2002). If left untreated, these underlying interpersonal difficulties frequently persist into adulthood. In addition, youth with untreated depression are at an increased risk for physical illness, substance abuse, recurrent episodes of depression, and suicidal behavior (NIMH, 2013, 2014). Consequently, there is a strong need to identify depressive symptoms early and make it possible for youth struggling with depression to get the help they need.

Suicide risk. The most severe problem associated with depression is the risk of suicide. Although most people who are depressed do not commit suicide, depressed youth, especially those dealing with what they perceive as a crisis, are at a greater risk for suicidal behaviors. The strongest risk factors for attempted suicide in young people are depression, substance abuse, and aggressive or disruptive behaviors (NIMH, 2013). The suicide rate among youth has increased dramatically during the past 3 decades, with suicide reported as the third leading cause of death among 15- to 24-year-olds (NIMH, 2014). More girls attempt suicide than boys; however, boys are four times as likely to actually kill themselves and tend to use more lethal means, such as firearms.

Suicide attempts are often preceded by signals, warnings, or actual threats. Some of the signs to watch for include verbal messages (e.g., "I wish I were dead," "There's only one way out," "I won't be around much longer"), a preoccupation with death, changes in sleeping and eating patterns, decline in school performance, or giving away possessions. Suicidal behaviors and threats represent a cry for help and must be taken seriously. Professional school counselors typically have been trained in suicide assessment, and most schools have policies and procedures related to crisis intervention. When a professional school counselor has reason to believe that a student is contemplating suicide, the counselor will want to assess the nature and intensity of the student's thoughts and follow up with a response that will keep the student safe (see Chapters 67 and 68).

Interventions

Professional school counselors have opportunities to intervene at multiple levels to help children and adolescents deal with depressive symptoms. Intervention can take the form of prevention, which is designed to reduce incidences of depression before problems begin, or direct counseling services for at-risk groups and individuals. Interventions at all levels need to be developmentally informed, with an overarching goal of enhancing resilience and external resources.

A number of factors, including school policy and size, may dictate the nature and type of interventions the professional school counselor implements. Professional school counselors are responsible for a wide range of services and work with a large number of students, teachers, and parents. If too much time is spent with only a few students, the larger proportion of the student body may be shortchanged (Erford, 2015c). Recognizing the challenge of balancing multiple responsibilities, professional school counselors play crucial roles in assessing, coordinating referrals, and, when needed, providing direct treatment or follow-up services for students with depression. They also are key leaders in planning and implementing prevention programs for students, parents, and teachers.

Assessment and Evaluation

Accurately assessing depression in children and adolescents can be challenging because the symptoms often cannot be observed directly and therefore may go unrecognized. By being aware of the signs, symptoms, and co-occurring conditions associated with child and adolescent depression, professional school counselors can help identify students who may be in need of services. The purpose of assessment is to inform treatment, which may involve direct counseling services at the school or elsewhere.

Typically, multiple sources of information are used to guide decision making and treatment planning. It helps to gather information from the child, parents, and teachers. Self-report instruments, structured or semi-structured interviews, and behavior rating scales are some of the methods that can be used in assessment. Professional school counselors who have been trained in appraisal procedures may choose to use assessment instruments designed for depression screening, such as the *Children's Depression Inventory* (CDI-2), the *Beck Depression Inventory* (BDI-II), and the *Center for Epidemiological Studies Depression Scale* (CES-D) (see Muller & Erford, 2012; NIMH, 2013). Professional school counselors who have not been trained to use a particular instrument should get supervision to ensure that the instrument is administered and interpreted properly. If the screening evaluation indicates the student has depressive symptoms and possibly a depressive disorder, the professional school counselor will want to provide referral information to parents so that a more comprehensive diagnostic evaluation can be conducted. In such cases, the professional school counselor can serve as a liaison between the referral agency and the family.

Direct Counseling Services

When helping students who have depression, direct counseling services are often warranted. These services may include individual counseling, referral, and group counseling.

Individual counseling. For some students, short-term individual counseling or group counseling may be warranted. Research has demonstrated the efficacy of certain types of counseling, especially cognitive-behavioral therapy (CBT), in alleviating depressive symptoms in young people (NIMH, 2013, 2014). The goal of CBT is to help children and adolescents develop cognitive structures that will positively influence their future experiences (Kendall, 2011). The cognitive component of CBT helps individuals identify and change negative, pessimistic thinking, biases, and attributions. The behavioral component, also important to the process, focuses on increasing positive behavior patterns and improving social skills.

Another type of counseling, interpersonal therapy for adolescents (IPT), was adapted from IPT for adults. Although it has not been researched as extensively as CBT with young people, studies have demonstrated that moderately to severely depressed adolescents who have undergone IPT treatment experienced a significant reduction in depressive symptoms and subsequent improvement in overall functioning (Mellin & Beamish, 2002). The two primary goals of IPT are to reduce depressive symptoms and to improve disturbed personal relationships that may contribute to depression. Both CBT and IPT were developed to treat depression but differ in theory and practice. Both approaches require training to be used effectively with students.

Professional school counselors who work individually with depressed students should collaborate with family members and teachers so that they can support the work that is being done with the child. By consulting with parents and teachers, counselors can help significant others in the student's environment learn how to encourage the student's use of new skills.

Referral. At times, professional school counselors will work with students whose problems are severe and chronic. When this occurs, the appropriate response may be to make referrals to mental health professionals in the community. In particular, if the required interventions cannot be implemented in the school, if medication is a possibility, or if the student appears to be in danger of harming anyone, making a referral may be the preferred course of action. In such cases, the professional school counselor will want to meet with the parents of the student to discuss concerns and determine their willingness to pursue outside help. If they are willing to consider outside help, a letter written by the professional school counselor to the referral source can facilitate treatment and collaboration (Merrell, 2008).

Group counseling. Group counseling provides another mode by which students with depressive symptoms can be helped. Numerous outcome studies have demonstrated the efficacy of implementing comprehensive intervention programs that emphasize cognitive behavioral

Table 42.4 Resources and Intervention Programs for Helping Students With Depression

Title	Description	Publishing information
Helping Students Overcome Depression and Anxiety: A Practical Guide (Merrell, 2008)	Provides comprehensive information about child and adolescent depression and other internalizing disorders. Offers practical guidelines for assessment and intervention. Describes more than 40 psychoeducational and psychosocial techniques that can be adapted for youth at different developmental levels. Provides reproducible worksheets for use with students.	Guilford Press 72 Spring Street New York, NY 10012 1-800-365-7006 www.guilford.com
Taking ACTION Program (Stark & Kendall, 1996)	A comprehensive intervention program designed for youth between ages 9 and 13 years, although activities can be adapted for younger or older students. Provides guidelines for 30 group counseling sessions that focus on affective education, problem-solving skills, social skills, coping skills, and cognitive interventions.	Workbook Publishing 298 Llanfair Road Ardmore, PA 19003 1-610-896-9797
Adolescent Coping With Depression Course (Rohde et al., 2005)	A comprehensive cognitive-behavioral intervention program designed for small-group work with adolescents ages 14 to 18 years, although it may be adapted for younger students. Provides directions for 16 2-hour psychoeducational sessions. Activities are highly structured. Length of sessions may be problematic in a school setting.	Castalia Publishing Co. P.O. Box 1587 Eugene, OR 97440 1-541-343-4433
Interpersonal Psychotherapy for Depressed Adolescents (Mufson et al., 2011)	Provides an overview of interpersonal therapy and depression, an in-depth description of applications of IPT for depressed adolescents, and a discussion of special issues related to working with youth. May be more appropriate for mature, insightful adolescents. Due to its clinical focus, it may be less applicable in a school setting.	Guilford Press 72 Spring Street New York, NY 10012 1-800-365-7006 www.guilford.com

techniques. (See Erford et al., 2011 for a meta-analytic review of outcome studies of interventions with depressed children and adolescents). Sources for depression programs and brief descriptions are listed in Table 42.4.

The intervention programs described in Table 42.4 range from a minimum of 12 sessions to as many as 30 sessions; consequently, in some schools it will not be feasible to implement them as designed. Merrell (2008) suggested devising a modified comprehensive group program, incorporating key elements that the programs have in common, which include the following:

- Developing a therapeutic relationship based on trust and respect
- Education regarding depression
- Activity scheduling (monitoring, increasing participation in pleasant events)
- Emotional education (identifying and labeling emotions, identifying situations in which emotions are likely to occur, recognizing the link between thoughts and feelings)
- Cognitive change strategies (challenging negative or irrational thoughts, practicing appropriate attributions, increasing the focus on positive thoughts and events)
- Problem solving, negotiation, and conflict resolution

- Relaxation training
- Social skills and communication skills
- Goal setting and relapse prevention (p. 76)

When conducting groups for students who are depressed or who are at risk for depression, professional school counselors will want to adapt activities so that they are developmentally appropriate and so that students' real-life concerns are integrated. Including homework assignments between sessions, involving parents, and adding booster sessions that occur after the program has been completed are ways to increase the efficacy of the experience. Attention should be given to age range, gender composition, and group size, with 4 to 10 students in a group being ideal (Merrell, 2008). Whereas individual and/or group counseling may be beneficial and necessary for some students, a way to reach even more students is through school-based prevention programs.

School-Based Prevention Programs

School-based prevention programs can be effective in preventing depression in school-age youth. These programs may include student-oriented programs and parent and teacher training programs.

Student-oriented programs. Professional school counselors can be instrumental in coordinating and leading life-skills training programs to promote positive mental health in young people. Because all youth are exposed to sources of stress, and many youth are at risk for experiencing depressive symptoms of some type, it is important for professional school counselors to enhance students' ability to respond adaptively and cope well. Prevention programs can be designed as classroom guidance, which is geared toward students, or as training programs, which are geared toward parents and/or school personnel. Topics for student-oriented prevention can include many of the elements that were described in the section on group counseling: emotional awareness, recognizing the link between thoughts and feelings, coping skills, problem-solving skills, interpersonal skills, conflict resolution, and relaxation training.

An example of a student-oriented prevention program—the Penn State Adolescent Study—was developed by Petersen et al. (1993) to promote mental health and increase coping skills among sixth-grade students. This 16-session psychoeducational program helped students develop positive emotional, cognitive, and behavioral responses to stressors and challenges. Each session emphasized a particular social skill, coping method, or challenge, and began with an activity that demonstrated the topic. Students were given opportunities to practice new problem-solving skills for issues such as peer pressure, making friends, and family conflict. Each session ended with a summary and discussion of major points that were then linked to upcoming sessions. Evaluation indicated that students' coping skills and problem-solving abilities improved after participating in the program, but the effects were not observable one year later, leading to the suggestion of following up with booster sessions throughout the school year would enhance the program's long-term effectiveness.

Parent and teacher training programs. In addition to planning student-oriented prevention programs, professional school counselors can initiate training programs for teachers and parents. Teachers and parents typically have more interaction with youth than any other adults. Training programs that facilitate the development of skills in communication, coping, and behavior management can be instrumental in promoting healthy interactions, thus helping prevent the development of depressive symptoms in young people. Also, programs designed to raise parent and teacher awareness about depression can help improve access to needed mental health care for children whose depression might otherwise go undetected. Many parents and teachers may feel reluctant or unprepared to relate children's academic or social difficulties with poor emotional health (Kirchner, Yoder, Kramer, Lindsey, & Thrush, 2000). Professional school counselors can collaborate with mental health providers in the community to lead workshops designed to disseminate information about depression, possible interventions, and community resources.

Kirchner et al. (2000) developed a pilot program, *Depression in the Classroom*, for K–12 teachers to educate participants about depression and suicide among children and adolescents. Program goals were to provide (a) information about the biological and psychosocial basis of depression; and (b) tools to increase educators' ability to detect depressive disorders, educate others about depression, and make referrals within the community. The program, led by mental health specialists from an academic medical center, combined didactic instruction with experiential activities (e.g., responding to video vignettes) and represented a collaborative effort between a medical academic center and school systems. Outcome results indicated that participants not only increased their own knowledge about depression but also shared their knowledge with colleagues and students. Also, a majority of the participants reportedly applied the skills learned in the course when interacting with depressed students in their classroom. This program represented a large collaborative effort between an academic medical center and several school systems. Similar programs, perhaps on a smaller scale, could be designed through the collaborative efforts of professional school counselors and community mental health practitioners.

Summary/Conclusion

Child and adolescent depression is a serious but treatable condition that has received considerable attention. Many youth will experience depressed mood and other depressive symptoms, even though they may not be clinically depressed. Depression and depressive symptoms can interfere with learning, psychosocial development, and interpersonal relationships. If untreated, depressive symptoms can lead to mood disorders that continue into adulthood. On the other hand, early identification and treatment of symptoms can help put young people on a healthy developmental trajectory.

Professional school counselors have the knowledge and skills needed to enhance the psychological development and well-being of youth. By understanding the signs, symptoms, and etiology of depression, professional school counselors can play crucial roles in identifying students who may be struggling with these disorders. They can intervene on multiple levels, both from a preventive and a remedial perspective. Prevention activities directed toward students can facilitate the development of positive coping and interaction skills. Programmatic efforts directed toward parents and teachers can increase their knowledge about depression and skill in adult–child interaction. Individual and group counseling can help students address dysfunctional cognitive processes, learn strategies for dealing with interpersonal concerns, and develop skills for coping with stress and negative emotions. Through such efforts, professional school counselors can be instrumental in helping students meet the challenges of development in ways that promote mental health.

CHAPTER 43

Helping Students Deal With Obsessive-Compulsive Disorder

*Bradley T. Erford**

Preview

Obsessive-compulsive disorder (OCD), a neurobiological disorder once thought to be rare in children, affects 1 out of every 200 children (American Psychiatric Association [APA], 2013). Professional school counselors knowledgeable about the signs of OCD can help ensure early detection, referral for appropriate services, and effective in-school interventions.

Obsessive-compulsive disorder (OCD), previously thought to be uncommon in students, affects approximately 1 out of 200 students (APA, 2013), so there are likely to be several students struggling with the debilitating effects of this disorder in most schools at any given time. Children with OCD are consumed by intrusive, repetitive, distressing thoughts and accompanying repetitive rituals. These symptoms can significantly interfere with academic, psychological, and social functioning.

Unfortunately, OCD in school-age children often goes undetected or is misdiagnosed. Even when detected, the treatments that students receive are often inappropriate (Adams, 2004; Heyman et al., 2004; International OCD Foundation, 2014). This leaves students and their families confused and hopeless. With the right psychological, behavioral, medical, social, and academic interventions, however, students with OCD and their families can find relief from the debilitating effects of this condition. Professional school counselors are in a key position to ensure that students with OCD are identified and receive effective resources. The purpose of this chapter is to aid professional school counselors in their efforts to help students with OCD, their families, and school personnel identify and better manage this condition.

What Is OCD?

OCD is a neurobiological disorder characterized by obsessions and compulsions, occurring either alone or in combination. An obsession is a persistent irrational thought, image, or impulse that causes distress for the student. The student generally recognizes that these thoughts are irrational but is not able to stop them. Obsessions cause the student significant anxiety,

---

*Special thanks to Gail Mears for outstanding contributions to the first two editions of this chapter.

which the student seeks to manage through the use of compulsions. Compulsions are behavioral or thinking rituals that reduce the anxiety caused by the obsession. The relief is temporary, however, and the student feels obliged to continue the use of rituals to manage the resulting anxiety (APA, 2013; Chansky, 2000). OCD is a chronic disorder with symptoms that worsen over time if left untreated. This disorder has many ups and downs. During periods of stress, students with OCD may notice a significant increase in symptoms. Although the symptoms of OCD are similar for children, adolescents, and adults, unlike adults and adolescents, young children may not view their obsessions as irrational.

Most young students engage in some form of ritualized behavior. These behaviors are not typically symptoms of OCD. Childhood rituals usually are in the service of helping children gain more mastery over their environment and they ultimately lead to a sense of competence. There is no excessive distress associated with these behaviors, and they do not interfere with social and academic functioning (Adams, 2004; Merlo & Storch, 2006a). Children who insist on a particular bedtime ritual, carry a special object, or want favored stories read over and over again are not suffering from OCD. They are engaging in normal childhood behaviors. The adolescent who takes a long time to get ready for a date or who spends major blocks of time practicing a sport or instrument is also not suffering from OCD. These behaviors, while sometimes vexing to adults, do not interfere with the child's academic, social, and psychological development. The student who needs to touch every object in his bedroom 10 times before leaving for school, however, is showing definite symptoms of OCD. The symptoms of OCD cause distress to students, are time-consuming, and likely interfere with social, emotional, and academic functioning. The following are examples of students with OCD.

- Mary, age 13 years, finds school harder and harder to attend. For the past 2 years she has been increasingly plagued by sexual images she finds offensive, and she worries that she is crazy. She recites prayers to deal with the anxiety these images cause. It is becoming harder for Mary to pay attention to her classwork. She is often preoccupied by the need to pray. Additionally, the proximity of the males in her classes seems to trigger these sexual images. Her grades are dropping, and her school attendance is erratic. She no longer likes to spend time with her friends, is irritable at home, and is feeling more and more despondent.
- Sammy, age 10 years, is in fourth grade. He worries constantly about germs and getting sick. He is particularly worried about getting AIDS. He is careful not to touch anything that he considers dirty, such as doorknobs, faucets, trash, and toilets. He also does not like to touch things that other students have handled. He is often late for school, as he needs to wash and rewash his hands many times during the course of getting ready in the morning. During the school day, he repeatedly asks to go to the bathroom to wash his hands after touching objects handled by other students. His hands are red and raw, and Sammy seems to be anxious most of the time. He does not play with the other children anymore.
- Jimmy, age 9 years, feels the need for things to be "just right." He spends hours arranging objects in his room at home to feel comfortable. In school he is having increasing difficulty with his written work and with reading. His papers are full of erasure marks, and he generally is unable to finish assignments. When reading, Jimmy needs to reread each word, making sure that he pronounces each one correctly. Jimmy has frequent anger outbursts in the classroom.

What Types of Obsessions Do Children Have?

Obsessions may take many forms, and it is the intrusive, irrational, and distressing nature of these thoughts, images, or impulses that mark them as obsessions (APA, 2013). Obsessions that are commonly reported by children include fear of contamination (worry about germs, getting sick, dying), fear of hurting oneself or others, obscene imagery or thoughts of inappropriate sexual behavior, fear of sinning, need for symmetry or the need to have objects arranged in certain ways, doubting (e.g., Did I really lock the door?), or the need to repeat actions a certain number of times (Chansky, 2000; Merlo & Storch, 2006b). Fear of dirt and germs is the most common obsession experienced by students and is reported by approximately 40% of students with OCD.

What Type of Compulsions Do Children Have?

Compulsions are behavioral or thinking rituals that the student feels compelled to perform to reduce the anxiety caused by the obsessions. To meet the criteria for a compulsion, the behavior or mental ritual must cause marked distress to the student, consume more than an hour a day, or interfere significantly with daily functioning (APA, 2013). Though rare, students can experience compulsions without accompanying obsessions. Common forms of compulsions include washing, checking, repeating behaviors, counting, hoarding, praying, and arranging things symmetrically. Washing rituals are the most frequent compulsions displayed by children, and boys are more likely than girls to engage in counting rituals.

What Causes OCD?

Historically, OCD was thought to be a disorder that resulted from poor parenting or some other form of environmental stress. Currently, OCD is understood to be a neurobiological disorder. OCD is associated with overactivity and structural abnormalities in multiple regions of the brain (Waltz, 2000). Students with OCD often have other neurological irregularities such as tics and nonverbal learning problems. Serotonin, a neurotransmitter, is the brain chemical most likely involved in OCD (Chansky, 2000). While it is not known if dysregulation of serotonin is the main causative factor in OCD, all medications effective in relieving OCD symptoms affect serotonin pathways.

Stress can precipitate or exacerbate symptoms of OCD, but students with OCD are in the grip of a brain malfunction. Chansky (2000) referred to the symptoms of OCD as a brain hiccup. The obsessions and compulsions are involuntary and intrusive, and students with OCD do not feel as if they have the ability to stop the intrusive obsessions or to not engage the resulting compulsions. Students with OCD are literally stuck in their respective obsessions and resulting behavioral or mental rituals. This information is very important for parents who often feel responsible (and may have been actually blamed!) for producing this condition in their children.

Heredity is a likely factor in the development of OCD. Students may inherit a vulnerability to OCD, but heredity alone does not explain the actual expression of the disorder. Higher rates of OCD have been observed in students who have family members diagnosed with OCD, depression, anxiety disorders, or Tourette's syndrome (APA, 2013). Research from the National Institute of Mental Health indicated that a group of students developed an acute and severe onset or exacerbation of OCD symptoms that is associated with a strep infection—Pediatric Autoimmune Neuropsychiatric Disorder Associated with Strep (PANDAS; Snider & Swedo, 2004). When a child presents with a sudden onset or increase in OCD symptoms, a referral should be made to a pediatrician to rule out PANDAS.

Who Gets OCD?

It is estimated that 1 in 200 students are diagnosed with OCD at any one time. This is likely an underestimate of the prevalence rate of OCD because students are often secretive about their symptoms and family members and professionals often don't understand that the troubling behaviors displayed by the student may be a result of OCD. The *Diagnostic and Statistical Manual of Mental Disorders* (5th ed.; *DSM-5*; APA, 2013) sets a lifetime prevalence rate of OCD in children at 1.0% to 2.3% and notes that the prevalence rate of OCD in students is consistent across cultures. Students diagnosed with OCD may also have other diagnosed disorders including ADHD, Tourette's syndrome, developmental disabilities, nonverbal learning disabilities, anxiety disorders, and depressive disorders. Ten percent to 30% of students diagnosed with ADHD and 40% to 60% of children diagnosed with Tourette's syndrome also qualify for a diagnosis of OCD. Males and females are diagnosed with OCD in equal numbers. However, OCD tends to occur at an earlier age in boys than in girls. The average age of onset for males is between the ages of 6 and 15 years, and the average age of onset for females is between the ages of 20 and 29 years (APA, 2013). Clinically, OCD is similar for boys and girls. There is some indication that there is an increased likelihood that boys have family members with OCD, and boys seem to have higher rates of tic disorders than do girls.

What Are the Signs That a Student May Have OCD?

Children's obsessions and compulsions are not always apparent to an observer. Young children are more open about their compulsions, but older children and adolescents often hide these symptoms. Whether visible or not, the symptoms of OCD weigh heavily on students. The stress of dealing with their symptoms may lead to other behavioral problems. Sometimes students are able to control their compulsions in school but not at home. Parent reports of OCD symptoms should be taken seriously, even if the student does not demonstrate the same behaviors in school (Chansky, 2000). There are multiple signs that might indicate a student is struggling with the symptoms of OCD. School personnel should be attentive to a number of common signs (Adams, 2004; Chansky, 2000; Chansky & Grayson, n.d.; see Table 43.1).

How Is OCD Diagnosed?

A professional qualified to diagnose and assess mental disorders should always make the diagnosis of OCD. This professional will want to gather information from the student, parents, and relevant school professionals. Standardized questionnaires are often used to help in the diagnosis and evaluate the extent to which OCD is interfering with the child's social, emo-

Table 43.1 Common Signs of OCD

Repeated requests to go to the bathroom. The child seeks to engage in washing rituals to manage the anxiety caused by contamination fears that get triggered in the normal course of the school day.

Repeated reassurance-seeking from teachers and other adult authorities. This goes well beyond the typical questioning that might be expected from any school child.

The appearance of daydreaming or disinterest in schoolwork. Students with OCD are preoccupied with their frightening obsessions and compensating ritual. When so much attention is focused internally, it is difficult to stay engaged with the classroom activity.

Bouts of anger or anxiety. This can be the result of being exposed to situations that trigger obsessions. A student with contamination fears may get quite upset when expected to share materials with another student. Anxiety and irritability may result when students are frustrated in their attempts to engage in compulsions. Therefore, the student whose request to go to the bathroom is denied may become quite agitated.

The need to do things in "just the right way." This can dramatically interfere with schoolwork. These types of obsessions can prevent students from finishing tasks in a timely manner. Students may suffer from reading or writing compulsions. OCD may prevent the students from finishing written or reading assignments as they struggle with the need to write or read perfectly, resulting in erasures and undone work. Students with OCD may resist writing or reading in an effort to avoid the associated obsessions and compulsions. As school becomes more and more burdensome, students may try to avoid school altogether.

Frequent tardiness for school or classes. Obsessions and resulting compulsions can make getting ready for school or the transition between classes very time-consuming. A student who needs to repeat behaviors over and over again, arrange and rearrange objects, or repetitively wash hands may be frequently tardy for school and classes.

Social isolation. The time students spend managing their OCD symptoms can greatly interfere with the time they have available for friends. Being with other students may reduce their ability to engage in compulsions or may risk triggering obsessions and compulsions (such as fear of hurting another). These students worry that their inability to control their compulsions will lead to being ridiculed by their peers. Social isolation is a way of managing these fears.

Depression and low self-esteem. The ongoing battle with obsessions and compulsions that students with OCD face is extremely discouraging, potentially leaving the student demoralized and hopeless.

tional, and academic functioning. The diagnosis of OCD is often complicated by the presence of other comorbid conditions such as anxiety disorders, oppositional defiant disorder, depression, eating disorders, ADHD, developmental disabilities, Tourette's syndrome, or nonverbal language disorders (APA, 2013). Acquaint yourself with experienced diagnosticians in your community who are equipped to evaluate students showing symptoms of OCD.

How Is OCD Treated?

Cognitive-behavior therapy (CBT) and behavior therapy are considered the most effective treatment for students with OCD (Merlo & Storch, 2006a). Cognitive and behavioral strategies are designed to help students delay and reduce compulsive rituals when they are exposed to situations that trigger obsessions. They are also designed to empower students by providing information regarding the neurobiological roots of OCD and by helping students develop cognitive strategies that empower them to feel in control of, rather than controlled by, OCD symptoms. Medication should be considered for students when symptoms are so severe that

CBT is too anxiety provoking or when there is little or no response to CBT alone. Treatment in these cases should be a combination of CBT and medication. Medication alone does not help students develop the behavioral and cognitive strategies so useful in minimizing the impact of OCD symptoms.

The medications most commonly prescribed for childhood OCD include clomipramine (Anafranil), fluoxetine (Prozac), fluvoxamine (Luvox), paroxetine (Paxil), and sertraline (Zoloft). Clomipramine, fluvoxamine, and sertraline have FDA approval for use with students diagnosed with OCD. All of these medications affect serotonin levels in the brain. All but clomipramine are in the family of drugs known as *selective serotonin reuptake inhibitors* (SSRIs).

Parents need to be involved in their child's treatment. Having a child with OCD is extremely stressful, and parents as well as children need support, information, and coping strategies. Sometimes, in an attempt to deal with their child's distress, parents become involved in their child's rituals. An example of this would be a parent who agrees to repeatedly wash the same article of clothing before the child agrees to wear it. Parents are important partners in their child's effort to learn strategies to better manage OCD.

How Can School Counselors Help?

Professional school counselors are key school resources for students struggling with the symptoms of OCD. According to experts (Adams, 2004; Adams & Torchia, 1998; Chansky, 2000), the following are actions that can help minimize the impact of OCD on students at school.

- Professional school counselors can educate school personnel about the signs of OCD. Statistics suggest that there are likely multiple children with OCD in any school. Educating teachers, principals, and parents about the signs of OCD will increase the likelihood that students will get the help that they need and avoid the academic, psychological, and social consequences of untreated OCD.
- Professional school counselors can consult with parents, teachers, the school psychologist, and outside mental health providers to ensure that students diagnosed with OCD receive appropriate in-school interventions. Some students with mild OCD symptoms will need no accommodations from the school. In fact, the school may not even be aware of the diagnosis. Students with moderate to severe OCD, however, may need help from professional school counselors and teachers to manage programs designed to delay or reduce compulsive rituals.
- Professional school counselors can provide a place where students with OCD get a reprieve from the stress of the classroom and the stress of delaying rituals. The treatment of OCD involves helping students develop a plan to delay participating in compulsive rituals. The goal is a reduction in these rituals, not necessarily the elimination of these rituals. Part of that plan will likely include a "safe place" where students can go to recover from the stress of dealing with OCD.
- Professional school counselors can be alert to both the positive and negative changes that result from medication. Negative effects may include, but are not limited to, dry mouth, increased irritability, upset stomach, drowsiness, insomnia, and headaches.
- Professional school counselors can help parents find the educational, psychological, and medical resources that they will need to help their child manage OCD. Understanding

that OCD is a neurobiological disorder and not the result of bad parenting can be an enormous source of support for parents.
- Professional school counselors can advocate that students with OCD get appropriate in-school accommodations. Students with OCD may be eligible for special educational services under Section 504 of the Rehabilitation Act of 1973 or, if educational functioning is severely compromised, under the Individuals with Disabilities Education Improvement Act of 2004.
- Professional school counselors can help create a positive classroom environment with peers. In more severe cases, it may be helpful to educate the student's classmates about OCD. In most cases, however, a more general classroom curriculum is recommended. Chansky (2000) suggested units on health issues that affect the body from head to toe. Most students will know someone struggling with a disabling condition and this identification may increase their ability to empathize with the student struggling with OCD in the classroom. Consent from the student and parents should always be secured before talking with classmates about an individual child's condition.

What Are Some Classroom Strategies That Will Help Children With OCD?

Students should not be punished for symptoms of OCD over which they have no control. Taking away recess or giving detentions may only worsen the behaviors these punishments are designed to eliminate. Some of the helpful classroom strategies identified by Adams and Torchia (1998) and Chansky and Grayson (n.d.) include:

- Find ways to accommodate the student's symptoms. Examples of supportive classroom accommodations include (a) allow students with writing compulsions to take tests orally; (b) grade students on the content, not the neatness, of their papers; (c) provide resources for a student with reading compulsions to listen to books on tape; (d) give extra time on tests; (e) develop signals and phrases with students to cue them when they appear stuck in OCD rituals that you are willing to help.
- Support students with OCD by identifying areas of strength. OCD is a demoralizing illness, and students need to be reminded of the things they do well.
- Help students with OCD manage social interactions. Set up opportunities for students to work collaboratively with peers. Avoid putting these students in situations in which they are likely to be ignored or left out.

Summary/Conclusion

Students can expect significant help with the debilitating symptoms of OCD. Though considered a chronic illness, with appropriate treatment and school and home support, students with OCD will likely experience a significant reduction in the distress and subsequent functional impairments associated with this condition. Unfortunately, educators and mental health practitioners are often misinformed about the cause of OCD and effective intervention strategies. Professional school counselors are in a key position to ensure that teachers and

Table 43.2 Additional Resources for Helping Students With OCD

Organizations

Anxiety Disorders Association of America, P.O. Box 631409, Silver Spring, MD, 21263-1409 (www.adaa.org)

National Alliance for the Mentally Ill, Child and Adolescent Network, 200 North Glebe Road, Suite 1015, Arlington, VA 22203-3754

National Institute of Mental Health, Building 10, Room 4N 208, Bethesda, MD 20892-1255 (www.nimh.nih.gov)

Obsessive–Compulsive Foundation, 337 Notch Hill Road, North Branford, CT 0697 (http://www.ocfoundation.org)

Obsessive Compulsive Information Center, Madison Institute of Medicine, 7617 Mineral Point Road, Suite 300, Madison, WI 53717 (http://www.healthtechsys.com)

Books

Adams, G. B., & Torchia, M. (1998). *School personnel: A critical link in the identification, treatment and management of OCD in children and adolescents* (3rd ed.). Milford, CT: OC Foundation.

Chanksy, T. E. (2000). *Freeing your child from obsessive-compulsive disorder: A powerful practical guide for parents of children and adolescents.* New York, NY: Three Rivers Press.

Dornbush, M. P., & Pruitt, S. K. (1995). *Teaching the tiger: A handbook for individuals involved in the education of students with attention deficit disorders, Tourette syndrome or obsessive-compulsive disorder.* Duarte, CA: Hope Press.

Johnston, H. F., & Fruehling, J. J. (2002). *Obsessive compulsive disorder in children & adolescents: A guide.* Madison, WI: University of Wisconsin, Child Psychopharmacology Information Center.

March, S., & Mulle, K. (1998). *OCD in children and adolescents: A cognitive behavioral treatment manual.* New York, NY: Guilford Press.

Rapoport, J. (1991). *The boy who couldn't stop washing.* New York, NY: Penguin Books.

Thomsen, P. H. (1999). *From thoughts to obsessions: Obsessive compulsive disorder in children and adolescents.* Philadelphia, PA: Jessica Kingsley.

Waltz, M. (2000). *Obsessive-compulsive disorder: Help for children and adolescents.* Cambridge, UK: O'Reilly.

Multimedia Instructional Kit

How to respond to obsessive-compulsive disorder in the classroom. Available online through the Obsessive-Compulsive Foundation: http://www.ocfoundation.org

other school personnel are informed and alert to the signs and symptoms of OCD. Through partnerships with teachers, school nurses, school psychologists, and qualified mental health professionals in the community, professional school counselors can promote in-school strategies that will support students with OCD in their academic, social, and emotional development. Professional school counselors play an important role in making school a satisfying experience that is not overshadowed by OCD. See Table 43.2 for additional resources for helping students with OCD.

CHAPTER 44

Separation Anxiety Disorder in the Schools

Henry L. Harris and Sejal Parikh Foxx

Preview

Separation anxiety is a common emotional reaction that some students experience daily. It becomes problematic, however, when the emotional reactions negatively affect normal academic or social activities. For some students, separation anxiety is the cause of school avoidance, poor academic performance, and other disruptive behaviors. Without appropriate treatment, these individuals could possibly encounter additional emotional difficulties. We discuss characteristics of students with separation anxiety disorder (SAD) and interventions that could be helpful to parents, teachers, school administrators, and professional school counselors during the remediation process.

Anxiety is an emotional response that students experience daily. It is considered an important part of social development and a helpful reaction to a variety of situations. Even so, anxiety is often negatively perceived and misunderstood (Huberty, 1990). For example, some parents and teachers perceive students with anxiety disorders as readily recognizable and not having serious problems. When asked to actually identify students with anxiety, however, parents and teachers seem to have a difficult time doing so. When descriptions are provided about the behaviors of anxious students, their ability to identify those students significantly increases (Walkup & Ginsberg, 2002). Many students with anxiety exhibit the following:

- Trouble leaving the car and entering the school in the mornings
- Trouble learning and sharing in group or social activities
- Regular visits to the school nurse with physical complaints
- Difficulty demonstrating knowledge on tests or through classroom participation; considered underachievers
- High rates of absences (Walkup & Ginsberg, 2002)
- Limited overall socialization experiences
- Greater risk of being teased by other students
- Tension within the family (Velting, Setzer, & Albano, 2004)

Given such negative consequences of anxiety, it is imperative that professional school counselors be proactive when addressing this serious issue.

Anxiety Disorders

The *Diagnostic and Statistical Manual of Mental Disorders* (5th ed.; *DSM-5*; American Psychiatric Association [APA], 2013) lists the following anxiety disorders that are sometimes diagnosed in children: Separation Anxiety Disorder, Simple Phobia, Social Phobia, and Generalized Anxiety Disorder. Much information is known about separation anxiety disorder (SAD). SAD is the most commonly diagnosed anxiety disorder in children with the median age of onset around 7 years of age. Furthermore, studies have illustrated that children diagnosed with SAD have an increased risk of developing other mental disorders into adulthood (In-Albon, Meyer, & Schneider, 2013).

For most children, normal separation anxiety intensifies during early childhood and then gradually decreases between 3 and 5 years of age (Masi, Mucci, & Millepiedi, 2001). Separation anxiety becomes an issue of concern for professional school counselors when (a) the normal functioning of the student is hampered by the intensity, length, and frequency of behavior; (b) the demonstrated behavior is inappropriate for the current situation; (c) the student lacks the ability to make the behaviorally appropriate transition; and (d) the behavior significantly affects how the student functions in society (Huberty, 1990).

Separation Anxiety Disorder

Separation anxiety disorder persists in individuals under the age of 18 years for at least 4 weeks. Further, those with SAD experience persistent anxiety at a level that is developmentally abnormal in response to a separation or impending separation from the attachment figure (APA, 2013). The prevalence rate of SAD has been broadly estimated between 3% and 13% (Doobay, 2008) with other researchers suggesting between 0.5% and 20%. (Kossowsky, Wilhelm, Roth, & Schneider, 2012). As one of the most frequently diagnosed disorders of early childhood, SAD also indicates a high risk factor for comorbidity with other childhood anxiety disorders (Herren, In-Albon, & Schneider, 2013). Previous research has also identified SAD as a predictor for adult panic disorder and generalized anxiety disorder in adulthood (Kossowsky et al., 2012).

SAD is characterized by excessive anxiety and worry about being separated from home or from a major attachment figure, and students with this disorder often believe that something tragic will happen to them or their parents (APA, 2013). Sometimes when students are asked what they are afraid of, students communicate a fear of being displaced and never finding their parents again. They may also be preoccupied with dreadful images of crooks, monsters, or other dangerous animals that could possibly harm them or their parents. Students with SAD were often described in one extreme as individuals who are intrusive, demanding, and in need of constant attention, and in the other extreme as being very conscientious and constantly desiring to please others. Furthermore, some young children with SAD may also "display disruptive, oppositional, and avoidance behaviors that cause significant family interference in child and family functioning" (Pincus, Eyberg, & Choate, 2005, p. 164).

Sleep could be another issue for some students with SAD because they are afraid to stay in a room by themselves and may insist that someone stay with them until they fall asleep. They may have repeated nightmares and report occurrences of seeing people in their room or peering eyes staring at them. Sometimes during the night when they awake, they seek comfort in their parent's bedroom. When this is not possible, they will either sleep next to their parent's bedroom door or seek the companionship of a sibling or family pet (American Academy of Child & Adolescent Psychiatry, 2011a). Even during the daytime hours, some students may refuse to let the major attachment figure out of their sight and at times become hysterical when that figure is physically in another room (APA, 2013). Similar reactions may occur when separation is anticipated, as when students are getting dressed and ready to go to school in the morning. They may cry, become angry, and even try to physically strike the individual who is causing the separation.

Some students with SAD experience excessive worry only when they are away from their home surroundings. If they participate in a camp, attend school, or visit relatives or friends, these students have a strong desire to return home. When this is not possible, they may make attempts to contact parents, feel sad, lose their ability to concentrate, fake illnesses, become contentious, or experience social withdrawal (Tongue, 1994).

Realize that older students with SAD have fewer symptoms than younger children, and they may report feeling faint or dizzy (APA, 2013). More often, unrealistic worry about major attachment figures and school refusal are behaviors reported by students from 5 to 8 years of age. Extreme worry and distress at the time of separation is more common in students ranging from age 9 to 12 years. Adolescents most often report somatic complaints and school refusal (Masi et al., 2001).

School Refusal

Often, SAD is the precursor to school refusal. About 30% to 38% of those children who refuse to attend school meet the diagnostic criteria for SAD (Doobay, 2008). There is a difference between school refusal and truancy. School refusal has emotional consequences and lacks the presence of antisocial behaviors. Jongsma, Peterson, and McInnis (2006) offered the following behavioral observations related to school refusal:

- Constant hesitancy or refusal to attend school because of the desire to stay at home with the parent. Some are preoccupied with thoughts that, if separated, something terrifying will happen to them or their parents.
- Emotional strains and complaints such as crying, temper outbursts, or begging the parents not to take them to school (when expecting separation from home to attend school or following arrival at school).
- Commonly expressed complaints of headaches, stomach pains, or feeling nauseated prior to attending school or following arrival.
- When departing home or arriving at school, the student may stay excessively close to the parent.
- Fear of the separation from the parents is accompanied by low levels of self-esteem and self-confidence.
- Students communicate and express a fear of failure and anxiety along with the refusal to attend school.

When students with SAD refuse to attend school, it could lead to academic problems and social isolation. Even when attending school, their excessive demands "often become a source of teacher and peer frustration, resulting in resentment, ridicule, and conflict within the classroom" (Deluty & DeVitis, 1996, p. 108).

Interventions

There are a number of interventions professional school counselors can use to help students, teachers, and families cope with SAD. The interventions designed and selected should ideally reflect a team effort involving the professional school counselor, parents, teachers, administrators, the school psychologist, and school nurse. Professional school counselors should first have adequate knowledge about separation anxiety and the behavioral characteristics associated with it. Professional school counselors must be aware of their personal feelings and biases toward students and parents who may be experiencing separation anxiety, for example, by exploring the following questions:

How do I honestly feel about students with SAD?

Am I able to accurately identify students with SAD?

Do I believe that the parents are solely responsible for their children's behavior?

Do I feel more discipline would solve the problem?

Is this child a "crybaby" and simply trying to gain attention?

Do I perceive this child's behavior as disruptive and caused by overprotective parents?

Am I displaying too much sympathy toward this child?

Do I have the time, skills, or available resources needed to help these students and their families?

The intervention team should also explore the same questions.

Once the questions have been thoroughly explored, the next phase should involve professional school counselors consulting with parents, teachers, and school administrators to provide information on students suspected of having anxiety-related issues, such as excessive worry, frequent absences, or somatic complaints (Scott, Culley, & Weissberg, 1995). During the consultation process, professional school counselors should make sure that parents, teachers, and school administrators are knowledgeable about various aspects of SAD and how it potentially affects the academic and social development of students. For teachers and administrators, in-service training focusing on separation anxiety issues would be helpful. Professional school counselors could additionally help students with SAD by creating a safe environment where students could go to reduce their anxiety during anxious moments, check in with them at the beginning of school to access their anxiety levels, teach them age-appropriate relaxation techniques, and possibly alter their arrival times to school if the separation anxiety becomes too extreme at the beginning of the day.

The school psychologist is often a valuable resource for the professional school counselor. The role played by the school psychologist will depend on the severity of the problem, the level of parental involvement, and school policy (some school systems may require outside help). The school nurse may contribute by conducting a preliminary physical on students experiencing somatic complaints. They are also in a position to recommend to parents that the student undergo a thorough physical examination. Eliminating physical ailments as causes of the student's pain and discomfort (Scott et al., 1995) allows the association to be made between anxiety and somatic issues. The process of creating a mental health or developmental plan can begin to help the student develop more effective coping skills.

Consulting With Parents

When discussing SAD with parents, professional school counselors should gather as much information as possible about the child and the family. Kearney, LaSota, Amie, and Vecchio (2007) contended that parents of children with SAD may unknowingly facilitate anxiety during their child's anxious moments by being overprotective, excessively reassuring, or having aversive parent–child interactions. It would therefore be helpful to genuinely explore with parents: (a) their parenting style; (b) whether they have experienced any form of anxiety themselves; (c) any recent sudden or negative life events or stressors; (d) their perspective on the student's personality and behavior; (e) the length of time the student has been experiencing separation anxiety; (f) whether or not other family members have previously encountered this problem; (g) whether the student's siblings have been affected by the behavior; and (h) their role in helping design and implement selected interventions.

Professional school counselors can also assist parents during consultation by helping them recognize their own feelings about SAD because some feelings could reveal personal, subconscious levels of anxiety and discomfort regarding the student. Professional school counselors should encourage parents to be aware of their child's personality and convey relevant information to school personnel. Furthermore, professional school counselors may assist parents in the following ways:

- Teaching parents appropriate ways to prepare the student before the separation occurs
- Making parents aware of appropriate transitional objects to use with the student, such as a picture or a small toy
- Encouraging parents to never make fun of their child or say things such as "Big boys and girls don't cry" or "Other kids are going to tease you if you cry" (Hewitt, 2011)
- Encouraging parents to leave school when it is time to leave, because sometimes the situation becomes more chaotic when the parents stay longer than normal
- Encouraging parents to never sneak away from their child, always say goodbye, and return at the expected time
- Encouraging parents to send their child a short e-mail message as a positive reinforcement for staying in school if access to computers is available in the school
- Encouraging parents to set up a morning and evening routine
- Helping parents set mandatory expectations for school attendance and limiting reassurance-seeking behavior

Systematic Desensitization

Systematic desensitization is a behavioral intervention designed by Wolpe (1958) to eliminate fear and anxiety by exposing the individual to the feared stimulus in a carefully graduated manner (Butcher, Hooley, & Mineka, 2013). The first step in this process consists of relaxation training. Children with SAD could be taught simple relaxation techniques such as learning how to breathe or tightening and relaxing different muscles in the body (progressive muscle relaxation training). Some students may be too young to fully understand this concept, so the professional school counselor should modify this technique according to the student's developmental level. The student is then instructed to practice relaxation skills daily, ranging from 10 to 20 minutes while listening to a tape of relaxation instructions. The next step

Table 44.1 Sample Hierarchy (Huberty, 1990)

Step 11.	Child is in the classroom with activities occurring.
Step 10.	Child is alone in the classroom.
Step 09.	Child is alone in the classroom with the teacher.
Step 08.	Child enters the classroom alone.
Step 07.	Child enters the classroom with a parent.
Step 06.	Child walks to the classroom alone.
Step 05.	Child walks to the classroom with the parent.
Step 04.	Child enters the school building alone.
Step 03.	Child enters the school building with the parent.
Step 02.	Child gets into the car with the parent.
Step 01.	Child gets dressed and prepares to go to school.

includes developing a hierarchy of fears, with situations producing the highest level of anxiety placed at the top graduating down to situations causing little or no anxiety at the bottom (see Table 44.1 for a sample hierarchy).

The student should be in a relaxed mood when each session begins. The professional school counselor asks the student to imagine the lowest anxiety-provoking situation on the hierarchy and signal by raising a finger if he or she experiences anxiety. If no anxiety is experienced, this format is followed until the student reaches the highest situation on the hierarchy without experiencing any anxiety (Huberty, 1990; Lee & Miltenberger, 1996). This approach may be more applicable for use with older children or adolescents.

Problem Solving

Professional school counselors could also use problem solving as an intervention to help students with SAD. Problem solving is known as a step-by-step process in which the student generates and tests a number of different methods for coping with specific anxiety problem situations. The student should be initially taught to identify a specific anxiety situation. Next, emphasis is placed on the student generating as many alternative actions to reduce the anxiety. The professional school counselor then encourages the student to explore the costs and benefits of each alternative action and decide which is most effective or appropriate. Finally, the student evaluates the outcome and tries a different solution if the desired effect was not achieved (Velting et al., 2004). Throughout the problem-solving process, it is important that professional school counselors help students remain as calm as possible if they hope to achieve the desired results.

In Vivo Desensitization

In vivo desensitization is an alternate form of systematic desensitization and may be more practical for professional school counselors to use in the school setting, especially for students who refuse to attend school. This approach requires the student and parent to be active participants (Huberty, 1990). The professional school counselor, parents, teachers, school nurse, and school psychologist cooperate in varying degrees to establish a hierarchy of tasks specifically designed to bring the student closer to the class or school environment where the most anxiety occurs. The professional school counselor, along with the help of the parent, is responsible for gradually exposing the student to each step in the hierarchy. When anxiety is reported, that particular step is repeated until the anxiety no longer exists. The process requires patience and continues until the student has completed all steps in the hierarchy without experiencing anxiety. (See the sample hierarchy developed by Huberty, 1990, in Table 44.1.)

This technique can also be taught to parents to use with children outside of school. For example, the hierarchy could include items for the anxious child such as playing outside in the backyard with the parent inside, playing alone in a room for 5 minutes, sleeping in his or her own room 1 night a week, or staying at home with a sitter (Phelps, Cox, & Bajorek, 1992).

Token Economies and Positive Reinforcement

The token economy is a type of positive reinforcement system. This intervention rewards students with tokens or points only when a level of desired behavior is reached. Parents should be involved in designing the reward system, which could range from using actual tokens for use at the local arcade or exchanging points for prizes. In some situations, this intervention could be paired with *in vivo* desensitization and tokens/points awarded when one of the steps in the hierarchy is completed.

Play Therapy

Play therapy is another form of counseling that professional school counselors should consider using when helping students with SAD. During the play sessions, students are provided the opportunity to express their emotions through what they do best: play. According to Landreth (1993) and Guerney (1979), play is the student's symbolic language of self-expression, and during the process of play therapy, students have the opportunity to fully experience all parts of the self because the play is self-directed and safe. Students with SAD are ideal candidates for this form of counseling because one of the major goals of play therapy is to help reduce anxiety and stress levels in the emotional mind of a vulnerable child (Landreth, 1993).

Art Therapy

Professional school counselors should also consider using art therapy as a form of counseling for students with SAD. Art therapy includes various activities such as drawing, using a sand tray, sculpting, finger painting, storytelling, and using music. This process provides individuals the opportunity to confront their concerns and unresolved issues through artwork. The goal of art therapy is to help students with SAD manage their anxiety more effectively through artistic expression of what lies within their inner world. This approach may be particularly useful for nonverbal children and for students who have difficulties expressing internal conflicts (Thompson, 2003).

Table 44.2 Books on Separation Anxiety for the Pre-K Through Sixth-Grade Levels

Benjamin Comes Back/Benjamin Regresa, by A. Brandt, 2000, Publisher: HarperCollins.
Don't Forget to Write, by M. Selway, 1994, Publisher: Ideal Children's Books.
Freddie's First Night Away, by D. Steele, 1992, Publisher: Dell.
I Don't Want to Go to School: Helping Children Cope With Separation Anxiety, by N. Pando, 2005, Publisher: New Horizon Press.
I'm Scared (Dealing With Feelings), by E. Crarey, 1996, Publisher: Parenting Press.
Into the Great Forest: A Story for Children Away From Parents for the First Time, by P. Marcus, 2001, Publisher: American Psychological Association.
Lester's Overnight, by K. Chorao, 1997, Publisher: Dutton/Plume.
Maybe She Forgot, by E. Kandoian, 1990, Publisher: Cobblehill/Dutton.
Mommy Don't Go, by E. Crarey, 1996, Publisher: Parenting Press.
Mommy, Daddy, Come Back Soon, by D. Pappas, 2001, Publisher: American Psychological Association.
My First Day at Nursery School, by B. Edwards, 2002, Publisher: Bloomsbury-USA Publishers.
My Somebody Special, by S. Weeks, 2002, Publisher: Harcourt.
Pinky & Rex Go to Camp, by J. Howe, 1999, Publisher: Simon & Schuster.
The Good-Bye Book, by J. Viorst, 1992, Publisher: Simon & Schuster.
The Kissing Hand, by A. Penn, 1995, Publisher: Child Welfare League of America.
The Runaway Bunny, by M. W. Brown, 1991, Publisher: HarperCollins Children's Books.
Wemberly Worried, by K. Henkes, 2000, Publisher: HarperCollins.
When Mommy and Daddy Go to Work, by J. Cole, 2001, Publisher: HarperCollins.
You Go Away, by D. Corey, 1999, Publisher: Albert Whitman.

Response to Intervention

Response to Intervention (RtI) is a three-tiered service delivery framework aimed at meeting the academic and behavioral needs of students. To support students who are at potential risk of SAD, school counselors can provide school-wide services as a tier 1 intervention on positive school supports, anti-bullying, and peer relationships in efforts to build a safe school environment. After conducting an assessment, school counselors can identify, through teacher and parent referrals, any students who meet some of the indicators of SAD. If any students are identified, tier 2 interventions, such as small group work, can be provided. Finally, after tier 2 effectiveness has been assessed and it is determined a student still needs interventions around SAD-related issues, tier 3 interventions can be implemented. This may consist of long term and intensive counseling which can be provided through referral services (Sulkowski, Joyce, & Storch, 2012).

Other Interventions

Professional school counselors should also consider conducting classroom guidance activities that focus on separation anxiety. Reading animated books to early elementary-age students

Table 44.3 Books and Web Sites for Parents, Teens, and Teachers

Books

Artful Therapy, by J. A. Rubin, 2005, Publisher: Wiley.

Child Art Therapy, 25th Anniversary Edition, by J.A. Rubing, 2005, Publisher: Wiley.

Everyday Goodbyes: Starting School and Early Care: A Guide to the Separation Process, by N. Balaban, 2006, Publisher: Teacher College Press.

Freeing Your Child From Anxiety: Powerful, Practical Solutions to Overcome Your Child's Fears, Worries and Phobias, by T. Chansky, 2004, Publisher: Broadway Books.

Helping Your Child Overcome Separation Anxiety or School Refusal: A Step-By-Step Guide for Parents, by A. R. Eisen and L. B. Engler, 2006, Publisher: New Harbinger.

Separation Anxiety in Children and Adolescents: An Individualized Approach to Assessment and Treatment, by A. R. Eisen and C. E. Schaefer, 2005, Publisher: Guilford Press.

Your Anxious Child, by J. S. Darcey and L. B. Fiore, 2000, Publisher: Jossey-Bass.

Web Sites

Anxiety Disorders Association of America (www.adaa.org)

Anxiety and Depression Association of America (http://www.adaa.org/living-with-anxiety/children)

Bright Horizons (http://www.brighthorizons.com/)

Childhood Anxiety Network (www.childhoodanxietynetwork.org)

Child Mind Institute (http://www.childmind.org/en/health/disorder-guide/separation-anxiety-disorder)

HELPGUIDE.ORG (http://www.helpguide.org/mental/separation_anxiety_causes_prevention_treatment.htm)

The Child Anxiety Network (www.childanxiety.net)

Medline Plus at National Institutes of Health (http://www.nlm.nih.gov/medlineplus) National Mental Health Association (www.nmha.org)

National Alliance for the Mentally Ill (www.nami.org)

Separation Anxiety Disorder (www.worrywisekids.org)

---

about characters confronting this sensitive issue could prove beneficial (see Table 44.2 for resources for students in the pre-K to sixth-grade level and Table 44.3 for resources for parents, teens, and teachers). Other appropriate cognitive behavioral interventions could include modeling, relaxation, cognitive restructuring, shaping, and flooding. Group counseling is another option professional school counselors should take into consideration for students, along with filial therapy training for parents (Guerney, 1997; Johnson, 1995). For students who do not respond to counseling, the addition of medication could prove beneficial (Bagnell, Kutcher, & Garcia-Ortega, 2011). If a decision is made to use medication along with traditional counseling to help students with SAD, parents should consult with a credible child psychiatrist and be thoroughly informed about the potential positive and negative effects of the medication. Ultimately, the type of counseling approach used will vary and depend on a number of different factors including the severity of the problem, available school resources, professional school counselor's training experience, school policies, time, and the level of parent involvement (Sulkowski et al., 2012).

Summary/Conclusion

Separation anxiety is an expected and healthy emotional reaction that is a part of normal development for many children and should only become a concern for professional school counselors when the anxiety begins to negatively affect the individual academically, emotionally, and socially. Professional school counselors must have accurate knowledge about the characteristics associated with SAD, including appropriate assessment tools and appropriate interventions. Professional school counselors should make the effort to work collaboratively with parents, teachers, administrators, school nurses, and school psychologists to formulate a plan to help families and students with SAD, always striving to convey patience, empathy, understanding, and a sense of hope.

CHAPTER 45

Test Anxiety

*Bradley T. Erford**

Preview

The importance of test scores continues to be a focal point for grade promotion and educational accountability, and anxiety can develop when a student feels pressure to perform. Professional school counselors who understand the physiological and psychological responses to anxiety can facilitate student development of positive coping strategies. Included in this chapter are suggestions for parents, teachers, and students to reduce test anxiety and increase test performance.

S*tress, fear,* and *anxiety* are terms that are often used interchangeably. An example of *eustress,* or good stress, is the anticipation of a happy upcoming event (e.g., a dance, an award; Seaward, 2011). Acute *distress* is instantaneous (e.g., being scared by a clap of thunder), while chronic stress or anxiety occurs slowly over time and results in a continued state of heightened anxiety. An example of chronic stress or anxiety would be the expectation of performing near-superior levels on tasks both at home and school.

Professional school counselors can often help to determine if the cause for concern is due to anxiety or a phobia. A *phobia* is an irrational fear that is specific to an identified source and extends beyond the normal fears associated with child and adolescent development (e.g., fear of heights). Extreme measures are often used to avoid the source of fear (e.g., repeatedly ill on testing days, emotional outbursts when testing occurs). Certainly, students can develop test phobias and in such instances, professional school counselors could be helpful in ameliorating symptoms or suggesting outside resources for consultation, evaluation, and intervention. In the current educational context, standardized tests continue to be a focal point for progress monitoring and grade promotion. When a student feels pressure to perform at exceptionally high levels, anxiety can develop. Basic human fears (Seaward, 2011) can be translated into test anxiety as follows:

- Fear of the unknown (What is the test about?)
- Fear of failure (What if I don't pass?)
- Fear of rejection (Will my family/friends still love me if I fail?)
- Fear of isolation (What if I am the only one who fails?)
- Fear of loss of self-control (What if I am so scared during the test that I can't think?)

A basic understanding of physiological responses to anxiety can assist professional school counselors in developing appropriate intervention strategies. Two categories of anxiety

---

*Special thanks to Vicki Brooks-McNamara for her outstanding contributions to the first two editions of this chapter.

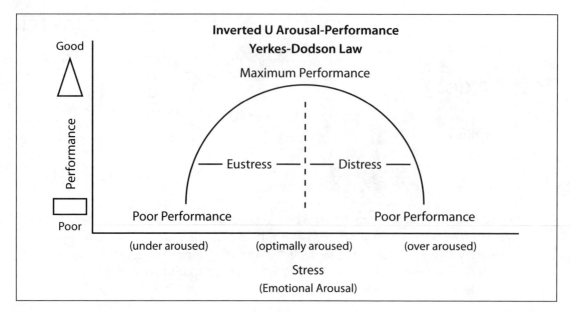

Figure 45.1. Inverted U arousal performance. *Note.* From *Managing Stress: Principles and Strategies for Health and Well Being* (p. 9), by B. L. Seaward, 2009, Sudbury, MA: Jones & Bartlett. Copyright 2009 by Jones & Bartlett. Reprinted with permission.

are evidenced in the literature: state (e.g., specific moment in time, result of an event) and trait (e.g., over time, personality characteristics; Williams, 2009). Anxiety affects all domains of the individual: spiritual, emotional, social, intellectual, and physical. Under stress/anxiety, the body responds physiologically by initiating the fight-or-flight syndrome. When the stress is continued over time, the body's systems begin to weaken. Visible external symptoms (e.g., sleeplessness, irritability) can appear. Sport performance research has identified the relationship between arousal and performance (see Figure 45.1). Simply put, as arousal increases from a minimal state (waking up) to a fully conscious and alert state, performance increases. However, if arousal continues and creates a heightened anxious state, performance begins to decline.

The optimal state of performance is called *eustress* (Seaward, 2011). Continued and heightened anxiety creates distress and a decline in performance occurs. Anxiety can create psychological roadblocks to learning (Slavin, 2011). Among the major student stressors are peer acceptance and classroom performance, including test results (Brooks, 2004). Tables 45.1 and 45.2 provide numerous tips for various stakeholders to help reduce test anxiety.

Relaxation Techniques

Relaxation techniques vary greatly, and they are subject to one's preferred style of learning and cognitive and affective abilities. Students with acute visualization and imagery capabilities are essentially unlimited with regard to relaxation and visualization development. Research has documented the positive effects of visualization, relaxation, and imagery in overall psychological and physiological function and performance. The study of psychoneuroimmunology (integration of mind, nerve, and immune systems) provides exciting data that support the interconnectedness of the body (Seaward, 2011).

Table 45.1 Suggestions for Parents/Guardians to Help Students Reduce Test Anxiety

Minimize your (positive or negative) personal feelings about tests and testing.
Reframe negative reactions (e.g., "I'm a failure") to one of hopeful reactions (e.g., "*We* can work together to do better").
Allow students to discuss their feelings about an upcoming test without judging.
Instill acceptance. Let students know that they are more than their performances on tests.
Keep *your* fears to yourself.
Avoid using words with a negative connotation (e.g., *scared*).
Have your child create and complete practice tests.
Ask for professional outside help when needed (e.g., trait anxiety, test phobia).
Teach positive coping strategies (see Chapter 52, *Helping Students Acquire Time-Management Skills*).
Help identify assets and resiliency characteristics (e.g., learning style).

Table 45.2 Tips for Students

Study at a regular time and place. Identify a location for study.
Plan study sessions with a group of successful students.
Study as soon after the class as possible. Make study checklists for each class.
Use hours during the day to study (1-hour intervals are excellent).
Limit blocks of time for studying to no more than 30 to 45 minutes on one course. Take a 3- to 5-minute break before moving to another subject.
Eat complex carbohydrates or protein on breaks, not high sugar foods (e.g., candy, cola).
Keep organized notes from class. Match and file assignments with each chapter.
Review your notes daily and weekly.
Do not re-write notes. Use a highlighter for identifying important points. Write in extensional ideas and descriptions, and review highlighted material for tests.
Write key words/phrases in margins; use these for last-minute review.
Study the most difficult or boring subjects first.
Identify the time of day when you learn the best (morning, afternoon, or evening).
Block this time for intensive study.
Sit in the front of the class.
If the teacher talks fast, learn to work with another student to share notes.
If the teacher is organized, take notes in outline form or use information from the board or overheads.
If the teacher is disorganized, take notes by leaving space between notes to fill in later.
If the class is mostly discussion, take bulleted notes and write key ideas or statements below the bullets.
If the class has a lab with it, make sure you have a lab notebook for recording all materials (e.g., drawings).
Try to incorporate all learning styles: auditory, visual, and kinesthetic. Hear the lecture (auditory), write the notes (kinesthetic), and review the notes/materials by reading (visual) and sharing with a study group (auditory).
Study by self-testing with note cards; divide pages length-wise (e.g., left side for questions and right side for answers); use a cover sheet to cover answers when studying from the book or notes.
Learn relaxation and visualization skills.
Develop short- and long-term goals.
Vocabulary is important on all standardized tests; read recreationally as well as academically.

Table 45.3 Additional Resources: Testing Information Web Sites

The Education Trust (http://www.edtrust.org/). Gives individual state results.
FairTest (www.fairtest.org). Advocacy group working to reduce flaws in standardized tests and equity for all students.
GWired (http://gwired.gwu.edu/counsel/). Search box at top of page, type *test anxiety*. "Tip of the month" has good tips/strategies and ways to reduce test anxiety.
KidsHealth (http://kidshealth.org/teen/homework/tips/test_anxiety.html). Great tips and strategies.
The Nation's Report Card (http://nces.ed.gov/nationsreportcard). Compares test results by state and includes exam questions.
Students First (http://www.student-affairs.buffalo.edu/shs/ccenter/stressstudy.php). Provides good explanation of cause and effect, reduction, coping strategies, study habits, and test anxiety. Click on "Self Help Materials" for resources on study skills and stress management.
Study Guide and Services (www.studygs.net). A wealth of information and links to guides on test-taking strategies, preparing for tests, learning, studying, classroom participation, specific subject help.
Sylvan Learning Centers (www.educate.com). Can help pinpoint weak academic areas. Has fees/costs attached.

Professional school counselors may want to inform or obtain consent from parents before sharing with the student visualization, imagery, and relaxation information or materials. Familial religious and personal preferences might preclude the professional school counselor from using relaxation, visualization, or imagery as coping strategies for reducing test anxiety (see Chapter 65).

Decreasing Test Anxiety Via Systematic Desensitization

Systematic desensitization requires that the individual be relaxed while he or she is introduced to small doses of the anxiety producing event (e.g., test). During daily relaxation practice, additional test anxiety factors can be introduced (e.g., smells and noises in the room, the teacher's voice, pencil in hand, reading the directions, taking the test). A minimum of 4 weeks should be allowed for the practice of systematic desensitization. As an alternative to real-life implementation, the gestalt of the entire test day can be replicated visually in the mind (covert desensitization) while consciously practicing the mastered relaxation exercise (Seaward, 2011).

A practice test could be given while the student is in a relaxed state and continues reinforcement of the learned skills (e.g., deep breathing). A support person may need to assist the student on the first several attempts to verbally encourage relaxation and deep breathing. The student may need verbal instructions (e.g., put the pencil down, close your eyes and complete 10 cycles of deep breathing before picking your pencil up and continuing with the test).

Summary/Conclusion

The pressure for students to achieve academically can lead to increased anxiety and fear. By first understanding the physiology of the fight-or-flight response and then applying successful strategies and interventions, all stakeholders can begin to feel a sense of control over the requirements and standards for academic success in school. Various Web sites (see Table 45.3) can also provide timely and updated information on testing tips, managing stress, and learning strategies.

CHAPTER 46

Helping Students Who Have Posttraumatic Stress Disorder

*Bradley T. Erford**

Preview

Students are increasingly exposed to traumatic events and diagnosed with posttraumatic stress disorder (PTSD). PTSD is characterized by a reexperiencing of the trauma, avoiding the trauma, and persistent physiological arousal. Familiarity of symptoms, how to conduct an assessment, and common treatment modalities are of paramount importance to the professional school counselor.

Current research suggests that students are increasingly exposed to traumatic events and consequently diagnosed with posttraumatic stress disorder (PTSD). There is substantial research suggesting that students may suffer significant psychological, social, and biological distress in relation to exposure to a traumatic event (Perrin, Smith, & Yule, 2000). Studies have investigated the sequelae of symptoms evident when students are exposed to major traumas, such as violence in the home or community, exposure to war, natural disasters, man-made disasters, serious medical illness, accidents, and sexual abuse (Horowitz, McKay, & Marshall, 2005). These studies also indicated that symptoms of PTSD, although similar in many respects to those observed in adults, are sometimes manifested differently by school-aged students. Therefore, assessment and treatment modalities must be shifted accordingly. Professional school counselors may see students present with exposure to any number of traumatic events. Familiarity with the types of symptoms likely to be seen, how to conduct an assessment, and the most common types of treatment modalities is important in helping students work through trauma.

History

PTSD was brought to public awareness during World War I, when it was named *combat neurosis*. In World War II, the symptoms of PTSD were defined as *traumatic neurosis* and manifested by consciously reliving and resolving traumatic memories associated with war experiences (Kardiner, 1941; Kardiner & Spiegel, 1947). The first large-scale studies of PTSD occurred as a

---

*Special thanks to Kelly M. Murray for her outstanding contributions to the first two editions of this chapter, may she rest in peace.

result of the Vietnam War (Egendorf, Kadushin, Laufer, Rothbart, & Sloan, 1981; Yager, 1976). It was also at this time that studies were conducted to document the prevalence of PTSD in the general population as a result of other traumatic stresses, such as rape, domestic violence, and childhood sexual abuse (Frank, Turner, & Steuwart, 1980). The *Diagnostic and Statistical Manual of Mental Disorders* (3rd ed.; *DSM-III*; American Psychiatric Association [APA], 1980) first recognized the constellation of posttraumatic symptoms as a disorder in 1980. There was initial skepticism about the diagnosis of PTSD being used for children, however (American Academy of Child and Adolescent Psychiatry [AACAP], 1998). Since that time there has been considerable research on how trauma affects children, how symptoms of PTSD are manifested in children, and how assessment and treatment may differ for children compared to adults.

Clinical Presentation

According to the *Diagnostic and Statistical Manual of Mental Disorders* (5th ed.; *DSM-5*; APA, 2013), for a child, adolescent, or adult to meet the criteria for PTSD, symptoms must follow exposure to an extreme traumatic stressor. The person must have experienced, witnessed, or been confronted with an event that involved actual or threatened death or serious injury or a threat to the physical integrity of self or others. The person's response must have involved fear, helplessness, or horror, and this may have been expressed by disorganized or agitated behavior. The way that a student reexperiences the trauma and manifests distress is likely to change with age and maturity, becoming more adult-like and closer to the *DSM-5* description of the disorder.

Students will often exhibit irritability, anger, and aggression, or they may be quite verbal about the trauma and their ensuing feelings, while others do not wish to discuss the incident or how they are feeling. Very young children who have experienced trauma may present with few symptoms listed in the *DSM-5*. This may be in part because they do not have the necessary verbal or cognitive skills to communicate their symptoms. Therefore, infants, toddlers, and preschoolers may present with anxiety symptoms such as fears of monsters and animals, separation anxiety, and fear of strangers. These children may avoid situations or circumstances that may or may not have a link with the trauma, have sleep disturbances, and have preoccupations with symbols or words that may or may not have a certain link with the traumatic event (Scheeringa, 2010). The student (like an adult) must express his or her symptoms for longer than 1 month to meet the criteria for PTSD. The disturbance must also cause clinically significant distress or impairment in social or academic functioning.

Epidemiology

The student's subjective appraisal of the situation appears to be an important factor in explaining why some are significantly affected by a traumatic event while others are not (Massad & Hulsey, 2006). Three factors have consistently been found in the development of PTSD in students: (a) the severity of the trauma exposure; (b) trauma-related parental distress; and (c) temporal proximity to the traumatic event.

Parental reaction to the traumatic event influences the student's PTSD symptomology. Numerous studies have reported the impact of familial support and parental emotional reaction to the trauma on the student's PTSD symptoms. These studies indicated that familial support across a broad range of traumas mitigated the development of PTSD in students. Parental distress about the trauma and/or the presence of parental psychiatric disorders also predicted higher levels of PTSD in the student. A study of Holocaust survivors and their offspring found that the offspring were more likely to respond to trauma with PTSD if their parents had PTSD (Yehuda, Schmeidler, Giller, Siever, & Binder-Brynes, 1998). Lyons (1987) postulated that the best predictor of outcome for students was the ability of parents and other significant adults to cope with the trauma. Another predictor for positive outcome was the student's intelligence quotient (IQ); higher IQ appears to protect people from developing PTSD (Saigh, Yasik, Oberfield, Halamandaris, & Bremmer, 2006) and is a strong predictor of resiliency (Silva et al., 2000).

Traumatized students often exhibit symptoms of co-occurring disorders in addition to PTSD. It is not always easy to diagnose PTSD as both the students and parents may minimize symptoms. For young children who do not have the cognitive or verbal skills to accurately self-report their symptoms, it is often difficult to get a clear diagnostic picture. Relying on parental report can also be problematic as parents may be dealing with their own trauma as well as trying to support their child. Parents may also not be aware of the existence or severity of their child's symptoms.

Students who present with PTSD may also exhibit symptoms of depression (APA, 2013). Major depressive disorder sometimes precedes and predisposes students to the onset of PTSD. The comorbidity of students with PTSD and other anxiety disorders is also common. Given the many manifestations of traumatization, it is not surprising that rates of comorbidity with PTSD are high. Many students develop fears associated with specific aspects of the trauma, which can eventually become phobic. Others find themselves extremely anxious much of the time and have difficulty controlling their worries. Panic disorder is not uncommon as children react to their own internal state of anxiety with physical symptoms. Some children experience "survivor guilt" and ruminate over cognitions that they should have done more to help others. Increased alcohol use by adolescents may also occur.

Assessment

PTSD is often difficult to diagnose. While the professional school counselor may not be directly involved in the diagnosis of PTSD, the following assessment procedures are helpful in understanding the diagnostic process. According to the *DSM-5* (APA, 2013), symptoms usually begin within 3 months after the trauma, although sometimes there may be a delay of months, or even years, before symptoms appear. The symptoms of the disorder and the relative predominance of reexperiencing, avoidance, and hyperarousal symptoms may vary with time. Duration of the symptoms varies, with complete recovery occurring within 3 months in approximately 50% of cases, while many others have persisting symptoms for longer than 12 months after the trauma. In some cases, the course is characterized by a waxing and waning of symptoms. Symptom reactivation may occur in response to reminders of the original trauma, life stressors, or new traumatic events.

A thorough and proper assessment requires a face-to-face interview with the student in which she is directly asked questions about the traumatic symptoms experienced. It is important to also interview the parents so as to gather as much information as possible. The use of empathy, establishment of rapport, and a safe environment where the student can discuss painful and angry feelings are very important to acquiring accurate information. Particular attention should be given to using developmentally appropriate language when assessing the student.

Both the parents and the student should be asked directly about the traumatic event and about PTSD symptoms in detail. Specific questions related to reexperiencing, avoidant, and hyperarousal symptoms as described in the *DSM-5* should be asked. Other symptoms that often present comorbidly with PTSD should be assessed, such as symptoms of depression, anxiety, substance abuse, and acting-out behaviors. Obtain reports of any preceding, concurrent, or more recent stressors in the student's life as well. Some examples of stressors may be child abuse, significant conflict within the family, frequent moves, death in the family, and exposure to community violence (AACAP, 1998).

The professional school counselor should be aware of developmental variations in the presentation of PTSD symptoms, especially with young children. For an accurate assessment, ask about developmentally specific symptoms when interviewing young children. AACAP (1998) reported that there are a few published semi-structured assessments available such as the Structured Clinical Interview for DSM-IV (SCID) and the Diagnostic Interview Schedule Clinician-Administered (DISC) PTSD Scale for Children and Adolescents. AACAP also reported that the following child–parent rating forms may be clinically useful for following the course of PTSD symptoms in children: (a) Child PTSD Reaction Index; (b) Trauma Symptom Checklist for Children; (c) Checklist of Child Distress Symptoms–Child and Parent Report Versions; (d) Children's Impact of Traumatic Events Schedule; (e) Child PTSD Symptom Scale; and (f) Impact of Event Scale. Two other assessment instruments with good score validity and reliability are the (a) Child PTSD Symptom Scale (Foa, Johnson, Feeny, & Treadwell, 2001) and (b) PTSD Index (Steinberg, Brymer, Decker, & Pynoos, 2004). Using a single instrument limits the type of information needed to make a PTSD diagnosis, however, as a student must have a certain number of symptoms from each of three different categories to meet *DSM-5* criteria. It is difficult for any single instrument to assess for all of these criteria. Therefore, there is no good substitute for a thorough and direct interview with both the student and parents. It is also sometimes useful to speak with the student's teacher(s) to get a history of symptomology manifested at school with a particular emphasis on changes in school behavior, interaction with peers, concentration, activity level, and academic performance since the traumatic stressor.

In addition, it is a good idea to initially meet with the parents without the student. When interviewing parents, the goal is to gather as much information as possible so that an understanding of the parents' perspective on the trauma and relationship with the child can be determined. Perrin et al. (2000) also stressed the importance of assessing information on the following:

- Family psychiatric and medical history
- Marital conflict, separation, divorce, abuse
- Developmental history, including the student's temperament and mood
- Academic history and performance in school prior to and after the trauma
- Student's current functioning
- Impact of the trauma on the family and parents
- Presence of parental PTSD symptoms
- The perception of how much support is available to the child from the family

In the interview, have the student recall as much of the trauma as possible. After the student has told his or her story, go back and clarify or prompt with additional questions.

Tracking the timeline of the trauma and subsequent symptoms is useful in making a diagnosis of PTSD. If unsure about the sequence of events or a particular symptom, ask about it directly. As much as possible, try to obtain the student's report of trauma-related attributions and perceptions. Query beliefs about the event, how the student feels subsequent to being exposed to the stressor, level of responsibility, and perception of family support (AACAP, 1998). The student's feelings, thoughts, and behaviors related to the event should be queried as well as his or her thoughts and feelings about the future. With very young children who find it difficult to developmentally discuss the trauma and their thoughts, feelings, and behaviors related to it, it is often useful to use other methods of gathering information. According to Perrin et al. (2000), giving the student pencil and paper and encouraging the student to draw something about which he or she can tell a story is useful in gathering information and helps the student feel comfortable enough to disclose. Encourage the student to elaborate on his or her story, and then try to link the story with some part of the traumatic event to facilitate emotional release. After the student has become more comfortable, ask him or her to draw the traumatic event. Discuss the picture, and ask the student to describe the sensory components, feelings, thoughts, and coping strategies used during and since the trauma. It is also important to help normalize the student's reactions to the traumatic event as well as to positively reinforce the student for having courage to draw about and discuss the traumatic event. While the professional school counselor is assessing the student for PTSD symptoms and the associated sequelae symptoms, he or she should also be asking the student about and noting other symptoms often associated with PTSD, such as depressive symptoms, suicidal ideations, anxiety symptoms, substance abuse, and conduct disorder behavior.

Treatment

To date there is limited empirical outcome research on the treatment of students with PTSD. Direct exploration of the event is likely to be more efficacious in older and more mature students. For younger children, more indirect methods of addressing traumatic issues, such as art and play therapy (use of drawings, puppets, dolls, etc.) may be indicated. The use of multiple informant assessment, especially with young children, is likely to elicit more information about the traumatic event and the manifestation of symptoms. For this reason, information collected from young children should be supplemented by parent reports.

A treatment plan should be based on the clinical presentation of the child and should address PTSD symptoms as well as other emotional–behavioral symptoms the student may be experiencing. Each student's course of PTSD and associated symptoms will be variable and may be extremely idiosyncratic in the nature, intensity, and length of symptoms. Therefore, different treatment modalities may be needed, depending on the student and the nature of the presenting symptoms and problems. Some will require short-term, long-term, or intermittent treatment. Others may require different levels of care (e.g., outpatient care, partial hospitalization, inpatient hospitalization). The professional school counselor may also need to decide which treatment modality will be the most efficacious for the student—individual, family, or group therapy (AACAP, 1998).

Psychoeducation for parents, teachers, and family members may help normalize PTSD symptoms and gain their support in treating the student who has PTSD. Education about the traumatic experience and subsequent symptoms may also be helpful to the student who has been exposed to a stressor. The student often has perceptions, feelings, and symptoms about the stressor that can be normalized to help increase self-efficacy and thereby decrease anxiety.

Individual counseling is another modality that can be extremely helpful to students who have been exposed to a stressor. There are many different theoretical orientations that are used by professional school counselors to help students with PTSD. Psychoanalytic or psychodynamic approaches are sometimes utilized and often help to expose defense mechanisms that are being used and also to redefine current significant relationships in the student's life. Play and art therapy are also often used to accommodate students who are developmentally incapable of benefiting from a direct verbal exchange with a professional school counselor. These indirect methods of addressing traumatic issues may be helpful to students so as not to retraumatize them as they think about and talk about the traumatic event.

There is also significant empirical support for cognitive-behavioral therapy (CBT) in the literature for the treatment of PTSD (Dalgleish, 2004; Feeny, Foa, Treadwell, & March, 2004). The goals of CBT treatment are the reduction of PTSD symptoms, the development of positive coping skills, and an increase in the individual's sense of well-being. It is helpful to provide both the parents and student with education and information on PTSD and its effects on all levels of functioning. Normalizing the student's, parents', and family's feelings and responses also may help to lessen anxiety and alleviate the severity of symptoms. This form of psychotherapy also focuses on the teaching of progressive muscle relaxation, thought-stopping, positive imagery, and deep breathing prior to having the student discuss the traumatic event. Mastering these skills gives the student a sense of control over thoughts and feelings rather than being overwhelmed by them and will help the student approach the discussion of the traumatic event with confidence, thereby reducing uncontrollable reexperiencing of fears and symptoms. At the center of CBT is also the use of in vivo exposure to help the emotional processing of traumatic memories. This process is done in such a way as to help the student process his or her emotional reactions to the event in a safe and trusting way to master and lessen feelings about the traumatic event.

Family therapy is a way to integrate the whole family into the student's treatment. Parental support and reaction to the student are likely to affect the student's symptomology. Most experts assert that inclusion of the parents and/or supportive others in treatment is important for resolution of students' PTSD symptoms. Including parents in treatment helps them to monitor their child's progress and symptomology and also helps them to resolve their emotional distress related to the trauma (Foa, Keane, Friedman, & Cohen, 2010).

Trauma-focused groups for students and parents can lead to beneficial open discussions of perceptions, attributions, and feelings about the traumatic event. Group therapy is often used after major traumas and disasters as a way to help debrief and normalize the event for the student. School-based group crisis intervention may be particularly useful after trauma and disaster situations.

Summary/Conclusion

As students are increasingly exposed to traumatic stressors and events, it is likely that the professional school counselor will be called upon to assess and intervene with a student with PTSD or PTSD-like symptoms. Familiarity and knowledge of *DSM-5* criteria for PTSD is essential for the professional school counselor to understand the complexity of this disorder. With a comprehensive assessment and proper treatment, most students will typically improve within 3 to 6 months, while others may need longer term treatment.

CHAPTER 47

Habits, Tics, and Self-Mutilation (Cutting): A Behavioral Approach to Assessment and Treatment

*Bradley T. Erford**

Preview

The purpose of this chapter is to provide an overview for identifying, assessing, and treating habits, tics, and self-mutilation (nonsuicidal self-injury). Information related to the etiology and epidemiology will also be provided.

Tics

Tics are sudden, brief, repetitive, rapid, stereotyped motor movements or vocalizations that are nonrhythmic and generally believed to be involuntary. Tics can be exacerbated by fatigue, stress, and medical conditions and may also be triggered by specific environmental events. Motor tics involve the singular or recurrent contraction of one or more of the body's muscle groups (e.g., eye blinking, head jerking, shoulder shrugging). Vocal tics involve singular or recurrent vocal sounds, words, and/or phrases (e.g., throat clearing).

Tics are categorized as either simple or complex. Simple tics are limited to individual muscle groups (e.g., eye blinking, facial grimacing) or utterances (e.g., sniffing, snorting). Complex motor tics involve recurrent coordinated patterns of motor movement such as retracing one's steps or twirling when walking. Complex vocal tics involve recurrent repetition of words, phrases, or complete sentences. Tics often emerge as simple tics and over time may develop into more complex patterns.

The average age of onset for tic disorders is approximately 7 years of age (Woods & Miltenberger, 2006). However, the onset of tic disorders has been observed in individuals as young as 1 year of age and as old as 18 years of age. Most often, motor tics appear before vocal tics. Typically, tics take a cephalo-caudal trajectory (head-downward) in that they begin in the face and gradually move downward to affect the neck, shoulders, and trunk.

---

*Special thanks to T. Steuart Watson, Brad A. Dufrene, and Kristi Hofstadter for their outstanding contributions to the previous edition of this chapter.

Diagnosis of Tic Disorder

An accurate diagnosis of tic disorders depends upon the length of time that tics have been present as well as the concurrent or independent presence of motor and/or vocal tics. Three classifications of tic disorders that occur across a continuum of severity are listed in the *Diagnostic and Statistical Manual of Mental Disorders* (5th ed.; *DSM-5*; American Psychiatric Association [APA], 2013). *Transient tics* are singular or recurrent episodes of motor or vocal tics that are present for at least 4 weeks but not longer than 12 months. *Chronic tics* are motor or vocal tics that are present for more than 1 year. *Tourette's disorder* (TD) is characterized by the presence of multiple motor and one or more vocal tics that have been present for more than 1 year. However, a diagnosis of TD does not require that motor and vocal tics occur concurrently.

Although tic disorders have been studied since the early 20th century, their exact etiology is unknown. Currently, the areas that are receiving the greatest attention are genetic and neurobiological influences, although some researchers have approached the etiology of tic spectrum disorders from a learning perspective. Each of these areas is discussed.

Genetics

Results of family and twin studies indicate that genetic factors may play an important role in the transmission and expression of tic disorders. Family genetic studies have found that the recurrence of tic disorders in affected families is higher than the expected rate (Pauls, Raymond, Leckman, & Stevenson, 1991). In studies of monozygotic twins, the concordance rate for TD and tic spectrum disorders has been found to range from 50% to 90% (Hyde, Aaronson, Randolph, Rickler, & Weinberger, 1992; Price, Kidd, Cohen, Pauls, & Leckman, 1993). Studies using dizygotic twins have found concordance rates for TD and tic disorders that range from 8% to 23%. Although these studies suggest that genetics may be responsible for tic spectrum disorders, no genetic markers have been identified to date.

Neurobiological

While evidence of genetic contributions to tic spectrum disorders is mounting, a body of research exists that implicates neurobiological factors. Neurochemical systems that have been implicated in tic disorders are the dopaminergic, serotonergic, noradrenergic, opiod, cholinergic, GABAergic, cAMP, arginine, vasopressin, and oxytocin systems (Cicchette & Cohen, 2006). Neurochemical explanations of tic disorders are based on EEGs and other brain-imaging techniques as well as the effects of specific drugs for treating tics.

Although tic spectrum disorders may be more common in students than previously thought, prevalence data suggests that Tourette's disorder remains a relatively rare disorder. TD affects more than three out of 10,000 school-age children (Apter et al., 1993). Boys are five times more likely to be diagnosed with TD while Caucasians are more likely than African-Americans and Hispanics to develop TD. Additionally, children are more likely than adults to be affected by TD as evidenced by substantially lower prevalence rates for adults (e.g., 1–2 per 10,000; APA, 2013). Prevalence rates for transient tic disorder in children have been reported between 12% and 16%. The prevalence rate for chronic tic disorder is likely somewhere in between.

Learning

Some researchers have approached the etiology of tic spectrum disorders from a learning perspective (Watson, Dufrene, Weaver, Butler, & Meeks, 2005); in some instances, tic behaviors may be the result of an interaction between neurobiology and learning. For example, an individual predisposed to tics and tic behavior may, due to a variety of environmental consequences (e.g., reduction in muscle tension, access to social attention), increase his or her rate of tics over time, and the tics may assume varied and unusual forms as a result of shaping and response generalization. In addition to explaining the origin of tics, a body of literature is emerging in which specific environmental stimuli that alter the rate of tic behaviors are being identified. Identifying such variables may allow practitioners to quickly develop effective and individually tailored interventions.

Habits

Habits are learned, benign, persistent, stereotyped behaviors that appear to serve no meaningful purpose for the individual. Habits may be maintained by positive reinforcement (attention), negative reinforcement (reduction of unpleasant physiological arousal), or automatic reinforcement (sensory stimulation) and elicited by many discriminative stimuli (e.g., transitional objects). Most individuals will engage in some habit behavior (e.g., foot tapping, thumb sucking, hair twirling) over the course of their lives. Because most habits are benign and often transient, most go untreated. However, some habits may result in substantial negative physical, social, academic, occupational, or psychological discomfort for the individual who exhibits them. For instance, habits may result in negative interactions with parents, teachers, or peers. The student who sucks her thumb may be teased by peers, scolded by parents, and suffer physical damage (e.g., malocclusions). Because habits may result in substantial negative consequences, they are an important concern for parents, professionals (e.g., professional school counselors, physicians, psychologists), and the student who engages in the habit. The most common habits seen in clinical settings are trichotillomania (hair pulling), bruxism (teeth grinding or clenching), nail biting, and thumb sucking.

Etiology and Epidemiology of Habit Disorders

Current research indicates that habits are learned behaviors that are not indicative of underlying psychopathology. Children who engage in habits do not significantly differ from children who do not on measures such as the *Achenbach System of Empirically Based Assessment* or *Eyberg Child Behavior Inventory*. It has been suggested that habits are caused by states of anxiety or tension, thus fostering the idea that individuals who exhibit habits are "nervous," and the anxiety or tension they feel causes them to exhibit these "nervous" habits. Support for the theory that individuals who exhibit habits experience significantly more anxiety and tension than others has been mixed (Woods & Miltenberger, 2006).

From a behavioral perspective, it is likely that some habits are directly reinforced while others become conditioned reinforcers (i.e., they are paired with either an unconditioned reinforcer like food or with another conditioned reinforcer like playing in the tub), and as a result, are maintained for long periods. For instance, a student who normally receives little social attention from parents may be reprimanded when he sucks his thumb. Social attention provided contingent upon thumb sucking might serve to increase the future likelihood of thumb sucking. Thumb sucking may also provide tactile and kinesthetic stimulation of the oral tissue during times of minimal stimulation which may also maintain the behavior (i.e., automatic reinforcement).

Because habit disorders cover such a wide range of topographically different behaviors, it is extremely difficult to obtain overall prevalence estimates. However, rough estimates for specific habits have been reported. Cichette and Cohen (2006) reported prevalence data for habits most commonly seen in clinics. Bruxism is estimated to occur in 7% to 88% of the population. The wide range in prevalence rates is due to the varied definitions used by researchers who study bruxism. Estimates for the prevalence of trichotillomania are only available for adults (0.6% to 1%; APA, 2013). Trichotillomania is more common in females, except for during the preschool years, when it is more common in males. Prevalence rates for nail biting increase from preschool to adolescence, where it peaks at roughly 45%, but then steadily declines to a rate of 4.5% in adults. Nail biting is most common in females. Thumb sucking occurs in 30% to 40% of preschool children and 10% to 20% of children 6 years and older.

Identification of Habits and Tics

Identifying, assessing, and treating habits and tics focuses on operationally defined, observable behaviors and employs a multimethod and a multi-informant approach for collecting data. Methods for accurately and operationally identifying habit and tic behaviors include interviews, direct observation, and permanent product measures (e.g., nails, hairs) where possible. Figure 47.1 presents a decision tree that may help the professional school counselor determine which method of data gathering is most appropriate in a given circumstance.

Interviews

Interviews should be conducted with parents, teachers, and the student (when appropriate). The purpose of the interview is to first gain general information related to the student's developmental, medical, social, and academic histories. During the medical portion of the interview (with parents), information related to current and past medications as well as physician evaluations should be gathered in order to determine if there are possible organic causes for the habit or tic.

After developmental, medical, social, and academic histories have been gathered, specific information regarding the habit or tic should be obtained. Questions related to when the behavior was first noticed, what the behavior looks like (having the student or parent perform the behavior may be appropriate), previous treatment attempts, and other areas of concern are important at this point. Following this, questions related to the times when the behavior is most frequently exhibited, events that precede the behavior (both physiological and environmental) and events that typically follow the behavior (e.g., social attention, reduction of unpleasant physiological stimulation) should be asked. Information gathered from such questions can facilitate the development of hypotheses regarding possible functions of the behavior (e.g., access to social attention, negative reinforcement). The function of behavior can generally be regarded as the "why" of behavior. See Figures 47.2, 47.3, and 47.4 for examples of abbreviated parent, student, and teacher interview forms, respectively.

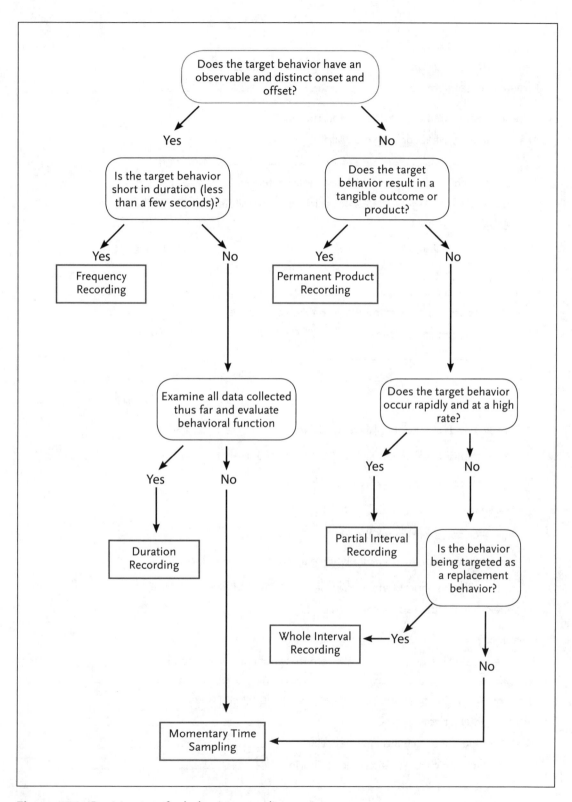

Figure 47.1. Decision tree for behavior recording.

Date: _____ Student Name: _____

Date of Birth: _____ Grade: _____

Parent/Guardian Name: _____

Developmental, Medical, and Social Information

At approximately what age did your child:

    Sit up _____ Walk _____ Say first words _____

    Potty train _____ Use simple sentences _____

Has your child been diagnosed by a physician with any medical condition?

    ❏ Yes ❏ No

Diagnosis	Date Diagnosed
_____	_____
_____	_____

Please list all past and current medications taken by your child.

Medication Name	Dates Taken
_____	From _____ To _____
_____	From _____ To _____

Does your child:

    have friends at school? ❏ Yes ❏ No

    have friends in the neighborhood? ❏ Yes ❏ No

    get teased by peers? ❏ Yes ❏ No

    get along well with adults? ❏ Yes ❏ No

    get along well with other children? ❏ Yes ❏ No

    use age-appropriate behavior when playing? ❏ Yes ❏ No

    play with age-appropriate toys/games? ❏ Yes ❏ No

Describe other health or social concerns: _____

Behavior

Describe in detail the behavior(s) of concern that your child is exhibiting.

_____

Please provide a demonstration of the behavior(s) described above.

When did you first notice this behavior? _____

What have you done to change this behavior? _____

How long has your child exhibited each behavior? _____

Figure 47.2. Abbreviated parent interview form.

> Has the behavior changed in any way over the course of occurrence?   ☐ Yes   ☐ No
>
> How?   When?   In response to what (in your opinion)?
>
> _____
>
> **Functional Hypothesis Development**
>
> In what situation or setting is your child most likely to perform the behavior(s)?
>
> _____
>
> During what time(s) of the day is your child most likely to exhibit the behavior(s)?
>
> _____
>
> In what situation(s) or setting(s) is your child least likely to perform the behavior(s)?
>
> _____
>
> During what time(s) of the day is your child least likely to exhibit the behavior(s)?
>
> _____
>
> What typically occurs before the behavior(s)? _____
>
> _____
>
> What typically follows the behavior(s)? _____
>
> _____
>
> How do others (for example, peers, teachers, and parents) respond to this behavior?
>
> _____
>
> **Hypothesized function (circle one):**
>
> tangible reinforcement   negative reinforcement   social attention
>
>   automatic reinforcement

Any student may exhibit a particular behavior for a number of reasons. Research indicates that there are four general classes of reasons (consequences) that account for the maintenance of problem behaviors: (a) tangible reinforcement, (b) social attention, (c) negative reinforcement, and (d) automatic reinforcement (Iwata, Dorsey, Slifer, Bauman, & Richman, 1994). However, social attention, negative reinforcement (escape or avoidance of an unpleasant activity or physiological state), and automatic reinforcement (sensory stimulation) appear to be the most common consequences that maintain habits or tics. In the function-based treatments section of this chapter, it will become apparent that determining the "why" of behavior (identifying maintaining consequences) can be extremely useful for developing treatment.

Direct Observation

Following interviews with parents, teachers, and the student, direct observations of the student should be conducted. Direct observations can be used to verify information gathered during interviews as well as to obtain additional information related to the presenting problem. Observation times may be selected based on information gathered during interviews

(text continues on page 530)

Date: _____ Student Name: _____
Date of Birth: _____ Grade: _____
Parent/Guardian Name: _____

Behavior

Describe in detail each of your habits or tics. _____
_____

Please provide a demonstration of the behavior(s) described above.

When did you first start doing this behavior(s)? _____
_____

How long have you been doing this behavior(s)? _____
_____

Do you notice a sensation or feeling that occurs before the behavior(s)? ❑ Yes ❑ No

If yes, which behavior? _____

Describe the sensation. _____

How do you feel AFTER you have done the habit or tic? _____

How do others respond to you when you do the habit or tic? _____

Functional Hypothesis Development

In what school and home situation are you most likely to do the habit(s)/tic(s)?
_____

During what time(s) of the day do you do the habit(s)/tic(s)? _____
_____

In what school and home situation(s) or setting(s) do you hardly ever perform the habit(s)/tic(s)?
_____

During what time(s) of the day do you hardly ever perform the habit(s)/tic(s)? _____
_____

What typically happens before your habit(s)/tic(s)? _____
_____

What typically happens after your habit(s)/tic(s)? _____
_____

Hypothesized function (circle one):

tangible reinforcement   negative reinforcement   social attention
          automatic reinforcement

Figure 47.3. Abbreviated student interview form.

Date: _____ Student Name: _____

Date of Birth: _____ Grade: _____

Teacher Name: _____

Academic Performance

Please indicate how the student is performing in the area of reading as compared to same-grade peers.

❑ Significantly above peers ❑ Above peers ❑ Comparable to peers

❑ Below peers ❑ Significantly below peers

Please indicate how the student is performing in the area of math as compared to same-grade peers.

❑ Significantly above peers ❑ Above peers ❑ Comparable to peers

❑ Below peers ❑ Significantly below peers

Please list any academic areas that are particularly *difficult* for the student:
_____

Please list any academic areas that are particularly *easy* for the student:
_____

Please list any academic areas that are of particularly *low* interest for the student:
_____

Please list any academic areas that are of particularly *high* interest for the student:
_____

Behavior

Describe in detail the behavior(s) of concern that the student is exhibiting.
_____

Please provide a demonstration of the behavior(s) described above.

How often is the behavior exhibited (per day)? _____
_____

Please describe any previously implemented interventions: _____
_____

What do you do when the student does the habit or tic? _____
_____

How do the other students respond? _____
_____

Figure 47.4. Abbreviated teacher interview form. *(continues)*

Functional Hypothesis Development

In what situation or setting is the child most likely to perform the behavior(s)?
_____

During what time(s) of the day is the child most likely to exhibit the behavior(s)?
_____

In what situation(s) or setting(s) is the child least likely to perform the behavior(s)?
_____

During what time(s) of the day is the child least likely to exhibit the behavior(s)?
_____

What typically occurs before the behavior(s)?
_____

What typically follows the behavior(s)?
_____

Does the behavior occur more often during a particular academic subject or task?
_____

Do any of the following occur after the behavior?

- ☐ Teacher attention   ☐ Peer attention   ☐ Task termination
- ☐ Assistance with work   ☐ Access to rewards   ☐ Self-stimulation
- ☐ Removal from social situations

Hypothesized function (circle one):

tangible reinforcement   negative reinforcement   social attention

automatic reinforcement

Figure 47.4. (*continued*)

that indicates when the habit or tic is most likely to occur. Ideally, direct observations should be conducted across a number of occasions and settings (again based upon information gathered during interviews). During direct observations, the professional school counselor should record the presenting problem on dimensions including frequency and duration. Such information can be useful in developing a baseline for which to evaluate treatment success and for developing and verifying hypotheses regarding the potential functions for a particular behavior. In addition, close attention should be paid to those events that precede (antecedents) and follow (consequences) the presenting problem. A number of published observation forms designed specifically for use in school settings are available to aid practitioners in recording antecedents, behaviors, and consequences (Watson & Steege, 2009).

Permanent Products

In some cases it may not be possible to directly observe habits. For instance, if the student engages in hair pulling only in private, then it would be impossible to observe the behavior. Additionally, some students may react to observation (referred to as "reactivity") such that the behavior may not be exhibited during observation times. Permanent products can serve as one means to overcome such hurdles. Permanent products refer to those relatively enduring "remnants" of behavior. With trichotillomania, it may be possible to measure bald spots on the scalp to determine if hair is being pulled from a particular region. The student may also be instructed to save pulled hairs in order to obtain an accurate count of the number of hairs pulled during a day. In the case of nail biting, the length of the nails on each hand can be measured. Permanent product measures provide information that can be used to verify behaviors reported by parents, teachers, or the student. Not all habit behaviors (e.g., thumb sucking, hair twirling) and tics are amenable to collecting permanent product measures because they do not leave enduring, measurable remnants.

Rating Scales

In addition to informant report, direct-observation, and permanent product measurement, rating scales may prove useful for evaluating symptom severity and client response to intervention. With regard to TD and tic disorders, the *Yale Global Tic Severity Scale* (YGTSS) is a semistructured, clinician-rated scale for measuring tic severity during the past week. Research indicates that the YGTSS yields reliable and valid scores, is sensitive to treatment gains (Storch et al., 2005), and may be a useful tool for evaluating student's level of tic severity prior to and following intervention.

Function-Based Treatments

Antecedent Interventions

Information gathered during interviews and direct observation may identify specific antecedent events that reliably precede the habit or tic. If a reliable antecedent is identified, then the following procedure may be implemented. First, identify similar antecedents that have not elicited the habit or tic in the past. Next, arrange the environment such that there are numerous opportunities for the nonelicited antecedent to occur and heavily reinforce all appropriate behaviors other than the habit or tic (differential reinforcement of other behavior). Finally, the event that elicited the habit or tic may be gradually reintroduced. For example, if assessment data indicated that a vocal tic is most often exhibited when a student is assigned difficult multiplication problems (e.g., double-digit multiplication with regrouping), then the student can be provided with simpler math problems (e.g., single-digit multiplication problems) and positive social attention contingent upon the absence of the vocal tic (e.g., "I really like the way you are quietly working on your math worksheet"). Difficult multiplication problems can be gradually reintroduced while continuing to provide positive social attention contingent upon the absence of the vocal tic.

Social Attention

If interview and direct observation data indicate that social attention is maintaining the occurrence of a habit or tic, the primary intervention is to withhold attention when the habit or tic is exhibited (extinction) and to provide social attention when appropriate behaviors other than the habit or tic are exhibited (differential reinforcement).

Negative Reinforcement

If interview and direct observation data indicate that escape from an unpleasant activity (negative reinforcement) is maintaining a habit or tic, then the practitioner must develop an intervention in which the student cannot escape the unpleasant activity. For example, in the case of a student who exhibited a vocal and motor tic primarily in the classroom setting, it was determined (from interview and observation data) that the student was able to escape academic demands following the exhibition of the vocal and motor tics by being directed by the teacher to go to the back of the class to "calm down." Thus, vocal and motor tics allowed the student to escape academic demands that were present in the classroom. After discovering why the student exhibited vocal and motor tics, it was rather easy to develop treatment based on this information. First, the student was no longer allowed to escape academic tasks following the vocal and motor tics (extinction). Next, the student was allowed to take breaks (escape academic tasks) following completion of gradually increasing work requirements (differential reinforcement and shaping).

Automatic Reinforcement

Quite often, habit and tic behaviors are maintained by automatic reinforcement (sensory stimulation). In such cases, the practitioner must develop an intervention that either blocks sensory stimulation or punishes the behavior. For instance, one could attach a stick to a child's thumb, thus preventing the child from receiving tactile–kinesthetic stimulation provided by thumb sucking (extinction). Sometimes, however, it may not be possible to simply prevent access to sensory stimulation gained by the habit or tic. In such cases, it may be necessary to punish the habit or tic. A very effective treatment for eliminating thumb sucking is to place an unpleasant tasting substance on the thumb (e.g., Stopzit, Thumbz, Ambisol) after the student is observed sucking his or her thumb (punishment) and rewarding behaviors other than thumb sucking (differential reinforcement). It is important to note that whenever punishment procedures are implemented, some sort of reinforcement should be provided for the nonoccurrence of the problem behavior (differential reinforcement).

General Treatment Procedures

Habit Reversal

Some treatment approaches are effective despite not being based on the function of the behavior. Habit reversal (HR) procedures represent one such approach. HR techniques are among the most effective nonpharmacological treatments for habits and tics (Watson, Howell, &

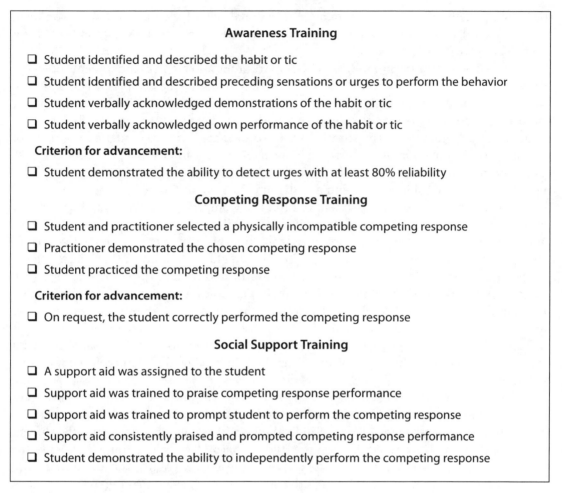

Figure 47.5. Treatment integrity checklist—habit reversal.

Smith, 2006). The original habit reversal procedure (Azrin & Nunn, 1973) contained 13 steps. Follow-up research indicated that all 13 steps were not necessary for the procedure to be effective. Three of the original 13 components are now considered sufficient for effective treatment: (a) awareness training, (b) competing response training, and (c) social support training. This approach to habit reversal has been labeled simplified habit reversal (SHR; see Figure 47.5).

The first step in SHR is *awareness training*. Awareness training involves the student becoming aware of the habit or tic and the sensations that precede it. Awareness is accomplished by having the student describe the habit or tic, describe the sensations that precede the habit or tic, acknowledge counselor demonstrations of the habit or tic, and acknowledge the student's own habit or tic. Awareness training should include multiple opportunities for the student to acknowledge counselor demonstrations and identify self-produced habits or tics. Counselors should praise the student for displaying awareness of the habit or tic and provide corrective feedback to the student when she does not display awareness of the habit or tic. Successful awareness training may be completed in one to two sessions with additional student practice outside of the session (e.g., at home). Successful completion of awareness training is necessary for teaching additional SHR components. Professional school counselors may be confident that a student has achieved awareness by observing the student acknowledge awareness for the habit or tic without prompting.

Competing response training follows awareness training and involves the student and therapist selecting a competing response, the therapist demonstrating the competing response, and finally the student practicing the competing response. Typically, the behavior chosen as the competing response is physically incompatible with the target response (e.g., hands in pockets or lap for trichotillomania). The student is trained to engage in the competing response for 1 minute, contingent upon the occurrence of the habit or tic. Initially, the professional school counselor may prompt the student to engage in the competing response immediately following exhibition of the habit or tic. Eventually though, the student should be expected to engage in the competing response independent of prompts. Competing response training typically occurs across one to two sessions with additional practice at home and throughout the day. During training, the student should experience multiple practice opportunities with the competing response. Professional school counselors should praise the student for engaging in the competing response prior to exhibiting the habit or tic and prompt the student to engage in the competing response if he performs the habit or tic. Professional school counselors should pay careful attention to the level of independence that the student attains with regard to independently engaging in the competing response. Acquisition of the competing response is evidenced by student engagement in the competing response prior to exhibition of the habit or tic (e.g., student folds hands prior to raising forearm, placing finger in mouth, and biting fingernail).

The final component of SHR is *social support training*. The purpose of social support training is to provide the student with an aid who will help implement SHR. Social support training involves three components. First, an individual who has regular contact with the student throughout the day is recruited to assist the student. Second, the aid is trained to praise the student following accurate display of the competing response. Finally, the aid is trained to prompt the student to engage in the competing response in the event that the student engages in the habit or tic. For a more detailed account of SHR, readers should refer to Woods and Miltenberger (2006).

Pharmacological Treatments

Pharmacological agents traditionally have been the treatment of choice for tic spectrum disorders. Neuroleptics are the most commonly used pharmacological agents and work by blocking the reuptake of the neurotransmitter dopamine. Neuroleptics are categorized into two types: typical and atypical. Typical neuroleptics include haloperidol (Haldol) and pimozide (Orap). Haloperidol and pimozide are equally effective in treating tic spectrum disorder. Although typical neuroleptics are effective in significantly reducing tic frequency, they possess a long list of possible side effects including those that range from mild (e.g., dry mouth, constipation, weight gain) to severe (e.g., extra-pyramidal symptoms, tardive dyskinesia, seizures).

Atypical neuroleptics are becoming increasingly popular and include olanzapine (Zyprexa), clozapine (Clozaril), and risperidone (Risperdal). The atypical neuroleptics are often as effective as the typical neuroleptics but carry less of a risk for serious side effects such as extra-pyramidal symptoms and tardive dyskinesia. The atypical neuroleptics may, however, cause less serious side effects (e.g., dry mouth, constipation, weight gain, restlessness, and incontinence).

Self-Mutilation and Nonsuicidal Self-Injury

Self-mutilation (SM) is the deliberate, direct destruction or alteration of body tissue without the presence of suicidal intent (Miller & DeZolt, 2004). The *DSM-5* (APA, 2013) refers to self-mutilation under the new diagnostic category on nonsuicidal self-injury. The most widely accepted classification system for SM was developed by Favazza (1996). In this classification, SM is divided into three categories: (a) *major*, which refers to infrequent but highly destructive behaviors such as enucleation, castration, and limb amputation; (b) *stereotypic*, which refers to behaviors such as head banging and self-biting; and (c) *superficial/moderate*, which refers to behaviors such as cutting, pinching, scratching, and nail biting. Superficial/moderate SM is the most common form of SM and typically occurs on the arms, wrists, inner thigh, and stomach. Superficial/moderate SM behaviors overlap with behaviors that are often classified as habits (e.g., trichotillomania, nail biting) since they are repetitive, volitional, and appear to serve no adaptive role. The remainder of this discussion will focus on superficial/moderate SM because it continues to be an important topic for school personnel.

Skin cutting may be the most common form of episodic superficial/moderate self-mutilation. Skin cutting is often a symptom, or an associated feature, of borderline, histrionic, and antisocial personality disorders, posttraumatic stress disorder, dissociative disorders, eating disorders, and depression. Research indicates that cutting behaviors appear most often during adolescence, may be more prevalent in girls, may sometimes, but not always, be precipitated by incidents of sexual and/or physical abuse, and have an underestimated prevalence (Ross & Heath, 2002). Recent estimates suggest that almost 14% of adolescents have engaged in self-mutilation, including cutting at some point, with females nearly twice as likely to have engaged in self-mutilation.

Skin cutting is often strategically performed in that areas chosen for cutting are easily hidden by clothes. Because individuals who engage in skin cutting are often secretive and reluctant to contact mental health services, identification, assessment, and treatment are often difficult. Furthermore, the lack of standardized instruments for assessing SM is problematic. A comprehensive assessment of skin cutting should include direct observations and interviews with the student suspected of cutting, caregivers, and other adults who frequently observe the individual (e.g., school personnel). Direct observations should include checking for cuts and the presence of heavy clothing that may serve to hide damage. When the student is interviewed, she should be asked directly whether or not she is engaging in skin cutting. If the student is engaging in skin cutting, then a suicide risk assessment should be immediately conducted.

Functional assessment techniques may also be employed in the assessment of skin cutting. While few empirically based assessment instruments are available for skin cutting, functional assessment techniques may be appropriate because skin cutting is topographically similar to other superficial/moderate SM behaviors (e.g., trichotillomania, nail biting) which are amenable to functional assessment procedures. During the assessment stage, information related to antecedents (e.g., triggers), specific behaviors (e.g., jagged lacerations to the thigh), and consequences (e.g., social attention, reduction of unpleasant physiological and emotional arousal) of skin cutting should be gathered. Precise definitions and reliable antecedents and consequences of skin cutting may be useful during the treatment stage. For example, one individual may frequently engage in skin cutting in response to anxiety-evoking events and may be maintained or negatively reinforced by anxiety reduction. Treatment for such an individual may involve teaching the individual to engage in diaphragmatic breathing and progressive muscle relaxation in the face of anxiety-evoking situations because such behaviors could produce similar consequences (i.e., anxiety reduction).

The empirical literature contains scant data regarding effective treatments for skin cutting for children and adolescents. Pharmacological treatment (e.g., SSRIs) may be effective for treating conditions (e.g., anxiety, depression) that are associated with skin cutting, thereby reducing the occurrence of cutting (Favazza, 1998). Additionally, behavioral techniques such as simplified habit reversal may be effective because skin cutting is topographically similar to other habit behaviors (e.g., trichotillomania, nail biting) that are effectively treated by simplified habit reversal. Finally, function-based treatments (e.g., modification of antecedent events, programming alternative responses, manipulating consequences) may prove effective for treating skin cutting. It is important to note that the discussion of SM provided here is cursory. Interested readers should refer to Favazza (1998, 1999) or Lieberman and Poland (2006) for a more detailed discussion of assessment and treatment for SM.

Summary/Conclusion

Although habits and tics appear to be benign disorders, there exists the possibility for significant social, educational–occupational, psychological, and physical damage. From a learning perspective, habits and tics represent learned behaviors that are affected by specific environmental events. The research literature supported the use of behavioral procedures for the assessment and treatment of habits, tics and self-mutilation (nonsuicidal self-injury). Those procedures appear to offer relatively quick and effective means for treating habit and tic disorders, and self-mutilation.

CHAPTER 48

Reactive Attachment Disorder in Schools: Recommendations for Professional School Counselors

Carl J. Sheperis, R. Anthony Doggett, and Robika M. Mylroie*

Preview

Children who experience pathogenic care prior to age 5 years can develop reactive attachment disorder (RAD). This disorder, which manifests in a host of behavioral problems, is of growing concern to professional school counselors. We discuss the characteristics of RAD, diagnostic criteria, issues related to the school system, and recommendations for professional school counselors.

When students transfer in and out of school systems, professional school counselors face a host of difficult administrative issues, including maintaining student records, gathering accurate evaluations of progress, and establishing relationships with families. No school population is more transitory than students from foster care. Some students in foster care experience as many as 50 or 60 placements across numerous school districts (Sheperis, Renfro-Michel, & Doggett, 2003). Many of these students also have mental health issues related to abuse or neglect that eventuated their foster care placement, thus creating more concerns for professional school counselors. In fact, some evidence suggests that students in foster care are more likely to receive behavioral health care services than any other group of Medicaid-eligible children. Often, these health care services are related to a disruption of healthy attachment patterns resulting in reactive attachment disorder (RAD).

A commonly misunderstood and underdiagnosed disorder, RAD is a growing concern for professional school counselors (Sonneborn Lawler, 2014). This disorder begins in early childhood and affects academic, behavioral, cognitive, affective, social, physical, and spiritual–moral development (Shi, 2014). RAD also can be positively treated through intervention (Hayes, 1997). Professional school counselors are in a unique position because of their prolonged interactions with these students to recognize symptoms of serious underlying problems and make appropriate referrals. We present professional school counselors with information about reactive attachment disorder, its development, some methods of treatment, and guidelines for intervention in a school system. However, before expounding upon the nature of RAD, it is important to explain the process of attachment and its function in a student's life.

---

*Special thanks to Angela R. Cole for her contribution to the previous edition of this chapter.

Attachment

Attachment is a process common to humans and many animal species. Disruptions in the process affect humans throughout their entire lives and can negatively affect the ability to form healthy relationships. Bowlby (1969) saw attachment as an instinctual, evolutionary process that occurs in four stages. He believed that the process of attachment functioned as a survival drive of the species. The process begins with an infant's communication of needs for proximity and physical contact through vocal and behavioral cues (e.g., crying, latching on, grasping). Acknowledgement and fulfillment of these needs by a caregiver begin to positively shape the infant's behavior. Infants begin the second stage of attachment between 8 and 12 weeks of age by establishing indicators of caregiver preference through behavioral cues such as reaching and scooting. According to Bowlby, the third stage of attachment occurs from 12 weeks through 24 months of age. This is the stage that Ainsworth, Blehar, Walters, and Wall (1978) believed to involve the true process of attachment. In this stage, infants and toddlers begin to anticipate caregiver actions and adjust their own behavior in accordance with these anticipated events. Thus, consistency of the primary caregiver's display of affection and attention to the needs of the child are critical components in the formation of healthy adjustments on the part of the child. An understanding of caregiver independence and the development of reciprocity in the infant–caregiver relationship characterized Bowlby's fourth stage of attachment development, thus moving into a more sophisticated aspect of the process. The key facet across all of these stages is consistency in the provision of behavioral reinforcement to infant and toddler basic emotional and physical needs. In essence, this reinforcement is a method of conditioning the child to use human relationships as a sense of security and comfort (Buckner, Lopez, Dunkel, & Joiner, 2008).

When the provision of infant and toddler basic needs is not conducted in a consistent fashion, attachment becomes disrupted, resulting in insecure attachment patterns and adverse reactions toward human relationships. In research, disrupted attachment has been linked to psychiatric syndromes, criminal behavior, and drug use (Allen, Hauser, & Borman-Spurrell, 1996; Rosenstein & Horowitz, 1996). Chronic inconsistency in meeting infant and toddler needs, as well as the introduction of early childhood trauma (i.e., abuse or neglect), may result in the formation of RAD.

Reactive Attachment Disorder

A personal difficulty that professional school counselors may face with regard to RAD is a lack of ability to prevent the development of the disorder. RAD develops from a lack of appropriate bonding between infant and primary caregiver, which ordinarily occurs well before a child comes of school age. Thus, the goal for professional school counselors is identification of problem behaviors and acquisition of appropriate resources (Hayes, 1997). The *Diagnostic and Statistical Manual of Mental Disorders* (5th ed.; *DSM-5*; American Psychiatric Association [APA], 2013) criteria for RAD changed with the new edition. The subtypes of RAD in the *DSM-IV* were split into two distinct disorders: RAD and disinhibited social engagement disorder (DSED). In the *DSM-5*, the diagnostic criteria for RAD now includes (a) disturbed and developmentally inappropriate social relatedness across contexts, beginning before age 5 years; (b) evidence of pathogenic care; and (c) a presumption that the pathogenic care is responsible for the disturbed behavior. Reactive attachment disorder is now more focused on the inhibited type, which is seen as a lack of response to social interactions.

Identification of RAD

Childhood psychological disorders often affect various areas of functioning (e.g., behavior, cognition, academic progress, and developmental processes; Achenbach, 1995). Many disorders also share similar symptoms. These commonalities make it difficult to differentiate RAD from disorders such as attention-deficit/hyperactivity disorder (ADHD), disinhibited social engagement disorder, intellectual developmental disorder (formerly mental retardation), major depression disorder, oppositional defiant disorder (ODD), conduct disorder (CO), autism spectrum disorder, learning disorders, and expressive and mixed receptive–expressive language disorders (Sheperis et al., 2003). To effectively coordinate academic services, it is necessary for professional school counselors to understand how to differentiate between a child with RAD and a child exhibiting behaviors characteristic of other disorders. Thus, an understanding of diagnostic criteria for the disorder is warranted.

The principle factor in accurate diagnosis is the presence of an abusive and neglectful environment (i.e., pathogenic care) prior to age 5 years (APA, 2013). However, this factor is not solely indicative of RAD (Sheperis et al., 2003). Children with RAD often have poor interpersonal skills and have difficulty establishing appropriate relationships with peers and adults (Levy & Orlans, 1998). These boundary issues manifest in an inability to interact with familiar people. For example, children with RAD may be very introverted and, similar to autism spectrum disorder, may not respond to familiar people or caregivers (Sheperis et al., 2003). These children may also respond to cordial interactions in an aggressive manner. Other indicators of RAD include poor hygiene, muscular rigidity, and/or lack of affection (Lake, 2005). To accurately diagnose RAD, the disturbed pattern of interaction must have begun prior to age 5 years (APA, 2013).

Similarities to Other Disorders

When psychological disorders share similar characteristics, a process of differential diagnosis is necessary. Differential diagnosis requires attention to exclusionary criteria of disorders with similar characteristics. For example, a child with RAD may appear very similar to a child with attention-deficit/hyperactivity disorder (ADHD). Specifically, both may exhibit little connection between cause-and-effect thinking. For example, a child may behave with unusual levels of impulsivity and hyperactivity. However, unlike children with RAD, children with ADHD will have formed relationships with caregivers and other supportive persons (APA, 2013). Also, the impulsive–hyperactive behavior of children with ADHD differs somewhat from disinhibited behavior exhibited by children with disinhibited social engagement disorder (DSED). In particular, the child with DSED displays inappropriate boundaries and may act as if a relationship exists with a complete stranger rather than being reserved and curious.

Children with RAD may also display behaviors and characteristics similar to intellectual developmental disorder (IDD). However, if criteria are met for IDD, the child cannot be diagnosed with RAD. Accurate assessment of a child's behavior requires a working knowledge of human developmental levels (e.g., cognitive functioning and age-appropriate behaviors). An accurate diagnosis of RAD requires that disruptive behavior must be a result of pathogenic care rather than IDD or other cognitive deficits (APA, 2013). RAD may, however, occur in conjunction with cognitive deficits and developmental delays. More specifically, although both RAD and IDD may result in a child's inability to form meaningful, healthy relationships with significant persons such as caregivers, failed relationships for a child with RAD result from pathogenic care rather than developmental issues.

Some behaviors exhibited by children diagnosed with RAD can also be characteristic of childhood depression. With either disorder, a sense of depression can be manifested in isolation and through a lack of pleasure from customary activities. The attitude of children with RAD is often pouty, sulky, and sullen (Sheperis et al., 2003). To further exacerbate depressive characteristics, children with RAD typically have a wide range of cognitive distortions and lack belief in fairness and good in the world. Considering the deprivation of basic needs that children diagnosed with RAD often suffer due to pathogenic care during infancy and early childhood, these distortions can be understood to some degree. However, they should not be accepted. This distorted belief system may result in a lack of belief about being able to influence the path their life will take. Such an extreme external locus of control in children with RAD may increase inhibition and decrease self-modulation related to more serious behavior (e.g., suicide, reactive and predatory behaviors, juvenile delinquency).

In the *DSM-5*, the disinhibited subtype of RAD was changed to DSED. Characteristic of either CD or ODD, a child with DSED may be both overtly and passively aggressive. Also characteristic of either disorder, children with DSED may be deceitful or lie to manipulate others (Sheperis et al., 2003). According to Levy and Orlans (1998), DSED also manifests in chronic lying and generalized delinquent behavior (e.g., stealing and fighting). Because the behaviors characteristic of DSED, CD, and ODD are so similar in nature, it is difficult to differentiate the disorders without an appropriate psychosocial history. The main differentiating criterion is the presence of pathogenic care prior to age 5 years.

Children with RAD may also share similarities with children who are diagnosed with autism spectrum disorder (APA, 2013). Both fail to make appropriate attachments to caregivers. The primary difference is that behaviors related to RAD must have developed within the framework of an abusive or detrimental environment while a child with autism spectrum disorder may have been raised in a supportive and caring environment. The *DSM-5* stated that children with autism spectrum disorder will present impairment in the quality of communication and will display patterned behavior consisting of restricted, repetitive, and stereotyped movements (e.g., overly preoccupied with a stereotyped and restricted pattern of abnormally intense or abnormally focused interest, need to perform a routine or ritual which has no apparent purpose, hand-flapping or wringing, and obsession with parts of objects).

Academic Issues Related to RAD

Repeated changes in foster care and school settings often lead to academic skills or performance deficits for children with RAD (Zirkie & Peterson, 2001). Professional school counselors can help establish effective learning environments in which teachers can recognize individual learning preferences and realize when a student needs assistance in learning a particular skill. A skill deficit can occur when a student has not met the mastery criteria of a curriculum but advances to the next grade (e.g., social promotion). This promotion becomes a problem because the child is expected to complete tasks at a more advanced level than his or her ability may allow. An example of an academic performance deficit occurs when behavior problems affect academic performance (e.g., a child with RAD who is unwilling to complete assignments because of a general dislike and mistrust of adults). Unlike children with reading and math disorders or expressive and mixed receptive–expressive language disorders, the academic difficulties of children with RAD may stem from a lack of stability and continuity of care rather than from a cognitive or neurological deficit. Professional school counselors can affect positive outcomes for these children through the acquisition and coordination of quality services (Sonneborn Lawler, 2014). The primary step in this process for a child exhibiting symptoms of RAD, particularly a foster child or an adopted child, is to review the child's academic record and to examine the frequency of school transfers with the length of stability in each school. The professional school counselor should also examine academic records for patterns of problems, both in academic behavior (e.g., previous grade retentions or advancements) and in social behavior (e.g., numerous suspensions, refusal to complete tasks or assignments, lying, and/or impulsive or aggressive behavior). One potential method of achieving this task is to conduct regularly scheduled meetings with the student.

RAD is most amenable to mental health intervention during early childhood (Zeanah & Gleason, 2010). Thus, early identification of problem behaviors and appropriate referral are key tasks for professional school counselors (Pfaller & Kiselica, 1996). Although early intervention programs such as Head Start are often warranted, appropriate academic services may not be identified until the child is of school age. Once in the schools, these children are in need of structure and order in a caring, supportive environment to succeed academically. By virtue of their knowledge of the school system, professional school counselors can identify and advocate assignment to appropriate teachers who could provide such an environment for these children.

Because of the multitude of school-related problems identified, children diagnosed with RAD are at-risk for academic failure. Professional school counselors may also establish dropout prevention services for these children. However, the efficacy of such programs with this population is yet to be tested. Early identification of academic difficulties is preferred to dropout prevention. If academic problems are identified early, professional school counselors can advocate for intervention in academic areas as needed. The school counselor may refer the student to be tested for special education services.

When Individualized Education Program (IEP) meetings are held for the student, the professional school counselor and special education coordinator should ensure that the appropriate personnel are present (e.g., legal guardian of the student, special education representative, administration representative, juvenile justice officer, an expert on RAD). The professional school counselor may also act as a liaison ensuring that appropriate services are provided for the student. This role would provide added success to IEP meetings, because the professional school counselor would have ongoing contact with mental health counseling agencies, other psychological service providers, juvenile justice officials, child welfare agencies, and other parties providing services to the student and family. The professional school counselor is in a good position to establish open communication with the student's guardian or guardians, ensuring that they are informed about the services being provided. Serving as a liaison also provides the family with a contact person for questions about the process.

Legal Issues

Children who are in foster care or who have been adopted often have complex custodial issues, and professional school counselors are in a unique position to ensure that the school is a safe and secure environment (Zirkie & Peterson, 2001). School officials must be aware of the custodial rights of each student and limit access to the disclosure of information to appropriate sources as dictated by the Family Educational Rights and Privacy Act of 1974 (FERPA) and the Individuals With Disabilities Education Improvement Act of 2004 (IDEA). For example, school officials must obtain appropriate consent for individualized assessment procedures, special education services, or any special treatment that is not provided to all students. Also, school officials must ensure that children are only released from school to those with custodial power. Custodial rights and the power to consent may be legally granted to a biological parent, adoptive parent, foster parent, guardian *ad litem*, or human services agency. Professional school counselors can ensure appropriate care in these matters through review of academic records and appropriate dissemination of information to school officials.

Recommendations for Professional School Counselors

Following are recommendations for best practice in working with students with RAD.

1. If a student is suspected of having RAD, refer the student for appropriate mental health assessment.
2. Establish a supportive relationship with the student.
3. Obtain accurate academic records from all previous school districts.
4. Examine academic records for evidence of a pattern of a problem behavior.
5. Obtain behavioral observation data.
6. Consult the school psychologist.
7. Establish an IEP and include all key players in the formation of the plan (i.e., foster parents, guardians *ad litem*, human services professionals, mental health counselors).
8. Identify appropriate services for the student.
9. Coordinate efforts with teachers and IEP team members.
10. Maintain continued contact with classroom teachers.
11. Conduct regularly scheduled parent meetings.
12. Maintain phone contact with parents or caregivers.

Professional school counselors may also use a cognitive behavioral intervention to aid the child with RAD. This process occurs in three phases: (a) identification of cognitive errors (such as self-blame), (b) assessment of cognitive distortions within the child's reasoning process, and (c) replacement of cognitive errors with accurate cognitions (Sheperis et al., 2003). More interventions may be used as the child becomes stable. The professional school counselor and teachers should develop reasonable goals and techniques as the intervention process takes place. For example, if the goal is to lessen anxiety, the technique should be as simple as stress management.

Summary/Conclusion

Attachment is an instinctual process that occurs between a child and his or her primary caregiver. When that process is disrupted, students have difficulty with self-regulation and forming healthy relationships. This disruption, under chronic abuse or neglect conditions (e.g., pathogenic care), can develop into reactive attachment disorder or disinhibited social engagement disorder. RAD and DSED affect many areas of a student's life, including school. Professional school counselors are in a unique position to help stabilize several domains through advocacy and targeted interventions. Because disrupted attachment has been linked to psychiatric syndromes, criminal behavior, and drug use (Allen et al., 1996; Rosenstein & Horowitz, 1996), it is important to intervene early and to work toward stabilization. Professional school counselors can help students and their families to access appropriate resources and ensure that appropriate academic interventions are in place.

CHAPTER 49

Students With Learning Disabilities: Counseling Issues and Strategies

Adriana G. McEachern

Preview

Approximately 42% of students in exceptional education classes have been diagnosed with a learning disability. Professional school counselors can help these students be successful academically and cope with personal and social issues stemming from their disability. Learning disability issues relevant to professional school counselors and counseling strategies that can be used to help these students will be discussed in this chapter.

Learning disabilities, intriguing and puzzling disorders, are of concern to educators, parents, researchers, professional school counselors, and students (Kirk, Gallagher, & Coleman, 2012; Leichtentritt & Shechtman, 2010). The intriguing aspects of learning disabilities are that there are multiple causes and multiple types, and even students with the same type of learning disabilities may have different sets of deficiencies with different sets of needs (Lambie & Milsom, 2010). Learning disabilities are puzzling because these students may have normal or even gifted intelligence, yet they are not always successful in school. Researchers have been studying learning disabilities since the 1800s, and the term *learning disabilities* was first proposed by parents and Samuel Kirk in 1963 to describe the condition (Kirk et al., 2012). Currently 2.4 million students are diagnosed with learning disabilities in the United States (Individuals with Disabilities Education Act [IDEA], Part B, Child Count, 2010). Although there has been a decline in the last 10 years in the number of students diagnosed with learning disabilities, learning disability is still the largest special education category of disability, comprising 42% of all children requiring school-based special education services (Cortiella & Horowitz, 2014). Two thirds of children with learning disabilities are males; Blacks and Hispanics are overrepresented in special education in some states with Whites and Asians underrepresented.

Definitions and Prevalence

A *specific learning disability* is the term used with the school-age population to refer to disorders that affect the understanding or use of language, written or spoken, that manifest in difficulties with listening, thinking, reading, writing, and mathematical calculations (IDEA, 2004). The term specific learning disability includes perceptual disabilities, brain injury, minimal brain dysfunction, dyslexia, and developmental aphasia, but does not include learning deficiencies resulting from visual, hearing, or motor disabilities; mental retardation; emotional disturbances; or environmental, cultural, or economic disadvantage. Specific learning disabilities affect students' ability to either interpret what they see and hear or link information from different parts of the brain. States must adopt criteria consistent with Sec. 300.309 of IDEA for determining whether a child has a specific learning disability. No longer does inclusionary criteria consist simply of a significant discrepancy between academic achievement and the capacity to learn (Cortiella & Horowitz, 2014). Many states have adopted criteria that require the use of Response to Intervention (RTI) to provide assistance to students with reading, mathematical, and learning deficiencies. RTI, included as part of the eligibility process in IDEA (2004), includes evidence-based intervention practices aimed at providing early intervention, the documentation of which can be used to identify students with a specific learning disability (Marshak, Dandeneau, Prezant, & L'Amoreaux, 2010). For example, a student's lack of progress in validated, evidence-based instruction can rule out inadequate instruction as the cause for learning deficiencies and can provide evidence that the learning deficiencies were caused by a disability. RTI is a multi-tiered system of support that can be used at all grade levels and with all students (Cortiella & Horowitz, 2014). It includes a number of school professionals (e.g., general and special education teachers, school psychologists, school counselors, reading specialists) making informed educational decisions on the type, intensity, and duration of the interventions while closely monitoring students' progress (U.S. Department of Education, 2014). Further, in determining eligibility for special education with a specific learning disability, information obtained on the student should be carefully considered and documented and should come from a variety of sources, including aptitude and achievement tests, parent input, teacher recommendations, as well as information about the child's physical condition, social or cultural background, and adaptive behavior.

The *Diagnostic and Statistical Manual of Mental Disorders, Fifth Edition* (American Psychiatric Association, 2013) refers to a learning disability as a specific learning disorder (SLD) with criteria similar to IDEA (2004) that include:

- Persistent difficulty with reading, writing, arithmetic, or mathematical reasoning not caused by developmental, neurological, visual, hearing, or motor disorders.
- Academic skills well below the average range based on culturally and linguistically appropriate assessments.
- An impairment that interferes with the individual's academic and work performance or activities of daily living.
- Determination through a review of various assessments, including medical, educational, test scores, family reports, educational observations, and RTIs.

Characteristics and Identification of Students with LD

A learning disability can manifest itself in several ways, such as specific difficulties with spoken and written language, coordination, self-control, or attention deficits. Students with learning disabilities may experience problems with learning tasks, memory, and paired-associate learning (Cortiella & Horowitz, 2014; Marshak et al., 2010; Trolley, Haas, & Patti, 2009). These impairments are due to subtle central nervous system dysfunction that causes the brain and the brain's perceptual systems to work differently from the way they function in students without LDs; in many cases, the disturbance starts before birth (Marshak et al., 2010; Trolley et al., 2009). Possible causes of LD have included genetic and hereditary factors, fetal brain development, environmental toxins, drug use, and problems during pregnancy or delivery (Trolley et al., 2009).

Characteristics of students with learning disabilities will differ among individuals who may exhibit deficits in the cognitive, motor, or social domains (Cortiella & Horowitz, 2014; Marshak et al., 2010). Those with cognitive difficulties will experience problems in reading, arithmetic, or thinking. Some have problems with gross or perceptual-motor skills while others have social deficiencies. Reading deficiencies are the most common among students with learning disabilities, and the term *dyslexia* has become synonymous with a reading disability (Cortiella & Horowitz, 2014). Those with reading problems may not be able to decode the sounds of the letters in the alphabet that result in slow oral reading and poor reading comprehension. Due to these difficulties, these students lack the motivation to read. The processing learning disability called dysgraphia results in problems with written composition, poor spelling, handwriting, and difficulty with grammar and punctuation (Cortiella & Horowitz, 2014; Orbin, 2010). A student with language deficits may have difficulty understanding what is said and expressing himself or herself verbally. Approximately two thirds of students with learning disabilities have mathematics difficulties referred to as dyscalculia. These students are unable to learn and understand math concepts, have difficulty memorizing basic number facts, and will have difficulty managing money (Cortiella & Horowitz, 2014). Students with dyscalculia are often not diagnosed and thus may not receive the services they need because most school special education programs are based on reading disabilities (Orbin, 2010). Dyspraxia, another form of learning disability, results in motor coordination, balance, and eye-hand coordination problems (Cortiella & Horowitz, 2014: Orbin, 2010). In spite of having normal hearing and vision, some students with learning disabilities may have auditory and visual processing problems that cause them difficulty in understanding and processing language; those with central auditory processing disorders are easily distracted, exhibit difficulty recalling auditory information, and discriminating important information if there is background noise. Students with nonverbal learning disabilities may often not be diagnosed because although they have verbal, reading, and writing skills, they demonstrate social skill deficits such as understanding social cues and others' body language. Although attention-deficit/hyperactivity disorder (ADHD), that results in hyperactivity and/or inattention, is not considered a learning disability, approximately one third of students with ADHD also have a learning disability.

Studies have shown that students with LDs have lower academic self-concepts than their normal achieving peers (Wei & Marder, 2012). They often experience difficulty making and keeping friends and may demonstrate inappropriate social behavior (Barber & Mueller, 2011). The lack of social skills and competence contributes to rejection by their peers and results in feelings of isolation and withdrawal from classroom activities. Students with learning disabilities may be more disruptive in class and have more classroom behavior problems and disciplinary referrals than their peers without learning disabilities (Cortiella & Horowitz, 2014). In addition, they may be more prone than their peers without learning disabilities to have family-related problems such as financial difficulties and lack of educational stimulation.

The federal government outlines specific procedures for identifying students with LDs and a process that must be followed in evaluating these students under the Education for All Handicapped Children Act of 1975, the Individuals With Disabilities Education Act

Amendments of 1997, and the Individuals With Disabilities Education Improvement Act of 2004 (Cortiella & Horowitz, 2014; Schmidt, J., 2010). Failure to follow this process can result in civil court actions, state and federal sanctions, and loss of funding for the school district. A multidisciplinary team (e.g., teacher, school psychologist, social worker, professional school counselor, behavioral specialist) must conduct the evaluation, and the child's parents must be involved and give consent. Professional school counselors often participate in the multidisciplinary team (Marshak et al., 2010; Trolley et al., 2009). Assessment instruments must be administered in the child's native language, and more than one criterion (e.g., verbal or written expression, listening comprehension, reading, mathematics reasoning and calculations) must be evident for the diagnosis. An Individualized Education Program (IEP) is developed if the assessment and evaluations of RTI results indicate the student meets the eligibility criteria for special education services (Marshak et al., 2010). The IEP is based on the unique needs of the student and specifies the educational and related services (e.g., counseling) that will be provided. The IEP acts as a monitoring device to assure the student is in fact receiving services as agreed to by the parents and school personnel. The IEP must include (a) assessments (e.g., medical, personal–social, behavioral functioning, current educational performance, academic achievement, cognitive and motor functioning); (b) a statement of the levels of academic achievement and functional performance that includes how the disability affects the student's ability to progress in the general education curriculum; (c) goals and short- and long-term objectives to meet student needs; (d) educational services and any auxiliary aids and accommodations that need to be provided, names of individuals who will provide such services, and specific timelines; and (e) annual evaluation procedures and IEP updates.

Personal, Social, and Educational Needs

Students with LDs often experience frustration in completing day-to-day tasks and assignments. They may display fear of failure, fear of learning, and approach tasks with reticence. They may say, "I can't do this," "I don't know how," or "I'll never learn this." In addition, they may demonstrate low frustration tolerance and be prone to exhibit temper tantrums and disruptive behavior when confronted with learning situations (Turnbull, Turnbull, Wehmeyer, & Shogren, 2012). Feelings of failure, worthlessness, and low self-esteem can further compound learning problems (Barber & Mueller, 2011); therefore, students with learning disabilities will need a variety of interventions, such as individualized counseling, group counseling, social skills training, behavioral strategies and contracting, and parent involvement and education, to help them cope with their feelings and adjust to their disability (Schmidt, J., 2010). They will need encouragement and support from parents, teachers, professional school counselors, and other significant adults in their lives. They will also need to develop academic strategies that will help them cope with the specific difficulties of their learning disabilities.

Students who have difficulty forming interpersonal relationships, or who may act socially inappropriately, will benefit from group counseling and social skills training. Students with behavior problems can be helped with behavior modification and contingency contracting strategies implemented by the professional school counselor as well as teachers in the classroom. High school-age students often need help developing career goals and plans (Lalor & Madaus, 2013). Students with learning disabilities also need professional school counselors to act as advocates for them to assure they receive the services identified in the IEP (American School Counselor Association [ASCA], 2009; Geltner & Leibforth, 2008; Trolley et al., 2009).

Counseling Strategies

Solution-focused counseling can be used with students with learning disabilities because of its focus on solutions rather than problems and its effectiveness with students who lack motivation, confidence, and perseverance (Saadatzaade & Khalili, 2012). This approach can be implemented in both individual and group counseling interventions. Daki and Savage (2010) found that using solution-focused counseling techniques can help students with reading difficulties become more involved in the reading process and develop improved reading skills.

Play techniques, art, music, and expressive writings can be used with elementary school students in individual and group counseling to elicit and express feelings toward the disability, school-related experiences, peer conflicts, and family difficulties (Trice-Black, Bailey, & Riechel, 2013). The use of bibliotherapy can also be helpful with students with learning disabilities to help them cope with the challenges of learning disabilities by providing a method for clarifying feelings and promoting self-expression (Parsons & Nord, 2013). These interventions provide a nonthreatening and creative outlet for students that can be adapted to their developmental levels, needs, and unique concerns. When using play techniques with children with hyperactivity who may become overstimulated by the toys and the playroom, Carmichael (2006) recommended limit setting. For example, the child is instructed to select five or six toys initially. If the child shows symptoms of overstimulation, the toys are reduced by one. Expressive writing activities such as journaling and timed writing exercises can encourage self-exploration and reflection (Gladding, 2011). Narrative therapy has been recommended for use with children and adolescents with learning disabilities because it empowers the child by focusing on the strengths, assets, and resources they possess to reconstruct a more preferable way of living with the disability (Lambie & Milsom, 2010). In narrative therapy, the child with a learning disability is the expert and the counselor a facilitative listener who assists minor clients in reframing their stories to make changes.

Group counseling has been proven to be successful with students with learning disabilities to increase self-esteem, social skills and competence, and improve behavior (Daki & Savage, 2010; Leichtentritt & Shechtman, 2010). Expressive-supportive group counseling, in particular, has been found to be effective because it helps students address social, personal, and self-esteem problems through interaction with others (Leichtentritt & Shechtman, 2010). The expressive supportive groups, conducted by professional school counselors in Leichtentritt and Shechtman's (2010) study, engaged students in activities that promoted the exploration and discussion of their concerns and difficulties aimed at eliciting commitment to change. Therapeutic games, bibliotherapy, phototherapy, art therapy, and therapeutic cards were used as activities for the younger-aged children. Small-group activities that include the use of role play and puppets with elementary-age children can also be used. Educational groups at all grade levels can help students with learning disabilities identify and use learning strategies and techniques to help them compensate for academic deficiencies (Trolley et al., 2009). Some of these strategies include checking for spelling errors before submitting assignments, using a calculator to assure accuracy, writing down all homework assignments, and finding alternative ways of learning (e.g., films, visitations, hands-on activities, use of technology). Students who have difficulty remembering can be taught mnemonic strategies (memory devices and strategies); memory strategies created by the students themselves are most effective.

Cognitive-Behavioral Approaches

Cognitive-behavioral counseling techniques can be applied in individual and group counseling to teach skills and coping strategies. These techniques can be especially useful for students with learning disabilities who demonstrate inattentiveness, impulsivity, and hyperactivity (Schmidt, J., 2010); however, these techniques can also be used with students who exhibit fear of learning and low self-concept. Designed for older elementary and adolescent students, cognitive-behavioral approaches can be most effective when combined with concurrent consultation and training for parents and teachers. The professional school counselor links the school and home components, thus providing an integrative, multimodal, holistic, collaborative approach to address the student's needs. Group sessions and parent and teacher training can occur simultaneously, and the professional school counselor may want to provide these opportunities. The objectives of this approach should include: (a) increasing knowledge of, and adjustment to, the learning disability; (b) teaching the cognitive-behavioral approach so that faulty beliefs and distorted thoughts can be disputed and new thoughts, feelings, and behavior can be generated; (c) changing self-defeating, self-deprecating, absolutist language; and (d) changing behaviors and feelings associated with negative thinking patterns. Behavioral self-management should be included along with contingency contracting and weekly cognitive–behavioral homework assignments to monitor students' motivation throughout the intervention process (Corey, 2013; Shillingford, Lambie, & Walter, 2007).

Stress Reduction, Imagery, and Relaxation Training

Professional school counselors can use visual imagery, relaxation, and stress reduction techniques in individual and group counseling sessions (Gladding, 2011). Visual imagery is a powerful technique that can be used to help students visualize beforehand situations that may be potentially threatening or stressful (e.g., speaking in front of the class, taking an exam, asking a peer to a social event). Autosuggestion or talking with oneself can also help these students build self-confidence and self-esteem. Students can combine self-talk with other relaxation methods such as progressive muscle relaxation or meditation. Some examples of self-talk are, "I can behave calmly in stressful situations," "I can perform to the best of my abilities," and "I am a happy and competent person." Students can make up their own self-affirmations and repeat them periodically throughout the day.

Career Counseling

In comparison to their peers without learning disabilities, students with learning disabilities tend to lack skills in identifying and attaining career choices and making postsecondary training and job related decisions can be challenging for them (Lalor & Madaus, 2013). Further, many students and their families are not aware of the contingencies of the school-to-work or school-to-postsecondary education transition processes and will need help from professional school counselors to understand how these processes work (Cheatham, Smith, Elliot, & Friedline, 2013; Niles & Harris-Bowlsbey, 2013). An important factor for professional school counselors to understand when providing career services is the effect of the disability on specific job requirements of chosen careers; these need to be presented realistically to students. Students with learning disabilities also need knowledge and skill development on the job search, completing employment applications and résumés, conducting effective job interviews, and following up with prospective employers (Lindstrom, Doren, & Miesch, 2011). Connecting students with mentors in the workforce who can serve as role models and offer support can facilitate the career decision and transition processes.

Students with LDs who are planning to attend postsecondary institutions following graduation need assistance with activities related to educational planning, such as evaluating available training prospects and materials, completing applications for postsecondary training, taking entrance examinations such as the *Scholastic Aptitude Test* (SAT) and the *American College Testing Program* (ACT), setting personal goals, and accessing self-help resources (Bassett & Dunn, 2012; Lalor & Madaus, 2013) Professional school counselors can empower students with LDs to take greater control of their lives by informing them about their legal rights related to discrimination in employment or educational settings (Gerber, 2012). It is important for these students to know that services from the Division of Vocational Rehabilitation may help defray the cost of educational training and provide job evaluation and placement assistance (Lindstrom et al., 2011; Marshak et al., 2010). Students with disabilities may need special accommodations (e.g., tutors, academic support, readers, books on tape, psychoeducational assessment, disability services, and counseling) and considerations on the job sites or educational facilities (ASCA, 2013c; Niles & Harris-Bowlsbey, 2013). Having students engage in group experiences during their junior and senior years can help facilitate transitions based on their career choices. McEachern and Kenny (2007) recommended two psychoeducational group models that can be used with high school students with disabilities to help transition from school-to-work and school-to-postsecondary education. Group interventions should be documented in the students' IEPs and written into their Transition Plans (Trolley et al., 2009).

Computer-assisted career guidance systems, such as the *System of Interactive Guidance and Information, SIGI 3* (Valpar International Corporation, 2011), and Internet-delivered career planning systems and resources can help high school students become more involved in the career awareness and exploration process (Niles & Harris-Bowlsbey, 2013). Students can work individually on computers and receive immediate feedback. Access to large databases at the local, state, and national levels can provide students with college admissions, financial aid, vocational–technical training, internships, and scholarship information. Professional school counselors can help students interpret and discuss the results of their searches along with helping them with résumé preparation, employment interviewing, conducting job searches, and learning other career-related skills by using computer-assisted guidance programs and the Internet. Professional school counselors may want to purchase the book *The Internet: A Tool for Career Planning* (Osborn, Dikel, & Sampson, 2011), published by the National Career Development Association.

Peer Facilitation Programs

Peer helpers can be used to work with students with learning disabilities to help them adjust to school situations and to act as special friends (ASCA, 2008; Schmidt, J., 2010). Professional school counselors can pair trained peer helpers with students with learning disabilities based on the students' special needs and interests. These helpers act as positive role models, conflict mediators, advisors to help students with learning disabilities navigate successfully in the school environment, and tutors to help them improve academically. One peer-assisted academic learning strategy, researched in kindergarten to secondary education classrooms, that has been shown to be efficacious in improving reading in students with learning disabilities is the Peer-Assisted Learning Strategies program (PALS; Rafdal, McMaster, McConnell, Fuchs, & Fuchs, 2011). Students with learning disabilities are paired with students with strong academic skills for about 30 minutes of instruction 3 to 5 days per week. Students helped by their PALS peers improved in word recognition, reading fluency, and reading comprehension. The professional school counselor can facilitate and monitor peer helper interactions and provide supervisory feedback during peer-helper classes and meetings.

Teacher and Parent Consultation

Professional school counselors partner and collaborate with teachers and parents to share strategies that support student achievement and personal, social, and career development (ASCA, 2012a). Professional school counselors can consult with teachers individually or in groups to assist in building skills and developing effective academic interventions. Professional school counselors can help teachers learn more about the effects of a learning disability on students' learning and classroom behavior by conducting workshops and in-service trainings during faculty meetings. Some classroom strategies that have worked with students with learning disabilities include the following:

- Rearranging seats so students face away from distractions and are seated in areas accessible to school personnel who can help them focus their attention
- Assigning smaller amounts of work (e.g., 8 math problems instead of 20)
- Providing demonstrations of expected tasks and giving explanations in brief, clear steps
- Organizing materials in color-coded folders
- Moving around the room to check on students' progress
- Having students write down instructions
- Using colored highlighters to emphasize important information
- Repeating important points
- Tape-recording directions
- Using written checklists
- Using individualized cues and prompts
- Presenting material in a variety of ways (e.g., visually, orally, kinesthetically)
- Rewarding students for demonstrating appropriate behaviors
- Using media and technology to enhance instruction
- Providing students with more time to take tests and making test-taking accommodations (Gregg & Nelson, 2012; Mastropieri & Scruggs, 2009; Orbin, 2010; Trolley et al., 2009)

Parents of students with learning disabilities experience many feelings, frustrations, and stressors while raising their children. They, like their children, must adjust to the disabling condition and the effects it has on their child and family (Danino & Schechtman, 2012). Professional school counselors can provide assistance to parents by meeting with them individually or in groups to help them understand their challenges and to strategize ways to help their children be successful (Marshak et al., 2010). Groups, focused on expression of emotions and stress reduction, can be effective interventions for parents with children with learning disabilities to help them relieve stress (Danino & Schechtman, 2012). Forming parent support groups before or after school or referring parents to existing community groups can help them connect with other parents facing similar experiences. One study showed that students of parents who participated in a 9-week parent effectiveness workshop improved their self-concept in comparison to students whose parents did not participate (Elbaum & Vaughn, 2001). In addition to parent effectiveness workshops, professional school counselors can also help parents by teaching them (a) behavior management techniques; (b) how to help their children with school assignments; (c) how to structure the home and study environment; and (d) how to communicate more effectively with their children and teachers (Marshak et al., 2010). Many parents need help understanding their children's behavioral reactions to their disability and the challenges these reactions present. Parents will need assistance in learning how to focus on their child's strengths rather than the disability.

Advocacy and Collaboration

Professional school counselors can advocate for students with learning disabilities to ensure that their special needs are being met (Geltner & Leibforth, 2008). Advocacy can occur on individual or systemic levels (Marshak et al., 2010). On an individual level, professional school counselors can begin by helping to ensure that students with learning disabilities are appropriately identified so that educational and counseling services can be provided to facilitate school success. On a systemic level, professional school counselors can facilitate the identification process by educating teachers, parents, and other school staff on the characteristics and needs of these students. It is critical that professional school counselors serve as members of their school improvement and strategic planning committees as other venues for systemic advocacy. Further, advocacy entails continuous, collaborative consultation with multidisciplinary team members to effectively pool resources, identify and resolve problems, and share decision making and responsibilities for the implementation of educational strategies. During the IEP process, advocacy should focus on the student's strengths and capabilities, and these should be incorporated into the plan (Geltner & Leibforth, 2008).

Professional school counselors can help parents become effective advocates for their children. Parents need information on the academic effects of learning disabilities, public policy and laws related to the disability and educational placement, the IEP process, and special educational programs that can help their children (ASCA, 2013c). Professional school counselors must work collaboratively with community agency personnel and appropriate specialists who can help students with learning disabilities and their families outside the school setting (ASCA, 2010b). In addition, professional school counselors need to demonstrate cultural sensitivity and understanding with parents who, because of their ethnicity or recent immigrant status, may not be fluent in English or knowledgeable about the expectations of the school or of their child's disability (ASCA, 2009). Finally, students with learning disabilities need to be taught to be their own advocates. Self-advocacy skills can help these students become more involved in decision making that affects their academic and career goals. Advocacy skills can be taught and practiced by students in small-group and large-group guidance interventions (Erford, 2015c).

Summary/Conclusion

Learning disabilities affect the understanding or use of language and can manifest in different ways for various students. These may include cognitive deficiencies in writing, spelling, reading, arithmetic, and thinking; gross or perceptual–motor skills may also be affected. Problems with hyperactivity, impulsivity, distractibility, problem solving, and social skills may be evident. Students coping with learning disabilities may experience low self-esteem, feelings of failure, frustration, and difficulty making and keeping friends.

Counseling strategies implemented through individual and group counseling can help students with learning disabilities at all levels to develop effective problem-solving, social, and academic skills that will help them be successful in school. Some of these strategies include brief solution-focused counseling, play techniques, expressive arts and writings, role-play, puppets (elementary age), bibliotherapy, cognitive-behavioral techniques, stress reduction, relaxation, guided visual imagery, and career exploration. To help these students compensate for academic difficulties, education-focused groups can be conducted to teach students specific techniques such as mnemonic strategies, organizing school materials, using calculators and computers to check for math and spelling errors, and the use of audiovisual and other instructional aids. Students with learning disabilities can be paired with their higher functioning peers for tutoring and social support.

The federal government has delineated specific procedures in the Education for All Handicapped Children Act of 1975 and IDEA (2004) that involve a multidisciplinary approach to identify and place students with learning disabilities in appropriate learning environments. An Individualized Educational Program is developed for each student that outlines the educational, social, and counseling services that will be provided. Professional school counselors can also conduct workshops with teachers and parents to assist them in dealing more effectively with the needs of these students in the classroom and at home. Support groups can help parents connect with others who share similar concerns. Advocacy and collaboration with school staff and community personnel is critical to ensure that the needs and rights of students with learning disabilities are met. Teaching students with learning disabilities self-advocacy skills can also help students become more self-sufficient in making academic and career choices.

CHAPTER 50

Helping Students With Severe Behavioral Problems

Gregory R. Janson and Jonathan Procter

Preview

Professional school counselors are often called on to provide support, crisis resolution, and treatment and prevention strategies for students with severe behavioral problems at every grade level. The interventions that offer the most promising approach to helping students are systemic in nature, in which the professional school counselor serves as both counselor and facilitator, bringing together students, teachers, parents, administrators, and staff. In this chapter, strategies for working with all these groups are presented within the context of the extended school community.

Teachers and administrators polled just 50 or 60 years ago reported their most significant behavioral challenges were gum chewing, cutting in line, running in hallways, talking out of turn or making noise, and violating the school's dress code. More recent studies show that these minor offenses have been replaced by robbery, assault, drug abuse, pregnancy, and sexually transmitted infections. Bullying, victimization, and the lingering terror created by school shootings are now part of the educational landscape. During this same time frame, experimentation with alcohol, drugs, smoking, and reckless behaviors have begun in early adolescence and sometimes even within the middle childhood period of development. Against this almost overwhelming backdrop, the professional school counselor is the one individual who has the skills and the mandate to facilitate a systemic approach to managing severe behavior that includes all constituent groups: teachers, students, administrators, staff, and parents.

School and Community Climate

The first step to managing severe behavior in a school setting is to understand the broader systems in which it occurs. When students live in environments that are dangerous or chaotic—at home, in school, or in the community—they become physically and emotionally reactive. A community–school climate assessment, conducted together with educator colleagues, puts student behaviors in context and helps to discriminate between violent reactions to difficult circumstances and more individual pathology. Is the community a safe one? Is the school a place where students *feel* safe, where they can learn without looking over their shoulder or worrying about being bullied in the restrooms or hallways? Do students look forward to coming to school? Are their lives at home safe? What looks like anger or depression in a classroom might well be an appropriate reaction to the stress of living in a dangerous environment. Some students cope by becoming the identified patient; others become the troublemaker.

Understanding Severe Behavior

A student's behavior serves a purpose, even when it does not seem to make sense. Behavior, when viewed externally, can appear self-destructive because it antagonizes others and isolates the student. However, gaining an understanding of maladaptive behavior patterns can help not only teachers and peers, but it can provide insight into why a student uses that particular behavioral repertoire. Severe behavior can be linked to power, control and significance, attention, self-protection, anger, hate, guilt, sadness, and resentment—knowing the motivation is a significant step toward diminishing the behaviors. In the absence of overt disruptive, aggressive behaviors, there may be symptoms of anxiety, dissociation, or depression or abuse (Allan et al., 2014; Maughan, Collishaw, & Stringaris, 2013; Somer, 2011). Severe behavior is often associated with a history of victimization, trauma, abuse, and neglect, which can make it challenging to separate issues that are developmental or environmental from more pathological issues (Hughes, 2010). It is that trauma which "freezes" or impairs emotional development. But when a 6-foot tall, 160-pound teenager is angrily looming, theory is not the first thing that comes to mind. The fact that a history of untreated trauma can lead a 16-year-old to act and respond with the emotional maturity of an 11-year-old is quickly forgotten.

Conceptually, severe behavior in all its forms is an expression of the limited cognitive, affective, and physical resources that students have available to them at any given developmental stage. The more distressed the individual, the more maladaptive the behavior and the greater its frequency, intensity, and duration. Severe behavioral problems are seldom limited to classrooms and are accompanied by a host of other problems that can include substance abuse, expressions of anger through vandalism or violence, depression, anxiety, suicidal thoughts or behaviors, self-mutilation, or inappropriate sexual activity.

Under many disciplinary codes, behaviors that are considered unacceptable are labeled *severe* and get lumped together. Smoking marijuana on school grounds and threatening another student with a knife both earn suspension or expulsion, but they are radically different acts. Dyeing one's hair black is not the same as bringing a pint of vodka to school. Fidgeting and refusing to follow instructions due to the anxiety of being homeless or because of familial stress may lead to the same behaviors in class as a student with attention-deficit/hyperactivity disorder, but the interventions will need to be radically different.

Good behavioral assessment is an ongoing process that should be broad based, be longitudinal, and should consider all the systems in which the student functions, as well as the student's character and temperament. Careful assessment can place behaviors in context and help to structure consequences that contribute to the student's growth and learning. This is where the professional school counselor's input is crucial to formulating an effective educational disciplinary policy.

Relationship and Guidance Are Curative

Teachers are in a unique and desirable position when it comes to providing support to students who face turmoil in their home environment, and they are likely to be the first to observe maladaptive behavioral patterns within the school setting (Martin, DeMarni Cromer, & Freyd,

2010). Changing a student's problematic behavior positively and permanently requires positive interpersonal relationships and guidance (Janson & King, 2006). Successful interventions adhere to the basic principles of guidance and provide a corrective emotional experience. Providing the student with empathetic understanding and unconditional positive regard can foster better communication without the fear of judgment or using punitive measures that ultimately inhibit the flow of the communicative process. Harsh discipline, behaviorally-based interventions, and behavior punishment–reward systems are seldom effective with difficult students because they rely on authority and power. Once the environment changes or the source of authority is out of sight, the student's behavior often reverts to "same old, same old." In effect, teachers can become part of the problem (Janson & King, 2006; McEachern, Aluede, & Kenny, 2008).

Culture and Language

When families immigrate to the United States, students who learn English are seldom taught feeling words, making it sometimes challenging to correctly interpret affective reactions. For example, a teacher could easily misinterpret a student response as anger when the real emotion is frustration. Students who learn English faster than their parents may become mediators between the family and the outside world, a position of power and control that may create problems in relating to adults and authority figures at school. Part of your intervention might involve helping a student's parents access the resources they need to master a new language. This can do a great deal to reduce stress at home and stabilize the family.

The Physiology of Anger and Stress-Management Techniques

Anger is a universal human emotion that serves a purpose; it is part of the fight/flight reflex. Anger can feel overwhelming, and few of us are trained to deal with angry confrontations, particularly with or among students. Our own fight/flight reflexes tend to kick in, along with the stress hormones that drive those reflexes, and we cannot simply "think them away." Awareness of how these reactions affect us, both physically and emotionally, and how they can be minimized with specific relaxation techniques, is a key component of dealing with any severe behavioral challenge. Educating others about anger, anger management, and relaxation techniques is a vital role for professional school counselors; moreover, this education allows students to cope better with stressors (Bothe, Grignon, & Olness, 2014).

Attend to the Physiological Aspects of Severe Behavior—Yours and Theirs

When confronted by severe behavior, defensiveness, fear, anger, and the activation of a fight–flight reflex, people breathe faster, feel their hearts thumping, and become dry-mouthed and sweaty palmed. Stomachs knot, jaws clench—sometimes hard enough to make the muscles bulge so that little vein that runs up one's forehead suddenly stands out in stark relief. An angry reaction can be seen by anyone and can raise the level of potential danger. Exercise self-awareness of bodily reactions when evaluating a potential threat. If you can sit, sit. Sitting interrupts and decreases the force directed against a person when the student suddenly has to look down at that person instead of going toe to toe. Lower voice volume so the other person must be silent to hear it. Breathe slowly, talk quietly and calmly, and offer choices. Acknowledge the student's emotion, communicate understanding, and identify an acceptable alternative course of action which can include self-monitoring behavior (Gaines & Barry, 2008).

Use Mindfulness and Meditation

Most students have trouble with impulse control and with regulating their emotional thermostats. Group training is useful because it does not single out students with behavioral problems. All students can benefit from mindfulness-based approaches that help them connect with their bodily sensations, gain a better awareness of emotional states, and learn to emotionally regulate (Burke, 2010). When severe behavior occurs, make the counseling office a safe haven. Keep a comfy chair in the office with a set of headphones and a quilt. Have older students put the headphones on and listen to an album like Enya's *The Very Best of Enya* or any slow music with a soothing rhythm. The relaxing music helps lessen anxiety and improve behavioral outcomes (Gold, Voracek, & Wigram, 2004). The quilt provides warmth to counter the drop in skin temperature that results from stress and gives a sense of comfort and security. For most students, 10 to 15 minutes is all that is required for the crisis to pass and their bodies and minds to settle down. Secondary benefits accrue in the form of a strengthened relationship; even with consequences, relationships grow stronger when boundaries are pushed to the limit and the relationship remains intact. Using Biodots, which measure skin temperature and are readily available from retailers like Amazon.com, is an inexpensive and enjoyable way to demonstrate to students that mindfulness and meditation work.

Counseling Interventions

An effective systemic approach requires building relationships with and between everyone in the system: students, parents, teachers, staff, and administrators. When these groups communicate with each other in meaningful ways, everyone wins. This is a challenging task under the best of circumstances and not always compatible with the minutiae of your everyday professional responsibilities. It means leaving your office for the uncertainty of the hallways, cafeteria, and other areas of the school where you can interact with people in genuine, personal ways that build relationships outside the confines of the school counselor's office, where relationships are more formally and strictly defined (Hazler, 1998). It also means helping others to leave their comfort zone and consider ways to enhance their ability to form positive relationships with difficult students and their parents. Successful interventions will depend in large part on their involvement and support for your efforts.

Counseling Interventions With Students: They Notice You Notice

A number of counseling interventions have been shown to help students with severe behavioral problems adjust to the academic environment. These include (a) accentuating the positive and personal; (b) not expecting gratitude or appreciation; (c) having faith in their ability to succeed; (d) providing encouragement; (e) using student interests; (f) self-disclosing; (g) experiencing real reactions; and (h) addressing hunger and homelessness.

Accentuate the Positive and Personal

Notice positive points, and comment on them! Can't find a positive point? Search until you do. Make enthusiasm and optimism contagious. An unexpected word of encouragement makes students feel acknowledged and valued, but is particularly effective with troubled students. They may seem unresponsive or indifferent, *but they will notice you noticed!*

Be Prepared to Drive on One-Way Streets

Effective relationship building with difficult students means being without expectations for gratitude or appreciation. Counselors are trained to give clients unconditional positive regard and empathy, regardless of the client's attitude. This may be more difficult for other professionals. Helping them see opportunities to build relationships even as students push the limits can be as simple as acknowledging students' underlying feelings when their behavior earns unpleasant consequences: "It must be tough to have people telling you what to do all the time and have to deal with these consequences." This reflection allows the student to feel heard and can help promote positive interpersonal relationships.

Have Faith in Students and Communicate That Faith

No one can predict future behavior with perfect accuracy, and to do so with a troubled student only reinforces a negative expectation that can become a self-fulfilling prophecy. Faith and encouragement counter discouragement and disaffection. Teachers who serve as a role model for students can see positive growth and development including decreased problematic behaviors like drug use (Yancey, Grant, Kurosky, Kravitz-Wirtz, & Mistry, 2011). Counselors may or may not see immediate positive results from actions, but it is not unusual for many counselors (and teachers) to hear from students long after they leave school. And what they often hear is, "You were the only person who believed in me," not "You really knew a lot about physics."

Provide Encouragement and Positive Reinforcement

Students attempt to find a balance between their individual identity, family norms, and societal notions, which can create inner turmoil, confusion and problematic behaviors (Arslan, 2009). Separate students from behaviors. Make it a point to share how effective encouragement and personal warmth can be. Be the person who says, "I know that you have everything you need to accomplish what you want to accomplish, and when you are ready, you will do it," or "I may not approve of the direction you are taking, but you can count on me to support you for you as long as it takes." There are a number of resources that provide the specific language and techniques of encouragement you can implement within the school setting or share with teachers and administrators (Mitchell & Bradshaw, 2013; Pisacreta, Tincani, Connell, & Axelrod, 2011).

Use What Students Are Interested in to Build Relationships

What do students care about? When you see them in the hall, are they wearing a university sweatshirt or team colors? In the cafeteria, do you see them in a shirt with the logo of a band that you or your own children like? Find small starting places to build your relationships. Getting on their level and being curious about their interests allows a starting point for dialogue, which can blossom into a therapeutic alliance.

Risk Sharing Yourself and Who You Are

Strategic and appropriate self-disclosure makes you real to young persons who pay far more attention to how you act and who you are rather than what you say. Counselors receive extensive training in self-disclosure and are able to practice these skills under supervision, but teachers, staff, and administrators may feel awkward, uncomfortable, or vulnerable making self-disclosures. Even a brief training can help others gain a degree of comfort and practice talking about themselves with difficult students. Good topics include revealing what they like, what they succeeded at, what they are not good at. What teams do they root for? What foods do they like? How about music, bands, cars, movies? These tidbits need not be major disclosures, but each interaction forms another strand of potential relationship, another possible connection that starts the process of reducing a student's isolation, anger, and loneliness.

Discomfort, Frustration, Anger, and Even Fear Are Appropriate Reactions to Feel

Students with behavioral problems can be frustrating, aggravating, difficult to work with, and hard to like. Daunting to engage, they are often intimidating, menacing, or scary to peers and teachers alike. Accepting your own discomfort and validating teachers' discomfort is a solid starting point. Many of these students are unaware of the impact they have on people, or they revel in the negative attention. When their behavior alienates others, it contributes to more isolation, anger, sadness, and withdrawal. We are entitled to our anger, but only at a student's behavior, never the personhood of the student. Interactions with students who are depressed, despondent, or who might be suffering from a self-destructive eating disorder can leave anyone feeling inadequate, unsure, and concerned about the possibility of self-injury or suicide. Have we done the right thing? Helped enough in ways that were helpful? Uncertainty, guilt, and worry are normal reactions. They are a part of working with at-risk students.

Hunger and Homelessness

Hunger and homelessness are chronic stressors for growing numbers of students and their families. Concentrating in math class may be impossible when you are hungry. Accepting a verbal reprimand from a teacher without lashing out may be hard if you are living in a car or have shuffled from couch to couch in the homes of friends and relatives. Does the school district need to develop contingency plans to help manage the emotional trauma of being homeless while at the same time helping with shelter, food, clothing, and hygiene? Loss of school and attendance records is a major challenge for homeless families.

Special Developmental Emphases With Students

Depending on work setting, different types of interventions may be necessary, based on the developmental stage of students. For elementary students, play therapy techniques are highly effective and can be adapted for use by teachers in the classroom and by parents at home. Every elementary school should have a playroom or special area where students can retreat to play through stressful experiences and difficult feelings. Time alone in a playroom or with a counselor teaches students the helpfulness of disengagement without the punitive aspects of a typical time-out. It teaches responsibility and pride in the ability to self-regulate emotions. The benefits of play therapy can be woven across curricula and used when developing functional behavioral plans (M. Schmidt, 2010). There are a number of books filled with techniques and ideas for working with students who do not respond to traditional approaches (e.g., Gil, 2012; Schaefer & Drewes, 2011; Shelby & Campos, 2011). If negative punishment measures such as time-outs are the only option, be mindful that longer time-outs are not always better (Donaldson, Vollmer, Yakich, & Van Camp, 2013). Many times, 5 minutes is all that is needed to allow the student to process what is going on and emotionally self-regulate.

For students in middle school, transitioning from the relative safety of an elementary school to a middle school can be harrowing. Bullying is commonplace and is likely to be a major issue as students begin to experiment with their physical and psychological power. Victims and bystanders often share experiences that are characterized by a full range of traumatic psychological and physiological reactions that follow many of them into later life (Janson, Carney, Hazler, & Oh, 2009; Janson & Hazler, 2004). Bullies, like their victims, are also more likely to experience future relationship problems and a past history of bullying is associated with later criminal behavior (Luukkonen, Riala, Hakko, & Räsänen, 2011). Counseling interventions that provide a comprehensive evaluation and are personalized to the concerns presented are most effective when working with the students and their families (Orpinas & Horne, 2006).

The predictable struggles of adolescence can be magnified by traumatic experiences from childhood that may reemerge in high school. Students may self-medicate with alcohol or other drugs or engage in risky sexual practices. When social skills are poorly developed, compensatory isolation, loneliness, self-injurious behaviors, aggression, and other severe behaviors may emerge. Teachers can help to identify students who would benefit from some kind of training in communication, assertiveness, problem solving, and anxiety or anger management. Teaching self-regulation and appropriate emotional reactivity can encourage long-term prosocial behavior across the lifespan (Carlo, Crockett, Wolff, & Beal, 2012).

Counseling Interventions That Help Teachers

Work closely with teachers to identify students at-risk for severe behaviors to lay the groundwork for preventive action. Again, rating scales and checklists can help identify patterns and symptoms and form a basis for discussion. When crises arise, you will already have in place the kind of relationships with teaching colleagues that are necessary for effective systemic interventions.

Make Time to Build Relationships

When teachers believe in a student, against the odds, the possibility of changing that student's behavior improves exponentially. When students lack positive relationships with teachers, students tend to respond to negative expectations. When a disruption occurs in class, returning to the lecture may be an effective way of calming down the rest of the students after the incident. However, when problems arise repeatedly, teachers must decide whether to ignore the issues, address a student privately, or devote class time to processing the issues. Severe behaviors affect the learning of everyone in the room. Although class time taken away from learning content material may be worrisome, we know that the most effective learning includes feelings as well as cognitive material (Rogers, Lyon, & Tausch, 2014). These types of learning have a place in classroom life.

Use the Same Hallway Techniques as Counselors

Teachers who are popular with students, who seem to have the least trouble managing lunch period in the cafeteria, or who give the fewest number of detentions are often teachers who have taken the time to form relationships with students outside of the classroom. Teacher–student relationships in classroom settings can be limited, but in the hallways, there is freedom to interact more openly as people. The most effective way to enhance relationships with students may be to take full advantage of the dozens of spontaneous interactions in hallways and chance encounters in cafeterias, the playground, playing fields, and other areas outside the classroom or office (Hazler, 1998).

Share Tricks of the Trade

Teachers may say, "I'm a teacher, not a counselor!" but teaching is the most ancient of helping professions. Counseling techniques and relationship-building can be taught to anyone willing to learn and can be highly effective when used by teachers. There is a personal incentive involved as well: Many teachers who learn and apply these skills report that their own relationships, self-confidence, and self-image improve (Kottler & Kottler, 2007). That is a significant payoff for them and a good use of your time!

Be Concrete and Predictable!

A predictable routine is essential for emotionally volatile students, and interventions as simple as using a calendar with events and requirements clearly written out can help provide structure. Straightforward, positive language may be the best way to communicate with students who have severe behavior issues. Humorous sarcasm is often lost on these students and is frequently misinterpreted. Here is an effective technique to suggest to teachers to improve communication. Have students repeat back to you what you have said to them, to make certain they understand. If you find yourself getting frustrated, stop and ask what the student is hearing. What they may be hearing may have little to do with what you were trying to say.

Touch Carefully, and Then Only in the Context of Affirmation

Share your knowledge about appropriate touch with teachers. It is not prudent to touch students without first having built a solid relationship. An affirming pat on the back or light touch on the forearm may be rejected; grabbing a student's arm, as a teacher may do with a younger child or even with an adolescent, may earn them a punch. Students who have been traumatized; sexually, physically, and emotionally abused; or placed in foster care may react violently to physical contact. Within the context of their experiences, this reaction may be appropriate. Don't assume!

Help Teachers Teach as They Are

It takes courage for teachers to stand up in front of a classroom and be themselves. It takes genuineness, openness, and a willingness to be vulnerable as a person that many of us understandably fear (Rogers et al., 2014). Addressing our defensiveness, our inadequacies, and our avoidance can make it easier to form positive relationships with difficult students once they realize that we, too, are far from perfect. Developing a clear teaching philosophy that embraces imperfection as well as achievement can also help us achieve our own potential, personally and professionally. Help teachers support each other by setting time aside to develop these beliefs more formally. A clear teaching philosophy should also include beliefs and biases about severe behavior and how to respond to students.

Support Beleaguered Teachers

It is not uncommon for teachers to have more than one student in a class with severe behaviors of differing types. These teachers often feel overwhelmed and unsupported. Your encouragement, professional expertise, and helpful techniques can turn a hopeless morning into a day with possibilities. Sometimes, placing a college student interested in service learning in the classroom can provide needed extra support.

Help Teachers Support Each Other

Organize regular gatherings that connect teachers with you and with each other in ways that enhance professional growth and development. Informal gatherings can be facilitated by the participants taking turns and by providing opportunities to debrief, brainstorm, and share ideas and techniques. It is also an opportunity to keep tabs on difficult students and their progress. An informal brown-bag lunch or short meeting can pay large dividends by building a sense of collegiality and decreasing feelings of isolation. These gatherings should be used for personal and professional support, not administrative tasks and agendas. Separate inservice trainings can give teachers opportunities to learn and practice crisis resolution skills, behavioral assessment, peer mediation, and alternative ways of resolving interpersonal differences. Some in-services may qualify for continuing education credits, making the time invested serve a dual purpose.

The Payoff for Forming Closer Relationships With Difficult Students May Not Be Academic

Teachers who build positive relationships with difficult students may not see advancement in academic classroom work, though behavior might improve. What the relationship can achieve is to improve quality of life, self-esteem, and sense of inclusion, all of which may have solid future payoffs. Students may not be able to form a positive school identity without some degree of academic success, but without the relationship connection that keeps difficult students engaged, academics are not likely to even appear on the radar.

Be Content With Less Than Perfection

Behavioral change is a painstakingly slow process for most of us. This is particularly true for a student with behavioral problems who has had a long history of negative reinforcement and a failure identity or "bad guy" reputation (better than no identity!). Look for slight improvements in attitude, interactions with peers, and in the way he or she relates to you. Small decreases in intensity, frequency, and duration of behavior represent solid progress. Students who are able to sit in class, rather than disrupt it, or participate in some minor way instead of looking at their hands for an hour have achieved an enormous success.

Avoid Reviewing Past Failures

The memory of past failures burns in our hearts and minds; we do not forget failure. Reminding students of their past mistakes is a counter-productive strategy. When not reacting defensively, most troubled students focus on negatives and pronounce harsher judgments on themselves than do adults. It is better to remind them of past successes. Even angry or disheartened students ready to give up and drop out in their junior year have successfully completed 10 grades. That is a lot more success than failure.

Special Treatment

Is a teacher willing to negotiate varying timelines, passing scores, or quiet places to take exams for students with behavioral problems? Where should students sit? Where can students go if they need to calm down? Will a student need a break before class ends? This can often be quietly accomplished by asking the student to run an errand. These likely challenges can be anticipated; however, teachers sometimes worry how others will view the appearance of special treatment for those students who "do not deserve it." These issues only apply if students are in competition with each other. In a school that encourages every student to do his or her personal best, providing extra consideration for those who need it is a community responsibility. Some students need little support from a teacher to work hard and excel. Others need more help and support to hang on. Providing the support that students need to thrive will model caring, consideration, and kindness. It also helps develop students' skills in negotiating (vs. "lawyering") to obtain what they need.

Impact of Assignments

Certain assignments that involve talking or writing about family and family experiences can be triggers for severe behavior. Students in foster care, or who have been abused or traumatized at home, often react by withdrawing or acting out. Assignments relating to personal experiences should be carefully considered for their impact on these students.

Meet the Student Wherever He or She Is

Reassure teachers that not liking a difficult student or being afraid of that student is a normal reaction. These are often the hardest students to reach. They may be violent, aggressive, anxious, isolated, indifferent, withdrawn, or depressed. Help make a realistic appraisal of any threat: safety comes first. Help teachers understand a student's context and put the student's behavior in perspective. Coming back to school from a suspension can create major problems for both teacher and student; these events are seldom well planned or structured by the system. As a professional school counselor, you are trained to anticipate these bumps in the road, putting you in the unique position of being able to advocate for students and support teachers at the same time.

Become a "Windtalker"

During World War II, Native Americans who spoke Navajo played a key role in transmitting information by talking in their unique language. Help teachers become *Windtalkers* by developing their own special language or code to communicate with difficult students. "Codes" can be used to communicate to students when to get back on task and used by students to signal when a time-out is needed. Signals can be discrete messages expressed in words or nonverbally that are unique and private to the two individuals. Just having such a code helps build a positive relationship.

Identify Hot Buttons

Many students have a marvelous ability to ferret out and push our hot buttons. Swearing or abusive language sends some teachers spiraling while others will have little or no reaction, leaving them freer to offer the student a choice: amend the behavior or deal with the consequences. Identifying and managing areas of personal reactivity reduces vulnerability and adds a measure of control, increasing response options for teachers.

Help Teachers Understand the Impact of Medications

Medications may cause students to fall asleep during class, suffer from reduced impulse control, or constantly feel irritated and angry. Ritalin is both addictive and overprescribed. Nearly all children improve focus and concentration with Ritalin since it stimulates that part of the brain that regulates impulse control. Prescription drugs used to treat asthma, allergies, epilepsy, depression, anxiety, and other common disorders of childhood and adolescence typically have side effects that include dry mouth, gastric complaints, headaches, stomachaches, bowel complaints, dizziness, sedation, irritability, and confusion (McVoy & Findling, 2013). Sucking on a sugar-free lozenge can help alleviate the discomfort of dry mouth, though the school's rules may prohibit the use of candies. As a counselor, you can help negotiate these issues. The other side of the medication issue is what to look for if a student stops taking prescribed medication. Could that be a contributing factor to behavior?

Counseling Interventions With Administrators and Staff

Many administrators find that their exercise of power is severely limited because they must answer to different groups with competing agendas. However, we also know that an involved and committed principal who is willing to lead by example can be the single most powerful and effective means of moving a school community from disaffection to involvement and connection. Building solid relationships with school administrators can gain you strong allies.

Explain and Promote a Systemic Approach

Solicit ideas and opinions from all constituents before making recommendations. Then develop a clear written plan that explains what you are proposing and why, supported by reasonable goals and objectives. Everyone's role should be detailed, as should some form of outcome measures. Demonstrate the clear advantages of what you propose, including economic advantages, if you can identify them. In practical terms, a school that students look forward to attending is a school with a high attendance rate, and that has real monetary benefits.

Administrators Can Create a Culture of Recognition and Appreciation

Schools characterized by cheerful cooperation, appreciation, and mutual respect are schools that students enjoy attending and places that teachers, staff, and administrators look forward to coming to work. They are the schools where principals know students by name and set policies that foster pride, inclusion, and cooperation. With little or no outlay of resources, administrators can develop programs that provide recognition and mutual appreciation (teacher of the week, most improved student or class, most friendly). There should be a number of awards that focus on relationships so that all students are included, not marginalized further. Time invested in creating a culture of appreciation pays off in better grades, enthusiastic students, better behavior, and fewer financial losses due to absenteeism, vandalism, detentions, and Saturday schools.

Recognize Administrators as Conduits to the School Board and Community at Large

Community resources are not always well coordinated with school resources. Administrators are ideally positioned to identify opportunities and make outside connections. These links can support your efforts and help students to learn new skills and competencies, develop their creativity, and enhance their physical well-being, particularly after school, when many students are on their own until their parents get home at 7 p.m. or 8 p.m.

Include Staff

Secretaries, office managers, support staff, cafeteria workers, and custodial staff can play important supportive roles in helping students and parents feel welcome and included. Involving these essential members of the school community in your trainings and activities help them react to severe behaviors in positive ways that provide understanding and avoid negative reinforcement. Inclusion and increased job satisfaction help make their school day more productive and enjoyable as well.

Disciplinary Codes

Educational discipline should focus on how to help students learn, negotiate, and have consequences that are logically connected to the offense (Mackenzie & Stanzione, 2010; Webster-Stratton, Reid, & Hammond, 2004). Harsh penalties and excessive rules actually reduce students' level of responsibility. Suspension and expulsion often serve as negative reinforcements for students. Sometimes a suspension can help break a student's cycle of behaviors. But more often than not, suspension serves to separate students from the school community and further isolate them. Suspensions also may be welcomed by students as legalized truancy. In-school consequences are always preferable to out-of-school consequences. Reviewing your school's discipline plan to ensure that it is educational rather than punitive and relies on consequences rather than punishment should top your agenda.

Dealing With Resistance

Like students with severe behaviors, other individuals in the system may have little hope that the future will be better. A teacher may say, "Don't waste your breath. Things around here never change." An administrator may tell you, "Sorry, there's nothing I can do." Students will look at you skeptically: "Yeah, riiiiiiiight." When faced with resistance, model qualities you want others to model for students: optimism, patience, understanding, openness, affirmation, a group ethic, and willingness to cooperate and negotiate. When students with severe behavioral problems cannot see a positive future for themselves, there is little motivation to listen to you or follow rules. Help them create a positive vision of the future by forging relationships in noncrisis times.

Corporal Punishment

Corporal punishment and harsh discipline are not effective in managing severe behaviors, though a number of school districts in the United States still use paddling (Dupper & Dingus, 2008; Han, 2011). You may have to address beliefs about discipline and corporal punishment with administrators and teachers and offer creative alternatives to parents, countering myths about spanking and corporal punishment. When constructing this conversation, it is important to take into consideration the institutional culture of the school and the cultural and religious beliefs of the parents and guardians.

Do Not Reinvent the Wheel!

Make connections with professionals in the community who can support your efforts. Invite educators from local colleges or universities to talk about suicide, sexuality, and violence. Make use of undergraduates in the fields of family studies, sociology, social work, and psychology who are looking for service learning opportunities. See if graduate programs may be willing to place practicum and internship students with you.

Counseling Interventions With Parents and Caregivers

Get parents on board! Behavioral change starts at home, so let parents do their share. Show them how to get the job done. Contact with parents prior to a behavioral crisis helps to prevent the relationship from turning adversarial when severe behavior erupts. Parents are a vital link in the process of managing severe behavior, and it is unlikely that interventions will succeed without them. Make sure parents hear from you when things go right, not just during a crisis!

Stress Calm, Assertive, Consistent Responses to Difficult Behavior

Clarity is important. Help parents avoid sarcasm and learn to state what they expect directly and calmly. If there are rules to be followed and chores to be done, the list should be posted in writing in a prominent place. Make sure that parents are prepared for the realities of slow change (their own as well as their child's). It is hard for exhausted parents to ignore negative behaviors and push themselves to develop creative learning consequences rather than punishment. Likewise, good behavior is often ignored, or not rewarded, and consistency seems elusive when parents are overwhelmed with work and dealing with their children and/or each other. Sometimes it is just easier to ignore behaviors that are inappropriate, dangerous, or aggressive. Punishment then tends to become arbitrary and dependent on the parents' mood, not on the child's behavior. Inconsistent parenting styles, or parenting styles that are overindulgent or extremely authoritarian, can create chaos in the lives of children. Communication patterns based on screaming, yelling, nagging, and threats foster oppositional and defiant behaviors. Corporal punishment often simply aggravates the severity and frequency of negative behaviors. The primary cause of treatment failure occurs when parents abandon the treatment plan too soon and do not stay the course of treatment (Allen & Warzak, 2000).

Help Parents and Caregivers Model the Behaviors They Want to See

Help parents understand the eventual payoff for ignoring bad behavior and modeling kindness, cooperation, and patience in the face of rudeness, defiance, and disobedience. With younger children who are having problems self-regulating their aggressive behavior, only nonviolent videos, games, and television programs should be permitted. To see positive change in young people, strive to promote openness and encourage individualized growth through empathy and genuineness (Bjerke, 2010; Gatongi, 2007). If the adults in the household are separated or divorced or have ended a relationship, advise them to not criticize their ex-partner in front of the children. They should avoid fighting in front of their children, and practice offering choices with well-thought-out consequences for negative behaviors.

Who's In Charge Here?

Parents often forget that they are the adults in a household. Students' behaviors at home often lead to fights between parents or between parents and teachers. The child who is "out of control" at home is all too often the one who is really running the show. Tip parents off that if they find themselves fighting over a child's behavior, they should stop and consider what is really happening. Once parents and teachers start arguing, the focus shifts off the student, who is often then "in the clear."

Let the Past Stay in the Past

Keep the focus in the present and future. Children are all too well aware of their failures and shortcomings, especially children with behavioral problems. When parents focus on failure, children become discouraged. Are parents optimistic about their child's future? When parents are not optimistic, that child is more likely to meet their negative expectation.

Create Consequences That Are Logical, Reasonable, Respectful and Connected to Behavior, Not Grades

With many students, a poor grade is a motivator to do better. Parental supports, such as assigned study times and mild restrictions can be effective in improving behavior and school performance. However, with children with severe behaviors, grades are an expected source of failure, and multiple consequences can create a cycle of increasing opposition or withdrawal and isolation. Consequences should be well understood by students in advance and should not be piggybacked. An "F" in English should not be compounded by adding social restrictions, grounding, removal of privileges, and other, harsher punishments. When too many consequences pile up, they lead to discouragement, and children simply give up. Most parents underestimate the tremendous emotional and social pressure on any child with multiple academic deficits. The consequences of a failure identity at school extend well beyond a poor grade.

Create Opportunities for Success

Work with parents to create situations in which their children can experience success at least two or three times a day. A simple task, properly executed—such as getting home on time, knowing the difference between one tool and another when helping with a project—each tiny success contributes to building self-esteem and reducing severe behavior. Do family members know how to express appreciation for each other? Do parents reward good behavior? Checklists and specific instructions about how to express appreciation and give encouragement are easily found in most counseling texts.

Create Immediate Symptom Relief at Home

Practice being indulgent and authoritative even when it seems difficult (Garcia & Gracia, 2009). When a student comes home with a failing grade and an attitude to go with it, take that child out for a favored excursion and provide empathy and support. Do not argue with an angry adolescent! Disengage from them, hard as that might be. Let them go to their rooms and stew over their predicament (which is theirs, not yours!). Give choices, and avoid ultimatums that only serve to escalate the level of tension. Whatever might be the parent's pattern of behavior, suggest a change and things will most likely improve (McMahon & Forehand,

2003). When parents break their pattern of interaction by acting positively and unexpectedly, children are often astonished and must change their own behavior to compensate.

Summary/Conclusion

A systemic process may be slow and often frustrating to implement, considering the logistics involved, but the changes accomplished will be more permanent and accepted by more people than changes established by harsh disciplinary policies or the frequent use of suspensions and expulsions. Finally, even as you care for others and struggle to create systemic change for students, families, schools, and community, make sure that you do not leave yourself out of the equation. Make certain your needs are met, that you have adequate peer supervision and support, and good nutrition, exercise, and adequate rest. The best example you can set for students with severe behavioral problems is the example of a satisfying and productive life, lived in close connection with others who care for you as you care for them.

CHAPTER 51

Counseling High-Functioning Students With Autism Spectrum Disorder

Henry L. Harris

Preview

Autism spectrum disorder (ASD) is a neurodevelopmental disorder that involves mild to severe deficits in a person's ability to communicate and socially interact with others. ASD is significantly more common in boys than in girls and affects all racial and ethnic groups regardless of socioeconomic level. ASD may develop before age 3 years and early diagnosis is an essential step to begin the intervention process. Individuals who have been diagnosed with ASD but who do not have intellectual disabilities are often referred to as having high-functioning autism (HFASD; Klin, Pauls, Schultz, & Volkmar, 2005). Currently there is no known specific cause of ASD nor is there a cure. In this chapter, I provide an overview of ASD, characteristics of students with HFASD, assessment and diagnostic information, suggestions for professional school counselors, and a list of resources.

Autism spectrum disorder (ASD) is a neurodevelopmental disorder that was at one time considered a rare condition that occurred in only one out of 2,500 persons (Matson & Kozlowski, 2011). Unfortunately, the rates of autism have drastically increased across multiple racial and ethnic groups. For example, since 2007 there has been a 110% increase in the diagnosis for Hispanic children, 91% increase for non-Hispanic Black children, and a 70% increase for non-Hispanic White children (Centers for Disease Control [CDC], 2012b); The most recent estimates from the CDC (2014a) have further indicated that for every 68 children, one individual is diagnosed with ASD. There is also a significant gender gap because the ASD rate is nearly five times higher in boys than girls (one in 42 boys compared to one in 189 girls). In addition, non-Hispanic White children are 50% more likely to be identified with ASD than Hispanic children and are 30% more likely to receive this diagnosis than non-Hispanic Black children (CDC, 2014a).

In the current *Diagnostic and Statistical Manual of Mental Disorders* (DSM-5; American Psychiatric Association [APA], 2013), there were significant revisions made to this disorder. First, the term was changed from *autistic disorder* to *autism spectrum disorder*. Next, Asperger's disorder, childhood disintegrative disorder (CDD), Rett's disorder, and pervasive development disorder—not otherwise specified (PDD-NOS) were eliminated and combined into one category, ASD. According to Gensler (2012), collapsing the disorders will impact many families and individuals as they will have to deal with the autism label that previously may not have specifically applied to them. Gensler further elaborated that the change in terminology would also require insurance companies and school systems to alter systems that align children's diagnosis with reimbursement entitlements and appropriate educational services. In order to meet the new criteria for ASD, the number of symptoms also increased from three to five (Beighley & Matson, 2014).

The majority of children born with ASD require long-term care and services. Estimates suggested that it costs $17,000 more annually to care for a child with ASD compared to one without ASD. If a child with ASD has an intellectual disability, then the cost increases (Lavelle, Weinstein, Newhouse, Kuhithau, & Prosser, 2014). From a national perspective, assuming that 40% of individuals with ASD have an intellectual disability (ID), the national cost of supporting children with ASD in the United States is $61 billion annually. Special education services, different forms of ASD-related therapy, and other indirect costs such as loss of parental wages were the largest contributors to the total costs (Buescher, Cidav, Knapp, & Mandell, 2014). Genetics and early prenatal exposures have been suggested as possible causes. While there is not cure for ASD, with early detection and intensive therapeutic interventions and education, these individuals will have the opportunity to develop skills that will help them reach their potential (Centers for Disease Control, 2014a).

General Characteristics of Autism Spectrum Disorder

ASD is a complex disorder characterized by the development of unusual behaviors in the areas of socialization, communication, and interest and activities before 3 years of age (Heflin & Alaimo, 2007). According to Bregman (2005) "the defining feature of autism is presence of a distinctive impairment in the nature and quality of social and communicative development (influenced by specific biological and environmental circumstances of the individual)" (p. 3). Parents are typically the first to notice autistic symptoms in their child, as they may observe their children not reaching appropriate developmental milestones (see Table 51.1). Jang, Matson, Cervantes, and Konst (2014) discovered in their study of over 1,478 toddlers that parents reported they initially recognized developmental problems in their children at 12–13 months of age. It is also important to note that while racial disparities exist with receipt of the ASD diagnosis, parents reported their first concerns close to the same time, regardless of race.

Children diagnosed with ASD may have difficulty interacting socially with others. From a very early age they may appear aloof and most comfortable when left alone, having little need for interaction with other people. In social settings, children with ASD may respond solely to adults or engage other children in one-sided scripted play in which they direct the action. As they grow older, rather than playing creatively with other children, they may spend their time gathering factual information on narrow topics or ask unusual, personal, and rhetorical questions to attain factual knowledge on a topic of interest (Bregman, 2005).

Some ASD individuals have abnormal communication skills, particularly delayed echolalia whereby they repeat language phrases previously heard months, sometimes years before. They may also speak with an abnormal pitch or volume in their speech, use rote language, and improperly use pronouns in a reverse manner at times referring to themselves in the first person (APA, 2013). Individuals with ASD may fail to orient to another person's voice or use other forms of communication such as gesturing. For example, an individual with ASD who wants something unattainable may take another person by the hand and lead the individual

Table 51.1 Counseling Resources

Autism Internet Modules from OCALI. www.autisminternetmodules.org

Autism Research Institute (ARI), 4182 Adams Avenue, San Diego, CA 92116 (www.autismresearch institute.com)

Autism Society of America, 7910 Woodmont Ave, Suite 300, Bethesda, MD 20814-3067 (www.autism-society.org)

Autism Speaks. http://www.autismspeaks.org/family-services/resource-guide

Center for Autism and Related Disorders (CARD), Corporate Headquarters, 19019 Ventura Blvd. Suite 300, Tarzana, CA 91356 (www.centerforautism.com)

Organization for Autism Research (OAR). www.researchautism.org

National Institute of Neurological Disorders and Stroke (NINDS), 6001 Executive Blvd, Bethesda, MD 20892-9663 (www.ninds.nih.gov)

The Center on Secondary Education for Students with Autism Spectrum Disorders (CSESA). http://csesa.fpg.unc.edu

Treatment and Education of Autistic & Related Communication Handicapped Children (TEACCH)–A Division of the UNC Department of Psychiatry; University of North Carolina at Chapel Hill, Chapel Hill, NC 27599 (www.teacch.com)

Wrightslaw—A legal resource for parents, educators, advocates, and attorneys providing accurate, reliable information about special education law, education law, and advocacy for children with disabilities. (www.wrightslaw.com)

---

to the desired object. This is a nonverbal method used to accomplish an end goal and is also referred to as using another person as a tool because normal communication skills may be lacking (Wetherby & Prizant, 2005).

Individuals with ASD may demonstrate a very narrow range of interest and activities, which limits their ability to reason and use their imagination. They may have unusual attachment to parts of an object rather than the complete object itself. Rather than roll a toy car around the floor, some ASD individuals may spend their time spinning the wheels on the car (Heflin & Alaimo, 2007). Some individuals with ASD also have an obsessive desire for the preservation of sameness and might become abnormally upset when a change is made in an established routine. If a routine change occurs in their schedule, such as taking a different route to school, sometimes these individuals may have temper tantrums until familiar order is restored (APA, 2013). Individuals with ASD may additionally have uncoordinated gross motor or fine motor skill development, be physically overactive or extremely underactive, display signs of distress for reasons others may not understand, and experience sensory integration problems related to certain sounds, noises, or textures of which others may not be aware (APA, 2013; Heflin & Alaimo, 2007; National Education Association [NEA], 2006). Individuals with ASD may also experience problems falling or staying asleep, gastrointestinal problems, and seizures that may be triggered by lack of sleep or high fever (National Institute of Mental Health [NIMH], 2011).

Although ASD is defined by a specific group of behaviors, it is important for professional school counselors to recognize that individuals diagnosed with ASD can act very differently from one another. They may display a combination of the behaviors ranging from mild to very severe. Two students with the same diagnosis may act very differently from one another because of the differences in their development (National Institutes of Child Health & Human Development [NICHD], 2014).

High-Functioning Autism Spectrum Disorder

High-functioning autism spectrum disorder (HFASD) is a label used to describe children who meet the diagnostic criteria for ASD, yet are able to speak and have an average or above-average IQ. They are also able to function close to or above a normal level in society. Individuals with HFASD have impaired social, communication, and imaginative skills associated with difficulties they experience in their social lives (Hiraiwa, 2011). Because of their inability to maintain socially appropriate interactions, they may also become isolated, manipulated, and possibly victimized by their peers (Little, 2001). According to Hiraiwa, (2011), approximately 70% of HFASD children experience bullying while in elementary or middle school. Because this bullying is often not witnessed, it is sometimes challenging to find out essential details of the actual situation.

The ability to accurately perceive social events and predict social behaviors in others is required for individuals who are HFASD to actively participate and become engaged in social situations. When such social communication skills are absent, these individuals may experience abnormal levels of anxiety and stress, which contributes to them experiencing frequent tantrums, and in some circumstances withdrawal or anger (Myles, 2003). Such behaviors are sometimes misinterpreted as defiant and willful rather than resulting from challenges to self-regulation (Laurent & Rubin, 2004).

Individuals with HFASD are extremely literal in their interpretations and often adhere rigidly to routine and order. When routine and order is changed, they may experience abnormal levels of discomfort that others may fail to understand. Individuals with HFASD also may become distracted before completing tasks and have difficulties transitioning between activities. Students with HFASD may be performing academically at or above their grade level in some or all of their subjects, yet their unusual behavioral mannerisms often interfere with their progress (Zager & Shamow, 2005). During situations of sensory overload, which could result from being in a class with too many students, walking down a crowded hallway, eating lunch in a noisy cafeteria, or having too many objects in a classroom setting (e.g., pictures on the wall), students with HFASD may not be able to self-regulate their sensory experiences. As a result, they may have a strong emotional reaction, appearing stressed or withdrawn (Laurent & Rubin, 2004). As Gutstein (2000) succinctly phrased it,

> the high functioning child with autism specializes in studying social relationships in a universe where the sheer amount of noise invading his brain constantly threatens to overwhelm him. He learns to specialize in avoiding chaos, by shutting out and avoiding most elements of variability and novelty. Instead he focuses on the non-changing aspects of his environment. Elements that remain the same provide him with the greatest experience of meaning and relation. He is obsessed by his search for stable patterns and unchanging relationships in his social universe like the immutable laws of mathematics, the unvarying progression of video games and other predictable sequences that occurs the same way over and over. He focuses on an interaction style which, for him, is a matter of survival. The only means he has for enjoying social encounters is to discover ways to predict and or control social events. Each time he participates in an interaction that progresses in a predictable manner is a victory for science. (pp. 37–38)

Assessment and Diagnosis

An accurate assessment of autism is imperative and should be completed as early as possible because this is the first step in developing an intervention plan (Van Bourgondien, 1996). It is also significant because some research has demonstrated that intensive behavioral therapy during preschool years can significantly improve language and cognitive skills of individuals with ASD (NIMH, 2011). Physicians play a critical role in this process because from birth to age 3 years they are primarily the only professionals that have routine contact with children before they enter school. While most physicians recognize the value of early assessment and intervention, for a variety of reasons many have a difficult time identifying children with developmental delays and disorders (Gabovitch & Wiseman, 2005). During office visits, both physicians and parents have the opportunity to monitor the child's physical, social, emotional, and cognitive development through developmental screening. This developmental screening identifies important milestones that children should accomplish at specific ages. Given the variation in how each child develops, some observed differences may indicate only a mild delay while other differences may indicate more serious concerns that should be addressed (Gabovitch & Wiseman, 2005).

When significant developmental delays are observed, a more formalized assessment is needed. The *Autism Diagnostic Observation Schedule* (ADOS; Lord, Rutter, DiLavore, & Risi, 2001), *Childhood Autism Rating Scale* (CARS; Schopler, Reichler, & Renner, 1988), and *TEACCH Transition Assessment Profile* (TTAP; Mesibov, Thomas, Chapman, & Schopler, 2007) are useful screening tools that require special training to administer and interpret. The *Autism Behavioral Checklist* (ABC; Krug, Arick, & Almond, 1980), the *Battelle Developmental Inventory, Second Edition* (BDI-2; Newborg, 2005), the *Modified Checklist for Autism in Toddlers* (M-CHAT; Robins, Fein, Barton, & Green, 2001), the *Social Responsiveness Scale* (SRS; Constantino, 2005), and the *Social Communication Questionnaire* (SCQ; Rutter, Bailey, & Lord, 2003) are additional screening tools that could be completed by parents and/or teachers.

Once the assessment is complete and a diagnosis made, the next phase of development is to create a treatment plan with a group of professionals knowledgeable about autism, as this could impact the overall process (Van Bourgondien & Mesibov, 1989). Because of the various services the child may need, professionals from multiple backgrounds could be helpful. This multidisciplinary assessment team may include some or all of the following professionals:

- *Developmental pediatrician*—Has specific training in the evaluation and care of children with developmental delays including autism spectrum disorders. May also help to locate resources for families within each community to provide additional support.
- *Child psychiatrist*—A medical doctor may be initially involved in the diagnosis and if needed can prescribe medication and provide help in other areas concerning behavior emotions and social relationships.
- *Psychologist*—Specializes in understanding the nature and impact of developmental disabilities including autism spectrum disorders. May perform psychological assessments and help with behavior modification planning and social skills training.
- *Occupational therapist*—Helps clients improve coordination of basic motor functions and reasoning skills that will help them accomplish common daily-living tasks such as dressing and eating; may also work on sensory integration.

- *Physical therapist*—Helps to improve the use of bones, muscles, joints, and nerves to develop muscle strength, coordination, and motor skills.
- *Speech–language pathologist*—Involved in the improvement of communication skills including speech and language.
- *Social worker*—May provide counseling services or act as case manager helping to arrange services for the family as needed (Autism Society of America, 2011).
- *Licensed professional counselor*—May provide social skills training to the individual or counseling to family members and also serve as a case manager.
- *Chiropractor*—Can provide series of chiropractic adjustments such as upper cervical adjustment and cranial sacral therapy.
- *Nutritionist*—Can monitor the child's nutritional concerns by evaluating feeding history, dietary intake, and suggest blood tests that reflect nutritional status to determine whether the child has nutritional deficiencies.
- *School teacher*—Responsible for helping develop and monitor the Individualized Education Program (IEP) for children in the school setting. Should have knowledge of ASD and training through Treatment & Education of Autistic and Related Communication Handicapped Children (TEACCH) organization.
- *Professional school counselor*—Can be an important voice of support for children with ASD and their families. Should attend IEP meetings, provide social-skills training and counseling services to students with ASD, and consult with other members of the team when necessary to help develop functioning social, emotional, and communication skills in the school setting.
- *School principal*—Responsible for creating a safe behavioral and learning environment for all children. Essential that they have an understanding of ASD and how HFASD students are impacted by the school environment. They can have an influential role helping develop an appropriate curriculum.

Parents and other professionals must work collaboratively and serve the best interests of the child. Opening lines of communication is paramount to monitor the child's progress. Parents must keep themselves informed about their child's disability, be organized, and always prepared to consult with members of the assessment team (Autism Society of America, 2011).

Suggestions for Professional School Counselors

Students with HFASD bring unique needs to the school setting, and there are a number of interventions that professional school counselors may provide to help them reach their maximum potential. Professional school counselors should first develop an awareness about their personal feelings and attitudes toward HFASD students and their families. Furthermore, professional school counselors should attain sufficient knowledge about ASD and the characteristics associated with HFASD. When knowledge about HFASD is lacking, professional school counselors are advised to attend conferences and workshops, read literature, and consult more experienced professionals. If professional school counselors discover themselves harboring negative attitudes toward students with HFASD and their families, they should explore reasons why the attitudes exist and attempt to resolve them.

Counseling HFASD Students

There are a number of counseling interventions that professional school counselors may use when working with HFASD students, and for this to be effective they must take into consideration the unique characteristics of each HFASD student. Even though many HFASD students perform well academically, issues related to anxiety, isolation, and depression many need to be addressed (Zager & Shamow, 2005). To confront anxiety, professional school counselors could use a variety of modified cognitive behavioral techniques such as guided imagery, relaxation, and modeling. For example, the anxiety experienced in some students with HFASD may be decreased by helping them become aware of what causes their anxiety and then teaching them appropriate relaxation techniques such as deep breathing. A modified structured version of guided imagery focusing on positive things they enjoy rather than things they fear may also help. Music therapy may also be a useful avenue for professional school counselors to explore (Stahmer, Collings, & Palinkas, 2005). Self-management consists of designed activities for students to maintain or change their own behavior. Wilkinson (2008) suggested using this as a strategy to help HFASD students practice and learn classroom rules and procedures that most of their peers learn intuitively.

Professional school counselors should consider using applied behavioral analysis (ABA) with some students with HFASD. The first step in ABA is to identify the behavior that needs to be changed. Once the behavior is identified, appropriate strategies should then be developed that will alter the behavior. During this time, the professional school counselor may provide reinforcements to elicit and maintain desired behavior. When an intervention is not successful, another technique is developed (Schoen, 2003). ABA also may be used by school psychologists and school social workers working with students with HFASD.

Video modeling is another technique that has been effective in teaching appropriate social behaviors to children with ASD. This approach involves videotaping another student performing the desired behaviors. The videotape is then shown repeatedly to the student that desires the skill (Carothers & Taylor, 2004). There are three basic steps needed to implement video modeling for HFASD students and the steps include: 1) define and identify the target skill; 2) determine the type of media to use (i.e., video DVD or iPad) and produce video; and 3) implement the video modeling intervention (Ganz, Earles-Vollrath, & Cook, 2011). Professional school counselors are encouraged to have the student role-play the newly observed behavior as a method of strengthening the new observation. It may also be helpful for the professional school counselor to participate by modeling the observed videotaped behavior for the student and then guide the student in using the desired behavior. Professional school counselors may further assist students with HFASD by (a) seeking a buddy with good social and communication skills who might accompany them to some less structured social situations; (b) helping them to be placed in classes that are interesting to them; (c) helping them create a daily schedule for school that should be written in a way that helps the child anticipate changes and remain calm when those changes occur; (d) helping HFASD develop appropriate skills to deal with impulsive behaviors that may be perceived as manipulative; and (e) providing individual counseling using a variety of approaches to help develop social skills and concrete problem solving (TEACCH Autism Program, 2014).

Integrated Play Group

Children who develop normally will typically engage in stimulating play that is imaginative, socially interactive, and pleasing. Unfortunately, many children with ASD do not engage in this type of play. Therefore integrated play groups (IPGs) could be used with children aged 3 to 11 years to decrease social isolation and improve social and symbolic play skills (Wolfberg, 2009). IPG consists of guides, expert players, and novice players. The guides are competent group leaders, the expert members are peers with good social, communication, and imaginative skills, and the novice players are children with ASD. The groups ordinarily consist of three to five members with a higher ratio of experts to novices, meet twice per week from 30 minutes to an hour, and are highly structured and follow consistent routines (Lantz, Nelson, & Loftin, 2004).

IPG has three levels of group leader support. Level one is modeled and directed play. During this time, the group leader directs the group interaction. Verbal guidance is the second level of support where the group interaction is developed from a distance. During the last level of support, the group leader does not interact with the children as they play, but is available for supervision (Lantz et al., 2004). According to Wolfberg (2003), children with ASD who have experienced IPG have improved their social language skills, ability to sustain social interactions, the quality of their play, and developed friendships.

Medication

Behavioral problems that keep individuals with ASD from effectively functioning at home or school—such as aggression, severe tantrums, and self-injurious behavior—are often addressed using medications developed to treat similar symptoms in other disorders. Unfortunately, many of these medications have not been officially approved for use in children, yet they are prescribed by the doctor as needed. The doctor prescribing the medication should have experience working with individuals with ASD, prescribe the lowest, most effective dose possible, and closely monitor the child while on the medication. Parents should also be aware of the possible side effects and realize that individuals with ASD may respond to medications differently than normally developing children. If a child is taking prescription medication, parents must consider whether school officials should be made aware of this. It is interesting to note that one small ($n = 13$) study by Andari et al. (2010) discovered that oxytocin had a positive effect on the social interaction skills of children with ASD, which suggested a therapeutic potential for this drug.

Consulting With Parents

Parental involvement has been identified as a key component in building a strong and effective educational experience for children with disabilities (Stoner et al., 2005). The Individuals with Disabilities Education Improvement Act of 2004 (IDEA) and No Child Left Behind Act of 2001 (NCLB) mandate that parents of children with disabilities have the legal right to be involved in aspects of their child's education. The interaction between parents and educational professionals, however, is often poorly organized and fragmented. The level of cooperation is also damaged sometimes because of the frustration, tension, and confusion created, and it ultimately affects the delivery of services and the well-being of the students being served (Lake & Billingsley, 2000).

When consulting with parents of children with ASD, professional school counselors should attempt to establish and build trust by genuinely listening to parental concerns, respecting their views, and following up on promises made. They should also strive to help parents understand the Individualized Education Program and prepare them for IEP meetings by discussing procedures, identifying members on the IEP team, and, if needed, attempting to make procedural changes that will equalize the role of all team members present at such meetings. Professional school counselors should also provide parents with information concerning other related services, make them aware of their legal rights, and develop a line of communication that recognizes and values their expertise as parents. Parents are empowered when educators value, recognize, and learn from parental expertise related to their child with ASD (Stoner et al., 2005).

Consulting With Teachers

When consulting with teachers on issues concerning students with HFASD, professional school counselors may find it helpful to follow guidelines outlined by the organization Treatment & Education of Autistic and Related Communication Handicapped Children (TEACCH). Hogan (2014) suggested placing high-functioning students with ASD in regular classrooms in which their classes are interesting to them and relate to their strengths. Their desk area should also be neatly organized and without clutter, because this could be distracting. Also, when directions are written on a test, it might prove beneficial if the directions are highlighted or bolded (NEA, 2006; Swanson, 2005).

If students are assisted by an individual aide, the aide should be knowledgeable about ASD and receive specific training regarding high-functioning autism. Knowledgeable professional school counselors may provide some of this training. The aide should not be considered a babysitter and is most useful to the student when assistance is provided throughout the day in developing and implementing the student's structure such as through developing schedules, modifying assignments, and completing checklists (Hogan, 2014; Swanson, 2005). Professional school counselors should also help teachers understand that because HFASD students often have difficulty processing language, it is helpful to slow down the pace of instruction and keep the language clear, including instructional language. Teachers are encouraged to be clear, brief, and concise about their expectations and even rehearse behaviors for new situations (Zager & Shamow, 2005). Finally, to help other students understand students with HFASD in their class or school, it might prove helpful if professional school counselors provide classroom guidance services explaining some general information about ASD. If needed, professional school counselors should also consult with teachers and help them find ways to effectively discuss ASD with their students.

Summary/Conclusion

The number of children diagnosed with ASD has significantly increased over the years. Many of these children are now students enrolled in public schools with the right to be included in regular classes whenever possible (IDEA, 2004). Professional school counselors are encouraged to become advocates for students with ASD and their families (Mulick & Butter, 2002). Effective advocacy requires accurate knowledge about ASD and associated characteristics, counseling, and psychoeducational interventions. Despite the challenges that many HFASD students encounter, they can be successful if school personnel are provided the appropriate support services. School administrators, professional school counselors, teachers, parents, and other support professionals must all work together to ensure that students with ASD have the opportunity to lead more productive and satisfying lives.

SECTION 7

Special Issues and Populations in School Counseling

CHAPTER 52

Helping Students Acquire Time-Management Skills

Bradley T. Erford

Preview

Developing and applying time-management strategies can help reduce frustration and missed deadlines. Examples of positive strategies, including goal setting, prioritization, development of timelines, action plans, and worksheets for accomplishing these strategies are provided.

Time management is probably a misnomer. We cannot manage time, but we can certainly manage ourselves with respect to time, which involves prioritizing and effectively carrying out the priorities for everyday work, play, and rest.

Symptoms of poor time management can include rushing, vacillation, missed deadlines, and feeling overwhelmed. Over time, poor time management can lead to burnout. Burnout occurs when the individual cannot effectively maintain normal routines or behaviors (see Chapter 59). Psychological symptoms of burnout include apathy, anxiousness, confusion, and noncompletion of tasks. Increased heart rate, altered sleep patterns, and increased blood pressure are physiological symptoms of burnout (Seaward, 2011).

Applying successful problem-solving strategies (e.g., goal setting) can help reduce time-management issues. For example, maintaining an overall 3.0 GPA can only be met by setting short- and long-term goals for each subject. For math, the short-term goal might be to obtain 80% or higher on tests. Short-term steps are needed to achieve the ultimate 80% goal and can include meeting with a study group three times per week or regularly reviewing homework with a checklist for completion. The time-management strategy of prioritization could assist in short-term goal achievement.

Professional school counselors' tasks include asking open-ended questions leading to the identification of both short- and long-term goals. After a goal is identified, the development of an action plan can begin. Progress checks and identifying available assets (e.g., parent or other adults) can increase the likelihood of goal achievement. Although the pace of everyday life has increased, the tested methods of time management remain the same.

Time management can be a learned familial or cultural trait (e.g., acceptance of late arrivals), and some behavior characteristics get in the way of effective time management (e.g.,

---

*Special thanks to Vicki Brooks-McNamara for her outstanding contributions to the first two editions of this chapter.

perfectionism and procrastination; Seaward, 2011). As such, effective management of time is a learned skill, and the keys to overall success revolve around planning and organization. An excellent beginning for student organization would be the purchase of a daily/weekly/monthly planner, and parents and teachers should be included in the student's efforts to use the planner.

Control of Time

Managing daily activities can be made easier by following simple guidelines that involve setting goals and getting organized. The guidelines have a built-in assumption: Success is the desired end result. Success, as referred to in this chapter, encompasses all aspects of life (e.g., school, home, friends).

Set Goals

One must set goals specific to each task or desired accomplishment. Short-term goals are essential for reaching the stated long-term goal. Both short- and long-term goals should be clearly defined with a plan of action and measurable outcomes including (a) *What do I want?* (goal); (b) *How I am going to get there?* (action plan); (c) *How will I know when I get there?* (measurable outcome).

The goal-setting worksheet in Figure 52.1 assists individuals in identifying the long-term goal (LTG; e.g., 3.0 GPA) while establishing short-term goals (STG) with specified action plans (P). Each STG has a measurable outcome (MO), indicating what a successful result is for specific goals. Finally, the summation of each STG's MO leads to LTG successful completion (e.g., attaining a 3.0 GPA).

Getting Organized

Attaining goals involves planning and organizing time. Organizational tips include the following:

1. *Keep a daily/weekly planner.* Write homework assignments and tasks down immediately upon receiving them, and transfer information to a monthly/semester calendar.
2. *Prioritize tasks using the prioritization worksheet* (see Figure 52.2). This worksheet can be used for daily, weekly, monthly, or semester prioritization. In the top section, no order or ranking should occur when listing tasks. Ranking occurs in the ABC Section. Using information from the ABC section, prioritize tasks as follows: *high urgency* with *high importance* (I); *low urgency* with *high importance* (II); *high urgency* with *low importance* (III); and *low urgency* with *low importance* (IV). The last section provides a list with (I) having the highest priority for immediate completion and (IV) the lowest priority for completion. Prioritization errors often occur when enjoyable tasks are ranked as urgent-important (e.g., calling my friend).
3. *Monitor one's use of time for 1 week.* The Time Allocation Worksheet in Figure 52.3 provides a means for recording time spent on individual activities. The right-hand column

(text continues on page 589)

GOAL SETTING

Long-Term Goal (LTG):

To get to the long-term goal (LTG), I must:

Short-Term Goals (STG):

1. _____   3. _____

2. _____   4. _____

My plan (P) for each short-term (STG) to be accomplished:

STG #1 (P)	STG #2 (P)	STG #3 (P)	STG #4 (P)

I will know when I have achieved each STG by this measurable outcome (MO):

STG # 1 _____

STG # 2 _____

STG # 3 _____

STG #4 _____

Figure 52.1. Goal Setting Worksheet.

©2016 by PRO-ED, Inc.   #14017

PRIORITIZATION WORKSHEET

Write down all tasks needing to be completed. Do not worry about order or rank.

1.	6.
2.	7.
3.	8.
4.	9.
5.	10.

ABC Rank Order

Under **Column A,** write the items that *MUST* be done. Under **Column C**, write the items that you would *LIKE* to get done but that are not essential (can wait). Under **Column B**, write all others.

Column A	Column B	Column C
_____	_____	_____
_____	_____	_____
_____	_____	_____
_____	_____	_____
_____	_____	_____

Now organize the list in the *important* versus *urgent* matrix.

		IMPORTANT	
		High Importance	Low Importance
URGENT	High Urgency	I. A. B. C.	III. A. B. C.
	Low Urgency	II. A. B. C.	IV. A. B. C.

Then, begin to work on these tasks in the following order:

    I. (A)   III. (A)
      (B)   (B)
      (C)   (C)

    II. (A)   IV. (A)
      (B)   (B)
      (C)   (C)

Figure 52.2. Prioritization Worksheet.

©2016 by PRO-ED, Inc.   #14017

TIME ALLOCATION WORKSHEET

My Time: Hours Per Day

	Mon	Tue	Wed	Thurs	Fri	Sat	Sun	Total
Sleep:								
School:								
Classes								
Lunch								
Clubs								
Sports								
Friends								
Free								
Dressing:								
School								
Date								
Other								
Study:								
Math								
English								
History								
Science								
Other								
Other:								
Total: 24 hours								

Figure 52.3. Time Allocation Worksheet.

©2016 by PRO-ED, Inc.   #14017

SCHEDULING TIME

Boxing Example (effective for weekends):

8:00–12:00	=	work on term paper (research)
12:00–1:00	=	lunch/exercise
1:00–5:00	=	2 hrs draft writing; other classes 2 hrs
5:00–7:00	=	time with family/dinner
7:00–9:00	=	movies
9:00–10:00	=	relax/bed

Time-Mapping Schedule (Saturday example):

9:00–9:30	=	eat breakfast; gather research materials
9:30–10:00	=	travel to library
10:00–10:30	=	determine how to locate needed reference using the librarian for assistance
10:30–11:00	=	gather first section of paper's research
11:00–11:30	=	take notes; write up outlines/narratives
11:30–12:00	=	organize for next section of research
12:00–12:30	=	gather second section references
12:30–1:00	=	take notes; write up outlines/narratives
1:00–1:30	=	travel home
1:30–2:00	=	lunch
2:00–2:30	=	reward for hard morning in library
2:30–3:00	=	review English
3:00–3:30	=	review science
3:30–4:00	=	math
4:00–	=	relax; dinner; fun with family or friends

Boxing & Time-Mapping Schedule (weekday example for study time):

7:30–3:00	=	classes (if free hour: library research)
3:00–6:00	=	sports/clubs
6:00–7:00	=	dinner
7:00–7:45	=	math homework (most difficult subject)
7:45–8:30	=	English homework
8:30–9:15	=	science homework
9:15–10:00	=	history homework (easiest)

Figure 52.4. Scheduling Time.

©2016 by PRO-ED, Inc. #14017

Table 52.1 Additional Tips for Managing and Scheduling Time

Calculate time needed per assignment.

Record the time it takes to read five pages of the textbook. Use this time as a measure for blocking out time needs by class.

Identify the best time of day for learning (e.g., early morning or early evening).

During each study session, review previous lecture notes or materials. Reread the notes highlighting the important word(s) or ideas. Review the highlighted material for the test.

Take breaks during study time (e.g., every 30 minutes, take a 5-minute break).

Predetermine a stop time for studying. Hold to it. This will provide a short-term goal with a reward at the end.

Break large tasks down into smaller tasks.

Identify the time of day in which you are most productive. Use this time for completing urgent and important tasks.

Let go of attempting low-priority items. Do not stop a high-priority task for a less ranked task.

Each day, review the daily/weekly/monthly/semester planner. Reassess and redirect if necessary.

Learn to speak up. Share with others (especially family) urgent and important tasks and goals with assigned timelines. By knowing these, others can support you in achieving your goals.

summarizes the total hours per week for each activity, while the bottom row summarizes daily totals. Time should only be recorded in half-hour increments. After tallying time-use over a week, a schedule of time can be created to assist with urgent-important task completion.

4. *Schedule time for task completion* (see the scheduling time worksheet in Figure 52.4). After completing the goal setting, prioritization, and time allocation worksheets, development of a schedule can begin. Several methods can be employed (e.g., boxing, time mapping). Table 52.1 provides additional time-management tips.

Table 52.2 (see next page) provides a listing of Web sites and additional information for aid in time management.

Summary/ Conclusion

Effective use and management of time can create opportunities for engaging in pleasurable and fun activities. Through development of positive habits (e.g., using a daily planner), organization can become a reality. Once essential tasks are identified and goals established, the process for attainment becomes a roadmap for success. Clearly, success can occur as a result of careful thought, planning, organization, and effective time management.

Table 52.2 Web Sites and Additional References

http://teacher.scholastic.com/professional/futureteachers/time_management.htm
    Tips for managing and creating effective teaching time

www.wannalearn.com/Academic_Subjects/Study_Skills
    Links to study skills information, videos, books (by age groups) for helping students learn to study

http://www.ucc.vt.edu/academic_support_students/study_skills_information/index.html
    Time scheduling suggestions from Virginia Tech

www.collegeboard.com/student/plan
    Links for homework tips, life outside of the classroom; personal time management tools, time management tips for high school students

http://ub-counseling.buffalo.edu/stresstime.shtml
    Time management with steps and other links for help

Davis, M., Eshelman, E. R., & McKay, M. (2000). *The relaxation and stress reduction workbook* (5th ed.). Oakland, CA: New Harbinger.

Gore, M. C., & Dowd, J. F. (1999). *Taming the timestealers: Tricks of the trade from organized teachers.* Thousand Oaks, CA: Corwin Press.

CHAPTER 53

Understanding Special Education Policies and Procedures

*Bradley T. Erford**

Preview

Professional school counselors are often members of multidisciplinary teams charged with determining student eligibility for special education and related services. In addition, students with disabilities are served within the framework of a comprehensive developmental counseling program. This chapter summarizes special education policies and procedures for the professional school counselor.

As the role of the professional school counselor has evolved and expanded over the past 50 years, so have the challenges, including the challenge of providing services to students with disabilities. Results of a survey of professional school counselors indicated that although they provide many services to students with disabilities, they felt only somewhat prepared (Milsom, 2002). To effectively meet this challenge, it is the professional school counselor's responsibility to acquire a basic knowledge of the disabilities that qualify students for special education and related services under the Individuals with Disabilities Education Improvement Act of 2004 (IDEA) and the policies and procedures followed by schools to ensure that students with disabilities receive a free and appropriate public education.

A Brief History and Description of Special Education Law

The Education for All Handicapped Children Act of 1975 (P.L. 94-142) was enacted by Congress to meet the needs of students with disabilities. The federal regulations implementing the law were put in place in 1977. In 1990, the name of the act changed to the Individuals with Disabilities Education Act of 1990 (IDEA; P.L. 101-476) and "people first" language was added (e.g., student with a disability, child with a specific disability) throughout (Yell, 2012). The act was again amended in 1991 (P.L.102-119), reauthorizing Part H, the section providing funding for the planning and implementation of early intervention programs and naming the section The Early Intervention Program for Infants and Toddlers With Disabilities (Murdick,

---

*Special thanks to Tracy C. Leinbaugh for her outstanding contributions to the first two editions of this chapter.

Gartin, & Crabtree, 2013). The 1997 IDEA Amendments (P.L. 105-17) included clarifications to the law and extended and restructured the original nine subchapters into four subchapters, or parts (Yell, 2012). The 2004 reauthorization of the act changed the name to the Individuals with Disabilities Education Improvement Act of 2004 (IDEA).

The first subchapter of IDEA is Part A, which provides the definitions, or general provisions, of the law. Part B provides detailed information regarding the grant program that requires every state receiving federal assistance under IDEA to ensure that a free and appropriate public education (FAPE) is provided to all qualified children and youth with disabilities within the state. Procedural safeguards protecting the interests of students with disabilities are also included here.

Parts C and D are discretionary support programs. Part C, originally Part H of the Education of All Handicapped Children Act Amendments of 1986 (P.L. 99-457), extends the protections in Part B to infants and toddlers with disabilities (birth to age 3 years). Part B has been permanently reauthorized, but Parts C and D are discretionary and support programs that are authorized on a limited basis and must be reauthorized approximately every 5 years. All 50 states are participants in federal funding and have developed policies and procedures to implement a free and appropriate education to all children and youth with disabilities.

Principles and Provisions of IDEA

It is important for professional school counselors to know that not all students with disabilities are included in the categories served by IDEA. Only those whose disability adversely affects their education and who require special education and related services to achieve are covered. IDEA specifies the following categories of disabling conditions (Turnbull, Turnbull, Wehmeyer, & Shogren, 2012; Yell, 2012): specific learning disabilities, speech or language impairments, intellectual disabilities, emotional disturbance, other health impairments, multiple disabilities, deafness, hearing impairments, orthopedic impairments, autism, visual impairments (including blindness), traumatic brain injury, development delay, and deafblindness. These categories are the minimum which states are required to serve. States do not have to adopt every category exactly as specified. They may combine categories, divide categories, use different terminology, or expand the definitions, but all students with disabilities who fall within the categories and meet the appropriate criteria as specified by the IDEA must be served for states to receive the federal funding provided by the law.

In addition, states must identify and evaluate all children and youth with disabilities from birth through the age of 21 years. If a state does not require that students without disabilities receive an education between the ages of 3 and 5, and 18 and 22 years, they are not required to provide an education for those with disabilities. IDEA contains provisions to ensure that all students with disabilities who qualify for special education and related services receive a FAPE and that procedural protections are granted to the students and their parents or guardians (Yell, 2012) including: zero reject; free and appropriate education (FAPE); least restrictive environment (LRE); identification and evaluation; confidentiality of information; procedural safeguards; technology-related assistance; personnel development; and placement in private schools. Following is a closer examination of each of these provisions and what each means.

Zero Reject

The zero reject principle means that all students who are eligible for special education and related services under IDEA are entitled to a FAPE. This entitlement is unconditional and without exception, and it extends to students attending private schools. The local public school district is responsible for identifying, assessing, evaluating, and providing services for all eligible students in private schools within the district's boundaries. Parents do not have to request that a school district do this. Each school district is legally responsible for locating all children and youth with disabilities. States generally meet this mandate through the establishment of Child Find programs.

Free and Appropriate Public Education

IDEA requires each state to have policies that ensure all students with disabilities a free and appropriate public education. Each state may establish its own special education standards to meet this mandate, but they must, at a minimum, meet those specified by IDEA. State standards may exceed those set by IDEA. Local school districts must meet their state's standards regardless of whether they meet or exceed IDEA's. To ensure that a FAPE is provided to each student with a disability receiving special services, an Individualized Education Program (IEP) must be developed.

Least Restrictive Environment

The provision of least restrictive environment mandates that all students with disabilities are to be educated with their peers without disabilities to the maximum extent *appropriate* for each student. This is determined by the multidisciplinary team, which includes the parents, educational professionals, and the student, when possible, during the development of the IEP.

Identification and Evaluation

IDEA mandates a nondiscriminatory (fair and unbiased) evaluation that serves two purposes: (a) to determine whether a student has a disability, and (b) if it is determined that a disability exists and the student is eligible, to decide the nature of the special education and related services the student needs to ensure that a free and appropriate public education is provided. This evaluation must be full and formal, consisting of many different procedures that are specified by IDEA. All procedures must conform to certain standards and are administered and interpreted by trained personnel. Protection is guaranteed in evaluation procedures by the following:

- Tests must be administered in the native language or mode of communication of the child.
- Standardized tests must be validated for the intended purpose and must be administered by trained personnel following the publisher's instructions.
- The evaluation must assess the child's specific areas of educational need. Useful information provided by the parents is included in the evaluation.

- Technically sound instruments must be used to assess multiple areas: cognitive, behavioral, physical, and developmental.
- No single test or procedure may serve as the sole criterion for determination of disability, programming, or placement.
- The evaluation team is multidisciplinary and includes at least one member who has knowledge in the suspected area of disability.
- All areas related to the suspected disability must be assessed.

Confidentiality

The privacy rights specified by IDEA are similar to those in the Family Educational Rights and Privacy Act of 1974 (FERPA), often referred to as the Buckley Amendment. IDEA extends protection to four areas: (a) the right of parental access to records, (b) the right of the parent or guardian to amend their child's records, (c) the right of protection from disclosure of information to others without permission from the parent or guardian (or the student if at the age of majority), and (d) the destruction of records.

Procedural Safeguards

IDEA includes procedural safeguards to protect the interests of students with disabilities. Included are general safeguards, the right to an independent educational evaluation, the right to the appointment of surrogate parents if needed, and dispute resolution. General safeguards of particular importance to the professional school counselor are the requirement of notification and consent and the stay-put provision. Schools must notify parents of any change in placement or program and must obtain consent from the parents before the initial evaluation and placement in special education. All parties on the multidisciplinary team must agree to any change in program.

Technology-Related Assistance

IDEA mandates that assistive technology devices and services must be provided and included in the IEP if necessary to provide a FAPE as special education or a related service or to maintain the student with a disability in the LRE.

Personnel Development

Personnel providing services to students with disabilities must be trained and licensed in their specific fields, and in-service training must be provided to all education personnel working with students with disabilities, including general education teachers. Professional school counselors should participate in opportunities to increase their knowledge and skills to effectively serve students with disabilities.

Private School Placement

When the local education agency is unable to provide a FAPE and places a student with a disability in a nonpublic school, the local education agency retains responsibility for seeing that the IEP is implemented, a FAPE is provided, and that all education expenses are provided. The parents or guardians of the student are not financially responsible for the costs of the placement.

Implementation of IDEA

Although states develop their own procedures for implementing IDEA, the basic process of identification of students with disabilities and provision of special education and related services is similar for each. As a member of the school-based team, the professional school counselor should be familiar with the basic procedures. The specific policies and provisions for each state are outlined in a manual with sample forms that are available from the special education directors of each school district or from the state's department of education. Following are the steps generally followed when implementing the provisions of IDEA.

Screening

Screening, although not required, is considered good practice. It helps identify which students might need further testing to determine whether they qualify for special education. Screening often is done through the administration of group tests.

Prereferral

Schools are prohibited from placing into special education students who have experienced lack of instruction or who have limited English proficiency and who, because of those educational needs, do not perform well in general education. Many schools have teams of teachers and other education specialists, including professional school counselors, for the purpose of providing immediate and necessary help to teachers experiencing challenges with students and to guard against misidentifying students as having disabilities, as this practice can have serious consequences. Accurate records of all interventions and the results are kept, often by professional school counselors, to document the need for a full evaluation, should the team decide that the next step is needed.

Referral

The prereferral intervention team may decide to submit to the child study team a formal, written request for a student to receive a full and formal nondiscriminatory evaluation. The form for this request usually asks for specific and comprehensive information regarding basic screening results, areas of education concerns that prompted the referral, the nature of prereferral interventions and results, and any concerns expressed by the student or the family.

Nondiscriminatory Evaluation

This requirement of IDEA is for the purpose of finding the answers to two questions: (a) does the student have a disability and, if so, (b) what is the nature of the specifically designed instruction and related services that the student needs? Parental consent is required for the evaluation to proceed. The evaluation consists of many different procedures that measure the student's cognitive, behavioral, physical, and developmental functional levels and must conform to certain standards and involve specified individuals. All areas related to the suspected disability must be assessed, including health, vision, hearing, social–emotional functioning, intelligence, academic performance, communicative ability, and motor ability.

Procedures used in the evaluation must be nondiscriminatory on a racial or cultural basis, must be valid for the purpose used, and must accurately reflect the student's aptitude and achievement level. All existing data on the student are reviewed, including school records, observations, work products, and information from the parents. The whole child is evaluated and a broad view is taken of the student's needs and strengths.

Evaluation Team

The multidisciplinary evaluation team includes, at a minimum, the student's parents; at least one of the student's general education teachers; at least one special education teacher; a representative of the school district who is qualified to provide or supervise instruction to meet the unique needs of students with disabilities and who has knowledge of the general education curricula and of the availability of local education resources; someone who can interpret the instructional implications of the evaluation results; related services personnel; and the student, when appropriate. The professional school counselor, who possesses many of the skills required by IDEA, is an important member of this team.

Each professional who administers a test compiles a written report of the instrument used and the findings and presents it at a team meeting. If the student is found to not have a disability and is ineligible for special education, the parents must be given a notice on ineligibility, and the student remains in general education without special education and related services. If the student has a disability and qualifies, the team determines specifically what kind of specially designed instruction and related services the student needs, keeping in mind that the school has a duty to provide an appropriate education and access to the general education curricula to the maximum extent appropriate. The school must provide a continuum of placements, from least to most restrictive, which can include regular class placement, special education resource services, a self-contained classroom, a special school, home instruction, or hospital or institution placement.

Developing the IFSP and IEP

Infants and toddlers with disabilities require an Individualized Family Services Plan (IFSP) which takes into consideration the strengths and needs of the family as well as the child. Schools that include preschool programs for children with disabilities may stipulate that the professional school counselor provide many of the services required by the family, including case management. Professional school counselors may also provide case management for elementary and secondary special education students. Students with disabilities ages 3 through 21 years require an Individualized Education Program (IEP) based on the student's development and needs and specifying outcomes for the student.

The IEP assures that the student will benefit from special education and have the opportunity for an equal education, independent living, economic self-sufficiency, and full participation and is often developed by the same team that conducted the evaluation. In the development of the IEP, the team must consider the student's strengths, the parents' concerns, the results of the evaluation, and any special factors, including the following:

- Appropriate strategies to address behavior for students whose behavior impedes the learning of self or others.
- Language needs as related to the IEP for the student with English as a second language.
- The use of Braille or other appropriate reading and writing media for the student who is blind or who has a visual impairment.
- Language and communication needs and opportunities to communicate with peers and professionals in their language and mode for students who are deaf or have hearing impairments.
- Assistive technology devices and services as appropriate (Turnbull et al., 2012).

The IEP must contain the following:

- The student's level of performance.
- How the disability affects the student's involvement in the general education curriculum.
- Measurable annual goals (short-term objectives).
- Special education and related services provided to the student, modifications to the program, and supports provided.
- Amount of participation in both academic and nonacademic activities with nondisabled peers.
- Individual modifications in the administration of state- and/or district-wide assessments of achievement given to all students.
- Dates for beginning services and anticipated frequency, location, and duration of services.
- Transition plans, including (a) beginning at the age of 14 years, a statement of needs related to transition services; (b) beginning at the age of 16 years, a statement of needed transition services; and (c) 1 year before the student reaches the age of majority, a statement that the student has been informed of his or her rights under IDEA.
- How progress toward annual goals will be measured and how the parents will be informed of the student's progress.

Movement in school must be promoted by the IEP related to seven adult outcomes: postsecondary education, vocational training, employment with others without disabilities, continuing and adult education, adult services, independent living, and community participation (Turnbull et al., 2012).

IEP team meetings must be scheduled at times that facilitate parental attendance. If the parents do not participate, the team must develop the IEP to serve the student. Parent consent is not required to implement the IEP, but the parents may challenge it at any point. The IEP must be in effect at the beginning of the school year. In cases where students are determined eligible for services at some time during the school year, the team may not wait until the beginning of the next school year to begin the development of the IEP. The IEP must be reviewed at least annually, and the team must review and revise it to address five matters: (a) any lack of expected progress; (b) the result of a reevaluation (required every 3 years); (c) information about the student provided to or by the parents; (d) anticipated needs; and (e) other matters related to the student's education.

The professional school counselor may write annual goals for the student with a disability related to social–personal development. Goals may address helping the student and the parents understand the nature of the student's disability and the possible effects on learning, socialization, and personal development and helping the student adjust to school and socialize with peers. Methods of achieving these goals may include parent education, parent support groups, individual counseling with the parents, individual counseling, group counseling and support groups, and classroom guidance activities involving the student. Among others, such student services may address issues such as personal adjustment, loss and grieving, social skills, family and peer relationships, conflict resolution, decision making and problem solving, goal setting, study skills, career planning, and self-esteem.

Summary/Conclusion

Students with disabilities are increasingly receiving special education in general education classrooms with their nondisabled peers. Professional school counselors are highly trained educational specialists who provide services to all students, including students with disabilities. These services may require serving as a member of a prereferral intervention team, response to intervention procedures, or a multidisciplinary team. The professional school counselor may write annual goals for the IEPs of students with disabilities and be responsible for the implementation of those goals. When implementing a developmental, comprehensive guidance and counseling program, students with disabilities are recipients of responsive services, core school counseling curriculum, and individual planning, just as students without disabilities are. A basic understanding of the federal laws, provisions, and procedures relating to special education are beneficial for the professional school counselor to understand and to ensure that each and every student may benefit from his or her education.

CHAPTER 54

Understanding Section 504 Policies and Procedures

Amy J. Newmeyer and Mark D. Newmeyer

Preview

Section 504 of The Rehabilitation Act of 1973 can be used to provide school accommodations for a variety of disabilities not covered under the Individuals with Disabilities Education Improvement Act of 2004 (IDEA) guidelines. It is important that professional school counselors understand this law and how it can be used to best serve students who need various accommodations in the school setting. We review Section 504 policies, discuss differences between policies and procedures for IDEA and Section 504, and conclude with two case examples.

Section 504 of The Rehabilitation Act of 1973 is a law that prohibits discrimination on the basis of disability in any program or activity that receives federal financial assistance. Thus, all public school systems are covered under the scope of this law. The U.S. Department of Education's Office for Civil Rights is responsible for enforcing this law in different areas including employment practices; program accessibility; and preschool, elementary, secondary, and postsecondary education. In a school setting, this means that students with disabilities should be able to access the same services as students without disabilities. Section 504 defines eligible students as those who have a physical or mental impairment, have a record of such impairment, or are perceived as having such an impairment (Schulzinger, 1999). The impairment must also substantially limit one or more major life activities, including caring for self, performing manual tasks, walking, seeing, speaking, breathing, learning, and working. The 2008 Americans with Disabilities Act Amendments expanded the list of major life activities to include reading, concentrating, thinking, sleeping, eating, and major bodily functions (Zirkel, 2009). Approximately 1–2% of students receive Section 504 accommodations, with a higher prevalence among secondary school students (Holler & Zirkel, 2008). There are several important differences between IDEA and Section 504:

- Section 504 applies to elementary, secondary, postsecondary, and work settings whereas IDEA applies only to elementary and secondary school settings (Betz, 2001).
- Section 504 does not list specific eligibility categories.
- Section 504 describes "appropriate education" as those services that meet the needs of the student with a disability as adequately as those students without a disability.
- Section 504 does not require that a diagnostic evaluation be performed to determine eligibility.

- Section 504 does not provide funds to the school system to provide services.
- Section 504 requires that the school district designate an employee who will ensure compliance with the law and handle any grievances.
- Section 504 requires the school district to ensure that tests and other evaluation measures are given in a way that reflects the student's skills and are not affected by impairment.
- Students eligible for Section 504 accommodations remain in a general education classroom because 504 guarantees access, not services or specialized instruction (Schulzinger, 1999).

Examples of students who may qualify for Section 504 accommodations include the following:

- Students who have a chronic medical condition that causes them to miss extended periods at school because of appointments for health care and therapies or symptoms of pain and fatigue.
- Students who have side effects from prescribed medications.
- Students who need an assistive communication device to participate in the classroom.
- Students who are evaluated for IDEA but may be ineligible. These conditions may include mild learning disabilities or attention-deficit/hyperactivity disorder.
- Students who cannot take written or oral tests because of impaired writing or communication skills (Schulzinger, 1999).

Reasonable accommodations for eligible students may include physical rearrangement of the classroom, lesson presentation, assignments, test taking, organizational skills, behaviors, or medication administration. Some examples include the following:

- Changing the volume of homework while maintaining the same educational standards.
- Allowing rest periods for children who are easily fatigued, or rearranging the classroom schedule to allow for a shortened academic day.
- Providing an extra set of materials for the student to use at home.
- Providing access to health care during field-trip and off-campus activities.
- Seating the student near the teacher to minimize distractions.
- Asking the teacher to repeat instructions or write them down for the student.
- Breaking assignments into smaller segments (Schulzinger, 1999).

Section 504 states that a group of professionals rather than an individual should decide placement and services. The referral for a Section 504 plan may come from a professional, parent, or the student. The school must have a designated 504 coordinator who is responsible for coordinating services and assembling the team (Betz, 2001). However, the law does not state which school personnel must be present as members of the team. The professional school counselor can play a vital role in assisting this team to determine appropriate services and to advocate for students with special needs. Other personnel who should be present include the student's teachers, parents, school nurse, and other related service providers. Although the law does not require a written document, it is generally encouraged to ensure that everyone involved is aware of the accommodations and plan for services. Many experts recommend the 504 plan follow the same format as an Individualized Education Program (IEP).

The Role of the Professional School Counselor

The professional school counselor is in a position to advocate for a student who may benefit from a 504 plan and can initiate a referral for a 504 plan by contacting the school's 504 coordinator. Additionally, by providing a linkage between the family, classroom, school, 504 coordinator, and other support systems, the professional school counselor often greatly facilitates the collaborative process and also plays a vital role by informing and educating principle individuals regarding the benefits of using 504 accommodations. That is to say, educators and families may not fully understand the importance that 504 accommodations may have in a student's educational development (Brady, 2004). Huefner (2006) cited examples of situations that may require consideration of a 504 plan:

1. A student has recently been diagnosed with ADHD or a mild learning disability, but is not eligible for an IEP.
2. A student with a medical illness has recently returned to school and may have requested extra help.
3. A student has a chronic health condition.
4. A family notifies school personnel of the presence of a physical or mental impairment for their child, of which the school was previously unaware.
5. When school personnel believe a child is at risk for falling behind in school because of a physical or mental condition.

Case Study 1

A 9-year-old female student in a third-grade classroom has recently been diagnosed with attention-deficit/hyperactivity disorder, predominantly inattentive presentation. She has normal intelligence and does not have any evidence of learning disabilities or a language disorder. She does not have any significant behavioral problems in the classroom setting. However, she is inattentive and distractible, and frequently forgets to write down assignments or turn them in, significantly affecting the grades that she receives. This student may qualify for accommodations under Section 504. Possible accommodations include the following:

- Changing her classroom seat so that she is close to the teacher and distractions from other students are minimized.
- Establishing an assignment book that is checked by her teacher at the end of the day to ensure that she has written down all assignments. Her parents can be responsible for checking the assignment book to ensure that assignments are completed and returned to school.
- Repeating directions if necessary to ensure that she has heard them correctly.
- Giving extra test-taking time, if needed.
- If medications are administered, excusing her from the classroom at the appropriate time to receive the medication.

Case Study 2

A 13-year-old male student has recently been diagnosed with cancer. He has always been a good student and has no known behavioral or academic problems. However, he has missed

Table 54.1 Online Resources about Section 504

www.wrightslaw.com/info/sec504.accoms.mods.pdf—contains a list of sample modifications and accommodations that can be written into a Section 504 document for a child with behavioral or learning difficulties in the classroom.

http://www.dcn-cde.ca.gov/504/Units/504index.htm—online module for review of Section 504 regulations.

http://www.hhs.gov/ocr/civilrights/resources/factsheets/504.pdf—fact sheet from the Office for Civil Rights of the U.S. Department of Health and Human Services.

http://www.greatschools.org/special-education/legal-rights/868-section-504.gs—parent handout on Section 504 regulations.

http://www2.ed.gov/about/offices/list/ocr/504faq.html—overview of Section 504 regulations.

---

several weeks of school because of hospitalization and is now on a medication regimen at home that also requires that medications be administered during the day at school. Although he wants to attend school, his teachers are noticing that he seems exhausted by the end of the school day and often falls asleep in class. Possible accommodations for this child include the following:

- Rearranging his class schedule so that all academic courses are scheduled during the morning so that he can be excused for the afternoon, if fatigued.
- Providing an extra set of books for use at home or in the hospital so he can keep up with homework.
- Allowing for more than the maximum number of absentee days if he is able to complete the missed work on time.
- Allowing for a note-taking buddy in his classes to send him notes when he is absent.
- Excusing him from class when necessary to administer medications.
- Allowing for use of a wheelchair for off-campus field trips if his participation is limited because of exhaustion.

Summary/Conclusion

Section 504 of The Rehabilitation Act of 1973 is a law ensuring that students with medical or psychological conditions have equal access to services in facilities and programs receiving federal financial assistance. However, many school and medical professionals are not fully aware of the regulations set forth in Section 504. This often results in confusion regarding the use of a 504 plan, and thus available services and accommodations may be overlooked (American Academy of Pediatrics, 2000). See Table 54.1 for some helpful online resources related to Section 504. The professional school counselor should be aware of the presence of the 504 statute, as it can be used to provide certain accommodations to students with disabilities who do not qualify for services under the IDEA regulations. Additionally, the professional school counselor is frequently called upon to be the 504 case manager for students and can also act as an advocate for the student with a disability by initiating the process of forming a 504 plan and serving as a member of the 504 team.

CHAPTER 55

School Support for Students Who Have Chronic Illnesses

Carol J. Kaffenberger

Preview

Information concerning ways in which a school counselor can facilitate school support for students with chronic illnesses and barriers faced by students with chronic illness was reviewed. A model for supporting students with chronic illness and strategies and resources for supporting students with chronic illness was offered.

It is estimated that 20% of all students have a chronic illness, and one third of this population experience consequences of their disease severe enough to interfere with school performance (Bloom, Jones, & Freeman, 2013; Van Cleave, Gortmaker, & Perrin, 2010). Chronic illnesses share three characteristics: they require medical interventions, are prolonged in duration, and are rarely cured (Stanton, Revenson, & Tennen, 2007; Van Cleave et al., 2010). Cancer, asthma, food allergies, heart disease, lupus, bowel disorders, sickle cell anemia, cystic fibrosis, type 1 and type 2 diabetes, obesity, juvenile rheumatoid arthritis, seizure disorder, chronic pain, mental illness, and HIV/AIDS are among the most common chronic illnesses affecting children (Compas, Jaser, Dunn, & Rodriguez, 2012; West, Denzer, Wildman, & Anhalt, 2013). The prevalence of many of these conditions (e.g., obesity, asthma) has increased in recent decades, and due to improved treatment protocols, children with certain conditions (e.g., sickle cell anemia, cystic fibrosis, cancer) are living longer (Van Cleave et al., 2010).

Students with chronic illness are more frequently absent from school than their healthy peers; experience psychosocial consequences including depression, difficulties with social and peer interaction, and lower academic achievement; have a higher incidence of cognitive disabilities as a result of their illness or its treatment; and have lasting consequences affecting future life opportunities (Compas et al., 2012; Layte & McCrory, 2013; Shaw & McCabe, 2008; Shiu, 2001). Students who are out of school for extended periods with chronic illness require support as they transition from the hospital or home back to school. This process is called *school reentry* or *school reintegration*. For the child with a chronic illness, being in school represents a return to normalcy; school is what students "do." Being in school as much as possible or making a successful transition back to school is associated with more positive long-term outcomes for students (Canter & Roberts, 2012; Hamlet, Gergar & Schaefer, 2011).

School reentry or support for students with chronic illness is a complex process. School support must be tailored to the individual needs of the student and the family as well as the specific characteristics of the student's illness (Canter & Roberts, 2012). School attendance and grading policies and homebound instruction regulations are often inflexible and serve as a barrier to successful school support (Kaffenberger, 2006b; Prevatt, Heffner, & Lowe, 2000). School personnel often feel unprepared to meet the individual needs of these students and lack information and resources concerning the disease or an understanding of the individual needs of the students and their families (Hamlet et al., 2011; Moore, Kaffenberger, Oh, Goldberg, & Hudspeth, 2009; West et al., 2013).

Models for Successful School Support

Model programs have been developed that describe strategies for supporting students with chronic illness and for helping them make the transition back to school when they have been out for extended periods (Canter & Roberts, 2012; Nabors & Lehmkuhl, 2004; Shaw & McCabe, 2008). Model comprehensive school support programs have the following features in common (Canter & Roberts, 2010; Kaffenberger, 2006a): They identify a coordinator of services, provide direct services to the student, consult with the family, educate and sensitize school personnel and classmates, and involve the medical team.

Coordination of School Support Programs

The success of programs to support students with chronic illness depends on the identification of a liaison who takes responsibility for coordinating the school support or school reentry process (Bradley-Klug et al., 2013; Harris, 2009; Kaffenberger, 2006b). The school counselor is ideally suited to provide the coordination services (Hamlet et al., 2011). The liaison oversees the first phases of the process by meeting with the family and the student and convening the support team. The liaison should have access to the family, the student, school staff, and members of the medical team.

The liaison meets with the parents to determine the student's continuing needs: to discuss how they want information about the child's illness communicated to teachers and the student's peers, to assess resources and available family support, and to obtain necessary parental permission to communicate with others about the student. The liaison begins the process by providing information to the family about available school services and the importance of involving the school from the time of diagnosis. With written permission from the parents, the liaison communicates with the medical team, gaining information about the diagnosis and treatment to identify support the student may need during the transition back to school.

Next, the liaison meets with the student to assess his or her understanding of the disease and treatment process and to talk about how the student wants peers to find out about the illness. The liaison determines student desires concerning involvement and communication with peers and the school and may discuss having a classroom lesson to educate classmates about the diagnosis.

The liaison works with the school to educate and inform school personnel. A workshop for teachers and administrators is recommended as the best vehicle for sensitizing school personnel to the unique needs of the student, informing the educators about how to handle the classroom responses to the sick student (Harris, 2009; West et al., 2013). The liaison may also be asked to coordinate a classroom lesson for peers (Hamlet et al., 2011; Kaffenberger 2006b). Research (West et al., 2013) indicates that when teachers and classmates are informed, the transition back to school is more successful. Finally, the liaison keeps the lines of communication open, passing along updated information and planning for school reentry.

While the benefits of a comprehensive school support program cannot be denied, the reality is that such programs are not available to serve most students with chronic illness (Canter & Roberts, 2012). Although there is general agreement that a comprehensive school support program is ideal, staffing issues, funding, and lack of supporting research data about the effectiveness of existing programs limit the number of programs being implemented.

The critical factor determining the success of the comprehensive school support program is the identification of a liaison to coordinate services. As Prevatt et al. (2000) recognized in their review of school reintegration programs, how the liaison is staffed and funded is one of the most significant barriers to the successful implementation of programs. While the literature underscores the importance of the liaison role, guidance about who is best suited to play this role is not offered.

A Role for School Counselors in the School Support Process

Typically, the return to school after a diagnosis is put together in a piecemeal fashion. Families are unsure of what their child's future holds and what their child will need, and they struggle to understand the school regulations and how to access services. Frequently, the school's response is slow. Schools scramble to educate themselves about the diagnosis, the needs of the student and family, and available resources. Well-meaning school personnel, lacking clarity about their role, knowledge about the illness, and available resources, feel unprepared to meet the needs of these children and their families (Moore et al., 2009; West et al., 2013). School counselors, however, by virtue of their training, skills, and leadership role in the school, are ideally suited to facilitate the school support or reentry for students with chronic illnesses and support the chronically ill student's siblings and family (Bauman, 2010; Hamlet et al., 2011; Kaffenberger, 2006b).

Strategies for Working With Students With Chronic Illnesses

The following are strategies professional school counselors can use to coordinate school support for students with chronic illnesses:

1. *Make early contact with the family* (see Table 55.1). As soon as you learn of the diagnosis of an illness, contact the parents. Recognize that the family is struggling to respond to the medical needs of the student and may postpone contact with the school (Case-Smith, 2004). Contacting the family early on provides to the family a sense of hope as well as additional resources. No matter how long the student is expected to be out of school, planning for school reentry should begin early.
2. *Form a school support team composed of stakeholders* (see Table 55.2). The purpose of a school support team is to coordinate services and implement the school support plan. The school support team may include the school counselor, public health or school nurse, social worker, teacher, and administrator. The school support team should consist

Table 55.1 Questions to Consider in Your Early Contact With the Family

At the time of the crisis, school personnel often postpone contact with the family. By taking the initiative, and making early contact with the family, you give the parent and child a sense of hope. You provide a resource outside the family circle, establish your role as an advocate for the sick child and siblings, and you facilitate school reentry.

- Tell me more about your child's diagnosis, treatment process, and how you expect these to affect him/her.
- Would you be willing to come to school for a meeting to share information, to hear about available school resources, and to help plan for school support?
- How might school performance/attendance be affected?
- How much does your child know/understand about the illness?
- What do you want school staff, your child's teacher, the school community, and other children to know about the illness? And who do you want to tell them about it?
- Is there someone on the medical team with whom you would like us to work?
- How can we communicate? Who can we contact? Who will contact us?
- What support would you like from the school when your child is out of school? Cards? Class work? Video of class? Calls? Visits? Web cam?
- Are you aware of resources/information/support groups dealing with this illness?
- Have you used the Internet to access information and materials regarding the illness? Are you willing to share what you learn with the school? Would you like me to help you find information?
- Who is helping *you* through this?
- What can we do to help you and your family?
- How is the sick child's sibling(s) doing? What role can we play in terms of supporting the siblings?

of three to four individuals who will assume responsibility for providing and coordinating services to the student and family. Members of this team should be determined by school district organization and staffing and by the unique situation of each student and family. The school support team should identify a liaison that will assume primary and on-going responsibility for contact with the family and the health care professionals; the liaison may be the school counselor or any member of the school support team. Consider documenting roles, responsibilities, and activities of the school support team (see Table 55.3).

3. *Hold a school support meeting with the parents as soon as possible.* Determine who should attend this meeting based on the needs of the student and family. Include the school support team members, the student's teacher, school nurse, a special education teacher (if appropriate), Section 504 coordinator, and an administrator. The purpose of this meeting is to coordinate the school reentry process and negotiate the way the school can support the student and family. Discuss the following with the parents:
   - Learn all you can from the parents about the illness, the expected course of treatment, and the psychological impact the experience is having on the student with the chronic illness and the student's parents and siblings.
   - Provide the parents with resources (see Table 55.4) and information about the services the school can provide, such as special education and Section 504 modifications, homebound instruction, and ways in which the student's peers can continue to have

Table 55.2 Suggested Checklist for School Support Teams

Convene the School Support Team. The purpose of a School Support Team is to oversee services and support for all students with chronic illnesses in the school. The School Support Team can consist of the school counselor, social worker, and public health nurse. Consider including an administrator, the student services director, and teachers for some meetings.

- ☐ Review the medical alert list for the school.
- ☐ Develop School Support Team goals based on the review of the medical alert list and particular needs of students in the school.
- ☐ Share expertise and set goals for needs and future response strategies.
- ☐ When a student is newly diagnosed:
    - Communicate with other members of the School Support Team
    - Identify the liaison with the family (school counselor, social worker, public health nurse, or teacher with strongest ties to the family)
    - Contact parent(s) of the identified student
    - Gather information, regarding the illness, from the parent and other sources.
    - Arrange for parent conference:
        - Educate parents about school resources
        - Refer student to Child Study Team
        - Consider a 504 plan
        - Negotiate a plan for school support
    - Conduct a workshop to educate and sensitize faculty.
    - Conduct a classroom lesson with the student's peers.
    - Meet with the ill student when appropriate and/or necessary.
    - Meet with sibling(s) and/or consult with their school counselor. Notify the siblings' school counselors.
    - Consult with a homebound teacher.
    - Consult with student's doctor, psychiatrist, and/or other medical personnel.

Table 55.3 School Support Team Planning

Suggested Intervention	Team Member	Date	Comments
Identify the school support team members			
Identify support team coordinator			
Contact family			
Convene school support team			
Facilitate parent conferences			
Develop school reentry plan			
Conduct faculty workshop			
Conduct classroom lessons			
Consult medical personnel			
Provide support for student			
Provide support for siblings & peers			
Follow-up			

Table 55.4 Resources

Recommended Reading for Parents, Counselors, and Educators

Clark, C. D. (2003). *In sickness and in play: Children coping with chronic illness.* New Brunswick, NJ: Rutgers University Press. [Coping with juvenile diabetes and asthma.]

Dempsey, S. (2008). *Extreme parenting: Parenting your child with a chronic illness.* London, UK: Jessica Kingsley Press. [One parent's story with tips for coping with any chronic illness.]

Edwards, M., & Titman, P. (2010). *Promoting psychological well-being in children with acute and chronic illness.* London, UK: Jessica Kingsley Publishers.

Heugel, K., & Verdick, E.(Eds.). (1998). *Young people and chronic illness: True stories, help and hope.* Minneapolis, MN: Free Spirit Publications.

Keene, N. (2003). *Educating the child with cancer.* New York, NY: The Candlelighters Foundation.

Meyer, D. J., & Vadasy, P. F. (2008). *Sibshops: Workshops for siblings of children with special needs* (Revised edition). Baltimore, MD: Paul Brookes Publ. Inc.

Singer, A. T. (2007). *Coping with your child's chronic illness.* San Francisco, CA: Robert D. Reed Publishers.

Recommended Reading for Children and Adolescents

Carney, K. L. (1998). *What is cancer anyway? Explaining cancer to children of all ages.* (Barklay and Eve Series, Book 5). Wethersfield, CT: Dragonfly Publishing Co.

Krementz, J. (1989). *How it feels to fight for your life.* New York, NY: Little Brown.

Meyer, D. (1997). *View from our shoes: Growing up with a brother or sister with special needs.* Bethesda, MD: Woodbine House.

Special Kids in School Series published by Jayjo Books LLC, Plainview, NY.
    Gosselin, K. (2001). *Taking cancer to school.*
    Gosselin, K. (2004). *Taking diabetes to school* (3rd ed.).
    Henry, C. S. (2000). *Taking cystic fibrosis to school.*
    Miller, D. D. L., & Dineen, T. (2002). *Taking arthritis to school.*
    Mitchelhill, B. & Gosselin, K. (1998). *Taking asthma to school.*
    Weiner, E. (2000). *Taking food allergies to school.*

Online Resources for Information and Support

Allergy and Asthma Network/Mothers of Asthmatics, Inc.—(703) 641-9595—http://www.aanma.org/

American Brain Tumor Association—www.abta.org/kids/home.htm

Arthritis Foundation—http://www.arthritis.org/conditions-treatments/disease-center/juvenile--arthritis/

Association of Cancer Online Resources—Provides access to 142 online communities and related resources. http://www.acor.org

Band-Aids and Blackboards—This child-friendly Web site was created by a nurse educator to help kids and teens cope with chronic illness and returning to school—http://www.lehman.cuny.edu/faculty/jfleitas/bandaides/

Brave Kids—Online resources for children with chronic and life-threatening illnesses—http://www.bravekids.org

American Childhood Cancer Organization—Provides support for children and families—http://www.acco.org/

The Childhood Brain Tumor Foundation—www.childhoodbraintumor.org

Children With Diabetes—Online community for children with diabetes and their families—http://www.childrenwithdiabetes.com/

Crohn's and Colitis Foundation of America—www.ccfa.org

Cystic Fibrosis Foundation—http://www.cff.org/

This website is sponsored by the American Academy of Pediatrics and offers information and resources and childhood chronic illnesses to parents—www.Healthychildren.org

Juvenile Diabetes Research Foundation—http://jdrf.org/

Kids With Heart National Association for Children's Heart Disorders—http://kidswithheart.org

Lymphoma & Leukemia Society—http://www.lls.org/

Starbright—Support for seriously ill children and their families—https://www.starbrightworld.org/

Students with Chronic Illnesses: Guidance for Families, Schools and Students. Two-page paper produced by National Institutes of Health http://www.nhlbi.nih.gov/health/resources/lung/asthma-guide-family

---

contact with the student. Provide information about the effect the illness may have on the siblings.
- Help the parents understand the needs of the siblings and offer assistance.
- Gain the parents' permission to discuss the student's illness with staff, peers, and the medical team treating the student.
- Develop a school support or reentry plan (see Table 55.3).

4. *Components of a school support or reentry* plan (see Table 55.2). Recognize that each student and family will require individualized services. Consider the following issues:
   - Identify a liaison who will be the point of contact between the school and family and the school and medical professionals.
   - Obtain the parents' permission to allow the liaison to coordinate services and have access to medical information or to communicate with a member of the student's medical team.
   - Decide how the staff will hear about the student's illness, who on the staff will be told, and how they will be told. Decide how school staff will receive updated information. Discuss how peers and classmates can stay in contact with the student.
   - Decide how the student's class and peers will hear about the illness, who will tell them, and what will they be told. Decide how they will receive updated information.
   - Decide what steps should be taken to continue the student's education. If the student will receive homebound services, provide the parents with the necessary information for gaining those services. If the student's attendance is expected to be irregular, decide how the student will receive schoolwork and who will supervise its completion.
   - Decide whether the student should be referred to the Child Study committee for consideration of special education or Section 504 modifications.
   - Discuss how the siblings will be supported.
   - Prepare for the student's return to school. Determine what medical and educational modifications will be required.

5. *Coordinate support services.* While the school counselor is not responsible for providing all of the services the student with a chronic illness might require, the school counselor can coordinate and facilitate those services. Support services could include a workshop for faculty and staff and a classroom presentation to students (see Table 55.5).
   - The purpose of the workshop for faculty and staff is to help them understand the medical and psychological needs of the student. Helping the school staff understand the

(text continues on page 612)

Table 55.5 School Support for Students With Chronic Illness: Presentation Guidelines

Purpose: The purpose of a staff workshop or class presentation is to provide accurate information to the staff and the classmates of the student with the chronic illness and to allay the fears of staff and classmates. It is believed that school support will be more successful when staff, peers, and classmates are informed about the illness and have had a chance to voice their concerns.

Who should facilitate: The workshop or classroom presentation could be conducted by school personnel (public health nurse, school counselor, social worker, teacher, or administrator); a member of the child/adolescent's medical team (social worker, psychologist, nurse practitioner, physician, child life specialist); or by the parent of the student. The facilitator should be knowledgeable about the specifics of the disease and able to provide age-appropriate information to the students.

Before conducting the session: Obtain permission of the family and student before conducting the workshop or presentation. Plan with the parents and the student concerning what is to be shared.

Who should participate in the staff workshop: At a small elementary school, the workshop could involve the entire faculty and staff. At a large elementary school or a middle school, the student's team (those faculty and staff members who have contact with the student) should participate. At the high school level, it is suggested that the workshop be conducted with the members of the faculty and staff who have contact with the adolescent.

Who should participate in the classroom presentation: At the elementary level the lesson should involve the student's classmates and peers. At the middle school level, the student's team should participate. At the high school level it is suggested that the lesson be conducted in the science class to discuss the medical aspects of the disease and in the homeroom to discuss the social and personal impact of the disease.

What to expect from the faculty, staff, and students: A discussion of serious medical issues will prompt memories of people in their lives who have been sick or died. The facilitator should expect to hear personal stories and questions. Faculty and staff will want to hear about how to treat the student, the ongoing medical concerns and responsibilities of the school, and what will be expected of the school staff. Students will have many questions about what it is like to have the disease and how they should treat the sick student. At the high school level, expect existential questions about life and death.

Faculty/Staff Workshop Outline

Suggested Procedures (30 minutes):

Opening:
1. Introduce the presenters, especially if they are unknown to the students.
2. Begin with an explanation about the purpose of the presentation:
    - To learn about the (name of the disease) that (name of the child/adolescent) has.
    - To understand why he/she is out of school.
    - To learn what we can expect when he/she comes back to school.
    - To talk about what we can do to help the child/adolescent.
3. Ask the staff what they know about (name of the disease)?

Information about the disease:
1. Provide information about the disease.
    - Definition of the disease, including types, prevalence among children/adolescents, general prognosis, medical treatment, and side effects.
2. Provide information about the particular medical needs of the student.

Describe the school support or school reentry plan:
1. Provide information about when the child/adolescent will be back in school.
   - Describe feelings and concerns of the child/adolescent and parents.
   - Present homebound instruction plan and/or 504 plan.
2. Discuss the responsibilities of faculty and staff for educational, medical and psychological support of the child/adolescent.
3. Identify a liaison, the point of contact, for updated information about the child/adolescent, and his/her medical/educational needs.

Discuss faculty responsibilities to help the sick student:
1. Brainstorm ideas of how to help the sick child/adolescent. How will contact with the school be continued while at home/hospital (e.g., cards, e-mails, visits, phone calls)?
   - Discuss ways to keep the child/adolescent involved in school activities.
   - Discuss issue of siblings of the sick child/adolescent and ways to support them.
   - Discuss faculty questions and concerns.

Presentation to Classmates Lesson Plan

Suggested Procedures (30–45 minutes):

Opening:
1. Introduce the presenters, especially if they are unknown to the students.
2. Begin with an explanation about the purpose of the lesson:
   - To learn about (the disease) that (name of the child/adolescent) has
   - To understand why he/she is out of school
   - To learn what we can expect when he/she comes back to school
   - To talk about what we can do to help the child/adolescent
3. Ask the children what they know about (name of the disease)?

Information about the disease:
1. Provide age-appropriate information about the disease.
   - Definition of the disease, including types, prevalence among children/adolescents, general prognosis, medical treatment, and side effects
   - Visuals including videos, overheads, worksheets may be used to reinforce the goals of the lesson.
2. Address the following typical concerns of classmates:
   - Can I catch this disease?
   - How did _____ get this disease?
   - Will _____ get better? Will _____ die?
   - How does _____ feel? Is it painful?

Discuss what to expect when the child/adolescent is back at school:
1. Provide information about when the child/adolescent will be back in school.
2. Describe the sick child/adolescent's feelings and concerns about returning to school.
3. Allow time for questions.

Discuss what classmates can do to help the sick child/adolescent:
1. Brainstorm ideas of how to help the sick child/adolescent.
2. Talk about what is helpful and what would be unhelpful.
3. Allow time for questions.

needs of the student will increase the chances of successful school support or school reentry. A member of the student's medical team, the public health or school nurse assigned to the student's school, the parents of the student, or the school counselor could conduct the workshop.

- The purpose of the classroom presentation is to increase peers' understanding of the medical and social needs of the student. At the high school level, a group session for peers who are close to the adolescent should be held. This session should help peers gain accurate information about the student's illness and sensitize them to his or her social needs. The information could also be provided in a science class that focuses on a scientific understanding of the illness. A teacher, a member of the student's medical team, the public health or school nurse assigned to the student's school, the parents of the student, or the school counselor could conduct the classroom presentation.

6. *Provide support for the siblings.* Siblings' needs are often overlooked (Barrera, Fleming, & Kahn, 2004). Well-meaning teachers who do not know how to address the issue of the student with chronic illness with the student's healthy siblings ignore the opportunity to provide direct support. The school counselor can provide both direct and indirect help to the siblings by helping the staff and the siblings' peers understand sibling needs. If the siblings attend a different school, contact their school counselor.

7. *Coordinate support to the student with a chronic illness.* Support for the sick student may include providing direct services, individual or small-group counseling concerning adjustment to illness, coping strategies, school reentry preparation, and peer or academic issues. The professional school counselor can maintain contact with the student while he or she is out of school and encourage peers and teachers to maintain contact as well. The school counselor could also facilitate communication between the homebound teacher and school. By making the school community aware of the ongoing needs of the student with chronic illness, the school counselor is providing necessary services.

Summary/Conclusion

The professional school counselor can play an important role by providing school support for students with chronic illnesses. By making early contact with the family, forming a school support team, negotiating a role for the school, providing information and resources, developing a school reentry plan, supporting the siblings of students with chronic illness, providing a classroom presentation to the student's peers, and helping the school community to understand the needs of these students and families, school counselors can effectively support reentry for students with chronic illnesses.

CHAPTER 56

Intervention Strategies for Physically or Sexually Abused Students

David J. Carter and Patricia Carter

Preview

In this chapter we discuss causes, symptoms, and treatment strategies regarding the physical and/or sexual abuse of students. We briefly discuss the legal responsibility and consequences and explore the recognition, intervention, and reporting of student physical and sexual abuse. The information we present in this chapter is especially important for the professional school counselor who works closely with students and serves as an advocate and a first line of defense against abuse. To address the abuse cycle, the professional school counselor must understand the misperceptions about such experiences, including misperceptions about self, the abuser, and the behavior or act that was forced upon the student.

Professional school counselors who believe that a student's physical or mental health and welfare has been or may be affected by physical or sexual abuse have a professional and legal responsibility to report the case immediately to a law enforcement agency or to the state's department of child protection services. Every school should have a designated protocol for reporting abuse, and the following information should be given in the initial report to the local department of social services:

1) Child's name, age, gender and address, 2) Parent's name and address, 3) Nature and extent of the injury or condition observed, 4) Prior injuries and when observed, 5) Actions taken by the reporter (e.g., talking with the child), 6) When the act occurred, and 7) Reporter's name, location, and contact information, sometimes not required but extremely valuable. (Crosson-Tower, 2013, p. 31)

In the past decade, 16.2% of cases referred to Child Protective Services have come from education personnel—the highest percentage from any profession (Bradly & McCarlie, 2012). This indicates that educators are a primary line of defense against child abuse because of their frequent contact and relationship to children and adolescents. Educators are trained observers and have knowledge of the wide range of behaviors children exhibit at each developmental stage. They can quickly recognize outlying behaviors that might indicate abuse. Professional school counselors, in particular, are critical to identifying, reporting, and intervening in suspected abuse because they work closely with teachers and students, and are likely to be the child's primary support system, advocate, and designer of preventative programs (Crosson-Tower, 2013).

In this chapter, we address the recognition, intervention, and reporting of student physical and sexual abuse. Child abuse is defined as

> any recent act or failure to act resulting in imminent risk of serious harm, death, serious physical or emotional harm, sexual abuse, or exploitation of a child (minor age as described by state statutes) by a parent or caretaker (including out-of-home care providers) who are responsible for the child's welfare. (Child Abuse Prevention and Treatment Act, 2010, p. 6)

The Child Abuse Prevention and Treatment Act (2010) defined sexual abuse as

> employment, use, persuasion, inducement, enticement, or coercion of any child to engage in, or assist any other person to engage in, any sexually explicit conduct or any simulation of such conduct for the purpose of producing any visual depiction of such conduct; or the rape, and in cases of caretaker or interfamilial relationship, statutory rape, molestation, prostitution, or other form of sexual exploitation of children or incest with children. (p. 31)

Physical abuse is defined specifically as any nonaccidental injury to a child while the child is under the supervision of a caretaker. An accurate way to detect physical abuse is by direct observations of outward physical signs:

- Adult-size human bite marks. All bite marks should be assessed.
- Burns, especially from objects such as cigarettes, irons, and other objects.
- Marks that represent hard blows from whip-like objects that make a burn around the body, such as electrical cords.
- Bruises in specific shapes, such as hangers, handprints, and paddles.
- Bald spots from severe hair pulling (rule out trichotillomania).
- Frequent bruising around the neck, face, or head; the abdomen; or along the arms, especially around the wrist.
- Extreme sensitivity to pain or complaints of soreness and stiffness or awkward movements as if caused by pain.

Professional school counselors working with abused students must be familiar with the complex dynamics that arise when the student experiences abuse. One of the most critical components of rapport building with any child is the comprehension of his or her internal frame of reference. This is often difficult to do in cases of sexual abuse. An abused child is often confused about the issue that is apparent to others.

There are many characteristics that profile a victim of sexual abuse. Engel (2005) identified the following:

- Demonstrates fearful behavior (cringe, flinch) around adults.
- Low self-esteem and loss of self-respect.
- A strong need for closeness, affection, and love.
- Believing that he or she doesn't deserve better care.
- Difficulty in setting and enforcing social boundaries.
- Struggles with forming healthy peer relationships.
- Belief that he or she is not validated without a relationship.

- Strong desire to avoid confrontation.
- Tendency to suppress anger or act out in aggressive ways.
- Denying the seriousness of a stressful situation.
- Taking on the needs and responsibilities of others.
- Blaming others for relationship problems.
- Fear of being abandoned and alone.
- Belief that he or she should be treated poorly.

Because sexual abuse is shame based, it sends the message that the child is worthless, unacceptable, and bad. The child might feel defective, unwanted, and alienated from others. Abused children will often try to overcompensate for these feelings by striving for control or perfection. If the child is able to be successful in gaining power, especially over others, he or she becomes increasingly less vulnerable to further shame and more likely to blame others. Other children strive for superiority in an attempt to overcome shame. Like power seeking, this is a way to compensate for an underlying sense of defectiveness. The perception is that if the child strives for perfection he or she is no longer vulnerable and will therefore overcome shame. Both of these defense mechanisms are destined to fail, and the student will reinforce the belief that nothing he does is good enough (Engel, 2005; Yates, Allardyce, & MacQueen, 2012).

An abused student will harbor many emotions arising from the abuse. Misperceptions about the experience, including those about self, the abuser, and the behavior or act that was forced upon the child linger and can be debilitating to the abused child. In many instances, total recovery from the emotional trauma never happens; rather, the abusee develops coping skills or defense mechanisms to help reduce the highly stressful recall of memories or ensuing flashbacks.

An abused student struggles to cope with abusive experiences while accomplishing common developmental tasks. After the abuse, the student may attempt to cope with the abuse rather than fulfill developmental tasks such as acquiring social skills, developing a sense of self, and learning to achieve. Although professionals have noted that a "loss of innocence" occurs when a student is abused, another loss may also occur—that of lost opportunities.

Rather than being free of mind to pursue playful, healthy, ego-strengthening activities, an abused student may struggle to survive emotionally and physically. In cases of long-standing, repeated familial abuse, an abused student must develop self-reliance and inner strength as a means of survival (Smith & Carlson, 1997). Not all children are able to achieve this, especially when sexual abuse is involved.

Students come to regard abuse and sexuality through their relationships with others. Fundamental sexual feelings and attitudes are based on early life experiences. There is nothing new in this concept; professional school counselors understand they may have to deal with students' physical and sexual abuse problems. Following are self-reflections professionals can ask themselves to explore their feelings and attitudes:

- How did your mother, father, and/or caretakers show affection and anger in the family?
- What kinds of punishment were used in your family or your ethnic group when you were a child?
- Remember and describe a time when you were punished physically as a child. What happened, and how did you feel at the time?

- Describe in your own words the relationship between corporal punishment and physical abuse?
- How do your personal experiences of corporal punishment affect your professional work on this issue? Do these experiences make it harder or easier to work with students who have been abused?

Childhood experiences that are based on trust and safe physical boundaries set the stage for the development of healthy coping skills (Babatsikos, 2010). When trust is violated, students develop defenses against being hurt. Defenses (e.g., attitudes of excessive self-sufficiency, self-love, self-hate, blame taking, blame giving) come together to form an individual's personality. It is the professional school counselor's responsibility to differentiate between student-demonstrated defense mechanisms and coping strategies and act accordingly.

Signs and Symptoms

Professional school counselors have regular contact with students and should be able to recognize indicators of abuse. Interaction with the student will acquaint personnel to his or her normal behavior and will thus alert counselors to the student's mood swings, withdrawal, and atypical acting-out behavior. Feelings of helplessness related to abuse could be acted out through an eating disorder (American Psychiatric Association, 2013). Physical signs include scratches, burns, welts, broken teeth, cuts, and bruises not associated with sports or skateboarding. Pay attention to students who don't want to sit down or who sit carefully, as if injured. Young students may exhibit precocious sex play with classmates or objects, may ask more questions than normal, or know sexual terminology inappropriate for their age group. Others may refuse to undress for physical education or not be allowed to spend the night at a friend's house.

Abused students can habitually be late to school or exhibit prolonged absences because the abusing parent wants to keep an injured child at home until the evidence of abuse disappears. In some cases, students frequently arrive early at school and remain after classes rather than return home. They might be inappropriately dressed for the weather; students who wear long-sleeve shirts and sweaters on hot days may be covering up bruises, burns, or other marks of abuse. The student may be wary of physical contact from adults and peers. Students may also try desperately to get attention from adult figures such as teachers and the professional school counselor (Bradly & McCarlie, 2012).

As a professional school counselor, keep in mind that abuse of students can be perpetuated by other students as well. For these reasons, become an expert at unmasking sexual con games that take place between students. The goal of any perpetrator is to successfully increase the trust and secrecy between himself or herself and the victim (Lantzman, Viljoen, Scalora, & Ullman, 2011). Be on the lookout for students who violate boundaries, such as by wearing revealing clothing, standing too close to others, saying too much about themselves too soon, making sexual comments about other students' body parts, asking very personal questions, touching another students' legs or other parts of the body, or saying or doing things that are offensive or vulgar.

Also watch for victim boundaries that may be too closed, such as students who have few friends, rarely share feelings with others, rarely ask for help, seek isolation, or are cautious about letting trustworthy adults appropriately touch them (i.e., hand shakes, pats on the back). With the professional school counselor's help, students who have been abused can learn to set appropriate boundaries and identify and avoid students who look out only for their own interests. Table 56.1 provides a developmental listing of symptoms of students who have been abused.

Helpful Strategies

Disclosure of abuse may be accidental or purposeful. Accidental disclosure occurs when others observe the abuse, when the student is injured, or when the student acts out sexually. Purposeful disclosure occurs when the student desires to end the abusive relationship. Whatever the circumstances of the disclosure, don't assume the student will be anxious to talk openly about the abuse. It is essential to evaluate the student's level of trust, emotional stability, memory skills, cognitive ability, social maturity, accuracy of recall of past events, and ability to verbalize accurately (Kagan, 1991).

The purpose of the initial meeting with the student is to determine the type of abuse that occurred and to ensure that the student is protected. The meeting should be conducted in a safe place, and the student should be comfortable in the setting. Remain flexible and follow the student's lead in regard to pace, breadth, and depth. Refrain from interrupting, and remain patient. Provide frequent praise for the student's bravery in disclosing (Saywitz & Faller, 2006). If the student gives any indication of experiencing high stress levels or retraumatization, make alternative strategies and arrangements to avoid revictimization of the student (Smith & Carlson, 1997):

- Set boundaries while giving the student a safe space for self-expression. Create an accepting environment by posing understandable questions sensitive to the developmental level of the student in terms of memory, language, reasoning, knowledge, and emotional maturity (Saywitz & Faller, 2006). The primary goal is to help the student merge self-expression with self-discovery, leading to an emotional catharsis.
- Be objective, and maintain a neutral stance. Pay careful attention to your body language, tone of voice, and facial expression and avoid leading, suggestive, coercive, or accusatory questions or content. Avoid close-ended questions; open-ended questions elicit the most accurate, unbiased information (Wurtele, Moreno, & Kenny, 2008).
- Empathy is of highest importance. It is permissible for you to self-disclose and show empathy in a warm and caring manner when appropriate and accurate to the situation. Express caring in a nonsexual manner. Remember that unconditional positive regard is a therapeutic process. Providing acceptance and understanding will help reduce the student's fears and anxiety (Allardyce, 2013).
- Address the abusive issues in a straightforward manner, and explore with the student his or her feelings and thoughts in a firm but warm and fair manner. Examination involves helping the student get in touch with the irrational beliefs that affect his or her self-esteem and confidence. Explore the student's behavior therapeutically as a result of the abusive situation.
- Use techniques incorporating art, music, role-playing, and talk therapy for changing the attributes in abused children of all ages. For example, a student can create a "warm fuzzy

Table 56.1 Symptoms of Abused Students

Elementary School

Withdrawn, fearful
Depressed or flat affect, cries easily
Passive, avoids eye contact, sinks down in chair
Squirms in seat, painful to sit
Suspicious or frequent bruises, welts, cuts, burns, bite makes, choke marks, grab marks, scratches, pinch marks
Somatic complaints (e.g., stomachaches, painful urination or bowel movements, headaches, dizziness)
Violent or sexual drawings or stories
Advanced sexual vocabulary
Imitating sexual or violent behavior alone or with other children during play, with toys
Hypersensitive to appropriate social touching (e.g., pats on the back, handshakes)
Restroom accidents (enuresis, encopresis)
Not allowed to spend the night at a friend's house
Behavioral problems (e.g., temper tantrums, regression, aggression, destructive behavior)
Verbal inhibition
Fear of adults
Arrives to school early and leaves late
Low achiever
Dressed inappropriately for the season
Poor hygiene
Difficulty staying awake
Extremely adaptable/flexible
Flashbacks

Middle School

In addition to symptoms displayed in elementary-age children, the residual effects of abuse create more complex symptoms in middle school.

Vandalism, destruction of property
Self-mutilation
Bullying, using force, or intimidating smaller children
Angry or violent outbursts
Withdrawal from physical contact from teachers or other students
Physical complaints of headaches, dizziness, muscle cramps
Poor peer relationships; few, if any, friends
Severe drop in grades
Precocious sex play
Won't undress for gym
Low self-esteem
Vacillates between being ultra-adult and ultra-immature
Dishonesty (e.g., cheats, lies, steals)
Fear of failure

High School
Due to higher cognitive abilities, high school students develop even more complex behaviors as a result of dysfunctional coping abilities. Self-destructive behavior (e.g., drugs, alcohol, cutting) Extreme moodiness Suicidal thoughts Withdrawal from friends and family School truancy, poor school performance Sexually vulgar conversations and behavior with opposite sex Obsessive cleanliness Compulsive behaviors

friend list" to identify people and places to go to for safety and support (Celano, Hazzard, Campbell, & Long, 2002).
- Do not attempt to intervene by contacting parents regarding suspected abuse, because it could give the perpetrator an opportunity to cover his or her actions. It is not unusual for a parent who is suspected of abuse to withdraw the student and move out of state with very little warning.

In the majority of cases, the professional school counselor becomes the first person that the student talks to about the abuse, and so the counselor becomes the "outcry witness." Because the counseling relationship is addressing such sensitive issues with legal consequences, professional school counselors must be well apprised of the legal and policy protocols within their state and school district as well as the child protective services process (Sandoval, 2013). Following is a list of strategies and techniques for addressing initial reports of abuse:

- Do not overreact.
- Sit facing the student, with no desk between the two of you.
- Stay calm, and use active listening.
- Remember, perpetrators rely on trust and secrecy to victimize, so be patient.
- Refrain from displaying anger, disapproval, or disgust toward the parents or perpetrator.
- Let the student know that you believe him or her.
- Refrain from asking leading questions or probing for information the student is unwilling to give.
- Help the student feel powerful by offering options.
- Place the blame on the offender and let students know it's not their fault.
- Ensure students' secrecy.
- Explain to the student, in age-appropriate language, mandated reporting and the steps that will be followed.
- Do not contact the student's parents.
- Ask the student if he or she feels safe returning home. If the student indicates feeling unsafe, contact CPS immediately for intervention.
- Report the abuse by contacting protective services or the police to come to the school for a written report.

Child Protection Services

Professional school counselors are required to contact the designated agency, including Child Protective Services (CPS) and/or law enforcement and provide information on suspected maltreatment when they recognize signs of child abuse or neglect. When the report is filed, CPS makes the following decisions:

1. CPS must decide if the report meets the statutory criteria for abuse or neglect, and then they must investigate to determine if the abuse or neglect can be substantiated.
2. CPS assesses the child's safety at home along with the need for emergency services or removal. CPS will also assess the risk factors involved for future abuse and neglect. If the investigation rules out abuse, the case is referred or the case is closed.
3. CPS assesses the family for strengths, needs, and factors contributing to the risk of child maltreatment.
4. During the planning phase (which includes strategies or services to achieve goals and outcomes along with specific time frames), CPS identifies outcomes and goals that will reduce or eliminate maltreatment.
5. Service provision includes both in- and out-of-house services such as family preservation, parenting education, foster care, and reunification services.
6. Evaluation, a critical step, involves assessing the safety of the child and the reduction of risks; the achievement of family outcomes, goals, and tasks; and reviewing progress and needs for continued services. If continued services are warranted, then CPS will return to the planning or service provision stages to reassess the needs of the case. If the evaluation is favorable, the case will be closed once it is determined that the family can protect their child without further CPS services.

Counselor and Organizational Liability

All states have laws requiring professional school counselors to report suspected abuse to the designated authorities, and they must follow rigid guidelines when they conduct counseling following disclosures or accusations of abuse from others. It is imperative for counselors to adhere to the ethical standards of the American Counseling Association and the American School Counselor Association and to follow the legal guidelines of their school system and respective district. If you are not sure what the protocol is in your school, immediately check with your building administrator. One professional school counselor had this to say: "I learned from a veteran counselor in my school that if I suspect abuse I am to immediately notify the principal, not the assistant principal, not the school psychologist, the principal." Other school districts require the professional school counselor to notify a law enforcement officer as the initial contact.

Consistent, effective reporting of abuse depends upon the professional school counselor understanding the dynamics of abuse and reporting procedures. Cooperation among the professional school counselor, staff, administration, law enforcement, and child protective services is essential. The following vignette is typical of the types of behavior students who have been physically abused will exhibit in the classroom.

Case Study

Kathy was 9 years old when her teacher became concerned about possible abuse. She was extremely shy and withdrawn and often took a great deal of time to comprehend information, although testing showed no significant physical or cognitive difficulties. Her mother, a professional nurse who had chosen to stay home with her four children, and her father, a store manager, found Kathy's slowness especially upsetting.

As Kathy's homework increased, she became more withdrawn and unhappy. The teacher suggested she seek help at home from her parents, especially with her English. At first Kathy began coming to school with peculiar marks on her hands and arms. On another day she arrived with burn marks covering a good part of her right hand. It had not been treated and had become infected. Using open-ended questions in a safe environment for self-expression, the teacher asked Kathy about her injuries. The teacher learned that Kathy was being abused by her father. After drinking, he would "help her" with her homework, become agitated by her slowness, and burn her with his lit cigarette.

The school district's protocol for abuse involved meeting with the crisis team at the academic site to discuss intervention options. As head of the crisis team, the school principal was responsible for contacting Child Protective Services and inviting a CPS official to the school for a written report. In conjunction with information from Kathy and the crisis team, CPS was successful in assessing that Kathy's safety was in jeopardy at home, and emergency services were initiated. Kathy was placed with her grandparents and continued attending classes at her neighborhood school to promote continuity, stability, and to reduce additional stressors. Kathy's teacher was instrumental in communicating academic accomplishments and socialization concerns to the grandparents. After ongoing family counseling, Kathy was returned to her home with periodic monitoring from her school and child protective services.

Summary/Conclusion

Students who are physically and sexually abused are robbed of more than innocence—they are robbed of emotional stability, rational thinking, and interactions built on trust and well-being. The ability to form and maintain protective and appropriate boundaries is exhausted. Emotional desires that need to be explored and fulfilled are stunted and go unattended or are repressed and can lead to depression or anger. A student's physical and mental welfare is a top priority in school, and the professional school counselor must serve as the student's safety advocate. With every interaction the professional school counselor can help the student take new steps toward an enhanced quality of life. In turn, the student becomes an empowered survivor by taking control of the issues.

CHAPTER 57

Counseling Sexual Minority Students in the Schools

Mark Pope, Lela Kosteck Bunch, and Michael S. Rankins*

Preview

We address the issues that are important for professional school counselors who counsel sexual minority students, including gay, lesbian, bisexual, transgender, intersex, queer, and questioning (GLBTIQQ) youth. The issues include developing a context in which to discuss these issues; "coming out," or the developmental aspects of sexual identity development; the extent of the problems that sexual minority youth face in the schools and society; the effects of negative attitudes and violence toward these youth; and ethical and legal issues in dealing with sexual minority youth in the schools. In addition, we discuss school-based interventions that focus on the role of the parents and schools, separation (e.g., separate schools for sexual minority youth) or culture change, deliberate psycho-affective education, valuing differences, and the power of subtle symbols.

Fag. Dyke. Wuss. Queer. Lezzie. These are some of the words that sexual minority youth often hear as they progress through elementary and secondary schools in the United States. Whether these terms are directed at them because they look and act different or at others who look and act different, the point has been made: "You are different, and that is bad." "You're different and not a member of our group." These statements occur at a time when sexual minority youth so desperately want and need to belong. This is the lexicon of adolescence in America. This verbal and physical harassment is designed to elicit conformity from those so targeted and security for the deliverer, "no matter how bad my life is, at least I'm not one of THEM."

> To be a boy or girl who is "different" from your peers' notions of what a male or female is supposed to do or be is to become the object of derisive comments challenging your sexual orientation. In the USA if you are a sensitive boy who cries at movies, or an athletic girl who wears jeans and no makeup, you are subject to whispers or catcalls from your peers. To be different during a time when conformity to your peer group is the norm is to be a target for verbal and physical harassment from that same group, especially about sexuality. (Pope, 2000, p. 285)

Professional school counselors are confronted regularly with elementary, middle, and high school students who are gay, lesbian, bisexual, transgender, intersex, queer, or simply

---

* *Special thanks to Dawn M. Szymanski for her contributions to a previous edition of this chapter.*

questioning (GLBTIQQ) if they are different. Fontaine (1998) surveyed professional school counselors and found that more than half (51%) of both middle and high school counselors had worked with at least one student who was questioning their sexual orientation, and 42% had worked with at least one self-identified lesbian or gay student. Twenty-one percent of elementary school counselors also reported that they were aware of students in their schools who were identifying as gay or lesbian or who were questioning their sexual orientation. Professional school counselors need to know what to do when that young person walks into the school counseling office and says, "I think I might be a lesbian."

Unfortunately, there are no easy answers. This chapter, however, does provide some guidelines to aid the professional school counselor in helping these courageous young people. Young people who are different face physical and verbal harassment because they are different or just perceived as being different from peers. In this chapter, we will address the following issues: developing a context in which to discuss sexual minority student issues; "coming out," or the developmental aspects of sexual identity development; the extent of the problems that sexual minority youth face in the schools and society; the effects of negative attitudes and violence toward these youth; and ethical and legal issues in dealing with sexual minority youth in the schools. In addition, we discuss school-based interventions that focus on the roles of parents and schools, separation (e.g., separate schools for sexual minority youth) or culture change, deliberate psycho-affective education, valuing differences, and the power of subtle symbols.

Developing a Context in Which to Discuss These Issues

In this chapter, we will discuss sex, sexuality, sexual orientation, and other related issues. Sex and sexuality in American society are taboo subjects. We know that we are supposed to know about it; we are excited about it; we talk about it in indirect ways; we sometimes even talk about it in direct ways, but that is generally considered unseemly. Perhaps our parents talked to us (rarely with us) about it. Our schools have had to fight hard to get an opportunity to teach about it. Socially, we are just not very comfortable with sex (LeVay & Valente, 2006).

Here, we will use the general term *sexual minority* to include a variety of young people who are in various stages of their psychosocial, gender, sexual, and cultural identity development processes, including gays (males who identify with a same-sex sexual or affectional orientation); lesbians (females who identify with a same-sex sexual or affectional orientation); bisexuals (males or females who identify with both a same-sex and opposite-sex sexual or affectional orientation); transgender (individuals who are physiologically one gender but who are psychologically the opposite gender); intersex (individuals who have biological characteristics of both males and females); queer (individuals who identify as "different" sexually than the majority culture); and questioning (individuals who are unsure of their sexual or affectional orientation or gender identity). This sometimes will be abbreviated as either GLBTIQQ or GLBT, as appropriate, in this chapter.

Further, there are a number of well-written articles and books on the etiology of sexual orientation (e.g., LeVay, 1991, 1999; see LeVay & Valente, 2006). The topic of sexual orientation is complex, evocative, and confusing. To date, it remains unclear exactly how sexual orientation is determined. Moreover, because conservative religious and political groups tend to view homosexuality as a moral issue while others see it as a civil rights issue, it cannot be separated easily from either context. A person's sexual orientation has both political and religious implications. Finally, given the lack of definitive answers from scientific research, confusion and uncertainty tend to underlie the often intense discussions about the sexual behavior and mental health needs of sexual minorities in our society (Barret & Logan, 2002; Barret & Robinson, 2000; Ciro et al., 2005; Pope & Barret, 2002a). Rarely does anyone agree on anything, yet it appears there is a growing research consensus about the roots of sexual orientation. It is imperative that this type of information be readily available to both parents and students. We make the assumption that the causes of sexual orientation are not known definitively but that sexual orientation is not mutable.

Social attitudes toward homosexuality have also undergone many changes: from the acceptance and integration of same-sex persons into the Native American tribes of North America (Roscoe, 1989); to the acceptance of same-sex unions by the Christian church in the middle ages (Boswell, 1995); to the persecution of homosexually oriented persons under the Victorians (Rowse, 1977); to the enlightened approaches of pre-Nazi Germany (Hirschfeld, 1935), pre-Stalinist Russia (Thorstad, 1974), and imperial China (Ruan, 1991); and finally to the removal of homosexuality from the psychiatric manual of mental disorders (Bayer, 1987). History has seen an ebb and flow in the social acceptance of same-sex orientations (Pope & Barret, 2002a).

In the past, sexual minority adults had to cope with active anger, religious hatred, psychiatric labels, and occupational discrimination. Pope and Barrett (2002b) described how aspects of this discrimination were reflected in the workplace:

> If they did not live in large cities such as New York, San Francisco, and Boston where vital lesbian and gay culture thrives, gay men and lesbians generally kept their sexual orientation a closely guarded secret. . . . Many of them fabricated social lives that included dates with persons of the opposite sex and rarely would share their vacation photographs with their co-workers. If there were a social event with co-workers, many would bring opposite sex "dates" that had been secured to help "cover" their secret. Some even chose careers on the basis of its "safety" in the event they did decide to come out. For example, it was not unusual to hear young gay men or lesbians speak of avoiding careers that involved working with children or commenting on "conservative" corporations that would not deal with their sexual orientation easily. Others carefully guarded their sexual orientation for fear that the promotions would be denied them if they were more "out." Fortunately today, for many lesbian and gay clients, much of this is changing, as it is not unusual to hear casual conversations about the social and relationship aspects of gay and lesbian co-workers in the workplace. (p. 215)

For today's sexual minority youth, there are many positive sexual minority role models available. GLBTIQQ individuals appear in virtually every aspect of daily life. They are more "out" to their families and coworkers, visible in their neighborhoods, assertive in demanding equal rights, and have moved beyond the fear and shame that used to keep most of them invisible. This change can be seen in all aspects of the media, gay-positive statements from national and local political candidates and in the debates within virtually all Christian denominations about the role of gay men and lesbians within the church (Barret & Logan, 2002).

"Coming out to self," or accepting one's own same-sex feelings, attraction, and orientation, is an important and necessary developmental task for anyone who is gay or lesbian, but it is especially important for the gay or lesbian adolescent (Pope, 1995). Males tend to define themselves as gay in the context of same-sex erotic contact, but females experience lesbian feelings in situations of romantic love and emotional attachment (Troiden, 1979). Coleman, Butcher, and Carson (1984) provided a good explanation of general developmental stages and the tasks associated with each stage:

> If developmental tasks are not mastered at the appropriate stage, the individual suffers from immaturities and incompetencies and is placed at a serious disadvantage in adjusting at later developmental levels—that is, the individual becomes increasingly vulnerable through accumulated failures to master psychosocial requirements. . . . Some developmental tasks are set by the individual's own needs, some by the physical and social environment. Members of different socioeconomic and sociocultural groups face somewhat different developmental tasks. (p. 111)

Pope (1995) stated that this developmental task of discovery and acceptance of whom one is and how one functions sexually plays an important role, especially in adolescence. This is, however, also the time for many gay males and lesbians when the greatest denial of differences exists from their peer group. Unfortunately, if the developmental tasks of sexual orientation identification are not accomplished during this critical time and are denied and delayed, then other tasks, such as relationship formation, are also delayed, causing a developmental chain reaction. It is very common to hear that gay men who came out when they were substantially past adolescence have all the problems associated with those of teenagers who have just begun dating. It is important to note that once the critical period has passed in the developmental task, it may be very difficult or impossible to correct the resulting psychological difficulties.

Adolescence is not an easy time in anyone's life because of the required psychosexual identity development. This tumultuous time is only made more difficult, however, when homophobic slurs and insults are hurled at young persons who may have already begun to realize that their sexual orientation is different from their heterosexual peers. Both verbal and physical harassment are designed to elicit conformity from those so targeted along with security for the deliverer ("No matter how bad my life is, at least I'm not one of THEM"). A large study of Minnesota junior and senior high school students found that approximately 11% were still unsure about their sexual orientation (Remafedi, Resnick, Blum, & Harris, 1992). Twenty percent of self-identified gay and bisexual men surveyed on college campuses knew about their sexual orientation in high school, and another 17% knew as far back as grade school that they were gay. The figures are 6% and 11%, respectively, for lesbians (Elliott & Brantley, 1997).

Coming to terms with one's sexual differences during the teen years makes forming a sexual identity a greater challenge (D'Augelli, 1992). This is because youth are socialized in the home and school, in the media, and throughout most of their lives to appreciate falling in love with members of the other gender (Rotheram-Borus & Fernandez, 1995). Though there is wide variation in sexual identity formation in adolescence, some common themes emerge for many gay teens: feeling different, experiencing confusion, and, finally, expressing acceptance (Mannino, 1999; Ponterotto, Utsey, & Pedersen, 2006). Chung and Katayama (1998) reported that the formation of sexual identity is a developmental process composed of the stages of awareness of same-sex feelings, feeling confused because one's assumed sexual orientation differs from one's perceived orientation, tolerance and acceptance of a lesbian or gay identity, and integration of a sexual identity with other aspects of one's life.

Gay men and lesbians often report feeling different from others during childhood. Many of these differences are in gender nonconformity—that is, play and sport interests are more congruent with the other gender (Mondimore, 1996). Boys may find they are quieter, less active, and more sensitive than other boys, while girls may find that they are more physically active, assertive, and more "tom-boyish" than their peers. Marinoble (1998) described the difficulties experienced by many such sexual minority youth, including identity conflict, feelings of isolation and stigmatization, peer relationship problems, and family disruptions. Omizo, Omizo, and Okamoto (1998) found that common sentiments among young sexual minority persons include confusion, fear of not being understood, fear of negative or violent reactions from others, concerns about what kind of a future they might have, poor self-esteem, and internalized feelings of self-hatred. Within especially conservative cultures or families, such as those of some Asian American youth, there are few if any positive role models with whom sexual minority youth may identify (Chung & Katayama, 1998). For such youth, it is likely that feelings of isolation and confusion are magnified.

Some gay youth cope with their confusion by concretizing their gay identity very quickly. This is sometimes initiated by puberty, where feeling different takes on a clearer, more precise feeling of sexual attraction. Herdt and Boxer (1996), in a study of 200 ethnically diverse lesbian, gay, and bisexual youth, found that awareness of same-sex attraction occurred between ages 11 and 12, on average. Other gay teens try to deny their same-sex feelings and become super-heterosexual in an effort to retrain themselves, and still others become bewildered, guilt ridden, and lonely, escaping into substance abuse, depression, and suicidal ideation.

Not all gay and lesbian teenagers accept themselves, which is understandable given the constant battering they receive from some cultures and religions as well as from their peers, family, and society (Mannino, 1999). Eventually, however, the majority of gay youth who do accept their sexuality begin to feel a need to disclose their sexual orientation to others. There are many strategies to such disclosure, but close friends are usually told first, with parents being told later. The fear of rejection and isolation, along with parental sanctions, tend to be ever present; therefore, some sexual minority youth decide not to disclose at all, especially if they are still in high school or living with their parents or other family members (Newman & Muzzonigro, 1993). When young people do decide to reveal their sexual orientation to their parents, having some idea of a "format" for such a coming out process is often helpful. Savin-Williams (1990) reported in a study of gay and lesbian youth that most of those who had successfully come out to self could be described as: (a) being politically and socially involved with other gays and lesbians, having numerous same-sex sexual encounters, regularly frequenting bars, and describing an early onset of same-sex sexual feelings that were beyond their control; (b) feeling accepted by family members and friends and feeling that they had even more friends than before they came out; (c) feeling they were accomplished and self-sufficient, but not feeling competitive and forceful or affectionate and compassionate; (d) being generally older and well-educated, coming from wealthy urban families; (e) measuring their self-esteem and sense of well-being by their relationships with friends and by their career and academic achievements rather than by their possessions and good looks; and (f) being politically liberal and supportive of the feminist movement.

Extent of the Problems That Sexual Minority Youth Face in the Schools and Society

Although we have already discussed a number of social and environmental difficulties that sexual minority youth may encounter, a more intensive focus on education and socialization issues is warranted because the schools are the workplace for young people. Owens (1998) captured the experience of sexual minority students in the schools:

> Schools are social molds where rigid expectations of conduct and behavior are reinforced. Conformity is tyrannical. The wrong clothes or the wrong comment can result in ostracism. Sexual conformity is enforced most rigidly. Those that do not conform are open to the physical, verbal, and mental bullying of the majority. Reports from lesbian and gay teens range from put-downs and "rude comments and jokes" through "profanities written on my locker" and threats to actual violence and physical abuse. The overall result is loneliness, fear, and self-loathing. (pp. 95–96)

Sexual minority youth face stigmatization and a significant number of stressors in the school environment, including ostracism, physical violence, and verbal harassment (Elze, 2003; Espelage, Aragon, Birkett, & Koenig, 2008; Horn & Nucci, 2006). The search for one's sexual identity (male or female) is an important part of adolescence, but when that search is intertwined with minority status—that is, either race or sexual orientation—it is even more complex (Chung & Katayama, 1998).

In the United States, there is still fear and loathing of gay and lesbian people. According to the FBI Hate Crime Statistics Report, the majority of reported offenses were due to anti-male homosexual bias (Federal Bureau of Investigation, 2013). Using a sample of 5,240 LGBT secondary school students, Kosciw, Greytak, and Diaz (2009) found that the indicators of a hostile school climate included frequency of homophobic remarks along with victimizations regarding sexual orientation and gender expression. They also reported that LGBT youth in communities with lower adult educational attainment and in rural communities may face particularly hostile school environments.

These negative feelings toward sexual minority youth are being reinforced by school workers' indifference to these issues. Derogatory remarks by fellow students directed at sexual minority students often go unchallenged by teachers, administrators, or professional school counselors, whereas a similar racist statement would likely prompt a reprimand (DePaul, Walsh, & Dam, 2009; Elze, 2003; Porreca, 2010; Varjas et al., 2007). The dynamics are complicated when sexual minority school employees are trying to hide their sexual orientation and distance themselves from sexual minority youth (Hardie, 2012). Reluctant or unable to support sexual minority youth, these sexual minority teachers, professional school counselors, administrators, or other school staff fail to provide the role modeling or safety that other cultural minority school workers (e.g., African American, Asian American, Native American, Hispanic American) provide for students from their own specific culture.

Effects of Negative Attitudes and Violence Toward GLBTIQQ Youth

Adolescents who are different from their peers face a variety of barriers to healthy psychological development, most of which are created and delivered by their peers, family, culture, and society (Pope, 2000). Besner and Spungin (1995) reported a variety of consequences for the lesbian and gay adolescent such as a high incidence of acting out in school; rebelling against authority; abusing alcohol and other substances; feeling depressed, isolated, and confused; engaging in prostitution; and attempting suicide. Jordan, Vaughan, and Woodworth (1997), in a study of 34 lesbian and gay high school students, reported a clear relationship between derogatory language directed against sexual minority students by their peers and adults in the school setting and self-harmful behavior, such as suicidal ideation, attempted suicide, running away, poor academic performance, and truancy. (Documentation of risk factors that increase the potential for suicide in sexual minority youth, titled "Factors Which Increase Risk of Suicide for Sexual Minority Youth," is posted at www.umsl.edu/~pope.)

Gay youth are from three to five times more likely to attempt suicide than are their heterosexual peers (Bailey & Phariss, 1996; Mondimore, 1996; Russell & Joyner, 2001). Gibson (1989) also found that gay male adolescents are six times more likely to attempt suicide than are their heterosexual counterparts. Currently, there is much discussion among researchers about these statistics, based on the skewed demographics of the populations sampled. The results of many of these studies have been criticized for the retrospective nature of the reports, the involvement of many of the youths in social service systems, and the recruitment of study participants from bars, which might inflate the actual numbers. It is quite difficult to gather generalizable data on this population because of the difficulty of operationalizing sexual orientation and the previously cited issues.

Ethical and Legal Issues in Dealing With Sexual Minority Youth in the Schools

The question of what is the ethical and legal role of the professional school counselor when counseling sexual minority students is an important and practical one. Ethically, the role is clear. Professional school counselors assist students in discovering who they truly and honestly are and help them develop a strong and positive personal and cultural identity.

Research conducted by Nicolosi (1991) described an approach called *reparative therapy* (RT) that claims to change sexual orientation (always from gay to straight, rather than the opposite). RT parallels another "treatment," *conversion therapy* (CT), hailed by conservative Christian groups as proof that prayer and meditation can "drive the sin out" and bring the "sick homosexual" back to health. Both RT and CT have received abundant attention, and both have been soundly condemned by the American Counseling Association, American Psychiatric Association, American Psychological Association, National Association of Social Workers, National Association of School Psychologists, American School Health Association, American Federation of Teachers, National Education Association, and American Academy of Pediatrics. Mental health workers are warned that research indicates both of these "treatments" are more likely to be harmful than helpful. Many believe it is unethical for mental health professionals to practice CT or RT (Barret, 1999; Just the Facts Coalition, 2000).

As to queries regarding whether sexual orientation is open to change, Money (1990) stated the following:

> The concept of voluntary choice is as much in error (as applied to sexual orientation) as in its application to handedness or to native language. You do not choose your native language as a preference, even though you are born without it. You assimilate it into

a brain prenatally made ready to receive a native language from those who constitute your primate troop and who speak that language to you and listen to you when you speak it. Once assimilated through the ears into the brain, a native language becomes securely locked in—as securely as if it has been phylogenetically preordained to be locked in prenatally by a process of genetic pre-determinism or by the determinism of fetal hormonal or other brain chemistries. So also with sexual status or orientation, which, whatever its genesis, also may become assimilated and locked into the brain as monosexually homosexual or heterosexual or as bisexually a mixture of both. (pp. 43–44)

Legally, the role of the professional school counselor is limited by school district policies as well as by state laws and regulations that govern the credentialing of professional school counselors in their state. Also, if the school counselor is licensed as a professional counselor or other mental health professional, the person must operate within the bounds of confidentiality as outlined in the state laws and judicial cases that govern the specialty. Some school districts may require parental disclosure and consent; others may not. Professional school counselors, therefore, must be knowledgeable of the specific policies, laws, and regulations that govern their conduct. It is, however, of the utmost importance to sexual minority students that professional school counselors be seen as their ally and their protector in the school. Clearly, the shift toward the protection of sexual minority students in the schools is gaining momentum.

School-Based Interventions

In order to protect sexual minority students, schools must take an active role in eliminating antigay harassment and creating a positive environment for these students. In this section, the role of parents and school workers will be explored along with specific issues dealing with separation (e.g., separate schools for sexual minority youth) or culture change, deliberate psycho-affective education, valuing differences, and the power of subtle signs.

Role of Parents and School Workers

Parents and school workers often teach homophobic attitudes in quite subtle, and sometimes not so subtle, ways (Kosciw et al., 2009). Some adults do this very consciously because they believe that this is the best way to eliminate such behavior in young people, that it will somehow persuade the student—through their disapproval—not to be gay or lesbian. For other adults, it is not a conscious process, only one that is ingrained and reinforced through others in their environment. Many never contemplate that they are, in fact, emotionally victimizing the sexual minority student.

Through persistent derogatory jokes, behavioral admonitions ("Don't be a sissy" or "Don't hold your hand that way; that's too gay" or "Girls don't sit like that"), and overheard homophobic conversations, gay and lesbian students absorb these negative attitudes regarding sexual minorities becoming victims of the adults they trust and who profess love for them. How do these gay and lesbian children deal with this incongruity?

Some respond by denying their sexual orientation and dating and engaging in sexual activities with members of the opposite sex, trying to pass as heterosexual. Others respond by developing a strong contempt for those gays and lesbians who are more open and obvious. They may take out their own sexual frustrations through varying degrees of aggression toward gay and lesbian members of the community. Other gay and lesbian teenagers respond by withdrawing from society and becoming shy and isolated. They are reluctant to join in social activities with friends and family and live in a world all their own. Some of these teenagers are so filled with self-hatred they cannot find anything acceptable or positive to say about themselves. Some seek out groups that believe their homosexual orientation can be changed. These individuals will go to great extremes and will be highly motivated to do whatever it takes to be straight (Besner & Spungin, 1995).

In Savin-Williams's (1990) study predicting self-esteem among lesbian and gay youth, the teenagers with the highest levels of self-esteem felt accepted by their mothers, male and female friends, and their academic advisors. Lesbian youth who had positive parental relationships felt comfortable with their sexual orientation. Satisfying parental relationships, maternal knowledge of their homosexuality, and having relatively little contact with fathers predicted positive self-esteem for gay men. Mothers are important for self-esteem for both gay men and lesbians and are viewed as considerably more supportive, warm, and compassionate than fathers. Early parent–child interactions, physical affection, childhood rearing practices, and family religious teachings are considered good predictors of the state of comfort students have with their sexual orientation.

Pope (2000) and Pope and Englar-Carlson (2001) reported that messages that parents give to their children are important in the child's developing self-esteem. Phrases such as "Be who you are and never be afraid to express your feelings" or "I love you for you" or "It's okay to talk about anything with me, even if I do not like what you have to say, I will always love you" convey a message of unconditional, positive acceptance—no matter the situation. Unfortunately, parental words spoken in haste and anger can destroy years of positive communication. The best parents weigh the impact of their words before speaking them to their children, never saying negative phrases, even in jest, because such phrases are powerful and will rarely be forgotten by the child.

Glazier (2010) analyzed data from the 2007 Youth Risk Behavior Survey for two of the largest school districts in Boulder County, Colorado. Of the 2,408 participants in this study, one of the most important findings was that supportive adults in the schools helped to reduce the impact of the negative experiences that high school youth have. This especially holds true when a student discloses his or her sexual minority status ("comes out") to school personnel. It is a major life event and deserves to be treated in a sensitive and caring way by the school worker. Some guidelines to help school personnel respond to students who disclose their sexual minority status are posted at http://www.umsl.edu/~pope/disclose.html.

Separation or Culture Change

During the 1980s and 1990s, between the political far-right's attempts to take control of school boards and the unionization of school workers, the schools became the battleground on which many of the tough political questions of the day were played. During this time, the issue of what to do with sexual minority students also came to the top of the school agenda.

Responses to these issues varied considerably among schools. In the New York City schools, the Harvey Milk School was established in 1985 for gay and lesbian students who were not succeeding. In Dallas, Texas, a private school for lesbian and gay youth opened in

1997 (Williams, 1997). In the Los Angeles Unified School District, Dr. Virginia Uribe established Project 10, a dropout prevention program offering emotional support, information, and resources to young people who self-identify as lesbian, gay, or bisexual or who wish to obtain information about sexual orientation (Uribe & Harbeck, 1992). Shortly thereafter, the San Francisco Unified School District, under the leadership of Kevin Gogin, began a similar program called Project 21 (Gustavsson & MacEachron, 1998). Most other school districts have established programs like Project 10 and have chosen not to go with the separate school that isolates sexual minority students from the mainstream.

Changing the school culture is imperative in this process of stopping school violence against sexual minority youth (Black, Fedewa, & Gonzalez, 2012; Glazier, 2010; Kosciw et al., 2009; Porreca, 2010). Each stakeholder in the school system has a vital role in solving this problem, including school-board members, administrators, teachers, professional school counselors, school nurses, school social workers, school psychologists, and school cafeteria, maintenance, and transportation workers. School stakeholders need tools to combat this violence that will enable them to at least promote an environment of tolerance and, ideally, to foster the creation of an environment in which sexual minority youth, like all other youth, are appreciated and valued. Merely being a sympathetic teacher is insufficient; teachers themselves need more training. School sponsored workshops on strategies in working with sexual minority students should provide up-to-date information along with more knowledge and skills regarding sexual orientation, sexual identity, and gender identity.

Craig (2013) described a supportive intervention within the schools focusing on multi-ethnic sexual minority youth. Affirmative Supportive Safe and Empowering Talk (ASSET) is a gay-affirmative, school- and strengths-based program using group counseling to promote resilience in this group.

The "Teaching Respect for All" workshop was created by the Gay, Lesbian, Straight Educators Network (GLSEN) and Parents, Family, and Friends of Lesbians and Gays (PFLAG) and is an important resource in combating violence against sexual minority students and transforming the school culture that tolerates such violence. Bauman and Sachs-Kapp (1998) outlined a "Hate Hurts" campaign to raise awareness of sexual minority youth issues among school stakeholders. As Principal McCallie said in the newspaper article, "You do not have to accept homosexuality as equal to heterosexuality, but you do have to accept that everyone should be safe in the schools" (p. B4). Professional school counselors must be in the forefront of such programs.

Deliberate Psycho-Affective Education

In American culture, boys are not taught how to handle feelings—not by their fathers nor by the schools (Pollack, 1998; Pope & Englar-Carlson, 2001). Pope (1998, 2000) stated that elementary and secondary schools in the United States do an acceptable job of cognitive education, excellent on information, and okay on critical thinking, but most schools fail when it comes to "affective" education. This is not what is being termed *moral education*, or *character education*; it is affective education, psychological education, or psycho-affective education. Teaching these important affective skills, such as interpersonal, social, and psychological skills, is rarely included in any school curriculum, even though such pioneers as Sprinthall (1984) have written about deliberate psychological education for many years.

The deliberate psycho-affective education of our children must become a priority or we will continue to see even more violence by young people who feel they have no hope, no place to turn, no one to talk to, no one who listens, and who have no perspective on life (Paphazy, 2003; Pope, 1998, 2000; Pope & Englar-Carlson, 2001). These students feel that any personal rejection or emotional hurt they experience is a tragedy from which they can never recover. Because they only have feelings of hurt and emotional pain and have no other interpersonal skills to cope with these overwhelming feelings, they attack people whom they believe have caused them that pain (and often innocent bystanders), but their rage is directed at the institution they know best. Their parents take their rage to their workplace because that is their primary institutional focus; their children take their rage to schools. For example, in the Jonesboro, Arkansas, massacre of 10 students and a teacher by an 11-year-old boy and a 13-year-old boy with semiautomatic weapons, shooting their victims as they exited school during a fire alarm, many of their classmates now tell how the boys had talked about doing this for awhile. What caused this? According to news reports, one of the boys was "enraged" over having been "dumped by his girlfriend."

Pope (1998, 2000) reported that many people in U.S. society and school systems undervalue psycho-affective education. Although the schools cannot cure all the ills of society, education is more than information and even more than critical thinking. It is also about who we are and who we love during a time in our lives (school age) when we have many questions about those issues. Not enough attention to these issues is given in our schools. We must educate the whole child, not just the cognitive part. What we are seeing is the effect of that omission.

Professional school counselors are important to the total care and education of students, from elementary school through high school (Pope, 1998, 2000). The following three types of professional school counselor activities are examples of deliberate psycho-affective education in the school: mental health counseling, career counseling, and providing a safe place to openly discuss sex (Pope & Barret, 2002b; Pope, Prince, & Mitchell, 2000). The more that homosexuality (and sexuality in general) is treated as taboo and not discussed openly, the greater the risk of homophobia and misinformation and the greater the risk of violence to sexual minority youth. Many of these issues are addressed in the personal–social domain of the American School Counselor Association's *National Standards for Students* (ASCA; 2004) and supported by other professions who work with youth including the Society for Adolescent Health and Medicine (2013) in their position paper, *Recommendations for Promoting Health and Well-Being of Lesbian, Gay, Bisexual, and Transgender Adolescents*.

Valuing Differences

Respect, appreciation, and valuing differences are essential to stopping the violence against sexual minority students (Pope, 2000). Teachers, counselors, administrators, and parents need to be more outspoken in their desire to teach their children about developing positive self-esteem and greater acceptance of differences. Inclusive diversity training workshops have been developed. *Inclusive* is used here to mean that "diversity" is inclusive of ethnic and racial minorities as well as sexual minorities (Pope, 1995). An excellent tool in teaching individuals to appreciate and value human differences is the *Myers-Briggs Type Indicator* (MBTI), a Jungian-based personality inventory. One of the most important outcomes of using the MBTI is to teach the importance of the individual's opposite personality traits. For example, although your personality preference may be for extraversion and others for introversion, there is no inherent hierarchy in which one is better than the other; in fact, both are required for successful functioning in the world.

Other tools are available for teaching multicultural and diversity lessons, including GLSEN's "Teaching Respect for All," Besner and Spungin's (1995) model workshop for educators on homophobia in their Appendix B, Bauman and Sachs-Kapp's (1998) sexual orientation workshops led by school counselors for GLB youth, and Pope, Pangelinan, and Coker's (2011) book on teaching multicultural competence. The National Coalition Building Institute, B'nai B'rith, and the American Friends Service Committee all offer excellent workshops on these topics and more.

In terms of the school curriculum, it is important to integrate and infuse gay and lesbian examples into all courses where appropriate (Ryan, Patraw, & Bednar, 2013). For example, when discussing U.S. history and the role of Native Americans, it would be appropriate to mention the revered position of *winktes* and *berdaches*, Native American terms for sexual minority persons, in the spiritual life of American Indians as the shaman or medicine person of the tribe as well as the many examples of female warriors (Katz, 1976). After reading "The Picnic," a short story by James Baldwin, a world famous African American author, teachers can discuss Baldwin's gay orientation and the consequences of having a double oppression (being gay and African American).

Sexual minority students consistently report feelings of isolation in their schools and communities. A program that was developed to combat such isolation is the Gay-Straight Alliance (GSA), a program developed by the Gay-Lesbian-Straight Education Network (GLSEN) in the late 1980s. GSAs are student clubs all around the world that work to improve the school environment for all students, regardless of sexual orientation or gender identity/expression. Two Web sites support these clubs: http://www.glsen.org/gsa and http://www.gsanetwork.org/. There are over 4,000 such clubs around the world with many of them being led by professional school counselors in their schools.

In research conducted on the effects of GSAs, it has been found that GSAs have many positive outcomes for both students and their schools. The positive outcomes for the students include providing individual support to sexual minority youth (Garcia-Alonso, 2004), "providing information about coming out or relationships, connecting with supportive counselors, faculty, and staff, finding counselors, faculty, and staff mentors; assisting youth to develop coping strategies for living in a frequently hostile world" (Walls, Kane, & Wisneski, 2010, p. 312); providing a safe place for the development of positive relationships; improving sexual minority students relationships with others as a direct result of their involvement in the GSA (Dietz, 1997; Hecht, 1998); having increased connections with supportive sexual minority faculty increases a sense of belonging and increases the likelihood that the student would officially report incidents of harassment or assault to school officials (Walls et al., 2010); improving mental health for sexual minority students (Goodenow, Szalacha, & Westheimer, 2006; Walls et al., 2010); increasing comfort with their sexual identity, greater self-efficacy, and increasing sense of identification with their school (Cooper-Nicols, 2007); decreasing risky health behaviors (Rhee, 2004); increasing their motivation for school and their grades. The positive outcomes for schools include GSA members in general (including allies) reported feeling safer at school and, at the same time, being harassed less frequently, as well as experiencing decreasing levels of homophobia in school environment (Szalacha,

2001). And such effects were found regardless of whether the sexual minority youth was involved in the GSA or not.

> GSAs in schools foster a more accepting climate toward sexual minority students or at least give the impression of institutional legitimacy for their presence. In this case, the presence of GSAs in schools should have a positive impact on sexual minority youth whether or not they are members or active participants in the student organization. (Walls et al., 2010, p. 313)

Finally, school workers who are sexual minorities themselves should be encouraged to disclose their sexual orientation or gender identity and be offered support and employment protection. One openly gay or lesbian teacher can affect the atmosphere of the entire school in a positive way (Munoz-Plaza, Quinn, & Rounds, 2002). The importance of sexual minority role models cannot be overstressed and open sexual minority school workers challenge the myths and stereotypes for all students, not just the GLBTIQQ ones (Owens, 1998).

The Power of Subtle Signs

There are many ways of letting sexual minority students know that professional school counselors, teachers, administrators, and other school workers are supportive of their struggle. If, because of your school district, you are unable as a teacher or professional school counselor to be as overtly supportive as you would like to be, there remains a number of other ways in which you can still relay to sexual minority students a message of your support. Following are a few of the more obvious ways to show your support:

- Have a "safe zone" or "safe space" sticker at the entrance to your office or classroom (available from the Bridges Project of the National Youth Advocacy Coalition or at www.glsen.org).
- Have available in your school guidance office and library literature on sexual minority youth concerns (see www.umsl.edu/~pope/bibliographies.html).
- Post online resources for sexual minority students:
  - International Lesbian, Gay, Bisexual, Transgender, Queer Youth and Student Organization (www.iglyo.com)
  - Parents, Family, and Friends of Lesbians and Gays (www.pflag.org)
  - Gay, Lesbian, and Straight Educators Network (www.glsen.org)
  - *Oasis* (teen magazine; www.oasisjournals.com)
  - The Cool Page for Queer Teens (www.bidstrup.com/cool.htm)
  - National Gay and Lesbian Task Force (http://www.thetaskforce.org/)
- Offer free family counseling services on campus to deal with the issues of sexual minorities.
- Use gay and lesbian positive examples in your teaching or counseling.
- Use inclusive, stigma-free language in the classroom and in all communication, such as using *partners* instead of *husbands and wives*.
- Post pictures of famous sexual minority people (see a list at www.umsl.edu/~pope/famous.html).

By demonstrating an accepting attitude, school workers can send a strong message to students and create a tolerant environment within the entire school. The issues of tolerance, acceptance, and value can all be explored under the umbrella of diversity.

Some Final Thoughts

The role of the professional school counselor in working with sexual minority students is clear. Professional school counselors assist students in discovering who they truly and honestly are and then help them develop a strong and positive personal and cultural identity so that they can live happy, successful, and productive lives in society.

Further, the professional school counselor is expected to take a leadership role in protecting and advocating for sexual minority students as well as developing and implementing school policies that eliminate the verbal and physical harassment of all students, including sexual minority students. This is especially important because research indicates that sexual minority students are more likely to disclose their sexual minority status to their professional school counselors than to any other school worker (Harris & Bliss, 1997). Professional school counselors must therefore be prepared for when sexual minority students present themselves for counseling (Ciro et al., 2005; Pope, 2000).

Further, the relationship is clear between derogatory language/harassment directed against sexual minority students by their peers and adults in the school setting and self-harmful behavior, such as attempted suicide, suicidal ideation, running away, poor academic performance, and truancy (Bontempo & D'Augelli, 2002; Ciro et al., 2005; Russell & Joyner, 2001). Professional school counselors must not allow such language or physical harassment for any student.

Clearly, the momentum is turning toward the protection of sexual minority students in the schools. In 1993, Massachusetts became the first state to ban antigay discrimination in its schools and create a statewide "safe schools" program. The U.S. Department of Education issued guidelines in March 1997 stating explicitly that lesbian and gay students are covered by federal prohibitions against sexual harassment.

Attitudes on sexuality and sexual orientation are indeed changing, and this should bode well for sexual minority students. Although the message is not as strong as many of us would like, it is becoming clear that although people can have their own private hatreds, expressing those hatreds publically as physical or verbal harassment or writing them into policy will not be allowed. The harassment of sexual minority students and teachers should not be tolerated in America or in any society.

Heterosexism, which according to Lorde (1984) is defined as a "belief in the inherent superiority of one pattern of loving and thereby its right to dominance" (p. 45), and homophobia, which is the fear of being gay and hatred of gays and lesbians (Herr, 1997), must be exposed just as racism and sexism have been.

The Massachusetts Governor's Commission on Lesbian and Gay Youth issued a report in 1993 that summarized succinctly a blueprint for ending violence in the schools against gay and lesbian youth. The recommendations included the following:

1. Promulgating school policies that protect gay and lesbian students through:
   - antidiscrimination policies that explicitly include sexual orientation for students and teachers, including teacher contracts;
   - policies that guarantee equal access to education and school activities;
   - antiharassment policies and guidelines that deal with handling incidents of antigay language, harassment, or violence; and

- multicultural and diversity policies that are inclusive of lesbian and gay culture (Pope, 1995, 2002);
2. Training teachers in multicultural issues (which are inclusive of lesbian and gay culture) and suicide and violence prevention as well as changing teacher certification requirements and school accreditation to include this training (Pope, 1995, 2002);
3. School-based support groups for gay and straight students;
4. Curriculum that includes gay and lesbian issues; and
5. Information in school libraries for gay and lesbian adolescents.

As a consequence of this report, the Massachusetts Board of Education unanimously adopted the nation's first state educational policy prohibiting discrimination against lesbian and gay elementary and secondary students and teachers (Besner & Spungin, 1995). Many cities in the United States have since adopted similar policies in their schools.

Summary/Conclusion

We have presented the issues that are important for professional school counselors who are counseling sexual minority students, including gay, lesbian, bisexual, transgender, intersex, queer, and questioning youth (GLBTIQQ). The issues included developing a context in which to discuss the issues; "coming out" or the developmental aspects of sexual identity development; the extent of the problems that sexual minority youth face in the schools and society; the effects of negative attitudes and violence toward these youth; and ethical and legal issues in dealing with sexual minority youth in the schools. In addition, we discussed school-based interventions that focus on the role of the parents and schools, separation (e.g., separate schools for sexual minority youth) or culture change, deliberate psycho-affective education, valuing differences, and the power of subtle symbols.

The lives of sexual minority students in the schools *are* getting better. It is important, however, not to minimize the detrimental effects of verbal and physical violence and harassment on sexual minority students' academic performance and social development. Professional school counselors must focus on the recommendations we have presented for improving the school environment and the quality of the life for sexual minority students. It just makes it better for all students.

CHAPTER 58

Helping Students From Changing Families

Qi Shi and Bradley T. Erford*

Preview

We provide practical interventions for professional school counselors who must address the needs of students from families with diverse living arrangements such as stepparents, single parents, and interracial parents, which in this chapter is referred to as the surface structure. We also provide general guidelines, assessment procedures, and case histories with interventions.

To be a professional school counselor is to be sensitive to the changing nature of families. Day in and day out, professional school counselors witness the transformations of families in diverse forms of living arrangements, which will be referred to as the *surface structure* of families. Professional school counselors are called upon to provide interventions for the challenges that family transformations and stress present in an atmosphere of rising levels of poverty, substance abuse, homelessness, and violence (Erford, 2015c).

The task of helping students and their families in often-stressful transformations through a landscape filled with mountains of substance abuse, poverty, and violence can be seen as dismal. It can also be seen as a great opportunity to take part in the creation of a new chapter in the history of human resiliency. This chapter includes specific examples and guidelines for helping students from families in transition (e.g., single-parent, stepparent, nontraditional families such as gay, lesbian, interracial, and homeless) in the interest of assisting professional school counselors determined to promote competency and resiliency in the face of these challenges.

Single Parenting, Stepparenting, and Cohabitating Surface Structures

How much are the surface structures of students and their families changing today? The Pew Research Center's (PRC; 2010) survey, along with demographic and economic data from the Population Resource Center, provides strong evidence that the American family is experiencing vast change. For example, in terms of surface structure, in the year 2010, only one fifth of U.S. households (20.2%) were made up of nuclear families (i.e., a married man and woman

---

*In the first edition of this book, this chapter was written by Dr. Estes J. Lockhart, may he rest in peace.

and their children), which significantly differed from the 1960s, when the nuclear family made up 45% of households (Jacobsen, Mather, & Dupuis, 2012).

Cohabitation (i.e., unmarried individuals living together as couples) increased by 41% in the 2000s, increasing from 5.5 million households in 2000 to about 7.7 million in 2010 (Jacobsen et al., 2012). Cohabitation is becoming a significant trend, with one third of cohabitants parenting children (Shattuck & Kreider, 2013). In 2010, about 8% of all children under the age of 18 years lived with cohabiting parents (Federal Interagency Forum on Child and Family Statistics, 2013). There has been a rapid increase in single-parent families over the past 40 years; 29% of children younger than 18 years resided in single-parent homes in 2010 (Mather, 2010). One of the reasons for many of the single-family homes was out-of-wedlock birth, which reached its highest rate in 2009, when 41% of all births in the United States were out of wedlock (Martin et al., 2012). However, one must not be quick to assume that single parenting or any other surface structure provides a simple cause-and-effect relationship with a student experiencing difficulty at school. For example, while children of divorce have a higher rate of adverse outcomes such as behavioral, emotional, mental, and physical health, and substance-abuse problems, these effects are likely related to other childhood adversity experienced by children whose parents divorce (Fergusson, McLeod, & Horwood, 2014). While children of divorced parents have lower academic performance than children from nondivorced families overall, this effect is not likely based on changed family surface structure alone. Youth in single-parent families show a negative effect academically, due to several related factors such as lower family socioeconomic status and education level (Fergusson et al., 2014), increased parental conflict, and the child's decreased psychosocial well-being (Potter, 2010).

While a professional school counselor can't directly alter the economic well-being or educational attainment of a single parent, they can provide resources for single parents, referring them to agencies and groups in the community that can provide economic support, educational opportunities, or mental health and physical health services. Professional school counselors can also assist single parents with parenting skills either through direct consultation or referral to parenting programs. Professional school counselors can also help students find the strength to rise above troubled backgrounds, in part by running loss groups in which students from families in transition can find needed support. Perhaps one of the most important things a professional school counselor can do is to be a person whom students know cares for them. In that role of trusted, caring significant other, the professional school counselor can help the student understand that the challenges facing his or her family were not caused by the student, nor are they the student's responsibility to correct. However, the student can learn to cope and have a successful, meaningful life.

Trauma in Changing Families

As the trend toward diverse surface structures in families grows, some of the patterns that are currently thought of as nontraditional will become more commonplace. For example, families are increasingly living in metropolitan areas. From 2000 to 2010, the majority of the U.S. population growth took place within metropolitan areas, and around 84% of the U.S. population lives in a metropolitan area (Wilson, Plane, Mackun, Fischetti, & Goworowska, 2012). In urban schools, 30% to 60% of students lived with caregivers other than their biological parents (Hampton, Rak, & Mumford, 1997). These caregivers may be foster parents, grandparents, stepparents, or adoptive parents. Many of the families in caregiving arrangements will require more services, because the students may present with the effects of traumatic early-life experiences (Schwartz, 1999).

Professional school counselors can support families who are experiencing trauma by helping them find social support and therapy in the community, by listening to the student and family in a caring way, and by helping the student and caregiver maintain a supportive relationship with each other. With parental permission, professional school counselors can also inform teachers and administrators of the situation and seek their support of the student, particularly in helping the student feel a sense of belonging and identification. Professional school counselors can help students who are experiencing trauma to use individual strengths and resources. Some crucial aspects of a recovery environment (resiliency) for students who are involved in traumatic family situations are parental distress, parental psychopathology, individual strengths and resources of the student, social and system resources and intelligence, communication skills, sense of self-efficacy, coping abilities, talents, and feelings of bonding (Meichenbaum, 2002).

Homeless, Interracial, and Gay and Lesbian Surface Structures

Professional school counselors are increasingly helping students from homeless families, interracial marriages, and gay and lesbian couples. Interracial and interethnic marriages have more than doubled over the past few decades. In 1980, interracial marriages accounted for less than 7% of all new marriages, and by 2010 they accounted for about 15% of all new marriages (Wang, 2012). This has led to a surge in interracial babies, as evidenced by the growing percent of the U.S. population identified as two or more races, which rose by 32% from 2000 to 2010 (Jones & Bullock, 2012). Estimates from the Annual Homeless Assessment Report [AHAR] to Congress state that families with children constitute 36% of the total homeless population, and nearly one quarter of all homeless people were children under the age of 18 years (U.S. Department of Housing and Urban Development [HUD], 2013). Approximately 45% of all homeless people live in major cities, and the remainder lives in smaller cities, counties, and rural areas, but the prevalence of homelessness in those areas is decreasing. Students from homeless, gay and lesbian, and interracial families will most often require help with acceptance and full inclusion.

Homelessness

Homeless students present with a specific set of difficulties, including frequent relocation, lack of a permanent address, lack of a place to study, lack of a place to store personal items including school items, difficulty attending or participating in school events, and the stress of living in shelters with strangers and no private space. Homeless students might carry in their backpacks everything that is important to them. Professional school counselors can help these students find a safe place to keep a few personal items. It is also helpful to assist these students to find a place to study or arrange for them to have a study period at school for completing homework that would otherwise be very difficult to complete, thus leading to the students' falling behind. Embarrassment about living arrangements is prevalent, and helping homeless students know how to speak about it with other students is valuable. Students who are homeless often have difficulty accessing special education programs; professional school counselors can be advocates for special education services where needed.

The most significant problems are perhaps those that homeless families experience on the street and in the shelters which the student may need to discuss with the professional school counselor. It is important to know that the student may be hesitant to discuss his or her family situation. Joining with the student so that the student will risk sharing his or her secrets is a key to providing help. Additional information on homelessness may be found at the U.S. Department of Housing and Urban Development Web site (www.hud.gov/homeless).

Gay or Lesbian Families

Students from gay or lesbian families most often need help coping with the issues of anger and embarrassment. They may be angry with one or both of their parents or because of society's perception and treatment of the family structure. It can be helpful for the student who is angry to take part in family counseling with a mental health counselor. The professional school counselor can deal with this anger at school as anger would be dealt with in counseling a student for loss. The embarrassment can be addressed through the cognitive technique of challenging assumptions. The student's belief that his or her peers will label the student on the basis of his or her gay or lesbian parents needs to be challenged. Existing data on students of lesbian mothers suggest that students may fare better when the mothers are in good psychological health and living with a lesbian partner with whom childcare is shared (Patterson, 2002). It is helpful for the student to normalize his or her situation as much as possible. It is supportive for children in lesbian and gay families to be able to interact with peers in similar situations. Additional information on gay and lesbian families can be found on the American Psychological Association Web site (www.apa.org/pi/parent.html).

Interracial Families

Many interracial families share close, caring relationships and strong parenting skills, which will be strengths to draw upon when intervening to help these students find acceptance and full inclusion. The professional school counselor is encouraged to search for strengths in the culture and race of students who present with a need for acceptance and inclusion. Professional school counselors need to be aware of different approaches families from diverse cultures and races may take in relation to issues such as parenting, spirituality, or the anger they may express toward outside agencies or even the practitioner (Cleek, Wofsy, Boyd-Franklin, Mundy, & Howell, 2012). For example, a family member who has experienced racism or who feels alienated by outside agencies may go to school meetings with a "chip on her shoulder." The professional school counselor can join with this parent prior to the school meeting and gain that parent's respect—or, at least, the beginning of trust—and can therefore make the parent feel she has an advocate within the system and feel more secure in the meeting.

The remainder of this chapter provides basic information a professional school counselor must consider when helping students from families with diverse surface structures, particularly those in transition. It provides specific examples of the kind of issues presented to professional school counselors by changing families in a landscape of high stress and suggests helpful interventions for students and families. These interventions not only focus on assessing needs and surface structures but also strengths, resources, and resiliency. For example, studies have concluded that interventions in which a student feels that someone in or outside the family truly cares promote resiliency in the face of substantial risk factors (Richaud, 2013).

Basic Considerations When Counseling Students From Changing Families

When counseling students from changing families, professional school counselors should consider several basic facets, including noting differences in families with similar surface structures, assessing comorbidity and premorbidity in the family, staying positive no matter how stressful the family challenge, being aware of general factors that are fostering family resilience, assessing family strengths and needs, and providing for the direct or indirect delivery of support.

Note Differences in Families With Similar Surface Structure

There are nearly infinite ways to be a family. While the considerations offered in this chapter for intervening with families based on their surface structure can be helpful, professional school counselors must use interventions wisely in the context of the actual family receiving the help. For example, according to the Current Population Survey (U.S. Census Bureau, 2012), 24% of all households are headed by single mothers, whereas only 3.9% of all households are headed by single fathers (Vespa, Lewis, & Kreider, 2013). Over 50% of single-parent households live below the poverty level, in comparison to less than 40% of households headed by two parents, and it is more common for single mothers to live below the poverty level (30.9%) than it is for single-father households (16.4%; Hokayem & Heggeness, 2014; Vespa et al., 2013).

A family that has become a single-parent family because of the separation of supportive and caring yet incompatible parents has different needs than a single-parent family in which the parents are angry with each other, poorly educated, and, prior to the divorce, were attempting to cope with alcoholism. As a third possibility, single-parent families often result from the death of a beloved parent and spouse. In the first family, the focus will be on ensuring that the student understands that he or she was neither the cause nor cure for the troubles between two very loving and supportive parents. In the second family, the focus likely will be on the possible traumatic effects resulting from living in a family filled with anger and alcoholism and making sure that the angry parents do not put the student in the middle of their anger. In the third family situation, the focus will be on loss. Professional school counselors who help single-parent families will have to be able to flexibly shift from one set of intervention skills to another.

Assess Comorbidity and Premorbidity in the Family

Attempting to cope with one stressor is very different from being forced to cope with a series of unexpected short-term traumas or a sustained series of traumatic events including a prolonged trauma (Jonkman, Verlinden, Bolle, Boer, & Lindauer, 2013). Clinicians refer to having more than one serious need as *comorbidity* and a significant need prior to the problem at hand as *premorbidity*.

Comorbidity and premorbidity must be considered when addressing the needs of a student from a family that is undergoing a challenging transition. For example, children who have witnessed domestic abuse have been shown to experience more adverse psychological and behavioral outcomes, such as control problems and more hostile cognitions about women (Moylan et al., 2010). Thus, a professional school counselor helping a student from a family that is transitioning through a difficult divorce in which there has been domestic abuse should be sensitive to the need for intervention or referral for additional clinical services to address a serious condition premorbid to the stress of the divorce. There may be a need to help the student through group work with social skills and control problems at school, but concurrently the family should seek clinical counseling to address the trauma of victimization and negative thoughts associated with women.

Stay Positive, No Matter How Stressful the Family Challenge

It is essential to stay positive. Stressful life events can also have long-term positive effects (Ramos & Leal, 2013). Consider the case of a young man who, 20 years earlier, had been a student in an alternative school. The young man said he remembered a counseling session in which the counselor had asked him to think about something positive he could take from his current situation to carry with him in life. He said that prior to his mother's separation from his father, he had experienced physical abuse and watched his mother be physically abused. He said looking back it was easy to see why he'd become aggressive enough to end up in the alternative school. He said that he had decided back then in response to the directive in the counseling session to always remind himself when tough situations faced him in life that he had already made it through worse than he would ever face. He told the counselor that when he was feeling upset about his recent employment situation, he said to himself, "I've been through much worse and handled it, so I know I'll make it through this fine." Thus, it is useful for professional school counselors helping families undergoing difficult transitions to remember the folk wisdom that says, "What doesn't kill me will make me stronger." It is important to communicate to students and families going through tough or even traumatic experiences that their ability to endure and continue to cope is impressive.

Be Aware of General Factors Fostering Family Resilience

Child-focused studies have pointed to the importance of 10 general factors in the family system in fostering resilience (McCubbin, McCubbin, Thompson, Han, & Allen, 1997). These include family problem-solving communication, equality, spirituality, flexibility, truthfulness, hope, family time and routine, social support, health, and family hardiness (in which the family steels itself and views itself as having a sense of control and influence over the outcome). Meichenbaum (2002) cited a list of studies that suggested protective factors characteristic of resilient children and adolescents, including close relationships to a caring parent figure, supportive extended kin, a sense of belonging and identification, warmth, structure and high expectations in parenting, cohesive families, socioeconomic advantages, and extended family networks. The effective professional school counselor helps students develop these resiliency characteristics through work with students and families.

Assess Basic Family Strengths and Needs

When you are assessing family strengths and needs, it is helpful to collapse the family resiliency factors mentioned by McCubbin et al. (1997) and the protective factors of resilient children and adolescents mentioned by Meichenbaum (2002) into the following five main categories: (a) Parenting, (b) Legal–Economic, (c) Structural–Social, (d) Beliefs, and (e) Health. *Parenting* includes decisions regarding schooling, academics, and discipline as well as warmth, structure, and high expectations. *Legal–Economic* refers to the custody, school records and alimony issues as well as financial well-being of the family. *Structural–Social* refers to all the structural relationship issues in a family such as hierarchy, leadership, alliances, coalitions, cohesion, boundaries, differentiation, extended kinship, social network support, family time, family hardiness, sense of belonging and identification and communication style (see Chapter 29, "Using Family Systems Interventions in Schools"). *Beliefs* include values, sense of equality, spiritual issues, sense of hope, and truthfulness. *Health* refers to mental and physical health issues.

Often, when intervening with high stress families in transition, the professional school counselor will have to assist the family in parenting issues around academics and will have to encourage teacher support for the student during times of crisis. After all, the bottom line for educators is academic performance.

Provide for the Direct or Indirect Delivery of Support

Most professional school counselor direct services will be in the parenting, academic support, and social support areas. The professional school counselor will often become a case manager or consultant for the family in the area of mental and physical health and economic support, providing referrals and liaison services to other professionals. The area of belief systems is a difficult one for the professional school counselor. Issues of truth, hope, trust and spirituality, when they are conceived as a search for meaning, are the stock and trade of a professional school counselor's work, and yet when applied to families in crisis, based on the family's view of these issues, the professional school counselor may choose to refer out for these services. However, even this decision is made complex by the work setting of the professional school counselor. A professional counselor working in a public school would generally stay away from spirituality, specifically in terms of religion, when it is approached by the family, while a professional counselor working in a parochial school might find the issue of religion appropriate and even central. The examples given throughout the remainder of this chapter come back to these general factors of resiliency and protection, giving specific guidelines in areas that are central to the surface structure of families.

Intervention Examples by Surface Structures

This section includes several examples of family interventions upon varying surface structures.

Single-Parent Family: Basic Guidelines

1. *Parenting.* Being a single parent can lead to work overload with accompanying high stress. While the health and safety of the children is the primary responsibility, the need

to provide and maintain a home environment that encourages learning and good behavior in school is also critical. This educational dimension of parenting can be very demanding for single parents because of the required amount of time that quality collaboration and coordination between home and school.
2. *Legal–Economic.* Single parents frequently must raise children with fewer financial resources. Custody battles, child-support payments, and alimony payments may cause financial, social, and other stresses. Also, there may be issues between custodial and noncustodial parents over visits and access to school meetings and records. The law is that noncustodial parents have the same access to school records as do custodial parents, unless a judge has ruled otherwise and that ruling with the judge's signature is in the student's record.
3. *Structural–Social.* A parent and child may become enmeshed or emotionally fused, thereby feeding each other's emotional problems. A child may assume the role of a spousal child, taking the place emotionally of the absent parent. Either of these situations can lead to conditions of anxiety or depression. Hierarchy issues can result in fights over who is in control, and coalitions of the child and one parent against the other parent may occur. At the same time, close relationships between parent and child in times of crisis can be helpful, and a child taking on an appropriate supportive role such as helping the parent with monitoring siblings for a limited time can be a growth experience for the student. In cases of divorce, it is important to help parents avoid putting the child in the middle of spousal disagreements or emotional upset. Professional school counselors should not witness fighting between angry couples, whether the child is present or not. The message should always be that, no matter what your interactions in other places, in the professional school counselor's office, everyone can feel safe and emotionally protected. This can be particularly important in gaining the respect of the parents. It can be helpful for the parents to see that for a brief time they are able to interact appropriately, and when the child is present, the child can observe them interact in a way that is appropriate, not hurtful.
4. *Belief Systems.* A single parent who starts dating can bring new individuals into the home and cause a host of difficulties, including the children feeling that the parent cares more for the new friend than for them. Children may also worry that someone they don't know will be making decisions for them, which can lead to conflicts of trust and loyalty. In single-parent families that occur because of separation or divorce, parents may believe they are guilty for not preventing the divorce. Children may worry that they helped to cause a separation or should be responsible for fixing it. Children may even imagine that their parents will reunite. In such cases, the Three Cs Maxim can be helpful. Parents tell children they didn't *cause* the separation and can't *correct* the situation, but they can learn to *cope* with the situation.
5. *Mental–Emotional and Physical Health Issues.* Parents and children may experience feelings of loss. Financial weakness may result in family members lacking proper health care, such as dental, vision, and medical services, which can seriously affect education. Community health services, service clubs, and helpful medical providers can often address the most serious problems.

Example 1: Single Parent With a Middle School Student

Tom was a student who grew up in a home with an abusive father and found it hard to understand why his mother continued to live with his father. When he stated these feelings to his mother, she always responded that she loved his father and hoped he would change. Tom's father frequently informed his mother and the children that he would change because he cared too much for them to continue hurting them. He was an alcoholic, however, and became very angry when drunk. The final straw for Tom's mother came when Tom was a middle school student and his father sexually abused Tom's sister. Tom's mother reported her husband to social services, and criminal charges were filed. At school, Tom evidenced much social anxiety. He missed school frequently, particularly on stressful occasions such as test days. He hung out with antisocial peers who verbally abused other students and teachers. One-on-one, Tom was very pleasant with adults but was frequently referred to the office for joining in verbal attacks on others.

Assessment. The professional school counselor began to work with Tom and witnessed the school avoidance, verbal threats and taunts, academic failure, and social anxiety. She decided to invite Tom's mother to the school for a brief family session. In the session she learned about the stressful family abuse Tom had witnessed. The mother said she barely could get by financially, because she was a clerk in a local department store and made just above minimum wage. Now with her husband in jail, the home was the most pleasant it had been in many years, but financially she was slipping and having to work an extra half job, which didn't give her the time to help Tom or his sister with their schoolwork. Parenting was stressful for Tom's mother, because she didn't have the time or energy to provide the high structure or academic help Tom needed. She and Tom had become close allies during his father's drunken rages.

The professional school counselor determined that Tom and his mother had an *enmeshed relationship*, meaning they were fused emotionally and were feeding into each other's anxiety. The professional school counselor figured that the enmeshment had much to do with Tom's social isolation and school avoidance. At the same time, the professional school counselor was aware that during the trauma suffered by the family it was normal for Tom and his mother to become extremely protective of each other as well as becoming the eyes and ears for each other's pain. The professional school counselor learned from Tom and his mother that Tom had very low self-esteem. He expected to be treated poorly and figured he got what he deserved. On the positive side, Tom felt that his mother and sister loved him. Even his father, while treating him horribly, nonetheless maintained that he cared for Tom. Tom had on-grade-level academic skills and loved to read. Also, in one-on-one interactions, he was very sociable and pleasant. Tom possessed some strengths, and it was essential for the professional school counselor to help him recognize and build on those strengths.

Intervention. To address parenting concerns about supervision, the professional school counselor suggested to Tom's mother that she ask social services to help arrange and pay for a slot in a YMCA afternoon program, where Tom would be supervised and would also get help with his homework. The professional school counselor, after receiving appropriate information releases, called social services and followed up with a short memo requesting the YMCA afternoon program for Tom. To address the possible trauma, enmeshment, and parenting skills, she also asked about the possibility of social services paying for mental health counseling. In the process, the professional school counselor learned that in criminal cases such as that of Tom's father, the court provided money for therapy for children through a state fund, and social services would recommend and pay for mental health counseling. The professional school counselor assured the social services caseworker that she would encourage the mother to make an appointment for Tom and herself for mental health counseling. The professional school counselor, after receiving appropriate information releases from Tom's mother, was able to inform the family counselor of the need for boundaries in the enmeshed relationship between Tom and his mother.

To address issues of self-esteem and personal trauma, the professional school counselor also let Tom know that she understood the pain he had suffered and that she wanted him to drop in for short meetings to get things off his chest, as needed. During these meetings, the professional school counselor learned that Tom had been traumatized by his father's behavior and made to feel worthless. Following suggestions by Meichenbaum (2002) for child-focused intervention in cases of trauma, the professional school counselor provided Tom an opportunity to appropriately talk about his experiences. She nurtured Tom's coping skills and worked on stress-related symptom reduction. She helped Tom value himself and find meaning in his experiences that he could take with him in life. She helped him combat his sense of isolation and encouraged him to have hope. The professional school counselor gave Tom's mother a 10-minute telephone check-in every 2 weeks to see how things were going and to reassure her that she was available to the mother, when needed.

Stepparent Surface Structure: Basic Guidelines

1. *Parenting.* Parenting issues are often the focus of difficulty in stepfamilies. Both parents may have had different parenting experiences in previous marriages. Ex-spouses of the two remarried parents may have been more supportive or less supportive. Children often expect to continue in a comfortable and habitual pattern. This can be a set-up for the stepparent who then ends up in a battle with the child resulting in stress for the entire family. Being a member of two different households, the child may have difficulty handling the parenting differences when he goes from one biological parent's home to the other.
2. *Legal–Economic.* Resentment about payments to the ex-spouse can become an issue in some families. Finances can become an issue when parent and stepparent have differing opinions about how to manage money for a stepchild, such as for buying clothes, automobiles, trips, and education. As with single parents, non-custodial parents might have problems with access to children from another marriage or to school records.
3. *Structural–Support.* Remarriage may increase or decrease prior support networks. For example, if an older stepparent didn't expect to parent a young child that his or her spouse brings to the marriage, different expectations about duties with children can lead to stress. Where children feel they are members of two different households, stressful relationships can result. It is important for parents to realize that it is not necessarily easy for children to bond with a stepparent, and doing so will take time.
4. *Beliefs.* Beliefs about religion, discipline, academics, dress, curfews, dating, and extracurricular activities can lead to stress for the family and children.
5. *Mental and Physical Health.* The emergence of feelings of loss is often a major issue in stepfamilies (e.g., the child may suffer the loss of a close relationship with a biological parent; the children may still be hoping that somehow their biological parents will get back together).

Example 2: Stepparent With a High School Student

Linda was a high school student who had lived with her father for 10 years after her parents' separation and divorce. Her father remarried a woman who felt very strongly that children should be parented using an authoritarian model. She had a daughter who was in college whom she pointed to as an example of high success with authoritarian parenting. The father, on the other hand, believed in a much looser, hands-off approach. He and his new wife were both intellectuals who constantly battled over authoritarian parenting versus what the father defined as humanitarian parenting. While the daughter in college and the one in high school didn't engage in sibling rivalry, the parents of the two fought over the differences in the two children. Linda, who had a good relationship with her stepmother when her father and her stepmother were dating, began to express extreme anger toward her stepmother when her stepmother began to discipline her.

Many of their battles were over issues such as 15- and 30-minute curfew violations, which her father felt should be ignored or merely mentioned and forgotten, while her stepmother demanded punishment. Other issues such as drunkenness after dates worried both parents. Even in this area, however, the father argued that these events happened only occasionally and should be punished mildly, while the stepmother felt the girl should be seriously monitored and sent for therapy. Additionally, Linda and her father both indicated a feeling of loss of the close relationship they had prior to the father's remarriage. The stepmother, on the other hand, felt that Linda and her father still had a close relationship, and that she, the new wife, was less important to her new husband than his daughter. The father stated that while he didn't want his new family to function this way, if he had to choose one over the other, it would have to be his child, "his blood."

Linda's decline in academic performance brought on additional battles between stepmother and father. The stepmother wanted the father to set tight limits and monitor his daughter's work. The father said that his work prevented rigorous monitoring because he frequently had business meetings at night. The stepmother said she could provide the necessary monitoring with the father's support. When the father agreed, Linda began a war with her stepmother and accused her father of abandoning her. Linda demanded to spend more time with her biological mother, who didn't have the wherewithal or desire to take on additional parenting duties. The non-custodial biological parent refused to level with Linda and instead led her to believe that at some time in the future Linda would be able to live with her.

Assessment. Much of Linda's decline in academic performance was directly related to structural issues in the family that interfered with the parents' ability to parent her. A battle raged constantly over the hierarchy and leadership of the family. The stepmother wanted a very authoritarian leadership style and expected to be at the top of the hierarchy. She had grown up in a family in which her father was mentally troubled, and her mother took charge and provided what little order existed. She vowed to herself that, in her life, there would not be the frustrations, anxiety, and embarrassment born of the chaos brought on by her father. Her role model had been a strong woman who led and protected the family from a weak man. The father had grown up in a liberal family in which any behavior was acceptable, and he became highly responsible because he chose to do so. He believed that being a family was essentially a task in democracy in which all family members, parents and children, had equal votes and voices.

In this situation, the daughter constantly used her alliance (and almost spousal relationship) with her father prior to the arrival of her stepmother to build a coalition against her stepmother. The daughter constantly complained to the father that her evil stepmother was victimizing her. The wife complained that Linda was in charge of the family and would send both Linda and the family into a tailspin if she were not stopped. The father felt caught in the middle of powerful forces, between his own beliefs about being a family, his loyalty to his daughter, his desire to succeed in his marriage, and his hope for his daughter to succeed academically.

When school teachers or the professional school counselor attempted to intervene with the family, the educators would experience the frustration of a family that meant well but could not agree on a plan for getting the daughter back in line academically. Also, it was clear that the family was not going to carry out a plan consistently, even if it was agreed upon.

Intervention. The main issues were parenting and academics, beliefs, and family structure, which all were intricately wound together, keeping the family stuck and the child in trouble. The initial approach in this situation is to determine whether there are any serious family problems such as alcoholism or mental illness and to address structural issues that keep the family from being able to make decisions or follow through on them. If there are serious problems (ruled out in this case), the professional school counselor should provide referral information. Clearly, in this family the structural issue is the daughter's coalition with the father that kept the stepmother feeling in a one-down position and that her husband was not supportive. This is a difficult situation, usually requiring couples counseling, because it is often accompanied by bitterness of a spouse who feels the expectations of the marriage are not being met. In this case, the stepmother also has differentiation issues from her family of origin, meaning she becomes very emotionally upset in the face of what she sees as the same loose, undependable, democratic leadership that wrecked her family. She is unable to stay in a cognitive problem-solving mode with her husband or anyone else who she feels represents this type of thinking—even a professional school counselor or family counselor.

The key for the professional school counselor is *not* to suggest couples counseling, because this will alienate the couple (although, if the couple mentions couples counseling, the professional school counselor should commend them on their wisdom and give them several good referrals). What *can* be done is to ask the parents if they would be willing to shelve their personal beliefs about parenting and academics in the interest of arriving at a compromise plan that everyone involved could carry out successfully. Getting that agreement, the professional school counselor would suggest that they simply list what is necessary for a young person to succeed in school, including proper study time in the evening, monitoring by a parent to ensure that homework and test reviews are being done appropriately, and communication between home and teachers to check on results and performance in class. The father and stepmother can agree to those things. The structured nature of the plan will appeal to the stepmother. The father can still have close discussions with his daughter, but ultimately he must require that the very simple plan be followed. He can talk with his daughter about her feelings but not about blaming anyone for anything.

The issue here is to get around the serious structural and belief issues that will require much commitment and counseling while going for a simple plan that will enable the daughter to perform in school. If the couple should ask how the professional school counselor feels about their beliefs, it is important to say that there are many ways to parent a child successfully, but all successful plans require consistency, commitment, and support. Do not try to resolve the stepmother and daughter issues. Do use the father and daughter relationship as a way to reward the girl for success, and suggest that the parents make certain to find individual time to have fun for themselves while enduring the stress of parenting a young adolescent in a stepfamily arrangement. Commend the parents on coming for help and caring enough to do the right thing.

Interracial Parent Surface Structure: Basic Guidelines

1. *Parenting.* Different cultures frequently have different beliefs about parenting. For example, Latinos typically place a high value on respect for parents from children. Adolescent rebellion or disrespect to parents can be horrifying to a Latino parent while it is fully acceptable as a stage of development to Western Europeans (Chapman & Stein, 2014).
2. *Legal–Economic.* Different cultures have differing beliefs about who should and should not work and under what conditions.
3. *Structural–Social.* The child with parents of different heritage may experience his or her identity as multiracial. Many of the positive or negative feelings that can be generated around this multiracial identity (especially as the young person enters adolescence) is influenced by parental attitudes about classifications of race and societal attitudes. When the child with a multiracial identity encounters strong racist attitudes toward her, the child's identity can be influenced in very negative ways. The child can become socially isolated in a community that lacks appreciation of diversity. Extended family problems between the grandparents and parents regarding racial issues also can bring tension to the home of the multiracial child.
4. *Beliefs.* Issues with the school system about classification can arise. It is important for the school system to honor the family's belief about how their child is to be identified.
5. *Health.* Where racial victimization or bullying exists, the professional school counselor will want to intervene to prevent future trauma. Schools can affirm students' feelings, take their concerns seriously, and enforce regulations against hate-bullying toward students. There are also programs for sensitizing the student body, staff, and parents about the effects of bullying and how to address it.

Consider the case of a male high school student with a multiracial identity. He lived in a town where he encountered strong racism almost daily, both among school classmates and from townspeople while simply walking down the street. The essential intervention was to help him build a couple of close relationships with kids in the town. He was to ignore taunting on the streets from adults and discuss it at school with his professional school counselor and at home with his parents, but not to retaliate. Several important student body leaders were invited and responded positively to coming to his defense at school when any bullying started.

Foster Parent, Adoptive Parent, and Grandparent Surface Structure: Basic Guidelines

1. *Parenting.* Foster children may have seen many different parenting styles and need help adapting to yet another one. In the case of grandparents, they may be a little behind on the parenting issues of the day and need help in updating their parenting skills. Also, grandparents and others who adopt or serve as foster parents may be doing so in the interest of friends, relatives, or their own children who may be divorcing or have died. In this case, the foster parents, grandparents, or adoptive parents will themselves be

grieving while attempting the new task of parenting. When a foster family takes on numerous children, their attention may be divided, and the neediest children tend to get the most attention. Where the child has moved from school to school, academic performance may be affected, students may lack good learning and study skills, or students may focus more on basic survival needs rather than education needs.
2. *Legal–Economic.* Legal issues are similar to single parenting and stepparenting.
3. *Structural–Social.* Finding afterschool programs for students so that guardians can rest may be helpful. The child may have trouble bonding with new parents, and this may result in conflict at home and worry on the part of the foster parent, grandparent, or adoptive parent.
4. *Beliefs.* Children who have lived in foster homes might believe they will not be able to remain with their adoptive parents. Foster and adoptive children may not believe they will remain at the school they are attending and therefore will not have a strong commitment to the school or teachers. These children may have guilty beliefs about why they do not have a stable home life and parents.
5. *Health.* Other children may ridicule foster or adoptive children. Also, these children might have suffered trauma, neglect, or serious emotional stress in previous settings and might therefore require psychotherapy.

Example 3: Interracial Parents With an Adopted Elementary Student

Terrence was a second-grader who was adopted by an interracial couple. The woman was Caucasian and the father was African American. They were both professionals but decided that the woman would stay home with the child. The woman was happy with this decision because she thought her husband could better provide economically, and she felt more competent to parent a young child than her husband. He agreed. The wife also looked forward to taking some classes during the day at a local college.

At school, Terrence was very active. When the parents were informed of this, they questioned if they should have the child assessed for attention-deficit/hyperactivity disorder. Teachers reported that Terrence was difficult to keep on task and had trouble gaining acceptance from the other children because of his overactive behavior. Though he was very active, Terrence did not hurt anyone. At home, the family reported having no trouble getting Terrence to bond with them, yet he spoke as though he would be leaving the home and that nothing in the house, including things in his room, belonged to him.

Assessment. Terrence had lived in many foster homes and was having trouble understanding that adoption meant he would stay forever with these parents. Also, Terrence had learned to bond quickly as a survival mechanism. He wanted the love and caring immediately and for as long as he could with the parents with whom he was placed. Terrence placed little value on the schoolwork or students because he believed that he would have to leave any friendships, school projects, or work fairly soon. He lost many relationships with friends, teachers, and parents and had developed a survival mechanism to protect himself. He never committed completely to friends and schoolwork. He was anxious because he never knew what would happen to him next, and he knew he could not perform in school as well as many of the other students.

Intervention. The main intervention was for the parents to convince Terrence that he would be with them forever. His adoptive father and mother informed him that the furniture in his room was his forever, and that he would never be leaving their home. At school the professional school counselor and teachers reinforced the stability of his placement. They said they expected him to stay with them, and they wanted to help him do well. Terrence's mother began helping him get on track academically. The professional school counselor suggested that the parents wait and see how Terrence did at the school before considering an evaluation for ADHD. The professional school counselor said it was natural for Terrence to be a little anxious, given his situation, and perhaps he was just a very active boy. The plan was to provide him with structure in the class to help him learn to follow class rules, and as he adjusted to parents and school, hopefully he would find friends and begin to replace his old survival skills with some new ones. The professional school counselor set up some times for the adoptive mother to visit the classroom and to become a parent volunteer to help Terrence make the adjustment. In addition, the professional school counselor made an appointment to meet with the family in a month and review how Terrence was adapting.

Summary/Conclusion

A key to helping changing families is to not get lost in their differences. It helps to be aware of issues that frequently arise with a particular type of family, and at the same time stay open and sensitive to the individual nature of the family. There are many ways to be a family, and a particular family, no matter the type in terms of surface structure, may not evidence the issues typically associated with that type of living arrangement. For example, there are gay and lesbian relationships in which children feel embarrassed and there are those in which they do not. Some interracial families receive tremendous support from their extended families and others do not. Some single, step, and cohabiting families have educational attainment, economic well-being, and social support which makes coping with family transitions much easier for them than for those families lacking in any of these three factors. Many individuals will experience traumatic events (about 50 to 60% of adults), but prevalence of posttraumatic stress disorder is quite low—in general, 5 to 10% among all adults (Meichenbaum, 2011). Individuals and the families in which they grow up may respond very differently to similar events and circumstances. It is important to keep an open mind when working with families in transition. Professional school counselors need to approach all changing families according to both their strengths and needs.

CHAPTER 59

Preventing Professional School Counselor Burnout

Gerta Bardhoshi and Bradley T. Erford*

Preview

Burnout and attrition from the field of school counseling are quite high. It is a condition that emerges as a function of the complex interplay of environmental stressors and individual differences. Burnout is a slow and corrosive condition that causes fatigue, cynicism, lack of motivation, and, possibly, depression.

As a professional school counselor or school counselor in training, you may have wondered about burnout and even questioned whether you may be suffering some of the symptoms associated with it. *Burnout* is a term often read about and learned during a training program. Because of professional training, it may be relatively easy to spot in other people. However, when it is the professional school counselor who is tired and feeling ineffective, it is often rationalized as being part of the job. In reality, burnout and attrition from the field of school counseling is quite high. A 1994 study by Grosch and Olsen suggested that the average counselor has a productive life span of 10 years before burnout becomes a substantial factor.

Burnout is a slow, corrosive condition that tends to get progressively worse. This is especially true for the professional school counselor who will often overlook his or her own needs in order to be available to others. For school counselors, as with counselors in general, empathy demands are high and the emotional challenges of working intensively with clients are considerable. In addition, counselors have to also deal with competing life demands. Not only must counselors be present daily for their clients and in their workplace, they are also attempting to balance multiple competing roles (e.g., spouse, parent, friendships, mentor relationships, community roles). This struggle for balance puts additional stress on mental and physical well-being, adding to the formula for burnout (Bryant & Constantine, 2006). As the professional school counselor continues to ignore or deny the extent of his or her burnout, symptoms get slowly worse and more pervasive.

In the past, definitions for burnout have been vague and all encompassing. Although there has been a good deal of research on burnout for human service workers, there has been relatively little research on burnout specifically for professional school counselors. The research that does exist for professional school counselors shows that the job is often stressful,

---

*Special thanks to Kelly M. Murray for her outstanding contributions to the first two editions of this chapter, may she rest in peace.

intense, and unrelenting. The demands placed upon a professional school counselor are often plentiful and, at times, conflicting (Burnham & Jackson, 2000). They are called upon to work with students who present with a host of issues, the families and parents of these students, administrators, teachers, other mental health professionals, and other school officials. The professional school counselor may work in many different domains and wear many hats, some of which may not align with professional standards (Scarborough & Culbreth, 2008). Professional school counselors are relied upon to make critical decisions about students which may affect those students for the rest of their lives.

Professional school counselors often experience a variety of on-the-job stressors, including an overabundance of work, insufficient pleasure at work, inadequate structure and poor management, role conflict and ambiguity, poor relationships with supervisory personnel, meager recognition for efforts, and the feeling of lacking control of one's situation. Other stressors that have been reported are a lack of time, excessive caseloads, high paperwork and other non-counseling duties, being unable to catch up on backlogs of work, a lack of support, lack of clinical supervision, unavailability of adequate testing and interview facilities, lack of funding to attend conventions, lack of in-service training, lack of opportunity for advancement and promotion, and isolation from peers. An important contributor to burnout is the absence of the opportunity to experience completion and follow through with students with whom professional school counselors work. Often the child or the counselor moves on, and, therefore, the counselor is unable to determine if the work he or she has done with the child has been truly effective. The stress and anxiety associated with these many demands may be intense and may take a toll on the professional school counselor.

Burnout has been defined as a prolonged exposure to chronic stressors on the job (Maslach, Schaufeli, & Leiter, 2001). Maslach, Jackson, and Leiter (1996) reported that burnout is a three-dimensional construct. The first component is described as *emotional exhaustion*. Frequently, as professionals try to sustain their efforts in dealing with high work demands, they report feelings of being tired and overwhelmed. As demands persist and emotional resources are further expended, professionals feel they are no longer able to maintain involvement with students (Lee & Ashforth, 1996). In this component, the professional school counselor may feel overwhelmed by his or her job demands. The second component involves *depersonalization*. Professionals suffering from burnout may attempt to purposefully distance themselves emotionally and cognitively from their job (Maslach et al., 2001). As a result, they develop impersonal attitudes and become indifferent in responding to students. They may have negative feelings and attitudes toward students. This distancing of others can lead professional school counselors to believe their students deserve their afflictions. The last component of burnout is a *reduced sense of personal accomplishment* that is often manifested in feelings of incompetence and helplessness toward helping students. It is no surprise that school counselors who are burned out face chronic, overwhelming job demands and have developed an indifference toward students, also experience lack of confidence in making a difference in the lives of others.

Symptoms of Burnout

Burnout can have serious and pervasive consequences for professional school counselors and the students they serve. Individual differences in burnout reactions emerge as a function of the complex interplay of environmental stressors, the supports available, and individual differences (Demerouti, Nachreiner, Bakker, & Schaufeli, 2001; Maslach et al., 2001). Kottler (2010) described burnout as the single most common personal consequence of practicing therapy. He believes that it is not a question of who will experience burnout, but how long the next episode will last. According to Kottler, symptoms of burnout include an unwillingness to discuss work in social and family circles, a reluctance to check messages or return calls, and an unseemly delight in canceled appointments. Daydreaming and escape fantasies occupy the professional counselor's thoughts. Symptoms of burnout may last even after the exposure to the on-the-job stressors has ended, negatively affecting daily well-being beyond the work environment (Söderström, Ekstedt, & Åkerstedt, 2006). Cynicism, loss of enthusiasm and spontaneity, procrastination, physical fatigue, and lack of family and social involvement predominate. There is also a reluctance to admit that a problem exists. The use of alcohol and other drugs has also been linked with burnout among groups of helping professionals.

In a classic empirical synthesis, Kahill (1988) grouped the symptoms of burnout into five major categories. The first reported category is *physical*. Burnout has been associated with general physical health and illness as well as with some somatic complaints such as sleep disturbance and high blood pressure. The second category of symptoms is *emotional*. Some of the most commonly reported emotional symptoms are emotional depletion, irritability, anger, anxiety, guilt, depression, and helplessness. Kahill found that burnout is most closely associated with depression. The third category of burnout symptoms is *behavioral*. A number of unproductive behaviors are associated with burnout. Such behaviors include job turnover, poor job performance, absenteeism, and substance abuse. The fourth category of symptoms is *interpersonal* and usually affects clients, friends, and family members. The final category of symptoms is *attitudinal*. Negative attitudes and cognitions may develop toward clients, work, family, oneself, and life.

Whereas high job demands may be a given in schools, resources seem to be more amenable to change in a short time period (Hakanen, Bakker, & Schaufeli, 2006). Important resources that may help professionals deal with high job demands and minimize burnout include the availability of quality support systems and job autonomy (Bakker, Demerouti, & Verbeke, 2004; Kim & Stoner, 2008; Lee & Ashforth, 1996). The supervisor can be a major source of stress or a significant figure in the prevention and management of burnout. Supervisors who respond effectively to professional school counselor needs increase feelings of confidence, competence, and control (Webber, 2004). Professional school counselors whose supervisors are not counselors may be at high risk of burnout, since such supervisors may possess neither the technical expertise nor the requisite emotional sensitivity to provide support related to some of the unique problems of professional school counselors. On the other hand, feelings of choice and control at work have been identified as minimizing burnout and promoting engagement with one's job (Demerouti et al., 2001). The school environment may itself hamper school counselors' professional autonomy due to limited opportunity for decision making and self-evaluation. School counselor leadership is an important call to action that, among other benefits, could also impact burnout.

Inadequate preparation for the job is also a crucial intrapersonal variable in burnout. Among professional school counselors, age has also been consistently associated with burnout. Modest inverse relationships have been reported, indicating that the likelihood of burnout decreases as age increases. It could be that idealistic young school counselors, who perhaps have not had the training to adequately prepare them for the realities of the job, are more susceptible to burnout. This relationship however suggests that professional school counselors eventually succeed in affecting the development of job satisfaction through changes in personal aspirations and needs, or in the job itself, or they leave the profession (Butler & Constantine, 2005). But burnout is not an endpoint; it is a process. If the trend is not corrected, symptoms that began in a minor way may lead to serious depression, substance abuse, and other severe emotional distress that can be expected to lead to critical impairment. Furthermore, burnout has the potential to be contagious between professionals in an organization, highlighting the importance of a proactive rather than simply a reactive approach (Bakker & Schaufeli, 2000).

Steps to Minimize and Eliminate Burnout

So, what are some steps that can be taken to minimize or, better yet, eliminate burnout? Maslach et al. (2001) contend that a focus on both the individual and their work environment is important in addressing burnout. Corey (2013) offered advice to look within yourself to determine what choices you are making (and not making) to keep yourself vibrant. This can go a long way in preventing what some people consider to be an inevitable condition associated with the helping professions. It is crucial to recognize that you have considerable control over whether you become burned out. Although you cannot always control stressful events, you do have a great deal of control over how you interpret and react to these events. It is important to realize that you cannot continue to give and give while getting little in return. There is a price to pay for always being available and assuming that you are able to control the lives and destinies of others. Become attuned to the subtle signs of burnout, rather than waiting for a full-blown condition of emotional and physical exhaustion to set in. Wilkerson and Bellini (2006) also identified the professional school counselor as having the specialized expertise to influence factors related to creating a work environment in their schools that minimizes burnout. Develop your own strategy for keeping yourself vibrant both professionally and personally, whether that includes reaching out to colleagues and supervisors, creating opportunities for professional development, or scheduling activities that keep you engaged and fully charged. Table 59.1 lists a number of suggestions for preventing burnout, and Table 59.2 (see page 660) provides a list of resources to help professional school counselors deal with job stress and burnout.

Summary/Conclusion

Burnout and attrition from the field of school counseling are quite high, and the symptoms of burnout can be insidious. Burnout often occurs slowly and tends to get worse over time. This is especially true if the professional school counselor ignores or overlooks his or her own needs. It can be relatively easy to rationalize the symptoms of burnout as being "just part of the job." With heavy caseloads, long hours, and a population that presents with difficult and plentiful issues and potential lack of resources, a professional school counselor's job can be extremely stressful, intense, and unrelenting. Burnout symptoms can be serious and pervasive. It is imperative for the professional school counselor to be aware of what the definitions of burnout are and how to spot it in oneself and colleagues. Engaging in self-care and prevention is also essential to decrease the risk of burnout and minimize symptoms.

Table 59.1 Suggestions for Preventing Burnout

Evaluate your goals, priorities, and expectations to see if they are realistic and if they are getting you what you want and need.

Recognize that you can be an active agent in your life.

Find other interests besides work, especially if work is not meeting your important needs.

Think of ways to bring variety into your work.

Take the initiative and start new projects that have personal meaning, and do not wait for the system to sanction this initiative.

Learn to monitor the impact of stress on the job and at home.

Attend to your health through adequate sleep, an exercise program, proper diet, and meditation or relaxation.

Develop new friendships that are characterized by a mutuality of giving and receiving.

Advocate for the role of the school counselor and share your successes.

Learn how to ask for what you want, though don't always expect to get it.

Learn how to work for self-confirmation and for self-rewards, as opposed to looking externally for validation.

Explore opportunities for shared decision making on initiatives that impact students.

Find meaning through play, travel, or new experiences.

Take the time to evaluate the meaningfulness of your projects to determine where you should continue to invest time and energy.

Avoid assuming burdens that are properly the responsibility of others. If you worry more about your clients than they do themselves, it would be wise for you to reconsider this investment.

Take classes and workshops, attend conferences, and read to gain new perspectives on old issues.

Rearrange your schedule to reduce stress.

Learn your limits, and learn to set limits with others.

Learn to accept yourself with your imperfections, including being able to forgive yourself when you make a mistake or do not live up to your ideals.

Exchange jobs with a colleague for a short period, or ask a colleague to join forces in a common work project.

Form a support group with colleagues to share feelings of frustration and to find better ways of approaching the reality of a difficult job situation.

Cultivate some hobbies that bring pleasure.

Make time for your spiritual growth.

Become more active in your professional organization.

Table 59.2 Resources to Help Professional School Counselors Deal With Job Stress and Burnout

Burnout: Symptoms, Antecedents, and Assessments

Cherniss, C. (1980). *Professional burnout in human service organizations*. New York, NY: Praeger.

Cordes, C. L., & Dougherty, T. W. (1993). A review and an integration of research on job burnout. *Academy of Management Review, 18,* 621–656.

Farber, B. A. (1991). *Crisis in education: Stress and burnout in the American teacher*. San Francisco, CA: Jossey-Bass.

Golemiewski, R. T., & Munzenrider, R. F. (1988). *Phases of burnout: Development in concepts and applications*. New York, NY: Praeger.

Grosch, W. N., & Oleson, D. C. (1994). *When helping starts to hurt: A new look at burnout among psychotherapists*. New York, NY: Norton.

Grosch, W. N., & Oleson, D. C. (1995). Therapist burnout: A self psychology and system perspective. *Innovations in Clinical Practice, 14,* 439–454.

Heubner, E. S. (1993). Professionals under stress—A review of burnout among the helping professions with implications for school psychologists. *Psychology in the Schools, 30,* 40–49.

Schaufeli, W. B., Maslach, C., & Marek T. (Eds.). (1993). *Professional burnout: Recent developments in theory and research*. Washington, DC: Taylor & Francis.

Burnout: Interventions and Prevention

Cherniss, C. (1995). *Beyond burnout: Helping teachers, nurses, therapists, and lawyers recover from stress and disillusionment*. New York, NY: Praeger.

Figley, C. R. (1995). *Compassion fatigue: Coping with secondary traumatic stress disorder in those who treat the traumatized*. New York, NY: Brunner/Mazelm.

Gold, Y., & Roth, R. A. (1993). *Teachers managing stress and preventing burnout: The professional health solution*. Washington, DC: Falmer Press.

Grosch, W. N., & Oleson, D. C. (1995). Prevention: Avoiding burnout. In M. B. Sussman (Ed.), *A perilous calling: The hazards of psychotherapy practice*. New York, NY: Wiley.

Jaffe, D. T., & Scott, C. D. (1988). *Take this job and love it: How to change your work without changing your job*. New York, NY: Simon & Schuster.

Lambie, G. W. (2006). Burnout prevention: A humanistic perspective and structured group supervision activity. *Journal of Humanistic Counseling, Education, and Development, 45(1),* 32–45.

O'Halloran, T. M., & Linton, J. M. (2000). Stress on the job: Self-care resources for counselors. *Journal of Mental Health Counseling, 22,* 354–364.

Osborn, C. (2004). Seven salutary suggestions for counselor stamina. *Journal of Counseling & Development, 82,* 319–328.

Paine, W. S. (Ed.). (1982). *Job stress and burnout: Research, theory and intervention perspectives*. Beverly Hills, CA: Sage.

Pines, A., & Aronson, E. (1988). *Career burnout: Causes and cures*. New York, NY: Free Press.

Pines, A., Aronson, E., & Kefry, D. (1981) *Burnout: From tedium to personal growth*. New York, NY: The Free Press.

Richardson, A. M., & Burke, R. J. (1995) Models of burnout: Implications for interventions. *International Journal of Stress Management, 2,* 31–43.

Spicuzza, F., & de Voe, M. W. (1982). Burnout in the helping professions: Mutual aid groups as self-help. *Personnel & Guidance Journal, 61,* 95–99.

Agencies, Organizations, and Advocacy Groups

American Institute of Stress (AIS): A nonprofit organization that serves as a resource and clearinghouse for information on stress-related matters. The Institute's services include newsletter reprints, monographs, and abstracts: 1-800-24-RELAX.

American Psychological Association (APA) Help Line: Call APA's help line at 1-800-964-2000 for information on resources and helping professionals in your area (choose the first option).

Internet Resources

Center for Anxiety and Stress Treatment (**www.stressrelease.com**); Phone: 619-542-0536. This site has a variety of resources that aid in stress reduction, including tips and techniques for reducing stress at work.

Teachers Helping Teachers (**www.pacificnet.net/~mandel**); Phone: 818-7801281. This is a networking site for teachers to ask and answer questions about the teaching field. They can also get information about special issues, such as burnout and job stress.

CHAPTER 60

The Professional School Counselor in the Rural Setting: Strategies for Meeting Challenges and Maximizing Rewards

Deborah L. Drew and Dorothy Breen

Preview

The rural setting presents challenges and rewards to the professional school counselor. We offer strategies to assist professional school counselors in creating and delivering programs that meet the needs of rural students.

The practice of school counseling in a rural setting is both rewarding and uniquely challenging. There is a sense of close community, caring, and trust and appreciation of skills and services offered, but circumstances such as isolation, cultural issues, and limited resources present challenges to the professional living and working in those settings. According to the National Center for Education Statistics (2011a), 13.4 % of elementary and secondary schools in the United States live in rural areas and 20.2% are in rural and small town locations.

Professional school counselors play a critical role in students' lives (Kuranz, 2002a), especially in rural settings. To be most effective, professional school counselors must recognize the challenges and thrive on the rewards of the rural setting. In this chapter, we discuss four prominent challenges presented in the literature: rural isolation, rural culture, limited resources, and ethical dilemmas. We offer strategies for meeting these challenges and maximizing the counseling benefits to the rural school setting. Admittedly, the earlier research was sparse regarding these strategies and is supplemented with findings from our ongoing research. However, in recent years, there seems to be more attention paid to rural school counseling (Bardhoshi & Duncan, 2009; Griffin, Hutchins, & Meece, 2011; Grimes, Haskins, & Paisley, 2013; Hann-Morrison, 2011). We present an updated literature review and added some suggestions from these authors to the strategies for rural school counselors.

Isolation

In rural settings, the professional school counselor may be the only counselor in the school, school district, and community. There is often a lack of contact with other professional school counselors (Breen & Drew, 2001). Consequently, there may not be peer support and access to professional colleagues for collaboration, supervision, or consultation available nearby. There are few opportunities for professional development and, those that are available may require the professional school counselor to drive long distances. The need for socialization is important, especially for young, unmarried professional school counselors. As one counselor stated, "Isolation is difficult—it's very difficult being a single person in this community" (Sutton & Pearson, 2002, p. 272). The impact of isolation has been identified as a contributor to high turnover rates among education specialists in rural schools.

The Rural Culture

Unique is a term used in the literature when describing the rural culture and the rural school environment (Breen & Drew, 2005; Hann-Morrison, 2011). The rural community offers close personal relationships, personal recognition, caring, involvement, traditional values, and independence. However, it takes time to get to know the people and become established. Other challenges include limited resources, distrust of the unfamiliar, and lack of privacy and anonymity (Breen & Drew, 2001). Rural schools tend to be smaller, more personal centers of community identity. By definition, rural schools are usually

> geographically isolated, [and] located in less densely populated areas. These conditions limit opportunities of rural youth for adequate health services, social and recreational activities, relevant educational experiences and exposure to vocational life styles which could be a means of changing their future. (Sweeney, 1971, p. 6)

Researchers have found that rural students are more likely to use tobacco, drugs, and alcohol, while "rural areas are less equipped to deal with the consequences" (Hines, 2002, p. 197).

Limited Resources

Lack of resources is one of the chief complaints that professional school counselors have about the rural setting. Financial resources are limited, and counseling resources may not be readily available (Hines, 2002). The professional school counselor may be expected to "wear many hats" and "be all things to all people" (Breen & Drew, 2001). The professional school counselor might take on the role of generalist: "In the small, understaffed school, the realities of limited resources demand that the counselor, or a few counselors, take responsibility for the total range of student needs" (Sutton & Pearson, 2002, p. 276).

The National Institute of Mental Health (2000) stated that "Americans living in rural and frontier areas have the same kinds of mental health problems and needs for services as individuals who live in urban and suburban areas. Yet, rural areas have unique characteristics that present barriers to mental health care" (p. 1). Furthermore, "for many students and families the school counselor is the first mental health provider they see" and "may be the only mental health provider they ever see" (Kuranz, 2002a, p. 173).

The unique circumstances of the rural setting affect career development. Rural high school juniors and seniors seek information about careers from teachers, parents, and friends, as well as the school counselor, indicating the need to share the resources of the school counselor with others (Griffin et al., 2011). With few resources in these communities, school counselor social justice advocates in rural areas need the partnerships of all available community members (Grimes et al., 2013).

Ethical Dilemmas

The unique characteristics of the rural setting also present dilemmas to the professional school counselor trying to maintain good ethical standards. Maintaining boundaries is especially difficult for counselors who may face expectations to be all things to all people (Breen & Drew, 2001). Both the American Counseling Association's (ACA; 2014) *Code of Ethics* and the American School Counselor Association's (ASCA; 2010a) *Ethical Standards for School Counselors* require counselors to practice within the bounds of individual professional competence. Though ethical standards require referral, resources for referral may be remote.

The professional school counselor keeps information confidential (ASCA, 2010a). Small-school expectations of "knowing" about students may challenge adherence to this standard. Teachers, administrators, and parents in rural settings are accustomed to knowing, and knowing about, students. In fact, these people may know much more about the student than the professional school counselor does because of their involvement in the rural community. School policies may not adhere to this ethical standard, and professional school counselors may be caught between school policy and ethics.

Dual or multiple relationships provide both the professional school counselor and the client and families with a sense of closeness, familiarity, and community, but they also can present ethical dilemmas. Meeting clients in a variety of roles and settings—at school, the store, church, the gym, the doctor's office, the bank, and so on—challenge basic ethical principles of confidentiality. ASCA (2010a) advises that professional school counselors avoid dual relationships that might impair objectivity and increase the risk of harm to students. If the dual relationship is unavoidable, then "the school counselor is responsible for taking action to eliminate or reduce the potential for harm to the student through use of safeguards which might include informed consent, consultation, supervision, and documentation" (Section A.4.a.). The rural setting makes avoiding multiple relationships virtually impossible. A professional school counselor who has worked or lived in the same community for several years may be familiar with siblings, cousins, aunts, uncles, parents, and grandparents of current students. It is possible that too much familiarity can compromise objectivity and challenge sound practice. High visibility, while at times a benefit, makes the analogy of "living in a fishbowl" quite applicable to the rural professional school counselor: "Particularly in small towns and rural communities it is difficult for school counselors to avoid overlap between their personal and professional lives." (Herlihy & Corey, 2006, p. 145)

The "counselor everywhere you go" phenomenon (Breen & Drew, 2001) can create an ethical dilemma by leading to stress and burnout, thus compromising good practice. The ACA *Code of Ethics* (2014) calls for counselors to "monitor themselves for signs of impairment from their own physical, mental, or emotional problems and refrain from offering or providing professional services when impaired" (C.2.g.). But, who takes over when the professional school counselor is impaired?

Strategies for Working in Rural Communities

There are many strategies available to address the needs of the rural professional school counselor. The following are designed to help deal with the isolation of working in a rural setting, understand the rural culture, enhance the limited available resources, and resolve ethical dilemmas.

Coping With Isolation

In order to cope with the professional isolation of working in rural communities, professional school counselors should take on a leadership role and develop support networks.

Lead the way. The rural professional school counselor may avoid working in isolation by becoming a leader and taking responsibility for meeting the needs created by the isolation of the rural community. Take a leadership role rather than a service provider role. Build networks and partnerships in your community. The proverb "It takes a village to raise a child" resonates with truth (Bunch & Gibson, 2002, p. 16). Look for opportunities *within* the rural setting to meet the needs created by the setting. Invite professionals from the community, county, state, and university or college faculty and graduate students to provide training, consultation, and services. Request that your state department of education hire counselors to work as consultants, supervisors, and mentors for rural professional school counselors.

Develop support networks. The school counselor may network with neighboring school districts and engage in consultation and supervision. The counselor may use structured group and peer supervision models, ask school administration to provide time and funding for supervision, mentoring and professional development, and become involved in state and regional professional counseling associations. Together, school counselors can advocate for the needs of rural professional school counselors.

Understanding the Rural Culture

The rural community is unique. Getting to know and appreciate the unique aspects of rural culture will contribute to the effectiveness of the professional school counselor (Breen & Drew, 2001, 2005; Sutton & Pearson, 2002). Become involved in the community in order to learn the cultural roles, norms, biases, and issues. Embrace the "communal notion of being" of the rural culture with a readiness to collaborate with the community (Hann-Morrison, 2011, p. 7). Volunteer in the community. Spend time talking with individuals and families in an effort to respect rural lifestyle and values. Take time to carefully plan the school counseling program for the rural setting. Administer a needs assessment to determine specific areas to address. Think about the way in which the rural setting affects you and your work (Breen & Drew, 2005). Table 60.1 offers questions for rural counselors to contemplate from our 2005 article. Today we would add two additional questions for rural school counselors to consider: How will I collaborate with my school and community?, and What does my principal perceive to be my most important role?

Enhancing Limited Resources

Collaboration is the key to school counseling in the rural setting. School counselors can collaborate with resource personnel who are available in the school, the local community, surrounding communities, and nearest cities (Breen & Drew, 2001; Griffin et al., 2011; Grimes et al., 2013; Hann-Morrison, 2011).

Think of school counseling services as a program, not a person: "Look at your school in a new light. It's an employer filled with highly qualified professionals in teaching, health

Table 60.1 Questions for Rural Counselors

- In what ways does the rural setting help your counseling practice?
- In what ways does it challenge your practice?
- How does it change your work?
- How does it change your concept of the role of a professional school counselor?
- How does your rural professional role challenge your personal life?
- What can you draw upon from your training that focuses on rural counseling?
- What kind of training do you need to look for that focuses on rural counseling?
- What kind of support do you have that focuses on rural counseling?
- What kind of support do you need to look for that focuses on rural counseling?

services, administration and support services, transportation, and food services" (Bunch & Gibson, 2002, p. 14). Work with teachers and students to provide them with education and information regarding career decision making so that they can better assist the students who come to them (Griffin et al., 2011).

According to results of a study on rural school principals' perceptions of the school counselor's role, principals value the work of school counselors in the personal/social domain: crisis intervention; enhancing relationships, coping strategies, and social skill building; understanding self; individual counseling; and identifying and resolving student issues, needs, and problems. Principals may look to school counselors as consultants, team members, and collaborators specifically addressing the personal/social needs of students (Bardhoshi & Duncan, 2009).

Encourage these professionals, staff, and community members to collaborate in the school counseling program. For example, enlist the help of administrators, teachers, nurses, custodians, cooks, secretaries, bus drivers, parents, grandparents, and students as peer counselors, mentors, and tutors. Work with teachers to integrate developmental counseling services into the classroom curriculum.

Use technology. Search Web sites for resources. In Table 60.2, we list several Web sites, some with links to other helpful programs and information.

Involve parents in the process. Help parents understand opportunities, deadlines, and expectations of career and college planning. Remember that people in rural areas are accustomed to solving their own problems—enlist their help. Empower and inform parents to help their children make career decisions (Griffin et al., 2011).

Involve the community. It is important for community members to rely on each other to meet the needs of students. School counselors can work collaboratively with community leaders and helpers such as faith-based organizations and their leaders, community parks and recreational programs, coaches, and political leaders. Organize community summits to discuss meeting the needs of students. Use community "asset-mapping" to identify resources (Grimes et al., 2013).

Use regional programs. Help plan regional programs with other professional school counselors to offer greater exposure to information on health issues, careers, and colleges. Engage

Table 60.2 Resources

American Counseling Association (www.counseling.org)
American Mental Health Counselors Association (www.amhca.org)
American School Counselor Association (www.schoolcounselor.org)
American Psychological Association (www.apa.org)
National Alliance for the Mentally Ill (www.nami.org)
National Association for Rural Mental Health (www.narmh.org)
National Career Development Association (www.ncda.org)
National Rural Health Association (www.nrharural.org)
College Board, Inc. (www.collegeboard.com)
Princeton Review (www.princetonreview.com)
Student Financial Aid Form (www.fafsa.ed.gov)

students in extracurricular activities that provide opportunities to interact with students from larger cities. Promote job shadowing.

Make appropriate referrals. Stay within your role as a professional school counselor and refer. Kuranz (2002a) stated that "the context of the school mission . . . is to support academic achievement" (p. 173). Form relationships with community agencies and mental health agencies and health professionals. In the rural community, professional school counselors need to think broadly when looking for mental health referrals and support services. See Table 60.3 for a list of ideas.

Resolving Rural Ethical Dilemmas

Keep ethical thinking in the forefront at all times. Be aware of ethical dilemmas presented by the rural setting. Provide school officials with a copy of codes of ethics (ACA, 2014; ASCA, 2010a) and educate them about their implications (Dansby-Giles, 2002).

Clarify, define, publicize, and communicate the professional school counselor role (Herlihy & Corey, 2006). Develop and use a disclosure statement. Update job descriptions (Dansby-Giles, 2002). Educate administrators and school board members about the boundaries of competence, time, and the need for ongoing training and supervision. Follow, but also influence, school policies.

Discuss multiple relationships and confidentiality. Talk with students and their families about familiarity in the rural setting and how to handle dilemmas such as confidentiality and multiple relationships.

Set clear boundaries. Set limits on your work. Stay within the bounds of your competence, time, and job description. Refer! Keep the welfare of your students and their families in the forefront of your thinking, but recognize that you cannot and should not be all things to all people.

Table 60.3 Potential Referral and Support Services in Rural Areas

- Physicians, physicians' assistants, nurse practitioners, community health nurses
- State and county agencies and local town offices
- Clergy and church programs
- Police and fire departments
- Funeral directors (for bereavement)
- United Way programs
- Regional and county assistance programs
- School-to-work programs
- State and national career resource centers
- TRIO programs
- Job service offices and offices for training and development
- State offices of substance abuse prevention and intervention and SAMHSA
- State department of behavioral health services
- Vocational rehabilitation
- Local or regional domestic violence programs and child abuse prevention programs
- Local transportation services
- Crisis services
- Red Cross training for Disaster Mental Health Response
- Political and government officials
- Parks and recreation departments
- County Community Action Programs
- Community Mental Health Agencies and Hospitals

Follow an ethical decision-making model. A variety of practice-based models for ethical decision making are available. Cottone and Claus (2000) summarized and compared nine models. Stone (2010) thoroughly discussed ethical issues faced by professional school counselors and offered a model for ethical decision making that encourages professional school counselors to consider the context of the school setting. Rural school counselors should consider the context and culture of the rural school and community.

Consult and seek supervision. Engage in regular consultation with other professionals. Use the telephone and Internet to overcome distances. Discuss ethical issues in ongoing supervision.

Engage in professional development. Stretch the boundaries of your competence through regular professional development. Attend workshops on ethics and ethical decision making to stay current. Codes are revised approximately every 10 years. Use online resources for information and questions (e.g., www.counseling.org, www.schoolcounselor.org).

Practice personal stress management. Take care of yourself, and implement relaxation strategies. Use your support system, and do not practice when impaired.

Purchase malpractice insurance. Even the best professional school counselors can be accused of ethical or legal violations. Help yourself by obtaining professional liability insurance. Your professional organization offers insurance for professional school counselors. Don't assume your school liability insurance will cover you (Remley & Herlihy, 2010).

Summary/Conclusion

Unique circumstances of the rural setting present both challenges and rewards to the professional school counselor. The rewards of close relationships, a sense of community, and appreciation of what the professional has to offer contrast with challenges that come from isolation, cultural issues, limited resources, and ethical dilemmas. More than one quarter of U.S. public school students attend rural and small-town schools. Professional school counselors play a critical role in the lives of these students. Employing effective strategies to maximize the benefits of the rural setting can help professional school counselors create school programs that truly meet the needs of rural students. Taking a leadership role, building networks, learning to value the rural culture, using the resources of the community, using technology, and practicing ethically are some of the ways that rural professional school counselors can meet the challenges and maximize the rewards.

CHAPTER 61

Counseling Multiracial Students

Henry L. Harris, Lyndon P. Abrams, and Edward A. Wierzalis

Preview

There is a growing number of interracial marriages and partnerships and, as a result, the number of multiracial children has increased. Although multiracial children's learning and developmental needs are similar to those of other children, multiracial children may encounter unique challenges because of their heritage. Gibbs and Moskowitz-Sweet (1991) defined a multiracial person as one who is a product of a union in which one parent is from one race and the other parent is from another race. The purpose of this chapter is to help professional school counselors understand some of the issues confronting multiracial students. We provide an overview of multiracial individuals, along with a brief history of interracial marriages, followed by a review of research concerning multiracial persons and professional school counselors' perceptions of multiracial individuals. The final section concludes with implications for professional school counselors and a list of resources for parents and teachers.

Multiracial individuals—historically described as mixed, biracial, or interracial—represent a unique and growing segment of the school-age population. Furthermore, they represent a visible symbol of society's racial divisions and ambiguities (Chiong, 1998). According to the U.S. Census (2010), multiracial individuals, also described as Two or More Races population, comprised 2.9% (9 million) of the nation's overall population of 308 million people. Of the total multiracial population, 92% (7 million) reported belonging explicitly to two races, 7.5% (410,000) indicated three races, and less than 1% (48,000) reported four or more races. The Black and White multiracial population experienced the greatest growth between 2000 and 2010 increasing by 134% to 1 million individuals. The Asian and White multiracial group increased 87% to a population total of 750,000, and the American Indian and Alaskan Native and White population experienced a 32% increase to 350,000 individuals (Humes, Jones, & Ramirez, 2011).

In terms of the region of the country, 38% of multiracial persons lived in the West, 31% lived in the South, 16% lived in the Midwest, and 16% lived in the Northeastern region of the United States. The percentage of individuals reporting belonging to more than one race in the 2010 Census also varied considerably depending upon race. For example, of 231 million Whites, only 3.2% (7.5 million) reported belonging to more than one race. There were 42 million African Americans reported in the 2010 Census, yet only 7.4% (3 million) indicated they belonged to more than one race, which is extremely low, as estimates suggest that between "75 percent and 95 percent of blacks could define themselves as something other than black because of their mixed heritage" (Valentine, 1995, p. 47). Furthermore, of the 5.21 million

American Indian and Alaska Natives, 44% (1.6 million) reported belonging to more than one race; of the nearly 12 million Asians, 14% (2.2 million) reported belonging to more than one race; of the 1.2 million Native Hawaiian and Other Pacific Islanders, 56% (85,000) reported belonging to more than one race; and of the 21.7 million "Some Other Race" category, 12% (2.6 million) reported belonging to more than one race (Humes et al., 2011).

Multiracial persons have traditionally been analyzed and judged from sociocultural and biological perspectives (Nakashima, 1992). The sociocultural perspective characterized them as social and cultural outcasts who were incapable of fitting in or gaining acceptance in any racial group. Park (1928) described multiracial individuals as strangers living in two different worlds. He envisioned their life experience as a period of crisis, resulting in restlessness, spiritual instability, and intensified self-consciousness. Stonequist (1937) asserted that multiracial persons were condemned to live in two different cultural societies that were hostile to each other and, as a result, they were destined to lead a life of loneliness and confusion because of the lower societal status to which they were assigned.

The biological perspective characterized multiracial individuals as depressive, moody, unhappy, aggressive, impulsive, and mentally and physically weak race-conscious beings destined to have a variety of social, emotional, and psychological problems because of their unnatural genetic blend (Caste, 1926; Krause, 1941). Fueled by the eugenics movement during the early 1900s, multiracial people were also perceived to have a shorter life span, be less fertile, have larger than normal skulls and teeth too big for their jaws, in addition to other complicated disabilities (Aikman, 1933). Some eugenicists believed that certain races were genetically superior to others, and the mixing of the races would dilute the superior White race, thus lowering the potential for future generations (Farber, 2003). The goal behind the sociocultural and biological perspective was to create a racially divisive climate by socially and legally discouraging Caucasians from marrying and/or having children with people of color (Nakashima, 1992).

History of Interracial Marriage

"I have nothing against interracial marriages, I just feel sorry for the children because they will not be accepted." "Marriage is difficult enough. Why would you want to marry someone from a different race?" "The children will not know who to identify with and will grow up confused." "The children are going to suffer." This may be one of many responses given by people from different racial and ethnic groups when the topic of interracial marriage is addressed. Interracial marriages and unions have been a controversial part of U.S. history dating from the 1600s. According to Greenberg (1999), prior to the institution of slavery, interracial sex was quite common, as well as some interracial unions; however, as race slavery began to replace servant labor in the South, the offspring of interracial unions began to blur the distinction between Black and White and free and slave. As a method to protect the economic interest of slave owners in the United States, Maryland, in 1664, became the first colony to create antimiscegenation laws designed purposely to discourage and prohibit interracial marriages and sexual relations between "freeborn English women" and "Negro Slaves" (Pascoe, 1991). Years later, in 1691, Virginia made it illegal for Caucasian women to marry Native Americans and Blacks and also made it illegal for them to bear mixed-race children (Greenberg, 1999). In addition to the creation of antimiscegenation laws, the one-drop rule was also established

(Zack, 1995). The one-drop rule stated that any person with one drop of Black blood in their body was considered Black, regardless of their physical appearance (Tatum, 2003). This rule was formally adopted by the U.S. Census in 1920 (Hickman, 1997).

Weinberger (1966) contended that 40 of the possible 50 states at some point had antimiscegenation laws, and the only racial minority group affected by all of the statutes was African Americans. Antimiscegenation laws were constitutionally upheld until 1967. In a landmark decision, the United States Supreme Court ruled in *Loving v. Virginia* (1967) that such laws banning interracial marriages were unconstitutional under the 14th Amendment. At that time, 16 other states had laws prohibiting interracial marriages (Taylor, Funk, & Craighill, 2006). Alabama was the last state to officially remove the language banning interracial marriages from the state's constitution, and close to half of the participants who voted did not want the language removed (Parker, 1999).

Following the 1967 Supreme Court decision, there was a significant rise in the number of interracial marriages. Consider the facts:

- Approximately 15% of all new marriages in the United States in 2010 were between people from different ethnic or racial groups, and from this group, 9% of Whites, 17% of Blacks, 26% of Hispanics, and 28% of Asians interracially married (Wang & Taylor, 2012).
- Overall, interracial couples made up 8.4% of all married couples in 2010 compared to 3.2% in 1980. Of Black males, 24%, compared to 9% of Black females, interracially married in 2010. With Asians, the opposite occurred with 36% of Asian females compared to 17% of Asian males interracially married during the same period (Wang & Taylor, 2012). Between 2008–2010, 22% of new marriages in the Western region of the United States were interracial marriages, compared to 14% in the South, 13% in the Northeast, and 11% in the Midwest.
- Median income earnings for White/Asian married couples were the highest for all couples at $71,000, regardless of race, between 2008–2010. Of Americans, 35% indicated that either a close relative or immediate member of their family was married to someone from a different race. Additionally 63% indicated they would be fine with a family member who was interracially married compared to 28% in 1986 (Wang & Taylor, 2012).
- Hispanics married outside of their ethnic group more than any other racial or ethnic groups (Wang, 2012).

The lower rates of interracial marriage among African Americans suggest that racial boundaries are more prominent, with racial prejudice being more noticeable for this group (Lee & Bean, 2004). Even though attitudes toward interracial marriages have improved, some social stigma against such marriages remains.

Research Associated With Multiracial Individuals

Multiracial individuals have constituted a segment of American society that has encountered various forms of prejudice and discrimination (Lee, 2005), and the research concerning this population has produced a variety of outcomes. Some studies have concluded that multiracial individuals were more likely to experience problems with depression, sexual conflicts, social marginality, interpersonal relationships, racial identity issues, substance abuse, delinquency, conduct problems, negative outcomes in schools such as being expelled or suspended, and social rejection (e.g., Choi, Harachi, Gillmore, & Catalano, 2006; Collins, 2000; Cooney & Radina, 2000; Milan & Keiley, 2000).

Other investigations of multiracial individuals have revealed more positive outcomes by discovering that multiracial individuals were (a) proud of their heritage; (b) emotionally secure with high levels of self-esteem; (c) comfortable dealing with issues relating to their identity; (d) independent, creative, and experienced good parental relationships similar to other single-race individuals; and (e) had less grade retention, higher GPA, and high test scores (e.g., Bracey, Bamaca, & Umana-Taylor, 2004; Hall, 2002; Minville, Constantine, Baysden, & So-Lloyd, 2005; Radina & Cooney, 2000; Rockquemore & Brunsma, 2002; Suzuki-Crumly & Hyers, 2004). In summary, Shin and Sanchez (2005) concluded in their review of multiracial research that investigations taken from clinical populations tended to find negative outcomes, while studies that sampled nonclinical multiracial populations found more positive results.

More recent research has indicated that diversity of the residential neighborhood influenced identity development (Holloway, Wright, Ellis, & East, 2009). In another study, Bratter and Heard (2009) found that the identity development of multiracial adolescents from Black/White mirrored the father's identity, particularly if the father was White. However, for Asian/White families, the identity of multiracial adolescents was influenced more by the mother, regardless of her race. Based upon the history of multiracial persons in the United States, Chen and Hamilton (2012) discovered that participants in their study took more time judging individuals as multiracial rather than from one particular racial group. The findings also revealed that their perceptions of multiracial persons were influenced by physical appearance. Similar results were revealed in the Young, Sanchez, and Wilton (2013) study. It is safe to assume that multiracial students may encounter certain forms of prejudicial behavior because of their heritage.

School Counselors and Multiracial Students

The multiracial population has typically been an underserved group in schools and, because of their increasing numbers, writers in the counseling profession specifically encouraged professional school counselors to address the counseling needs of multiracial students more effectively in the school setting (Herring, 1992; Nishimura, 1995; Wardle, 1992). Nishimura and Bol (1997) collected data investigating the perceptions of the counseling needs of multiracial children from 120 professional school counselors. They did not report that multiracial children experienced any more or fewer problems compared to other children; however, middle school counselors were more likely to report that multiracial students experienced more behavioral problems. The professional school counselors also indicated that multiracial students presented both unique and general counseling issues, and the majority believed they were able to meet the counseling needs of multiracial students without changing their current counseling program.

Harris (2002) expanded the Nishimura and Bol (1997) study of professional school counselors' perceptions of multiracial students by increasing the sample size from a larger geographic region. The results indicated that (a) elementary school counselors perceived multiracial students to have more behavioral problems compared to other children; (b) secondary school counselors perceived minorities to be more accepting of multiracial children than nonminorities; (c) professional school counselors with 1 to 5 years of counseling experience were more likely to automatically categorize multiracial students specifically with the minority parent and also more likely to believe that presenting problems that multiracial students experienced were caused by identity conflicts; and (d) male school counselors perceived multiracial students to experience more academic problems compared to other students and were also more likely than female school counselors to perceive minorities as more accepting of multiracial students compared to nonminorities (Harris, 2002).

The Harris (2002) study also demonstrated how actively promoting cultural diversity and awareness programs in schools affected school counselors' perceptions of multiracial students. It is interesting to note that the majority of professional school counselors who indicated they were uncertain whether multiracial students exhibited more behavioral problems compared to other students were in schools that *somewhat* promoted cultural diversity and awareness programs. Professional school counselors who were employed in schools that *did not* actively promote cultural diversity and awareness programs believed that multiracial students were more likely to attribute problems to identity confusion and automatically categorized multiracial students with the minority parent. They also believed that multiracial students should identify most with the minority parent and perceived minorities to be more accepting of multiracial students compared to nonminorities (Harris, 2002).

Using additional analysis from Harris' (2002) data, Harris and Durodoye (2006) explored how the race of the professional school counselor affected perceptions of multiracial students. Statistically significant relationships were found in the following areas:

- Caucasian school counselors were more likely than African American school counselors to believe that multiracial students would experience more difficulties adjusting to society when compared to students of other racial and ethnic backgrounds.
- Caucasian school counselors compared to African American school counselors were more likely to perceive multiracial children as displaying more negative social skills and attitudes toward adults compared to students of other racial and ethnic backgrounds.
- African American school counselors compared to Caucasian school counselors were more likely to believe it is socially and psychologically best for multiracial students to live in a neighborhood mirroring the minority parent.
- African American school counselors compared to Caucasian school counselors were more likely to perceive minorities as being more accepting of multiracial students.
- A larger number of African American school counselors compared to Caucasian school counselors believed that multiracial children should racially identify most with the minority parent.
- African American school counselors were more likely than Caucasian school counselors to believe that the presenting problems multiracial children experienced were the result of a racial identity conflict.
- While African American school counselors reported that they had taken a multicultural counseling course more frequently than Caucasian school counselors, African American school counselors were more likely to work in racially nondiverse schools and even less likely to promote cultural diversity and awareness programs compared to Caucasian school counselors (Harris & Durodoye, 2006).

More recently, Harris (2013), using a national sample of 1,627 school counselors from all 50 states, including the District of Columbia, explored school counselors' personal perceptions of multiracial individuals. Results indicated that school counselors who had 1 to 5 years of experience were more likely to believe that multiracial students experienced more academic and behavioral problems. In addition, middle school counselors were more likely to believe that multiracial students would have a more difficult time adjusting to society. School counselors who were unsure if the physical appearance of multiracial students affected how they racially identified themselves were also unsure whether cultural diversity and awareness programs were promoted in their school. When exploring the element of a diverse student body, school counselors employed in schools with a "very diverse" student body believed that multiracial students would experience fewer problems related to identity development if they lived in a diverse community. It was also interesting that the same participants believed that the problems experienced by multiracial students were related to identity conflicts.

Suggestions for Professional School Counselors

The number of multiracial students enrolled in schools is likely to increase, so it is imperative for professional school counselors to examine their own lives and explore how race, ethnicity, and culture have shaped their attitudes, values, and personal feelings about multiracial students and their families if professional school counselors hope to create a culturally responsive school environment (Nishimura, 1995). Harris (2002, 2013) suggested professional school counselors begin this self-analysis by asking the following questions:

- How do I feel about interracial marriages and partnerships?
- Do I perceive some more favorably than others?
- How do I feel about multiracial children?
- How do I feel or react when I see a member from my own racial group romantically involved or married to someone from another racial group?
- What preconceived thoughts come to my mind when I see a multiracial student having academic or behavioral problems?
- Does the gender or physical appearance of the multiracial student affect my perceptions?
- Do I assume the problems multiracial students experience are a result of a confused identity?
- How do teachers, students, and administrators treat multiracial students in my school?
- How are multiracial students identified on school forms? Who makes that decision?
- Do I believe multiracial students can be just as successful as other students?
- What impact does my gender or socioeconomic status have on my perceptions?
- If I have negative or inaccurate perceptions of multiracial individuals, what must I personally do to do overcome them?

This self-analysis is helpful for professional school counselors seeking to become culturally competent professionals.

Research in the counseling profession has addressed identity formation concerning multiracial individuals (Bowles, 1993; Poston, 1990; Rockquemore & Brunsma, 2002), and in a pluralistic society where race is such a determining factor, identity formation can be a challenging task for all children. When one is a member of a minority group, the identity formation challenge deepens, and the task is much greater (Chiong, 1998). It would therefore be helpful for professional school counselors to become aware of six important environmental factors needed to facilitate the development of a healthy identity for multiracial students (McRoy & Zurcher, 1983).

1. Parents should acknowledge and discuss their racial heritage with their children. If multiracial children inquire about skin color or hair texture, receive strange looks from people, or hear negative comments because they are multiracial, parents must be willing to openly address these matters in a caring manner.

2. Parents must be flexible in promoting the development of a positive racial identity. Ladner (1984) identified three methods used by parents of multiracial children to confront the issue of racial identity: (a) deny that race is important and implore "my child is human above all else" (p. 7); (b) promote one parent's racial identity over the other; and (c) teach their children to promote a multiracial identity. Parents should not encourage multiracial children to choose one parent's racial identity over the other. When they are forced to disown part of their heritage, their sense of self may not be firmly grounded, which impedes the healthy development of their identity. Failure to identify with one parent means that identification with the other parent cannot be truly integrated as part of the multiracial child's self-identity (Bowles, 1993). According to the American Academy of Child and Adolescent Psychiatry (2011b), multiracial individuals who culturally identify with both parents tend to grow up much happier compared to multiracial children embracing a monoracial identity. Multiracial children may also experience massive feelings of guilt and shame if they are forced to choose one parent's racial identity over the other (Winn & Priest, 1993).

3. Multiracial families should live in a racially diverse neighborhood so their children will have the opportunity to develop relationships with a culturally diverse group of peers and attend a culturally diverse school (McRoy & Zurcher, 1983). When multiracial children live in a racially segregated neighborhood, they may be more inclined to adopt the racial identity of the neighborhood. Consider multiracial individuals from Black/White unions; regardless of their physical appearance, they were identified as Black and lived in the Black community because it was the most accepting. While this perception bears some truth, professional school counselors should not automatically assume that minorities are always more accepting of multiracial children or believe it is best socially or psychologically for them to live in a neighborhood reflecting the minority parent. According to Buttery (1987) and Dhooper (2003), this is sometimes a difficult issue for both the minority and majority communities.

4. McRoy and Zurcher (1983) encouraged multiracial families to have frequent contact and social interactions with racially diverse organizations and institutions. Frequent contact with diverse groups and organizations allows people from all racial backgrounds the opportunity to form more realistic perceptions of each other.

5. Multiracial children are encouraged to avoid forming stereotypical attitudes toward other racial, ethnic, and culturally diverse groups. Parents are role models for their children, and if they have prejudicial attitudes of which they are unaware, their children may be influenced as well. Just because two people are in an interracial relationship does not mean they have resolved all of their issues concerning race. Winn and Priest (1993) discovered in their study that multiracial children consistently expressed the belief that their parents had not sufficiently prepared them to deal with prejudice and racism. They also believed they were experienced negatively by White society and experienced prejudice from their parent's minority culture as well.

6. McRoy and Zurcher (1983) suggested that the family identify itself is a multiracial unit, based upon the integration of the five previous recommendations.

Professional school counselors must understand the role of one's physical appearance and its impact on multiracial students. Some multiracial students who are a combination of

Native American and some other race may worry they do not look Native American enough to claim it. In addition, multiracial youth of African American and some other race display similar views. Many visibly wear their African American heritage, yet other parts of their background are not always seen in their appearance or formally acknowledged. Multiracial students, particularly in high school, are generally aware of their physical appearance and how others perceive them. In this way, their appearance can influence how they self-identify (Lopez, 2004). Root (1998) discovered multiracial females endured more ridicule and rejection because of their appearance than multiracial males for body size, hair texture, hairstyles, hair color, bust size, eye shape, and eye color. Such experiences potentially reinforce feelings of "not belonging." Because schools are one of the most important social environments for acceptance and rejection, professional school counselors must recognize the impact of physical appearance when working with multiracial students.

Teachers, administrators, and other support personnel may have more contact with multiracial students than some professional school counselors. Wehrly, Kenney, and Kenney (1999) encouraged professional school counselors to help educators become more culturally competent through training and in-service workshops. Some of this training should specifically include information on knowledge and skills needed to work with multiracial students and other children raised in multiracial families. Harris (2002, 2013) noted professional school counselors who worked in schools that actively promoted cultural diversity and awareness programs held more accurate perceptions about multiracial individuals and their families.

Professional school counselors are also encouraged to increase their knowledge concerning identity development when assessing multiracial students. Poston (1990) and Rockquemore and Brunsma (2002) offered more accurate concepts of identity development for multiracial individuals than previous models. Regardless of which group multiracial students choose to identify with publicly, conflicts may exist over how they privately identify themselves (Chiong, 1998). Also, when consulting with parents of multiracial students, it is helpful for professional school counselors to provide support and understanding. It might be beneficial to know the racial or ethnic background of each parent because certain combinations of multiracial offspring experience differential acceptance levels in different communities. Black/White multiracial persons are more racially polarized by society and likely to experience greater challenges in dealing with both communities (Chiong, 1998; Dhooper, 2003). Professional school counselors should also sensitively explore how the parents view their child's racial identity at home, how they would like to see their child's racial identity incorporated in the school, the level of involvement of the extended family, the racial make-up of the family neighborhood, socioeconomic status of the family, and the types of coping skills they provide to their multiracial children for dealing with issues concerning prejudice and racism.

In counseling situations, professional school counselors should be aware of themes which may arise for multiracial children, including uniqueness, physical appearance, acceptance and belonging, and self-esteem (Root, 1994). Furthermore, professional school counselors are encouraged to take into consideration the developmental age of multiracial children. While role playing, art therapy, and music therapy are appropriate therapeutic tools, multiracial students from pre-K through elementary age may be best suited for play therapy. Play therapy is a form of counseling that allows children to demonstrate what they are experiencing through play. When working with adolescents, counselors must be able to tell the dif-

Table 61.1 List of Resources Supporting Multiracial Populations

- **Mavin Foundation (founded 1998);** www.mavinfoundation.org; A nonprofit organization that empowers multiracial, multiethnic, and transracially adopted youth, families, and communities
- **Musing Momma;** http://www.musingmomma.com/p/101-resources.html
- **Project RACE (founded 1991);** www.projectrace.com; Nonprofit organization responsible for advocating for multiracial children and adults
- **Resources for Multiracial Families;** http://www.multiracialsky.com/
- **Teaching Tolerance;** http://www.tolerance.org/about; Provides educators with free educational materials that promote respect for differences and appreciation of diversity in the classroom and beyond

ference between typical adolescent behaviors and behaviors resulting from their multiracial heritage (Gibbs & Moskowitz-Sweet, 1991). During counseling sessions, if multiracial clients display negative behaviors because of racial and ethnic factors, they must be allowed to act out or verbalize their feelings in a safe environment.

Professional school counselors should genuinely explore how multiracial students feel about their identity and realize that, for some multiracial adolescents, how others perceive them in society may influence how they identify themselves racially (Lopez, 2004). In addition, professional school counselors should (a) strive to build a trusting relationship with multiracial students who are sensitive to racial factors; (b) help multiracial students explore multiple sides of their heritage; (c) help multiracial students see the connection (if any) between the presenting issue and their multiracial heritage; (d) involve the family and community resources when necessary (Dhooper, 2003); and (e) share with parents of multiracial students and school teachers information on appropriate multiracial resources (see Table 61.1) and school activities, such as those included in the curriculum titled "Serving Children in Biracial/Biethnic Families" (Gerstenblatt, 2000).

Summary/Conclusion

Multiracial students need and deserve broader support from schools and communities; however, before this support becomes a reality, the way society perceives and classifies multiracial students must also change. The possibility of this change occurring increases only after professional school counselors, teachers, administrators, and communities become more aware of some of the unique issues faced by multiracial students (Chiong, 1998). Professional school counselors are in a unique position to become advocates for multiracial students, and while they have developmental and learning needs similar to those of single-race children, they also encounter unique challenges because of their heritage, which represents a visible symbol of society's racial divisions. Professional school counselors must beware of the challenges encountered by multiracial students and their families and strive to become social change agents for this growing population.

CHAPTER 62

Emotional Safety in the Classroom

Gregory R. Janson and Margaret A. King

Preview

Emotional security in the classroom is vital to students' positive growth and development, yet classrooms may become emotionally dangerous when sanctioned behavioral management practices lead to a repetitive pattern of negative interactions between teachers and students, creating a negative school climate. Younger children in elementary school classrooms may be at the greatest risk for this type of emotional maltreatment, which is largely unrecognized by teachers. This chapter discusses the effects of emotional maltreatment in school settings and presents professional school counselors with preventive strategies to raise awareness of the issues, improve the emotional lives of students, and foster a more positive learning environment.

Research has established that an affirming relationship between teachers and students creates a safe learning environment conducive to academic achievement and students' positive growth and development (Hamre & Pianta, 2005). Conversely, that same relationship can interfere with learning and development when exchanges between teacher and student are characterized by repetitive negative interactions. The damage done by these negative relationships is often unintentional and almost invisible to the teacher, since the basis of the exchange is frequently embedded in sanctioned behavior management practices. These practices pose serious threats to students' cognitive development and mental and emotional well-being when they become part of the culture of the classroom (Shumba, 2002a). For some students, the culture of the classroom becomes so negative that the interactions between the teacher and the student escalate to the level of emotional maltreatment and qualify as a form of child abuse (Janson & King, 2010). In these situations, the student is seldom recognized as a victim, but instead becomes the "identified patient."

In practice, teachers believe that emotional maltreatment is harmful to children, but tend not to recognize it when they see it (Shumba, 2002b) and are unaware of the role that they, as teachers, may play in creating schooling environments that are emotionally unsafe for children. Behavioral strategies that may constitute emotional maltreatment include forcing, shaming, singling out individual children to criticize or punish, threatening children with the loss of recess if they fail to complete all of their work, withholding bathroom visits, isolating children through the excessive use of timeouts or punitively seating them away from the group, modeling inappropriate behaviors and a lack of self-control (such as yelling or screaming at children who do not act appropriately), and failing to show unconditional positive regard for every student. These strategies are commonly employed in the name of classroom management or discipline, and when conceptualized as such, make it difficult for teachers to recognize the element of emotional maltreatment implicit in the interactions. Some researchers have described this dynamic as a form of hidden trauma or bullying (Twemlow, Fonagy, Sacco, & Brethour, 2006). The picture is further complicated because victims are unlikely to complain. Younger children are doubly at risk because they are most likely to be maltreated by teachers and staff as well as bullied by peers (Benbenishty, Zeira, Astor, & Khoury-Kassabri, 2002). They are also least likely to recognize emotional maltreatment because they so often see these strategies as appropriate discipline and believe that teachers have the absolute right to punish any child who is not complying with group rules. Many children may also believe that they deserve to receive this kind of discipline because it is the type of discipline that is used in their homes. Older children and adolescents may see teachers' discipline strategies as unfair and object to them, but they may still fail to recognize them as emotional maltreatment. Teachers of younger children may also be more isolated than teachers at the high school level, because adolescents interact with many different teachers; the negative climate in one classroom may be counterbalanced by positive experiences in other classrooms, mitigating the negative effects. Younger children tend to remain in a single classroom, and if that classroom is characterized by a negative emotional climate, the effects can be pervasive and the impact significant.

Emotional maltreatment has serious consequences for students' physical health as well as their psychological well-being. Students who experience emotional maltreatment by school personnel may display the same range of symptoms and behaviors as those who experience more overt and dramatic forms of interpersonal violence such as peer-on-peer bullying and community violence. These negative effects include problems with behavior (both acting out and inwardly directed anxiety and depression), emotional adjustment, school avoidance, self-esteem, personality development, and academic accomplishment (Geiger & Fischer, 2006; Kairys, Johnson, & Committee on Child Abuse and Neglect, 2002). Somatic symptoms such as stomachaches, headaches, asthmatic attacks, bowel upsets, respiratory ailments, and other stress-related illnesses are common. Equally important, when a student cannot rely on his or her teacher to be emotionally safe, that student loses the single most important human resource outside the home: a trusted teacher (Doyle, 2003). Without that source of support, reassurance, and validation, students living dangerous lives outside of school may have nowhere to turn.

Even though teachers and administrators are highly trained, certified professionals, they may have difficulty understanding emotional maltreatment and how to prevent it. They may not have adequate training and experience in guidance strategies that rely on the relationship between teacher and student to affect change as opposed to behavioral strategies that rely on the teacher's superior size, power, and authority to enforce compliance. On the other hand, professional school counselors have the training, credibility, and professional mandate to consult regarding behavior management and to counter the negative effects of emotional maltreatment, not just through their one-on-one work with students but through education and prevention that ensures both the physical and emotional safety of students. Through a process of assessment, raised awareness, prevention, and intervention, professional school counselors can support educators and administrators and make schools safer, more affirming, student-centered environments that enhance the positive growth and development of every student.

Is Your School a Safe School?

Safe schools are environments where children *feel* safe, both physically and psychologically. This makes the prime question: Is your school a safe school? Such a question can be threatening to school personnel, so it makes sense to begin with a low-key approach that perhaps addresses groups of teachers, administrators, and staff separately as part of a wider initiative on school climate. Sitting down with small groups of teachers may be the best place to begin any kind of assessment, and talking about school climate in broad terms may be a less threatening way to initiate a dialog than focusing on individuals' behavior or even self-reflection. Later, as comfort levels rise, a spirit of joint cooperation evolves, and defensiveness becomes less of an issue, a more self-reflective/self-evaluative approach can be considered. Once a sufficient degree of trust and safety is established, administrators and teachers can be invited to joint discussions. Being sensitive to the power dynamics of your school and how well teachers relate to each other and to administrators and staff is essential to a positive outcome.

Initial questions can be simple: What defines our "school climate?" Is our school a safe haven for the students who come here? Do students feel as though they are valued? Are their experiences generally positive? Do you feel students look forward to coming to school? Are there students who regard school with dreadful anticipation? Why? Who are they and how might we help them? Do our students see us as reliable, predictable adults who can be counted on to provide the emotional support and affirmation needed to create a strong learning environment as well as content and instruction? How do we know? How might we do better? The guiding principle for all these questions and the behaviors examined is the most basic principle of all helping professions: first, do no harm. Above all, we must ensure that practices within the classroom and the school do not violate this fundamental protection for children (King & Janson, 2009).

Physical Safety

When most educators and parents sit down to talk about a "safe school," they generally talk about the physical safety of children, and it is likely that this is where your own discussions would begin. Physical safety is far easier to gauge than psychological safety because it is measured using observable, external factors: (a) making sure the physical environment of the school is safe and (b) implementing disciplinary policies and procedures to deal with attendance, drugs, alcohol, weapons, fighting and student conduct. Unfortunately, schools that pride themselves on safety often promote zero tolerance for prohibited behaviors; harsh suspension and expulsion policies; and security procedures that can include metal detectors, security officers, and identification cards. While adults may feel safer with metal detectors and punitive disciplinary policies, many of these procedures have the opposite effect on students. They create alarm, serving as constant, fearful reminders that danger is ever present. This reduces students' sense of responsibility and community and creates a low-grade, persistent level of emotional turmoil and uncertainty. Harsh disciplinary procedures can also lead to alienation and disrupted relationships as opposed to an educational discipline approach that stresses relationships, structures consequences that encourage responsibility, and provides opportunities for students to remain engaged with their peers, the school, and the teacher (King,

2004). The tone and timbre of these policies and procedures have a significant influence on the degree of affirmation and emotional security that students feel.

The corporal punishment of children through paddling or other physical means is presently legal in 19 states and represents a major form of child assault that remains unrecognized by many parents and educators. The United Nations Convention on the Rights of the Child (United Nations General Assembly, 1989) requires educators and schools to respect the dignity and physical person of the child and specifically forbids corporal punishment in schools. This may be one of the reasons that only two of the 194 member nations have failed to ratify the Convention. One nation is Somalia, which lacks a recognized government. The other is the United States. If your school practices corporal punishment, this is a place to begin.

In settings where corporal punishment is illegal or is not used, school personnel may employ closely related disciplinary actions that are physical in nature and that have the same negative effects as corporal punishment. These actions include pushing, shoving, grabbing, "propelling" a student (i.e., grabbing an arm or an elbow and forcing the student to move from one place to another), throwing things, and intimidation through nonverbal gestures and expressions that are based on physicality and power. These are all forms of emotional maltreatment. Regardless of how free from physical harm a child may be, the relationship between physical safety and psychological safety is deeply intertwined. Environments that are both secure and stable depend on trust, warmth and affirmation, not just physical safety. Discussions should center not only on whether children feel safe *in their person* but *emotionally safe* as well. Do existing policies and procedures at your school foster a sense of safety, inclusion, and well-being?

Emotional Security: Sticks and Stones Will Break My Bones, But Names Will Never Hurt Me

Research on children's emotional and social development concludes that name-calling does hurt children and adolescents, often affecting them as powerfully as "sticks and stones," and play a key role in rising levels of school violence (Astor, Benbenishty, Zeira, & Vinokur, 2002; Garbarino & Delara, 2002; Geiger & Fischer, 2006). Emerging research on brain development and emotional maltreatment shows that emotional abuse can be as damaging as physical abuse, leading to lifelong psychological and physiological consequences for children and adolescents (Janson, Carney, Hazler, & Oh, 2009; Viallancourt, Hymel, & McDougall, 2013). School personnel might need to initially discuss their beliefs regarding corporal punishment, emotional maltreatment, discipline, and the nature of children. Subsequent conversations should focus on (a) how to recognize emotional maltreatment and (b) how to create emotional security for children. Adolescents are often victims of emotional maltreatment in schools; however, the younger the student, the greater the risk, suggesting that professional school counselors focus their initial efforts on younger students.

Emotional Maltreatment: How Do We Recognize It?

Emotional maltreatment is a form of child abuse defined as a repeated pattern of damaging interactions between children and adults (Kairys et al., 2002). The behaviors associated with emotional maltreatment include forcing, shaming, rejecting, isolating, ignoring, terrorizing, and corrupting, with research suggesting that these interactions and behaviors frequently occur in schools between teachers and students, not just in homes (Griffith & Zigler, 2002; Shone & Parada, 2005). This may be a surprise to many teachers who view themselves as mandated reporters of child abuse but assume that "accepted practice" means that disciplinary practices cannot be abusive, simply because it occurs within a school classroom. In reality, a quiet classroom that appears ordered and disciplined may be a place where desperate children are too terrified to do anything but sit and comply with the teacher's instructions (King & Janson, 2009, 2011; Janson & King, 2010). Consider the following cases.

> John, age 5 years, is often isolated from his classmates because he frequently speaks out of turn. His teacher repeatedly states to the whole class that when John can control his tongue, he will be able to join the group. When John's behavior does not improve, he is moved farther and farther away from the group. John spends much of his kindergarten year in isolation, does not acquire the necessary skills to successfully complete kindergarten, and is retained for a second year in kindergarten.

> Sara, a third grader, is obese. The other children in her class will not play with her and call her names. When Sara complains to her teacher, she is told that if she didn't eat so much and wasn't so fat she would have friends. When Sara's parents attempt to intervene, the teacher uses information she has gathered on childhood obesity as the reason for her response and reminds the parents that they should not allow Sara to eat so much. The taunting continues with no intervention from the teacher.

> Robert, a second grader, likes math but does not like to take timed tests. He becomes scared and is unable to focus. He is never able to finish a math test in the designated time. On Tuesday and Thursday, Robert's teacher gives timed tests. Each Tuesday and Thursday, Robert complains of a stomachache before leaving home for school. When the teacher begins the test, Robert begins to cry. The teacher tells Robert to stop acting like a baby, and if he continues she will send him to the preschool classroom.

In each of the preceding situations, the teacher is using a strategy that is institutionalized in many classrooms. In the case of John, a child is isolated from the group because the child is demonstrating behaviors that are either annoying or difficult for the teacher to handle. The isolation may include moving the desk or work space to a corner of the classroom, making the child sit in the hall alone, sending the child to sit in the principal's office, or keeping the child in at recess. In Sara's case, the teacher used information about childhood obesity to justify not intervening when other children were verbally abusing and rejecting Sara. In addition, the teacher used scapegoating and blaming the victim as a technique for rationalizing Sara's situation. If Sara didn't eat so much, she wouldn't be obese and her peers would not reject and humiliate her. Sara learns that it is her fault and that she deserves the treatment she is receiving; this becomes part of her belief system and self-image. Robert's teacher has inappropriate academic expectations of Robert. She uses name-calling, verbal threats, and public humiliation as a means to gain control and force Robert to change his behavior. Simply stated, these forms of maltreatment constitute a form of "invisible" bullying in the classroom. However, the consequences for children are anything but invisible. The impact of emotional maltreatment, the shaming and humiliation presented in these examples, is not limited to Robert,

John, and Sara. Bystanders to the abuse of others learn hard lessons that stay with them, negatively affecting their feelings and beliefs about life and relationships long after they have left the classroom (Janson et al., 2009; Janson & Hazler, 2004).

Teachers are often insensitive to issues of emotional maltreatment because they are taught to believe that almost any measure is justified to maintain order and to control children. Many teachers and parents may believe that the best way to ensure a child's compliance and obedience is not through guidance and relationship but through shaming, belittling, and humiliating, and/or with the implicit threat of physical force. They also believe that abuse occurs in the home and not in the school—teachers simply do not believe that they are capable of abuse, even though many teachers will view the behaviors of colleagues as emotional maltreatment, yet do nothing about it when they witness it (Janson, 2014). Professional school counselors, on the other hand, are familiar with the subtleties of abuse and the multiple facets of emotional maltreatment. As such, they are in a strong position to provide the appropriate guidance and support to teachers to help create emotionally safe classroom environments.

Emotionally Safe Classrooms

The most successful classrooms are those in which children believe they are valued, included, and emotionally supported (Hamre & Pianta, 2005; Hyson, 2004). The quality of the student–teacher relationships has a direct bearing not only on the emotional security of the student but on that student's academic performance, sense of self-confidence, self-esteem, and positive growth and personality development (Klem & Connell, 2004). Classrooms should be a place where students can openly express their feelings. In such emotionally secure classroom environments, students learn and grow into socially competent individuals. Strategies used to create this inner security must be based on reflective practice and a personal and ethical commitment to teaching that is characterized by positive teacher–student interactions, personal warmth and affirmation, and unconditional positive regard for children. This does not suggest that negativity can be avoided, but rather that students need to learn how to deal with negativity in relationships and regulate their emotions in a safe environment where they *feel* securely attached to adults who respond to their needs in developmentally appropriate ways (Janson & King, 2010; Twemlow, Fonagy, & Sacco, 2002). This is the essential characteristic of a positive school climate. When children feel as though they belong, and when they can depend on their teachers to be reliable and predictable, they have the best possible opportunity to learn and develop healthy personalities. Through consultation, in-service training, and the facilitation of discussion groups, professional school counselors can assist teachers in creating emotionally safe classrooms in a supportive, nonthreatening manner. The following seven-step process is offered as one model of this type of facilitation, training and discussion.

Seven Steps Toward Creating Emotionally Safe Classrooms

Systemic change is needed to create emotionally safe classrooms; professional school counselors are well-situated to facilitate the necessary dialog and discussion that can lead to greater emotional security for children. Systemic change may be slow, and there needs to be buy-in and commitment by the participants. The payoff for patience and a commitment to the principles of affirmation is not just for students. However, emotionally safe classrooms are places where teachers thrive as well. The seven steps to creating emotionally safe classrooms are as follows:

1. *Study, prepare, present:* Examine your own beliefs. Study about safe schools, what constitutes a positive school climate, and how to recognize and counter emotional maltreatment and abuse. As you educate yourself, you will be better able to educate others about the significance of emotional security to learning and the growth and development of healthy, well-adjusted children. Use your knowledge to engage teachers and administrators at your school about emotional maltreatment in schools. Become an expert!
2. *Prioritize:* Make students' emotional security your priority and help to make it a priority in your school. Develop a network of educators in your school who can share information with others at local, state, and national meetings and conferences. Write about the issues related to emotional maltreatment in school publications, newspapers, and professional journals. Seek funding for projects to expand the work.
3. *Make time to network and collaborate:* You will need time to discuss these issues, to allow ideas to settle, and to give sufficient opportunity to try new strategies. Brainstorming with colleagues and offering your services for consultation makes managing a difficult student's behavior everyone's concern and helps take the pressure off of individual teachers to "have all the answers." Encourage your school and district to set aside time as a part of the professional development plan to talk about emotional maltreatment in schools and to develop strategies for change. Meet regularly.
4. *Create materials:* Develop handouts, research summaries, tip sheets, worksheets, and other resources and materials to help teachers create and implement strategies to support emotionally safe classrooms. Assist teachers in using the materials in their individual classrooms. School counselors are well-known for providing valuable resource materials; take advantage of this!
5. *Tap administrators:* Involve school and district administrators in the work. They are in a position to create policy and provide resources to make emotionally safe classrooms and a positive school climate a priority. They can also help recruit participants and organize training activities. One of the most effective interventions you can make is to bring your school principal on board (King & Janson, 2011).
6. *Involve parents:* Parents want what is best for their children, so encourage them to participate in the training. Encourage them to communicate with school personnel regarding their views on creating emotionally safe classrooms. Urge them to form parent groups to support the development of emotionally safe schools. This can have a significant payoff for children at home as well as at school.
7. *Engage the community:* Raise awareness in the community. Hold meetings and forums where teachers, parents, and community members can interact and identify strategies that can be used in the larger community to promote emotionally safe schools. Seek support from local businesses, libraries, and mental health organizations.

Summary/Conclusion

Professional school counselors can help foster a culture of affirmation and inclusion in their schools by raising awareness of the negative impact of punitive behavioral practices and facilitating discussions that explore self-reflective practices and creative guidance alternatives, thus encouraging the implementation of emotionally safe classrooms and contributing to the creation of a positive school climate. Emotionally safe classrooms are inclusive places where children are valued, affirmed, and accepted by their teachers, even when their behaviors are inappropriate. A secure environment helps children foster a healthy sense of self, learn to effectively self-regulate their behavior, and develop social and academic competence. By using the power of the relationship and the principles of guidance and inclusion, educators will better deal with difficult behaviors and situations without shaming, humiliating, ridiculing, or isolating.

CHAPTER 63

Counseling Children of Poverty

Donna S. Sheperis and Belinda J. Lopez

Preview

In this chapter, we address the implications of poverty on the lives of children, the measures professional school counselors take to mediate those effects, and the challenges faced when working with children of poverty. The concept of resiliency is discussed along with specific interventions used by professional school counselors working with this population.

Children live in an everchanging combination of family, environmental, and social systems. As of 2011, estimates indicated that over one fifth of American children under 18 years of age lived in poverty, and that number includes greater than one half of children living with single mothers (Federal Interagency Forum on Child and Family Statistics, 2013). Poverty has affected families and children as the economy has stagnated, the job climate has offered limited opportunities for lower skilled workers, and access to insurance or other benefits has decreased (Vernon, 2009b). Numerous conditions affect children living below the poverty threshold, including inadequate housing, low educational attainment, and limited access to health care.

Poverty, or low socioeconomic status, carries a stigma in modern society. Higher class status in U.S. culture is associated with feelings of power, security, and privilege. Families who remain in poverty are often viewed as lazy or inferior by those in higher socioeconomic brackets. In addition to judgments about behavioral or initiative differences, perceived intellect is also linked to class. The poor in our society are regularly stigmatized in school, employment, and other settings as being intellectually inferior.

From a developmental perspective, research has indicated a direct link between poverty and subsequent effects on the developing child. Mothers living in poverty receive fewer prenatal services, have children with higher levels of disability and morbidity, and find their ability to obtain services and opportunities limited by financial constraints (Feerick & Silverman, 2006; Peterson, Mayer, Summers, & Luze, 2010; Rauch & Lanphear, 2012). In addition, links existed between poverty and what are often termed *at risk* children, including those with low self-esteem, lower educational aims, and more frequent delinquent behaviors (Gross & Capuzzi, 2014). In essence, counseling children who are poor has inherent implications that are not typical of the overall child and adolescent population.

Counseling Issues

Children of poverty are often lumped into a category known as at-risk children. But what does *at risk* really mean? The literature defines *at risk* children as those who come from a deprived background; that is, with high rates of poverty and unemployment as well as low rates of educational achievement (Glossary of Education Reform, 2013). Additionally, these children are considered to be at-risk of some form of failure or negative life event because of the adversities in their young lives (Gross & Capuzzi, 2014). Children of poverty experience higher rates of substance use, juvenile delinquency, involvement in gangs, unsafe sexual practices, and teenage pregnancy (Azzi-Lessing, 2010; Gonsoulin, Darwin, Read, & National Evaluation and Technical Assistance Center for the Education of Children and Youth Who Are Neglected, 2012; Wadsworth, Wolff, Santiago, & Moran, 2008).

Research has linked the reality of children growing up in poverty with interpersonal, psychosocial, school, and community consequences. The Multicultural Counseling Competencies adopted by the American Counseling Association in 1992 acknowledge that poverty, along with related socioeconomic status concerns, affect the client and influence the counseling process (Arrendondo et al., 1996). Children of poverty are more likely to suffer low self-esteem and self-image. Children who need but cannot afford essential services such as glasses, routine medication, or hearing aids understandably find the simple act of participating in a school environment more frustrating, and thus less desirable.

Constant comparison to a middle or upper class standard of living creates unique feelings of inferiority for the children of poverty. Consider a child who lives in a transitional shelter with multiple families and attends school with children who live in single family homes in the surrounding community. Placement in a transitional shelter indicates an unstable housing history, which may not be true for the other children in the school setting. Unstable housing and an often mobile way of life opens the door to educational hardship. As a professional school counselor, one of the chapter authors found that loss of educational records, improper grade placement, and the inability to keep up with school work strongly affected the students' motivation to achieve. This community-based concern becomes a school concern as multiple moves from home to shelter to other housing affect a child's constancy and stability in a school setting.

Other school-based concerns exist for children who are poor. Children of poverty are more likely to underachieve according to middle-class standards, perform poorly in school, and/or drop out before graduation. They have greater incidences of tardiness and absenteeism, factors often linked to problems of healthcare access because children who are sick are less likely to go to school. For example, when young children are ill, parents often use the older children to stay at home to care for the younger child. In addition, tardiness and absenteeism are linked to family values and beliefs surrounding the importance of education. Because financial hardships place a strain on the family, parents often depend on all members, including children, to work and contribute to the family income. Given their situation, education is much lower priority. These family values and behaviors affect the values and behaviors of children. Formal education is often valued less and is less accessible in families of poverty. Because adults in poverty are rarely well educated, they are less likely to value formal education, and their children are therefore less motivated to attend or complete school. Home environments of children living in poverty are not always conducive to the completion of homework, which subsequently affects a child's ability and willingness to attend school (Southworth, 2010). As a result, children who drop out of school are more likely to be involved in the juvenile justice system, be unemployed, become young parents, and continue to live in poverty than are their counterparts who graduate from high school (Alexander, 2010; Bilchik, 2008).

Delinquency is a prevailing community consequence of poverty. Children who live at or below the poverty level are more likely to become involved in the juvenile court system as they seek ways to achieve status that are in violation of social rules (Bilchik, 2008). There are higher rates of theft, violence, and substance use in this population. Substandard housing and communities with high rates of crime and violence further contribute to a child's psychosocial and interpersonal concerns. Children who live in poor neighborhoods may not have access to healthy and safe outdoor play areas. Because of increased risk in the community, parents and caregivers may prohibit their children from playing outside or socializing with other neighborhood families; this, in turn, limits social opportunities, and the child's primary source of entertainment becomes a television or video game. Because the ability to communicate, get along with others, and learn social skills is a result of these types of childhood experiences, children of poverty may bring inferior or even maladaptive interpersonal skills to the school environment.

Does poverty cause delinquency or any of the other behaviors or consequences mentioned thus far? Not directly. Regardless, we know that children of poverty are at a greater risk for such problems and that counselors—especially those in a school setting—need to be aware of these possibilities.

Interventions

While the impact of poverty on the lives of children is substantial and the consequences potentially severe, research indicates that some children of poverty are able to avoid its devastating effects; indeed, many are able to thrive. The risk of poverty to children can be mediated or minimized through intervention (Chung, Hawkins, Gilchrist, Hill, & Nagin, 2002). A discussion of the resiliency of children is warranted to address the efficacy of interventions. Resiliency is a child's capacity to persist despite facing obstacles associated with identified risk factors such as poverty (Taylor & Karcher, 2009). A number of factors contribute to a student's resiliency including a strong support network of primary and extended family, teachers, mentors, counselors and other competent, committed adults (Sink & Edwards, 2008). Professional school counselors are afforded a unique opportunity to promote resiliency in students by being one of these competent adults and by creating a committed support network for the students they serve.

It is clear that a focus on education is primary in addressing children of poverty. Education, which increases skills and employment opportunities, is an important route for children of poverty to take to counteract the potential consequences of these identified risks (Taylor & Karcher, 2009). Professional school counselors historically address the academic, personal, and career needs of the students they serve. School counselors work as a link between the child's stakeholders including teachers, parents, and the community resources to facilitate successful student development. With an at-risk population, such as children of poverty, the professional school counselor becomes an essential force in providing opportunities that facilitate resiliency and subsequent success.

To reach the students, professional school counselors must first reach the family. Families in poverty tend to focus on day-to-day issues to meet the basic survival needs of housing and nutrition. They are less likely to see the relevance in education that has no immediate impact on the families' well-being and lack the resources to connect education to long-term consequences and career potential (Children's Aid Society, 2012). Because families of poverty may not value education the same as families who are not poor, the task of the professional school counselor is often to educate families about the role of education in advancing the lives of children. Families in poverty are not always aware that education can actually mediate negative outcomes such as delinquency and ongoing poverty.

In addition to educating families, the professional school counselor may be in a position to educate faculty and staff about the role and impact of poverty on students. Professional school counselors serve as a bridge to faculty. Often, educators fall prey to cultural misunderstandings and view children of poverty from a deficit perspective believing them to be innately unmotivated or unable to make decisions (Amatea & West-Olatunji, 2007). Counselors can work with faculty to assist their understanding of concerns about a student's absences or a seeming lack of ambition in an otherwise academically competent student (Cross & Burney, 2005). Professional school counselors constantly serve as advocates for students and their families, and providing valuable information to the people involved in the lives of children of poverty is a form of that advocacy.

A third area for professional school counselors is to enlighten students to the role of education. Many children of poverty do not enter the educational domain with the middle-class values and aspirations espoused by a school system. By design, school systems expect students to complete a secondary education and then enter into a skilled workforce or postsecondary institution (Cross & Burney, 2005). A primary role of the professional school counselor is college and career preparatory activities. With children of poverty, this role is even more essential, as many of these children lack appropriate family role models related to completing a high school education, considering higher education, and exploring related career opportunities. Vocational choices are often linked to class status, suggesting that professional school counselors are in a position to link children of poverty to resources beyond the minimally skilled or trade occupations that might be expected by others. In fact, professional school counselors may find themselves serving as the only voice of high expectation related to postsecondary educational opportunities (Gillespie & Starkey, 2006).

Another area of influence afforded the professional school counselor is in the development and implementation of wraparound services; that is, services that include community, family, health, social services, and educational perspectives. Such partnerships ensure greater involvement with at-risk children while distributing the burden for tending to these students' needs since the professional school counselor may not be able to address them all (Bryan, 2005). The involvement of committed networks of supportive and influential adults in the lives of children of poverty serves as a substantial force in mediating negative effects and providing children with the greatest potential for success.

In addition to individual and systemic intervention, professional school counselors are able to form and conduct group counseling and classroom guidance opportunities for the students they serve. Children of poverty may feel out of place in a school setting comprised of higher socioeconomic status children. Bringing children together who have experienced similar circumstances, such as children whose families have moved recently or multiple times, can provide a safe opportunity for children of poverty to find their place in the school environment. Building on the concept of resiliency, group opportunities afford children the chance to try out new styles of interacting and shape the social and emotional skills needed for successfully navigating the academic community.

Challenges for Professional School Counselors

Just as children of poverty face substantial challenges in achieving academic success, breaking the poverty cycle, and growing into well-adjusted, healthy adults, the professional school counselors who work with these students face their own set of challenges. As identified in the early 1990s, counselor training programs have been built on research containing inherent middle-class biases, which frequently results in counselors entering the workforce with their own set of biases. Professional counselors view students as having greater likelihood for success when they are articulate, educated, and interpersonally attractive (Bachelor, Laverdiere, Gamache, & Bordeleau, 2007). As such, some professional school counselors may view students from low socioeconomic backgrounds as less desirable and less likely to benefit from or succeed in counseling due to differences in communication styles and behaviors.

As in all counseling settings, professional school counselors take care not to impose their own values and beliefs onto their students. Master's level school counselors have invested in substantial education and may carry similar expectations into their work with students. Such expectations may not match the expectations or abilities of the students they serve. For example, professional school counselors working in career preparatory activities could find that they link vocational choices to class status as the result of such expectations and biases. Similarly, children of poverty may find themselves uncomfortable working with professional school counselors they view as not being like themselves or of a noticeably different socioeconomic class. Professional school counselors must work to create an inviting presence for students through an interpersonal and professional presentation that makes students feel comfortable and is attentive to the diversity of the student population.

One of the greatest challenges is working within an impoverished social and education system. Children of poverty live in school districts that may be likewise impoverished. This, in turn, affects the resources afforded professional school counselors as well as the number of school counseling positions available to serve the population, resulting in high student-to-counselor ratios (Cross & Burney, 2005). With the American School Counseling Association (2014) reporting the national student-to-counselor ratio average at 471 to 1, professional school counselors in impoverished areas are likely to find themselves with an even higher assigned student population.

Counselors working in any school setting must be creative and flexible in order to provide services. Working with children of poverty is no exception. Because counseling occurs when and where it is needed, professional school counselors may find themselves setting up briefcase offices or rolling offices in order to most effectively bring services to their students. Professional school counselors must be sensitive to the diverse racial and ethnic backgrounds present in children of poverty and ensure that the tools they use to work with students are reflective of that diversity. This may require multiracial toys and games that better fit the student populations. For example, multiple families of dolls from a variety of ethnic backgrounds allow children of stepfamilies and blended families to more closely approximate their own family system in play therapy (Kottman, 2003).

A subtle yet important distinction in working with children of poverty is the use of inclusive language. Professional school counselors attempting to understand a student's home life can ask students to draw or talk about where they sleep rather than assuming the children have their own bedrooms. Discussing adults in the home in terms of who takes care of the students is more inclusive than using traditional *mother* and *father* references. Because children of poverty often live in complex and sometimes chaotic family systems (Vernon, 2009b), genograms may prove useful in discovering how the system affects the student. Additionally, the use of timelines may help professional school counselors understand the transient history of many children of poverty.

Summary/Conclusion

Professional school counselors successfully working with children of poverty serve as change agents. They are aware of poverty's potentially lasting effects and consequences. Professional school counselors are in the unique position to provide interventions that will help mediate the negative consequences of poverty. Educating school personnel, families, and children is critical to the success of children of poverty. Professional school counselors link children and their families to critical resources through targeted career and postsecondary preparation as well as wraparound services. An understanding of the biases against children of poverty allows the professional school counselor to act as an advocate for a population that, with intervention, has greater potential to break out of poverty. Professional school counselors are aware of the inherent challenges in this work and plan accordingly to foster the success of the students they serve.

CHAPTER 64

Parent Involvement in Schools

Henry L. Harris and Edward A. Wierzalis

Preview

In this chapter, we focus on various aspects of parent involvement in schools. Different types of parent involvement, barriers that might prevent involvement, and recommendations to increase parent involvement and partnerships will be examined. Brief descriptions of successful parental involvement programs and Internet resources are provided.

Parents and school personnel collaboratively play an important role in educating children. Parents are responsible for being involved in their children's lives by raising them in warm, nurturing, safe, and secure environments that stimulate social, emotional, and intellectual development. According to Topor, Keane, Shelton, and Calkins (2010) children with parents more involved in their education, compared to children with lesser involved parents, had higher levels of academic performance. Some have considered parent involvement "an important ingredient for the remedy of many ills in education today" (Shute, Hansen, Underwood, & Razzouk, 2011, p. 1). Parents who are uninvolved may provide for the basic needs of their children, but are emotionally absent, often placing their needs above the needs of their children (Baumrind, 1991).

Public schools, in part, are responsible for providing children the opportunity to pursue a quality education. Pursuit of a quality education has proven to be more challenging for some students, particularly disadvantaged and minority students. As a result, public schools have been required by the No Child Left Behind Act of 2001 (NCLB) to close the achievement gap between disadvantaged and minority students and their peers (U.S. Department of Education, 2001). NCLB attempts to close the achievement gap by requiring schools to (a) help students meet challenging academic standards by testing them in math, science, and reading; (b) collect and report student achievement data by race, poverty level, children with disabilities, and English language learners; (c) make annual adequate yearly progress (AYP) reports that demonstrate how all students are meeting state goals in math and reading; and (d) ensure that all teachers are highly qualified.

NCLB (U.S. Department of Education, 2001) also recognizes the importance of parent involvement because parents are allowed to have access to schools, perhaps more now than ever before. For example, when schools are identified as "In Need of Improvement," they must establish activities and programs to increase parent involvement and schedule regular meetings to discuss parents' concerns when requested by parents. Parents also have input into writing a parental involvement plan, and once it is adopted they must receive a copy of the plan. The ultimate goal is to increase the level of parent involvement and make parents full partners in the educational development of their children. This is a significant partnership that must be continuously nurtured because of the relationship between education and income. Individuals with higher levels of education tend to earn higher salaries, are less likely to be unemployed, and live overall healthier lifestyles (Baum, Ma, & Payea, 2013).

Parent Involvement

Parent involvement refers to behaviors that parents display at home and in the school settings that support the educational progress of their children (Nokali, Bachman, & Votruba-Drzal, 2010). When students feel support from both environments, these students experience more self-confidence, believe school is more important, and perform better (Thigpen & Freedberg, 2014). Parental involvement also motivates students when they observe their parents taking an active interest in school (Gonzalez-DeHass, Willems, & Holbein, 2005). Helping students become more goal oriented has also been associated with parental involvement. While investigating parental involvement with kindergarten children, McWayne, Hampton, Fantuzzo, Cohen, and Sekino (2004) found that involved parents provided a rich learning environment at home with activities that included talking to their children about the value of school and helping them practice things they had learned in school. When compared to the children of less involved parents, these children displayed higher levels of social skills and greater achievement in mathematics and reading. In a study by Topor et al. (2010), teachers defined parent involvement as their perception of the positive attitude parents had toward their children's education, teachers, and schools. The results indicated that increased parent involvement was significantly related to increased levels of academic performance as assessed by teacher evaluations of the child's academic performance in the classroom and by standardized achievement test scores. Williams and Sanchez (2012) conducted a qualitative study that explored parental involvement at an inner city high school that involved 15 parents and 10 school officials. The results indicated that school officials and parents agreed that participation outside of school and at school were definitive indicators of parent involvement. However, they disagreed on their descriptions of uninvolved parents and the importance of communication between home and school.

In summary, the research on the benefits of parent involvement indicated improved student behaviors including attendance and attitudes, student mental health, improved parent–teacher relationships, higher teacher morale, more positive school climate, and increased parent satisfaction, confidence, and interest in their own education (Hornby & Lafaele, 2011). Given the positive benefits of parent involvement, it seems imperative that all schools attempt to build effective partnerships with parents. Schools may also need to revise their definition of parent involvement to include other variables such as home-based learning activities (Bower & Griffin, 2011).

Types of Parent Involvement

Parent involvement entails a variety of parenting behaviors including discussing homework with children, attending Parent–Teacher Organization/Association (PTO/PTA) meetings, serving as assistants in the classroom, participating as school volunteers, participating in parental school advisory councils, or engaging in active communication with teachers and other school officials regarding the educational concerns of their children (Hornby & Lafaele, 2011). Epstein's (2010) framework outlined six methods of parent involvement partnerships:

1. *Parenting:* Helping all families establish home environments to support children as students. Activities include: (a) family support programs to help families with nutrition, health, and other services; (b) suggestions for a home environment that supports learning at each grade level; (c) neighborhood meetings to help families and schools understand each other; and (d) home visits during transitional phases to preschool, elementary, middle, and high school.
2. *Communication:* Design effective forms for school-to-home and home-to-school communications about school programs and children's progress. Activities include: (a) annual conferences with every parent; (b) weekly or monthly folders of student work sent home for parental review and comments; (c) language translators to help families when needed; and (d) regularly scheduling useful notices, phone calls, newsletters, and other forms of communication.
3. *Volunteering:* Recognize and organize parental help and support. Activities include: (a) parental patrols or other activities to help provide safety and operation of various school programs; (b) school and classroom volunteer programs to assist teachers, students, administrators, other school personnel, or other parents; and (c) yearly postcard survey to identify all available talents, times, and locations of volunteers.
4. *Learning at home:* Provide information and ideas to families about how to help students with homework and other curriculum-related activities, decisions, and planning. Activities include: (a) information on homework policies; (b) how to monitor and discuss school-related work at home; (c) information for families on required skills for students at each grade level and in all subjects; and (d) summer learning packets.
5. *Decision making:* Include parents in school decisions; develop new parent leaders and representatives. Activities include: (a) active PTA/PTO advisory councils, advocacy groups, school review boards, and various other committees for parental leadership and participation; (b) information on school or local elections for school representatives; (c) networking that will connect all families with parental representatives; and (d) advocacy groups to campaign and lobby for school reform and improvements.
6. *Collaboration with community:* Identify and integrate resources and services from the community to strengthen school programs, family practices, and student learning. Activities include: (a) information for students and families on community health, cultural, recreational, social support, and other programs or services; (b) service to the community by families, students, and the schools; (c) providing information that connects with learning skills and talents, including summer programs for students; and (d) participation in school programs for students.

There may be difficulties that parents, schools, and communities encounter when they work together to increase parent involvement. However, all groups must be willing to listen, understand, and diligently strive to overcome any potential barriers. Children are supported most effectively when families and schools have shared goals and work collaboratively to accomplish the goals (Epstein, 2010). Table 64.1 provides some suggested parental involvement

Table 64.1 Effective Parent Involvement Activities

1. *Parent Visitation/Observation Days.* Send personalized invitations for parents to sit with their child in the classroom (Benson & Martin, 2003).
2. *Parent/Student Switch Day.* A process in which students are excused one day from class only if a parent volunteers to take their place at school. The parent is responsible for following the student's daily schedule (with some exceptions; Loucks, 1992).
3. *Newsletters.* Inform parents about various topics, including homework strategies, reports about special school projects, teacher features, and parenting tips. The newsletters should be well designed and sent out to parents monthly or quarterly, depending on school needs (Loucks, 1992).
4. *Parent Classes.* Classes offered at school focus on topics such as how to help students with homework, tutoring strategies, parenting skills, drug education, and improving communications skills (Loucks, 1992).
5. *Lunch With Professional School Counselors.* Program designed by professional school counselors that involves going to the parents' places of employment (Evans & Hines, 1997).
6. *Parent Computer Day.* Invite parents to be instructed in the use of computers by their children (Benson & Martin, 2003).
7. *Coffee With the Principal.* Invite parents to participate in informal discussions with the principal on a regular basis (Benson & Martin, 2003).
8. Provide a meal along with some form of entertainment (e.g., talent show, song, dance) as an activity to involve parents in schools (Ippolito, 2012).

activities, and Table 64.2 provides some Internet resources for more information on parental involvement.

Barriers to Parent Involvement

Most parents care about their children's educational experience, but their level of involvement might be affected by a number of different barriers, including personal beliefs. For example, some parents may believe their primary role is to ensure that their children attend school. When this perception occurs, parents are less inclined to be involved and the role of education becomes the sole responsibility of the school. Parents' personal beliefs about their communication skills and intellectual ability to help their children succeed in school could also hinder parent involvement (Hornby & Lafaele, 2011). In addition, educational level of parents, race, ethnicity, and age of children are other significant factors that affect parent involvement. Unfortunately, for many students and schools, parent involvement decreases with student age and reaches the lowest levels during the secondary school years, arguably a time when parent involvement is needed most. When perceived barriers that impact parent involvement are not confronted, students may not reach their academic, social, and emotional potential.

The Parent–Teacher Relationship

Parents and teachers sometimes have a difficult time working together because they do not trust each other. Teachers sometimes perceive parents as outsiders who lack the basic educational skills needed to help children learn. This perspective could cause some parents to develop negative feelings and attitudes toward school personnel (Anderson, 1999). Parents may also not fully understand the kind of role the school would like them to fill regarding their

Table 64.2 Internet Resources

American School Counselor Association Parent Resources (http://schoolcounselor.org/parents-public/parent-resources)
Education World (http://www.educationworld.com/a_special/parent_involvement.shtml)
National Coalition for Parent Involvement in Education (www.ncpie.org)
National Education Association (http://www.nea.org/)
National Parent Teacher Association (http://www.pta.org/)
National Network of Partnership Schools (http://www.csos.jhu.edu/p2000/)
Pacer Center Champions for Children with Disabilities (http://www.pacer.org/leadership/)
Parents as Teachers (http://www.parentsasteachers.org/)
Parent Educational Advocacy Training Center (www.peatc.org)
Technical Assistance ALLIANCE for Parents Centers (www.taalliance.org)
Wrightslaw (www.wrightslaw.com)

involvement at home and school. Furthermore, parents may question whether school officials are sincerely concerned about the educational welfare of their children.

Some parents had negative experiences during their educational years and feel intimidated by school personnel, sometimes believing that teachers, professional school counselors, or administrators call them only to deliver negative news about their children or blame them personally for the problems their children are experiencing at school. Some parents also fear reprisals from teachers if they are perceived as too vocal when offering suggestions or expressing criticism (Minority Community Outreach, 2010).

It is possible that the relationship between teachers and parents is further strained because of their misperceptions of parent involvement. In a study conducted by Barge and Loges (2003), parents identified (a) monitoring student academic progress, (b) cultivating personal relationships with teachers, (c) using extracurricular school programs, and (d) developing community support systems as important aspects to positive parental involvement. On the other hand, teachers perceived helpful parent involvement as (a) communicating with the child and the school; (b) participation in the child's schooling and life, in general; (c) fundamental parenting duties including supervision of the child; and (d) discipline, particularly support for punishment administered by the school. Halsey's (2005) investigation of parental involvement in junior high schools revealed that a majority of teachers believed that many parents were not interested in participating in their children's education. Parents, on the other hand, believed that teachers only wanted a limited amount of involvement because they often did not receive personalized individual communication about how they could become involved.

Reynolds, Crea, Medina, Degnan, and McRoy (2014) found that teachers and parents agreed that better communication was needed from both sides. All too often, particularly for minorities, parents do not feel like their opinions are welcomed or valued and as a result do not return to school or go to meetings unless absolutely necessary. As a result of the low parent involvement, school officials interpret this as lack of interest from the parents and subsequently believe it is the responsibility of the school to plan and decide on all school-related matters for students. Parents perceive this lack of engagement from the school as an indicator that participating in school-related events is a waste of their time (Minority Community Outreach, 2010).

The Issue of Race

Race may be another factor contributing to mistrust because of the history of racial discrimination. Lareau and Horvat (1999) contended that some minority parents may approach the schools with challenges and criticism rather than deference and support. School officials must understand the sociopolitical history of parents who have children of color attending schools and recognize within racial group perspectives. Some may not completely trust school personnel for a number of reasons, including lack of a diverse, understanding teaching staff. For example, Reynolds et al. (2014) discovered that teachers serving urban high school minority students needed to include more positive feedback about students when they communicated with parents. Parents on the other hand wanted to hear from teachers before it was too late in the process for an intervention to occur. Furthermore, both groups indicated a need for an organized and systemic approach to parent involvement to enhance parent–teacher interactions. In addition, because of compelling cultural barriers, a need for assistance to accommodate for cultural differences was acknowledged.

Within traditional Latino culture, parents may not become involved with the school because of the high level of respect given to educators. Latino parents perceive educators as competent professionals and often believe it would be counterproductive to interfere with schools (Quezada, Diaz, & Sanchez, 2003). However, more recent research indicated that Latino parents are more actively involved, particularly at home, in supporting their children's learning. In addition these parents are motivated to become more involved when they receive specific invitations from teachers and students (Walker, Ice, Hoover-Dempsey, & Sandler, 2011).

Language and Poverty

School officials should be aware of how language could be a barrier limiting parental involvement. According to Sue and Sue (2013), European American culture places a strong emphasis on a person's ability to understand and speak English. As a result, individuals who are bilingual or from lower class backgrounds who do not use Standard English while communicating may be unfairly treated or perceived as inferior. In addition, their own sense of self-worth may be diminished because they may not be able to help their children complete their homework assignments or understand forms sent home (Quezada et al., 2003). During academic year 2002–2003, 8.7% of public school students were English language learners (ELL), and in 2011–2012 that number had slightly increased to 9.1% (U.S. Department of Education, 2014). This is important to acknowledge because some research has demonstrated that immigrant minority parents encountered more barriers regarding parent involvement and were less likely to be involved in schools compared to Caucasian parents (Turney & Kao, 2009). In another study, more encouraging results by Reynolds et al. (2014) discovered that immigrant parents had higher self-efficacy and held stronger beliefs in their ability to impact their child's educational experience when compared to native-born parents, second, and third generation parents.

Many U.S. families are deeply affected by poverty; in 2012, 20% of families, including 16.1 million children, were considered poor. In addition, over 40% of these poor children (7.1 million) lived in extreme poverty at less than half of the poverty level; for a family of four, this translates to $11,746 annually, $976 monthly, $226 weekly, and $8 individually or $32 daily (Children's Defense Fund, 2014). It is also important to note that children in single parent families were almost four times more likely to live in poverty compared to children who live within married couple families. While 70% of all children lived in two parent homes in 2012, more than 50% of African American children and nearly 33% of Hispanic children lived in single parent homes, compared to only 20% of White children. Regionally, poverty rates were also highest in the South (25%). However, in urban areas the rates were slightly higher at 29%, compared to 27% in small towns and rural areas (Children's Defense Fund, 2014). It is crucial for schools to encourage parents from low-income families to become involved in their children's education. School officials should also be aware that some parents are living from paycheck to paycheck. In order to survive, these parents often hold multiple jobs with rigid work schedules that prevent frequent participation in school-related events.

While numerous positive benefits of parental involvement have been demonstrated, the level of parental involvement can decrease as students progress from elementary through middle and high schools (Hornby & Lafaele, 2011; Minority Community Outreach, 2010). Schools must maintain positive and open communication with parents to offset this decline in involvement. Parents, school officials, and community residents and leaders must learn to build cooperative educational partnerships if students are to be provided with necessary educational skills.

Diverse Parent Involvement Models

School personnel must be respectful of the variety of nontraditional family structures that exist in today's culture. Children may not come from the model of a traditional family but may be from single-parent homes, same-sex couples, or living with and raised by their grandparents or some other kinship care arrangement (i.e., students raised by an extended family member). Schools need to be sensitive to nontraditional family needs and work diligently to provide them with support and create ways for them to be involved in their children's education. Grandparents raising grandchildren is a growing trend (Edwards & Daire, 2006), and it is imperative that their rights to be appropriately involved in their grandchildren's education be recognized by the school.

Same-sex parents are confronted with the prejudices and stereotypes of society, thus making their parental rights particularly challenging. Gay and lesbian parents and their children operate under different societal sanctions compared to those offered to families headed by heterosexual parents (Goldberg, 2010). School personnel may be uncomfortable and unsure how to incorporate same-sex parents into many of the activities that will foster parental involvement. However, same-sex parents have the right to be a part of their children's education and, as a result, schools must positively engage these parents in all school–parent partnerships. Same-sex parents share the same concerns for their children's emotional and physical safety and education as any other parent.

Recommendations to Increase Parent Involvement

School officials should seriously explore ways to overcome barriers and develop a school environment that facilitates parental involvement. Chavkin and Garza-Lubeck (1990) originally outlined six critical steps needed for successful parent involvement programs, and within this chapter, two additional steps are included. The steps consist of: (1) motivation; (2) accurate assessment; (3) training of staff; (4) community outreach programs; (5) networking with community businesses and agencies; (6) parent–teacher partnerships; (7) role of school boards; and (8) role of the professional school counselor.

The first step required is *motivation*. School officials must be highly motivated and have a genuine desire to create a parent involvement initiative that welcomes parents from all racial, ethnic, and economic backgrounds to become valued partners in the education of students. School officials must have the desire, ability, and willingness to establish open lines of communication with parents to make them feel welcome.

Motivation also calls for flexibility, demonstrated by scheduling programs during times more convenient to parents, providing daycare to younger siblings for major school programs, conducting home visits to invite parents to school, offering to bring school-related functions to the site of parents' employers, and seeking parental input regarding workshops or training sessions (Quezada et al., 2003). Schools should be especially committed to creating an open-school and open-classroom policy for low-income parents because, compared to middle-class parents, they are far less likely to run into their children's teachers in their neighborhood settings (Lott, 2003; Minority Community Outreach, 2010). The school mission should also reflect the importance of parent involvement and establish a clear foundation for parent engagement in school activities (Centers for Disease Control and Prevention, 2012a).

Step two calls for an *accurate assessment* of parental involvement. This helps establish accurate information reflecting the interest level and needs of the community. The assessment process could include methods such as informal observations; town-hall meetings with parents and school officials; examining preexisting data (e.g., number of parents attending PTA meetings, looking at the current number of parent volunteers, previous school history); reviewing current policies regarding parental involvement programs; and organizing focus groups, mailed surveys, random telephone surveys, and local radio call-in programs (Pryor, 1996). When accurate knowledge is developed, specific programs can be designed to better address concerns.

Step three calls for continuous *training and staff development*, a vital component of successful parent involvement programs. In-service training could initially begin by exploring school officials' views of parent involvement and past experiences. School officials should be made aware that some parents (e.g., parents who lack education, have low incomes, are from culturally diverse backgrounds) may feel unwelcome in the educational environment and avoid schools. Workshops addressing these types of issues could prove beneficial in helping school officials become more aware of their own personal biases and also help them develop a better understanding of individuals from culturally different groups. This need has been consistently deemed necessary throughout the literature (Bower & Griffin, 2011; Hornby & Lafaele, 2011; Minority Community Outreach, 2010; Williams & Sanchez, 2012). Superintendents and school boards should encourage school principals to develop a welcoming environment by posting signs in multiple languages and by providing customer service training to front office staff (Minority Community Outreach, 2010).

Step four involves school officials venturing out into the community to *establish a relationship* with its various members. Recreational facilities, churches, and cultural gatherings provide unique opportunities for educators to familiarize themselves with key community members who also may be able to further assist them in developing strong parent–school relationships (Chavkin & Garza-Lubeck, 1990). Employers should also be targeted during this step and encouraged to use family- and student-friendly business practices such as providing leave time for parents to volunteer in school or attend conferences, and, when possible, offer parental training and child care. Employers could potentially benefit by having better public and community relations, improved worker morale and loyalty, and a more qualified workforce for the future (U.S. Department of Education, 1996).

Step five involves schools *networking with social services agencies*. Chavkin and Garza-Lubeck (1990) suggested helping to arrange services for families in need is a significant part of the effort required to involve parents. Student achievement and attendance is based on more than just instruction, because factors such as health, housing, transportation, nutrition, and clothing play influential roles in determining student success.

Step six focuses on the quality of *parent–teacher partnerships*. Parents and teachers must, for the benefit of the children and the success of the school, work to create effective home–school partnerships. Parents and teachers must be willing to develop open lines of communication with one another and start perceiving each other as partners rather than adversaries. Using emerging technology as a means of communication may be another source schools may consider using to improve communication between parents and teachers (Olmstead, 2013).

Step seven focuses on the role of the *school board* in helping to encourage parent involvement. Devlin-Sherer and Devlin-Sherer (1994) suggested that school boards could be more proactive in promoting parent involvement by influencing administrators to establish meaningful parent involvement programs, requiring administrators to create realistic plans for parent involvement that would be reviewed periodically, and helping establish and promote guidelines for parent involvement initiatives. Schools could also host a class for parents about the role and function of the school board, encourage parents to attend school board meetings, and invite school board members to speak with parents about their role in education (Minority Community Outreach, 2010).

Step eight involves the role of the *professional school counselor* in facilitating parent involvement. Epstein and Van Voorhis (2010) suggested that professional school counselors should spend one fifth of their time strengthening family and community engagement programs. Furthermore they should also strive to teach parents how to interpret various progress reports, offer workshops that are of interest to parents, and organize parent forums. Professional school counselors, because of their unique training, could offer workshops to bolster parental communication skills and help school personnel become more aware of diverse parental models.

Summary/Conclusion

Parents are stakeholders in educational reform and should have a role in the delivery of programs intended to enhance and improve the outcomes of their children's education. They must become more actively involved in their children's education and provide their children, regardless of circumstances, with a nurturing environment conducive to academic success. Professional school counselors, teachers, administrators, and other staff members must equally strive to do more to encourage parental involvement, especially from fathers and parents from low-income families. Schools must work to eliminate barriers that prevent parental involvement and realize that most parents would like to become full partners in the educational process. Finally, parents, school professionals, and members of the community should understand that it really does "take a village" to educate a child. Educated children are more likely to grow up and become educated adults. Adults with higher levels of education tend to be more active citizens than other adults and, as previously stated, earn higher wages and live healthier life styles (Baum et al., 2013).

CHAPTER 65

Helping Students Manage Stress

*Bradley T. Erford**

Preview

Stress is a pervasive problem that affects students at all grade levels. Within recent decades, youth have exhibited more stress-related difficulties than in the past. The pressures of living in an increasingly complex society, accompanied by declining coping skills and social support, contribute to the increase in numbers of students facing stress-related health issues. Sources of stress, outcomes associated with stress, and resources that help students cope more effectively with stressful events are addressed. Prevention suggestions that professional school counselors can initiate in classrooms and intervention strategies for group and individual counseling are provided.

"I don't know how I'm going to get it all done," lamented Abby, a 14-year-old high school freshman. "I have two big projects, three tests, and a ton of math homework. Mrs. Cook is going insane; I think she's mad at all of us. And soccer tryouts are tomorrow after school. Tiffany is acting all moody again and won't talk to me. Nobody understands—it's just too much."

Abby's concerns reflect what many young people experience on a regular basis. Time demands, relationships, and developmental transitions are just a few of the many stressors that are an ongoing part of students' lives. Do youth today feel more stressed than in previous generations? What exactly is stress, and how does it affect students' mental and physical well-being? Why is it that some individuals seemingly handle pressure and change with ease, while others suffer deleterious effects? What can professional school counselors do to help young people develop strategies to manage stress effectively? In this chapter, stress, its effects on young people, and examples of prevention and intervention activities that can be implemented by professional school counselors are described.

Stress

The number of youth experiencing stress-related disorders, including depression, eating disorders, anxiety, social dysfunction, and substance abuse, has increased over the past few decades (McNamara, 2011). Increased pressures faced by youth, coupled with declining coping

---

*Special thanks to Debbie W. Newsome, Nancy H. Whitlatch, and Julia A. Southern for their outstanding contributions to previous editions of this chapter.

skills and decreased social support, represent a challenge to professional school counselors and others who work with children and adolescents.

Stress can be defined in multiple ways. Lazarus and Folkman (1984) defined stress as "a particular relationship between the person and the environment that is appraised by the person as taxing or exceeding his or her resources and endangering his or her well-being" (p. 19). Stress can refer to an internal state, an external event, or the interaction between a person and the environment (McNamara, 2011). Perceptions of what is stressful vary widely among individuals. Indeed, something perceived as stressful by one person may be seen as trivial or even positive by another.

Stress can be viewed as a relationship between the events that happen to individuals and the individual's physical, cognitive, emotional, and behavioral responses to the events (McNamara, 2011). Several models describing the stress process have been proposed. Psychological models of stress focus on the reciprocal interactions between an individual and the environment. An example of such a model is presented in Figure 65.1. The model is comprised of the following components: environmental stressors, an individual's subjective perceptions of the stressors, short-term responses, and long-term effects. Frequency, intensity, and timing of stressors can affect mental health, with outcomes being moderated by parental and peer support, individual psychological traits, and coping skills. Coping with stress is the process by which a person handles stressful situations and the emotions they generate.

Types of Stressors

Childhood and adolescence may be marked by extremely stressful events and transitions as well as daily aggravations that require responses. Chronic demands or stressors are enduring aspects of the environment that involve deprivation or hardship and create ongoing challenges for an individual. Wadsworth, Raviv, Compas, and Connor-Smith (2005) found that chronic stress can cause an individual to become more susceptible to additional stressors and hinder their ability to employ effective coping mechanisms. Poverty, physical disability, and family dysfunction are examples of chronic stressors. In contrast, acute stressors, sometimes referred to as life events, involve changes or disruptions in existing conditions, such as those caused by accidents or illnesses. Chronic and acute stressors can be further classified as normative life events, non-normative events, and daily hassles (McNamara, 2011).

- *Normative life events:* Generic developmental challenges that everyone encounters. Normative events include physical changes, school transitions, emerging sexuality, changing peer and family relationships, and changes in cognitive levels.
- *Non-normative life events:* Unexpected, demanding events that may challenge the transitional experience. Examples include catastrophic phenomena (sudden, powerful events requiring major adaptive responses from the groups sharing the experience, including natural disasters, accidents, and terrorism) and unexpected changes such as parental divorce, injury, unemployment, or a family member's death or major illness.
- *Daily hassles:* Stable, repetitive stressors that tend to be irritating or annoying. Examples include parent–child conflict, academic demands, peer pressure, interpersonal concerns, and financial concerns. Ongoing hassles, in some ways, are more predictive of psychological symptoms than acute, episodic stressors and are associated with depression, anxiety, and conduct problems.

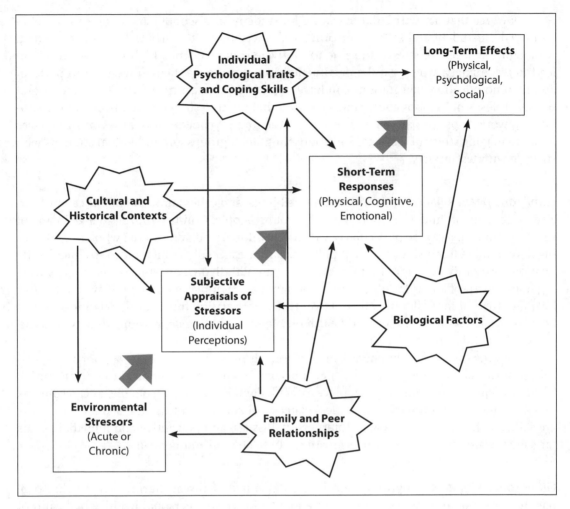

Figure 65.1. The stress process.

Normative, non-normative, and daily stressors can occur in multiple contexts, including school, home, and neighborhood.

School. Normative educational transitions, such as entering school for the first time, changing schools, or moving from one level to another (e.g., elementary school to middle school) can be significant sources of stress for young people. School-related factors that are unrelated to such transitions also can be stressful. Concerns about grades, teachers, homework, exams, extracurricular activities, and fitting in with peers are ongoing challenges that can be potentially taxing. Specific stressors in the school environment include impatient teachers, fear of failure, unclear assignments, work overload, expectations to achieve, and peer pressure, to name just a few. In an ongoing research study, middle school and high school students cited poor facilities, perceived unfair grading policies, uncommitted teachers, and negative school reputations as factors that impeded learning, thus serving as significant sources of stress.

One area that has particular relevance for students and school personnel is the emphasis placed on student and school performance, especially as it relates to high-stakes testing. Although low levels of stress can serve to motivate some students, high levels of stress can lead to test anxiety, which can be detrimental to performance. Being pressured to perform and then not meeting expectations can have upsetting, long-lasting effects. There are several things professional school counselors can do to help with test-related stress, including conducting workshops for parents and teachers, teaching psychoeducational lessons to classes about managing stressful feelings, and counseling small groups and individual students who struggle with test anxiety.

Family and peers. Relationships with parents, siblings, and other family members can be both a source of support and a source of stress for young people. Conflict and/or change in any of these relationships can be particularly stressful. Children and adolescents who are undergoing developmental transitions such as puberty may be especially vulnerable to strained family relationships or dysfunctional family systems. Parental divorce or remarriage, siblings leaving home, birth of a new family member, or parental unemployment are life events that can be quite stressful for children and adolescents. Distress arising from family relationships has been associated with several mental health problems, including depression, anxiety, and eating disorders (McNamara, 2011).

As in the case of family interactions, relationships with peers can be supportive, stressful, or both. As children grow older, peers become increasingly important and influential. Cliques, prejudice, and bullying can place difficult demands on young people, as can conflicts in values, increased intimacy, and issues related to sexuality. Professional school counselors are skilled at helping students with interpersonal issues, and preventive and remedial efforts targeted toward improving peer relationships can benefit all young people.

Other sources of stress. Anything perceived as a source of threat, harm, loss, or challenge has the potential to be stressful for children and adolescents. Personal health, the health of friends and family members, and planning for the future are among the many additional, yet common, sources of stress. Dealing with poverty and ongoing financial issues can serve as a chronic stressor for children and parents (Wadsworth et al., 2005), as can minority group status and prejudice. The timing of puberty and its accompanying physiological changes can be quite stressful, especially for girls. When numerous stressors are experienced simultaneously, or when the timing of events departs significantly from the norm, youth are more likely to experience distress. Indeed, students who perceive combinations of school, family, peer group, and other life situations as stressful are likely to display symptoms of emotional and physical distress (McNamara, 2011).

People of all ages must deal with catastrophic events. Following the September 11th, 2001, terrorist attacks on New York City and Washington, DC, the American sense of safety and security was shaken to the core. Emotional distress associated with those attacks and other tragic events, including natural disasters and accidents, is expected. All youth should be watched for signs of emotional distress in the wake of exposure to any type of catastrophe. Helping young people cope with their distress is one of the most important challenges a mental health professional can face (National Institute of Mental Health, 2013b).

Stress-Related Outcomes

Exposure to stress triggers physical, emotional, and cognitive changes in the body. Immediate, short-term reactions to stress can motivate people to action; however, long-term exposure can lead to physical and psychosocial difficulties. Of critical interest to mental health professionals is the manner in which stress is appraised, because subjective appraisals affect the nature and intensity of stress-related responses.

Physiological responses. When someone perceives an event as acutely stressful (e.g., harmful, threatening, challenging), automatic physiological responses are activated. Blood pressure, heart rate, respiration rate, and perspiration increase, helping mobilize the body's resources for action (McNamara, 2011). The chemical messengers dopamine and norepinephrine are released in the sympathetic nervous system. The adrenal hormones cortisol and epinephrine, responding to signals passed from the hypothalamus, begin to circulate. Muscles tense and blood sugar increases as the body prepares for an anticipated emergency.

As short-term responses, these physiological reactions to stress are not harmful and indeed may be helpful in cases of actual emergency. However, when exposure to stress is chronic and the stress response is overactivated, health-related problems occur. Gastrointestinal, circulatory, respiratory, and musculoskeletal disorders have been linked to stress, as have migraine, heartburn, diabetes, certain cancers, and rheumatoid arthritis (McNamara, 2011). Chronic stress can alter the immune system and hypothalamic-pituitary-adrenal (HPA) axis activity, leaving individuals more susceptible to physical illness and mental health disorders such as depression, alcoholism, and certain anxiety disorders.

Most of the research on physiological responses to stress has been conducted with adults, although children's responses are thought to be comparable. Children may not describe or interpret their physical symptoms in the same way as adults, however. In a study focusing on children's responses, second- through sixth-grade students were asked to describe the way their bodies felt during a past stressful event (Sharrer & Ryan-Wenger, 2002). The five most common physiological symptoms listed were headache, stomachache, getting sweaty, heart beating fast or feeling "funny," and feeling sick. Children also mentioned having tight muscles, being shaky, and tingling. Because people experience symptoms in different ways, professional school counselors will want to give students opportunities to describe the physiological responses they have to stressful situations. Physiological symptoms serve as signals that let youth know they are dealing with something stressful that may require action (e.g., active problem-solving, relaxation exercises).

Cognitive and emotional responses. Just as people respond physiologically to perceived stress, they also respond cognitively and emotionally. These responses, which are dependent on the individual's appraisal of the situation, are directly related to the process of coping, which is discussed in the next section. Immediate, short-term cognitive responses to stress include increased arousal and alertness and increased cognition and vigilance (McNamara, 2011). Initial emotional responses can include anger, fear, nervousness, and anxiety. Sharrer and Ryan-Wenger (2002) reported that children described feeling mad, worried, sad, nervous, and afraid when they were in stressful situations, with "mad" being the most common response.

As in the case of physiological stress responses, short-term cognitive and emotional reactions to stress typically serve a purpose and are not, in and of themselves, harmful. However, exposure to long-term stress can have negative effects on psychological well-being. Some of the cognitive problems associated with too much stress include concentration difficulties, distractibility, and disorganization. For adolescents, the most common psychological outcome associated with stress overload is depression. Other mental health conditions linked to stress include posttraumatic stress disorder (PTSD), obsessive–compulsive disorder, panic disorder, other anxiety disorders, substance abuse, and eating disorders (McNamara, 2011). Symptoms associated with these conditions can interfere severely with students' self-esteem, interpersonal relationships, and academic functioning.

Coping With Stress

Lazarus and Folkman (1984) defined coping as cognitive and behavioral efforts directed toward managing any demands that are appraised as taxing or exceeding one's available resources. Personality and situational factors influence the ways in which people cope with these demands (McNamara, 2011). Conflict is commonly experienced in everyday life, and the degree to which young people are able to employ effective coping strategies can transform a conflict into a problem that can be solved productively, rather than result in negative outcomes. A person's subjective appraisal of a situation affects the selection of coping strategies, which differ depending on the situation.

One way researchers categorize coping responses is based on whether the response is *problem-focused* or *emotion-focused* (see McNamara, 2011). Problem-focused coping strategies attempt to alter the source of stress whereas emotion-focused coping strategies attempt to reduce the emotional distress associated with a given situation. Generally, problem-focused strategies are associated with adaptive coping, reduced depression, and other positive outcomes, whereas relying exclusively on emotion-focused strategies can lead to maladaptive functioning. With problem-focused coping, individuals take active steps to deal with the situation, thus enhancing one's sense of control over the environment. Emotion-focused coping, in contrast, may involve avoidance, which provides temporary symptom relief but, over time, is less effective in reducing symptoms associated with stress. Professional school counselors can implement stress management interventions that are tailored toward helping students use active, problem-focused coping strategies. Examples of stress management interventions are described later in this chapter.

Many types of coping strategies are used by children and adolescents. Typically, young people use a combination of problem-focused and emotion-focused strategies to cope with stressful situations. Coping strategies used by youth form the foundation for coping strategies used in adulthood (Plunkett, Radmacher, & Moll-Pharana, 2000). Young people differ in their use of coping styles based on a number of factors (see Table 65.1), including age and gender (McNamara, 2011). Girls tend to use a wider range of coping styles and are more likely to seek social support. They also are more likely to vent feelings, seek spiritual support, positively reframe situations, and engage in wishful thinking. Boys, on the other hand, show a stronger preference for using humor, engaging in sports, and seeking other diversions, both positive and negative. Males may come across as more stable and difficult to irritate, whereas girls may ruminate and self-evaluate more. By being aware of these potential differences in

Table 65.1 Coping Strategies Used By Young People (Plunkett et al., 2000)

Accessing Support—staying connected with family, friends, school personnel, church
Enhancing Self-Reliance—making decisions, problem solving, reframing
Ventilating Feelings—may be appropriate or inappropriate ventilation
Seeking Diversions—relaxing, engaging in activities or exercise
Avoidance—escaping, denying, or avoiding issues and/or people; substance use

coping style, professional school counselors can be better prepared to help all students develop and practice strategies that will facilitate adaptive adjustment.

Protective Resources

What factors help students cope effectively with stressful situations, thereby avoiding the negative psychological and physical effects of stress? Research on resilience in young people indicates that protective resources, including social support and personal attributes or dispositions, seem to help people cope with stress more constructively, even in adverse circumstances (D'Imperio & Dubow, 2000; McNamara, 2011).

Social support. Supportive relationships with family members, peers, and other significant people play an important role in helping students cope with negative events. Supportive relationships can have a buffering effect on stress by preventing stressful events and hassles from occurring in the first place; making individuals feel less vulnerable when they do occur; reducing the impact and intensity of stress-related symptoms; and providing help, advice, and support to remove the stressor (McNamara, 2011).

Supportive families characterized by warmth, high levels of communication, involvement, and appropriate structure help promote positive adjustment and self-efficacy in children. Professional school counselors have the unique opportunity to help parents understand the connection between a child's life at home and life at school. Toward this end, professional school counselors can lead workshops designed to teach effective parenting practices and healthy family interaction patterns.

Similarly, positive relationships with peers can help buffer the negative effects of stress. Class guidance lessons and small-group sessions focusing on peer relationships can provide children with the skills needed to develop and maintain healthy friendships. Beyond this, professional school counselors can facilitate the development of a positive, supportive school climate by leading in-service workshops and providing consultation for teachers and other school personnel who work with students.

Personal attributes. Several personal characteristics can serve as protective factors against stressful events, including self-esteem, self-competence, optimism, and a sense of control (McNamara, 2011). Young people who view themselves as worthy and competent are less vulnerable to stress-related problems. Likewise, youth who approach life with expectations of favorable outcomes tend to cope more competently with stress. An internal locus of control, characterized by beliefs that outcomes are contingent upon personal effort, also appears to have a buffering effect against stressors. Students who believe that their efforts can influence the outcome in a given situation are more likely to engage in proactive coping strategies when faced with difficulties. When internalized control is taken to the extreme, however, uncontrollable events may evoke maladaptive coping efforts rather than buffer against stress.

By overseeing the delivery of comprehensive developmental guidance programs, professional school counselors work to promote the personal attributes of self-esteem, positive outlook, and sense of control. By ensuring that all students receive systematic, developmentally appropriate instruction in these domains, professional school counselors facilitate the bolstering of student resiliency.

Interventions in Schools

If we are going to help young people cope in an increasingly demanding world, it is crucial to invest in primary prevention methods (McNamara, 2011), the goal of which is to help all children develop the psychosocial skills needed for meeting life's challenges. For those students who have been exposed to trauma or excessive stress, and for other students who may not be coping well, additional interventions in the form of group counseling, individual counseling, parent or teacher consultation, and/or referral to outside resources may be warranted. In this section, preventive measures that can be initiated by professional school counselors are described. Attention is also given to ways professional school counselors can help vulnerable students through group and individual counseling.

Psychoeducational Interventions for Students

Initiating preventive measures *before* stress becomes a problem prepares students to deal with demanding situations more effectively. Professional school counselors can influence the largest number of students through classroom psychoeducational activities. Depending on school size and policy, professional school counselors may personally teach the lessons or may train classroom teachers to do so. Equipping students with generalizable coping strategies can help curtail many of the problems associated with stress overload (McNamara, 2011).

Stress management programs for children and adolescents, which can be a part of a comprehensive developmental guidance program, typically focus on (a) identifying sources of stress, (b) recognizing the physical and emotional consequences of stress, and (c) learning and implementing adaptive coping responses. Recommended components for preventive programs (McNamara, 2011) include education about the causes and consequences of stress; training in methods to reduce psychological and physical arousal; general problem-solving and decision-making skills; general cognitive skills (including cognitive restructuring); physical ways of coping with stress; study skills and time management; skills for increasing self-control and self-esteem; and social skills, including effective communication, conflict resolution, and assertiveness training. Numerous resources for professional school counselors describe developmentally appropriate activities for each of these topics, and several of the components (i.e., social skills, self-esteem, problem solving) are already part of the scope and sequence that comprise comprehensive guidance programs. In this section, general suggestions related to the components that have particular relevance to stress management are

Table 65.2 Recognizing Stress

How does it feel when you are stressed?
How can you know that you are stressed?
What sorts of thoughts do you have?
How do you feel in your body?
How does stress affect your behavior?
How do you act toward other people when you are stressed? How do they act toward you?
How can you tell when other people are stressed?
Who do you know that is stressed?

Table 65.3 Stinkin' Thinkin'—4 Steps for Reducing Negative Thoughts

STOP: Stop before you react.
BREATHE: Belly breathe to keep from getting tense. It is impossible to be tense and relaxed at the same time.
REFLECT: Examine the situation. What is the concern? Am I threatened? What thoughts and feelings am I having? What's the worst that could happen? Can I handle it? Am I jumping to conclusions? Is there another way to look at the situation?
CHOOSE: What do I want to happen? What can I do? What coping behaviors will work? Do I have the time, skills, and desire to achieve a solution? Am I avoiding? DECIDE!

provided. These suggestions are broad, and professional school counselors will want to ensure that the related activities are developmentally appropriate for their student population.

Education about the stress process. It is important for students to be able to identify stressors and recognize their own personal physical and emotional responses to stress. McNamara (2011) offered some "starting questions" that can help students recognize their own responses to stress (see Table 65.2).

To help students develop self-awareness, ask them to keep a stress-awareness diary in which they record stress-triggering events as well as their symptoms and reactions. When the stress diaries are discussed, encourage students to describe their personal appraisals of the events. The discussion can provide an opportunity to teach ways to restructure negative thoughts (see Table 65.3).

Physical ways to manage stress. Nutrition, physical activity, and sleep quality all affect people's mental health (McNamara, 2011). Professional school counselors can share information about the relationship between good health and coping with stressors. Unfortunately, many students do not eat nutritionally balanced meals at home or at school. Also, insufficient sleep and exercise contribute to feelings of fatigue and irritability. Studies have shown that physical activity, in addition to strengthening muscles, bones, the cardiovascular system, and the respiratory system, helps decrease fatigue and moodiness (Lau, 2002). Regular physical exercise can boost self-confidence, increase resilience, and make students better able to handle frustration. Similarly, sleeping well helps people cope with life, manage stress, and achieve well-being (McNamara, 2011). Children and adolescents, as well as adults, often spend far fewer hours than necessary getting quality sleep (Lau, 2002). Helping young people determine how much sleep they need and encouraging them to make commitments toward meeting that need can facilitate the stress-management process.

Learning how to relax is another important stress-management tool. Relaxation helps prevent some of the damaging physiological effects of stress and also helps prepare people to cope with stress more effectively. Being relaxed is both an outlook on life (e.g., calm, laid back) and a skill that can be learned. Developing relaxation techniques can help replace depleted energy resources and prevent the build-up of tension. Listening to music, taking a hot bath, drawing or painting, working in the yard, and participating in imagery exercises are all ways of relaxing. Help students explore ways of relaxing that are helpful to them, and encourage them to participate in at least one relaxation activity daily. Abdominal breathing (or "belly breathing"), progressive relaxation, and imagery are relaxation techniques that are easily taught and can be used by students in virtually any surrounding. It may be helpful to tell students that some people feel silly when trying out these relaxation skills, especially at the beginning. With time and practice, the techniques become more comfortable and can be employed easily to help reduce tension (see Figure 65.2).

Guided imagery or visualization can be used in conjunction with deep breathing to enhance relaxation. Imagery can be used with classes, small groups, or individuals. To normalize the process and ensure that students do not confuse it with hypnosis, explain that commercials use visualization to sell products and that athletes use visualization to improve performance. Begin with abdominal breathing. See Figure 65.3 for an example of an imagery exercise that can be read aloud after students have closed their eyes and started the breathing activity. After the students have completed the visualization exercise, tell them that when they feel stress in their bodies or have disturbing thoughts to imagine this safe place again and to practice breathing deeply. Depending on the age of the students, you might encourage them to draw what they visualized, talk about their pictures, and/or discuss when they might imagine this safe place again.

Study skills and time management. Assignments, tests, and the pressure to succeed can all be sources of stress for students of all ages. Developing good study skills and time management skills are essential to academic success and stress reduction. Students can be taught to handle academic tasks in ways that are efficient and effective. Suggestions that promote effective use of study time include:

- Practice active studying.
- Read the summary at the end of textbook chapters first. This will help you know what the author considers important.
- Read the questions at the end of the passage and all picture captions in advance. Try to answer the questions as you read.
- If you encounter a section that doesn't make sense, keep reading. Many times, questionable areas become clear with further reading.
- Review what you have read.
- Use mnemonics, a technique for improving the memory, to help remember important facts. (Adults will need to teach children how to use this tool.)

> Abdominal breathing can be done in a sitting or standing position. Speaking slowly and quietly, ask students to close their eyes and do the following:
>
> > Take a deep breath through your nose, very slowly. Pull the breath deeply into the bottom of your stomach (count 1-2-3-4). Then breathe out slowly through your mouth to the count of 8. (Repeat the breathing cycle) Place your hand on your stomach. You should be able to feel it move as you breathe. You will notice that as you continue breathing like this, you become very relaxed. (Repeat the breathing cycle) Now open your eyes. Notice the feelings you have in your body.

Figure 65.2. Abdominal breathing.

> First, help the students move to a relaxed state through abdominal breathing. The counselor continues to speak slowly and quietly:
>
> > Your whole body feels more relaxed. I am going to ask you to picture something in your mind's eye. If at any time you feel uncomfortable, open your eyes. Now, picture a place where you feel safe and cared for. (Wait several seconds) Look around this safe, safe place. (Wait several seconds) What is around you? (Wait several seconds) Is this place inside or outside? (Wait several seconds) Are there people or pets around you? (Wait several seconds) What do you hear? (Wait) Do you smell anything? (Wait) Now, stay in this safe place for a few minutes. (Wait a few minutes) When you are ready, take a deep, deep breath and open your eyes.

Figure 65.3. Guided imagery.

- Find an ideal study environment.
- Establish a regular place to study. This can help with structure and motivation. Keep it attractive and organized.
- Control internal and external distractions.
- Be aware of your own body clock. Choose times to study when your energy level is high.
- Take breaks.
- Use time management tools.
- Clarify your goals. What is most important and why?
- Avoid procrastination. Establish a routine and reward yourself for completing tasks on time (e.g., invite a friend over, participate in a favorite activity).
- Keep a calendar or day-timer. Write down assignments, due dates, and other scheduled events.
- Break down large tasks into manageable units and plan for their completion.
- Keep a daily and weekly to-do list to help prioritize activities and assignments. Check off completed tasks.
- Recognize the need for balance and flexibility.

- Keep things in perspective. Worry saps time and energy and is nonproductive. If you find yourself getting anxious about schoolwork, take time to relax and practice deep breathing. By simply breathing deeply, anxiety decreases.

Working With Parents and Teachers

Parent workshops. Parents or caregivers are experts on their children and interact with them daily. By offering parent-education workshops, which might be titled, "Helping Your Student Deal With Stress," parents can be given tools to help children manage stress more effectively and learn ways to reduce stress in the home. Any of the topics listed in the section titled *Psychoeducational Interventions for Students* can be included in a parent workshop. Professional school counselors may also want to share the following with parents:

- Teach parents deep breathing techniques to use when they feel stressed so that they can reinforce the practice with their children.
- Television, movies, and computer viewing of virtual violence can create stress.
- Sharing adult worries with children can contribute to children's stress.
- Overly high expectations can be stressful. Many times, parents are not aware of the expectations their children perceive. Although parents may not require straight As, children hear what is not said. A parent who expects perfection in him- or herself delivers a strong message that perfection is expected from each member of the family.
- Encourage parents to establish routines. Routines provide structure, eliminate uncertainty, and reduce chaos. Chaos creates stress (Lau, 2002).
- Parents can be sensitive to overload on their families or their children and take steps to remove stressors. Parents have the responsibility of intervening on their children's behalf when necessary.
- Parents can be reminded of the importance of nutrition, exercise, and quality sleep to combat stress.
- Parents are essential in helping children at all levels with the study skills and time management skills described in the previous section.
- Parents can help children appraise stressful situations constructively and then implement appropriate coping strategies.

Many parents need to realize that *they* must be in control of the family. Parents, with the best of intentions, often allow children to make adult decisions. Children suffer stress if they are asked to make these decisions before they are developmentally able. The mantra "Our family is a benign and loving monarchy" allows children to know that they are being cared for, loved, and protected.

Working with teachers. In addition to working with parents, professional school counselors will want to consult with teachers and offer in-service training on topics related to stress management. Teachers need information that will help them identify students who are suffering from stress. Behaviors that may indicate problems with stress in students include nail biting, fidgeting, separation anxiety, school phobia, bullying, violent and/or disruptive behaviors, obsessive–compulsive behaviors, social problems, crying, and excessive worry. Helping teachers understand the links between thoughts, feelings, and behaviors promotes understanding, if not acceptance, of student behaviors and can pave the way for making necessary interventions. Teachers need to be reminded that the professional school counselor is available for individual and small-group counseling as well as whole-class guidance to help students cope with stress more effectively.

In-service workshops for teachers on stress management can focus on the same topics that are listed as psychoeducational topics for students. In particular, professional school counselors will want to provide information to school personnel about the stress process, stress symptoms, and associated consequences. It may be helpful to engage the group in deep breathing or progressive relaxation exercises as tools to use themselves and with their students.

Numerous stressors exist in schools—some are unavoidable and others are not. Professional school counselors can work with school personnel to identify stressors that are part of the school environment and find ways to eliminate or ameliorate those stressors that are amenable to change. For example, high-stakes testing has added stress to the school environment. Anxiety and stress surrounding educational evaluation is considerable. Teachers sometimes unknowingly add to this pressure by reminding students throughout the year, "This will be on the final exam." During in-service workshops, it might be beneficial to have teachers brainstorm other wordings that might be less anxiety provoking. Most teachers want students to understand the importance of tests but unwittingly add to student anxiety and stress by focusing too strongly on that importance. Test anxiety can impair performance and negatively affect test results.

Group and Individual Counseling

Group counseling. Children who experience traumatic life events can suffer fear-related problems that impede their normal functioning and cause them to become disengaged in learning. These students may benefit from interacting with peers and adults in a group setting to enhance their self-worth, security, and control (Robinson, Rotter, Robinson, Fey, & Vogel, 2003). Professional school counselors can help these students explore the self in relation to the life events that have affected them. Also, therapeutic stress reduction skills and coping strategies can be shared in counseling groups that deal with family changes, relationships, anger management, inappropriate behaviors, anxiety, and depression. When planning for group counseling, professional school counselors can use the following procedures:

- Ensure that proper, school-regulated procedures for obtaining parental permission for students to participate in a counseling group are followed.
- Explain the nature of the group to teachers, and request the names of students who might benefit.
- Interview selected students to identify appropriate candidates for group participation and assess their level of interest.
- Notify or seek permission from parents. If a note is sent home, state the type of group, length and number of sessions, and activities that will take place in the group. Include a phone number where the professional school counselor can be reached if there are questions.
- Plan for the group, including time, place, and number of sessions. Include the activities that will take place in each session. Consider students' developmental levels as activities are planned.
- Proceed with group sessions. During the first session, describe the purpose of the group and include an explanation of confidentiality and its limits in age-appropriate terms.

- Provide information about stress, its causes, and typical responses. Ask students to think of a situation that stresses them, then ask, "Where in your body do you feel that worry or stress?" and "What are your thoughts when you have those feelings?"
- Teach students relaxation techniques, including deep breathing, progressive relaxation, and visualization.
- In subsequent sessions, focus on learning and implementing coping strategies (mental strategies, physical ways of coping, interpersonal skills, problem solving, etc.). Provide students with opportunities to "rehearse" (through role play or other methods) their responses to anticipated stressful experiences.
- Encourage students to use their new skills and to teach them to family members.
- At the conclusion of the group, give students an opportunity to evaluate their experience.

Individual counseling. When stress is a significant problem for a particular student, individual counseling may be warranted. Students may self-refer or be referred by teachers or parents. In many schools, long-term individual counseling is discouraged, and it may be necessary to make an outside referral so that the student gets the necessary help.

When working with any student individually, professional school counselors will want to explain confidentiality and its limits. Take time to build a therapeutic relationship and give the student an opportunity to tell his or her story. This will aid in assessing the severity of the problem and making decisions about next steps. Is the stress fear-based, and, if so, is the fear specific or generalized? What is the students' sense of control, security, and self-worth? Recommended interventions to help individuals deal with stress while increasing his or her sense of self-worth and control. Include relaxation training, systematic desensitization, guided imagery, interpersonal communication skills training, decision-making and life-skills training, creating success experiences, bibliocounseling, and encouragement (Robinson et al., 2003). In particular, professional school counselors should give students the opportunity to talk about what is stressful, identify their reactions to the stressful situation, explore effective coping strategies, and implement those strategies. If the student continues to manifest symptoms of distress or if the counselor suspects a more chronic condition (e.g., anxiety, PTSD, depression, abuse), it would be appropriate to suggest individual or family counseling in the community.

Summary/Conclusion

Stress is a pervasive problem that affects students at all grade levels. It seems that youth are experiencing more adverse reactions to stress than they have in the past. Stressors can come in many forms, including developmental transitions, life events, catastrophic events, and daily hassles. Indeed, change of any type can be stressful. When students experience stress, physical, cognitive, and emotional responses are likely. Chronic, long-term exposure to stress can be detrimental to physical and emotional health and well-being.

People cope with stress in numerous ways, with some coping strategies being more adaptive than others. Active, problem-focused coping tends to yield better outcomes than emotion-focused coping, particularly when the coping style is characterized by avoidance. In addition to individual coping styles, protective factors such as family and peer support, self-confidence, and an internal sense of control appear to affect the manner in which young people manage stress.

Professional school counselors can intervene on multiple levels to help students manage stress more effectively. Primary prevention methods include classroom guidance lessons, parent workshops, and teacher training sessions and consultation on topics related to stress management. In cases where students are at risk for stress-related problems or have evidenced poor coping skills, professional school counselors can offer group and individual counseling as well as coordinate services for those students who need outside professional help. Professional school counselors play instrumental roles in helping create safe, supportive schools and in teaching students and their caregivers life skills that will help them cope effectively with present and future stressors.

CHAPTER 66

Helping Students Manage Anger

*Carol Z. A. McGinnis and Bradley T. Erford**

Preview

The purpose of this chapter is to provide an introduction to anger management interventions, with specific focus on applications and techniques that professional school counselors can use in providing individual and group counseling to students with anger-related problems. Classroom guidance topics and activities for educating students about anger and effective anger management are also discussed.

Definitions for state and trait anger vary in the field of counseling and psychology. For example, Pascual-Leone, Gilles, Singh, and Andreescu (2013) focused on the internal processing of this emotion in their definition of "dysfunctional anger [as] a complex human experience resulting from an underlying cognitive-affective dysfunction and often resulting in a wide range of affective and interpersonal difficulties" (p. 92). Berkowitz and Harmon-Jones (2004), however, shifted that focus to include actions pertinent to perceived external sources in their definition of anger as "a syndrome of relatively specific feelings, cognitions, and physiological reactions linked associatively with an urge to injure some target" (p. 108).

Although mental health practitioners and researchers have discussed the lack of conceptual clarity of anger and its related processes (Smith, Larson, DeBaryshe, & Salzman, 2000), it is commonly accepted that anger is a normal human emotion that can be viewed at three levels: (1) *physical symptoms* of feelings of anger may include increased heart rate, muscular tension, and adrenaline flow; (2) *cognitive experiences* of anger frequently include distorted negative perceptions and interpretations of others' behaviors; and (3) *behavioral indications* of anger may include a variety of physical and verbal outbursts such as yelling, screaming, kicking, and fighting (Feindler & Engel, 2011). These reactions to anger can be directed toward others or self.

Anger is generally perceived negatively because, unmanaged, it can lead to aggression and violence. Yet anger can also serve an adaptive, positive function (McGinnis, 2008). Anger can stimulate us to take action when we or loved ones are under the threat of attack and can serve as an impetus for us to take appropriate actions to bring about needed changes, such as better or more equitable rules or laws (Lochman, Powell, Clanton, & McElroy, 2006).

Because anger is an emotion that can have adverse consequences for both self and others, it is important that the problem be addressed early on. Childre and Rozman (2003) noted

---

**Special thanks to John R. Charlesworth for his outstanding contribution to the first two editions of this chapter.*

that the problem is not anger itself but that individuals frequently do not know how to manage anger. Nowhere has the problem of anger management been more evident than with school-age students. Because these students spend the majority of the day at school, access to an anger management program during these hours is a significant element to implement (Candelaria, Fedewa, & Ahn, 2012).

Professional school counselors are in a unique position to help individuals understand and effectively cope with feelings of anger because they can provide students with needed classroom guidance and individual and group counseling anger-management programs and services, beginning with their entrance into elementary schools. The purpose of this chapter is to provide an introduction to anger management interventions, with specific emphasis on practical applications and techniques that professional school counselors can use while working with students in individual and small-group counseling. Instruction and activities that can be incorporated into guidance classroom lessons that educate students about anger and anger awareness will be introduced, and methods for reducing the development of anger-related problems will also be discussed.

Cognitive-Behavioral Interventions

The most frequently used individual and group treatment approaches for anger (and those considered to be most effective) have a basis in cognitive-behavioral therapy (Childre & Rozman, 2003; Kassinove & Tafrate, 2002; Smith et al., 2000). Sukhodolsky, Kassinove, and Gorman (2004) conducted a meta-analysis of cognitive-behavioral therapy (CBT) treatment outcomes for children and adolescents with anger-related problems. This comprehensive review included 21 published and 19 unpublished articles with a medium mean effect size (Cohen's $d = 0.67$). This review provided professional school counselors with an understanding of the types and content of CBT anger-management programs contained in the professional literature. Skills training, problem solving, affective education, and multimodal interventions were found in the 40 articles. Of these intervention types, skills training and multimodal treatments were more effective in reducing aggressive behavior and improving social skills, whereas problem-solving treatments were more effective in reducing subjective anger experiences. Also helpful to the positive treatment outcomes for these children were techniques of modeling, feedback, and homework often implemented as a part of CBT treatment planning.

The two most recognized theoretical cognitive-behavioral approaches to anger management are Beck's (2000) cognitive-behavioral therapy (CBT), and Ellis's (2002) rational-emotive behavior therapy (REBT). Although each of these approaches has distinctive features, both have much in common. Both approaches require students to identify the situations/ events in which they experience anger. Emphasis is then placed on helping students to identify the thoughts/cognitions that precede anger. The major intervention common to both approaches is to help students determine whether these cognitions (thoughts) are rational or irrational (Ellis, 2002), correct or false, distorted or inaccurate (Beck, 2000) and to replace irrational, inaccurate thoughts with more rational, accurate ones.

From his approach, Ellis attempts to change students' false assumptions by confronting their irrational thoughts, demonstrating how illogical the thoughts are, and teaching students how to replace the irrational thoughts with more rational ones that can result in students changing basic philosophical assumptions and values. In a recent study conducted by Flanagan, Allen, and Henry (2010), researchers found that anger management treatment with an added REBT component reduced both anger and aggression in a public school population of 9- to 11-year-olds. This 10-week lunchtime intervention model with pre-post design highlighted the value of teaching anger coping strategies and problem solving to children who process this emotion in negative ways.

In contrast to Ellis's REBT, which is often highly directive, persuasive, confrontational, and didactically oriented, Beck's CBT emphasizes the importance of the student–counselor relationship, and primarily uses open-ended Socratic questioning to help students reflect upon and discover the inaccuracies of their own thinking. Creed, Reisweber, and Beck (2011) presented many specific school-based interventions for this more collaborative approach that is oriented toward cognitive case conceptualization. Some of these interventions included the use of thought bubbles, coping cards, and reverse role-play as well as the introduction of replacement behaviors and relaxation techniques. It is important to note that both REBT and CBT value homework assignments, have students engage in behaviors designed to test the validity of cognitions, and frequently draw upon a wide range of behavioral techniques.

The following brief scenario illustrates some examples of the irrational, inaccurate thoughts that both Ellis and Beck believed frequently lead to inappropriate feelings of anger, and how a counselor might intervene:

Tom asked his best friend and classmate, Jason, to wait for him so they could walk home together after school. When Tom discovered that Jason wasn't waiting for him after school, Tom had the following thoughts that created feelings of anger for him:

"Jason *should have* waited for me."

"It is *terrible* and *awful* that Jason didn't wait."

"You can *never* count on Jason for anything."

Given this scenario, both Ellis and Beck would help Tom see that his thoughts are irrational or inaccurate and help him to replace them with more rational, accurate thoughts. Ellis would be more likely to didactically teach Tom that his thoughts are irrational by confronting and telling him something like: "Although it would have been nice if Jason had waited for you, there is no law that says that he *must, has to, or should have* waited for you," "Although Jason didn't meet you, it isn't terrible or awful, your world isn't collapsing, but this is a minor annoyance because he didn't do what you wanted," and finally "Jason has done many things for you, and not doing that one thing doesn't mean you can't count on him for other things."

In contrast to Ellis's intervention in the scenario, Beck would be more likely to achieve the same ends by using Socratic questions, such as "Other than that you wanted Jason to wait for you, is there any reason why he *should have* waited for you? Was Jason's not waiting for you terrible or awful, or merely disappointing or annoying for you?" And, "Does Jason's not waiting for you in this one instance mean that you can never count on him or does it just mean that he didn't wait this one time?"

Meichenbaum's (2002) cognitive behavior modification (CBM) is another major cognitive-behavioral therapy that has been successfully used in treating anger. Like REBT and CBT, CBM shares the assumption that distressing emotions are typically due to maladaptive thoughts. CBM focuses on making students aware of and training them to develop more effective self-talk that will enable them to cope more effectively in problematic situations. Stress inoculation training (SIT) was developed as a particular coping-skills program (Meichenbaum, 2002) to aid in stress reduction and is effective with a number of problems, including anger. SIT appears to be particularly beneficial when the student experiences anger in relatively specific situations. In addition to helping the student learn helpful behavioral techniques, the student is taught a number of specific coping thoughts to assist in working through the anger provoking situation.

In addition to these approaches for anger management and coping skills, Meichenbaum (2006) recommended that treatment may need to be gender specific when working with adolescent girls with aggression issues due to limitations in research that has been designed for boys. Meichenbaum noted that aggressive behaviors may be unique for girls due to differential incidence, expression types, developmental course, risk factors, and implications for assessment, treatment, and prevention of aggressive behaviors.

Behavioral Interventions

Cognitive-behavior approaches differentially incorporate a wide variety of behavioral techniques in treating anger problems, including the following:

- *Relaxation training.* Students can be taught to relax using a variety of modalities, including progressive relaxation (learning to systematically tighten and then relax the muscle groups of the body), yoga exercises, or meditation.
- *Homework assignments.* Students may be assigned to engage in self-monitoring of their thoughts and/or behaviors, keep an anger log, practice engaging in new behaviors, or participate in bibliotherapy.
- *Assertiveness training.* Before students are taught behavioral assertiveness skills, students are frequently taught the difference between nonassertive, assertive, and aggressive behavior. In addition, any cognitive distortions or irrational thoughts impeding assertive behavior are replaced. Students can then learn assertiveness skills through modeling, role-playing, and graded task assignments in real-life situations.
- *Distraction techniques.* After learning to identify cognitive and/or bodily cues that are precursors of anger, students can be taught a variety of distraction techniques, including counting to 10, removing themselves from the environment, or using humor (e.g., picturing an aggressor in his or her underwear or wearing a clown's costume).
- *Imagery.* Students can use imagery to learn relaxation and as another distraction technique by envisioning themselves in calm, peaceful scenes. Professional school counselors can also use imagery to help students see themselves effectively using their learned cognitive and behavioral skills in what previously were anger-provoking situations.
- *Problem-solving skills.* Students can be taught a general problem-solving model to assist in identifying a wider repertoire of methods for coping with anger-provoking situations.
- *Social skills training.* Students can be taught a wide range of social skills, such as smiling and providing eye contact, to assist in developing interpersonal skills.
- *Communication skills.* Students can be taught how to actively listen and produce "I messages."

Cole, Treadwell, Dosani, and Frederickson (2013) determined that there has been a paucity of cognitive-behavioral research in anger management programs designed for preadolescent children despite the need for them (Joughin, 2006). In the effort to fill that gap, Cole et al. evaluated a 6-week, group-delivered program, *Learning How to Deal With Our Angry Feelings*, for 7- to 11-year-olds in a no treatment/treatment and treatment/no treatment cohort format. In this study, 70 children were randomly assigned to 13 different groups in three schools and were exposed to short term, 45 minute weekly sessions. Based on Sharp and Herrick's (2000) "firework model" of anger, these sessions covered topics of: Getting to know each other; What things make us angry?; Getting angry; Calming down—"thinking differently"; and Calming down—"putting out the fuse." As a result, these researchers found that the children in the no treatment/treatment cohort benefitted from increased understanding of anger and a change in the way this emotion was managed as rated by teachers after the intervention was completed.

Professional school counselors who come from more of a pure behavioral counseling approach also use many of the behavioral techniques just described. As opposed to cognitive-behavioral-oriented counselors who see the main benefit of the behavioral techniques as producing changes in cognition, traditional behaviorists see the main benefit of these techniques as producing changes in behavior. Traditional behaviorists are also more likely to use positive reinforcement for students engaging in appropriate behavior and use extinction or punishment when needed to help eliminate aggressive behavior.

Play Therapy

Another viable method for reducing anger problems is individual play therapy (Fischetti, 2001). Rather than accepting that one standardized play-therapy approach is the most effective for all clients and situations, Fischetti preferred a prescriptive approach that enabled a professional school counselor to choose one they believe will be most effective. Fischetti (2001) identified three approaches useful for planning treatment for students with anger management problems. *Client-centered play therapy* is a nondirective approach that is a viable choice when the clinician can provide the student time to pursue their issues and personal growth. *Release play therapy* is a structured approach to assist clients in reenacting a stressful event and working through the pain and anger associated with it. Finally, *cognitive-behavioral play therapy* enables the clinician to use a wide range of behavioral techniques, such as antecedents, reinforcers, contingencies, modeling, relaxation training, systematic desensitization, and cognitive interventions such as learning to identify and replace dysfunctional thoughts, to best meet the treatment goals jointly developed with the student. A frequent component of cognitive-behavioral play therapy is student homework.

In addition to describing play-therapy approaches, Fischetti (2001) provided a number of case examples intended to demonstrate their treatment effectiveness. Kaduson and Shaefer (2010) provided a variety of individual and group play-therapy techniques and activities that can be incorporated into appropriate play-therapy approaches to assist students in working through anger-management issues. One example of such a technique would include:

- *Relaxation Training: Bubble Breaths* (Cabe, 2001, p. 346) is used in play therapy to help students learn relaxation training that can be used to reduce feelings of anxiety and anger, and the accompanying physical reactions. Students fill the room with bubbles and "pop" them as they fall. Students are then invited to pop the bubbles one at a time, which is more challenging but can be done with practice. Attention is then directed toward the deep breathing and controlled exhaling involved. The counselor follows this with instruction on how to breathe from the belly. Students are taught how they can use a series of three bubble breaths to relax when they begin to feel anxious or angry. This approach has been used successfully with all age ranges and with individuals as well as large groups.

Group Therapy

The implementation of group therapy is a popular way to address anger management issues within the school environment because they incorporate psychoeducation and role-play that can be useful in building many different types of prosocial behaviors. One program that has been designed for group implementation is as follows:

- *Seeing Red: An Anger Management and Peacemaking Curriculum for Kids* (Simmonds, 2013) is a group therapy activity for use with six to eight elementary- to middle school-aged students who have difficulty controlling their anger and making healthy choices. This curriculum incorporates a framework of lesson plans that are successive in skill-building and relate to key concepts, key activities, and the facilitation of effective group facilitation. The key concepts include identifying anger triggers, taking responsibility for mistakes, exploring how more painful feelings can be covered up with anger, and empowering group members as peacemakers. Key activities involve establishing trust, practicing feeling statements, developing practical problem-solving skills, controlling anger, and exploring natural consequences for anger choices. Guidelines for effective group facilitation for this curriculum include development of leadership, social skills, and self-esteem; heterogeneous group composition with no more than two years span in age; and consistency in the same meeting time and group members over time.

Classroom Guidance

There are many ways that professional school counselors can incorporate anger, anger prevention, and anger management into their classroom guidance and psychoeducational efforts. A combination of age-appropriate direct instruction, activities, and exercises (Golden, 2006) can be used to help students learn (a) what anger is; (b) the physiological cues associated with angry feelings; (c) the relationship between thoughts and feelings; (d) the difference between thoughts, feelings, and behavior; (e) cognitive and behavioral strategies for reducing arousal; (f) healthy versus unhealthy anger; (g) consequences of anger; and (h) general problem-solving and coping skills. An example of classroom guidance might also include activities and instruction relevant to bibliotherapy used in individual or group sessions:

- *How to Take the Grrrr Out of Anger* (Verdick & Lisovskis, 2003) is a book geared toward normalizing anger for children age 9 through 12 years through the identification of healthy versus unhealthy expression choices. Children learn how to deal with their own anger as well as with others who struggle with this emotion using a variety of strategies that range from choosing non-violent behaviors to finding safer conflict resolution resources. Cute graphics and steps help children to identify anger buttons, warning signs, and ways to solve anger problems with accompanying tips for using "anger radar" and "taming your temper." This book was the recipient of the National Parenting Publication's (NAPPA) 2003 Gold Award in the ages 9 and up category and the Children's Resources Honors Award.

Summary/Conclusion

Anger is a normal human emotion that can stimulate people to engage in constructive acts or lead to destructive behaviors. Frequently, anger problems first become apparent during a student's school years. Professional school counselors, particularly elementary counselors, are in a unique position to proactively help students better understand anger and learn effective anger management through classroom guidance classes. In addition, with knowledge and skill using cognitive-behavioral, behavioral, play-, and group-therapy interventions, professional school counselors can provide students with effective, age-appropriate individual and group counseling services.

CHAPTER 67

Bereavement in Schools: How to Respond

Susan Norris Huss and Melissa Nowicki

Preview

We will describe how the professional school counselor can take a leadership role in making a school "grief friendly." An overview of children's perceptions of death and typical grief reactions of different age groups is provided, followed by a brief description of the stages of grief and how these stages are experienced as age and individual specific. The major focus involves individual and group techniques, but brief attention will be given to preventive programs that can be included in a comprehensive developmental counseling program.

Bereavement is present in many forms in every school. Grief occurs any time a student experiences a loss. One out of every 20 American students under the age of 15 loses at least one parent to death (Dougy Center, 2014). It is also estimated that in a secondary school of 800 students, 24 students will experience the death of a family member (Selekman, Busch, & Kimble, 2001). There are no estimates of how many children experience the death of a grandparent, sibling, close friend, or even a pet. Grief also occurs through non-death-related losses (e.g., not making the football team, losing a homework assignment, moving to a new building, or anytime there is a major change in one's life). Suicide is also becoming more prevalent in schools. The Dougy Center (2014) stated that the third leading cause of death for 10- to 24-year-olds is suicide. This prevalence of bereavement dictates that professional school counselors must understand bereavement and its manifestations in students as well as be able to provide the security, continuity, and support that bereaved students need.

Students from preschool to late adolescence experience grief when a loss occurs. This is a relatively new belief. At one time it was believed that children did not have the capacity to grieve (Freud, 1957; Miller, 1971). This belief has changed. Bereavement and grief are very much a part of students' school experience and thus it becomes important for professional school counselors to be able to assist students and school personnel in the bereavement process. The goal should be to create a "grief-friendly" school environment. This environment is one that not only responds in a healthy way to a crisis but is also sensitive to the numerous and various losses students experience throughout a school year. Table 67.1 provides several characteristics of a grief-friendly school.

Beliefs About Death

Age is a major contributing factor to how a student perceives death. Although past experience and cognitive ability also affect these beliefs for each individual, there are some general

Table 67.1 McGlauflin's (2002) Grief-Friendly School Characteristics

Supportive crisis action team
Knowledgeable about grief
Recognition of the uniqueness of every crisis, death, and loss in the school
Open and honest communication with students about any loss
Respect for all feelings
Acceptance of the consciousness of grief
Acknowledgment and respect of all the good-byes in the school throughout the year
Remembering that education is the mission of the school
Maintenance of standards in a compassionate manner
Collective support for each other

Table 67.2 General Age-Related Perceptions of Death

Ages 3–5	Reversible; Temporary; Magical; Sense of security is threatened; May regress in behavior; May cry and become clingy
Ages 6–9	Permanence is understood; Universality belief begins; Personifies death; Wider social network; Models adult reactions; Curious about rituals; Very concrete questions
Ages 10–13	Overwhelmed; Wants facts; Believes he or she may have caused the death; Begins to understand finality of death; Begins to realize "I could die;" May have psychosomatic symptoms; Grieves more like adults and "want to get on with life"
Ages 14–18	Accepts that death is universal; Intense feelings of adolescence carries over to grief; Turns to friends for support more so than adults; May be suicidal; May feel pressure to assume more adult roles

perceptions about and general reactions to death for different age groups (see Table 67.2; Christ, 2000; Selekman et al., 2001; Worden, 2008). It is important for professional school counselors to understand these differences in order to provide appropriate interventions for the student.

When working with bereaved students, it is essential to understand the developmental nature of the grieving process in children and adolescents. As students develop cognitively, their level of understanding of a death experience changes. With this new understanding comes a new set of questions related to the death as well as the possibility that they will grieve again for the death of a loved one. It is important not only to remember that anniversaries (deaths, birthdays) and significant events (graduation, prom, parents' night) may cause a reoccurrence of some grieving but also that simply a new level of understanding can bring about the same reoccurrence of grief.

The generally accepted concept of "stages of grief" takes on a new meaning when working with children. Those stages are generally shock and denial, anger, bargaining, depression, and acceptance (Kubler-Ross, 1969). Generally, one thinks of moving through one stage and into another; however, stages of grief can also be seen as a roller coaster, because they go up and down in intensity. Other students' experiences may be more like a coil—they grieve again and again in a spiral manner as their understanding increases. The major implications of this spiraling effect is to be aware that interventions such as loss support groups should not be limited only to recently bereaved students. The resolution of grief often requires cyclical processing as students grow up.

Although each person grieves in a unique way, there are some general reactions that could be considered normal grieving processes (Perry, 2001). These may include (but are not limited to) denial; emotional numbing; anger, irritability, episodic rage; fear and characteristic rushes of anxiety; confusion; difficulty sleeping; regressive behaviors; physical complaints such as stomachaches or headaches; and changes in appetite. All stakeholders need to acquire an understanding of common student bereavement characteristics.

Proactive Programming

A grief-friendly school provides opportunities (e.g., workshops, seminars, in-services) for all stakeholders in the school (e.g., teachers, staff, parents) to be informed about the common characteristics of grief in students as well as what is considered to be normal grief reactions. There should also be an updated, functioning crisis-response plan in place for those crisis situations that create losses in schools. There is not space in this chapter to detail these two preventive programs, but a professional school counselor can play an instrumental role in ensuring that these aspects are in place.

The comprehensive developmental school counseling program in a grief-friendly school should include classroom guidance activities related to bereavement and the grieving process. Since this form of "death education" may be questioned, it can be positively marketed as helping students to develop loss-coping skills to deal with the many losses commonly experienced in schools. The information students learn in these sessions provides the basis for student belief that the school is grief friendly. Learning loss-coping skills can provide a resource of learned behavior for major losses such as the death of a parent. It is important to remember that the mission of the school is to educate students and impart life skills. Loss-coping skills are an example of these life skills. Some resources for the development of these activities have been produced by the Dougy Center (http://www.dougy.org), the National Alliance for Grieving Children (http://childrengrieve.org), and the National Center for School Crisis and Bereavement (http://www.stchristophershospital.com/pediatric-specialties-programs/specialties/693).

Interventions

When a student has suffered a loss, interventions should provide opportunities to share feelings and memories; assist in identifying support systems; assist in the development of coping mechanisms to help them process as they go through the grieving experience; normalize their feelings; and provide a safe environment to do all the above (Huss, 1997).

Group Counseling

Group work is one way of providing interventions (Jacobs, Harvill, & Masson, 2012; Johnson-Schroetlin, 2000; Sharpnack, 2000). Group work is efficient because it serves more than one student at a time, there are more resources and viewpoints within the group, and groups provide the needed sense of universality and commonality for the bereaved child. Detailed group program plans are available from Haasl (2000), Lehmann (2001a, 2001b), and Webb (2010).

Expressing, acknowledging, and owning one's feelings are extremely important when working with a bereaved student, who is often confused by conflicting feelings (e.g., relief and sadness if the death was after a prolonged illness). Having never experienced a feeling before may be frightening, and the student needs to understand that any feeling is okay and normal for someone experiencing grief. Most of the interventions discussed here can be used to assist in the understanding of feelings, expression of feelings, and understanding of the universality and commonality of feelings. This understanding of the universality and commonality allows bereaved students to move through the grieving process. In addition, the interventions described in the rest of this chapter can be used in group settings as well as when working with individuals.

Artistic activities. Art in many forms (e.g., music, drawing, sculpture) can be an effective means of expressing feelings about a loss. Students can draw pictures of how they feel or pictures of the loved one who has died (or of the loss), and share pictures and stories with the group. Students can express how they felt about the activity, whether or not it helped them to talk about the loss, what the picture means to them, or how it relates to the way they feel. They can also use modeling clay to create images that express feelings. Another good activity is to have students draw a picture of their family before and after the loss. This provides a basis for discussing family differences and similarities after the loss. It also provides an opportunity to discuss the student's remaining support system.

Bibliotherapy. Books provide a wide variety of opportunities for intervention with bereaved students. Books can be read to the student, with the student, or by the student and then discussed at a later session. A book about death can also be read to a class that is anxious about a classmate who has experienced death, and preparing a list of recommended books can provide support for families as they strive to assist in the bereavement process. The professional school counselor should develop a resource library, preferably in the media center. Reading or creating poetry that expresses feelings of grief concerning the loss can also help the student during the grieving process.

Playing. Toys and playing with young students may be helpful as a means of expressing feelings that are hard to express and hard to understand. Dolls, aggressive toys, animals (stuffed or plastic), and other toys and games can be used by the student in playing out anxieties and emotions involved with issues related to grief or loss. Puppets are especially helpful for reluctant participants.

Storytelling. Students from preschool through middle school may benefit from storytelling. Students can be given sentence starters that they can use to either tell or write a story. Examples of sentence starters are: Someday I would like to . . . ; I wish I would have . . . ; If I could . . . ; Whenever I see . . . ; and When I think about. . . . Sentence starters can be created to meet the specific circumstances of the student's loss.

Letter writing. Writing a letter to the person who died can be a powerful tool for saying goodbye or to share something that was left unsaid because of the death. A letter written to someone with whom the student desires to share feelings concerning the loss can be the beginning of communication. Families often send unintentional messages that it is not okay to talk about a loss. Writing a letter can begin the much needed communication process.

Journaling. Encourage students to keep a journal of their feelings as well as questions they may have. Journal entries can be used to facilitate discussion with students to assist them during this transitional time. Keeping a journal allows students to express feelings and can be a record of their bereavement journey. They can reflect about feelings and see that feelings change during their journey in intensity, type, and duration.

Celebrating life through memory work. Memory work is a way of expressing feelings and normalizing what has happened. Group or individual collages can be made from pictures of the deceased loved one. Students can bring items belonging to the deceased person and share something about the relevance of the item or the memory of the person to whom the item belonged. Individual or group memory books can be made that include pictures, drawings, and letters. Memory books provide a way to keep the person who died in the student's life in an appropriate manner. By creating a memory book, the student is honoring the deceased without obsessing, thereby providing a mechanism for moving forward through the grieving process.

Closure. It is very important to plan events to provide closure when the grieving student is ready. This does not mean that the deceased is forgotten; it means the child is ready to move forward. Use balloons and bubbles in concluding activities by presenting them as methods of releasing or letting go. This could include letting go of someone, a feeling, an attitude, or other emotions connected to loss.

Special Circumstances

A great many students will experience the death of a close family member. The professional school counselor is often confused about the appropriate role to play. Some specific suggestions follow.

Death of a Family Member

When a member of a student's family dies, the professional school counselor should make contact with the family, if possible. Depending on the religion/culture of the family, the professional school counselor should participate in an appropriate manner. An example would be to visit the funeral home and talk with the student. That discussion could include the following:

- An expression of sympathy.
- Informing the student that the professional school counselor will be visiting his or her classroom(s), asking for input into what he or she would like to be said, and telling the student exactly what will be shared. This eases the mind of the student and gives direction to the professional school counselor.
- What kind of support the professional school counselor will provide once the student returns to school (e.g., opportunities to talk, providing a quiet place when needed, talking with other students).

The professional school counselor should then visit the classroom(s) of the bereaved student and talk about how to be a good friend to a bereaved student. This visit should include the following:

- Setting the record straight. This is particularly needed if it is a violent death, since there may be many rumors.
- Helping the class decide how they will express their sympathy to the bereaved family (e.g., flowers, cards, visit to the funeral home or funeral).
- A discussion of how the student wishes to be treated when he or she returns to school. This often assures the other students that the bereaved student is doing okay because he or she has talked with the professional school counselor.
- A general discussion of grief and bereavement.
- A discussion about the feelings students are experiencing and why (e.g., fear that their parent may die, reoccurring feelings from a loss they have experienced in the past). It may be helpful to encourage students to tell their families that a friend has experienced this loss or, with younger students, to send a note home. This gives the families the opportunity to be alert to any needs that may arise from this experience.
- Awareness that this is a "teachable moment." It is an opportunity to either reinforce what was taught in a developmental guidance unit presented before the loss occurred or to teach those concepts now. It is much easier to work with grieving children if they have learned something previously to which you can relate.

Of concern for many professional school counselors when a family death occurs is the religious or spiritual questions that are often asked by the bereaved student (e.g., "Do you believe that when someone dies, they go to heaven?"). These questions should be redirected to what the student and student's family believes. The same is true of certain rituals associated with the funeral. These kinds of questions may also be asked during the classroom visit.

Suicide Situations

Educators may be unsure how to talk with students about suicide. Goodman (2010) suggested the following:

- Define suicide as when "someone chooses to make their body stop working."
- Give age-appropriate facts and explanations.
- Dispel myths about suicide.
- Retell good memories.
- Model feelings and thoughts for students.
- Emphasize suicide is a mistake because there "is always another way out."

Get the message out to all students that suicide is not a good choice, and provide other choices to prevent a "copycat" suicide.

Complicated Grief

Determining when a referral is needed is difficult because of the developmental nature of student bereavement. If the symptoms persist for an extended period of time or do not lessen in intensity, it could be cause for alarm. McIntire (2003) recommended counseling for children who exhibit several of the following over an extended period: depressions so severe that a child shows little interest in daily activities; inability to sleep, eat normally, or be alone; regression in behavior to that of a less-mature child; imitation of the deceased parent; repeatedly wishing to join the deceased; loss of interest in friends or play and refusal to attend school; or a persistent and marked drop in school achievement. Cases involving complicated grief should be immediately referred to mental health professionals specializing in the treatment of such cases.

Summary/Conclusion

This has been a brief description of some of the more important aspects of working with bereaved children in a grief-friendly school. The school may be and should be the most stable place in a student's life during the time immediately following the death of the loved one. This stability is supported by remembering the educational mission of the school and maintaining the usual discipline, expectations, and academic standards. At the same time, it is important to create an environment that respects the needs of the bereaved child, whether the loss involves a low grade, a lost friendship, or the death of a parent. It should also be the place that understands the developmental nature of childhood bereavement and thus provides ongoing support for the bereaved student. The professional school counselor needs to stay informed about available resources inside and outside of school to use not only for the bereaved students but also for those within the school. The grief-friendly school has both proactive and reactive programming in place to assist all stakeholders in the bereavement process. Dealing with grief may be one of the most challenging aspects of the school counseling program, but because there is such a prevalence of grief in school, it is also one of the most important.

CHAPTER 68

Crisis Intervention With Individuals in the Schools

Gerta Bardhoshi and Bradley T. Erford*

Preview

Crisis work with students in the schools is becoming more common. Professional school counselors need to gain knowledge about the various physical, cognitive, emotional, and behavioral manifestations of crises in children so that they can recognize, assess, and intervene with students. Development of positive characteristics and skills along with an understanding and practice of some intervention and assessment models provide the needed resources for a crisis counselor to plan the appropriate course of intervention with the individual student in crisis.

Pressures of violence and abuse, bullying, terrorism, family discord, economic depression, loss, disease, and addiction bombard children who are either victims of or witness crises. Gratuitous violence in the media makes children regular bystanders to crisis. Situational crises often appear unexpectedly, and the effects of this exposure impact children's lives at school, where they are expected to learn and grow in a structured academic setting. In addition, children are developing and growing, and thus they often experience developmental crises as they work to master life tasks and progress through life transitions (Jackson-Cherry & Erford, 2014). Acknowledging the prominent role of safety in the learning environment, schools across the country have developed crisis plans in the hopes of containing the effects of a crisis on students. In this fast-changing world, knowledge of support, intervention, and coping strategies in crisis situations may not have kept pace with what is required to truly help students in crisis. In addition, the application of a culturally sensitive lens in school-based crisis intervention plans may also be lagging (Annandale, Heath, Dean, Kemple, & Takino, 2011). This chapter is an overview of the work needed within the life of an individual student in crisis in a school setting. It deals with the systemic crisis work that is needed when the entire school ecology is affected by crisis.

First, we define crisis and then explore in general some pivotal crisis concepts, including the physical, mental, emotional, and behavioral components to crisis, and specific reactions of students. Next, we examine the training, characteristics, and qualities of effective crisis professionals. This is followed by appropriate intervention and assessment models that have been shown effective in the school setting. A special emphasis on understanding suicidal ideation,

---

*Special thanks to Fran Steigerwald for her outstanding contributions to the first two editions of this chapter.

behavior, and intervention is stressed because of the destructive risks involved. The chapter ends with a summary of effective guidelines for working with school children in crisis.

A Look at Crisis

There are many definitions of crisis. James and Gilliland (2012) worked these definitions into a consolidated, easy-to-understand idea that encompassed the major points: "Crisis is a perception or experiencing of an event or situation as an intolerable difficulty that exceeds the person's current resources and coping mechanisms" (p. 8). Key in this definition is the importance of the "perception" of the crisis, the response of the person exposed to it. This concept is illustrated in the Chinese word for crisis that is composed of two symbols, one representing *danger* and the other *opportunity*. How an individual is helped to perceive the crisis will provide much information as to whether he or she will cope well and grow from it, be overwhelmed and immobilized by it, or survive by protecting and blocking but have negative after-effects.

Mitchell and Everly (1993) defined a crisis event as "an event which produces a temporary state of psychological disequilibrium and a subsequent state of emotional turmoil" (p. 5). This disequilibrium or turmoil has been commonly referred to as *stress*, a phenomenon identified in the classic work of Selye (1956) as a mind–body reaction that causes wear and tear upon the person. Stress has been defined as "a response characterized by physical and psychological arousal arising as a direct result of an exposure to any demand or pressure on a living organism" (Mitchell & Everly, 1993, p. 5).

Crisis can be developmental, situational, existential, or ecosystemic in nature (James & Gilliland, 2012). Whatever is the nature of the crisis, stress is always a major component. This stress is deeply personal, and its corresponding impairment is dependent upon the individual's perception of the crisis situation. When children perceive stressful experiences as severe, unpredictable, and recurring, they are more likely to experience disequilibrium that impacts their self-regulating capabilities (Thompson, 2014). Crisis stress is often observed as a combination of symptoms that are cognitive, emotional, physical, and behavioral. Researchers have worked to synthesize the many signs and symptoms of crises and stress. Tables 68.1, 68.2, 68.3, and 68.4, respectively, list general physical, mental or cognitive, emotional, and behavioral symptomology information gathered from the classic research of Girdano, Dusek, and Everly (2011), Mitchell and Everly (1993), and Myer (2001). Additional information from Greenstone and Leviton (2010) and Thompson (2014) has been added pertaining to age-related and developmental reactions of students to stress and crises. The level of symptomology should be individually considered on a continuum ranging from *no impairment* to *severe impairment* in each area. Additional contextual factors such as the nature of the occurring event, students' vulnerability and resiliency, support from caregivers, and the effects of previous experiences on student coping skills should also be considered to inform a clearer picture of symptomology (Thompson, 2014).

A crisis in an individual's life typically lasts for a maximum of 6 to 8 weeks (Hendricks & McKean, 2003). After that, symptoms are usually expected to diminish along with the obvious discomforts they caused. However, recent research points out that the aftereffects of stressful events in childhood can be longer in duration, possibly extending into adolescence and adulthood, and even having the potential for multigenerational impact (Carlisle & Rofes, 2007; Thompson, 2014; van der Kolk, Roth, Pelcovitz, Sunday, & Spinazzola, 2005). Helping

Table 68.1 Physical (Age-Related) Symptoms of Crisis and Stress

The body strongly reacts to crisis and stress. Repeated or prolonged stress can cause exhaustion, decreased immunity, and psychosomatic illness throughout an individual's life. Common symptoms include the following:
- secreted stress hormones (cortisol, aldosterone, epinephrine)
- increased neural excitability (rapid breathing, dizziness)
- increased cardiovascular activity (heart rate, blood pressure, stroke volume, cardiac output)
- increased metabolic activity (gluconeogenesis, protein mobilization, muscle wasting, decreased antibody production, fat mobilization)
- increased sodium retention and neurological sweating
- change in salivation and in gastrointestinal system tonus and motility
- suppression of the immune system
- under-reaction to stress (hyporesponsiveness)

Symptoms common in preschool children (1–5 years)
- loss of bladder or bowel control, constipation
- speech difficulties, such as stammering
- loss of or increase in appetite

Symptoms common in school-age students (5–11 years)
- headaches or other physical complaints as stated above

Symptoms common in preadolescent students (11–14 years)
- appetite disturbances
- physical pain, such as headaches, vague pain, bowel problems, psychosomatic complaints
- skin eruptions

Symptoms common in adolescent students (14–18 years)
- physical complaints such as headaches, psychosomatic symptoms, bowel problems, rashes, asthma
- appetite and sleep disturbances
- hypochondriasis
- amenorrhea or dysmenorrhea
- loss of sexual interest
- agitation or decrease in energy levels

the student during the immediate aftermath of the crisis is of great importance in determining whether he or she is able to soon resume the normalcy of life or whether there are resulting residual complications and long-term effects in affective, behavioral, and cognitive functioning from the crisis.

Posttraumatic Stress Disorder

Trauma can produce persistent symptoms that cause a diagnosable condition of stress and anxiety called *posttraumatic stress disorder* (PTSD). PTSD is a complex disorder that is often comorbid and requires specialized help, and new crises can exacerbate and complicate PTSD. It is important for crisis workers to understand this disorder to make appropriate referrals.

Table 68.2 Mental or Cognitive (Age-Related) Symptoms of Crisis and Stress

There are always beliefs, attitudes, perceptions, and cognitions that go along with crisis. The negativity and intensity of these cognitions help determine the psychological interpretation of the crisis and the subsequent level of the stress response and/or impairment. These cognitive impairments reduce coping ability.

- thought overload
- confused thinking
- difficulty making decisions
- difficulty controlling impulses
- lowered concentration
- memory dysfunction
- intrusive thoughts
- nightmares
- reduced problem solving
- mental orientation toward threat
- lowering of all higher cognitive functions

Symptoms common in preschoolers (1–5 years)
- night terrors
- confusion

Symptoms common in school-age students (5–11 years)
- night terrors, nightmares, fear of darkness
- poor concentration
- loss of interest in school

Symptoms common in preadolescent students (11–14 years)
- loss of interest in peer activity
- denial

Symptoms common in adolescent students (14–18 years)
- confusion
- poor concentration
- tendency to blame

Refer to Chapter 46, "Helping Students Who Have Posttraumatic Stress Disorder," for further information on this topic.

Understanding and Structuring Crisis Work

Crisis intervention or management work requires quick and immediate action to provide the support and direction that the student in crisis cannot provide for him- or herself. Crisis counseling may be appropriate once a person has been stabilized from the initial crisis.

Lindemann (1944, 1956) was the first to offer a theory of crisis work to help professionals and paraprofessionals to understand the needs of clients in crisis. He clearly provided a new framework for normalizing, not pathologizing, behaviors specific to people suffering from loss and trauma who felt unbalance or disequilibrium. Lindemann's proposed process

Table 68.3 Emotional (Age-Related) Symptoms of Crisis and Stress

Emotions are immediate triggers in crisis. Expression of emotions in a crisis is healthy and should be encouraged. In crisis situations, it is normal for emotions to rise to uncomfortable levels as
- emotional shock
- fear
- anger
- grief or sadness
- depression
- feeling overwhelmed (helpless or hopeless)
- emotional flattening or denial
- moodiness and irritability
- decompensation
- depersonalizing

Symptoms common in preschoolers (1–5 years)
- fears of darkness, animals, strangers, or abandonment

Symptoms common in school-age students (5–11 years)
- generalized anxiety
- irritability
- withdrawal from peers
- fears about weather, safety, harm, loss or abandonment
- depression

Symptoms common in preadolescent students (11–14 years)
- depression
- loss of interest in peers and social activities
- anger
- fear of loss of family, friends, home, or personal harm

Symptoms common in adolescent students (14–18 years)
- depression
- indifference or apathy
- anger at perceived unfairness of crisis
- fear of loss
- guilt

took the clients through their disrupted state with brief intervention and grief work, to problem solving or working through the loss, and finally to a return to equilibrium. Lindemann's (1956) model is presented in Figure 68.1.

Today, brief solution-focused therapy follows much the same format. Crisis work focuses on facilitating an understanding of the crisis and its manifestations while not working on any ongoing problems as brief therapy would. It is important to remember that crisis intervention is not a long-term counseling approach. It is short-term problem or solution-focused work to get the client back to a state of balance where they can employ coping skills to deal with the crisis (Myer, 2001). Regardless of the approach, it is clear that crisis intervention involves an established procedure (Greenstone & Leviton, 2010).

Table 68.4 Behavioral (Age-Related) Symptoms of Crisis and Stress

Emotional energy prepares for action, and, in times of crisis, behaviors may be the first things seen and attended to. Behaviors are purposeful. They are often manifestations of the intent of working out the discomfort caused by the crisis, no matter how misdirected it may seem to the observer. Such behaviors include the following:
- changes in ordinary behavior patterns or regression
- inability to perform daily functions
- changes in eating, drinking, or sleeping habits
- self-harming behaviors
- changes in personal hygiene
- hyperarousal
- withdrawal, prolonged silences
- rebellion, fighting

Symptoms common in preschoolers (1–5 years)
- bed-wetting
- clinging to parents
- thumb-sucking
- cries or screams for help
- immobility with trembling and frightening expressions
- running either toward an adult or in aimless motion

Symptoms common in school-age students (5–11 years)
- thumb-sucking
- whining
- clinging
- aggressive behaviors
- competition with siblings for parental attention
- school avoidance
- regressive behaviors

Symptoms common in preadolescent students (11–14 years)
- sleeplessness or too much sleeping
- fighting
- attention-seeking behaviors
- withdrawing behaviors
- refusal to do chores

Symptoms common in adolescent students (14–18 years)
- poor or reduced performance
- aggressive behaviors
- withdrawing or isolating behaviors
- changes in peer group or friends
- irresponsibility
- delinquent behaviors
- rebellion
- refusal to do chores
- attention-seeking behaviors
- decline in struggling with parents

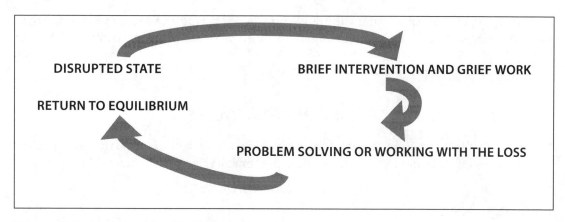

Figure 68.1. Lindemann's crisis intervention process.

A Look at Crisis Professionals

Since crisis intervention and management is time limited, the ability to quickly establish rapport and an environment of trust and caring is essential. Rogers (1957) established the core conditions for successful counseling: empathic understanding, unconditional positive regard, and congruence. These basic conditions are necessary in crisis work to gain an understanding of the client's perception of the crisis; however, the crisis worker must be able to quickly exhibit these conditions with the student in crisis while being supportive and often directive and in control of the crisis event. In crisis intervention, the crisis worker is extremely active in working through the set phases, and it is this needed structure that helps the student in crisis proceed to balance.

Effective communication skills are essential, including listening, clarifying, understanding nonverbal cues, asking questions to obtain accurate information, legitimizing feelings, and responding well to the client's feelings and perceptions. These skills, along with withholding judgment, shame, and advice-giving, are skills that develop rapport and begin to help manage the student's crisis (Greenstone & Leviton, 2010).

Training in crisis theory, symptomology, intervention, and assessment are necessary for a competent crisis worker. It is also vital to understand the referral process, state and local law, legal implications of working with minors, parental notification, and commitment or hospitalization procedures. In addition, Myer and Hanna (1996) have included quick thinking, tolerance of medical trauma, sense of reconciliation with death, and sense of humor. Because counselors who provide crisis intervention may be at risk to also experience symptoms, especially when the crisis is a shared trauma (e.g., natural disaster or school violence), an ability to recognize personal vulnerabilities, maintain healthy boundaries, and practice self-care is essential (Bell & Robinson, 2013).

Awareness of multicultural perspectives, culturally biased assumptions of crisis, and the client's worldview of the events are necessary for correct assessment and intervention. Misinterpretation because of lack of sensitivity to cultural values, social or political backgrounds, and cultural behaviors in crisis can unfairly label clients and result in inappropriate interventions (Hays & Erford, 2014). Seeking representation from diverse stakeholder groups in developing and implementing culturally-competent crisis intervention strategies may be an important step for school professionals involved in crisis planning (Annandale et al., 2011).

A Look at What Works

Successful crisis intervention requires that professional school counselors plan ahead, become familiar with effective models of intervention, and practice age-specific school interventions.

Planning Ahead

For professional school counselors, it is important to realize that crisis work will be part of the routine. Planning ahead through knowledge of crisis and stress, training in handling these events, and ongoing self-preparation is essential. In the moment of the crisis, there is no time to contemplate, refer to a manual, or look up a step-by-step process in the files. Determine state law and school policy for parental notification, clients who are minors, and confidentiality. Make clear your ethical practice on involving family and guardians in crisis situations. Your plans need to be known, practiced, handy, and visible. Several models are clear, well-established, and proven effective. Two models of intervention and one model for assessment are outlined and discussed, with the emphasis on working with students. It is important to decide which model of intervention will be employed and make the necessary preparation. All three of these models offer practical interventions that can be implemented by a professional school counselor when an individual crisis erupts in a child's day.

Models

Roberts (1996; see Table 68.5) outlined a seven-stage crisis intervention model that "can facilitate early identification of crisis, problem-solving, and effective crisis resolution" (p. 26). It is important to maintain close contact and provide the student and family with resource information and community assistance as needed. Greenstone and Leviton (2010; see Table 68.6) have a similar crisis intervention plan that calls for six major components along with some practical suggestions.

Myer (2001) worked to expand the concept of assessment as paramount in effective intervention in his triage assessment model. This assessment begins by listening to the crisis story to determine the catalyst and the student's unique view. Next, assessment takes place within three domains: *affective* (identify and rank anger–hostility, or anxiety–fear, or sadness–melancholy); *cognitive* (identify and rank whether there is perceived physical, psychological, social–relationship, or moral–spiritual transgression, threat or loss); and *behavioral* (identify and rank behaviors as approach, avoidance, or immobility). There are always reactions to crisis in these three domains, and it is vital to determine and rank severity of impairment in each area. Next, crisis workers are encouraged to utilize the triage assessment as a guide to appropriate intervention in the domains that appear with most impairment: affective (awareness, support, and catharsis); cognitive (clarifying, delimiting and ordering); or behavioral (guiding, protecting, and mobilizing).

Table 68.5 Roberts's Seven-Stage Crisis Model

Beginning with a thorough assessment.

Stage 1—ASSESS LETHALITY, examines how dangerous the student is to self and others and looks at the immediate psychosocial needs.

Stage 2—ESTABLISH RAPPORT, stresses the need to rapidly bond with the student using respect, acceptance, and reassurance.

Stage 3—IDENTIFY MAJOR PROBLEMS, allows for the student to vent about the precipitating event and helps the student rank the problems by harm or potential threat.

Stage 4—DEAL WITH FEELINGS, uses active listening skills and communicates warmth, respect, reassurance, and nonjudgmental validation.

Stage 5—EXPLORE ALTERNATIVES, uses the calmness and rationality of the crisis worker, since the student is often distressed and unable to function clearly. Ideally the student and the crisis worker can join collaboratively; however, the crisis worker may often need to initiate discussion of adaptive coping mechanisms.

Stage 6—DEVELOP ACTION PLAN, develops and implements actions to help restore the student to balance and functionality. Reasonableness, encouragement, and supportiveness are essential ingredients in successful implementation.

Stage 7—FOLLOW-UP, completes the crisis resolution and sets times to meet (daily, weekly or monthly) to gauge the student's success in functioning.

Table 68.6 Greenstone and Leviton's (2010) Crisis Intervention Model

IMMEDIACY—Work "to relieve anxiety, prevent further disorientation [and] ensure that sufferers do not harm themselves or cause harm to others" (p. 8).

CONTROL—Work to "be clear about what and whom you are attempting to control, enter the crisis scene cautiously, [and] be clear in your introductory statements, do not promise things that might not happen. . . . direct and arrange the pattern of standing or sitting to gain the victim's attention, guide the sufferer with your eyes and voice rather than through physical force, use physical force only as a last resort and only if you are trained and authorized, [and] remove the victim from the crisis situation" (pp. 8–10).

ASSESSMENT—Work to "evaluate on the spot . . . make the evaluation quick, accurate, and comprehensive . . . focus your assessment on the present crisis and events . . . what are the precipitating events . . . ask short, direct questions . . . one at a time . . . allow enough time for the victim to answer . . . allow the crisis to be the victim's crisis . . . assess actual and symbolic meaning . . . listen for what is not being said . . . allow the victim to speak freely and to ventilate feelings . . . see the crisis as temporary . . . [and] return control to the victim as soon as possible" (pp. 10–13).

DISPOSITION—Work to "help the victim identify and mobilize personal resources . . . mobilize social resources . . . hold out hope that solutions are possible . . . develop options . . . [and] help the parties to the crisis make an agreement" (p. 13).

REFERRAL—Much preplanning is needed for this component. As a crisis worker, you need to have a comprehensive list of referral sources (agencies, community professionals, doctors, lawyers, clergy, hospitals, transporters, and law enforcement) with hours of operation, telephone numbers, and names, always accurate and available to you for immediate use. Provide the information (if a minor to the parent or guardian) clearly and in writing, asking for verification of information.

FOLLOW-UP—Work to determine whether follow up procedures have been done, providing further help or re-referrals, if necessary.

Table 68.7 Age-Appropriate Interventions for Students Recovering From Crisis

Interventions for preschoolers (1–5 years)
- play reenactment
- verbal and physical comforting and attention
- expression of feelings and concerns
- suggestions for comforting bedtime routines and support

Interventions for school-age students (5–11 years)
- patience and tolerance
- play reenactment; discussing emotions
- discussion about crisis experience with peers and adults with expectations that occur in crisis
- temporary relaxation of expectations in school and home
- opportunities for undemanding structure and routine

Interventions for preadolescent students (11–14 years)
- group activities geared toward resuming routine
- same-age activities
- undemanding but structured routine
- individual attention and consideration

Interventions for adolescent students (14–18 years)
- letter writing
- participation in the community
- discussion of feelings and concerns
- temporary reduction of expectations
- encourage discussion of crisis fears with family

Age-Specific Interventions in the Schools

Remember that crisis is in the eye of the person who perceives it. It is paramount that crisis workers suspend their judgment about the appropriateness of the student's reactions to the crisis. Working to understand the crisis and validating reactions from the student's perspective is essential. Students exhibit behaviors as a result of their emotional states. In school situations, these behaviors may be the first things noticed and attended to. School personnel must understand what the student really needs before they discipline the student's behaviors (Kohn, 2006). Table 68.7 provides age-appropriate interventions to help the student regain balance and reach pre-crisis levels of stress (Greenstone & Leviton, 2010).

A Special Look at Suicide

One of the most devastating things that can happen in crisis is loss of life. When that loss of life is a student's, everyone involved asks what could have been done to prevent it, or why no signs were seen. For youth 15 to 19 years of age, suicide rates peaked in 1994 and have steadily declined since, comprising 12.3% of all teen deaths. But suicide is still the third leading cause of death for youth between the ages of 10 and 24 years, after homicides and accidents. In this age group, the male to female ratio of completed suicides is 5 to 1, with girls however being more likely to report attempting suicide. Native American/Alaskan Native youth have

Table 68.8 Basic Steps in Addressing Suicidal or Homicidal Intent

Step 1: Assess for predictors

- A. Sex and age
- B. Previous attempts
- C. Familiarity with someone who has attempted or completed suicide or family history of suicide
- D. Use of drugs and/or alcohol
- E. Depression and/or medical conditions
- F. Warning signs, such as suicide talk, giving away personal items, sudden change in behavior and patterns, preoccupation with death (in music or reading)
- G. Sexual orientation and gender identity (gay, lesbian, bisexual, and transgender adolescents exhibit more self-harm and suicidal thoughts and behaviors)

Step 2: Determine the seriousness of the intent

- A. Solicit suicidal or homicidal thoughts
- B. Determine whether there is a plan, and solicit details to determine feasibility with the higher risk in specific details and actions. Regarding homicide, if specific individuals are named, there is a duty to protect and warn.
- C. Determine lethality, and check out the means and access. A gun is the most dangerous and commonly used lethal method, and if a loaded gun is kept available in the home, there is high risk

Step 3: Determine life stressors and life resources. If life is lately filled with many stressors and few supports, the likelihood of completed suicide is greater.

---

the highest rates of suicide-related death, with Hispanic youth being more likely to report attempting suicide (Centers for Disease Control and Prevention, 2014b). Professional school counselors must be able to assess the danger of suicide or homicide and know the steps to take in these emergency situations. If a professional school counselor reasonably suspects that a student may take his or her own life or the life of someone else, referral and/or commitment to a psychiatric facility is vitally necessary. While this topic certainly warrants more expanded coverage, Table 68.8 provides the basic steps in the assessment of suicide or homicide risk that is needed to determine the level of risk (compiled from Farberow, Heilig, & Litman, 1968; Glaitto & Rai, 1999; Gould & Kramer, 2001).

If there is any risk of suicide or homicide, always consult with supervisors or experienced clinicians before releasing a student from your office. Never leave such a student unattended. *Always* bring in another individual to assist and consult. If you detect a moderate or high risk of suicide or homicide, know the steps in your community that are necessary for referral for further assessment or to hospitalize if necessary. Have these emergency names, numbers, and modes of transport readily available.

Some short-term interventions include:

- Write up a safety contract with the student, specifying actions when ideations occur.
- Make plans to remove the means.
- Make others aware, and get the support of family and significant others such as clergy or community resources.

- Contact mental health counselors for increased visitation or advise any counselor currently working with the student.
- Use further suicide assessment instruments to acquire more information or refer for psychiatric evaluation.
- Call police if imminent (homicidal) danger is suspected.

Summary/Conclusion

The following list summarizes the ideas discussed in this chapter:

- Work to keep yourself grounded and healthy and your skills effective and developed.
- Understand the crisis through the perception of the person in the crisis. Actively listen to the story.
- Work to establish rapport and trust.
- Plan ahead with appropriate and adequate referral source information, allocated space for intervention, and an accessible model of intervention.
- Remember to be holistic. Observe and assess the physical, behavioral, emotional, and cognitive manifestations.
- Begin work where there is most impairment.
- Determine whether the effects are long-lasting and if referral for PTSD assessment is needed.
- Keep a multicultural awareness of the student's expressions of emotions, perspectives, and behaviors.
- Student misbehaviors are immediately noticeable. Ask yourself what the student needs rather than fall into the compliance/conformance trap.
- Make yourself an expert in suicidology. Know what to assess, how to do it, and how to refer in lethal cases.
- Never work in isolation. Involve the student's support system, and always involve a consultant/supervisor.
- Continue to develop and practice your art.

CHAPTER 69

Systemic Crisis Intervention in the Schools

Bradley T. Erford*

Preview

Systemic crisis intervention in schools needs to be seriously addressed system wide, with the system being the school, the families, and the community. Many crises affect large numbers of people and must be addressed with a systemic developmental–ecological approach to facilitate optimal recovery for everyone, as well as to effectively solve problems and facilitate needed changes to prevent further incidents. Development of a comprehensive crisis plan is a large undertaking, but many of the elements are generic and can be universally incorporated, along with adaptations that need to be made for specific system needs. Understanding these components and having a plan in place to quickly activate can be the difference between extended problems and effective solutions. Professional school counselors play a pivotal role in systemic crisis intervention.

A junior high school student commits suicide. A kindergarten student disappears, and kidnapping is suspected. A family on vacation with their three elementary-age children is killed in an airplane crash. Gang slogans and activity spring up in the school hallways. A suspected gay student is beaten up behind the school. Two 15-year-olds overdose over the weekend. Four seniors are fatally injured on prom night in a car accident involving alcohol. A drive-by shooting kills the star basketball player. Five girls report being fondled and groped in the hallway by sixth-grade boys. In addition to these many possible school-life crises, more than two dozen real incidents of school shootings occurred in the United States from 1996 to 2013, causing the media to call school violence a "deadly pattern" (Infoplease, 2014). While media make these incidents feel all too common, Collins and Collins (2005) defined these events further: "Crises are rare and unexpected events, and it is daunting to anticipate and prepare for the circumstances and special challenges associated with various potential crisis events. This is true whether a crisis affects one individual or the entire school community" (p. 410).

Schools have installed metal detectors, used armed police, enacted policies of zero tolerance, and insisted that students use transparent mesh book bags to help control the seemingly escalating violence. Still, crises seem an uncontrollable part of school life. What can be controlled is the school's professionals' knowledgeable and quick response to crises in order to prevent further exacerbation, trauma, and harm. All the above scenarios require a systemic

---

*Special thanks to Fran Steigerwald for her outstanding contributions to the first two editions of this chapter.

crisis plan that is comprehensive, well organized, mobilizes many resources, and operates quickly.

What Is Systemic Crisis Intervention?

Systemic crisis intervention is based in systems theory, which emerged in the 1940s. Goldenberg and Goldenberg (2001) summarized the development of systems theory as a new way to look at a problem, event, situation, or organization from the perspective of the interaction of all the components and of how the entire unit operates. Later, family therapy applied these concepts and elaborated the movement from looking at individual characteristics to interactions among individuals. The study became the system. Previously, scientific thinking was infused with "linear causality: A causes B, which acts upon C, causing D to occur" (p. 21). The circular causality of systems work stresses reciprocity. Forces do not move in a linear direction, but rather they are influenced by and are influencing other components in the system. Systems theory is more holistic, understanding that the whole is greater than the sum of its parts, and that each part continually impacts and is mutually affected by the others. Solutions are seen as the responsibility of everyone involved rather than one person's duty. The maintenance of positive change is more possible and effective with multiple input and change occurring at the interactional level.

Collins and Collins (2005) proposed a developmental–ecological model for crisis intervention. Students perceive and handle crises according to their age and developmental background. The many levels of systems that impact the students must also be considered for a comprehensive crisis intervention approach. Ecosystems theory examines interactions among students' various systems. Knoff (2003) provided the concept of ecology to graphically explain how all levels of systems interface and provide reciprocal influences.

Cavaiola and Colford (2006) examined crisis intervention as a process whereby the victim or affected persons need to be restored to precrisis levels. The focus needs to be on preparedness, with emphasis on choosing a crisis team and developing a crisis plan.

The stated crises that began this chapter do not affect just one individual. Many people are affected, many need to be considered, and many resources need to be mobilized in crisis intervention. The National Education Association (2014) stated that in crises, communication is often the problem:

> The overall communication objective in a crisis is to quickly adjust . . . the school community position from one of response and reaction to one of relative control, and an ability to take proactive steps toward healing and a return to learning. (p. 4)

Caplan's (1964) classic crisis intervention model proposed the following three levels of response in times of crisis. These three components are used as a backbone for many crisis intervention plans.

1. Prevention works to stimulate the environment and foster health so that crises are less likely to occur.
2. Intervention works to contain the crises and reduce negative impact once the crises have occurred.
3. Postvention provides long-term care and support after the crises, also allowing feedback to improve future crisis responses.

A Systemic Approach to Individual Crisis

In systemic intervention, the professional school counselor knows that the problem does not reside in the student alone but in the student's interactions with others in the system. It may be determined that this student was bullied and harassed on the playground, or that in the morning the student overheard his parents speaking of divorce. Resolution involves intervention with all the involved parties and resources.

Techniques to assess and intervene systematically, such as mapping, are important to know. Mapping can be conducted with the student, parents, or persons the professional school counselor determines to be close to the student. In their classic books, Minuchin (1974) and Minuchin and Fishman (1981) applied the concept of mapping in family work. It is this type of diagramming that examines through drawing the family structure and patterns of interaction, observing distances, connections, coalitions, repetitive sequences, and boundaries. Creative questioning by the professional school counselor elicits vital information regarding open and closed systems, negative or positive feedback loops, enmeshed or disengaged subsystems, boundaries, and power.

Mapping can be extended to include the classroom, teachers, school, and community. This more global approach has been referred to as *ecosystemic mapping*. In ecosystemic mapping, the diagrams include the larger social system and outer world of the child. Using community organizations and institutions—as well as the child, family, classroom, and school community—problematic symptoms and resiliency resources can be identified (Sherman & Fredman, 1986).

Cerio (1995) discussed other techniques that professional school counselors can use, such as worldview, hierarchy, and triangles. In *worldview*, the professional school counselor works to illicit the values that influence the interactions of the students with parents and others in their environment. A clash of values between home and school can create a problem. Examining the *hierarchical structure* often leads to an understanding of the power and influence dynamics as well as getting a clearer picture of the roles that are played out in the system. *Triangulation* refers to the process of involving a third party to take sides against another. Triangle work looks at the interaction of three members or parties as a way of resisting, sabotaging, or impeding change, since alliances influence the other member in the triangle and increase the degree of difficulty of arriving at and agreeing to solutions. Cerio summarized these techniques with five basic questions that a professional school counselor should ask to get a systems perspective:

1. What are the world views of the family and the school personnel?
2. What are the positions of the family members and school personnel in the family–school hierarchy?
3. What subsystems are involved with the problem?
4. What is the nature of the boundaries of the subsystems?
5. What triangles are in play related to the problem? (p. 43)

Individual crises can benefit from systems intervention by assessing the crisis and formulating the interventions from a more holistic perspective. A crisis that has gained public attention can be perpetuated by a member of the school community's mishandling of a situation. System-wide, school and community involvement in the plan outlining expected roles and duties can only help the crisis situation.

A Systemic Approach to School-Wide Crisis

Systemic counseling is needed when the school or school system is more visibly affected by the crisis, such as with a student suicide or homicide, because many parts of the system will be affected. Best friends, neighbors, classmates, fellow students, and friends of friends all form concentric circles of varying closeness around the victim, and all experience some stress from the crisis. A general plan must be in place prior to the crisis to mobilize resources as needed and to involve the community for effective prevention–intervention action, and the students' developmental–ecological needs and levels need to be considered.

The school needs a comprehensive guide to systemic crisis intervention that is available for immediate action. Professional school counselors should assist in the formulation and use of such a plan or be instrumental in beginning the dialogue to formulate such a plan.

A Comprehensive School Crisis Plan

James and Gilliland (2012) explained that although comprehensive crisis plans take a great deal of time and resources to create, they are essential to effectively respond to crises. Plans all need to involve generic elements, so using an available outline as a template is helpful. But these plans also need to be specific to the school community's particular needs and demands. Beginning with a needs assessment is vital. James and Gilliland suggested a two-tiered team, the first involving the school–community resources for the larger planning picture, and a second tier composed of building response teams with information on the physical plant and its occupants. Some suggested roles for the crisis response team are the crisis response coordinator, the crisis intervention coordinator, the media liaison, the security liaison, the community–medical liaison, the parent liaison, crisis interveners, and the resource person.

James and Gilliland (2012) suggested the following elements be spelled out in a crisis response plan: (a) physical requirements set up for counseling, communications, operations, information, first-aid, and break centers; (b) logistics involving how communication will flow, procedural checklists, provisions, and building plans; and (c) the crisis response of getting and verifying the facts; assessing the impact of the crisis to determine the degree of mobilization; providing triage assessment to determine those who are most affected and in need of immediate intervention; providing psychological first-aid; having a model of intervention in place; providing crisis interviews; and the briefing, debriefing, and demobilizing phase.

In a school-wide crisis, the systemic crisis intervention plan is a very comprehensive project that involves the entire community. The National Education Association (NEA; 2014) provided information and guidance for developing and using a crisis plan. Their *School Crisis Guide: Help and Healing in a Time of Crisis* can lead the professional school counselor and crisis planning team through assessing the system's needs; developing a crisis response team and plan; and building local, state, and national crisis networks. The guide is organized into three main sections: being prepared before a crisis, being responsive during a crisis, and being diligent in moving beyond crisis.

In the first section, the NEA (2014) provides assistance by giving guiding principles for crisis response and prevention plans. These plans must be inclusive and collaborative among school community, staff, administrators, teachers, associations, law enforcement, fire department, mental health agencies, PTAs, and other community partners; have as a goal to be supportive of students and staff; provide strategies for information dissemination of the plan to all involved and know that members know what to do in case of an emergency; and be practiced and updated. This section also provides a checklist to assess how the system measures up to meeting crisis needs in terms of policy and procedure, operations, and aftermath.

In the second section, critical response actions are outlined and organized by the action to be taken each day and the media or communications challenges that may need to be addressed (NEA, 2014). Day one is focused on response. Day two is focused on information. Day three and beyond is focused on communication. Detailed responses are given in this useful resource, from reminders to mobilize resources to sending follow-up letters.

In the third section, attention is given to support for long-term healing, building partnerships, striving to achieve a "new normal," and dealing with the media (NEA, 2014). Information on handling donations and memorials and managing anniversaries and physical reminders is outlined.

As a response to school tragedies, the U.S. Department of Education, Office of Special Education Programs (2000a) and the Department of Justice produced a guide to help make schools safer. *Early Warning, Timely Response: A Guide to Safe Schools* was published based on research and proven practical strategies. A follow-up publication (U.S. Department of Education, Office of Special Education Programs, 2000b), *Safeguarding Our Children: An Action Guide*, was also developed to help schools implement safety plans. (A full text of these public domain publications can be accessed online; see U.S. Department of Education, Office of Special Education Programs, 2000a, 2000b). Professional school counselors should become familiar with these valuable resources.

Critical Incident Stress Debriefing (CISD) Model

"Critical Incident Stress Debriefing (CISD) is a form of structured psychological debriefing conducted in small groups. It was originally developed . . . as a direct, action-oriented crisis intervention process designed to prevent or mitigate traumatic stress" (Mitchell & Everly, 1993, p. 3). CISD was first formulated and used with emergency and public service personnel, but its use has expanded and it is now used with most populations that have experienced a natural disaster, accident, trauma, or event critical enough to tax the coping skills of the people involved. It has been used successfully worldwide and with all ages, including school-aged children. Most areas of the United States have trained CISD personnel available to assist commercial, industrial, and community groups.

When a crisis hits a school community, systematic crisis intervention assumes that all members of the community are affected to some degree and need attention. Students and their parents can be the beneficiaries of CISD work. However, often the professional staff, teachers, and crisis personnel are overlooked because all the focus is on the students. The caregivers also need care. Burnout is especially severe if caregiver needs in a crisis are unattended. CISD is one way to provide staff, faculty, crisis workers, and witnesses with an effective way to help them cope. Professional school counselors need to attend to the needs of the helpers (including themselves) following the immediate phases of a crisis.

CISD was the result of study and research by Mitchell and Everly (1993): "CISD is a crisis intervention process designed to stabilize cognitive and affective processes and to further mitigate the impact of a traumatic event" (p. 15). Some of the basic principles of CISD include:

1. It is not therapy and should only be done by a team of people specifically trained in CISD.

2. It is a group process with the purpose of reducing stress and enhancing recovery.
3. Not all problems will be solved; referrals may be necessary.
4. A person can attend a meeting and not speak and still gain benefit.
5. It is best to have voluntary participation, but attendance is required for all to benefit.
6. CISD should take place after 24 hours and before 72 hours of the crisis (with variations depending upon the event).
7. CISD teams are "multiorganizational and multijurisdictional in structure" (p. 15).
8. CISD should be taken as one option of critical incident stress management.
9. Consult Chapter 68, "Crisis Intervention With Individuals in the Schools," for a basic understanding of the symptomology and signs of stress in people during crises. It is important that people who have suffered from a crisis or trauma know that many physical, affective, cognitive, and behavioral manifestations are "normal" under the circumstances. There is a specific stage in the CISD intervention when this material needs to be shared with the participants.

The CISD response team for a regional response is usually made up of about 40 people, with about 12 mental health professionals and the rest being peer support personnel made up of community workers in emergency or stress-related fields, such as nursing, law enforcement, or first response teams. Once the need for CISD has been determined, team membership is formed from this community pool and is composed of three to five members, depending on the number and nature of the participants. A clergyman trained in CISD can also be present to act as a listener and a guide, although preaching or praying is not a part of CISD. The optimal number of participants is 4 to 20, but up to 30 participants can be handled if the time is lengthened to give everyone an opportunity to share. Detailed descriptions of each member's duties, preparation and set-up, and procedures for the debriefing are specific and prescribed. The normal time required for an intervention is from 1 to 4 hours. During each stage, participants as a whole are asked directed questions to help tell their story and usually take turns responding. People are allowed to pass if they choose not to say anything. Each stage has specific questions to move the process along. Leaders typically do not provide feedback after individuals share.

Table 69.1 presents a description of the seven stages of CISD (Mitchell & Everly, 1993). Post-debriefing activities include one-on-one time with members who expressed or exhibited a need for extra attention during the CISD intervention. This connection can be a supportive word or a suggested referral for therapy. This one-on-one time can occur during refreshments following the CISD intervention. A post-debriefing meeting for the intervention team itself must occur to provide good mental health and prevent against stress overload for the team. Professional school counselors need to know how to access a CISD team or seek out specialized training or community support to start a CISD project. Knowledge and skill enhancement through CISD training and participation can greatly benefit a professional school counselor's sense of competency at times of crisis.

The NOVA Model

The NOVA model (National Organization for Victim Assistance, 1997) has been used successfully with older students in group crisis intervention. It is similar to the CISD model but requires less structure and allows for more interactions between the facilitator and the participants. A session generally lasts approximately 2 hours and should include enough students to

Table 69.1 Seven Stages of Critical Incident Stress Debriefing (CISD)

Stage	Description/Purpose
1. Introduction	To introduce team members, explain process, set expectations.
2. Fact Phase	To describe the traumatic event from each participant's perspective on a cognitive level.
3. Thought Phase	To allow participants to describe cognitive reactions and to transition to emotional reactions.
4. Reaction Phase	To identify the most traumatic aspect of the event for the participants.
5. Symptom Phase	To identify personal symptoms of distress and transition back to the cognitive level.
6. Teaching Phase	To educate regarding what are normal reactions and adaptive coping mechanisms (i.e., stress management). Provide cognitive anchor.
7. Reentry Phase	To clarify ambiguities and prepare for termination.

provide good interaction but small enough to be able to identify for assessment the students who may need further help. The NOVA model session includes the following:

1. Introductions and safety and security statements; descriptions of physical, emotional, and cognitive reactions at the time of the event
2. Ventilation and validation of emotional upheaval
3. Descriptions of the aftermath and present reactions or feelings
4. Ongoing facilitation of validation, refraining from judgment, and drawing and bonding students together to normalize thoughts and feelings
5. Questions about the future with a discussion of coping strategies
6. Referral sources
7. Summarization to reaffirm experiences
8. Postgroup sessions (30 minutes) to distribute handouts, answer questions, or follow-up

This more informal group process is used to help all students affected by the crisis and also should highlight those students who need further assessment and assistance.

Student Death and Suicide

When a student dies, the entire school community is affected because of the interpersonal nature of the ecosystem and because the death of a child is commonly considered unnatural. Developmentally, students are deeply connected with their peer group to master the tasks of industry and identity formation. They often see themselves as invincible. The death of a peer shakes students emotionally and cognitively. When schools are confronted with such a serious loss, sensitive, supportive, and prepared handling of the crisis is paramount. Proper handling of the crisis can influence the school community's emotional response as well as reduce harmful consequences. Collins and Collins (2005) discussed some of the tasks that are involved in this process:

1. Verifying the information and details
2. Dispensing of the information to the students

3. Stabilizing the situation and providing student safety
4. Helping the school community cope with the loss (students, parents, teachers, staff)
5. Protecting the privacy of the family
6. Communicating with the media
7. Planning ongoing support and counseling

Preparing how information will be dispensed to the students involves knowing which students or groups of students may be most deeply affected. This can be accomplished by eco-mapping the deceased student to determine interactions and levels of points of contact and relationships. Closest friends, associates, and teachers need to be told individually as quickly as possible to prevent speculation and rumors. Closer friends like those involved in clubs, homeroom, or activities need to be told in smaller groups, with two adult helpers present. Class-size groups for the remaining school community can similarly best handle the sharing of the information. Sharing details surrounding the death, allowing for questions, providing time to talk, providing available resources in the school or after school activities, and providing referral services for those students who request them are essential components. Memorials and follow-up can best be handled knowing the culture of the school community (Cavaiola & Colford, 2006; Collins & Collins, 2005; James & Gilliland, 2012).

A special note on student suicide needs to be clarified: "Student suicides differ from other school-based crises because of the self-initiated behavior, the complex underlying motivations, and the various cultural values and interpretations associated with the suicide" (Collins & Collins, 2005, p. 427). Information on suicide prevention, assessment, intervention, and postvention is vital to professional school counselors and personnel. There is serious evidence of contagion and cluster suicides occurring in school settings. The processing of a student suicide needs to be informed with this fact. Sensationalizing the suicide action and the student, encouraging media coverage, and memorializing or commemorating the suicide are inappropriate. Supportive groups for those who are deeply affected and for survivors are encouraged.

Students' grief reactions are developmental and affect academics, emotions, and cognitions. Providing a safe supportive environment with understanding individuals where students can explore their reactions and reach some level of resolution or be referred for additional support are key functions of a crisis plan that involve the death of a student.

Summary/Conclusion

In summary, the following are 10 things to remember in systemic crisis intervention:

1. A systems approach to crisis is more holistic than individual work alone.
2. A systems approach to crisis broadens the scope of assessment and available resources.
3. Communication is essential in resolving systemic crises.
4. Systems intervention recognizes that problems reside in the interactions.
5. Being able to use systems techniques such as mapping, discovering subsystems and boundaries, hierarchy, worldview, and triangulation work enhance individual crisis intervention.
6. A comprehensive plan involving school and community needs to be in place before a crisis occurs, with all members of the team knowing their functions.

7. The professional school counselor plays a vital role in the formulation and implementation of such a plan.
8. Physical requirements, logistics, and crisis responses all need to be planned out.
9. Training in a systemic crisis intervention model (e.g., CISD, NOVA) is important for the professional school counselor.
10. Always remember to attend to the needs of the caregivers, professionals, and crisis workers.

References

Achenbach, T. M. (1986). *The direct observation form of the child behavior checklist* (rev. ed.). Burlington, VT: University of Vermont, Department of Psychiatry.

Achenbach, T. M. (1995). Behavior problems in 5- to 11-year-old children from low-income families. *Journal of the American Academy of Child & Adolescent Psychiatry, 34,* 536–537. doi:10.1097/00004583-199505000-00003

Achenbach, T. M., & Rescorla, L. A. (2000). *Manual for the ASEBA preschool forms and profiles*. Burlington, VT: University of Vermont, Department of Psychiatry.

Achenbach, T. M., & Rescorla, L. A. (2001). *Manual for the ASEBA school-age forms and profiles*. Burlington, VT: University of Vermont, Department of Psychiatry.

Achieve. (2013) *Implementing the common core state standards: The role of the school counselor.* Retrieved from http://www.achieve.org/publications/implementing-common-core-state-standards-role-school-counselor-action-brief

Adams, G. B. (2004). Identifying, assessing, and treating obsessive–compulsive disorder in school-aged children: The role of school personnel. *Teaching Exceptional Children, 37*(2), 46–53. doi:10.1177/1053451209353447

Adams, G. B., & Torchia, M. (1998). *School personnel: A critical link in the identification, treatment and management of OCD in children and adolescents* (3rd ed.). Milford, CT: OC Foundation.

Adelman, C. (1999). *Answers in the tool box: Academic intensity, attendance patterns, and bachelor's degree attainment.* Retrieved from http://www.ed.gov/pubs/Toolbox/Title.html

Adelman, H. S., & Taylor, L. (2002). School counselors and school reform: New directions. *Professional School Counseling, 5,* 235–248.

Aikman, K. B. (1933). Race mixing. *Eugenics Review, 25,* 161–166.

Ainsworth, M. D., Blehar, M. C., Walters, E., & Wall, S. (1978). *Patterns of attachment*. Hillsdale, NJ: Erlbaum.

Akos, P. (2000). Building empathy in elementary school children through group work. *Journal for Specialists in Group Work, 25,* 214–223. doi:10.1080/01933920008411462

Akos, P., & Levitt, D. H. (2002). Promoting healthy body image in middle school. *Professional School Counseling, 6,* 138–144.

Akos, P., & Martin, M. (2003). Transition groups for preparing students for middle school. *The Journal for Specialists in Group Work, 28,* 139–154. doi:10.1177/0193392203028002005

Alberto, P. A., & Troutman, A. C. (2012). *Applied behavior analysis for teachers* (9th ed.). Columbus, OH: Merrill.

Alexander, K., & Alexander, M. D. (2012). *American public school law* (8th ed.). Belmont, CA: Thomson West.

Alexander, R. (2010). The impact of poverty on African American children in the child welfare and juvenile justice systems. *Forum on Public Policy Online, 2010*(4).

Alexander-Roberts, C. (1995). *The parents' guide to making it through the tough years: ADHD & teens.* Lanham, MD: Gaylor.

Allan, N. P., Capron, D. W., Lejuez, C. W., Reynolds, E. K., MacPherson, L., & Schmidt, N. B. (2014). Developmental trajectories of anxiety symptoms in early adolescence: The influence of anxiety sensitivity. *Journal of Abnormal Child Psychology, 42,* 589–600. doi:10.1007/s10802-013-9806-0

Allardyce, S. (2013). Assessing risk of victim crossover with children and young people who display harmful sexual behaviours. *Child Abuse Review, 22,* 255–267.

Allen, D., & Dadgar, M. (2012). Does dual enrollment increase students' success in college? Evidence from a quasi-experimental analysis of dual enrollment in New York City. *New Directions for Higher Education, 158,* 11–19. doi:10.1002/he.20010

Allen, J. (1992). *Action-oriented research: Promoting school counseling advocacy and accountability.* (Report No. EDO-CG-92-11). Washington, DC: Office of Education Research and Improvement. (ERIC Document Reproduction Service No. ED 347477)

Allen, J. P., Hauser, S. T., & Borman-Spurrell, E. (1996). Attachment theory as a framework for understanding sequelae of severe adolescent psychopathology: An 11-year follow-up study. *Journal of Consulting and Clinical Psychology, 64,* 254–263. doi:10.1037/0022-006X.64.2.254

Allen, K. D., & Warzak, W. J. (2000). The problem of parental nonadherance in clinical behavioral analysis: Effective treatment is not enough. *Journal of Applied Behavior Analysis, 33,* 373–391. doi:10.1901/jaba.2000.33-373

Amatea, E. S., & West-Olatunji, C. A. (2007). Joining the conversation about educating our poorest children: Emerging leadership roles for school counselors in high-poverty schools. *Professional School Counseling, 11,* 81–89. doi:10.5330/PSC.n.2010-11.81

America's Career Resource Network. (2014). *National career development guidelines.* Retrieved from http://acrn.ovae.org/ncdg.htm

American Academy of Child and Adolescent Psychiatry. (1998). Practice parameters for the assessment and treatment of children and adolescents with posttraumatic stress disorder. *Journal of American Child and Adolescent Psychiatry, 737*(Suppl. 10), 4S–26S. doi:10.1097/00004583-199810001-00002

American Academy of Child and Adolescent Psychiatry. (2011a). *Facts for families: Children who won't go to school (Separation Anxiety)*, No. 7. Retrieved from http://www.aacap.org/AACAP/Families_and_Youth/Facts_for_Families/Facts_for_Families_Pages/Children_Who_Wont_Go_To_School_07.aspx

American Academy of Child and Adolescent Psychiatry. (2011b). *Facts for families: Multiracial children.* Retrieved from http://www.aacap.org/aacap/Families_and_Youth/Facts_for_Families/Facts_for_Families_Pages/Multiracial_Children_71.aspx

American Academy of Pediatrics. (2000). Provision of educationally related services for children and adolescents with chronic diseases and disabling conditions: Committee on children with disabilities. *Pediatrics, 105,* 448–451. doi:10.1542/peds.2007-0885

American College Testing Program (ACT). (2008). *Career planning survey, inventory of work-relevant abilities.* Iowa City, IA: Author

American College Testing Program (ACT). (2010). *The condition of college & career readiness 2010.* Iowa City, IA: Author.

American College Testing Program (ACT). (2013). *Class profile report.* Retrieved from http://www.act.org/products.html

American Counseling Association. (1995). *Counselor credentialing laws: Scopes of practice, language and tiers.* Alexandria, VA: Author.

American Counseling Association. (2004). *Position statement on high-stakes testing.* Alexandria, VA: Author.

American Counseling Association. (2013). *United States student-to-counselor ratios for elementary and secondary schools—2010-2011 data year.* Retrieved from http://www.counseling.org/PublicPolicy/PDF/2010-2011_Student_to_Counselor_Ratio.pdf

American Counseling Association. (2014). *ACA code of ethics.* Alexandria, VA: Author.

American Counseling Association. (2015a). *A guide to state laws and regulations on professional school counseling.* Retrieved from http://www.aca.org

American Counseling Association. (2015b). *Licensing requirements* (5th ed.). Alexandria, VA: Author

American Counseling Association, Task Force on School Counseling. (2013). *Common core standards: Essential information for school counselors.* Retrieved from http://www.counseling.org/docs/resources---school-counselors/common-core-state-standards.pdf?sfvrsn=2

American Educational Research Association. (2002). *AERA position statement concerning high-stakes testing in pre K–12 education.* Washington, DC: Author.

American Educational Research Association, American Psychological Association, & National Council on Measurement in Education. (1999). *Standards for educational and psychological testing.* Washington, DC: APA.

American Psychiatric Association. (1980). *Diagnostic and statistical manual of mental disorders* (3rd ed.). Washington, DC: Author.

American Psychiatric Association. (1987). *Diagnostic and statistical manual of mental disorders* (3rd ed., text rev.). Washington, DC: Author.

American Psychiatric Association. (1994). *Diagnostic and statistical manual of mental disorders* (4th ed.). Washington, DC: Author.

American Psychiatric Association. (2013). *Diagnostic and statistical manual of mental disorders* (5th ed.). Washington, DC: Author.

American Psychological Association. (2014). *Code of Fair Testing Practices in Education prepared by the Joint Committee on Testing Practices.* Washington, DC: Author.

American Psychological Association Zero Tolerance Task Force. (2006). *Are zero tolerance policies effective in schools?* Washington, DC: American Psychological Association.

American School Counselor Association. (2000). *School counselor competencies* [Brochure]. Alexandria, VA: Author.

American School Counselor Association. (2002a). ASCA study examines counselor-to-student ratios. *ASCA School Counselor, 39*(5), 50. doi:10.5330/PSC.n.2010-12.34

American School Counselor Association. (2002b). Hot topics for school counselors. *ASCA School Counselor, 39*(5), 51.

American School Counselor Association. (2003a). *The ASCA national model: A framework for school counseling programs.* Alexandria, VA: Author.

American School Counselor Association. (2003b). *Learn about RAMP.* Retrieved from http://www.ascanationalmodel.org/learn-about-ramp

American School Counselor Association. (2004). *ASCA national standards for students.* Alexandria, VA: Author.

American School Counselor Association. (2005). *The ASCA national model: A framework for school counseling programs* (2nd ed.). Alexandria, VA: Author.

American School Counselor Association. (2008). *The professional school counselor and peer helping.* Alexandria, VA: Author.

American School Counselor Association. (2009). *Position statement: Cultural diversity.* Alexandria, VA: Author.

American School Counselor Association. (2010a). *Ethical standards for school counselors.* Retrieved from http://www.schoolcounselor.org/asca/media/asca/Resource%20Center/Legal%20and%20Ethical%20Issues/Sample%20Documents/EthicalStandards2010.pdf

American School Counselor Association. (2010b). *The professional school counselor and school-family-community partnerships.* Alexandria, VA: Author.

American School Counselor Association. (2011a). *School-to-counselor ratios.* Retrieved from http://www.schoolcounselor.org/asca/media/asca/home/ratios10-11.pdf

American School Counselor Association. (2011b). *Position statement: The professional school counselor and the promotion of safe schools through conflict resolution and bullying/harassment prevention.* Retrieved from http://www.schoolcounselor.org/asca/media/asca/home/position%20statements/PS_Bullying.pdf

American School Counselor Association. (2012a). *The ASCA national model: A framework for school counseling programs* (3rd ed.). Alexandria, VA: Author.

American School Counselor Association. (2012b). *School counseling competencies*. Retrieved from http://www.schoolcounselor.org/asca/media/asca/home/SCCompetencies.pdf

American School Counselor Association. (2013a). *Certification requirements*. Retrieved from http://www.schoolcounselor.org/school-counselors-members/careers-roles/state-certification-requirements

American School Counselor Association. (2013b). *Position statement: Comprehensive school counseling programs*. Alexandria, VA: Author.

American School Counselor Association. (2013c). *The professional school counselor and students with disabilities*. Alexandria, VA: Author.

American School Counselor Association. (2014). *Student-to-school counselor ratios 2010-2011*. Retrieved from http://www.schoolcounselor.org/asca/media/asca/home/Ratios10-11.pdf

Americans With Disabilities Act of 1990, 42 U.S.C. § 12101 et seq. (1990)

Amstutz, L. S., & Mullet, J. H. (2005). *The little book of restorative discipline for schools. Teaching responsibility; Creating caring climates*. Philadelphia, PA: Good Books.

Andari, E., Duhamel, J. R., Zalla, T. Herbrecht, E. Leboyer, M. & Sirigu, A. (2010). Promoting social behavior with oxytocin in high-functioning autism spectrum disorders. *Proceedings of the National Academy of Sciences of the United States of America, 107*, 4389–4394. doi:10.1073/pnas.0910249107

Anderson, S. A. (1999). How parental involvement makes a difference in reading achievement. *Reading Improvement, 60*, 61–86.

Andringa, J. W., & Fustin, M. (1991). Learning to plan for and implement change: School building faculty responds. *Journal of Educational Research, 84*, 233–238.

Annandale, N., Heath, M., Dean, B., Kemple, A., & Takino, Y. (2011). Assessing cultural competency in school crisis plans. *Journal of School Violence, 10*(1), 16–33. doi:10.1080/15388220.2010.519263

Apter, A., Pauls, D. L., Bleich, A., Zohar, A. H., Kron, S., Ratzoni, G . . . Gadot, N. (1993). An epidemiologic study of Gilles de la Tourette's syndrome in Israel. *Archives of General Psychiatry, 50*, 734–738. doi:10.1001/archpsyc.1993.01820210068008

Arbuckle, D. S. (1970). Does the school really need counselors? *The School Counselor, 17*, 325–330.

Arman, J. F., & McNair, R. (2000). A small group model for working with elementary school children of alcoholics. *Professional School Counseling, 3*, 290–293.

Armstrong, T. (1993). *Seven kinds of smart: Identifying and developing your many intelligences*. New York, NY: Penguin.

Arrendondo, P., Toporek, M. S., Brown, S., Jones, J., Locke, D. C., Sanchez, J., & Stadler, H. (1996). *Operationalization of the multicultural counseling competencies*. AMCD: Alexandria, VA

Arslan, C. (2009). Anger, self-esteem, and perceived social support in adolescence. *Social Behavior and Personality, 37*, 555–564. doi:10.2224/sbp.2009.37.4.555

Association for Assessment in Counseling and Education. (2004). *Responsibilities of users of standardized tests* (3rd ed.). Alexandria, VA: Author.

Association for Counselor Education and Supervision. (2007). *ACES technology competencies 2007*. Retrieved from http://files.acesonline.net/doc/2007_aces_technology_competencies.pdf

Association for Specialists in Group Work. (2007). *Best practices guidelines*. Retrieved from http://www.asgw.org/pdf/best_practices.pdf

Astor, R. A., Benbenishty, R., Zeira, A., & Vinokur, A. (2002). School climate, observed risky behaviors, and victimization as predictors of high school students' fear and judgments of school violence as a problem. *Health Education & Behavior, 29*, 716–736. doi:10.1177/109019802237940

Athanasiou, M. S., Geil, M., Hazel, C. E., & Copeland, E. P. (2002). A look inside school-based consultation: A qualitative study of the beliefs and practices of school psychologists and teachers. *School Psychology Quarterly, 17*, 258–298. doi:10.1521/scpq.17.3.258.20884

Aubrey, R. F. (1991). A house divided: Guidance and counseling in 20th century America. In D. R. Coy, C. G. Cole, W. G. Huey, & S. J. Sears (Eds.), *Towards the transformation of secondary school counseling* (pp. 4–26). Ann Arbor, MI: ERIC Counseling and Personnel Services Clearinghouse.

Auerbach, A. H., & Johnson, M. (1977). Research on the therapist's level of experience. In A. S. Gurman, & A. M. Razin (Eds.), *Effective psychotherapy: A handbook of research* (pp. 84–102). New York, NY: Pergamon Press.

Autism Society of America. (2011). *Facts and statistics*. Retrieved from http://www.autism-society.org/about-autism/facts-and-statistics/

Aydin, N. G., Bryan, J. A., & Duys, D. K. (2012). School counselors' partnerships with linguistically diverse families: An exploratory study. *School Community Journal, 22*(1), 145–166.

Ayllon, T., & Azrin, N. (1968). *The token economy: A motivational system for therapy and rehabilitation*. New York, NY: Appleton-Century-Crofts.

Azrin, N. H., & Nunn, R. G. (1973). Habit reversal: A method of eliminating nervous habits and tics. *Behavior Research and Therapy, 11*, 619–628. doi:10.1016/0005-7967(73)90119-8

Azzi-Lessing, L. (2010). Meeting the mental health needs of poor and vulnerable children in early care and education programs. *Early Childhood Research & Practice, 12*(1).

Babatsikos, G. (2010). Parents' knowledge, attitudes and practices about preventing child sexual abuse: A literature review. *Child Abuse Review, 19*, 107–129. doi:10.1002/car.1102

Bachelor, A., Laverdiere, O., Gamache, D., & Bordeleau, V. (2007). Client's collaboration in therapy: Self-perceptions and relationships with client psychological functioning, interpersonal relations, and motivation. *Psychotherapy: Theory, Research, Practice, Training, 44*, 175–192. doi:10.1037/0033-3204.44.2.175

Bagnell, A., Kutcher, S., & Garcia-Ortega, I. (2011). *Identification, diagnosis, & treatment of adolescent anxiety disorders: A package for first contact health providers*. Retrieved from http://www.teenmentalhealth.org/images/resources/Child_Anxiety_FINAL_2012.pdf

Bailey, D. F., & Bradford-Bailey, M. (2004). Respecting differences: Racial and ethnic groups. In R. Pérusse & G. E. Goodnough (Eds.), *Leadership and advocacy in school counseling* (pp. 157–186). Pacific Grove, CA: Brooks/Cole.

Bailey, N. J., & Phariss, T. (1996). Breaking through the wall of silence: Gay, lesbian, and bisexual issues for middle level educators. *Middle School Journal, 27*, 38–46. doi:10.2307/23023281

Baker, C. A., & Cato, S. (2010). The foundation component. In J. R. Studer & J. F. Diambra (Eds.), *A guide to practicum and internship for school counselors-in-training* (pp. 95-105). New York, NY: Routledge/Taylor & Francis Group.

Baker, S. B. (1994). Mandatory teaching experience for school counselors: An impediment to uniform certification standards for school counselors. *Counselor Education & Supervision, 33*, 314–326. doi:10.1002/j.1556-6978.1994.tb00297.x

Baker, S. B. (2001). Reflections of forty years in the school counseling profession: Is the glass half full or half empty? *Professional School Counseling, 5*, 75–83.

Baker, S. B., & Gerler, E. R. (2007). *School counseling for the twenty-first century* (5th ed.). Upper Saddle River, NJ: Prentice Hall.

Baker, S., Swisher, J., Nadenichek, P., & Popowicz, C. (1984). Measured effects of primary prevention strategies. *The Personnel and Guidance Journal, 62*, 459–464. doi:10.1111/j.2164-4918.1984.tb00255.x

Bakker, A. B., Demerouti, E., & Verbeke, W. (2004). Using the job demands-resources model to predict burnout and performance. *Human Resource Management, 43*(1), 83–104. doi:10.1002/hrm.20004

Bakker, A. B., & Schaufeli, W. B. (2000). Burnout contagion processes among teachers. *Journal of Applied Social Psychology, 30*, 2289–2308. doi:10.1111/j.1559-1816.2000.tb02437.x

Banerjee, R., Robinson, C., & Smalley, D. (2010). *Evaluation of the Beatbullying Peer Mentoring Programme. Report for Beatbullying*. Sussex, UK: University of Sussex.

Barber, C., & Mueller, C. T. (2011). Social and self-perceptions of adolescents identified as gifted, learning disabled, and twice-exceptional. *Roeper Review, 33*, 109–120. doi:10.1080/02783193.2011.554158

Bardhoshi, G., & Duncan, K. (2009). Rural school principals' perception of the school counselor's role. *Rural Educator, 30*(3), 16–24.

Bardick, A. D., Bernes, K. B., McCulloch, A. R. M., Witko, K. D., Spriddle, J. W., & Roest, A. R. (2004). Eating disorder intervention, prevention, and treatment: Recommendations for school counselors. *Professional School Counseling, 8*, 168–175. doi:10.1375/ajgc.17.1.60

Barge, J. K., & Loges, W. E. (2003). Parent, student, and teacher perceptions of parental involvement. *Journal of Applied Communication Research, 31*, 140–163. doi:10.1080/0090988032000064597

Barkley, R. A. (2006). *Attention-deficit hyperactivity disorder: A handbook for diagnosis and treatment* (3rd ed.). New York, NY: Guilford Press.

Barr, J., & Higgins-D'Alessandro, A. (2009). How adolescent empathy and prosocial behavior change in the context of school culture: A two-year longitudinal study. *Adolescence, 44*, 751–772. doi:10.1007/s10964-012-9900-6

Barrera, M., Fleming, C. F., & Kahn, F. S. (2004). The role of emotional social support in the psychological adjustment of siblings of children with cancer. *Child: Care, Health & Development, 30*, 103–111.

Barret, B. (1999, March). Conversion therapy. *Counseling Today, 12*.

Barret, B., & Logan, C. (2002). *Counseling gay men and lesbians: A practice primer*. Pacific Grove, CA: Brooks/Cole.

Barret, R. L., & Robinson, B. E. (2000). *Gay fathers*. San Francisco, CA: Jossey-Bass.

Barrington, B. L., & Hendricks, B. H. (1989). Differentiating characteristics of high school graduates, dropouts, and nongraduates. *Journal of Educational Research, 82*, 309–319. doi:10.3200/JOER.102.1.3-14

Barrish, H. H., Saunders, M., & Wolf, M. M. (1969). Good behavior game: Effects of individual contingencies for group consequences on disruptive behavior in a classroom. *Journal of Applied Behavior Analysis, 2*, 119–124. doi:10.1901/jaba.1969.2-119

Baskin, T. W., & Slaten, C. D. (2014). Contextual school counseling approach: Linking contextual psychotherapy with the school environment. *The Counseling Psychologist, 42*, 73–96. doi:10.1177/0011000012473664

Bassett, D., & Dunn, C. (2012). Introduction to special issue on transition and students with learning disabilities and emotional–behavior disorders. *Intervention in School and Clinic, 48*(1), 3–5. doi:10.1177/1053451212443128

Bauer, S. R., Sapp, M., & Johnson, D. (2000). Group counseling strategies for rural at-risk high school students. *High School Journal, 83*(2), 41–51.

Baum, S., Ma, J., & Payea, K. (2013. *Education pays 2013: The benefits of higher education for individuals and society*. Retrieved from http://trends.collegeboard.org/sites/default/files/education-pays-2013-full-report.pdf

Bauman, S., & Sachs-Kapp, P. (1998). A school takes a stand: Promotion of sexual orientation workshops by counselors. *Professional School Counseling, 1*(3), 42–45.

Baumrind, D. (1991). The influence of parenting style on adolescent competence and substance use. *Journal of Early Adolescence, 11*(1), 56–95. doi:10.1177/0272431691111004

Bayer, R. (1987). *Homosexuality and American psychiatry: The politics of diagnosis*. Princeton, NJ: Princeton University Press.

Beale, A. V. (1986). Trivial pursuit: The history of guidance. *The School Counselor, 34*, 14–17.

Beane, J. A. (1998). Reclaiming a democratic purpose for education. *Educational Leadership, 56*, 8–11.

Beck, A. T. (1989). *Love is not enough*. New York, NY: Harper & Row.

Beck, A. T. (2000). *Prisoners of hate: The cognitive basis of anger, hostility, and violence*. New York, NY: Perennial.

Beck, A. T., Rush, A. J., Shaw, B. F., & Emery, G. (1987). *Cognitive therapy of depression.* New York, NY: Guilford Press.

Beck, J. S., Beck, A. T., & Jolly, J. B. (2005). *Beck Youth Inventories* (2nd ed.). San Antonio, TX: Pearson.

Beers, C. W. (1908). *A mind that found itself.* Pittsburgh, PA: University of Pittsburgh Press.

Beighley, J. S., & Matson, J. L. (2014). Comparing social skills in children diagnosed with autism spectrum disorder according to the DSM-IV-TR and the DSM-5. *Journal of Developmental and Physical Disabilities, 26,* 193–202. doi:10.1007/s10882-014-9382-4

Bell, C. H., & Robinson, E. H. (2013). Shared trauma in counseling: Information and implications for counselors. *Journal of Mental Health Counseling, 35,* 310–323.

Bellotti v. Baird, 443 U.S. 622 (1979).

Bemak, F. (2000). Transforming the role of the counselor to provide leadership in educational reform through collaboration. *Professional School Counseling, 2,* 323–331.

Benbenishty, R., Zeira, A., Astor, R. A., & Khoury-Kassabri, M. (2002). Maltreatment of primary school students by educational staff in Israel. *Child Abuse & Neglect, 26,* 1291–1309. doi:10.1016/S0145-2134(02)00416-7

Bennett, G. K., Seashore, H. G., & Wesman, A. G. (1992). *Technical manual: Differential aptitude tests* (5th ed.). San Antonio, TX: The Psychological Corporation.

Bennis, W. (1994). *On becoming a leader.* Cambridge, MA: Perseus Books.

Benson, F., & Martin, S. (2003). Organizing successful parent involvement in urban schools. *Child Study Journal, 33,* 187–193.

Berg, I. K., & Miller, S. (1992). *Working with the problem drinker.* New York, NY: Norton.

Berkowitz, L., & Harmon-Jones, E. (2004). Toward an understanding of the determinants of anger. *Emotion, 4*(2), 107. doi:10.1037/1528-3542.4.2.107

Bernard, J. M., & Goodyear, R. K. (2013). *Fundamentals of clinical supervision* (5th ed.). Upper Saddle River, NJ: Pearson.

Bernard, M. E. (2001). *Program ACHIEVE: A curriculum of lessons for teaching students how to achieve and develop social–emotional–behavioral well being, Vols. 1–6.* Laguna Beach, CA: You Can Do It! Education.

Bernard, M. E., Ellis, A., & Terjesen, M. (2006). Rational-emotive behavioral approaches to childhood disorders: History, theory, practice, and research. In A. Ellis & M. E. Bernard (Eds.), *Rational emotive behavioral approaches to childhood disorders: Theory, practice, and research* (pp. 384). New York, NY: Springer.

Besner, H. F., & Spungin, C. I. (1995). *Gay & lesbian students: Understanding their needs.* Washington, DC: Taylor & Francis.

Betz, C. (2001). Use of 504 plans for children and youth with disabilities: Nursing application. *Pediatric Nursing, 27,* 347–352.

Beutler, L. E., Crago, M., & Arizmendi, T. G. (1994). Research on therapist variables in psychotherapy. In S. L. Garfield & A. E. Bergin (Eds.), *Handbook of psychotherapy and behavior change* (4th ed., pp. 270–310). New York, NY: Wiley.

Beutler, L. E., Machado, P. P. P., & Neufeldt, S. A. (1994). Therapist variables. In A. E. Bergin, & S. L. Garfield (Eds.), *Handbook of psychotherapy and behavior change* (4th ed., pp. 229–269). New York, NY: Wiley.

Bigler, R. S., Averhart, C. J., & Liben, L. S. (2003). Race and the workforce: Occupational status, aspirations, and stereotyping among African American children. *Developmental Psychology, 39,* 572–580. doi:10.1037/0012-1649.39.3.572

Bilchik, S. (2008). Is racial and ethnic equity possible in juvenile justice? *Reclaiming Children and Youth, 17*(2), 19–23.

Biskupic, J. (1999, May 25). Davis v. Monroe County Board of Education et al. *The Washington Post,* A1:1.

Bjerke, J. J. (2010). Qualities of mental health professionals preferred by mid-adolescents. *Dissertation Abstracts International, 71.*

Blacher, J. H., Murray-Ward, M., & Uellendahl, G. E. (2005). School counselors and student assessment. *Professional School Counseling, 8,* 337–343.

Black, W. W., Fedewa, A. L., & Gonzalez, K. A. (2012). Effects of 'safe school' programs and policies on the social climate for sexual minority youth: A review of the literature. *Journal of LGBT Youth, 9,* 321–339. doi:10.1080/19361653.2012.714343

Bloom, B. S. (1956). *Taxonomy of educational objectives, Handbook 1: The cognitive domain.* New York, NY: David McKay.

Bloom, B., Jones, L. I., & Freeman, G. (2013). *Summary health statistics for U.S. children: National Health Interview Survey, 2012, National Statistics.* Retrieved from http://www.cdc.gov/nchs/data/series/sr_10/sr10_258.pdf

Bolman, L. G., & Deal, T. E. (2013). *Reframing organizations: Artistry, choice and leadership* (5th ed.). San Francisco, CA: Jossey-Bass.

Bontempo, D. E., & D'Augelli, A. R. (2002). Effects of at-school victimization and sexual orientation on lesbian, gay, or bisexual youths' health risk behavior. *Journal of Adolescent Health, 30,* 364–374. doi:10.1016/S1054-139X(01)00415-3

Borders, D. L., & Drury, R. D. (1992). Comprehensive school counseling programs: A review for policy makers and practitioners. *Journal of Counseling & Development, 70,* 487–498. doi:10.1002/j.1556-6676.1992.tb01643.x

Boshoven, J. (2003, December). McIntosh University vs. Burlington College: The college search (AKA: College is like a Coat...). *School Counselor Connections, 1,* 8–9.

Boswell, J. (1995). *Same-sex unions in premodern Europe.* New York, NY: Vintage Books.

Bothe, D. A., Grignon, J. B., & Olness, K. N. (2014). The effects of a stress management intervention in elementary school children. *Journal of Developmental and Behavioral Pediatrics, 35*(1), 62–67. doi:10.1097/DBP.0000000000000016

Boutwell, D. A., & Myrick, R. D. (1992). The go for it club. *Elementary School Guidance & Counseling, 27,* 65–72.

Bower, H. A., & Griffin, D. (2011). Can the Epstein model of parental involvement work in a high-minority, high poverty elementary school? A pilot study. *Professional School Counseling, 15,* 77–87. doi:10.5330/PSC.n.2011-15.77

Bowlby, J. (1969). *Attachment and loss* (Vol. 1). New York, NY: Basic Books.

Bowles, D. D. (1993). Biracial identity: Children born to African-American and White couples. *Clinical Social Work Journal, 21,* 417–428. doi:10.1007/BF00755575

Bracey, J. R., Bamaca, M. A., & Umana-Taylor, A. J. (2004). Examining ethnic identity and self-esteem among biracial and monoracial adolescents. *Journal of Youth and Adolescence, 22,* 123–132. doi:10.1023/B:JOYO.0000013424.93635.68

Bradley, C. (2001). A counseling group for African-American adolescent males. *Professional School Counseling, 4,* 370–373.

Bradley-Klug, K. L., Jeffries-DeLoatche, K. L., Walsh, A., Bateman, L. P., Nadeau, J., Powers, D. J., & Cunningham, J. (2013). School psychologists' perceptions of primary care partnerships: Implications for building the collaborative bridge. *Advances in School Mental Health Promotion, 6,* 51–67. doi:10.1080/1754730X.2012.760921

Bradly, A., & McCarlie, C. (2012). *Embracing diversity—Risk management and risk reduction: A practice model for children and young people and the system around them.* Dorset, UK: Russell House, Lyme Regis.

Bradshaw, C., Sawyer, A., & O'Brennan, L. (2009). A social disorganization perspective on bullying-related attitudes and behaviors: The influence of school context. *American Journal of Community Psychology, 43*(3/4), 204–220. doi:10.1007/s10464-009-9240-1

Brady, K. P. (2004). Section 504 student eligibility for students with reading disabilities: A primer for advocates. *Reading & Writing Quarterly, 20,* 305–329. doi:10.1080/10573560490446349

Braskamp, L. A., & Maehr, M. L. (1985). *School Administrator Assessment Survey.* Retrieved from https://www.ets.org/test_link/find_tests/

Bratter, J., & Heard, H. E. (2009). Mother's, father's, or both? Parental gender and parent-child interactions in the racial classification of adolescents. *Sociological Forum, 24,* 658–688. doi:10.1111/j.1573-7861.2009.01124.x

Breen, D., & Drew, D. (2001, September). *Interviews with rural school counselors.* Paper presented at the meeting of the North Atlantic Association for Counselor Education and Supervision, Amherst, MA.

Breen, D., & Drew, D. L. (2005). Professional counseling in rural settings: Raising awareness through discussion and self-study with implications for training and support. In R. K. Yep, & G. R. Waltz (Eds.), *VISTAS: Compelling perspectives on counseling* (pp. 247–250). Alexandria, VA: American Counseling Association.

Bregman, J. D. (2005). Definitions and characteristics of the spectrum. In D. Zaeger (Ed.), *Autism spectrum disorders: Identification, education, and treatment* (pp. 3–46). Mahwah, NJ: Erlbaum.

Brewer, J. M. (1942). History of vocational guidance. New York, NY: Harper & Brothers.

Bridges.com. (2006). *CX online* [Computer program]. Kelowna, British Columbia: Author.

Bridges Transitions. (2014). *Choices planner.* Retrieved from http://www.bridges.com/us/prodnserv/choicesplanner_hs/index.html

Brigman, G., & Campbell, C. (2003). Helping students improve academic achievement and school success behavior. *Professional School Counseling, 7,* 91–98.

Bristow-Braitman, A. (1995). Addiction recovery: 12-step programs and cognitive-behavioral psychology. *Journal of Counseling & Development, 73,* 414–449. doi:10.1002/j.1556-6676.1995.tb01774.x

Brookover, W. B. (1978). Elementary school social climate and school achievement. *American Educational Research Journal, 15,* 301–318. doi:10.3102/00028312015002301

Brooks, V. (2004). Stress management: The school counselor's role. In R. Pérusse, & G. E. Goodnough (Eds.), *Leadership and advocacy in school counseling* (pp. 328–352). Pacific Grove, CA: Brooks/Cole.

Brown, D., & Brooks, L. (1990). *Career choice and development: Applying contemporary theories to practice* (2nd ed.). San Francisco, CA: Jossey-Bass.

Brown, D., Pryzwansky, W. B., & Schulte, A. C. (2010). *Psychological consultation and collaboration: Introduction to theory and practice* (7th ed.). Upper Saddle River, NJ: Pearson Education.

Brown, D., & Trusty, J. (2005). School counselors, comprehensive school counseling programs, and academic achievement: Are school counselors promising more than they can deliver? *Professional School Counseling, 9,* 1–8.

Brown-Chidsey, R., Andren, K. J., & Harrison, P. L. (Eds.). (2013). *Assessment for intervention: A problem-solving approach* (2nd ed.). New York, NY: Guilford Press.

Brown-Chidsey, R., & Steege, M. W. (2005) *Response to intervention: Principles and strategies for effective practice.* New York, NY: Guilford Press.

Brown-Chidsey, R., & Steege, M. W. (2010). *Response to intervention: Principles and strategies for effective practice* (2nd ed.). New York, NY: Guilford Press.

Bryan, J. (2005). Fostering educational resilience and achievement in urban schools through school-family-community partnerships. *Professional School Counseling, 8,* 219–227.

Bryan J., Moore-Thomas, C., Day-Vines, N. L., & Holcomb-McCoy, C. (2011). School counselors as social capital: The effects of high school college counseling on college application rates. *Journal of Counseling & Development, 89,* 190–199. doi:10.1002/j.1556-6678.2011.tb00077.x

Bryant, R. M., & Constantine, M. G. (2006). Multiple role balance, job satisfaction, and life satisfaction in women school counselors. *Professional School Counseling, 9,* 265–271.

Buck, J. (1964). *Manual for the House-Tree-Person test.* Los Angeles, CA: Western Psychological Services.

Buckner, J. D., Lopez, C., Dunkel, S., & Joiner, T. R. (2008). Behavior management training for the treatment of reactive attachment disorder. *Child Maltreatment, 13,* 289–297. doi:10.1177/1077559508318396

Buescher, A. V. S., Cidav, Z., Knapp, M., & Mandell, D. S. (2014). Costs of autism spectrum disorders in the United Kingdom and the United States. *JAMA Pediatrics, 168*(8), 721–728. doi:10.1001/jamapediatrics.2014.210

Bulach, C. R. (2001). Reshaping school culture to empower its partners. *Education Digest, 67,* 8–11.

Bunch, C., & Gibson, M. J. (2002). School-to-career models: Some assembly (and assistance) required. *ASCA School Counselor, 39*(4), 12–17.

Bundy, M., & Boser, J. (1987). Helping latchkey children: A group guidance approach. *School Counseling, 35,* 58–65.

Burke, C. A. (2010). Mindfulness-based approaches with children and adolescents: A preliminary review of current research in an emergent field. *Journal of Child and Family Studies, 19,* 133-144. doi:10.1007/s10826-009-9282-x

Burnam, W. H. (1926). *Great teachers and mental health: A study of seven educational hygienists.* New York, NY: Appleton.

Burnham, J. J., & Jackson, C. M. (2000). School counselor roles: Discrepancies between school practice and existing models. *Professional School Counseling, 4,* 16–24.

Burns, D. D. (2008). *Feeling good: The new mood therapy.* New York, NY: Morrow, Williams.

Butcher, J. N., Graham, J. R., Ben-Porath, Y. S., Tellegen, A., Dahlstrom, W. G., & Kaemmer, B. (1989). *The Minnesota Multiphasic Personality Inventory* (2nd ed.). Minneapolis, MN: University of Minnesota Press.

Butcher, J. N., Hooley, J. M., & Mineka, S. M. (2013). *Abnormal psychology* (16th ed.). Upper Saddle River, NJ: Pearson.

Butler, D. L. (2002). Individualizing instruction in self-regulated learning. *Theory Into Practice, 41,* 81–92. doi:10.1207/s15430421tip4102_4

Butler, D. L., & Winne, P. H. (1995). Feedback and self-regulated learning: A theoretical synthesis. *Review of Educational Research, 65,* 245–281. doi:10.3102/00346543065003245

Butler, S. K., & Constantine, M. G. (2005). Collective self-esteem and burnout in professional school counselors. *Professional School Counseling, 9,* 55–62.

Buttery, T. J. (1987). Biracial children: Racial identification, self-esteem and school adjustment. *Delta Phi Record, 22,* 50–53. doi:10.1080/00228958.1987.10517805

Byely, L., Archibald, B., Graber, J., & Brooks-Gunn, J. (2000). A prospective study of familial and social influences on girls' body image and dieting. *International Journal of Eating Disorders, 28,* 155–164. doi:10.1002/1098-108X(200009)28:2<155::AID-EAT4>3.0.CO;2-K

Cabe, N. (2001). Relaxation training: Bubble breaths. In H. G. Kaduson, & C. E. Schaefer (Eds.), *101 more favorite play therapy techniques* (pp. 346–349). Northvale, NJ: Aronson.

Camizzi, E., Clark, M. A., Yacco, S., & Goodman, W. (2009). Becoming "difference makers:" School-university collaboration to create, implement, and evaluate data-driven counseling interventions. *Professional School Counseling, 12,* 471–479. doi:10.5330/PSC.n.2010-12.471

Campbell, C., & Dahir, C. (1997). *Sharing the vision: The national standards for school counseling programs.* Alexandria, VA: American School Counselor Association.

Campbell, D. T., & Stanley, J. C. (1963). *Experimental and quasi-experimental designs for research.* Boston, MA: Houghton Mifflin.

Candelaria, A. M., Fedewa, A. L., & Ahn, S. (2012). The effects of anger management on children's social and emotional outcomes: A meta-analysis. *School Psychology International, 33,* 596–614. doi:10.1177/0143034312454360

Canter, K. S., & Roberts, M. C., (2012). A systematic and quantitative review of interventions to facilitate school reentry for children with chronic health conditions. *Journal of Pediatric Psychology, 37,* 1065–1075.

Caplan, G. (1964). *Principles of preventive psychiatry.* New York, NY: Basic Books.

Carey, J., & Dimmitt, C. (2012). School counseling and student outcomes: Summary of six statewide studies. *Professional School Counseling, 16*(2), 146–153. doi:10.5330/PSC.n.2012-16.146

Carey, J. C., & Harrington, K. M. (2010a). *Nebraska school counseling evaluation report*. Amherst, MA: Center for School Counseling Outcome Research and Evaluation.

Carey, J. C., & Harrington, K. M. (2010b). *Utah school counseling evaluation report*. Amherst, MA: Center for School Counseling Outcome Research and Evaluation.

Carey, J., Harrington, K., Martin, I., & Stevenson, D. (2012). A statewide evaluation of the outcomes of the implementation of ASCA National Model school counseling programs in Utah high school. *Professional School Counseling, 16*(2), 89–99. doi:10.5330/PSC.n.2012-16.89

Carlisle, N., & Rofes, E. (2007). School bullying: Do adult survivors perceive long-term effects? *Traumatology, 13*(1), 16–26. doi:10.1177/1534765607299911

Carlo, G., Crockett, L. J., Wolff, J. M., & Beal, S. J. (2012). The role of emotional reactivity, self-regulation, and puberty in adolescents' prosocial behaviors. *Social Development, 21*, 667–685. doi:10.1111/j.1467-9507.2012.00660.x

Carlson, J., & Sperry, L. (2001). Adlerian counseling theory and practice. In D. C. Locke, J. E. Myers, & E. L. Herr (Eds.), *The handbook of counseling* (pp. 171–179). Thousand Oaks, CA: Sage.

Carmichael, K. D. (2006). *Play therapy: An introduction*. Upper Saddle River, NJ: Pearson, Merrill.

Carnevale, A. P. (2008). College for all? *Change: The Magazine of Higher Learning, 40*, 22–31. doi:10.3200/CHNG.40.1.22-31

Carney, J., & Scott, H. (2012). Eating issues in schools: Detection, management, and consultation with allied professionals. *Journal of Counseling & Development, 90*, 290–297. doi:10.1002/j.1556-6676.2012.00037.x

Carothers, D. E., & Taylor, R. L. (2004). How teachers and parents can work together to teach daily living skills to children with autism. *Focus on Autism and Other Developmental Disabilities, 2*, 102–104. doi:10.1177/10883576040190020501

Carr, E. (1994). Emerging themes in functional analysis of problem behavior. *Journal of Applied Behavior Analysis, 27*, 393–400. doi:10.1901/jaba.1994.27-393

Carr, E., & Durand, V. M. (1985). Reducing behavior problems through functional communication training. *Journal of Applied Behavior Analysis, 18*, 111–126. doi:10.1901/jaba.1985.18-111

Carter, S. L. (2009). Recent trends in conducting school-based experimental functional analyses. *International Journal of Behavioral Consultation and Therapy, 5*(2), 185–191.

Case-Smith, J. (2004). Parenting a child with a chronic medical condition. *American Journal of Occupational Therapy, 58*, 551–560.

Caste, W. E. (1926). Biological and social consequences of race crossing. *American Journal of Physical Anthropology, 9*, 145–156. doi:10.1002/ajpa.1330090212

Cattell, R. B. (1987). *Intelligence: Its structure, growth and action*. Amsterdam, Netherlands: North-Holland.

Cavaiola, A. A., & Colford, J. E. (2006). *A practical guide to crisis intervention*. Boston, MA: Houghton Mifflin/Lahaska Press.

Celano, M., Hazzard, A., Campbell, S., & Long, C. (2002). Attributions retraining with sexually abused children: Review of techniques. *Child Maltreatment, 7*, 65–76. doi:10.1037/0033-3204.43.2.201

Center for Public Education. (2012). *The United States of education: The changing demographics of the United States and their schools*. Retrieved from http://www.centerforpubliceducation.org/Main-Menu/Staffingstudents/Changing-Demographics-At-a-glance/The-United-States-of-education-The-changing-demographics-of-the-United-States-and-their-schools.html

Centers for Disease Control and Prevention. (2011). *Youth risk behavior surveillance 2011*. Retrieved from http://www.cdc.gov/mmwr/pdf/ss/ss6104.pdf

Centers for Disease Control and Prevention. (2012a) *Parent engagement: Strategies for involving parents in school health*. Retrieved from http://www.cdc.gov/healthyyouth/protective/pdf/parent_engagement_strategies.pdf

Centers for Disease Control and Prevention. (2012b). *Prevalence of autism spectrum disorders (ASDs)*. Retrieved from http://www.cdc.gov/mmwr/preview/mmwrhtml/ss6103a1.htm

Centers for Disease Control and Prevention. (2014a). *Prevalence of autism spectrum disorders among children aged 8 years*. Retrieved from http://www.cdc.gov/mmwr/pdf/ss/ss6302.pdf

Centers for Disease Control and Prevention. (2014b). *Suicide prevention*. Retrieved from http://www.cdc.gov/violenceprevention/pub/youth_suicide.html

Cerio, J. (1995). Systems troubleshooting for school counselors. *The Journal for the Professional Counselor, 10*(2), 39–47.

Chafouleas, S., Riley-Tillman, T. C., & Sugai, G. (2007). *School-based behavioral assessment: Informing intervention and instruction*. New York, NY: Guilford Press.

Chansky, T., & Grayson, J. (n.d.). *Teacher's guidelines for helping children with obsessive-compulsive disorder in the classroom*. Milford, CT: The Obsessive-Compulsive Foundation.

Chansky, T. E. (2000). *Freeing your child from obsessive-compulsive disorder: A powerful practical guide for parents of children and adolescents*. New York, NY: Three Rivers Press.

Chapman, M. V., & Stein, G. L. (2014). How do new immigrant Latino parents interpret problem behavior in adolescents? *Qualitative Social Work, 13*, 270–287. doi:10.1177/1473325012468478

Chavkin, N. F., & Garza-Lubeck, M. (1990). Multicultural approaches to parent involvement: Research and practice. *Social Work in Education, 13*, 22–34. doi:10.1093/cs/13.1.22

Cheatham, G. A., Smith, S. J., Elliot, W., & Friedline, T. (2012). Family assets, postsecondary education, and students with disabilities: Building on progress and overcoming challenges. *Children and Youth Services Review, 35*, 1078–1086. doi:10.1016/j.childyouth.2013.04.019

Chen, J. M., & Hamilton, D. L. (2012). Natural ambiguities: Racial categorization of multiracial individuals. *Journal of Experimental Social Psychology, 48*(1), 152-164. doi:10.1016/j.jesp.2011.10.005

Chen, P., & Vazsonyi, A. T. (2013). Future orientation, school contexts, and problem behaviors: A multilevel study. *Journal of Youth and Adolescence, 42*(1), 67–81. doi:10.1007/s10964-012-9785-4

Child Abuse Prevention and Treatment Act. (2010). Retrieved from http://www.acf.hhs.gov/sites/default/files/cb/capta2010.pdf

Childre, D., & Rozman, D. (2003). *Transforming anger: The HeartMath solution for letting go of rage, frustration, and irritation*. Oakland, CA: New Harbinger.

Children and Families In Need of Services Act of 2000, Ch. 984.085. Retrieved from http://www.leg.state.fl.us/statutes/index.cfm?App_mode=Display_Statute&URL=0900-0999/0984/0984ContentsIndex.html

Children's Aid Society. (2012). *Inspire /aspire: Annual report 2012*. Retrieved from ERIC database (ED540953).

Children's Defense Fund. (2014). *The state of America's children*. Retrieved from http://www.childrensdefense.org/child-research-data-publications/data/2014-soac.pdf

Chiong, J. A. (1998). *Racial categorization of multiracial children in schools*. Westport, CT: Bergin & Garvey.

Choi, Y., Harachi, T. W., Gillmore, M. R., & Catalano, R. F. (2006). Are multiracial adolescents at greater risk? Comparison of rates, patterns, and correlates of substance use and violence between monoracial and multiracial adolescents. *American Journal of Orthopsychiatry, 76*, 86–97. doi:10.1037/0002-9432.76.1.86

Cholewa, B., Smith-Adcock, S., & Amatea, E. (2010). Decreasing elementary school children's disruptive behaviors: A review of four evidence-based programs for school counselors. *Journal of School Counseling, 8*(4), 1–35.

Christ, G. H. (2000). Impact of development on children's mourning. *Cancer Practice, 8*, 72–81.

Christenson, A., & Jacobson, N. S. (1993). Who (or what) can do psychotherapy: The status and challenge of nonprofessional therapies. *Psychological Science, 5*(1), 8–14. doi:10.1111/j.1467-9280.1994.tb00606.x

Christner, R. W., Stewart, J. L., & Lennon, L. (2012). Parent consultation: A cognitive-behavioral perspective. In R. B. Mennuti, A. Freeman, & R. W. Christner (Eds.), *Cognitive-behavioral interventions in educational settings: A handbook for practice* (pp. 345–365). New York, NY: Routledge.

Choy, S. P. (2001). *Students whose parents did not go to college: Postsecondary access, persistence, and attainment.* Retrieved from http://nces.ed.gov/pubs2001/2001126.pdf

Chung, I. J., Hawkins, J. D., Gilchrist, L. D., Hill, K. G., & Nagin, D. S. (2002). Identifying and predicting offending trajectories among poor children. *Social Service Review, 76,* 663–685. doi:10.1086/342999

Chung, Y. B., & Katayama, M. (1998). Ethnic and sexual identity development of Asian-American lesbian and gay adolescents. *Professional School Counseling, 1*(3), 21–25.

Cicchette, D., & Cohen, D. J. (2006). *Manual of developmental psychopathology* (2nd ed.). New York, NY: Wiley.

Ciro, D., Surko, M., Bhandarkar, K., Helfgott, N., Peake, K., & Epstein, I. (2005). Lesbian, gay, bisexual, sexual-orientation questioning adolescents seeking mental health services: Risk factors, worries, and desire to talk about them. *Social Work in Mental Health, 3,* 213–234. doi:10.1300/J200v03n03_01

Claassen, R., & Claassen, R. (2008). *Discipline that restores. Strategies to create respect, cooperation, and responsibility in the classroom.* Charleston, SC: BookSurge.

Cleek, E. N., Wofsy, M., Boyd-Franklin, N., Mundy, B., & Howell, T. J. (2012). The Family Empowerment Program: An interdisciplinary approach to working with multi-stressed urban families. *Family Process, 51,* 207–217. doi:10.1111/j.1545-5300.2012.01392.x

Cloninger, S. C. (2000). *Theories of personality: Understanding persons* (3rd ed.). New York, NY: Prentice Hall.

Cohane, G. H., & Pope, H. G. (2001). Body image in boys: A review of the literature. *International Journal of Eating Disorders, 29,* 373–379. doi:10.1002/eat.1033

Cohen, D. K., & Loewenberg Ball, D. (2001). Making change: Instruction and its improvement. *Phi Delta Kappan, 83,* 73–78.

Cohen, J. (1988). *Statistical power analysis for the behavioral sciences* (2nd ed.). Hillsdale, NJ: Erlbaum.

Cohen, R. J., Swerdlik, M. E., & Sturman, E. (2012). *Psychological testing and assessment: An introduction to test and measurement* (8th ed.). Boston, MA: McGraw-Hill.

COIN Educational Products. (2007). *COIN career community.* Toledo, OH: Author.

Coker, K. (2004). Alcohol and other substance abuse: The school counselor's role. In R. Pérusse, & G. E. Goodnough (Eds.), *Leadership and advocacy in school counseling* (pp. 284–327). Pacific Grove, CA: Brooks/Cole.

Cole, C. L., Marder, T., & McCann, L. (2000). Self-monitoring. In E. S. Shapiro & T. R. Kratochwill (Eds.), *Conducting school-based assessments of child and adolescent behavior* (2nd ed., pp. 121–149). New York, NY: Guilford Press.

Cole, R. L., Treadwell, S., Dosani, S., & Frederickson, N. (2013). Evaluation of a short-term, cognitive-behavioral intervention for primary age children with anger-related difficulties. *School Psychology International, 34,* 82–100. doi:10.1177/0143034312451062

Coleman, J. C., Butcher, J. N., & Carson, R. C. (1984). *Abnormal psychology and modern life* (7th ed.). Glenview, IL: Scott Foresman.

College Board. (2014). *Scholastic Assessment Test (SAT) Reasoning Test.* Retrieved from http://www.collegeboard.com

Collie, R. J., Shapka, J. D., & Perry, N. E. (2011). Predicting teacher commitment: The impact of school climate and social–emotional learning. *Psychology in the Schools, 48,* 1034–1048. doi:10.1002/pits.20611

Collins, B. G., & Collins, T. M. (2005). *Crisis and trauma: Developmental-ecological intervention.* Boston, MA: Houghton Mifflin/Lahaska Press.

Collins, J. F. (2000). Biracial Japanese American identity: An evolving process. *Cultural Diversity & Ethnic Minority Psychology, 6*, 115–133. doi:10.1037/1099-9809.6.2.115

Colvin, G. (2002). Designing classroom organization and structure. In K. L. Lane, F. M. Gresham, & T. E. O'Shaughnessy (Eds.), *Interventions for children with or at risk for emotional and behavioral disorders* (pp. 159–174). Boston, MA: Allyn & Bacon.

Combs, J. L., Pearson, C. M., & Smith, G. T.(2011). A risk model for preadolescent disordered eating. *International Journal of Eating Disorders, 44*, 596–604. doi:10.1002/eat.20851

Combs, J. L., Pearson, C. M., Zapolski, T. B., & Smith, G. T. (2013). Preadolescent disordered eating predicts subsequent eating dysfunction. *Journal of Pediatric Psychology, 38*(1), 41–49. doi:10.1093/jpepsy/jss094

Common Core Standards. (2009). *What parents should know*. Retrieved from http://www.corestandards.org/what-parents-should-know/

Compas, B. E., Jaser, S. S., Dunn, M. J., & Rodriquez, E. M. (2012). Coping with chronic illness in childhood and adolescence. *Annual Review of Clinical Psychology, 8*, 455–480.

Conant, J. B. (1959). *The American high school today: A first report to interested citizens*. New York, NY: McGraw-Hill.

Conley, D. (2013). *College and career ready and the Common Core: What everyone needs to know*. Portland, OR: Educational Policy Improvement Center.

Conley, D. T. (2010). *College and career ready: Helping all students succeed beyond high school*. San Francisco, CA: Jossey-Bass.

Conners, C. K. (2008). *Manual for the Connors' Rating Scales* (3rd ed.). North Tonawanda, NY: Multi Health Systems.

Constantino, J. N. (2005). *Social Responsiveness Scale*. Los Angeles, CA: Western Psychological Services.

Consulting Psychologists Press. (2014). *Strong Interest Inventory assessment*. Retrieved from https://www.cpp.com/products/strong/index.aspx

Cooney, T. M., & Radina, M. E. (2000). Adjustment problems in adolescence: Are multiracial children at-risk? *American Journal of Orthopsychiatry, 70*, 433–444. doi:10.1037/h0087744

Cooper, B. (2004). Empathy, interaction and caring: Teachers' roles in a constrained environment. *Pastoral Care in Education, 22*, 12–21. doi:10.1111/j.0264-3944.2004.00299.x

Cooper, J. O., Heron, T. E., & Heward, W. L. (2007). *Applied behavior analysis* (2nd ed.). Columbus, OH: Merrill.

Cooper-Nicols, M. (2007). Exploring the experiences of gay, lesbian, and bisexual adolescents in school: Lessons for school psychologists. *Dissertation Abstracts International, 67*, 7B. (UMI No. 3225315)

Copa, G. H. (1999). *New designs for learning: K–12 schools*. Berkeley, CA: National Center for Research in Vocational Education.

Corey, G. (2013). *Theory and practice of counseling and psychotherapy* (9th ed.). Pacific Grove, CA: Brooks/Cole.

Corey, G., Corey, M. S., & Callanan, R. (2010). *Issues and ethics in the helping profession* (8th ed.). Pacific Grove, CA: Brooks/Cole.

Cortiella, C., & Horowitz, S. H. (2014). *The state of learning disabilities facts, trends and emerging issues* (3rd. ed.). New York, NY: National Center for Learning Disabilities.

Cottone, R. R., & Claus, R. E. (2000). Ethical decision-making models: A review of the literature. *Journal of Counseling & Development, 78*, 275–283. doi:10.1002/j.1556-6676.2000.tb01908.x

Council for Accreditation of Counseling and Related Educational Programs (CACREP). (2009). *CACREP 2009 standards*. Retrieved from http://www.cacrep.org/wp-content/uploads/2013/12/2009-Standards.pdf

Council for Accreditation of Counseling and Related Educational Programs (CACREP). (2014). *Council for Accreditation of Counseling and Related Educational Programs (CACREP): CACREP/CORE Updates* Retrieved from http://www.cacrep.org/news-and-events/cacrepcore-updates/

Covey, S. (1991). *Principle-centered leadership.* New York, NY: Simon & Schuster.

Craig, S. L. (2013). Affirmative Supportive Safe and Empowering Talk (ASSET): Leveraging the strengths and resiliencies of sexual minority youth in school-based groups. *Journal of LGBT Issues in Counseling, 7,* 372–386. doi:10.1080/15538605.2013.839342

Crawford, D., & Bodine, R. (1997). *Conflict resolution education: A guide to implementing programs in schools, youth-serving organizations, and community and juvenile justice settings.* Washington, DC: U.S. Department of Justice.

Creed, T. A., Reisweber, J., & Beck, A. T. (2011). *Cognitive therapy for adolescents in school settings.* New York, NY: Guilford Press.

Crites, J. O. (1978). *Theory and research handbook for the Career Maturity Inventory.* Monterey, CA: CTB/McGraw-Hill.

Crites, J. O., & Savickas, M. L. (1996). Revision of the Career Maturity Inventory. *Journal of Career Assessment, 4,* 131–138. doi:10.1177/106907279600400202

Crone, D. A., & Horner, R. H. (2003). *Building positive behavior support systems in schools.* New York, NY: Guilford Press.

Cross, T. L., & Burney, V. H. (2005). High ability, rural, and poor: Lessons from Project Aspire and implications for school counselors. *The Journal of Secondary Gifted Education, 16,* 148–156.

Crosson-Tower, C. (2013). *Understanding child abuse and neglect* (9th ed.). Boston, MA: Pearson.

Cunningham, W. G., & Cresso, D. W. (1993). *Cultural leadership: The culture of excellence in education.* Boston, MA: Allyn & Bacon.

Dahir, C. (2001). The national standards for school counseling programs: Development and implementation. *Professional School Counseling, 4,* 320–327.

Dahir, C. A., Sheldon, C. B., & Valiga, M. J. (1998). *Vision into action: Implementing the national standards for school counseling programs.* Alexandria, VA: American School Counselor Association.

Dahir, C. A., & Stone, C. B. (2003). Accountability: A M.E.A.S.U.R.E. of the impact school counselors have on student achievement. *Professional School Counseling, 6,* 214–221.

Daki, J., & Savage, R. S., (2010). Solution focused brief therapy: Impacts on academic and emotional difficulties. *The Journal of Educational Research, 103,* 309–326. doi:10.1080/00220670903383127

Dalgleish, T. (2004). Cognitive approaches to posttraumatic stress disorder: The evolution of multi-presentational theorizing. *Psychological Bulletin, 130,* 228–260. doi:10.1037/0033-2909.130.2.228

Danino, M., & Schechtman, Z. (2012). Superiority of group counseling to individual coaching for parents of children with learning disabilities. *Psychotherapy Research, 22,* 592–603. doi:10.1080/10503307.2012.692953

Dansby-Giles, G. (2002). Ethics: Handling requests for confidential information is not always as simple as black and white. *ASCA School Counselor, 39*(3), 22–25.

D'Augelli, A. R. (1992). Teaching lesbian/gay development: From oppression to exceptionality. In K. Harbeck (Ed.), *Coming out of the classroom closet* (pp. 213–227). New York, NY: Harrington Park Press.

Davis v. Monroe County Board of Education et al., 120 S. Ct. F.3d 1390 (1999).

Davis, K. M., & Garrett, M. T. (1998). Bridging the gap between school counselors and teachers: A proactive approach. *Professional School Counseling, 1*(5), 54–55.

Davis, T. (2005). *Exploring school counseling: Professional practices and perspectives.* Boston, MA: Lahaska Press/Houghton Mifflin.

Deck, M., Cecil, J., & Cobia, D. (1990). School counselor research as perceived by ASCA leaders: Implications for the profession. *Elementary School Guidance and Counseling, 25*(1), 12–20.

Delinquency; Interstate Compact on Juveniles Act (985.2065), 2000. Retrieved from http://www.leg.state.fl.us/statutes/index.cfm?App_mode=Display_Statute&URL=0900-0999/0985/0985ContentsIndex.html

Deluty, R. H., & DeVitis, J. L. (1996). Fears in the classroom: Psychological issues and pedagogical implications. *Educational Horizons, 2,* 108–113.

Demerouti, E., Nachreiner, F., Bakker, A. B., & Schaufeli, W. B. (2001). The job demands-resources model of burnout. *Journal of Applied Psychology, 86,* 499–512. doi:10.1037/0021-9010.86.3.499

Deming, W. E. (1993). *The new economics for industry, government, and education.* Cambridge, MA: MIT Press.

Deming, W. E. (2000). *Out of crisis.* Cambridge, MA: MIT Press.

Deno, E. (1970). Special education as developmental capital. *Exceptional Children, 37,* 229–237. doi:10.1177/00224669940270040

Deno, S. L. (2013). Problem-solving assessment. In R. Brown-Chidsey, K. J. Andren, & P. L. Harrison (Eds.), *Assessment for intervention: A problem-solving approach* (2nd ed., pp. 10–36). New York, NY: Guilford Press.

DePaul, J., Walsh, M. E., & Dam, U. C. (2009). The role of school counselors in addressing sexual orientation in schools. *Professional School Counseling, 12,* 300–308. doi:10.5330/PSC.n.2010-12.300

Dervarics, C. (2011). *Study: Minority, low-income students lack adequate access to educational opportunities.* Retrieved from http://diverseeducation.com/article/16180/

deShazer, S. (1985). *Keys to solution in brief therapy.* New York, NY: Norton.

DeThorne, L. S., & Schaefer, B. A. (2004). A guide to child nonverbal IQ measures. *American Journal of Speech-Language Pathology, 12,* 275–290. doi:10.1044/1058-0360(2004/029)

Devlin-Sherer, R., & Devlin-Sherer, W. L., (1994). Do school boards encourage parent involvement? *Education, 114,* 535–542.

DeVoss, J. A., & Andrews, M. F. (2006). *School counselors as educational leaders.* Boston, MA: Lahaska Press/Houghton Mifflin.

DeWit, D. J., Offord, D. R., Sanford, M., Rye, B. J., Shain, M., & Wright, R. (2000). The effect of school culture on adolescent behavioural problems: Self-esteem, attachment to learning, and peer approval of deviance as mediating mechanisms. *Canadian Journal of School Psychology, 16,* 15–38. doi:10.1177/082957350001600102

Dhooper, S. S. (2003). Social work response to the needs of biracial Americans. *Journal of Ethnic & Cultural Diversity in Social Work, 12,* 19–47. doi:10.1300/J051v12n04_02

Dietz, T. J. (1997). The impact of membership in a support group for gay, lesbian, and bisexual students. *Journal of College Student Psychotherapy, 12,* 57–72. doi:10.1300/J035v12n01_06

DiGiuseppe, R. (2007). Rational emotive behavior therapy. In H. T. Prout & D. T. Brown (Eds.), *Counseling and psychotherapy with children and adolescents: Theory and practice for school settings* (pp. 252–301). New York, NY: Wiley.

DiGiuseppe, R. A., Doyle, K. A., Dryden, W., & Backx, W. (2014). *A practitioner's guide to rational emotive behavior therapy* (3rd ed.). New York, NY: Oxford University Press.

Dimmitt, C. (2009). Why evaluation matters: Determining effective school counseling practices. *Professional School Counseling, 12,* 395–399. doi:10.5330/PSC.n.2010-12.395

Dimmitt, C., & Wilkerson, B. (2012). Comprehensive school counseling in Rhode Island: Access to services and student outcomes. *Professional School Counseling, 16*(2), 125–135. doi:10.5330/PSC.n.2012-16.125

Dimmitt, C. A., Carey, J. C., & Hatch, P. A. (2007). *Evidence-based school counseling: Making a difference with data-driven practices.* Thousand Oaks, CA: Corwin Press

D'Imperio, R. L., & Dubow, E. F. (2000). Resilient and stress-affected adolescents in an urban setting. *Journal of Clinical Child Psychology, 29,* 129–142. doi:10.1207/S15374424jccp2901_13

Dinkmeyer, D., Carlson, J., & Dinkmeyer, D. C. (2005). *Consultation: Creating school-based interventions* (3rd ed.). Oxford, UK: Routledge.

Dinkmeyer, D. C., Dinkmeyer, D. C., Jr., & Sperry, L. (1987). *Adlerian counseling and psychotherapy* (2nd ed.). Columbus, OH: Merrill.

Dixon, D. N. (1987). From Parsons to profession: The history of guidance and counseling. In J. A. Glover, & R. R. Ronning (Eds.), *Historical foundations of educational psychology* (pp. 107–119). New York, NY: Plenum Press.

Dixon, P. N., & Johnson, W. L. (1991). Revising the Charles F. Kettering, Ltd. School Climate Profile: Further analysis of the subscale structure. *Educational & Psychological Measurement, 51,* 135–141. doi:10.1177/0013164491511012

Dobson, K. S. (1989). A meta-analysis of the efficacy of cognitive therapy for depression. *Journal of Consulting & Clinical Psychology, 57,* 414–419. doi:10.1037/0022-006X.57.3.414

Doggett, R. A., Edwards, R. P., Moore, J. W., Tingstrom, D. H., & Wilczynski, S. M. (2001). An approach to functional assessment in general education classroom settings. *School Psychology Review, 30,* 313–328.

Doggett, R. A., Mueller, M. M., & Moore, J. W. (2002). Functional assessment informant record for teachers: Creation, evaluation, and future research. *Proven Practice: Prevention & Remediation Solutions for Schools, 4,* 25–30.

Doll, B., Zucker, S., & Brehm, K. (2004). *Resilient classrooms: Creating healthy environments for learning.* New York, NY: Guilford Press.

Dollarhide, C. T., & Saginak, K. A. (2012). *Comprehensive school counseling programs: K–12 delivery systems in action.* Upper Saddle River, NJ: Pearson.

Domaleski, C., & Hall, E. (2013). *Assessment transition and implications for accountability.* Dover, NH: Center for Assessment.

Donaldson, J. M., Vollmer, T. R., Yakich, T. M., & Van Camp, C. (2013). Effects of a reduced time-out interval on compliance with the time-out instruction. *Journal of Applied Behavior Analysis, 46,* 369–378. doi:10.1002/jaba.40

Donnay, D. A. C., Morris, M. L., Schaubhut, N. A., Thompson, R. C., Grutter, J., & Hammer, A. L. (2005). *Strong Interest Inventory* [Newly revised]. Mountain View, CA: CPP, Inc.

Doobay, A. F. (2008). School refusal behavior associated with separation anxiety disorder: A cognitive-behavioral approach to treatment. *Psychology in the Schools, 45,* 261–272. doi:10.1002/pits.20299

Dougherty, A. M. (2013). *Psychological consultation and collaboration in school and community settings* (6th ed.). Belmont, CA: Brooks/Cole.

Dougy Center. (2014). The National Center for Grieving Children and Families. Retrieved from http://www.dougy.org

Doyle, C. (2003). Child emotional abuse: The role of educational professionals. *Education & Child Psychology, 20*(1), 8–21.

Drasgow, E., & Yell, M. L. (2001). Functional behavioral assessments: Legal requirements and challenges. *School Psychology Review, 30,* 239–251.

Drechsler, R., Straub, M., Doehnert, M., Heinrich, H., Steinhausen, H. C., & Brandeis, D. (2007). Controlled evaluation of a neurofeedback training of slow cortical potentials in children with attention deficit/hyperactivity disorder (ADHD). *Behavioral and Brain Functions, 3*(35), 1–13. doi:10.1186/1744-9081-3-35

Drefs, M. (2003). Developmental considerations for school-wide comprehensive guidance and counseling programs. *Guidance & Counselling, 18,* 153–160.

Dreikurs, R., & Stolz, V. (1991). *Children: The challenge.* New York, NY: Hawthorn.

Dryden, W., David, D., & Ellis, A. (2010). Rational emotive behavior therapy. In K. S. Dobson (Ed.), Handbook of cognitive behavioral therapies (pp. 226–276). New York, NY: Guilford Press.

Dubrin, A. J. (2004). *Leadership: Research findings, practice, and skills.* Boston, MA: Houghton Mifflin.

Dugger, S. M. (in press). *Foundations of career counseling: A case-based approach.* Upper Saddle River, NJ: Pearson.

Duncan, A. (2014). *Key policy letters from the Education Secretary and Deputy Secretary.* Retrieved from http://www2.ed.gov/policy/elsec/guid/secletter/140630.html

Dunlap, G., & Fox, L. (2011). Function-based interventions for children with challenging behavior. *Journal of Early Intervention, 33,* 333–343. doi:10.1177/1053815111429971

Dunlap, G., Kern, L., dePerczel, M., Clarke, S., Wilson, D., & Childs, K. (1993). Functional analysis of classroom variables for students with emotional and behavioral disorders. *Behavioral Disorders, 18,* 275–291.

Dunn, R. (1999). How do we teach them. *Teaching PreK-8, 29*(7), 50–53.

Dunn, R., & DeBello, T. C. (Eds.). (1999). *Improved test scores, attitudes and behaviors in America's schools: Supervisors' success stories.* Westport, CT: Bergin & Garvy.

Dunn, R., Denig, S., & Lovelace, M. K. (2001). Two sides of the same coin, or different strokes for different folks. *Teacher Librarian, 28*(3), 9–15.

Dunn, R., & Dunn, K. (1992). *Teaching elementary students through their individual learning styles.* Boston, MA: Allyn & Bacon.

Dunn, R., & Dunn, K. (1993). *Teaching secondary students through their individual learning styles.* Boston, MA: Allyn & Bacon.

Dunn, R., Dunn, K., & Price, G. E. (1989). *Learning Style Inventory manual.* Lawrence, KS: Price Systems.

Dupper, D. R. (2010). Does the punishment fit the crime? The impact of zero tolerance discipline on at-risk youth. *Children & Schools, 32*(2), 67–69. doi:10.1093/cs/32.2.67

Dupper, D. R., & Dingus, A. (2008). Corporal punishment in U.S. public schools: A continuing challenge for school social workers. *Children & Schools, 30,* 243–250. doi:10.1093/cs/30.4.243

Durand, V. M., & Crimmins, D. B. (1988). Identifying the variables maintaining self-injurious behavior. *Journal of Autism and Developmental Disorders, 18,* 99–117. doi:10.1007/BF02211821

Ediger, M. (1997). Improving school culture. *Education, 118,* 36–41.

EdITS. (1995). *Career occupational preference system.* San Diego, CA: Author.

EdITS. (2014). *COPSystem.* Retrieved from http://www.edits.net/products/copsystem.html

Edmonson, J. H., & White, J. (1998). A tutorial and counseling program: Helping students at-risk of dropping out of school. *Professional School Counseling, 1*(4), 43–51.

Education for All Handicapped Children Act of 1975, 20 U.S.C. § 1400 et seq. (1975)

Education for All Handicapped Children Act of 1975, 20 U.S.C. § 1400 et seq. (1975) (amended 1986)

Education Trust. (1997). *The national guidance and counseling reform program.* Washington, DC: Author.

Education Trust. (1999). *Transforming school counseling initiative* [Brochure]. Washington, DC: Author.

Education Trust. (2000) *What we do. Transforming school counseling. Working definition of school counseling.* Retrieved from http://www.edtrust.org/dc/tsc/vision

Education Trust. (2003). *Transforming school counseling initiative.* Retrieved from http://www.edtrust.org/dc/tsc

Edwards, M., Adams, E. M., Waldo, M., Hadfield, O.D., & Biegel, G. (2014). Effects of a mindfulness group on Latino adolescent students: Examining levels of perceived stress, mindfulness, self-compassion and psychological symptoms. *Journal of Specialists in Group Work, 39,* 145–163. doi:10.1080/01933922.2014.891683

Edwards, O. W., & Daire, A. P. (2006). School-age children raised by their grandparents: Problems and solutions. *Journal of Instructional Psychology, 33,* 113–119.

Edwards, R. P. (2002). A tutorial for using the Functional Assessment Informant Record for Teachers. *Proven Practice, 4,* 31–38.

Egan, G. (1975). *The skilled helper.* Monterey, CA: Brooks/Cole.

Egendorf A., Kadushin, C., Laufer, R. S., Rothbart, G., & Sloan, L. (1981). *Legacies of Vietnam: Comparative adjustment of veterans and their peers, Vols I–IV.* Washington, DC: U.S. Government Accounting Office.

Ehly, S., & Dustin, R. (1989). *Individual and group counseling in schools.* New York, NY: Guilford Press.

Ehren, B. J. (2013). Expanding pockets of excellence in RTI. *The Reading Teacher, 69,* 449–458. doi:10.1002/TRTR.1147

Eisenberg, M. E., Neumark-Sztainer, M. S., & Perry, C. (2005). The role of social norms and friends' influences on unhealthy weight-control behaviors among adolescent girls. *Social Science & Medicine, 60,* 163–173. doi:10.1016/j.socscimed.2004.06.055

Ekstrom, R. B., Elmore, P. B., Schafer, W. D., Trotter, T. V., & Webster, B. (2004). A survey of assessment and evaluation activities of school counselors. *Professional School Counseling, 8*, 24–30.

Elbaum, B., & Vaughn, S. (2001). School-based interventions to enhance the self-concept of students with learning disabilities? A meta-analysis. *Elementary School Journal, 101*, 303–329. doi:10.1086/499670

Elliott, L., & Brantley, C. (1997). *Sex on campus: The naked truth about the real sex lives of college students.* New York, NY: Random House.

Elliott, L., Orr, L., Watson, L., & Jackson, A. (2005). Secondary prevention interventions for young drug abusers: A systematic review of the evidence. *Adolescence, 40*(157), 1–23.

Ellis, A. (1975). *How to live with a neurotic: At home and at work* (rev. ed.). New York, NY: Crown.

Ellis, A. (2001a). *Feeling better, getting better, staying better.* Atascadero, CA: Impact.

Ellis, A. (2001b). *Overcoming destructive beliefs, feelings, and behaviors.* Amherst, NY: Prometheus Books.

Ellis, A. (2002). *Anger: How to live with and without it.* New York, NY: Citadel Press.

Ellis, A., & Poppa, S. (2001). Interview with Albert Ellis: The "cognitive revolution" in psychotherapy. *Romanian Journal of Cognitive and Behavioral Psychotherapies, 1*(1), 7–16.

Elze, D. (2003) Gay, lesbian, and bisexual youth's perceptions of their high school environments and comfort in school. *Children and Schools, 25*, 225–239. doi:10.1093/cs/25.4.225

Engel, B. (2005). *Breaking the cycle of abuse.* Hoboken, NJ: Wiley.

Epstein, J. L. (2010). *School, family, and community partnerships: Preparing educators and improving schools* (2nd ed.). Boulder, CO: Westview Press.

Epstein, J. L., & McPartland, J. M. (1976). *Quality of School Life Scale.* Chicago, IL: Riverside.

Epstein, J. L., & Van Voorhis, F. L. (2010). School counselors' roles in developing partnerships with families and communities for student success. *Professional School Counseling, 14*, 1–14.

Equit, M., Pälmke, M., Becker, N., Moritz, A., Becker, S., & Gontard, A. (2013). Eating problems in young children—a population-based study. *Acta Paediatrica, 102*, 149–155. doi:10.1111/apa.12078

Erford, B. T. (1999). The comparative effectiveness of a modified time-out procedure for oppositional and defiant children. *The Professional School Counselor, 2*, 205–210.

Erford, B. T. (Ed.). (2010). *Group work in the schools.* Columbus, OH: Pearson Merrill Prentice Hall.

Erford, B. T. (2013). *Assessment for counselors* (2nd ed.). Boston, MA: Cengage.

Erford, B. T. (Ed.). (2014). *Research and evaluation in counseling.* Boston, MA: Cengage.

Erford, B. T. (2015a). *40 techniques every counselor should know* (2nd ed.). Columbus, OH: Pearson Merrill.

Erford, B. T. (2015b). *Clinical experiences in counseling.* Columbus, OH: Pearson Merrill.

Erford, B. T. (2015c). *Transforming the school counseling profession* (4th ed.). Columbus, OH: Pearson Merrill.

Erford, B. T., Erford, B. M., Lattanzi, G., Weller, J., Schein, H., Wolf, E . . . Peacock, E. (2011). Counseling outcomes from 1990 to 2008 for school-age youth with depression: A meta-analysis. *Journal of Counseling & Development, 89*, 439–457. doi:10.1002/j.1556-6676.2011.tb02841.x

Erford, B. T., Moore-Thomas, C., & Mazzuca, S. (2004). Improving academic achievement through an understanding of learning styles. In R. Pérusse & G. E. Goodnough (Eds.), *Leadership and advocacy in school counseling* (pp. 34–70). Pacific Grove, CA: Brooks/Cole.

Erickson, L. (1987). Conceptions of school culture. *Educational Administration Quarterly, 23*, 11–24.

Erickson, L. (1991). Conceptions of school culture: An overview. In N. B. Wyner (Ed.), *Current perspectives on the culture of schools* (pp. 1–12). Cambridge, MA: Brookline Books.

Erwin, J. (2006). Boosting students' intrinsic motivation: A choice theory approach. *International Journal of Choice Theory, 1*(1), 11–13.

Eschenauer, R., & Chen-Hayes, S. (2005). The transformative individual school counseling model: An accountability model for urban school counselors. *Professional School Counseling, 8*, 244–248.

Espelage, D. L., Aragon, S. R., Birkett, M., & Koenig, B. W. (2008). Homophobic teasing, psychological outcomes, and sexual orientation among high school students: What influence do parents and schools have? *School Psychology Review, 37*, 202–216.

Evans, E. H., Tovée, M. J., Boothroyd, L. G., & Drewett, R. F. (2013). Body dissatisfaction and disordered eating attitudes in 7- to 11-year-old girls: Testing a sociocultural model. *Body Image, 10*(1), 8–15. doi:10.1016/j.bodyim.2012.10.001

Evans, J. E., & Hines, P. L. (1997). Lunch with school counselors: Reaching parents through their workplace. *Professional School Counseling, 1,* 45–48.

Everett, G. E., Olmi, D. J., Edwards, R. P., Tingstrom, D. H., Sterling-Turner, H. E., & Christ, T. J. (2007). An empirical investigation of time-out with and without escape extinction to treat escape maintained noncompliance. *Behavior Modification, 31,* 412–434. doi:10.1177/0145445506297725

Eyberg, S. M., & Robinson, E. A. (1982). Conduct problem behavior: Standardization of a behavioral rating scale with adolescents. *Journal of Clinical Child Psychology, 12,* 347–354. doi:10.1080/15374418309533155

Fairchild, T. (1993). Accountability practices of school counselors: 1990 national survey. *The School Counselor, 40,* 363–374.

Family Educational Rights and Privacy Act of 1974, 20 U.S.C. § 1232g; 34 CFR Part 99 (1974)

Fan, W. A., Williams, M., & Corkin, D. A. M. (2011). A multilevel analysis of student perceptions of school climate: The effect of social and academic risk factors. *Psychology in the Schools, 48,* 632–646. doi:10.1002/pits.20579

Faraone, S., & Biederman, J. (1998). Neurobiology of attention-deficit/hyperactivity disorder. *Biological Psychiatry, 44,* 122–131. doi:10.1016/S0006-3223(98)00240-6

Farber, P. (2003). Race-mixing and science in the United States. *Endeavor, 27,* 166–170. doi:10.1016/j.endeavour.2003.08.007

Farberow, N. L., Heilig, S. M., & Litman, R. (1968). *Techniques in crisis intervention: A training manual.* Los Angeles, CA: Los Angeles Suicide Prevention Center.

Farmer, E., & Farmer, T. (1999). The role of schools in outcomes for youth: Implications for children's mental health services research. *Journal of Child and Family Studies, 8,* 377–396. doi:10.1023/A:1021943518480

Favazza, A. R. (1996). *Bodies under siege: Self-mutilation and body modification in culture and psychiatry* (2nd ed.). Baltimore, MD: Johns Hopkins University Press.

Favazza, A. R. (1998). The coming of age of self-mutilation. *The Journal of Nervous and Mental Disease, 186,* 259–268. doi:10.1097/00005053-199805000-00001

Favazza, A. R. (1999). Self-mutilation. In D. G. Jacobs (Ed.), *The Harvard Medical School guide to suicide assessment and interventions* (pp. 125–145). San Francisco, CA: Jossey-Bass.

Federal Bureau of Investigation. (2013, November 25). *Latest hate crime statistics: Annual report shows slight decrease.* Retrieved from http://www.fbi.gov/news/stories/2013/november/annual-hate-crime-statistics-show-slight-decease/annual-hate-crime-statistics-show-slight-decrease

Federal Interagency Forum on Child and Family Statistics. (2013). *America's children: Key national indicators of well-being, 2013.* Retrieved from http://www.childstats.gov/pdf/ac2013/ac_13.pdf

Feeny, N. C., Foa, E. B., Treadwell, K. R. H., & March, J. (2004). Posttraumatic stress disorder in youth: A critical review of the cognitive and behavioral treatment outcome literature. *Professional Psychology: Research and Practice, 35,* 466–476. doi:10.1037/0735-7028.35.5.466

Feerick, M. M., & Silverman, G. B. (2006). *Children exposed to violence.* Baltimore, MD: Brookes.

Feindler, E. L., & Engel, E. C. (2011). Assessment and intervention for adolescents with anger and aggression difficulties in school settings. *Psychology in the Schools, 48,* 243–253. doi:10.1002/pits.20550

Fergusson, D. M., McLeod, G. F. H., & Horwood, L. J. (2014). Parental separation/divorce in childhood and partnership outcomes at age 30. *Journal of Child Psychology and Psychiatry, 55,* 352–360. doi:10.1111/jcpp.12107

Fergusson, D. M., McLeod, G. F. H., & Horwood, L. J. (2014). Parental separation/divorce in childhood and partnership outcomes at age 30. *Journal of Child Psychology and Psychiatry, 55,* 352–360. doi:10.1111/jcpp.12107

Ferrance, E. (2000). *Themes in education.* Retrieved from http://www.brown.edu/academics/education-alliance/sites/brown.edu.academics.education-alliance/files/publications/act_research.pdf

Fischetti, B. (2001). Use of play therapy for anger management in the school setting. In A. A. Drewes, C. E. Schaefer, & L. Carey (Eds.), *School-based play therapy* (pp. 238–255). New York, NY: Wiley.

Fitch, T., Newby, E., Ballestero, V., & Marshall, J. L. (2001). Future school administrators' perceptions of the school counselor's role. *Counselor Education & Supervision, 41,* 89–99. doi:10.1002/j.1556-6978.2001.tb01273.x

Flanagan, R., Allen, K., & Henry, D. J. (2010). The impact of anger management treatment and rational emotive behavior therapy in a public school setting on social skills, anger management, and depression. *Journal of Rational-Emotive & Cognitive-Behavior Therapy, 28*(2), 87–99. doi:10.1007/s10942-009-0102-4

Foa, E. B., Johnson, K., Feeny, N. C., & Treadwell, K. R. T. (2001). The child PTSD symptom scale (CPSS): Preliminary psychometrics of a measure for children with PTSD. *Journal of Clinical Child Psychology, 30,* 376–384. doi:10.1207/S15374424JCCP3003_9

Foa, E. B., Keane, T. M., Friedman, M. J., & Cohen, J. A. (Eds.). (2010). *Effective treatments for PTSD* (2nd ed.). New York, NY: Guilford Press.

Fontaine, J. H. (1998). Evidencing a need: School counselors' experiences with gay and lesbian students. *Professional School Counseling, 1*(3), 8–14.

Foxx, R. M., & Azrin, N. H. (1972). Restitution: A method of eliminating aggressive–disruptive behavior of retarded and brain damaged patients. *Behavior Research and Therapy, 10,* 15–27. doi:10.1016/0005-967(72)90003-4

Foxx, R. M., & Azrin, N. H. (1973). The elimination of autistic self-stimulatory behavior by overcorrection. *Journal of Applied Behavior Analysis, 6,* 1–14. doi:10.1901/jaba.1973.6-1

Frank, E., Turner, S. M., & Steuwart, B. D. (1980). Initial response to rape: The impact of stressors within the rape situation. *Journal of Behavioral Assessment, 2,* 39–53. doi:10.1007/BF01321431

Franko, D. L., & Omori, M. (1999). Subclinical eating disorders in adolescent women: A test of the continuity hypothesis and its psychological correlates. *Journal of Adolescence, 22,* 389–396. doi:10.1006/jado.1999.0230

Freeman, A., Pretzer, F., Fleming, B., & Simon, K. M. (2004). *Clinical applications of cognitive therapy* (2nd ed.). New York, NY: Kluwer Academic/Plenum.

Freud, F. (1957). *On narcissism. The complete psychological works of Sigmund Freud.* New Haven, CT: Yale University.

Freud, S. (1916). *Introductory lectures on psychoanalysis* (Vols. 15 and 16, standard ed.). London, UK: Hogarth.

Freud, S. (1923). *The ego and the id* (Vol 19, standard ed.). London, UK: Hogarth.

Freud, S. (1924). *A short account of psychoanalysis* (Vol. 19, standard ed). London, UK: Hogarth.

Frey K. S., Hirschstein, M. K., Edstrom, L. V., & Snell, J. L. (2009). Observed reductions in school bullying, nonbullying aggression, and destructive bystander behavior: A longitudinal evaluation. *Journal of Educational Psychology, 101,* 466–481. doi:10.1037/a0013839

Frick, T. W. (1990). Analysis of patterns in time: A method of recording and quantifying temporal relations in education. *American Educational Research Journal, 27,* 180–204. doi:10.3102/00028312027001180

Fulkerson, M. (2013). *Treatment planning from a reality therapy perspective.* Owensboro, KY: Self-Publication.

Gabel, K. A., & Kearney, K. (1998). Promoting reasonable perspectives of body weight: Issues for school counselors. *Professional School Counseling, 1,* 32–35.

Gabovitch, E. M., & Wiseman, N. D. (2005). Early identification of autism spectrum disorders. In D. Zaeger (Ed.), *Autism spectrum disorders: Identification, education, and treatment* (pp. 145–172). Mahwah, NJ: Erlbaum.

Gaines, T., & Barry, L. M. (2008). The effect of a self-monitored relaxation breathing exercise on male adolescent aggressive behavior. *Adolescence, 43*(170), 291–302.

Gani, C., Birbaumer, N., & Strehl, U. (2008). Long term effects after feedback of slow cortical potentials and of theta-beta amplitudes in children with attention. *International Journal of Bioelectromagnetism, 10*, 209–232.

Gansle, K. A., & Noell, G. H. (2008). Consulting with teachers regarding academic skills: Problem solving for basic skills. *International Journal of Behavioral Consultation and Therapy, 4*, 199–211.

Ganz, J. B., Earles-Vollrath, T. L., & Cook, K. E. (2011). Video modeling: A visually based intervention for children with autism spectrum disorder. *Teaching Exceptional Children, 43*, 8–19.

Garbarino, J., & Delara, E. (2002). *And words can hurt forever: How to protect adolescents from bullying, harassment and emotional violence.* New York, NY: The Free Press.

García, F., & Gracia, E. (2009). Is always authoritative the optimum parenting style? Evidence from Spanish families. *Adolescence, 44*(173), 101–131.

Garcia-Alonso, P. M. (2004). From surviving to thriving: An investigation of the utility of support groups designed to address the special needs of sexual minority youth in public high schools. *Dissertation Abstracts International, 65*, 3A. (UMI No. 3126026)

Garcia-Grau, E., Fuste, A., Miro, A., Saldana, C., & Bados, A. (2004). Coping styles and vulnerability to eating disorders in adolescent boys. *European Eating Disorders Review, 12*, 61–67. doi:10.1002/erv.550

Gardner, H. (2011). *Frames of mind: The theory of multiple intelligences* (3rd ed.). New York, NY: Basic Books.

Garner, D. M., Garfinkel, P. E., & Irvine, M. J. (1986). Integration and sequencing of treatment approaches for eating disorders. *Psychotherapy and Psychosomatics, 46*, 67–75. doi:10.1159/000287963

Garner, N. E. (1996, March). *A multiple intelligences approach to conflict resolution.* Workshop presented at the National Conference on Conflict Management and Peer Mediation in a Residential Setting, Bronx, NY.

Gatongi, F. (2007). Person-centered approach in schools: Is it the answer to disruptive behavior in our classrooms. *Counselling Psychology Quarterly, 20*(2), 205–211. doi:10.1080/09515070701403406

Geiger, B., & Fischer, M. (2006). Will words ever harm me? *Journal of Interpersonal Violence, 21*, 337–357. doi:10.1177/0886260505282886

Geltner, J. A., & Leibforth, T. N. (2008). Advocacy in the IEP process: Strengths-based school counseling in action. *Professional School Counseling, 12*, 162–165. doi:10.5330/PSC.n.2010-12.162

Gensler, D. (2012). Autism spectrum disorder in DSM-V: Differential diagnosis and boundary conditions. *Journal of Infant and Adolescent Psychotherapy, 11*, 86–95. doi:10.1080/15289168.2012.676339

Gerber, P. S. (2012). The impact of learning disabilities on adulthood: A review of the evidenced-based literature for research and practice in adult education. *Journal of Learning Disabilities, 45*(1), 31–46. doi:10.1177/0022219411426858

Gerber, S., & Terry-Day, B. (1999). Does peer mediation really work? *Professional School Counseling, 2*, 169–171.

Gerler, E. (1985). Elementary school counseling research and the classroom learning environment. *Elementary School Guidance & Counseling, 20*, 39–40.

Gerler, E., & Anderson, R. (1986). The effects of classroom guidance on children's success in school. *Journal of Counseling & Development, 65*, 78–81. doi:10.1002/j.1556-6676.1986.tb01236.x

Gerler, E. R., & Herndon, E. Y. (1993). Learning how to succeed academically in middle school. *Elementary School Guidance and Counseling, 27*, 186–197.

Gerstenblatt, P. (Ed.). (2000). *Serving children in biracial/biethnic families: A supplementary diversity curriculum for the training of child care providers.* Unpublished manuscript, Oakland, CA. (ERIC Document Reproduction Service No. ED 461425)

Gevensleben, H., Holl, B., Albrecht, B., Schlamp, D., Kratz, O., Studer, P... Heinrich, H. (2010). Neurofeedback training in children with ADHD: 6-month follow-up of a randomized controlled trial. *European Child and Adolescent Psychiatry, 19*, 715–724. doi:10.1007/s00787-010-0109-5

Gibbs, J. T., & Moskowitz-Sweet, G. (1991). Clinical and cultural issues in the treatment of biracial and bicultural adolescents. *The Journal of Contemporary Human Services, 12,* 579–592.

Gibson, P. (1989). Gay male and lesbian youth suicide. In M. R. Feinleib (Ed.), *Report of the Secretary's task force on youth suicide. Volume 3: Preventions and interventions in youth suicide* (pp. 110–142, U.S. Department of Health and Human Services Pub. No. ADM 89-1623). Washington, DC: U.S. Government Printing Office.

Gil, E. (2012). Trauma-focused integrated play therapy (TF-IPT). In P. Goodyear-Brown (Ed.), *Handbook of child sexual abuse: Identification, assessment, and treatment* (pp. 251–278). Hoboken, NJ: John Wiley & Sons.

Giles, M., & Hass, M. (2008). Fostering a healthy body image: Prevention and intervention with adolescent eating disorders. *Journal of School Counseling, 6*(13).

Gillespie, A., & Starkey, D. S. (2006). The role of the rural school counselor in preparing high school students for college. *Delta Education Journal, 3*(2), 24–28.

Girdano, D. A., Dusek, D. E., & Everly, G. S. (2011). *Controlling stress and tension* (9th ed.). Upper Saddle River, NJ: Pearson.

Gladding, S. T. (2011). *The creative arts in counseling* (4th ed.). Alexandria, VA: American Counseling Association.

Gladding, S. T. (2012). *Groups: A counseling specialty.* Upper Saddle River, NJ: Pearson.

Gladding, S. T. (2013). *Counseling: A comprehensive profession* (7th ed.). Upper Saddle River, NJ: Pearson.

Glaitto, M. F., & Rai, A. K. (1999). *Evaluation and treatment of patients with suicide ideation.* Retrieved from http://www.aafp.org/afp/1999/0315/p1500.html

Glass, C., Arnkoff, D., & Shapiro, S. (2011). Expectations and preferences. *Psychotherapy, 38,* 455–461. doi:10.1037/0033-3204.38.4.455

Glasser, C. (2004). *Choice theory class meetings flash card kit for elementary school students.* Chatsworth, CA: The William Glasser Institute.

Glasser, W. (1998). *The quality school: Managing students without coercion.* New York, NY: Harper Perennial.

Glasser, W. (2001). *Every student can succeed.* Chatsworth, CA: The William Glasser Institute.

Glasser, W. (2005). *Defining mental health as a public health problem.* Chatsworth, CA: The William Glasser Institute.

Glasser, W. (2011). *Take charge of your life.* Bloomington, IN: iUniverse.

Glazier, R. P. (2010). Sexual minority youth and risk behaviors: Implications for the school environment. *Dissertation Abstracts International, Section A: Humanities and Social Sciences, 70*(9-A), 3403.

Glossary of Education Reform. (2013). *At-risk.* Retrieved from http://edglossary.org/at-risk/

Goertz, M. E. (2001). Redefining government roles in an era of standards-based reform. *Phi Delta Kappan, 83,* 62–66.

Goh, H. L., Iwata, B. A., & DeLeon, I. G. (1996, May). *The functional analysis screening tool.* Poster presented at the meeting of the Association for Behavior Analysis, San Diego, CA.

Gold, C., Voracek, M, & Wigram, T. (2004). Effects of music therapy for children and adolescents with psychopathology: A meta-analysis. *Journal of Child Psychology and Psychiatry, 45,* 1054–1063. doi:10.1111/j.1469-7610.2004.t01-1-00298.x

Goldberg, A. E. (2010). *Lesbian and gay parents and their children: Research on the family life cycle.* Division 44: Contemporary perspectives on lesbian, gay, and bisexual psychology. Washington, DC, US: American Psychological Association. doi:10.1037/12055-000

Golden, B. (2006). *Healthy anger: How to help children and teens manage their anger.* Oxford, UK: University Press.

Goldenberg, H., & Goldenberg, I. (2001). *Counseling today's families* (4th ed.). Pacific Grove, CA: Brooks/Cole.

Gonsoulin, S. S., Darwin, M. J., Read, N. W., & National Evaluation and Technical Assistance Center for the Education of Children and Youth Who Are Neglected. (2012). *Providing individually tailored academic and behavioral support services for youth in the juvenile justice and child welfare systems. Practice guide*. Retrieved from ERIC database (ED533051).

Gonzalez-DeHass, A. R., Willems, P. P., & Holbein, M. F. D. (2005). Examining the relationship between parental involvement and student motivation. *Educational Psychology Review, 2*, 99–123. doi:10.1007/s10648-005-3949-7

Goodenow, C., Szalacha, L., & Westheimer, K. (2006). School support groups, other school factors, and the safety of sexual minority adolescents. *Psychology in the Schools, 43*, 573–589. doi:10.1002/pits.20173

Goodman, R. F. (2010). Art as a component of grief work with children. In N. B. Webb (Ed.), *Helping bereaved children: A handbook for practitioners* (2nd ed., pp. 297–322). New York, NY: Guilford Press.

Goodnough, G., Perusse, R., & Erford, B. T. (2015). Developmental classroom guidance. In B. T. Erford (Ed.), *Transforming the school counseling profession* (4th ed., pp. 221–239). Columbus, OH: Pearson Merrill.

Goodnough, G. E., & Ripley, V. (1997). Structured groups for high school seniors making the transition to college and to military service. *The School Counselor, 44*, 230–234.

Gore, S. A., Vander Wal, J. S., & Thelen, M. H. (2009). Treatment of eating disorders in children and adolescents. In J. K. Thompson, & L. Smolak (Eds.), *Body image, eating disorders, and obesity in youth: Assessment, prevention, and treatment* (2nd ed., pp. 293–311). Washington, DC: American Psychological Association.

Gottfredson, L. S. (1981). Circumscription and compromise: A developmental theory of occupational aspirations. *Journal of Counseling Psychology, 28*, 545–579. doi:10.1037/0022-0167.28.6.545

Gould, M. S., & Kramer, R. A. (2001). Youth suicide. *Suicide and Life-Threatening Behavior, 31*, 6–30. doi:10.1521/suli.31.1.5.6.24219

Green, A., & Keys, S. (2001). Expanding the developmental school counseling paradigm: Meeting the needs of the 21st century student school. *Professional School Counseling, 5*, 84–95.

Greenberg, D. (1999). *White weddings: The incredible staying power of the laws against interracial marriage*. Retrieved from http://www.slate.com/id/30352/

Greenstone, J. L., & Leviton, S. C. (2010). *Elements of crisis intervention: Crises and how to respond to them* (3rd ed.). Pacific Grove, CA: Brooks/Cole.

Gregg, N., & Nelson, J. M. (2012). Meta-analysis on the effectiveness of extra time as a test accommodation for transitioning adolescents with learning disabilities: More questions than answers. *Journal of Learning Disabilities, 45*, 128–138. doi:10.1177/0022219409355484

Gresham, F. M., & Elliot, S. G. (2008). *Social Skills Improvement System Rating System* (2nd ed.). Minneapolis, MN: Pearson.

Gresham, F. M., & Kendell, G. K. (1987). School consultation research: Methodological critique and future research direction. *School Psychology Review, 16*, 306–316.

Gresham, F. M., Watson, T. S., & Skinner, C. H. (2001). Functional behavioral assessment: Principles, procedures, and future directions. *School Psychology Review, 30*, 156–172.

Griffin, D., Hutchins, B. C., & Meece, J. L. (2011). Where do rural high school students go to find information about their futures? *Journal of Counseling & Development, 89*, 172–181. doi:10.1002/j.1556-6678.2011.tb00075.x

Griffith, N. H., & Zigler, J. (2002). *The unkindest cut: The emotional maltreatment of children*. Nashville, TN: Red Clay & Vinegar.

Griggs, S. A. (1985). Counseling for individual learning styles. *Journal of Counseling & Development, 64*, 202–206. doi:10.1002/j.1556-6676.1985.tb01074.x

Griggs, S. A. (1991). *Learning styles counseling*. Ann Arbor, MI: Educational Resources Information Center for Counseling and Personnel Services.

Grimes, L. E., Haskins, N., & Paisley, P. O. (2013). So I went out there: A phenomenological study on the experiences of rural school counselor social justice advocates. *Professional School Counseling, 17*(1), 40–51. doi:10.5330/PSC.n.2013-17.40

Grosch, W. N., & Olsen, D. C. (1994). *When helping starts to hurt: A new look at burnout among psychotherapists.* New York, NY: Norton.

Gross, D. R., & Capuzzi, D. (2014) Defining youth at risk. In D. Capuzzi, & D. R. Gross (Eds.), *Youth at risk: A prevention resource for counselors, teachers, and parents* (6th ed.). Alexandria, VA: American Counseling Association.

Guerney, L. F. (1979). Play therapy with learning disabled children. *Journal of Clinical Child Psychiatry, 3*, 242–244. doi:10.1080/15374417909532929

Guerney, L. F. (1997). Filial therapy. In K. O'Conner, & M. L. Braverman (Eds.), *Play therapy theory and practice: A comparative presentation* (pp. 131–159). New York, NY: Wiley.

Guilford, J. P. (1982). Cognitive psychology's ambiguities: Some suggested remedies. *Psychological Review, 89*, 48–59. doi:10.1037/0033-295X.89.1.48

Gustavsson, N. S., & MacEachron, A. E. (1998). Violence and lesbian and gay youth. In L. M. Sloan, & N. S. Gustavsson (Eds.), *Violence and social injustice against lesbian, gay and bisexual people* (pp. 41–50). New York, NY: Harrington Park Press.

Gutstein, S. E. (2000). *Autism/Aspergers: Solving the relationship puzzle.* Arlington, TX: Future Horizons.

Guttmacher Institute. (2013). *State policies in brief: Minors access to contraceptive information.* Retrieved from http://www.guttmacher.org/statecenter/spibs/spib_MACS.pdf

Gysbers, N. (1988). Major trends in career development theory and practice: Implications for industrial education and guidance personnel. *Journal of Industrial Teacher Education, 25*, 5–14.

Gysbers, N. C. (2001). School guidance and counseling in the 21st century: Remember the past into the future. *Professional School Counseling, 5*, 96–105.

Gysbers, N. C. (2005). Comprehensive school guidance programs in the United States: A career profile. *International Journal for Educational and Vocational Guidance, 5*, 203–215. doi:10.1007/s10775-005-8800-7

Gysbers, N. C. (2013). Career-ready students: A goal of comprehensive school counseling programs. *Career Development Quarterly, 61*, 283–288. doi:10.1002/j.2161-0045.2013.00057.x

Gysbers, N. C., & Henderson, P. (2012). *Developing and managing your school guidance program* (5th ed.). Alexandria, VA: American Counseling Association.

Gysbers, N. C., & Moore, E. J. (1981). *Improving guidance programs.* Englewood Cliffs, NJ: Prentice Hall.

Gysbers, N. C., & Stanley, B. (2014). From position to program. *ASCA School Counselor, 51*(3), 22–27.

Gysbers, N. C., Stanley, J. B., Kosteck-Bunch, L., Magnuson, C. S., & Starr, M. F. (2011). *Missouri comprehensive guidance and counseling program: A manual for program development, implementation, evaluation and enhancement.* Warrensburg, MO: University of Central Missouri, Missouri Center for Career Education.

Haasl, B. (2000). *Bereavement support group program for children: Participant workbook* (2nd ed.). Philadelphia, PA: Accelerated Development.

Hagborg, W. (1993). Middle-school student satisfaction with group counseling: An initial study. *Journal for Specialists in Group Work, 18*, 80–85. doi:10.1080/01933929308413740

Hakanen, J. J. Bakker, A. B., & Schaufeli, W. B. (2006). Burnout and work engagement among teachers. *Journal of School Psychology, 43*, 495–513. doi:10.1016/j.jsp.2005.11.001

Haley, J. (1973). *Uncommon therapy: The psychiatric techniques of Milton H. Erickson, MD.* New York, NY: Norton.

Hall, A. S., & Lin, M. J. (1994). An integrative consultation framework: A practical tool for elementary school counselors. *Elementary School Guidance & Counseling, 29*, 16–27.

Hall, K. R., Rushing, J. L., & Khurshid, A. (2011). Using the solving problems together psychoeducational group counseling model as an intervention for negative peer pressure. *Journal for Specialists in Group Work, 36*, 97–110. doi:10.1080/01933922.2011.562344

Hall, R. E. (2002). Biracial sensitive practice: Expanding social services to an invisible population. *Journal of Human Behavior in the Social Environment, 5*, 29–44. doi:10.1300/J137v05n02_03

Halpin, A. W. (1966). *Organizational climate description questionnaire.* (Available from Dr. Andrew E. Hayes, Department of Educational Design and Management, UNC–Wilmington, 601 S. College Road, Wilmington, NC 28403-3297)

Halsey, P. A. (2005). Parent involvement in junior high schools: A failure to communicate. *American Secondary Education, 34*, 57–69.

Hambleton, R. (2013). *Setting performance standards on educational assessments and criteria for evaluating the process: Laboratory of Psychometric and Evaluative Research Report 377.* Amherst, MA: School of Education University of Massachusetts.

Hamilton, M. L., & Richardson, V. (1995). Effects of the culture in two schools on the process and outcomes of staff development. *Elementary School Journal, 95*, 367–385. doi:10.1086/461809

Hamlet, H. S., Gergar, P. G., & Schaefer, B. A. (2011). Students living with chronic illness: The school counselor's role. *Professional School Counseling, 14*, 202–210.

Hampton, F. M., Rak, C., & Mumford, D. A. (1997). Children's literature reflecting diverse family structures: Social and academic benefits for early reading programs. *ERS Spectrum, 15*(4), 10–15.

Hamre, B. K., & Pianta, R. C. (2005). Can instructional and emotional support in the first-grade classroom make a difference for children at risk of school failure? *Child Development, 76*, 949–967. doi:10.1111/j.1467-8624.2005.00889.x

Han, S. (2011). Probability of corporal punishment: Lack of resources and vulnerable students. *The Journal of Educational Research, 104*, 420–430. doi:10.1080/00220671.2010.500313

Hann-Morrison, D. (2011). The varied roles of school counselors in rural settings. *Georgia School Counselors Association Journal, 18*(1), 26–33.

Hardie, A. (2012). Lesbian teachers and students: Issues and dilemmas of being 'out' in primary school. *Sex Education, 12*, 273–282. doi:10.1080/14681811.2011.615595

Hargrove, L., Godin, D., & Dodd, B. (2008). *College outcomes comparison by AP and non-AP high school experiences.* Retrieved from http://research.collegeboard.org/sites/default/files/publications/2012/7/researchreport-2008-3-college-outcomes-ap-non-ap-high-school-experiences.pdf

Harrington, J. C., & Harrington, T. F. (2006). *Ability explorer.* St. Paul, MN: JIST Works.

Harris, H. L. (2002). School counselors' perceptions of biracial children: A pilot study. *Professional School Counseling, 6*, 120–129.

Harris, H. L. (2013). A national survey of school counselors' perceptions of multiracial students. *Professional School Counseling, 17*, 1–19. doi:10.5330/PSC.n.2013-17.1

Harris, H. L., & Durodoye, B. A. (2006). School counselor perceptions of multiracial students. *Research in the Schools, 13*, 13–24.

Harris, M. B., & Bliss, G. K. (1997). Coming out in a school setting: Former students' experiences and opinions about disclosure. In M. B. Harris (Ed.), *School experiences of gay and lesbian youth* (pp. 85–100). New York, NY: Harrington Park Press.

Harris, M. S. (2009). School reintegration and adolescents with cancer: The role of school psychologists. *Psychology in the Schools, 46*, 579–592.

Hart, P. J., & Jacobi, M. (1992). *From gatekeeper to advocate: Transforming the role of the school counselor.* New York, NY: College Entrance Examination Board.

Hartman, T., & Bowman, J. (1996). *Think fast, the ADD experience.* Grass Valley, CA: Underwood Books.

Hassel, B., Raack, L., Burkhardt, G., Chapko, M., & Blaser, S. (2000). *Making good choices: Districts take the lead.* Oak Brook, IL: North Central Regional Educational Laboratory.

Hatch, T. (2002). When improvement programs collide. *Phi Delta Kappan, 83*, 626–634.

Hatch, T. (2008). Professional challenges in school counseling: Organizational, institutional and political. *Journal of School Counseling, 6*(22). Retrieved from http://jsc.montana.edu/articles/v6n22.pdf

Hatch, T. (2014). *The use of data in school counseling: Hatching results for students, programs and the professions*. Thousand Oaks, CA: Corwin Press.

Hatch, T., & Bowers, J. (2002). The block to build on. *ASCA School Counselor, 39*(5), 13–17.

Haycock, K. (2002, June). *Dispelling the myth: A role for school counselors*. Paper presented at the annual meeting of The Education Trust on Transforming School Counseling, Chicago, IL.

Hayden, L., Poynton, T., & Sabella, R. (2008). School counselor's use of technology. *Journal of Technology and Counseling, 5*(1).

Hayes, S. H. (1997). Reactive attachment disorder: Recommendations for school counselors. *School Counselor, 44*, 353–361.

Hays, D. G., Arrendondo, P., Gladding, S., & Toporek, R. L. (2010). Integrating social justice in group work: The next decade. *Journal for Specialists in Group Work, 35*, 177–206. doi:10.1080/01933921003706022

Hays, D. G., & Erford, B. T. (Eds.). (2014). *Developing multicultural competence: A system's approach* (2nd ed.). Columbus, OH: Pearson Merrill.

Hazler, R. J. (1998). *Helping in the hallways: Advanced strategies for enhancing school relationships*. Thousand Oaks, CA: Corwin Press.

Health Insurance Portability and Accountability Act of 1996 (HIPAA), Public Law 104-191, Stat. 1936.

Hecht, J. B. (1998). Suicidality and psychological adjustment in a community sample of lesbian, gay, and bisexual youth. *Dissertation Abstracts International, 58*, 7-B. (UMI No. 9738659)

Heflin, L. J., & Alaimo, D. F. (2007). *Students with autism spectrum disorders: Effective instructional practices*. Upper Saddle River, NJ: Pearson, Merrill, Prentice Hall.

Heinrich, H., Gevensleben, H., Freisleder, F. J., Moll, G. H., & Rothenberger, A. (2004). Training of slow cortical potentials in attention-deficit/hyperactivity disorder: Evidence for positive behavioral and neurophysiological effects. *Biological Psychiatry, 55*, 772–775. doi:10.1016/j.biopsych.2003.11.013.

Helwig, A. A. (1998). Gender-role stereotyping: Testing theory with a longitudinal sample. *Sex Roles, 38*, 403–423. doi:10.1023/A:1018757821850

Hembree-Kigin, T. L., & McNeil, C. B. (1995). *Parent–child interaction therapy*. New York, NY: Plenum Press.

Hendricks, J. E., & McKean, J. B. (2003). *Crisis intervention: Contemporary issues for on-site interveners* (3rd ed.). Springfield, IL: Thomas.

Henington, C., & Skinner, C. H. (1998). Peer monitoring. In K. Toping & S. Ehly (Eds.), *Peer-assisted learning* (pp. 237–253). Mahwah, NJ: Erlbaum.

Herdt, G., & Boxer, A. (1996). *Children of horizons: How gay and lesbian teens are leading a new way out of the closet* (2nd ed.). New York, NY: Beacon Press.

Herlihy, B., & Corey, G. (2006). *Boundary issues in counseling. Multiple roles and responsibilities* (2nd ed.). Alexandria, VA: American Counseling Association.

Herlihy, B., & Corey, G. (2014). *ACA ethical standards casebook* (7th ed.). Alexandria, VA: American Counseling Association.

Herr, E. L. (2001). The impact of national policies, economics, and school reform on comprehensive guidance programs. *Professional School Counseling, 4*, 236–245.

Herr, E. L. (2002). School reform and perspectives on the role of school counselors: A century of proposals for change. *Professional School Counseling, 5*, 220–234.

Herr, E. L., Cramer, S. H., & Niles, S. G. (2004). *Career guidance and counseling through the lifespan* (5th ed.). New York, NY: HarperCollins.

Herr, K. (1997). Learning lessons from school: Homophobia, heterosexism, and the construction of failure. In M. B. Harris (Ed.), *School experiences of gay and lesbian youth* (pp. 51–64). New York, NY: Harrington Park Press.

Herren, C., In-Albon, T., & Schneider, S. (2013). Beliefs regarding child anxiety and parenting competence in parents of children with separation anxiety disorder. *Journal of Behavior Therapy and Experimental Psychiatry, 44*, 53–60. doi:10.1016/j.jbtep.2012.07.005

Herring, R. D. (1992). Biracial children: An increasing concern for elementary and middle school counselors. *Elementary School Guidance & Counseling, 27*, 123–130.

Hersey, P. (1984). *The situational leader.* Escondido, CA: Center for Leadership Studies.

Hersey, P., & Blanchard, K. (1969). Life-cycle theory of leadership. *Training and Development Journal, 23*, 26–34.

Hess, K., & Gong, B. (2014). *Ready for college and career? Achieving the common core standards and beyond through deeper, student-centered learning.* Quincy, MA: Nellie Mae Education Foundation.

Hess, R. T., & Robbins, P. (2012). *The data toolkit: Ten tools for supporting school improvement.* Thousand Oaks, CA: Corwin Press.

Hewitt, D. (2011). *So this is normal too?* (2nd ed.). Beltsville, MD: Redleaf Press.

Heyman, I., Fombonne, E., Simmons, H., Ford, T., Meltzer, H., & Goodman, R. (2004). Prevalence of obsessive-compulsive disorder in the British nationwide survey of child mental health. *International Review of Psychiatry, 15*(1/2), 178–185. doi:10.1192/bjp.179.4.324

Hickman, C. B. (1997).The devil and the one drop rule: Racial categories, African Americans, and the U.S. census. *Michigan Law Review, 95*, 1161–1266.

Hines, P. L. (2002). Transforming the rural school counselor. *Theory into Practice, 41*, 192–201. doi:10.1207/s15430421tip4103_8

Hines, P. L., & Fields, T. H. (2004). School counseling and academic achievement. In R. Pérusse & G. E. Goodnough (Eds.), *Leadership and advocacy in school counseling* (pp. 3–26). Belmont, CA: Brooks/Cole.

Hines, P. L., Lemons, R., & Crews, K. (2011) *Poised to lead: How school counselors can drive college and career readiness.* Retrieved from http://www.edtrust.org/sites/edtrust.org/files/publications/files/Poised_To_Lead_0.pdf

Hinton, D., & Warnke, B., & Wubbolding, R. (2011). Choosing success in the classroom by building student relationships. *International Journal of Choice Theory Reality Therapy, 31*(1), 90–96.

Hiraiwa, M. (2011). High-functioning autistic children: From a physician's perspective. *Journal of the Japan Medical Association, 140*, 589–592.

Hirschfeld, M. (1935). *Men and women: The world journey of a sexologist.* New York, NY: Putnam.

Hirschi, A., & Lage, D. (2007). The relation of secondary students' career choice readiness to a six-phase model of career decision making. *Journal of Career Development, 34*, 164–191. doi:10.1177/0894845307307473

Hixson, J., & Tinzmann, M. B. (1990). *What changes are generating new needs for professional development?* Chicago, IL: North Central Regional Educational Laboratory.

H. L. Etc., Appelant v. Scott M. Matheson, 101 S. Ct. 2727. (1982).

Hodges, E. E., & Perry, D. G. (1999). Personal and interpersonal antecedents and consequences of victimization by peers. *Journal of Personality & Social Psychology, 76*, 677–685. doi:10.1037/0022-3514.76.4.677

Hoff, K. E., Ervin, R. A., & Friman, P. C. (2005). Refining functional behavioral assessment: Analyzing the separate and combined effects of hypothesized controlling variables during ongoing classroom routines. *School Psychology Review, 34*, 45–57.

Hogan, K. (2014). *Recommendations for students with high functioning autism.* Retrieved from http://teacch.com/educational-approaches/recommendations-for-students-with-high-functioning-autism-kerry-hogan

Hogan, M. J. (2000). Diagnosis and treatment of teen drug use. *Medical Clinics of North America, 84*, 927–966. doi:10.1016/S0025-7125(05)70268-6

Hokayem, C., & Heggeness, M. L. (2014). *Living in near poverty in the United States: 1966-2012. Current population reports.* U.S. Census Bureau. Retrieved from http://www.census.gov/prod/2014pubs/p60-248.pdf

Holcomb-McCoy, C. (2004). Assessing the multicultural competence of school counselors: A checklist. *Professional School Counseling, 7*, 178–183.

Holcomb-McCoy, C., & Bryan, J. (2010). Advocacy and empowerment in parent consultation: Implications for theory and practice. *Journal of Counseling & Development, 88,* 259–268. doi:10.1002/j.1556-6678.2010.tb00021.x

Holcomb-McCoy, C.,& Chen-Hayes, S. (2015). Culturally competent school counselors: Affirming diversity by challenging oppression. In B. T. Erford (Ed.), *Transforming the school counseling profession* (4th ed., pp. 173–193). Columbus, OH: Pearson, Merrill.

Holland, J. L. (1985). *Making vocational choices: A theory of vocational personalities and work environments* (2nd ed.). Englewood Cliffs, NJ: Prentice Hall.

Holland, J. L. (1994). *Self-directed search*. Lutz, FL: Psychological Assessment Resources.

Holland, J. L., & Powell, A. B. (1994). *Self-Directed Search Career Explorer*. Odessa, FL: Psychological Assessment Resources.

Holland, J. L., Powell, A. B., & Fritzsche, B. A. (1997). *Self-Directed Search* (4th ed.). Odessa, FL: Psychological Assessment Resources.

Holler, R. A., & Zirkel, P. A. (2008). Section 504 and public schools: A national survey concerning "Section504-only" students. *NASSP Bulletin, 92,* 19–43. doi:10.1177/0192636508314106

Holloway, S. R., Wright, R., Ellis, M., & East, M. (2009). Place, scale and the racial claims made for multiracial children in the 1990 US census. *Ethnic and Racial Studies, 32,* 522–547. doi:10.1080/01419870802021120

Honos-Webb, L. (2010). *The gift of ADHD: How to transform your child's problems into strengths* (2nd ed.). Oakland, CA: New Harbinger.

Horn, S. S., & Nucci, L. (2006). Harassment of gay and lesbian youth and school violence in America: An analysis and directions for intervention. In C. Daiute (Ed.), *International perspectives on youth conflict and development* (pp. 139–155). New York, NY: Oxford University Press.

Hornby, G., & Lafaele, R. (2011). Barriers to parental involvement in education: An explanatory model. *Educational Review, 61,* 37–52. doi:10.1080/00131911.2010.488049

Horowitz, K., McKay, M., & Marshall, R. (2005). Community violence and urban families: Experiences, effects, and directions for intervention. *American Journal of Orthopsychiatry, 75,* 356–368. doi:10.1037/0002-9432.75.3.356

House, R. M. (2002, June). *MetLife national school counselor training initiative*. Paper presented at the annual meeting of The Education Trust on Transforming School Counseling, Chicago, IL.

House, R. M., & Hayes, R. (2002). School counselors: Becoming key players in school reform. *Professional School Counseling, 5,* 249–256.

House, R. M., & Martin, P. J. (1998). Advocating for better futures for all students: A new vision for school counselors. *Education, 119,* 284–291.

House, R. M., & Sears, S. (2002). Preparing school counselors to be leaders and advocates: A critical need in the new millennium. *Theory Into Practice, 41,* 154–162. doi:10.1207/s15430421tip4103_3

Hovland, J., Peterson, T., & Smaby, M. (1996). School counselors as conflict resolution consultants: Practicing what we teach. *The School Counselor, 44*(1), 71–79.

Hubbard, L., & Hands, C. M. (2011). *Including families and communities in urban education*. Charlotte, NC: Information Age.

Huberty, T. J. (1990). Reducing academic related anxiety. *Special Services in the Schools, 5,* 261–276. doi:10.1300/J008v05n03_14

Huefner, D. S. (2006). *Getting comfortable with special education law: A framework for working with children with disabilities* (2nd ed.). Norwood, MA: Christopher-Gordon.

Hughes, D. (2010). Reasons for misbehavior. In A. Becker-Weidman, & D. Shell (Eds.), *Attachment parenting: Developing connections and healing children* (pp. 67–81). Lanham, MD: Jason Aronson.

Hughes, K. L., & Karp, M. M. (2004). *School-based career development: A synthesis of the literature*. New York, NY: Columbia University, Institute on Education and the Economy.

Hughey, K. J., Lapan, R. T., & Gysbers, N. C. (1993). Evaluation of a high school guidance-language arts career unit: A qualitative approach. *The School Counselor, 41,* 96–101.

Humes, K. R., Jones, N. A., & Ramirez, R. R. (2011). *Overview of race and Hispanic origin: 2010.* Washington, DC: U.S. Census Bureau.

Hurst, D., & Eggert, J. (2006, June). *The successful first year school counselor.* Presentation at the American School Counselor Association Conference, Chicago, IL.

Huss, S. N. (1997). The effect of peer bereavement support groups on the self-esteem, depression, and problem behavior of parentally bereaved children. (Doctoral dissertation, University of Toledo, OH). *Dissertation Abstracts International, 58*/04 (UMI No. 9729145).

Hyde, T. M., Aaronson, B. A., Randolph, C., Rickler, K. C., & Weinberger, D. R. (1992). Relationship of birth weight to the phenotypic expression of Gilles de la Tourette's syndrome in monozygotic twins. *Neurology, 42,* 652–658. doi:10.1212/WNL.42.3.652

Hyson, M. (2004). *The emotional development of young children: Building an emotion-centered curriculum.* New York, NY: Teachers College Press.

Hyun, M., Chung, H., & Lee, Y. (2005). The effect of cognitive-behavioral group therapy on the self-esteem, depression, and self-efficacy of runaway adolescents in a shelter in South Korea. *Applied Nursing Research, 18,* 160–166. doi:10.1016/j.apnr.2004.07.006

Imai, C., & Berry, M. (2001). *Follow your true colors to the work you love* [Instructor's guide]. Riverside, CA: True Colors.

Imber, M., & Van Geel, T. (2009). *Education law* (4th ed.). Mahway, NJ: Erlbaum.

In-Albon, T., Meyer, A. H., & Schneider, S. (2013). Separation anxiety avoidance inventory-child and parent version: Psychometric properties and clinical utility in a clinical and school sample. *Child Psychiatry and Human Development, 44,* 689–697. doi:10.1007/s10578-013-0364-z

Indiana Department of Education. (1999). *Standards, assessment, school improvement, and accountability.* Retrieved from http://www.in.gov/edroundtable/2394.htm

Individuals with Disabilities Education Act of 1990, 20 U.S.C. § 1400 et seq. (1990) (amended 1991)

Individuals with Disabilities Education Improvement Act of 2004, 20 U.S.C. § 1400 et seq. (2004) (reauthorization of IDEA 1990)

Individuals with Disabilities Education Act, Part B Child Count, 2010, Students ages 6-21. Retrieved from https://explore.data.gov/Education/2012-IDEA-Part-B-Child-Count-and-Educational-Envir/5t72-4535

Infoplease. (2014). *A timeline of recent worldwide school and mass shootings.* Retrieved from http://www.infoplease.com/ipa/A0777958.html

International OCD Foundation. (2014). *What you need to know about obsessive compulsive disorder.* Retrieved from http://www.ocfoundation.org/uploadedFiles/WhatYouNeed_09.pdf

Ioannidis, J. P. A., Cappelleri, J. C., & Lau, J. (1998). Issues in comparisons between meta-analyses and large trials. *JAMA, 279,* 1089–1093. doi:10.1001/jama.279.14.1089

Ippolito, J. (2012). Bringing marginalized parents and caregivers into their children's schooling. What works? *Research into Practice, 43,* 1–4.

Israel, A. C., & Ivanova, M. Y. (2002). Global and dimensional self-esteem in preadolescent and early adolescent children who are overweight: Age and gender differences. *International Journal of Eating Disorders, 31,* 424–429. doi:10.1002/eat.10048

Iwata, B., Dorsey, M. F., Slifer, K. J., Bauman, K. E., & Richman, G. S. (1994). Toward a functional analysis of self-injury. *Journal of Applied Behavior Analysis, 27,* 197–209. doi:10.1901/jaba.1994.27-197

Iwata, B. A., Pace, G. M., Dorsey, M. F., Zarcone, J. R., Vollmer, T. R., & Smith, R. G. (1994). The functions of self-injurious behavior: An experimental-epidemiological analysis. *Journal of Applied Behavior Analysis, 27,* 215–240. doi:10.1901/jaba.1994.27-215

Jackson, M., & Grant, D. (2004). Equity, access, and career development: Contextual conflicts. In R. Pérusse, & G. E. Goodnough (Eds.), *Leadership and advocacy in school counseling* (pp. 125–153). Pacific Grove, CA: Brooks/Cole.

Jackson-Cherry, L., & Erford, B. T. (Eds.). (2014). *Crisis assessment, intervention, and prevention* (2nd ed.). Columbus, OH: Pearson Merrill.

Jacobs, E. E., Harvill, R. L., & Masson, R. L. (2012). *Group counseling: Strategies and skills* (7th ed.). Pacific Grove, CA: Brooks/Cole.

Jacobsen, L. A., Mather, M., & Dupuis, G. (2012). *Household change in the United States.* Retrieved from http://www.prb.org/Publications/Reports/2012/us-household-change.aspx

James, R. K., & Gilliland, B. E. (2012). *Crisis intervention strategies* (7th ed.). Belmont, CA: Brooks/Cole.

Jang, J., Matson, J. L., Cervantes, P. E., & Konst, M. J. (2014). The relationship between ethnicity and age of first concern in toddlers with autism spectrum disorder. *Research in Autism Spectrum Disorders, 8,* 925–932. doi:10.1016/j.rasd.2014.04.003

Janson, G. R. (2014). Emotional maltreatment by teachers: The hidden curriculum of bullying in the classroom. In J. E. Barlett (Ed.), *School bullying: Predictive factors, coping strategies and effects on mental health.* New York, NY: Nova Science.

Janson, G. R., Carney, J. S., Hazler, R. J., & Oh, I. (2009). Bystanders' reactions to witnessing repetitive abuse experiences. *Journal of Counseling & Development, 87,* 319–326. doi:10.1002/j.1556-6678.2009.tb00113.x

Janson, G. R., & Hazler, R. J. (2004). Trauma reactions of bystanders and victims to repetitive abuse experiences. *Violence and Victims, 19,* 239–255. doi:10.1891/vivi.19.2.239.64102

Janson, G. R., & King, M. A. (2006). Emotional security in the classroom: What works for children. *Journal of Family & Consumer Sciences, 98*(2), 70–74.

Janson, G. R., & King, M. (2010). Creating emotionally healthy learning environments: Eliminating emotional maltreatment in classrooms. *Journal for the Association for Childhood Education International, 23,* 1–7.

JIST. (2014). *New guide for occupational exploration.* Retrieved from http://jist.emcp.com/new-guide-for-occupational-exploration-hardcover.html

Johansson, C. B. (1986). *Career Assessment Inventory.* Minneapolis, MN: NCS.

Johnson, C. D., & Johnson, S. K. (2001). *Results-based student support programs: Leadership academy workbook.* San Juan Capistrano, CA: Professional Update.

Johnson, C. D., & Johnson, S. K. (2002). *Building stronger school counseling programs: Bringing futuristic approaches into the present.* Greensboro, NC: CAPS Press.

Johnson, D. W., & Johnson, R. T. (1991). *Teaching students to be peacemakers.* Edina, MN: Interaction Book.

Johnson, J., Lambright, P., Sparks, E., Stiff, L., & Taft, M. E. (2006, June). *Top thirteen ways to prepare your school or district to implement the ASCA national model.* Presentation at the American School Counselor Association Conference, Chicago, IL.

Johnson, J., Rochkind, J., Ott, A., DuPont, S., & Hess, J. (2011). *Can I get a little advice here? How an overstretched high school guidance system is undermining students' college aspirations.* Retrieved from http://www.publicagenda.org/media/can-i-get-a-little-advice-here

Johnson, J. H. (1997). *Data-driven school improvement* (ERIC digest No. ED401595). Retrieved from http://eric.ed.gov/

Johnson, L. (1995). Filial therapy: A bridge between individual child therapy and family therapy. *Journal of Family Psychotherapy, 6,* 55–70. doi:10.1300/j085V06N03_03

Johnson, W. L., & Johnson, A. M. (1992a). A study on the Kettering School Climate Scale. *Education, 112,* 635–642.

Johnson, W. L., & Johnson, A. M. (1992b). Validity of the Quality of School Life Scale: A primary and second order factor analysis. *Educational & Psychological Measurement, 53,* 145–153. doi:10.1177/0013164493053001016

Johnson, W. L., & Johnson, A. M. (1995). A Rasch analysis of factors derived from the Charles F. Kettering Ltd. School Climate Profile. *Educational & Psychological Measurement, 55,* 456–467. doi:10.1177/0013164495055003013

Johnson, W. L., Snyder, K. J., Anderson, R. H., & Johnson, A. M. (1997). Assessing school work culture. *Research in the Schools, 4,* 35–43.

Johnson-Schroetlin, C. A. (2000). Childhood grief: Are bereavement support groups beneficial for latency age children?. *Dissertation Abstracts International, 61,* 2764.

Joint Committee on Testing Practices. (2004). *Code of fair testing practices in education.* Retrieved from http://www.apa.org/science/fairtestcode.html

Jones, N. A., & Bullock, J. (2012). *The two or more races population: 2010.* Retrieved from http://www.census.gov/prod/cen2010/briefs/c2010br-13.pdf

Jongsma, A., Peterson, M. L., & McInnis, W. P. (2006). *The child and adolescent psychotherapy treatment planner* (4th ed.). New York, NY: Wiley

Jonkman, C. S., Verlinden, E., Bolle, E. A., Boer, F., & Lindauer, R. J. L. (2013). Traumatic stress symptomatology after child maltreatment and single traumatic events: Different profiles. *Journal of Traumatic Stress, 26,* 225–323. doi:10.1002/jts.21792

Jordan, K. M., Vaughan, J. S., & Woodworth, K. J. (1997). I will survive: Lesbian, gay, and bisexual youths' experience of high school. In M. B. Harris (Ed.), *School experiences of gay and lesbian youth* (pp. 17–34). New York, NY: Harrington Park Press.

Joughin, C. (2006). *Cognitive behaviour therapy can be effective in managing behavioural problems and conduct disorder in pre-adolescence. What works for children group: Evidence nugget.* Retrieved from http://www.whatworksforchildren.org.uk/docs/Nuggets/pdfs/CBT%20nugget.pdf

Jung, J., & Forbes, G. (2012). Body dissatisfaction and characteristics of disordered eating among black and white early adolescent girls and boys. *Journal of Early Adolescence, 33,* 737–764. doi:10.1177/0272431612468504

Just the Facts Coalition. (2000). *Just the facts about sexual orientation & youth: A primer for principals, educators & school personnel.* Washington, DC: Author.

Juvonen, J., & Graham, S. (2014). Bullying in schools: The power of bullies and the plight of victims. *Annual Review of Psychology, 65*(1), 159–185. doi:10.1146/annurev-psych-010213-115030

Kaduson, H., & Schaefer, C. (2010). *101 favorite play therapy techniques* (Vol. 3). Northvale, NJ: Jason Aronson.

Kaffenberger, C. (2006a). Caring for students with chronic illness. *Principal, 85,* 34–37.

Kaffenberger, C. (2006b). School reentry for students with chronic illness: A role for professional school counselors. *Professional School Counseling, 9,* 223–230.

Kagan, S. (1991). *United we stand, collaboration for child care and early education services.* New York, NY: Teachers College Press.

Kahill, S. (1988). Symptoms of professional burnout: A review of the empirical evidence. *Canadian Psychology, 29,* 284–297. doi:10.1037/h0079772

Kairys, S., Johnson, C., & Committee on Child Abuse and Neglect. (2002). The psychological maltreatment of children (Tech. Rep.). *Pediatrics, 109*(4), e68.

Kalil, C., & Lowery, D. (1999). *Follow your true colors to the work you love: The workbook: A journey in self-discovery & career decision-making.* Riverside, CA: True Colors.

Kallestad, J. H. (2010). Changes in school climate in a long-term perspective. *Scandinavian Journal of Educational Research, 54,* 1–14. doi:10.1080/00313830903488429

Kalodner, C. R. (2011). Cognitive-behavioral theories. In D. Capuzzi & Doug Gross (Eds.), *Counseling and psychotherapy: Theories and interventions* (pp. 193–213). Alexandria, VA: American Counseling Association.

Kamphaus, R. W., & Reynolds, C. R. (2007). *BASC-2 behavior and emotional screening system.* San Antonio, TX: Pearson.

Kampwirth, T. J. (2011). *Collaborative consultation in the schools: Effective practices for students with learning and behavior problems* (4th ed.). Upper Saddle River, NJ: Pearson Education.

Kandor, J. R., & Bobby, C. L. (1992). Introduction to a special feature. *Journal of Counseling & Development, 70,* 666. doi:10.1002/j.1556-6676.1992.tb02142.x

Kardiner, A. (1941). *The traumatic neuroses of war.* New York, NY: Hoeber.

Kardiner, A., & Spiegel, H. (1947). *War, stress and neurotic illness.* New York, NY: Hoeber.

Kärnä, K. A., Voeten, M., Little, T. D., Poskiparta, E., Kaljonen, A., & Salmivalli, C. (2011). A large-scale evaluation of the KiVa antibullying program: Grades 4-6. *Child Development, 82*(1), 311–330. doi:10.1111/j.1467-8624.2010.01557.x

Kassinove, H., & Tafrate, R. C. (2002). *Anger management: The complete treatment guide for practitioners.* Atascadero, CA: Impact

Katz, J. (1976). *Gay American history.* New York, NY: Thomas Y. Crowell Company.

Kaufman, A. S., & Kaufman, N. L. (2004a). *Kaufman Assessment Battery for Children* (2nd ed.). Circle Pines, MN: American Guidance Services.

Kaufman, A. S., & Kaufman, N. L. (2004b). *Kaufman Brief Intelligence Test* (2nd ed.). Circle Pines, MN: American Guidance Services.

Kazdin, A. (1993). Psychotherapy for children and adolescents: Current progress and future research directions. *American Psychologist, 48,* 644–657. doi:10.1037/0003-066X.48.6.644

Kearney, C. A., LaSota, M. T., Amie, L-M, & Vecchio, J. (2007). Parent training in the treatment of school refusal behavior. In J. M. Briemeister, & C. E. Schaefer (Eds.), *Handbook of parent training: Helping parents prevent and solve problems* (3rd ed., pp. 164–202). New York, NY: Wiley.

Keat, D. B. (1974). *Fundamentals of child counseling.* Boston, MA: Houghton Mifflin.

Kehle, T. J., Bray, M. A., Theodore, L. A., Jenson, W. R., & Clark, E. (2000). A multi-component intervention designed to reduce disruptive classroom behavior. *Psychology in the Schools, 37,* 475–481. doi:10.1002/1520-6807(200009)37:5<475::AID-PITS7>3.0.CO;2-P

Kellough, R. D., & Roberts, P. L. (2010). *A resource guide for elementary school teaching* (7th ed.). Upper Saddle River, NJ: Pearson Merrill.

Kelley, M. L. (1990). *School–home notes: Promoting children's classroom success.* New York, NY: Guilford Press.

Kelley, M. L., & Jurbergs, N. (2009). Daily report cards: Home-based consequences for classroom behavior. In A. Akin-Little, S. G. Little, M. A. Bray, & T. J. Kehle (Eds.), *Behavioral interventions in schools: Evidence-based positive strategies* (pp. 221–230). Washington, DC: American Psychological Association.

Kendall, P. C. (2011). *Child and adolescent therapy: Cognitive-behavioral procedures* (4th ed.). New York, NY: Guilford Press.

Kern, L., & Clemens, N. H. (2007). Antecedent strategies to promote appropriate classroom behavior. *Psychology in the Schools, 44*(1), 65–75. doi:10.1002/pits.20206

Kern, L., Dunlap, G., Clarke, S., & Childs, K. E. (1994). Student-assisted functional assessment interview. *Diagnostique, 19,* 29–39. doi:10.1177/073724779401900203

Kerwin, K., Ponterotto, J. G., Jackson, B. L., & Harris, A. (1993). Racial identity in biracial children: A qualitative investigation. *Journal of Counseling Psychology, 40,* 221–231. doi:10.1037/0022-0167.40.2.221

Kiersey, D. (1998). *Please understand me II: Temperament, character, intelligence.* Del Mar, CA: Prometheus Nemesis.

Kiewra, K. A. (2002). How classroom teachers can help students learn and teach them how to learn. *Theory Into Practice, 41,* 71–80. doi:10.1207/s15430421tip4102_3

Kim, H. & Stoner, M. (2008). Burnout and turnover intention among social workers: Effects of role stress, job autonomy and social support. *Administration in Social Work, 32*(3), 5–25. doi:10.1080/03643100801922357

King, M. (2004). Guidance with boys in early childhood classrooms. In D. Gartrell (Ed.), *The power of guidance: Teaching social-emotional skills in early childhood classrooms* (pp. 106–124). Clifton Park, NY: Thomson/Delmar Learning.

King, M., & Janson, G. R. (2009). First do no harm: Emotional maltreatment in the classroom. *Early Childhood Education Journal, 37,* 1–4. doi:10.1007/s10643-009-0330-3

King, M., & Janson, G. R. (2011, September/October). Beware emotional maltreatment. *Principal Magazine,* 18–21.

King, N., Madsen, E. R., Braverman, M., Paterson, C., & Yancey A. K. (2008). Career decision-making: Perspectives of low-income urban youth. *Spaces for Difference: An Interdisciplinary Journal, 1*, 21–41.

Kirchner, J. E., Yoder, M. C., Kramer, T. L., Lindsey, M. S., & Thrush, C. R. (2000). Development of an educational program to increase school personnel's awareness about child and adolescent depression. *Education, 121*, 235–246.

Kirk, S. A., Gallagher, J. J., & Coleman, M. R.. (2012). *Educating exceptional children* (14th ed.). Stamford, CT: Cengage Learning.

Kizner, L. R., & Kizner, S. R. (1999). Small group counseling with adopted children. *Professional School Counseling, 2*, 226–229.

Klem, A. M., & Connell, J. P. (2004). Relationships matter: Linking teacher support to student engagement and achievement. *Journal of School Health, 74*, 262–273. doi:10.1111/j.1746-1561.2004.tb08283.x

Klin, A., Pauls, D., Schultz, R., & Volkmar, F. (2005). Three diagnostic approaches to Asperger syndrome: Implications for research. *Journal of Autism & Developmental Disorders, 335*, 221–234. doi:10.1007/s10803-004-2001-y

Kluck, A. S. (2010). Family influence on disordered eating: The role of body image dissatisfaction. *Body Image, 7*(1), 8–14. doi:10.1016/j.bodyim.2009.09.009

Knaus, W. (1974). *Rational–emotive education: A manual for elementary teachers*. New York, NY: Institute for Rational Living.

Knoff, H. (Ed.). (2003). *The assessment of child and adolescent personality*. New York, NY: Guilford Press.

Knotek, S. E. (2003). Making sense of jargon during consultation: Understanding consultees' social language to effect change in student study teams. *Journal of Educational and Psychological Consultation, 14*, 181–207. doi:10.1207/s1532768xjepc1402_5

Kohn, A. (1993). Choices for children: Why and how to let students decide. *Phi Delta Kappan, 75*(1), 8–20.

Kohn, A. (2006). *Beyond discipline: From compliance to community*. Alexandria, VA: Association for Supervision and Curriculum Development.

Kosciw, J. G., Greytak, E. A., & Diaz, E. M. (2009). Who, what, where, when, and why: Demographic and ecological factors contributing to hostile school climate for lesbian, gay, bisexual, and transgender youth. *Journal of Youth and Adolescence, 38*, 976–988. doi:10.1007/s10964-009-9412-1

Kossowsky, J., Wilhelm, F. H., Roth, W. T., & Schneider, S. (2012). Separation anxiety disorder in children: Disorder-specific responses to experimental separation from the mother. *Journal of Child Psychology and Psychiatry, and Allied Disciplines, 53*, 178–87. doi:10.1111/j.1469-7610.2011.02465.x

Kottler, J. (2010). *On being a therapist* (4th ed.). San Francisco, CA: Jossey-Bass.

Kottler, J. A., & Kottler, E. (2007). *Counseling skills for teachers* (2nd ed.). Thousand Oaks, CA: Corwin Press.

Kottman, T. (2003). *Partners in play: An Adlerian approach to play therapy* (2nd ed.). Alexandria, VA: American Counseling Association.

Kottman, T., & Johnson, V. (1993). Adlerian play therapy: A tool for school counselors. *Elementary School Guidance & Counseling, 28*, 42–51.

Kouzes, J. M., & Posner, B. Z. (1995). *The leadership challenge*. San Francisco, CA: Jossey-Bass.

Kouzes, J. M., & Posner, B. Z. (2001). *Leadership practices inventory facilitator's guide*. San Diego, CA: Jossey-Bass/Pfeiffer.

Kovacs, M. (2010). *The Children's Depression Inventory-2*. San Antonio, TX: Pearson.

Kowalski, R. M., Giumetti, G. W., Schroeder, A. N., & Lattanner, M. R. (2014). Bullying in the digital age: A critical review and meta-analysis of cyberbullying research among youth. *Psychological Bulletin, 140*, 1073–1137. doi:10.1037/a0035618

Krause, W. W. (1941). Race crossing in Hawaii. *Journal of Heredity, 32*, 371–378.

Krug, D. A., Arick, J. R., & Almond, P. (1980). Behavioral checklist for identifying severely handicapped individuals with high levels of autistic behavior. *Journal of Child Psychology & Psychiatry & Allied Disciplines, 21*, 221–229. doi:10.1111/j.1469-7610.1980.tb01797.x

Krumboltz, J. D., & Worthington, R. (1999). The school-to-work transition from a learning theory perspective. *The Career Development Quarterly, 47,* 312–325. doi:10.1002/j.2161-0045.1999.tb00740.x

Kubler-Ross, E. (1969). *On death and dying.* New York, NY: MacMillan.

Kuder. (2014). *Career assessment, planning, and development services.* Retrieved from http://www.kuder.com

Kuder, Inc. (2012). *Kuder Career Interests Assessment* (KCIA). Adel, IA: Author.

Kuranz, M. (2002a). Cultivating student potential. *Professional School Counseling, 5,* 172–179.

Kuranz, M. (2002b, June). *The new ASCA national model for school counseling programs.* Presentation at the Education Trust 2002 Summer Academy, Chicago, IL.

Kush, K., & Cochran, L. (1993). Enhancing a sense of agency through career planning. *Journal of Counseling Psychology, 40,* 434–451. doi:10.1037/0022-0167.40.4.434

Ladner, J. (1984). Providing a healthy environment for interracial children. *Interracial Books for Children Bulletin, 15,* 7–8.

LaFountain, R. M., Garner, N. E., & Eliason, G. T. (1996). Solution-focused counseling groups: A key for school counselors. *The School Counselor, 43,* 256–267.

Lake, J., & Billingsley, B. (2000). An analysis of factors that contribute to parent–school conflict in special education. *Remedial and Special Education, 21,* 240–252. doi:10.1177/074193250002100407

Lake, P. (2005, September–October). Recognizing reactive attachment disorder. *Behavioral Health Management, 25*(5), 41–44.

Lalor, A. R., & Madaus, J. W. (2013). Helping students with learning disabilities search for colleges: Tips for professionals. *Insights on Learning Disabilities, 10*(1), 53–72.

Lambert, M. J. (1986). Some implications for psychotherapy research for eclectic practice. *International Journal of Eclectic Psychotherapy, 5,* 16–46.

Lambert, M. J. (1991). Introduction to psychotherapy research. In L. E. Beutler & M. Crago (Eds.), *Psychotherapy research: An international review of programmatic studies* (p. 123). Washington, DC: American Psychological Association.

Lambert, M. J., & Barley, D. E. (2001). Research summary on the therapeutic relationship and psychotherapy outcome. *Psychotherapy: Theory, Research, Practice, Training, 38,* 357–361. doi:10.1037/0033-3204.38.4.357

Lambert, M. J., & Bergin, A. E. (1983). Therapist characteristics and their contribution to psychotherapy outcome. In C. E. Walker (Ed.), *The handbook of clinical psychology: Theory, research and practice* (pp. 205–241). Homewood, IL: Dow Jones-Irwin.

Lambie, G., & Milsom, A. (2010). A narrative approach to supporting students with learning disabilities. *Journal of Counseling & Development, 88,* 196–203. doi:10.1002/j.1556-6678.2010.tb00009.x

Lancioni, G. E., Singh, N. N., O'Reilly, M. F., Sigafoos, J., & Didden, R. (2012). Function of challenging behaviors. In J. L. Matson (Ed.), *Functional assessment for challenging behaviors* (pp. 45–64). New York, NY: Springer.

Landreth, G. L. (1993). Child-centered play therapy. *Elementary School Guidance and Counseling, 28,* 17–29.

Lane, K. L., Gresham, F. M., & O'Shaughnessy, T. E. (2002). *Interventions for children with or at risk for emotional and behavioral disorders.* Boston, MA: Allyn & Bacon.

Lantz, J. F., Nelson, J. M., & Loftin, R. L. (2004, November–December). Guiding children with autism in play: Applying the integrated play group model in school setting. *Teaching Exceptional Children,* 8–14. doi:10.1177/004005990403700201

Lantzman, N., Viljoen, J., Scalora, M., & Ullman, D. (2011). Sexual offending in adolescence: A comparison of sibling offenders and nonsibling offender across domains of risk and treatment need. *Journal of Child Sexual Abuse, 20,* 245–263. doi:10.1080/10538712.2011.571233

Lapan, R. T. (2001). Results-based comprehensive guidance and counseling programs: A framework for planning and evaluation. *Professional School Counseling, 4,* 289–299.

Lapan, R., Gysbers, N., Cook, A., Bragg, S., & Robbins, J. (2006, June). *Improving school counseling programs and school counselor training*. Presentation at the American School Counselor Association Conference, Chicago, IL.

Lapan, R. T., Gysbers N. C., & Kayson, M. (2006). *How implementing all Missouri guidance programs improves academic achievement for all Missouri students*. Jefferson City, MO: Missouri Department of Elementary and Secondary Education.

Lapan, R. T., Gysbers, N. C., & Petroski, G. F. (2003). Helping seventh graders be safe and successful: A statewide study of the impact of comprehensive guidance and counseling programs. *Professional School Counseling, 6*, 186–197.

Lapan, R. T., Gysbers, N. C., & Sun, Y. (1997). The impact of more fully implemented guidance programs on the school experiences of high school students: A statewide evaluation study. *Journal of Counseling & Development, 75*, 292–302. doi:10.1002/j.1556-6676.1997.tb02344.x

Lapan, R. T., Harrington, K., Brown, J., & Manley, R. (2009, July). *Professional school counseling makes a difference in Chicago*. Presentation at the American School Counselor Association National Conference, Dallas, TX.

Lareau, A., & Horvat, E. N. (1999) Moments of social inclusion and exclusion: Race, class, and cultural capita in family-school relationships. *Sociology of Education, 72*, 37–53. doi:10.2307/2673185

Lau, B. W. K. (2002). Stress in children: Can nurses help? *Pediatric Nursing, 28*, 13–19. doi:35400010030667.0010

Laurent, A. C., & Rubin, E. (2004). Challenges in emotional regulation in Asperger syndrome and high functioning autism. *Topics in Language Disorders, 24*, 286–297.

Lavelle, T. A., Weinstein, M. C., Newhouse, J. P., Kuhithau, K. A., & Prosser, L. A. (2014). Economic burden of childhood autism spectrum disorders. *Pediatrics, 133*, e520-529. doi:10.1542/peds.2013-0763

Lavoritano, J. E., & Segal, P. B. (1992). Evaluating the efficacy of short-term counseling on adolescents in a school setting. *Adolescence, 27*(107), 535–543. doi:35400003057628.0040

Lawlis, F. (2005). *The ADD answer*. New York, NY: A Plume Book.

Layte, R., & McCrory, C. (2013). Paediatric chronic illness and educational failure: The role of emotional and behavioural problems. *Social Psychiatry and Psychiatric Epidemiology, 48*, 1307–1316. doi:10.1007/s00127-012-0609-3

Lazarus, R. S., & Folkman, S. (1984). *Stress, appraisal and coping*. New York, NY: Springer.

Lee, J., & Bean, D. F. (2004). American's changing color lines: Immigration, race/ethnicity, and multiracial identification. *Annual Review of Sociology, 30*, 221–242. doi:10.1146/annurev.soc.30.012703.110519

Lee, M., & Miltenberger, R. G. (1996). School refusal behavior: Classification, assessment, and treatment issues. *Education and Treatment of Children, 19*, 474–483.

Lee, R. S. (1993). Effects of classroom guidance on student achievement. *Elementary School Guidance & Counseling, 27*, 163–171.

Lee, R. T., & Ashforth, B. E. (1996). A meta-analytic examination of the correlates of the three dimensions of burnout. *Journal of Applied Psychology, 81*, 123–133. doi:10.1037/0021-9010.81.2.123

Lee, S. M. (2005). *New marriages, new families: U.S. racial and Hispanic intermarriage*. Population Bulletin, 60. Washington, DC: Population Reference Bureau.

Lee, V. V. (2004). Violence prevention and conflict resolution education in the schools. In R. Pérusse & G. E. Goodnough (Eds.), *Leadership and advocacy in school counseling* (pp. 222–261). Pacific Grove, CA: Brooks/Cole.

Lee, V. V., & Goodnough, G. E. (2015). Systemic, data-driven school counseling practice and programming for equity. In B. T. Erford (Ed.), *Transforming the school counseling profession* (4th ed., pp. 66–91). Upper Saddle River, NJ: Pearson Merrill.

Lehmann, L. (2001a). *Mourning child grief support group curriculum: Early childhood edition: Kindergarten–grade 2*. New York, NY: Brunner-Routledge.

Lehmann, L. (2001b). *Mourning child grief support group curriculum: Middle childhood edition: Grades 3–6*. New York, NY: Brunner-Routledge.

Leichtentritt, J., & Shechtman, Z. (2010). Children with and without learning disabilities: A comparison of processes and outcomes following group counseling. *Journal of Learning Disabilities, 43*, 169–179. doi:10.1177/0022219409345008.

Leithwood, K. (2002). Organizational conditions to support teaching and learning. In W. D. Hawley & D. L. Rollie (Eds.), *The keys to effective schools: Educational reforms as continuous improvement* (pp. 97–110). Thousand Oaks, CA: Corwin Press.

Lemberger, M. E., & Clemens, E. V. (2012). Connectedness and self-regulation as constructs of the student success skills program in inner-city African American elementary school students. *Journal of Counseling & Development, 90*, 450-458. doi:10.1002/j.1556-6676.2012.00056.x

Leuwerke, W. C., Walker, J., & Shi, Q. (2009). Informing principals: The impact of different types of information on principals' perceptions of professional school counselors. *Professional School Counseling, 12*, 263–271. doi:10.5330/PSC.n.2010-12.263

LeVay, S. (1991). A difference in hypothalamic structure between heterosexual and homosexual men. *Science, 253*, 1034–1037. doi:10.1126/science.1887219

LeVay, S. (1999). *Queer science*. New York, NY: McGraw-Hill.

LeVay, S., & Valente, S. M. (2006). *Human sexuality* (2nd ed.). Sunderland, MA: Sinauer Associates.

Levenson, G. (2006). *The educational benefits of origami*. Retrieved from http://home.earthlink.net/~robertcubie/origami/edu.html

Levine, M. P., & Smolak, L. (2009). Primary prevention of body image disturbances and disordered eating in childhood and early adolescence. In J. K. Thompson, & L. Smolak (Eds.), *Body image, eating disorders, and obesity in youth: Assessment, prevention, and treatment* (2nd ed., pp. 237–260). Washington, DC: American Psychological Association.

Lewis, M. W., & Lewis, A. C. (1996). Peer helping programs: Helper role, supervisor training, and suicidal behavior. *Journal of Counseling & Development, 74*, 307–313. doi:10.1002/j.1556-6676.1996.tb01871.x

Lewis, T. (2007). *Environmental Inventory*. Retrieved from http://www.pbis.org/resource/192/classroom-checklists-effective-classroom-plan-environmental-inventory-checklist

Lewis, T. J., Scott, T. M., & Sugai, G. (1994). The problem behavior questionnaire: A teacher-based instrument to develop functional hypotheses of problem behavior in general education classrooms. *Diagnostique, 19*, 103–115. doi:10.1177/073724779401900207

Levy, T. M., & Orlans, M. (1998). *Attachment, trauma, and healing: Understanding and treating attachment disorder in children and families*. Washington, DC: Child Welfare League of America.

Li, Q. (2007). New bottle but old wine: A research of cyberbullying in schools. *Computers in Human Behavior, 23*, 1777–1791. doi:10.1016/j.chb.2005.10.005

Lieberman, R., & Poland, S. (2006). Self-mutilation. In G. G. Bear, & K. M. Minke (Eds.), *Children's needs III: Development, prevention, and intervention* (pp. 965–976). Bethesda, MD: National Association of School Psychologists

Liechty, J. (2010). Body image distortion and three types of weight loss behaviors among nonoverweight girls in the United States. *Journal of Adolescent Health, 47*, 176–182. doi:10.1016/j.jadohealth.2010.01.004

Likert, R. & Likert, J. G. (1972). *The Likert profile of a school*. Ann Arbor, MI: Likert Associates.

Linde, L. (2015). Ethical, legal, and professional issues in school counseling. In B. T. Erford (Ed.), *Transforming the school counseling profession* (4th ed., pp. 146–172). Columbus, OH: Pearson Merrill.

Lindemann, E. (1944). Symptomatology and management of acute grief. *American Journal of Psychiatry, 101*, 141–148.

Lindemann, E. (1956). The meaning of crisis in individual and family. *Teachers College Record, 57*, 310.

Lindsay, P. (1998). Conflict resolution and peer mediation in public schools: What works? *Mediation Quarterly, 16*(1), 85–99. doi:10.1002/crq.3890160109

Lindstrom, L., Doren, B., & Miesch, J. (2011). Waging a living: Career development and long-term employment outcomes for young adults with disabilities. *Exceptional Children, 77,* 423–434.

Linquanti, R. (2011). *Strengthening assessment for English learner success: How can the promise of the common core standards and innovative assessment systems be realized?* Sacramento, CA: Policy Analysis for California Education and Rennie Center for Education Research and Policy.

Litow, L., & Pumroy, D. K. (1975). A brief review of classroom group–oriented contingencies. *Journal of Applied Behavior Analysis, 8,* 341–347. doi:10.1901/jaba.1975.8-341

Little, L. (2001). Peer victimization of children with Aspergers spectrum disorders. *Journal of the American Academy of Child and Adolescent Psychiatry, 40,* 995–996.

Littrell, J. M., Malia, J. A., & Vanderwood, M. (1995). Single-session brief counseling in high school. *Journal of Counseling & Development, 73,* 341–458. doi:10.1002/j.1556-6676.1995.tb01779.x

Littrell, J. M., & Peterson, J. S. (2001). Transforming the school culture: A model based on an exemplary counselor. *Professional School Counseling, 4,* 310–319.

Litwin, G. H., & Stringer, R. A., Jr. (1968). *Motivation and organizational climate.* Cambridge, MA: Harvard University Press.

Lochman, J. E., Powell, N. R., Clanton, N., & McElroy, H. K. (2006). Anger and aggression. In G. G. Bear, & K. M. Minke (Eds.), *Children's needs III: Development, prevention, and intervention* (pp. 115–134). Washington, DC: National Association of School Psychologists.

Lockwood, A. T. (1998). *Comprehensive reform: A guide for school leaders.* Oak Brook, IL: North Central Regional Educational Lab.

Lombardi, A., Murray, C., & Gerdes, H. (2012). Academic achievement of first generation college students with disabilities. *Journal of College Student Development, 53,* 811–826. doi:10.1353/csd.2012.0082

Lopez, A. M. (2004). Fluidity and multiplicity in mixed heritage students' racial/ethnic identifications: Implications for research. In K. R. Wallace (Ed.), *Working with multiracial students* (pp. 25–50). Greenwich, CT: Information Age Publishing.

Lord, C., Rutter, M., DiLavore, P. C., & Risi, S. (2001). *Autism Diagnostic Observation Scale.* Los Angeles, CA: Western Psychological Services.

Lorde, A. (1984). *Sister outsider.* Freedom, CA: The Crossing Press.

Lorion, R. P. (2011). Understanding Sarason's concepts of school cultures and change: Joining a community in school improvement efforts. *American Journal Community Psychology, 48,* 147–156. doi:10.1007/s10464-010-9359-0

Lott, B. (2003). Recognizing and welcoming the standpoint of low-income parents in the public schools. *Journal of Educational and Psychological Consultation, 14,* 91–104.

Loucks, H. (1992). Increasing parent/family involvement: Ten ideas that work. *NASSP Bulletin, 4,* 19–23.

Lougy, R., DeRuvo, S., & Rosenthal, D. (2009). *The school counselor's guide to ADHD: What to know and what to do to help your students.* Thousand Oaks, CA: Corwin Press

Loving v. Virginia, 388 U.S. 1 (1967).

Lowry, D. (1990). *True Colors training manual.* Corona, CA: True Colors.

Luke, M., & Bernard, J. M. (2006). The school counseling supervision model: An extension of the discrimination model. *Counselor Education and Supervision, 45,* 292–295. doi:10.1002/j.1556-6978.2006.tb00004.x

Lund, E. M., Blake, J. J., Ewing, H. K., & Banks, C. S. (2012). School counselors' and school psychologists' bullying prevention and intervention strategies: A look into real-world practices. *Journal of School Violence, 11,* 246-265. doi:10.1080/15388220.2012.682005

Luukkonen, A. H., Riala, K., Hakko, H., & Räsänen, P. (2011). Bullying behaviour and criminality: A population-based follow-up study of adolescent psychiatric inpatients in northern Finland. *Forensic Science International, 207*(1–3), 106–110. doi:10.1016/j.forsciint.2010.09.012

Luzzo, D. A., & Pierce, G. (1996). Effects of DISCOVER on the career maturity of middle school students. *The Career Development Quarterly, 45,* 170–172. doi:10.1002/j.2161-0045.1996.tb00267.x

Lyons, J. A. (1987). Posttraumatic stress disorder in children and adolescents: A review of literature. *Journal of Developmental and Behavioral Pediatrics, 8,* 349–356. doi:10.1097/00004703-198712000-00007

Mackenzie, R. J., & Stanzione, L. E. (2010). *Setting limits in the classroom* (3rd ed.). New York, NY: Random House.

Maehr, M. L., & Midgley, G. (1996). *Transforming school cultures.* Boulder, CO: Westview Press.

Mager, R. F. (1997). *Preparing instructional objectives: A critical tool in the development of effective instruction.* Atlanta, GA: The Center for Effective Performance.

Magnuson, C. S., & Starr, M. F. (2000). How early is too early to begin life career planning? The importance of the elementary school years. *Journal of Career Development, 27,* 89–101. doi:10.1023/A:1007844500034

Maine, M. (2000). *Body wars: Making peace with women's bodies.* Carlsbad, CA: Gurze Books.

Mannino, J. D. (1999). *Sexual themes and variations: The new millennium.* New York, NY: McGraw-Hill.

Marchant, G. J., Paulson, S. E., & Rothlisberg, B. A. (2001). Relations of middle school students' perceptions of family and school contexts with academic achievement. *Psychology in the School, 38,* 505–519. doi:10.1002/pits.1039

Marion, S. (2013). *The common core in the context of standards-based reform.* Dover, NH: Center for Assessment.

Marinoble, R. M. (1998). Homosexuality: A blind spot in the school mirror. *Professional School Counseling, 1*(3), 4–7.

Marshak, L. E., Dandeneau, C. J., Prezant, F. P. & L'Amoreaux, N. A. (Eds.). (2010). *The school counselor's guide to helping students with disabilities.* San Francisco, CA: Jossey-Bass.

Martens, B. K., & McIntyre L. L. (2009). The importance of treatment integrity in school-based behavioral intervention. In A. Akin-Little, S. G. Little, M. Bray, & T. J. Kehle (Eds.), *Behavioral interventions in schools: Evidence-based positive strategies* (pp. 59–72). Washington, DC: American Psychological Association.

Martens, B. K., Witt, J. C., Daly, E. J., & Vollmer, T. R. (1999). Behavior analysis: Theory and practice in educational settings. In C. R. Reynolds & T. B. Gutkin (Eds.), *The handbook of school psychology* (pp. 638–663). New York, NY: Wiley.

Martin, C. G., DeMarni Cromer, L., & Freyd, J. J. (2010). Teachers' beliefs about maltreatment effects on student learning and classroom behavior. *Journal of Child & Adolescent Trauma, 3,* 245–254. doi:10.1080/19361521.2010.523061

Martin, J. A., Hamilton, B. E., Ventura, S. J., Osterman, M. J. K., Wilson, E. C., & Matthews, T. J. (2012). Births: Final data for 2010. *National vital statistics reports, 61*(1). Retrieved from http://www.cdc.gov/nchs/data/nvsr/nvsr61/nvsr61_01.pdf

Martin, J., & Hoshmand, L. (1995). Research on psychological practice. In L. Hoshmand, & J. Martin (Eds.), *Research as praxis: Lessons from programmatic research in therapeutic psychology* (pp. 48–80). New York, NY: Teachers College Press.

Martin, P. (2015). Transforming the school counseling profession. In B. T. Erford (Ed.), *Transforming the school counseling profession* (4th ed.; pp. 35–49). Columbus, OH: Pearson Merrill.

Martinez v. School Board, 861 F2d 1502 (11th Cir. 1988), on remand, 711 F. Supp. 1066 (M.D. Fla. 1989).

Masi, G., Mucci, M., & Millepiedi, S. (2001). Separation anxiety disorders in children and adolescents. *CNS Drugs, 15,* 93–104. doi:10.2165/00023210-200115020-00002

Maslach, C., Jackson, S. E., & Leiter, M. P. (1996). *The Maslach Burnout Inventory* (3rd ed.). Palo Alto, CA: Consulting Psychologists Press.

Maslach, C., Schaufeli, W. B., & Leiter, M. P. (2001). Job burnout. *Annual Review of Psychology, 52,* 397–422.

Maslow, A. H. (1968). *Toward a psychology of being* (2nd ed.). Princeton, NJ: Van Nostrand.

Mason, E. (2010). Leadership practices of school counselors and counseling program implementation. *NASSP Bulletin, 94,* 274–285. doi:10.1177/0192636510395012

Massad, P. M., & Hulsey, T. L. (2006). Causal attributions in posttraumatic stress disorder: Implications for clinical research and practice. *Psychotherapy: Theory, Research, Practice, Training, 43*, 201–215. doi:10.1037/0033-3204.43.2.201

Mastropieri, M. A., & Scruggs, T. E. (2009). *The inclusive classroom: Strategies for effective instruction* (4th ed.). Upper Saddle River, NJ: Pearson Merrill.

Mather, M. (2010). *U.S. children in single-mother families.* Population Reference Bureau. Retrieved from http://www.prb.org/pdf10/single-motherfamilies.pdf

Mathews, J. (2003). *Harvard schmarvard: Getting beyond the Ivy League to the college that's best for you.* New York, NY: Prima.

Mathewson, R. H. (1949). *Guidance policy and practice.* New York, NY: Harper.

Matson, J. L., & Kozlowski, A. M. (2011). The increasing prevalence of autism spectrum disorders. *Research in Autism Spectrum Disorders, 5*, 418–425. doi:10.1016/j.rasd.2010.06.004

Maughan, B., Collishaw, S., & Stringaris, A. (2013). Depression in childhood and adolescence. *Journal of the Canadian Academy of Child and Adolescent Psychiatry, 22*(1), 35–40. doi:10.1007/s00787-012-0318-1

Maxis, S. (2013). The relationship between school counselor self-efficacy and the rate of graduation for males at urban, predominantly African American, underperforming high schools. *Dissertation Abstracts International Section A, 74.*

McCabe, M. P., & Ricciardelli, L. A. (2001). Parent, peer, and media influences on body image and strategies to both increase and decrease body size among adolescent boys and girls. *Adolescence, 36*, 225–240. doi:35400009950230.0030

McCarney, S. B., & Arthaud, T. J. (2004). *Attention Deficit Disorders Evaluation Scale* (3rd ed., home version technical manual). Columbia, MO: Hawthorne Educational Services.

McChesney, J. (1998). *Whole school reform.* Retrieved from ERIC database. (ED427388).

McClung, C., & Hoglund, R. (2013). A Glasser quality school leads to choosing excellence. *International Journal of Choice Theory and Reality Therapy, 32*(2), 54–64.

McComas, J. J., Hoch, H., & Mace, F. C. (2000). Functional analysis. In E. S. Shapiro & T. R. Kratochwill (Eds.), *Conducting school-based assessments of children and adolescent behavior* (pp. 78–120). New York, NY: Guilford Press.

McConaughy, S. H. (2013). *Clinical interview for children and adolescents: Assessment to intervention* (2nd ed.). New York, NY: Guilford Press.

McCrae, R. R., & Costa, P. T., Jr. (2010). *NEO Inventories for the NEO-PI-3, NEO-FFI-3, NEO PI-R, professional manual.* Lutz, FL: Psychological Assessment Resources.

McCubbin, H., McCubbin, M., Thompson, A., Han, S., & Allen, C. (1997). Families under stress: What makes them resilient. *Journal of Family and Consumer Sciences, 89*, 2–11.

McCurdy, K. (2003). *School counseling: A scope of practice for the 21st century.* Canton, OH: Malone College.

McCurdy, M., Coutts, M. J., Sheridan, S. M., & Campbell, L. M. (2013). Ecological variables in school-based assessment and intervention planning. In R. Brown-Chidsey, K. J. Andren, & P. Harrison (Eds.), *Assessment for intervention: A problem-solving approach* (2nd ed., pp. 39–61). New York, NY: Guilford Press.

McDaniels, C., & Gysbers, N. C. (1992). *Counseling for career development: Theories, resources, and practice.* San Francisco, CA: Jossey-Bass.

McEachern, A. G., Aluede, O., & Kenny, M. C. (2008). Emotional abuse in the classroom: Implications and interventions for counselors. *Journal of Counseling & Development, 86*, 3–10. doi:10.1002/j.1556-6678.2008.tb00619.x

McEachern, A. G., & Kenny, M. C. (2007). Transition groups for high school students with disabilities. *Journal for Specialists in Group Work, 32*, 165–177. doi:10.1080/01933920701227190

McEvoy, A., & Welker, R. (2000). Antisocial behavior, academic failure, and school climate: A critical review. *Journal of Emotional and Behavioral Disorders, 8*, 130–140. doi:10.1177/106342660000800301

McGinnis, C. Z. A. (2008). Using anger productively: "Amazon" warrior theory. *Psychology Journal, 5*(2), 73–91.

McGlauflin, H. (2002). The Dominoes: A metaphor for helping grieving children, teens and their families. *Healing Ministry, 9*(2), 53–56.

McGrath, E. P., & Repetti, R. L. (2002). A longitudinal study of children's depressive symptoms, self-perceptions, and cognitive distortions about the self. *Journal of Abnormal Psychology, 111*(1), 77–87. doi:10.1037/0021-843X.111.1.77

McIntire, N. (2003). *Children and grief*. Retrieved from http://www.ericdigests.org/2003-5/grief.htm

McIntosh, K., Brown, J. A., & Borgmeier, C. J. (2008). Validity of functional behavior assessment within a response to intervention framework: Evidence, recommended practice, and future directions. *Assessment for Effective Intervention, 34*(1), 6–14. doi:10.1177/1534508408314096

McMahon, J. & Woo, C. S. (2012). Introduction to counseling couples. In A. Vernon (Ed.), *Cognitive and rational-emotive behavior therapy with couples* (pp. 1–15). New York, NY: Springer.

McMahon, R. R., & Forehand, R. L. (2003). *Helping the noncompliant child*. New York, NY: Guilford Press.

McMillan, J. H. (2013). *Classroom assessment: Principles and practice for effective instruction*. Needham Heights, MA: Allyn & Bacon.

McNamara, S. (2011). *Stress in young people: What's new and what can we do?* New York, NY: Continuum.

McRoy, R. G., & Zurcher, L. A. (1983). *Transracial and inracial adoptees: The adolescent years*. Springfield, IL: Thomas.

McVoy, M., & Findling, R. L. (2013). *Clinical manual of child and adolescent psychopharmacology* (2nd ed.). Arlington, VA: American Psychiatric.

McWayne, C., Hampton, V., Fantuzzo, J., Cohen, H. L., & Sekino, Y. (2004). A multivariate examination of parent involvement and the social and academic competencies of urban kindergarten children. *Psychology in the Schools, 41*, 363–377. doi:10.1002/pits.10163

Meichenbaum, D. (1977). *Cognitive-behavior modification: An integrative approach*. New York, NY: Plenum Press.

Meichenbaum, D. (2002). *Treating individuals with anger control problems and aggressive behavior*. Waterloo, ON: Institute Press.

Meichenbaum, D. (2006). *Comparison of aggression in boys and girls: A case for gender-specific interventions*. Unpublished manuscript.

Meichenbaum, D. (2011). *Important facts about resilience: A consideration of research findings about resilience and implications for assessment and treatment*. Retrieved from http://www.melissainstitute.org/documents/facts_resilience.pdf

Mellin, E. A., & Beamish, P. M. (2002). Interpersonal theory and adolescents with depression: Clinical update. *Journal of Mental Health Counseling, 24*(2), 110–125.

Mennuti, R. B., Freeman, A., & Christner, R. W. (2012). *Cognitive-behavioral interventions in educational settings: A handbook for practice* (2nd ed.). New York, NY: Routledge.

Merlo, L. J. E., & Storch, E. (2006a). Obsessive-compulsive disorder: Strategies for using CBT & pharmacotherapy. *Journal of Family Practice, 55*, 329–333. doi:35400015684039.0050

Merlo, L. J. E, & Storch, E. A. (2006b). Obsessive-compulsive disorder: Tools for recognizing its many expressions, *Journal of Family Practice, 55*, 217–222.

Merrell, K. W. (2000). Informant report: Rating scale measures. In E. S. Shapiro, & T. R. Kratochwill (Eds.), *Conducting school-based assessments of child and adolescent behavior* (pp. 203–234). New York, NY: Guilford Press.

Merrell, K. W. (2008). *Helping students overcome depression and anxiety: A practical guide* (2nd ed.). New York, NY: Guilford Press.

Merrell, K. W., Ervin, R. A., & Gimpel-Peacock, G. A. (2012). *School psychology for the 21st century: Foundations and practices* (2nd ed.). New York, NY: Guilford Press.

Merrell, K. W., Gueldner, B. A., Ross, S. W., & Isava, D. M. (2008). How effective are school bullying intervention programs? A meta-analysis of intervention research. *School Psychology Quarterly, 23*(1), 26–42. doi:10.1037/1045-3830.23.1.26

Mesibov, G., Thomas, J. B., Chapman, S. M., & Schopler, E. (2007). *TEACCH transition assessment profile* (2nd ed.). Austin, TX: PRO-ED.

Milan, S., & Keiley, M. K. (2000). Biracial youth and families in therapy: Issues and interventions. *Journal of Marital and Family Therapy, 26,* 305–315. doi:10.1111/j.1752-0606.2000.tb00300.x

Mildon, R. L., Moore, D. W., & Dixon, R. S. (2004). Combining noncontingent escape and functional communication training for negatively reinforced disruptive behavior. *Journal of Positive Behavior Interventions, 6,* 92–102.

Miller, D. N., & DeZolt, D. M. (2004). Self-mutilation. In T. S. Watson & C. H. Skinner (Eds.), *Comprehensive encyclopedia of school psychology* (pp. 291–293). New York, NY: Kluwer Press.

Miller, G. (1968). *Guidance: Principles and services.* Columbus, OH: Merrill.

Miller, J. B. (1971). Children's reactions to the death of a parent: A review of the psychoanalytic literature. *Journal of American Psychoanalytic Association, 19,* 697–719. doi:10.1177/000306517101900405

Milsom, A. S. (2002). Students with disabilities: School counselor involvement and preparation. *Professional School Counseling, 5,* 331–338.

Milstein, M. M. (1993). *Restructuring schools: Doing it right.* Newbury Park, CA: Corwin Press.

Miltenberger, R. (2004). *Behavior modification: Principles and procedures* (3rd ed.). Belmont, CA: Wadsworth Thompson Learning.

Miltenberger, R. G. (2011). *Behavior modification: Principles and procedures* (5th ed.). Belmont, CA: Wadsworth/Thomson Learning.

Minkoff, H. B., & Terres, C. K. (1985). ASCA perspectives: Past, present, and future. *Journal of Counseling & Development, 63,* 424–427. doi:10.1002/j.1556-6676.1985.tb02824.x

Minor Consent Law, 42 U.S.C. §§290dd-3.

Minority Community Outreach. (2010). *Minority parent and community engagement: Best practices and policy recommendations for closing the gaps in student achievement.* Retrieved from http://www.maldef.org/assets/pdf/mco_maldef%20report_final.pdf

Minuchin, S. (1974). *Families and family therapy.* Cambridge, MA: Harvard University Press.

Minuchin, S., & Fishman, H. (1981). *Family therapy techniques.* Cambridge, MA: Harvard University Press.

Minuchin, S., & Nichols, M. P. (1998). *Family healing: Strategies for hope and understanding.* New York, NY: The Free Press.

Minville, M. L., Constantine, M. G., Baysden, M. F., & So-Lloyd G. (2005). Chameleon changes: An exploration of racial identity themes of multiracial people. *Journal of Counseling Psychology, 52,* 507–516. doi:10.1037/0022-0167.52.4.507

Mitchell, J. T., & Everly, G. S. (1993). *Critical incident stress debriefing (CISD): An operations manual for the prevention of traumatic stress among emergency services and disaster workers.* Retrieved from http://www.info-trauma.org/flash/media-e/mitchellCriticalIncidentStressDebriefing.pdf

Mitchell, M. M., & Bradshaw, C. P. (2013). Examining classroom influences on student perceptions of school climate: The role of classroom management and exclusionary discipline strategies. *Journal of School Psychology, 51,* 599–610. doi:10.1016/j.jsp.2013.05.005

Mondimore, F. M. (1996). *A natural history of homosexuality.* Baltimore, MD: Johns Hopkins University Press.

Money, J. (1990). Agenda and credenda of the Kinsey scale. In D. P. McWhirter, S. A. Sanders, & J. M. Reinisch (Eds.), *Homosexuality/heterosexuality: Concepts of sexual orientation* (pp. 41–60). New York, NY: Oxford University Press.

Monte, C. F. (1998). *Beneath the mask: An introduction to theories of personality* (6th ed). New York, NY: Wiley.

Monteiro-Leitner, J., Asner-Self, K. K., Milde, C., Leitner, D. W., & Skelton, D. (2006). The role of the rural school counselor: Counselor, counselor-in-training, and principal perceptions. *Professional School Counseling, 9*, 248–251.

Moore, J. B., Kaffenberger, C., Oh, K. M., Goldberg, P., & Hudspeth, R. (2009). School reentry for children with cancer: Perceptions of health care professionals, school personnel and parents. *Journal of Pediatric Oncology, 26*, 86–89.

Moore, J. W., Tingstrom, D. H., Doggett, R. A., & Carlyon, W. D. (2001). Restructuring an existing token economy in a psychiatric facility for children. *Child & Family Behavior Therapy, 23*, 53–59. doi:10.1300/J019v23n03_04

Moyer, S. M., Sullivan, R. J., & Growcock, D. (2012). When is it ethical to inform administrators about student risk-taking behaviors? Perceptions of school counselors. *Professional School Counseling, 15*, 98–109. doi:10.5330/PSC.n.2012-15.98

Moylan, C. A., Herrenkohl, T. I., Sousa, C., Tajima, E. A., Herrenkohl, R. C., & Russo, M. J. (2010). The effects of child abuse and exposure to domestic violence on adolescent internalizing and externalizing behavior problems. *Journal of Family Violence, 25*, 53–63. doi:10.1007/s10896-009-9269-9

Mufson, L., Dorta, K. P., Moreau, D. & Weissman, M. M. (2011). *Interpersonal psychotherapy for depressed adolescents* (2nd ed.). New York, NY: Guilford Press.

Mulick, J. A., & Butter, E. M. (2002). Educational advocacy for children with autism. *Behavioral Interventions, 17*, 54–74. doi:10.1002/bin.106

Muller, B. E., & Erford, B. T. (2012). Choosing assessment instruments for depression outcome research with school-aged youth. *Journal of Counseling & Development, 90*, 208–220.

Mullis, F., & Edwards, D. (2001). Consulting with parents: Applying family systems concepts and techniques. *Professional School Counseling, 5*, 116–123.

Mullis, F., & Otwell, P. S. (1998). Who gets the kids? Consulting with parents about child custody decisions. *Professional School Counseling, 2*, 103–109.

Munoz-Plaza, C., Quinn, S. C., & Rounds, K. A. (2002). Lesbian, gay, bisexual and transgender students: Perceived social support in the high school environment. *High School Journal, 85*(4), 52–63. doi:10.1353/hsj.2002.0011

Murdick, N., Gartin, B., & Crabtree, T. (2013). *Special education law* (3rd ed.). Upper Saddle River, NJ: Merrill.

Muris, P., Meesters, C., Vincken, M., & Eijkelenboom, A. (2005). Reducing children's aggressive and oppositional behaviors in the schools: Preliminary results on the effectiveness of social-cognitive group intervention program. *Child & Family Behavior Therapy, 27*(1), 17–32. doi:10.1300/J019v27n01_02

Murphy, J. J. (2008). *Solution-focused counseling in middle and high schools* (2nd ed.). Alexandria, VA: American Counseling Association.

Murphy, J. J. (2009). Common factors of school-based change. In B. L. Duncan, S. D. Miller, B. E. Wampold, & M. A. Hubble (Eds.), *The heart and soul of change: What works in therapy* (pp. 361–386). Washington, DC: American Psychological Association.

Murphy, S. (2004). Professional training and regulation in school counseling. In B. T. Erford (Ed.), *Professional school counseling: A handbook of theories, programs and practices* (pp. 71–77). Austin, TX: PRO-ED.

Murray, H. A., & Bellak, L. (1973). *Thematic Apperception Test*. San Antonio, TX: Harcourt Assessment.

Murray, K. (2010). Preventing professional school counselor burnout. In B. T. Erford (Ed.), *Professional school counseling: A handbook of theories, programs and practices* (2nd ed., pp. 982–988). Austin, TX: PRO-ED.

Mussell, M. P., Binford, R. B., & Fulkerson, J. A. (2000). Eating disorders: Summary of risk factors, prevention programming, and prevention research. *The Counseling Psychologist, 28*, 764–796. doi:10.1177/0011000000286002

Musser, E. H., Bray, M. A., Kehle, T. J., & Jenson, W. R. (2001). Reducing disruptive behavior in students with serious emotional disturbance. *School Psychology Review, 30*, 294–304.

Mutch, C., & Collins, S. (2012). Partners in learning: Schools' engagement with parents, families, and communities in New Zealand. *School Community Journal, 22*, 167–187.

Muuss, R. E. (1996). *Theories of adolescence* (6th ed.). New York, NY: McGraw-Hill.

Myer, R. A. (2001). *Assessment for crisis intervention: A triage assessment model*. Belmont, CA: Brooks/Cole.

Myer, R. A., & Hanna, F. J. (1996). Working in hospital emergency departments: Guidelines for crisis intervention workers. In A. R. Roberts (Ed.), *Crisis management & brief treatment* (pp. 16–30). Chicago, IL: Nelson-Hall.

Myers, G. E. (1935). Coordinated guidance: Some suggestions for a program of pupil personnel work. *Occupations, 13*, 804–807. doi:10.1002/j.2164-5892.1935.tb00163.x

Myers, I. B., McCaulley, M. H., Quenk, N. L., & Hammer, A. L. (2003). *MBTI manual: A guide to the development and use of the Myers-Briggs Type Indicator* (3rd ed.). Palo Alto, CA: CPP.

Myles, B. S. (2003). Behavioral forms of stress management for individuals with Asperger syndrome. *Child and Adolescent Psychiatric Clinics of North America, 12*, 123–141. doi:10.1016/S1056-4993(02)00048-2

Myrick, R. D. (2010). *Developmental guidance and counseling: A practical approach* (5th ed.). Minneapolis, MN: Educational Media Corporation.

Myrick, R., Merhill, H., & Swanson, L. (1986). Changing students' attitudes through classroom guidance. *School Counselor, 33*, 244–252.

Nabors, L., Weist, M., Shugarman, R., Woeste, M., Mullet, E., & Rosner, L. (2004). Assessment, prevention, and intervention activities in a school-based program for children experiencing homelessness. *Behavior Modification, 28*, 565–578.

Nabors, L. A., & Lehmkuhl, H. D. (2004). Children with chronic medical conditions: Recommendations for school mental health clinicians. *Journal of Developmental and Physical Disabilities, 16*, 1–15.

Naglieri, J. A., LeBuffe, P. A., & Pfeiffer, S. I. (1994). *Devereux Scales of Mental Disorders*. New York, NY: The Psychological Corporation.

Nagaoka, J., Farrington, C. A., Roderick, M., Allensworth, E., Keyes, T. S., Johnson, D. W., & Beechum, N. O. (2013). Readiness for college: The role of noncognitive factors and context. *Voices in Urban Education, 38*, 45–51.

Nakashima, C. J. (1992). An invisible monster: The creation and denial of racially mixed people in America. In M. P. P. Root (Ed.), *Racially mixed people in America* (pp. 162–180). Newbury Park, CA: Sage.

National Association of State Directors of Special Education. (2005). *Response to intervention: Policy considerations and implementation*. Alexandria, VA: Author.

National Board for Certified Counselors. (2013). *Code of ethics*. Retrieved from http://www.nbcc.org/assets/ethics/nbcc-codeofethics.pdf

National Board for Certified Counselors. (2014). *Apply for certification*. Retrieved from http://www.nbcc.org/Certification/ApplyForCertification

National Board for Professional Teaching Standards. (2014). *NBPTS school counseling standards*. Retrieved from http://www.nbpts.org/sites/default/files/documents/certificates/nbpts-certificate-ecya-sc-standards.pdf

National Center for Education Statistics. (2011a). Digest of Education Statistics, Table 205.40. Retrieved from http://nces.ed.gov/programs/digest/d13/tables/dt13_205.40.asp

National Center for Education Statistics. (2011b). *Student reports of bullying and cyber-bullying: Results from the 2009 school crime supplement to the national crime victimization survey*. Retrieved from http://nces.ed.gov/pubs2011/2011336.pdf

National Center for Education Statistics. (2013). *State nonfiscal survey of public elementary and secondary education," 2001–02 and 2011–12; and projections of education statistics to 2023*. Washington, DC: Author.

National Center for Learning Disabilities. (2014). *Accommodations vs. modifications: What's the difference?* Retrieved from http://www.ncld.org/students-disabilities/accommodations-education/accommodations-vs-modifications-whats-difference

National Center on Response to Intervention. (2014). *What is RTI?* Retrieved from http://rtinetwork.org/learn/what

National Education Association. (2006). *The puzzle of autism.* Washington, DC: Author.

National Education Association. (2014). *School crisis guide: Help and healing in a time of crisis.* Retrieved from http://crisisguide.neahin.org/crisisguide/images/SchoolCrisisGuide.pdf

National Education Goals Panel. (1993). *Promises to keep: Creating high standards for American students.* Washington, DC: Author.

National Education Goals Panel. (1994). *Building a nation of learners.* Washington, DC: Author.

National Governors Association and the Council of Chief State School Officers. (2014). *Common core state standards initiative.* Retrieved from http://www.corestandards.org

National Institutes of Child Health & Human Development. (2014). *Autism spectrum disorder: Overview.* Retrieved from http://www.nichd.nih.gov/health/topics/autism/Pages/default.aspx

National Institute of Mental Health. (2000). *Rural mental health research fact sheet* (Publication No. 00-4741). Bethesda, MD: Author

National Institute of Mental Health. (2011). *A parent's guide to autism spectrum disorder.* Retrieved from http://www.nimh.nih.gov/health/publications/a-parents-guide-to-autism-spectrum-disorder/index.shtml

National Institute of Mental Health. (2012). *Attention deficit hyperactivity disorder.* Retrieved from http://www.nimh.nih.gov/health/publications/attention-deficit-hyperactivity-disorder/index.shtml?utm_source=REFERENCES_R7

National Institute of Mental Health. (2013a). *Depression in children and adolescents: Fact sheet.* Retrieved from http://www.nimh.nih.gov/health/publications/depression-in-children-and-adolescents/index.shtml

National Institute of Mental Health. (2013). *Helping children and adolescents cope with violence and disasters.* Retrieved from http://www.nimh.nih.gov/health/publications/helping-children-and-adolescents-cope-with-violence-and-disasters-parents-trifold/index.shtml

National Institute of Mental Health. (2014). *What is depression?* Retrieved from http://www.nimh.nih.gov/health/publications/depression/index.shtml

National Institute on Drug Abuse. (2014). *Monitoring the Future Study: Trends and statistics.* Retrieved from http://www.drugabuse.gov/related-topics/trends-statistics/monitoring-future

National Occupational Information Coordinating Committee. (2004). *National career development guidelines.* Washington, DC: Author.

National Office for School Counselor Advocacy. (2012). *Best practices for implementing NOSCA's eight components of college and career readiness counseling.* New York, NY: College Board.

National Organization for Victim Assistance. (1997). *Community crisis response team training manual* (2nd ed.). Retrieved from https://www.ncjrs.gov/ovc_archives/reports/crt/welcome.html

N.C. ex rel M.C. v. Bedford Cent. Sch. Dist., 348 F. Supp. 2d 32, 35 (S.D.N.Y. 2004)

Nearpass, G. (1990). Counseling and guidance effectiveness in North American high schools: A meta-analysis of the research findings (Doctoral dissertation, University of Colorado at Boulder, 1989). *Dissertation Abstracts International, 49,* 1948-A.

Nelson, J. R., & Dykeman, C. (1996). The effects of group counseling interventions on students with behavioral adjustment problems. *Elementary School Guidance & Counseling, 31*(1), 21–34.

Neumark-Sztainer, D., Wall, M., Larson, N. I., Eisenberg, M. E., & Loth, K. (2011). Dieting and disordered eating behaviors from adolescence to young adulthood: Findings from a 10-year longitudinal study. *Journal of the American Dietetic Association, 111,* 1004–1011. doi:10.1016/j.jada.2011.04.012

Newborg, J. (2005). *Battelle Developmental Inventory* (2nd ed.). Itasca, IL: Riverside.

Newcomer, L. (2008). *Positive behavior support for the classroom.* Retrieved from http://opi.mt.gov/pdf/mbi/Newcomer2008classroom.pdf

Newcomer, L. L., & Lewis, T. J. (2004). Functional behavior assessment: An investigation of assessment reliability and effectiveness of function-based interventions. *Journal of Emotional and Behavioral Disorders, 12,* 168–181.

Newman, B. S., & Muzzonigro, P. G. (1993). The effects of traditional family values on the coming out process of gay male adolescents. *Adolescence, 28,* 213–226. doi:35400003694602.0170

Nichols, M. (2012). *Family therapy: Concepts and methods* (10th ed.). New York, NY: Allyn & Bacon.

Nicholson, C., & Hibpshman, T. (1998). *Slosson Intelligence Test–Revised.* East Aurora, NY: Slosson Educational.

Nickerson, A. B., Singleton, D., Schnurr, B., & Collen, M. H., (2014). Perceptions of school climate as a function of bullying involvement. *Journal of Applied School Psychology, 30,* 157–181. doi:10.1080/15377903.2014.888530

Nicolosi, J. (1991). *Reparative therapy of male homosexuality: A new clinical approach.* Northvale, NJ: Aronson.

Niles, S. G., & Goodnough, G. E. (1996). Life-role salience and values: A review of recent research. *The Career Development Quarterly, 45,* 65–86. doi:10.1002/j.2161-0045.1996.tb00463.x

Niles, S. G., & Harris-Bowlsbey, J. (2013). *Career development interventions in the 21st century* (4th ed.). Upper Saddle River, NJ: Pearson Education.

Nishimura, N. (1995). Addressing the needs of biracial children: An issue for school counselors in a multicultural school environment. *The School Counselor, 43,* 52–57.

Nishimura, N., & Bol, L. (1997). School counselors' perceptions of the counseling needs of biracial children in an urban educational setting. *Research in the Schools, 4*(2), 17–23.

No Child Left Behind Act of 2001, 20 U.S.C. 70 § 6301 et seq. (2002). Retrieved from http://www.ed.gov/policy/elsec/leg/esea02/index.html

Nokali, N. E., Bachman, H. J., & Votruba-Drzal, E. (2010). Parent involvement and children's academic and social development in elementary school. *Child Development, 72,* 988–1005. doi:10.1111/j.1467-8624.2010.01447.x

Nunez, A., & Cuccaro-Alamin, S. (1998). *First generation students: Undergraduates whose parents never enrolled in postsecondary education.* Retrieved from http://nces.ed.gov/pubs98/98082.pdf

Nystul, M. S. (2006). *Introduction to counseling: An art and science perspective* (3rd ed.). Boston, MA: Allyn & Bacon.

Obama, M. L. R. (2014, July). *Remarks by the first lady to the American School Counselor Association Annual Conference* Orlando, Florida. Retrieved from http://www.whitehouse.gov/the-press-office/2014/07/01/remarks-first-lady-american-school-counselor-association-annual-conferen

O'Dea, J. (2000). School-based interventions to prevent eating problems: First do no harm. *Eating Disorders, 8,* 123–130. doi:10.1080/10640260008251219

O'Dea, J. A. (2004). Evidence for a self-esteem approach in the prevention of body image and eating problems among children and adolescents. *Eating Disorders, 12,* 225–239. doi:10.1080/10640260490481438

O'Dea, J. A., & Abraham, S. (1999). Onset of disordered eating attitudes and behaviors in early adolescence: Interplay of pubertal status, gender, weight, and age. *Adolescence, 34,* 671–679. doi:35400008188584.0040

O'Hanlon, W. H., & Weiner-Davis, M. (2003). *In search of solutions: A new direction in psychotherapy* (rev.). New York, NY: W. W. Norton.

Ohring, R., Graber, J. A., & Brooks-Gunn, J. (2002). Girls' recurrent and concurrent body dissatisfaction: Correlates and consequences over 8 years. *International Journal of Eating Disorders, 31,* 404–415. doi:10.1002/eat.10049

O'Kelly, M. (2010). *CBT in action: A practitioner's toolkit.* Melbourne, AU: CBT Australia.

Oliver, L. W., & Spokane, A. R. (1988). Career-intervention outcome: What contributes to client gain? *Journal of Counseling Psychology, 35,* 447–462. doi:10.1037/0022-0167.45.2.150

Ollendick, T. H., & Hersen, M. (1984). An overview of child behavioral assessment. In T. H. Ollendick & M. Hersen (Eds.), *Child behavioral assessment: Principles and procedures* (pp. 3-19). New York, NY: Pergamon Press.

Ollendick, T. H., & King, N. J. (2004). Empirically supported treatments for children and adolescents: Advances toward evidence-based practice. In P. M. Barrett & T. H. Ollendick (Eds.), *Handbook of interventions that work with children and adolescents: Prevention and treatment* (pp. 3-25). New York, NY: Wiley.

Olmstead, C. (2013). Using technology to increase parent involvement in schools. *TechTrends, 57*(6), 28-37. doi:10.1007/s11528-013-0699-0

Olson, L. (1979). *Lost in the shuffle: A report on the guidance system in California secondary schools.* Santa Barbara, CA: Citizens Policy Center, Open Road Issues Research.

Olweus, D. (1993). *Bullying at school: What we know and what we can do.* Cambridge, MA: Blackwell.

Omizo, M. M., & Omizo, S. A. (1988). The effects of participation in group counseling sessions on self-esteem and locus of control among adolescents from divorced families. *The School Counselor, 36,* 54-60.

Omizo, M. M., Omizo, S. A., & Okamoto, C. M. (1998). Gay and lesbian adolescents: A phenomenological study. *Professional School Counseling, 1*(3), 35-37.

O'Neill, R. E., Horner, R. H., Albin, R. W., Sprague, J. R., Storey, K., & Newton, J. S. (1997). *Functional assessment and program development for problem behavior. A practical handbook* (2nd ed.). Pacific Grove, CA: Brooks/Cole.

Orbin, A. (2010). Learning disabilities. In L. E. Marshak, C. J. Dandeneau, F. P. Prezant, & N. A. L'Amoreaux (Eds.), *The school counselor's guide to helping students with disabilities,* (pp. 271-274). San Francisco, CA: Jossey-Bass.

Orpinas, P., & Horne, A. M. (2006). Persistent bullying: Counseling interventions. In P. Orpinas, & A. M. Horne (Eds.), *Bullying prevention: Creating a positive school climate and developing social competence* (pp. 181-202). Washington, DC: American Psychological Association. doi:10.1037/11330-008

Osborn, D,, Dikel, M. R., & Sampson, J. P. (2011). *The internet: A tool for career planning* (3rd ed.). Columbus, OH: National Career Development Association.

Otwell, P. S., & Mullis, F. (1997). Counselor-led staff development: An efficient approach to teacher consultation. *Professional School Counseling, 1,* 25-30.

Owens, R. E. (1998). *Queer kids: The challenges and promise for lesbian, gay, and bisexual youth.* New York, NY: Harrington Park Press.

Page v. Rotterdam-Mohonasen Central School District 109 Misc. 2d 1049, 441 N.Y. S. 2d 323 (1981).

Paisley, P. (2001). Maintaining and enhancing the developmental focus in school counseling programs. *Professional School Counseling, 4,* 271-277.

Paisley, P., & Peace, S. D. (1995). Developmental principles: A framework for school counseling programs. *Elementary School Guidance and Counseling, 30,* 85-93.

Paisley, P. O., & Borders, L. D. (1995). School counseling: An evolving specialty. *Journal of Counseling & Development, 74,* 150-153. doi:10.1002/j.1556-6676.1995.tb01840.x

Paisley, P. O., & McMahon, G. H. (2001). School counseling for the 21st century: Challenges and opportunities. *Professional School Counseling, 5,* 106-115.

Palmer, S., & Cochran, L. (1988). Parents as agents of career development. *Journal of Counseling Psychology, 35*(1), 71-76. doi:10.1037/0022-0167.35.1.71

Paone, T. R., Packman, J., Maddux, C., & Rothman, T. (2008). A school-based group activity therapy intervention with at-risk high school students as it relates to their moral reasoning. *International Journal of Play Therapy, 17,* 122-137. doi:10.1037/a0012582

Paphazy, J. E. (2003). Resilience, the fourth R: The role of schools in this promotion. In E. H. Grotberg (Ed.), *Resilience for today: Gaining strength from adversity* (pp. 105-140). Westport, CT: Praeger/Greenwood.

Parents Against Child Abuse in School v. Williamsport Area School District, 594 A.2d 796 (Pa. Commw. Ct. 1991).

Park, R. (1928). Human migration and the marginal man. *American Journal of Sociology, 33*, 881–893. doi:10.1086/214592

Parker, S. (1999, March 23). Erasing a remnant of Jim Crow South from law books. *The Christian Science Monitor, 3*, 3.

Parikh, S. B. (2013). Urban high school students' experiences in an afterschool college readiness program. *The Urban Review, 45*, 220-231. doi:10.1007/s11256-012-0213-6

Parsad, B., Alexander, D., Farris, E., & Hudson, L. (2003). *High school guidance counseling* (NCES Publication #2003015). Washington, DC: National Center for Educational Statistics.

Parsons, F. (1909). *Choosing a vocation*. Boston, MA: Houghton Mifflin.

Parsons, J., & Nord, C. (2013, May/June). By the book. *ASCA School Counselor*, 10–13.

Partnership for Assessment of Readiness for College and Careers. (2013). *About PARCC*. Retrieved from http://www.parcconline.org/about-parcc

Pascoe, P. (1991). Race, gender, and intercultural relations: The case of interracial marriage. *Frontiers: A Journal of Women's Studies, 12*, 5–18.

Pascual-Leone, A., Gilles, P., Singh, T., & Andreescu, C. A. (2013). Problem anger in psychotherapy: An emotion-focused perspective on hate, rage, and rejecting anger. *Journal of Contemporary Psychotherapy, 43*(2), 83–92. doi:10.1007/s10879-012-9214-8

Patterson, C. J. (2002). *Research summary on lesbian and gay parenting*. Retrieved from http:/apa.org/pi/parent.html

Pauls, D. L., Raymond, C. L., Leckman, J. F., & Stevenson, J. M. (1991). A family study of Tourette's syndrome. *American Journal of Human Genetics, 48*, 154–163.

Pearson Education. (2014a). *CDM-R: Harrington-O'Shea career decision-making system–Revised*. Retrieved from http://www.pearsonclinical.com/education/products/100000512/harrington-oshea-career-decision-making-systemrevised-cdm-r.html

Pearson Education. (2014b). *Differential Aptitude Tests*. Retrieved from http://www.pearsonassessments.com/learningassessments/products/100000564/differential-aptitude-tests-fifth-edition-dat-dat.html?Pid=015-4060-47X

Pearson Education. (2014c). *Otis-Lennon School Ability Test*. Retrieved from http://www.pearsonassessments.com/learningassessments/products/100000003/otis-lennon-school-ability-test-eighth-edition-olsat-8-olsat-8.html?Pid=OLSAT

Pearson Education. (2014d). *Stanford Achievement Test series*. Retrieved from http://www.pearsonassessments.com/learningassessments/products/100000415/stanford-achievement-test-series-tenth-edition.html?Pid=SAT10C

Pedro-Carroll, J. L., & Alpert-Gillis, L. J. (1997). Preventive interventions for children of divorce: A developmental model for 5 and 6 year old children. *Journal of Primary Prevention, 18*, 5–23. doi:10.1023/A:1024601421020

Pedro-Carroll, J. L., Sutton, S. E., & Wyman, P. A. (1999). A two-year follow-up of a preventive intervention for young children of divorce. *School Psychology Review, 28*, 467–476.

Perrin, S., Smith, P., & Yule, W. (2000). Review: The assessment and treatment of post-traumatic stress disorder in children and adolescents. *Journal of Child Psychology and Psychiatry, 41*, 277–289.

Perry, B. D. (2001). Death & loss: Helping children manage their grief. *Early Childhood Today, 15*, 22–23.

Pérusse, R., & Goodnough, G. E. (2001). A comparison of existing school counselor program content with The Education Trust initiatives. *Counselor Education and Supervision, 41*, 100–110. doi:10.1002/j.1556-6978.2001.tb01274.x

Pérusse, R., & Goodnough, G. E. (2002, October). *Multiple perspectives: Shaping our future in school counselor education*. Paper presented at the Association of Counselor Education and Supervision Conference, Park City, UT.

Pérusse, R., Goodnough, A., & Noel, C. (2001). Use of the national standards for school counseling programs in preparing school counselors. *Professional School Counseling, 5*, 49–55.

Pesa, J. A., Syre, T. R., & Jones, E. (2000). Psychosocial differences associated with body weight among female adolescents: The importance of body image. *Journal of Adolescent Health, 26*, 330–337. doi:10.1016/S1054-139X(99)00118-4

Petersen, A. C., Compas, B. E., Brooks-Gunn, J., Stemmler, M., Ey, S., & Grant, K. E. (1993). Depression in adolescence. *American Psychologist, 48*, 155–168. doi:10.1037/0003-066X.48.2.155

Peterson, C. A., Mayer, L., Summers, J., & Luze, G. J. (2010). Meeting needs of young children at risk for or having a disability. *Early Childhood Education Journal, 37*, 509–517. doi:10.1007/s10643-010-0375-3

Pew Research Center. (2010). *The decline of marriage and rise of new families.* Retrieved from http://www.pewsocialtrends.org/files/2010/11/pew-social-trends-2010-families.pdf

Pfaller, J. E., & Kiselica, M. S. (1996). Implications of attachment theory for the role of school counselors. *School Counselor, 43*, 208–217.

Phelps, L., Cox, D., & Bajorek, E. (1992). School phobia and separation anxiety: Diagnostic and treatment comparisons. *Psychology in the Schools, 29*, 384–394. doi:10.1002/1520-6807(199210)29:4<384::AID-PITS2310290412>3.0.CO;2-1

Phelps, L., Sapia, J., Nathanson, D., & Nelson, L. (2000). An empirically supported eating disorder prevention program. *Psychology in the Schools, 37*, 443–452. doi:10.1002/1520-6807(200009)37:5<443::AID-PITS4>3.0.CO;2-8

Piedmont, R. L. (1998). *The Revised NEO Personality Inventory: Clinical and research applications.* New York, NY: Plenum Press.

Pincus, D. B., Eyberg, S. M., & Choate, M. L. (2005). Adapting parent-child therapy for young children with separation anxiety disorder. *Education and Treatment of Children, 28*, 163–181.

Pinder, F. A., & Fitzgerald, P. W. (1984). The effectiveness of a computerized guidance system in promoting career decision making. *Journal of Vocational Behavior, 24*, 123-131. doi:10.1016/0001-8791(84)90071-X

Pisacreta, J., Tincani, M., Connell, J. E., & Axelrod, S. (2011). Increasing teachers' use of a 1:1 praise-to-behavior correction ratio to decrease student disruption in general education classrooms. *Behavioral Interventions, 26*, 243–260. doi:10.1002/bin.341

Pittman, F. (1987). *Turning points: Treating families in transition and crisis.* New York, NY: Norton.

Plucker, J. A. (1998). The relationship between school climate conditions and student aspirations. *Journal of Educational Research, 91*, 240–246. doi:10.1080/00220679809597549

Plunkett, S. W., Radmacher, K. A., & Moll-Pharana, D. (2000). Adolescent life events, stress, and coping: A comparison of communities and genders. *Professional School Counseling, 3*, 356–367.

Pollack, W. (1998). *Real boys: Rescuing our sons from the myths of boyhood.* New York, NY: Random House.

Ponterotto, J. G., Utsey, S. O., Pedersen, P. B. (2006). *Preventing prejudice: A guide for counselors, educators, and parents* (2nd ed.). Thousand Oaks, CA: Sage.

Pope, M. (1995). The "salad bowl" is big enough for us all: An argument for the inclusion of lesbians and gays in any definition of multiculturalism. *Journal of Counseling & Development, 73*, 301–304. doi:10.1002/j.1556-6676.1995.tb01752.x

Pope, M. (1998, March 25). School counselors and whole person education. Message posted to The Education Forum online electronic mailing list, archived at http://educationreform.ipbhost.com

Pope, M. (2000). Preventing school violence aimed at gay, lesbian, bisexual, and transgender youth. In D. S. Sandhu, & C. B. Aspy (Eds.), *Violence in American schools: A practical guide for counselors* (pp. 285–304). Alexandria, VA: American Counseling Association.

Pope, M. (2002). Incorporating gay and lesbian culture into multicultural counseling. In J. Trusty, E. J. Looby, & D. S. Sandhu (Eds.), *Multicultural counseling: Context, theory and practice, and competence* (pp. 203–218). Hauppauge, NY: Nova Science Publishers.

Pope, M., & Barret, B. (2002a). Counseling gay men toward an integrated sexuality. In L. D. Burlew, & D. Capuzzi (Eds.), *Sexuality counseling* (pp. 149–176). Hauppauge, NY: Nova Science.

Pope, M., & Barret, B. (2002b). Providing career counseling services to gay and lesbian clients. In S. G. Niles (Ed.), *Adult career development: Concepts, issues, and practices* (3rd ed., pp. 215–232). Tulsa, OK: National Career Development Association.

Pope, M., & Englar-Carlson, M. (2001). Fathers and sons: The relationship between violence and masculinity. *The Family Journal, 9,* 367–374. doi:10.1177/1066480701094003

Pope, M., Pangelinan, J. S., & Coker, A. D. (Eds.). (2011). *Experiential activities for teaching multicultural competence in counseling.* Alexandria, VA: American Counseling Association.

Pope, M., Prince, J. P., & Mitchell, K. (2000). Responsible career counseling with lesbian and gay students. In D. A. Luzzo (Ed.), *Career counseling of college students: An empirical guide to strategies that work* (pp. 267–284). Washington, DC: American Psychological Association.

Porreca, K. A. (2010). The leadership of the high school principal in providing a supportive environment for lesbian, gay, bisexual and transgender students. *Dissertation Abstracts International, Section A: Humanities and Social Sciences, 71*(6-A), 1869.

Poston, W. S. C. (1990). The biracial identity development model: A needed addition. *Journal of Counseling & Development, 69,* 152–155. doi:10.1002/j.1556-6676.1990.tb01477.x

Potter, D. (2010). Psychosocial well-being and the relationship between divorce and children's academic achievement. *Journal of Marriage and Family, 72,* 933–946. doi:10.1111/j.1741-3737.2010.00740.x

Prediger, D. J. (1999). Basic structure of work-relevant abilities. *Journal of Counseling Psychology, 46,* 173–184.doi:10.1037/0022-0167.46.2.173

Premack, D. (1959). Toward empirical behavior laws: I. Positive reinforcement. *Psychological Review, 66,* 219–233. doi:10.1037/h0040891

Prevatt, F. F., Heffer, R. W., & Lowe, P. A. (2000). A review of school reintegration programs for children with cancer. *Journal of School Psychology, 38,* 447–467.

Price, R. A., Kidd, K. K., Cohen, D. J., Pauls, D. L., & Leckman, J. E. (1993). Human basal ganglia volume asymmetries in magnetic resonance images. *Magnetic Resonance Imaging, 11,* 493–498. doi:10.1016/0730-725X(93)90468-S

Protection of Pupil Rights Amendment (PPRA), 20 U.S.C. §1232h. (2002)

Prout, H., & DeMartino, A. (1986). A meta-analysis of school-based studies of psychotherapy. *Journal of School Psychology, 24,* 285–292. doi:10.1016/0022-4405(86)90061-0

Prout, S., & Prout, H. (1998). A meta-analysis of school-based studies of counseling and psychotherapy: An update. *Journal of School Psychology, 36,* 121–136. doi:10.1016/S0022-4405(98)00007-7

Pryor, C. (1996). Techniques for assessing family school connections. *Social Work in Education, 18,* 85–94. doi:10.1093/cs/18.2.85

Pryor, D. B., & Tollerud, T. R. (1999). Applications of Adlerian principles in school settings. *Professional School Counseling, 4,* 299–304.

Psychological Assessment Resources. (2014). *Vocational Preference Inventory.* Retrieved from http://www4.parinc.com/Products/Product.aspx?ProductID=VPI

Psychological Corporation. (1992). *Manual for the Differential Aptitude Tests* (5th ed.). San Antonio, TX: Author.

Putnam, R. F., Handler, M. W., Rey, J., & McCarty, J. (2005). The development of behaviorally based public school consultation services. *Behavior Modification, 29,* 521–538. doi:10.1177/0145445504273286

Quellmalz, E., Shield, P. M., & Knapp, M. S. (1995). *School-based reform: Lessons from a national study.* Washington, DC: U.S. Department of Education.

Quezada, R. L., Diaz, D. M., & Sanchez, M. (2003). Involving Latino parents. *Leadership, 10,* 32–38.

Quinn, M. M., Gable, R. A., Fox, J., Rutherford, R. B., Jr., Van Acker, R., & Conroy, M. (2001). Putting quality functional assessment into practice in school: A research agenda on behalf of E/BD students. *Education and Treatment of Children, 24,* 261–275.

Radford, P. M., Aldrich, J. L., & Ervin, R. A. (2000). An annotated bibliography of 102 school-based functional assessment studies. *Proven Practice: Prevention & Remediation Solutions for Schools, 3*, 24–43.

Radina, M. E., & Cooney, T. M. (2000). Relationship quality between multiracial adolescents and their biological parents. *American Journal of Orthopsychiatry, 70*, 445–454. doi:10.1037/h0087763

Rafdal, B. H., McMaster, K. L., McConnell, S. R., Fuchs, D., & Fuchs, L. S. (2011). The effectiveness of kindergarten peer-assisted learning strategies for students with disabilities. *Exceptional Children, 77*, 229–316.

Ramos, C., & Leal, I. (2013). Posttraumatic growth in the aftermath of trauma: A literature review about related factors and application contexts. *Psychology, Community & Health, 2*(1), 43–54. doi:10.5964/pch.v2i1.39

Rathvon, N. (1999). *Effective school interventions*. New York, NY: Guilford Press.

Rauch, S., & Lanphear, B. (2012). Prevention of disability in children: Elevating the role of environment. *The Future of Children, 22*(1), 193–217. doi:10.1353/foc.2012.0006

Reckase, M. D. (2011). *Computerized adaptive assessment (CAA): The way forward*. Sacramento, CA: Policy Analysis for California Education and Rennie Center for Education Research and Policy.

Reeder, J., Douzenis, C., & Bergin, J. J. (1997). The effects of small group counseling on the racial attitudes of second grade students. *Professional School Counseling, 1*(2), 15–22.

Reese, R. J., Prout, H. T., Zirkelback, E. A., & Anderson, C. R. (2010). Effectiveness of school-based psychotherapy: A meta-analysis of dissertation research. *Psychology in the Schools, 47*, 1035–1045. doi:10.1002/pits.20522

Rehabilitation Act of 1973, 29 U.S.C. § 701 et seq.

Reichgott Junge, E. (2014, February) Charter school path paved with choice, compromise, common sense. *Phi Delta Kappan, 95*(5), 13–17.

Remafedi, G. J., Resnick, M., Blum, R., & Harris, L. (1992). Demography of sexual orientation in adolescents. *Pediatrics, 89*, 714–721.

Remley, T. P., & Herlihy, B. (2010). *Ethical, legal, and professional issues in counseling* (3rd ed.). Upper Saddle River, NJ: Pearson Merrill.

Remley, T. P., Jr., & Herlihy, B. (2013). *Ethical, legal, and professional issues in counseling* (4th ed.). Upper Saddle River, NJ: Merrill/Prentice Hall.

Reschly, D. J. (2008). School psychology paradigm shift and beyond. In A. Thomas & J. Grimes (Eds.), *Best practices in school psychology* (5th ed., vol. 1, pp. 3–15). Bethesda, MD: National Association of School Psychologists.

Reynolds, A. D., Crea, T. M., Medina, J., Degnan, & McRoy, R. (2014). A mixed-method case study of parental involvement in an urban high school serving minority students. *Urban Education*, 1–26. doi:10.1177/0042085914534272

Reynolds, C. R., & Kamphaus, R. W. (2004). *Behavior Assessment System for Children* (2nd ed.). San Antonio, TX: Pearson.

Reynolds, C. R., & Richmond, B. O. (2008). *Revised Children's Manifest Anxiety Scale*. Los Angeles, CA: Western Psychological Services.

Reynolds, W. M. (2001). *Manual for the Reynolds Adolescent Depression Scale* (2nd ed.). Lutz, FL: Psychological Assessment Resources.

Reynolds, W. M. (2002). *Manual for the Reynolds Adolescent Depression Scale* (2nd ed., RADS-2). Lutz, FL: Psychological Assessment Resources.

Rhee, S. S. (2004). School violence victimization, coping, social support, and health-risk behaviors of lesbian, gay, and bisexual youth: A report of recent high school graduates. *Dissertation Abstracts International, 65*, 1B. (UMI No. 3120374)

Rhode, G., Jenson, W. R., & Reavis, H. K. (2010). *The tough kid book: Practical classroom management strategies* (2nd ed.). Eugene, OR: Pacific Northwest.

Rhodes, J. E., Camic, P. M., Milburn, M., & Lowe, S. R. (2009). Improving middle school climate through teacher-centered change. *Journal of Community Psychology, 37*, 711–724. doi:10.1002/jcop

Rhodes, V., Stevens, D., & Hemmings, A. (2011). Creating positive culture in a new urban high school. *The High School Journal, 94*(3), 82–94. doi:10.1353/hsj.2011.0004

Rhyne-Winkler, M. C., & Hubbard, G. T. (1994). Eating attitudes and behavior: A school counseling program. *The School Counselor, 41,* 195–198.

Ricciardelli, L. A., & McCabe, M. P. (2001). Children's body image concerns and eating disturbance: A review of the literature. *Clinical Psychology Review, 21,* 325–344. doi:10.1016/S0272-7358(99)00051-3

Richaud, M. C. (2013). Contributions to the study and promotion of resilience in socially vulnerable children. *American Psychologist, 68,* 751–758. doi:10.1037/a0034327

Riddle, J., Bergin, J. J., & Douzenis, C. (1997). Effects of group counseling on self-concepts of children of alcoholics. *Elementary School Guidance & Counseling, 31,* 192–202.

Ripley, V. V., & Goodnough, G. E. (2001). Planning and implementing group counseling in a high school. *Professional School Counseling, 5,* 62–65.

Riverside. (2014a). *Cognitive Abilities Test.* Retrieved from http://www.riverpub.com/products/cogAt/

Riverside. (2014b). *Iowa Tests of Basic Skills.* Retrieved from http://www.riversidepublishing.com/products/itbs/

Roberts, A. R. (1996). Epidemiology and definitions of acute crisis. In A. R. Roberts (Ed.), *Crisis management & brief treatment* (pp. 3–15). Chicago, IL: Nelson-Hall.

Roberts, R. F., & Doggett, R. A. (2011, November). *Evaluating the effects of consultation methods in the school setting.* Poster presented at the National Association of School Psychologists Annual Conference, San Francisco, CA.

Robins, D. K., Fein, D., Barton, M. L., & Green, L. A. (2001). The Modified Checklist for Autism in Toddlers: An initial study investigating the early detection of autism and pervasive development disorders. *Journal of Autism & Developmental Disorders, 31,* 131–144. doi:10.1023/A:1010738829569

Robinson, C. M. (1996). Alcoholics anonymous as seen from the perspective of self-psychology. *Smith College Studies in Social Work, 66,* 129–145. doi:10.1080/00377319709517484

Robinson, E. H., Rotter, J. C., Robinson, S. L., Fey, M. A., & Vogel, J. E. (2003). *Fears, stress and trauma: Helping children cope* (Rep. No. EDD00036). Washington, DC: Office of Educational Research and Improvement. (ERIC Document Reproduction Service No. ED482770).

Robinson, L. A., Berman, J. S., & Neimeyer, R. A. (1990). Psychotherapy for the treatment of depression: A comprehensive review of controlled outcome research. *Psychological Bulletin, 108,* 30–49. doi:10.1037/0033-2909.108.1.30

Rockquemore., K. A., & Brunsma, D. L. (2002). Socially embedded identities: Theories, typologies, and processes of racial identity among Black/White biracials. *The Sociological Quarterly, 43,* 335–356. doi:10.1111/j.1533-8525.2002.tb00052.x

Roderick, M., Nagaoka, J., & Coca, V. (2009). College readiness for all: The challenge for urban high schools. *The Future of Children, 19,* 185–210. doi:10.1353/foc.0.0024

Rodgers, R. F., Paxton, S. J., & Chabrol, H. (2009). Effects of parental comments on body dissatisfaction and eating disturbance in young adults: A sociocultural model. *Body Image, 6,* 171–177. doi:10.1016/j.bodyim.2009.04.004

Rofes, E. (1989). Opening up the classroom closet: Responding to the educational needs of gay and lesbian youth. *Harvard Educational Review, 59,* 443–453.

Rogers, C. R. (1942). *Counseling and psychotherapy: Newer concepts in practice.* New York, NY: Houghton Mifflin.

Rogers, C. R. (1951). *Client-centered therapy: Its current practice, implications, and theory.* Boston, MA: Houghton Mifflin.

Rogers, C. (1957). *Client-centered therapy.* Boston, MA: Houghton Mifflin.

Rogers, C. (1980). *A way of being.* Boston, MA: Houghton Mifflin.

Rogers, C. R., Lyon, H. R., & Tausch, R. (2014). *On becoming an effective teacher: Person-centered teaching, psychology, philosophy, and dialogues with Carl R. Rogers and Harold Lyon.* New York, NY: Routledge/Taylor & Francis Group.

Rohde, P., Lewinsohn, P. M., Clarke, G. N., Hops, H. & Seeley, J. R. (2005). The adolescent coping with depression course: A cognitive-behavioral approach to the treatment of adolescent depression. In E. D. Hibbs, & P. S. Jensen (Eds.), *Psychosocial treatments for child and adolescent disorders: Empirically based strategies for clinical practice* (2nd ed., pp. 219–237). Washington, DC: American Psychological Association.

Roid, G. H. (2003) *The Stanford-Binet Intelligence Scale* (5th ed., Technical manual). Itasca, IL: Riverside.

Rollins, J. (2006, August 10). Charter schools: Threat or opportunity? *Counseling Today, Features*. Retrieved from ct.counseling.org/2006/08/charter-schools-threat-or-opportunity

Root, M. P. P. (1994). Mixed-race women. In L Comas-Diaz, & B. Greene (Eds.), *Women of color: Integrating ethnic and gender identities in psychotherapy* (pp. 455–478). New York, NY: Guilford Press.

Root, M. P. P. (1998). Experiences and processes affecting racial identity development: Preliminary results from the Biracial Sibling Project. *Cultural Diversity and Mental Health, 4*, 237–247. doi:10.1037/1099-9809.4.3.237

Rorschach, H. (1921/1998). *The Rorschach Inkblot Test*. Kirkland, WA: Hogrefe & Huber.

Roscoe, W. (1989). Strange country this: Images of berdaches and warrior women. In W. Roscoe (Ed.), *Living the spirit: A gay American Indian anthology* (pp. 48–76). New York, NY: St. Martin's Press.

Rose, L. C. (2001). Grades for schools reach all-time high. *Phi Delta Kappan, 83*, 2.

Rosenstein, D. S., & Horowitz, H. A. (1996). Adolescent attachment and psychopathology. *Journal of Consulting and Clinical Psychology, 64*, 244–253. doi:10.1037/0022-006X.64.2.244

Ross, J. A., & Sibbald, T. M. (2010). The role of external diagnosis in school improvement in an Ontario school district. *The Alberta Journal of Educational Research, 56*, 403–418.

Ross, S., & Heath, N. (2002). A study of the frequency of self-mutilation in a community sample of adolescents. *Journal of Youth and Adolescence, 31*, 67–77. doi:10.1023/A:1014089117419

Rotheram-Borus, M. J., & Fernandez, I. (1995). Sexual orientation and developmental challenges experienced by gay and lesbian youths. *Suicide & Life Threatening Behavior, 25*, 26–34. doi:10.1111/j.1943-278X.1995.tb00487.x

Rounds, J. B., Jr., Henly, G. A., Dawis, R. V., & Lofquist, L. H. (1981). *Manual for the Minnesota Importance Questionnaire: A measure of needs and values*. Minneapolis, MN: University of Minnesota, Vocational Psychology Research.

Rowse, A. L. (1977). *Homosexuals in history: A study in ambivalence in society, literature and the arts*. New York, NY: Carroll & Graf.

Ruan, F. F. (1991). *Sex in China: Studies in sexology in Chinese culture*. New York, NY: Plenum Press.

Russell, S. T., & Joyner, K. (2001). Adolescent sexual orientation and suicide risk: Evidence from a national study. *American Journal of Public Health, 91*, 1276–1281. doi:10.2105/AJPH.91.8.1276

Rutter, M., Bailey, A., & Lord, C. (2003). *SCQ: The social communication questionnaire*. Los Angeles, CA: Western Psychological Services.

Ryan, C. L., Patraw, J. M., & Bednar, M. (2013). Discussing princess boys and pregnant men: Teaching about gender diversity and transgender experiences within an elementary school curriculum. *Journal of LGBT Youth, 10*(1-2), 83–105. doi:10.1080/19361653.2012.718540

Rye, D. R., & Sparks, R. (1999). *Strengthening K–12 school counseling programs: A support system*. Philadelphia, PA: Accelerated Development.

Saadatzaade, R., & Khalili, S. (2012). Effects of solution focused group counseling on student's self-regulation and academic achievement. *International Journal for Cross-Disciplinary Subjects in Education, 3*, 780–787.

Saigh, P. A., Yasik, A. E., Oberfield, R. A., Halamandaris, P. V., & Bremmer, J. D. (2006). The intellectual performance of traumatized children and adolescents with or without posttraumatic stress disorder. *Journal of Abnormal Psychology, 115*, 332–340. doi:10.1037/0021-843X.115.2.332

Sailor, W., Doolittle, J., Bradley, R., & Danielson, L. (2009). Response to intervention and positive behavior support. In W. Sailor, G. Dunlap, G. Sugai, & R. Horner (Eds.), *Handbook of positive behavior support* (pp. 729–753). New York, NY: Springer.

Sailor, W., Dunlap, G., Sugai, G., & Horner, R. (2009). *Handbook of positive behavior support*. New York, NY: Springer.

Salmivalli, C., & Pöyhönen, V. (2012). Cyberbullying in Finland. In Q. Li, D. Cross, & P. K. Smith (Eds.), *Cyberbullying in the global playground: Research from international perspectives* (pp. 57–72). Chichester, UK: Wiley-Blackwell.

Salvia, J., Ysseldyke, J., & Bolt, S. (2013). *Assessment: In special and inclusive education* (12th ed.). Boston, MA: Cengage.

Sandhu, D. H. (Ed.). (2001). *Elementary school counseling in the new millennium*. Alexandria, VA: American Counseling Association.

Sandoval, J. (2013). *Crisis counseling, intervention and prevention in the schools* (3rd ed.). New York, NY: Routledge.

Sandy, S. V. (2001). Conflict resolution education in the schools: "Getting there." *Conflict Resolution Quarterly, 19*, 237–250. doi:10.1002/crq.3890190207

Saphier, J., Haley-Speca, M. A., & Gower, R. (2008). *The skillful teacher: Building your teaching skills* (6th ed.). Carlisle, MA: Research for Better Teaching.

Sapp, M. (1997). *Counseling and psychotherapy: Theories, associated research, and issues*. Lanham, MD: University Press of America.

Sarason, S. B. (1995). *School change: The personal development of a point of view*. New York, NY: Teachers College Press.

Saterstrom, M. H., & Steph, J. A. (Eds.). (2014). *Educators guide to free guidance materials*. Randolph, WI: Educators Progress Service.

Sattler, J. M. (2006). *Assessment of children: Behavioral, social, and clinical foundation* (5th ed.). San Diego, CA: Author.

Saudargas, R. A. (1992). *State-event classroom observation system*. Knoxville, TN: University of Tennessee, Department of Psychology.

Savickas, M. L. (1990). The career decision-making course: Description and field test. *The Career Development Quarterly, 38*, 275–284. doi:10.1002/j.2161-0045.1990.tb00388.x

Savickas, M. L. (1993). Predictive validity criteria for career development measures. *Journal of Career Assessment*, 93–104. doi:10.1177/106907279300100109

Savickas, M. L. (1999). The transition from school to work: Developmental perspective. *The Career Development Quarterly, 47*, 326–336. doi:10.1002/j.2161-0045.1999.tb00741.x

Savickas, M. L., Stilling, S. M., & Schwartz, S. (1984). Time perspective in vocational maturity and career decision-making. *Journal of Vocational Behavior, 25*, 258–269. doi:10.1016/0001-8791(84)90049-6

Savin-Williams, R. C. (1990). *Gay and lesbian youth: Expressions of identity*. New York, NY: Hemisphere.

Savitz-Romer, M. (2012). The gap between influence and efficacy: College readiness training, urban school counselors, and the promotion of equity. *Counselor Education & Supervision, 51*, 98–111. doi:10.1002/j.1556-6978.2012.00007.x

Saywitz, K., & Faller, K. C. (2006). *Interviewing child witnesses and victims of abuse*. Washington, DC: U.S. Department of Justice, Juvenile Justice Resource Center.

Scarborough, J. L., & Culbreth, J. R. (2008). Examining discrepancies between actual and preferred practice of school counselors. *Journal of Counseling and Development, 86*, 446–459. doi:10.1002/j.1556-6678.2008.tb00533.x

Schaefer, C. E., & Drewes, A. A. (2011). The therapeutic powers of play and play therapy. In C. E. Schaefer (Ed.), *Foundations of play therapy* (2nd ed., pp. 15–25). Hoboken, NJ: John Wiley & Sons.

Schaffer, D., Fisher, P. W., & Lucas, C. (1999). Respondent-based interviews. In D. Schaffer, C. P. Lucas, & J. E. Richters (Eds.), *Diagnostic assessment in child and adolescent psychopathology* (pp. 3–33). New York, NY: Guilford Press.

Scheeringa, M. J. (2010). Posttraumatic stress disorder. In C. H. Zeanah (Ed.), *Handbook of infant mental health* (3rd ed., pp. 345–361). New York, NY: Guilford Press.

Schellenberg, R. (2012). *A new era in school counseling: A practical guide* (2nd ed.). Lanham: MD: Rowman & Littlefield Education.

Schmidt, J. J. (Ed.). (2010). *The elementary/middle school counselor's survival guide* (3rd ed.). San Francisco, CA: Jossey-Bass.

Schmidt, J. J., & Ciechalski, J. C. (2001). School counseling standards: A summary and comparison with other student services' standards. *Professional School Counseling, 4*, 328–333.

Schmidt, M. (2010). Using play therapy assessment in an elementary and intermediate school setting. In A. A. Drewes, & C. E. Schaefer (Eds.), *School-based play therapy* (2nd ed., pp. 107–122). Hoboken, NJ: John Wiley & Sons.

Schoen, A. A. (2003). What potential does the applied behavioral analysis approach have for treatment of children and youth with autism? *Journal of Applied Psychology, 30*, 125–130.

Schoon, I., Gutman, L. M., & Sabates, R. (2012). Is uncertainty bad for you? It depends . . . *Directions for Youth Development, 135*, 65–75. doi:10.1002/yd.20029

Schopler, E., Reichler, R. J., & Renner, B. R. (1988). *The Childhood Autism Rating Scale*. Los Angeles, CA: Western Psychological Services.

Schulzinger, R. (1999). *Understanding the 504 statute: The role of state Title V programs and health care providers*. Gainesville, FL: The Institute for Child Health Policy.

Schwartz, W. (1999). *Family diversity in urban schools*. Retrieved from http://www.ericdigests.org/2000-2/urban.htm

Schwartz, W. (2001). *Closing the achievement gap: Principles for improving the educational success of all students* Retrieved from ERIC database. (ED460191).

Schweiger, W. K., Henderson, D. A., McCaskill, K., Clawson, T. W., & Collins, D. R. (Eds.). (2011). *Counselor preparation: Programs, faculty, trends* (13th ed.). New York, NY: Routledge.

Scott, E. S. (2001). *The legal construction of adolescence*. Retrieved from http://www.hofstra.edu/PDF/law_lawrev_esscott.pdf

Scott, J., Culley, M., & Weissberg, E. (1995). Helping the separation anxious school refuser. *Elementary School Guidance & Counseling, 29*, 289–296.

Scruggs, M. Y., Wasielewski, R. A., & Ash, M. J. (1999). Comprehensive evaluation of a K–12 counseling program. *Professional School Counseling, 2*, 244–247.

Sears, S. J. (1995). Career and educational planning in the middle level school. *National Association of Secondary School Principals, 79*, 36–42. doi:10.1177/019263659507957008

Sears, S. J., & Granello, D. H. (2002). School counseling now and in the future: A reaction. *Professional School Counseling, 5*, 164–171.

Sears. S., Wood, C., & Hinkelman, L. (2010). Improving student achievement. In B. T. Erford (Ed.), *Professional school counseling; A handbook of theories, programs, and practices* (2nd ed., pp. 902–913) Austin, TX: PRO-ED.

Seaward, B. L. (2011). *Managing stress: Principles and strategies for health and well-being* (7th ed.). Sudbury, MA: Jones & Bartlett.

Selekman, J., Busch, T., & Kimble, C. (2001). Grieving children: Are we meeting the challenge? *Pediatric Nursing, 27*, 414–419.

Self-Directed Search. (2014). *Self-Directed Search*. Retrieved from http://www.self-directed-search.com/

Selye, H. (1956). *The stress of life*. New York, NY: McGraw-Hill.

Senge, P. (1990). *The fifth discipline: The art and practice of the learning organization*. New York, NY: Doubleday.

Sergiovanni, T. J. (1992). *Moral leadership: Getting to the heart of school improvement*. San Francisco, CA: Jossey-Bass.

Sergiovanni, T. J. (2001). *The principalship*. Boston, MA: Allyn & Bacon.

Sexton, T. L. (1996). The relevance of counseling outcome research: Current trends and practical implications. *Journal of Counseling & Development, 74*, 590–600. doi:10.1002/j.1556-6676.1996.tb02298.x

Sexton, T. L. (1999). *Evidence-based counseling: Implications for counseling practice, preparation, and professionalism.* Greensboro, NC: ERIC Clearinghouse on Counseling and Student Services. (ERIC Document Reproduction Service No. ED435948)

Sexton, T. L., & Whiston, S. C. (1991). A review of the empirical basis for counseling: Implications for practice and training. *Counselor Education and Supervision, 30,* 330–354. doi:10.1002/j.1556-6978.1991.tb01215.x

Sexton, T. L., Whiston, S. C., Bleuer, J. C., & Walz, G. R. (1997). *Integrating outcomes research into counseling practice and training.* Alexandria, VA: American Counseling Association.

Shadish, W. R. (1996). Meta-analysis and the exploration of causal mediating processes: A primer of examples, methods, and issues. *Psychological Methods, 1,* 47–65. doi:10.1037/1082-989X.1.1.47

Shapiro, E. S. (1996). *Academic skills problems workbook.* New York, NY: Guilford Press.

Shapiro, E. S., & Kratochwill, T. R. (2000). Introduction: Conducting a multidimensional behavioral assessment. In E. S. Shapiro & T. R. Kratochwill (Eds.), *Conducting school-based assessments of child and adolescent behavior* (pp. 1–20). New York, NY: Guilford Press.

Shapiro, S., Newcomb, M., & Loeb, T. B. (1997). Fear of fat, disregulated-restrained eating, and body-esteem: Prevalence and gender differences among eight- to ten-year-old children. *Journal of Clinical Child Psychology, 26,* 358–365. doi:10.1207/s15374424jccp2604_4

Sharp, P., & Herrick, E. (2000). Promoting emotional literacy: Anger management groups. In N. Barwick (Ed.), *Clinical counselling in schools* (pp. 124–141). London, UK: Routledge.

Sharpe, D. (1997). Of apples and oranges, file drawers and garbage. Why validity issues in meta-analysis will not go away. *Clinical Psychology Review, 17,* 881–901. doi:10.1016/S0272-7358(97)00056-1

Sharpnack, J. D. (2000). The efficacy of group bereavement interventions: An integrative review of the research literature. *Dissertation Abstracts International, 61,* 6721.

Sharrer, V. W., & Ryan-Wenger, N. A. (2002). School-age children's self-reported stress symptoms. *Pediatric Nursing, 28,* 21–27. doi:35400010030667.0020

Shattuck, R. M., & Kreider, R. M. (2013). *Social and economic characteristics of currently unmarried women with a recent birth: 2011.* American Community Survey Reports, U.S. Census Bureau. Retrieved from http://www.census.gov/prod/2013pubs/acs-21.pdf

Shaw, J., & Reyes, P. (1992). School cultures: Organizational value orientation and commitment. *Journal of Educational Research, 85,* 295–302. doi:10.1080/00220671.1992.9941129

Shaw, S. R., & McCabe, P. C. (2008). Hospital-to-school transition for children with chronic illness: Meeting the new challenges of an evolving healthcare system. *Psychology in the Schools, 45,* 74–87. doi:10.1002/pits.20280

Shechtman, Z. (1993). School adjustment and small-group therapy: An Israeli study. *Journal of Counseling & Development, 72*(1), 77–81. doi:10.1002/j.1556-6676.1993.tb02281.x

Shelby, J., & Campos, K. G. (2011). Cognitive-behavioral play therapy for traumatized children: Narrowing the divide between ideology and evidence. In A. A. Drewes, S. C. Bratton, & C. E. Schaefer (Eds.), *Integrative play therapy* (pp. 107–128). Hoboken, NJ: John Wiley & Sons. doi:10.1002/9781118094792.ch7

Sheperd, K. K. (1994). Stemming conflict through peer mediation. *School Administrator, 51,* 14–17.

Sheperis, C. J., Renfro-Michel, E., & Doggett, R. A. (2003). In home treatment of reactive attachment disorder in a therapeutic foster care system: A case example. *Journal of Mental Health Counseling, 25*(1), 76–88.

Sheridan, S. M., Kratochwill, T. R., & Bergan, J. R. (1996). *Conjoint behavioral consultation: A procedural manual.* New York, NY: Plenum Press.

Sherman, R., & Fredman, N. (1986). *Handbook of structured techniques in marriage and family therapy.* New York, NY: Brunner/Mazel.

Shi, L. (2014). Treatment of reactive attachment disorder in young children: Importance of understanding emotional dynamics. *American Journal of Family Therapy, 42*(1), 1–13. doi:10.1080/01926187.2013.763513

Shillingford, M., & Lambie, G. (2010). Contribution of professional school counselors' values and leadership practices to their programmatic service delivery. *Professional School Counseling, 13*, 208–217.

Shillingford, M. A., Lambie, G. W., & Walter, S. M., (2007). An integrative, cognitive-behavioral, systemic approach to working with students diagnosed with attention deficit hyperactive disorder. *Professional School Counseling Journal, 11*(2), 105–112. doi:10.5330/PSC.n.2010-11.105

Shin, M., & Sanchez, D. T. (2005). Perspectives and research on the positive and negative implications of having multiple racial identities. *Psychological Bulletin, 131*, 569–591. doi:10.1037/0033-2909.131.4.569

Shin, R. Q., Rogers, J., Stanciu, A., Silas, M., Brown-Smythe, C., & Austin, B. (2010). Advancing social justice in urban schools through the implementation of transformative groups for youth of color. *Journal for Specialists in Group Work, 35*(3), 230–235. doi:10.1080/01933922.2010.492899

Shiu, S. (2001). Issues in the education of students with chronic illness. *International Journal of Disability, Development and Education, 48*, 269–281.

Shone, B., & Parada, H. (2005). Emotional maltreatment of children and child welfare intervention: A position paper for Peel Children's Aid. *Ontario Association of Children's Aid Societies Journal, 49*(4), 17–22.

Short, P. M., & Rinehart, J. S. (1993). Teacher empowerment and school climate. *Education, 113*, 592–595.

Shumba, A. (2002a). The nature, extent and effects of emotional abuse on primary school pupils by teachers in Zimbabwe. *Child Abuse & Neglect, 26*, 783–791. doi:10.1016/S0145-2134(02)00351-4

Shumba, A. (2002b). Teacher conceptualization of child abuse in schools in the new millennium. *Journal of Interpersonal Violence, 17*, 403–415. doi:10.1177/0886260502017004004

Shute, V. J., Hansen, E. G., Underwood, J. S., & Razzouk, R. (2011). A review of the relationship between parental involvement and secondary school students' academic achievement. *Education Research International*, 1–10. doi:10.1155/2011915326

Siegel, D. (2012). *Pocket guide to interpersonal neurobiology*. New York, NY: W. W. Norton & Company.

Sill, A. C. (1995). Four years at a glance: A simple course work planning sheet. *The School Counselor, 43*, 88–92.

Silva, R., Alpert, M., Munoz, D., Singh, S., Matzner, F., & Dummit, S. (2000). Stress and vulnerability to posttraumatic stress disorder in children and adolescents. *American Journal of Psychiatry, 157*, 1229–1235. doi:10.1176/appi.ajp.157.8.1229

Simmonds, J. (2013). *Seeing red: An anger management and peacemaking curriculum for kids*. Gabriola Island, BC: New Society.

Sink, C., & Stroh, H. (2003). Raising achievement test scores of early elementary school students through comprehensive school counseling programs. *Professional School Counseling, 6*, 350–364.

Sink, C. A. (2005). Fostering academic development and learning: Implications and recommendations for middle school counselors. *Professional School Counseling, 9*, 128–135.

Sink, C. A. (2009). School counselors as accountability leaders: Another call for action. *Professional School Counseling, 13*(2), 68–74.

Sink, C. A., Akos, P., Turnbull, R. J., & Mvududu, N. (2008). An investigation of comprehensive school counseling programs and academic achievement in Washington State middle schools. *Professional School Counseling, 12*(1), 43–53. doi:10.5330/PSC.n.2010-12.43

Sink, C. A., & Edwards, C. (2008). Supportive learning communities and the transformative role of professional school counselors. *Professional School Counseling, 12*(2), 108–114.

Skinner, B. F. (1953). *Science and human behavior*. New York, NY: Macmillan.

Skinner, C. H., Belfiore, P. J., & Pierce, N. (1992). Cover, copy, and compare: Increasing geography accuracy in students with behavior disorders. *School Psychology Review, 21*, 73–81.

Skinner, C. H., McLaughlin, T. F., & Logan, P. (1997). Cover, copy, and compare: A self-managed academic intervention effective across skills, students, and settings. *Journal of Behavioral Education, 7*, 295–306. doi:10.1023/A:1022823522040

Skinner, C. H., Rhymer, K. N., & McDaniel, C. E. (2000). Naturalistic direct observation in educational settings. In E. S. Shapiro & T. R. Kratochwill (Eds.), *Conducting school-based assessments of child and adolescent behavior* (pp. 21–54). New York, NY: Guilford Press.

Skinner, C. H., Shapiro, E. S., Turco, T. L., & Cole, C. L. (1992). A comparison of self- and peer-delivered immediate corrective feedback on multiplication performance. *Journal of School Psychology, 30*, 101–116. doi:10.1016/0022-4405(92)90024-Y

Skinner, C. H., Turco, T. L., & Beatty, K. L. (1989). Cover, copy, and compare: A method for increasing multiplication performance. *School Psychology Review, 18*, 412–420.

Sklare, G. B. (2014). *Brief counseling that works: A solution-focused approach for school counselors* (3rd ed.). Thousand Oaks, CA: Corwin.

Slavin, R. E. (2011). *Educational psychology: Theory and practice* (10th ed.). Upper Saddle River, NJ: Pearson.

Slavin, R. E., & Madden, N. A. (2000). Roots and wings: Effects of whole-school reform on student achievement. *Journal for Students Placed at Risk, 5*(1/2), 109. doi:10.1080/10824669.2000.9671383

Slavin, R. E., Madden, N. A., & Wasik, B. A. (1996). Roots & wings. In S. Stringfield, S. Ross, & L. Smith (Eds.), *Bold plans for school restructuring: The new American schools design* (pp. 207–232). Hillsdale, NJ: Erlbaum.

Slonje, R., Smith, P. K., & Frisen, A. (2013). The nature of cyberbullying, and strategies for prevention. *Computers in Human Behavior, 29*(1), 26–32. doi:10.1016/j.chb.2012.05.024

Smarter Balanced Assessment Consortium. (2014). *K–12 education.* Retrieved from http://www.smarterbalanced.org/k-12-education

Smead, R. (1995). *Skills and techniques for group work with children and adolescents*. Champaign, IL: Research Press.

Smith, C., & Carlson, B. (1997). Stress, coping and resilience in children and youth. *Social Service Review, 71*, 231–257.

Smith, D., Larson, J., DeBaryshe, B., & Salzman, M. (2000). Anger management for youths: What works and for whom? In D. S. Sandhu, & C. B. Aspy (Eds.), *Violence in American schools: A practical guide for counselors* (pp. 217–230). Alexandria, VA: American Counseling Association.

Smith, J. D., Schneider, B. H., Smith, P. K., & Ananiadou, K. (2004). The effectiveness of whole-school antibullying programs: A synthesis of evaluation research. *School Psychology Review, 33,*547–560.

Smith, P. K. (2012). Cyberbullying and cyber aggression. In S. R. Jimerson, A. B. Nickerson, M. J. Mayer, & M. J. Furlong (Eds.), *Handbook of school violence and school safety: International research and practice* (pp. 93–103). New York, NY: Routledge.

Smith, S. D., & Chen-Hayes, S. F. (2004). Leadership and advocacy for lesbian, bisexual, gay, transgendered, and questioning (LBGTQ) students: Academic, career, and interpersonal success strategies. In R. Pérusse & G. E. Goodnough (Eds.), *Leadership and advocacy in school counseling* (pp. 187–221). Pacific Grove, CA: Brooks/Cole.

Smith, S. L. (2001). Teaching experience for school counselors: Counselor educators' perceptions. *Professional School Counseling, 4*, 216–224.

Smith, T. J., Dittmer, K. I., & Skinner, C. H. (2002). Enhancing science performance in students with learning disabilities using cover, copy and compare: A student shows the way. *Psychology in the Schools, 39*, 417–426. doi:10.1002/pits.10037

Snider, L. A., & Swedo, S. E. (2004). PANDAS: Current status & directions of research. *Molecular Psychiatry, 9*, 900–907. doi:10.1038/sj.mp.4001542

Snow, B. M. (1981). Counselor licensure as perceived by counselors and psychologists. *The Personnel and Guidance Journal, 60*, 80–83. doi:10.1002/j.2164-4918.1981.tb00645.x

Snow, B. M. (1982). Counselor licensure: What activities should be allowed? *Counselor Education and Supervision, 21*, 237–244. doi:10.1002/j.1556-6978.1982.tb01707.x

Society for Adolescent Health and Medicine. (2013). Recommendations for promoting the health and well-being of lesbian, gay, bisexual, and transgender adolescents: A position paper of the Society for Adolescent Health and Medicine. *Journal of Adolescent Health, 52*, 506–510.

Söderström, M., Ekstedt, M., & Åkerstedt, T. (2006). Weekday and weekend patterns of diurnal cortisol, activation and fatigue among people scoring high for burnout. *Scandinavian Journal of Work, Environment & Health, 2*, 35–40.

Sohn, D. (1997). Questions for meta-analysis. *Psychological Reports, 81*, 3–15. doi:10.2466/pr0.1997.81.1.3

Somer, E. (2011). Dissociation in traumatized children and adolescents. In V. Ardino (Ed.), *Posttraumatic syndromes in childhood and adolescence: A handbook of research and practice* (pp. 157–174). Chichester, UK: Wiley-Blackwell.

Sonna, L. (2005). *The everything parent's guide to children with ADD/ADHD*. Avon, MA: Adams Media.

Sonneborn Lawler, D. (2014). Addressing attachment disorganization and reactive attachment disorder in maltreated youth: Development of an introductory guide outlining best practices for school psychologists. *Dissertation Abstracts International, Section A, 74*.

Southworth, S. (2010). Examining the effects of school composition on North Carolina student achievement over time. *Education Policy Analysis Archives*, (1829). Retrieved from ERIC database (EJ913483).

Spokane, A. R., & Oliver, L. W. (1983). Research integration: Approaches, problems and recommendations for research reporting. *Journal of Counseling Psychology, 30*, 252–257. doi:10.1037/0022-0167.30.2.252

Sprick, R. S., & Howard, L. S. (1995). *The teacher's encyclopedia of behavior management*. Longmont, CO: Sopris West.

Sprinthall, N. (1981). A new model for research in the science of guidance and counseling. *The Personnel and Guidance Journal, 59*, 487–493. doi:10.1002/j.2164-4918.1981.tb00602.x

Sprinthall, N. A. (1984). Primary prevention: A road paved with a plethora of promises and procrastinations. *Personnel & Guidance Journal, 62*, 491–495. doi:10.1111/j.2164-4918.1984.tb00262.x

Stahmer, C. A., Collings, N. M., & Palinkas, L. A. (2005). Early interventions practices for children with autism: Descriptions from community providers. *Focus on Autism and Other Developmental Disabilities, 20*, 66–79. doi:10.1177/10883576050200020301

Stanton, A. L., Revenson, T., & Tennen, H. (2007). Health psychology: Psychological adjustment to chronic disease. *Annual Review Psychology, 58*, 565–592. doi:10.1146/annurev.psych.58.110405.085615

Stark, K. D., & Kendall, P. C. (1996). *Treating depressed children: Therapist manual for ACTION*. Ardmore, PA: Workbook.

Starr, M. F. (1996). Comprehensive guidance and systematic educational and career planning: Why a K–12 approach? *Journal of Career Development, 23*, 9–22. doi:10.1007/BF02471265

Staub, E. (2005). The roots of goodness: The fulfillment of basic human needs and the development of caring, helping and non-aggression, inclusion, inclusive caring, moral courage, active bystandership, and altruism born of suffering. *Nebraska Symposium on Motivation, 51*, 37–64.

St. Clair, K. (1989). Middle school counseling research: A resource for school counselors. *Elementary School Guidance and Counseling, 23*, 219–226.

Steege, M. W., & Watson, T. S. (2009). *Conducting school-based functional assessments* (2nd ed.). New York, NY: Guilford Press.

Steen, S. (2009) Group counseling for African American elementary students: An exploratory study. *The Journal for Specialists in Group Work, 34*(2), 101-117. doi:10.1080/01933920902791929

Steen, S., Henfield, M. S., & Booker, B. (2014). The Achieving Success Everyday Group Counseling Model: Implications for professional school counselors. *Journal for Specialists in Group Work, 39*(1), 29–46. doi:10.1080/01933922.2013.861886

Steering Committee. (2002). Empirically supported therapy relationships: Conclusions and recommendations of the Division 29 Task Force. In J. C. Norcross (Ed.), *Psychotherapy relationships that work: Therapist contribution and responsiveness to patients* (pp. 441–443). Oxford, UK: Oxford University Press.

Stein, D. M., & Lambert, M. J. (1995). Graduate training in psychotherapy: Are therapy outcomes enhanced? *Journal of Consulting & Clinical Psychology, 63,* 182–196. doi:10.1037/0022-006X.63.2.182

Steinberg, A. M., Brymer, M. J., Decker, K. B., & Pynoos, R. S. (2004). The University of California at Los Angeles post-traumatic stress disorder reaction index. *Current Psychiatry Reports, 6,* 96–100. doi:10.1007/s11920-004-0048-2

Sterling, H. E., & Watson, T. S. (1999). An empirically based guide for the use of time–out in the preschool and elementary classroom. *Psychology in the Schools, 36,* 135–148.

Sterling-Turner, H. E., Robinson, S. L., & Wilczynski, S. M. (2001). Functional assessment of distracting and disruptive behaviors in school settings. *School Psychology Review, 30,* 211–226.

Sterling-Turner, H. E., Watson, T. S., & Moore, J. W. (2000). The effects of direct training and treatment integrity on treatment outcomes in school consultation: Applications of direct behavioral consultation. *School Psychology Quarterly, 17,* 47–77.

Stern, G. G., & Richman, J. (1964). *High School Characteristics Index.* (Available from Dr. Joel L. Richman, 770 James Street, Suite 215, Syracuse, NY 13203)

Sternberg, R. J. (1998). Principles of teaching for successful intelligence. *Educational Psychologist, 33*(2/3), 65–72. doi:10.1080/00461520.1998.9653291

Sternberg, R. J. (2007). *Wisdom, intelligence, and creativity synthesized.* New York, NY: Cambridge University Press.

Stewart, J. L., Christner, R., & Freeman, A. (2007). An introduction to cognitive-behavior group therapy with youth. In R. Christner, J. L Stewart, & A. Freeman (Eds.), *Handbook of cognitive-behavior group therapy with children and adolescents: Specific settings and presenting problems* (pp. 3–21). New York, NY: Routledge.

Stone, C. (2004). School counselors as leaders and advocates in addressing sexual harassment. In R. Pérusse, & G. E. Goodnough (Eds.), *Leadership and advocacy in school counseling* (pp. 353–377). Pacific Grove, CA: Brooks/Cole.

Stone, C., & Dahir, C. (2012). *The transformed school counselor.* Boston, MA: Houghton Mifflin.

Stone, C., & Turba, R. (1999). School counselors using technology for advocacy. *The Journal of Technology in Counseling, 1*(1). Retrieved from http://jtc.colstate.edu/vol1_1/advocacy.htm

Stone, C. B. (2010). *School counseling principles: Ethics and law* (2nd ed.). Alexandria, VA: American School Counselor Association.

Stone, C. B., & Dahir, C. A. (2011). *School counselor accountability: A measure of student success* (3rd ed.). Upper Saddle River, NJ: Pearson.

Stone, J. R., & Lewis, M. V. (2012). *College and career ready in the 21st century.* New York, NY: Teachers College Press.

Stone, L. A., & Bradley, F. O. (1994). *Foundations of elementary and middle school counseling.* White Plains, NY: Longman.

Stonequist, E. V. (1937). *The marginal man: A study in personality and culture and conflict.* New York, NY: Russell & Russell.

Stoner, J. B., Bock, S. J., Thompson, J. R., Angell, M. E., Heyl, B. S., & Crowley, E. P. (2005). Welcome to our world: Parent perceptions of interactions between young children with ASD and educational professionals. *Focus on Autism and Other Developmental Disabilities, 1,* 39–51. doi:10.1177/10883576 050200010401

Storch, E. A., Murphy, T. K., Geffken, G. R., Sajid, M., Allen, P., Roberti, J. W., et al. (2005). Reliability and validity of the Yale Global Tic Severity Scale. *Psychological Assessment, 17,* 486–891. doi:10.1037/1040-3590.17.4.486

Studer, J. R., & Diambra, J. F. (2010). *A guide to practicum and internship for school counselor trainees.* New York, NY: Routledge Press.

Studer, J. R., Diambra, J. F., Breckner, J. A., & Heidel, R. E. (2011). *Obstacles and successes in implementing the ASCA National Model in schools.* Retrieved from http://files.eric.ed.gov/fulltext/EJ914272.pdf

Substance Abuse and Mental Health Services Administration. (2005). SAMSHA makes available treatment program guide. *Alcoholism and Drug Abuse Weekly, 17*(19), 4–6.

Substance Abuse and Mental Health Services Administration. (2013). *Results from the 2012 national survey on drug use and health: National findings.* Retrieved from http://www.samhsa.gov/data/sites/default/files/NSDUH-DetTabs2012/NSDUH-DetTabs2012/PDFW/NSDUH-DetTabsSect6pe-Tabs47to66-2012.pdf

Sue, D. W., & Sue, D. (2013). *Counseling the culturally and ethnically different client* (6th ed.). New York, NY: Wiley.

Sukhodolsky, D., Kassinove, H., & Gorman, B. (2004). Cognitive-behavioral therapy for anger in children and adolescents: A meta-analysis. *Aggression and Violent Behavior, 9,* 247–269. doi:10.1016/j.avb.2003.08.005

Sulkowski, M. L., Joyce, D. K., & Storch, E. A. (2012). Treating childhood anxiety in schools: Service delivery in a response to intervention paradigm. *Journal of Child and Family Studies, 21,* 938–947. doi:10.1007/s10826-011-9553-1

Super, D. E. (1955). Transition: From vocational guidance to counseling psychology. *Journal of Counseling Psychology, 2,* 3–9. doi:10.1037/h0041630

Super, D. E. (1957). *A psychology of careers.* New York, NY: Harper & Row.

Super, D. E. (Ed.). (1974). *Measuring vocational maturity for counseling and evaluation.* Washington, DC: National Vocational Guidance Association.

Super, D. E. (1983). Assessment in career guidance: Toward truly developmental counseling. *Personnel and Guidance Journal, 61,* 555–562. doi:10.1111/j.2164-4918.1983.tb00099.x

Super, D. E. (1990). Career and life development. In D. Brown, & L. Brooks (Eds.), *Career choice and development: Applying contemporary theories to practice* (2nd ed., pp. 197–261). San Francisco, CA: Jossey-Bass.

Super, D. E., Osborne, W. L., Walsh, D. J., Brown, S. D., & Niles, S. G. (1992). Developmental assessment and counseling: The C-DAC model. *Journal of Counseling & Development, 71,* 74–80. doi:10.1002/j.1556-6676.1992.tb02175.x

Super, D. E., Savickas, M. L., & Super, C. M. (1996). The life span, life-space approach to careers. In D. Brown, & L. Brooks (Eds.), *Career choice and development: Applying contemporary theories to practice* (3rd ed., pp. 121–178). San Francisco, CA: Jossey-Bass.

Super, D. E., Thompson, A. S., & Lindeman, R. H. (1988). *Adult career concerns inventory: Manual for research and exploratory use in counseling.* Palo Alto, CA: CPP.

Sutter, J., & Eyberg, S. M. (1984). *Sutter-Eyberg Student Behavior Inventory.* Gainesville, FL: University of Florida.

Sutton, J. M., Jr., & Fall, M. (1995). The relationship of school climate factors to counselor self-efficacy. *Journal of Counseling & Development, 73,* 331–336. doi:10.1002/j.1556-6676.1995.tb01759.x

Sutton, J. M., & Pearson, R. (2002). The practice of school counseling in rural and small town schools. *Professional School Counseling, 5,* 266–276.

Suzuki-Crumly, J., & Hyers, L. L. (2004). The relationship among ethnic identity, psychological well-being, and intergroup competence: An investigation of two biracial groups. *Cultural Diversity & Ethnic Minority Psychology, 10,* 137–150. doi:10.1037/1099-9809.10.2.137

Swanson, T. C. (2005). Provide structure for children with learning and behavior problems. *Intervention and School Clinic, 40,* 182–187.

Sweeney, T. J. (1971). *Rural poor students and guidance. Guidance Monograph Series, Series VI: Minority Groups and Guidance.* Boston, MA: Houghton Mifflin.

Sweeney, T. J. (2009). *Adlerian counseling and psychotherapy: A practitioner's approach* (5th ed.). New York, NY: Routledge.

Symonds, W. C., Schwartz, R. B., & Ferguson, R. (2011). *Pathways to prosperity: Meeting the challenge of preparing young Americans for the 21st century.* Retrieved from http://www.gse.harvard.edu/news/11/02/pathways-prosperity-meeting-challenge-preparing-young-americans-21st-century

Szalacha, L. A. (2001). The sexual diversity climate of Massachusetts' secondary schools and the success of the safe school program for gay and lesbian students. *Dissertation Abstracts International, 62,* 1327. (UMI No. 3012938)

Talbert, J. E., & McLaughlin, M. W. (1999). Assessing the school environment: Embedded context and bottom-up research strategies. In S. L. Friedman & T. D. Wachs (Eds.), *Measuring environment across lifespan: Emerging methods and concepts* (pp. 197–227). Washington, DC: American Psychological Association.

Talleyrand, R. M. (2010). Eating disorders in African American girls: Implications for counselors. *Journal of Counseling & Development, 88*, 319–324. doi:10.1002/j.1556-6678.2010.tb00028.x

Tartakovsky, M. (2011). *9 myths, misconceptions and stereotypes about ADHD*. Retrieved from http://psychcentral.com/blog/archives/2011/06/24/9-myths-misconceptions-and-stereotypes-about-adhd/

Tatum, B. D. (2003). *"Why are all the black kids sitting together in the cafeteria?"* (5th anniversary ed.). New York, NY: Basic Books.

Tauriac, J. J., Kim, G. S., Lambe Sarinana, S., Tawa, J., & Kahn, V. D. (2013) Utilizing affinity groups to enhance intergroup dialogue workshops for racially and ethnically diverse students. *The Journal for Specialists in Group Work, 38*, 241–260. doi:10.1080/01933922.2013.800176

Taylor, E. R., & Karcher, M. (2009). Cultural and developmental variations in the resiliencies promoted by school counselors. *Journal of Professional Counseling: Practice, Theory & Research, 37*(2), 66–87.

Taylor, P., Funk, C., & Craighill, P. (2006). *Guess who's coming to dinner?* Retrieved from http://pewresearch.org/pubs/304/guess-whos-coming-to-dinner

TEACCH Autism Program. (2014). *Information on autism*. Retrieved from http://www.teacch.com/highfunction.html

Teske, S. C. (2011). A study of zero tolerance policies in schools: A multi-integrated systems approach to improve outcomes for adolescents. *Journal of Child and Adolescent Psychiatric Nursing, 24*(2), 88–97. doi:10.1111/j.1744-6171.2011.00273.x

Thayer, P. B. (2000, May). Retention of students from first generation and low income backgrounds. *Opportunity Outlook*, 2–8.

Thigpen, D., & Freedberg, L. (2014, January 1). *The power of parents*. Retrieved from http://edsource.org/wp-content/uploads/Power-of-Parents-Feb-2014.pdf

Thompson, R. A. (2012). *Professional school counseling: Best practices for working in the schools* (3rd ed.). New York, NY: Brunner-Routledge.

Thompson, R. A. (2014). Stress and child development. *The Future of Children, 24*(1), 41–59. Retrieved from http://futureofchildren.org/futureofchildren/publications/docs/24_01_02.pdf

Thompson, R. M. (2003). *Counseling techniques* (2nd ed.). New York, NY: Brunner-Routledge.

Thorstad, D. (1974). *The Bolsheviks and the early homosexual rights movement*. New York, NY: Times Change Press.

Thurstone, L. L. (1938). Primary mental abilities. *Psychometric Monographs*, 1.

Tingstrom, D. H. (2002). The good behavior game. In M. Hersen & W. Sledge (Eds.), *The encyclopedia of psychotherapy* (Vol. 1, pp. 879–884). New York, NY: Academic Press.

Title IX of the Education Amendments of 1972. Retrieved from http://www.dol.gov/oasam/regs/statutes/titleix.htm

Tollerud, T. R., & Nejedlo, R. J. (2009). Designing a developmental counseling curriculum. In A. Vernon (Ed.), *Counseling children and adolescents* (4th ed.). Denver, CO: Love.

Tongue, B. (1994). Separation anxiety disorder. In T. H. Ollendick, N. J. King, & W. Yule (Eds.), *International handbook of phobic and anxiety disorders in children and adolescents* (pp. 145–168). New York, NY: Plenum Press.

Topdemir, C. (2013). School counselors' beliefs about accountability. *Practitioner Scholar: Journal of Counseling & Professional Psychology, 2*(1), 12–22.

Topor, D. R., Keane, S. P., Shelton,, T. L., & Calkins, S. D. (2010). Parent involvement and student academic performance: A multiple mediational analysis. *Journal of Prevention Intervention Community, 38*, 183–197. doi:1080/108552352352.2010.486297

Traxler, A. E., & North, R. D. (1966). *Techniques of guidance*. New York, NY: Harper & Row.

Trice-Black, S., Bailey, C. E., & Riechel, M. E. K. (2013). Play therapy in school counseling. *Professional School Counseling Journal, 16*, 303–312.

Troiden, R. R. (1979). The formation of homosexual identities. *Journal of Homosexuality, 17*, 362–373. doi:10.1300/J082v17n01_02

Trolley, B. C., Haas, H. S., & Patti, D. C. (2009). *The school counselor's guide to special education*. Thousand Oaks, CA: Corwin Press.

Trusty, J. (1996). Relationship of parental involvement in teens' career development to teens' attitudes, perceptions, and behavior. *Journal of Research and Development in Education, 30*, 317–323. doi:35400006076963.0070

Trusty, J. (1998). Family influences on educational expectations of late adolescents. *Journal of Educational Research, 91*, 260–270. doi:10.1080/00220679809597553

Trusty, J. (1999). Effects of eighth-grade parental involvement on late adolescents' educational expectations. *Journal of Research and Development in Education, 32*, 224–233. doi:35400008991516.0030

Trusty, J. (2002). African Americans' educational expectations: Longitudinal causal models for women and men. *Journal of Counseling & Development, 80*, 332–345. doi:10.1002/j.1556-6678.2002.tb00198.x

Trusty, J. (2004). *Effects of students' middle-school and high-school experiences on completion of the bachelor's degree*. Retrieved from http://www.umass.edu/schoolcounseling/uploads/ResearchBrief2.1.pdf

Trusty, J., & Ng, K. (2000). Longitudinal effects of achievement perceptions on choice of postsecondary major. *Journal of Vocational Behavior, 57*, 123–135. doi:10.1006/jvbe.1999.1735

Trusty, J., & Niles, S. G. (2003). High-school math courses and completion of the bachelor's degree. *Professional School Counseling, 7*, 99–107.

Trusty, J., & Niles, S. G. (2004). Realized potential or lost talent: High-school variables and bachelor's degree completion. *Career Development Quarterly, 53*, 2–15. doi:10.1002/j.2161-0045.2004.tb00651.x

Trusty, J., & Pirtle, T. (1998). Parents' transmission of educational goals to their adolescent children. *Journal of Research and Development in Education, 32*, 53–65. doi:35400007141428.0070

Trusty, J., Robinson, C., Plata, M., & Ng, K. (2000). Effects of gender, SES, and early academic performance on post-secondary educational choice. *Journal of Counseling & Development, 76*, 463–472.

Trusty, J., Watts, R. E., & Crawford, R. (1996). Career information resources for parents of public school seniors: Findings from a national study. *Journal of Career Development, 22*, 227–238. doi:10.1007/BF02259992

Trusty, J., Watts, R. E., & Erdman, P. (1997). Predictors of parents' involvement in their teens' career development. *Journal of Career Development, 23*, 189–201. doi:10.1007/BF02359189

Tuckman, B. W. (1965). Developmental sequence in small groups. *Psychological Bulletin, 63*, 384–399. doi:10.1037/h0022100

Turnbull, R., Turnbull, A., Wehmeyer, M. L., & Shogren, K. A. (2012). *Exceptional lives: Special education in today's schools* (7th ed.). Upper Saddle River, NJ: Merrill.

Turney, K., & Kao, G. (2009). Barriers to school involvement: Are immigrant parents disadvantaged? *The Journal of Educational Research, 102*, 257–271. doi:10.3200/JOER.102.4.257-271

Twemlow, S. W., Fonagy, P., & Sacco, F. C. (2002). Feeling safe in school. *Smith College Studies in Social Work, 72*, 303–326. doi:10.1080/00377310209517660

Twemlow, S. W., Fonagy, P., Sacco, F. C., & Brethour, J. R., Jr. (2006). Teachers who bully students: A hidden trauma. *International Journal of Social Psychiatry, 52*, 187–198. doi:10.1177/0020764006067234

Tyler, J. M., & Sabella, R. M. (2004). *Using technology to improve counseling practice: A primer for the 21st century*. Alexandria, VA: American Counseling Association.

Unger, H. G. (2006). *But what if I don't want to go to college? A guide to success through alternative education* (3rd ed.). New York, NY: Ferguson.

United Nations General Assembly. (1989). *Adoption of a convention on the rights of the child* (UN Doc. A/Res/44/25). New York, NY: Author.

United Way. (2005). *2-1-1. Get connected. Get answers.* Retrieved from http://national.unitedway.org/211/

Unverferth, A. R., Talbert-Johnson, C., & Bogard, T. (2012). Perceived barriers for first generation college students: Reforms to level the terrain. *International Journal of Educational Reform, 21*, 238–252.

Uribe, V., & Harbeck, K. (1992). Addressing the needs of lesbian, gay, and bisexual youth: The origins of project 10 and school-based intervention. In K. Harbeck (Ed.), *Coming out of the classroom closet* (pp. 9–28). New York, NY: Harrington Park Press.

U.S. Bureau of Labor Statistics. (2014). *Occupational outlook handbook 2014 edition.* Retrieved from http://www.bls.gov/ooh/home.htm

U.S. Census Bureau. (2010). *Mapping census 2010: The geography of U.S. diversity.* Washington, DC: U.S. Government Printing Office.

U.S. Census Bureau. (2012). *Current population survey, annual social and economic supplement.* Retrieved from http://www.census.gov/cps/

U.S. Congress. (2009). American Recovery and Reinvestment Act of 2009. Public Law, (111-5), 111.

U.S. Department of Defense. (2005). *ASVAB exploring careers: The ASVAB career exploration guide.* Washington, DC: U.S. Government Printing Office.

U.S. Department of Education. (1994). *Goals 2000: The Educate America Act.* Washington, DC: Author.

U.S. Department of Education. (1996). *A new understanding of parent involvement: Family-work school.* Washington, DC: U.S. Government Printing Office.

U.S. Department of Education. (1998). *Tools for schools: School reform models.* Washington, DC: Author.

U.S. Department of Education. (2001). *No Child Left Behind Act.* Retrieved from http://www.ed.gov/legislation/ESEA02/

U.S. Department of Education. (2009). *Thirty-first annual report to Congress on the implementation of the Individuals with Disabilities Education Act: Results.* Washington, DC: Author.

U.S. Department of Education. (2011). *Race to the Top Act of 2011.* Retrieved from http://www2.ed.gov/programs/racetothetop/index.html

U.S. Department of Education. (2014). *Building the legacy: IDEA.* Retrieved from http://idea.ed.gov/explore/view/p/%2Croot%2Cregs%2C300%2CD%2C300%252E306%2C

U.S. Department of Education, National Center for Educational Statistics. (2014). *The condition of education* (NCES Publication No. 2014-083). Retrieved from http://nces.ed.gov/pubs2014/2014083.pdf

U.S. Department of Education, Office of Special Education Programs. (2000a). *Early warning, timely response: A guide to safe schools.* Retrieved from http://cecp.air.org/guide/guide.pdf

U.S. Department of Education, Office of Special Education Programs. (2000b). *Safeguarding our children: An action guide.* Retrieved from http://www2.ed.gov/admins/lead/safety/actguide/action_guide.pdf

U.S. Department of Housing and Urban Development. (2013). *The 2013 Annual Homeless Assessment Report (AHAR) to Congress.* Retrieved from https://www.onecpd.info/resources/documents/ahar-2013-part1.pdf

U.S. Department of Labor Employment and Training Administration. (2001). *O*NET Work Importance Locator.* Washington, DC: Author.

Valentine, G. (1995). Commentary-shades of gray: The conundrum of color categories. *Teaching Tolerance, 49*, 47.

Valpar International Corporation. (2011). *SIGI 3.* Tucson, AZ: Author.

Valpar. (2014). *SIGI 3.* Retrieved from http://www.sigi3.org/

Van Bourgondien, M. E. (1996). Interventions for adults with autism. *Journal of Rehabilitation, 11*, 65–71.

Van Bourgondien, M. E., & Mesibov, G. B. (1989). Diagnosis and treatment of adolescents and adults with autism. In G. Dawson (Ed.), *Autism* (pp. 367–385). New York, NY: Guilford Press.

Van Cleave, J., Gortmaker, S. L., & Perrin, J. M. (2010). Dynamics of obesity and chronic health conditions among children and youth. *Journal of American Medical Association, 303,* 623–630.

van den Berg, P. A., Mond, J., Eisenberg, M., Ackard, D., & Neumark-Sztainer, D. (2010). The link between body dissatisfaction and self-esteem in adolescents: Similarities across gender, age, weight status, race/ethnicity, and socioeconomic status. *Journal of Adolescent Health, 47,* 290–296. doi:10.1016/j.jadohealth.2010.02.004

van der Kolk, B. A., Roth, S., Pelcovitz, D., Sunday, S., & Spinazzola, J. (2005). Disorders of extreme stress: The empirical foundation of a complex adaptation to trauma. *Journal of Traumatic Stress, 18,* 389–399. doi:10.1002/jts.20047

Van Ryzin, M. J. (2011). Protective factors at school: Reciprocal effects among adolescents' perceptions of the school environment, engagement in learning, and hope. *Journal of Youth and Adolescence, 40,* 1568-1580. doi:10.1007/s10964-011-9637-7

VanZandt, Z., & Hayslip, J. (2001). *Developing your school-counseling program: A handbook for systemic planning.* Belmont, CA: Wadsworth/Thomson Learning.

Varjas, K., Graybill, E., Mahan, W., Meyers, J., Dew, B., Marshall, M., Singh, A., & Birckbichler, L. (2007). Urban service providers' perspectives on school responses to gay, lesbian, and questioning students: An exploratory study. *Professional School Counseling, 11*(2), 113–119. doi:10.5330/PSC.n.2010-11.113

Vassilopoulos, S., Brouzos, A., Damer, D., Mellou, A., & Mitropoulou, A. (2013). A psychoeducational school-based group intervention for socially anxious children. *Journal for Specialists in Group Work, 38,* 1–23. doi:10.1080/01933922.2013.819953

Velting, O. N., Setzer, N. J., & Albano, A. M. (2004). Update on and advances in assessments and cognitive-behavioral treatment of anxiety disorders in children and adolescents. Research and Practice, 35, 42–54. doi:10.1037/0735-7028.35.1.42

Verdick, E., & Lisovskis, M. (2003). *How to take the grrrr out of anger.* Minneapolis, MN: Free Spirit.

Vernon, A. (1989). *Thinking, feeling, behaving: An emotional education curriculum for adolescents, grades 7–12.* Champaign, IL: Research Press.

Vernon, A. (1998a). *The PASSPORT program: A journey through social, emotional, cognitive, and self-development (Grades 1–5).* Champaign, IL: Research Press.

Vernon, A. (1998b). *The PASSPORT program: A journey through social, emotional, cognitive, and self-development (Grades 6–8).* Champaign, IL: Research Press.

Vernon, A. (1998c). *The PASSPORT program: A journey through social, emotional, cognitive, and self-development (Grades 9–12).* Champaign, IL: Research Press.

Vernon, A. (2002). *What works when with children and adolescents: A handbook of individual counseling techniques.* Champaign, IL: Research Press.

Vernon, A. (2004). Applications of rational-emotive behavior therapy. In A. Vernon (Ed.), *Counseling children and adolescents* (3rd ed., pp. 163–187). Denver, CO: Love.

Vernon, A. (2006a). *Thinking, feeling, behaving: An emotional education program for adolescents.* Champaign, IL: Research Press.

Vernon, A. (2006b). *Thinking, feeling, behaving: An emotional education program for children.* Champaign, IL: Research Press.

Vernon, A. (2007). Applications of REBT in groups. In R. W. Christner, J. L. Stewart, & A. Freeman (Eds.), *Handbook of cognitive-behavioral group therapy for children and adolescents: Specific settings and presenting problems.* New York, NY: Routledge.

Vernon, A. (2009a). *More of what works when with children and adolescents: A handbook of individual counseling techniques.* Champaign, IL: Research Press.

Vernon, A. (2009b). *Counseling children & adolescents* (4th ed.). Denver, CO: Love.

Vernon, A. (2011). Rational emotive behavior therapy. In D. Capuzzi & D. Gross (Eds.), *Counseling and psychotherapy: Theories and interventions* (pp. 237–251). Alexandria, VA: American Counseling Association.

Vespa, J., Lewis, J. M., & Kreider, R. M. (2013). *America's families and living arrangements: 2012: Population characteristics.* Retrieved from http://www.census.gov/prod/2013pubs/p20-570.pdf

Viallancourt, R., Hymel, S., & McDougall, P. (2013). The biological underpinnings of peer victimization: Understanding why and how the effects of bullying can last a lifetime. *Theory Into Practice, 52,* 241–248. doi:10.1080/00405841.2013.829726

Villalba, J. A., & Sheperis, S. F. (2004). Special education identification and placement. In T. S. Watson (Ed.), *Comprehensive encyclopedia of school psychology* (pp. 135–149). Hingman, MA: Kluwer Academic.

Vilhjalmsson, R., Kristjansdottir, G., & Ward, D. S. (2012). Bodily deviations and body image in adolescence.*Youth & Society, 44,* 366–384. doi:10.1177/0044118X11402850

Vollmer, T. R., & Northup, J. (1996). Some implications of functional analysis for school psychology. *School Psychology Quarterly, 11,* 76–92. doi:10.1037/h0088922

Vreeman, R. C., & Carroll, A. E. (2007). A systematic review of school-based interventions to prevent bullying. *Archives of Pediatrics & Adolescent Medicine, 161*(1), 78–88. doi:10.1001/archpedi.161.1.78

Wadsworth, M. E., Raviv, T., Compas, B. E., & Connor-Smith, J. K. (2005). Parent and adolescent responses to poverty-related stress: Tests of mediated and moderated coping models. *Journal of Child and Family Studies, 14,* 283–298. doi:10.1007/s10826-005-5056-2

Wadsworth, M. E., Wolff, B., Santiago, C., & Moran, E. G. (2008). Adolescent coping with poverty-related stress. *Prevention Researcher, 15*(4), 13–16.

Waehler, C., Kalodner, C., Wampold, B., & Lichtenberg, J. (2000). Empirically supported treatments (ESTs) in perspective: Implications for counseling psychology training. *The Counseling Psychologist, 28,* 657–671. doi:10.1177/0011000000285004

Walker, J. M. T., Ice, C. L., Hoover-Dempsey, K. V., & Sandler, H. M. (2011). Latino parents' motivations for involvement in their children's schooling. *The Elementary School Journal, 111,* 409–429.

Walkup, J. T., & Ginsberg, G. S. (2002). Anxiety disorders in children and adolescents. *International Review of Psychiatry, 14,* 85–86.

Wallace, R. C., Jr., Engel, D. E., & Mooney, J. E. (1997). *The learning school: A guide to vision-based leadership.* Thousand Oaks, CA: Corwin Press.

Walls, N. E., Kane, S. B., & Wisneski, H. (2010). Gay-straight alliances and school experiences of sexual minority youth. *Youth & Society, 41,* 307–332. doi:10.1177/0044118X09334957

Walter, J. L., & Peller, J. E. (1992). *Becoming solution-focused in brief therapy.* New York, NY: Brunner/Maxel.

Waltz, M. (2000). *Obsessive compulsive disorder: Help for children and adolescents.* Cambridge, UK: O'Reilly.

Walz, G. R., & Benjamin, L. (1984). A systems approach to career guidance. *Vocational Guidance Quarterly, 33,* 26–34. doi:10.1002/j.2164-585X.1984.tb01599.x

Wang, W. (2012). *The rise of intermarriage: Rates, characteristics vary by race and gender.* Washington, DC: Pew Social & Demographic Trends. Retrieved from http://www.pewsocialtrends.org/files/2012/02/SDT-Intermarriage-II.pdf

Wang, W., & Taylor, P. (2012). *The rise of intermarriage: Rates, characteristics vary by race and gender.* Retrieved from https:// www.pewsocialtrends.org/files/2012/02/SDT-Intermarriage-II.pdf

Wardle, F. (1992). Supporting biracial children in the school setting. *Education and Treatment of Children, 15,* 163–172.

Ware, J. N., Ohrt, J. H., & Swank, J. M. (2012). A phenomenological exploration of children's experiences in a social skills group. *The Journal for Specialists in Group Work, 37,* 133–151. doi:10.1080/01933922.2012.663862

Warters, J. (1946). *High school personnel work today.* New York, NY: McGraw Hill.

Watsford, C., & Rickwood, D. (2014). Young people's expectations, preferences, and experiences of therapy: Effects on clinical outcome, service use, and help-seeking intentions. *Clinical Psychologist, 18*(1), 43–51. doi:10.1111/cp.12034

Watson, T. S., Dufrene, B. A., Weaver, A. D., Butler, T., & Meeks, C. (2005). Brief antecedent assessment and treatment of tics in the regular education classroom: A preliminary investigation. *Behavior Modification, 29*, 839857. doi:10.1177/0145445505279252

Watson, T. S., Howell, L. A., & Smith, S. L. (2006). Behavioral interventions for tic disorders. In D. W. Woods, & R. G. Miltenberger (Eds.), *Tic disorders, trichotillomania, and other repetitive disorders: Behavioral approaches to analysis and treatment* (pp. 73–96). Boston, MA: Kluwer.

Watson, T. S., & Steege, M. (2009). *Conducting school-based functional behavioral assessments: A practitioner's guide* (2nd ed.). New York, NY: Guilford.

Webb, L., & Brigman, G. (2005). Student success skills: Tools and strategies for improved academic and social outcomes. *Professional School Counseling, 10*, 112–120.

Webb, L. D., Brigman, G. A., & Campbell, C. (2005). Linking school counselors and student success: A replication of the student success skills approach targeting the academic and social competence of students. *Professional School Counseling, 8*, 407–413.

Webb, L. D., & Myrick, R. D. (2003). A group counseling intervention for children with attention deficit hyperactivity disorder. *Professional School Counseling, 7*, 108–115.

Webb, N. B. (2010). *Helping bereaved children: A handbook for practitioners* (2nd ed.). New York, NY: Guilford Press.

Webber, J. (2004). Factors affecting burnout in school counselors. *Dissertation Abstracts International Section A: Humanities and Social Sciences, 66*(9), 3224.

Webb-Landman, E. (2012). Using group counseling to improve the attendance of elementary school students with high rates of absenteeism: An action research study. *Georgia School Counselors Association Journal, 19*(1), 37–64.

Webster-Stratton, C., Reid, M. J., & Hammond, M. (2004). Treating children with early-onset conduct problems: Intervention outcomes for parent, child, and teacher training. *Journal of Clinical Child and Adolescent Psychology, 33*(1), 105–124. doi:10.1207/S15374424JCCP3301_11

Wechsler, D. (2008). *Manual for the Wechsler Adult Intelligence Scale* (4th ed.). San Antonio, TX: The Psychological Corporation.

Wechsler, D. (2014). *Manual for the Wechsler Intelligence Scale for Children* (5th ed.). San Antonio, TX: The Psychological Corporation.

Wehrly, B., Kenney, K. R., & Kenney, M. E. (1999). *Counseling multiracial families*. Thousand Oaks, CA: Sage.

Wei, X., & Marder, C. (2012). Self-concept development of students with disabilities: Disability category, gender, and racial differences from early elementary to high school. *Remedial and Special Education, 33*, 247–257. doi:10.1177/0741932510394872

Weinberger, A. D. (1966). Interracial intimacy. *Journal of Sex Research, 2*, 157–168.

Weinstein, C. S., & Mignano, A. J., Jr. (1997). *Elementary classroom management* (2nd ed.). New York, NY: McGraw-Hill.

Weiss, K., & Wertheim, E. H. (2005). An evaluation of a prevention program for disordered eating in adolescent girls: Examining responses of high- and low-risk girls. *Eating Disorders, 13*, 143–156. doi:10.1080/10640260590918946

Wells, G., & Claxton, G. (2008). *Learning for life in the 21st century: Sociocultural perspectives on the future of education*. Malden, MA: Blackwell.

West, A. M., Denzer, A. Q., Wildman, B. G., & Anhalt, K. (2013). Teacher perception of burden and willingness to accommodate children with chronic health conditions. *Advances in School Mental Health Promotion, 6*, 35–50. doi:10.1080/1754730X.2012.760920

Wetherby, A. M., & Prizant, B. M. (2005). Enhancing language and communication development in autism spectrum disorders. Assessment and intervention guidelines. In D. Zager (Ed.), *Autism spectrum disorders* (3rd ed., pp. 327–365). Mahwah, NJ: Erlbaum.

Whiston, S., Feldwisch, R., & James, B. (2015). Outcomes research on school counseling interventions and programs. In B. T. Erford (Ed.), *Transforming the school counseling profession* (4th ed., pp. 132–145). Columbus, OH: Pearson, Merrill, Prentice Hall.

Whiston, S., & Sexton, T. (1998). A review of school counseling outcome research: Implications for practice. *Journal of Counseling & Development, 76,* 412–426. doi:10.1002/pits.20372

Whiston, S. C. (2002). Response to the past, present, and future of school counseling: Raising some issues. *Professional School Counseling, 5,* 148–155.

Whiston, S. C., Brecheisen, B. K., & Stephens, J. (2003). Does treatment modality affect career counseling effectiveness? *Journal of Vocational Behavior, 62,* 390–410. doi:10.1016/S0001-8791(02)00050-7

Whiston, S. C., Eder, K., Rahardja, D., & Tai, W. L. (2005, June). *Research supporting school counseling: Comprehensive findings.* Paper presented at the annual meeting of the American School Counselor Association, Orlando, FL.

Whiston, S. C., & Quinby, R. F. (2009). Review of school counseling outcome research. *Psychology in Schools, 46,* 267-272. doi:10.1002/pits.20372

Whiston, S. C., Sexton, T. L., & Lasoff, D. L. (1998). Career-intervention outcome: A replication and extension of Oliver and Spokane (1988). *Journal of Counseling Psychology, 45,* 150–165. doi:10.1037/0022-0167.45.2.150

Whiston, S. C., Tai, W. L., Rahardja, D., & Eder, K. (2011). School counseling outcome: A meta-analytic examination of interventions. *Journal of Counseling & Development, 89,* 37–55. doi:10.1002/j.1556-6678.2011.tb00059.x

White, F. A. (2007). The professional school counselor's challenge: Accountability. *Journal of Professional Counseling: Practice, Theory & Research, 35*(2), 62–70.

Wiggins, J. D., & Wiggins, A. H. (1992). Elementary students' self-esteem and behavioral ratings related to counselor time-task emphases. *The School Counselor, 39,* 377–381.

Wilkerson, K., & Bellini, J. (2006). Intrapersonal and organizational factors associated with burnout among school counselors. *Journal of Counseling & Development, 84,* 440–450. doi: 10.1002/j.1556-6678.2006.tb00428.x

Wilkerson, K., Pérusse, R., & Hughes, A. (2013). Comprehensive school counseling programs and students achievement outcomes: A comparative analysis of RAMP versus Non-RAMP schools. *Professional School Counseling, 16,* 172–184. doi:10.5330/PSC.n.2013-16.172

Wilkinson, L. A. (2008). Self-management for children with high-functioning autism spectrum disorders. *Intervention in School and Clinic, 43,* 150–157. doi:10.1177/1053451207311613

Willard, N. E. (2007). *Cyberbullying and cyberthreats: Responding to the challenge of online social aggression, threats, and distress.* Champaign, IL: Research Press.

Williams, C. U., McMahon, H.G., McLeod, A., & Rice, R. (2013). An exploration of secondary school counselors' experiences engaging in group work. *Journal for Specialists in Group Work, 38*(2), 96–120. doi:10.1080/01933922.2013.775205

Williams, J. M. (Ed.). (2009). *Applied sport psychology: Personal growth to peak performance* (6th ed.). New York, NY: McGraw-Hill.

Williams, M. (1997, September 21). Nations' first private school for gays opens in Dallas education facility is run by two teachers as a haven from the harassment that occurs on traditional campuses. So far, enrollment totals seven. *The Los Angeles Times,* p. 35.

Williams, T. T., & Sanchez, B. (2012) Parental involvement (and uninvolvement) at an inner-city high school. *Urban Education, 47,* 625–652. doi:10.1177/0042085912437794

Williamson, C. G. (1939). *How to counsel students.* New York, NY: McGraw-Hill.

Wilson, N. (1986). Effects of a classroom guidance unit on sixth graders' examination performance. *Journal of Hispanic Education and Development, 25*(2), 70–79.

Wilson, S. J., Lipsey, M. W., & Derzon, J. H. (2003). The effects of school-based intervention programs on aggressive behavior: A meta-analysis. *Journal of Consulting & Clinical Psychology, 71,* 136–149. doi:10.1037/0022-006X.71.1.136

Wilson, S. G., Plane, D. A., Mackun, P. J., Fischetti, T. R., & Goworowska, J. (2012). *Patterns of metropolitan and micropolitan population change: 2000 to 2010.* Retrieved from http://www.census.gov/prod/cen2010/reports/c2010sr-01.pdf

Winn, N. N., & Priest, R. (1993). Counseling biracial children: A forgotten component of multicultural counseling. *Family Therapy, 20,* 29–35.

Wolfberg, P. J. (2003). *Peer play and the autism spectrum: The art of guiding children's socialization and imagination.* Shawnee Mission, KS: Autism Asperger.

Wolfberg, P. J. (2009). *Play and imagination in children with autism* (2nd ed.). New York, NY: Teachers College Press.

Wolpe, J. (1958). *Psychotherapy by reciprocal inhibition.* Stanford, CA: Stanford University Press.

Woodcock, R., McGrew, K., & Mather, N. (2001). *Woodcock-Johnson: Tests of Cognitive Ability* (3rd ed.). Itasca, IL: Riverside.

Woodcock, R., Mather, N., & McGrew, K. (2001). *Woodcock-Johnson: Tests of Achievement* (3rd ed.). Itasca, IL: Riverside.

Woods, D. W., & Miltenberger, R. G. (Eds.). (2006). *Tic disorders, trichotillomania, and other repetitive behavior disorders: Behavioral approaches to analysis and treatment.* Boston, MA: Kluwer.

Woodward, K. S. (1999). *Alignment of national and state standards: A report by the GED testing service.* Washington, DC: American Council on Education & GED Testing Service.

Worden, J. W. (2008). *Grief counseling and grief therapy: A handbook for the mental health professional.* New York, NY: Springer.

World Health Organization. (2007). *International statistical classification of diseases and related health problems* (10th rev., version for 2007). New York, NY: Author.

Wren, D. J. (1999). School culture: Exploring the hidden curriculum. *Adolescence, 34,* 593–596.

Wrenn, C. G. (1962). *The counselor in a changing world.* Washington, DC: American Personnel and Guidance Association.

Wubbolding, R. (2000). *Reality therapy for the 21st century.* Philadelphia, PA: Brunner-Routledge.

Wubbolding, R. (2005). The power of belonging. *International Journal of Reality Therapy, 24*(2), 43–44.

Wubbolding, R. (2006). Searching for mental health. *International Journal of Choice Theory, 1*(1), 5–6.

Wubbolding, R. (2011). *Reality therapy: Theories of psychotherapy series.* Washington, DC: American Psychological Association.

Wubbolding, R. (2015). *Reality therapy training manual* (16th rev.). Cincinnati, OH: Center for Reality Therapy.

Wubbolding, R., & Brickell, J. (2001). *A set of directions for putting and keeping yourself together.* Minneapolis, MN: Educational Media Corporation.

Wubbolding, R., & Brickell, J. (2005). Purpose of behavior: Language and levels of commitment. *International Journal of Reality Therapy, 25*(1), 39–41.

Wurtele, S., Moreno, T., & Kenny, M. (2008). Evaluation of a sexual abuse prevention workshop for parents of young children. *Journal of Child and Adolescent Trauma, 1,* 331–340. doi:10.1080/19361520802505768

Yager, J. (1976). Postcombat violent behavior in psychiatrically maladjusted soldiers. *Archives of General Psychiatry, 33,* 1332–1335.

Yalom, I. D., & Leszcz, M. (2005). *The theory and practice of group psychotherapy* (5th ed.). New York, NY: HarperCollins.

Yancey, A. K., Grant, D., Kurosky, S., Kravitz-Wirtz, N., & Mistry, R. (2011). Role modeling, risk, and resilience in California adolescents. *Journal of Adolescent Health, 48,* 36–43. doi:10.1016/j.jadohealth.2010.05.001

Yates, P., Allardyce, S., & MacQueen, S, (2012). Children who display harmful sexual behavior: Assessing the risks of boys abusing at home, in the community or across both settings. *Journal of Sexual Aggression, 18,* 23–35. doi:10.1080/13552600.2011.634527

Yehuda, R., Schmeidler, J., Giller, E. L., Jr., Siever, L. J., & Binder-Brynes, K. (1998). Relationship between posttraumatic stress disorder characteristics of holocaust survivors. *American Journal of Psychiatry, 155,* 841–843.

Yell, M. L. (2012). *The law and special education* (3rd ed.). Upper Saddle River, NJ: Pearson Merrill.

Yeung Thompson, R. S., & Leadbeater, B. J. (2013). Peer victimization and internalizing symptoms from adolescence into young adulthood: Building strength through emotional support. *Journal of Research on Adolescence, 23*, 290–303. doi:10.1111/j.1532-7795.2012.00827.x

Young, A., & Kaffenberger, C. (2009). *Making DATA work* (2nd ed.). Alexandria, VA: American School Counselor Association.

Young, A., & Miller-Kneale, M. (2013). *School counselor leadership: An essential practice.* Alexandria, VA: American School Counselor Association.

Young, D. M., Sanchez, D. T., & Wilton, L. S. (2013). At the crossroads of race: Racial ambiguity and biracial identification influence psychological essentialist thinking. *Cultural Diversity and Ethnic Minority Psychology, 19*, 461–467. doi:10.1037/a0032565

Young, H. (2006). REBT assessment and treatment with adolescents. In A. Ellis & M. E. Bernard (Eds.), *Rational emotive behavioral approaches to childhood disorders: Theory, practice, and research* (pp. 115–132). New York, NY: Springer.

Young, M. A., & Basham, A. (2014). Consultation and supervision. In B. T. Erford (Ed.), *Orientation to the counseling profession: Advocacy, ethics, and essential professional foundations* (2nd ed., pp. 423–451). Upper Saddle River, NJ: Pearson.

Young, R. A. (1994). Helping adolescents with career development: The active role of parents. *The Career Development Quarterly, 42*, 195–203. doi:10.1002/j.2161-0045.1994.tb00934.x

Zack, N. (1995). Mixed black and white race and public policy. *Hypatia, 10*, 120–132. doi:10.1111/j.1527-2001.1995.tb01356.x

Zager, D., & Shamow, N. (2005). Teaching students with autism spectrum disorders. In D. Zaeger (Eds.), *Autism spectrum disorders: Identification, education, and treatment* (3rd ed., pp. 295–326). Mahwah, NJ: Erlbaum.

Zeanah, C. H., & Gleason, M. M. (2010). *Reactive attachment disorders: A review for DSM-5.* Washington, DC: American Psychiatric Association.

Zehr, H. (2002). *The little book of restorative justice.* Philadelphia, PA: Good Books.

Ziffer, J. M., Crawford, E., & Penney-Wietor, J. (2007). The boomerang bunch: A school-based multifamily group approach for students and their families recovering from parental separation and divorce. *The Journal for Specialists in Group Work, 32*(2), 154–164. doi:10.1080/01933920701227141

Zimmerman, B., Bonner, S., & Kovach, R. (1996). *Developing self-regulated learners: Beyond achievement to self-regulation.* Washington, DC: American Psychological Association.

Zimmerman, B. J., & Schunk, D. H. (Eds.). (2001). *Self-regulated learning and academic achievement: Theoretical perspectives* (2nd ed.). Mahwah, NJ: Erlbaum.

Zinck, K., & Littrell, J. M. (2000). Action research shows group counseling effective with at-risk adolescent girls. *Professional School Counseling, 4*(1), 50–60.

Zins, J. E. (1993). Enhancing consultee problem-solving skills in consultative interactions. *Journal of Counseling & Development, 72*, 185–190. doi:10.1002/j.1556-6676.1993.tb00919.x

Zirkel, P. A. (2009). Section 504: Student eligibility update. *The Clearing House, 82*, 209–211. doi:3200/TCHS.82.5.209-211

Zirkie, D. S., & Peterson, T. L. (2001). The school counselor's role in academic and social adjustment of late adopted children. *Professional School Counseling, 4*, 366–369.